# Criminal Law and Procedure

## Eighth Edition

# Criminal Law and Procedure

## Eighth Edition

Daniel E. Hall, J.D., Ed.D.

 CENGAGE

Australia • Brazil • Canada • Mexico • Singapore • United Kingdom • United States

***Criminal Law and Procedure,* Eighth Edition**
**Daniel E. Hall**

SVP, Higher Education Product Management:
Erin Joyner

VP, Product Management, Learning Experiences:
Thais Alencar

Product Director: Jason Fremder

Product Manager: Abbie Schultheis

Product Assistant: Nick Perez

Creative Studios Designer: Erin Griffin

Content Manager: Arul Joseph Raj, Lumina
Datamatics, Inc.

Production Service: Lumina Datamatics, Inc.

Digital Delivery Quality Partner: Mark Hopkinson

Intellectual Property Analyst: Ashley Maynard

Intellectual Property Project Manager: Ilakkiya
Jayagopi, Lumina Datamatics, Inc.

Cover image(s): Fer Gregory/Shutterstock.com

Library of Congress Control Number: 2021915920

Student Edition:
ISBN: 978-0-357-61933-9

Loose-leaf Edition:
ISBN: 978-0-357-61934-6

**Cengage**
200 Pier 4 Boulevard
Boston, MA 02210
USA

Cengage is a leading provider of customized learning solutions with
employees residing in nearly 40 different countries and sales in more
than 125 countries around the world. Find your local representative at
**www.cengage.com.**

To learn more about Cengage platforms and services, register or access
your online learning solution, or purchase materials for your course, visit
**www.cengage.com.**

Printed in Mexico
Print Number: 01          Print Year: 2021

# Dedication

Few people are blessed with having a lifelong friend. I am one.
Kevin, thanks for five decades of friendship.

# PART I
## CRIMINAL LAW   1

# PART II
## CRIMINAL PROCEDURE   289

# Part 1

## Criminal Law

### Chapter 1

## Introduction to the Legal System of the United States 2

### Chapter 2

## Introduction to Criminal Law 24

## Chapter 3

# The Ingredients of Crime: Thinking and Acting 41

## Chapter 4

# Crimes Against the Person 74

## Chapter 5

# Crimes Involving Property   **119**

## Chapter 6

# Crimes Against the Public   **149**

## Chapter 7

# Parties and Incomplete Crimes                                          211

## Chapter 8

# Factual and Legal Defenses                                          223

## Chapter 9

# Constitutional Defenses                                          251

# Part 2

## Criminal Procedure

## Chapter 10

## The Criminal Justice System                                290

## Chapter 11

## The Constitution and Criminal Procedure            309

## Chapter 12

## Searches and Seizures: Fundamentals                330

## Chapter 13

# Searches and Seizures: Exceptions 372

## Chapter 14

# Interrogation, Surveillance, and Forensic Practices 405

## Chapter 15

# The Pretrial Process 447

## Chapter 16

# Trial                                                                    475

## Chapter 17

# Sentencing and Appeal                                                    503

## Appendix

# The Constitution of the United States of America | 543

It is a privilege to offer you the eighth edition of *Criminal Law and Procedure*. Now 30 years on the market, I am humbled in the knowledge that tens of thousands of students, and thousands of professors, at universities and colleges throughout the United States and Canada have relied on *Criminal Law and Procedure* to support their classroom learning and teaching.

This revision is more than an update. It is the largest and most comprehensive revision the book has undergone in a decade. The basic organization, approach, and pedagogy are the same as in previous editions. But rapid and significant changes in technology and society have resulted in an additional chapter, new sections in existing chapters, new cases, new graphics, and new textual discussion throughout.

## Organization of the Text

If you are new to this book, welcome. What follows are its organizational and pedagogical features. If you have used the text in the past, rest assured that the revisions, while large, won't disrupt your learning plan. I have detailed what is new, what has been revised, and what has been eliminated in the *Changes in the Eighth Edition* section, which appears below.

The organization, content, and pedagogy are the same as before. My highest priorities are to present the material in a manner that is accessible to the undergraduate student and to get the law right. All of the pedagogical features of the earlier editions have been retained, including the hybrid textbook/casebook approach, highlighted definitions, glossary of terms, table of cases, and a thorough index. The distinction between chapter questions and chapter problems continues in this text, the former testing content knowledge and the latter testing the students' problem-solving, critical thinking, and analytical skills.

Keeping in mind the diverse audience of students and instructors who use this text, I have designed two general methods of use. The first is as a combination text and casebook. The second method is to omit the cases and use the text alone. Both methods are possible because I do not use any case to exclusively teach a point of law. Instead, the cases are used to illustrate a point in practice and to develop the cognitive skills of students. Accordingly, if time does not permit it or the educational goals of an instructor are focused elsewhere, the cases may be omitted without losing substantive content. As always, I take liberties with case editing. String citations and other non-content matter are often omitted,

sometimes without indication, to make the reading of the cases smoother. Readers are advised to find the official case for the full, unedited version.

The first half of the text covers substantive criminal law, and the second half of the text discusses both the constitutional dimensions of criminal procedure and the practical dimensions of the criminal justice process.

## Key Features

**Ethical Considerations** that expose students to ethical questions in criminal law and general ethical principles and laws that apply to players in the criminal justice system

**Writing Style** that challenges but does not overwhelm undergraduate students

**Key Terms** that are in bold on first use and clearly defined in the margin

**Oyez Feature,** which offers edited cases that reinforce content and promote the development of case analysis skills

**Sidebars** that can be used to spark class discussion and student interest in issues involving the criminal justice system and criminal law. To provide context for the frequency of the crimes and topics discussed, a sidebar labeled CrimeStats appears throughout.

**Exhibits** that reinforce textual material and help illustrate important ideas

**Review Questions** that call for content-related answers to reinforce and retain chapter concepts

**Chapter Problems & Critical Thinking Exercises** that are intended to develop critical thinking and problem-solving skills

## Changes in the Eighth Edition

I have added new material and updated existing material to keep abreast of changes in both the law and the criminal justice disciplines. The changes and additions include, inter alia, the following:

- For the first time, the book is offered in full color.
- The Fourth Amendment chapter is divided into two chapters, one covering foundational material and the second covering the many exceptions to the warrant and probable cause requirements.

- Several new subchapters have been added.
- The law has been updated throughout. This includes United States Supreme Court opinions issued as late as June 2021.
- Many new Oyez case excerpts have been added and several older cases removed. The new cases cover, among other subjects, mens rea, murder, cybercrime, sexual assault, civil rights, duress, dual sovereignty (*Gamble v. United States*), Third-Party Doctrine and cell data (*Carpenter v. United States*), Fourth Amendment seizure (*Torres v. Madrid*), unanimous jury verdicts (*Ramos v. Louisiana*), and jury impeachment for racial bias (*Pena v. Colorado*).
- Over a dozen new exhibits and a dozen new photos have been added.
- The number of additions, edits, and deletions from the text narrative are too many to be listed. The more significant changes include the following:
  o New material on civil rights crimes and equal protection
  o An expanded discussions of the fundamental elements of crimes, mens rea, actus reus, and concurrence, and a new discussion of attendant circumstances
  o New material on police liability, particularly qualified immunity
  o Recent developments in felony murder
  o A discussion of the evolving definition of rape
  o New material on the various forms of cyber and computer crime
  o New material on crimes involving animals
  o The issue of wrongful convictions, particularly the role of false memories and eyewitness misidentification
  o An expanded examination of crimes against the public, using the Capitol insurrection of January 6, 2021, for illustrations
  o Dual sovereignty
  o Free Speech issues that are hot now, including True Threats and Fighting Words
  o An expanded discussion of self-defense, including Stand Your Ground laws
  o An enlarged discussion of electronic and digital surveillance
  o An enlarged discussion of interrogation techniques, including police deception
  o New material on plea bargaining
  o New material on legislative amelioration and executive commutations and pardons

I love to hear from professors and students about my books. If there is material that you want to see added, or there is something that can be improved, please write to me at hallslawbooks@gmail.com.

# Cengage Instructor Center

Additional instructor resources for this product are available online. Instructor assets include an Instructor's Manual, PowerPoint® slides, and a test bank powered by Cognero®. Sign up or sign in at www.cengage.com to search for and access this product and its online resources.

The Cengage Instructor Center is an all-in-one resource for class preparation, presentation, and testing. The instructor resources available for download include:

- **Instructor's Manual.** Provides activities and assessments for each chapter (including business cases with corresponding assessment activities) and their correlation to specific learning objectives, an outline, key terms with definitions, a chapter summary, and several ideas for engaging with students with discussion questions, ice breakers, case studies, and social learning activities that may be conducted in an on-ground, hybrid, or online modality.
- **Test Bank.** A comprehensive test bank, offered in Blackboard, Moodle, Desire2Learn, and Canvas formats, contains learning objective-specific true-false, multiple-choice, and essay questions for each chapter. Import the test bank into your LMS to edit and manage questions and to create tests.
- **PowerPoint Slides.** Presentations are closely tied to the Instructor's Manual, providing ample opportunities for generating classroom discussion and interaction. They offer ready-to-use, visual outlines of each chapter that may be easily customized for your lectures.
- **Transition Guide.** Highlights all of the changes in the text and in the digital offerings from the previous edition to this edition.

## Cengage Testing Powered by Cognero

Cognero is a flexible online system that allows you to author, edit, and manage test bank content from multiple Cengage solutions; create multiple test versions in an instant; and deliver tests from your LMS, your classroom, or wherever you want.

# Acknowledgments

I would like to thank the Product Manager Abbie Schultheis and the Vendor Content Manager, Arul Joseph Raj of Lumina Datamatics, for their continued support and belief in this text.

# About the Author

Daniel E. Hall is a Professor of Justice and Community Studies and Political Science at Miami University. He is also visiting professor of law at Sun Yat-sen University in Guangzhou, China. He earned his B.S. at Indiana University, J.D. at Washburn University, and Ed.D. in Higher Education at the University of Central Florida. In addition to experience as a defense attorney in the United States and assistant attorney general of the Federated States of Micronesia, he has more than 20 years of experience teaching criminal law and procedure in higher education. He has authored a dozen journal articles and 28 books (including subsequent editions) on public law subjects. You may email Daniel at hallslawbooks@gmail.com.

# Part 1

# Criminal Law

# Introduction to the Legal System of the United States

## Federalism

Learning Objective: Describe federalism and explain its impact on criminal law and procedure.

In this textbook, you will be introduced to two important and high-profile areas of U.S. law: criminal law and criminal procedure. As the idiom *If it bleeds, it leads* expresses, crime and the criminal justice system are popular fodder for journalists. Unfortunately, however, much of what appears in the news is wrong. As is commonly said today, it is "fake news." The objective of this book—obviously—is to help you learn criminal law and procedure. But it is more than that. You should be a more informed member of the community and a more discerning observer of the criminal justice system when you complete this book.

Criminal law doesn't spring from the Cloud. It is part of a larger legal and political system that dates back nearly a thousand years. Therefore, this chapter begins by framing criminal law in its larger historic and political context. This can be complicated, both because the history is long and because contemporary criminal law and procedure exists at several levels and in many forms. These include federal and state constitutional law, the common law, and statutory law. It will be easier to understand modern criminal law if we first explore the basic structure of American government. Let's return to your high school civics class.

The United States is divided into two sovereign forms of government—this is referred to as **federalism**. Think of federalism as a vertical division of power with the national government resting above the state governments. This doesn't mean the states are subservient to the federal government. Often, the states are independent or "sovereign." The Framers of the Constitution of the United States established these two levels of government in an attempt to prevent the centralization of power. The belief that "absolute power corrupts absolutely" was the catalyst for the division

**federalism**

A system of political organization with two or more levels of government (for example, city, state, and national) coexisting in the same area, with the lower levels having some independent powers.

## Sidebar

At trial, a *sidebar* is a meeting between the judge and the attorneys, at the judge's bench, outside the hearing of the jury. Sidebars are used to discuss issues that the jury is not permitted to hear. In this text, the sidebars will appear periodically. This periodic feature contains information relevant to the legal subject being studied.

of governmental powers and the many checks and balances between them that are baked into the three branches of the federal government.

In theory, the national government, commonly referred to as the *federal government,* and the state governments each possess authority over citizens, as well as over particular policy areas, free from the interference of the other government. This is known as **dual sovereignty**. But the Framers of the Constitution intended to establish a limited federal government. That is, most governmental powers were to reside in the states, with the federal government being limited to the powers expressly delegated to it by the U.S. Constitution. This principle is found in the Tenth Amendment, which reads: "The powers not delegated to the United States by the Constitution, nor prohibited to it by the States, are reserved to the States respectively, or the people."

A very important responsibility of the states is to regulate for the health and welfare of its citizens. This is known as the **police power**. In spite of its name, the police power isn't only about criminal justice. It refers to any effort to improve the welfare of the people. Consider, for example, the COVID-19 pandemic. The responsibility, and authority, to control the spread of the virus and to protect the public from infection fell mostly to the states. That is why governors and state health officials, not federal officials, issued orders about social distancing, masking, and closing businesses. It is through the police power that the states protect people from one another. Murder, rape, arson, burglary, and thefts are state crimes. The primacy of the states in protecting for the general welfare is reflected in the work of the courts. About 95% of all crimes are tried in state courts.

But there are small zones of authority that are exclusively federal. These authorities are specifically listed by the U.S. Constitution. They include:

1. Coin money, punish counterfeiters, and fix standards of weights and measures.
2. Establish a post office and post roads.
3. Promote the progress of science and useful arts by providing artists and scientists exclusive rights to their discoveries and writings.
4. Punish piracy and other crimes on the high seas.
5. Declare war and raise armies.
6. Conduct diplomacy and foreign affairs.
7. Regulate interstate and foreign commerce.
8. Make laws necessary and proper for carrying into execution other powers expressly granted in the Constitution.

The last two of these powers—the regulation of interstate commerce and the making of all necessary and proper laws—have proven to be significant sources of federal authority. Through the **Commerce Clause**, the federal government asserts criminal law jurisdiction over crimes that occur in more than one state, such as kidnapping and the trafficking of persons across state lines. The Necessary and Proper Clause enables the federal government to create criminal laws to support its other specifically listed powers, such as the criminalization of mail fraud under its power to create a post office. Also important is the Supremacy Clause of Article VI, which provides that

**dual sovereignty**
When multiple governments have concurrent authority over people or policy.

**police power**
The government's authority and power to set up and enforce laws to provide for the safety, health, and general welfare of the people.

**Commerce Clause**
Found in Article I, sec. 8 of the Constitution, this clause empowers the federal government to regulate commerce between the states, with foreign governments, and Indian tribes.

This Constitution, and the Laws of the United States which shall be made in Pursuance thereof; and all Treaties made, or which shall be made, under the Authority of the United States, shall be the supreme Law of the Land; and the Judges in every State shall be bound thereby, any Thing in the Constitution or Laws of any State to the Contrary notwithstanding.

The Supremacy Clause declares federal law, if valid, to be a higher form of law than state law. Of course, if the federal government attempts to regulate an area belonging to the states, its law is invalid and the state law is controlling. But if the federal government possesses **jurisdiction** or concurrent state and federal jurisdiction exists, federal law reigns supreme. If concurrent jurisdiction exists, state law is set aside if (1) it conflicts with federal law or (2) Congress has declared that federal law shall exist alone. The latter is known as "preemption." This relationship, which clearly distinguishes federal and state authorities, is known as **dual federalism**. Federal law rarely invalidates state criminal law because state and federal criminal laws are more likely to be parallel or complementary. In such cases, a state government and the federal government have **concurrent jurisdiction** (see Exhibit 1–1) and engage is what is known as **cooperative federalism**.

Cooperative federalism, which is not a third jurisdictional model, but instead, a relational descriptor, is characterized by significant interaction between the states and federal government (and local forms of government) in an effort to effectively regulate and administer laws and programs. Cooperative federalism is focused on federal and state collaboration, not on drawing lines of authority between the two.

There are many illustrations of successful federal-state alliances. The government's response to COVID-19 is an example. The states took the lead with regulating businesses and individuals while the federal government led the effort to control the borders, support research, and fund the development and distribution of a vaccine. The War on Terror that has been fought since the 9-11 attacks is another example. The states and federal government have developed information sharing and other joint law enforcement and intelligence processes. In terms of the law, both state and federal **terrorism** laws exist. You may find it odd, or unfair, but the Supreme Court had decided on a couple of occasions (the most recent being in 2019) that it does not violate double jeopardy for an individual to be tried and punished by both the federal and a state government. You will learn more about this in Chapter 9.[1]

As you learned earlier, a few policy areas belong exclusively to the federal government. Punishing counterfeiters is an example. Although the expansion of federal authority is likely to continue to increase as people and goods become

**jurisdiction**
The geographical area within which a court (or a public official) has the right and power to operate. Or the persons about whom and the subject matters about which a court has the right and power to make decisions that are legally binding.

**dual federalism**
A model of governance where the federal government and states have distinct, separate authorities.

**concurrent jurisdiction**
Two or more jurisdictions or courts possessing authority over the same matter.

**cooperative federalism**
A model of governance where the federal government and the states share in governing.

**terrorism**
The definition of terrorism is the subject of ongoing debate. However, one federal statute defines it as activities that involve violence or acts dangerous to human life that are violations of law and appear to be intended to intimate or coerce a civilian population, to influence a policy of government by intimidation or coercion, or to affect the conduct of government through mass destruction, assassination, or kidnapping.[2] 18 U.S.C. §2331.

## Exhibit 1–1 Federal and State Criminal Jurisdiction

| State Jurisdiction | Concurrent Jurisdiction | Federal Jurisdiction |
|---|---|---|
| 1. States may regulate for the health, safety, and morals of their citizens | 1. Those acts that fall into both federal and state jurisdictions | 1. Acts in interstate or international commerce and that stem from an enumerated federal power |
| 2. Those acts that involve a state government, its officials, and property<br><br>Examples: Murder; rape; theft; driving under the influence of a drug; gambling | Examples: Bank robbery of a federally insured institution; an act of terrorism against the United States that harms an individual, state property, or individual property | 2. Crimes involving the government of the United States, including its officials and property<br><br>Examples: Murder of a federal official or murder on federal land; interstate kidnapping; interstate flight of a felon |

## Sidebar

### How to Brief a Case

You are about to read the first judicial decision found in this text. Decisions of courts are often written and are commonly referred to as *judicial opinions* or *cases*. These cases are published in law reporters so they may be used as precedent. Many cases appear in this text for your education. Your instructor may also require that you read other cases, often from your jurisdiction. The cases included in your book have been edited, citations have been omitted, and legal issues not relevant to the subject discussed have been excised. There is a common method that students of the law use to read and analyze (also known as briefing) cases.

Most judicial opinions are written using a similar format. First, the name of the case appears with the name of the court, the cite (location where the case has been published), and the year. When the body of the case begins, the name of the judge or judges responsible for writing the opinion appears directly before the first paragraph. The opinion contains an introduction to the case, which normally includes the procedural history of the case. This is followed by a summary of the facts that led to the dispute, the court's analysis of the law that applies to the case, and the court's conclusions and orders, if any.

Most opinions used here are from appellate courts, where many judges sit at one time. After the case is over, the judges vote on an outcome. The majority vote wins, and the opinion of the majority is written by one of those judges. If other judges in the majority wish to add to the majority opinion, they may write one or more concurring opinions. Concurring opinions appear after majority opinions in the law reporters. When judges who were not in the majority feel strongly about their position, they may file dissenting opinions, which appear after the concurring opinions, if any. Only the majority opinion is law, although concurring and dissenting opinions are often informative.

Here is a suggested format for briefing cases:

1. Read the case. On your first reading, do not take notes; simply attempt to get a *feel* for the case. Then read the case again and use the following suggested method of briefing.

2. State the *relevant* facts. Often, cases read like little stories. You need to weed out the facts that have no bearing on the subject you are studying.

3. Identify the legal issue of the case. The issue is the legal question that is being answered by the court.

4. Identify the applicable rules, standards, or other laws, as they apply to the issues you have identified.

5. Explain the court's decision and analysis. Why and how did the court reach its conclusion? Note whether the court affirmed, reversed, or remanded the case. You may also want to do the same for concurring or dissenting opinions.

more national and international in character, the Supreme Court has reaffirmed the central role of states in protecting the people, and it has conversely made it clear that the federal government can only make laws when the Constitution expressly authorizes it to do so.

For example, the Supreme Court invalidated the federal Gun-Free Zone Act of 1990 because it found no genuine connection between guns around schools and interstate commerce. This case is featured in your first Oyez.

## Oyez

About This Feature: Oyez (pronounced O-Yay) is a Latin word that found its way into French and eventually into English. The word means "hear ye" and is used to attract attention. Traditionally, it is called out three times to open court sessions. The Supreme Court of the United States continues to open its sessions with it. Specifically, the Marshall of the Court calls out the following:

The Honorable, the Chief Justice and the Associate Justices of the Supreme Court of the United States. Oyez! Oyez! Oyez! All persons having business before the Honorable, the Supreme Court of the United States, are admonished to draw near and give their attention, for the Court is now sitting. God save the United States and this Honorable Court.

Oyez is used in this book to announce that you are about to read a court case that illustrates the subject you are studying. The cases, which can be dozens of pages long, are "excerpted," or reduced, to their most relevant parts. Both state and federal cases are featured. Your first Oyez case is *Lopez v. United States*. In it, the Supreme Court of the United States discusses whether the federal government has the authority to control guns in and around schools.

(continued)

United States v. Lopez
514 U.S. 549 (1995)

Chief Justice Rehnquist delivered the opinion of the Court

In the Gun-Free School Zones Act of 1990 [Act], Congress made it a federal offense "for any individual knowingly to possess a firearm at a place that the individual knows, or has reasonable cause to believe, is a school zone." The Act neither regulates a commercial activity nor contains a requirement that the possession be connected in any way to interstate commerce. We hold that the Act exceeds the authority of Congress "[t]o regulate Commerce ... among the several States ...." U.S. Const., Art. I, § 8, cl. 3.

On March 10, 1992, respondent, who was then a 12th-grade student, arrived at Edison High School in San Antonio, Texas, carrying a concealed .38-caliber handgun and five bullets. Acting upon an anonymous tip, school authorities confronted respondent, who admitted that he was carrying the weapon. He was arrested and charged under Texas law with firearm possession on school premises. The next day, the state charges were dismissed after federal agents charged respondent by complaint with violating the Gun-Free School Zones Act of 1990. ...

We start with first principles. The Constitution creates a Federal Government of enumerated powers. See Art. I, § 8. As James Madison wrote: "The powers delegated by the proposed Constitution to the federal government are few and defined. Those which are to remain in the State governments are numerous and indefinite." ...

"Just as the separation and independence of the coordinate branches of the Federal Government serve to prevent the accumulation of excessive power in anyone branch, a healthy balance of power between the States and the Federal Government will reduce the risk of tyranny and abuse from either front." ...

Consistent with this structure, we have identified three broad categories of activity that Congress may regulate under its commerce power. First, Congress may regulate the use of the channels of interstate commerce. '[T]he authority of Congress to keep the channels of interstate commerce free from immoral and injurious uses has been frequently sustained, and is no longer open to question.' Second, Congress is empowered to regulate and protect the instrumentalities of interstate commerce, or persons or things in interstate commerce, even though the threat may come only from intrastate activities. Finally, Congress' commerce authority includes the power to regulate those activities having a substantial relation to interstate commerce and those activities that substantially affect interstate commerce.

Within this final category, admittedly, our case law has not been clear whether an activity must "affect" or "substantially affect" interstate commerce in order to be within Congress' power to regulate it under the Commerce Clause. ...

We now turn to consider the power of Congress, in the light of this framework, to enact [Act]. The first two categories of authority may be quickly disposed of: [Act] is not a regulation of the use of the channels of interstate commerce, nor is it an attempt to prohibit the interstate transportation of a commodity through the channels of commerce; nor can [Act] be justified as a regulation by which Congress has sought to protect an instrumentality of interstate commerce or a thing in interstate commerce. Thus, if [Act] is to be sustained, it must be under the third category as a regulation of an activity that substantially affects interstate commerce. ...

Section 922(q) is a criminal statute that by its terms has nothing to do with "commerce" or any sort of economic enterprise, however broadly one might define those terms. Section 922(q) is not an essential part of a larger regulation of economic activity, in which the regulatory scheme could be undercut unless the intrastate activity were regulated. ...

Under our federal system, the "'States possess primary authority for defining and enforcing the criminal law. ...

The Government's essential contention, *in fine*, is that we may determine here that § 922(q) is valid because possession of a firearm in a local school zone does indeed substantially affect interstate commerce. The Government argues that possession of a firearm in a school zone may result in violent crime and that violent crime can be expected to affect the functioning of the national economy in two ways. First, the costs of violent crime are substantial, and, through the mechanism of insurance, those costs are spread throughout the population. Second, violent crime reduces the willingness of individuals to travel to areas within the country that are perceived to be unsafe. The Government also argues that the presence of guns in schools poses a substantial threat to the educational process by threatening the learning environment. A handicapped educational process, in turn, will result in a less productive citizenry. That, in turn, would have an adverse effect on the Nation's economic well-being. ...

The possession of a gun in a local school zone is in no sense an economic activity that might, through repetition elsewhere, substantially affect any sort of interstate commerce. Respondent was a local student at a local school; there is no indication that he had recently moved in interstate commerce, and there is no requirement that his possession of the firearm have any concrete tie to interstate commerce.

To uphold the Government's contentions here, we would have to pile inference upon inference in a manner that would bid fair to convert congressional authority under the Commerce Clause to a general police power of the sort retained by the States. Admittedly, some of our prior cases have taken long steps down that road, giving great deference to congressional action. The broad language in these opinions has suggested the possibility of additional expansion, but we decline here to proceed any further. To do so would require us to conclude that the Constitution's enumeration of powers does not presuppose something not enumerated and that there never will be a distinction between what is truly national and what is truly local. This we are unwilling to do.

Two years later, the Brady Handgun Violence Protection Act was invalidated in *Printz v. United States*[3] because it required state officials to conduct background checks on gun purchasers. The Court held that Congress was without the authority to direct local enforcement officers in this way. In yet another case favoring state authority, *United States v. Morrison*,[4] the Supreme Court struck down part of the Violence Against Women Act because it held that it was a state, not federal, authority to provide victims of sex crimes with civil remedies against their attackers. In another 2000 case, *Jones v. United States*,[5] the Court invalidated the application of a federal arson statute to the prosecution of a man for firebombing his cousin's home. The Court rejected the United States' theory that it had jurisdiction because the home's mortgage, its insurance, and its natural gas were all purchased in interstate commerce. The Court penned that if it were to accept the government's position, "hardly a building in the land would fall outside the federal statute's domain."

Philip Lange/Shutterstock.com

However, a connection was found in the 2005 case *Gonzales v. Raich*.[6] In that case, the federal government's prohibition of the possession of marijuana was upheld, although state law allowed its possession and use for medical purposes. The interstate nature of marijuana production and sales made for an easy case of federal jurisdiction. In fact, the plaintiffs conceded this point. Their theory that California's law permitting limited use of marijuana should trump federal law failed, largely because the federal government had a "rational basis" to believe that the state law would undermine the intention of the federal law by providing a stream through which interstate drug trafficking could occur.

In 2010, the Court affirmed a federal statute that delegated the authority to seek civil commitment of federal sex offenders after their sentences were served to federal prosecutors. Similar state laws were previously upheld, but in the 2010 case *United States v. Comstock*,[7] the defendant complained that civil commitment was a traditional state authority and accordingly, the federal law was invalid. Relying on the Necessary and Proper Clause, the Court rejected the argument. That the statute required the federal government to give the appropriate state officials the first opportunity to file for commitment in state court also reduced the Court's concerns that state autonomy was threatened.

Local governments have not been mentioned so far. This is because the Constitution does not recognize the existence of local governments. However, state constitutions and laws establish local forms of government, such as counties, cities, and districts. These local entities are often empowered by state law with limited authority to create criminal law. These laws, usually in the form of ordinances, are discussed in Chapter 2.

The result of this division of power is that the states (as well as other jurisdictions, such as the District of Columbia), the federal government, territories and local governments each have a separate set of criminal laws. For this reason, you must keep in mind that the principles you will learn from this book are general. It is both impossible and pointless to teach the specific laws of every jurisdiction of the United States in this textbook.

# Separation of Powers

Learning Objective: Describe the separation of powers with an emphasis on how it impacts criminal law and criminal procedure.

Another division of governmental power is known as **separation of powers**. This is the division of governmental power into three branches—the executive, legislative, and judicial—making a horizontal division of power, just as federalism is the vertical division (see Exhibit 1–2). Each branch is delegated certain

**separation of powers**
Division of the federal government (and state governments) into legislative (lawmaking), judicial (law interpreting), and executive (law enforcement) branches.

## Exhibit 1–2 Division of Governmental Power

|  | Legislative Branch | Executive Branch | Judicial Branch |
|---|---|---|---|
| The Government of the United States (Federal Government) | U.S. Congress | President of the United States | Federal Courts |
| State Governments | State Legislatures | Governors | State Courts |

**statute**
A law passed by a legislature.

functions that the other two may not encroach upon. The executive branch consists of the president of the United States, the president's staff, and the various administrative agencies that the president oversees. Generally, it is the duty of the executive branch to enforce the laws of the federal government. In criminal law, the executive branch investigates alleged violations of the law, gathers the evidence necessary to prove that a violation has occurred, and prosecutes alleged criminals. The president does this through the various federal law enforcement and administrative agencies.

The legislative branch consists of the U.S. Congress, which creates the laws of the United States. Congressionally created laws are known as **statutes**. Finally, the judicial branch comprises the various federal courts of the land. That branch is charged with the administration of justice. A more comprehensive discussion of the judicial branch follows later in this chapter.

In a further attempt to diffuse governmental power, the framers designed a system of checks and balances that prevents any one branch from exclusively controlling most functions. Several checks can be found in the Constitution.

For example, Congress is responsible for making the law. This function is checked by the president, who may veto legislation. The president is then checked by Congress, which may override a veto with a two-thirds majority. The president is responsible for conducting foreign affairs and making treaties and for serving as commander in chief of the military. The Senate, however, must approve the treaties negotiated by the executive branch, and Congress has been delegated the authority to make the rules that regulate the military. In the context of criminal law, this means that Congress, state legislatures, and local councils declare what acts are criminal; for their part, the president, state governors, prosecutors, and law enforcement agencies detect and respond to criminal acts, prosecute violators, and administer judicially ordered punishments. The judicial branch interprets criminal law, oversees criminal adjudications, sentences offenders, and to a limited extent oversees the entire system of adjudication and punishment.

Through the power of judicial review, the judiciary may invalidate actions of the president or Congress that violate the Constitution. In contrast, the political branches select federal judges through the nomination (president) and confirmation (Senate) process. Unpopular judicial decisions may be changed either by statute, if the issue is one of statutory interpretation, or by constitutional amendment, if the issue is one of constitutional interpretation. Rogue judges, even though appointed for life, can be impeached and removed by Congress.

Even though the U.S. Constitution does not establish three branches of government for the many states (the U.S. Constitution designs the structure of the federal government only but also demands that states have republican forms of government), all state constitutions do, in varying forms, model the federal constitution. The result is a two-tiered system with each tier split into three parts.

In this form of government, the legislature defines what acts are criminal, what process must be used to ensure that a wrongdoer answers for an act, and what punishment should be imposed for the act.

The duty of the executive branch is to enforce and implement the laws created by the legislature, as well as to enforce the orders of courts. This is done by two independent law enforcement agencies; police and prosecutors. For example, if a state legislature prohibits cyberstalking, state or law enforcement officers will investigate a suspect and turn them over to a local or state prosecutor, who will decide whether to prosecute. There are over 18,000 law enforcement agencies in the United States. The vast majority of these agencies are found in the states. State and municipal law enforcement agencies are known by a variety of names (e.g., highway patrol, state police, bureau of investigation, county sheriff, township constables, and city police). Many state and local agencies have overlapping jurisdiction. A city police officer, for example, shares jurisdiction with both the county sheriff and state police.

Although federal law enforcement comprises a small number of the 18,000 agencies, there are many law enforcement agencies, including the Federal Bureau of Investigation, Drug Enforcement Administration, U.S. Marshal Service, Department of Homeland Security, Immigration and Customs Enforcement, U.S. Secret Service, U.S. Coast Guard, Transportation Security Administration (including the Air Marshal Service), and the Department of the Treasury. Many federal agencies that don't have law enforcement as their primary responsibility have law enforcement officers. For example, the U.S. Post Office has a large number of officers in its Postal Inspection Service and the Food and Drug Administration employs a large cadre of investigators.

When a law enforcement agency has completed its investigation, the case is turned over to a prosecutor. The prosecutor is the attorney who represents the people. The prosecutor leads every aspect of the prosecution; the filing of the charge, conducting grand juries, negotiating plea agreements, trying the case, recommending punishment, and representing the state during appeals. In the federal system, the prosecutor is referred to as a U.S. Attorney. In the states and localities, prosecutors are known as district attorneys, county attorneys, state attorneys, city attorneys, or, simply, prosecutors. U.S. Attorneys are appointed by the president of the United States, subject to confirmation by the U.S. Senate, and state prosecutors are either elected by the people or appointed by an executive officer.

Finally, the judicial branch is charged with the administration of justice. The courts become involved after the executive branch has arrested or accused an individual of a crime as well as at certain points during criminal investigations. The duties of the judicial branch are explored further in the next section of this chapter. Lawyers, legal assistants, and law enforcement officials are likely to have significant contacts with state and federal courts; therefore, it is important to understand the structure of the court system.

# Courts

Learning Objective: Describe the organization and role of courts in the American criminal justice system.

Of the three branches of government, attorneys and other legal professionals have the most interaction with the judicial branch. For that reason, the judicial branch is singled out for a deeper discussion.

Within the federal and state judiciaries, a hierarchy of courts exists. All state court systems, as well as the federal court system, have at least two types of courts: trial courts and appellate courts. However, because each state is free to structure its judiciary in any manner, significant variation is found in the different court systems. What follows are general principles that apply to all states and the federal system.

**trial court**
A court that hears and determines a case initially, as opposed to an appellate court. A court of general jurisdiction.

Trial courts are commonly featured in movies, television, and streaming dramas. A criminal case begins at a trial court. This is where witnesses testify, the bloody hand and axe are presented—often to a jury as well as a judge—and where verdicts and sentences are announced. In the federal system, trial courts are labeled as U.S. District Courts. The United States is divided into 94 judicial districts, using state boundaries to establish district limits. Each state constitutes at least one district, although larger states are divided into several districts. For example, Kansas has only one district, and the federal trial court located in Kansas is known as the U.S. District Court for the District of Kansas. California, in contrast, is made up of four districts; the Northern, Eastern, Central, and Southern Districts of California.

State trial courts are known by various names, such as district, superior, county, and circuit courts. Despite variations in name, these courts are similar.

**appellate court**
A higher court that can hear appeals from a lower court.

**brief**
A written document filed with a court through which a party presents a legal claim, legal theory, supporting authorities, and requests some form of relief.

**record on appeal**
A formal, written account of a case, containing the complete formal history of all actions taken, papers filed, rulings made, opinions written, and so forth.

**remand**
The return of a case from a higher court to a lower court with instructions for the lower court to act in some manner, e.g. conduct a new trial or rehear an issue.

Appellate courts review the decisions and actions of trial courts and lower appellate courts for error. Appellate courts do not conduct trials; no witnesses are called and the bloody knife is not introduced as evidence. Instead, the judges review the **briefs** submitted by the parties and examine the **record** from the trial court for mistakes, known as trial court error. Often, but not always, appellate courts will hear arguments from the attorneys involved in the case. After the appellate court has reviewed the record and examined it for error, it will issue a written opinion. An appellate court can reverse, affirm, or remand the lower court decision. To *reverse* is to determine that the lower court has rendered a wrong decision and to change that decision. An affirmation leaves the lower court opinion unchanged.

In some cases, an appellate court will remand the case to the lower court. A **remand** is an order to return the case to a lower court, often with instructions, such as to reconsider the case without specific evidence that was determined to have been unlawfully considered the first time. If a mistake can't be corrected, a new trial may be ordered. For example, if an appellate court decides that a judge acted in a manner or made a decision that prevented a criminal defendant from having

## Sidebar

### The Workload of U.S. Courts

The court system is actually many court systems composed of the federal system and the many state systems. In 2018, approximately 84 million cases were filed in state and local trial courts. Of these, 53% were traffic offenses, 20% were criminal cases, 20% were civil cases, 6% were domestic cases, and 1% were juvenile cases.

*Source of state statistics:* State Court Caseload Digest. (National Center for State Courts 2019). Retrieved from courtstatistics.org on December 28, 2020.

In 2019, the federal system was composed of 1 Supreme Court, 13 appellate courts, and 94 district courts. The district courts had 390,555 total cases, of which 92,678 were criminal cases. The regional courts of appeals saw 48,486 appeals. A total of 776,674 bankruptcies were filed in the U.S. bankruptcy courts. In 2018, 6,442 cases were filed, 73 were heard, and 69 cases terminated in the Supreme Court.

*Source of federal statistics: 2019 Judicial Business of the United States Courts,* Administrative Office of the United States Courts: *http://www.uscourts.gov/ and Chief Justice's Year-End Summary of the Federal Judiciary (2019) found at supremecourt.gov.*

a fair trial, and the defendant was convicted, an appellate court may reverse the conviction and remand the case to the trial court for a new trial with instructions that the judge not act in a similar manner.

In the federal system and many states, there are two levels of appellate courts, an intermediate and highest level. The intermediate level courts in the federal system are the U.S. Courts of Appeal.[8] There are 11 judicial circuits in the United States, with 1 court of appeals in each circuit. Additionally, there is a court of appeals for Washington, D.C., and for the federal circuit. Therefore, there are 13 U.S. Courts of Appeal in total (see Exhibit 1–3). Appeals from the district courts are taken to these courts.

The highest court in the country is the U.S. Supreme Court. Appeals from the circuit courts are taken to the Supreme Court. Also, appeals of federal issues from state supreme courts go to the U.S. Supreme Court. Although an appeal to a circuit court and to a state's first appellate court (and often its second level of appeal as well) is generally a right any litigant has, the Supreme Court is not required to hear most appeals, and it does not. In recent years, the Supreme Court has denied review of approximately 97% of the cases appealed. Therefore, the states' supreme courts and federal circuit courts are often a defendant's last chance to be heard.

Many states have two levels of appeals; some have only one. Most states label their high courts "supreme court" and their intermediate level court the court of appeals. An example of an exception is New York, which has named its highest court the Court of Appeals of New York and refers to its trial courts as supreme courts, county courts, city courts, and district courts.

In states that have only one appellate court, appeals are taken directly to that court. New Hampshire is such a state, so appeals from New Hampshire's trial courts are taken directly to the Supreme Court of New Hampshire. In most instances, a first appeal is an appeal of right. This means that the appellate court is required to hear the case. However, second appeals are more likely to be discretionary; the appellate court can decide to hear, or not hear, these cases. To have a case heard by the U.S. Supreme Court and most state supreme courts, the person appealing must seek **certiorari**, an order from an appellate court to the lower court requiring the record to be sent to the higher court for review. When "cert." is granted, the appellate court will hear the appeal; and when certiorari is denied, it will not.

Finally, be aware that a number of **inferior courts** exist. These are courts that fall under trial courts in hierarchy. As such, appeals from these courts do not usually go to the intermediate-level appellate courts, as described earlier, but to the trial level court first. Municipal courts, police courts, and justices of the peace are examples of inferior courts. An appeal from one of these courts is initially heard by a state trial level court before an appeal is taken to a state appellate court. The federal system also has inferior courts. The U.S. Bankruptcy Courts are inferior courts because appeals from the decisions of these courts go to the district courts, in most cases, and not to the courts of appeals. Only after the trial court has rendered its decision may an appeal be taken to an appellate court.

Many inferior courts in the state system are not **courts of record**. No digital, audio, or stenographic recording of the trial or hearing at the inferior court is made. As such, when an appeal is taken to the trial level court, it is normally **de novo**. This means that the trial level court conducts a new trial, rather than reviewing a record as most appellate courts do. Federal district courts do not conduct new trials, as all federal courts, including bankruptcy courts, are courts of record. State inferior courts have limited jurisdiction; for example, municipal courts usually hear municipal ordinance violations and only minor state law violations. The amount of money that a person may be fined and the amount of time that a defendant may be sentenced to serve in jail are also limited. Generally, no juries are used at the inferior court level.

**certiorari**
(Latin) "To make sure." A request for certiorari (or "cert." for short) is like an appeal, but one that the higher court is not required to take for decision. It is literally a writ from the higher court asking the lower court for the record of the case.

**inferior court**
A court with special, limited responsibilities, such as a probate court.

**court of record**
Generally, another term for trial court.

**de novo**
Anew. For a case to be tried again as if there had not been a prior trial.

**Exhibit 1–3** The 13 Federal Judicial Circuits

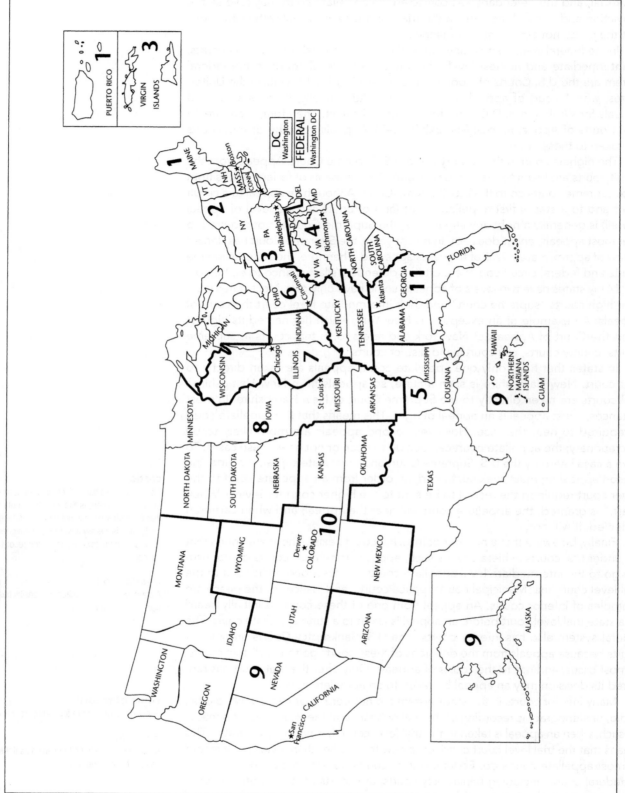

*Source:* http://www.uscourts.gov/court_locator.aspx

## Exhibit 1–4 State and Federal Court Structures

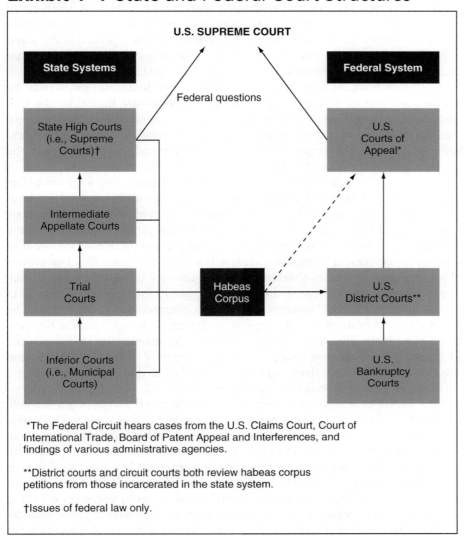

*The Federal Circuit hears cases from the U.S. Claims Court, Court of International Trade, Board of Patent Appeal and Interferences, and findings of various administrative agencies.

**District courts and circuit courts both review habeas corpus petitions from those incarcerated in the state system.

†Issues of federal law only.

Exhibit 1–4 is a basic diagram of the federal and state court systems. The appellate routes are indicated by lines drawn from one court to another. Later in this book you will learn how the appeals process works and how the federal and state systems interact in criminal law. Note where this diagram is located so that you may refer to it later.

Most state trial courts are **courts of general jurisdiction**. Courts of general jurisdiction possess the authority to hear a broad range of cases, including civil law as well as criminal. In contrast, **courts of limited jurisdiction** hear only specific types of cases. You have already been introduced to one limited jurisdiction court, the municipal court. Inferior courts, such as municipal courts, are always courts of limited jurisdiction. Some states employ systems that have specialized trial courts to handle domestic, civil, or criminal cases. These may be in the form of a separate court (e.g., Criminal Court of Harp County) or may be a division of a trial court (e.g., Superior Court of Harp County, Criminal Division). Drug courts, Military Veteran courts, and juvenile courts are other examples. Appellate courts may also be limited in jurisdiction to a particular area of law, such as the Oklahoma Court of Criminal Appeals.

The federal government also has special courts. As previously mentioned, a nationwide system of bankruptcy courts is administered by the national government.

**court of general jurisdiction**
Another term for trial court; that is, a court having jurisdiction to try all classes of civil and criminal cases except those that can be heard only by a court of limited jurisdiction.

**court of limited jurisdiction**
A court whose jurisdiction is limited to civil cases of a certain type, or that involve a limited amount of money, or whose jurisdiction in criminal cases is confined to petty offenses and preliminary hearings.

In addition, the U.S. Claims Court, Tax Court, and Court of International Trade are part of the federal judiciary, and each has a specific area of law over which it may exercise jurisdiction. Often, those cases over which they have jurisdiction are exclusive of district courts. However, the jurisdiction of those courts is outside the scope of this book, as they deal only with civil law. Criminal cases in federal court are heard by district courts, and criminal appeals are heard by the U.S. Courts of Appeals.

Let's turn from the organization of courts to their function. First, it must be emphasized that all courts—local, state, and federal—are bound by the U.S. Constitution. Consequently, all courts have a duty to apply federal constitutional law. This is important in criminal law because the criminal procedure rights found in the U.S. Constitution are much broader and deeper today than in the past. You will learn a lot more about these rights in the second half of this book.

As previously mentioned, the judicial branch is charged with the administration of justice. The courts are the place where civil and criminal disputes are resolved, if the parties cannot reach a resolution themselves. In an effort to resolve disputes, courts must apply the laws of the land. To apply the law, judges must **interpret** the legislation and constitutions of the nation. To *interpret* means to read the law in an attempt to understand its meaning. This nation's courts are the final interpreters of law. If a court interprets a statute's meaning contrary to the intent of a legislature, the legislature may rewrite the statute to make its intent clearer. This type of revision has the effect of "reversing" the court's interpretation of the statute. The process is much more difficult if a legislature desires to change a judicial interpretation of a constitution. At the national level, the Constitution has been amended 27 times. The amendment process is found in Article V of the Constitution and requires action by the federal legislature as well as by the states. Amending a constitution is more difficult than amending legislation.

The judicial branch is independent from the other two branches of government. It is the duty of the courts of this nation to remain neutral and apply the laws fairly and impartially. At the federal level, the judiciary is shielded from interference from the other two branches. For example, the Constitution prohibits Congress from reducing the pay of federal judges after they are appointed. This prevents Congress from coercing the courts into action under the threat of no pay. The Constitution also provides for lifetime appointments of federal judges, thereby keeping the judicial branch from being influenced by political concerns or the waves of public opinion. Judicial independence permits courts to make decisions that are disadvantageous to the government or unpopular with the people, but are required by law.

The need for an independent judiciary is particularly important when one considers the role courts play as the guardians of constitutional principles, including civil rights. **Judicial review** is the power of courts to invalidate legislation and the acts of the executive branch that are unlawful. To strike a law or to tell the police or a state governor that they have violated the law requires tremendous will. At the federal level, judges have the security of lifetime appointment, so they judge without worrying about angering the president or Congress. Alexander Hamilton wrote of the power of judicial review, and of the importance of an independent judiciary, in the *Federalist Papers,* where he stated:

> Permanency in office frees the judges from political pressures and prevents invasions on judicial power by the president and Congress.

■ ■ ■

The Constitution imposes certain restrictions on the Congress designed to protect individual liberties, but unless the courts are independent and have the power to declare the laws in violation of the Constitution null and void these protections amount to nothing. The power of the Supreme Court to declare laws unconstitutional leads some to assume that the judicial branch will be superior to the legislative branch. Let us look at this argument.

**interpret**
Studying a document *and* surrounding circumstances to decide the document's meaning.

**judicial review**
The authority of a court to review and invalidate legislation and executive action that are unlawful.

Only the Constitution is *fundamental* law; the Constitution establishes the principles and structure of the government. To argue that the Constitution is not superior to the laws suggests that the *representatives of the people* are superior *to the people* and that the Constitution is inferior to the government it gave birth to. The courts are the arbiters between the legislative branch and the people; the courts are to interpret the laws and prevent the legislative branch from exceeding the powers granted it. The courts must not only place the Constitution higher than the laws passed by Congress, they must also place the intentions of the people ahead of the intentions of the representative. . . .

The landmark case dealing with judicial review is *Marbury v. Madison,* 1 Cranch 137, 2 L. Ed. 60 (1803). Writing for the Court, Chief Justice Marshall wrote that even though the Constitution does not contain explicit language providing for the power of judicial review, Article III of the Constitution implicitly endows the judiciary with the authority. Although seldom used by the Supreme Court for over a hundred years following the *Marbury* decision, it is now well established that courts possess the authority to review the actions of the executive and legislative branches and to declare any law, command, or other action void if it violates the U.S. Constitution. The power is held by both state and federal courts.

The power to invalidate statutes is rarely used, for two reasons. First, the judiciary is aware of how awesome the power is; consequently, courts invoke the authority sparingly. Second, many rules of statutory construction exist and have the effect of preserving legislation. For example, if two interpretations of a statute are possible, one that violates the Constitution and one that does not, one rule of statutory construction requires that the statute be construed so that it is consistent with the Constitution. Although rarely done, statutes are occasionally determined invalid. In Chapters 8 and 9, on defenses, you will learn many constitutional constraints on government behavior. These defenses often rely on the authority of the judiciary to invalidate statutes or police conduct to give them teeth.[9]

# Comparing Civil Law and Criminal Law

Learning Objective: Compare and contrast civil and criminal law.

Now that you are familiar with the larger governmental context within which criminal law fits, let's take a look at how it relates to other areas of law. A common categorization of the law is to break it into subject areas. The largest categories are civil and criminal law. The differences between criminal law and civil law are significant. Yet, there are also many similarities and areas of overlap. Exhibit 1–5 compares criminal and civil law.

The biggest difference between criminal law and civil law is their differing objectives. There are at least five purposes or objectives of criminal law. First, criminal law is intended to deter undesirable behavior. A second purpose is to offer victims and the community at large a sense of retribution. A third purpose is to incapacitate offenders; to reduce their opportunity to reoffend. This is done through imprisonment, electronic monitoring, death, and other methods. Fourth, the rehabilitation of offenders is also an objective in many cases. A fifth and growing purpose is restoration. Restorative justice focuses on healing victims and to making the offender whole again, in the community. You will dig deeper into each of these in this chapter.

Civil law, on the other hand, has as its primary purpose the compensation of people who are injured by someone else's conduct. Many definitions of civil law exist. This author prefers a negative definition—civil law is everything but criminal

## Exhibit 1–5  Criminal and Civil Law Compared

|  | **Criminal Law** | **Civil Law** |
|---|---|---|
| Purposes | Retribution, deterrence, incapacitation, rehabilitation, restoration | Compensation and deterrence |
| Remedies | Fines, restitution, imprisonment, counseling, rehabilitation, injunctions, capital punishment | Damages and equitable relief |
| Parties | Government and individual defendant | Individual plaintiff and defendant (or government as individual) |
| Standard of Proof | Beyond a reasonable doubt | Preponderance of evidence |
| Burdens | Government bears burden of proof and process designed to protect rights of defendant (due process) | Plaintiff bears burden of proof and parties treated equally in process |

**contract**
An agreement that affects or creates legal relationships between two or more persons. To be a *contract*, an agreement must involve at least one promise, consideration, persons legally capable of making binding agreements, and a reasonable certainty about the meaning of the terms.

**damages**
Money that a court orders paid to a person who has suffered damage (a loss or harm) by the person who caused the injury (the violation of the person's rights).

**tort**
A civil (as opposed to a criminal) wrong, other than a breach of contract.

**negligence**
The failure to exercise a reasonable amount of care in a situation that causes harm to someone or something.

**intentional**
Determination to do a certain thing.

**strict liability**
The legal responsibility for damage or injury, even if you are not at fault or negligent.

**compensatory damages**
Damages awarded for the actual loss suffered by a plaintiff.

law. There are many areas of civil law, including tort, contract, property, intellectual property, and family law. Contract law and tort law are two of the largest areas of civil law.

Contract law is a branch of civil law that deals with agreements between two or more parties. You probably have already entered into a contract. Apartment leases, credit card agreements, and book-of-the-month club agreements are all contracts. To have a **contract**, two or more people must agree to behave in a specific manner. If you violate your obligation under a contract, you have committed a civil wrong called a breach of contract. The landlord may sue you for your breach and receive **damages**. *Damages* are monetary compensation for loss.

Tort law is a branch of civil law that is concerned with civil wrongs but not contract actions. You have likely seen television ads for personal injury attorneys. These attorneys are practicing in the tort law area. A civil wrong, other than a breach of contract, is known as a **tort**. Torts are different from contracts in that the duty owed another party in contract law is created by the parties through their agreement. In tort law, the duty is imposed by the law. For example, Donald Triden heaves a beer bottle across a dance floor at a bar, hitting and injuring Joe Bump. Donald has committed a tort. Even though they have not entered into an agreement to not harm each other, Donald is liable because the law requires that we all act reasonably in situations where it is possible to harm people or property.

When a person fails to act reasonably and unintentionally injures another, that person is responsible for a **negligence**. Automobile accidents and medical malpractice are examples of negligent torts. When a person intentionally injures another person, an **intentional** tort has occurred. Many intentional torts are also crimes, and this is one zone where criminal and common law overlap. If at that fraternity party Donald makes Joe angry, and as a result Joe intentionally strikes Donald with the bottle, Joe has committed both a crime and an intentional tort. Although criminal law may impose a jail sentence (or other punitive measures), tort law would normally only seek to compensate Donald for his injuries.

The final type of tort is the **strict liability** tort. In these situations, liability exists even though the tortfeasor acted with extreme caution and did not intend to cause harm. An example of a strict liability tort is blasting. Whenever a mining or demolition company uses blasting, it is liable for any injuries or damages it causes to property, even if the company exercises extreme caution.

Damages that are awarded (won) in a lawsuit to compensate a party for actual loss are **compensatory damages**. Compensatory damages do just what the name states—compensate the injured party. However, another type of damages exists—**punitive damages**. Contrary to what you have learned so far, punitive damages are awarded in civil suits and are intended to deter undesirable behavior. Punitive damages are often requested by plaintiffs but are rarely awarded. If punitive damages appear to you to be more of a criminal law tool than a civil tool, you are right. It is an oddity in the law.

Trial courts have considerable discretion in awarding punitive damages. There is a limit, however. In the 1996 case *BMW v. Gore*,[10] a jury verdict in actual damages of $4,000 accompanied by a punitive damages award of $4 million, which was reduced to $2 million by the state Supreme Court, was set aside by the U.S. Supreme Court because it found that the plaintiff wasn't on notice, a due process requirement, that it could be penalized by such a sum. As such, the judgement was arbitrary. Because it was a civil case, not a criminal case, the court couldn't turn to the Eighth Amendment's bar on excessive fines to review the award. Instead, it held that due process, the basic fairness clause that applies to all governmental conduct and decisions, expects punitive damages awards to be reasonable, considering three factors: (1) the degree of reprehensibility of conduct, (2) the disparity between actual harm and the punitive award, and (3) a comparison of the award to similar civil or criminal penalties. What was plaintiff Gore's injury? He had not been told that the car he purchased had been repainted to cover damage from acid rain. On remand, the trial court gave the plaintiff the choice between a new trial or accepting $50,000 in punitive damages.

In *State Farm v. Campbell*[11] a plaintiff sued an insurance company over a $50,000 liability policy. The jury awarded the plaintiff $2.6 million and actual damages of $145 million in punitive damages. The trial judge reduced the punitive award to $1 million. The Supreme Court, applying the *BMW* criteria, found the 9:1 ratio of actual to punitive damages excessive and remanded the case to the state court with an order to reduce the award.

In the well-known case involving the massive oil spill in Alaskan waters by one of Exxon's oil tankers, *Exxon Shipping Co. v. Baker*,[12] the jury award of $2.5 billion in punitive damages and $507 million in actual damages, a 5:1 ratio, was found to be excessive. Unlike the earlier cases, *Exxon* was not decided on due process grounds but, rather, upon maritime law. Regardless, the Court's rejection of the 5:1 ratio is instructive in all cases.

The last major case in which the Supreme Court reviewed a punitive damages award was *Philip Morris U.S.A. v. Williams*.[13] The jury award of $821,485.50 in actual damages and $79.5 million in punitive damages—which had been reduced by the trial judge to $32 million in punitive damages—was reversed and remanded to the trial court to reduce the punitive damages figure. In addition to being excessive, the Court rejected the award because it punished the company for harm caused to third parties, people not involved in the litigation. On remand, the award was reinstated with a different theory. Philip Morris appealed this decision to the U.S. Supreme Court, which denied certiorari.

Finally, a few other differences between criminal law and civil law should be mentioned. First, in civil law the person who brings the lawsuit (the plaintiff) is the person who was injured. For example, suppose you are at the grocery store doing your shopping and request the assistance of a checkout person who has recently divorced a spouse who looks very much like you. The checker immediately becomes enraged and vents all of his anger for his ex-wife on you by striking you with a box of cereal. He has committed a possible assault and battery in both tort law (these are intentional torts) and criminal law. However, in tort law, you must sue the checker yourself to recover any losses you suffer.

In criminal law, on the other hand, the government—whether national, state, or local—always files criminal charges. At some point in your life you may have read a sign in a store that threatened to prosecute shoplifters to the fullest extent

**punitive damages**
Damages that are awarded over and above compensatory damages or actual damages because of the wanton, reckless, or malicious nature of the wrong done by the plaintiff.

## Sidebar

### About Case Names, Titles, and Captions

Cases filed with courts are given a case title, also known as a case name. The title consists of the parties to the action. In civil cases the title is *citizen v. citizen*, for example, *Joe Smith v. Anna Smith*. In criminal actions the title is in the form of *The Government v. Defendant*. For example, *United States of America v. Joe Smith* or *State of New Mexico v. Rul Aman*.

Cases also have captions. The caption appears at the top of the title page of all documents filed with a court and includes the case name, the court name, the case number, and the name of the document being filed with the court. The illustration in Exhibit 1–6 is an example of both a criminal case caption and a civil case caption.

**culpable**

Blamable; at fault. A person who has done a wrongful act (whether criminal or civil) is described as "culpable."

of the law. Well, the store can't do it. What the store can do is to file a complaint with the police or prosecutor.  The government will then determine whether to file criminal charges. This is because a violation of criminal law is characterized as an attack on the citizens of a state (or the federal government) and, as such, is a violation of public, not private, law. Because it is public, the decision to file—or not to file—is made by the prosecutor.

Civil cases are entitled *Sue Yu v. Ima Innocent;* in criminal law, it is *government* (i.e., *State of Montana) v. Ima Sued.* In some jurisdictions, criminal actions are brought under the name of the people. This is done in New York, where criminal cases are entitled *The People of the State of New York v. Ima Guilty.*

There is no difference between a criminal action brought in the name of the state and a criminal action brought in the name of the people of a state. All prosecutions at the national level are brought by the United States of America. Note that governments may become involved in civil disputes. For example, if the state of South Dakota enters into a contract with a person, and a dispute concerning that contract arises, the suit will be titled either *citizen v. South Dakota* or *South Dakota v. citizen.*

The two fields also differ in what is required to have a successful case. In civil law one must show actual injury to win. If, in our grocery store example, the box of cereal missed your head and you suffered no injury (damages), you would not have a civil suit. However, a criminal action for assault or battery may still be brought, as no injury is required in criminal law. This is because the purpose of criminal law is to prevent this type of conduct, not to compensate for actual injuries.

To turn this idea around, there are many instances in which a person's negligence could be subject to a civil cause of action, but not to a criminal action. If a person accidentally strikes another during a game of golf with a golf ball, causing injury, the injured party may sue for the concussion received; but no purpose would be served by prosecuting the individual who hit the ball. No deterrent effect is achieved, as there was no intent to cause the injury. In most cases, society has made the determination (through its criminal laws) that a greater amount of **culpability** should be required for criminal liability than for civil. Criminal law is usually more concerned with the immorality of an act than is tort law. This is consistent with the goals of the two disciplines, as it is easier to prevent intentional acts than accidental ones. These concepts will be discussed later in the chapter on mens rea.

# The Social Contract

Learning Objective: Describe the social contract and explain its relationship to criminal law.

In 2020, Hong Kong residents were jailed for peacefully demanding more rights from the Chinese government, Thai protestors were arrested for criticizing

## Exhibit 1–6 Simple Caption—Criminal Case and Civil Case

```
              IN THE UNITED STATES DISTRICT COURT FOR
                    THE DISTRICT OF MARYLAND
                        NORTHERN DIVISION

UNITED STATES OF AMERICA)          )
_____ Plaintiff,          )
         v.                        )          Case No. _____
                                   )
IMA CRIMINAL,                      )
_____ Defendant           )

                    Motion to Suppress Evidence
```

```
              IN THE UNITED STATES DISTRICT COURT FOR
                    THE DISTRICT OF MARYLAND
                        NORTHERN DIVISION

RASHEED D. JONES                   )
Plaintiff,                         )
                                   )
         v.                        )          Case No.
                                   )
LING WONG,                         )
Defendant                          )

                Defendant's Motion for Summary Judgment
```

Thailand's king, and journalists across the globe were punished for reporting stories or expressing political opinions that offended governments. In spite of the stresses of a deep political divide, increasing distrust of once trusted institutions, a pandemic, demonstrations calling for racial justice, and violence in the streets, the United States has remained largely free of government censorship and arbitrary detention and punishment.

This is true, in part, because freedom and liberty are part of this nation's DNA. It was, in part, the longing for freedom of religious thought that caused the English Puritan emigration from England to what was to become Plymouth, Massachusetts, in 1620. Later, the desire for freedom from the oppressive crown of England was the catalyst for the Declaration of Independence and the American Revolution. Finally, the fear that all governments tend to abuse their power led to the creation of a constitution that contains specific limits on governmental power and specific protections of individual rights. But what exactly is freedom?

*Freedom*, or liberty, is the ability to act without interference. In a political and legal sense, it means the ability to act free from the interference of government. However, even in the freest societies, personal behavior is limited. This is because the actions of every member of society have the potential, at times, to affect other members. The total absence of government is anarchy. Without government, there would be little control over behavior. The strong and cunning would prey on the weak and unintelligent; the licentious on the decent. Although it is true that to live in such a world would be living free from government interference, it would not be a life free of oppression and arbitrary harm.

To prevent anarchy and to protect people from one another, the people have entered into a **social contract** that defines the respective rights and responsibilities of

**social contract**
An implied agreement between all people that they will obey the laws and relinquish a measured amount of liberty in exchange for security.

**Exhibit 1–7** Maximizing Security and Liberty: The Tension Between Freedom and the Need for Governmental Protection

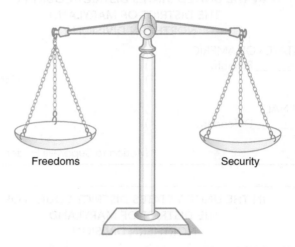

Freedoms                    Security

To reach the greatest individual freedom & personal security, unchecked individual freedom must be balanced with security to prevent & punish harmful behaviour.

the people and government. People implicitly agree to relinquish a measured amount of liberty, to obey the laws, and to be engaged in self-governance in exchange for a collective protection from one another and foreign threats. Maintaining the "right" balance between liberty and security is a perennial challenge (see Exhibit 1–7).

The Social Contract is expressed in the Preamble to the U.S. Constitution. It states:

> "We, the People of the United States, in order to form a more perfect union, establish justice, insure domestic tranquility, provide for the common defense, promote the general welfare, and secure the blessings of liberty to ourselves and our posterity, do ordain and establish this Constitution for the United States of America."

The idea is also found in the Declaration of Independence, where Thomas Jefferson penned:

> . . . that all Men are created equal, that they are endowed by their Creator with certain unalienable Rights, that among these are Life, Liberty, and the Pursuit of Happiness—That to secure these Rights, Governments are instituted among Men, deriving their just Powers from the Consent of the Governed."

Inherent in the Social Contract are limits on liberty. Per the common expression, "One person's liberty ends at the tips of the noses of other people." On the other hand, government must be controlled. As the British historian Lord Acton observed, absolute power corrupts absolutely. The Constitution establishes a zone of freedom over which government is prohibited from, or at least must have a very good reason for, regulating. The individual freedoms that comprise this zone are known as individual rights, civil rights, or **civil liberties**.

In nearly all nations, governmental involvement in the affairs of people is increasing. This is due in part to the increasing interdependence of the people. That is, members of society now depend on one another to provide goods and services that were once commonly self-provided. In addition, the staggering increase in world population has caused people to have much more contact with one another

**civil liberties**
Individual liberties guaranteed by the Constitution and, in particular, by the Bill of Rights.

than they did in the past. The larger the population, contact between people, and dependence of people on one another, the greater the number of conflicts and problems that will arise. These problems often demand governmental responses that can threaten liberty.

Crisis also tends to alter the security/liberty balance. This has been true during wars, when the government is given more latitude to restrict freedoms in the interest of national security. This isn't a new phenomenon. There is a Latin phrase that dates back a couple thousand years to express it, *inter arma enim silent leges*, which translates to "in times of war, law falls silent." War isn't the only crisis that leads to increases in governmental power. Consider, for example, the COVID-19 pandemic. The governmental response to the spread of the disease led to losses in liberty. The restrictions on social gatherings, the closure of businesses, mandatory masking, and the impact of those measures on speech, religion, and other rights would be quickly invalidated by the courts in normal circumstances. But the threat of an easily transmitted, quickly spreading, deadly disease was found by most courts to justify temporary suspensions of individual rights.

## Ethical Considerations

### Basics on Ethics in Criminal Law

This feature, which appears in every chapter of this book, examines a particular ethical issue or dilemma that attorneys, judges, legal assistants, law enforcement officers, and parties confront in criminal cases.

In criminal cases, the various parties are governed by different sets of rules. Attorneys are regulated by state bar authorities. Most state bar authorities have adopted a modified version of the American Bar Association's (ABA) model rules. The ABA first issued a set of rules, the Canons of Professional Ethics, in 1908. In the 1960s, the ABA issued a new set of rules under the title Model Code of Professional Responsibility. Then, 20 years later, the Model Rules of Professional Conduct were issued. Today, it is the Model Rules that most states have adopted, typically with modifications. Accordingly, the Model Rules will be referenced in this book.

State bar authorities, not the ABA, enforce ethics rules. Typical sanctions for violations are reprimands, suspensions of the right to practice, restitution, and disbarment, which is the permanent removal from the practice of law. Additionally, judges possess the authority to discipline violations by attorneys (actually anyone appearing before the court) and contemptuous behavior with fines, temporary incarceration, and other penalties. Although not regulated by state or federal governmental authorities, paralegals are guided by the National Association of Legal Assistants and the National Federation of Paralegal Association codes of professional conduct. More significantly, paralegals are indirectly regulated by state bars through their supervising attorneys, who are ultimately accountable for the research conducted by, and documents drafted by, their paralegals. Law enforcement officers are bound by state and federal laws and departmental rules.

Above all of these rules are the U.S. Constitution and the 50 state constitutions. Today, there is considerable constitutional case law that looks, smells, and tastes like ethics rules. Prosecuting attorneys, for example, are required to disclose evidence that tends to prove innocence to defendants. A violating prosecutor may be disciplined by a court, regardless of the bar's rules on the subject.

In each of the following chapters, a different dimension of ethics in criminal law will be explored more fully.

# Key Terms

appellate courts
Bill of Rights
briefs
certiorari
civil liberties
Commerce Clause
compensatory damages
concurrent jurisdiction
contract
cooperative federalism
court of record
courts of general jurisdiction

courts of limited jurisdiction
culpability
damages
de novo
dual federalism
federalism
inferior courts
intentional
interpret
judicial review
jurisdiction
negligence

police power
punitive damages
record
remand
separation of powers
social contract
statute
strict liability
terrorism
tort
trial courts

# Review Questions

1. What is the primary duty of the executive branch of government in criminal law?

2. Define the term "court of record."

3. Define jurisdiction and distinguish between a court of general jurisdiction and a court of limited jurisdiction.

4. What are the goals of criminal law? Civil law?

5. Who may file a civil suit? A criminal suit? How are these different?

6. What are compensatory damages? Punitive damages?

7. Should punitive damages be permitted in civil law? Explain your position.

8. Define culpability.

# Problems & Critical Thinking Exercises

1. In 1973, the U.S. Supreme Court handed down the famous case *Roe v. Wade*, 410 U.S. 113 (1973), wherein the Court determined that the decision to have an abortion is a private decision that is protected from government intervention, in some circumstances, by the U.S. Constitution. Suppose that a state legislature passes legislation (a state statute) that attempts to reverse the *Roe* decision by prohibiting all abortions in that state. Which is controlling in that state, the statute or the decision of the U.S. Supreme Court? Explain your answer.

2. Assume Congress responds to the COVID-19 pandemic with the following legislation. What are the constitutional arguments in favor of, and opposed to, the authority granted by Congress in each section?

Viral Disease Response and Recovery Act

*Section 1*

The President of the United States shall have the emergency authority to close the borders of the United States to commerce, immigration, and emigration, if needed to control the spread of disease that threatens the health and welfare of the people.

*Section 2*

The Director of the Center for Disease Control shall have the emergency authority to redirect the agency's appropriations to research and programs that are determined to be needed to address the outbreak of an infectious disease or other public health emergency.

*Section 3*

The President of the United States shall have the authority to close businesses, order the people into quarantine, and to regulate travel and commerce on all roads and highways in the United States to address the outbreak of an infectious disease or other public health emergency.

3. Assume that the U.S. Supreme Court has previously determined that regulation of traffic on county roads is a power reserved exclusively to the states. In reaction to this opinion, the U.S. Congress enacts a statute providing that the regulation of county roads will be within the jurisdiction of the U.S. Congress from that date forward. Your law office represents a client who is charged with violating the federal statute that prohibits driving on all roads while intoxicated. Do you have a defense? If so, explain.

4. In theory, people can increase their "freedom" by establishing a government and relinquishing freedoms (civil liberties) to that government. Explain why this paradox is true.

5. A bomb is exploded in a crowded shopping mall, killing 50 people and injuring hundreds of others. A written message is received at the local police station claiming that the attack was perpetrated by Foreigners for a New United States (FNUS), an established organization that has as its purpose the "destruction of the government of the United States and its citizens who support their government." Agents of the Federal Bureau of Investigation, working with local police, traced the message to Terry Ist, a leader of FNUS. Terry Ist was charged, convicted, and sentenced pursuant to the following federal statute:

**Terrorism**

   i. Terrorist organization: The Attorney General, upon credible evidence that an organization has as a purpose to bring harm to the United States or its citizens, may declare such organization a terrorist organization by publishing notice of such declaration in the *Federal Register*.

   ii. Any individual who is a member of a terrorist organization, as declared by the Attorney General in the previous section of this law, and who causes harm to person or property with the intent of (i) intimidating or coercing a civilian population; (ii) influencing the policy of a government by intimidation or coercion; or (iii) affecting the conduct of a government by mass destruction, assassination or kidnapping is guilty of terrorism, a felony.

   iii. The government of the United States shall have exclusive jurisdiction to prosecute individuals for all crimes arising from acts of terrorism, as defined by this law herein.

   After Terry Ist's conviction, the state where the bombing took place requested that Terry be turned over to it, where he was to be tried for murder and other offenses. The United States refused, citing section iii of the above law. Further, the U.S. Attorney filed a motion to have the case removed to federal court, along with an accompanying motion to dismiss the criminal action, asserting that section iii prohibits the state prosecution. Discuss the federalism issue, making the best case for both the state and federal governments. Conclude by explaining who should prevail and why.

# Endnotes

1. *Gamble v. United States*, 587 U.S. (2019)
2. 18 U.S.C. §2331.
3. *Printz v. United States*, 521 U.S. 98 (1997)
4. *United States v. Morrison*, 529 U.S. 598 (2000)
5. *Jones v. United States*, 529 U.S. 848 (2000)
6. *Gonzales v. Raich*, 545 U.S. 1 (2005)
7. *United States v. Comstock*, 560 U.S. 126 (2010)
8. 28 U.S.C. § 41 *et seq.*
9. For more on the separation of powers and federalism, See Daniel E. Hall and John P. Feldmeier, *Constitutional Law: Governmental Power and Individual Freedoms*, 4th ed. (Upper Saddle River, NJ: Prentice Hall Publishing, 2021), chapters 1–7. Chapter 1 contains a discussion of judicial review authority.
10. 517 U.S. 559 (1996).
11. 538 U.S. 408 (2003).
12. 554 U.S. 571 (2008).
13. 549 U.S. 346 (2007).

# Chapter 2

# Introduction to Criminal Law

## Criminal Law and Criminal Procedure Compared

Learning Objective: Define, compare, and contrast criminal law and criminal procedure.

This text is divided into two parts. The first part covers criminal law and the second part, criminal procedure. In all areas of legal study, a distinction is made between substance and procedure. Substantive law defines rights and obligations. Procedural law establishes the methods used to enforce legal rights and obligations. The substance of tort law defines what a tort is and what damages an injured party is entitled to recover from a lawsuit. Substantive contract law defines what a contract is, tells whether it must be in writing to be enforceable, who must sign it, what the penalty for breach is, and other such information. The field of civil procedure sets rules for how to bring the substance of the law before a court for resolution of a claim. To decide that a client has an injury that can be compensated under the law is a substantive decision. The question then becomes how injured clients get the compensation to which they are entitled. Procedural law tells you how to file a lawsuit, where to file, when to file, and how to prosecute the claim. Such is the case for criminal law and procedure.

**Criminal law**, as a field of law, defines what constitutes a crime and what punishment can be imposed for committing crimes. Criminal law also defines the defenses that a defendant may raise. So, in the first half of this book you will study a variety of crimes, such as murder, theft, and sexual assault, as well as several defenses, including mistake, insanity, and self-defense.

**criminal law**
The branch of the law that specifies what conduct constitutes crime, sets out the defenses to criminal accusations, and establishes punishments for such conduct.

Criminal procedure puts substantive criminal law into action. It is concerned with the processes used to bring criminals to justice, beginning with police investigation and continuing throughout the process of administering justice. When and under what conditions may a person be arrested? How and where must the criminal charge be filed? When can the police conduct a search? How does the accused assert a defense? How long can a person be held in custody by the police without charges being filed? How long after charges are filed does the accused have to wait before a trial is held? These are all examples of criminal procedure questions that you will learn in the latter half of this book.

In the remainder of the book, the term "criminal law" is used often. Often this refers to general criminal law, including both substantive criminal law and criminal procedure.

**criminal procedure**
The rules of procedure by which criminal prosecutions are governed.

# Why Punish?

Learning Objective: Compare and contrast the seven common purposes of punishing offenders.

There are two overarching philosophies to explain why conduct is criminalized and punished. The first is retributivism and the second, utilitarianism. To a retributivist, punishment is both needed and earned. For an offender to be right with themselves and the community, they need to "pay for their crimes." To the utilitarian, punishment isn't about retribution. It is about maximizing the greatest good for the greatest number of people. These two philosophies manifest in six commonly recognized objectives, or purposes, of criminal law. The first objective, retribution, is obviously retributivist. The other five—deterrence, rehabilitation, incapacitation, restitution, and restoration—are utilitarian. We begin by looking at deterrence.

## Specific and General Deterrence

There are two forms of **deterrence**. *Specific deterrence* seeks to deter individuals from reoffending. It is a negative reward theory. It assumes that people will make the rational choice to avoid being punished again. Of course, there are many factors at play, including whether the actor engages in rational thinking, the perceived likelihood of getting caught again, and the severity of the punishment when compared to the expected benefit of reoffending.

*General deterrence* attempts to deter all members of society from engaging in criminal activity. In theory, when the public observes Mr. X being punished for his actions, the public is deterred from behaving similarly for fear of the same punishment. Of course, individuals will react differently to the knowledge of Mr. X's punishment. Individuals weigh the risk of being caught and the level of punishment against the benefit of committing the crime. All people do this at one time or another. Have you ever intentionally run a stoplight? Jaywalked? If so, you have made the decision to violate the law. Neither crime involves a severe penalty. That fact, in addition to the likelihood of not being discovered by law enforcement agents, probably affected your decision.

Presumably, if conviction of either crime was punished by incarceration (time in jail), then the deterrent effect would be greater. Would you be as likely to jaywalk if you knew that you could spend time in jail for such an act? Some people would; others would not. It is safe to assume, however, that as the punishment increases, so does compliance. However, one author observed that it is not as effective to increase the punishment as it is to increase the likelihood of being punished.[1] It is unknown how much either of these factors influences behavior, but it is generally accepted that they both do.

**deterrence**
To prevent an individual from committing a crime.

## Incapacitation

*Incapacitation,* also referred to as restraint, is the third purpose of criminal punishment. Incapacitation does not seek to deter criminal conduct by influencing people's choices, but prevents criminal conduct by restraining those who have committed crimes. Criminals who are restrained in jail or prison—or in the extreme, executed—are incapable of causing harm to the general public. This theory is often the rationale for long-term imprisonment of individuals who are believed to be beyond rehabilitation. It is also promoted by those who lack faith in rehabilitation and believe that all criminals should be removed from society to prevent the chance of repetition.

Crimes that are caused by mental disease or occur in a moment of passion are not deterred because the individual does not have the opportunity to consider the punishment that will be inflicted for committing the crime before it is committed. Deterrence methods are effective only for individuals who are sufficiently intelligent to understand the consequences of their actions, are sane enough to understand the consequences of their actions, and who are not laboring under such uncontrollable feelings that an understanding that they may be punished is lost.

## Rehabilitation

*Rehabilitation* is another purpose for punishing offenders. The theory of rehabilitation is that if the criminal is subjected to educational and vocational programs, treatment and counseling, and other measures, it is possible to alter the individual's behavior to conform to social norms. As expressed by another author:

> To the extent that crime is caused by elements of the offender's personality, educational defects, lack of work skills, and the like, we should be able to prevent him from committing more crimes by training, medical and psychiatric help, and guidance into law-abiding patterns of behavior. Strictly speaking, rehabilitation is not "punishment," but help to the offender. However, since this kind of help is frequently provided while the subject is in prison or at large on probation or parole under a sentence that carries some condemnation and some restriction of freedom, it is customary to list rehabilitation as one of the objects of a sentence in a criminal case.[2]

The concept of rehabilitation has come under considerable scrutiny in recent years, in part because the success of rehabilitative programs is questionable. Advocates of rehabilitation point out, however, that these programs would be more successful if better funded.

## Retribution

*Retribution,* or societal vengeance, is the fourth purpose. Simply put, punishment through the criminal justice system is society's method of avenging a wrong. The idea that one who commits a wrong must be punished is an old one. The Old Testament speaks of an "eye for an eye." However, many people question the place of retribution in contemporary society. In reality, rarely is retribution the sole purpose. In most instances, society's desire for revenge can be satisfied while fulfilling one of the other purposes of punishment, such as incapacitation.

It has also been asserted that public retribution prevents private retribution.[3] That is, when the victim (or anyone who might avenge a victim) of a crime knows that the offender has been punished, the victim's need to seek revenge is lessened or removed. Therefore, punishing wrongdoers promotes social order by preventing vigilantism. Retribution in such instances has a deterrent effect, as victims of crimes are less likely to seek revenge. This is a good example of how the various purposes discussed are interrelated.

# Restitution

As you learned earlier, courts occasionally order offenders to compensate their victims for their actual losses. An accountant, for example, who embezzled $25,000 from a client may be ordered to repay the money, saving the victim from undergoing the expense and inconvenience of suing in civil court.

# Restoration

Restorative justice focuses on healing victims and restoring the offender to the community. The victim-in-fact, the victim's family, offender, offender's family, and the larger community are involved in the process. Inclusive open dialogue, mutual respect, and understanding are characteristics of restoration. Actions that are taken include financial restitution, an apology by the offender, forgiveness by the victim, community service, and possibly, incarceration. Restorative justice is commonly found in traditional communities. Although there is little history of restorative justice in the United States, interest in it is growing as the nation searches for alternatives to imprisonment. You will dig deeper into each of these objectives later in this chapter. But this provides us with enough information about the purposes of criminal law to compare with civil law.

See Exhibit 2–1 for a summary of purposes of the outcomes of both the criminal and civil law systems.

Finally, a sociological note. The criminal law isn't the only, nor is it always the best, form of social control. Education, at home and at school, is an important tool; religion and humanism, with their respective emphases on distinguishing between good and evil and respecting life, are others. The human desire to acquire and keep the affection and respect of family, friends, and associates no doubt has a great influence in deterring most people from bad conduct. The civil side of the law, which forces one to pay damages for the harmful results that one's undesirable conduct has caused to others, or which in inappropriate situations grants injunctions against bad conduct or orders the specific performance of good conduct, also plays a part in influencing behavior along desirable lines.[4]

# Where Does Criminal Law Come From?

Learning Objective: Define, describe, and apply the various sources of criminal law.

Criminal law exists in many forms, from many sources. Today, most law is made by legislatures. That is the U.S. Congress, state legislatures, and municipal councils and commissions. Further, administrative regulations now make up a much larger percentage of criminal law than in the past. This hasn't always been the case. This discussion begins with another form of law, judge-made law.

## The Common Law

The oldest form of criminal law in the United States is the **common law**. The common law developed in England and was brought to the United States by the English colonists.

> The common law, as it exists in this country, is of English origin. Founded on ancient local rules and customs and in feudal times, it began to evolve in the King's courts and was eventually molded into the viable principles through which it continues to operate. The common law migrated to this continent with the first English colonists, who claimed the system as their birthright; it continued in full force in the 13 original colonies until the American Revolution, at which time it was adopted by each of the states as well as the national government of the new nation.[5]

**common law**
The legal system that originated in England and is composed of case law and statutes that grow and change, influenced by ever-changing custom and tradition.

**Exhibit 2–1** The Purposes of Criminal and Civil Law Compared

| Purpose | Philosophy | Criminal Law | Civil Law |
|---|---|---|---|
| Deterrence | Utilitarianism | ✓ | ✓ |
| Retribution | Retributivism | ✓ | |
| Rehabilitation | Utilitarianism | ✓ | |
| Incapacitation | Utilitarianism | ✓ | |
| Restitution | Utilitarianism | ✓ | ✓ |
| Restoration | Utilitarianism | ✓ | |

**stare decisis**
Latin for "let the decision stand. The doctrine that judicial decisions stand as precedents for cases arising in the future.

**precedent**
Prior decisions of the same court, or a higher court, that a judge must follow in deciding a subsequent case presenting similar facts and the same legal problem, even though different parties are involved and many years have elapsed.

Simply stated, the common law is judge-made law. To understand how the common law developed, a bit of English legal history, particularly the concepts of precedence and **stare decisis**, is important. Beginning with William the Conqueror in 1066 (the "Norman Conquest"), the English monarchy began using law to reinforce the authority of the monarchy, to displace the preexisting system of feudal law, to promote economic stability and development, and to unify the kingdom. Prior to 1066, all law in England was feudal; it was local and varied between counties, which were known as the shires and hundreds. In the early years after the Norman Conquest, the king sent his judges to hear cases throughout the nation. These judges returned to London, where they discussed their decisions. This process, along with the creation of royal courts, led to the development of rules of court and legal doctrines that would be applied in all cases.

One such doctrine, intended to make the law consistent and predictable, held that a legal decision of a court was binding on itself and its inferior courts in the future. The specific decision of a court is known as a **precedent**. The idea that a court's precedent is binding going forward is expressed in Latin as *stare decisis et non quieta movera*. In English, this translates to "stand by precedents and do not disturb settled points." The Supreme Court of Indiana expressed its view of stare decisis:

> Under the doctrine of stare decisis, this Court adheres to a principle of law which has been firmly established. Important policy considerations militate in favor of continuity and predictability in the law. Therefore, we are reluctant to disturb longstanding precedent which involves salient issues. Precedent operates as a maxim for judicial restraint to prevent the unjustified reversal to a series of decisions merely because the composition of the court has changed.[6]

The impact of having royal courts with national authority issuing decisions that bound lower courts was that England, for the first time in its history, had a set of laws that were *common to all people*. Hence, it became known as the Common Law. This didn't happen overnight. It took hundreds of years for the courts and the Common Law to fully develop.

> The common law, as frequently defined, includes those principles, usages, and rules of action applicable to the government and security of persons and property which do not rest for their authority upon any express or positive statute or other written declaration, but upon statements of principles found in the decisions of courts. The common law is inseparably identified with the decisions of the courts and can be determined only from such decisions in former cases bearing upon the subject under inquiry. As distinguished from

statutory or written law, it embraces the great body of unwritten law founded upon general custom, usage, or common consent, and based upon natural justice or reason. It may otherwise be defined as custom long acquiesced in or sanctioned by immemorial usage and judicial decision. . . .

In a broader sense the common law is the system of rules and declarations of principles from which our judicial ideas and legal definitions are derived, and which are continually expanding. It is not a codification of exact or inflexible rules for human conduct, for the redress of injuries, or for protection against wrongs, but is rather the embodiment of broad and comprehensive unwritten principles, inspired by natural reason and an innate sense of justice, and adopted by common consent for the regulation and government of the affairs of men.[7]

As expressed in the above quotation, the common law is dynamic, adapting to meet contemporary challenges. As one court stated, "The common law of the land is based upon human experience in the unceasing effort of an enlightened people to ascertain what is right and just between men."[8]

While courts (and the monarch) were responsible for making law in the early years of the common law, the situation changed with the advent of Parliament in the thirteen and fourteenth centuries. Although early Parliament had very limited authority, it eventually evolved into the general lawmaking body of England, displacing courts in the lawmaking function. Today, legislatures in all common law nations are the primary lawmakers. In the United States, the Congress of the United States is the federal lawmaker and the legislatures of the states are each responsible for making state laws. However, for reasons detailed later, courts continue to play an important role in the development of the common law.

What this meant for criminal law is that judges created crimes and defenses, as they heard cases. As time passed, established "common law crimes" developed. First the courts determined what acts should be criminal, and then the specifics of each crime developed; what exactly had to be proved to establish guilt, what defenses were available, and what punishment was appropriate for conviction. Let's imagine how this happened. At some point in time, nearly a thousand years ago, a man killed his neighbor who insulted him. A local official known as a shire-reeve (today, a sheriff) brought the man who committed the homicide to a court. That court declared the homicide to be a crime, naming it murder and ordering the defendant's death. A precedent was set; murders were to be punished by death. But years later the court is faced with a different case. A defendant is brought before the court for killing a man who inexplicably attacked him with an axe. In this case, the court decides that a person may use deadly force in self-defense and sets the defendant free. A new precedent, building on what came before, has been established. This process continues in perpetuity.

The 13 original states all adopted the common law. Most did so through their state constitutions. Today, nearly all of the states have forbidden courts from creating new crimes. This responsibility falls to democratically elected legislatures, which have the authority to amend or abolish judge-made law. Subject to these limitations, courts occasionally recognize new defenses, interpret statutory law, and continue to interpret and define old Common Law doctrines. One caveat on the authority of legislatures to set aside judge-made law is needed. Legislatures don't have the authority to change judicial interpretations of constitutional law. These can only be changed by a higher court or through constitutional amendment.

## The Principle of Legality

Whether common law crimes should continue to exist is debated. Those who favor permitting common law crimes believe courts to need the authority to "fill in the gaps" left by the legislatures when those bodies either fail to foresee all potential crimes or simply forget to include a crime that was foreseen. However, a separation of powers question is raised by this scenario: namely, should the judicial branch actively second-guess or clean house for the legislative branch? Such conduct does appear to be the exercise of legislative authority. However, few people want intentionally dangerous or disruptive behavior not to be criminalized, and it appears to be impossible for legislatures to foresee all possible acts that are dangerous and disruptive.

Those who oppose a common law of crimes point to the concept embodied in the phrase *nullum crimen sine lege*, which translates roughly to "there is no crime if there is no statute." Similarly, *nulla poena sine lege* has come to mean that "there shall be no punishment if there is no statute." These concepts, when considered in concert, insist that the criminal law must be written, that the written law must exist at the time that the accused committed the act in question, and that criminal laws be more precise than civil laws.[9] This is the *principle of legality*.

The legality principle is premised on the common sense idea that people are entitled to know, prior to committing an act, that the act may be punished. This is commonly referred to as *notice*. The idea is consistent with general notions of fairness and justice, not only in the United States but to peoples around the world. All that is required is notice of the law, not that every individual prosecuted under the law have actual knowledge of it. The law imposes a duty on all people to be aware of written law. As is commonly said, "ignorance of the law is no excuse." The *Keeler* case discusses the legality principle.

The *Keeler* is an opinion of the California Supreme Court; therefore, it is not the law of all of the United States. Similar decisions have been made in other states, however.

## Oyez

### Keeler v. Superior Court
#### 2 Cal. 3d 619, 470 P.2d 617 (Ca. Supreme Court 1970)

**Mosk, J.**

In this proceeding for writ of prohibition, we are called upon to decide whether an unborn viable fetus is a "human being" within the meaning of the California statute defining murder. We conclude that the legislature did not intend such a meaning, and that for us to construe the statute to the contrary and apply it to this petitioner would exceed our judicial power and deny petitioner due process of law.

The evidence received at the preliminary examination may be summarized as follows: Petitioner and Teresa Keeler obtained an interlocutory decree of divorce on September 27, 1968. They had been married for sixteen years. Unknown to the petitioner, Mrs. Keeler was then pregnant by one Ernest Vogt, whom she had met earlier that summer. She subsequently began living with Vogt in Stockton, but concealed the fact from petitioner. Petitioner was given custody of their two daughters, aged 12 and 13 years, and under the decree Mrs. Keeler had the right to take the girls on alternate weekends.

On February 23, 1969, Mrs. Keeler was driving on a narrow mountain road in Amador County after delivering the girls to their home. She met petitioner driving in the opposite direction; he blocked the road with his car, and she pulled over to the side. He walked to her vehicle and began speaking to her. He seemed calm, and she rolled down her window to hear him. He said, "I hear you're pregnant. If you are, you had better stay away from the girls and from here." She did not reply, and he opened the car door; as she later testified, "He assisted me out of the car . . . [I]t wasn't rough at this time." Petitioner then looked at her abdomen and became "extremely upset." He said, "You sure are. I'm going to stomp it out of you." He pushed her against the car, shoved his knee into her abdomen, and struck her in the face with several blows. She fainted, and when she regained consciousness, petitioner had departed.

Mrs. Keeler drove back to Stockton, and the police and medical assistance were summoned. She had suffered substantial facial injuries, as well as extensive bruising of the abdominal wall. A Caesarian section was performed, and the fetus was examined in utero. Its head was found to be severely fractured, and it was delivered stillborn. The pathologist gave as his opinion that the cause of death was skull fracture with consequent cerebral hemorrhaging, that death would be immediate, and that the injury could have been the result of force applied to the mother's abdomen. There was no air in the fetus' lungs, and the umbilical cord was intact. . . .

The evidence was in conflict as to the estimated age of the fetus; the expert testimony on the point, however, concluded "with reasonable medical certainty" that the fetus had developed to the stage of viability, i.e., that in the event of premature birth on the date in question, it would have had a 75 percent to 96 percent chance of survival.

(continued)

An information was filed charging petitioner, in count I, with committing the crime of murder. . . .

Penal Code section 187 provides: "Murder is the unlawful killing of a human being, with malice aforethought." The dispositive question is whether the fetus which petitioner is accused of killing was, on February 23, 1969, a "human being" within the meaning of the statute. If it was not, petitioner cannot be charged with its "murder". . . .

■  ■  ■

We conclude that in declaring murder to be the unlawful and malicious killing of a "human being," the Legislature of 1850 intended that term to have the settled common law meaning of a person who had been born alive, and did not intend the act of feticide—as distinguished from abortion—to be an offense under the laws of California.

■  ■  ■

The People urge, however that the sciences of obstetrics and pediatrics have greatly progressed since 1872, to the point where, with proper medical care, a normally developed fetus prematurely born . . . is "viable" . . . since an unborn but viable fetus is now fully capable of independent life. . . . But we cannot join in the conclusion sought to be deduced: we cannot hold this petitioner to answer for murder by reason of his alleged act of killing an unborn—even though viable—fetus. To such a charge there are two insuperable obstacles, one "jurisdictional" and the other constitutional.

Penal Code section 6 declares in relevant part that "No act or omission" accomplished after the code has taken effect "is criminal or punishable, except as prescribed by this code. . . ." This section embodies a fundamental principle of our tripartite form of government, i.e., that subject to the constitutional prohibition against cruel and unusual punishment, the power to define crimes and fix penalties is vested exclusively in the legislative branch. Stated differently, there are no common law crimes in California. . . . In order that a public offense be committed, some statute, ordinance or regulation prior in time to the commission of the act, must denounce it.

■  ■  ■

Applying these rules to the case at bar, we would undoubtedly act in excess of the judicial power if we were to adopt the People's proposed construction of section 187. As we have shown, the Legislature has defined the crime of murder in California to apply only to the unlawful and malicious killing of one who has been born alive. We recognize that the killing of an unborn but viable fetus may be deemed by some to be an offense of similar nature and gravity; but as Chief Justice Marshall warned long ago: "It would be dangerous, indeed, to carry the principle that a case which is within the reason or mischief of a statute, is within its provisions, so far as to punish a crime not enumerated in the statute, because it is of equal atrocity, or of kindred character, with those which are enumerated." . . . Whether to thus extend liability for murder in California is a determination solely within the province of the Legislature. For a court to simply declare, by judicial fiat, that the time has now come to prosecute under section 187 one who kills an unborn but viable fetus would indeed be to rewrite the statute under the guise of construing it. . . . to make it "a judicial function". . . "raises very serious questions concerning the principle of separation of powers."

The second obstacle to the proposed judicial enlargement of section 187 is the guarantee of due process of law. . . .

The first essential of due process is fair warning of the act which is made punishable as a crime. "That the terms of a penal statute creating a new offense must be sufficiently explicit to inform those who are subject to it what conduct on their part will render them liable to its penalties, is a well-recognized requirement, consonant alike with ordinary notions of fair play and the settled rules of law."

Also note that the court determined that the common law violates "ordinary notions of fair play" and that no warning or notice was given to Keeler that his act could be defined as murder. As the court noted, these requirements are embodied in the **due process** clauses of the U.S. Constitution and the constitutions of the many states. There are two dimensions to due process, procedural and substantive. Procedural due process, in both civil and criminal law, requires that individuals be put on notice of impending government action, be given an opportunity to be heard and to present evidence, and in some cases, benefit from other rights, such as having counsel appointed and having the case heard by a jury. Substantive due process recognizes individual rights to act or not to act. For example, privacy is not explicitly protected in the Constitution of the United States. Regardless, the Supreme Court has found an implicit right to privacy in the due process clauses' protection of liberty. Through this implicit right, the Court has invalidated laws prohibiting interracial marriage, prohibiting the use of contraception by married persons, and prohibiting women from ending pregnancies in some circumstances.

**due process**
The *due process* clauses of the Fifth and Fourteenth Amendments to the U.S. Constitution require that no persons be deprived of life, liberty, or property without having notice and a real chance to present their side in a legal dispute.

### Other Uses of the Common Law

Even in those jurisdictions that have abandoned use of the common law to create crimes, the common law continues to be important for many reasons.

First, many statutes mirror the common law in language. That is, legislatures often simply codify the common law's criminal prohibitions. Hence, when a question arises concerning whether a particular act of a defendant is intended to fall under the intent of a criminal prohibition, the case law handed down prior to codification of the common law may answer the question. The result is that the crime remains the same, but the source of the prohibition has changed. It is also possible for a legislature to change only part of a common law definition and leave the remainder the same. If so, prior case law may be helpful when considering the unaltered portion of the definition.

Second, many of the concepts developed at the common law are still recognized. For example, the distinction between felonies and misdemeanors continues today. Although jurisdictions vary in definition, a felony is a serious crime usually punishable by more than one year in prison. A misdemeanor is less serious and usually is punishable by one year or less in jail.

Third, legislatures occasionally enact a criminal prohibition without establishing the potential penalty for violation. In such cases, courts will often look to the penalties applied to similar common law crimes for guidance.

Fourth, in addition to defining crimes, the common law established many procedures that were used to adjudicate criminal cases. These procedures most often dealt with criminal defenses. What defenses could be raised, as well as how and when, were often answered by the common law. For example, the various tests to determine if a defendant was sane when an alleged crime was committed were developed under the common law. If a legislature has not specifically changed these procedural rules, they remain in effect, even if the power of courts to create common law crimes has been abolished.

## Statutory Law

As you have already learned, the legislative branch is responsible for the creation of law. You have also learned that legislatures possess the authority to modify, abolish, or adopt the common law, in whole or in part. During the nineteenth century, the codification of criminal law began.[10] This effectively displaced the role of the judiciary in defining crimes.

Although the power of the legislative branch to declare behavior criminal is significant, there are limits. The U.S. Constitution and many state constitutions contain limits on such state and federal authority. Most of these limits are found in the Bill of Rights. For example, the First Amendment to the federal Constitution prohibits government, with few exceptions, from punishing an individual for exercising choice of religion and for expressing opinions and thoughts. If a legislature enacts a law that violates a constitutional right, a court will strike it down. This is the power of judicial review, which you studied in Chapter 1. You will learn much more about the rights that apply in criminal cases in later chapters.

## Ordinances

**ordinance**
A local or city law, rule, or regulation.

**Ordinances** are laws enacted by city, county, and other local governments. Most ordinances are administrative or civil. But most municipalities are also empowered by their states to make criminal laws. In some instances, criminal ordinances simply mirror state statutes. For example, many cities have assault and battery ordinances, just as their states have assault and battery statutes. Traffic and parking violations may also be criminal, although some cities pursue these as civil violations, which permits enabling the state to pursue criminal charges for the same act. But cities and counties also enact laws unique to their settings and needs.

Ordinances may not conflict with state or federal law. Any ordinance that is inconsistent with higher law may be invalidated by a court. States limit the power of cities to punish for ordinance violations, and most city court trials are to the bench, not to a jury.

## Constitutional Law

Finally, constitutional law is included in this list of sources of criminal law, not because it defines what conduct is criminal but because of its significant impact on criminal law. Specifically, the U.S. Constitution, primarily through the Bill of Rights, is responsible for establishing many of the rules governing criminal procedure. You will become more aware of why this is true as you learn more about criminal law and procedure. See Exhibit 2–2 for a listing of a few of the most important events in the history of the U.S. Constitution.

Although it is common for courses in criminal procedure to focus on the U.S. Constitution, state constitutions are also important. Most state constitutions protect the same rights that are found in the U.S. Constitution. The right to be free from unreasonable searches and seizures, for example, is found in the U.S. Constitution and every state constitution. Although the U.S. Constitution is the highest form of law and the states may not infringe on the rights it protects, the states may enlarge their counterpart rights, and they may create rights not expressly found in the U.S. Constitution. You will see examples of state protections that extend beyond the U.S. Constitution in future chapters.

## Exhibit 2–2 Important Dates in the History of the U.S. Constitution

| | |
|---|---|
| May 25, 1787 | Constitutional Convention opens in Philadelphia. |
| September 17, 1787 | Constitutional Convention closes, delegates sign the Constitution, and it is sent to the states for ratification. This is recognized as Constitution (and Citizenship) Day by federal law. |
| December 6, 1787 | Delaware is the first state to ratify the Constitution. |
| June 21, 1788 | New Hampshire is the ninth state to ratify and thereby provides the requisite number of ratifying states to adopt the Constitution for the entire United States. |
| May 29, 1790 | Rhode Island is the thirteenth (last) state to ratify the Constitution. |
| December 15, 1791 | Bill of Rights is ratified. |
| December 6, 1865 | Thirteenth Amendment, abolishing slavery, is ratified. |
| July 28, 1868 | Fourteenth Amendment, providing for due process, equal protection, and privileges and immunities, is ratified. |
| February 3, 1870 | Fifteenth Amendment, prohibiting the vote from being withheld for race, color, or previous servitude, is ratified. |
| May 7, 1992 | The Twenty-seventh Amendment, the last to date, was ratified. Addressing the raises for members of Congress, the amendment is the last to be ratified even though it was one of the original 12 amendments to be proposed. |

Independence Hall in Philadelphia, PA, served as the Pennsylvania State House, venue for the Second Continental Congress, and where the Declaration of Independence and Constitution were both debated and drafted.

## Administrative Law

It is likely that you have already had business with a government agency. Agencies are governmental units, federal, state, and local, that administer the affairs of the government. There are two types of agencies: social welfare and regulatory. The two names reflect the purposes behind each type. Social welfare agencies put into effect government programs. For example, in Indiana, the State Department of Public Welfare administers the distribution of public money to those deemed needy. In contrast, state medical licensing boards are regulatory, because their duty is to oversee and regulate the practice of medicine in the various states. Regulatory and administrative agencies both receive their delegation of authority from the legislative branch.

Because legislatures do not possess the time or the expertise to write detailed law, they often enact general statutes with delegations to one or more administrative agencies to further detail the law. Just as legislative enactments are known as statutes (or codes), administrative laws are known as **regulations** or rules. The extent to which a legislature may delegate its lawmaking authority, if at all, has been a continuing source of disagreement. Some scholars argue that legislatures may not grant such an important legislative function to agencies. Doing so is believed to be a violation of the principle of separation of powers, because agencies typically fall into the executive branch of government.

In spite of the separation of powers problem, the U.S. Supreme Court has determined that agencies may create regulations that have the effect of law. This includes criminal prohibitions. The Court's opinion on how much authority may be delegated to administrative agencies has undergone a few changes over the years. In 1911, the U.S. Supreme Court handed down the opinion in the *Grimaud* case, the subject of your next Oyez.

*Grimaud* is the law today. Agencies may be delegated penal rulemaking authority. However, the Supreme Court has said that Congress may not delegate the responsibility of establishing penalties to an agency, with the possible exception of small fines. Congress must either set the precise penalty or set a range from which an agency can further determine the appropriate penalty.

An interesting question concerns how much guidance Congress must give an agency in its delegation. Because Congress is delegating its power to create law

**regulation**
Law created by governmental administrative agencies.

# Oyez

## United States v. Grimaud
### 220 U.S. 506 (1911)

The defendants were indicted for grazing sheep on the Sierra Forest Reserve without having obtained the permission required by the regulations adopted by the Secretary of Agriculture. They demurred on the ground that the Forest Reserve Act of 1891 was unconstitutional, insofar as it delegated to the Secretary of Agriculture power to make rules and regulations and made a violation thereof a penal offense.

■ ■ ■

From the various acts relating to the establishment and management of forest reservations it appears that they were intended "to improve and protect the forest and to secure favorable conditions to water flows." . . . It was also declared that the Secretary "may make such rules and regulations and establish such service as will insure the objects of such reservation, namely, to regulate their occupancy and use to prevent the forests thereon from destruction; *and any violation of the provisions of this act or such* rules and regulations shall be punished," as is provided in [the statute].

Under these acts, therefore, any use of the reservations for grazing or other lawful purpose was required to be subject to the rules and regulations established by the Secretary of Agriculture. To pasture sheep and cattle on the reservation, at will and without restraint, might interfere seriously with the accomplishment of the purposes for which they were established. But a limited and regulated use for pasturage might not be inconsistent with the object sought to be attained by the statute. The determination of such questions, however, was a matter of administrative detail. What might be harmless in one forest might be harmful to another. What might be injurious at one stage of timber growth, or at one season of the year, might not be so at another.

In the nature of things, it was impracticable for Congress to provide general regulations for these various and varying details of management. Each reservation had its peculiar and special features; and in authorizing the Secretary of Agriculture to meet these local conditions, Congress was merely conferring administrative functions upon an agent, and not delegating to him legislative power.

■ ■ ■

It must be admitted that it is difficult to define the line which separates the legislative power to make laws from the administrative authority to make regulations. This difficulty has often been recognized [as] referred to by Chief Justice Marshall . . . : "It will not be contended that Congress can delegate to the courts, or to any other tribunals, powers which are strictly and exclusively legislative. But Congress may certainly delegate to others, powers which the legislature may rightfully exercise itself." What were these non-legislative powers which Congress could exercise but which also might be delegated to others was not determined, for he said: "The line has not been exactly drawn which separates those important subjects, which must be entirely regulated by the legislature itself, from those of less interest, in which a general provision may be made, and power given to those who are to act under such general provisions to fill up the details."

From the beginning of the Government, various acts have been passed conferring upon the executive officers power to make rules and regulations—not for the government of their departments but for administering the laws which did govern. None of these statutes could confer legislative power. But when Congress had legislated and indicated its will, it could give to those who were to act under such general provisions "power to fill up the details" by the establishment of administrative rules and regulations, the violation of which could be punished by fine or imprisonment fixed by Congress, or by penalties fixed by Congress or measured by the injury done.

■ ■ ■

It is true that there is no act of Congress which, in express terms, declares that it shall be unlawful to graze sheep on a forest reserve. But the statutes, from which we have quoted, declare that the privilege of using reserves for "all proper and lawful purposes" is subject to the proviso that the person shall comply "with the rules and regulations covering such forest reservation." The same act makes it an offense to violate those regulations.

■ ■ ■

The Secretary of Agriculture could not make rules and regulations for any and every purpose. As to those here involved, they all regulate matters clearly indicated and authorized by Congress.

to an agency, it is expected to give the agency some guidance as to what it wants. This limits the discretion of the agency and prevents it from becoming a substitute legislature.[11] Normally, Congress must provide an intelligible principle or sufficient standards to guide an agency.[12] It takes little congressional guidance to satisfy these tests. Due to the special nature of criminal law (i.e., the deprivation to liberty that may result from a criminal conviction), defendants have argued that Congress must be more specific, or give an agency less discretion, when delegating the authority to create penal rules, as opposed to non-penal rules. The Supreme Court refused to answer that question in *Touby v. United States*.

*Touby* illustrates that an agency may be delegated the authority to declare acts criminal and that Congress must provide at least an "intelligible principle," and possibly more, when making this type of delegation. Congress may not delegate the authority to set a penalty to an agency, although it may allow the agency to set the penalty for a violation from within statutory guidelines. An agency may not, however, establish more serious penalties, such an imprisonment, even if the sentences fall within statutory limits.

While agencies may not sentence individuals to imprisonment, legislatively endorsed, noncriminal deprivations of freedom may be ordered by agencies in rare circumstances, such as during quarantines, for psychiatric evaluations and treatment, and to detain illegal immigrants.

An interesting contemporary issue is the extent to which private parties may be delegated governmental powers. For example, in some states, fines levied by homeowner and condominium associations are enforceable in courts. While this area of law is in development and much remains to be defined, a few general principles can be deduced. First, private parties may not, or have very limited authority to, punish individuals. Second, when private parties are acting on the behalf of a government, they are bound by the same rules that apply to the government.[13]

## Sidebar

### Finding Administrative Regulations

Federal administrative rules are found in the Code of Federal Regulations (C.F.R.). New rules that have not yet been added to the C.F.R. may be found in the *Federal Register*. Each state has its counterpart publications. For example, in Florida they are the Florida Administrative Code and the *Florida Administrative Weekly*, respectively.

## Oyez

### Touby v. United States
### 500 U.S. 160 (1991)

O'CONNOR, J., delivered the opinion for a unanimous Court.

Petitioners were convicted of manufacturing and conspiring to manufacture "Euphoria," a drug temporarily designated as a schedule I controlled substance pursuant to § 201(h) of the Controlled Substances Act. We consider whether § 201(h) unconstitutionally delegates legislative power to the Attorney General and whether the Attorney General's subdelegation to the Drug Enforcement Administration (DEA) was authorized by statute. . . .

[T]he Controlled Substances Act (Act) . . . establishes five categories or "schedules" of controlled substances, the manufacture, possession, and distribution of which the Act regulates or prohibits. Violations involving schedule I substances carry the most severe penalties, as these substances are believed to pose the most serious threat to public safety. Relevant here, § 201(a) of the Act authorizes the Attorney General to add or remove substances, or to move a substance from one schedule to another. . . .

When adding a substance to a schedule, the Attorney General must follow specified procedures. First, the Attorney General must request a scientific and medical evaluation from the Secretary of Health and Human Services (HHS), together with a recommendation as to whether the substances should be controlled. A substance cannot be scheduled if the Secretary recommends against it. . . . Second, the Attorney General must consider eight factors with respect to the substance, including its potential for abuse, scientific evidence of its pharmacological effect, its psychic or physiological dependence liability, and whether the substance is an immediate precursor of a substance already controlled. . . . Third, the Attorney General must comply with notice-and-hearing provisions of the Administrative Procedure Act . . . which permit comment by interested parties. . . . In addition, the Act permits any aggrieved person to challenge the scheduling of a substance by the Attorney General in a court of appeals. . . .

It takes time to comply with these procedural requirements. From the time when law enforcement officials identify a dangerous new drug, it typically takes 6 to 12 months to add it to one of the schedules. . . . Drug traffickers were able to take advantage of this time gap by designing drugs that were similar in pharmacological effect to scheduled substances but differing slightly in chemical composition, so that existing schedules did not apply to them. These "designer drugs" were developed and widely marketed long before the Government was able to schedule them and initiate prosecutions. . . .

To combat the "designer drug" problem, Congress in 1984 amended the Act to create an expedited procedure by which the Attorney General can schedule a substance on a temporary basis when doing so is "necessary to avoid an imminent hazard to the public safety." . . . Temporary scheduling under § 201(h) allows the Attorney General to bypass, for a limited time, several of the requirements for permanent scheduling. The Attorney General need consider only three of the eight factors required for permanent scheduling. . . . Rather than comply with the APA notice-and-hearing provisions, the Attorney General need provide only a 30-day notice of proposed scheduling in the Federal Register. . . . Notice also must be transmitted to the Secretary of HHS, but the Secretary's prior approval of a proposed scheduling is not required. . . . Finally . . . an order to schedule a substance temporarily "is not subject to judicial review."

Because it has fewer procedural requirements, temporary scheduling enables the government to respond more quickly to the threat posed by dangerous new drugs. A temporary scheduling order can be issued 30 days after a new drug is identified, and the order remains valid for one year. During this 1-year period, the Attorney General presumably will initiate the permanent scheduling process. . . .

The Attorney General promulgated regulations delegating to the DEA his powers under the Act, including the power to schedule controlled substances on a temporary basis. Pursuant to that delegation, the DEA Administrator issued an order scheduling . . . "Euphoria" as a schedule I controlled substance. . . .

While the temporary scheduling order was in effect, DEA agents, executing a valid search warrant, discovered a fully operational drug laboratory in Daniel and Lyrissa Touby's home. The Toubys were indicted for manufacturing and conspiring to manufacture Euphoria. They moved to dismiss the indictment on the grounds that § 201(h) unconstitutionally delegates legislative power to the Attorney General. . . . The United States District Court for the District of New Jersey denied the motion to dismiss . . . and the Court of Appeals for the Third Circuit affirmed. . . . We granted certiorari . . . and now affirm.

The Constitution provides that "all legislative Powers herein granted shall be vested in a Congress of the United States." From this language the Court has derived the nondelegation doctrine: that Congress may not constitutionally delegate its legislative power to another Branch of government. "The nondelegation doctrine is rooted in the principle of separation of powers that underlies our tripartite system of Government." . . .

We have long recognized that nondelegation does not prevent Congress from seeking assistance, within proper limits, from its coordinate Branches. . . . Thus, Congress does not violate the Constitution merely because it legislates in broad terms, leaving a certain degree of discretion to executive or judicial actors. So long as Congress "lay[s] down by legislative act an intelligible principle to which the person or body authorized to [act] is directed to conform, such legislative action is not a forbidden delegation of legislative power." . . .

Petitioners wisely concede that Congress has set forth in § 201(h) an "intelligible principle" to constrain the Attorney General's discretion to schedule controlled substances on a temporary basis. . . . Petitioners suggest, however, that something more than an "intelligible principle" is required when Congress authorizes another Branch to promulgate regulations that contemplate criminal sanctions. They contend that regulations of this sort pose a heightened risk to individual liberty and that Congress must therefore provide more specific guidance. Our cases are not entirely clear as to whether or not more specific guidance is in fact required. . . . We need not resolve the issue today. We conclude that § 201(h) passes muster even if greater congressional specificity is required in the criminal context.

Although it features fewer procedural requirements than the permanent scheduling statute, § 201(h) meaningfully constrains the Attorney General's discretion to define criminal conduct. . . .

It is clear that in § 201(h) and § 202(b), Congress has placed multiple restrictions on the Attorney General's discretion to define criminal conduct. These restrictions satisfy the constitutional requirements of the nondelegation doctrine.

## Court Rules

Just as administrative agencies need the authority to "fill in the gaps" of legislation because statutes are not specific enough to satisfy all of an agency's needs, so do courts. The U.S. Congress and all of the state legislatures have enacted some form of statute establishing general rules of civil and criminal procedure. However, to fill in the gaps left by legislatures, courts adopt **court rules**, which also govern civil and criminal processes. Although court rules deal with procedural issues (such as service of process, limits on the length of briefs and memoranda, and timing of filing) and not substantive issues, they are important. Of course, court rules may not

**court rules**
Rules promulgated by the court, governing procedure or practice before it.

conflict with legislative mandates. If a rule does conflict with a statute, the statute is controlling. One exception to this rule may be when the statute is unconstitutional and the rule is a viable alternative, but discussion of this situation is best left to a course on constitutional law and judicial process.

Most court rules are drafted under the direction of the highest court of the state and become effective by either vote of the court or presentation to the state legislature for ratification. In the federal system, the rules are drafted by the Judicial Conference under the direction of the Supreme Court and then presented to Congress. If Congress fails to act to nullify the rules, they become law. Of course, Congress may amend the rules at will. Many jurisdictions also have local rules, that is, rules created by local courts for practice in those courts. The rules cannot conflict with either statutes or higher court rules. In the federal system, district courts adopt local rules. Being familiar with the rules of the courts in your jurisdiction is imperative. If you are not, you may miss important deadlines, file incomplete documents, or have your filings stricken.

## The Model Penal Code

**Model Penal Code**
A proposed criminal code prepared jointly by the Commission on Uniform State Laws and the American Law Institute.

On occasion, the **Model Penal Code** and Commentaries (MPC) will be referenced in this text. Commissioned by the American Law Institute (ALI) and drafted by criminal law scholars and practitioners, the MPC was issued in 1962. The MPC was intended to establish a uniform approach to criminal law. The MPC isn't law until adopted by a legislature. It has been highly influential, having been adopted, in varying degrees, by nearly every state. The ALI periodically revises sections of the MPC. In 2020, the ALI was considering updates to the sexual offenses sections to bring them into alignment with contemporary standards. Because its provisions have been made law is so many states, the MPC is often referenced in the first half of this book. See Exhibit 2-3 for a summary of the sources of criminal law.

## Exhibit 2–3 Sources of Criminal Law

| Source | Comment |
| --- | --- |
| Constitutions | The United States and every individual state have a constitution. The U.S. Constitution is the supreme law of the land. Amendment of the federal Constitution requires a two-thirds vote by both houses of the U.S. Congress and approval by three-fourths of the states, or in the alternative, for two-thirds of the states to call for a constitutional convention and approval of three-fourths of the states of any suggested amendments. All existing amendments were enacted using the first method. |
| Statutes | The written law created by legislatures, also known as codes. State statutes may not conflict with either their own constitution or the federal Constitution. State statutes also are invalid if they conflict with other federal law, and the federal government has concurrent jurisdiction with the states. Statutes of the United States are invalid if they conflict with the U.S. Constitution or if they attempt to regulate outside federal jurisdiction. Legislatures may change statutes at will. |
| Common Law | Law that evolved, as courts, through judicial opinions, recognized customs, and practices. Legislatures may alter, amend, or abolish the common law at will. In criminal law, the common law is responsible for the creation of crimes and for establishing defenses to crimes. |
| Regulations | Created by administrative agencies under a grant of authority from a legislative body. Regulations must be consistent with statutes and constitutions and may not exceed the legislative grant of power. The power to make rules and regulations is granted to "fill in the gaps" left by legislatures when drafting statutes. |
| Ordinances | Written law of local bodies, such as city councils. Must be consistent with all higher forms of law. |
| Model Penal Code | Written under the direction of the American Law Institute. It was drafted by experts in criminal law to be presented to the states for adoption. It is not law until a state has adopted it, in whole or in part. More than half of the states have adopted at least part of the Model Penal Code. |
| Court Rules | Rules created by courts to manage their cases. Court rules are procedural and commonly establish deadlines, lengths of filings, and so on. Court rules may not conflict with statutes or constitutions. |

## Ethical Considerations

### Defending Individuals Charged with Horrendous Crimes

Defense attorneys are not held in the highest regard by all people, many of whom assume that a defense attorney's willingness to defend individuals charged with horrendous crimes is a reflection of the attorney's values. In actuality, this conclusion is correct, but there is a disconnect between the value that motivates an attorney to defend an individual charged with a horrendous crime and the value that many individuals apply in judging the attorney for the decision. Defense attorneys are often judged by individuals who apply personal values to them, while the attorneys must apply professional values.

The two model codes from which the states have enacted their rules that govern attorney ethics, the Model Rules of Professional Conduct and Model Code of Professional Responsibility, require attorneys to zealously represent their clients, regardless of the alleged crime. This requirement does not exist in a vacuum. The entire U.S. system of justice is built upon the idea that if you have two opposed parties, each with a loyal, zealous advocate, the truth will be unveiled to the fact finder. This *adversarial system* was developed in England and exists, in various forms, in all common law nations.

The obligation of defense attorneys to zealously represent their clients and to maintain their clients' confidentiality is not without a price. Defense attorneys are the subject of public disdain and ridicule. In some circumstances, their professional and personal lives are injured when they are called upon to defend unpopular defendants. An example of this is the attorney featured in the case *People v. Belge,* which you will find in Chapter 10 of this book. In this case, two attorneys, Francis R. Belge and Frank H. Armani, represented a man accused of murder. During their conversations with the accused, he claimed to have committed three other murders. The attorneys confirmed two of the murders of young women by visiting the locations where his client had buried the bodies of his victims. After viewing the bodies, the attorneys discussed whether they should disclose the location of the bodies. They concluded that their duty to their client to maintain his confidence did not permit disclosure. They continuously denied knowing the location of the bodies throughout the case, even when asked by the families of the missing girls. When their client disclosed having told them, there was public outrage. Although accord was not universal, most ethics scholars agreed that the attorneys made the correct decision.

But the decision came at a high price. Both men received death threats and began to carry guns. Belge was charged with the health crime of not reporting a dead body for burial, Belge's family life was injured, and his practice diminished. He ultimately moved to another state. Armani's experience was similar, but he remained in the region and his practice eventually recovered. Armani said of the decision they made:

> God only knows that this thing drove me crazy; it really bothered me. And if there was any way I could have, I would have told Mr. and Mrs. Hauck. But my hands were tied. And as a result, this thing has cost me dearly. My law practice failed. I spent nearly $40,000 defending Garrow. . . . I've lost about every friend I have. But there was nothing else I could do. Please believe that!

Unquestionably, if the attorneys had not visited the scene, they would have been correct in maintaining their client's confidence. However, the prosecutor who obtained the grand jury indictment against Belge alleged that the attorneys' presence at the crime scene changed matters. The court hearing the case, however, held that "Belge conducted himself as an officer of the Court with all the zeal at his command to protect the constitutional rights of his client. Both on the grounds of privileged communication and the interests of justice the Indictment is dismissed."

*Source:* Mark Gado, *Robert Garrow: The Predator,* Court TV, Crime Library, at *http://www.crimelibrary.com/serial_killers /predators/robert_garrow/1.html* (March 11, 2008).

## Key Terms

common law
court rules
criminal law
criminal procedure

deterrence
due process
Model Penal Code
ordinance

precedent
regulation
stare decisis

## Review Questions

**1.** What are civil liberties? Give two examples of civil liberties that are protected by the U.S. Constitution.

**2.** What is the common law? How do the concepts of stare decisis and precedent relate to the common law?

3. The common law is different in every state. Why?

4. What does the Latin phrase *nullum crimen sine lege* translate to? Explain the significance of that phrase.

5. Explain how the common law can violate the principle of legality.

6. State three uses the common law has in criminal law in those jurisdictions that do not permit common law creation of crimes.

7. What is the source of most criminal law today? Where does that law come from?

8. What is an ordinance?

9. What is a regulation?

10. What is a court rule?

11. Place the following sources of law in order of authority, beginning with the highest form of law and ending with the lowest. Notice that both state and federal sources of law are included: U.S. Code, state constitutions, federal administrative regulations, ordinances, U.S. Constitution, state administrative regulations, state statutes.

## Problems & Critical Thinking Exercises

1. List the various purposes for punishing criminal law violators. Using your answers, discuss whether each of the purposes can be achieved for the following acts in problems 2–5:

2. John, having always wanted a guitar, stole one from a fellow student's room while that student was out.

3. Jack suffers from a physical disease of the mind that causes him to have violent episodes. Jack has no way of knowing when the episodes will occur. However, the disease is controllable with medication. Despite this, Jack often does not take the medicine, as he finds the injections painful and inconvenient. One day, when he had not taken the medicine, Jack had an episode and struck Mike, causing him personal injury.

4. The same facts apply, as in problem 3, except there is no treatment or medication that can control Jack's behavior. He was diagnosed as having the disease years before striking Mike and has caused such an injury before during a similar violent episode.

5. Unknown to Kevin, he has epilepsy. One day, while he was driving his automobile, he suffered his first seizure. The seizure caused him to lose control of his car and strike a pedestrian, inflicting a fatal injury.

## Endnotes

1. See E. Puttkammer, *Administration of Criminal Law*, 16–17 (1953).

2. Schwartz and Goldstein, *Police Guidance Manuals* (Charlottesville: University of Virginia Press, 1968), Manual No. 3, at 21–32, reprinted in *Cases, Materials, and Problems on the Advocacy and Administration of Criminal Justice* 173 by Harold Norris (unpublished manuscript available in the Detroit College of Law library).

3. See Note, 78 *Colum. L. Rev.* 1249, 1247–59 (1978); LaFave and Scott, *Criminal Law* 26 (Hornbook Series, St. Paul: West, 1986).

4. LaFave and Scott at 23.

5. 15A Am. Jur. 2d *Common Law* 6 (1976).

6. *Marsillett v. State*, 495 N.E.2d 699, 704 (Ind. 1986) (citations omitted).

7. 15A Am. Jur. 2d *Common Law* 1 (1976).

8. *Helms v. American Security Co.*, 22 N.E.2d 822 (Ind. 1986).

9. P. Robinson, *Fundamentals of Criminal Law* (Boston: Little, Brown, 1988).

10. Today in the United Kingdom, where the common law originated, most law is created by Parliament (which dates to the 1300s), not by courts.

11. See *Schechter Poultry Corp. v. United States,* 2nd ed., 295 U.S. 495 (1935).

12. See D. Hall, *Administrative Law: Bureaucracy in a Democracy*, 7th ed., ch. 5 (Upper Saddle River, NJ: Prentice Hall, 2020).

13. *Id.*

# Chapter 3

# The Ingredients of Crime: Thinking and Acting

## Chapter Outline

## Mens Rea Past

Learning Objective: Compare and contrast general, specific, strict, vicarious, and corporate mens rea under the common law.

Nearly every crime consists of two essential elements: the mental and the physical. This chapter examines, in depth, those elements. You will also learn about the related matters of concurrence and attendant circumstances.

The late Supreme Court Justice Oliver Wendell Holmes wrote that

*[e]ven a dog distinguishes between being stumbled over and being kicked.*[1]

This pithy statement expressed a fundamental law of nature. The difference between intentional and unintentional conduct is so instinctive that its truth extends into the animal kingdom. Maybe you have heard it said that there are two natural responses to a threat; fight or flight. The dog doesn't flee or bite the person who accidentally steps on its tail because it is not threatened.

For humans, distinguishing between intended and accidental harm informs a common understanding of fairness. Indeed, many of the earliest laws known to humanity, dating back thousands of years, punished intended harm more severely than unintended harm. Modern criminal law follows this model; that is, people are often held accountable for intentional behavior and not, or at least less, for unintended conduct, even though the consequences may be the same.

**mens rea**
(Latin) A state of mind that produces a crime.

**Mens rea** is the mental of a crime. It is often defined as "a guilty mind." It is best defined as the state of mind required to be criminally liable for a certain act. In modern law, it is sometimes the case that no intent whatsoever is required to be guilty of a crime, although most criminal laws require intent to some degree before criminal liability attaches to an act.

Mens rea is an important concept in criminal law. It is also a confusing one, largely because of the lack of uniformity between criminal statutes and judicial decisions of the states, federal government, and territories. One author found 79 words and phrases in the U.S. Criminal Code used to describe mens rea.[2] Malicious, mischievous, purposeful, unlawful, intentional, with specific intent, knowing, fraudulent, with an evil purpose, careless, willful, negligent, and reckless are examples. Often, when courts or legislatures use the same term, they do so assuming different meanings for the term. For this reason, the drafters of the Model Penal Code (MPC) attempted to establish uniform terms and definitions for those terms. The MPC approach is examined later. First, you will learn how mens rea was defined at the common law.

## Mens Rea and the Common Law

One principle under the common law was that there should be no crime if there was no act accompanied by a guilty mind. The Latin phrase that expresses this principle is *actus non facit reum nisi mens sit rea*. As you just learned, intent is no longer a universal element. Despite this, the principle that "only conscious wrong-doing constitutes crime is deeply rooted in our legal system and remains the rule, rather than the exception."[3]

## General, Specific, and Constructive Intent

In the earliest years of the common law, the mens rea requirement was simple; a defendant had to be morally culpable, to have acted with a malicious, evil mind. This early conception of culpability had moral roots. Over a long period of time, the courts developed a more cognitively focused approach, eventually distinguishing between **general intent** and **specific intent**.

**general intent**
The desire to commit a prohibited act but not the outcome of that act.

**specific intent**
An intent to commit the exact crime charged or the precise outcome of the act, not merely an intent to commit the act without an intention to cause the outcome.

If a defendant's purpose was to cause the *result* of the act, the defendant possessed specific intent. If the defendant intended only the act, and not the result of that act, then the defendant possessed general intent. For example, Don Defendant throws a large rock at Victoria Victim, inflicting a fatal wound. If Defendant only intended to injure Victim, not kill her, he possessed general intent. However, if Defendant threw the rock hoping it would kill Victim, he possessed specific intent. The distinction between general and specific intent is an important one because many statutes require specific intent for a higher level crime and general intent for a lower crime. In this example, many state statues would allow Defendant to be charged with first-degree murder if he intended to kill Victim, but with second-degree murder if he only intended to injure Victim.

So long as a defendant intends to cause the result, it is irrelevant that the means used to achieve the result are likely to fail. For example, assume

Defendant desires to cause the death of Victim. One day, while walking down a street, Defendant notices Victim far away. Defendant picks up a rock and hurls it toward Victim, hoping it will strike and kill her. But because of the distance, he does not expect the rock to strike its intended target. However, all of those afternoons practicing his baseball pitch paid off, and the rock hits Victim in the head, killing her instantly. The fact that Defendant threw the rock with an intent to kill is enough to establish Defendant's specific intent. That the outcome is is unlikely is no defense.

Specific intent may also be proved, in some jurisdictions, by showing that the defendant possessed knowledge of a particular fact or illegality. This requirement of knowledge is known as **scienter**. Although scienter and mens rea are commonly treated as synonyms, they are not. Scienter is a specific form of mens rea. If an individual commits a crime that has a scienter element while believing that the act engaged in is lawful or without the specific knowledge required, scienter is lacking and only general intent exists.[4]

Scienter often does not require proof of subjective knowledge. Rather, it can be established by proving that the defendant should have known the fact in question. For example, assume that Abina recently emigrated to the United States. In her home country, uniforms are common. Security guards, cab drivers, and hotel employees all wear uniforms that are difficult to distinguish from police. Not fully acclimated to the United States, she ignored the warning of a police officer to not jaywalk. She didn't give the officer much thought because she was accustomed to ignoring people in uniform. The officer approached her, threatened to arrest her, and she struck the officer in the face. She was arrested and charged with battery of a peace officer, a felony. Returning to our police officer example, a jury could find that a reasonable person should have known that the individual was an officer even if the jury believes that Abina didn't subjectively know the assaulted individual was a police officer.

Consider the crime of receiving stolen property. If an individual received stolen property, but did so without knowledge that it was stolen, no crime has been committed. For some crimes that require scienter, the absence of scienter may leave a general intent crime. If a man strikes a person whom he believes is obstructing traffic, he has committed an assault. If he knew, or should have known, that the person was a police officer attempting to direct traffic, then he may be accountable for the higher crime of assault on a police officer. However, if the police officer was not wearing a uniform and did not announce himself as an officer, then the defendant is liable only for simple assault. Possession of burglary tools and obstruction of justice are also examples: the former requiring knowledge of the tools' character and the latter requiring knowledge of obstruction.

At common law, specific intent could be found in a third type of situation, whenever **constructive intent** could be proven. A legal fiction, constructive intent applies when a defendant does not intend to cause the result, but it is likely to occur. If John fires a handgun at close range at Sally, aiming at her torso, and kills her as a result, he could be charged with the specific-intent crime of first-degree murder, even though he only intended to injure her. This is because the possibility of killing someone under those circumstances is significant. However, liability may not exist if he had aimed at her leg and the weapon discharged improperly, causing the bullet to strike her in the torso. The bullet entered the victim's torso as a result of the malfunction of the gun; it was not Defendant's desire to shoot her in the upper body. As to the amount of probability necessary to prove constructive intent, only "practical or substantial" probability is required, not absolute.[5]

**scienter**
(Latin) Knowingly; with guilty knowledge. [pronounce: si-*en*-ter]

**constructive intent**
Inferred, implied, or presumed from the circumstances.

Specific intent can be found in a fourth situation, whenever a defendant intends a result beyond the act taken. This doctrine applies to uncompleted crimes. For example, if a man attacks a woman intending to rape her, but she is able to free herself and escape, he may be charged with assault with intent to rape. To prove this charge, the prosecution must show that he assaulted the victim with the specific intent of raping her. Proving that the defendant had a specific intent to assault her is not enough to sustain the intent-to-rape charge, although it would justify a conviction for assault, a lesser crime.

Another example is the crime of breaking and entering with the intent to burglarize. Again, the prosecution must prove that the actor intended to steal from the home after breaking into it, even though the plan was thwarted for some reason outside of the actor's control. Proving that the actor broke in and entered, but had no intent to steal, will support a conviction for breaking and entering, but not the more serious crime of breaking and entering with the intent to commit burglary.

General intent is much easier to define, as it is simply the desire to act. In most situations, if the prosecution can show that a defendant intended to take the act that resulted in the prohibited outcome, then general intent is proved. Generally, no desire to cause a particular consequence is required. So, if you fire a gun without a desire to kill someone, but the bullet does kill a person, you possess a general intent and may be prosecuted for a general-intent homicide.

Some jurisdictions require more than simply a desire to act to prove general intent. In those states, some level of negligence must be proven. Consider the following two examples:

> Rural Defendant has lived on a farm for more than 20 years. Defendant's nearest neighbor is over three miles away, and Defendant routinely target shoots in his backyard. He has never encountered anyone in the area where he shoots, and everyone who lives in the community knows of his practice. One day, while target shooting, he accidentally shoots and kills a trespasser he did not know was on his property.

> Metro Defendant likes to hunt on weekends. One weekend, Metro and his friend were hunting and Metro lost sight of his friend. Eager to capture his first deer of the season, Metro fired into a bush in which he observed bushes move. But Metro's friend was in the bush, and Metro's gunshot inflicted a fatal wound.

In both examples, the defendants had no desire to harm the individuals who were shot, and both possessed the intent to fire the weapon. A strict construction of general and specific intent results in both defendants committing a general-intent murder. However, in some jurisdictions, Rural may be free from liability because he appears to have been less reckless or negligent than Metro, who should have considered the possibility that it could have been his friend who was causing the disturbance in the bush.

This discussion has not exhausted the many definitions and distinctions that exist for specific and general intent. In the *Carson* case, it appears that the Court of Appeals for the District of Columbia has created a hybrid general-specific intent for the crime of cruelty to children.

## Malum in Se and Malum Prohibitum

Often, crimes are characterized as either malum in se or malum prohibitum. Acts that are inherently evil are malum in se. If a crime is not evil in itself, but is only criminal because it is declared so by a legislature, it is characterized as malum prohibitum. Examples of crimes that are malum in se are murder, rape, arson, and mayhem. Failure to file your quarterly tax report or to get the proper building permit are malum prohibitum.

## Oyez

## Janet A. Carson, Appellant v. United States, Appellee
### 556 A.2d 1076, 1989 (D.C. 1989)

**MACK, Associate Judge:**

On June 4, 1985, Janet Carson arrived home from work at about 3:45 P.M. and was informed by one of her children that a fuse needed replacement. While looking for a fuse, appellant noticed that eight dollars were missing from her dresser drawer. She called her children—thirteen-year-old Cornell, six-year-old Everett, five-year-old Angelica, and eight-year-old Charmaine Schmidt—to her bedroom; each child denied knowing anything about the missing money. At that point she went downstairs, and as she returned upstairs she picked up an electrical cord; she later testified that she routinely used the cord to discipline the children. She again asked the children about the missing money, and they again denied any knowledge of the money's disappearance. Appellant then whipped each of the children several times.

The next day at the school attended by Everett, Angelica, and Charmaine, school officials noticed marks and bruises on the children. Detective Harmon of the Metropolitan Police Department went to the school and took the three children to Children's Hospital. Everett's abrasions were cleaned and bandaged; the other two children received no treatment.

Appellant was subsequently charged with three counts of cruelty to children. . . . [Ms. Carson was convicted and sentenced to thirty days on each count, which was suspended to one year's probation. She appealed the conviction and this is the opinion of the appellate court.]

Before considering appellant's claim that the evidence was insufficient to support her conviction, we must first determine the mens rea required for conviction under D.C. Code § 22–901. We conclude that the offense is a general intent crime, which also requires a showing of malice. . . .

Section 22–901 provides in pertinent part:

Any person who shall torture, cruelly beat, abuse, or otherwise willfully maltreat any child under the age of 18 years . . . shall be deemed guilty of a misdemeanor, and, when convicted thereof, shall be subject to punishment by a fine of not more than $250, or by imprisonment for a term not exceeding 2 years, or both.

The [D.C. Jury Instructions] define the elements of the offense as follows:

1. that the defendant tortured, cruelly beat, abused or otherwise maltreated a child;
2. that at the time of the incident, the child was under the age of 18 years; and
3. that the defendant acted willfully, that is, with an evil intent or with bad purpose to maltreat the child. It is not enough that you find that the defendant exercised bad judgement or acted unreasonably. Rather, it is necessary that you find that the defendant was motivated by an evil intent or state of mind in committing the acts which constitute the offense.

■ ■ ■

Judicial interpretation of D.C. Code § 22–901 has been limited . . . [T]he United States Court of Appeals for the District of Columbia held that the terms "abuse" and "willfully mistreat" as used in the statute "call for something worse than good intentions coupled with bad judgment," and incorporate "the requirement of an evil state of mind." . . . The cases would seem to teach that cruelty to children is something more than a general intent crime and something less than a specific intent crime.

■ ■ ■

In other contexts, this court has equated the terms "evil intent" and "malice." This court has noted that a showing of bad or evil purpose is "necessary to distinguish the mental state required for malice-based offenses from that involved in crimes the conviction for which demands proof no more than general intent or criminal negligence." Thus, if cruelty to children requires proof of something more than general intent, that something more would seem to be malice.

■ ■ ■

Having determined the mens rea required for conviction of cruelty to children, we must now determine whether the government's proof was sufficient to establish the requisite mens rea in this case. Appellant concedes that the record supports the trial court's finding of general intent. However, she argues that the government failed to prove that she acted with malice. She argues that, according to her undisputed testimony, she was motivated not by an evil intent but, rather, by a "concern for [her] children's welfare and upbringing." At first blush, the record supports her argument as to motivation.

The government argues, however, that to find malice "all that is required [is] a conscious disregard of a known and substantial risk of the harm. . . ."

(continued)

Malice is a rather slippery concept, not amenable to precise definition. . . . Simply put, we believe that a parent acts with malice when a parent acts out of a desire to inflict pain rather than out of genuine effort to correct the child, or when the parent, in a genuine effort to correct the child, acts with a conscious disregard that serious harm will result.

■  ■  ■

In this case, appellant's testimony regarding her motive was not directly contradicted. The government relied basically on the nature of the wounds and the manner of the punishment to establish malice. The government introduced pictures of the injuries sustained by the children and also pointed to the ages of the children, and the fact that appellant used an electrical cord to whip the children as evidence that appellant acted with evil intent, or at least as evidence that appellant acted with a conscious disregard that serious harm (of the nature which would flow from an evil intent) would result.

From our perspective in this court, we cannot conclude that the evidence justifies the inference that appellant acted out of a desire to inflict pain. . . .

The trial court also noted that appellant had "high standards" for her children—"she didn't want them to steal; she didn't want them to use drugs." The court found that appellant had worked hard to make a good life for herself and her children. She had left the welfare rolls and become a policewoman, "supporting all those children on her own." We echo the trial court's sentiment that appellant had a genuine and deep-felt love and concern for her children.

Further, we do not believe that the punishment was so excessive or the manner so egregious as to lead to the conclusion that appellant acted with a conscious disregard of the serious harm which would result. The mother testified that the whippings lasted perhaps a minute. As to the manner of discipline, reasonable people might disagree as to whether whipping with an electrical cord is in itself offensive or no more offensive than the use of commonly employed devices or methods used to exact discipline. We would only note that appellant testified that because the children were jumping around and that because she was eight months pregnant and therefore awkward, the cord made contact on the children's bodies where it otherwise may not have done so.

However, when the manner of punishment, the length of punishment, the nature of the injuries and the ages of the children are viewed as a whole, we cannot say that the trial court was plainly in error in concluding that appellant acted with conscious disregard of the harm which resulted. . . .

Conviction AFFIRMED.

The distinction between malum in se and malum prohibitum is used throughout criminal law. The distinction is important because it influences legislators and judges in the creation and interpretation of crimes. Crimes malum in se, for example, commonly require an evil intent whereas crimes malum prohibitum don't. Some crimes may be both malum in se and malum prohibitum, depending upon the degree of violation. For example, driving "a little over the speed limit" may be malum prohibitum, but significantly exceeding the speed limit is malum in se."[6] In this example, the threat to life is the operative fact. Speeding slightly over the limit is not likely to cause another's death, whereas racing through a city at 30 miles over the speed limit, or even 10 miles an hour over the limit in a school zone, can foreseeably kill someone. If while driving 4 miles over the speed limit, the defendant strikes and kills a pedestrian who walks into the driver's path from behind another car, the act is likely to be determined malum prohibitum, and a manslaughter charge is not likely to follow. However, the same may not be true if the driver is traveling at 30 miles over the speed limit when the accident occurs.

### Transferred Intent

Whenever a person intends a harm but, because of bad aim or other cause, the intended harm befalls another, the intent is transferred from the intended victim to the unintended victim. This is the doctrine of **transferred intent**. If John Defendant observes a neighbor burning the American flag and in anger shoots at him, missing him but killing William, the doctrine of transferred intent permits prosecution of Defendant as if he intended to kill William.

There are limits on the doctrine of transferred intent. First, the harm that actually results must be similar to the intended harm. If the harms are

**transferred intent**
The principle that if an unintended illegal act results from the intent to commit a crime, that act is also a crime.

substantially different, then the intent does not transfer. For example, if A throws a baseball at B's window, hoping to break it, and the ball instead hits C in the head and kills him, it cannot be said that the intent to break the window transfers to C and that A can be punished for intentionally killing C. Person A may be criminally liable for a lesser crime, such as involuntary manslaughter, depending upon the amount of negligence involved, but he is not responsible for intentionally causing C's death.

A second limitation on the doctrine is that the transfer cannot increase the defendant's liability. In other words, any defenses the defendant has against the intended victim are transferred to the unintended victim. For example, A shoots at B in self-defense but hits C, inflicting a fatal wound. Because A had a valid defense if B had been killed by the shot, then A also has a defense as to C. In this case, A has committed no crime.

In some situations, a defense may only limit a person's criminal liability to a lesser charge. You will learn later that certain defenses negate specific intent, but not general intent. One such defense is intoxication. Assault is a general-intent crime, whereas assault with an intent to kill is a specific-intent crime. Intoxication may be a defense to the higher assault with an intent to kill, but not assault. So if A, while intoxicated, hurls a knife at B but hits C, A may be charged with assault because intoxication would be no defense if she hit B. Person A would have a defense against the specific-intent crime of assault with intent to kill, so the same defense is available for harm to C.

## Strict Liability

At the beginning of this chapter you read that some crimes don't require an evil intent. These crimes are proven simply by showing that the act was committed; no particular mental state has to be proven. Known as *strict liability*, this approach is an exception to the common law requirement that there be both an evil mind and an evil act. The term *strict liability* is not used in all jurisdictions. Further, the term also has a tort meaning. Do not confuse criminal liability without fault with tort strict liability.

**Strict liability crimes** usually are minor violations, punished by fines and not incarceration. However, strict liability is permitted as the mental element, or lack thereof, for felonies and may be punished with incarceration.

Most traffic violations, such as running a stoplight and speeding, are examples of strict liability crimes. Laws intended to protect minors are often silent on knowledge of the age of the victim. Statutory rape, for example, is treated as a strict liability crime in most states; therefore, a mistaken belief, even if it is the result of a fraudulent representation of age by the victim, does not relieve the defendant of criminal responsibility for having consensual sex with a minor. Similarly, selling drugs or alcohol or otherwise contributing to the delinquency of minors often does not have a mens rea requirement, at least in regard to the age of the victim. It is common for crimes that are malum prohibitum to be strict liability, whereas crimes malum in se usually require proof of some mental state. It is also generally true that violation of crimes malum prohibitum is not punished as severely as violation of crimes malum in se.

**strict liability crimes**
Crimes or offenses in which mens rea or criminal intent is not an element.

Often, "public offenses" or "regulatory offenses" are strict liability. The term "regulatory" is often used because the criminal prohibition has been established by an administrative agency through rulemaking, is enforced by an administrative agency, or is part of a comprehensive regulatory scheme established by a legislature.

There are an increasing number of regulatory offenses in the United States. Indeed, there has been a significant rise in the number of strict liability crimes, both regulatory and other, in recent decades. According to one study, 40% of nonviolent federal offenses created during a two-year period had no, or weak, mens rea requirements.[7]

Strict liability crimes, particularly those that impose serious penalties, have been challenged on many grounds. Some jurists believe that the expansion of strict liability beyond infractions and regulatory violations are undemocratic. But the U.S. Supreme Court has upheld strict liability statutes in most instances, affording legislatures wide latitude in defining criminality.[8] Even so, there are limits, and if a legislature eliminates proof of mens rea for a crime that has traditionally required proof of specific intent or purpose or omits mens rea for a crime that is punished severely, due process is implicated and may be the basis for invalidating the change.

In the *Morissette* case, found in your next Oyez, the Supreme Court addressed the omission of mens rea for the traditional crime of converting (theft) spent bomb casings. The defendant was convicted at the trial level, but the U.S. Supreme Court reversed the conviction.

# Oyez

## Morissette v. United States
### 342 U.S. 246 (1952)

**Mr. Justice JACKSON delivered the opinion of the Court.**

This would have remained a profoundly insignificant case to all except its immediate parties had it not been so tried and submitted to the jury as to raise questions both fundamental and far-reaching in federal criminal law, for which reason we granted certiorari.

On a large tract of uninhabited and untilled land in a wooded and sparsely populated area of Michigan, the Government established a practice bombing range over which the Air Force dropped simulated bombs at ground targets. These bombs consisted of a metal cylinder about forty inches long and eight inches across, filled with sand and enough black powder to cause a smoke puff by which the strike could be located. At various places about the range signs read Danger—Keep Out—Bombing Range. Nevertheless, the range was known as good deer country and was extensively hunted.

Spent bomb casings were cleared from the targets and thrown into piles 'so that they will be out of the way.' They were not sacked or piled in any order but were dumped in heaps, some of which had been accumulating for four years or upwards, were exposed to the weather and rusting away.

Morissette, in December of 1948, went hunting in this area but did not get a deer. He thought to meet expenses of the trip by salvaging some of these casings. He loaded three tons of them on his truck and took them to a nearby farm, where they were flattened by driving a tractor over them. After expending this labor and trucking them to market in Flint, he realized $84.

Morissette, by occupation, is a fruit stand operator in summer and a trucker and scrap iron collector in winter. An honorably discharged veteran of World War II, he enjoys a good name among his neighbors and has had no blemish on his record more disreputable than a conviction for reckless driving.

The loading, crushing and transporting of these casings were all in broad daylight, in full view of passers-by, without the slightest effort at concealment. When an investigation was started, Morissette voluntarily, promptly and candidly told the whole story to the authorities, saying that he had no intention of stealing but thought the property was abandoned, unwanted and considered of no value to the Government. He was indicted, however, on the charge that he "did unlawfully, wilfully and knowingly steal and convert" property of the United States of the value of $84, in violation of 18 U.S.C. 641, 18 U.S.C.A. § 641, which provides that "whoever embezzles, steals, purloins, or knowingly converts" government property is punishable by fine and imprisonment. Morissette was convicted and sentenced to imprisonment for two months or to pay a fine of $200. The Court of Appeals affirmed, one judge dissenting ...

The contention that an injury can amount to a crime only when inflicted by intention is not a provincial or transient notion. It is universal and persistent in mature systems of law, as belief in freedom of the human will and a consequent ability and duty of the normal individual to choose between good and evil. A relationship between some mental element and punishment for a harmful act is almost as instinctive as the child's familiar exculpatory "but I didn't mean to," and has afforded the rational basis for a tardy and unfinished substitution of deterrence and reformation in place of retaliation and vengeance as the motivation for public prosecution. . . .

Crime, as a compound concept, generally constituted only from concurrence of an evil-meaning mind with an evil-doing hand, was congenial with an intense individualism and took deep and early root in American soil. As the states codified the common law of crimes, even if their enactments were silent on the subject, their courts assumed that the omission did not signify disapproval of the principle but merely recognized that intent was so inherent in the idea of the offense that it required no statutory definition.

However, [some crimes fall into a] category of another character, with very different antecedents and origins. The crimes there involved depend on no mental element but consist only of forbidden acts or omissions. . . . The industrial revolution multiplied the number of workmen exposed to injury from increasingly powerful and complex mechanisms, driven by freshly discovered sources of energy, requiring higher precautions by employers. Traffic of velocities, volumes and varieties unheard of came to subject the wayfarer to intolerable casualty risks if the owners and drivers were not to observe new cares and uniformities of conduct. Congestion of cities and crowding of quarters called for health and welfare regulations undreamed of in simpler times. Wide distribution of goods became an instrument of wide distribution of harm when those who dispersed food, drink, drugs, and even securities, did not comply with reasonable standards of quality, integrity, disclosure and care. Such dangers have engendered increasingly numerous and detailed regulations which heighten the duties of those in control of particular industries, trades, properties, or activities that affect public health, safety or welfare.

. . . Many violations of such regulations result in no direct or immediate injury to person or property but merely create the danger or probability of injury which the law seeks to minimize.

■ ■ ■

Stealing, larceny, and its variants and equivalents, were among the earliest offenses known to the law that existed before legislation [common law]. . . . State courts of last resort, on whom fall the heaviest burden of interpreting criminal law in this country, have consistently retained the requirement of intent in larceny-type offenses. If any state has deviated, the exception has neither been called to our attention nor disclosed by our research.

We hold that the mere omission from [the conversion statute] of any mention of intent will not be construed as eliminating that element from the crimes denounced.

## Strict Liability and Statutory Construction

Strict liability crimes are controversial. For decades, civil libertarians have sounded the alarm of overcriminalization and easy criminalization. Strict liability is an example of the latter. The problem addressed by the Supreme Court in *Morissette* occurs often; what is the mens rea requirement when a statute doesn't have one? Some state legislatures have responded by adding mens rea to existing crimes. Another approach is illustrated by the following Ohio statute:

**O.R.C. 2901.21 Criminal liability, culpability.**

(A) Except as provided in division (B) of this section, a person is not guilty of an offense unless both of the following apply:

(1) The person's liability is based on conduct that includes either a voluntary act, or an omission to perform an act or duty that the person is capable of performing;

(2) The person has the requisite degree of culpability for each element as to which a culpable mental state is specified by the language defining the offense.

(B) When the language defining an offense does not specify any degree of culpability, and plainly indicates a purpose to impose strict criminal liability for the conduct described in the section, then culpability is not required for a person to be guilty of the offense. The fact that one division of a section plainly indicates a purpose to impose strict liability for an offense defined in that division does not by itself plainly indicate a purpose to impose strict criminal liability for an offense defined in other divisions of the section that do not specify a degree of culpability.

(C)

(1) When language defining an element of an offense that is related to knowledge or intent or to which mens rea could fairly be applied neither specifies culpability nor plainly indicates a purpose to impose strict liability, the element of the offense is established only if a person acts recklessly.

Under this statute, strict liability only exists when the legislature "plainly" intends it. If a statute is silent on mens rea, the legislature directs the courts to impute recklessness.

In jurisdictions without such a mandate, courts consider many factors when making the mens rea decision. First, the **legislative history** of the statute may indicate whether the crime was intended to have a mens rea requirement. The statements of members of legislatures while debating the law (before it became law and was a bill), reports of committees of Congress, and other related materials may indicate whether the legislature intended a mens rea requirement.

Second, courts look to whether the crime existed under the common law. If so, the mens rea used under the common law may be adopted by the court. Third, the mens rea standards for related crimes is considered. Fourth, the seriousness of the punishment. The greater the punishment, the more likely a court will expect at least a minimum level of culpability. Fifth, the burden that would be placed on the prosecution if mens rea were required. Sixth, any applicable rules of statutory construction. These are known as *canons* of **statutory construction**.

You previously learned one of these canons: whenever a statute can be construed as either constitutional or unconstitutional, it must be read as constitutional. Some jurisdictions follow the rule, either by judicial rule (canon) or by statute, that if a criminal statute does not specifically impose strict liability, then the court is to impose a mens rea requirement. Ohio did this, as you read earlier, and this is what the Supreme Court did in *Morrisette*. And *Troiano* is a case from New York, a state jurisdiction where such a rule is applied. See Exhibit 3–1 for examples of other canons that are applied in criminal cases.

There is an important exception to the presumption of mens rea when a statute is silent on the subject: public welfare cases. The Supreme Court has long recognized that public welfare, or regulatory, laws are often intended to impose strict liability because of the large risk that legislatures and administrative agencies are attempting to manage. In such cases, courts are not to impose mens rea when the law, statute, or administrative regulation is silent on state of mind. For example, strict liability for corporate officials who injure consumers who purchased misbranded drugs was upheld.[9] Similarly the Court refused to impute mens rea for the crime of possessing a hand grenade because of the public safety rationale of the law.[10] For a law to qualify as a public welfare statute, the harm that it seeks to prevent must seriously threaten health or life. In addition, the history of how the act is regulated is important. If the threat is not widespread and significant, the law will not be characterized as public welfare and a court will be more likely to impose mens rea.[11]

Another factor is implicit in the public welfare cases—the nature of the act regulated. If the act was a crime at the common law that required the government to prove state of mind, as opposed to being a recent regulatory creation, it is more likely that a court will want to impose mens rea.

**legislative history**
The background documents and records of hearings related to the enactment of a bill.

**statutory construction**
Guidelines employed by judges in the interpretation of statutes that have developed and evolved over hundreds of years.

**Exhibit 3–1** Examples of Canons of Construction
That Apply In Criminal Cases

| Canon | Description |
|---|---|
| Narrow Construction | Criminal statutes are to be narrowly construed by courts. |
| Ambiguous Language | Ambiguous language in a statute is to be construed in the defendant's favor or, if too ambiguous, the statute is void. |
| Legislative Prerogative | Courts are to be mindful that the source of penal law should be legislatures, not courts. Criminal statutes are to be narrowly construed. This is also known as the Rule of Lenity. |
| Constitutionality Presumption | Statutes are presumed constitutional, and if a court can construe a statute as constitutional or unconstitutional without causing unfairness to the defendant, the statute is to be construed as constitutional. |
| Plain Meaning | The plain meaning of a statute shall be enforced unless the result is absurd. If absurd, the court may turn to other evidence (e.g., legislative intent) to assist in interpreting the statute. |

## Oyez

### People v. Alicia Troiano
### 552 N.Y.S.2d 541 (1990)

**UTE WOLFF LALLY, J.**

[Defendant was charged with having insufficient brakes on her car and the following facts were stipulated to by the parties:]

On May 1, 1987 at approximately 11:35 P.M. the defendant was involved in a two-car accident. . . . Defendant was the owner and operator of a 1972 Oldsmobile station wagon. . . . The driver of the other vehicle died as a result of injuries suffered in that accident. The decedent failed to yield the right of way at a stop sign at that intersection. The decedent's blood alcohol level was .10%. Both vehicles were impounded. The defendant's vehicle was inspected by Al Stern of Al's Towing Corporation, and as a result of that inspection, the instant charge was brought. [Mr. Stern testified that the defendant's right rear brake was insufficient under state law guidelines.]

The defendant testified that she had not experienced any problems with the braking system of the car. She did not hear any squeaks or other noises. She did not notice any leaking of brake fluid and was able to stop properly at a stop sign just minutes before the accident. Further, the car had been inspected in September, 1986 and had a proper inspection sticker affixed to the windshield.

The defense also called Mr. Troiano, defendant's husband, who had been employed as an automobile mechanic until 1983. Following Stern's inspection, Mr. Troiano towed the vehicle in question back to his house. He pulled off all four wheels and examined the brake shoes and lining and found the brake lining on the right rear wheel to be a little more than 1/16 of an inch at its thinnest point and, consequently adequate.

■  ■  ■

[The statute] provides in pertinent part, that "every motor vehicle, operated or driven on the highways of the State, shall be provided with adequate brakes. . . ."

The court will first deal with the question of whether the statute is one of strict liability. The plain language of [the brake statute] does not require a mens rea or a culpable mental state as an element of the crime and in reliance thereon the People have made no attempt to make a prima facie showing that defendant knew or had reason to know of the defect.

(continued)

"Culpable mental state" means intentional, knowing, reckless or criminally negligent conduct. . . . If the commission of a particular offense or some material element thereof does not require a culpable mental state on the part of the actor, such an offense is one of "strict liability."

It is a well-known principle of statutory construction that absent the legislature's clear indication of an intent to impose strict liability, a statute should be construed to require mens rea. . . . [The Court determined that the defendant had to have had knowledge of the defect to be liable and that no such showing had been made. Accordingly, defendant's motion for dismissal was granted.]

## Vicarious Liability

**vicarious liability**
Legal responsibility for the acts of another person because of some relationship with that person.

The term **vicarious liability** refers to situations in which one person is held accountable for the actions of another. Under vicarious liability, there is no requirement of mens rea as there is for strict liability, and in addition, there is no requirement for an act, at least not by the defendant. The person who is liable for the actions of another need not act, encourage another to act, or intend any harm at all. As is true with vicarious liability in tort law, this situation is most common between employers and employees.

Employers may be liable for the actions of their employees when criminal laws relating to the operation of the business are violated. For example, the owner of a business may be prosecuted for failure to comply with product safety regulations, even though that was a duty delegated to an employee and the owner had no knowledge that the products manufactured were substandard. Vicarious liability is often imposed on those who market food and drugs.[12] This is because of the significant public welfare interest in the quality of these products.

## Corporate Liability

**corporate liability**
The liability of a corporation for the acts of its directors, officers, shareholders, agents, and employees.

**Corporate liability** is a form of vicarious liability. Under the common law, corporations could not be convicted of crimes. However, this is no longer the law.

Corporations, partnerships, and other organizations can be held criminally accountable for the acts of their employees and agents under traditional respondeat superior theory. Agents must be working within the scope of their employment for the company to be liable. If an employee of Starbucks strikes an enemy while on break in the parking lot of the store, the company is not liable for battery. However, if officers of a corporation send employees into a workplace knowing that it is dangerous and represent to the employees that it is safe, the company may be liable for battery to the employee, or even manslaughter, if death results.

One legal scholar identified three theories under which corporations can be found criminally liable today. The first is traditional principal-agent theory, which developed at the common law. Second, corporations should be liable for the actions of their policymakers but not their employees. The third theory holds that corporations are liable for their agents and employees when corporate policy or practices fail to prevent the crime from happening.[13]

The MPC provides for corporate liability when the agent is acting within the scope of employment. In addition, it must be shown that the corporation had a duty under the law to act, and the act was not done or the act taken by the agent was authorized, requested, commanded, performed, or recklessly tolerated by the board of directors or other high management.[14]

Today, in most jurisdictions, corporations can be held criminally liable for any act that is criminal for a natural person. This includes crimes against the person, such as rape, murder, and battery. *People v. Warner-Lambert Co.*, which appears later in this chapter, is an example of when a company was charged with negligent homicide. In a subsequent case in Illinois, a corporation was convicted of involuntary manslaughter and several of its officers were convicted of murder for the death of an employee that could have been prevented.[15] The most common criminal actions against corporations, however, are not crimes against person. They are property and regulatory crimes.[16]

Obviously, companies cannot be incarcerated, so fines are usually imposed. In some instances, **injunctions** may be imposed or a company's status may be altered, suspended, or terminated. Finally, note that corporate liability does not free the agent from criminal liability. In most cases, the agents or employees remain criminally liable for their acts. Indeed, proving corporate mens rea can be more difficult than proving individual mens rea. Two prominent cases illustrate this point.

**injunctions**
A judge's order to a person to do or to refrain from doing a particular thing.

One of the most famous cases of alleged corporate crime involved the Ford Motor Company. In the late 1960s, Ford designed a new subcompact car, the Pinto. To maximize trunk space, the Pinto's fuel tank was located behind the rear axle rather than above it, which was the common design. However, this new design made the car more vulnerable to fire and explosions in rear-end accidents. Other design decisions, including lack of reinforcement of the rear of the car and a poorly designed fuel filler pipe, accentuated the risk. Following several deaths from fires resulting from rear-end collisions, civil suits were filed against Ford in different states. During discovery in one of those actions, a report that detailed the costs of correcting the problem ($11 per car, 12.5 million cars, totaling $137 million) in comparison to the costs of the expected number of deaths and injuries (180 deaths, 180 injuries, totaling $49.5 million) was produced. This and other evidence led prosecutors in Indiana to charge Ford with negligent homicide.[17]

Many civil actions also were filed by individuals who were harmed. Ultimately, Ford was not convicted of the charged crime but was found liable in several civil actions. Although an unsuccessful criminal prosecution, the Ford case continues to be prominent in discussions of corporate criminal liability because the underlying premise of the prosecution—namely, that a corporation can be charged with traditional crimes—was generally accepted.

The 2002 Enron debacle is another example. As a result of misrepresentations about Enron's financial status by Enron officers and Enron's accounting firm, Arthur Andersen, LLP, investors were not aware of Enron's financial distress. Employees and investors lost millions of dollars when the company went bankrupt in December 2001. In addition to criminal charges against Enron officials, Enron's accounting firm, Arthur Andersen, LLP, was charged with obstruction of justice for destroying Enron documents and computer files that were sought by federal authorities. The government alleged that Andersen employees destroyed files containing unfavorable information about Enron that had not been made available to investors. Andersen, a top-five accounting firm, had 85,000 employees and offices the world over at the time of its indictment. Many commentators were critical of the indictment, asserting that the focus of corporate crime should be the responsible individuals, not companies. A conviction of Andersen, it was alleged, could lead to more than a fine (as provided for by statute). Andersen faced demise by losing its Securities and Exchange status and its corporate status. This would result in 85,000 unemployed individuals, most of whom were not parties to the crime.

Ultimately, Andersen was convicted of obstruction of justice and was sentenced to five years' probation and a $500,000 fine. The terms of its probation included additional fines if it committed new crimes, and the firm was required to obtain approval before it sold its assets. Andersen appealed, and in 2005 a unanimous Supreme Court set aside the conviction.[18] However, as a result of the scandal, Andersen had lost nearly all of its clients, had surrendered its license to practice before the Securities and Exchange Commission, had its license revoked in many states, its total staffing had fallen to just a few hundred, and the firm was defending against more than a hundred civil actions by the time the Supreme Court issued its decision in 2005. Today, only a small part of Arthur Anderson continues to offer consultancy services, but not accountancy, under the name Accenture.

# Mens Rea Present

## The MPC and States of Mind

Learning Objective: Explain the four states of mind recognized under the MPC.

The drafters of the MPC chose to reject most of the common law terms when they addressed mens rea. The result is that the MPC recognizes four states of mind: purposely, knowing, reckless, and negligent (see Exhibit 3–2).[19]

**purposely**
Intentionally; knowingly.

**knowingly**
With full knowledge and intentionally; willfully.

To act **purposely**, a defendant must have a desire to cause the result. *Purposely* most closely equates with the common law's *specific intent* standard.

To act **knowingly**, a defendant must be aware of the nature of the act and be practically certain that his or her conduct will cause a particular result—which is not the defendant's objective. The difference between purposeful acts and knowing acts is that to be purposeful, one must act intending to cause the particular result. To act knowingly, the defendant must be practically certain (nearly 100% positive) that the result will occur, but the defendant is not taking the act to cause that result. For example, if a legitimate moving company owner leases a van to an illegal drug dealer knowing that the van will be used to transport drugs across the country, the

## Exhibit 3–2 Mens Rea Under the MPC

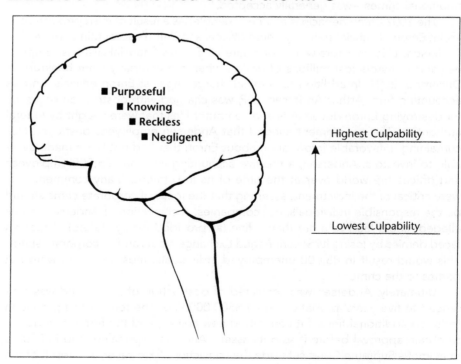

owner has acted knowingly. He has not acted with purpose, because it is not the owner's objective to transport the contraband.

The third state of mind recognized by the MPC is **recklessness**. Individuals act recklessly when they consciously disregard a substantial and unjustifiable risk that the result will occur. The difference between a knowing act and a reckless act is in the degree of risk. "A person acts 'knowingly' with respect to a result if he is nearly certain that his conduct will cause the result. If he is aware only of a substantial risk, he acts 'recklessly' with respect to the result."[20] The Code says that the risk taken must be one that involves a "gross deviation from the standard of conduct that a law-abiding person would observe in the actor's situation."[21]

The final state of mind is **negligence**. The definition of negligence is similar to recklessness; that is, there must be a "substantial and unjustifiable risk" taken by the defendant. However, a person acts negligently when there is no conscious awareness of the risk, when there should have been. To act recklessly, one must take a risk that amounts to a "gross deviation from the standard of conduct that a law-abiding person would observe in the actor's situation." When defendants have acted negligently, they have failed to perceive (be aware of) the risk altogether, and that failure is a gross deviation from a law-abiding person's standard.

**recklessness**
Indifference to consequences; indifference to the safety and rights of others. Recklessness implies conduct amounting to more than ordinary negligence.

**negligence**
Under the MPC, a defendant acts negligently when the resulting harm or material element of a crime occurs because of the defendant has taken a substantial and unjustifiable risk, even if the risk is not perceived, so long as the risk involves a gross deviation from the standard of conduct that a law-abiding person would observe.

## Proving Mens Rea

At trial, the prosecution has the burden of establishing that the defendant possessed the required mental state when the act was committed. Proof of intent can be troublesome to prosecution, especially when subjective intent has to be proven. *Subjective intent* refers to the motives, intentions, and desires that were in the defendant's mind at the time the act took place. Subjective intent is a defendant's actual intent.

In most cases, defendants do not admit to committing the acts in question. Even when defendants do admit to some acts, they commonly deny intent. For crimes that require intent, admission of the act is not enough to sustain a conviction. How does a prosecutor prove subjective intent? The answer is by using **inferences**.

An *inference* is a conclusion that a judge or jury is permitted to make after considering the facts of a case. Imagine that a man walks up to another man and strikes him in the head with a hammer, using great force in his swing. The wound is fatal, and the attacker is charged with first-degree murder. To sustain a first-degree murder charge in this jurisdiction, it must be shown that the man intended to cause the victim's death. The defendant disavows such intent, admitting only that he intended to hit and injure the victim. In such a case, the jury would be permitted to infer the defendant's intent to kill the victim from the seriousness of the act. In a jurisdiction that uses the objective standard, the jury could conclude that a reasonable person would have known that the blow from a hammer would cause the victim's death, and the subjective intent of the defendant would not matter.

A **presumption** is a conclusion that must be made by a judge or jury. Most people have heard of the presumption of innocence in criminal law. This presumption is a *rebuttable presumption*. Rebuttable presumptions are conclusions that must be made by a judge or jury, unless disproven by the facts. Hence, defendants are innocent until proven guilty. *Irrebuttable presumptions* are conclusions that must be made by the judge or jury and cannot be disproved. Regardless of what the evidence shows, an irrebuttable presumption stands as a fact.

**inference**
A fact (or proposition) that is *probably* true because a true fact (or proposition) leads you to believe that the *inferred* fact (or proposition) is also true.

**presumption**
A presumption *of law* is an automatic assumption required by law that whenever a certain set of facts shows up, a court must automatically draw certain legal conclusions.

# Motive

**motive**
The reason why a person does something.

The reason a person commits a crime is **motive**. More precisely, an actor's rationale for wanting a desired result or to commit a specific act is the actor's motive.

Motive is different from mens rea. Motive leads to mens rea. Mens rea, in contrast, is concerned with whether a person intended to act. For example, greed is a motive for many acts. A bank robber's motive for robbing a bank is greed (or even, possibly, the challenge). The robber's mens rea is neither greed nor the emotional thrill resulting from the risk; rather, it is the intent to take money using force or threat. Said another way, the robber's mens rea (intent) is used to satisfy the motive (greed).

Motive is rarely an element of a crime. Therefore, prosecutors do not have to prove motive to be successful in a prosecution. As a practical matter, however, the trier of fact will want to know why the defendant committed the alleged crime. In many crimes, the motive will be apparent. Greed is easily understood and is imputed by juries to accused thieves. In other crimes, such as murder, there may be no apparent motive, and the prosecutor may need to introduce evidence explaining why a defendant would commit such a heinous crime. Was the murder motivated by greed (e.g., to gain an inheritance), or by passion (e.g., in revenge for infidelity), or by some other emotion? Usually, the prosecutor will prove motive; but in a case in which the defendant has pleaded insanity, the defendant bears the burden of providing either that there was no motive (e.g., the defendant did not want this to happen, but a mental disease or defect made her do it) or that the motive was the product of insanity (e.g., he believed the decedent was Godzilla).

A bad motive does not make an otherwise lawful act criminal. Conversely, a good motive does not excuse the commission of a crime. The issue is simply whether the prosecution has proven, beyond a reasonable doubt, that all the elements of the crime were committed.

Motive plays a role at sentencing. A good motive may justify a mitigation of sentence, whereas a bad motive may act in the reverse.

In some instances, a good motive may prevent charges from being filed at all. Police and prosecutors do not pursue some cases, even though a crime has been committed, when a person acted with good intentions. Conversely, law enforcement officials may pursue a case more passionately if the defendant acted from an evil motive. Although uncommon, prosecutors must sometimes prove motive. An example are hate crimes, where an actor's racial, religious, or gender motive for committing a crime (e.g. battery) is an element of the offense. Exhibit 3–3 summarizes mens rea versus motive.

# Actus Reus: Acting

Learning Objective: Define actus reus and explain whether thought, speech, personal status, and possession are treated as acts.

Earlier in this chapter, you learned the Latin phrase *actus non facit reum nisi mens sit rea*. The phrase expresses the common law requirement that two essential elements must be present to have a crime: a guilty mind and a guilty act. **Actus reus** is the physical part of a crime; it is the act. An act , or conduct in the words of the MPC, is a physical movement. If Mrs. X shoots and kills Mrs. T, the act is pulling the trigger of the gun.

**actus reus**
(Latin) An act. For example, an *actus reus* is a "wrongful deed" (such as killing a person), which, if done with mens rea, a "guilty mind" (such as *malice aforethought*), is a crime (such as *first-degree* murder).

The MPC states that a "person is not guilty of an offense unless his liability is based on conduct that includes a voluntary act."[22]

## Exhibit 3–3  Mens Rea v. Motive

|  | Mens Rea | Motive |
|---|---|---|
| Defined | The level of intentionality to commit an act that is required to prove a crime. | The reason a person acted. |
| Trial | An element of nearly all crimes that must be proven at trial beyond a reasonable doubt. | Not an element of any crime and doesn't have to be proved. However, a prosecutor may need to establish voluntariness motive in order to persuade a fact finder to convict. |
| Sentencing | May be considered in mitigation or aggravation. | May be considered in mitigation or aggravation. |

## Voluntariness

A person is only criminally liable for voluntary acts. To be voluntary, an act must occur as a result of the actor's conscious choice. The MPC requires that acts be voluntary and specifically lists the following as being involuntary:

1. reflexes and convulsions;
2. bodily movements during unconsciousness or sleep;
3. conduct during hypnosis or resulting from hypnotic suggestion; and
4. other movements that are not a product of the effort or determination of the actor.[23]

It is important to distinguish mens rea and actus reus. Actus reus only requires a voluntary choice of movement. No evil intent is required to have an act; that is a question of mens rea. Imagine that Jim chooses to swing his arm. As a result, he hits Tom. The level of intent required to prove battery and whether Jim possessed that intent are questions of mens rea. For actus reus, all that needs be known is whether Jim voluntarily chose to swing his arm.

In the *Cogdon* case, a woman was acquitted of murdering her daughter because it was determined that her acts were not voluntary.[24] No defense of insanity was raised in this case. If it had been, the analysis would have been different. Read about Ms. Cogdon's tragic crime in your next Oyez.

## Oyez

### King v. Cogdon
#### Supreme Court of Victoria (1950)

Mrs. Cogdon was charged with the murder of her only child, a daughter called Pat, aged 19. Pat had for some time been receiving psychiatric treatment for a relatively minor neurotic condition of which, in her psychiatrist's opinion, she was now cured. Despite this, Mrs. Cogdon continued to worry unduly about her. Describing the relationship between Pat and her mother, Mr. Cogdon testified: "I don't think

(continued)

a mother could have thought any more of her daughter. I think she absolutely adored her." On the conscious level, there was no doubt [of] Mrs. Cogdon's deep attachment to her daughter.

To the charge of murdering Pat, Mrs. Cogdon pleaded not guilty. Her story, though somewhat bizarre, was not seriously challenged by the Crown, and led to her acquittal. She told how on the night before her daughter's death, she had dreamt that their house was full of spiders and that these spiders were crawling all over Pat. In her sleep, Mrs. Cogdon left the bed she shared with her husband, went into Pat's room, and awakened to find herself violently brushing at Pat's face, presumably to remove the spiders. This woke Pat. Mrs. Cogdon told her she was just tucking her in.

At the trial, she testified that she still believed, as she had been told, that the occupants of a nearby house bred spiders as a hobby, preparing nests for them behind the pictures on their walls. It was these spiders that in her dreams had invaded their home and attacked Pat. There had also been a previous dream in which ghosts had sat at the end of Mrs. Cogdon's bed and she had said to them, "Well, you have come to take Pattie." It does not seem fanciful to accept the psychological explanation of these spiders and ghosts as the projections of Mrs. Cogdon's subconscious hostility toward her daughter, a hostility which was itself rooted in Mrs. Cogdon's own early life and marital relationship.

The morning after the spider dream, she told her doctor of it. He gave her a sedative and, because of the dream and certain previous difficulties she had reported, discussed the possibility of psychiatric treatment. That evening, Mrs. Cogdon suggested to her husband that he attend his lodge meeting, and asked Pat to come with her to the cinema. After her husband had gone, Pat looked through the paper, not unusually found no tolerable programme, and said that as she was going out the next evening, she thought she would rather go to bed early. Later, while Pat was having a bath preparatory to retiring, Mrs. Cogdon went into her room, put a hot water bottle in the bed, turned back the bedclothes, and placed a glass of hot milk beside the bed, ready for Pat. She then went to bed herself. There was some desultory conversation between them about the war in Korea, and just before she put out her light, Pat called out to her mother, "Mum, don't be so silly worrying about the war, it's not on our front step yet."

Mrs. Cogdon went to sleep. She dreamt that "the war was all around the house," that the soldiers were in Pat's room, and that one soldier was on the bed attacking Pat. This is all of the dream that she could later recapture. Her first "waking" memory was of running from Pat's room, out of the house to the home of her sister who lived next door. When her sister opened the front door, Mrs. Cogdon fell into her arms crying, "I think I've hurt Pattie."

In fact, Mrs. Cogdon had, in her somnambulistic state, left her bed, fetched an axe from the woodheap, entered Pat's room, and struck two accurate forceful blows on the head with the blade of the axe, thus killing her.

■ ■ ■

At all events the jury believed Mrs. Cogdon's story . . . [Mrs. Cogdon] was acquitted because the act of killing itself was not, in law, regarded as her act at all . . .

Ms. Cogdon isn't alone in causing harm while asleep. The film *Sleepwalk with Me*[25] documents the danger of extreme sleepwalking through the life of comedian Mike Birbiglia. More than once, Mr. Birbiglia has injured himself while performing his dreams. Once, while on tour, he dreamed that a missile was heading for him in his hotel room. After consulting the military experts in the room with him, he decided to end his life by throwing himself out of the window in his room, which he did, in reality. Unfortunately, the window was closed and he was on the second floor of the hotel. He jumped through the glass, fell two stories, screaming all the way, landed, got up, and began running. A short time later he woke, returned to the hotel, asked the reception clerk for another key to his room, and was treated for his wounds. To reduce the possibility of a repeat performance, he sedates himself, wears mittens, and sleeps in a sleeping bag that closes all the way to his face.

Imagine that in Mr. Birbiglia's dream he was ordered to detain the hotel reception clerk because he was about to commit an act of terrorism. Birbiglia would not be guilty of battery or false imprisonment if he grabbed the man and held on to him until he woke because he wouldn't be acting voluntarily. On the other hand, some courts have rejected this defense when the actor knows of their disease and doesn't take reasonable measures to control it. In one case, a man who knew he suffered from epilepsy was found guilty of manslaughter when his seizure caused him to lose control of his car, causing him to hit and kill several children.[26] Returning to Birbiglia, if he doesn't take remedial action to control his sleepwalking, he could be criminally culpable for future criminal conduct.

There is a close relationship between insanity and involuntary action. In most jurisdictions, one cannot plead both lack of a voluntary act and insanity. In those situations, the rules of the insanity defense apply. See Chapter 8 for a complete discussion of insanity as a defense.

## Thoughts and Statements as Acts

Thoughts alone are not acts, so they not be criminalized. People are free to dream about running their professors over with tractors or poisoning the local barista who insulted them when they asked for soy milk. It is not until they translate those evil thoughts into acts that they can be punished.

Generally, people are also free to speak. The First Amendment to the U.S. Constitution protects freedom of speech. There are, however, limits to First Amendment protection of speech. Inciting riots, treason, solicitation, conspiracy, and inciting imminent lawlessness are examples of speech that may be prohibited. You will learn more about the First Amendment protection of speech later.

## Personal Status as an Act

Generally, a person's status cannot be punished. Illness, financial status, race, sex, and religion are examples of human conditions and statuses. Some conditions are directly related to illegal behavior. For example, being addicted to illegal narcotics is a condition that cannot be criminalized. However, using and selling prohibited narcotics are acts that may be punished.

Vagrancy is one area over which there is a split in legal opinion. Some courts have held that vagrancy may be prohibited; others have determined that vagrancy is a condition and does not constitute a crime. One author noted that there is a "growing body of authority" holding such statutes unconstitutional.[27]

In *Robinson v. California,* the U.S. Supreme Court was called upon to review a California statute that made it a crime "either to use narcotics, or to be addicted to the use of narcotics." The Court reversed Robinson's conviction, and in the opinion stated:

> This statute, therefore, is not one which punishes a person for the use of narcotics, for their purchase, sale or possession, or for antisocial or disorderly behavior resulting from their administration. It is not a law which even purports to provide or require medical treatment. Rather, we deal with a statute which makes the "status" of narcotic addiction a criminal offense, for which the offender may be prosecuted "at any time before he reforms." California has said that a person can be continuously guilty of this offense, whether or not he has ever used or possessed any narcotics within the state, and whether or not he has been guilty of any antisocial behavior there.
>
> It is unlikely that any State at this moment in history would attempt to make it a criminal offense for a person to be mentally ill, or a leper, or to be afflicted with a venereal disease. A State might determine that the general health and welfare require that the victims of these and other human afflictions be dealt with by compulsory treatment, involving quarantine, confinement, or sequestration. But in the light of contemporary human knowledge, a law which made a criminal offense of such a disease would doubtless be universally thought of to be

an infliction of cruel and unusual punishment in violation of the Eighth and Fourteenth Amendments. . . .

We cannot but consider the statute before us as of the same category . . . . We hold that a state law which imprisons a person thus afflicted as a criminal, even though he has never touched any narcotic drug within the State or been guilty of any irregular behavior there, inflicts a cruel and unusual punishment in violation of the Fourteenth Amendment. . . .[28]

While personal status may not be criminalized, it may be subject to the regulatory authority of the state. Individuals who are mentally ill and who pose a danger to themselves or others may be civilly committed, for example. This includes the commitment of sexual predators.

## Possession as an Act

Possession of certain items, such as narcotics or burglary tools, may be made criminal. Possession of deadly weapons is both a federal and a state crime. Following the terrorist attacks of September 11, 2001, for example, Congress made it unlawful to possess biological agents or delivery systems for biological agents that are intended to be used as weapons.[29] Possession is not, strictly speaking, an act. Possession does not involve an active body movement; rather, possession is a passive state of being. Even so, most possession laws have been upheld.

Jurisdictions differ in what is required to prove possession. Some require that actual possession be shown; others allow proof of constructive possession. Constructive possession is used to extend criminal liability to those who never exercised actual possession but had dominion and control over the contraband. An example is a familiar scenario to police. A car has a driver and passenger. The passenger is carrying illegal drugs. This this is known to the driver, they are responsible in some jurisdictions for possession, even though they are not in direct possession, have not used, and don't own the drugs. In essence, the law imposes a duty on people to remove illegal items from the area over which they have dominion and control. Failure to comply with such a duty is treated as an act and can lead to criminal liability.

One problem with crimes of possession is the possibility of convicting people who had no knowledge of the existence of illegal items in an area under their dominion and control. An owner of a house has dominion and control over the guest room but may not be aware that a guest has brought illegal items into the room. Most jurisdictions have remedied this problem by requiring knowledge of the presence of the goods. The MPC also uses such a test. The Code states that possession is an act as long as the "possessor knowingly procured or received the thing possessed or was aware of his control thereof for a sufficient period to have been able to terminate his possession." Under the Code, possession can be actual or constructive. However, if constructive, the possessor must have known of the items for a period of time long enough to permit the possessor to terminate possession. So, if the owner of the house discovered the cocaine only minutes before the police arrived to search the premises, no possession could be found on the owner's behalf.

Finally, one person or many people can be in possession of items. Using the preceding example, assume that two or more people jointly owned the home in question. All of the owners could be liable, if it was determined that all had constructive possession and adequate time to remove the cocaine from the house. It is possible that fewer than all of the owners knew of the cocaine and, as such, did not have constructive possession. Each person who is alleged to have dominion and control (constructive possession) must be examined individually, and separate decisions as to their individual liability must be made.

# Actus Reus: Not Acting

Learning Objective: Identify and describe three or more occasions when inaction is criminal.

In 2011, allegations of sexual abuse of children by former Penn State University assistant football coach Jerry Sandusky went viral. Sandusky was convicted and sentenced in 2012 to 30 to 60 years in prison for abusing many young men.[30] But this wasn't the end of the story. Several other Penn State officials were charged with crimes resulting from Sandusky's crimes, including perjury and failure to report abuse of a minor. Rape and perjury are acts. Failing to report a crime does not involve an act. It is just the opposite— it is the failure to act. Generally, only acts are prohibited by criminal law. However, in some situations, failing to act is criminal. An **omission** is a failure to act when required to do so by criminal law.

**omission**
Failing to do something that is required by law.

It is often the case that a person who may have a moral duty to act does not have a legal duty to act. In most instances, for example, people do not have a legal duty to assist one another in times of need. It would not be criminal in most jurisdictions for an excellent swimmer to watch another drown. Nor would it be criminal to watch another walk into a dangerous situation, such as a bank robbery in progress, if the observer had no connection with the criminal event. There are exceptions to this rule. To be liable for a failure to act, a person must have a "duty" to act. The duty to act may come from the common law or statutory law.

## Duty Imposed by Statute

Under the common law, people had no duty to assist others whose lives were in danger. This continues to be the general rule, but today, some states impose a duty, and criminal liability for failing, to help others. Even when expected, rescue isn't required if it puts the rescuer's life at risk. Statutory duty to others occurs in two forms:

1. Duty to report
2. Duty to act

All of the states and the federal government impose a duty to report harm, or potential harm, in some circumstances. It is common for medical and mental health professionals, law enforcement officers, teachers, and caregivers to be obliged to report elder, child, and spousal abuse to some legal authority. Failure to comply is a crime of omission.

There are other specific reporting requirements found in state and federal laws. Businesses that store or dispose of toxic materials are required to maintain records and file reports, taxpayers are required to file tax returns, drivers of automobiles involved in accidents are required to stop at their accident scenes, and some states require individuals to report wild animals that are loose. Ohio is unique in criminalizing the failure to report any felony that has been, or is being, committed. The same law requires health care professionals to report stab wounds, gunshot wounds, and burn injuries that appear to be the result of violence.[31]

Sometimes the duty transcends reporting; a person must act to protect others. Most commonly, both forms of duty are imposed on people who are in special relationships with the victims. As mentioned earlier, the doctors, teachers, and mental health professionals who have a duty to report child abuse have no obligation to act; they, for example, aren't compelled to remove a child from a dangerous home. A parent or guardian, on the other hand, is different. They are expected to proactively protect their children.

The Penn State sex abuse scandal, mentioned earlier, and the Parkland School massacre illustrate the difference between the two duties. The Penn State case involved multiple rapes of juveniles by Gerald Sandusky, assistant coach of the Penn State football team. The assaults took place on the Penn State campus, in Sandusky's car, and in other locations. One of the assaults, which occurred in a shower at the university, was witnessed by an employee of the football team. He reported the incident to the football coach, Joe Paterno. Paterno is alleged to have passed on the report to his superiors, Tim Curley and Gary Schultz. Pennsylvania law required knowledge of sexual abuse by an employee to be reported to the "person in charge," who in turn had an obligation to pass the report along to "authorities." While there was disagreement about whether Paterno reported all that he knew, whether he should have reported the incident to authorities, and whether Curley and Schultz made the required reporting to authorities, there was no doubt that the initial employee did what was expected of him. He reported the incident to his superiors; he had no obligation to intervene in the crime.

In the Parkland case, Scot Peterson, a sheriff's deputy and school resource officer at the Marjory Stoneman Douglas High School in Parkland, Florida, remained outside of the school, handgun drawn, while a gunman murdered 17 people and injured 17 more. Allegedly, he dissuaded other police officers from entering the building. Pinellas County Sheriff Bob Gualtieri referred to Mr. Peterson as "a coward, a failure and a criminal."[32] Peterson was criminally charged in 2019 for child abuse and neglect on the theory that he owed the students and employees a duty of protection, by virtue of being both a law enforcement and school resource officer. There is no statute in Florida requiring police to respond in such massacres, so Peterson was charged under a law creating a duty for "caregivers." One of Peterson's defenses is that the law, which clearly applies to health care and similar providers, doesn't apply to police officers. The case was pending when this book went to press.

## Duty by Relationship

Even when a statute doesn't expressly create a duty to act, the law will sometimes impose one when a special relationship of care exists. The most common examples are parent-to-child and spouse-to-spouse. In such personal relationships, a level of dependence exists that gives rise to criminal liability for failure to assist the party who is in danger.

Generally, any time a joint enterprise is undertaken by two or more parties, it can be assumed that a duty to assist one another during that enterprise is created. For example, if two people decide to go river rafting, they must rescue one another during that rafting trip, provided that the rescuer is not endangered by attempting the rescue.

In the parent–child relationship, a parent can be guilty of manslaughter if the child dies as a result of the parent's failure to seek medical attention for the child when the child is sick, or for failing to pull the child out of a pool when the child is drowning. The same would be true of a spouse. If a wife permitted her husband to die when she could have saved his life by calling 911 or handing him an EpiPen, she could be criminally liable. In addition, it has been held that employers owe a duty to assist their employees. For example, the master of a ship must attempt to rescue a seaman who has fallen overboard.

## Duty by Contract

A duty to act can be created in a third way—by contract. For example, physicians are hired to care for the health of their patients. If a doctor watches as a patient slowly dies, doing nothing to save the patient's life when there were measures that could have been taken, the doctor is liable for homicide. The same is true of a lifeguard. The lifeguard is hired to save those who are drowning, and if a lifeguard sits and watches a swimmer drown when the swimmer could have been saved, the lifeguard is liable for homicide.

Remember, the general rule is that people owe no duty to rescue others. So, if an Olympic swimmer happens to be on the beach when another person is drowning, the Olympian can watch the person drown without risking criminal liability.

## Assumption of Duty

Even though the general rule is that people do not have a duty to rescue strangers, it is possible, either expressly or by one's actions, to make an *assumption of duty*. The assumption is express if it is stated orally or in writing. Assumption is different from duty premised on contract, in that assumptions are gratuitous. If Sidney is at a pool and agrees to care for another's child while the parent uses the restroom, Sidney has assumed the duty expressly. If the child falls into the pool, and Sidney takes no action to save the child, Sidney is liable for murder if the child drowns.

It is possible through one's actions to assume the duty to rescue someone. Assume that Sidney is now at a lake. One person, David, is swimming, and three other people are relaxing on the beach. David begins to scream for help. Sidney jumps up and dives into the water to rescue David. Halfway out to David, she changes her mind and returns to shore. By the time she returns to shore, it is too late for someone else to make the swim to David, and David dies. In this case, Sidney assumed the duty of the rescue by beginning the rescue attempt. However, whether Sidney is liable for murder depends on what condition the drowning person was left in after Sidney changed her mind. If Sidney's actions caused the other three people on the beach to fail to attempt a rescue, Sidney's actions left David in a worse condition than he would have been in had Sidney not begun the rescue. However, if Sidney's actions did not prevent anyone else from attempting a rescue, Sidney's action did not put David in a worse situation and Sidney is not liable for murder, even if the other person fails in the rescue attempt.

Finally, note that we can easily change this last example into an express assumption. All that has to be added is a statement by Sidney to the others on the beach that she will swim out and rescue David. Such a statement, if it caused others to forgo a rescue attempt, is an express assumption of duty.

## Creating Danger

Any time a person creates the circumstance that endangers a stranger, a duty to save the stranger is created. This is true whether the danger was caused intentionally or negligently. So, if an arsonist sets fire to a house that is believed to be empty and is discovered not to be, the arsonist must attempt to save anyone inside. If not, the arsonist is also a murderer. The same would be true of a negligently caused fire. If an electrician begins a fire in a home and does nothing to warn the inhabitants, the electrician is also liable for murder.

## Causation

For crimes that require a particular result, the act must be the "cause" of the result. In criminal law, two forms of causation exist: factual and legal. If either of these is missing, no specific intent crime has been committed. Even if so, the actor may be convicted of a lesser included offense that doesn't require an intent to cause the outcome.

An act is the *cause in fact* of the result if the result would not have occurred unless the act occurred. This is known as the *sine qua non* test, which means that "but for" the conduct, the harm would not have resulted.

**legal cause**
The proximate cause of an injury; probable cause; cause that the law deems sufficient.

**proximate cause**
The "legal cause" of an accident or other injury (which may have several actual causes). The *proximate cause* of an injury is not necessarily the closest thing in time or space to the injury, and not necessarily the event that set things in motion, because "proximate cause" is a legal, not a physical concept.

**foreseeable**
The degree to which the consequences of an action *should* have been anticipated, recognized, and considered beforehand. *Not* hindsight.

**intervening cause**
A cause of an accident or other injury that will remove the blame from the wrongdoer who originally set events in motion.

**Legal cause** must also be proved. Legal causation focuses on the degree of similarity between the defendant's intended result and the actual result. It also examines the similarity between the intended manner used to bring about a result and the actual manner that caused the result. Generally, the greater the similarity between the purpose and the result, and the manner intended and the manner that actually caused the result, the more likely that the defendant is the legal cause. Legal cause is also commonly referred to as **proximate cause**. *Proximate* means "nearly, next to, or close." In the context of criminal causation, it refers to the relationship between the act and the result. The result must be a consequence of the act, not a coincidence. An outcome is proximately caused by an act if a reasonable person would have foreseen and expected the result. This is known as **foreseeability**.

Most problems raised in this area involve legal causation, not factual causation. This is because, to prove factual causation, it must be shown that the defendant's action set into motion the events that led to the prohibited result. This is not difficult to prove. Determining legal causation is more troublesome, however.

Let us examine a few examples. Hank shoots Mark, intending to kill him. Mark dies from the gunshot wound. Hank is the factual cause of the murder because he set into motion the events that killed Mark. To state it another way, "but for" Hank's act, Mark would not have died. Hank is also the legal cause of Mark's death because the resulting death is identical to Hank's intention.

Now assume that Hank intended only to injure Mark, not to kill him. Accordingly, he stabbed Mark in the foot with a knife and promptly called 911, which dispatched an ambulance. The paramedics negligently administered a dangerous medication, causing Mark's death. Hank continues to be the factual cause of Mark's death, because if he had not injured Mark, the medical attention that ended Mark's life would not have been necessary. However, Hank is not the legal cause of Mark's death because the result wasn't foreseeable. But don't worry, Hank isn't walking free. He is liable for aggravated battery and likely, a lower form of homicide. You will learn more about these crimes in upcoming chapters.

Note that it is common for legal cause to be lacking when an **intervening cause** exists, as it does in the previous example. An *intervening cause* is a happening that occurs after the initial act and changes the outcome. Intervening causes function to block the connection between an act and the result, because the intervening cause changes what would have been the result if the result had flowed freely from the act. Intervening causes can negate or lower criminal liability for the particular result. However, lower crimes may continue to be punishable. In the preceding example, the intervening cause is the negligent medical care of the paramedics. Hank's intent was not to cause Mark's death, and, as such, he was not the legal cause of Mark's death. Of course, Hank may also have a mens rea defense.

Assume that Hank shot Mark intending to kill him, but because Hank is a poor shot, he only injured Mark. As before, the paramedics who treat Mark negligently administer the wrong medication and cause his death. Again, Hank is the factual cause of Mark's death. Whether he is the legal cause is debatable. Even though the intended result occurred, it occurred in a manner entirely unintended. If the manner in which the result occurs differs significantly from the manner that was intended, the defendant may not be liable. This appears consistent with common notions of fairness: Why should Hank be liable for murder when at least part of the blame belongs to the paramedics? Courts are split on this issue. Some would find that Hank is liable for intent murder, whereas others would hold Hank liable for a lower murder.

If a victim suffers the intended injury while attempting to avoid the injury, the defendant is liable for the crime, even though the manner is entirely different than intended. So, if Mark is struck and killed by a bus while running from Hank, who intends to stab Mark to death, Hank is considered both the legal and the factual cause of Mark's death. There is a limit to this theory; that is, there must be some nexus between the unintended manner and the act. If a reasonable person would not have expected the result to occur, the defendant is not liable. So, if Mark was not killed by a passing bus but, rather, by a hit on the head by a piano accidentally dropped by movers, Hank is not the legal cause of his death. This is true even though Mark would not have happened to be under the piano if he were not running from Hank.

In the rare instance where two events happen simultaneously, and both could be the legal cause of the outcome, both are treated as the legal cause. This is true even if only one event was the actual cause. For example, if two people shoot a victim at the same moment, both are liable for murder. However, it is possible that only one actually caused the death. If it is not possible to determine which bullet was the actual cause of death, both people are liable. If it can be determined which bullet was responsible for killing the victim, the other party is relieved of responsibility for murder (although not attempted murder).

Even though the preceding examples dealt with purposeful crimes, remember that the principle applies to all crimes that require a particular result. The result need not be one that comes about purposely or intentionally. Crimes of recklessness and negligence may require a specific result to be criminal. Reckless homicide requires that the behavior that is reckless actually cause a death.

The MPC requires that the conduct in question be the actual result or cause of the result. Section 2.03 of the MPC provides that if a particular result is necessary to prove a crime, the "element is not established unless the actual result is a probable consequence of the actor's conduct." Further, the Code states that the crime is not proven if the actual result is different from the defendant's purpose, unless:

1. The resulting harm is the same; however, it occurred to the wrong person or thing (transferred intent).

2. The actual harm is not as great or as serious as intended.

3. The actual harm involves the same kind of injury or harm as intended and is not *too remote or accidental* in its occurrence to have a bearing on the actor's liability.

These requirements apply to all levels of culpability under the Code—that is, purposeful, knowing, reckless, and negligent—and must be adjusted accordingly. Accordingly, if the crime is one of recklessness or negligence, then the Code's criteria should be viewed in light of risks and probable results and not purpose.

The phrase "too remote or accidental" is the Code's proximate cause requirement. It is the same as discussed earlier, except that the drafters of the Code chose not to use the phrase "proximate cause." In *People v. Warner-Lambert Co.*, a company and some of its officers were indicted for manslaughter and negligent homicide. The charges stemmed from an industrial accident at one of Warner-Lambert's plants. The high court of New York dismissed the indictments, finding that the defendants were not the proximate cause of the plant employees' deaths because the explosion that caused their deaths was not foreseeable. This case is featured in your next Oyez.

## Oyez

### People v. Warner-Lambert Co.
### 51 N.Y.2d 295, 414 N.E.2d 660 (1980), cert. denied, 450 U.S. 1031 (1981)

**Opinion by Judge Jones**

Defendant Warner-Lambert Co. is a manufacturing corporation which produces, among other items, Freshen-Up chewing gum. The individual defendants were officers or employees of the corporation. Defendant Kraft was vice-president in charge of manufacturing; defendant Harris was the director of corporate safety and security; defendants O'Mahoney and O'Rourke were, respectively, plant manager and plant engineer of the Warner-Lambert facility located at 30-30 Thompson Avenue in Long Island City, New York, which was the situs of the events out of which this indictment arose. The indictment charges each defendant with six counts of manslaughter . . . and six counts of criminally negligent homicide . . . in consequence of the deaths of six employees which resulted from a massive explosion and fire at the Long Island City Warner-Lambert plant about 2:30 a.m. on November 21, 1976.

On the day on which the explosion occurred, Freshen-Up gum, which is retailed in the shape of a square tablet with a jelly-like center, was being produced at the Warner-Lambert plant by a process in which filled ropes of the gum were passed through a bed of magnesium stearate (MS), a dry, dustlike lubricant which was applied by hand, then into a die-cut punch (a Uniplast machine) which was sprayed with a cooling agent (liquid nitrogen), where the gum was formed into the square tablets. Both the MS (normally an inert, organic compound) and the liquid nitrogen were employed to prevent the chicle from adhering to the sizing and cutting machinery, the tendency to adhere being less if a dry lubricant was used and the punch was kept at a low temperature. The process produced a dispersal of MS dust in the air and an accumulation of it at the base of the Uniplast machine and on overhead pipes; some also remained ambient in the atmosphere in the surrounding area.

Both MS and liquid nitrogen are considered safe and are widely used in the industry. In bulk, MS will only burn or smolder if ignited; however, like many substances, if suspended in the air in sufficient concentration the dust poses a substantial risk of explosion if ignited. . . . Liquid nitrogen is highly volatile, is easily ignited and, if ignited, will explode. Among possible causes of such ignition of either liquid oxygen or ambient MS are electrical or mechanical sparks.

■ ■ ■

There was proof that an inspection of the plant by Warner-Lambert's insurance carrier in February, 1976, had resulted in advice to the insured that the dust condition in the Freshen-Up gum production area presented an explosion hazard and that the MS concentration was above the [low point where explosion could occur], together with recommendations for installation of a dust exhaust system and modification of electrical equipment to meet standards for dust areas. Although a variety of proposals for altering the dust condition were considered by the individual defendants in consultations and communications with each other and some alterations in the MS application were made, both ambient and settled MS dust were still present on November 21, 1976.

■ ■ ■

The issue before us, however, is whether defendants could be held criminally liable for what actually occurred, on theories of reckless or negligent conduct, based on the evidence submitted to this Grand Jury, viewed in the light most favorable to the People. The focus of our attention must be on the issue of culpability, taking into account the conduct of the defendants and the factors of foreseeability and of causation, all of which in combination constitute the ultimate amalgam on which criminal liability may or may not be predicated.

First, we look at the evidence as to the actual event or chain of events which triggered the explosion—evidence which may only be characterized as hypothetical and speculative. . . . The prosecution hypothesizes that under what it describes as "the most plausible of theories," the initial detonation was attributable to mechanical sparking. . . .

Another explanation for the initial explosion was offered by an expert called by the prosecution who hypothesized that liquid oxygen . . . dripped onto settled MS dust at the base of the Uniplast, became trapped there, and then, when subjected to the impact caused by a moving metal part, reacted violently, causing ignition of already dispersed MS.

Viewed most favorably to the People, the proof with respect to the actual cause of the explosion is speculative only, and as to at least one of the major hypotheses—that involving oxygen liquefaction—there was no evidence that the process was foreseeable or known to any of the defendants. In sum, there was no proof sufficient to support a finding that defendants foresaw or should have foreseen the physical cause of the explosion. This being so, there was not legally sufficient evidence to establish the offenses charged or any lesser included offense.

[The grand jury indictment is therefore, invalid and dismissed.]

## The "Year-and-a-Day Rule"

At common law, a person could not be charged with murder if the victim did not die within one year and one day after the act. The rule addressed the issue of causation. It was developed to prevent a conviction for murder at a time in history when medical science could not precisely determine the actual cause of a person's death. If a person lived for more than a year and a day after being injured by a defendant's acts and then died, it was assumed that medical science could not adequately attribute the victim's death to the defendant's act.

It is questionable, in light of the advances in medicine, whether the rule should continue. It has been abolished in many states and in a few, it has been modified. In California, for example, if a death occurs more than three years and day after an act, it is presumed that the act isn't the cause of death. The state bears the burden of overcoming the presumption.[33] In *Rogers v. Tennessee* (2001), the Supreme Court reviewed a conviction in Tennessee that was allowed to stand because the Tennessee courts announced the abrogation of the rule in the case. The court was asked to invalidate the conviction as *ex post facto* and contrary to due process.

## Oyez

### Rogers v. Tennessee
### 532 U.S. 451 (2001)

**Justice O'Connor delivered the opinion of the Court.**

This case concerns the constitutionality of the retroactive application of a judicial decision abolishing the common law "year-and-a-day rule." At common law, the year-and-a-day rule provided that no defendant could be convicted of murder unless his victim had died by the defendant's act within a year and a day of the act. . . . The Supreme Court of Tennessee abolished the rule as it had existed at common law in Tennessee and applied its decision to petitioner to uphold his conviction. The question before us is whether, in doing so, the court denied petitioner due process of law in violation of the Fourteenth Amendment.

Petitioner Wilbert K. Rogers was convicted in Tennessee state court of second-degree murder. According to the undisputed facts, petitioner stabbed his victim, James Bowdery, with a butcher knife on May 6, 1994. One of the stab wounds penetrated Bowdery's heart. During surgery to repair the wound to his heart, Bowdery went into cardiac arrest, but was resuscitated and survived the procedure. As a result, however, he had developed a condition known as "cerebral hypoxia," which results from a loss of oxygen to the brain. Bowdery's higher-brain functions had ceased, and he slipped into and remained in a coma until August 7, 1995, when he died from a kidney infection (a common complication experienced by comatose patients). Approximately 15 months had passed between the stabbing and Bowdery's death, which, according to the undisputed testimony of the county medical examiner, was caused by cerebral hypoxia "secondary to a stab wound to the heart." . . .

Based on this evidence, the jury found petitioner guilty under Tennessee's criminal homicide statute. The statute, which makes no mention of the year-and-a-day rule, defines criminal homicide simply as "the unlawful killing of another person, which may be first degree murder, second degree murder, voluntary manslaughter, criminally negligent homicide or vehicular homicide." . . . Petitioner appealed his conviction to the Tennessee Court of Criminal Appeals, arguing that, despite its absence from the statute, the year-and-a-day rule persisted as part of the common law of Tennessee and, as such, precluded his conviction.

The Court of Criminal Appeals rejected that argument and affirmed the conviction. The court held that Tennessee's Criminal Sentencing Reform Act of 1989 (1989 Act), which abolished all common law defenses in criminal actions in Tennessee, had abolished the rule. The court also rejected petitioner's further contention that the legislative abolition of the rule constituted an *ex post facto* violation, noting that the 1989 Act had taken effect five years before petitioner committed his crime. . . .

The Supreme Court of Tennessee affirmed on different grounds. The court observed that it had recognized the viability of the year and a day rule in Tennessee in *Percer v. State*, 118 Tenn. 765, 103 S.W. 780 (1907), and that, "[d]espite the paucity of case law" on the rule in Tennessee, "both parties . . . agree that the . . . rule was a part of the common law of this State." Turning to the rule's present status,

(continued)

the court noted that the rule has been legislatively or judicially abolished by the "vast majority" of jurisdictions recently to have considered the issue. The court concluded that, contrary to the conclusion of the Court of Criminal Appeals, the 1989 Act had not abolished the rule. After reviewing the justifications for the rule at common law, however, the court found that the original reasons for recognizing the rule no longer exist. Accordingly, the court abolished the rule as it had existed at common law in Tennessee. The court disagreed with petitioner's contention that application of its decision abolishing the rule to his case would violate the *Ex Post Facto* Clauses of the State and Federal Constitutions. Those constitutional provisions, the court observed, refer only to legislative Acts. . . .

Although petitioner's claim is one of due process, the Constitution's *Ex Post Facto* Clause figures prominently in his argument. The Clause provides simply that "[n]o State shall . . . pass any . . . ex post facto Law" (Art. I, § 10, cl. 1). The most well-known and oft-repeated explanation of the scope of the Clause's protection was given by Justice Chase, who long ago identified, in dictum, four types of laws to which the Clause extends:

1st. Every law that makes an action done before the passing of the law, and which was innocent when done, criminal; and punishes such action. 2d. Every law that aggravates a crime, or makes it greater than it was, when committed. 3d. Every law that changes the punishment, and inflicts a greater punishment, than the law annexed to the crime, when committed. 4th. Every law that alters the legal rules of evidence, and receives less, or different, testimony, than the law required at the time of the commission of the offense, in order to convict the offender.

Strict application of *ex post facto* principles [to courts] would unduly impair the incremental and reasoned development of precedent that is the foundation of the common law system. The common law, in short, presupposes a measure of evolution that is incompatible with stringent application of *ex post facto* principles. It was on account of concerns such as these that *Bouie* restricted due process limitations on the retroactive application of judicial interpretations of criminal statutes to those that are "unexpected and indefensible by reference to the law which had been expressed prior to the conduct in issue." Bouie v. City of Columbia, . . . .

We believe this limitation adequately serves the common law context as well. It accords common law courts the substantial leeway they must enjoy as they engage in the daily task of formulating and passing upon criminal defenses and interpreting such doctrines as causation and intent, reevaluating and refining them as may be necessary to bring the common law into conformity with logic and common sense. It also adequately respects the due process concern with fundamental fairness and protects against vindictive or arbitrary judicial lawmaking by safeguarding defendants against unjustified and unpredictable breaks with prior law. Accordingly, we conclude that a judicial alteration of a common law doctrine of criminal law violates the principle of fair warning, and hence must not be given retroactive effect, only where it is "unexpected and indefensible by reference to the law which had been expressed prior to the conduct in issue." . . .

Turning to the particular facts of the instant case, the Tennessee court's abolition of the year-and-a-day rule was not unexpected and indefensible. The year-and-a-day rule is widely viewed as an outdated relic of the common law. Petitioner does not even so much as hint that good reasons exist for retaining the rule, so we need not delve too deeply into the rule and its history here. Suffice it to say that the rule is generally believed to date back to the thirteenth century, when it served as a statute of limitations governing the time in which an individual might initiate a private action for murder known as an "appeal of death"; that by the eighteenth century, the rule had been extended to the law governing public prosecutions for murder; that the primary and most frequently cited justification for the rule is that thirteenth-century medical science was incapable of establishing causation beyond a reasonable doubt when a great deal of time had elapsed between the injury to the victim and his death; and that, as practically every court recently has noted to have considered the rule as to render it without question obsolete. . . . For this reason, the year-and-a-day rule has been legislatively or judicially abolished in the vast majority of jurisdictions recently to have addressed the issue. . . .

[The Court then discussed the small number of Tennessee cases that mention the Rule and concluded that in no case did the Supreme Court of Tennessee ever apply the Rule.]

In short, there is nothing to indicate that the Tennessee court's abolition of the rule in petitioner's case represented an exercise of the sort of unfair and arbitrary judicial action against which the Due Process Clause aims to protect. Far from a marked and unpredictable departure from prior precedent, the court's decision was a routine exercise of common law decisionmaking in which the court brought the law into conformity with reason and common sense. It did so by laying to rest an archaic and outdated rule that had never been relied upon as a ground of decision in any reported Tennessee case.

The judgement of the Supreme Court of Tennessee is accordingly affirmed.

## Cause Not Coincidence: Concurrence

For crimes that have both a mental and a physical element, an additional requirement of concurrence must be proved. *Concurrence* is the joining of mens rea and the act. The mens rea must be the cause of the actus reus. Stated another way, the mental state must be formed before the act is taken. For example, Sandira hates Andy and desires to see him dead. Because of this feeling, Sandira waits for Andy to leave the house one night and runs him down with her car. In such a case, Sandira's mens rea set into motion the act that caused Andy's death. Now imagine that Sandira accidentally kills Andy in an auto accident. After the accident, she exclaims her happiness over Andy's demise. In this case, the mens rea is a coincidence, not the cause of the act.

The mere fact that the mental state happens before the act does not mean that there is concurrence. There must be a connection between the intent and the act; the mens rea must set the act into motion. So, if Doug forms the desire to kill Andy today but takes no action to further the desire, he cannot be charged with murder a year later when he accidentally shoots Andy while hunting.

As stated by the Court of Appeals of Indiana:

> Unless statutorily stated otherwise, it is black letter law that in order to constitute a crime "criminal intent" . . . must unite with an overt act, and they must concur in point of time. There must be a criminal act or omission as well as criminal intent. A felonious intent unconnected with an unlawful act constitutes no crime. . . . A person can only be punished for an offense he has committed and never for an offense he may commit in the future. A crime cannot be predicated upon future acts or upon contingencies or the taking effect of some future event.[34]

## Attendant Circumstances and Element Analysis

For conviction, a prosecutor must prove every element of a crime beyond a reasonable doubt. As you have learned, most crimes require prosecutors to prove mens rea and actus reus. But that isn't everything. Prosecutors also have to prove facts or conditions that are essential to the crime that are not acts, nor are they states of mind. **Attendant circumstances**, as they are known, tend to be objects or subjects in a sentence, while the actus reus is typically a verb. Consider the crime of battery—the intentional harmful or offensive touching of another person without consent. The mens rea is the intention to touch another person. The actus reus is the touching. But the crime also includes a requirement that the touching be unconsensual. This is neither a state of mind, nor is it an act. It is an attendant circumstance. The same is true of the harmful or offensive element. Both must be proven beyond a reasonable doubt, just like the mens rea and act. The outcome or result of an act is also a form of attendant circumstance. It is not an "act," but it surely must be proven in many crimes. Murder, for example, requires that the victim's death be proven.

**attendant circumstances**
Facts or conditions that must be proven, along with the mens rea and actus reus, for a defendant to be convicted.

In future chapters you will study the elements of specific crimes. In the very early common law, a person was legally liable for a harmful act if they were morally culpable; they possessed an evil or malicious mind. As you learned earlier, the courts refined this idea of general culpability into general and specific intent, each reflecting a different level of culpability. Each crime, however, continued to have one mens rea. This was known as **offense analysis**.

The MPC continues to recognize offense analysis as the default approach. But it also introduced an alternative approach, known as **element analysis**. When clearly intended in the legislation, the MPC provides for mentes reae, or multiple states of mind, in a single crime. Under this approach, each act, attending circumstance, and result may have their own mens rea. Let's return to the crime of battery. Applying offense analysis, the mens rea is intentionality. But what must be intended? Clearly, the touching must be intended. What about the harmful or offensive element? Must the defendant intend harm or offense? And if so, does the same mens rea apply to both elements? The MPC recognizes four states of mind and sometimes inserts more than one into the same crime.

**offense analysis**
The assignment of a single mens rea to an offense.

**element analysis**
The assignment of separate mens rea to each element of an offense.

Let's apply element analysis to Nebraska's burglary statute, which declares that "[a] person commits burglary if such person willfully, maliciously, and forcibly breaks and enters any real estate or any improvements erected thereon with intent to commit any felony or with intent to steal property of any value."[35]

A person commits burglary if such person

willfully, maliciously, and forcibly [mens rea of the acts of breaking and entering]

breaks [actus reus] and

enters [actus reus]

any real estate or any improvements erected thereon [attendant circumstance]

with intent to commit [mens rea for felony or to steal property]

any felony [attendant circumstance] OR

to steal property of any value [attendant circumstance]

Both offense and element analysis are applied today, depending on the jurisdiction and the specific crime.

In Exhibit 3–4, all of the elements of crimes that prosecutors must prove beyond a reasonable doubt are shown.

## Exhibit 3–4  Crime Formula

## Ethical Considerations

### Overzealous Representation

In Chapter 2's Ethical Considerations feature, you learned that attorneys have an obligation to zealously represent clients. But how far can an attorney take this obligation? What if a defense attorney intentionally hides the evidence of a client's crime from the government? This is precisely what happened in *In Re Ryder*. The attorney in that case hid the gun that his client used in a robbery, along with the stolen cash. Interestingly, the attorney had previously been a federal prosecutor!

Well, there is a limit to zealous representation. The Model Rules qualify the zealous representation requirement to behavior that is *within the bounds of the law*. In the case of the attorneys in the Chapter 2 feature, their decision not to disclose the location of the buried victims of their client's murders was held to be ethical, because the ethical obligation not to disclose client communications trumped the administrative violation of not reporting the location of human remains. An attorney, however, may not intentionally mislead a court or fabricate evidence. Advising or coaching witnesses to testify falsely—known as the crime of suborning perjury—is also overzealous conduct. Harboring a client fugitive, filing false documents with a court, allowing evidence within one's control to spoil without notifying the opposing party or court, harassing and bribing jurors and witnesses, and destroying or hiding evidence, as occurred in *In Re Ryder* are other examples of excessively zealous conduct.

Although defense attorneys and prosecutors share an obligation to zealously represent their clients, they have different constitutional missions. For the defense attorneys, the constitutional mission is the same as their general ethical obligation. For prosecutors, however, the duty is to seek justice. Accordingly, prosecutors are not to focus exclusively on obtaining convictions. Instead, they are to continuously reflect on whether justice is served by their decisions and actions. You will learn later in this book how this obligation creates obligations for the prosecutors that do not exist for defense attorneys.

## Key Terms

actus reus
attendant circumstances
constructive intent
corporate liability
element analysis
foreseeability
general intent
inferences
injunctions
intervening cause

knowingly
legal cause
legislative history
mens rea
motive
negligence
offense analysis
omission
presumption
proximate cause

purposely
recklessness
scienter
specific intent
statutory construction
strict liability crimes
transferred intent
vicarious liability

# Review Questions

1. In criminal law, causation is broken down into two forms. Name and briefly describe each.

2. Can a person be prosecuted for failing to save a stranger from danger? Why or why not?

3. What is concurrence?

4. What is an omission?

5. The MPC recognizes four types of mens rea. Name and briefly describe each.

6. What is vicarious liability?

7. What is a rebuttable presumption? An irrebuttable presumption?

8. Can corporations and other associations be guilty of crimes?

9. Distinguish mens rea from motive.

10. Define attendant circumstance.

11. Compare and contrast offense and element analysis.

# Problems & Critical Thinking Exercises

1–6. Many prisoners in the state and federal correctional systems are held at minimum-security "farms." Only inmates considered not to be dangerous are housed at these facilities because of the minimal security. In fact, in many cases it is possible for inmates to simply walk off. Of course, most do not leave the premises, because to do so results in an increased sentence (either due to a conviction for escape or a decrease in "good time") and a likelihood that the sentence will be spent in prison rather than the more desirable farm. Despite this practice, prisoners of these facilities do escape. Problems 1 through 6 present several different sets of facts involving a fictitious inmate, Spike Vincelli. Read each problem and discuss the defenses, if any, that Spike may have against a charge of escape. Discuss each in light of the following two statutes:

*Statute I*

It shall be unlawful for any person committed to any correctional facility to escape from that facility. Escape is defined as passing beyond the borders of a facility with an intent to never return or being lawfully beyond the borders of the facility and not returning when required to do so with an intent to never return. Violation of this statute constitutes a felony.

*Statute II*

It shall be unlawful for any person committed to any correctional facility to leave the premises of the facility. Leaving is defined as passing over the boundary lines of the facility. Violation of this statute constitutes a misdemeanor.

1. On June 21, Spike Vincelli received a telephone call from a hospital informing him that his mother had been involved in a serious accident. That evening, Spike left to see his mother, intending to return in the morning.

2. On June 21, Spike Vincelli had his first epileptic seizure. The seizure caused Spike to fall outside the boundary line surrounding the facility.

3. On June 21, Spike Vincelli decided that he was bored with living on the farm. That night he walked off the premises and fled for a friend's house 300 miles away, intending never to return.

4. On June 21, Spike Vincelli became involved in a fight with Ben Ichabod. In a fit of rage, Ben picked Spike up and threw him over the fence surrounding the farm. Spike was caught outside the fence by a guard before Spike had an opportunity to return.

5. In early April, Spike Vincelli decided that he was going to escape. He developed a plan that called for him to leave in July and meet his brother, who was passing through the area. As part of the plan, Ben Ichabod, a fellow inmate, was enlisted to pick Spike up off the ground and throw him over the fence that surrounded the facility. However, Ben, who is not very bright, threw Spike over the fence on June 21.

6. On June 21, Spike Vincelli became involved in a fight with Ben Ichabod. Ben, in a fit of rage, picked Spike up and threw him over the fence surrounding the facility. While outside the fence, Spike became overcome with a sense of freedom and ran from the facility.

7. Fred failed to show up for a date he had made with Penni. Penni, who was angered by Fred's actions, decided to vent her anger by cutting the tires of Fred's automobile. However, Penni did not know what make of automobile Fred drove and mistakenly cut the tires of a car owned by Fred's neighbor, Stacey. Penni is now charged with the

"purposeful destruction of personal property." Penni claims that her act was not purposeful because she did not intend to cut the tires of Stacey's car. Discuss this defense.

8. William, an experienced canoeist, was hired by a Boy Scout troop to supervise a canoe trip. While on the trip, two boys fell out of their canoe and began to drown. William watched as the boys drowned. Is William criminally liable for the deaths?

9. Sherri, who was near bankruptcy, decided to burn her house down and make an insurance claim for the loss. Sherri started the fire, which spread to a neighbor's house located 20 feet from Sherri's home. Unknown to Sherri, her neighbor was storing massive quantities of dynamite in the home. The fire at the neighbor's house spread to the room where the explosives were being stored, and the resulting explosion caused such vibrations that a construction worker one block away fell off a ladder and subsequently died from the fall. Sherri is charged with arson and murder. She has pled guilty to arson but maintains that she is not liable for the death of the worker. Is she correct?

10. The following statute was enacted by State Legislature:

It shall be unlawful for any person to be a pedophile. Pedophilia is defined as a condition where a person over the age of 17 years possesses a sexual desire for a person under the age of 8 years.

While attending a group therapy session, Jane admitted that she had sexual interest in boys under 8 years of age. A member of the group contacted the local police and reported Jane's statement. Jane was subsequently arrested and charged with violating the quoted statute. Discuss her defenses, if any.

11. Ashley, Amy, and Karen are roommates in college. They occupy a four-bedroom apartment, and all share in the bills and household duties. One weekend, a friend of Karen's, Janice, came to visit. Janice arrived on Thursday and was scheduled to stay until Monday. She stayed in the extra bedroom. On Thursday evening, Ashley discovered, while she was watching Janice unpack, that Janice had a significant amount of cocaine in one suitcase. Later that night, Ashley discussed this matter with Karen, who stated, "I'm sure she does—why does it matter to you?" Ashley immediately confronted Janice and told her that she would have to remove the cocaine from the premises or Ashley would call the police. Janice picked up the suitcase, carried it to her car, and placed it in the trunk. The next morning, when Karen learned what Ashley had done, Karen encouraged Janice to bring the suitcase back into the apartment. On Sunday morning, the police arrived with a warrant to search the apartment. The search uncovered the suitcase in the extra bedroom. Later, at the police station, the suitcase was opened and the drugs were discovered. All four women were charged with possession. Do Amy, Ashley, or Karen have a defense? The jurisdiction where they live applies the MPC.

12. In some nations, vicarious criminal liability is much broader than in the United States. For example, parents may be vicariously liable for the criminal acts of their children until the children reach adulthood. Should such laws be adopted in the United States? Explain your answer.

13. Develop your own fact scenarios, one demonstrating specific intent and another demonstrating general intent. Explain why each is an example of specific intent or general intent.

14. Using the two fact scenarios you created in problem 13, change the facts so the general-intent crime becomes a specific-intent crime and the specific-intent crime becomes a general-intent crime.

# Endnotes

1. Oliver Wendell Holmes. *The Common Law* (1881).

2. J. Goldstein et al., *Criminal Law: Theory and Process* (New York: Free Press, 1974).

3. 21 Am. Jur. 2d, *Criminal Law* 129 (1981).

4. See *United States v. Birkenstock*, 823 F.2d 1026 (7th Cir. 1987); *United States v. Pompanio*, 429 U.S. 10 (1976).

5. LaFave & Scott, *Criminal Law* (Hornbook Series, St. Paul: West, 1986), at 217.

6. LaFave & Scott at 34.

7. Gary Fields and John R. Emshwiller, As Federal Crime List Grows, Threshold of Guilt Declines, *The Wall Street Journal*, September 27, 2011.

8. See *Lambert v. California*, 355 U.S. 225 (1957), in which the U.S. Supreme Court found that a strict liability statute was violative of the due process clause of the U.S. Constitution.

9. *United States v. Dotterweich*, 320 U.S. 277 (1943).

10. *United States v. Freed*, 401 U.S. 601 (1971).

11. For a thorough discussion of mens rea and public welfare rationale, see J. Manly Parks, "The Public Welfare Rationale: Defining Mens Rea in RCRA," 18 *Wm. & Mary Envtl. L.& Pol'y Rev.* 219 (1993), http://scholarship.law.wm.edu/wmelpr/vol18/iss1/6

12. *United States v. Dotterweich*, 320 U.S. 277 (1943).

13. Jeffrey P. Cogin, "Corporations Can Kill Too: After Film Recovery, Are Individuals Accountable for Corporate Crimes," *Loyola of Los Angeles Law Review* 19 (1986): 1411, 1413–1414, http://digitalcommons.lmu.edu//llr/vol19/iss4/12

14. MPC § 2.07 deals with liability of corporations and unincorporated associations.

15. For more on the original cases, see Cogin, *infra*. For the reversals, see *People v. O'Neil, 194 Ill. App.3d 79*, 550 N.E.2d 109 (1990). The convictions of the individuals were reversed and remanded for retrial on appeal. The defendants pled guilty to involuntary manslaughter to avoid retrial. William Presecky, *2 Bosses Plead Guilty in 83 Death of Plant Worker, Chicago Tribune*, September 8, 1993, http://articles.chicagotribune.com/1993-09-08/news/9309080122_1_charles-kirschbaum-job-related-death-film-recovery-systems

16. See Jeffrey S. Parker, "Criminal Sentencing Policy for Organizations: The Unifying Approach of Optimal Penalties," 26 *Am. Cr. Law R.* 513 (1989).

17. For more on this case, see Francis T. Cullen, William J. Maakestad, and Gray Cavender, *Corporate Crime Under Attack: The Ford Pinto Case and Beyond* (Cincinnati: Anderson Publishing, 1987). See also G. Schwartz, "The Myth of the Ford Pinto Case," 43 *Rutgers Law R.* 1013 (1991).

18. Arthur Andersen v. United States, 544 U.S. 696 (2005)

19. MPC § 2.02, General Requirements of Culpability.

20. Kaplan & Weisberg, *Criminal Law* (Boston: Little, Brown, 1986).

21. MPC § 2.02(2)(c).

22. MPC § 2.01.

23. *Id.*

24. *King v. Cogdon* (Vict. 1950).

25. *Sleepwalk with Me*. Directed by Mike Birbiglia. Produced by Bedrock Media and WBEZ Chicago 2012.

26. *People v. Decina*, 138 N.E.2d 799 (N.Y. 1956).

27. A. Loewy, *Criminal Law*, 2nd ed. (Nutshell Series) (St. Paul: West, 1987).

28. *Robinson v. California*, 370 U.S. 660 (1962).

29. MPC §2.01(4).

30. Tim Rohan, *Sandusky Gets 30 to 60 Years for Sexual Abuse, New York Times*, October 8, 2012, http://www.nytimes.com/2012/10/10/sports/ncaafootball/penn-state-sandusky-is-sentenced-in-sex-abuse-case.html

31. O.R.C. sec. 2921.22.

32. Max Matza, Parkland shooting: Should school officer be jailed for child neglect? BBC News. June 6, 2019. Retrieved from BBC.com on December 28, 2020.

33. Cal. Crim. Code §194.

34. *Gebhard v. State*, 484 N.E.2d 45, 48 (Ind. Ct. App. 1985).

35. Nebraska Revised Statute 28-507.

# Chapter 4

# Crimes Against the Person

## Chapter Outline

## Studying Crimes

In the next three chapters, you will study crimes: their elements, how they are proved, and contemporary questions about them. It is not possible to examine every crime that appears in the criminal codes of the states, territories, municipalities, and federal government. What follows is a discussion of the most common crimes recognized, in some form, in most jurisdictions.

The crimes have been grouped as crimes against the person, crimes against property, and crimes against the public. This classification is common, but not scientific. Many of the crimes fit into more than one category. These classifications are made to give your learning structure, not because the labels have legal meaning. A witness' lies while testifying—perjury—is a crime against the administration of justice. But they also personally harm a party in the case.

Sometimes when one crime is proven, a **lesser included offense** is also proven. For example, if a defendant is convicted of murdering someone with a hammer, he has also committed a battery of the victim. In this circumstance, the battery is absorbed into the murder. This is referred to as **merger**. Under the merger doctrine, both crimes may be charged; but if the defendant is convicted of the more serious crime, the lesser is absorbed by the greater, and the defendant

**lesser included offense**
A crime whose elements are found completely within the elements of a more serious crime. If the more serious offense is proven, the lesser included offense merges into it and only the more serious offense is punished.

**merger**
When a person is charged with two crimes (based on exactly the same acts), one of which is a lesser included offense of the other. The lesser crime *merges* because, under the prohibition against double jeopardy, the person may be tried for only one crime.

is not punished for both. If acquitted of the greater charge, the defendant may be convicted of the lesser.

A closely related idea to lesser included offense is **predicate offense**, or predicate act. In this context, predicate means to base a crime on a specific act or underlying crime. As you will learn in a later chapter, proof that a defended intended commit a felony after breaking and entering a building is required to establish burglary in some states.. If an actor who breaks into a home doesn't intend to commit a felony when inside, there has been no burglary, although the lesser crime of breaking and entering has been committed. The predicate offense of burglary, therefore, is the intended felony. It can be, for example, theft, murder, arson, or rape. What makes these crimes different from others is that both the crime itself, burglary, and the intention to commit the predicate offense must be proven. In some cases, the predicate offense may be a lesser included offense. But in others, such as in our example, the predicate offense is independent. Proving one doesn't prove the other.

**predicate offense**
An act or offense that is an element of another crime.

# Homicide

Learning Objective: Define, compare, and contrast the various forms of murder and manslaughter at the common law.

## Sidebar

### Crime Statistics

There are many different ways to measure crime. Some methods, such as observation and experimentation, are impractical, or even more, immoral. The Federal Bureau of Investigation collects crime data from police departments all over the United States. These data are compiled and reported yearly under the title *Uniform Crime Reports* (UCR). Although a good comprehensive source of crime data since 1929, UCR data have some flaws. The most significant flaw concerns underreporting. Many crimes are not reported to the police. Even when a crime is reported, most police agencies report only the most serious offense committed. Hence, many crimes go unreported by individuals and police agencies. Also, because UCR data are aggregate data, no detail about the number of victims, offenders, or offenses per incident are provided. To remedy some of these problems, there is an ongoing effort to redesign the UCR system. This effort, known as the National Incident-based Reporting System, asks local law enforcement officers to move beyond aggregate data to providing information about each criminal incident.

Since 1991, colleges and universities that receive federal monies have been required to collect statistics on campus crime. The Campus Security Act requires that the collected data be made available to current and prospective faculty, staff, and students.

The second major system of crime data collection is the National Crime Victimization Survey (NCVS), administered by the U.S. Census Bureau on behalf of the U.S. Department of Justice. The NCVS is a large random survey of U.S. households. Respondents are asked whether they have been victimized by one or more of the listed violent and nonviolent crimes. The NCVS touts an impressive 95% response rate to its survey. The NCVS has its flaws as well. Some victims, particularly of certain crimes, are reluctant or ashamed to report the crime. Also, some people may not know that they have been victimized (e.g., embezzlement or fraud).

UCR data are presented in this text, most often in a boxed feature called Crime Stats. For additional information, NCVS data should be examined. Also, most local and state law enforcement agencies and courts have data available that are not provided by either the UCR or NCVS, such as data on arrests and crimes not included in the UCR or NCVS systems.

*Sources:* The FBI's UCR reports can be found in many locations, including *http://www .Ucr.fbi.gov* and NCVS data can be found in many locations, including *http://www.bjs.gov*

Homicide is the killing of one human being by another. Not all homicides are crimes. Assume, for example, that a COVID-19 vaccine can be fatal to people with shellfish allergies. Mr. Gower, a pharmacist, injects Blaine with the vaccine. Prior to the injection, Gower asks Blaine if he is allergic to shellfish. Blaine answers no, fearing that if tells Gower the truth he will not receive the vaccine. Blaine dies from the vaccine. No crime has been committed, even though a homicide occurred. Distinguishing between homicides where there is moral culpability and those where there isn't is a central feature of criminal law.

As you will see in this chapter, there are levels of culpable homicide today. That hasn't always been true. In the earliest years of the common law, a homicide was either murder, or not.

## Express Murder

Murder, at the common law, was defined as

1. the unlawful killing of a
2. human being with
3. malice aforethought

The first element is the actus reus—the unlawful killing of a human being. *Unlawful* incorporates a number of exceptions, known as excuses and justifications, that you will learn about later. For example, a person may kill an attacker in self-defense. Excuses and justifications have the effect of either totally absolving or reducing the liability of the actor.

Causation was discussed in the last chapter. An actor is criminally liable for homicide when they are the legal cause of death. You may recall that causation has two aspects; an act must be both the "but for" cause and the proximate cause, with the latter occurring when a victim's death is reasonably foreseeable.

Homicide by any means satisfies the actus reus. It can be direct through the use of poison, a knife, gun, crossbow, or other object. It is also possible to be liable for the death of a person who causes their own death. In one case, for example, a husband who repeatedly hit his wife and commanded her to jump into a river was convicted of murder when she drowned.[1]

## Exhibit 4–1 Crime Clock 2019

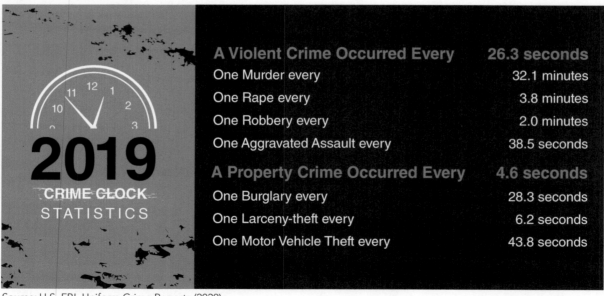

| A Violent Crime Occurred Every | 26.3 seconds |
|---|---|
| One Murder every | 32.1 minutes |
| One Rape every | 3.8 minutes |
| One Robbery every | 2.0 minutes |
| One Aggravated Assault every | 38.5 seconds |
| A Property Crime Occurred Every | 4.6 seconds |
| One Burglary every | 28.3 seconds |
| One Larceny-theft every | 6.2 seconds |
| One Motor Vehicle Theft every | 43.8 seconds |

*Source:* U.S. FBI, Uniform Crime Reports (2020)

One of the attendant circumstances of murder is the victim's death. The definition of death has evolved. For a long time, death was defined as the cessation of blood flow and respiration. This definition proved inadequate when medicine developed the ability to maintain blood circulation and respiration, but the patient had no hope of recovering brain function. Consequently, either brain death or a combination of the cessation of brain, circulation, and respiration functions are used to determine death.

The mens rea of murder was malice aforethought. There are two parts to this element, malice and aforethought. Once defined in an entirely moral way—to act out of an evil or ill will—malice developed into a cognitive, mental construct. Malice was a form of specific intent; the defendant's purpose had to be cause of the victim's death. The morality of the act became largely irrelevant.

The timing of this intent was important. It had to occur "aforethought," or before the act. The aforethought requirement is often expressed as acting with premeditation. An actor who spends weeks watching a victim's movements to identify the best moment to shoot them is acting with premeditation. But there are harder cases. Consider the following scenario. Jaylen recently lost a child to COVD-19. As she is exiting a courthouse, where she just completed paperwork concerning the child's death, she unexpectedly encounters a group of people protesting COVID-19 restrictions. They are unmasked and carrying signs expressing that the virus is a hoax. Full of grief and anger, she becomes enraged, grabs one of the signs and delivers a fatal blow to one of the protestors. Only seconds pass from the moment when she first sees the protestors to when she kills her victim. Was her act premeditated? As is so often in the law, it depends. Most courts have deemphasized the importance of the quantity of time in favor of examining whether Jaylen had adequate time to develop a malicious state of mind. Other doctrines, such as provocation, may also apply. These are discussed in greater detail later. The following are examples of express murder.

> Margaret believes Dorothy is flirting with her wife. Insanely jealous, Margaret decides to kill Dorothy. Margaret sits outside of Dorothy's home four consecutive nights, tracking her daily movements. She discovers that Dorothy walks her dog between 10 p.m. and 10:30 p.m. every night. The route of the walk is along a dark and lonely road. On the fifth night, Margaret shoots Dorothy, and her little dog too, during their walk.

> Lance is a professional cyclist. He is consistently ranked second in the world behind Eddy. Tired of being second, he slips poison into Eddy's water bottle when he isn't looking, killing him.

See Exhibit 4–2 for the formal charge against one of the United States' most notorious serial murderers, Jeffrey Dahmer.

## Implied Murder

The definition of murder proved to be so rigid that culpable defendants went unpunished. For example, no murder occurred if a victim died from a violent attack that was intended to seriously harm, but not kill, the victim. This and other holes led to the creation of new forms of murder. These are known as implied murders, to be contrasted with malice aforethought, or express murder. There were three:

1. When the defendant intended to cause serious bodily harm, and death resulted.

2. When the defendant created an unreasonably high risk of death that caused the victim's death. This was known as "depraved-heart murder."

3. Felony murder.

## **Exhibit 4–2** Circuit Court/Criminal Division

STATE OF WISCONSIN — CIRCUIT COURT CRIMINAL DIVISION — MILWAUKEE COUNTY

STATE OF WISCONSIN, Plaintiff — INFORMATION

vs.

Jeffrey L. Dahmer 05/21/60
924 N. 25th St.
Milwaukee, WI

Defendant.

CRIME(S):
See Charging Section Below
STATUTE(S) VIOLATED
See Charging Section Below
COMPLAINING WITNESS:
Donald Domagalski
CASE NUMBER:
F-912542

FILED 33 SEP 10 1991 GARY J. BARCZAK CLERK OF COURTS

I, E. MICHAEL MC CANN, DISTRICT ATTORNEY FOR MILWAUKEE COUNTY, WISCONSIN, HEREBY INFORM THE COURT THAT THE ABOVE NAMED DEFENDANT IN THE COUNTY OF MILWAUKEE, STATE OF WISCONSIN,

COUNT 01: FIRST DEGREE MURDER

COUNT 12: FIRST DEGREE INTENTIONAL HOMICIDE

on or about June 30, 1991, at 924 North 25th Street, City and County of Milwaukee, did cause the death of another human being, Matt Turner a/k/a Donald Montrell, with intent to kill that person contrary to Wisconsin Statutes section 940.01(1).

Upon conviction of each count of First Degree Intentional Homicide and each count of First Degree Murder, Class A Felonies, the penalty is life imprisonment.

DATED 9/10/91

E. MICHAEL MC CANN
DISTRICT ATTORNEY

E. Michael McCann
District Attorney

Jeffrey L. Dahmer
9.10.91

Jeffrey L. Dahmer 9.10.91
x The statement on page 1 is accurate as it applies to this page
Jeffrey L. Dahmer
9.10.91

(3)

### Intent to Cause Serious Bodily Harm Murder

The first form of implied murder is Intent to Cause Seriously Bodily Harm Murder. This crime filled in the hole that was discussed earlier: an actor could intentionally harm another, in very serious ways, causing the victim's death but be acquitted of murder if the prosecutor was unable to prove that the actor specifically intended to cause the victim's death.

Assume, back in the day when only express murder existed, Jonas decides to sever the hand of the man who stole his plow. Plows were essential and valuable tools in early farming communities. Jonas's objective is to teach the thief a lesson by disabling the offending hand. However, the offender dies of blood loss. Jonas can produce several witnesses who will testify that injuring a thief's hand is a common punishment in his community and that they heard Jonas express his intent to disable the thief in a way that he will "always remember the wrong he did." In this case, Jonas's purpose wasn't to cause death, so he wasn't guilty of murder. There being no other form of criminal homicide, the only prosecutorial options are battery and mayhem. Yet, the people of the time believed that this type of conduct was so dangerous, and the actor so culpable, that it should be treated as murder. So, Intent to Cause Serious Bodily Harm Murder was created. Its elements are

1. an act
2. taken with the specific intent
3. to cause the victim serious bodily harm
4. that results in the death of the victim

Like express murder, this crime's mens rea is specific intent. But the actor must specifically intend serious bodily injury, not death. Proving intention is tricky business. Short of a confession, how does any person know what someone else is thinking? As discussed earlier, this is where inferences come into play. Juries (or judges, if the court is acting as the finder of fact) are permitted to view the facts surrounding the murder and determine what the defendant's state of mind was when the act occurred. A jury may conclude from the facts that the defendant did intend to cause the death of the victim and convict the defendant of first-degree murder. If a jury concludes that the defendant did not intend to cause the death of the victim, but that the defendant did intend to cause serious bodily injury, then the crime is second-degree murder.

A related inference used in murder cases is the **deadly weapon doctrine**. This rule permits juries to infer that a defendant intended to kill his or her victim if a deadly weapon was used in the killing. It is only an inference; the fact finder can decide differently.

Any device or item may be a deadly weapon if, from the manner used, it is calculated or likely to produce death or serious bodily injury.[2] The Model Penal Code (MPC) defines a deadly weapon as "any firearm, or other weapon, device, instrument, material, or substance, whether animate or inanimate, which in the manner it is used or is intended to be used is known to be capable of producing death or serious bodily injury."[3] Under these definitions, some items that are not normally considered deadly may be deadly weapons if their use is calculated to cause serious bodily injury or death. The opposite is also true; some items that are normally considered deadly may not be, if used in a manner that does not pose a threat of serious harm or death. Hence, a bowling ball may be transformed from recreational equipment device into a deadly weapon when it is used to crush a person's skull. A gun, probably the most obvious example of a deadly device, may not be deemed deadly if used to hit someone over the head. A person's hands and feet are not normally deadly weapons. However, if it can be shown that a victim was significantly smaller than the defendant or that a defendant was especially expert in the use of their body to cause injury, the defendant's body is a deadly weapon. In the *Labelle* case, which appears in your next Oyez, the inference created by the deadly weapon doctrine was used to affirm a trial court conviction of attempted murder.

**deadly weapon doctrine**
A rule that permits juries to infer an actor's intent to cause the death of a victim when an instrument of death has been used in a manner that is likely to cause death or serious bodily injury.

## Depraved Heart Murder

Eventually, a second form of implied murder was recognized. So-called depraved heart murder, or depraved indifference murder, refers to a homicide that results

## Oyez

### Labelle v. State
### 550 N.E.2d 752 (Ind. 1990)

**DeBRULER, Justice.**

Appellant waived his right to a jury trial and was tried to the court and found guilty of attempted murder . . . and carrying a handgun without a license. . . .

The evidence produced at trial which tended to support the determination of guilt shows that members of the Outlaws motorcycle gang, who refer to themselves as "brothers," sometimes frequent the Beehive Tavern in Indianapolis. On February 2, 1987, appellant was a patron of the Beehive. He asked Oliphant, the bartender and co-owner of the bar, whether the Outlaws had come into the bar before, and Oliphant informed him that they had. Appellant remained at the Beehive until closing time and returned the next night. By 11:00 P.M., at least three employees and several patrons were in the bar. Three members of the Outlaws, including the victim, Allen Mayes, were there shooting pool. Sometime after 11:00, appellant threw a beer can at the stage, whereupon Oliphant asked him to leave, and appellant spat in his face. Oliphant testified, "[appellant said] that we're going to a funeral[,] to get my brothers together because we were going to a funeral. . . . [Appellant] told me I wasn't worth killing but a few of them—a few people in here were. And he proceeded to walk out the door." Oliphant stated that the three Outlaws were standing by the bar about ten feet from the door as he followed appellant out and that they were in roughly the same place when he came back in. Two or three minutes later, a shot rang out and Mayes was struck in the neck by a bullet and fell to the floor.

Fifteen to twenty minutes after the shooting, appellant was found under a truck which was parked across the street from the Beehive. A crowd which included the victim's two companions stood outside the bar and watched as appellant was being placed under arrest, and one of the Beehive's managers testified that appellant shouted at the two men, "Scumbags, you tell your brothers the angels are on their way[.] I got your brother." The door to the bar has a diamond-shaped window, which is taped to leave unobstructed only a two- or three-inch peephole. Looking into the bar from the outside, the peephole is approximately five feet, seven inches off the ground. Police found a bullet hole in the taped area to the right of the peephole. . . . [the police] searched the underneath side of the truck and found a .38 caliber revolver on the transmission brace, above the approximate spot appellant's head had been when he was under the truck. . . . [The medical expert] testified that, based on test results, it was his opinion that the bullet in Mayes's neck was from a .38 caliber weapon. . . .

Appellant also claims that there was insufficient evidence of intent to kill to support a conviction for attempted murder. . . . This court held there [in a previous case] that intent may be inferred from the use of a deadly weapon in a manner likely to cause injury or death and upheld the conviction. This Court has repeatedly upheld convictions for murder and attempted murder where the State sought to carry its burden of proof on the issue of intent by producing evidence that the defendant fired a gun in a crowd or at a group of people.

Appellant conceded in his testimony that he did fire a shot at the Beehive, but maintained that he was trying to hit a light over the door to the bar. He testified that he could not see into the bar because of the tape on the window and his distance from the door and that he had no intention of shooting any person, but intended only to aggravate Oliphant. . . .

State of mind can be established by the circumstances surrounding an incident. Appellant questioned the bartender the night before the shooting as to whether the Outlaws frequented the Beehive. . . . The eye-level location of the peephole and the proximity of the bullet hole to it would support an inference that the shot was fired into this inhabited barroom in a manner calculated to strike anyone standing at the bar in the upper body or head. This constitutes utilization of a deadly weapon in a manner likely to cause injury or death. There was sufficient evidence to support the trial court's verdict.

The judgement of the trial court is affirmed.

from an act that demonstrates a callous disregard for a high risk to the victim's life. No intent to kill, or even to harm, the victim is required. Broken down into its elements, depraved heart murder is

1. an act that
2. poses a high risk to life
3. a reasonable person would have been aware of the risk
4. the defendant disregarded the risk
5. death resulted

Depraved heart murder is more than accidental death. The act must ignore a risk that is so great that the act can be characterized as wanton. Some jurisdictions quantify the risk; they hold that death must be probable. The actor need not subjectively know the risk exists, but a prosecutor must show that a reasonable person would have seen it.

## Felony murder

In 2018, Lakeith Smith was convicted of murdering 16-year-old A'Donte Washington. But Mr. Smith neither intended to kill Mr. Washington, nor did he commit the act that caused his death. The conviction wasn't a mistake. It is an example of the third form of implied murder: **felony murder**.

Felony murder is a form of accomplice liability. The felony murder doctrine holds that co-felons are equally responsible for any death that occurs during a felony, regardless of who committed the act and the co-conspirators mens rea in regards to the homicide. In the case of Smith, he, Washington, and two other men conspired to burglarize homes. During the commission of one of the burglaries, a police officer arrived and exchanged gunfire with Washington, who was killed by the officer.  Because the death occurred during the commission of the felony, the three surviving offenders were convicted of murder. Smith was sentenced to 55 years in prison for the burglary, theft, and murder. Thirty years of the sentence were for the murder of Washington. Smith was 15 years old at the time of the crime.[4]

A prosecutor must prove each of the following elements for felony murder:

1. the killing of a human being by any person (not just the defendant or a co-conspirator)

2. during the commission of a named felony and

3. the felony is the proximate cause of the homicide, or the co-felons are acting in agency with one another

The felony murder rule acts to impute the required mens rea to the defendant and to create a form of agency liability between co-felons. The rule imputes mens rea because it applies in situations of unintended death; however, murder in the first degree is a specific-intent crime. The rationale is that one who engages in inherently dangerous crimes should be aware of the high risk to human life created by the crime. Vicarious liability is also imposed in some states; that is, all the individuals involved in the perpetration of the crime may be criminally liable for the resulting death.

For example, Grace and Eva decid to rob the First National Bank. They agreed to use whatever amount of violence is necessary to carry out the robbery. During the robbery, a bank teller summoned the police by use of a silent alarm. As Grace and Eva are leaving the bank, the police shout to them, ordering their surrender. Grace fires a shot from her gun , fatally wounding a police officer. Using the felony murder rule, Grace and Eva are equally criminally liable for the death of the police officer, even though Eva did not fire the weapon, nor did she conspire with Grace to kill the officer.

In some states, the act that causes the death of the victim need not be taken by one of the co-felons. For example, if Grace and Eva become involved in a shoot-out with the police after they rob the First National Bank, and a police officer accidentally shoots an innocent bystander, Grace and Eva are guilty of felony murder. However, if a police officer (or another person) kills one of the co-felons of the crime, the states are split on whether the surviving co-felons are guilty of felony murder.[5] The Lakeith Smith case is an example of a jurisdiction that holds co-felons liable.

In most jurisdictions, the legislature has specified the predicate offenses of felony murder. A few jurisdictions have limited the application of the rule to crimes that were felonies at common law, and others have limited the rule to felonies that involve a threat to human life. Robbery, rape, burglary, felony theft, arson, drug trafficking, and burglary are common.

**felony murder**
All co-felons are responsible for all homicides that occur during their crime, regardless of who committed the homicide and their individual mens rea.

As to "during the commission" element, the beginning and end of a crime is not always clear. Suppose that a robber knew that a large sum of money was being transferred between a bank and an armored car at a particular time and intended to steal the money during that transfer. Also assume that on the day of the robbery, the traffic was heavier than anticipated by the robber, and in an effort to arrive at the bank on time, the robber ran a stop sign. While passing through the intersection, the robber struck another vehicle, killing the driver. Was this death during the commission, or attempted commission, of the robbery? What if a police officer who is chasing an individual from the scene of a felony is shot 15 minutes and one mile away from the scene of the crime? Is this during the commission, or attempted commission, of the felony? It is likely that no felony murder would be found in the first example, because the death was too far removed from actual commission of the crime. The result would be different if the robber struck and killed the motorist while fleeing from the police immediately after commission of the holdup. This answers the second question. Courts have generally held that deaths that occur during the flight of a felon are "during the commission of the felony." However, the chase must be immediate, and the rule does not apply if there is a gap between the time the crime occurred, or was attempted, and the time the chase begins.

The third element can also be troublesome. In many ways this requirement is similar to the causation requirement discussed in Chapter 3. That is, the commission, or attempted commission, of the felony must be the legal cause (proximate cause) of the death. The death must be a "consequence, not coincidence" of the act; the resulting death must have been a foreseeable consequence of the act. So, if a patron of a store suffers a heart attack during a robbery, which was precipitated by the crime, the robbers are guilty of felony murder if the patron dies. However, if a patron who is unaware of an ongoing robbery suffers a heart attack and dies, the robbers are not liable for the death. The mere fact that the death and the crime occurred simultaneously does not mean that the robbers were the legal cause of the death.

In the *Losey* case, a defendant appealed his conviction of involuntary manslaughter (a form of felony murder) and aggravated burglary. The Ohio Court of Appeals applied a statute that read, "No person shall cause the death of another as a proximate result of the offender's committing or attempting to commit a felony." The statute named the crime involuntary manslaughter. The case is interesting from a causation perspective. Read the case and decide for yourself if the defendant should be punished for the death that occurred.

## Oyez

## State v. Losey
### 23 Ohio App. 3d 93, 491 N.E.2d 379 (1985)

**Per Curiam**

Defendant testified that he approached a house located at 616 Whitehorne Avenue shortly after 11:00 P.M. on November 25, 1983; that he knocked at the front door and, upon receiving no response, forced open the door and proceeded to attempt to remove a bicycle. His friend, who had been waiting outside, yelled that a car was slowly approaching. The defendant then placed the bicycle beside the front door and departed, leaving the front door open behind him. James Harper, the owner of 616 Whitehorne Avenue, testified that he heard a noise at approximately 1:00 A.M. Shortly thereafter, his mother, with whom he resided, appeared at his bedroom door inquiring about the noise. They proceeded together to the living room, whereupon they discovered the open front door and the bicycle standing near the door. James Harper stated that he told his mother to go back to her bedroom while he went to check the rest of the house. After so checking, he returned to the living room and was calling the police when his mother appeared in the hallway looking very upset and then collapsed. He called an emergency squad, which attempted to revive Mrs. Harper for almost an hour when the squadmen pronounced her dead. Prior to the burglary, Mrs. Harper had returned from bingo at approximately 10:00 P.M. that evening and had gone to bed. Based on these facts, the trial court found defendant guilty of aggravated burglary and involuntary manslaughter.

■  ■  ■

The doctor's testimony established that defendant's conduct was a cause of Mrs. Harper's death in the sense that it set in motion events which culminated in her death. However, it still must be determined whether defendant was legally responsible for her death—whether the death was the proximate result of his conduct. It is not necessary that the accused be in a position to foresee the precise consequence of his conduct; only that the consequence be foreseeable in the sense that what actually transpired was natural and logical in that it was within the scope of the risk created by his conduct. . . .

By the same token, in this case, the causal relationship between defendant's criminal conduct and Mrs. Harper's death was not too improbable, remote, or speculative to form a basis for criminal responsibility. Although the defendant did not engage in loud or violent conduct calculated to frighten or shock, his presence was nevertheless detected by Mrs. Harper. . . . [Conviction affirmed.]

In most jurisdictions, felony murder is treated as first-degree murder for the purpose of sentencing. Other statutes provide that felony murders that occur during named felonies are to be treated as first-degree murder and that murders during "all other felonies" are to be treated as second-degree murder. Even if the statute that creates this "all other felony" category does not expressly state that the felony must involve a danger to human life, it is common for courts to impose the requirement.

The Supreme Court has erected a few limits in the use of felony murder. In the 1982 case *Enmund v. Florida*,[6] the Court held that capital punishment violates the Eighth Amendment's prohibition of cruel and unusual punishments for someone who aided and abetted but did not themselves kill, attempt to kill, or intend to kill. The Court subsequently adjusted this decision in *Tison v. Arizona*, where it held that a conspirator who is a major participant in a felony and who acted with at least a reckless disregard for life may be punished as a murderer.[7] However, juveniles may not be executed for felony murder.[8]

Concerns about moral culpability for accomplice liability and whether African Americans are disproportionately impacted by the felony murder doctrine are likely to receive legislative and judicial attention in the years to come.

## Misdemeanor Manslaughter

Similar to the felony murder rule, one may be guilty of misdemeanor manslaughter if a death results from the commission of a misdemeanor, not a felony. Conviction of misdemeanor manslaughter results in liability for manslaughter, often involuntary manslaughter, and not murder.

Just as the felony murder doctrine has been limited in recent years, so has the crime of misdemeanor manslaughter. This is due largely to the significant increase in the creation of nonviolent crimes by legislatures and administrative bodies. Many states require that the misdemeanor be *malum in se*, and crimes that are *malum prohibitum* cannot be a basis for misdemeanor manslaughter. Requiring that the misdemeanor have a mens rea element is another limitation; that is, strict liability crimes may not be the basis for misdemeanor manslaughter. There is a trend to

## Sidebar

**Crime Stats: Homicide in the United States:**

In 2019, a total of 14,014 people were murdered or the subject of a nonnegligent manslaughter. This was 5 of every 100,000 persons in the United States. Most people are murdered with guns, primarily handguns. Knives, poisons, fists, and other weapons are also used to commit homicides.

*Source: Uniform Crime Reports,* U.S. Department of Justice, Federal Bureau of Investigation, 2020.

reject the misdemeanor manslaughter rule (as there is with the felony murder rule) and require that one of the four types of culpability recognized by the MPC (purposeful, knowing, negligent, or reckless) be present before imposing liability.

### Communicable Diseases and Murder

Communicable diseases, such as COVID-19, acquired immunodeficiency syndrome (AIDS), and anthrax, raise interesting criminal law situations. First, the intentional transmission of a disease can be criminal. For example, passing a disease to another, if intentional, is either attempted murder, if the disease is not passed to the victim or it is passed and the victim doesn't die, or murder, if the disease is successfully passed to, and causes the death of, the victim. This was what happened following the September 11, 2001, terrorist attacks on the World Trade Center and Pentagon. One week after the attacks, letters containing deadly anthrax spores were mailed to two U.S. senators and several media outlets. Five people were killed and many more were injured. The attacks led to the largest bioterrorism investigation in U.S. history. The key suspect in the case committed suicide in 2008, as the filing of charges against him became imminent. Although no one was ever charged, the highly contagious nature of the material and the obvious intentionality of the act would have easily supported a high mens rea homicide charge.[9]

Second, the unintentional but criminally negligent or reckless passing of such a disease may also be criminal under negligent manslaughter statutes. Sharing a needle with another, knowing that it has been used by an HIV-infected individual, falls into this category, as does the passing of the disease by a prostitute, who knows of her infection, to a client.

Third, due to the nature of the disease, it is often not discovered until long after it is contracted, and death may not occur for many years. This poses problems in jurisdictions that continue to follow the year-and-a-day rule (discussed later in this book) or other similar rules.

Fourth, in some situations, defendants have claimed that, because of the low probability of infecting another person, it is a factual impossibility to commit murder using AIDS. Fifth, AIDS may be characterized as a deadly weapon, and therefore, a charge of assault may be elevated to assault with a deadly weapon. Similarly, attacks leading to death may be treated as murder under the deadly weapon doctrine.

In most states, preexisting laws (e.g., murder, attempted murder, and intentional transmission of venereal disease) are relied upon to prosecute AIDS-related crimes. However, a few states have enacted statutes specifically directed at the intentional or negligent transmission of AIDS.

# Manslaughter

Originally all murders were punished equally: the murderer was executed.[10] Because of the harshness of this punishment, courts sometimes looked for ways to avoid convicting a person of murder. But this wasn't ideal because it freed defendants who were thought to be blameworthy—just not so blameworthy that they should be executed. Consequently, the courts developed a lesser form of homicide that was punished with life imprisonment: manslaughter.

**manslaughter**
A crime, less severe than murder, involving the wrongful but nonmalicious killing of another person.

**Manslaughter** was an unlawful killing without malice aforethought. Just as was the case with murder, the common law did not divide manslaughter into degrees. Whenever the states began codifying homicides, it was common for manslaughter to be divided into degrees, commonly referred to as voluntary and involuntary, although a few jurisdictions used first- and second-degree language. Today, many jurisdictions continue to recognize two forms of manslaughter.

Generally, it is the level of blameworthiness that distinguishes murder from manslaughter. In many cases, this is mens rea defense; the defendant lacked the intent to cause death. In others, there may be an intent to kill, but the circumstances warrant a reduction in the crime. These circumstances come in two forms, excuses and justifications. We begin with the mens rea defense of provocation.

## Provocation

At the common law, an actor who killed in response to a **provocation** committed manslaughter, rather than murder. The theory of provocation, also known as "heat-of-passion manslaughter," is that a defendant was operating under such an anger or passion that it was impossible for the defendant to have formed the intent to kill. The defense of provocation applies to instances when a person acts impulsively, when they "lose control."

As you have seen before, an objective test is used to determine if an actor was provoked. To satisfy this test, it must be shown that the provocative act was so severe that a reasonable person may also have killed. It does not require that a reasonable person would have killed, only that a reasonable person would have been so affected by the act that homicide was possible.

Catching one's spouse in the act of adultery is the classic example of provocation. This rule applies only to marriages and not to other romantic relationships. The traditional rule was that the cheating spouse had to be caught *in fragrante delicto*—actually engaged in extramarital sexual relations. If infidelity was discovered in any other way, a resulting homicide was punished as murder. So, being told of infidelity by a spouse or friend or discovering a hotel receipt and love notes in the pocket of a spouse's jacket were inadequate to establish the defense. The rationale for allowing the defense when a spouse witnesses the infidelity but not allowing it in other cases is that the former is more shocking and so provocative that a reasonable person would likely lose control.

In your next Oyez, a trial judge refused to instruct a jury on the alternative of manslaughter in a murder provoked by a cheating spouse. The trial judge applied the rule that statements are never adequate provocation. The appellate court reversed the trial judge, holding that the wife's statements and their timing were uniquely provocative and therefore may have justified a finding of manslaughter by the jury.

**provocation**
An act by a victim that reasonably causes another to respond with violence. Provocation has the effect of mitigating a crime.

## Oyez

### Commonwealth v. Schnopps
### 383 Mass. 178, 417 N.E.2d 1213 (1981)

**Abrams, J.**

On October 13, 1979, Marilyn R. Schnopps was fatally shot by her estranged husband George A. Schnopps. A jury convicted Schnopps of murder in the first degree, and he was sentenced to the mandatory term of life imprisonment. Schnopps claims that the trial judge erred by refusing to instruct the jury on voluntary manslaughter. We agree. We reverse and order a new trial. . . .

Schnopps testified that his wife had left him three weeks prior to the slaying. He claims that he first became aware of the problems in his 14-year marriage at a point about six months before the slaying. According to the defendant, on that occasion he took his wife to a club to dance, and she spent the evening dancing with a coworker. On arriving home, the defendant and his wife argued over her conduct. She told him that she no longer loved him and that she wanted a divorce. Schnopps became very upset. He admitted that he took out his shotgun during the course of this argument, but he denied that he intended to use it. . . . [The defendant and his wife continued to have marital problems for the next few months.]

On the day of the killing, Schnopps had asked his wife to come to their home and talk over their marital difficulties. Schnopps told his wife that he wanted his children at home, and that he wanted the family to remain intact. Schnopps cried during the conversation and begged his wife to let the children live with him and to keep their family together. His wife replied, "No, I am going to court, you are going to give me all the furniture, you are going to get the Hell out of here, and you won't have nothing." Then, pointing to her crotch, she said, "You will never touch this again, because I have got something bigger and better for it."

(continued)

On hearing those words, Schnopps claims that his mind went blank, and that he went "berserk." He went to a cabinet and got out a pistol he had bought the day before, and he shot his wife and himself. . . . [Schnopps lived and his wife died.]

Schnopps argues that "[t]he existence of sufficient provocation is not foreclosed absolutely because a defendant learns of a fact from oral statements rather than from personal observation," and that a sudden admission of adultery is equivalent to a discovery of the act itself, and is sufficient evidence of provocation.

Schnopps asserts that his wife's statements constituted a "peculiarly immediate and intense offense to a spouse's sensitivities." He concedes that the words at issue are indicative of past as well as present adultery. Schnopps claims, however, that his wife's admission of adultery was made for the first time on the day of the killing and hence the evidence of provocation was sufficient to trigger jury consideration of voluntary manslaughter as a possible verdict.

The Commonwealth quarrels with the defendant's claim, asserting that the defendant knew of his wife's infidelity for some months, and hence the killing did not follow immediately upon the provocation. Therefore, the Commonwealth concludes, a manslaughter instruction would have been improper. The flaw in the Commonwealth's argument is that conflicting testimony and inferences from the evidence are to be resolved by the trier of fact, not the judge.

Withdrawal of the issue of voluntary manslaughter in this case denied the jury the opportunity to pass on the defendant's credibility in the critical aspects of his testimony. The portion of Schnopps' testimony concerning provocation created a factual dispute between Schnopps and the Commonwealth. It was for the jury, not the judge, to resolve the factual issues raised by Schnopps' claim of provocation.

Reversed and remanded for new trial on the manslaughter issue.

Any act of provocation that prevents a person from forming a malicious intent can reduce a homicide from murder to manslaughter. Consider the following example:

Edgar and his children are walking from a restaurant to their car in the parking lot. At the same time, Randal is driving through the parking lot. Distracted by a text, Randal doesn't see the family and hits one of the children, propelling her into the air, to land 20 feet away. Edgar, overcome by emotion, grabs ahold of Randal as he exits his car, pushes him to the ground, and bangs his head on the pavement. The blow is fatal. Edgar is guilty of manslaughter, not murder.

Finally, the provocation defense will not be available if there was a sufficient "cooling-off" period. That is, if the time between the provocation and the homicide was long enough for a defendant to regain self-control, then the homicide will be treated as murder and not manslaughter.

## Mutual Combat

The defense of mutual combat is closely related to the defense of provocation. Mutual combat was once common. Boys and men, in particular, fought in school yards and bars. Dueling was once used to restore a man's honor if impeached. If two people engaged in consensual combat resulting in assaults and batteries, neither was guilty of a crime. Death, on the other hand, was different. By the 1800s, dueling was illegal and deaths resulting from a duel were criminal homicide. However, if both parties agreed to duel to death and one died, the crime was reduced to manslaughter.

Finally, the defense will not be available if there was a sufficient "cooling-off" period. That is, if the time between the provocation and the homicide was long enough for a defendant to regain self-control, then the homicide will be treated as murder and not manslaughter.

## Imperfect Self-Defense and Defense of Others

If Aryana harms Ita while defending herself from Ita's attack, Aryana has acted in self-defense. Self-defense, when valid, normally works to negate criminal liability entirely. So, if Aryana kills Ita to avoid serious bodily harm or death, she has committed an excusable homicide. What happens if Aryana was incorrect in her belief that her life was endangered by Ita? This is known as an imperfect self-defense and does not negate culpability entirely. It may, however, reduce her liability to voluntary manslaughter. For Aryana to be successful in her claim, she must prove that she had a good-faith belief that her life was in danger and that the killing appeared to be necessary to protect herself.

A person may also have an imperfect self-defense when an excessive amount of force is used as protection. So, if Aryana was correct in her belief that she needed to use force for her protection, but used excessive force, she is again liable for the lesser crime, provided she has a reasonable, although incorrect, belief that the amount of force used was necessary.

The concept of self-defense is extended to the defense of others. So, if Aryana kills Jamie while defending Thea, Kevin, Lisa, and Haris from apparent imminent harm, Aryana is no more liable than if she were defending herself. As is true of imperfect self-defense, if Aryana has a mistaken, but reasonable, belief that these people are in danger, her liability is reduced. Also, if an actor uses deadly force when a lesser amount of force would have been sufficient to stay the attack, liability is limited to manslaughter, provided that the belief that deadly force was necessary was reasonable under the circumstances.

## Modern Murder and Manslaughter

For many centuries, murder , in the three forms discussed earlier, and manslaughter were the only homicide crimes.

The MPC proposed a new , more nuanced, model for classifying criminal homicide. It begins by stating that "[a] person is guilty of criminal homicide if he purposely, knowingly, recklessly, or negligently causes the death of another human being."[11] The MPC follows by classifying all criminal homicides as murder, manslaughter, or negligent homicide. The MPC's four mens rea elements (purposeful, knowing, reckless, and negligent) are then assigned to these crimes. There is some overlap; for example, under some conditions a reckless homicide is murder, and under other conditions it is manslaughter. While the new approach has more levels of homicide, most of the common law's murder and manslaughter doctrines are found in it. While there is some new rules in the MPC, it is in many ways, a more coherent organization of what was a messy patchwork of rules. Let us look at the specifics of the MPC.

It is unsurprising that all purposeful and knowing homicides are classified as murder under the MPC. Additionally, a reckless homicide is murder when committed "under circumstances manifesting extreme indifference to the value of human life." The MPC then incorporates a "felony murder" type rule by stating that recklessness and indifference to human life are presumed if the accused was engaged in the commission or attempted commission of robbery, rape, arson, burglary, kidnapping, or felonious escape. So, if the accused are involved in one of those crimes, and a death results, they may be charged with murder under the MPC. Note that the MPC creates only a presumption of recklessness and indifference, which may be overcome at trial. Murder is the highest form of homicide, and the MPC declares it to be a felony of the first degree.

Manslaughters are felonies of the second degree under the MPC. All reckless homicides, except those previously described, are manslaughters. As at common law, the MPC contains a provision that reduces heat-of-passion murders to manslaughter. Specifically, the MPC states that a homicide, which would normally be murder, is manslaughter when it is "committed under the influence of extreme mental or emotional disturbance for which there is reasonable explanation or excuse. The reasonableness of such explanation or excuse shall be determined from the viewpoint of a person in the actor's situation under the circumstances as he believes them to be."

Last, negligent homicides are just as their title expresses—negligent. They are felonies of the third degree. For a summary of the Common Law and MPC approaches to the mens rea of murder and manslaughter, see Exhibit 4–3.

## Exhibit 4–3 Homicide Under the Common Law and MPC

| Common Law | MPC Mens Rea/Crime Label |
|---|---|
| Express Murder | Purposeful/Murder |
| Depraved Heart Murder | Knowing, Reckless with extreme indifference/ Murder |
| Intent to Do Serious Bodily Harm Murder | Knowing, Reckless/Murder |
| Felony Murder | Presumption of reckless or indifference to life if homicide occurs during or flight from sex crimes, robbery, arson, burglary, kidnapping, or felonious escape/Murder |
| Provocation | Yes, if extreme mental or emotional disturbance/ Manslaughter |
| Manslaughter | Reckless/Murder |
| Wasn't criminalized | Negligence |

**first-degree murder**
The highest form of homicide. The killing of another person with malice and premeditation, cruelty, or done during the commission of a major felony is typically murder in the first degree.

**second-degree murder**
Murder without premeditation.

Most states have followed the MPC model by creating degrees of murder and manslaughter. **First-degree murder** is the highest form of murder and is punished more severely than second-degree murder. **Second-degree murder** is a higher crime than manslaughter.

For a murder to be of the first degree, the highest crime, it must be shown that the homicide was willful, deliberate, and premeditated. Generally, first-degree murder applies whenever the murderer has as a goal the death of the victim. *Willful*, as used in first-degree murder, is a specific-intent concept. To be willful, the defendant must have specifically intended to cause the death.

*Deliberate* is usually defined as "a cool mind, not acting out of an immediate passion, fear, or rage." The term *premeditated* means "to think beforehand." Similar to *deliberate*, it eliminates impulsive acts from the grasp of first-degree murder. It is commonly said that there must be a gap in time between the decision to kill and the actual act. Of course, the length of the gap is the critical issue. Most courts hold that the gap in time must be "appreciable." Again, this term does little to define the length of time. The fact is that courts differ greatly in how they define *appreciable*. There are many reported cases where a lapse of only seconds was sufficient.[12] Some courts have held that all that need be shown is that the defendant had adequate time to form the intention before taking the act; the length of time is not determinative of the question.[13]

Those murders that result from poisoning, follow torture, or are traditional felony murders are often designated first-degree murder. Following the attacks of September 11, 2001, some states amended their statutes to include deaths resulting from terrorist activity in the classification of first-degree murders.[14] Second-degree murder is commonly given the negative definition "all murders that are not of the first degree are of the second." Second-degree murders differ from first in that the defendant lacked the specific intent to kill or lacked the premeditation and deliberation element of first-degree murder. A highly publicized case of unintentional murder was the conviction of former Minneapolis police officer Derek Chauvin for the death of George Floyd. Chauvin, who was on duty, restrained Floyd during an arrest by pressing his knee down on his neck and back for more than nine minutes. Although it could not be shown that Chauvin intended to cause Floyd's death, Chauvin was convicted of two counts of unintentional (depraved heart, being one) murder and one count of negligent manslaughter.

The lowest form of criminal homicide in most jurisdictions is involuntary manslaughter, sometimes named second-degree manslaughter. In most instances involuntary manslaughter is a form of negligent or reckless manslaughter. Two examples of involuntary manslaughter are *Commonwealth v. Carter* and *Roberson v. Texas*. In the former case, Michelle Carter was convicted by a juvenile court of involuntary manslaughter for encouraging her boyfriend to commit suicide. Before his death, the boyfriend and Ms. Carter discussed suicidal feelings several times. Each time, she discouraged him from committing suicide. Finally, however, she

Derek Chauvin, the former police officer who was convicted of the unintentional and negligent homicide of George Floyd.

not only encourages him but assists him in planning his death. Because they had a long-distance relationship, their communications were almost entirely by texts.[15] The second case, *Roberson*, is featured in your next Oyez.

## Oyez

### Roberson v. Texas
#### Court of Appeals of Texas – Ft. Worth (2010)

**Memorandum Opinion**

A jury convicted Appellant Tracy Denise Roberson of manslaughter and assessed her punishment at five years confinement. [she appealed]

Appellant was involved in a sexual relationship with Devin LaSalle. Appellant's husband, Darrell Roberson, shot and killed LaSalle sometime after midnight in the early morning hours of December 11, 2006, either before, when, or after Appellant yelled to Darrell that she was being raped. Those are the only facts that are clear and unequivocal. The remainder of the record is conflicting and contradictory.

It is unclear whether Darrell was aware of his wife's infidelity at the time he shot LaSalle. Darrell told detectives that he had driven to Oak Cliff in Dallas County for a card game. He said that Appellant called him a little after midnight to tell him that the house phone had been off the hook and that she was planning to take a bath. The State argues that this was Appellant's attempt to buy herself some intimate time in the car with LaSalle so that she could later claim to Darrell that the phone had been off the hook if Darrell called and got no answer

Darrell nevertheless tried to call Appellant around 1:30 A.M. on the house phone and got no answer because she was outside in LaSalle's vehicle. Darrell then repeatedly called the house phone, his daughter's cell phones, and Appellant's cell phone for the next half hour between 1:38 A.M. and 2:12 A.M. He told police that he became more and more concerned when he could not reach anyone. Finally, he managed to reach his seven-year-old daughter, J.R., at 2:12 A.M. She told Darrell that she could not find her mother in the home. Darrell told J.R. to make sure that the front door was locked and started driving toward home. He continued to talk to J.R. on the telephone as he drove. As Darrell drove up to his home, he saw LaSalle's truck parked in front of the house.

In Darrell's videotaped interview, he admitted that his first suspicion as he drove up and saw LaSalle's truck was that Appellant was with another man. Darrell told Detective Dishko that he did not see the man in the truck when he drove up, but during the 911 telephone call reporting the shooting, Darrell was overheard telling Appellant that he had seen LaSalle kissing her breasts.

In her interview, Appellant indicated that she saw Darrell get out of his vehicle with a gun in his hand. She told investigators,

So when the car just stopped, the one that's in front of us, I see it's Darrell, so I start screaming, Darrell, Darrell, Darrell, he's trying to rape me, he's trying to rape me, he's trying to rape me. But by then, Darrell is out of the Expedition, he has a gun, he's telling the person to stop.

After further questioning, Appellant changed her story slightly regarding whether Darrell was armed when he got out of his truck.

Detective Dishko testified that Appellant told him that Darrell had a very, very, very violent temper. Detective Dishko testified that Appellant told him that when she and LaSalle saw Darrell, LaSalle said Oh, shit, and immediately shifted into reverse gear, backing up the truck at a high rate of speed, laying rubber. Detective Dishko stated that Darrell's shoes, pants, and shirt all had rubber on them, which indicated that at some point in time he was in the vehicle's path [while] the tires were spinning, [and] the rubber was flying on him.

Appellant told Detective Dishko that she moved down onto the floorboard before the shot. Appellant also told investigators that Darrell had yelled at her to get out of LaSalle's truck and accused her of cheating on him when she got out of the truck after Darrell had shot LaSalle.

Both Appellant and Darrell agreed that Appellant began to scream rape while she was still in LaSalle's truck. The two also appeared to agree that Darrell did not begin firing at the truck until after he heard Appellant yell that LaSalle was raping her. During her interview, however, the officers pointed out to Appellant that she was in the line of Darrell's fire and in danger of being shot.

And Appellant stated in another interview that she believed Darrell shot at the truck not because she was being raped but because he was angry. . . .

In her first point, Appellant contends that the evidence is legally insufficient to sustain her conviction. In reviewing the legal sufficiency of the evidence to support a conviction, we view all of the evidence in the light most favorable to the prosecution in order to determine whether any rational trier of fact could have found the essential elements of the crime beyond a reasonable doubt.[2] Appellant was charged by indictment with

recklessly caus[ing] the death of Devin LaSalle by causing Darrell Roberson to shoot Devin LaSalle by falsely accusing Devin LaSalle of attempting to rape her. The Defendant's false accusation was reckless because it was made at a time when she knew that Darrell Roberson was armed with a firearm and Darrell Roberson, upon hearing the Defendant's false accusation, did cause the death of Devin LaSalle by shooting him with a deadly weapon, to wit: a firearm; and, in paragraph two, with criminally negligent homicide under the same circumstances. The jury convicted Appellant of manslaughter by recklessly causing LaSalle's death.

(continued)

While this is an unusual approach to a manslaughter accusation, it is supported by the law. A person commits the offense of manslaughter if he recklessly causes the death of an individual.[3] The penal code provides that

[a] person acts recklessly, or is reckless, with respect to circumstances surrounding his conduct or the result of his conduct when he is aware of but consciously disregards a substantial and unjustifiable risk that the circumstances exist or the result will occur. The risk must be of such a nature and degree that its disregard constitutes a gross deviation from the standard of care that an ordinary person would exercise under all the circumstances as viewed from the actor's standpoint.[4]

The issue of causation is addressed in section 6.04 of the penal code:

(a)  A person is criminally responsible if the result would not have occurred but for his conduct, operating either alone or concurrently with another cause, unless the concurrent cause was clearly sufficient to produce the result and the conduct of the actor clearly insufficient.

(b)  A person is nevertheless criminally responsible for causing a result if the only difference between what actually occurred and what he desired, contemplated, or risked is that:

   1.  different offense was committed; or
   2.  different person or property was injured, harmed, or otherwise affected.[5]

The jury was presented with a swearing match. Either Darrell shot and killed LaSalle because he was angry over the adulterous relationship between his wife and LaSalle, or he shot and killed LaSalle in response to Appellant's cries of rape; that is, he acted in defense of a third person. The jury chose to believe that Darrell shot and killed LaSalle in response to Appellant's shouts of rape. The jury also chose to believe that Appellant knew that Darrell had a hot temper and saw or knew that Darrell was armed when she created the unjustifiable risk that he would shoot LaSalle. Applying the appropriate standard of review, we hold that the evidence is legally sufficient to support Appellant's conviction  . . . .

You have already learned the misdemeanor manslaughter rule. In jurisdictions that recognize the rule, the person who commits the misdemeanor that results in an unintended death is responsible for the lowest form of criminal homicide.

Involuntary manslaughter also refers to negligent homicide, vehicular homicide, and similar statutes that punish for unintended, accidental deaths. The classic vehicular homicide is when a motorist runs a red light, strikes another car, and causes the death of the driver or passenger of that automobile. Some states, such as Illinois, make vehicular homicide a separate crime from involuntary manslaughter and impose a lesser punishment for vehicular homicide.[16] Deaths resulting from intoxicated drivers are always punished more severely than simple negligence.

## Life, Death, and Homicide

The actus reus of murder and manslaughter is the taking of a human life. Determining when life begins and ends can be a problem in criminal law, especially when dealing with fetuses.

At common law it was not a crime to destroy a fetus, unless it was "born alive." To be born alive, the fetus must leave its mother's body and exhibit some ability to live independently. Some courts have required that the umbilical cord be cut and that the fetus show its independence thereafter before it was considered a human life. Breathing and crying are both proof of the viability of the child.

Today, many states have enacted feticide statutes that focus on the viability of the fetus. Once it can be shown that the fetus is viable—that is, could live independently if it were born—then anyone who causes its death has committed feticide. Of course, this does not apply to abortion. Since the U.S. Supreme Court decision in *Roe v. Wade*, 410 U.S. 113 (1973), a woman possesses a limited right to abort a fetus she carries. Thus, states may not prohibit abortions that are protected under that decision. The primary purpose of feticide statutes is to punish individuals who kill fetuses without the mother's approval, as occurred in the *Keeler* case (see Chapter 2).

At the other end of the life continuum is death. Medical advances have made the determination of when death occurs more complex than it was only years ago. For a long time, people were considered dead when they ceased breathing and no longer had a heartbeat. Today, artificial means can be used to sustain both heart action and respiration. That being so, should one be free of criminal homicide in cases where the victim is being kept "alive" by artificial means and there is no reasonable hope of recovery? Should a physician be charged with murder for ending life support for a patient who has irreversible brain damage and is in a coma? Using the respiration and heart-function test, it would be criminal homicide to end such a treatment. However, many states now use brain death, rather than respiration and heartbeat, to determine when life has ended. In states that employ a brain death definition, it must be shown that there is a total cessation of brain function before legal death exists. The importance of defining death is illustrated by the *Fierro* case.

## Oyez

### State v. David Fierro
### 124 Ariz. 182, 603 P.2d 74 (1979)

**CAMERON, Chief Justice.**

The facts necessary for a resolution of this matter on appeal are as follows. Between 8 and 9 o'clock on the evening of 18 August 1977, Victor Corella was given a ride by Ray Montez and his wife Sandra as they were attempting to locate some marijuana. In the vicinity of 12th Street and Pima, Ray Montez heard his name called from another car. He stopped his car, walked over to the other car and saw that the passenger who had called his name was the defendant Fierro. Defendant told Ray Montez that his brother in the "M," or "Mexican Mafia," had instructed the defendant to kill Corella. Ray Montez told defendant to do it outside the car because he and his wife "did not want to see anything."

Montez returned to his car. Defendant followed and began talking with Corella. Corella got out of the car. Montez started to drive away when defendant began shooting Corella. Corella was shot once in the chest and four times in the head. Following the shooting, Corella's body was taken to the emergency room at Maricopa County Hospital. His blood pressure was very low due to secondary bleeding from the gunshot wound to the chest area. Surgery was performed in an effort to control the bleeding. He was then taken to the surgical intensive care unit, where a follow-up examination and evaluation revealed that he had suffered brain death. Corella was maintained on support systems for the next three days while follow-up studies were completed which confirmed the occurrence of brain death. The supportive measures were terminated and he was pronounced dead on 22 August 1977. . . .

CAUSE OF DEATH

At the trial, Dr. Hugh McGill, a surgical resident at the Maricopa County Hospital, testified that:

> After surgery he was taken to the intensive-care unit. He was evaluated by a neurosurgeon who felt there was nothing we could do for his brain, he had brain death. He remained somewhat stable over the next two or three days. We had follow-up studies that confirmed our impression of brain death and because of that supportive measures were terminated and he was pronounced dead, I believe, on the 22nd. . . .

Defendant initially argues that the termination of support systems by attendant doctors three days after Corella suffered "brain death" was the cause of Corella's death [and as such, he could not be responsible for Corella's death]. . . .

By the phrase "unchanged by human action" in Drury, we meant human action that changes or breaks the chain of natural events and of itself causes the death of the victim. In the instant case, the removal of life support systems did not change nor alter the natural progression of the victim's physical condition from the gunshot wounds in the head to his resulting death. There was no change "by human action." . . .

In the instant case, the body of the victim was breathing, though not spontaneously, and blood was pulsating through his body before the life support mechanisms were withdrawn. Because there was an absence of cardiac and circulatory arrest, under the common-law rule, he would not have been legally dead. Under the Harvard Medical School test and Proposal of the National Conference of Commissioners on Uniform State Laws, he was, in fact, dead before the life supports were withdrawn as he had become "brain" or "neurologically" dead prior to that time.

(continued)

We believe that while the common-law definition of death is still sufficient to establish death, the [brain death test] is also a valid test for death in Arizona. In the instant case, expert testimony was received, which showed that the victim suffered irreversible "brain death" before the life supports had been withdrawn. In effect, the doctors were just passively stepping aside to let the natural course of events lead from brain death to common-law death. In either case, the victim was legally dead for the purpose of the statute. . . .

## Suicide

Successful suicide was a crime under the common law of England. The property of a person who committed suicide was forfeited to the Crown and the deceased was buried on a public highway after having a stake driven through his body. Attempted suicide was also a crime, usually punished as a misdemeanor. Suicide is no longer criminalized. However, it is possible to involuntarily restrain, examine, and provide psychiatric treatment to individuals who have attempted to commit suicide under civil commitment laws.

It continues to be criminal to encourage or aid another to commit suicide. Attempts to establish a liberty right to die have failed. The U.S. Supreme Court held in 1997 that the Fourteenth Amendment doesn't protect the right to die.[17]

The legal issue most often arises in the context of physician-assisted suicide. Some states punish people who help another person die, as murderers. Other jurisdictions have laws that specifically address the act. These typically punish the act less severely than murder.

The most notorious examples of physician-assisted suicide involve Dr. Jack Kevorkian of Michigan. Dr. Kevorkian, a physician, assisted 20 terminally ill persons in committing suicide between 1990 and 1994, earning him the nickname Dr. Death. Dr. Kevorkian's license to practice medicine was suspended in 1991 for his behavior, and criminal charges were filed against him on several occasions. The first three cases were dismissed because the statute under which he was charged was held unconstitutional.

The Michigan legislature enacted a law in February 1993 that provided for as much as 4 years imprisonment and a $2,000 fine for providing the physical means by which another attempts or commits suicide or participates in a physical act by which another attempts or commits suicide. The person charged must have had knowledge that the other person intended to commit suicide.[18]

In 1999, Dr. Kevorkian allowed the news program *60 Minutes* to nationally broadcast his act of assisting his patient, Thomas Youk, to die. However, Dr. Kevorkian went further than he had in previous cases. Rather than providing a machine to the patient that could assist in death, Dr. Kevorkian administered a lethal injection to Mr. Youk. He then challenged Michigan prosecutors to charge him again. They did, and Dr. Kevorkian was convicted of murder and sentenced to 10 to 25 years in prison. He was paroled in 2007 after serving 8 years in prison and died 4 years later.

While Dr. Kevorkian may have gone too far in committing euthanasia, his first three acquittals suggested that there was public support for physician-assisted suicide. A few states have responded. In 1997, Oregon enacted the Death with Dignity Act. This law, which decriminalizes physician-assisted suicide under certain circumstances, was the first law of its type in U.S. history.[19] In 2019, a similar law, the Death with Dignity Act, became effective in Hawaii. For the Hawaii law to apply, the patient

- shall be at least 18 years old
- shall have a terminal, incurable, and irreversible disease that will result in death within 6 months, confirmed by two physicians
- shall make two oral requests to die, at least 20 days apart
- shall make a signed, written request that is witnessed by two people (one unrelated to the patient)

- shall be not suffering from depression or another condition that might interfere with the patient's ability to make an informed decision

## Corpus Delicti

**Corpus delicti** is a Latin phrase that translates as "the body of a crime." Prosecutors have the burden of proving the corpus delicti of crimes at trial. Every crime has a corpus delicti. It refers to the substance of the crime. For example, in murder cases the corpus delicti is the death of a victim and the act that caused the death. In arson, the corpus delicti is a burned structure and the cause of the fire.

A confession of an accused is never enough to prove corpus delicti. There must be either direct proof or circumstantial evidence supporting a confession.

In murder cases, the corpus delicti can usually be proved by an examination of the victim's corpse. After an autopsy, a physician is usually prepared to testify that the alleged act either did cause, or could have caused, the death. In some instances, the body of the alleged victim hasn't been found. Such "no body" cases make the job of the prosecution harder. Even so, if evidence—such as blood stains and discovered personal effects—establishes that the person is dead, then murder may be proven. Of course, the prosecution must also show that the defendant caused the death. So, if a defendant confesses to a murder, or makes other incriminating statements, and no other evidence is found, then no corpus delicti exists, and the defendant cannot be convicted. However, if blood matching the victim's is discovered where the defendant stated the murder occurred, then a murder conviction can be sustained.

**corpus delicti**
(Latin) "The body of the crime." The material substance upon which a crime has been committed; for example, a dead body (in the crime of murder) or a house burned down (in the crime of arson).

## Assault and Battery

Learning Objective: Compare and contrast the elements for assault and battery.

**Assault** and **battery** are two different crimes, although they may occur together. As with homicide, all states have made assaults and batteries criminal by statute.

A *battery* is an

1. intentional touching
2. of another
3. without consent
4. that is either offensive or harmful.

The mens rea element varies among the states; however, most now provide for both intentional and negligent battery. Of course, negligence in criminal law involves a greater risk than in civil law. To be negligent in criminal law, there must be a disregard of a high risk of injury to another; in tort law, one need only show a disregard of an ordinary risk. The MPC provides for purposeful, knowing, and reckless batteries. In addition, if one uses a deadly weapon, negligence may give rise to a battery charge. Otherwise, negligence may not provide the basis for a battery conviction.

The actus reus of battery is a touching. An individual need not touch someone with his or her actual person to commit a battery. Objects that are held are considered extensions of the body. If Sam strikes Doug with an iron, she has battered him even though her person never came into contact with his. Likewise, items thrown at another are extensions of the person who took the act of propelling them into the air. So, Sam also commits a battery by hitting Doug with the iron she has thrown at him.

A touching must be either offensive or harmful to be a battery. Of course, any resulting physical injury is proof of harm. The problem arises when one touches another in a manner found offensive to the person being touched, but there is

**assault**
An intentional threat, show of force, or movement that could reasonably make a person feel in danger of physical attack or harmful physical contact.

**battery**
An intentional, unconsented to, physical contact by one person (or an object controlled by that person) with another person.

no apparent physical injury. For example, a man who touches a woman's breast without her consent has committed a battery because the touching is offensive. If a person touches another in an angry manner, a battery has been committed, even though the touching was not intended to injure the party and in fact does no harm.

There are two varieties of assault. First, when a person puts another in fear or apprehension of an imminent battery, an assault has been committed. For example, if Gary attempts to strike Terry, but Terry evades the swing by ducking, Gary has committed an assault. The rule does not require that the victim actually experience a physical blow; apprehension of an impending battery is sufficient. Apprehension is simply an expectation of an unwanted event. Also, the threat must be imminent to rise to the level of an assault. A threat that one will be battered in the future is not sufficient. So, if Terry told Gary that he was "going to kick the shit out of him in one hour," there is no assault.

Because apprehension by the victim is required, there is no assault under this theory if the victim was not aware of the assault. For example, if X swings his arm at Y intending to scare Y, but Y has her back turned and does not see X's behavior, there is no assault. This is not true of batteries. If X strikes Y, a battery has been committed, regardless of whether Y saw the punch coming.

The second type of assault is an attempted battery. This definition remedies the problem just discussed. Any unsuccessful battery is an assault, regardless of the victim's knowledge of the act. Of course, it must be determined that the act in question would have been a battery if it had been completed.

To prove battery, it must be shown that a contact was made. Making contact is not necessary to prove an assault. However, it is possible to have both an assault and a battery. If John sees Henry swing the baseball bat that strikes John, there has been an assault and battery. However, due to the doctrine of merger, the defendant will be punished only for the higher crime of battery.

## Aggravated Assault and Battery

Under special circumstances, an assault or battery can be classified as aggravated. If aggravated, a higher penalty is imposed. The process of defining such crimes as more serious than simple assaults and batteries varies. Statutes may call such crimes aggravated assault or battery; or they may refer to specific crimes under a special name, such as assault with intent to kill; or they may simply use the facts at the sentencing stage to enhance (increase) the sentence; or they may refer to such crimes as a higher assault, such as felony assault rather than misdemeanor assault. In any event, the following facts commonly aggravate an assault or battery.

The assault is aggravated if the assault or battery is committed while the actor is engaged in committing another crime. So, if a man batters a woman while possessing the specific intent to rape her, he has committed an aggravated battery. This is true regardless of whether the rape was completed. If a defendant is stopped before he has committed the rape, but after he has assaulted or battered the victim, there has been an aggravated battery. Hence the crime may be titled "assault with intent to commit rape" or "assault with intent to murder."

It is also common to make assault and battery committed on persons of some special status more serious. Law enforcement officers or other public officials often fall into this category. Of course, the crime must relate to the performance or status of the officer to be aggravated. For example, if an off-duty police officer is struck by an angry neighbor over a boundary dispute, the battery is not aggravated. Examples of other protected classes of individuals are minors and the mentally disabled.

The extent of injury to the victim may also lead to an increased charge. Usually, a battery may be aggravated if the harm rises to the level of "serious bodily injury." Some statutes specifically state that certain injuries aggravate the crime of battery, such as the loss of an eye. Mayhem, a related crime, is discussed next.

# Mayhem

**Mayhem**, originally a common law crime, is the act of intentionally dismembering or disfiguring a person. The crime has an interesting origin. In England, all men were to be available to fight for the king. It was a serious crime to injure a man in such a manner as to make him unable to serve the crown in war. Early punishments for mayhem were incarceration, death, and the imposition of the same injury that had been inflicted on the victim. Originally, only dismemberment that could prevent a man from fighting for the king was punished as mayhem. As such, cutting off a man's leg or arm was punishable, whereas cutting off an ear was not.

Today, both disfigurement and dismemberment fall under mayhem statutes. Many jurisdictions specifically state what injuries must be sustained for a charge of mayhem. Causing another to lose an eye, ear, or limb are examples, as is castration.

Some states no longer have mayhem statutes. They have chosen to treat such crimes as aggravated batteries.

**mayhem**
The crime of violently, maliciously, and intentionally giving someone a serious permanent wound. In some states, a type of aggravated assault. Once, the crime of permanently wounding another (as by dismemberment) to deprive the person of fighting ability.

# Rape and Sex Offenses

This section examines sex crimes. More specifically, acts that are punished under specific sex crime statutes. Not all sexually motivated crimes are punished under sex crime laws. For example, the unwelcomed touching of a woman's breast is battery. This act may be prosecuted under a general battery statute or a more specific sexual battery statute.

The term "sex crimes" actually encompasses a variety of sexually motivated crimes. Rape, sodomy, incest, and sexually motivated batteries and murders are included. Obscenity, prostitution, abortion, distribution of child pornography, and public nudity are examples of other sex-related offenses.

## Rape

Learning Objective: Describe the evolution of the crime of rape into modern sexual assault laws.

At common law, the elements of **rape** were (1) sexual intercourse with (2) a woman, not the man's wife (3) committed without the victim's consent and by using force. This definition has evolved to be quite different today, as a result of advances in women's rights and other changes in American cultural values.

First, the common law definition required that the rapist be a man. Hence, women and male minors could not commit rape. Second, only women could be the victims of rape. Third, the *marital rape exception* provided that men could not be convicted of raping their wives. Similarly, a man could not be charged with battering his wife if the battery was inflicted in an effort to force sex. This exception was founded upon the theory that women implicitly consented to sex with their husbands upon demand. Additionally, many courts wrote that to permit a woman to charge her husband with such a crime would lead to destruction of the family unit. Fourth, the common law required that rape occur with force and without consent. This led many courts to require victims to resist the attack to the utmost and to continue to resist during the rape. Finally, the mens rea of rape was the intention to have intercourse with knowledge that the victim didn't consent. In the earliest years of the crime, the sex act was limited to penis-vagina. The "slightest penetration" of the woman's vulva is sufficient. The man need not ejaculate. Other sex acts, including anal sex and fellatio, were usually punished under sodomy statutes.

Progress in women's rights, a greater understanding of the psychological and physical harm caused by rape, and an appreciation that men and boys can also be sexually harmed have led to many changes in rape and sexual assault laws across the

**rape**
The crime of imposing sexual intercourse by force or otherwise without legally valid consent.

nation. First, most states have worded their statutes to permit minors and women to be charged with rape. While there are few cases of women actually raping men, or other women, there are several cases where women have been convicted as principals to the crime.[20] The Model Penal Code (MPC) is gender neutral regarding all sex crimes except rape.[21] But as late as 2020, the American Law Institute was considering several amendments to the MPC's outdated rape provisions, including gender neutrality.

The marital rape exception has been abolished in most states. A minority of states, however, have retained the rule in modified form. Ohio, for example, provides immunity to a husband except when he is separated from his wife.[22]

The use of force requirement is also changing. Historically, a victim was expected to resist an attack. Force, or at least a threat of serious bodily injury or death to overcome resistance, was required. Many states have moved away from requiring force to focusing on victim consent. Even in those states that continue to require force, sex with a person who is unconscious or for some other reason is unable to consent is rape.

The mens rea of rape is the intention to have sex with knowledge that the victim hasn't consented. Utah's rape law illustrates both the consent approach and the elimination of the spousal exception:

76-5-402. Rape.

(1) A person commits rape when the actor has sexual intercourse with another person without the victim's consent.

(2) This section applies whether or not the actor is married to the victim. . . .

Virginia, on the other hand, continues to require force or threat, except in cases of incapacity of the victim:

§ 18.2-61. Rape.

A. If any person has sexual intercourse with a complaining witness, whether or not his or her spouse, or causes a complaining witness, whether or not his or her spouse, to engage in sexual intercourse with any other person and such act is accomplished (i) against the complaining witness's will, by force, threat or intimidation of or against the complaining witness or another person; or (ii) through the use of the complaining witness's mental incapacity or physical helplessness; or (iii) with a child under age 13 as the victim, he or she shall be guilty of rape.

See Exhibit 4–4 for a summary of how rape is different today from the common law.

## Exhibit 4–4 How the Crime of Rape Has Evolved

| Common Law Element | Modern Element |
|---|---|
| Sexual Intercourse | In some manner all states have laws that cover all sex acts. |
| by a man | Gender neutral |
| with a woman | Gender neutral |
| not his wife | A minority approach; marital rape recognized in a majority of states |
| without consent | True today |
| by force | States are split between requiring force/threat or focusing on consent; if consent is element, then knowledge that the victim didn't consent is required |

Some states grade rape according to the extent of injuries that the victim received and whether the victim knew the rapist. The MPC punishes rape as a felony in the second degree, unless serious bodily injury occurs or the victim was not a social companion of the rapist, in which case the rape is of the first degree.

## Nonforcible Rape

It is possible to commit rape even when all the parties to the sex act consent. The elements of **statutory rape** are:

1. sex with a
2. person under a statutorily defined age
3. by another person, sometimes over a statutorily defined age

**statutory rape**
The crime of having sexual intercourse with a person under a certain state-set age, regardless of consent.

The actus reus was once sexual intercourse. Today, it is common for states to include all sex acts in their statutory rape prohibitions. In addition to the age element, what distinguishes statutory rape from other sex crimes is mens rea; statutory rape is a strict liability crime. The act of having sex with someone below the specified age is proof alone of guilt. No showing of mens rea is required. A few states impose a knowledge requirement. In those states, if the accused can convince the jury that there was reason to believe that the other party was "of age," then the accused is acquitted. For example, if a 15-year-old girl tells a boy that she is 17, she indeed looks 17, and she shows the boy a falsified identification bearing that age, he would have a defense to statutory rape.

At one time, statutory rape laws only protected girls, and this continues to be the law in a few states. Claims that this treatment is violative of the Equal Protection Clause of the U.S. Constitution were rejected by the Supreme Court. It found that because females can be impregnated, states have a legitimate interest in protecting girls but not boys.[23] However, many acts by adult females (or adult males to young males) may be prosecuted under another law, such as child molestation or criminal deviate conduct.

Statutory rape laws vary in their approach to age. Some make all sex with minors a crime, even if both actors are minors. In so-called Romeo and Juliet states, consensual sex by minors, or by a minor and an adult who is close in age, is not a crime, or is a lesser crime. Some states require the ages of the actors vary by a minimum number of years. For example, there must be at least three years difference between the victim and the offender.

**Crime Stats: Rape**

In 2019, there were 139,815 reported rapes in the United States. This number includes attempted rapes and assaults with intent to rape; however, statutory rapes are not included. The actual number of rapes is likely much higher, as rape is believed to be one of the most underreported crimes.

*Source: Uniform Crime Reports,* U.S. Department of Justice, Federal Bureau of Investigation, 2020.

Similar to statutory rape, having sex with those who are incapable of consenting due to mental or emotional disability is also rape, regardless of consent.

# Rape Shield Laws

**shield laws**
A state law that prohibits use of most evidence of a rape (or other sexual crime) victim's past sexual conduct at trial.

So-called **shield laws** were enacted in the 1970s and 1980s in an effort to protect rape victims from harassment by defense attorneys at trial. Before such laws existed, defense attorneys often would use evidence of a victim's prior sexual conduct to infer that the victim had consented to the act. It is believed that the humiliation of the rape itself, matched with the threat of harassment at trial, accounted for the nonreporting of many rapes.

**Do Civil Law Nations Better Protect Victims of Sex Crimes?**

The United States is of the common law tradition because of its roots in England, where the common law originated. Other examples of common law nations include Angola, Australia, Belize, India, and New Zealand. Many nations fall into the Civil Law tradition, including Angola, France, Italy, Germany, Mexico, Costa Rica, and Venezuela. Common Law nations employ different versions of an adversarial and accusatorial form of adjudicating cases. Civil Law nations employ inquisitorial forms of adjudication. Adversarial forms emphasize truth through contest, that is, two competing parties developing the facts and competing to persuade the court that their versions of the truth are correct. Adversarial systems also highly value the rights of criminal defendants. Inquisitorial systems are less confrontational and more concerned with the truth than with protecting the rights of defendants. So, adversarial systems emphasize both factual and legal guilt, the latter reflecting an expectation that police and prosecutors respect the rights of a defendant in the process. Inquisitorial systems put a premium on factual guilt.

When operationalized, the adversarial system can be more emotionally difficult for victims because of the rights of a defendant to confront the accusers, to cross-examine witnesses, and to have a public jury trial are paramount. Trials are highly technical, and rules of evidence are designed to keep unreliable, duplicative, and illegally obtained evidence from juries. Victims possess few or no rights. In inquisitorial systems, on the other hand, a case progresses as a continuous investigation wherein a dossier (case file) is prepared. Both the state and the defendant contribute to development of the dossier. There are few rules of evidence, and it is the dossier that is reviewed for the guilt/innocence determination at trial.

Testifying to a crime can be difficult for anyone, but it is particularly different for many victims of sex crimes. In the past, rape victims in adversarial trials were subjected to harassing cross-examination by defense attorneys, often intended to call their sexual character into question. Although many states in the United States have enacted rape shield laws intended to limit the breadth of what may be examined (e.g., the sexual history of a victim may be explored only if directly relevant), the adversarial system demands that accusers be physically present and subject to examination, in public trials. In the United States, this demand in embodied in the Sixth Amendment to the Constitution of the United States and the constitutions of all of the states.

The inquisitorial system, on the other hand, permits written statements (hearsay and inadmissible in the United States) of victims to be included in the dossier. For this reason, at least one scholar has posited that inquisitorial systems are less traumatic to victims of sex crimes.[24] Of course, this reason transcends sex crime victims to all victims, as well as to nonvictim witnesses who are intimidated by courtrooms and defendants.

Inquisitorial systems offer another advantage to victims. They permit victims to directly participate in the process. In many inquisitorial nations, victims are allowed to have counsel and to sue, in the same proceeding, their victims. In adversarial systems, victims must file a separate civil lawsuit to recover any damages resulting from the crime.

To protect victims from unwarranted abuse at trial, rape shield laws were enacted. Evidence of prior sexual conduct, except with the defendant, is not permitted at trial. Also, evidence of a victim's reputation in the community is inadmissible.

## Sex Offenses Against Children

Most states have a number of statutes specifically aimed at protecting children from sexual abuse and exploitation. Indiana has five statutes that directly pertain to sexual activity with children. Those statutes are as follows:

*Indiana Code § 35-42-4-3 Child Molesting*

(a) A person who, with a child under twelve (12) years of age, performs or submits to sexual intercourse or deviate sexual conduct commits child molesting, a Class B felony. However, the offense is a Class A felony if it is committed by using or threatening the use of deadly force, or while armed with a deadly weapon, or if it results in serious bodily injury.

(b) A person who, with a child under twelve (12) years of age, performs or submits to any fondling or touching, of either the child or the older person, with intent to arouse or to satisfy the sexual desire of either the child or the older person, commits child molesting, a Class C felony. However, the offense is a Class A felony if it is committed by using or threatening the use of deadly force, or while armed with a deadly weapon.

(c) A person sixteen (16) years of age or older who, with a child of twelve (12) years of age or older but under sixteen (16) years of age, performs or submits to sexual intercourse or deviate sexual conduct commits child molesting, a Class C felony. However, the offense is a Class A felony if it is committed by using or threatening the use of deadly force, or while armed with a deadly weapon.

(d) A person sixteen (16) years of age, or older who, with a child twelve (12) years of age or older but under sixteen (16) years of age, performs or submits to any fondling or touching, of either the child or the older person, with intent to arouse or to satisfy the sexual desires of either the child or the older person, commits child molesting, a Class D felony. However, the offense is a Class B felony if it is committed by using or threatening the use of deadly force, or while armed with a deadly weapon.

(e) It is a defense that the accused person reasonably believed that the child was sixteen (16) years of age or older at the time of the conduct.

(f) It is a defense that the child is or has ever been married.

*Indiana Code § 35-42-4-4 Child Exploitation*

(b) Any person who knowingly or intentionally:

(1) manages, produces, sponsors, presents, exhibits, photographs, films, or videotapes any performance or incident that includes sexual conduct by a child under sixteen (16) years of age; or

(2) disseminates, exhibits to another person, offers to disseminate or exhibit to another person, or sends or brings into Indiana for dissemination or exhibition matter that depicts or describes sexual conduct by a child under sixteen (16) years of age; commits child exploitation. . . .

(c) A person who knowingly or intentionally possesses:

(1) a picture;

(2) a drawing;

(3) a photograph;

(4) a negative image;

(5) undeveloped film;

(6) a motion picture;

(7) a videotape; or

(8) any pictorial representation; that depicts sexual conduct by a child who is, or appears to be, less than sixteen (16) years of age and that lacks serious literary, artistic, political or scientific value commits possession of child pornography. . . .

*Indiana Code § 35-42-4-5 Vicarious Sexual Gratification*

(a) A person eighteen (18) years of age or older who knowingly or intentionally directs, aids, induces, or causes a child under the age of sixteen (16) to touch or fondle himself or another child under the age of sixteen (16) with intent to arouse or satisfy the sexual desires of a child or the older person commits vicarious sexual gratification. . . .

(b) A person eighteen (18) years of age or older who knowingly or intentionally directs, aids, induces, or causes a child under the age of sixteen (16) to:

(1) engage in sexual intercourse with another child under sixteen (16) years of age;

(2) engage in sexual conduct with an animal other than a human being; or

(3) engage in deviate sexual conduct with another person . . . commits vicarious sexual gratification. . . .

*Indiana Code § 35-42-4-6 Child Solicitation*

A person eighteen (18) years of age or older who knowingly or intentionally solicits a child under twelve (12) years of age to engage in:

(1) sexual intercourse;

(2) deviate sexual conduct; or

(3) any fondling or touching intended to arouse or satisfy the sexual desires of either the child or the older person; commits child solicitation. . . .

*Indiana Code § 35-42-4-7 Child Seduction*

(e) If a person who is:

(1) at least eighteen (18) years of age; and

(2) the guardian, adoptive parent, adoptive grandparent, custodian . . . of a child at least sixteen (16) years of age but less than eighteen (18) years of age; engages in sexual intercourse or deviate sexual conduct with the child, the person commits child seduction. . . .

Note that statutory rape falls under the child molestation statute in Indiana. Also, the defense of a good-faith and reasonable belief that a child is of statutory age is recognized by statute.

The number of people charged with committing sex crimes against children is increasing. Many of those charged are nonbiological guardians. This trend has led to statutes such as Ind. Code § 35-42-4-7, "Child seduction," which was added to Indiana's sex offenses statutes in 1987.

## Megan's Laws, Commitment, and Castration

In New Jersey in 1994, Megan Kanka, a 7-year-old girl, was kidnapped, raped, and murdered by a recidivist sex offender who had been released from prison.

In response, New Jersey enacted what has become known as Megan's Law. The statute requires sex offenders to register with local law enforcement agencies. These agencies, in turn, make the registration information available to the public.

Today, every state has some form of Megan's Law.[25] In some states, registration is required and the information is not generally available. In other states, the public may request the information. And in others, law enforcement officials are required to disseminate the information. The rapid adoption of such laws by the states is due in part to the federal government. In 1996, a federal statute became effective that encouraged the states to adopt such laws and threatened loss of federal funds to those states that did not participate.[26]

In addition to registration and notification laws, some states have turned to civil or regulatory law to control sex offenders. Kansas law, for example, provides for the civil commitment of sexual predators who are "mentally abnormal" or suffer a "personality disorder," who lack control over their behavior, and who pose a danger to others. The law may be applied to any individual who meets these standards, regardless of whether charged, convicted, or previously punished. The Supreme Court found this law constitutional in *Kansas v. Hendricks* (1997).[27]

Subsequently, in the 2002 case *Kansas v. Crane*,[28] the Court again reviewed the Kansas law against a challenge that it violates due process to require anything less than total loss of control. The Court rejected this theory while reaffirming the *Hendricks* requirement of some loss of control.

A similar Washington state statute was upheld by the Supreme Court in *Seling v. Young* (2001).[29] The Court reasoned that the law is not criminal in nature, it is regulatory, and there is a long history of civil detention of individuals who are both mentally ill and dangerous. Federal law also provides for the civil commitment of sex offenders who are released from federal prison. The Supreme Court upheld the law against federalism challenges in 2010 in *United States v. Comstock*.[30]

Critics allege that these laws are unconstitutional efforts by states to bypass the criminal justice system by using civil commitment to punish sexual offenders. They also contend that individuals are not being punished for their actual behaviors but for their status. While the Supreme Court rejected these claims in the *Hendricks* case, it also emphasized that only individuals who are both mentally ill and dangerous may be committed and that the state must prove these elements in an adversarial hearing by at least clear and convincing evidence.

California has one of the most aggressive offender mental illness programs in the nation. The California Mentally Disordered Offender program (MDO) requires all corrections inmates to be screened for illness. If illness is found, inmates receive treatment while in prison. At the end of a prison term, an inmate is examined, and if determined to have a severe mental disorder that poses a danger to others, treatment is ordered as a condition of parole. Treatment is residential until an offender is determined to be no longer dangerous. Parolees in the MDO program are entitled to annual review and a hearing to determine dangerousness.

So-called chemical castration is also used to control sex offenders. Drugs such as Depo-Provera are used to inhibit the sex drive and sexual function of male sex offenders. Actual surgical castration is provided for by Texas law in lieu of taking the drugs. Texas leaves the choice to the offender. Castration is criticized for not addressing the underlying motivation of sex crimes—the need to control others. It is argued that castration will only lead to the commission of some other form of violent crime.[31]

# Kidnapping and False Imprisonment

## Kidnapping

Learning Objective: Define, describe, and apply the elements of kidnapping and false imprisonment.

**kidnapping**
Taking away and holding a person illegally, usually against the person's will or by force.

**Kidnapping** was a misdemeanor at common law, although it was regarded as a very serious crime, often resulting in life imprisonment. Felonies were often punished by death at the early common law. Today, kidnapping is a felony and carries a severe penalty in most states. Additionally, if the kidnapping takes the victim across state lines, the crime is a violation of the Federal Kidnapping Act.[32] The federal government, usually the Federal Bureau of Investigation, may become involved in any kidnapping 24 hours after the victim has been seized, by virtue of the Federal Kidnapping Act, which creates a presumption that the victim has been transported across state lines after that period of time.[33]

The elements of kidnapping are

1. the unlawful
2. taking and confinement and
3. asportation of
4. another person
5. by use of force, threat, fraud, or deception.

The taking of the victim must be unlawful. Thus, arrests made by police officers while engaged in their lawful duties are not kidnappings. Neither is it kidnapping for a guardian to take a ward from one place to another, as long as the action is lawful. However, when officers, or others, act completely without legal authority, they are not shielded from liability.

There must be a taking and confinement. Confinement is broadly construed. If Pat puts a gun to Craig's back and orders him to walk a half mile to Pat's home, there has been a confinement. Generally, there must be a restriction of the victim's freedom to take alternative action.

This taking and confinement must occur as a result of threat, force, fraud, or deception. Of course, Pat's gun in the example is ample threat to satisfy this requirement. Deception may also be used to gain control over the victim. For example, if Jon convinces his estranged wife to enter a house under the pretense of discussing their marital difficulties and then locks the door, he has fraudulently gained control over her.

Finally, there must be an asportation of the victim. *Asportation* means movement. The issue of the amount of movement necessary to meet this requirement is the most controversial question concerning kidnapping as a crime. The MPC

## Sidebar

### Amber Alerts

In 1996, Amber Hagerman, age 9, was kidnapped while riding her bicycle. Her abductor murdered her. In response, local news agencies, concerned citizens, and local law enforcement agencies partnered to create a public notification system of abducted children. Because time is critical in child abduction cases, the system is intended to provide expeditious and widespread notification of abductions. At the initiation of President George W. Bush, Congress enacted a national Amber Alert system in 2003. Although named for Amber Hagerman, AMBER is also an acronym for America's Missing: Broadcast Emergency Response. Today, all 50 states are participants in the system and various methods of disseminating the alerts are used, including radio, telephone, television, leaflets, and websites. Beginning in 2012, a national wireless system was established to text, free of charge, Amber Alerts to wireless users. The U.S. Department of Justice reports that hundreds of children have been recovered as a result of the AMBER system.

and most states now hold that if the kidnapping is incidental to the commission of another crime, there is insufficient asportation; some courts speak in terms of a movement of a "substantial distance."[34] To be incidental, a kidnapping must simply be a product of an intent to commit another crime. If a bank robber orders a teller to move from her window to the safe to fill a bag with money, four of the elements of kidnapping are present; however, the third element, asportation, has not been established because the movement was only incidental to the robbery. The result may be different if the teller was ordered to move to the safe for the purpose of raping her. The issue of substantial distance was raised in *Commonwealth v. Hughes.* In that case, the court focused on whether the movement substantially increased the risk of harm to the victim.

Many statutes specifically state that if the acts of asportation and confinement occur in furtherance of predicate crimes, then there is a kidnapping. Such statutes commonly include kidnapping for ransom, political reasons, rape, and murder. It is also common to upgrade kidnappings for these reasons. One type of kidnapping that is usually graded low is the taking of a child by a parent in violation of a court order.

## Parental Kidnapping

With a dissolution of marriage comes the separation of property owned by the couple, as well as a custody order if the couple has children. Often, costly and bitter custody disputes are also the result of divorce. In recent years "childnapping," or kidnapping of one's own child in violation of a custody order, has received much public attention.

### Oyez

#### Commonwealth v. Hughes
#### 399 A.2d 694 (Pa. Super. Ct. 1979)

**CERCONE, Judge:**

The appellant approached the victim, Ms. Helfrich, who was seated on a park bench. Appellant asked Ms. Helfrich if she wanted to go for a ride or smoke some marijuana with him. When Ms. Helfrich refused, appellant left. Minutes later, the appellant returned, placed a sharp kitchen knife to her throat, and stated, "I think you are going for a ride." Appellant forced Ms. Helfrich to walk to his car one and one-half blocks away and threatened to kill her if she resisted. Once in the car, he drove around the Media area in a reckless manner for approximately two miles and stopped his car in an abandoned lot surrounded by trees. He then forced Ms. Helfrich into the wooded area where he raped her. . . .

"A person is guilty of kidnapping if he unlawfully removes another a substantial distance, under the circumstances, from the place where he is found or if he unlawfully confines another for a substantial period in a place of isolation" . . . .

The framers of the MPC were aware of the experience of other jurisdictions when they drafted the model kidnapping statute. They recognized that "[w]hen an especially outrageous crime is committed there will be a public clamor for the extreme penalty and it is asking too much of public officials and juries to resist such pressures" . . . . To combat the undesirable situation of charging kidnapping to obtain a higher permissible sentence, the framers of the MPC drafted the kidnapping statute restrictively. . . . The drafters made explicit their "purpose to preclude kidnapping convictions based on trivial changes of location having no bearing on the evil at hand."

Drawing from the experience of other jurisdictions, the comments to the Model Code, and the fact that the Pennsylvania statute is similar to the MPC statute of kidnapping, it is clear to us that the legislature intended to exclude from kidnapping the incidental movement of a victim during the commission of a crime which does not substantially increase the risk of harm to the victim.

Turning to the case at hand, we find that the movement of the victim was not a trivial incident to the other crime charged. Although the victim was removed only a distance of 2 miles, the wooded area to which she was brought was in an isolated area, seemingly beyond the aid of her friends and police. Under the circumstances, two miles is a substantial enough distance to place the victim in a completely different environmental setting removed from the security of familiar surroundings. (In addition, the movement itself seriously endangered the victim as she was subject to a knife poised at her throat and to the reckless driving of appellant. At one point, appellant drove onto a one-way street in the wrong direction.) . . . Accordingly, the conviction is sustained.

Due to the rise in the number of such acts, new statutes specifically aimed at parental kidnapping have been adopted. The federal government entered this arena in 1980 by enacting the Parental Kidnapping Prevention Act.[35] Although this statute does not concern itself with criminal sanctions for childnapping, it does require that all states respect child custody orders of other states. That is, a person cannot escape a court order concerning custody of the child by kidnapping the child and fleeing to another jurisdiction. Interestingly, the federal government has left the actual punishment of parental kidnapping to the states. The federal kidnapping act specifically excludes such acts from its reach. Thus, kidnapping by a parent must be punished in a state court. This may occur in the state from which the child is taken or in any state where the parent takes the child.

Kidnapping of one's own child is often punished less severely than other kidnappings. This is sensible because many childnappings do not create a risk to the child's welfare; rather, they are the result of an overzealous, loving parent or a parent who is trying to hurt the other parent. Obviously, the crime should be punished because of the harm to the custodial parent, but the crime does not have the same evil motive a kidnapping with an intent to rape or murder does.

## False Imprisonment

**false imprisonment**
The unlawful restraint by one person of the physical liberty of another.

The crime of **false imprisonment** is a lesser included offense of kidnapping. The opposite is not true. Not all false imprisonments are kidnappings. A false imprisonment occurs when

1. one person
2. interferes
3. with another's liberty
4. by use of threat or force
5. without authority.

The primary distinction between the two crimes is the absence of asportation as an element of false imprisonment.

Today, some states have one statute that encompasses both false imprisonment and kidnapping. Such statutes are drafted so that the crime is graded, often elevating the crime if the motive is ransom, rape, serious bodily injury, or murder.

# True Threat

Learning Objective: Identity, define, and apply the elements of true threat.

In addition to actual harm, threatened harm can also be punished, subject to free speech limitations. Threatened harm is criminalized in an effort to both deter it and to incapacitate dangerous people. As a child, you may have heard the idiom *sticks and stones may break my bones, but words won't harm me*. Parents express this in an effort to help children deal with bullies—to give them the social tools to shrug off insensitive and nasty comments. It may also serve to reduce childhood violence. But the expression isn't always true. Words can be emotionally hurtful, and they can cause fear. At the common law, words, even if threatening, were not punished. Even today, much hurtful and offensive language is protected by the Free Speech Clause of the First Amendment. But there is a boundary to free speech. One form of speech that is not protected by the First Amendment is the **true threat**.

**true threat**
A threatening statement that is not protected by the Free Speech Clause of the First Amendment.

The starting place to understand what speech is protected is the 1966 case *Watts v. United States*. In *Watts*, the defendant, who was involved in a protest against police brutality, stated that "[t]hey always holler at us to get an education. And now I have already received my draft classification as 1-A and I have got to report for my physical this Monday coming. I am not going. If they ever make me carry a rifle the first man I want to get in my sights is L.B.J. . . . They are not going to make me kill my black brothers." By L.B.J., he was referring to U.S. President Lyndon B. Johnson. Mr. Watts was arrested, charged, and convicted of violating a federal statute that made it a crime to "knowingly and willfully . . . [make] any threat to take the life of or to inflict bodily harm upon the President of the United States." He appealed, eventually reaching the Supreme Court. The Court reversed his conviction on free speech grounds. While the Court acknowledged the nation's interest in protecting its president, it didn't find Mr. Watt's words to be a true threat. The Court wrote:

> For we must interpret the language Congress chose "against the background of a profound national commitment to the principle that debate on public issues should be uninhibited, robust, and wide-open, and that it may well include vehement, caustic, and sometimes unpleasantly sharp attacks on government and public officials."
>
> The language of the political arena, like the language used in labor disputes is often vituperative, abusive, and inexact. We agree with petitioner that his only offense here was "a kind of very crude offensive method of stating a political opposition to the President." Taken in context, and regarding the expressly conditional nature of the statement and the reaction of the listeners, we do not see how it could be interpreted otherwise.[36]

Although the decision didn't draw a clear line between lawful and criminal speech, a few workable rules came out of the case. First, hyperbole, particularly in political speech, is protected. Second, threats that are conditioned upon unlikely events are also protected. And finally, the reaction of listeners is important. The Court viewed them as indicators of context, of the speaker's intentions and apparent ability to follow through on the threat.

In some circumstances, the status of the person receiving the threat may also change the outcome. Lower courts have held, for example, that police officers are expected to tolerate more inflammatory and foul language than other people.

In a long line of cases, the Supreme Court has made clear that offensive and hateful statements may not be criminalized. The use of racial, religious, or gender epithets, for example, is protected speech in nearly all circumstances. This is discussed in greater detail in the following section on civil rights crimes.

The most recent Supreme Court case of any significance on true threat was issued in 2015. While the Supreme Court decided the case on statutory, not constitutional, grounds, the case illustrates how far a threat may have to go before it may be criminalized. The case is *Elonis v. United States* and it appears in the OYEZ feature.

## Oyez

### Elonis v. United States
### 575 U.S. 723 (2015)

**Chief Justice Roberts delivered the opinion of the Court.**

Federal law makes it a crime to transmit in interstate commerce "any communication containing any threat . . . to injure the person of another." Petitioner was convicted of violating this provision under instructions that required the jury to find that he communicated what a reasonable person would regard as a threat. The question is whether the statute also requires that the defendant be aware of the threatening nature of the communication, and—if not—whether the First Amendment requires such a showing.

Anthony Douglas Elonis was an active user of the social networking Web site Facebook. Users of that Web site may post items on their Facebook page that are accessible to other users, including Facebook "friends" who are notified when new content is posted. In May 2010, Elonis's wife of nearly seven years left him, taking with her their two young children. Elonis began "listening to more violent

(continued)

music" and posting self-styled "rap" lyrics inspired by the music. Eventually, Elonis changed the user name on his Facebook page from his actual name to a rap-style nom de plume, "Tone Dougie," to distinguish himself from his "on-line persona." The lyrics Elonis posted as "Tone Dougie" included graphically violent language and imagery. This material was often interspersed with disclaimers that the lyrics were "fictitious," with no intentional "resemblance to real persons." Elonis posted an explanation to another Facebook user that "I'm doing this for me. My writing is therapeutic. . . ."

Elonis's co-workers and friends viewed the posts in a different light. Around Halloween of 2010, Elonis posted a photograph of himself and a co-worker at a "Halloween Haunt" event at the amusement park where they worked. In the photograph, Elonis was holding a toy knife against his co-worker's neck, and in the caption Elonis wrote, "I wish." Elonis was not Facebook friends with the co-worker and did not "tag" her, a Facebook feature that would have alerted her to the posting. But the chief of park security was a Facebook "friend" of Elonis, saw the photograph, and fired him. . . .

"Moles! Didn't I tell y'all I had several? Y'all sayin' I had access to keys for all the f***in' gates. That I have sinister plans for all my friends and must have taken home a couple. Y'all think it's too dark and foggy to secure your facility from a man as mad as me? You see, even without a paycheck, I'm still the main attraction. Whoever thought the Halloween Haunt could be so f***in' scary?" . . .

Elonis's posts frequently included crude, degrading, and violent material about his soon-to-be ex-wife. . . . [He posted]

"Hi, I'm Tone Elonis.

Did you know that it's illegal for me to say I want to kill my wife? . . .

It's one of the only sentences that I'm not allowed to say. . . .

Now it was okay for me to say it right then because I was just telling you that it's illegal for me to say I want to kill my wife. . . .

Um, but what's interesting is that it's very illegal to say I really, really think someone out there should kill my wife. . . .

But not illegal to say with a mortar launcher.

Because that's its own sentence. . . .

I also found out that it's incredibly illegal, extremely illegal to go on Facebook and say something like the best place to fire a mortar launcher at her house would be from the cornfield behind it because of easy access to a getaway road and you'd have a clear line of sight through the sun room. . . .

Yet even more illegal to show an illustrated diagram.

[diagram of the house]. . . ."

. . .

After viewing some of Elonis's posts, his wife felt "extremely afraid for [her] life." . . .

A state court granted her a three-year protection-from-abuse order against Elonis (essentially, a restraining order). Elonis referred to the order in another post on his "Tone Dougie" page, also included in Count Two of the indictment:

"Fold up your [protection-from-abuse order] and put it in your pocket

Is it thick enough to stop a bullet?

Try to enforce an Order

that was improperly granted in the first place

Me thinks the Judge needs an education

on true threat jurisprudence

And prison time'll add zeros to my settlement . . .

And if worse comes to worse

I've got enough explosives

to take care of the State Police and the Sheriff's Department."

At the bottom of this post was a link to the Wikipedia article on "Freedom of speech. . . ."

[Elonis also posted:]

"That's it, I've had about enough

I'm checking out and making a name for myself

Enough elementary schools in a ten mile radius

to initiate the most heinous school shooting ever imagined

And hell hath no fury like a crazy man in a Kindergarten class

The only question is . . . which one?"

[The F.B.I. was contacted and two agents visited Elonis.]

Following their visit, during which Elonis was polite but uncooperative, Elonis posted another entry on his Facebook page, called "Little Agent Lady," which led to Count Five:

"You know your s***'s ridiculous

when you have the FBI knockin' at yo' door

Little Agent lady stood so close

Took all the strength I had not to turn the b**** ghost

Pull my knife, flick my wrist, and slit her throat

Leave her bleedin' from her jugular in the arms of her partner

[laughter]

So the next time you knock, you best be serving a warrant

And bring yo' SWAT and an explosives expert while you're at it

Cause little did y'all know, I was strapped wit' a bomb

Why do you think it took me so long to get dressed with no shoes on?

I was jus' waitin' for y'all to handcuff me and pat me down

Touch the detonator in my pocket and we're all goin'

[BOOM!]

Are all the pieces comin' together?

S***, I'm just a crazy sociopath

that gets off playin' you stupid f***s like a fiddle

And if y'all didn't hear, I'm gonna be famous

Cause I'm just an aspiring rapper who likes the attention

who happens to be under investigation for terrorism

cause y'all think I'm ready to turn the Valley into Fallujah

But I ain't gonna tell you which bridge is gonna fall

into which river or road

(continued)

And if you really believe this s***

I'll have some bridge rubble to sell you tomorrow

[BOOM!][BOOM!][BOOM!]"

[At trial, the jury was not instructed to find that Elonis intended to cause fear and the prosecutor argued that his mental state was immaterial. He was convicted.]

The fact that the statute does not specify any required mental state, however, does not mean that none exists. We have repeatedly held that "mere omission from a criminal enactment of any mention of criminal intent" should not be read "as dispensing with it." This rule of construction reflects the basic principle that "wrongdoing must be conscious to be criminal." As Justice Jackson explained, this principle is "as universal and persistent in mature systems of law as belief in freedom of the human will and a consequent ability and duty of the normal individual to choose between good and evil." The "central thought" is that a defendant must be "blameworthy in mind" before he can be found guilty, a concept courts have expressed over time through various terms such as *mens rea*, scienter, malice aforethought, guilty knowledge, and the like. Although there are exceptions, the "general rule" is that a guilty mind is "a necessary element in the indictment and proof of every crime." We therefore generally "interpret[ ] criminal statutes to include broadly applicable scienter requirements, even where the statute by its terms does not contain them." . . .

Elonis's conviction cannot stand. The jury was instructed that the Government need prove only that a reasonable person would regard Elonis's communications as threats, and that was error. Federal criminal liability generally does not turn solely on the results of an act without considering the defendant's mental state. That understanding "took deep and early root in American soil" and Congress left it intact here: Under Section 875(c), "wrongdoing must be conscious to be criminal."

There is no dispute that the mental state requirement in [the statute] is satisfied if the defendant transmits a communication for the purpose of issuing a threat, or with knowledge that the communication will be viewed as a threat. In response to a question at oral argument, Elonis stated that a finding of recklessness would not be sufficient. Neither Elonis nor the Government has briefed or argued that point, and we accordingly decline to address it. Given our disposition, it is not necessary to consider any First Amendment issues. . . .

The judgment of the United States Court of Appeals for the Third Circuit is reversed, and the case is remanded for further proceedings consistent with this opinion. [On remand, the appellate court affirmed Elonis' conviction because it found that the evidence supported a finding that Elonis' had a knowing, and therefore also reckless, state of mind.]

---

The Court avoided the First Amendment question by basing its *Elonis* decision on general criminal law principles. So, it is unknown whether the First Amendment requires subjective intent by a speaker.

True threat is early in its development. It lacks a precise formulation. The following is an amalgam of the caselaw defining the true threat doctrine.

1. The speaker intends, purposely, knowingly, or recklessly, to
2. communicate a
3. serious expression of an intent to
4. commit an act of unlawful violence to a particular individual or group of individuals that would cause a
5. reasonable person to fear serious bodily harm or death
6. and the threat is communicated to, and received by, the target individual or group.

The power of social media to rapidly communicate statements to millions of people, to any location, puts the problem of threats on steroids. New issues are also presented by digital communication. Does a threatening social media posting need to be communicated directly to the target of the threat? What about passive communication, such as when the speaker and target are friends on Facebook, but the target wasn't called out or tagged in the posting? Is it enough to communicate a threat, even though it never reaches the target? The answer to the last question appears to be no; a threat must reach its target in order for that person to be objectively fearful. These are hard questions yet to be answered by the Supreme Court.

# Stalking

Learning Objective: Define, describe, and apply the elements of stalking.

In recent years, **stalking** has received a lot of media, public, and legislative attention. Public awareness of stalking increased when prominent public figures who were the victims of stalkers, including politicians, actors, and law enforcement officials, began to speak out.

Stalking posed unique problems to law enforcement officials, prosecutors, and judges. Before 1990, no state had a law specifically aimed at combating stalking. Therefore, preexisting criminal laws, such as assault, battery, and threats, as well as the use of restraining orders, were relied upon in dealing with stalkers. But these laws proved ineffective. Often there is no assault, battery, or provable threat until the victim has been injured or murdered. Even when one of these crimes could be proven, sentences were short. Restraining orders also proved to give victims little protection.

In response to the growing public interest in stalking, California enacted the nation's first stalking law in 1990. By 1993, another 46 states had enacted similar laws.[37]

Stalking laws vary in their elements, but most include a list of acts that satisfy the actus reus of the crime. These include following, harassing, threatening, lying in wait, or conducting surveillance of another person. Usually, one act does not amount to stalking; rather, there must be a pattern of acts.

It is not enough that the acts happen. They must cause the victim to subjectively and objectively experience fear. Most laws have a double mens rea requirement; the defendant must intend the predicate acts and must either purposely or knowingly cause the victim's fear.

The state of Washington's stalking law is typical of what is found around the country:

RCW 9A.46.110; Stalking

(1) A person commits the crime of stalking if, without lawful authority and under circumstances not amounting to a felony attempt of another crime:

    (a) He or she intentionally and repeatedly harasses or repeatedly follows another person; and

    (b) The person being harassed or followed is placed in fear that the stalker intends to injure the person, another person, or property of the person or of another person. The feeling of fear must be one that a reasonable person in the same situation would experience under all the circumstances; and

    (c) The stalker either:

        (i) Intends to frighten, intimidate, or harass the person; or

        (ii) Knows or reasonably should know that the person is afraid, intimidated, or harassed even if the stalker did not intend to place the person in fear or intimidate or harass the person.

Even before stalking laws, many states criminalized harassment. Personal harassment, telephone harassment, and other specific forms of harassment are commonly included in these laws. However, as mentioned earlier, these statutes were not effective in stopping stalkers, primarily because of the short sentences violators usually received.

**stalking**
The crime of repeatedly following, threatening, or harassing another person in ways that lead to a legitimate fear of physical harm. Some states define *stalking* more broadly as any conduct with no legitimate purpose that seriously upsets a targeted person, especially conduct in violation of a protective order.

# Cyberstalking

A new type of stalker has emerged in recent years, the cyberstalker. **Cyberstalking** is the crime of using communication technology to transmit obscene, abusive, or harassing language intended to harass or threaten another person. Because of the impersonal and seemingly anonymous nature of electronic communications, it is easier to harass other persons than it has been in the past. In recent years, stalking using another person's identity has increased. Known as "spoofing," this crime has two victims: the individual receiving the messages and the individual whose identity has been stolen.

Both state and federal statutes exist that criminalize cyberstalking. For example, the Communications Decency Act, 47 U.S.C. § 223(a)(1)(A), provides for criminal prosecution of any person who "by means of a telecommunications device knowingly makes, creates, or solicits, and initiates the transmission of any comment, request, suggestion, proposal, image, or other communication which is obscene, lascivious, filthy, or indecent, with the intent to annoy, abuse, threaten or harass another person." Another federal statute, 18 U.S.C. § 875(c), makes it a federal crime to "transmit in interstate or foreign commerce any communication containing any threat to kidnap any person or any threat to injure the person of another." Other federal and state laws that were originally intended to apply to telephone harassment may apply as well.

The federal government extended its reach over stalking in 18 U.S.C. §2261(A) to include "harassment" and the use of computers to commit stalking. That statute criminalizes any act "to kill, injure, harass, or place under surveillance with intent to kill, injure, harass, or intimidate, or cause substantial emotional distress to a person" using "mail, any interactive computer service, or any facility of interstate or foreign commerce. . . ."

Although the Supreme Court has not spoken on the issue, lower courts have. In *United States v. Cassidy*, presented in your next Oyez, a federal trial court found the defendant's offensive tweeting to be protected by the First Amendment's free speech guarantee.

47 U.S.C. § 223(a)(1)(A) and similar statutes have been challenged as overbroad because they prohibit not only obscene speech, which clearly may be regulated, but also "indecent" speech that is intended to annoy. The jury is still out on this question.[38]

## Oyez

### United States v. Cassidy
#### 814 F. Supp.2d 574 (D.C. District of Maryland 2011)

Titus, J.

The Indictment in this case alleges that the Defendant, William Lawrence Cassidy, violated a federal stalking statute, 18 U.S.C. § 2261A(2)(A), when, with the intent to harass and cause substantial emotional distress to a person in another state, he used an interactive computer service to engage in a course of conduct that caused substantial emotional distress to a person whose initials are A.Z. by posting messages on www.Twitter.com and other Internet websites. . . .

[According to the FBI agent who investigated] A.Z. is an enthroned tulku or reincarnate master who was enthroned in 1988 as a reincarnate llama. Following the enthronement ceremony, the Supreme Head of this particular Sect of Buddhism renamed the center where A.Z. taught as Kunzang Odsal Palyou Changchub Choling ("KPC" or the "Center"). KPC was designated as the Supreme Head's seat in the West, and A.Z. is believed by members of the KPC to be the only American-born female tulku. . . .

[According to the FBI agent] Defendant, who was then known as William Sanderson, befriended one of the monks of the KPC in 2007; he claimed he was also a Buddhist American tulku and expressed an interest in meeting A.Z. Those close to A.Z. encouraged her to meet with Defendant. Thereafter, A.Z. invited Defendant to join her at her retreat in Arizona and Defendant asked to ride alone with her in her vehicle. While in the vehicle, Defendant proposed to A.Z., and she declined. He also asked her to pretend they were married. A.Z. confided in Defendant and shared details of her personal life, including the sexual abuse she had endured as a child and particulars of the failed relationship with her ex-husband. In response, Defendant asked A.Z. if she wanted him to kill her ex-husband, and A.Z. requested that her ex-husband not be harmed.

[The FBI agent's] affidavit also alleges that when Defendant claimed to have Stage IV Lung Cancer, members of the KPC took care of him, as if these were his final days. At that time, it came to light that Defendant's real name was William Cassidy. KPC members and A.Z. also began to notice that Defendant's conduct was inconsistent with this Sect's teachings. For example, he would gossip even though the Sect considers gossip offensive. These incidents led A.Z. to investigate Defendant's lineage to assess whether he was in fact a tulku.

Despite these concerns, however, KPC promoted Defendant in February 2008 to the position of Chief Operating Officer of KPC. Defendant held this position for only 2 weeks. On February 23, 2008, A.Z. learned that Defendant was never a tulku and confronted him. Defendant immediately left the retreat, taking with him a Buddhist nun, Nydia Alexandra. The [FBI agent's] affidavit asserts that, in the wake of his departure, the Defendant used Twitter and logs to harass KPC and A.Z. . . . [The court explained that tweets and blogs are not messages to specific individuals. They are the equivalent of a colonial bulletin board.] . . . the Twitter account "Vajragurl" frequently posts tweets.

As of July 5, 2010, over 350 tweets were posted on "Vajragurl" that allegedly were directed at A.Z. KPC believes that all but a few hundred of the alleged 8,000 tweets on the "Vajragurl" account pertain to A.Z. and KPC. [Defendant posted these posts anonymously and, while critical of A.Z. when written about her directly, they were not threatening. There were many disturbing posts concerning violence that were not specifically directed at A.Z., and when read in conjunction with the posts specifically about A.Z., her sect, and beliefs, were offensive or harassing to her.]

Defendant's tweets and blog postings have caused A.Z. substantial emotional distress. She fears for her own safety and that of her fellow KPC members. As a result of the alleged harassment, A.Z. has not left her house for a year and a half, except to see her psychiatrist. A.Z. was in such fear for her safety that she did not go to an October 2010 retreat. . . .

[T]he First Amendment protects speech even when the subject or manner of expression is uncomfortable and challenges conventional religious beliefs, political attitudes or standards of good taste. . . . Indeed, the Supreme Court has consistently classified emotionally distressing or outrageous speech as protected, especially where that speech touches on matters of political, religious, or public concern. This is because "in public debate our own citizens must tolerate insulting, and even outrageous, speech in order to provide 'adequate' 'breathing space' to the freedoms protected by the First Amendment'" . . . .

Even though numerous court decisions have made a point to protect anonymous, uncomfortable speech and extend that protection to the Internet, not all speech is protected speech. There are certain "well-defined and narrowly limited classes of speech" that remain unprotected by the First Amendment. . . . [I]t is clear that the Government's Indictment is directed at protected speech that is not exempted from protection by any of the recognized areas just described. First, A.Z. is a well-known religious figure who goes by the names Alyce Zeoli or Catherine Burroughs. Martha Sherrill, a *Washington Post* journalist wrote a critical nonfiction book about A.Z. entitled *The Buddha from Brooklyn* (Random House 1st ed. 2000). Second, although in bad taste, Mr. Cassidy's tweets and blog posts about A.Z. challenge her character and qualifications as a religious leader. And, while Mr. Cassidy's speech may have inflicted substantial emotional distress, the Government's Indictment here is directed squarely at protected speech: anonymous, uncomfortable Internet speech addressing religious matters.

Tellingly, the Government's Indictment is not limited to categories of speech that fall outside of First Amendment protection — obscenity, fraud, defamation, true threats, incitement or speech integral to criminal conduct. Because this speech does not fall into any of the recognized exceptions, the speech remains protected. . . .

Here, A.Z. had the ability to protect her "own sensibilities simply by averting" her eyes from the Defendant's blog and not looking at, or blocking his tweets. [The court distinguished posts from telephone calls, which are directed at specific individuals.]

[The court dismissed the indictment against Defendant.]

# Civil Rights and Hate Crimes

Learning Objective: Describe the constitutional limitations on when hate may be criminalized or used in a criminal case.

Police shootings, particularly of African Americans, and acts of violence by private individuals against others due to race, religion, and sexual orientation are contemporary problems with old roots. The states and federal government have laws that provide for

People demonstrating against Asian hate crimes, which increased during the COVID pandemic.

(1) civil and criminal remedies for harmful acts that are motivated by race, sex, religion, and other bias; and

(2) civil and criminal remedies for violations of constitutionally protected rights.

Before we discuss specific hate crimes, let's review the First Amendment's free speech limitations on criminalizing bias. As you learned earlier, most hate speech is protected by the First Amendment's Free Speech Clause. There are a couple of widely accepted purposes for protecting speech from government control and punishment. The first is that through a free market of ideas, scientific discovery, innovation, medicine, social understanding, and creative thought and expression will flourish. Free expression also advances the constitutional republicanism—only uninhibited, open, and robust debate about the most controversial subjects will enable society to remain free. Criticism and disagreement over policy, law, government, public officials, technology, and social conditions are necessary to accomplish these goals. As Justice Robert Jackson wrote, "If there is any fixed star in our constitutional constellation, it is that no official ... can prescribe what shall be orthodox in politics, nationalism, religion, or other matters of opinion or force citizens to confess by word or act their faith therein."[39]

*Brandenburg v. Ohio* (1969)[40] is an example. Brandenburg was a Ku Klux Klan (KKK) leader in Ohio charged with advocating violence at a rally held on private property that was witnessed by a reporter. At the rally, he and other men who were dressed in Klan robes, burned a cross, and made racist statements. Brandenburg said there would be "revengeance" against N\*\*\*ers and Jews and he claimed that Congress, Supreme Court, and the president were oppressing the Caucasian race. He continued by calling for African Americans to return to Africa and Jewish Americans to Israel. Brandenburg was charged under Ohio's Criminal Syndicalism statute, which forbade "advocat[ing] . . . sabotage, violence, or unlawful methods of terrorism as a means of accomplishing industrial or political reform" and for "voluntarily assembl[ing] with any society, group, or assemblage of persons formed to teach or advocate the doctrines of criminal syndicalism."

The Supreme Court held that threatening speech may only be regulated if (1) it is likely to result in (2) imminent lawlessness and (3) the speaker intends to cause that lawlessness. Applying this standard, the Court struck down Ohio's law as too broad. This formulation, known as the Brandenburg Test, remains the law today.

In a related case from 1992, *R.A.V. v. St. Paul*,[41] several teenagers who burned a cross on the lawn of a black family were charged and convicted of violating the following ordinance:

Whoever places on public or private property a symbol, object, appellation, characterization or graffiti, including, but not limited to a burning cross or Nazi swastika, which one knows or has reasonable ground to know arouses anger, alarm, resentment in others on the basis of race, color, creed, religion, or gender, commits disorderly conduct and shall be guilty of a misdemeanor.

Like Brandenburg, these convictions were reversed and overturned because the ordinance singled-out a specific belief, or viewpoint, for punishment. It didn't, for example, make it unlawful to arouse anger, alarm, or resentment on the basis of advancing love of all races, political beliefs, clothing style, or sexual orientation. Fundamental to the First Amendment is the idea that the government is not the overlord of morality; it is not permitted to decide what ideas, or the expression of them, are permissible.

In 1989, the Court heard another case in this line, *Wisconsin v. Mitchell*. But the bias law at issue in this case could be distinguished from both *Brandenburg* and *R.A.V.* because it didn't regulate speech. Instead, it acted as punishment enhancement for harmful conduct that was racially motivated. The defendant, Mitchel, was one of a group of African American men who beat a Caucasian teen, leaving the victim in a coma for four days. Mitchell was convicted of aggravated battery, and his punishment was increased from a maximum of two years in prison to an actual sentence of four years because he acted out of racial hatred. The applicable law permitted the punishment enhancement if the crime was motivated by "race, religion, color, disability, sexual orientation, national origin, or ancestry." Because the law was focused on conduct, not speech, and because motive had long been a consideration in sentencing, the Supreme Court upheld the law and affirmed the sentence.

Subsequently, the Court heard three cross-burning cases in tandem. These cases are collectively known as *Virginia v. Black*. The three defendants had all burned crosses on private property. Two defendants in all three cases burned crosses on the property of African Americans, without their consent, and the third defendant, Black, burned his cross on private property with the consent of the owner. All three defendants were charged with burning a cross with an intent to intimidate others. The law also created a presumption that cross burning was intended to intimidate other people. Although similar in facts, the legal issue in this case was different than in *Brandenburg*. Brandenburg was prosecuted for his speech. In this case, Black and the other defendants were prosecuted for the act of cross-burning. But the law also included the intended message. This combination of speech and act is known as expressive conduct. Expressive conduct falls within the protections of the First Amendment, but not the extent of pure speech.

The Supreme Court held that the state may punish conduct that is intended to intimidate, provided it does so in a viewpoint neutral manner. The law under review was determined to be viewpoint neutral because any cross-burning intended to intimidate, regardless of the motive or the identities of the persons involved, was prohibited. It didn't protect, for example, one racial group and not others.

While it upheld that portion of the law, the Court invalidated the law's presumption of intent because it was possible for a person to intend a benign message. Even the KKK used cross-burning to convey multiple messages. The group burns crosses to intimidate others, to express solidarity, as a symbol of ideology, and ritualistically. The first of these three may be criminalized; the last three are protected activities. The Court noted that there have been cases where crosses were burned for reasons that have nothing to do with race whatsoever. As such, Black's conviction was overturned.

To put this line of cases together, laws that punish hate speech are unconstitutional. But conduct that is otherwise illegal may be punished more severely when it is motivated by specific forms of hatred.

With an understanding of how the First Amendment limits the criminalization of bias, let's discuss civil rights laws. Some civil rights law criminalize civil rights violations. Other civil rights laws offer civil relief for violations. Because of the importance of one specific form of federal civil relief, we will begin with it.

The law, a part of the Civil Rights Act of 1871, was originally enacted to combat the terrorism of the Ku Klux Klan during Reconstruction in the south, by holding state officials who supported the KKK, accountable. Today, it is used to protect all people from civil rights violations by state and local officials. Codied today at 18 U.S.C. sec. 1983, the law provides that

1. any person who
2. "under color of state law"
3. deprives another person of a
4. legally protected right

is liable in damages, and possibly, subject to injunctive relief. This type of civil case is commonly known as a "1983 action." The federal government and state governments can't be sued under §1983. To be liable under §1983, an *individual* must act under color of state law. States create and empower local governments, so anyone acting under city, township, county, or state authority is subject to §1983. Territories and Washington, D.C. are included within the law's grasp. The following are examples of when an official can be liable under §1983.

A city police officer arbitrarily stops and searches a car and its occupants.

A corrections officer refuses to give an inmate who is seriously injured access to medical care.

However, an agent of the federal Bureau of Alcohol, Tobacco, and Firearms who breaks down a door to home without a warrant or probable cause is acting under color of federal law and therefore is not subject to liability under §1983. Similarly, the federal and state governments themselves can't be held liable. But difficult, federal officials can sometimes be held to account as well, but under different laws.

Civil rights plaintiffs must overcome a couple of immunities to succeed. The first is sovereign immunity. Under this doctrine, governments may only be sued when they allow it. Most states and the federal government have waived this immunity, in limited ways.

In recent years, police shootings have brought light to a controversial doctrine; individual immunity. There are two forms of this: absolute immunity and qualified immunity. In rare cases, officials are absolutely immune from both liability and the trouble of defending against a lawsuit. Judicial immunity, for example, provides that a judge is totally exempt from civil liability for judicial acts. This immunity extends to anyone acting under a judge's order. The rationale underpinning absolute immunity is that judges must make difficult decisions in close cases. To hold judges accountable for their mistakes would bring the judiciary to a halt.

The second, and more controversial defense, is qualified immunity. An official is liable only if she violates a clearly established right. Even if a right is violated, there is no liability if it is not clearly established at the time the act was committed. The qualified immunity standard has been criticized in recent years, particularly in the context of police shootings of African Americas, because the manner in which courts have applied the standard. They have interpreted the clearly established

## Sidebar

### Crime Stats: Hate Crime

There were 7,314 reported incidents involving 8,559 hate crimes in the United States in 2019. Of these crimes, 56% were racially motivated, 21% were motivated by religious beliefs, 17% by sexual orientation, 3% by gender identity, 12% by ethnicity, 2% by disability, and 1% by gender. A few were attributable to multiple factors. Most of these crimes were committed against the person, with intimidation and assault being the most common offense. A sizeable minority of hate offenses were committed against property, private and public.

*Source:* Uniform Crime Reports, Hate Crime Statistics, U.S. Department of Justice, Federal Bureau of Investigation, 2020.

standard to require hyper-identical precedent. For example, a prior finding that beating a suspect with a baton violated the Fourth Amendment didn't clearly establish a right to be free from an unprovoked beating in a later case because the police used a fire extinguisher, not a baton, to beat a suspect. The clearly established standard was created by the Supreme Court. It is not of constitutional origin. There is a possibility that the Court will revisit and revise it in the future.

Both the federal and state governments have civil rights criminal statutes. The signature federal law makes it a crime for two or more persons to conspire to injure, oppress, threaten, or intimidate a person for exercising a federally secured right.[42]

In addition to civil liability, civil rights offenders can face criminal charges. civil rights crimes. As mentioned earlier, many of these laws are quite old, having been enacted to combat the KKK's terrorization of African Americans, Catholics, and Jews in the late 19th century.

In addition, any person acting pursuant to state law or authority (under color of law) who deprives a person of a federally secured right due to alienage, race, or color is guilty of a federal civil rights crime.[43] The "color of law" requirement mirrows Section 1983. Consequently, defendants are usually state or local officials. It was under this statute that the police officers who beat Rodney King in Los Angeles were tried and convicted in federal court. In addition to criminal remedies, victims may seek civil remedies under a separate civil rights statute.[44] Other federal statutes criminalize interfering with voting rights, public education, jury service, and travel. States have similar civil rights laws.

## Ethical Considerations

### Can an Outspoken Racist Join the Bar?

Matthew F. Hale graduated from the Southern Illinois University School of Law in 1988 and passed the Illinois bar exam in the same year. However, he was not admitted to membership because the Illinois Bar authority questioned whether he was morally fit to be an attorney. Like all bar authorities, the Illinois Bar requires more than competence, as proved by passing the bar exam, to join the bar. It also requires good moral character and fitness. Hale's character was questioned by the Committee on Character and Fitness of the Illinois Bar because he was discovered to be a vocal and vehement racist. This was the first time since 1950 that the Illinois Bar had denied the admission of an applicant because of moral character. In that case, the applicant was denied admission because he was alleged to be a communist, and he refused to respond to an inquiry about his support for the Communist Party when asked by the Bar. Although he went on to be a law professor, Hale lost his appeal, eventually at the Supreme Court of the United States; therefore, he never obtained admission to the Illinois Bar.

At Hale's appeal of the decision of the Committee on Character and Fitness to an appeals panel of the Bar, examples of the depth of his hatred for black people and Jewish people and his disruptive and disrespectful protests were presented, as well as evidence that he lied to the Bar, had been arrested for assault and battery, failed to disclose a minor conviction in his application, and evidence that he had been suspended by his undergraduate college (Bradley University) for violating its policies, including referring to a member of the university community as "Jew Boy." Also, he wrote the following response to a woman who supported affirmative action:

> Your comments appearing in the Saturday, July 22nd issue of *The Journal Star* were as pathetic as they were asinine. When in the hell are people of your ilk going to face the fact that the nigger race is inferior in intellectual capacity. And I underline inferior. You have examples all around you, and yet you continue to cling to the misbegotten equality myth, which is not only destroying our universities but also our whole country. Is it going to take your rape at the hands of a nigger beast or your murder before you become aware of the problem. . . . I'm looking forward to the day when our people's eyes are opened and when people who believe in the equality myth no longer have any power to promote this garbage to others.

The appellate panel also discovered that one of Hale's past girlfriends had obtained a protective order against him because of his verbal abuse. His membership in the World Church of the Creator (WCOTC) was also significant. The doctrine of the church, which he led for a time as its Pontifex Maximus, asserts that the Jewish race is inferior, is an enemy of the church, and called for the destruction of all Jews. The church's beliefs about all nonwhites were similar. Although not emphasized by Hale for fear of turning away white member prospects, WCOTC doctrine also assaulted Christianity. Significant to the Bar was the church's

(continued)

requirement that Hale put his race above all other loyalties. Through his role as Pontifex Maximus, he preached racial hatred to both congregants and others.

Although Hale insisted that he could separate his beliefs from his duties as an attorney, he lost on appeal. The Bar concluded that he was not fit for a variety of reasons. One rule, for example, requires attorneys not to discriminate against those in the legal system because of sex, race, religion, or national origin. The Bar reaffirmed his First Amendment right to hold and express his racist beliefs—but not as an officer of the court. His beliefs were likely not enough to justify his exclusion from the Bar. It was the combination of the extremity of his beliefs when accompanied with his apparent disregard for the law, as evinced by his prior conduct, that excluded him from membership.

Two days after Hale's appeal was denied, a member of WCOTC began a two-day shooting spree. He ultimately killed two and injured nine people. He focused his deeds on racial minorities. The shooter committed suicide at the end of his killing spree. Hale indicated that the shooter was angry about the Bar's decision and said other violence could occur if he was not admitted to the Bar. Later, law enforcement officers would acquire a recording of Hale laughing about the spree and the lives that were taken.

Eventually, Hale also lost his appeal to the Illinois Supreme Court, and he was never admitted to the Bar. Subsequently, the WCOTC found itself embroiled in a trademark battle with another church that claimed WCOTC had stolen its name. Enraged at the judge in the case for ordering the WCOTC to stop using the name, Hale planned the judge's murder. The plot was discovered before the judge was harmed, and Hale was charged with soliciting the murder of the judge. He was convicted of soliciting the murder (and three counts of obstruction of justice) and sentenced to 40 years in prison in 2005.

*Sources:* Emelie East, "The Case of Matthew F. Hale: Implications for First Amendment rights, social mores and the direction of bar examiners in an era of intolerance of hatred," 13 *Geo. J. Legal Ethics* 741 (2000); the process and the Hale quote are from this source.

Anti-Defamation League (*http://www.adl.org/learn/ext_us/Hale.asp? xpicked=2&item=6*); the information on the trademark case and Hale's conviction are from this source.

## Key Terms

| | | |
|---|---|---|
| assault | first-degree murder | provocation |
| battery | kidnapping | rape |
| corpus delicti | lesser included offense | second-degree murder |
| cyberstalking | manslaughter | shield laws |
| deadly weapon doctrine | mayhem | stalking |
| false imprisonment | merger | statutory rape |
| felony murder | predicate offense | true threat |

## Review Questions

1. What is the primary distinction between first- and second-degree murder?

2. What is felony murder?

3. What is the difference between an assault and a battery?

4. What is the marital rape exception?

5. John caught his wife having sex with another man. In a fit of rage, he killed his wife. What crime has been committed?

6. What is meant by the phrase "imperfect self-defense"?

7. What is the primary distinction between false imprisonment and kidnapping?

8. Under the common law, if a person cut another's limb off, what crime was committed?

9. Give an example of a nonforcible rape.

10. What was the common law definition of murder?

# Problems & Critical Thinking Exercises

1. State statute reads: "Any act of 1. sexual intercourse 2. with another person 3. against that person's will and 4. by use of force or under such a threat of force that resistance would result in serious bodily injury or death, is rape." Explain how this statutory definition of rape differs from the common law definition.

2. On May 5, Mark and Sam, who had been neighbors for three years, argued over Sam's construction of a ditch, which diverted water onto Mark's property. Mark told Sam to stop construction of the ditch or he "would pay with his life." The following day, Mark and Sam met again in Sam's garage. Within minutes Mark became very angry and cut Sam's leg with an axe he found in Sam's garage. After cutting Sam, he panicked and ran home. Sam attempted to reach a telephone to call for help, but the cut proved fatal.

   Mark has been charged with first-degree murder. He claims that he had no intent to kill Sam; rather, he only intended to hit him on the leg with the dull, flat side of the axe in an effort to scare Sam. Discuss the facts and explain what crimes could be proved and why.

3. On July 1, 2013, Jeff shot Megan during a bank robbery. Megan remained on life-support systems until September 4, 2014. At that time the systems were disconnected and she ceased breathing. On June 15, 2014, her physician had declared her brain dead. It was not until September 4, 2014, that her family decided to stop the life-support system. Jeff is charged with murder. Discuss any defenses he may have.

4. Penelope and Brenda had been enemies for years. One evening, Penelope discovered that Brenda had attempted on many occasions to "pick up" Penelope's boyfriend. Penelope told a friend that she was "going to fix Brenda once and for all—that she was going to mess her face up bad." That evening, Penelope waited for Brenda outside her home and attacked her with a knife. Penelope slashed her in the face four times and cut off one ear. Brenda reported the event to the police, who have turned it over to the county prosecutor's office. As the office legal assistant, you have been assigned the task of determining what crime can be charged.

5. State statute reads: "It shall be a felony for any person to purposefully, knowingly, or recklessly cause the death of another person by the use of poison or other toxins." Eddie Farmer spread a toxic insecticide on his crops, which eventually mixed with rainwater and made its way into his neighbor's well. The insecticide was new, but it had been recommended by other farmers who had used it successfully. His neighbor's seven-year-old son, Mikey, died from the poisons in the water. Eddie has been charged with violating the state statute. Is he liable?

6. One evening after a play, Tracy was approached by a woman who pointed a pistol at her and ordered her to "give me all your money and jewelry." Tracy removed her jewels and handed them over, but told the robber that her money was in her purse, which was in the trunk of her car. The robber asked her where her car was parked, and Tracy pointed to a car 30 feet away. Tracy was then ordered to go to the automobile, remove the purse, and give it to the robber. She complied, and the woman ran off. The thief was eventually captured and tried for aggravated robbery and kidnapping. She was convicted of both and has appealed the kidnapping conviction. What do you think her argument would be to reverse the kidnapping conviction?

7. Do you believe that prostitution and solicitation of prostitution are victimless crimes? If so, does the threat of AIDS and other communicable diseases change your decision?

8. Make your best argument in support of legalizing (decriminalizing) prostitution.

9. Consider your life experiences. Have you ever committed a technical stalking (such as repeatedly seeking the affection of an uninterested person)?

# Endnotes

1. *State v. Myers*, 7 N.J. 465, 81 A.2d 710 (1951)

2. *Labelle v. State*, 550 N.E.2d 752 (Ind. 1990); *see also* LaFave & Scott at § 7.2(b).

3. MPC § 210.0(4).

4. Krista Johnson, Accomplice law case of Lakeith Smith, sentenced to 55 years, gains renewed interest. Montgomery Advertiser. June 11, 2020. Retrieved from montgomeryadvertiser.com on December 10, 2020.

5. *See Commonwealth v. Redline*, 391 Pa. 486, 137 A.2d 472 (1958).

6. *Enmund v. Florida*, 458 U.S. 782 (1982).

7. *Tison v. Arizona*, 481 U.S. 137, 158 (1987).

8. *Roper v. Simmons*, 543 U.S. 551 (2005).

9. The Federal Bureau of Investigation's prime suspect in the case committed suicide before he was charged. A microbiologist with a Ph.D. from the University of Cincinnati, Bruce Ivins had been employed by the U.S. Army Medical Research Institute of Infectious Diseases. See *http://www.fbi.gov/about-us/history/famous-cases/anthrax-amerithrax/amerithrax-investigation*

10. A. Loewy, *Criminal Law*, 2d ed. (Nutshell Series; St. Paul: West, 1987).

11. The MPC addresses homicide at § 210.0 *et seq.*

12. *See* LaFave & Scott, *Criminal Law* § 7.7 (Hornbook Series; St. Paul: West, 1986).

13. *State v. Corn*, 278 S.E.2d 221 (N.C. 1981).

14. See, for example, N.Y. Penal Law § 125.27(a)(xiii).

15. Note. *Commonwealth v. Carter*: Trial Court Convicts Defendant of Involuntary Manslaughter Based on Encouragement of Suicide, 131 *Harv. L. Rev.* 918 (2018).

16. See Ill. Rev. Stat. ch. 38, para. 9–3.

17. *Washington v. Glucksberg*, 521 U.S. 702 (1997).

18. Mich. Comp. Laws Ann. § 752.1027.

19. Robert Hardaway, Miranda Peterson, and Cassandra Mann, "The Right to Die and the Ninth Amendment: Compassion and Dying After *Glucksberg* and *Vacco*," 7 *George Mason L. Rev.* 313 (1999).

20. See 65 Am. Jur. 2d *Rape* 28 (1976).

21. MPC § 213.

22. Ohio Rev. Code § 2907.

23. *Michael M. v. Superior Court*, 450 U.S. 464 (1981).

24. Louise Elaine Ellison (July 1997), *A Comparative Study of Rape Trials in Adversarial and Inquisitorial Criminal Justice Systems*, Dissertation: University of Leeds, Faculty of Law.

25. Steven I. Friedland, "On Treatment, Punishment, and the Civil Commitment of Sex Offenders," 70 *U. Colo. L. Rev.* 73 (1999).

26. 42 U.S.C. § 14071.

27. *Kansas v. Hendricks*, 521 U.S. 346.

28. 534 U.S. 407 (2002).

29. 531 U.S. 250 (2001).

30. 560 U.S. 126 (2010).

31. Jean Peters-Baker, "Challenging Traditional Notions of Managing Sex Offenders: Prognosis Is Lifetime Management," 66 *U. Mo. at Kansas City L. Rev.* 629 (1997).

32. 18 U.S.C. § 1201.

33. 18 U.S.C. § 1201(b).

34. MPC § 212.1.

35. 28 U.S.C. § 1738A.

36. *Watts v. United States*, 394 U.S. 705 (1969).

37. Karen Brooks, "The New Stalking Laws: Are They Adequate to End Violence?" 14 *Hamline J. Pub. L. & Pol'y*. 259 (1993).

38. *ApolloMedia v. Reno*, 19 F. Supp. 2d 1081 (1998), aff'd, 119 S. Ct. 1450 (1999); and *ACLU v. Reno* 521 U.S. 844 (1997).

39. *West Virginia State Board of Education v. Barnette*, 319 U.S. 624 (1943).

40. *Brandenburg v. Ohio*, 395 U.S. 444 (1969).

41. *R.A.V. v. City of St. Paul*, 505 U.S. 377.

42. 18 U.S.C. § 241.

43. 18 U.S.C. § 242.

44. 42 U.S.C. § 1983.

# Chapter 5

# Crimes Involving Property

Michael Marin, former Wall Street trader, Yale University School of Law graduate, and a believed-to-be millionaire, called the Phoenix emergency line on July 5, 2009, to report that his estate mansion was ablaze. He reported having escaped the fire by wearing scuba gear to avoid the inhalation of smoke and scaling down a rope ladder from the second floor. Later, it was discovered that Marin was bankrupt. Police also discovered, thanks in part to a well-trained canine, that the fire was set intentionally. Marin was charged with arson and convicted in 2012.

Moments after the verdict was read, Marin was seen on a court television monitor drinking from a sports bottle. He immediately collapsed and died. Subsequent testing revealed that he ingested cyanide. Oddly, the day Marin set fire to his home is the day of the greatest number of arsons in U.S. history, according to one source.[1]

Arson is one of several crimes you will study in this chapter. Broadly, there are two types of crimes discussed in this chapter. First, where property is unlawfully used or harmed, and second, when property is taken from its rightful owner or possessor. Trespass, mischief, theft, arson, and burglary are examples of the first group. Larceny, fraud, extortion, and so-called white-collar crimes fall into the second group. The discussion begins with arson.

# Arson

Learning Objective: Define, describe, and apply the elements of arson.

**arson**
The malicious and unlawful burning of a building.

As originally defined, **arson** was a crime involving habitation. In England and the United States, the concept that a "person's home is their castle" continues to have great influence. A home is more than property, it is a person's refuge from the rest of the world. For this reason, common law crimes developed to protect this important sanctuary. Arson and burglary are two examples.

At common law, arson was defined very narrowly. It was the

1. malicious
2. burning of a
3. dwelling house of
4. another.

This definition was so narrowly construed that a property owner who burned down her own home to collect the insurance benefit didn't commit arson because she did not burn the dwelling of another.[2] In addition, the structure burned had to be a *dwelling.* Over time, the definition of a dwelling widened from only homes to any structure inhabited by people. Outhouses and the areas directly around the homes (*curtilage*) were included, provided the area was used frequently by people. However, the burning of businesses and other structures was not arson.

To have been a "burning," the building must have sustained damage, although slight damage was sufficient. However, if the structure was only smoke-damaged or discolored by the heat of a fire that never touched the building, there wasn't arson. Finally, blowing up a home was not arson unless part of the structure that was left standing after the explosion caught fire.

Malice was the historic mens rea of arson. As was true of murder, *malice* was defined as an evil intent. However, an intentional or extremely reckless burning was arson too.

Today, the definition of arson has been broadened by statute in most, if not all, states. Many have followed the lead of the Model Penal Code (MPC), which defines arson in this way:

### Section 220.1. Arson and Related Offenses.

(1) Arson.  A person is guilty of arson, a felony of the second degree, if he starts a fire or causes an explosion with the purpose of:

   (a) destroying a building or occupied structure of another;  or

   (b) destroying or damaging any property, whether his own or another's, to collect insurance for such loss.  It shall be an affirmative defense to prosecution under this paragraph that the actor's conduct did not recklessly endanger any building or occupied structure of another or place any other person in danger of death or bodily injury.

(2) Reckless Burning or Exploding.  A person commits a felony of the third degree if he purposely starts a fire or causes an explosion, whether on his own property or another's, and thereby recklessly:

   (a) places another person in danger of death or bodily injury;  or

   (b) places a building or occupied structure of another in danger of damage or destruction.

Today, it is common to prosecute property owners for burning their own buildings, if the purpose is to defraud an insurer or to cause injury. Be aware that the underlying fraud may constitute a separate offense. So, the homeowner who burns their own home to claim insurance money is guilty of both arson and fraud.

Another change in the law of arson is that the structure burned need not be a dwelling, though most statutes aggravate the crime if the structure is inhabited by people. Although the common law did not recognize explosions as a burning, you can see in the MPC provision above that it does, and most state statutes do too.[3]

The mens rea for arson under the MPC is purposeful and reckless. If a person starts a fire or causes an explosion with the purpose of destroying the building or defrauding an insurer, a felony of the second degree has been committed. It is a felony of the third degree to purposely start a fire or cause an explosion and thereby recklessly endanger a person or structure.[4] Note that under the MPC, the fire need not touch the structure, as was required by the common law. Setting the fire is enough to satisfy the burning requirement.

The MPC broadened the attendant circumstance element "dwelling" to include any occupied structure or any structure that is burned or destroyed for purposes of collecting insurance monies. Regardless, state laws often include the dwelling element or at least punish arson of homes more severely.

# Burglary

Learning Objective: Define, describe, and apply the elements of burglary.

Another old common law habitation crime is **burglary**, which was defined as the

1. breaking and entering
2. of another's dwelling
3. at night
4. for the purpose of committing a felony once inside.

> **burglary**
> Unlawfully entering the house of another person with the intention of committing a felony (usually theft).

The first element, a breaking, can be satisfied by either an actual break-in or by a constructive break-in. If an actor enters a dwelling by simply passing through an open door or window (a trespass), there is no breaking. To constitute a breaking, there has to be an act that changes the condition of the house in a way that enables entry. For example, opening an unlocked door or window is a breaking, while passing through an open door or window is not. Of course, picking a lock and breaking a window or door satisfy this element.

As you have seen in other crimes, burglary uses a fiction to broaden the scope of acts that satisfy the actus reus element. In this case, the fiction alters the breaking element. A constructive breaking occurs when one uses fraud or force to gain entry. So, if a burglar poses as a telephone repair worker to gain entry, then the breaking element has been satisfied. The same is true if the owner consents to the burglar's entry under threat or the use of force.

Once the breaking occurs, there must be an entry of the home. The burglar does not need to fully enter the structure; an entry occurs if any part of the burglar's body enters the house. So, the individual who breaks a window and reaches in to grab an item has entered the house.

Modern statutes have eliminated the breaking requirement, although most still require some form of "unlawful entry." Because trespasses, frauds, and breakings are unlawful, they satisfy modern statutory requirements.

The second element required is that the breaking and entry be of another person's dwelling. As with arson, at common law the structure had to be a dwelling. The person who lives in the dwelling does not have to be the owner, only an occupant. As such, rental property is included. Interestingly, at least one court has held that churches are dwellings, regardless of whether a person actually resides in the church, premised on the theory that churches are God's dwellings.[5] The dwelling had to belong to another person, so one could not burglarize one's own property. A few states continue to require that the property be a home. Many have broadened this element to include other structures.[6] However, if the structure burglarized is a dwelling, most states punish the crime more severely than if it were another type of building.

The third element at the Common Law was that burglary occur at night. This continues to be an element in some states; others have eliminated it while continuing to aggravate the crime if it happens at night. In those states that continue to require that the crime occur at night, sunrise and sunset are commonly used to distinguish night from day. To doubly ensure that an actor has committed the crime during the night, many statutes require the breaking to occur a set period of time after sunset and before sunrise. Connecticut, for example, defines "night" as "the period between thirty minutes after sunset and thirty minutes before sunrise."[7]

The fourth element was that the actor specifically intend to commit a felony when inside. If the actor's intent is to commit a misdemeanor, or to commit no crime at all, there was no burglary. If Jay's intent is to murder Mark, there is a burglary. It is not a burglary if Jay's intent is to punch Mark in the nose or get out of the rain.

Of course, many burglaries are not completed. A burglar may be caught by surprise by someone who was not known to be inside and flee from the property. It also happens that burglars are caught in the act by occupants who return. That the intended felony is not completed is immaterial. All that needs to be proven is that the accused entered with an intent to commit a felony. As is always true, proving a person's subjective mental state is nearly impossible. Thus, juries are permitted to infer intent from the actions of the defendant. A jury did just that in the *Lockett* case, the subject of your next Oyez.

## Oyez

### State of Illinois v. Gerry Lockett
### 196 Ill. App. 3d 981, 554 N.E.2d 566 (1990)

**JUSTICE O'CONNOR delivered the opinion of the court:**

Gerry Lockett was charged with residential burglary, convicted after a jury trial, and sentenced to 8 years imprisonment. . . .

At about 3:00 A.M. on November 27, 1987, Allan Cannon entered his apartment, which he shared with his sister. Cannon noticed a broken window in his sister's bedroom. He then saw a man, whom he did not know, standing about six feet away from him in the apartment hallway. The only light came from the bathroom off the hallway. The man said to Cannon, "I know your sister." Cannon fled the apartment to call the police from the nearby El station. Outside his apartment, Cannon saw the man running down an alley. Cannon described the man to police as a dark black man with curly hair, about 5'5" weighing about 200 pounds.

Cannon returned to his apartment and noticed that his bicycle had been placed on his bed, and that his sister's baby clothes, which had been packed in bags, had been thrown all over. Although the apartment was in a general state of disarray, which Cannon admitted was not uncommon, nothing had been taken. . . .

Lockett also argues, without merit, that the evidence could not support an inference of his intent to commit a theft. But when Cannon entered his apartment, he found a broken window and later noticed a rock and broken glass on the floor, indicating that the window had been broken from outside. Cannon also discovered contents of the apartment had been rearranged and thrown about. Even assuming that Lockett was, as he said, an acquaintance of Cannon's sister, and that the Cannons, as defense counsel implied, were less than diligent housekeepers, Lockett's presence, without permission, in the dark, empty apartment, at 3 A.M., supported the jury's inference of intent to commit a theft.

Some statutes now provide that intent to commit any crime is sufficient, regardless of misdemeanor or felony status. However, many continue to require an intent to commit either felony or any theft.

Putting all of these changes together, the common elements of burglary today are the

1. unlawful entry
2. of a dwelling (or any structure or building in some jurisdictions)
3. at night (or anytime in some jurisdictions)
4. for the purpose of committing a felony or theft
5. when inside.

As mentioned, burglary may be graded and higher penalties imposed if the act occurred at night, involved a dwelling, was perpetrated at a dwelling that was actually inhabited at the time of the crime, or was committed by a burglar with a weapon. See Exhibit 5–1 for an illustration of the Common Law and modern elements of arson and burglary.

## Exhibit 5–1 Arson and Burglary: Past and Present

| Crime | Past | Present |
|---|---|---|
| Arson | Malicious | Purposeful or reckless |
| | burning | Expanded to include destruction by explosives |
| | dwelling | Any building |
| | of another | Any building, including one's own if intent is to commit fraud |
| Burglary | Breaking and entering | Any unlawful entry |
| | dwelling | of any building |
| | of another | owned by oneself or another |
| | at night | at any time, although night burglaries are graded higher |
| | with specific intent | with the purpose of |
| | to commit a felony inside | committing a felony inside |

# Trespass and Mischief

Learning Objective: Define, describe, and apply the elements of trespass and criminal mischief.

**trespass**
The unlawful touching of personal property or entry onto, or remaining on, real property.

At some point in your life, you may have seen a "no trespassing" or "stay of the property" sign. **Trespass** is the unlawful touching of personal property or entry of real property. Remaining on, or maintaining control of, property beyond the time allowed by the owner is also trespass. There are both civil and criminal forms of trespass. Criminal trespass relies on property law to define the who, what, and where of rights to property. Sometimes, trespass to personal property is treated as a theft, known as larceny in criminal law. This is discussed later in this chapter.

The MPC, §221, recognizes two forms of trespass. The first is when a person enters or surreptitiously remains in a building with knowledge that he has no legal right (no "privilege" or "license") to be there. This offense is more serious if the act occurs at night, for the same reason burglaries at night are considered more serious than during the day. The second form of trespass occurs when the actor is informed of his trespass by actual communication, such as by fencing or a "No Trespassing" sign. The MPC characterizes a person who commits this act as a defiant trespasser. Exceptions to criminal trespass are recognized, such as for abandoned property.

Many states follow the MPC, requiring actual knowledge that the person had no right to be on the property. So, the backpacker who inadvertently hikes onto private property that adjoins a public wilderness area has not committed trespass. But the outcome would be different if the backpacker jumped a fence or ignored a private property sign.

There are exceptions to the prohibition of trespass. Landlords, for example, have limited rights to enter their properties to make repairs, inspect damage, and to show the property to future tenants or buyers. Of course, these rights are subject to restrictions that respect the privacy of the tenant, such as advanced notice of an

Philipp Borris/Shutterstock.com

intent to enter. Another example is businesses that are open to the public. With a few exceptions, such as when anti-discrimination laws require that a person be served and when code inspectors, police, and other officials are conducting official business, property owners are free to exclude people from their premises. A patron who refuses to leave, or comes onto property when directed not to, is committing trespass.

It is possible to trespass on public lands as well. Taxpayer or citizenship status doesn't give an individual the right to use or be on government property. Access to public spaces is more complicated than private spaces because individuals sometimes have First Amendment rights to speak, assemble, and to petition their government on public lands. But these rights aren't absolute. The First Amendment employs **forum analysis** to decide whether individuals have a right to speak or assemble in public spaces. Under this analysis, free speech and assembly rights are their highest on sidewalks and in public parks and are nearly zero in spaces that have historically been restricted, such as military bases, jails, and prisons. A person can't demand, for example, access to a sensitive military area to protest.

**forum analysis**
A framework for deciding whether an individual possesses free speech or association rights on public property.

Even in areas where First Amendment rights are at their highest, governments may enact laws to restrict the time, place, and manner of use. These laws must be reasonable. Laws typically restrict noise levels at night and require that demonstrators not block sidewalks, access to buildings, or interfere with the free flow of traffic. Governments may also restrict speech at public meetings, provided it does so in content and viewpoint neutral ways. For example, a City Council holds a hearing about a proposed improvement to its water treatment facility. The rules of the hearing allow for public comments, not to exceed three minutes per resident. The individual who refuses to step away from the podium after three minutes is a trespasser because the time limit is reasonable, and it doesn't discriminate against the resident's viewpoint. On the other hand, if a resident were to be silenced because she is critical of the proposal, the First Amendment would be violated and any prosecution for trespass would be invalid.

Every year, a significant amount of financial loss is the result of destruction of property. Arson accounts for much of this total, but not all. Most states have statutes making the destruction of another's property criminal. These laws may be part of the statute covering arson or may be a separate section of the criminal code.

Destruction of property, commonly called **criminal mischief**, is most often a specific intent crime that includes any form of destruction that reduces the value, dignity, or integrity of the property. For example, defacing a Jewish tombstone by painting a swastika on it would be criminal mischief, even though the paint may be removed. Tampering with property is also mischief, and special statutes criminalizing the tampering with critical infrastructure, life sustaining, and other sensitive equipment can be found in criminal codes around the nation.

**malicious (malicious) mischief**
The criminal offense of intentionally destroying another person's property.

Mischief is often graded so that the most heavily penalized offenses against public property are those resulting in damage in excess of a stated dollar amount or involving a danger to human life. The most serious mischiefs are usually low-grade felonies, and the rest are misdemeanors. For example, the Kentucky mischief statutes read:

*Ky. Rev. Stat. § 512.020*

> (1) A person is guilty of criminal mischief in the first degree when, having no right to do so or any reasonable ground to believe that he has such right, he intentionally or wantonly defaces, destroys, or damages any property causing pecuniary loss of $1,000 or more.

(2) Criminal mischief in the first degree is a Class D felony.

*Ky. Rev. Stat. § 512.030*

(1) A person is guilty of criminal mischief in the second degree when, having no right to do so or any reasonable ground to believe that he has such a right, he intentionally or wantonly defaces, destroys, or damages any property causing pecuniary loss of $500 or more.

(2) Criminal mischief in the second degree is a Class A misdemeanor.

*Ky. Rev. Stat. § 512.040*

(1) A person is guilty of criminal mischief in the third degree when:

(a) Having no right to do so or any reasonable ground to believe that he has such right, he intentionally or wantonly defaces, destroys, or damages any property; or

(b) He tampers with property so as knowingly to endanger the person or property of another.

(2) Criminal mischief in the third degree is a Class B misdemeanor.

# Theft and White-Collar Crimes

There are many types of theft. It is theft to take a pack of gum from a grocery store and not pay for it; for a lawyer to take a client's trust fund and spend it on a trip to a tropical island; for a bank officer to use a computer to make a transfer of a customer's funds to the bank officer's account; and to hold a gun on a person and demand that property and money be surrendered. However, these are fundamentally different crimes.

Some thefts are more violative of the person, such as robbery, and others are more violative of a trust relationship, such as the attorney and bank officer who absconded with their clients' money. The crimes also differ in the methods by which they are committed. A robbery involves an unlawful taking by force. Embezzlement, however, involves no force and a lawful taking—with a subsequent unlawful conversion.

Larceny was the first theft crime. The elements of larceny were very narrow and didn't cover many forms of stealing. Eventually, other forms of theft were created to fill in the gaps. This was not a fluid, orderly development, for two reasons. First, when larceny was first created, well over 600 years ago, the purpose of making theft criminal was more to prevent breaches of the peace (fights over possession of property) than to protect owners' interests. For example, larceny did not prohibit fraudulent takings of another's property. The rationale for this limitation was that violence was less likely than in a true larceny because the owner wouldn't be aware of the taking until time had passed. Second, larceny was punishable by death. The draconian punishment caused judges to be reluctant to expand its reach.[8]

## Sidebar

**Crime Stats: Larceny-Theft**

The U.S. Department of Justice includes the following as larceny for the purpose of the Uniform Crime Reporting Program: shoplifting, pocket-picking, purse-snatching, thefts from automobiles, thefts of motor vehicles, and all other thefts of personal property that occur without the use of force. The program shows that there were 5,086,096 million reported larcenies in the United States in 2019. This represents 1,550 thefts per 100,000 people. Of all property crimes, 73% were thefts. The average loss for a victim was $1,162, with nearly $6 billion dollars in total loss to all victims of larceny.

*Source: Crime in the United States,* U.S. Department of Justice, Federal Bureau of Investigation, 2020.

But eventually, the crimes of embezzlement and false pretenses were created. But this didn't fill-in all of the gaps and many theft acts continued to go unpunished. Some courts attempted to remedy this problem by broadening the definitions of the three crimes. However, computers, electronic banking, and other technological advances have led to new methods of stealing money and property, posing problems not anticipated by the judges who created the common law theft crimes. Some states have changed their definitions of larceny, false pretenses, and embezzlement to be more contemporary. Other states have simply abandoned the common law crimes and have enacted consolidated theft statutes. The common law theft crimes, modern consolidated theft statutes, and the MPC approach to theft are discussed here.

## Larceny

Learning Objective: Define, describe, and apply the elements of larceny.

At Common law, the elements of **larceny** were

1. the trespassory taking
2. and carrying away (*asportation*)
3. personal property
4. of another
5. with an intent to permanently deprive the owner of possession.

**larceny**
Stealing of any kind. Some types of larceny are specific crimes, such as *larceny by trick* or grand larceny.

The first element required that the thief obtain the property unlawfully, by trespass. As you have seen before, this is an area of intersection between property and criminal law. Property law defines when a person has rights to property. Obviously, if an actor has a legal right to take control of property, there is no trespass. As mentioned earlier, this element left a big hole in the law of theft. If property was lawfully acquired and then stolen, there was no crime. So, if Gill Bates loans Jobe Steves a laptop and Jobe subsequently refuses to return it, he would not be guilty of larceny at the old Common Law.

In an effort to protect employers (masters) from theft by their employees (servants), the legal fiction of *constructive possession* was created. This fiction held that when an employee received actual possession of the employer's property as part of the job, the employer maintained "constructive possession" while the employee had "custody" of the property. Since the employer retained possession, any subsequent taking of the property was trespassory. If this theory had not been developed, employees would have been free to steal property entrusted to them, as larceny required a trespassory taking. Of course, if an employee took property that was not under his or her care, there was a trespassory taking.

The courts never extended constructive possession to other relationships. This led to the creation of a new crime—embezzlement. This will be discussed a bit later in this chapter.

After acquiring the property, the defendant must carry away the property. The act of moving the property is called *asportation*. Generally, any asportation, even the slightest movement, satisfies this requirement. Although the word *asportation* implies that the actor will "carry" the property away, other methods of locomotion are satisfactory. For example, riding a stolen horse or driving a stolen automobile. Many states have done away with the asportation requirement by statute.

The third element is an attendant circumstance; the stolen item must be personal property. Land and items attached to land (e.g., houses) are considered real property. Theft of real property was not larceny. Objects that are movable property are personal property. In the early years of larceny, there was a further requirement that the item stolen be tangible personal property. Tangible personal property includes items that had inherent value and use, such as a plow, horse, and clothing. Documents that represent ownership were considered intangible property. A deed to property and stock notes are examples. It was not larceny to steal intangible personal property. Under modern statutes, all forms of personal property are protected by theft laws.

The fourth element is that the personal property must be owned by another. A person can't steal from themselves. However, the rule was extended to prohibit prosecution of a partner for taking partnership assets and joint tenants from taking each other's things; also, because husband and wife were one person under the Common Law, it was not possible for spouses to steal from one another.

Finally, the mens rea element: It is required that the defendant intend to permanently deprive the owner of possession of the property. In short, to be a thief one must have an intent to steal. If Jamar takes Eddie's lawn mower, intending to return the mower when he has completed his mowing, he has not committed larceny because didn't possess an intent to permanently deprive Eddie of the mower. Also, if an accused has a good faith belief that he had lawful right to the property, the requisite mens rea is absent.

Courts have held that if the property is held for such a long period, or it is used or damaged in some manner, that it loses a significant amount of its value, a larceny has occurred. Further, if an actor takes property intending to use it in a manner that threatens to devalue it, even if the actor intends to return it, larceny has occurred. To illustrate, imagine a pilot, Sully, who takes a plane owned by another person, intending to return it after using it in a daredevil show. In such a case, Sully is subjecting the property to substantial risk. Therefore he has committed larceny, even though he intends to return the plane.

## Embezzlement

Learning Objective: Define, describe, and apply the elements of embezzlement.

As you learned earlier, the trespassory taking element left some thefts unpunished. Courts addressed it in the employment context by creating the constructive possession doctrine. However, this fiction was never extended further. Consequently, there was no criminal punishment to steal property that was lawfully obtained. This limitation in the law of larceny was problematic. People commonly entrust money and property to others. The intent is not to transfer ownership (title), but to give the other person possession. A depositor of a bank gives possession of money to the bank; a client may give an attorney money to hold in a trust account; investment managers hold client funds; and friends and family often hold property for one another. In all of these situations, the property is taken lawfully, so there was no larceny at the Common Law if the property was taken after being handed over. The process of stealing property that is obtained lawfully is referred to as **conversion**.

This theory was carried to an extreme in a case in which a bank teller converted money handed to him by a depositor to himself, by placing the money in his own pocket. It was held that there was no larceny, because the teller acquired the money lawfully. The court also determined that there was no larceny under the theory of constructive possession, because the employer (bank) never had possession of the money. If the teller had put the money in the drawer and then taken it, the bank would have had constructive possession, and he would have committed larceny. The result was that the teller was guilty of no crime.[9] Unsatisfied with this situation, the English Parliament created a new crime: **embezzlement**.

The elements of embezzlement are

1. conversion
2. of personal property
3. of another
4. by one who has acquired lawful possession
5. with an intent to defraud the owner.

**conversion**
Any act that deprives an owner of property without that owner's permission and without just cause.

**embezzlement**
The fraudulent and secret taking of money or property by a person who has been trusted with it. This usually applies to an employee's taking money and covering it up by faking business records or account books.

To prove embezzlement, the prosecution must first show that an act of conversion occurred. Conversion is the unauthorized control over property with an intent to permanently deprive the owner of its possession or which substantially interferes with the rights of the owner.

As was the case with larceny, only tangible personal property was included. Today, nearly all forms of personal property may be embezzled. Like common law burglary and arson, the property had to belong to another. One could not embezzle one's own property.

The element that distinguished embezzlement from larceny was the taking requirement. Whereas larceny required a trespassory taking, embezzlement required lawful acquisition. Accountants, lawyers, bailees, executors of estates, and trustees are examples of those who can commit embezzlement.

To satisfy the mens rea requirement of embezzlement, it must be shown that the defendant possessed an "intent to defraud." Mere negligent conversion of another's property is not embezzlement. Because the mens rea requirement is so high, bona fide claims of mistake of fact and law are valid defenses. If an accountant makes an accounting error and converts a client's money, there is no embezzlement. This is a mistake of fact. If a friend you loaned money to keeps the money with the mistaken belief that he is allowed to in order to offset damage you caused to his property last year (when the law requires that he sue you for the damage), there is no embezzlement. This is a mistake of law and negates the intent required, as does a mistake of fact.

Embezzlement is prohibited in all states. Some states have retained the name *embezzlement*; others have renamed it theft and included it in a consolidated theft statute. Embezzlement, which occurs in interstate commerce, federally insured banks, and lending institutions, or involves officers and agents of the federal government, is also made criminal by the statutes of the United States.[10] Statute 18 U.S.C. § 641 is the embezzlement of public monies, property, and records statute. Violation of that provision, if the property embezzled has a value of $100 or greater, results in a fine of up to $10,000 and 10 years in prison. The remainder of that statute deals with embezzlement of nonpublic property that occurs in interstate commerce or by federal officials. The penalties vary for each provision.

## False Pretenses and Check Fraud

Learning Objective: Define, describe, and apply the elements of false pretenses.

At Common Law, it was not larcenous to use lies (false representations) to gain ownership or title to property. The early judges believed deeply in the concept of *caveat emptor*, which translates as "let the buyer beware."

As it had done with embezzlement, Parliament decided to make lies used to steal from others criminal. You already learned one crime that was intended to address this problem, larceny by trick. Its close cousin is **false pretenses**. The elements of false pretenses are

**false pretenses**
A lie told to cheat another person out of his or her money or property. It is a crime in most states, though the precise definition varies.

1. a false representation of

2. a material present or past fact

3. made with knowledge that the fact is false

4. with an intent to defraud the victim

5. thereby causing the victim to pass title to property to the actor.

To prove the first element, it must be shown that the actor made a false representation. This representation may be made orally, or in writing, or may be implied by one's actions. The law does not require the disclosure all relevant information during a business transaction—*caveat emptor* still exists in that regard. The law does, however, require that any affirmative statements (or implications from actions) be true. So, if a buyer fails to ask if property has a lien against it, there is no false pretense if the seller does not inform the buyer of such. The opposite is true if a buyer inquires about existing liens and encumbrances and is told there are none.

The false representation must be important to the transaction. If the statement is important, the law says that it is *material*. Generally, a representation is material if it would have had an impact on the victim's decision-making had the victim known the truth at the time the transaction took place.

The fact conveyed by the actor must not only be material, but it must also concern a present or past fact. In this context, *present* refers to the time of the transaction. Statements of expected facts, promises, predictions, and expectations cannot be the basis of false pretenses. So, if Aaron buys an automobile from Kathy and promises to pay her in six months, it is no crime if he fails to pay because he loses his source of income during that period. To permit breaches of such promises to be criminal would be the same as having a debtor's prison, which is not allowed in the United States. The same is not true if Aaron made the promise but had no intent of paying the debt. Some states treat this as false pretenses under the theory that his state of mind at the time of the sale was fraudulent. Some states do not treat his action as criminal and place the burden on Kathy to seek her own remedy in a civil cause of action. It is also necessary that the representation be one of fact. Accordingly, opinions are not included. Of course, the line between fact and opinion is often unclear.

It must also be proved that the defendant knew the statement was false. An unintentional misrepresentation is not sufficient to establish this element in most jurisdictions, although most jurisdictions will find knowledge if the lower mens rea standard, recklessness, is proved.

The defendant must have the additional mens rea of "intent to defraud." As with other theft crimes, if persons have a bona fide belief that a particular property belongs to them, there is a defense. In addition to intending to defraud the victim, it must also be shown that the victim was defrauded. Hence, if the victim was aware of the falsity of the statement and entered into the bargain anyway, there has been no crime.

Finally, the misrepresentation must be the cause of the victim passing title to property to the defendant. This is the element that distinguishes larceny by trick from false pretenses. Larceny by trick involves a transfer of possession of property, while false pretenses protects a victim from having title to property stolen. *Title* is ownership. Title can be acquired in one of two ways, either by obtaining the legal title that represents ownership of property or by acquiring possession with an intention by the seller to transfer title. Here are examples of both:

> Raygen offers to trade her state-of-the-art virtual reality headset for Grace's used car. Raygen has no intention to give up her headset. Grace signs the title to her car over to Raygen, but as planned, Raygen doesn't give up her VR headset. Raygen has committed false pretenses because she acquired legal title to the car through fraud.

> Grace offers to sell Maya her virtual reality headset for $200. She tells Maya that it has over $100 in software installed. Grace knows it doesn't. Maya gives Grace the money and receives the headset. Grace has committed both larceny by trick and false pretenses. The latter is true because Maya transferred possession and ownership of the money.

Just as with larceny and embezzlement, only tangible personal property was included within the grasp of false pretenses at early Common Law. Today, false pretenses protects all property that is subject to the protection of larceny. In most instances, this includes all forms of personal property.

Related to the crime of false pretenses is the crime of acquiring property or money by writing a check from an account that has insufficient funds to cover the draft. The act appears to fall into the category of false pretenses. Even though a check appears to be a promise of future payment, and, accordingly, it would appear to not meet the "representation of present or past fact" requirement of false pretenses, most courts have decided that a check writer is representing that there are adequate funds in the checking account at the time the check was uttered.

Today, bad check statutes are common. A conviction of a bad check law, in most cases, results in a less serious punishment than conviction on false pretenses.[11] Three common material elements are found in bad-check statutes. First, the mens rea may be proven by showing either an intent to defraud the payee or knowledge that there were insufficient funds in the account. Second, the check must be taken in exchange for something of value; third, there must have been insufficient funds in the account.

## Receiving and Selling Stolen Property

Learning Objective: Define, describe, and apply the elements of receiving stolen property.

Not only is it a crime to steal another's property, but it is also a crime to receive property that is known to be stolen, if the intent is to keep that property. In essence, one who buys or receives as a gift property that is known to be stolen is an accessory (after the fact) to the theft. Although the law applies to anyone who violates its prohibitions, the primary focus of law enforcement is *fences*, people who purchase stolen property with the intent of reselling the property for a profit. They act as the retailers of stolen property, with the thieves acting as suppliers.

The elements of **receiving stolen property** are

1. receiving property
2. that has been stolen
3. with knowledge of its stolen character
4. with an intent to deprive the owner of the property.

**receiving stolen property**
The criminal offense of getting or concealing property known to be stolen by another.

Receipt of the property may be shown by showing either actual possession or constructive possession of the property. Constructive possession occurs any time the defendant has control over the property, even though the defendant does not have actual possession. For example, if one makes arrangements for stolen property to be delivered to one's home, there is receipt once the property is in the house, even if the defendant was not present when the property was delivered. Receiving includes not only purchases of stolen property but also other transfers, such as gifts.

The property must have been stolen. In this context, stolen property includes that property acquired from larcenies, robberies, embezzlement, extortion, false pretenses, and similar crimes.

The final two elements deal with the mens rea of the crime of receiving stolen property. First, knowledge of the property's stolen character is required. At one time, many jurisdictions required subjective knowledge. Today, the objective test is more common.

The last element requires that the receiver of the property intends to deprive the owner of the property. Of course, if a defendant intends to keep the property, then this requirement is met. The language of the crime is broader, however, and includes any intent to deprive the owner of the use, ownership, or possession of the property. Thus, if one receives the property intending to destroy it or to give it as a gift, this element has been satisfied. Consider these two examples:

John posts an advertisement on BuyBay, a platform used by individuals to buy and sell personal property, offering to sell a piece of art for $200. Percel looks up the item on a website that estimates the value of art. The piece is valued at approximately $250. John likes the piece and the price, so he buys it. He later learns that it is stolen. John hasn't committed the crime of receiving stolen property because a reasonable person wouldn't have known it was stolen.

John is standing next to his car on the corner of a bad area of town. His trunk is open and full of boxed computers. Each box has the remnant of sticky labels that have been torn off of it. Using his cell phone, Percel discover the computers retail at $1,000 each. John is selling them for $200 each, "cash only." Percel purchases two. They are stolen. Percel has committed the crime of receiving stolen property because a reasonable person would have known they were stolen.

Not only do the states prohibit receiving stolen property, but the federal government also makes it a crime to receive stolen property that has traveled in interstate commerce or to receive stolen property while on lands controlled by the United States.[12]

# Robbery

Learning Objective: Define, describe, and apply the elements of robbery.

The material elements of **robbery** are

**robbery**
The illegal taking of property from the person of another by using force or threat of force.

1. a trespassory taking
2. and carrying away (asportation)
3. of personal property
4. from another's person or presence
5. using either force or threat
6. with an intent to steal the property.

Robbery is actually a type of assault mixed with a type of larceny. Because of the immediate danger created by the crime of robbery, it is punished more severely than either larceny or simple assault. Robbery was a crime under the common law and is a statutory crime in all states today.

The elements of trespassory taking—asportation, intent to steal, and that the property belongs to another—are the same as for larceny. However, robbery also requires that the property be taken from the victim's person or presence. So, property taken from another's hands, off another's body, or from another's clothing is taken from the person. Property that is taken from another's presence, but not from the person, also qualifies. For example, if a bank robber orders a teller to stand back while the thief empties the cash drawer, there has been a robbery. The states differ in their definitions of "from another's presence," but it is generally held that property is in a victim's presence any time the victim is in control of the property. This is true in the bank robbery example, as the teller was exercising control over the cash drawer at the time of the robbery.

Robbery is committed with the use of force or threat. This element is the feature that most distinguishes robbery from larceny. As far as the amount of force is concerned, the point of reference is the victim. Any force used against the person to obtain the property converts the larceny to robbery. For example, it is larceny, not robbery, if a pickpocket steals a wallet free of the owner's knowledge. Only the force necessary to take the wallet was used. It is robbery, however, if the victim catches the pickpocket, and an altercation ensues over possession of the wallet. The same result is true when dealing with purse snatchers. If the snatcher makes a clean grab and gets away without an altercation, it is larceny from the person. If the victim grabs the bag and fights to keep it, then it is robbery. A threat of force may also satisfy this requirement. If the robber states to the victim, "Give me your wallet or I'll blow your head off," there is a robbery, even though there was no physical contact between the robber and victim.

In most jurisdictions, the threatened harm must be immediate; threats of future harm are not adequate. Threats to third parties satisfy the threat element. The thief who holds a man's wife and threatens to harm her if the man does not give up his money is not free from the charge of robbery just because the person giving up the money is not the one threatened.

The mens rea of robbery is the specific intent to take the property and deprive the owner of it. As with the other theft crimes, a good faith, but incorrect, claim of right to the property is a defense. In *Richardson v. United States*, 403 F.2d 574 (D.C. Cir. 1968), a defendant's claim of right to money was a gambling debt. The trial court did not permit the illegal debt to be used as a defense, but the appellate court reversed. It stated in its opinion that:

> The government's position seems to be that no instruction on a claim of right is necessary unless the defendant had a legally enforceable right to the property he took. But specific intent depends upon a state of mind, not upon a legal fact. If the jury finds that the defendant believed himself entitled to the money, it cannot properly find that he had the requisite specific intent for robbery.

Robbery is typically a state law crime, but the United States has also prohibited certain robberies. Robbery of a federally insured bank is an example.[13]

Robbery is usually, if not always, graded. Robbery is graded higher if it results in serious injury to the victim or is committed using a deadly weapon.

# Extortion

Learning Objective: Define, describe, and apply the elements of extortion.

**Extortion**, also known in the law as **criminal coercion**, is more commonly known as *blackmail*. Extortion is similar to robbery because both acts involve stealing money under threat. However, the threat in a robbery must be of immediate harm. Extortion involves a threat of future harm. At common law, extortion applied only against public officers. Today, extortion is much broader. The elements of extortion are

1. the taking or acquisition of property or compelling an act or omission
2. of/by another person
3. using a threat
4. with an intent to permanently deprive the owner of the property or cause the act or omission to occur.

**extortion**
To acquire property or money using threats of harm to person, property, or reputation.

**criminal coercion**
A synonym for extortion.

Florida's extortion law is similar to what is found in many states:

> **836.05** **Threats; extortion.**—Whoever, either verbally or by a written or printed communication, maliciously threatens to accuse another of any crime or offense, or by such communication maliciously threatens an injury to the person, property or reputation of another, or maliciously threatens to expose another to disgrace, or to expose any secret affecting another, or to impute any deformity or lack of chastity to another, with intent thereby to extort money or any pecuniary advantage whatsoever, or with intent to compel the person so threatened, or any other person, to do any act or refrain from doing any act against his or her will, shall be guilty of a felony of the second degree,

The actus reus of extortion is twofold: the actor must intentionally communicate a threat and specifically intend to take property or money or to compel the victim to act, or to not act. Unlike robbery where the threat has to be immediate, a threat of future physical harm satisfies this element.

The objective of the threat must be to either (a) extract something of value, such as money or property or (2) coerce the victim to act, or not act.

A threat to injure the victim's reputation, business, financial status, or family relationship are examples. **Sextortion**, or the use of sexual images of a person to extort money or sex, is a growing phenomenon. In one case, an adult man who posed as a teenage boy convinced a 15-year-old girl to expose her breasts on camera. He recorded the incident and threatened to make the images public unless she agreed to perform sex acts on camera for him. He then used recordings of those acts to coerce her to involve a 14-year-old friend, who he also recorded and blackmailed into performing additional sex acts that were increasingly invasive of her privacy. When the girls attempted to step away, the defendant sent photos and video recordings to one of the girls' parents, a school principal, and over 80 members of a church where one of the victim's family attended. The extortionist was identified, a warrant issued, and a search of his computer revealed no less than 50 women and girls who had been victimized. He was convicted of several federal crimes.[14]

As is true of robbery, the threat may be directed at one person and the demand for property made from another. For example, if Gary states to Chris, "Give me $100,000 or I will kill your brother, Scott," Gary is an extortionist, even though he has not threatened Chris.

An interesting example of possible extortion involves Jeff Bezos, the founder of Amazon. In 2019 the *National Enquirer* reported that Mr. Bezos had an extramarital affair. The story referred to text messages between Bezos to his lover. In an effort to determine how the *National Enquirer* obtained the texts, Bezos hired a private investigator. He also went public with the scandal. In his public statements, Bezos alleged that the tabloid published the story for political reasons. The parent company of the *National Enquirer*, American Media, Inc. (AMI), replied to Bezos' allegation that it had political motives by threatening to release intimate photos of Bezos and his lover if he didn't agree to several terms, including a "public, mutually-agreed upon acknowledgement" from Bezos stating he didn't have evidence that the story was politically motivated or influenced by political forces."

In response, Bezos alleged that AMI was attempting to blackmail him.[15] One of the questions raised by the situation is whether the threatened action, the release of the photos, crossed the line from legitimate negotiations to extortion. After all, coercion is often a legitimate feature of business. For example, it is not unlawful for an employer to demand that an employee arrive on time, lest the employee will be fired. And attorneys engage in coercion when they negotiate settlements for their clients. There isn't a universal test to draw the line between negotiations and coercion. Many courts look to the truth of the allegations, whether the money or relief sought is reasonable, and whether what is demanded is designed to remedy the harm alleged. That the disclosure of the photos appears to be unrelated to the underlying question (whether AMI acted politically) and therefore won't right their alleged wrong, weighs against AMI.

**Sextortion**
The use of sexual images of a person to commit extortion.

In addition to state prohibitions, the federal government has made it a crime for federal officers to extort the public, to be involved in an extortion that interferes with interstate commerce, and to extort another by threatening to expose a violation of federal law.

# Consolidating Traditional Theft Crimes

Learning Objective: Describe how the MPC consolidates theft crimes.

The distinctions between the various forms of larceny are idiosyncratic. Consequently, the drafters of the MPC proposed a comprehensive consolidation of larcenies, uniformly labeled as theft.[16] Provided that a defendant is not prejudiced by doing so, the specification of one theft crime by the prosecution does not prohibit a conviction for another. So, if a defendant is specifically charged with larceny, they may be convicted of false pretenses or embezzlement.

The MPC recognizes the following forms of theft:

1. Theft by taking (includes common law larceny and embezzlement).
2. Theft by deception (includes common law false pretenses).
3. Theft by extortion.
4. Theft of property known to be mislaid, misdelivered, or lost, and no reasonable attempt to find the rightful owner is made.
5. Receiving stolen property.
6. Theft of professional services by deception or threat.
7. Conversion of entrusted funds.
8. Unauthorized use of another's automobile.

Under the MPC, thefts are felonies of the third degree if the amount stolen exceeds $500 or if the property stolen is a firearm, automobile, airplane, motorcycle, motorboat, or other vehicle; and, in cases of receiving stolen property, if the receiver of the property is a fence, then it is a felony of the third degree regardless of the value of the property. All unauthorized uses of automobiles are misdemeanors.

Because robbery involves a danger to people, it is treated as a separate crime.[17] If during the commission of a theft the actor inflicts serious bodily injury upon another, threatens serious bodily injury, or threatens to commit a felony of the first or second degree, there is a robbery. It is a felony of the second degree unless the actor attempts to kill or cause serious bodily injury, in which case it is a felony of the first degree.

Forgery is also treated as a separate offense.[18] Forgery is treated as a felony of the second degree if money, securities, postage stamps, stock, or other documents issued by the government are involved. It is a felony of the third degree if the forged document affects legal relationships, such as wills and contracts. All other forgeries are misdemeanors. See Exhibit 5–1, The Model Penal Code Past and Present, for a summary of the Common Law and modern approaches to theft.

Following the MPC's lead, the states have consolidated their theft laws, although in different ways. Most criminal codes have a general statement of consolidation followed by independent provisions that define the various forms of theft and their punishments. The following is New Hampshire's general statement of consolidation:

> **637:1 Consolidation**. – Conduct denominated theft in this chapter constitutes a single offense embracing the separate offenses such as those heretofore known as larceny, larceny by trick, larceny by bailees, embezzlement, false pretense, extortion, blackmail, receiving stolen property. An accusation of theft may be supported by evidence that it was committed in any manner that would be theft under this chapter, notwithstanding the specification of a different manner in the indictment or information.

Consistent with the MPC, most states give robbery separate treatment. Additionally, most states have specific theft-related crimes that they single out for special treatment. These include the trespassory, but temporary use of property and shoplifting are examples.

## Mail and Wire Fraud

Two federal crimes related to false pretenses are mail and wire fraud.[19] The U.S. Post Office was created by the federal government in the earliest days of the Republic. Stealing the mail was a problem at the time, and Congress enacted criminal laws to protect the mail, post officers, and mail carriers. In the early years, theft of the mail was punished with death. In 1872, Congress added the crime of mail fraud in response to a growing problem of thieves using the mails to dupe people, particularly America's rural population. As the Supreme Court expressed, the mail fraud statute was enacted "to prevent the frauds which are mostly gotten up in the large cities ... by thieves, forgers, and rapscallions generally, for the purpose of deceiving and fleecing the innocent people in the country."[20]

In 1952, mail fraud was enlarged to include wire fraud.[21] The elements of the two crimes are the same, except for the means by which they are committed. Wire fraud includes radio, television, and wire communications.

The elements of mail fraud (wire fraud) are for a person to

1. devise or intend to devise a scheme to defraud (or to perform specified fraudulent acts) and

2. the use of the mail (wire, radio, or television) for the purpose of executing, or attempting to execute, the scheme (or specified fraudulent acts).

To commit mail or wire fraud, the actor must intent to defraud the victim. The misrepresentation must be "material." To be material, the misrepresentation shall be so important that it influenced the victim's decision to buy, sell, or act.

These laws are very popular with federal prosecutors because few crimes are committed without the use of the mail or telephone. Any use of either satisfies the requirement. This includes communications between conspirators in planning and executing a crime and between the victim and thief. One prosecutor said that

"[t]o federal prosecutors of white-collar crime, the mail fraud statute is our Stradivarius, our Colt .45, our Louisville Slugger, our Cuisinart—and our true love. We may flirt with RICO, show off with 10b-5, and call the conspiracy law 'darling,' but we always come home to the virtues of 18 U.S.C. 1341, with its simplicity, adaptability, and comfortable familiarity."[22]

The prosecutor in the quote mentioned RICO. Quite often, mail fraud and wire fraud are the predicate offenses of a RICO count.

## RICO

Learning Objective: Define, describe, and apply the elements of RICO.

**Racketeer Influenced and Corrupt Organizations Act**
(19 U.S.C. 1961). A broadly applied 1970 federal law that creates certain "racketeering offenses" that include participation in various criminal schemes and conspiracies and that allows government seizure of property acquired in violation of the act.

RICO is an acronym for the **Racketeer Influenced and Corrupt Organizations Act**.[23] The U.S. Congress enacted RICO in the early 1970s in an attempt to curb organized crime. RICO has both criminal and civil provisions. Corrupt organizations and their leaders can be criminally charged and their victims can sue for damages.

Judicial interpretation of RICO has led to much controversy in recent years. Some attorneys contend that the effect of court opinions has been to extend the prohibition of RICO beyond Congress's original intent. Today, all businesses, not just traditional organized crime, are subject to RICO.

To establish a RICO violation, the United States must prove that the

1. defendant received money or income
2. from a pattern of racketeering activity
3. invested that money in an enterprise (business)
4. which operates in interstate commerce or affects interstate commerce.

The second element is the key to proving a RICO violation. A *pattern* is "two or more acts," referred to as the predicate acts. Those acts must fall into the definition of a "racketeering activity." The statute lists the state and federal crimes that are considered to be racketeering. Murder, kidnapping, extortion, and drug sales and transportation are examples of the state crimes included in the list. Mail fraud, wire fraud, "white slave traffic," or the transport of women across state boundaries for immoral purposes, securities fraud, and bribery are a few examples of the federal crimes included. Mail fraud is often the basis of a RICO violation, because the mails are often used by such enterprises. Here are examples of fraudulent schemes and their predicate acts:

- Terri sets up a fake corporation and sends thousands of letters inviting people to invest in the faux enterprise. The predicate acts are each instance of mail fraud.

- Tommy is an evangelist. He asks his congregants, by mail and television, to give to a charity to help people who have lost their jobs and incurred large medical bills resulting from a pandemic. Tommy directs his listeners to a webpage on the HelpFundMe website, a service that allows individuals to set up accounts to solicit and receive cash support. Tommy set up the site and keeps all of the donated monies. The predicate acts are each instance of mail and wire fraud.

- Rocko is the head of a crime family in New York. The family sells drugs, coordinates a prostitution business, and routinely bribes public officials. The predicate acts are each instance of the controlled substances law, prostitution, and bribery.

One criticism of RICO is that it has been interpreted in a manner that is inconsistent with Congress' intent. While intended to address a problem with organized crime, it has been used on many occasions against legitimate businesses. For example, the Supreme Court announced in a 1994 decision that RICO could apply to a coalition of antiabortion groups that were alleged to have conspired, through a pattern of racketeering, to shut down abortion clinics.[24] In that case, extortion, including alleged threats of assault, was used to satisfy this element.

Violation of RICO can result in serious criminal penalties. In addition, victims of such activity may sue civilly and receive treble damages, costs, and attorney fees. RICO also provides for **forfeiture** of property in criminal proceedings. *Forfeiture* is the taking of property and money of a defendant by the government. Many crimes have forfeiture provisions. A forfeiture is not the same as a fine. Forfeitures and fines are both levied as punishment, but the focus of a fine is generally to hurt a defendant's pocketbook. Forfeitures are specifically aimed at getting the property or money connected to the crime for which the individual was convicted. So, in a RICO situation, a convicted party could stand to lose the enterprise itself, as well as all profits from that activity.

However, many aspects of civil RICO are identical to criminal RICO. One example is the pattern requirement. The U.S. Supreme Court addressed the pattern question because the various appellate courts of the United States were divided on how to define that phrase. In *H.J., Inc. v. Northwestern Bell Telephone Co.*, 492 U.S. 229 (1989), the Supreme Court defined a pattern as more than one predicate act that are

**forfeiture**
A deprivation of money, property, or rights, without compensation, as a consequence of a default or the commission of a crime.

related to one another and the facts pose a threat of continued racketeering activity. *H.J.* is also a good illustration of how "legitimate businesses" are subject to RICO.

## Money Laundering

Learning Objective: Define, describe, and apply the elements of money laundering

Investigators have a maxim to solve white collar crimes; follow the money. It is a reality that thieves have to do something with their ill-gotten gains. This can be challenging. Spending, investing, depositing, and gifting large amounts of money attracts attention. Often, law enforcement attention. So, large criminal enterprises attempt to hide their profits. They do this in one of two ways. The money is channeled through legitimate businesses or they conceal the origins of the money through complex schemes of deposits, withdrawals, and transfers between multiple shell (fraudulent) and legitimate corporations. These techniques are known as money laundering. See Exhibit 5–2, Money Laundering, for a visual representation of the money laundering process.

An example of money laundering is found in the highly popular TV drama, *Breaking Bad*. Walter White, a protagonist in the series, concealed his drug money earnings by laundering them through a car wash. To do this, he inflated his car wash sales to cover for the drug money he was channeling through the business.

## Exhibit 5–2

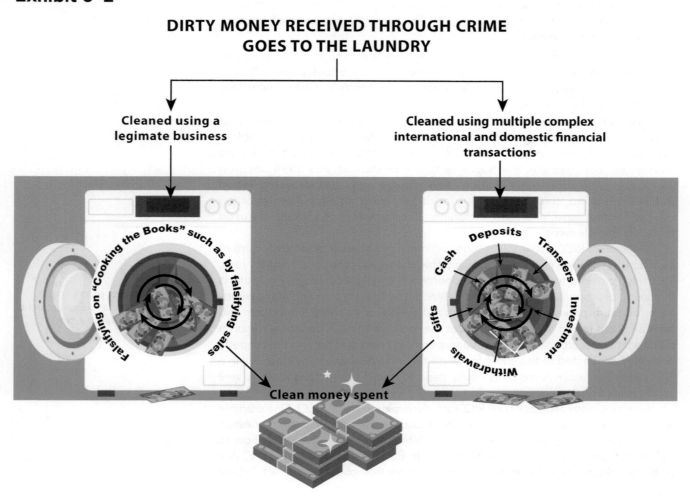

**DIRTY MONEY RECEIVED THROUGH CRIME
GOES TO THE LAUNDRY**

**Cleaned using a legimate business**

**Cleaned using multiple complex international and domestic financial transactions**

Falsifying on "Cooking the Books" such as by falsifying sales

Cash    Deposits    Transfers
Gifts    Investment
Withdrawals

**Clean money spent**

The federal Money Laundering Control Act, found at 18 U.S.C. §§ 1956 and 1957, criminalizes more than traditional laundering. It is a violation of this law for a person to:

1. conduct, or attempt to conduct, a financial transaction
2. knowing the money involved in the transaction is the product of illegal activity
3. with the intent to one of the following:

    a. carry on a "specified unlawful activity"
    b. commit tax evasion or tax fraud
    c. conceal or disguise the nature, location, source, ownership or control of proceeds of the specified unlawful activity
    d. avoid a financial transaction reporting requirement

"Financial transaction" includes bank transactions, such as a loan, deposit, withdrawal, and the transfer of funds. But it is more than banking business. All purchases, gifts, and pledges fall within the grasp of the law. The laundered money must be earned through "specified unlawful" acts. The list of unlawful activities is long; over 250 federal, state, and local crimes qualify. In practical terms, nearly all crimes qualify. A handful of examples are murder, sex crimes, tax crimes, extortion, fraud, immigration violations, espionage, firearms violations, kidnapping, obscenity, criminal mischief, and obstruction of justice.

A prosecutor must prove two states of mind. First, knowledge that the money is a product of unlawful activity and the second, specific intent to commit one of the four acts listed in element number 3 from the Money Laundering Control Act cited above: to carry on, evade taxes, conceal, or avoid reporting.

Violating the federal Money Laundering Control Act is punished with confiscation of the monies, huge fines, and long prison sentences. Many states have their own money laundering laws.

# Forgery and Counterfeiting

Learning Objective: Define, describe, and distinguish the elements of forgery and counterfeiting.

Another crime related to fraud is **forgery**. *Forgery* is

1. making, using, or changing
2. a false document (or the alteration of existing documents making them false)
3. that is passed
4. to another
5. with an intent to defraud.

**forgery**
Making a fake document (or altering a real one) with intent to commit a fraud.

The purpose of forgery statutes is both to prevent fraud and to preserve the value of written instruments. These functions are important because if forgery were to become common, people would no longer trust commercial documents, such as checks and contracts. The effect that would have on commerce is obvious.

The actus reus of forgery is the making of a false document, the altering of a genuine document, and the use of such a document. "Use" refers to actors who didn't create or alter false documents. Of course, they must be aware of the fraudulent nature of them and possess the mens rea. The second aspect of the actus reus is that the document must be passed, or "uttered," to another person. As is true throughout most of criminal law, person is defined to include people and businesses. The MPC, §224.1, defines the mens rea of forgery as purpose to defraud or knowledge that a fraud is being perpetuated.

Many states have updated their laws to include computer forgery. Under these laws, digital documents are included in the definition of document, which was formerly restricted to tangible documents, and the uttering requirement includes cyber uttering: computer uploads, postings, and transfers. Georgia, for example, added this to its forgery law:

> O.C.G.A §16-9-93(d)
>
> Computer Forgery. Any person who creates, alters, or deletes any data contained in any computer or computer network, who, if such person had created, altered, or deleted a tangible document or instrument would have committed forgery under Article 1 of this chapter, shall be guilty of the crime of computer forgery. The absence of a tangible writing directly created or altered by the offender shall not be a defense to the crime of computer forgery if a creation, alteration, or deletion of data was involved in lieu of a tangible document or instrument.

In many jurisdictions, forgery and uttering are separate crimes. In those states, one must only make the false instrument and possess an intent to defraud. The defendant need not present the document (utter) to the victim. That act, when accompanied with an intent to defraud, is the crime of *uttering*.

**counterfeiting**
The creation or passing of an imitation.

A closely related crime to forgery is **counterfeiting**. The elements of the two are similar. They both require, for example, an intent to defraud. What distinguishes the two crimes is that forgery is an alteration of an authentic document or the creation of a false, but new, document. A counterfeit, on the other hand, is an imitation of an authentic object. Generally, the elements of counterfeiting look something like this:

1. The creation of a
2. copy of an original item of value
3. with sufficient similitude to convince a person of ordinary caution that it is real
4. uttered or used
5. with intent to defraud.

Federal law criminalizes counterfeiting U.S. money. There are also laws that address counterfeit art and merchandise. Consider these two scenarios.

> Samuel Upman creates $100 bills in his basement using a digital graphics program. Using a high-quality printer and paper that feels like U.S. paper currency, he prints the bills and uses them to buy a car. Samuel has committed the crime of counterfeiting.

> Samuel Upman creates and prints U.S. currency of different denominations and donates it to his nearby Community Center to replace the worn and tattered money in the Center's Monopoly boardgame. Monopoly is one of several games that are played by youth and senior groups at the Center. Samuel didn't commit counterfeiting because he lacked an intent to defraud anyone.

## Identity Theft

Learning Objective: Define, describe, and apply the elements of identity theft.

It is possible to steal a person's identity as well as a person's property. The advent of the computer has made identity theft more common. Identity theft occurs whenever an individual uses a victim's name, Social Security number, e-mail address, or other identifying items in an effort to represent himself or herself as the victim. The mens rea of most identity theft statutes is an intention either to gain something of value through the deceit or to commit any other crime. This is the text of the Washington identity theft statute:

*RCW 9.35.020 Identity theft.*

(1) No person may knowingly obtain, possess, use, or transfer a means of identification or financial information of another person, living or dead, with the intent to commit, or to aid or abet, any crime.

(2) (a) Violation of this section when the accused or an accomplice uses the victim's means of identification or financial information and obtains an aggregate total of credit, money, goods, services, or anything else of value in excess of one thousand five hundred dollars in value shall constitute identity theft in the first degree. Identity theft in the first degree is a class B felony.

    (b) Violation of this section when the accused or an accomplice uses the victim's means of identification or financial information and obtains an aggregate total of credit, money, goods, services, or anything else of value that is less than one thousand five hundred dollars in value, or when no credit, money, goods, services, or anything of value is obtained shall constitute identity theft in the second degree. Identity theft in the second degree is a class C felony.

(3) A person who violates this section is liable for civil damages of five hundred dollars or actual damages, whichever is greater, including costs to repair the victim's credit record, and reasonable attorneys' fees as determined by the court.

(4) In a proceeding under this section, the crime will be considered to have been committed in any locality where the person whose means of identification or financial information was appropriated resides, or in which any part of the offense took place, regardless of whether the defendant was ever actually in that locality.

(5) The provisions of this section do not apply to any person who obtains another person's driver's license or other form of identification for the sole purpose of misrepresenting his or her age.

(6) In a proceeding under this section in which a person's means of identification or financial information was used without that person's authorization, and where there has been a conviction, the sentencing court may issue such orders as are necessary to correct a public record that contains false information resulting from a violation of this section.

An offender may be charged and convicted of both identity theft and the underlying crime. The defendant in the next Oyez case was convicted under the Washington statute. On appeal, she alleged that her conviction of both identity theft and forgery put her in double jeopardy.

The federal government also has an **identity theft** statute, the Identity Theft and Assumption Deterrence Act of 1998 (Identity Theft Act). Specifically, the Act[25] makes it a federal crime when anyone

> knowingly transfers or uses, without lawful authority, a means of identification of another person with the intent to commit, or to aid or abet, any unlawful activity that constitutes a violation of federal law, or that constitutes a felony under any applicable state or local law.

**identity theft**
The act of assuming another person's identity by fraud.

# Cybercrime

Learning Objective: Define, describe, and apply the elements of cybercrime.

Cybercrime is ubiquitous and huge business, or more accurately, anti-business. The total losses from cybercrime reached nearly $6 trillion in 2010 and were projected to pass $10 trillion by 2025. In 2010, this translated to nearly $200,000 in losses per second. If treated as a national economy, cybercrime would be the third largest in

## Oyez

### State v. Baldwin
### 45 P.3d 1093 Wash. App. Div. 1, 2002.

**Alexander, C.J.**

Jeanne Baldwin was found guilty of three counts of identity theft and two counts of forgery. The trial court imposed an exceptional sentence premised on the crimes being "major economic offenses" because Baldwin had utilized a complicated scheme to purchase a home and several automobiles with the stolen identities. Baldwin's central argument is that her convictions for both identity theft and forgery violate double jeopardy principles. We disagree, and affirm because the offenses involved different victims.

**I**

Baldwin, representing herself as "Kaytie Allshouse," purchased a house, forging Allshouse's name to two deeds of trust. The first deed of trust secured the interest of an institutional lender, Global Holdings; the second, subordinate, deed was in favor of the sellers, Diane Masin and David Swadberg. The deeds secured payment of $45,500, and $6,500, respectively.

Two months later, Baldwin rented a mailbox at the Mail Room, a mailbox-rental outlet in Everett. Baldwin presented herself as "Monica Schultz" and produced a Washington driver's license bearing that name. She signed Schultz's name to the mailbox application and began receiving mail in some fifteen other names. Baldwin later rented a mailbox from Jerald Landwehr at Cascade Storage, another mailbox-rental outlet. Baldwin again rented under a false name, this time as "Carol Hopey." She produced two pieces of identification, including a Washington driver's license. Baldwin told Landwehr the mailbox was for "Econo Accounting," and a number of her "employees" would be receiving mail. Letters and packages in a number of names were received at that mailbox.

Meanwhile, a U.S. postal inspector acting on a complaint placed a thirty-day mail cover on the Cascade Storage box address. Under a mail cover, all mail to a specific address is recorded by postmark, addressee, sender, and class of mail. The mail cover revealed mail in numerous names being sent to the rented box. The inspector then contacted a Detective who investigates financial crimes for the Snohomish County Sheriff's Office.

The detective traced the telephone number listed on the Cascade Storage rental paperwork to Baldwin. His suspicions that Baldwin had stolen Hopey's identity were confirmed when Cascade Storage manager Jerald Landwehr picked Baldwin's picture out of a photomontage.

As the detective and inspector proceeded to attempt to locate and call individuals whose names had been gleaned from the Cascade Storage mail cover, they learned the Everett Police Department had been independently investigating allegations of similar multiple name use at the Mail Room in Everett. The detective showed the same photomontage to the Mail Room's manager who immediately picked out Baldwin's picture.  . . .

■   ■   ■

A search of the Granite Falls property yielded a wallet containing a Washington driver's license in the name of "Kaytie Allshouse" bearing Baldwin's picture, and two VISA cards, also in the name of "Kaytie Allshouse." The search also uncovered vehicle titles and registrations for four different vehicles in the names of "Kaytie Allshouse" and "Carol Hopey," and auto insurance policies or cards in the names of "Kaytie Allshouse," "Carol Hopey," and "Monica Schultz." Officers also found a social security card for "Kaytie Allshouse" as well as homeowner's insurance correspondence and a utility bill, all addressed to "Kaytie Allshouse" at the Granite Falls address.

Baldwin was charged with six counts: (1) theft of Kaytie Allshouse's identity; (2) theft of Monica Schultz's identity; (3) theft of Carol Hopey's identity; (4) forgery of a deed in Allshouse's name; (5) forgery of Allshouse's name on an adjustable rider; and (6) forgery of a junior deed in Allshouse's name.

At trial, Kaytie Allshouse testified that she did not sign her name to the two trust deeds on the Granite Falls property. When asked how she felt about finding that someone had used her name to buy a house, she stated, "I don't want this in my name. It's not mine. I do not own it. . . . I just can't afford it. I don't want it." Likewise, Hopey testified she did not know Baldwin, had never lived in Snohomish County, had never rented a private mailbox, and had given no one permission to use her name. The jury found Baldwin guilty on all counts except the alleged forgery of the adjustable rate rider. . . .

Baldwin next contends that separate convictions and punishments for counts 1, 4, and 6 twice expose her to jeopardy. Her contention fails because each offense, as charged, includes elements not included in the other and each offense includes different victims.

The double jeopardy clause is not violated if the Legislature specifically authorizes multiple punishments. Washington applies the "same evidence" test to determine legislative intent. By this test, a defendant cannot be convicted of offenses that are identical both in fact and in law. The convictions stand, however, if there is an element in each offense which is not included in the other, and if proof of one offense would not necessarily also prove the other. . . .

Proof of theft of identity does not ipso facto prove forgery. Forgery requires the making, completion, or alteration of a written instrument. Theft of identity, on the other hand, requires use of a means of identification with the *intent* to commit an unlawful act. Thus, a jury could find Baldwin guilty of theft of identity, but not forgery. Because the elements of the two crimes are not the same, there is a strong presumption that the Legislature authorized multiple punishments for the same crime.

In addition to the three crimes not being the same in law, they are not the same in fact. As noted in *State v. McJimpson*, two crimes may not be the same in fact even though they arose from the same transaction. The court in *McJimpson* held that because each offense harmed a different victim, they were not the same in fact. Thus, the two offenses were not the same offense under the "same evidence" test. The same reasoning applies to this case. Baldwin was not subjected to double jeopardy because counts 1, 4 and 6 each has different victims.

Nor are we persuaded by Baldwin's assertion that the convictions for theft of identity and forgery merge. The merger doctrine applies only when the Legislature has clearly indicated that to prove a particular degree of a crime, "the State must prove not only that a defendant committed that crime . . . but that the crime was accompanied by an act which is defined as a crime elsewhere in the criminal statutes. . . . " It is relevant only when a crime is "elevated to a higher degree by proof of another crime proscribed elsewhere in the criminal code."

Here, neither of these crimes are crimes of degree; thus, neither crime elevates the other. Baldwin counters that to be convicted of identity theft, the State had to prove forgery. She claims that forgery is therefore an element of and merely incidental to the central crime of theft of identity, thus merging the two offenses. This "lesser included" offense argument fails because the State was not required to prove forgery in order to convict of theft of identity. Accordingly, the two crimes do not merge. . . . [Conviction affirmed].

the world, behind the United States and China. The "dark web," an underground web that is largely shielded from law enforcement, is estimated to be 5,000 times larger than the surface web that people commonly use.[26]

In addition to its economic impact, cybercrime can threaten the integrity of elections and democratic institutions through tampering of election results, altering website postings, and overwhelming the public with fake news; hacked implanted medical devices and hospital equipment can cause death and injury, and personal privacy is continually at risk through computers, phones, and other "smart" devices.

Cybercrime is a large and complex problem for law enforcement.

Gorodenkoff/Shutterstock.com

Computer crimes take two general forms. First, a computer can be the target of a crime. Theft of hardware and software is an example. Destruction and vandalism of computers is another crime where the computer is itself the target of an unlawful act. Viruses are also used to destroy computer programs.

A second form of computer crime, cybercrime, involves using a computer as a tool in the commission of a crime. Accessing confidential information, stealing intellectual property, threat and harassment, and the illegal distribution of obscenities fall into this category. Cybertheft is a very common offense. Obtaining illegal entry into a bank's computer records from a personal computer in order to steal money is an example, as is using another person's personal identification number and bank card to access an automatic teller machine.

Many computer-related crimes are punishable without special computer crimes laws. Standard larceny, embezzlement, fraud, and criminal mischief laws are often applicable. For example, stealing funds from a bank through a computer can usually be prosecuted under existing state and federal theft laws. Similarly, criminal mischief statutes could be used to prosecute the intentional destruction of computer programs by viruses.

In addition, the federal government and all of the states have enacted special legislation to deal with computers and crimes. There are several federal laws that address various forms of cybercrime. The most comprehensive statute is the Computer Fraud and Abuse Act, found at 18 U.S.C. §1830. It criminalizes the following acts:

1. Obtaining national security information through unauthorized computer access and sharing or retaining it;

2. Obtaining certain types of information through unauthorized computer access;

3. Trespassing in a government computer;

4. Engaging in computer-based frauds through unauthorized computer access;

5. Knowingly causing damage to certain computers by transmission of a program, information, code, or command;

6. Trafficking in passwords or other means of unauthorized access to a computer;

7. Making extortionate threats to harm a computer or based on information obtained through unauthorized access to a computer.

In everyday language, Section 1030 criminalizes hacking (unauthorized access), phishing (attempts to obtain personal information from recipients), denial of service attacks (acts intended to cause systems to shut down or fail), spreading viruses (implanting damaging software), and extortion (using a computer to express a threat intended to compel someone to transfer property). Because the Internet is by its nature interstate in character and the harm to commerce around the nation is so great, establishing federal jurisdiction is easy under the Commerce Clause.

These crimes are a mix of misdemeanors and felonies. One of the other federal cybercrime laws is a federal electronic espionage statute. 18 U.S.C. § 1831 protects corporate propriety information. It reads, in part:

In General—

Whoever, intending or knowing that the offense will benefit any foreign government, foreign instrumentality, or foreign agent, knowingly—

(1) steals, or without authorization appropriates, takes, carries away, or conceals, or by fraud, artifice, or deception obtains a trade secret;

(2) without authorization copies, duplicates, sketches, draws, photographs, downloads, uploads, alters, destroys, photocopies, replicates, transmits, delivers, sends, mails, communicates, or conveys a trade secret;

(3) receives, buys, or possesses a trade secret, knowing the same to have been stolen or appropriated, obtained, or converted without authorization;

(4) attempts to commit any offense described in any of paragraphs (1) through (3); or

(5) conspires with one or more other persons to commit any offense described in any of paragraphs (1) through (3), and one or more of such persons do any act to effect the object of the conspiracy, shall, except as provided in subsection (b), be fined not more than $500,000 or imprisoned not more than 15 years, or both.

Violations of Section 1830 and 1831 are commonly charged together.

One of the elements of a Section 1830 offense is to get into a computer in a manner that "exceeds authorized access."

The states all have similar laws. Because of the Doctrine of Dual Sovereignty, most cybercrimes can be punished by the state where they occur, the states where victims reside, and the federal government.

On the other side, computer technology has advanced law enforcement in some respects. The **National Crime Information Center** (NCIC) is used by law enforcement agencies nationwide in the reporting and detection of wanted persons. Computers are used to organize and manage case files. They are also used to investigate crimes and to hunt fugitives. Graphics programs are used to project a fugitive's appearance after donning a disguise or after having aged, to illustrate crime scenes, and to track the trajectory of bullets. Obviously, they are used to detect and document cybercrime. The use of computers by law enforcement raises interesting search and privacy questions. This topic is discussed in Chapter 12.

**National Crime Information Center**
Computerized records of criminals, warrants, stolen vehicles, etc.

## Ethical Considerations

### The Ineffective Assistance of Counsel

Criminal defendants are entitled to the effective assistance of counsel. So, what is the remedy for convictees who believe that their defense counsel committed professional malpractice? First, convictees may appeal their conviction. Second, the attorney may be sued in civil court for malpractice. Third, convictees may file a complaint with the bar authority. However, the standard of proof for convictees is high and, accordingly, most do not prevail.

To get a conviction remanded for new trial because of ineffective counsel in most jurisdictions, convictees must show that the representation was extremely inadequate, and as a consequence, the appellants were convicted. As plaintiffs in malpractice suits (where money damages, but not remand or reversal of the conviction, are sought), convictees have a similar expectation. They must obtain appellate relief from the conviction because of the ineffective assistance of counsel or must prove their innocence, separate from the criminal court judgment. This is commonly known as the exoneration rule because the bar is so high to prove criminal malpractice that few cases are filed. The trend is toward adoption of the exoneration rule in the states.

The final avenue of remedy for a victim of malpractice is to file a complaint against a convictee with the bar authority. The exoneration rule doesn't apply in these proceedings. For example, a plaintiff-convictee can report a violation of the rule of confidentiality, even if the breach didn't impact the outcome of the defendant's criminal case. For more on criminal malpractice, see Johanna M. Hickman, "Recent Developments in the Area of Criminal Malpractice," 18 Geo. *J. Legal Ethics*. 797 (2005).

## Key Terms

arson
burglary
conversion
counterfeiting
criminal coercion
criminal mischief
embezzlement

extortion
false pretenses
forfeiture
forgery
forum analysis
identity theft
larceny

National Crime Information Center
Racketeer Influenced and Corrupt
    Organizations Act
receiving stolen property
robbery
Sextortion
trespass

## Review Questions

1. What is a constructive breaking, when referring to the crime of burglary?

2. Define larceny.

3. What is criminal mischief?

4. Embezzlement is often punished more severely than simple larceny. Why?

5. What does the acronym RICO represent? What are the basic elements of RICO?

6. What are "fences"? At common law, what crime do fences commit?

7. How is destruction of a building by explosion treated by the MPC? At common law?

8. Brogan runs by a woman on the street and grabs her purse as he passes her. The purse is easily pulled from her arm, and Brogan's intent is to keep the contents. What crime has been committed?

9. Brogan runs by a woman on the street and grabs her purse as he passes her. The woman catches the strap and fights to keep the purse; however, the strap breaks, and Brogan is successful. He keeps the contents of the purse. What crime has been committed?

10. What is the difference between forgery and uttering?

## Problems & Critical Thinking Exercises

1. Arson is quite different today than it was at Common Law. What are the major differences?

2. Burglary is quite different today than it was at Common Law. What are the major differences?

3. Doug and Peggy are an elderly couple who are retired and residing in Florida. Both have suffered substantial physical deterioration, including vision loss and poor memory. Ned, who had coveted their 1962 Corvette for years, told the couple that they should trust him with their financial affairs, including giving him title to their vehicle. He told the two that he would drive them to the places they needed to go, but that state law required that his name appear on the title of the car, as he would be the sole driver. Doug and Peggy agreed to his request, believing that his statement concerning Florida law was correct.

   Subsequently, the couple created a trust account and named Ned as trustee. The purpose of the account was to provide Ned with a general fund from which he was to pay the household bills. Ned withdrew all the money and placed it into his personal account. When this occurred, the couple contacted Ned, who claimed to know nothing of the account. Peggy contacted the local prosecutor, who conducted an investigation. Through that investigation, it was discovered that Ned held title to the Corvette.

   You work for the prosecutor. Your assignment is to determine what crimes have been committed, if any. Your state has no theft statute, but recognizes common law theft crimes.

4. Imani and Paige were friends until they discovered that they shared an interest in Tracy. After Paige won her affection, Imani became enraged and took a key and ran it down the side of Paige's car. He then poured gasoline over the car and set it on fire. What crimes has Imani committed?

5. Kevin was walking down the sidewalk that passed in front of Sean's home. As he passed Sean's house, he looked in a front window and noticed a bottle of EnerJump, a sports drink, sitting on a table in the kitchen. Thirsty and tired, Kevin broke the front window and crawled into Sean's house. Once inside, he poured himself a glass of EnerJump and took a seat at the dining room table. While seated, he discovered and picked up a ring with a value in excess of $1,000, and put it into his pocket. When he finished his drink, he placed the empty glass in the sink and left. He later sold the ring and bought a stereo with the proceeds. What crimes have been committed, using common law theft crimes?

6. Brogan has an affair with Janice, who is married. After Janice ends the affair, Brogan threatens to tell Janice's husband about their sexual involvement unless Janice pays Brogan $5,000. Janice complies. What crime has been committed?

7. Penni is working the night shift at a local convenience store when Craig and Guido come in. Craig states to Penni, "Give us all the money in the register and we will not hurt you. Give us any trouble and we will knock the #?!@ out of you!" Penni complies. What crime has been committed? What if they had been brandishing weapons?

8. Discuss what crimes you think should be included in consolidated theft statutes and why. Explain why particular crimes should be left out of such a statute.

9. Mai Wong uses a 3-D printer to create a three-foot-tall duplicate of the famous Michelangelo Statue of David. She displays it in her living room. Mai's state has a counterfeit statute that applies to artwork. The elements of that statute are as you learned in the discussion in this chapter. Is she a counterfeiter? Explain your answer.

# Endnotes

1. Davenport, P., Michael Marin, Ex-Wall Street Trader, Took Cyanide After Arson Guilty Verdict, *Huffington Post*, July 27, 2012, found at http://www.huffingtonpost.com/2012/07/27/michael-marin-cyanide_n_1710731.html and Arson in America: The Odd Tale of Michael Marin, IndependentMail.com (April 23, 2013).
2. 5 Am. Jur. 2d *Arson* 2 (1962).
3. Model Penal Code § 220.1.
4. Model Penal Code § 220.1(1) and (2).
5. *People v. Richards*, 108 N.Y. 137, 15 N.E. 371 (1888).
6. LaFave & Scott, *Criminal Law* 797 (Hornbook Series; St. Paul: West, 1986).
7. Conn. Gen. Stat. §952-53a-100.
8. A. Loewy, *Criminal Law*, 2d ed. (Nutshell Series; St. Paul: West, 1987).
9. *Bazeley's Case*, 2 East P.C. 571 (Cr. Cas. Res. 1799); *see* LaFave & Scott, *Criminal Law* § 8.1 (Hornbook Series; St. Paul: West, 1986).
10. 18 U.S.C. § 641 *et seq.*
11. LaFave & Scott, *Criminal Law* § 8.9 (Hornbook Series; St. Paul: West, 1986).
12. 18 U.S.C. § 2311 *et seq.*
13. 18 U.S.C. § 2113.
14. *United States v. Fontana*, 869 F.3d 464 (2017).
15. Angel Au-Yeung, Jeff Bezos Details Blackmail Attempt by Publisher of "National Enquirer." *Forbes*, February 7, 2019. Retrieved from Forbes.com on December 21, 2020.
16. Model Penal Code § 223 *et seq.* deals with theft offenses.
17. *Id.* § 222.1.
18. *Id.* § 224.1.

**19.** 18 U.S.C. § 1341.

**20.** *McNally v. United States*, 483 U.S. 350, 356 (1987).

**21.** 18 U.S.C. § 1343.

**22.** Jed S. Rakoff, "The Federal Mail Fraud Statute (Part 1)." 18 *Duquesne L. Rev.* 771 (1980).

**23.** 18 U.S.C. § 1961 *et seq.*

**24.** *N.O.W. v. Scheidler*, 510 U.S. 249 (1994)

**25.** 18 U.S.C. § 1028.

**26.** Steve Morgan, Cybercrime to Cost the World $10.5 Trillion Annually by 2025, *Cybercrime Magazine*, November 13, 2020. Retrieved from cybersecurityventures.com on January 4, 2020.

# Chapter 6

# Crimes Against the Public

## Chapter Outline

On January 6, 2021, the United States witnessed the first attack on its iconic Capitol Building, located in Washington, D.C., since the British ransacked and burned it during the War of 1812. The invasion of the Capitol occurred when Congress was fulfilling its Twelfth Amendment responsibility to count the votes of the Electoral College in the 2020 election. This process is the last step in certifying the president-elect and vice-president-elect.

Prior to the session, President Donald J. Trump, who had lost re-election to former Vice President Joseph Biden, actively attempted to reverse the outcome of the election through dozens of court challenges, pleas for the electors to change their votes when the Electoral College met, pressure on state officials to change their popular vote counts, demands that Vice President Mike Pence and members of Congress declare that the election was fraudulently won by Joseph Biden and therefore, to reject several electoral votes cast for Biden, and an intense appeal to his supporters in a "Stop the Steal" campaign.

As part of the "Stop the Steal" campaign, thousands of people attended a rally in front of the White House that was timed to coincide with Congress' electoral vote counting session. President Trump and other speakers delivered speeches in which they restated the claim that the election was stolen, and they encouraged the attendees to march to the Capitol.

Subsequently, thousands of people walked to the Capitol, where a mob formed and stormed the building. The rioters overwhelmed the Capitol police, forcing their way into the building through doors and windows, with several scaling the walls and scaffolding that had been erected for the upcoming presidential inauguration. They roamed the building, entered members' offices, and eventually some of the invaders found their way onto the floors of both the House of Representatives and the Senate, only minutes after the members of both bodies had been evacuated. Videos, photos, and social media postings that surfaced in the days following the insurrection showed that some members of the mob had expressed intentions to murder Vice President Mike Pence, Speaker of the House of Representatives Nancy Pelosi, and other members of Congress. One Capitol police officer died and three officers later committed suicide in an apparent reaction to the events, an insurrectionist was killed, and four other peopled died as a result of the riot. The sight of the U.S. Capitol, a symbol of democracy, under siege shocked not only Americans but people the world over.

In criminal law terms, a plethora of crimes that are the subject of this chapter—crimes against the "state," or against the "people"—occurred that day. Some are crimes you learned in the last chapter. There are, for example, special federal trespass and mischief laws that apply. A few of the rioters stole items, including a lectern and laptop computer that belonged to the Speaker of the House. They will be charged with federal larceny. Other actors will face illegal entry, assault on a federal officer, mischief, sedition, and possibly, felony murder charges. A few of these crimes will be discussed in this chapter.

# Defining a "Crime Against the Public"

Chapters 4 and 5 were concerned with crimes that victimize individuals and private organizations. This chapter examines crimes that do not have individual victims. These are crimes involving the public welfare, social order, and society's morals. The crimes included in this chapter have been divided into five subsections: crimes against public morality; crimes against the public order; crimes against the administration of government; crimes against sovereignty and security; and crimes against the environment.

As to the first group, morality crimes, religion has long played a role in the "criminalization" of "victimless" crimes. Of course, religious groups do not dictate such policy—this would violate the First Amendment's Establishment Clause. Religion does, however, influence the moral values of the members of a society. In the United States, this influence is predominantly Christian. This is the reason that some acts that directly harm no one are prohibited.

Some critics call for an end to "victimless crimes." Despite this opposition, many victimless crimes exist and are likely to continue to be prohibited. However, regulating decency can easily run afoul of free speech, equal protection, and other rights, especially in an increasingly diverse nation.

**Exhibit 6–1** Types of Crimes Against the Public

| Morality | Public Order | Administration of Justice | Sovereignty and Security | Environment and Animals |
|----------|--------------|---------------------------|--------------------------|-------------------------|
| Prostitution | Riot | Perjury | Treason | Pollution |
| Solicitation of Prostitution | Trespass | Bribery | Sedition | Dangerous Chemicals and Toxins |
| Deviate Sex | Disturbing the Peace | Tax | Espionage | Larceny of Natural Resources |
| Incest | Incitement of Violence | Obstruction of Justice | Terrorism | Animal Neglect and Cruelty |
| Obscenity | Weapons | Contempt | | |
| Indecent Conduct | Drug and Alcohol Crimes | | | |

# Crimes Against Public Morality

## Prostitution and Solicitation

Learning Objective: Define, describe, and apply the elements of prostitution and solicitation of prostitution.

Often said to be the oldest profession, **prostitution** is prohibited in every state except Nevada, where each county of less than 700,000 residents is given the authority to determine whether it should be permitted. Ironically, state law also forbids prostitution in Sin City itself—Las Vegas.

Prostitution is defined as

1. providing
2. sexual services
3. in exchange for compensation.

In a few states, only intercourse is included in the definition of sexual services. In most states, however, sexual services include sodomy, fellatio, cunnilingus, and the touching of another's genitals.

The service must be provided in exchange for compensation. The person who is sexually promiscuous, but unpaid, goes unpunished. Typically, prostitutes are paid in cash, but compensation can come in the form of anything of value. Thus, the prostitute who accepts legal services from a lawyer in exchange for sexual services has received compensation. Where prostitution is illegal, it is common for prostitutes to use businesses, such as massage parlors and escort services, as fronts. Large crime organizations typically launder their prostitution proceeds.

Solicitation is a related crime. Any person who engages in selling sex, buying sex, or attempting to buy sex is guilty of solicitation. Note that a prostitute may be guilty of both solicitation and prostitution, if the prostitute makes the first contact with the buyer. There need not be the actual sale of sex for solicitation—only an attempt to sell sexual services. The clients of prostitutes, when prosecuted, are charged with solicitation.

The Modal Penal Code (MPC) states that "[a] person commits a violation if he hires a prostitute to engage in sexual activity with him, or if he enters or remains in a house of prostitution for the purpose of engaging in sexual activity."[1]

Those who promote prostitution (*pimps*) are usually punished more severely than prostitutes and customers. The MPC makes knowingly promoting prostitution a felony of the third degree if a child under 16 years of age is prostituted; the defendant's wife, child, or other ward is prostituted; the

**prostitution**
A person offering their body for sexual purposes in exchange for money. A crime in most states.

defendant forces or encourages another to engage in prostitution; or the defendant owns, controls, or manages a house of prostitution. In all other cases, promotion is a misdemeanor.

Nearly all sex-for-hire cases fall under state jurisdiction. However, the federal government may be involved in prosecution when a prostitute is transported in interstate commerce, or any other person is transported in interstate commerce for an immoral purpose.[2]

In recent years, evidence that many prostitutes, particularly foreign nationals, are victims of human trafficking has led to changes in enforcement and law. Police, for example, are trained to detect trafficking, separate the victims from their oppressors, and connect victims to social services, rather than treat them as criminals.

## Deviate Sexual Conduct and Incest

Learning Objective: Describe deviate sexual conduct crimes and explain how the right to privacy bounds what sex may be criminalized.

Rape and related crimes were discussed in Chapter 4. That chapter focused on sexual behavior that results in harm to a victim. This discussion is different, as there is usually no victim in fact, rather, the offense is to society's morals.

**sodomy**
A general word for an "unnatural" sex act or the crime committed by such act. While the definition varies, *sodomy* can include oral sex, anal sex, homosexual sex, or sex with animals.

Deviate sexual conduct, also known as **sodomy**, was historically defined as noncoital sex with a person of the opposite sex, same-sex sex of any form, or sex with an animal.

Many forms of sodomy have been decriminalized, in part because of the recognition of the liberty rights of adults to engage in whatever form of consenting sexual activity they choose. In 2003, the Supreme Court found the prohibition of private sex, in any form, between consenting adults to be violative of the right to privacy found in the Due Process Clauses in *Lawrence v. Texas*.[3] And in 2015, the Court found that same sex couples have a liberty right to marry in *Obergefell v. Hodges*.[4] Regardless of these decisions, some states continue to carry archaic sodomy laws on their books. These laws are unconstitutional and therefore unenforceable. Certain forms of sodomy, such as bestiality, continue to be criminalized. They are commonly referred to by other names, including deviate sex.

Incest is sex between family members. Generally, law enforcement is most concerned with abuse of children in the home. That topic was discussed in Chapter 4. It is also a crime for two consenting adult family members to engage in sex.

The actus reus of incest is intercourse, or other sexual conduct, between family members. Normally, incest laws parallel marriage laws for a definition of *family*. That is, if two people are permitted to marry under state law, then they are also permitted to engage in sex, regardless of marriage. It is common for states to prohibit marriage of individuals of first cousin affinity and closer.

## Marriage, Contraception, and Abortion

Marriage is a state-coopted institution. States regulate marriage in a number of ways. All states specify how many people may marry (two in each marriage is uniform), who may marry (no close relatives), who has the authority to perform the marriage ceremony, when couples may marry (some states require a waiting period and/or blood tests), and the payment of a fee for the issuance of a license. Additionally, states and the federal government have built marriage into their tax schemes. There are limits, however, to the regulation of marriage. For example, for many years, states prohibited, and even criminalized, marriages between people of different races and people of the same sex. As you learned earlier and will learn more about in Chapter 9, the Supreme Court invalidated these laws as violating one's right to liberty, as protected by due process. Similarly, criminal prohibitions of the use of contraceptives and early term abortions were invalidated.

## Indecent Exposure and Lewdness

Learning Objective: Define, describe, and apply the elements of indecent exposure.

Indecent exposure, or the exposure of one's "private parts" in public, was a Common Law misdemeanor. Today, the crime is usually criminalized by state statute or local ordinance.

Most indecent exposure laws require

1. an intentional exposure
2. of the private areas of the body
3. in a public place or public way.

In some jurisdictions, it is required that the exposure be done in an "offensive manner." As to the third element, the act must be committed in a public space, or in a private space that is easily visible to people. For example, a homeowner may not stand nude in front of a window, easily seen from the street or a neighbor's home.

In 1991, the U.S. Supreme Court examined a public nudity statute in the context of nude barroom dancing. In *Barnes v. Glen Theater, Inc.*,[5] the Court determined that nude dancing to be expressive conduct. It nonetheless upheld a law requiring the genital area and nipples of the breast to be covered because the State had a neutral and legitimate interest in regulating nudity. The Court penned that

> Likewise, the requirement that the dancers don pasties and a G-string does not deprive the dance of whatever erotic message it conveys; it simply makes the message slightly less graphic. The perceived evil that Indiana seeks to address is not erotic dancing, but public nudity. The appearance of people of all shapes, sizes and ages in the nude at a beach, for example, would convey little if any erotic message, yet the state still seeks to prevent it. Public nudity is the evil the state seeks to prevent, whether or not it is combined with expressive activity.

A similar restriction was subsequently affirmed in *Pap's A.M. v. City of Erie*,[6] where the Court applied the O'Brien Test to public nudity cases. The elements of the O'Brien Test are:

1. the regulation must be within the constitutional power of the government
2. the regulation furthers an important or substantial governmental interest
3. the interest must be unrelated to the suppression of free expression
4. any incidental restriction on speech must be no greater than is essential to the furtherance of the governmental interest

Applying these factors, the Court concluded that the State didn't intend to suppress expression, that requiring only the most private areas be covered to a minimal restriction, and that the government had a substantial interest in protecting public order and morality.

The MPC prohibits public indecency. The Code goes further with a provision proscribing all lewd acts that the defendant knows are likely to be observed by others who would be "affronted or alarmed" by the acts.[7]

## Obscenity

Learning Objective: Describe the First Amendment test used to determine if expression may be regulated because it is obscene.

David by Michelangelo, censored

MisterStock/Shutterstock.com/Ket4up/Shutterstock.com

Congress shall make no law respecting the establishment of religion, or prohibiting the free exercise thereof; *or abridging the freedom of speech,* or of the press; or the right of the people peaceably to assemble, and to petition the Government for a redress of grievances.

This is the First Amendment to the U.S. Constitution. Most, if not all, states have a similar provision in their constitutions. The italicized portion represents the only protection of speech in the Constitution. Because it is brief and broad, courts must interpret it to give it meaning. Freedom of speech encompasses far more than will be examined in this chapter. What will be discussed here is the extent of governmental power to regulate conduct that it deems to be indecent. Specifically, this section addresses sexually explicit materials, including films, books, and erotic dancing. It is well established that the term *speech*, as used in the First Amendment, means more than spoken utterances. It includes all forms of expression.

Both the federal and state governments regulate conduct, speech, books, movies, and other forms of expression that are believed to be "obscene." State governments are the most involved with regulating obscenity, due to general police power (the power to regulate for the health, welfare, and safety of citizens). However, the federal government is also involved; for example, it has criminalized sending obscene materials through the mail.[8]

Not all indecencies may be criminalized. Simply because something strikes one person as indecent does not mean that it should be prohibited. People have differing values, and to allow governments to prohibit all conduct (or other things) that is found offensive by some member of society would be to allow our government to criminalize all aspects of life. In addition, people perceive things differently. For example, in 1990 the Cincinnati Arts Center was charged with obscenity for displaying photographs taken by a respected artist, Robert Mapplethorpe. Included in the photos were depictions of nude children. The prosecutor contended that the pictures were obscene. A jury did not agree. The Arts Center and its director were acquitted, and many of the jurors commented that the testimony of art experts convinced them that the pictures had serious artistic value and were not obscene.[9]

It is important that the First Amendment be flexible and tolerant of new ideas and methods of expression. Simply because the majority of citizens would not see value in a form of expression does not mean it has no value. This is not to say that there is no limit on the freedom of expression. When considering sexually oriented expression, that line is drawn when the expression becomes obscene.[10]

Obscenity has proven to be an elusive concept for the Supreme Court. Through a series of decisions, from 1957 to the present, the Court has attempted to define *obscenity*. The famous quotation from Justice Potter Stewart—"I shall not today attempt further to define [obscenity]; and perhaps I could never succeed in intelligibly doing so. But I know it when I see it."[11] is a testament to the difficulty in defining such a concept. It also reflects what many people believe—that they may not be able to define obscenity, but they recognize it when they see it.

In *Roth v. United States,*[12] it was held that because it lacks redeeming social importance, obscenity is not protected by the First Amendment. The Court then established a test for determining whether something was obscene and, as such, not protected by the First Amendment. That test was "whether to the average person, applying contemporary community standards, the dominant theme of the material taken as a whole appeals to prurient interest." In addition, the material had to be "utterly without redeeming social value." Simply because "literature is dismally unpleasant, uncouth, and tawdry is not enough to make it 'obscene.'"[13]

In 1973, the Supreme Court reexamined the *Roth* obscenity test in *Miller v. California*.[14] In *Miller*, the Court rejected the requirement that the material be "utterly without redeeming social value" and lowered the standard to lacking "serious literary, artistic, political, or scientific value." The test under *Miller* has three parts:

1. The average person, applying contemporary community standards, would find that the work, taken as a whole, appeals to the prurient interest and

2. the work must depict or describe, in a patently offensive manner, sexual conduct specifically defined by the applicable state law, and

3. the work, when taken as a whole, must lack serious literary, artistic, political, or scientific value.

The *Miller* test makes it easier for states to regulate sexual materials. An "average person" has been equated with a reasonable person, as used in tort law.[15] The material must appeal to "prurient interest." Materials that have a tendency to excite a lustful, "shameful or morbid interest in nudity, sex or excretion" meet the prurient interest element.[16] Material that provokes normal, healthy, sexual desires is not obscene because it does not appeal to prurient interest.[17]

The Court gave examples in *Miller* of "patently offensive" materials that included depictions or descriptions of "ultimate sex acts, normal or perverted, actual or simulated . . . of masturbation, excretory functions, and lewd exhibition of the genitals."

One area where the states have substantially more power to regulate obscenity is when minors are involved. The Court has held that all child pornography is unprotected because of the special need to protect children from exploitation.[18] Similarly, governments may prohibit the distribution and sale of erotic materials to minors, even if such materials are not obscene.[19] Also, in *Osborne v. Ohio*,[20] the Supreme Court held that a person may be convicted for possession of child pornography in the home. This is an exception to the general rule that a person may possess obscene material in the home.[21]

Obscenity is a complex area of law. Many different criminal prohibitions exist throughout the states and federal government that focus on the sale, distribution, and possession of sexually oriented materials, performance of erotic dance, and public nudity. So long as minors are not involved, the activity is protected unless it is obscene. To determine whether pornography is obscene, one must apply the three-part *Miller* test. The states are free to regulate if children are involved, either as participants in the erotic materials (or performance) or as buyers of erotic materials, even if the material is not obscene.

In 2010, the Supreme Court invalidated a federal statute that regulated films that depicted animal cruelty on First Amendment grounds.

## Oyez

### United States v. Stevens
### (559 U.S. 460 (2010))

#### Chief Justice Roberts delivered the opinion of the Court

[The federal statute in question] establishes a criminal penalty of up to five years in prison for anyone who knowingly "creates, sells, or possesses a depiction of animal cruelty," if done "for commercial gain" in interstate or foreign commerce. A depiction of "animal cruelty" is defined as one "in which a living animal is intentionally maimed, mutilated, tortured, wounded, or killed," if that conduct violates federal or state law where "the creation, sale, or possession takes place." In what is referred to as the "exceptions clause," the law exempts from prohibition any depiction "that has serious religious, political, scientific, educational, journalistic, historical, or artistic value."

(continued)

The legislative background of [the law] focused primarily on the interstate market for "crush videos." According to the House Committee Report on the bill, such videos feature the intentional torture and killing of helpless animals, including cats, dogs, monkeys, mice, and hamsters. Crush videos often depict women slowly crushing animals to death "with their bare feet or while wearing high heeled shoes," sometimes while "talking to the animals in a kind of dominatrix patter" over "[t]he cries and squeals of the animals, obviously in great pain." Apparently these depictions "appeal to persons with a very specific sexual fetish who find them sexually arousing or otherwise exciting." The acts depicted in crush videos are typically prohibited by the animal cruelty laws enacted by all 50 States and the District of Columbia. . . .

This case, however, involves an application of [the law] to depictions of animal fighting. Dogfighting, for example, is unlawful in all 50 States and the District of Columbia. . . .

Stevens moved to dismiss the indictment, arguing that [the law] is facially invalid under the First Amendment. The District Court denied the motion. It held that the depictions subject to §48, like obscenity or child pornography, are categorically unprotected by the First Amendment. . . .

The First Amendment provides that "Congress shall make no law . . . abridging the freedom of speech." "[A]s a general matter, the First Amendment means that government has no power to restrict expression because of its message, its ideas, its subject matter, or its content. . . .

"From 1791 to the present," however, the First Amendment has "permitted restrictions upon the content of speech in a few limited areas," and has never "include[d] a freedom to disregard these traditional limitations." These "historic and traditional categories long familiar to the bar,"—including obscenity, defamation, fraud, incitement, and speech integral to criminal conduct,—are "well-defined and narrowly limited classes of speech, the prevention and punishment of which have never been thought to raise any Constitutional problem."

The Government argues that "depictions of animal cruelty" should be added to the list. . . .

The Government contends that "historical evidence" about the reach of the First Amendment is not "a necessary prerequisite for regulation today," and that categories of speech may be exempted from the First Amendment's protection without any long-settled tradition of subjecting that speech to regulation. Instead, the Government points to Congress's 'legislative judgment that . . . depictions of animals being intentionally tortured and killed [are] of such minimal redeeming value as to render [them] unworthy of First Amendment protection,' and asks the Court to uphold the ban on the same basis. The Government thus proposes that a claim of categorical exclusion should be considered under a simple balancing test: "Whether a given category of speech enjoys First Amendment protection depends upon a categorical balancing of the value of the speech against its societal costs."

As a free-floating test for First Amendment coverage, that sentence is startling and dangerous. The First Amendment's guarantee of free speech does not extend only to categories of speech that survive an ad hoc balancing of relative social costs and benefits. The First Amendment itself reflects a judgement by the American people that the benefits of its restrictions on the Government outweigh the costs. . . .

When we have identified categories of speech as fully outside the protection of the First Amendment, it has not been on the basis of a simple cost-benefit analysis. In *Ferber*, for example, we classified child pornography as such a category. We noted that the State of New York had a compelling interest in protecting children from abuse, and that the value of using children in these works (as opposed to simulated conduct or adult actors) was *de minimis*. But our decision did not rest on this "balance of competing interests" alone. We made clear that *Ferber* presented a special case: The market for child pornography was "intrinsically related" to the underlying abuse, and was therefore "an integral part of the production of such materials, an activity illegal throughout the Nation."

Our decisions in *Ferber* and other cases cannot be taken as establishing a freewheeling authority to declare new categories of speech outside the scope of the First Amendment. . . .

[The Court then found the law to be too broad. Not only could crush videos be prosecuted under the law, but bull fights, hunting, and other protected speech could as well.] Our construction of [the law] decides the constitutional question; the Government makes no effort to defend the constitutionality of [the law] as applied beyond crush videos and depictions of animal fighting. It argues that those particular depictions are intrinsically related to criminal conduct or are analogous to obscenity (if not themselves obscene), and that the ban on such speech is narrowly tailored to reinforce restrictions on the underlying conduct, prevent additional crime arising from the depictions, or safeguard public mores. But the Government nowhere attempts to extend these arguments to depictions of any other activities—depictions that are presumptively protected by the First Amendment but that remain subject to the criminal sanctions of [the law].

Nor does the Government seriously contest that the presumptively impermissible applications of [the law] (properly construed) far outnumber any permissible ones. However "growing" and "lucrative" the markets for crush videos and dogfighting depictions might be, they are dwarfed by the market for other depictions, such as hunting magazines and videos, that we have determined to be within the scope of [the law]. We therefore need not and do not decide whether a statute limited to crush videos or other depictions of extreme animal cruelty would be constitutional. We hold only that [the law] is not so limited but is instead substantially overbroad, and therefore invalid under the First Amendment.

Let's look at the MPC for an example of a prohibition of obscenity. The MPC makes it a misdemeanor to knowingly or recklessly do any of the following:[22]

1. Sell, deliver, or provide (or offer to do one of the three) any obscene writing, picture, record, or other obscene representation.

2. Present or perform in an obscene play, dance, or other performance.

3. Publish or exhibit obscene materials.

4. Possess obscene materials for commercial purposes.

5. Sell or otherwise commercially distribute materials represented as obscene.

The Code presumes that anyone who distributes obscene materials in the course of business has done so knowingly or recklessly.

Material is considered obscene under the Code if "considered as a whole, its predominant appeal is to prurient interest, that is, a shameful or morbid interest, in nudity, sex, or excretion, and if in addition it goes substantially beyond customary limits of candor in describing or representing such matter." Note that the Code's definition is similar to the Supreme Court's definition. The Code does add the requirement that the material go beyond "customary limits of candor." The Code makes it an affirmative defense that the obscene material was possessed for governmental, scientific, educational, or other justified causes. It also is not a crime for a person to give such materials to personal associates in noncommercial situations. The Code focuses on punishing commercial dissemination of obscene material.

## Regulating the Internet

The ability of the World Wide Web to penetrate every home and community across the globe has both positive and negative implications—while it can be an invaluable source of information and means of communication, it can also override community values and standards, subjecting them to whatever more may or may not be found online. . . . [T]he Internet is a challenge to the sovereignty of civilized communities, States, and nations to decide what is appropriate and decent behavior.[23]

According to Internetworldstats.com, Internet use around the world reached nearly 5 billion people by 2020. The greatest number of users are found in Asia, followed by Europe and North America. However, the greatest penetration of computers in daily life is in North America, followed by Oceana/Australia and Europe. The digital world presents both benefits and threats. Computers can be great social equalizers, tearing down class, education, and economic barriers. Information that was once held by few is now widely available. Instant, ubiquitous communication can fuel positive social and political change. It also unites lone wolves into dangerous packs. Law enforcement is more effective with digital tools. It is also more of a threat to privacy and liberty.

Today, there is a plethora of laws that regulate the Internet and digital information. One area of regulation is the presentation and hosting of obscenity. The first major national attempt to protect children from adult-oriented information on the Internet was the Communications Decency Act of 1996.[24] This statute limited the transmission of "obscene" and "indecent" materials to children. However, this statute was held unconstitutional by the Supreme Court in *Reno v. ACLU* (1997).[25] "The Supreme Court held that the law was overbroad because it prohibited both protected speech (indecent materials) and unprotected speech (obscene materials)." Obscene material, as defined by *Miller* and other cases, may be regulated but indecent material may not. In addition, the Court found that the law was overbroad because it limited access, both adult and juvenile. While it is lawful to limit the access of children to indecent materials (even if not obscene), the law limited the access of everyone because under current technology there is not a way to create zones that children cannot enter. In real space, it is possible to create such zones. Adult bookstores, for example, are zones where children may not enter.

Congress attempted again to protect children from the dangers of the Internet in 1998 through the Child Online Protection Act.[26] This law limited regulation to material that is harmful to minors. The law specifically incorporates the *Miller* test into its definition of what is prohibited. In a narrowly drafted decision, the Supreme Court upheld this law in 2002.[27] The court made it clear, however, that other constitutional issues may need to be examined in an attempt to correct the error of the Communications Decency Act. It remains to be seen if this law is constitutional.

In addition to shielding minors from adult content, Congress and the states have attempted to protect children from being used in sexually explicit films. While there is no question that the use of children can be criminalized, as can the possession of child pornography itself, modern technology has changed the landscape considerably. Today, it is possible to alter genuine photos of children to make them appear as if they are nude or engaged in sexual conduct. Photos of adults can be merged with those of children, and other computer graphic techniques can be employed to create virtual child pornography.

In the Child Pornography Prevention Act of 1996, Congress prohibited not only images of actual children in pornography but also "virtual" images created with the use of computers. As was true of the Communications Decency Act, the Supreme Court found the law to be contrary to First Amendment principles in *Ashcroft v. Free Speech Coalition.*

## Oyez

### Ashcroft v. Free Speech Coalition
### 535 U.S. 234 (2002)

**Justice Kennedy delivered the opinion of the Court**

We consider in this case whether the Child Pornography Prevention Act of 1996 (CPPA), 18 U.S.C. § 2251 *et seq.*, abridges the freedom of speech. The CPPA extends the federal prohibition against child pornography to sexually explicit images that appear to depict minors but were produced without using any real children. The statute prohibits, in specific circumstances, possessing or distributing these images, which may be created by using adults who look like minors or by using computer imaging. The new technology, according to Congress, makes it possible to create realistic images of children who do not exist. . . .

By prohibiting child pornography that does not depict an actual child, the statute goes beyond *New York v. Ferber*, 458 U.S. 747 (1982), which distinguished child pornography from other sexually explicit speech because of the State's interest in protecting the children exploited by the production process. As a general rule, pornography can be banned only if obscene, but under *Ferber*, pornography showing minors can be proscribed whether or not the images are obscene under the definition set forth in *Miller v. California*, 413 U.S. 15 (1973). *Ferber* recognized that "[t]he *Miller* standard, like all general definitions of what may be banned as obscene, does not reflect the State's particular and more compelling interest in prosecuting those who promote the sexual exploitation of children." . . .

The principal question to be resolved, then, is whether the CPPA is constitutional where it proscribes a significant universe of speech that is neither obscene under *Miller* nor child pornography under *Ferber*.

Before 1996, Congress defined child pornography as the type of depictions at issue in *Ferber*, images made using actual minors. 18 U.S.C. § 2252 (1994 ed.). The CPPA retains that prohibition at 18 U.S.C. § 2256(8)(A) and adds three other prohibited categories of speech, of which the first, § 2256(8)(B), and the third, § 2256(8)(D), are at issue in this case. Section 2256(8)(B) prohibits "any visual depiction, including any photograph, film, video, picture, or computer or computer-generated image or picture" that "is, or appears to be, of a minor engaging in sexually explicit conduct." The prohibition on "any visual depiction" does not depend at all on how the image is produced. The section captures a range of depictions, sometimes called "virtual child pornography," which include computer-generated images, as well as images produced by more traditional means. For instance, the literal terms of the statute embrace a Renaissance painting depicting a scene from classical mythology, a "picture" that "appears to be, of a minor engaging in sexually explicit conduct." The statute also prohibits Hollywood movies, filmed without any child actors, if a jury believes an actor "appears to be" a minor engaging in "actual or simulated . . . sexual intercourse."

These images do not involve, let alone harm, any children in the production process; but Congress decided the materials threaten children in other, less direct, ways. Pedophiles might use the materials to encourage children to participate in sexual activity. "[A] child who is reluctant to engage in sexual activity with an adult, or to pose for sexually explicit photographs, can sometimes be convinced by viewing depictions of other children 'having fun' participating in such activity." Furthermore, pedophiles might "whet their own sexual appetites" with the pornographic images, "thereby increasing the creation and distribution of child pornography and the sexual abuse and exploitation of actual children." Under these rationales, harm flows from the content of the images, not from the means of their production. In addition, Congress identified another problem created by computer-generated images: Their existence can make it harder to prosecute pornographers who do use real minors. As imaging technology improves, Congress found, it becomes more difficult to prove that a particular picture was produced using actual children. To ensure that defendants possessing child pornography using real minors cannot evade prosecution, Congress extended the ban to virtual child pornography.

Section 2256(8)(C) prohibits a more common and lower tech means of creating virtual images, known as computer morphing. Rather than creating original images, pornographers can alter innocent pictures of real children so that the children appear to be engaged in sexual activity. Although morphed images may fall within the definition of virtual child pornography, they implicate the interests of real children and are in that sense closer to the images in *Ferber*. Respondents do not challenge this provision, and we do not consider it.

Respondents do challenge § 2256(8)(D). Like the text of the "appears to be" provision, the sweep of this provision is quite broad. Section 2256(8)(D) defines child pornography to include any sexually explicit image that was "advertised, promoted, presented, described, or distributed in such a manner that conveys the impression" it depicts "a minor engaging in sexually explicit conduct." One Committee Report identified the provision as directed at sexually explicit images pandered as child pornography. ("This provision prevents child pornographers and pedophiles from exploiting prurient interests in child sexuality and sexual activity through the production or distribution of pornographic material which is intentionally pandered as child pornography"). The statute is not so limited in its reach, however, as it punishes even those possessors who took no part in pandering. Once a work has been described as child pornography, the taint remains on the speech in the hands of subsequent possessors, making possession unlawful even though the content otherwise would not be objectionable.

Fearing that the CPPA threatened the activities of its members, respondent Free Speech Coalition and others challenged the statute. . . .

The First Amendment commands, "Congress shall make no law . . . abridging the freedom of speech." The government may violate this mandate in many ways, but a law imposing criminal penalties on protected speech is a stark example of speech suppression. The CPPA's penalties are indeed severe. A first offender may be imprisoned for 15 years. § 2252A(b)(1). A repeat offender faces a prison sentence of not less than 5 years and not more than 30 years in prison. While even minor punishments can chill protected speech, this case provides a textbook example of why we permit facial challenges to statutes that burden expression. With these severe penalties in force, few legitimate movie producers or book publishers, or few other speakers in any capacity, would risk distributing images in or near the uncertain reach of this law. The Constitution gives significant protection from overbroad laws that chill speech within the First Amendment's vast and privileged sphere. Under this principle, the CPPA is unconstitutional on its face if it prohibits a substantial amount of protected expression.

The sexual abuse of a child is a most serious crime and an act repugnant to the moral instincts of a decent people. Congress also found that surrounding the serious offenders are those who flirt with these impulses and trade pictures and written accounts of sexual activity with young children.

Congress may pass valid laws to protect children from abuse, and it has. The prospect of crime, however, by itself does not justify laws suppressing protected speech. . . .

As a general principle, the First Amendment bars the government from dictating what we see or read or speak or hear. The freedom of speech has its limits; it does not embrace certain categories of speech, including defamation, incitement, obscenity, and pornography produced with real children. . . .

The CPPA prohibits speech despite its serious literary, artistic, political, or scientific value. The statute proscribes the visual depiction of an idea—that of teenagers engaging in sexual activity—that is a fact of modern society and has been a theme in art and literature throughout the ages. Under the CPPA, images are prohibited so long as the persons appear to be under 18 years of age. 18 U.S.C. § 2256(1). This is higher than the legal age for marriage in many States, as well as the age at which persons may consent to sexual relations.

(continued)

Both themes—teenage sexual activity and the sexual abuse of children—have inspired countless literary works. William Shakespeare created the most famous pair of teenage lovers, one of whom is just 13 years of age. See Romeo and Juliet, act I, sc. 2, l. 9 ("She hath not seen the change of fourteen years"). In the drama, Shakespeare portrays the relationship as something splendid and innocent, but not juvenile. The work has inspired no less than 40 motion pictures, some of which suggest that the teenagers consummated their relationship. *E.g.*, Romeo and Juliet (B. Luhrmann director, 1996). Shakespeare may not have written sexually explicit scenes for the Elizabethan audience, but were modern directors to adopt a less conventional approach, that fact alone would not compel the conclusion that the work was obscene.

Contemporary movies pursue similar themes. Last year's Academy Awards featured the movie, Traffic, which was nominated for Best Picture. . . . The film portrays a teenager, identified as a 16-year-old, who becomes addicted to drugs. The viewer sees the degradation of her addiction, which in the end leads her to a filthy room to trade sex for drugs. The year before, American Beauty won the Academy Award for Best Picture. . . . In the course of the movie, a teenage girl engages in sexual relations with her teenage boyfriend, and another yields herself to the gratification of a middle-aged man. The film also contains a scene where, although the movie audience understands the act is not taking place, one character believes he is watching a teenage boy performing a sexual act on an older man.

Our society, like other cultures, has empathy and enduring fascination with the lives and destinies of the young. Art and literature express the vital interest we all have in the formative years we ourselves once knew, when wounds can be so grievous, disappointment so profound, and mistaken choices so tragic, but when moral acts and self-fulfillment are still in reach. Whether or not the films we mention violate the CPPA, they explore themes within the wide sweep of the statute's prohibitions. If these films, or hundreds of others of lesser note that explore those subjects, contain a single graphic depiction of sexual activity within the statutory definition, the possessor of the film would be subject to severe punishment without inquiry into the work's redeeming value. This is inconsistent with an essential First Amendment rule: The artistic merit of a work does not depend on the presence of a single explicit scene. For this reason, and the others we have noted, the CPPA cannot be read to prohibit obscenity, because it lacks the required link between its prohibitions and the affront to community standards prohibited by the definition of obscenity.

[I]n *Osborne v. Ohio*, 495 U.S. 103 (1990), the Court ruled that these same interests justified a ban on the possession of pornography produced by using children. "Given the importance of the State's interest in protecting the victims of child pornography," the State was justified in "attempting to stamp out this vice at all levels in the distribution chain." . . . Osborne also noted the State's interest in preventing child pornography from being used as an aid in the solicitation of minors. . . . The Court, however, anchored its holding in the concern for the participants, those whom it called the "victims of child pornography." . . . It did not suggest that, absent this concern, other governmental interests would suffice. . . .

In contrast to the speech in *Ferber*, speech that itself is the record of sexual abuse, the CPPA prohibits speech that records no crime and creates no victims by its production. Virtual child pornography is not "intrinsically related" to the sexual abuse of children, as were the materials in *Ferber*. While the Government asserts that the images can lead to actual instances of child abuse, . . . the causal link is contingent and indirect. The CPPA, for reasons we have explored, is inconsistent with *Miller* and finds no support in *Ferber*. The Government seeks to justify its prohibitions in other ways. It argues that the CPPA is necessary because pedophiles may use virtual child pornography to seduce children. There are many things innocent in themselves, however, such as cartoons, video games, and candy, that might be used for immoral purposes, yet we would not expect those to be prohibited because they can be misused. The Government, of course, may punish adults who provide unsuitable materials to children, see *Ginsberg v. New York*, 390 U.S. 629 (1968), and it may enforce criminal penalties for unlawful solicitation. The precedents establish, however, that speech within the rights of adults to hear may not be silenced completely in an attempt to shield children from it. . . .

The Government submits further that virtual child pornography whets the appetites of pedophiles and encourages them to engage in illegal conduct. This rationale cannot sustain the provision in question. The mere tendency of speech to encourage unlawful acts is not a sufficient reason for banning it. . . .

The Government next argues that its objective of eliminating the market for pornography produced using real children necessitates a prohibition on virtual images as well. Virtual images, the Government contends, are indistinguishable from real ones; they are part of the same market and are often exchanged. In this way, it is said, virtual images promote the trafficking in works produced through the exploitation of real children. The hypothesis is somewhat implausible. If virtual images were identical to illegal child pornography, the illegal images would be driven from the market by the indistinguishable substitutes. Few pornographers would risk prosecution by abusing real children if fictional, computerized images would suffice.

In sum, § 2256(8)(B) covers materials beyond the categories recognized in *Ferber* and *Miller*, and the reasons the Government offers in support of limiting the freedom of speech have no justification in our precedents or in the law of the First Amendment. The provision abridges the freedom to engage in a substantial amount of lawful speech. For this reason, it is overbroad and unconstitutional.

States also have laws regulating the Internet. Of course, these laws must be crafted to avoid First Amendment and state-law free speech barriers. Additionally, the interstate character of the Internet can create jurisdictional problems for states. In *American Library Association v. Pataki* (S.D. N.Y. 1997),[28] a New York statute that regulated the Internet in much the same manner as the federal Communications Decency Act was invalidated not on First Amendment grounds but on jurisdictional grounds. The federal court that heard the case ruled that New York was without the authority to regulate conduct outside its borders. Congress responded to the *Free Speech Coalition* decision by enacting an amended version of the law that was upheld. The new statute, known as PROTECT, criminalizes soliciting, distributing, promoting, or presenting images with the belief, or that is intended to cause another to believe, that they are depictions of minors. To avoid the overbreadth problem of *Free Speech Coalition*, PROTECT did not include a ban on all virtual child pornography. The Court found the subtle distinction between banning all virtual child pornography and those depictions intended to convince others that they are actual minors adequate to uphold the law in *United States v. Williams*.[29]

Due to the plethora of cases addressing pornography and obscenity, it is strongly recommended that thorough research be conducted. There is a good chance that precedent with similar facts may be found. Beware, however, that this is an issue that often leaves courts split. Be sure that the opinions you find reflect the law of your jurisdiction.

# Crimes Against the Public Order

Crimes against the public order are crimes that involve **breaches of the peace**. The phrase *breaches of the peace* refers to all crimes that involve disturbing the tranquility or order of society. Breaches of the peace as a crime has its roots in early English Common Law. In England, breaches of the peace by individuals were criminal, as were breaches by groups.

> **breaches of the peace**
> A vague term for any illegal public disturbance; sometimes refers to the offense known as "disorderly conduct." It is defined and treated differently in different states.

Three groups of breaches were recognized; all were punished as misdemeanors. If three or more people met with an intention of causing a disturbance, they committed the common law offense of unlawful assembly. If the group took some action in an attempt to breach the peace, they were guilty of rout; if they were successful, the crime was riot.

Today, all jurisdictions prohibit breaches of the peace in some form by statute. These crimes are labeled disorderly conduct, unlawful assembly, riot, inciting violence, unlawful threat, and vagrancy. There are First Amendment limits to these crimes. For example, there is a line between criminal assembly and First Amendment protected assembly, association, and speech. The constitutional aspects of the crimes in this section will be explored in greater detail in chapter 9.

## Riot and Unlawful Assembly

Learning Objective: Define, describe, and apply the elements of riot and unlawful assembly.

Most states now have legislation that prohibits groups of people from meeting with the purpose of committing an unlawful act or committing a lawful act in an unlawful manner. This crime may be named unlawful assembly or riot. A group, or "assembly," is a specified minimum number of people, often three or five. Some jurisdictions continue to recognize the distinctions between unlawful assembly, rout, and riot.

The MPC recognizes two related crimes: riot and failure to disperse. Both crimes require an assembly of two or more persons who are behaving in a disorderly manner. If the purpose of the assembly is to commit a crime (felony or

Protestors and insurrectionists at the U.S. Capitol on January 6, 2021.

misdemeanor), to coerce public officials to act or not act, or if a deadly weapon is used, then the crime is riot.[30]

Failure to disperse occurs when a law enforcement officer, or other official, orders the members of a group of three or more to disperse and someone refuses. The disorderly conduct that the assembly is engaged in must be "likely to cause substantial harm or serious inconvenience, annoyance, or alarm," before an officer may order the group to disperse. This provision is included because the freedoms to associate and assemble are protected by the First Amendment to the U.S. Constitution, and such activity may be regulated only when it poses a threat to person, property, or society.

Most jurisdictions punish these crimes as misdemeanors. However, they may be elevated to felony if committed with a dangerous weapon, if someone is injured as a result of the activity, or if law enforcement officers are obstructed from performing their duties. The MPC makes rioting a felony of the third degree and failure to disperse a misdemeanor.

The federal government's anti-riot statute defines a riot as a public disturbance that involves either

(1) an act by a person who is part of a group of three or more that either harms people or property or presents a clear and present danger of such harm or

(2) a threat, matched with the immediately ability to execute the threat, by such a person and group.

Riot is a felony punishable up to five years for any person who has traveled in, or used telephony, television, radio, mail, or other facilities in interstate commerce, to incite, organize, participate, or aid and abet the riot.[31]

## Disturbing the Peace

Learning Objective: Define, describe, and apply the elements of disturbing the peace.

As mentioned, individuals may also commit crimes against the public order. Disturbing the peace is such a crime. This crime is also known as disorderly conduct, threat, excessive noise, and affray. In essence, any time the public order or tranquility is unreasonably interrupted by an individual, disturbance of the peace has occurred. States may have one law that encompasses all such acts or separate statutes for each.

lev radin/Shutterstock.com

Disturbances may occur in hundreds of forms. One may disturb the peace by making loud noises in a residential area at midnight, by attempting to cause fights with others, or by encouraging others to engage in similar conduct. Statutes often also prohibit indecent language and gestures.

As you have learned, the First Amendment protects all forms of expression. This protection prohibits government from making expression criminal. However, exceptions to the First Amendment have been created. Words that have a likelihood of causing a riot are such an exception. That is, even though the words are expression, they may be punished. The reason is obvious: riots lead to property damage, personal injuries, and sometimes death. As such, the interest of the government to control such behavior outweighs the First Amendment interest.

The **fighting words** doctrine is another exception. The Supreme Court has defined *fighting words* as those that inflict injury, tend to incite an immediate breach of the peace, or by their nature will cause a violent reaction by a person who hears them.[32] Laws that regulate speech that may be regulated, such as fighting words, must be drafted narrowly. If a law is drawn so broadly that both fighting words and legitimate speech are criminalized, it is unconstitutional and void. Although still applied in lower courts, Supreme Court precedent of recent years appeals to have greatly limited the doctrine, if not de facto overruled it. Today, to be criminalized, words must rise to the level of a true threat, which was previously discussed, or a speaker's words must be directed at, and are likely to produce, an imminent lawlessness. True threats were discussed in Chapter Four and speech that incites imminent lawlessness is discussed next.

The defendant in the *Witucki* case was convicted of disorderly conduct. The court found that his speech was unprotected because he used fighting words.

**fighting words**
Speech that is not protected by the First Amendment to the U.S. Constitution because it is likely to cause violence by the person to whom the words are spoken.

# Oyez

## City Of Little Falls v. Edwin George Witucki
### 295 N.W.2d 243 (Minn. 1980)

**Otis, Justice**

On December 11, 1978, a Morrison County Court jury found defendant guilty of disorderly conduct in violation of Little Falls, Minnesota, Ordinances. . . .

At approximately 11:00 P.M. on September 19, 1978, defendant Edwin George Witucki and a few of his friends entered the West Side Bar in Little Falls, Minnesota. Just outside the building defendant found a cat which he carried into the building and placed on the bar. Pursuant to defendant's request, one bartender served the cat some beef jerky and a shotglass of cream and served defendant a drink.

About five minutes later, the other bartender, Paula Erwin, told defendant to take the cat outside. He refused. She told him he was cut off from being served until the cat was removed. He responded, "I let you slip once too many times, I'm not going to let you slip again." Erwin, for the third time, told defendant to remove the cat. He responded by saying, "Hey, Butch, I don't have to take any of your crap." She then turned to return to the other end of the bar, and Witucki called her a "black-haired witch," a "cocksucker," and a "son-of-a-bitch."

When asked at trial about her reaction to the words, Erwin testified, "I didn't care for them very well. It scared me. There was nothing I could do about it. There were no guys around so I thought the best thing for me to do, because I was really mad at the time, was just to walk away from him." She also testified that calling the police or any sort of violent action on her part would not be wise or safe because he might wait for her outside after hours and because he was much larger than she and there were no men around to help her.

■ ■ ■

The question is, did defendant's words in the circumstances in which they were uttered constitute "those personally abusive epithets which, when addressed to the ordinary citizen, are as a matter of common knowledge, inherently likely to provoke violent reaction." . . .

In *In re S.L.J.* the appellant was a fourteen-year-old girl who yelled "fuck you pigs" at two police officers. . . . The court noted that although "no ordered society would condone the vulgar language" and although "her words were intended to, and did, arouse resentment in the officers, the constitution requires more before a person can be convicted for mere speech." The court held that where the words

(continued)

were spoken in retreat by a small teenage girl who was between fifteen and thirty feet from the two police officers sitting in their squad car, "there was no reasonable likelihood that [the words] would tend to incite an immediate breach of the peace or to provoke violent reaction by an ordinary, reasonable person.

In *Cohen v. California*, 403 U.S. 15, 91 S.Ct. 1780, 29 L. Ed. 2d 284 (1971), the defendant wore a jacket on which the words "Fuck the Draft" were plainly visible. The words were not directed against the person of any possibly offended person; they were directed against the draft.

The instant case is readily distinguishable from both *In re S.L.J.* and *Cohen v. California*. Unlike the defendant's language in *Cohen*, Witucki's language was directed at and was intended to be about a person, namely Erwin. The abusive language hurled by defendant at Erwin could readily be found by a jury to be inherently likely to incite violence. Defendant was not, as in *Cohen*, merely expressing a controversial political opinion in a vulgar way; he was directly insulting and intimidating an innocent person.

■   ■   ■

The fact that the words used by appellant are vulgar, offensive, and insulting, and that their use is condemned by an overwhelming majority of citizens does not make them punishable under the criminal statutes of this state unless they fall outside the protection afforded to speech by the First Amendment.

■   ■   ■

Defendant's speech in this case is not a "trifling and annoying instance of individual distasteful abuse of a privilege." He addressed such abusive, vulgar, insulting and obscene language toward the bartender that his language was properly found to be within the fighting words category of unprotected speech. . . . [Conviction affirmed.]

Several of the defendants in the Capitol insurrection cases were charged under a federal disorder statute.

(a) Whoever—

(1) knowingly enters or remains in any restricted building or grounds without lawful authority to do so;

(2) knowingly, and with intent to impede or disrupt the orderly conduct of Government business or official functions, engages in disorderly or disruptive conduct in, or within such proximity to, any restricted building or grounds when, or so that, such conduct, in fact, impedes or disrupts the orderly conduct of Government business or official functions;

(3) knowingly, and with the intent to impede or disrupt the orderly conduct of Government business or official functions, obstructs or impedes ingress or egress to or from any restricted building or grounds; or

(4) knowingly engages in any act of physical violence against any person or property in any restricted building or grounds;

(5) knowingly and willfully operates an unmanned aircraft system with the intent to knowingly and willfully direct or otherwise cause such unmanned aircraft system to enter or operate within or above a restricted building or grounds.

Another trespass and disorder prohibition, which applies specifically to the Capitol building and its grounds, was also used to prosecute many of the insurrectionists. The Violent Entry and Disorderly Conduct statute makes it a crime, among other acts, to willfully and knowingly

enter or remain on the floor of either House of Congress or in any cloakroom or lobby adjacent to that floor, in the Rayburn Room of the House of Representatives, or in the Marble Room of the Senate, unless authorized to do so pursuant to rules adopted, or an authorization given, by that House or

enter or remain in the gallery of either House of Congress in violation of rules governing admission to the gallery adopted by that House or pursuant to an authorization given by that House.[33]

The former crime is punished with as much as a year in prison and fine, except when committed with a dangerous weapon or significant bodily injury results. In those instances, the punishment is elevated to as much as ten years imprisonment. Conviction of the Capitol trespass statute is punished with as much as six months imprisonment and a fine.

## Inciting Lawlessness

Learning Objective: Define, describe, and apply the elements, and constitutional limits, of inciting lawlessness.

Whenever one person, acting independently, encourages another to commit an unlawful act or intends to cause a riot, the crimes of incitement of unlawful behavior or incitement of riot may be charged. Unlike riot, which requires a group, one person may commit this crime. Unlike disturbing the peace, it may be committed in a peaceful manner.

However, because the First Amendment applies, such statutes must be narrowly drawn. In fact, only speech that is intended, and is likely to, incite imminent lawless action may be regulated. This is known as the **Brandenburg Test**, named for the case where it was announced by the Supreme Court.[34] Under Brandenburg, speech may be regulated if it

1. intentionally directed at
2. inciting
3. imminent
4. lawless action
5. and it is likely to produce such action.

Hence, merely advocating unlawful conduct in the abstract is protected. Advocating future unlawful conduct is also protected, as it poses no imminent threat. Let's apply Brandenburg to two scenarios. In the first, Rebecca Rightman is the founder of A-Earth, a group that believes aliens from a distant planet inhabit the earth, taking the form of powerful people who have the colonization of the earth and the enslavement of humans as their goal. Rebecca is asked to speak at the local bookstore. A group of 11 people gather to hear her talk. None of the 11 attendees knew she was scheduled to speak. They were in the bookstore shopping for cooking, romance, and self-help books. During her presentation, Rebecca states that "We, and by we, I mean people, need to act now to save humanity. We must kill our leaders—our members of Congress and the president—and develop the technology to resist the alien armies when they arrive." Rebecca is arrested for incitement. While her statement may have been intended to incite lawless action, the context of where it was delivered, the audience, and their number of people in attendance, all weigh against the speech producing lawlessness.

The facts are the same in the second scenario, except that Rebecca is speaking in front the U.S. Capitol to 215 adherents of A-Earth. She knows that four of the attendees have been arrested for assaulting and threatening members of Congress, who they believed were aliens. Addressing the crowd, Rebecca states, "I have evidence that the alien invasion is imminent. We, and by we, I mean people, need to act now to save humanity. Tomorrow is too late. We must kill our leaders—our members of Congress and the president—and develop the technology to resist the alien armies when they arrive." As she speaks, the crowd grows increasingly restless, eventually repeatedly chanting "Kill them now. Save us all!" Rebecca is guilty of incitement because she intended to incite imminent, lawless action that is likely to occur, given who is in the audience, their reaction, the setting, and the content of her speech.

**Brandenburg Test**
An exception to free speech. Speech that is directed at causing imminent lawless action and is likely to cause such action may be regulated.

## Vagrancy and Panhandling

Learning Objective: Describe various ways vagrancy is criminalized and the constitutional limitations on these laws.

Vagrancy, as a criminal law issue, has received considerable attention. Most states and municipalities have statutes that forbid vagrancy. At Common Law, a *vagrant* was one who wandered from place to place with no means of support, except the charity of others. At one time, in early English law, vagrancy applied to disorderly persons, rogues (a dishonest wanderer), and vagabonds (a homeless person with no means of support).

Beginning in the 1880s, it was common in the United States for statutes to prohibit a wide range of behavior as vagrancy. These statutes were drafted broadly to give law enforcement officers considerable discretion in their enforcement. This discretion was used to control the "undesirables" of society. Many statutes made the status of being homeless, a gambler, and a drug addict a crime.

Today, states may not make personal status, such as drug addiction or alcoholism, a crime. The United States held that doing so violates the Eighth Amendment's prohibition of cruel and unusual punishment.[35] However, until 1972, people found undesirable by the police could be arrested under broadly worded vagrancy statutes for "wandering," or walking around a city, because this was an act, not a status. This situation ended in 1972 when the U.S. Supreme Court handed down *Papachristou v. City of Jacksonville,* 405 U.S. 156 (1972). The Court announced in that case that vagrancy statutes that prohibit walking around, frequenting liquor stores, being supported by one's wife, and similar behavior to be "too precarious for a rule of law" and violative of the Due Process and Cruel and Unusual Clauses of the Constitution.

The result of *Papachristou* has been more narrowly drawn vagrancy statutes. Today, such laws focus on more particularized behavior, and in many instances a mens rea element has been added. This addition prevents simple acts, such as walking at night, from being criminal. For example, a vagrancy law may prohibit "loitering or standing around with an intent to gamble," or "loitering or standing in a transportation facility [e.g., bus station] with the intent of soliciting charity."

In recent years, panhandling (begging) has been a problem in many cities. Panhandlers often choose to congregate in and near public transportation egresses and ingresses, because of the large number of people who use such facilities. Because panhandlers are sometimes aggressive and intimidating to patrons of such facilities, some jurisdictions have chosen to prohibit begging at public transportation sites.

As the number of homeless persons grows in the United States, so will the problems associated with vagrancy and panhandling. Examine statutes and ordinances that prohibit such activities with an awareness that they must be drawn carefully to avoid a First Amendment speech problem. Also be aware that other constitutional provisions may be implicated, such as the First Amendment's freedom of association and the Due Process and Equal Protection Clauses of the Fifth and Fourteenth Amendments.

## Weapons Crimes

Learning Objective: Describe the Second Amendment's limitation on the regulation of arms.

A discussion of the regulation of firearms properly begins with the Second Amendment to the U.S. Constitution, which reads:

A well regulated Militia, being necessary to the security of a free State, the right of the people to keep and bear Arms, shall not be infringed.

One of the most controversial Second Amendment issues is whether it has one clause or two independent clauses. If only one, the right to bear arms is connected to participation in a "well regulated militia." If the Amendment is read to have two independent clauses, an individual's right to bear arms is not dependent on serving in a militia.

For most of history, the Militia Clause of the Amendment was read as prefatory and Bear Arms Clause as operative, meaning the two were connected. For example, in the 1939 Supreme Court case, *United States v. Miller*,[36] a defendant who had been charged under a federal law prohibiting possession of short-barreled shotguns and rifles challenged the law as violating his Second Amendment right to possess a firearm. The Court stated:

> The Constitution as originally adopted granted to the Congress power — "To provide for calling forth the Militia to execute the Laws of the Union, suppress Insurrections and repel Invasions; To provide for organizing, arming, and disciplining, the Militia, and for governing such Part of them as may be employed in the Service of the United States, reserving to the States respectively, the Appointment of the Officers, and the Authority of training the Militia according to the discipline prescribed by Congress." U.S.C.A. Const. art. § 8. With obvious purpose to assure the continuation and render possible the effectiveness of such forces the declaration and guarantee of the Second Amendment were made. It must be interpreted and applied with that end in view.
>
> The Militia, which the States were expected to maintain and train, is different than Troops, which the States were forbidden to keep without the consent of Congress. The sentiment of the time strongly disfavored standing armies; the common view was that adequate defense of country and laws could be secured through the Militia—full-time civilians; part-time soldiers.
>
> Discussions of Militia occurred during the Constitutional Convention and evidence of the significance of Militias appear in the history and legislation of Colonies and States and the writings of the Framers. These show plainly enough that the Militia was to be comprised of all males physically capable of acting in concert for the common defense. 'A body of citizens enrolled for military discipline' that when called for service, were expected to appear bearing arms supplied by themselves and of the kind in common use at the time.

The Supreme Court affirmed this interpretation of the Second Amendment in the 1980 case *United States v. Lewis*.[37] The Court did not pass on the question if the Second Amendment establishes an individual right, as opposed to connecting the right to arms to the militia right, again until 2008 when it invalidated a Washington, D.C., ordinance forbidding the possession of handguns in the home in *District of Columbia v. Heller*. The Court explicitly found an independent, individual right to possess arms under the Second Amendment for the first time.

Note that the Court expressly acknowledged several limitations on the right to bear arms that may be imposed. The first concerns weapon type. The Second Amendment doesn't protect the right to bear firearms; it protects arms. This includes arms in common use by law-abiding people, such as firearms and knives. "Unusual" weapons aren't protected. The line between common and unusual is not well drawn. A grenade launcher is unusual. Whether a knife with a six-inch blade or a gun that can fire one round per second is common

# Oyez

## District Of Columbia v. Heller
### 554 U.S. 570 (2008)

**Justice Scalia delivered the opinion of the Court.**

We consider whether a District of Columbia prohibition on the possession of usable handguns in the home violates the Second Amendment to the Constitution.

The District of Columbia generally prohibits the possession of handguns. It is a crime to carry an unregistered firearm, and the registration of handguns is prohibited. Wholly apart from that prohibition, no person may carry a handgun without a license, but the chief of police may issue licenses for 1-year periods. District of Columbia law also requires residents to keep their lawfully owned firearms, such as registered long guns, "unloaded and dissembled or bound by a trigger lock or similar device" unless they are located in a place of business or are being used for lawful recreational activities. . . .

Respondent Dick Heller is a D. C. special police officer authorized to carry a handgun while on duty at the Federal Judicial Center. He applied for a registration certificate for a handgun that he wished to keep at home, but the District refused. . . .

The Second Amendment provides: "A well regulated Militia, being necessary to the security of a free State, the right of the people to keep and bear Arms, shall not be infringed." In interpreting this text, we are guided by the principle that "[t]he Constitution was written to be understood by the voters; its words and phrases were used in their normal and ordinary as distinguished from technical meaning." Normal meaning may of course include an idiomatic meaning, but it excludes secret or technical meanings that would not have been known to ordinary citizens in the founding generation.

The two sides in this case have set out very different interpretations of the Amendment. Petitioners and today's dissenting Justices believe that it protects only the right to possess and carry a firearm in connection with militia service. Respondent argues that it protects an individual right to possess a firearm unconnected with service in a militia, and to use that arm for traditionally lawful purposes, such as self-defense within the home. . . .

The Second Amendment is naturally divided into two parts: its prefatory clause and its operative clause. The former does not limit the latter grammatically, but rather announces a purpose. The Amendment could be rephrased, "Because a well regulated Militia is necessary to the security of a free State, the right of the people to keep and bear Arms shall not be infringed." . . . Although this structure of the Second Amendment is unique in our Constitution, other legal documents of the founding era, particularly individual-rights provisions of state constitutions, commonly included a prefatory statement of purpose. . . .

1. Operative Clause.

    a. "Right of the People." The first salient feature of the operative clause is that it codifies a "right of the people." The unamended Constitution and the Bill of Rights use the phrase "right of the people" two other times, in the First Amendment's Assembly-and-Petition Clause and in the Fourth Amendment's Search-and-Seizure Clause. The Ninth Amendment uses very similar terminology ("The enumeration in the Constitution, of certain rights, shall not be construed to deny or disparage others retained by the people"). All three of these instances unambiguously refer to individual rights, not "collective" rights, or rights that may be exercised only through participation in some corporate body.

    Three provisions of the Constitution refer to "the people" in a context other than "rights"—the famous preamble ("We the people"), §2 of Article I (providing that "the people" will choose members of the House), and the Tenth Amendment (providing that those powers not given the Federal Government remain with "the States" or "the people"). Those provisions arguably refer to "the people" acting collectively—but they deal with the exercise or reservation of powers, not rights. Nowhere else in the Constitution does a "right" attributed to "the people" refer to anything other than an individual right.

    What is more, in all six other provisions of the Constitution that mention "the people," the term unambiguously refers to all members of the political community, not an unspecified subset. . . .

    This contrasts markedly with the phrase "the militia" in the prefatory clause. As we will describe below, the "militia" in colonial America consisted of a subset of "the people"—those who were male, able bodied, and within a certain age range. Reading the Second Amendment as protecting only the right to "keep and bear Arms" in an organized militia therefore fits poorly with the operative clause's description of the holder of that right as "the people."

    We start therefore with a strong presumption that the Second Amendment right is exercised individually and belongs to all Americans.

    b. "Keep and bear Arms." We move now from the holder of the right—"the people"—to the substance of the right: "to keep and bear Arms."

    Before addressing the verbs "keep" and "bear," we interpret their object: "Arms." . . .

    Some have made the argument, bordering on the frivolous, that only those arms in existence in the 18th century are protected by the Second Amendment. We do not interpret constitutional rights that way. Just as the First Amendment protects modern forms of communications, *e.g., Reno* v. *American Civil Liberties Union*, 521 U. S. 844, 849 (1997), and the Fourth Amendment applies to modern forms of search, *e.g., Kyllo v. United States*, 533 U. S. 27, 35–36 (2001), the Second Amendment extends, prima facie, to all instruments that constitute bearable arms, even those that were not in existence at the time of the founding.

We turn to the phrases "keep arms" and "bear arms." Johnson defined "keep" as, most relevantly, "[t]o retain; not to lose," and "[t]o have in custody." Johnson 1095. Webster defined it as "[t]o hold; to retain in one's power or possession." No party has apprised us of an idiomatic meaning of "keep Arms." Thus, the most natural reading of "keep Arms" in the Second Amendment is to "have weapons." . . .

At the time of the founding, as now, to "bear" meant to "carry." . . .

c. Meaning of the Operative Clause. Putting all of these textual elements together, we find that they guarantee the individual right to possess and carry weapons in case of confrontation. This meaning is strongly confirmed by the historical background of the Second Amendment. We look to this because it has always been widely understood that the Second Amendment, like the First and Fourth Amendments, codified a *pre-existing* right. The very text of the Second Amendment implicitly recognizes the pre-existence of the right and declares only that it "shall not be infringed." . . .

There seems to us no doubt, on the basis of both text and history, that the Second Amendment conferred an individual right to keep and bear arms. Of course the right was not unlimited, just as the First Amendment's right of free speech was not, see, *e.g., United States* v. *Williams*, 553 U. S. ___ (2008). Thus, we do not read the Second Amendment to protect the right of citizens to carry arms for *any sort* of confrontation, just as we do not read the First Amendment to protect the right of citizens to speak for *any purpose*. Before turning to limitations upon the individual right, however, we must determine whether the prefatory clause of the Second Amendment comports with our interpretation of the operative clause.

2. Prefatory Clause.

The prefatory clause reads: "A well regulated Militia, being necessary to the security of a free State . . . ."

a. "Well-Regulated Militia." In *United States* v. *Miller*, 307 U. S. 174, 179 (1939), we explained that "the Militia comprised all males physically capable of acting in concert for the common defense." That definition comports with founding-era sources.

Petitioners take a seemingly narrower view of the militia, stating that "[m]ilitias are the state- and congressionally-regulated military forces described in the Militia Clauses (art. I, §8, cls. 15–16)." Although we agree with petitioners' interpretive assumption that "militia" means the same thing in Article I and the Second Amendment, we believe that petitioners identify the wrong thing, namely, the organized militia. Unlike armies and navies, which Congress is given the power to create ("to raise . . . Armies"; "to provide . . . a Navy," Art. I, §8, cls. 12–13), the militia is assumed by Article I already to be *in existence*. Congress is given the power to "provide for calling forth the militia," §8, cl. 15; and the power not to create, but to "organiz[e]" it—and not to organize "a" militia, which is what one would expect if the militia were to be a federal creation, but to organize "the" militia, connoting a body already in existence. This is fully consistent with the ordinary definition of the militia as all able-bodied men. From that pool, Congress has plenary power to organize the units that will make up an effective fighting force. That is what Congress did in the first militia Act, which specified that "each and every free able-bodied white male citizen of the respective states, resident therein, who is or shall be of the age of eighteen years, and under the age of forty-five years (except as is herein after excepted) shall severally and respectively be enrolled in the militia." Act of May 8, 1792, 1 Stat. 271. To be sure, Congress need not conscript every able-bodied man into the militia, because nothing in Article I suggests that in exercising its power to organize, discipline, and arm the militia, Congress must focus upon the entire body. Although the militia consists of all able-bodied men, the federally organized militia may consist of a subset of them.

Finally, the adjective "well-regulated" implies nothing more than the imposition of proper discipline and training. . . .

b. "Security of a Free State." The phrase "security of a free state" meant "security of a free polity," not security of each of the several States as the dissent [argues]. . . .

3. Relationship between Prefatory Clause and Operative Clause

We reach the question, then: Does the preface fit with an operative clause that creates an individual right to keep and bear arms? It fits perfectly, once one knows the history that the founding generation knew and that we have described above. That history showed that the way tyrants had eliminated a militia consisting of all the able-bodied men was not by banning the militia but simply by taking away the people's arms, enabling a select militia or standing army to suppress political opponents. This is what had occurred in England that prompted codification of the right to have arms in the English Bill of Rights. . . .

It is therefore entirely sensible that the Second Amendment's prefatory clause announces the purpose for which the right was codified: to prevent elimination of the militia. The prefatory clause does not suggest that preserving the militia was the only reason Americans valued the ancient right; most undoubtedly thought it even more important for self-defense and hunting. But the threat that the new Federal Government would destroy the citizens' militia by taking away their arms was the reason that right—unlike some other English rights—was codified in a written Constitution. . . .

(continued)

Our interpretation is confirmed by analogous arms-bearing rights in state constitutions that preceded and immediately followed adoption of the Second Amendment. . . .

Like most rights, the right secured by the Second Amendment is not unlimited. From Blackstone through the 19th-century cases, commentators and courts routinely explained that the right was not a right to keep and carry any weapon whatsoever in any manner whatsoever and for whatever purpose. For example, the majority of the 19th-century courts to consider the question held that prohibitions on carrying concealed weapons were lawful under the Second Amendment or state analogues. Although we do not undertake an exhaustive historical analysis today of the full scope of the Second Amendment, nothing in our opinion should be taken to cast doubt on longstanding prohibitions on the possession of firearms by felons and the mentally ill, or laws forbidding the carrying of firearms in sensitive places such as schools and government buildings, or laws imposing conditions and qualifications on the commercial sale of arms.

We also recognize another important limitation on the right to keep and carry arms. *Miller* said, as we have explained, that the sorts of weapons protected were those "in common use at the time." 307 U. S., at 179. We think that limitation is fairly supported by the historical tradition of prohibiting the carrying of "dangerous and unusual weapons." . . .

We turn finally to the law at issue here. As we have said, the law totally bans handgun possession in the home. It also requires that any lawful firearm in the home be disassembled or bound by a trigger lock at all times, rendering it inoperable.

In sum, we hold that the District's ban on handgun possession in the home violates the Second Amendment, as does its prohibition against rendering any lawful firearm in the home operable for the purpose of immediate self-defense. Assuming that Heller is not disqualified from the exercise of Second Amendment rights, the District must permit him to register his handgun and must issue him a license to carry it in the home. . . .

We are aware of the problem of handgun violence in this country, and we take seriously the concerns raised by the many *amici* who believe that prohibition of handgun ownership is a solution. The Constitution leaves the District of Columbia a variety of tools for combating that problem, including some measures regulating handguns. But the enshrinement of constitutional rights necessarily takes certain policy choices off the table. These include the absolute prohibition of handguns held and used for self-defense in the home. Undoubtedly some think that the Second Amendment is outmoded in a society where our standing army is the pride of our Nation, where well-trained police forces provide personal security, and where gun violence is a serious problem. That is perhaps debatable, but what is not debatable is that it is not the role of this Court to pronounce the Second Amendment extinct.

[The vote of the Court was 5-4. Two vigorous dissents were filed. Find and read them if you are interested in a different interpretation of the Second Amendment.]

or unusual is not clear, and the U.S. Courts of Appeals are not in agreement. The courts are also split on the appropriate standard of review to apply to arms restrictions, strict scrutiny or substantial relationship.[38] Oddly, at least one court has found that a small kitchen paring knife is not protected but larger, more dangerous knives are protected under the theory that the paring knife didn't advance the purposes of the State Constitution's protection of arms, which is to defend oneself or the State.[39]

Other limitations mentioned by Justice Scalia include sensitive location bans, such as in and around schools and government buildings, prohibiting certain classes of people from buying and possessing firearms, such as the mentally ill and felons, and reasonable commercial regulations. Presumably, registration, taxing, and background checks fall into the latter category.

Washington, D.C., is federal territory. As such, *Heller* did not address whether the Second Amendment's right to possess firearms applies against the states. Indeed, several cases from the late 1800s stood for the principle that the Second Amendment, whatever its meaning, only limited federal authority. The Supreme Court accepted *certiorari* in a case involving state regulation of arms only a year after *Heller*. In *McDonald v. Chicago*,[40] the Court incorporated Heller's individual right to possess a firearm.

## Possession, Sale, and Transfer Laws

*McDonald* and *Heller* apply to possession of handguns in the home. There is nothing in those decisions to limit the authority of government to require the registration of firearms, background checks prior to firearms purchases, or to more thoroughly regulate larger and more dangerous firearms, or the possession of any firearm outside of the home. One of the most common forms of weapons regulation is possession. Both federal and state laws prohibit a variety of possession-related offenses. These include improper possession of a weapon that is otherwise permitted (e.g., concealed possession); possession of altogether prohibited weapons (e.g., machine guns); and possession by certain classes of persons (e.g., possession by ex-felons, aliens, fugitives, mental incompetents, individuals who were dishonorably discharged from the military, those under stalking-related court orders, and individuals convicted of misdemeanor domestic violence). The possession of firearms is also prohibited in certain areas designated by statute. Near schools, in public buildings, in airports, in national and state parks, and on airplanes are examples.

One of the most significant federal firearms statutes is the National Firearms Act.[41] Enacted in reaction to the organized crime problem of the 1930s, this law prohibited the sale and possession of automatic weapons (machine guns). Another important federal law is the Gun Control Act of 1968. Among its many provisions are a prohibition of mail order guns and the prohibition of the possession, transfer, or receipt of firearms by felons, aliens, and certain other persons. Many of the limitations of the Gun Control Act were repealed or reduced in the Firearm Owners Protection Act of 1986,[42] such as lifting the ban on the interstate sales of long guns and the use of the U.S. Post Office mail to ship ammunition.

The federal Brady Handgun Violence Prevention Act of 1993—named for President Ronald Reagan's White House Press Secretary James Brady, who was shot during an attempted assassination of the president—requires all federally licensed gun dealers to conduct background checks of firearms purchasers to ensure that purchasers do not fall into one of the categories of ineligible buyers under the Gun Control Act of 1968. Records checks are now being implemented through the National Instant Background Check System (NICS). Another federal statute, the Violent Crime Control and Law Enforcement Act of 1994, prohibits the sale of semiautomatic weapons and large ammunition magazines. Additionally, the Bureau of Alcohol, Tobacco, Firearms and Explosives, the federal agency charged with enforcing federal gun laws, has promulgated a large set of regulations interpreting and further regulating firearms.

## Firearms Use Laws

Many jurisdictions forbid the discharge of firearms in urban areas, absent good cause. Arizona's unlawful discharge statute (A.R.S. § 13-3107) reads:

(A) A person who with criminal negligence discharges a firearm within or into the limits of any municipality is guilty of a class 6 felony. . . .

(C) This section does not apply if the firearm is discharged:

(1) As allowed pursuant to the provisions of Chapter 4 of this title.

(2) On a properly supervised range.

(3) In an area recommended as a hunting area by the Arizona game and fish department, approved and posted as required by the chief of police, but any such area may be closed when deemed unsafe by the chief of police or the director of the game and fish department.

(4) For the control of nuisance wildlife by permit from the Arizona game and fish department or the U.S. fish and wildlife service.

(5) By special permit of the chief of police of the municipality.

(6) As required by an animal control officer in the performance of duties as specified in section 9-499.04.

(7) Using blanks.

(8) More than one mile from any occupied structure as defined in section 13-3101.

(9) In self-defense or defense of another person against an animal attack if a reasonable person would believe that deadly physical force against the animal is immediately necessary and reasonable under the circumstances to protect oneself or the other person.

Other law forbids the use of certain weapons for hunting and fishing. For example, shotguns may not be permitted in the hunting of certain game. Some statues prohibit "aiming," "pointing," and otherwise threatening people with firearms.

The use of a weapon in the commission of a crime is sometimes a separate crime from the underlying offense. Nearly all jurisdictions require or permit enhancement of sentences for crimes committed while in possession of a firearm.

## Registration and Licensing

In addition to background checks, many states require guns to be registered. In some instances, licenses must be obtained to carry or use weapons.

The National Firearms Act[43] requires national registration of all firearms manufactured or transferred in the United States, and it prohibits the sale of automatic weapons (machine guns).

## Explosive and Incendiary Weapons

In May 2020, two attorneys, Colinford Mattis and Urooj Rahman, allegedly constructed and threw a homemade bomb, known as Molotov Cocktail, into a police car in New York City.[44] The crimes occurred during a Black Lives Matter protest of the killing of an African American man, George Floyd, by police in Minneapolis, Minnesota. The protest, which turned violent, resulted in about two hundred arrests. But Mattis and Rahman, along with a third defendant charged with using an incendiary device, Samantha Shader, were facing the most serious charges.

Federal and state laws criminalize the use of explosives and other incendiaries to cause harm. Mattis and Urooj were charged with several related crimes. One, for example, forbids an individual from maliciously damaging or destroying, or attempting to damage or destroy, by means of fire or an explosive property owned, in whole or part, rented, or leased by either the federal government or an agency that receives funding from the federal government.[45] The federal government asserted jurisdiction over the acts because the New York City Police Department receives financial support from the United States. Because the alleged acts involve a risk of life, the penalties for the crime are enhanced. When all of the charges are combined, the two defendants are facing 30 years to life imprisonment.

Courtesy of U.S. Attorney's Office, Eastern District of New York.

Urooj Rahman on the night she is alleged to have thrown a molotov cocktail into a police car.

# Drug and Alcohol Crimes

Learning Objective: Define, describe, and apply the elements of drug and alcohol use and possession crimes.

Crimes that involve the use of narcotics and alcohol may be classified in many ways. In one sense, such activity offends many people in society and appears to be an offense against the public morality. Whenever a pimp uses a young woman's drug addiction to induce her to become involved in prostitution, there is a crime against an individual. In the states, drug and alcohol crimes are universally regulated, although definitions and punishments vary considerably.

Drug and alcohol crimes are included in this section because of their impact on the order of society. Alcohol-related driving accidents are the cause of many fatalities. Drug addiction often is the cause of other crimes, such as theft, assaults, and prostitution. Police report that a number of domestic problems are caused by alcohol and drugs and that much of the violence directed toward law enforcement officers is drug related. Large cities, such as Detroit and Washington, D.C., have experienced a virtual drug boom, which has led to increased assaults, batteries, and drug-related homicides. Many addicts, desperate for a "fix," steal for drug money.

Drug and alcohol use are also expensive. Corporate America has recently awakened to the expenses associated with employee drug use. Employees who use drugs have high absenteeism and low productivity. Decreased performance caused by drug use can be costly, in both human and dollar terms. This is true especially in positions that require great concentration or pose risks to others, such as that of commercial pilots. In addition to business expenses, the high cost of rehabilitation can disable a family financially, and the price of drug-abuse detection and prosecution is high.

## Alcohol Crimes

Let it not be mistaken, alcohol is a drug. However, the law treats alcohol differently than it does other drugs. Alcohol may be legally possessed, consumed, and sold, subject only to a few restrictions. Narcotics, on the other hand, are significantly restricted. Their sale, possession, and consumption are limited to specific instances, such as for medical use. The federal government, as well as every state, has statutes that spell out what drugs are regulated.

There are many alcohol-related crimes. Public drunkenness laws make it criminal for a person to be intoxicated in a public place. This crime is a minor misdemeanor and rarely prosecuted, as many law enforcement agencies have a policy of allowing such persons to "sleep it off" and then releasing them.

All states have a minimum age requirement for the sale or consumption of alcohol. Those below the minimum age are minors. Any minor who purchases or consumes alcohol is violating the law. Additionally, any adult who knowingly provides alcohol to a minor is also guilty of a crime, commonly known as contributing to the delinquency of a minor.

Merchants holding liquor licenses may be subject to criminal penalties for not complying with liquor laws, such as selling alcohol on holidays, Sundays, or election day, as well as for selling alcohol to minors. A merchant who violates liquor laws may also suffer the civil penalty of revocation of liquor license.

Alcohol and automobiles have proven to be a deadly and expensive combination. All states have laws that criminalize driving while under the influence of alcohol or drugs. Driving while under the influence of alcohol or drugs, driving while intoxicated, and driving with an unlawful blood-alcohol level are the names of these crimes.

These statutes are generally of two genres. One type of law generally prohibits the operation of a motor vehicle while under the influence of any drug, including alcohol. To prove this charge, the quantity of the drug or alcohol in the defendant's system is not at issue; the defendant's ability to operate the vehicle safely is. In such cases, field sobriety tests are often required of the suspect. These are tests that the suspect usually performs at the location where the police made the stop. Coordination, spatial relations, and other driving-related skills are tested by field sobriety tests.

The second type of law prohibits driving a motor vehicle any time a person's blood-alcohol level is above a stated amount. The states vary in the quantity required, although 8 hundredths of a percent (0.08) and 10 hundredths of a percent (0.10) are common. The effect of these laws is that an irrebuttable presumption is created. The law presumes that anyone with the stated blood-alcohol level or above cannot safely operate a motor vehicle. Under such statutes, evidence that a person can safely operate a motor vehicle with a blood-alcohol level greater than the maximum allowed is not permitted.

In recent years, drunk driving has received considerable public and legislative attention. The result has been stricter laws and greater punishment for offenders. The once-common police practice of driving drunk drivers home is virtually nonexistent today.

First offenses are usually misdemeanors. Second or third offenses are felonies. In many jurisdictions, there has been a move toward alcohol treatment rather than incarceration. This often involves house arrest, alcohol treatment, and defensive driving education. Also, while in these programs, convicted persons are commonly required to submit to periodic blood or urine screening.

For first-time offenders, these programs have many advantages over prison. First, the focus is on curing the alcohol problem. If successful, the possibility of repetition is eliminated. Second, convicted persons are often permitted to continue to work and maintain family relationships. Finally, the cost of administration of alcohol programs is lower than the cost of incarceration. The value of such programs for repeat offenders is questionable, and in many jurisdictions jail time is required as early as a second conviction.

## Drug Crimes

Unlike possession of alcohol, possession of other drugs is a crime. Every state and the federal government have enacted some variation of the Uniform Controlled Substance Act, a model act (similar to the MPC) drafted by the Commissioners on Uniform Laws. These statutes establish schedules of drugs that categorize drugs based on their danger, potential for abuse, and medical benefits. These factors then determine a drug's allowed usage. For example, one schedule exists for drugs that may not be used under any condition, and another schedule permits use for medical and research purposes only. There are three basic drug crimes: possession, sales/distribution, and use.

Possession of prohibited drugs is a crime. Of course, actual possession is sufficient actus reus, but some jurisdictions also make constructive possession criminal. Constructive possession permits conviction of those people who exercise dominion and control over property where the illegal drug is located, even though the person has no "actual physical possession" of the prohibited narcotic. However, the MPC[46] and most jurisdictions require knowledge that the drug was present before culpability is imposed. As such, if a guest stays in Robert's home, Robert is not criminally liable for any drugs the guest has stowed away, unless Robert is aware of their presence. Once Robert becomes aware, he must see that the drugs are removed within a reasonable time or risk a possession charge.

First-time conviction of possession, if the quantity is small, is a misdemeanor and normally results in probation. In many states, if a person pleads guilty, submits to a term of probation, and successfully completes the probation, then no adjudication of guilt is entered; so, no record of conviction exists. Probation terms usually include drug counseling, periodic drug testing, and no other arrests during the period. This type of procedure is known as *deferred sentencing or suspended imposition of sentence*. See Chapter 16 for a discussion of sentencing.

The sale or distribution of prohibited drugs is the second primary drug offense. Generally, it is punished more severely than possession. Not only are sales

## Sidebar

### Drug Courts

Drug cases began to clog court dockets in the 1980s. As a result, legislators, judges, and others searched for alternatives to deal with drug offenders. One alternative that has proven to be popular is the drug court. The first drug court opened in Miami, Florida, in 1989. By 1997, there were 161 programs in existence in 38 states, the District of Columbia, and Puerto Rico. Forty percent of those courts were in Florida and California. Additionally, nearly every state without a drug court was in the process of developing one.

As the name implies, the drug court hears only drug cases. In most drug courts, only non-violent drug offenders are eligible for admission. The time of admission varies between programs. In some courts, the offender is deferred into the program. If the offender successfully completes the program, no conviction results. In others, offenders are channeled into the program after a plea of guilty or postconviction.

The drug court specializes in the treatment and monitoring of drug offenders. All programs have a treatment component, although the form of treatment varies significantly among programs. In addition, drug court programs are characterized by intensive monitoring. Participants are required to submit to daily or weekly drug screenings, and they are required to frequently appear in court. Many programs also use a system of "graduated sanctions" to punish participants who fail to meet program requirements.

The data concerning the success of drug programs are not clear. Unfortunately, one study indicates that 48% of the participants do not successfully complete their programs. It is too early to know the degree to which these programs decrease recidivism as compared to processing individuals through other courts, but at least one researcher has found that graduated sanctions programs may be successful in this regard.

*Sources:* Drug Courts: Overview of Growth, Characteristics, and Results Report of the General Accounting Office (GAO/GGD 97–106), July 31, 1997; and Adele Harrell, U.S. Department of Justice, National Institute of Justice (1998).

---

prohibited, but any "delivery" or "distribution" of drugs is also illegal. "Possession with an intent to deliver or sell" is similar to simple possession, except a mens rea of intending to sell must be proven. Possession with an intent to sell or deliver is punished more severely than possession; often, such possession is punished equally with actual sale or delivery.

The quantity of the drug involved affects the level of punishment for both possession and sale/distribution offenses. Other factors, such as selling to minors, may aggravate the sentence.

Unauthorized use of a controlled substance is also a crime. The mens rea is knowing use. So, if a person takes a pill containing a controlled substance that someone—who represented it to be an aspirin—gives him or her, there is no crime. Of course, the taking must be voluntary. If a person is forced down and injected with an illegal drug, he or she has committed no crime.

Recall from the earlier discussion of actus reus that addiction to controlled substances may not be made criminal. The U.S. Supreme Court has held that criminalizing a person's status as an addict is cruel and unusual punishment, as prohibited by the Eighth Amendment to the U.S. Constitution.[47] It is permitted, however, to punish a person for the act of taking a controlled substance.

## RICO and CCE

You have already learned that the Racketeer Influenced and Corrupt Organizations Act (RICO) was enacted to fight organized crime in all its forms. Another federal statute, Continuing Criminal Enterprise (CCE),[48] was enacted specifically to combat drug trafficking. The statute is aimed at prosecuting the people at the top of the drug-dealing and smuggling pyramid, and, accordingly, it has become known as the "Drug Kingpin statute."

A person engages in a criminal enterprise if (1) he/she is an administrator, organizer, or other leader (2) of a group of five or more people (3) who are involved in a series of drug violations. A *series* of violations means three or more drug convictions.[49]

Conviction of CCE results in stern punishment. A general violation receives 20 years to life in prison. Second convictions carry 30 years to life. If a person is determined to be a "principal leader," the amount of drugs involved was enormous, or the enterprise made $10 million or more in one year from drugs, then life imprisonment is mandatory. Fines may also be imposed. Also, the statute provides for imprisonment or death when murder results from the enterprise.[50]

Finally, the Comprehensive Forfeiture Act of 1984[51] applies to both RICO and CCE violations. This statute permits the government to seize property and money that is used in the commission of the crimes and that is a product of the crimes. So, if a drug dealer uses a boat to smuggle drugs, the boat can be seized, even though it may have been purchased with "honest" money. Any items acquired with drug money may be seized, as can bank accounts and trusts.

## Possession of Drug Paraphernalia

Another tool in the government's arsenal against drug use are laws that prohibit the sale, use, and possession of drug paraphernalia. These laws are often aimed at retailers who sell the devices that are used to take drugs. Needles, roach clips, and specialized pipes are examples of the type of paraphernalia that are proscribed.

These laws have been challenged on many fronts. One challenge asserts that such laws are vague because they do not adequately describe what is proscribed. In addition, it has been asserted that these laws are overly broad because they include devices that may be used for both legitimate and illegal purposes.[52] These issues were considered by the U.S. Supreme Court in the 1994 case *Posters 'N' Things, Ltd. v. United States*.[53] In this case, the Court held that a law proscribing items "primarily intended" or "designed for" drug use was neither too vague nor overly broad and, accordingly, found it constitutional.

# Respect, Honor, and Valor

Learning Objective: Describe how the First Amendment limits the authority of governments to protect the dignity and honor of objects and recognitions.

Governments enact laws intended to preserve the dignity and promote respect for sacred objects and institutions. But America is a free Republic. The authority of a government to prevent or punish speech is very limited. A government may not impose a belief upon a person, nor may it punish expressions that are unpopular or offensive. These principles create guardrails on how far a government can go to preserve the dignity of objects and ideas. For example, the Supreme Court invalidated laws that made it a crime to desecrate the flag of the United States. Of course, the state has the authority, if the not the duty, to protect private property. Stealing and burning a neighbor's flag can be prosecuted under ordinary criminal laws. Specifically, in this scenario, the neighbor committed trespass on land, larceny, and possibly, illegal burning. But a state or federal law that punishes a person for disrespecting or desecrating the flag violates the First Amendment. In short, government may not impose a belief upon a person, nor may it punish expressions it disfavors. But it may enforce viewpoint neutral laws to otherwise protected speech. If the larceny statute applies to the theft of all property, the neighbor isn't privileged to steal his neighbor's flag because he intends to burn it as a form of political expression. You will learn more about free speech and criminal law in Chapter 9.

The federal and state governments have legislation to protect the dignity and honor of more than flags. Many states and the federal government, for example, protect the valor of members of the military. These laws commonly forbid "stolen valor," or the false claims of military awards and honors. Your next Oyez features a valor thief's claim that he had a free speech right to lie about having earned military honors.

## Oyez

### United States v. Alvarez
### 567 U.S. 709 (2012)

**Justice Kennedy delivered the opinion of the Court.**

Lying was his habit. Xavier Alvarez, the respondent here, lied when he said that he played hockey for the Detroit Red Wings and that he once married a starlet from Mexico. But when he lied in announcing he held the Congressional Medal of Honor, respondent ventured onto new ground; for that lie violates a federal criminal statute, the Stolen Valor Act of 2005. 18 U. S. C. §704.

In 2007, respondent attended his first public meeting as a board member of the Three Valley Water District Board. The board is a governmental entity with headquarters in Claremont, California. He introduced himself as follows: "I'm a retired marine of 25 years. I retired in the year 2001. Back in 1987, I was awarded the Congressional Medal of Honor. I got wounded many times by the same guy." None of this was true. For all the record shows, respondent's statements were but a pathetic attempt to gain respect that eluded him. The statements do not seem to have been made to secure employment or financial benefits or admission to privileges reserved for those who had earned the Medal.

Respondent was indicted under the Stolen Valor Act for lying about the Congressional Medal of Honor at the meeting. . . .

It is right and proper that Congress, over a century ago, established an award so the Nation can hold in its highest respect and esteem those who, in the course of carrying out the "supreme and noble duty of contributing to the defense of the rights and honor of the nation," have acted with extraordinary honor. And it should be uncontested that this is a legitimate Government objective, indeed a most valued national aspiration and purpose. This does not end the inquiry, however. Fundamental constitutional principles require that laws enacted to honor the brave must be consistent with the precepts of the Constitution for which they fought.

The Government contends the criminal prohibition is a proper means to further its purpose in creating and awarding the Medal. When content-based speech regulation is in question, however, exacting scrutiny is required. Statutes suppressing or restricting speech must be judged by the sometimes inconvenient principles of the First Amendment. By this measure, the statutory provisions under which respondent was convicted must be held invalid, and his conviction must be set aside. . . .

"[A]s a general matter, the First Amendment means that government has no power to restrict expression because of its message, its ideas, its subject matter, or its content." As a result, the Constitution "demands that content-based restrictions on speech be presumed invalid . . . and that the Government bear the burden of showing their constitutionality."

In light of the substantial and expansive threats to free expression posed by content-based restrictions, this Court has rejected as "startling and dangerous" a "free-floating test for First Amendment coverage . . . [based on] an ad hoc balancing of relative social costs and benefits." Instead, content-based restrictions on speech have been permitted, as a general matter, only when confined to the few " 'historic and traditional categories [of expression] long familiar to the bar.'" Among these categories are advocacy intended, and likely, to incite imminent lawless action, obscenity, defamation, speech integral to criminal conduct, so-called "fighting words," child pornography, fraud, true threats, and speech presenting some grave and imminent threat the government has the power to prevent, although a restriction under the last category is most difficult to sustain.

Absent from those few categories where the law allows content-based regulation of speech is any general exception to the First Amendment for false statements. This comports with the common understanding that some false statements are inevitable if there is to be an open and vigorous expression of views in public and private conversation, expression the First Amendment seeks to guarantee. . . .

The Court has never endorsed the categorical rule the Government advances: that false statements receive no First Amendment protection. Our prior decisions have not confronted a measure, like the Stolen Valor Act, that targets falsity and nothing more. . . .

[The Court distinguished the Stolen Valor Act from lying to government officials and perjury, which cause serious harm.]

The Act by its plain terms applies to a false statement made at any time, in any place, to any person. . . .

Permitting the government to decree this speech to be a criminal offense, whether shouted from the rooftops or made in a barely audible whisper, would endorse government authority to compile a list of subjects about which false statements are punishable. That governmental power has no clear limiting principle. Our constitutional tradition stands against the idea that we need Oceania's Ministry of Truth. See G. Orwell, Nineteen Eighty-Four (1949) (Centennial ed. 2003). Were this law to be sustained, there could be an endless list of subjects the National Government or the States could single out. . . .

The Government is correct when it states military medals "serve the important public function of recognizing and expressing gratitude for acts of heroism and sacrifice in military service," and also " 'foste[r] morale, mission accomplishment and esprit de corps' among service members." . . .

But to recite the Government's compelling interests is not to end the matter. The First Amendment requires that the Government's chosen restriction on the speech at issue be "actually necessary" to achieve its interest. . . .

(continued)

The Government points to no evidence to support its claim that the public's general perception of military awards is diluted by false claims such as those made by Alvarez. . . . As one of the Government's amici notes "there is nothing that charlatans such as Xavier Alvarez can do to stain [the Medal winners'] honor. . . .

The Government has not shown, and cannot show, why counterspeech would not suffice to achieve its interest. The facts of this case indicate that the dynamics of free speech, of counterspeech, of refutation, can overcome the lie. Respondent lied at a public meeting. Even before the FBI began investigating him for his false statements "Alvarez was perceived as a phony," Once the lie was made public, he was ridiculed online, see Brief for Respondent 3, his actions were reported in the press, and a fellow board member called for his resignation. . . .

The remedy for speech that is false is speech that is true. This is the ordinary course in a free society. The response to the unreasoned is the rational; to the uninformed, the enlightened; to the straight-out lie, the simple truth. . . .

In addition, when the Government seeks to regulate protected speech, the restriction must be the "least restrictive means among available, effective alternatives." There is, however, at least one less speech-restrictive means by which the Government could likely protect the integrity of the military awards system.  A Government-created database could list Congressional Medal of Honor winners. Were a database accessible through the Internet, it would be easy to verify and expose false claims. . . .

The Nation well knows that one of the costs of the First Amendment is that it protects the speech we detest as well as the speech we embrace. Though few might find respondent's statements anything but contemptible, his right to make those statements is protected by the Constitution's guarantee of freedom of speech and expression. The Stolen Valor Act infringes upon speech protected by the First Amendment.

[The reversal of Alvarez' conviction by the Court of Appeals was affirmed.

## Academic Crimes

Learning Objective: Define, describe, and apply the elements of academic fraud.

In most colleges and universities, student cheating, if innocent, is treated as a teachable moment. If intentional, or reckless, the violator may be disciplined with a lower grade on the assignment, failing the class, suspension, and in the most serious cases, expulsion from the institution. But in a few states, academic fraud is also a crime. Connecticut declares that

> [n]o person shall prepare, offer to prepare, cause to be prepared, sell or offer for sale any term paper, thesis, dissertation, essay, report or other written, recorded, pictorial, artistic or other assignment knowing, or under the circumstances having reason to know, that said assignment is intended for submission either in whole or substantial part under the name of a student other than the author of the term paper, thesis, dissertation, essay, report or other written, recorded, pictorial, artistic or other assignment in fulfillment of the requirements for a degree, diploma, certificate or course of study at any university, college, academy, school or other educational institution which is chartered, incorporated, licensed, registered or supervised by this state.[54]

North Carolina has a similar law. It reads:

> It shall be unlawful for any person, firm, corporation or association to assist any student, or advertise, offer or attempt to assist any student, in obtaining or in attempting to obtain, by fraudulent means, any academic credit, grade or test score, or any diploma, certificate or other instrument purporting to confer any literary, scientific, professional, technical or other degree in any course of study in any university, college, academy or other educational institution. The activity prohibited by this subsection includes, but is not limited to, preparing or advertising, offering, or attempting to prepare a term paper, thesis, or dissertation for another; impersonating or advertising, offering or attempting to impersonate another in taking or attempting to take an examination; and the giving or changing of a grade or test score or offering to give or change a grade or test score in exchange for an article of value or money.[55]

Both Connecticut and North Carolina grade these crimes as misdemeanors.

From these statutes, the general elements of academic fraud are for a person

1. to prepare, assist, or sell (or receive)
2. a paper or other assignment
3. for (from) another person
4. knowing (intending) it will be submitted for academic credit.

# Crimes Against the Administration of Government

## Perjury

Learning Objective: Define, describe, and apply the elements of perjury.

**Perjury** was a crime at common law and continues to be prohibited by statute in all states.

The basic elements of perjury are

1. the making of a
2. false statement
3. with knowledge that it is false
4. while under oath.

To be successful, the prosecution has the tough burden of proving the mens rea: that the person who made the statement knew that it was false. As with other crimes, juries are permitted to infer a defendant's knowledge from surrounding facts.

In addition, the statement must be made while under oath. This requirement includes far more than testifying in court. Most laws cover all statements made before a person authorized to administer oaths. Therefore, perjury laws apply to people who sign affidavits before notary publics and appear as witnesses before a court reporter (e.g., for deposition), a grand jury, and all others who have the authority to administer oaths. For those individuals who have a religious objection to "swearing," the law permits an affirmation. This is simply an acknowledgment by the witness that the testimony he or she renders is truthful. The law treats an affirmation in the same manner as it does an oath.

Some jurisdictions require that the false statement be "material," or important to the matter. This requirement prevents prosecutions for trivial matters. Some jurisdictions have defined *materiality* as any matter that may affect the outcome of a case. If a statement is not material, even if untrue, then a perjury conviction is not permitted.

A related crime is **subornation of perjury**. This crime occurs when one convinces or procures another to commit perjury. One who commits subornation is treated as a perjurer for the purpose of sentencing.

In addition to being a crime in every state, perjury has been made criminal by statute in the United States. 18 U.S.C. § 1621 reads:

> Whoever (1) having taken an oath before a competent tribunal, officer, or person, in any case in which a law of the United States authorizes an oath to be administered, that he will testify, declare, depose, or certify truly . . . is true, willfully and contrary to such oath states or subscribes any material matter which he does not believe to be true. . . .

**perjury**
Lying while under oath, especially in a court proceeding. It is a crime.

**subornation of perjury**
The crime of asking or forcing another person to lie under oath.

## Sidebar

### The Problems of President Clinton: A Case Study in Crimes Against the Public

One of the most public cases of crimes against the public occurred in the late 1990s. For several years independent Counsel Kenneth Starr investigated President William J. Clinton and many of his associates for activities that transpired before and after Clinton assumed the presidency. In December 1998, the House of Representatives of the United States impeached President Clinton after receiving a referral from Mr. Starr. The House issued a two-count impeachment alleging both perjury and obstruction of justice.

In the impeachment, the president was accused of committing perjury to a grand jury. The House alleged that Mr. Clinton lied about the nature of his relationship with a White House intern, Monica Lewinsky. He was also accused of lying about a prior perjury he committed in a deposition in a sexual harassment action filed by Paula Jones, who had been an employee of the State of Arkansas when Mr. Clinton was governor of that state. In addition, he was charged directly with perjury in the Paula Jones sexual harassment lawsuit, with suborning perjury in that case, and with obstructing justice in that case.

Perjury can be a tricky affair because language can be a tricky affair. Proving perjury requires actual knowledge of falsity, materiality, and an oath. The mens rea is the difficult part, as demonstrated in the Clinton case. In response to questions concerning whether he had sexual relations with Ms. Lewinsky, Mr. Clinton answered in the negative. Later, it was discovered that these answers were true using Mr. Clinton's definition of sex, which he narrowly defined as intercourse. He later admitted to having oral and other forms of sexual contact with Ms. Lewinsky. Mr. Clinton also used semantics to evade disclosing other facts. For example, he relied on distinctions in tense when responding to certain questions. Mr. Clinton responded to one question by stating "[I]t depends on what the meaning of the word 'is' is. If the, if he, if is means is and never has been, that is not, that is one thing. If it means there is none, that was a completely true statement."

Another problem prosecutors faced in the Clinton case was his inability to recall facts. In response to many details, the president answered that he was unable to remember; or he would provide a qualified answer (e.g., I believe, but I'm not sure). In such cases, a prosecutor must prove that the witness did know the answer in order to prove perjury—a very difficult task.

Concerning the obstruction of justice charges, Mr. Starr alleged that Mr. Clinton attempted to retrieve gifts he had given to Ms. Lewinsky in an attempt to prevent them from falling into the hands of investigators. In addition, Mr. Starr accused the president of attempting to coach witnesses into testifying in a certain manner. For example, his secretary testified that the president met with her, told her that there were several things she needed to know, and that he had been asked about Monica Lewinsky in a deposition the day before. He then posed these questions and statements to the secretary: "You were always there when she was there, right? We were never really alone. Monica came on to me, and I never touched her, right? You can see and hear everything, right?"

On February 12, 1999, the Senate of the United States voted 45 to 55 in favor of conviction on the perjury count and 50–50 on the obstruction of justice count, in both cases falling short of the 67 votes necessary to convict and remove the president. Because Kenneth Starr (as well as many constitutional scholars) was of the opinion that a president must be impeached and removed before a criminal action may be filed against the president, Mr. Starr did not file criminal charges against Mr. Clinton. Mr. Clinton may now be charged and tried for both the perjury and obstruction allegations. In 1999, the trial judge in the Paula Jones case held Mr. Clinton in contempt of court for "giving false, misleading and evasive answers that were designed to obstruct the judicial process. . . . Simply put, the president's deposition testimony regarding whether he had ever been alone with Ms. Lewinsky was intentionally false, and his statements regarding whether he had ever engaged in sexual relations with Ms. Lewinsky likewise were intentionally false, notwithstanding tortured definitions and interpretations of the term 'sexual relations.'" The court ordered Mr. Clinton to pay plaintiff's expenses resulting from efforts to disprove his statements, as well as related court costs.

*Source: for contempt information: http://www.foxnews.com/news/packages/president/side0414a99.sml*

Of course, truth is a complete defense to a charge of perjury. What is truthful is not always easy to determine, and in most questionable cases prosecutors choose not to pursue the matter. This decision is largely due to the mens rea element.

## Bribery

Learning Objective: Define, describe, and apply the elements of bribery.

**bribery**
The offering, giving, receiving, or soliciting of anything of value in order to influence the actions of a public official.

As is true of perjury, **bribery** was a crime at English Common Law. Actually, bribery was initially a violation of biblical law, because it was wrong to attempt to influence judges, who were considered to be God's earthly representatives. Eventually, the crime was recognized by the courts of England.

Today, bribery is a statutory crime in the states and in the United States. The essential elements of the crime are

1. soliciting or accepting

2. anything of value

3. with the purpose of

4. violating a duty or trust.

Two primary forms of bribery are that of a public official and commercial bribery.

As mentioned, bribery began as a prohibition of influencing a judge. The crime was eventually extended to include bribery of all public officials and public servants. Statutes make it bribery to be the one accepting or giving the "thing of value." Hence, if a corporate official gives a public official money in exchange for awarding a contract to the company, both the corporate officer and the public official have committed bribery.

Most bribery statutes declare that unsuccessful offers are bribes. Thus, if the public official rejects the offer of the corporate officer, there is still a bribery violation. The offer need not be of money in exchange for a favor; anything of value is sufficient. Automobiles, tickets to a St. Louis Cardinals baseball game, and a promise of sexual favors all satisfy this requirement.

The offer must be made to a *public official or servant*. Both terms are defined broadly. Further, the offeror must be seeking to influence the official in a matter over which the official has authority. Most courts have held that whether the officer actually had the authority to carry out the requested act is not dispositive; the issue is whether the offeror believes that the official possesses the authority. Awarding of government contracts, setting favorable tax assessments, and overlooking civil and criminal violations are examples of corrupt acts.

The offer alone makes the offeror guilty of bribery. For the public official to be convicted, there must be an acceptance. This usually means that the official does the requested act; however, it is widely held that an acceptance is all that is necessary to support a conviction.

Bribery has been extended beyond the public affairs realm to commercial life. Whenever a person who is engaged in business activities breaches a duty or trust owed to someone (or something, such as a business organization) in exchange for something of value, bribery has been committed.

The MPC declares that commercial bribery is a misdemeanor. The Code applies to people in specific positions, such as lawyers, accountants, trustees, and officers of corporations.[56] Anyone who makes an offer to someone in one of these positions to violate the trust or duty created by the position is guilty of bribery. Of course, any person holding such a position who accepts such an offer is also guilty of bribery. The Code specifically states that any person who holds himself or herself out to the public to be in the business of appraising the value of services or commodities is guilty of bribery if he or she accepts a benefit to influence the decision or appraisal. Knowing that one is violating the trust is the mens rea under the Code.

If a seller for the Widgcom Company were to offer the purchasing agent of Retailers, Inc., money in exchange for receiving the contract to supply Retailers with Widgets for the next year, commercial bribery has occurred. A corporate officer who accepts free personal air travel in exchange for buying all corporate airline tickets from the same airline has committed bribery.

Finally, note that there are statutes that prohibit "throwing" athletic contests for pay. That is, any player, coach, owner, or official who accepts a benefit to cause one participant to win or lose commits bribery. These laws often apply to both professional and amateur sports.

# Tax Crimes

Learning Objective: Define, describe, and apply the elements of tax evasion.

You may have heard the quip, "In life, only two things are certain, death and taxes." Indeed, tax revenues are the lifeblood of government. In the United States, people are taxed at the federal, state, and local levels (county, municipal, and school district taxes). These taxes come in many forms, including income tax, property tax, gift and estate tax, sales tax, and excise taxes. Tax laws apply to individuals, estates, and business entities.

All taxing authorities have statutes that impose both civil and criminal penalties for violation of tax laws. Common violations of tax laws are tax evasion, failing to file a required tax return, filing a fraudulent return, and unlawful disclosure of tax information. These are not the only crimes related to taxes, however, as shown by the applicable federal statutes, which embody 16 tax-related crimes.[57]

**Tax evasion** involves paying less tax than required or underreporting one's income with the intent of paying less tax. The federal statute covering tax evasion reads:

> *26 U.S.C. § 7201 Attempt to evade or defeat tax*
>
> Any person who willfully attempts in any manner to evade or defeat any tax imposed by this title or the payment thereof shall, in addition to other penalties provided by law, be guilty of a felony and, upon conviction thereof, shall be fined not more than $100,000 ($500,000 in the case of a corporation), or imprisoned not more than 5 years, or both, together with the costs of prosecution.

**Tax fraud**, a crime closely related to evasion, involves using fraud or false statements to avoid a tax obligation. This crime may occur in many ways, including falsifying statements that are provided to a revenue agency, such as fraudulent receipts used for deductions. Filing false tax returns is also a form of tax fraud.

Failure to file a required tax return is also criminal. The relevant federal statute reads:

> *26 U.S.C. § 7203 Willful failure to file return, supply information, or pay tax*
>
> Any person required under this title to pay any estimated tax or tax, or required by this title or by regulations made under authority thereof to make a return, keep any records, or supply any information, who willfully fails to pay such estimated tax or tax, make such return, keep such records, or supply such information . . . [shall] be guilty of a misdemeanor and, upon conviction thereof, shall be fined not more than $25,000 ($100,000 in the case of a corporation), or imprisoned not more than 1 year, or both, together with the costs of prosecution.

Note that § 7203 applies to anyone who is required to file a tax return, pay a tax, or supply information. Therefore, this provision can be the basis of a prosecution of an employer who pays his or her employees in cash and makes no report to the Internal Revenue Service. Likewise, although some entities are not taxed, such as partnerships, they are required to file informational returns, and failure to do so violates this provision.

Tax evasion, filing fraudulent tax returns, and the unauthorized disclosure of information are crimes of commission. That is, an affirmative act is required to commit these crimes.

Failing to file a required return, or other information, is an act of omission. Proving such crimes requires not proof of an illegal act but that a required act was not taken. The quoted statutes require willful violations. Negligence in preparing a tax return or in filing the return is not criminal. However, such errors may lead to civil penalties.

The willfulness requirement was considered by the Supreme Court in *Cheek v. United States*.

**tax evasion**
The deliberate nonpayment or underpayment of taxes that are legally due. Criminal tax evasion has higher fines than civil fraud and the possibility of a prison sentence upon the showing of "willfulness."

**tax fraud**
The deliberate nonpayment or underpayment of taxes that are legally due.

## Oyez

### Cheek v. United States
### 498 U.S. 192 (1991)

**White, Justice, delivered the opinion of the Court**

Willfulness, as construed by our prior decisions in criminal tax cases, requires the Government to prove that the law imposed a duty on the defendant, that the defendant knew of this duty, and that he voluntarily and intentionally violated this duty. We deal first with the case where the issue is whether the defendant knew of the duty purportedly imposed by the provision of the statute or regulation he is accused of violating, a case in which there is no claim that the provision at issue is invalid. In such a case, if the Government proves actual knowledge of the pertinent legal duty, the prosecution, without more, has satisfied the knowledge component of the willfulness requirement. But carrying this burden requires negating a defendant's claim of ignorance of the law or a claim that because of a misunderstanding of the law, he had a good-faith belief that he was not violating any of the provisions of the tax laws. This is so because one cannot be aware that the law imposes a duty upon him and yet be ignorant of it, misunderstand the law, or believe that the duty does not exist. In the end, the issue is whether, based on all the evidence, the Government has proved that the defendant was aware of the duty at issue, which cannot be true if the jury credits a good-faith misunderstanding and belief submission, whether or not the claimed belief or misunderstanding is objectively reasonable.

In this case, if Cheek asserted that he truly believed that the Internal Revenue Code did not purport to treat wages as income, and the jury believed him, the Government would not have carried its burden to prove willfulness, however, unreasonable a court might deem such a belief. . . .

We thus disagree with the Court of Appeals' requirement that a claimed good-faith belief must be objectively reasonable if it is to be considered as possibly negating the Government's evidence purporting to show a defendant's awareness of the legal duty at issue. Knowledge and belief are characteristically questions for the fact finder.

Tax laws require the disclosure of all income and profits. This includes income from illegal sources. Gamblers are required to report their winnings, prostitutes their income, and drug dealers the profits derived from their sales. Failure to report income from illegal acts is the same as failure to report legally earned income. Because requiring people to report income from illegal activities raises a self-incrimination problem, tax laws require that all information obtained be kept confidential. Tax officials are not permitted to disclose such information to law enforcement authorities, and to do so is *unlawful disclosure*. The privilege against self-incrimination is discussed more thoroughly in Chapter 8.

## Obstruction of Justice

Learning Objective: Define, describe, and apply the elements of obstruction of justice.

*Obstruction of justice* refers to any number of unlawful acts. As a general proposition, any act that interferes with the performance of a public official's duties obstructs justice. However, the crime is most commonly associated with law enforcement and judicial officials.

The types of acts that fall under such statutes include tampering with witnesses or jurors, interfering with police officers, destroying evidence needed for a court proceeding, and intentionally giving false information to a prosecutor in an effort to hinder a prosecutorial effort. However, obstruction statutes are drafted broadly, thereby permitting creative prosecutions. For example, it is common for women who are physically abused by their husbands to contact the police during a violent episode and demand the husband's arrest, usually in an effort to get the man out of the house. Once the husband is arrested, many women lose interest in prosecuting and often refuse to testify against their husbands in court. In such a case, a prosecutor could charge the wife with obstruction of justice because of her refusal to testify.

Resisting arrest is a similar crime. At Common Law, one could resist an unlawful arrest. Although a few jurisdictions have retained this rule, this is not presently the law in most jurisdictions. Most states have followed the MPC approach, which prohibits even moderate resistance to any arrest.[58] It is a wise rule, considering the remedies that are available if a police officer makes an unlawful arrest. If the arrest is unlawful, but in good faith, the arrestee will be released either at the police station or after the first judicial hearing. If the arrest was unlawful and made maliciously, the arrestee not only will be released but also has a civil cause of action for false imprisonment and violation of civil rights.

## Contempt

Learning Objective: Compare and contrast civil, criminal, direct, and indirect contempt.

Failure to comply with a court order is contemptuous, as is taking any act with the purpose of undermining a court's authority or intending to interfere with its administration and process. Although statutes provide for contempt, it is widely accepted that the contempt power is inherent.

**Contempt** is divided into direct and indirect criminal contempt and direct and indirect civil contempt. *Direct contempt* refers to acts that occur in the presence of the judge. Although contempt usually occurs in the courtroom, the judges' chambers and office area are included. *Indirect contempt* refers to actions taken outside the presence of a court but that are violative of a court order.

Criminal contempt is imposed to punish a person for violating a court order. Civil contempt, by contrast, does not have punishment as its purpose. It is intended to coerce a person into complying with a court order. For example, if Mary refuses to testify at a trial despite an order to testify, the judge may order her confined until she complies. Once she testifies, she is free. Consequently, civil contemnors hold the keys to their jail cells; criminal contemnors do not. In theory, one who has been held in civil contempt can be punished for criminal contempt after complying with the court order. In practice, this seldom occurs, presumably because judges and prosecutors feel that the civil punishment imposed is adequate.

The contempt power is significant. Indirect criminal contemnors are entitled to all the protections of other criminal defendants, such as a right to a trial, assistance of counsel, and proof beyond a reasonable doubt. Direct criminal contemnors

**contempt**
A willful disobeying of a judge's command or official court order. Contempt can be *direct* (within the judge's notice) or *indirect* (outside the court and punishable only after proved to the judge). It can also be *civil contempt* (disobeying a court order in favor of an opponent) or *criminal contempt.*

## Sidebar

### Two Cases of Contempt

Contempt of court orders are common in domestic law cases. One case, which received considerable media attention, involved Dr. Elizabeth Morgan, who refused to obey a court order to disclose the location of her child, Heather, claiming that her ex-husband had molested the child. The judge ordered that she disclose the location of the child so her ex-husband could exercise his court-ordered visitation rights. She refused, and the judge ordered that she be incarcerated until she disclosed the child's whereabouts. Dr. Morgan spent a total of 759 days in jail and was released only after an act of Congress limited the amount of time a civil contemnor could spend in jail to one year.

A case from Houston, Texas, teaches that the contempt power of judges is powerful. Houston attorney John O'Quinn was found in criminal contempt by a federal district judge for sleeping in a jury room. The basis for the contempt citation was an order from the judge that O'Quinn (and others) "stay out of the facilities up here on this floor unless you get prior permission." The Fifth Circuit Court of Appeals reversed the conviction, finding that the judge's order was too vague. However, this is a good example of the breadth of the contempt power; had the judge's order been more specific, it would have been upheld.

*Source*: "A Hard Case of Contempt," *Time*, Sept. 18, 1989; "A Mother's 759 Days of Defiance," *U.S. News & World Report*, Oct. 9, 1989.

have no such rights, as the act took place in the presence of a judge. However, any sentence imposed may be appealed and reviewed for fairness.

Civil contemnors have few rights. They do not possess the rights of those accused of crimes, because civil contempt is not considered a criminal action. In most instances, they enjoy no right to appeal. A civil contemnor holds his or her own key; he or she must comply with the court's order. Of course, if an appellate court determines that the underlying order is unlawful, the civil contemnor is released. However, the individual may be charged with criminal contempt for failure to comply with the order before it was held unlawful by an appellate court. The fact that a court order may be nullified at some future date does not justify noncompliance. Court orders must be obeyed to ensure the orderly administration of justice.

Legislatures also have the power to cite for contempt. Legislatures, usually through committees, conduct hearings and other proceedings when considering bills and amendments to statutes. The contempt power serves the same function for legislatures that it does for courts. It furthers the orderly performance of legislative duties. Refusal to testify before a legislative body (usually a committee) or to produce documents or other items, and disruption of a proceeding are examples of legislative contempt. Persons charged with legislative contempt possess the same rights as defendants charged with other crimes. In most instances, legislative bodies refer contempt cases to prosecutors, rather than adjudicating such cases themselves.

# Crimes Against Sovereignty and Security

In the last section, you read about crimes that interfere with public administration. Those crimes may—but not necessarily—be intended to destroy the government or to make a political statement. This section examines the very serious crimes of treason, sedition, espionage, and terrorism.

## Treason

Learning Objective: Define, describe, and apply the elements of treason.

In Dante's imagination, the deepest region of hell is reserved for people who betray their God, country, and family. In the early Common Law, treason was considered more serious than murder. Although both were punished with death, traitors were treated to disembowelment, quartering, and other horrific forms of death while murderers and other felons received a quick death, often by beheading. The family of traitors also suffered corruption of blood; all family property was forfeited to the crown, and no titles or other family rights were passed on to heirs.

While the Framers also wrote and spoke about how detestable and dishonorable treason is, they were also wary of it. The British had used treason as a weapon to suppress dissent both before and during the American Revolution. Indeed, the Framers were traitors to the British Crown. So, they included treason in the Constitution—the only crime to appear there—not to emphasize its importance but to limit its use. Article III, section 3 reads:

> Clause 1: Treason against the United States, shall consist only in levying War against them, or in adhering to their Enemies, giving them Aid and Comfort. No Person shall be convicted of Treason unless on the Testimony of two Witnesses to the same overt Act, or on Confession in open Court.
>
> Clause 2: The Congress shall have Power to declare the Punishment of Treason, but no Attainder of Treason shall work Corruption of Blood, or Forfeiture except during the Life of the Person attainted.

Congress implemented Clause 1,[59] and the resulting elements of the offense are as follows:

1. A person who owes an allegiance to the United States,
2. *Levies* war or *Adheres* to an enemy of the United States and
3. commits an overt act and
4. possesses treasonable intent.

As to the first element, who may be a defendant, both the Treason Clause and the treason statute apply to people who owe allegiance to the United States. Undoubtedly, this includes citizens of the United States. Presumably, certain classes of non-citizens, such as members of the military and permanent residents, are included because they owe allegiance, by law and oath, to the United States. Short-term resident aliens are less clear.

There are two forms of treason; (1) levying war against the United States and (2) adhering to an enemy of the United States, giving them aid and comfort. The second requires adhering to an enemy state, a foreign power. The first doesn't.

Proof of either must be supported by an "overt act." The Supreme Court has interpreted this requirement narrowly. By requiring an overt act, the Framers rejected the British use of treason to punish speech. In addition to one overt act, the Treason Clause requires either the testimony of two witnesses to the overt act or a confession in open court.

Although the Constitution doesn't explicitly define the mens rea of treason, the specific intent to betray the Nation is presumably required. It is possible, therefore, to provide aid and comfort to an enemy and not commit treason. Imagine, for example, a U.S. soldier who offers food to starving enemy soldiers. Although the soldier is providing aid and comfort, there is no intent to betray the United States.

What acts amount to levying war was tested shortly after the Constitution was ratified. Aaron Burr, vice president under President Thomas Jefferson and murderer of Alexander Hamilton, was tried for treason in 1807. He is alleged to have plotted to seize part of the United States and Mexico to create a new nation. Burr and several alleged conspirators were arrested, charged, and tried for treason. Burr was acquitted at a trial that was presided over by the Chief Justice of the United States, John Marshall. Two of his alleged conspirators, Erick Bollman and Samuel Swartwout, were acquitted for the same reasons as Burr. Their appeal to the Supreme Court resulted in a written opinion, *Ex Parte Bollman and Ex Parte Swartwout* (1807).[60]

In *Ex Parte Bollman*, the Supreme Court held that planning an insurrection doesn't satisfy the overt act requirement. Even traveling to the place where the co-conspirators are to gather isn't adequate. Chief Justice John Marshall wrote, on behalf of the Court, that an "actual assemblage of men for the purpose of executing a treasonable design" must occur. Because the alleged conspirators hadn't reached this point in the plot, if real, they were acquitted.

In a WWII era case, *Cramer v. United States*,[61] the Supreme Court issued a similarly narrow interpretation of the second form of treason, providing the enemy with aid and comfort. Mr. Cramer was born in Germany and served in the German military during WWI. After the war, he moved to the United States, obtained citizenship, was gainfully employed and crime free. During his years in the United States, he remained close to his family and friends in Germany and sympathized with Germany in its conflicts with other European nations.

Cramer had been friendly with two German men, who returned to Germany shortly before war broke out between Germany and the United States. They returned to support the Nazis. During the war, subsequently, Cramer was contacted by the men, who had returned to the United States. Although suspicious of their intentions, he denied having ever been told why or how they returned to the United States. As it turned out, they were in the United States to commit sabotage. There was no evidence that he did anything to support their efforts. He testified that even when they met, he didn't even pay for their drinks. Cramer was charged and convicted of treason. His sentence was a fine of $10,000 and 45 years in prison. On appeal, the Supreme Court reversed his conviction. After discussing the history of treason in England and the United States, the Court penned

> Thus the crime of treason consists of two elements: adherence to the enemy; and rendering him aid and comfort. A citizen intellectually or emotionally may favor the enemy and harbor sympathies or convictions disloyal to this country's policy or interest, but so long as he commits no act of aid and comfort to the enemy, there is no treason. On the other hand, a citizen may take actions which do aid and comfort the enemy — making a speech critical of the government or opposing its measures, profiteering, striking in defense plants or essential work, and the hundred other things which impair our cohesion and diminish our strength — but if there is no adherence to the enemy in this, if there is no intent to betray, there is no treason. . . .

As this quote expresses, in addition to the strict interpretation of what amounts to levying war or offering aid and comfort, the Court has held that subjective intent must be proven, even if by inference. The Court found insufficient evidence that Cramer committed an overt act or that he harbored a specific intent to betray the United States.

Finally, the Clause addressed how treason may be punished. While Congress may punish treason with death, imprisonment, and fines, it may not issue an attainder or impose corruption of blood or forfeiture beyond the life of the traitor. The attainder language forbids Congress from declaring a person guilty of treason, a power that Parliament exercised. Rather, a defendant is entitled to a judicial trial. The corruption of blood prohibition means that punishment ends with the traitor; it doesn't extend forward to her children or heirs.

The overt act and double witness requirement make treason a difficult crime to prove. Consequently, there have been few treason convictions in all U.S. history and none whatsoever in several decades.

At the time of the writing of this edition, the rampage on the U.S. Capitol had just occurred, and many facts are yet to be found. For the actors who entered the building and assaulted officers, the overt act has been satisfied, even applying Justice Marshall's requirement that there be an "assemblage" of people. But establishing an intent to betray the United States will prove to be more difficult. If history is any guide, prosecutors will pursue other crimes over treason.

Federal law also punishes **Misprision of Treason**, or the failure to report known treason, with as many as seven years in prison. As is true of treason, this law applies to people who owe allegiance to the United States.

**Misprision of Treason**
The crime of failing to report known treason to authorities.

## Sedition and Espionage

Learning Objective: Define, describe, and apply the elements of sedition and espionage.

In the final weeks of Donald Trump's presidency, after the Electoral College declared Joe Biden the winner of the 2020 presidential election, but before the storming of the Capitol, a meeting, later dubbed the Sedition Summit, was held in the White House. In attendance were the president, former National Security Advisor and subsequently pardoned Michael Flynn, attorney to the president, attorney Sidney Powell, Chief of Staff Mark Meadows, White House counsel Pat Cipollone, and advisor to the president, Rudy Giuliani. The group is alleged to have discussed using the military, at gunpoint, to declare martial law, seize voting machines, and rerun the elections in Georgia, Pennsylvania, Michigan, and Wisconsin. At least two in the meeting, Cipollone and Meadows, objected to the plan. When news of the meeting went public, a frenzy of media stories and opinion pieces raised concerns about the anti-democratic and seditious nature of the discussion.[62]

Sedition has been recognized as a crime since the first days of the Republic. The misuse of sedition laws dates back as far. The Alien and Seditions Acts of the late eighteenth century made it a crime to write false, scandalous, or malicious stories about the government; increased the residency period required to become a citizen; and increased the president's authority to deport dangerous aliens.

The provisions of the sedition laws prohibiting free speech were controversial, and many prominent Americans opposed them—including Thomas Jefferson and James Madison. After the law expired by its own sunset provision, Congress reimbursed the paid fines for all those who had been convicted under its authority.[63]

Today there are several sedition laws, including a prohibition of seditious conspiracies to overthrow the government;[64] the Logan Act, which prohibits individuals from corresponding with foreign governments in relation to disputes such governments may have with the United States; and a prohibition of recruiting members of the U.S. armed forces to act against the United States.[65] These laws were drafted to focus on acts, thereby avoiding the free speech problems of the original sedition laws.

Seditious conspiracy is committed when

1. two or more persons

2. in any State or Territory, or in any place subject to the jurisdiction of the United States,

   a. conspire to overthrow, put down, or to destroy by force the Government of the United States, or

   b. to levy war against them, or to oppose by force the authority thereof, or

   c. by force to prevent, hinder, or delay the execution of any law of the United States, or

   d. by force to seize, take, or possess any property of the United States contrary to the authority thereof.

Applying this statute to the Capitol siege, any individual charged with seditious conspiracy will have to be shown to have acted in concert with another person. This is plausible, as it appears, at the time of this writing, that many participants acted together to overwhelm police, break windows, and push open doors. In other cases, e-mail and other correspondence, before, during, and after the incident, can be used to prove this element. As for the mens rea, proving that the actors intended to overthrow the government or to wage war against the United States may be difficult. But proving that they intended to possess property of the United States or to prevent, hinder, or delay Congress' electoral vote will be easier, given the nature of the "Stop the Steal" rally.

Riot and sedition involve violence. But nonviolent acts can also be disloyal and injurious to the Nation. Spies do this. The crime of spying is known as espionage. Julius and Ethel Rosenberg, Aldrich Ames, and Robert Hanssen are only a few of the many Americans who have been convicted of spying for other countries.

There are several federal espionage crimes, including *inter alia* the following:

18 U.S.C. § 793 applies to activities such as gathering, transmitting to an unauthorized person, or losing, information pertaining to the national defense, and to conspiracies to commit such offenses.

18 U.S.C. § 794 applies to: (1) persons who deliver, or attempt to deliver, information pertaining to the national defense of the United States to agents or subjects of foreign countries, with intent or reason to believe that it is to be used to the injury of the United States or to the advantage of a foreign nation; (2) wartime espionage; and (3) conspiracy to commit espionage.

18 U.S.C. § 1030(a)(1). Section 1030(a)(1) of Title 18, U.S.C., makes it unlawful to knowingly access a computer without authorization, or beyond the scope of one's authorization, and thereby obtain information that has been classified for national defense or foreign relations reasons, with intent or reason to believe that such information is to be used to the injury of the United States or to the advantage of a foreign nation.

50 U.S.C. § 783. Section 783 of Title 50, U.S.C., makes it unlawful for any officer or employee of the United States, or of any federal department or agency, to communicate to any person whom he or she knows or has reason to believe to be an agent of a foreign government, any information classified by the President or by the head of such department or agency as affecting the security of the United States, knowing or having reason to know that such information has been so classified. *See* 50 U.S.C. § 783(b). Conversely, it is unlawful for a foreign agent knowingly to receive classified information from a United States government employee, unless special authorization has been obtained. *See* 50 U.S.C. § 783(c).

50 U.S.C. § 421. The Intelligence Identities Protection Act (50 U.S.C. § 421) prohibits the unauthorized disclosure of information identifying certain United States intelligence officers, agents, informants or sources.

18 U.S.C. § 951. Section 951 of Title 18, United States Code, makes it unlawful for foreign agents to act as such without notifying the Attorney General, unless the agent is entitled to a statutory exemption from the registration requirement.

8 U.S.C. § 1185(b); 18 U.S.C. § 1542 et seq. The Internal Security Section has jurisdiction over prosecutions under 8 U.S.C. § 1185(b) and 18 U.S.C. §§ 1542 to 1544 when the defendants have subversive connections, or when travel to a restricted country is involved.

Most of these offenses require either intentionality or reason to believe the United States will be injured and an overt act in furtherance of the crime.

## Terrorism

Learning Objective: Define, describe, and apply the elements of terrorism.

The January 6, 2021, riot at the U.S. Capitol, the riots on America's west coast in 2020 and 2021, largely in response to the killing of George Floyd, and the rise of dangerous fringe groups have reminded the Nation that domestic terrorism is a continuing threat. And, of course, international terrorism is a continuing threat as well. Several acts of terrorism that predate the events of 2020 and 2021 have framed modern terrorism law. The Boston Bombings of 2013, The Oklahoma City Bombing of 1995, and the attacks on the United States of September 11, 2001 (9/11), are examples.

In 1995, Timothy McVeigh, with accomplices, bombed the federal building in Oklahoma City, Oklahoma, killing 167 people, including several children, and injuring over 600 others.[66] It would be the worst act of terror, in terms of loss of life, in the modern United States until the attacks of September 11, 2001. McVeigh was eventually executed for the deaths resulting from the bombing. See Exhibit 6–2 for a copy of McVeigh's death certificate. Unhappy with the lack of rights of the victims during the trial of McVeigh and with the right of defendants to repeated habeas corpus appeals on the same subjects, Congress, with President Clinton's approval, enacted the Antiterrorism and Effective Death Penalty Act of 1996. Through this statute habeas corpus relief was limited, *inter alia*, by requiring petitions to be filed within one year and limiting the number of petitions that may be filed in any one case. The Act also requires victim compensation and requires courts to provide closed-circuit television access to victims in instances where the venue of trial is changed from the location of the crime.

Just as Oklahoma City bombing caused change, the attacks of 9/11, the Uniting and Strengthening America by Providing Appropriate Tools Required to Intercept and Obstruct Terrorism Act of 2001 was enacted, commonly known as the Patriot Act. The Patriot Act was reauthorized, with amendments, in 2006. Many of its provisions expired in 2020, but at the time of the writing of this edition, there was a small movement to restore some of its provisions in response to the Capitol siege. For that reason, the Act's major provisions are listed here:

- Federal law enforcement authority to monitor e-mail and other forms of communication was expanded. Examples include treating stored voice-mail messages like e-mail, not as telephone conversations. E-mail enjoys less protection than telephone conversations do.

- Federal court authority to issue pen register and trap orders (devices used to determine the origin of electronic communications) was broadened to include the entire nation.

- Prior to the Patriot Act, law enforcement officers did not have to establish probable cause to obtain a court order to a telephone company to trace (using pen register/traps). Because the content of telephone conversations was not being intruded upon, law enforcement officers were only required to show that the data are "relevant to an ongoing investigation." The Patriot Act extended this procedure to obtaining a record of Web addresses that a suspect visits, even though identification of a Web address also identifies content.

- The Patriot Act authorizes "roving wiretaps." A roving wiretap is authorization to move a wiretap from one telephone or form of communication to another in order to follow the communications of the person under surveillance.

- Several new crimes were created, including money laundering of cybercrime and terrorism, overseas use of fraudulent U.S. credit cards, terrorist attacks on mass transit, and harboring terrorists, and it increased the penalties for counterfeiting.

- The Attorney General of the United States was delegated greater authority to deport suspected alien terrorists.

- Law enforcement agencies were given the authority to share grand jury and wiretap information that constitutes "foreign intelligence" with intelligence agencies. Previously, this action was not permitted.

The 9/11 attacks also led to the creation of a new law enforcement agency, the Department of Homeland Security (DHS). It is a household agency name today. Much of the federal government's arsenal in the War on Terror was consolidated under DHS. The Federal Emergency Management Agency, U.S. Coast Guard, Customs, Border Patrol, Secret Service, Transportation Security Administration, and Citizenship and Immigration Services (previously Immigration and Naturalization Service) are all units reporting to DHS. In total, DHS has nearly 200,000 employees under its umbrella.

These new laws are not without their critics. The most common criticism is that they tip the security/rights balance too far in favor of national security.

### The Crimes of Terrorism

The Federal Terrorism statute, 18 U.S.C. § 2331, defines international terrorism as follows:

**Exhibit 6–2** Official Copy, Vigo County Health Department Certificate of Death

Vigo County, Indiana Health Department Death Certificate for Timothy McVeigh, who was executed for the 1995 bombing of the Murrah Federal Building in Oklahoma City, OK.

OFFICIAL COPY
VIGO COUNTY HEALTH DEPARTMENT
CERTIFICATE OF DEATH

ATTENTION ESTATE: The Social Security # is being requested by this state agency in order to pursue its statutory responsibility. Disclosure is voluntary and there will be no penalty for refusal.

Local No. ...... 5.99

THE RECORDS IN THIS SERIES ARE CONFIDENTIAL PER IC 16-37-1-10

TYPE/PRINT IN PERMANENT BLACK INK

| 1 DECEASED—NAME (First, Middle, Last) Timothy James McVeigh | 2 SEX Male | 3a TIME OF DEATH 7:14 A.M. | 3b DATE OF DEATH June 11, 2001 |

| 4. SOCIAL SECURITY NUMBER 129-58-4709 | 5a AGE—Last Birthday (Years) 33 | 5b UNDER 1 YEAR | 5c UNDER 1 DAY | 6 DATE OF BIRTH April 23, 1968 | 7 BIRTHPLACE Lockport, NY |

DECEDENT

8a WAS DECEDENT A U.S. VETERAN? Yes
8b YEAR LAST SERVED IN U.S. ARMED FORCES 1991
9a PLACE OF DEATH — HOSPITAL □ Inpatient □ ER/Outpatient □ DOA — OTHER □ Nursing Home ☒ Other (Specify) U S Penitentiary

9b. FACILITY NAME (If not institution, give street and number) U S Penitentiary, 4200 Bureau Road
9c. CITY, TOWN, OR LOCATION OF DEATH Terre Haute
9d. COUNTY OF DEATH Vigo

10. MARITAL STATUS (Specify) Never Married
11. SURVIVING SPOUSE N/A
12a. DECEDENT'S USUAL OCCUPATION Soldier
12b. KIND OF BUSINESS/INDUSTRY US Army

13a. RESIDENCE—STATE New York
13b. COUNTY Niagara
13c. CITY, TOWN, OR LOCATION Lockport
13d. STREET AND NUMBER 6289 Campbell Blvd

13e. ZIP CODE 14094
13f. INSIDE CITY LIMITS □ No ☒ Yes
13g. ON A FARM? ☒ No □ Yes
14. CITIZEN OF WHAT COUNTRY? USA
15. WAS DECEDENT OF HISPANIC ORIGIN? ☒ No □ Yes
16. RACE White
17. DECEDENT'S EDUCATION Elementary/Secondary (0-12) 12  College (1-4 or 5 +)

PARENTS

18. FATHER'S NAME William McVeigh
19. MOTHER'S NAME Mildred Noreen Hill

INFORMANT

20a. INFORMANT'S NAME (Type/Print) Robert Nigh
20b. MAILING ADDRESS 2 West 6th St Tulsa, OK 74119
20c. Relationship Attorney

DISPOSITION

21a. METHOD OF DISPOSITION □ Entombment □ Burial ☒ Cremation □ Removal from State □ Donation □ Other (Specify)
21b. DATE AND PLACE OF DISPOSITION June 11, 2001 Terre Haute Crematory
21c. LOCATION—City or Town, State Terre Haute, IN

22a. EMBALMER'S NAME No Embalming
22b. EMBALMER'S LICENSE NO. N/A
23. WAS DEATH REPORTED TO CORONER? □ No ☒ Yes

24a. SIGNATURE OF FUNERAL DIRECTOR
24b. LICENSE NUMBER (of Licensee) FD09200035
25. NAME, ADDRESS, AND LICENSE NUMBER OF FUNERAL HOME Mattox Ryan Funeral Home 602 S 7th Street Terre Haute, IN 4780 FH19900001

CAUSE OF DEATH

26. PART I. Enter the diseases, injuries, or complications that caused the death. Do not enter nonspecific terms, such as cardiac or respiratory arrest, shock, or heart failure. List only one cause on each line.

IMMEDIATE CAUSE (Final disease or condition resulting in death) a. Lethal Injection
DUE TO (OR AS A CONSEQUENCE OF):
b.
DUE TO (OR AS A CONSEQUENCE OF):
c.
DUE TO (OR AS A CONSEQUENCE OF):
d.

Approximate Interval Between Onset and Death

PART II. Other significant conditions - Conditions contributing to death but not previously stated in Part I.

27. WAS DECEDENT PREGNANT ON 90 DAYS POSTPARTUM? NO
28a. WAS AN AUTOPSY PERFORMED? NO
28b. WERE AUTOPSY FINDINGS AVAILABLE PRIOR TO COMPLETION OF CAUSE OF DEATH? NO

CERTIFIER

29a. CERTIFIER (Check only one) □ CERTIFYING PHYSICIAN □ HEALTH OFFICER ☒ CORONER On the basis of examination and/or investigation, in my opinion, death occurred at the time, date, and place, and due to the cause(s) and manner as stated.

29b. SIGNATURE AND TITLE OF CERTIFIER Susan L. Amos MD VigoCounty Coroner
29c. MEDICAL LICENSE NO 01031117
29d. DATE SIGNED June 11, 2001

30. NAME AND ADDRESS OF PERSON WHO COMPLETED CAUSE OF DEATH (ITEM 26) Susan Amos Coroner 501 Hospital Lane Terre Haute, IN 47802

HEALTH OFFICER

31. HEALTH OFFICER'S SIGNATURE
32. DATE FILED JUN 11 2001

33. MANNER OF DEATH □ Natural □ Pending Investigation □ Accident □ Suicide □ Could not be Determined ☒ Homicide
34a. DATE OF INJURY June 11, 2001
34b. TIME OF INJURY 7:14 A.M.
34c. INJURY AT WORK? No
34d. DESCRIBE HOW INJURY OCCURRED Judicial Execution by lethal injection

34e. PLACE OF INJURY U.S. Penitentiary
34f. LOCATION 4200 Bureau Rd. Terre Haute, IN

34g. DATE PRONOUNCED DEAD June 11, 2001
34h. MOTOR VEHICLE ACCIDENT? No

SDH06-004 State Form 10110 (R5/1-99)

(1) the term "international terrorism" means activities that—

(a) involve violent acts or acts dangerous to human life that are a violation of the criminal laws of the United States or of any State, or that would be a criminal violation if committed within the jurisdiction of the United States or of any State;

(b) appear to be intended—

(i) to intimidate or coerce a civilian population;

(ii) to influence the policy of a government by intimidation or coercion; or

(iii) to affect the conduct of a government by mass destruction, assassination, or kidnapping; and

(c) occur primarily outside the territorial jurisdiction of the United States, or transcend national boundaries in terms of the means by which they are accomplished, the persons they appear intended to intimidate or coerce, or the locale in which their perpetrators operate or seek asylum;

(2) the term "national of the United States" has the meaning given such term in section 101(a)(22) of the Immigration and Nationality Act;

(3) the term "person" means any individual or entity capable of holding a legal or beneficial interest in property;

(4) the term "act of war" means any act occurring in the course of—

(a) declared war;

(b) armed conflict, whether or not war has been declared, between two or more nations; or

(c) armed conflict between military forces of any origin; and

(5) the term "domestic terrorism" means activities that—

(a) involve acts dangerous to human life that are a violation of the criminal laws of the United States or of any State;

(b) appear to be intended—

(i) to intimidate or coerce a civilian population;

(ii) to influence the policy of a government by intimidation or coercion; or

(iii) to affect the conduct of a government by mass destruction, assassination, or kidnapping; and

(c) occur primarily within the territorial jurisdiction of the United States.

Another statute, 18 U.S.C. § 2332, prohibits the following acts:

**(a) Prohibited acts.—**

(1) **Offenses.**—Whoever, involving conduct transcending national boundaries and in a circumstance described in subsection (b)—

(a) kills, kidnaps, maims, commits an assault resulting in serious bodily injury, or assaults with a dangerous weapon any person within the United States; or

(b) creates a substantial risk of serious bodily injury to any other person by destroying or damaging any structure, conveyance, or other real or personal property within the United States or by attempting or conspiring to destroy or damage any structure, conveyance, or other real or personal property within the United States; in violation of the laws of any State, or the United States, shall be punished as prescribed in subsection (c).

(2) **Treatment of threats, attempts and conspiracies.**—Whoever threatens to commit an offense under paragraph (1), or attempts or conspires to do so, shall be punished under subsection (c).

**(b) Jurisdictional bases.**—

(3) **Circumstances.**—The circumstances referred to in subsection (a) are—

(a) the mail or any facility of interstate or foreign commerce is used in furtherance of the offense;

(b) the offense obstructs, delays, or affects interstate or foreign commerce, or would have so obstructed, delayed, or affected interstate or foreign commerce if the offense had been consummated;

(c) the victim, or intended victim, is the U.S. government, a member of the uniformed services, or any official, officer, employee, or agent of the legislative, executive, or judicial branches, or of any department or agency, of the United States;

(d) the structure, conveyance, or other real or personal property is, in whole or in part, owned, possessed, or leased to the United States, or any department or agency of the United States;

(e) the offense is committed in the territorial sea (including the airspace above and the seabed and subsoil below, and artificial islands and fixed structures erected thereon) of the United States; or

(f) the offense is committed within the special maritime and territorial jurisdiction of the United States.

(4) **Co-conspirators and accessories after the fact.**—Jurisdiction shall exist over all principals and co-conspirators of an offense under this section, and accessories after the fact to any offense under this section, if at least one of the circumstances described in subparagraphs (A) through (F) of paragraph (1) is applicable to at least one offender.

**(c) Penalties . . .**

Yet another definition of terrorism can be found in the Homeland Security Act, 6 U.S.C. § 101(15):

(15) The term "terrorism" means any activity that—

(a) involves an act that—

(i) is dangerous to human life or potentially destructive of critical infrastructure or key resources; and

(ii) is a violation of the criminal laws of the United States or of any State or other subdivision of the United States; and

(b) appears to be intended—

(i) to intimidate or coerce a civilian population;

(ii) to influence the policy of a government by intimidation or coercion; or

(iii) to affect the conduct of a government by mass destruction, assassination, or kidnapping.

Federal law authorizes the Secretary of State to designate any foreign group of two or more persons that commit terrorist activities or plan or prepare to commit terrorist activities. Once designated, those who support the organization are in violation of federal law, noncitizens who are members of these organizations are immediately deportable, and the financial resources of the organizations may be seized by the United States.

Additionally, other federal statutes address specific acts of terrorism, such as bioterrorism; bombing public places; attacking mass transportation systems; harboring terrorists; supporting and financing terrorism, terrorist organizations, and nations that support terrorism; and using weapons of mass destruction. For example, 18 U.S.C. § 2332(a) prohibits the use of a weapon for mass destruction

1. against a national of the United States while such national is outside of the United States;

2. against any person or property within the United States, and the mail or any facility of interstate or foreign commerce is used in furtherance of the offense; such property is used in interstate or foreign commerce or in an activity that affects interstate or foreign commerce; any perpetrator travels in or causes another to travel in interstate or foreign commerce in furtherance of the offense; or the offense, or the results of the offense, affect interstate or foreign commerce, or, in the case of a threat, attempt, or conspiracy, would have affected interstate or foreign commerce;

3. against any property that is owned, leased, or used by the United States or by any department or agency of the United States, whether the property is within or outside of the United States; or

4. against any property within the United States that is owned, leased, or used by a foreign government. *Weapon of mass destruction* is defined as "any destructive device as defined in this law, any weapon that is designed or intended to cause death or serious bodily injury through the release, dissemination, or impact of toxic or poisonous chemicals, or their precursors, any weapon involving a biological agent, toxin, or vector (as those terms are defined in section 178 of this title), any weapon that is designed to release radiation or radioactivity at a level dangerous to human life."

Following the tragic attacks of September 11, 2001, Zacarias Moussaoui was charged with being the intended twentieth hijacker. Moussaoui could not board any of the hijacked flights on September 11 because he was in federal custody. Exhibit 6–3 is an excerpt of his indictment.

## Exhibit 6–3 Indictment of the Twentieth Hijacker in the September 11, 2001, Attacks on the United States

| IN THE UNITED STATES DISTRICT COURT FOR THE EASTERN DISTRICT OF VIRGINIA ALEXANDRIA DIVISION | | |
|---|---|---|
| UNITED STATES OF AMERICA | ) | CRIMINAL NO: |
| | ) | |
| -v- | ) | Conspiracy to Commit Acts of Terrorism |
| | ) | Transcending National Boundaries |
| ZACARIAS MOUSSAOUI, | ) | (18 U.S.C. §§ 2332b(a)(2) & (c)) |
| a/k/a "Shaqil," | ) | (Count One) |
| a/k/a "Abu Khalid al Sahrawi," | ) | |
| | ) | Conspiracy to Commit Aircraft Piracy |
| Defendant. ) | | (49 U.S.C. §§ 46502 (a)(1)(A) and (a)(2)(B)) |
| | ) | (Count Two) |
| | ) | |
| | ) | Conspiracy to Destroy Aircraft |
| | ) | (18 U.S.C. §§ 32(a)(7) & 34) |
| | ) | (Count Three) |

```
                    )
                    )          Conspiracy to Use Weapons of Mass
                               Destruction
                    )          (18 U.S.C. § 2332a(a))
                    )          (Count Four)
                    )
                    )          Conspiracy to Murder United States
                               Employees
                    )          (18 U.S.C. §§ 1114 & 1117)
                    )          (Count Five)
                    )
                    )          Conspiracy to Destroy Property
                    )          (18 U.S.C. §§ 844(f), (i), (n))
                    )          (Count Six)
```

DECEMBER 2001 TERM AT ALEXANDRIA INDICTMENT

THE GRAND JURY CHARGES THAT:

<u>COUNT ONE</u>

(Conspiracy to Commit Acts of Terrorism Transcending National Boundaries)

<u>Background: al Qaeda</u>

1. At all relevant times from in or about 1989 until the date of the filing of this Indictment, an international terrorist group existed which was dedicated to opposing non-Islamic governments with force and violence. This organization grew out of the "mekhtab al khidemat" (the "Services Office") organization which had maintained offices in various parts of the world, including Afghanistan, Pakistan (particularly in Peshawar), and the United States. The group was founded by Usama Bin Laden and Muhammad Atef, a/k/a "Abu Hafs al Masry," together with "Abu Ubaidah al Banshiri," and others. From in or about 1989 until the present, the group called itself "al Qaeda" ("the Base"). . . .

2. Bin Laden and al Qaeda violently opposed the United States for several reasons. First, the United States was regarded as an "infidel" because it was not governed in a manner consistent with the group's extremist interpretation of Islam. Second, the United States was viewed as providing essential support for other "infidel" governments and institutions, particularly the governments of Saudi Arabia and Egypt, the nation of Israel, and the United Nations organization, which were regarded as enemies of the group. Third, al Qaeda opposed the involvement of the United States armed forces in the Gulf War in 1991 and in Operation Restore Hope in Somalia in 1992 and 1993. In particular, al Qaeda opposed the continued presence of American military forces in Saudi Arabia (and elsewhere on the Saudi Arabian peninsula) following the Gulf War. Fourth, al Qaeda opposed the United States Government because of the arrest, conviction and imprisonment of persons belonging to al Qaeda or its affiliated terrorist groups or those with whom it worked. For these and other reasons, Bin Laden declared a jihad, or holy war, against the United States, which he has carried out through al Qaeda and its affiliated organizations.

3. One of the principal goals of al Qaeda was to drive the United States armed forces out of Saudi Arabia (and elsewhere on the Saudi Arabian peninsula) and Somalia by violence. Members of al Qaeda issued *fatwahs* (rulings on Islamic law) indicating that such attacks were both proper and necessary.

4. Al Qaeda functioned both on its own and through some of the terrorist organizations that operated under its umbrella, . . .

7. Since at least 1989, until the filing of this Indictment, Usama Bin Laden and the terrorist group al Qaeda sponsored, managed, and/or financially supported training camps in Afghanistan, which camps were used to instruct members and associates of al Qaeda and its affiliated terrorist groups in the use of firearms, explosives, chemical weapons, and other weapons of mass destruction. In addition to providing training in the use of various weapons, these camps were used to conduct operational planning against United States targets around the world and experiments in the use of chemical and biological weapons. . . .

(continued)

### The September 11 Hijackers

9. On September 11, 2001, co-conspirators Mohammed Atta, Abdul Alomari, Wail al-Shehri, Waleed al-Shehri, and Satam al-Suqami hijacked American Airlines Flight 11, bound from Boston to Los Angeles, and crashed it into the North Tower of the World Trade Center in New York. (In this Indictment, each hijacker will be identified with the flight number of the plane he hijacked.)

10. On September 11, 2001, co-conspirators Marwan al-Shehhi, Fayez Ahmed, a/k/a "Banihammad Fayez," Ahmed al-Ghamdi, Hamza al-Ghamdi, and Mohald al-Shehri hijacked United Airlines Flight 175, bound from Boston to Los Angeles, and crashed it into the South Tower of the World Trade Center in New York.

11. On September 11, 2001, co-conspirators Khalid al-Midhar, Nawaf al-Hazmi, Hani Hanjour, Salem al-Hamzi, and Majed Moqed hijacked American Airlines Flight 77, bound from Virginia to Los Angeles, and crashed it into the Pentagon.

12. On September 11, 2001, co-conspirators Ziad Jarrah, Ahmed al-Haznawi, Saaed al-Ghamdi, and Ahmed al-Nami hijacked United Airlines Flight 93, bound from Newark to San Francisco, and crashed it in Pennsylvania.

### The Defendant

13. ZACARIAS MOUSSAOUI, a/k/a "Shaqil," a/k/a "Abu Khalid al Sahrawi," was born in France of Moroccan descent on May 30, 1968. Before 2001 he was a resident of the United Kingdom. MOUSSAOUI held a masters degree from Southbank University in the United Kingdom and traveled widely.

### The Charge

16. From in or about 1989 until the date of the filing of this Indictment, in the Eastern District of Virginia, the Southern District of New York, and elsewhere, the defendant, ZACARIAS MOUSSAOUI, a/k/a "Shaqil," a/k/a "Abu Khalid al Sahrawi," with other members and associates of al Qaeda and others known and unknown to the Grand Jury, unlawfully, wilfully and knowingly combined, conspired, confederated and agreed to kill and maim persons within the United States, and to create a substantial risk of serious bodily injury to other persons by destroying and damaging structures, conveyances, and other real and personal property within the United States, in violation of the laws of States and the United States, in circumstances involving conduct transcending national boundaries, and in which facilities of interstate and foreign commerce were used in furtherance of the offense, the offense obstructed, delayed, and affected interstate and foreign commerce, the victim was the United States Government, members of the uniformed services, and officials, officers, employees, and agents of the governmental branches, departments, and agencies of the United States, and the structures, conveyances, and other real and personal property were, in whole or in part, owned, possessed, and leased to the United States and its departments and agencies, resulting in the deaths of thousands of persons on September 11, 2001.

### Overt Acts

In furtherance of the conspiracy, and to effect its objects, the defendant, and others known and unknown to the Grand Jury, committed the following overt acts:

### MOUSSAOUI Trains at Al Qaeda Training Camp

\* \* \*

### MOUSSAOUI Inquires About Flight Training

34. On or about September 29, 2000, ZACARIAS MOUSSAOUI contacted Airman Flight School in Norman, Oklahoma using an e-mail account he set up on September 6 with an internet service provider in Malaysia. . . .

### MOUSSAOUI Comes to the United States

46. Between on or about February 26, 2001, and on or about May 29, 2001, ZACARIAS MOUSSAOUI attended the Airman Flight School in Norman, Oklahoma, ending his classes early.

### MOUSSAOUI Contacts a Commercial Flight School

51. On or about May 23, 2001, ZACARIAS MOUSSAOUI contacted an office of the Pan Am International Flight Academy in Miami, Florida via e-mail.

<u>Hijackers Open Bank Accounts</u>

52. In Summer 2001, Fayez Ahmed (#175), Saeed al-Ghamdi (#93), Hamza al-Ghamdi (#175), Waleed al-Shehri (#11), Ziad Jarrah (#93), Satam al-Suqami (#11), Mohald al-Shehri (#175), Ahmed al-Nami (#93), and Ahmed al-Haznawi (#93) each opened a Florida Sun Trust bank account with a cash deposit.

<u>MOUSSAOUI Inquires About Aerial Application of Pesticides</u>

53. In or about June 2001, in Norman, Oklahoma, ZACARIAS MOUSSAOUI made inquiries about starting a crop dusting company.

<u>MOUSSAOUI Purchases Flight Training Equipment</u>

56. On or about June 20, 2001, ZACARIAS MOUSSAOUI purchased flight deck videos for the Boeing 747 Model 400 and the Boeing 747 Model 200 from the Ohio Pilot Store.

<u>MOUSSAOUI Pays for Flight Lessons</u>

60. On or about July 10 and July 11, 2001, ZACARIAS MOUSSAOUI made credit card payments to the Pan Am International Flight Academy for a simulator course in commercial flight training.

<u>MOUSSAOUI Purchases Knives</u>

68. On or about August 3, 2001, ZACARIAS MOUSSAOUI purchased two knives in Oklahoma City, Oklahoma.

<u>MOUSSAOUI Travels from Oklahoma to Minnesota</u>

70. On or about August 9 and August 10, 2001, ZACARIAS MOUSSAOUI was driven from Oklahoma to Minnesota.

<u>MOUSSAOUI Takes Commercial Flying Lessons in Minnesota</u>

71. On or about August 10, 2001, in Minneapolis, Minnesota, ZACARIAS MOUSSAOUI paid approximately $6,300 in cash to the Pan Am International Flight Academy.

72. Between August 13 and August 15, 2001, ZACARIAS MOUSSAOUI attended the Pan Am International Flight Academy in Minneapolis, Minnesota, for simulator training on the Boeing 747 Model 400.

<u>MOUSSAOUI Possesses Knives and Other Items</u>

\* \* \*

<u>MOUSSAOUI Lies to Federal Agents</u>

74. On or about August 17, 2001, ZACARIAS MOUSSAOUI, while being interviewed by federal agents in Minneapolis, attempted to explain his presence in the United States by falsely stating that he was simply interested in learning to fly.

<u>Final Preparations for the Coordinated Air Attack</u>

\* \* \*

<u>The September 11, 2001 Terrorist Attacks</u>

100. On or about September 11, 2001, the hijackers possessed a handwritten set of final instructions for a martyrdom operation on an airplane using knives.

101. On or about September 11, 2001, Mohammed Atta (#11) and Abdulaziz Alomari (#11) flew from Portland, Maine to Boston, Massachusetts.

102. On or about September 11, 2001, Mohammed Atta (#11) possessed operating manuals for the Boeing 757 and 767, pepper spray, knives, and German travel visas.

103. On or about September 11, 2001, Ziad Jarrah (#93) possessed flight manuals for Boeing 757 and 767 aircraft.

104. On or about September 11, 2001, Mohammed Atta, Abdul Aziz Alomari, Satam al-Suqami, Waleed M. al-Shehri, and Waleed al-Shehri hijacked American Airlines Flight 11, a Boeing 767, which had departed Boston at approximately 7:55 A.M. They flew Flight 11 into the North Tower of the World Trade Center in Manhattan at approximately 8:45 A.M., causing the collapse of the tower and the deaths of thousands of persons.

(continued)

105. On or about September 11, 2001, Hamza al-Ghamdi, Fayez Ahmed, Mohald al-Shehri, Ahmed al-Ghamdi, and Marwan al-Shehhi hijacked United Airlines Flight 175, a Boeing 767, which had departed from Boston at approximately 8:15 A.M. They flew Flight 175 into the South Tower of the World Trade Center in Manhattan at approximately 9:05 A.M., causing the collapse of the tower and the deaths of thousands of persons.

106. On or about September 11, 2001, Khalid al-Midhar, Majed Moqed, Nawaf al-Hazmi, Salem al-Hazmi, and Hani Hanjour hijacked American Airlines Flight 77, a Boeing 757, which had departed from Virginia bound for Los Angeles, at approximately 8:10 A.M. They flew Flight 77 into the Pentagon in Virginia at approximately 9:40 A.M., causing the deaths of 189 persons.

107. On or about September 11, 2001, Saeed al-Ghamdi, Ahmed al-Nami, Ahmed al-Haznawi, and Ziad Jarrah hijacked United Airlines Flight 93, a Boeing 757, which had departed from Newark, New Jersey bound for San Francisco at approximately 8:00 A.M. After resistance by the passengers, Flight 93 crashed in Somerset County, Pennsylvania at approximately 10:10 A.M., killing all on board.

### COUNT TWO

#### (Conspiracy to Commit Aircraft Piracy)

1. The allegations contained in Count One are repeated.

2. From in or about 1989 until the date of the filing of this Indictment, in the Eastern District of Virginia, the Southern District of New York, and elsewhere, the defendant, ZACARIAS MOUSSAOUI, a/k/a "Shaqil," a/k/a "Abu Khalid al Sahrawi," and other members and associates of al Qaeda and others known and unknown to the Grand Jury, unlawfully, wilfully and knowingly combined, conspired, confederated and agreed to commit aircraft piracy, by seizing and exercising control of aircraft in the special aircraft jurisdiction of the United States by force, violence, threat of force and violence, and intimidation, and with wrongful intent, with the result that thousands of people died on September 11, 2001.

#### Overt Acts

3. In furtherance of the conspiracy, and to effect its illegal objects, the defendant, and others known and unknown to the Grand Jury, committed the overt acts set forth in Count One of this Indictment, which are fully incorporated by reference.

(In violation of Title 49, United States Code, Sections 46502(a)(1)(A) and (a)(2)(B).)

### COUNT THREE

#### (Conspiracy to Destroy Aircraft)

1. The allegations contained in Count One are repeated.

2. From in or about 1989 until the date of the filing of this Indictment, in the Eastern District of Virginia, the Southern District of New York, and elsewhere, the defendant, ZACARIAS MOUSSAOUI, a/k/a "Shaqil," a/k/a "Abu Khalid al Sahrawi," and other members and associates of al Qaeda and others known and unknown to the Grand Jury, unlawfully, wilfully and knowingly combined, conspired, confederated and agreed to willfully destroy and wreck aircraft in the special aircraft jurisdiction of the United States, and to willfully perform acts of violence against and incapacitate individuals on such aircraft, so as likely to endanger the safety of such aircraft, resulting in the deaths of thousands of persons on September 11, 2001.

#### Overt Acts

3. In furtherance of the conspiracy, and to effect its illegal objects, the defendant, and others known and unknown to the Grand Jury, committed the overt acts set forth in Count One of this Indictment, which are fully incorporated by reference.

(In violation of Title 18, United States Code, Sections 32(a)(7) and 34.)

### COUNT FOUR

#### (Conspiracy to Use Weapons of Mass Destruction)

1. The allegations contained in Count One are repeated.

2. From in or about 1989 until the date of the filing of this Indictment, in the Eastern District of Virginia, the Southern District of New York, and elsewhere, the defendant, ZACARIAS MOUSSAOUI, a/k/a "Shaqil," a/k/a "Abu Khalid al Sahrawi," and other members and associates of al Qaeda and others known and unknown to the Grand Jury, unlawfully, wilfully and knowingly combined, conspired, confederated and agreed to use weapons of mass destruction, namely, airplanes intended for use as missiles, bombs, and similar devices, without lawful authority against persons within the United States,

with the results of such use affecting interstate and foreign commerce, and against property that was owned, leased and used by the United States and by departments and agencies of the United States, with the result that thousands of people died on September 11, 2001.

<u>Overt Acts</u>

3. In furtherance of the conspiracy, and to effect its illegal objects, the defendant, and others known and unknown to the Grand Jury, committed the overt acts set forth in Count One of this Indictment, which are fully incorporated by reference.

(In violation of Title 18, United States Code, Section 2332a(a).)

<u>COUNT FIVE</u>

(Conspiracy to Murder United States Employees)

1. The allegations contained in Count One are repeated.

2. From in or about 1989 until the date of the filing of this Indictment, in the Eastern District of Virginia, the Southern District of New York, and elsewhere, the defendant, ZACARIAS MOUSSAOUI, a/k/a "Shaqil," a/k/a "Abu Khalid al Sahrawi," and other members and associates of al Qaeda and others known and unknown to the Grand Jury, unlawfully, wilfully and knowingly combined, conspired, confederated and agreed to kill officers and employees of the United States and agencies and branches thereof, while such officers and employees were engaged in, and on account of, the performance of their official duties, and persons assisting such employees in the performance of their duties, in violation of Section 1114 of Title 18, United States Code, including members of the Department of Defense stationed at the Pentagon.

<u>Overt Acts</u>

3. In furtherance of the conspiracy, and to effect its illegal objects, the defendant, and others known and unknown to the Grand Jury, committed the overt acts set forth in Count One of this Indictment, which are fully incorporated by reference.

(In violation of Title 18, United States Code, Sections 1114 and 1117.)

<u>COUNT SIX</u>

(Conspiracy to Destroy Property of the United States)

1. The allegations contained in Count One are repeated.

2. . . .

<u>Overt Acts</u>

3. In furtherance of the conspiracy, and to effect its illegal objects, the defendant, and others known and unknown to the Grand Jury, committed the overt acts set forth in Count One of this Indictment, which are fully incorporated by reference.

(In violation of Title 18, United States Code, Sections 844(f), (i), and (n).)

_____
FOREPERSON

_____
MICHAEL CHERTOFF
ASSISTANT ATTORNEY GENERAL

_____
PAUL J. McNULTY
UNITED STATES ATTORNEY EASTERN
DISTRICT OF VIRGINIA

_____
MARY JO WHITE
UNITED STATES ATTORNEY SOUTHERN
DISTRICT OF NEW YORK

**PUBLICATION DATE:**
January 15, 2002

Source: http://www.justice.gov/ag/moussaouiindictment.htm

**Sidebar**

**Crime Stats: Terrorism**

According to the Center for Strategic and International Studies (CSIS), there were 893 terrorist incidents in the United States between 1994 and May 8, 2020. CSIS divided the incidents into five groups: right-wing, left-wing, ethnonationalist, religious, and other; 57% of all plots and attacks were perpetrated by right-wing, 25% by left-wing, and 15% by religious terrorists. Although fewer in number, religious terrorists killed the greatest number of people; nearly all occurring during the attacks of 9-11.

*Source:* Center for Strategic and International Studies. *The Escalating Terrorism Problem in the United States.* June 17, 2020. Retrieved from CSIS.org on December 26, 2020.

Finally, terrorists are subject to all the "traditional" penal laws of the states and nation. Terrorists that steal can be prosecuted for larceny, and those that kill can be prosecuted for murder. States also have terrorism laws, similar to the federal laws discussed next.

# Crimes Against the Environment and Animals

Learning Objective: Identify and describe three or more environmental crimes or crimes involving animal welfare or cruelty.

With the modernization of the United States has come a threat to the environment. The air and water that people depend upon for life and health have become polluted. Many species of flora and fauna have been lost, and many more are threatened.

Modernization threatens the environment in several ways. In the process of "developing" land, habitats are lost. Also, the use of dangerous chemicals and toxins has become commonplace. In many industries, toxic by-products of manufacturing are common. Toxic wastes and substances pose use, transportation, and disposal problems. The release of dangerous substances into the air or into water endangers public health and safety. The world's increased population aggravates the problem. Greater numbers of people place greater stress on natural systems. Resources are depleted faster, and nature's cleansing process becomes strained and less effective.

The first major federal environmental law was the Refuse Act of 1899, a law that prohibits, with criminal penalties, dumping refuse into waterways.[67] It continues in effect today. Today, there is a large body of environmental law that, to some extent, addresses many of the nation's environmental problems. The federal government's policy is to create and maintain conditions in which man and nature can exist in productive harmony. Both the federal and state governments play a role in regulating the environment, although the federal government is playing the larger part currently.

Several federal administrative agencies are charged with overseeing the enforcement and administration of environmental laws, including the Environmental Protection Agency, Coast Guard, Department of the Interior, Occupational Health and Safety Commission, and Department of Justice. Federal law provides for administrative, civil, and criminal sanctions on environmental law violators.

There are two classes of environmental laws. One class of laws is intended to further the public health and safety. The Clean Air Act, the Clean Water Act, and similar statutes are examples of this type of environmental regulation. A second class of laws is intended to protect the environment itself, for its aesthetic and recreational values. The Endangered Species Act is an example of a conservation law. Of course, many laws serve both objectives.

Until recently, environmental offenses were not usually treated as criminal; rather, they were classified as civil or administrative infractions. The federal government relied almost exclusively on administrative and civil processes to enforce environmental laws. Fines were the most common penalty sought by the government against offenders.

The belief that environmental violations are serious enough to be prosecuted as criminal offenses is a recent development. For example, one of the most notorious environmental cases was that of the Love Canal neighborhood in Niagara Falls, New York, where it was discovered in 1978 that the improper disposal of toxins was causing death and illness to local residents. An entire community was forced to relocate to escape the danger—yet not one person was prosecuted in the Love Canal case.

The fear of another Love Canal—or an accident like the one involving Union Carbide in Bhopal, India, where 2,000 people were killed and 200,000 people were injured—and the dangers posed by other environmental wrongs led Congress to strengthen environmental laws. The measures included added criminal sanctions. Relying on civil remedies alone had proved ineffective. Individuals were not being held accountable, and corporations found it more cost-effective to violate the law and pay any fines than to comply with the law.

Therefore, although most violations continue to be handled through civil and administrative proceedings, the number of environmental criminal cases is increasing. Of the 500 largest corporations in the United States, one-fourth have been convicted of an environmental crime or have been subject to civil penalties for violating environmental laws.[68] The Department of Justice has a special division charged with prosecuting environmental law crimes.

Unlike at Common Law, today, business entities such as corporations may be charged with crimes. Fines and dissolution of a corporation are examples of the penalties that may be imposed. Charging corporations for environmental violations is common. Of course, individuals may also be charged with violating environmental laws, and corporate employees may be charged for actions taken on behalf of a corporation. It is not a defense for an employee to claim that he or she was following a supervisor's directive, nor may it be a defense for the supervisor to claim that he or she is innocent because he or she delegated performance of the act to an employee.

Some environmental crimes are strict liability. Others, and of course those that can be punished with jail time, require some mens rea, usually a knowing violation.

Several federal environmental laws contain criminal sanctions. The most significant of these laws are the Clean Water Act; the Clean Air Act; the Comprehensive Environmental Response, Compensation, and Liability Act; the Resource Conservation and Recovery Act; the Occupational Safety and Health Act; the Toxic Substances Control Act; the Federal Insecticide, Fungicide, and Rodenticide Act; the Emergency Planning and Community Right-to-Know Act; and the Endangered Species Act. All statutes are examples of regulation for the public health, except for the final statute, which is a conservation law. These laws provide for administrative and civil remedies and procedures, in addition to criminal sanctions.

## Clean Water Act

The Clean Water Act (CWA)[69] regulates the discharge of pollutants into the nation's navigable waters. The CWA establishes a scheme of permits and reporting. The contamination of water with a pollutant, without a permit or exceeding the limits of a permit, is criminal under the Clean Water Act.

Both negligent and knowing acts are criminalized and may be punished with fines and imprisonment. A knowing act is punished more severely than a negligent act. Offenders who have acted negligently may be sentenced to one year in prison, whereas knowing offenders may be sentenced to three years in prison.[70] Fines may also be imposed for both, in addition to any civil remedies.

Also, the CWA contains a "knowing endangerment" provision. If a person violates the CWA with knowledge that the violation "places another person in imminent danger of death or serious bodily injury," the offender may be sentenced to up to 15 years in prison, and significant fines may be imposed.

Finally, false reporting under the Act is criminal and may be punished by up to two years in prison, in addition to a fine.

## Clean Air Act

The goal of the Clean Air Act (CAA) is to preserve air quality. It does this by regulating emissions of dangerous substances into the air.

Similar to the CWA in its criminal aspects, the CAA criminalized negligent and knowing violations of its mandates, punishing the latter more severely.[71] Further, it contains knowing endangerment and false reporting provisions.

## Comprehensive Environmental Response, Compensation, and Liability Act

The Comprehensive Environmental Response, Compensation, and Liability Act (CERCLA) is commonly known as *Superfund*. The purpose of CERCLA is to identify and clean up existing hazardous waste sites.

Any person who knowingly falsifies or destroys any required record or who fails to report a spill of hazardous materials may be punished with fines and imprisonment.[72]

## Resource Conservation and Recovery Act

The Resource Conservation and Recovery Act (RCRA) is similar to CERCLA in that they regulate the same subject matter: hazardous materials. However, CERCLA is an after-the-fact regulation intended to clean up existing sites, whereas RCRA is intended to regulate the day-to-day use, storage, transportation, handling, and disposal of hazardous materials.

There are no negligent violations under RCRA; rather, the mens rea for conviction of its prohibitions is knowledge. For example, the knowing transportation of hazardous waste to an unlicensed facility; the knowing treatment, storage, or disposal of hazardous waste without a permit; and the knowing violation of a permit are criminal and may be punished with both imprisonment and fines. As with the CWA and the CAA, knowingly endangering another enhances the punishment for a violation of RCRA.[73]

## Occupational Safety and Health Act

The Occupational Safety and Health Act (OSHA) regulates the work environment of the American worker. The objective of the law is to create safe working conditions. There is a plethora of regulations enforcing this mandate.

Any employer who causes the death of an employee as a result of noncompliance with OSHA may be prosecuted and sentenced to imprisonment and a fine. Of course, the employer may also be liable under other criminal laws, such as negligent manslaughter.

Additionally, OSHA requires employers to notify their employees of potential exposure to dangerous chemicals and to provide information and resources to protect the employees. Failure to notify employees of this risk is a criminal omission under OSHA. False reporting is also a crime under this statute.

## Toxic Substances Control Act

The Toxic Substances Control Act (TSCA) is the most comprehensive federal law concerning dangerous substances. The Environmental Protection Agency (EPA) is delegated considerable authority under the TSCA to regulate the sale, manufacture, development, processing, distribution, and disposal of toxic substances. Under the TSCA, the EPA is empowered to ban, or otherwise control, the production and distribution of chemicals. Asbestos and radon are examples of chemicals that the EPA has heavily regulated under the TSCA.

Any person who knowingly or willfully violates the TSCA concerning the manufacture, testing, or distribution of a chemical may be punished with both a fine and imprisonment. Also, false reporting, failing to maintain records, and failing to submit records as required by law are criminal acts under the TSCA.[74]

## Federal Insecticide, Fungicide, and Rodenticide Act

Chemicals that are lethal to pests may also be lethal or at least harmful to humans. In addition to being inhaled, pesticides find their way into human drinking water and food.

The Federal Insecticide, Fungicide, and Rodenticide Act (FIFRA) delegates to the EPA the task of regulating the manufacture, sale, distribution, and use of these chemicals. Some chemicals are forbidden; there are limits on the use of others. There are labeling and reporting requirements.

Knowing violations of any of FIFRA's requirements are criminal and may be punished with fines and imprisonment.[75]

## Emergency Planning and Community Right-to-Know Act

Bhopal, India; Chernobyl; and closer to home, Three Mile Island—all three are reminders that accidents happen, or that the actions of one person, such as a terrorist, can cause a tragedy of enormous proportion. In both the Chernobyl and Bhopal incidents, there was no planning or preparation for an accident.

The purpose of the Emergency Planning and Community Right-to-Know Act is to better prepare the community in which a facility is sited for disaster and to inform the community about emissions of hazardous substances by the facility. The Act requires facilities that use or produce chemicals to report both accidental and routine releases of substances into the air or water. Further, facilities are required to provide local officials (e.g., hospitals) with information about the chemicals used.

Knowing or willful failure to give notice of a release may be punished by both imprisonment and a fine.

## Endangered Species Act

The Endangered Species Act (ESA)[76] and the Marine Mammal Protection Act represent a different form of environmental law from those discussed so far. The purpose of these laws is not to protect the public health; rather, the intent is to preserve the integrity of the environment itself.

The ESA establishes a program of conservation of threatened and endangered species of plants and animals and the habitats where they are found. The law is coadministered by the Departments of Interior, Commerce, Agriculture, and Justice.

The ESA prohibits the sale, taking, possession, importation, and exportation of endangered species and the products of those species. Violations of the law are punishable by both fines and imprisonment.

## Marine Mammal Protection Act

Similar to the ESA, the Marine Mammal Protection Act (MMPA)[77] is intended to protect and conserve marine mammals. The taking of such creatures without a permit by a U.S. flag vessel while on the high seas is a crime. The taking, possession, and trade of animals protected under the law are prohibited within the United States unless a permit has been obtained. Fines and imprisonment may be imposed on violators.

These are but a few of the federal environmental laws. Also, many states have similar laws. In some instances, the states have been delegated the authority to enforce federal law. Environmental laws affect every person, not just businesses that use or trade in hazardous materials.

Because of overpopulation, high-density urbanization, industrialization, resource exploitation, and technological advances, every person has a duty to be environmentally aware, and the laws of the nation impose environmental obligations on the individual. The proper disposal of trash, car batteries, and motor oil, and the regulation of hunting and fishing, are examples of environmental laws that affect the daily lives of members of the public.

## Other Animal Protection Laws

Not long ago, law didn't protect animals. Owners were free to neglect and cruelly treat animals. This began to change about a hundred years ago, as social values concerning the humane treatment of animals gained traction. The pace of change accelerated in recent decades, a consequence of both animal rights concerns and an increasing concern that animal abuse is a precursor to violence against people.

Today, there are many other forms of animal protection laws. Animal cruelty and welfare laws vary considerably between the states. Many of the laws are regulatory, others criminal. They differ in language, acts criminalized, and punishment. The following offenses are commonly recognized:

- Cruelty
- Abandonment
- Neglect
- Bestiality

Many states, such as Wisconsin, make dognapping and catnapping a crime. It is common for states to exempt farming, meat, and the entertainment industries from animal treatment laws. Three of the listed acts are crimes of commission. The fourth, neglect, is a crime of omission. As an example of a modern law, Ohio criminalizes animal fighting, abandonment, injuring, poising, and other specific inhumane acts, in addition to cruelty:

O.R.C. §959.13: No person shall:

(1) Torture an animal, deprive one of necessary sustenance, unnecessarily or cruelly beat, needlessly mutilate or kill, or impound or confine an animal without supplying it during such confinement with a sufficient quantity of good wholesome food and water;

(2) Impound or confine an animal without affording it, during such confinement, access to shelter from wind, rain, snow, or excessive direct sunlight if it can reasonably be expected that the animals would otherwise become sick or in some other way suffer. Division (A)(2) of this section does not apply to animals impounded or confined prior to slaughter. For the purpose of this section, shelter means a man-made enclosure, windbreak, sunshade, or natural windbreak or sunshade that is developed from the earth's contour, tree development, or vegetation.[;]

(3) Carry or convey an animal in a cruel or inhuman[e] manner;

(4) Keep animals other than cattle, poultry or fowl, swine, sheep, or goats in an enclosure without wholesome exercise and change of air, nor or feed cows on food that produces impure or unwholesome milk;

(5) Detain livestock in railroad cars or compartments longer than twenty-eight hours after they are so placed without supplying them with necessary food, water, and attention, nor permit such stock to be so crowded as to overlie, crush, wound, or kill each other.

The federal government also regulates the treatment of animals, the Animal Welfare Act of 1966 (AWA) being the most prominent. The AWA applies to the use of specific listed animals in research, entertainment, and exhibition, and that are traded, sold, and transported in interstate or international commerce. Dogs, cats, rabbits, and primates all fall under the statute's protections. Farm animals, fish, horses, birds, and other animals are excluded from the statute's mandates. The AWA requires dealers, researchers, and people who exhibit protected animals to provide adequate housing, nutrition, veterinary care, and protection from the natural elements.

The estate of the author Ernest Hemingway was the subject of an AWA investigation in the early 2000s. The Hemingway home in the Florida Keys operates as a museum. In addition to leaving the home, Hemingway left cats. Specifically, polydactyly, or six- or seven-toed, cats who are descendants of the cats that Hemingway owned when he lived on the property. The cats roam freely and have proven popular with museum guests and locals. Concerned for the welfare of the cats after one wondered off the property, a volunteer of the museum contacted the United States Department of Agriculture (USDA), the agency responsible for enforcing the AWA.

The USDA inspectors concluded that the cats were covered by the AWA and ordered the museum to obtain an exhibition license and to erect a higher fence, install electric wire, or, in the alternative, hire a night watchperson to ensure that the cats didn't leave the property. The Agency also demanded that the museum provide the cats with separate sleeping cages and elevated resting surfaces. It issued these order in spite of the evidence that the cats were living good. The most compelling evidence of this conclusion came from an investigator from the nonprofit organization People for the Ethical Treatment of Animals (PETA), which had been hired by the USDA to assess the situation. The investigator wrote that "[w]hat I found was a bunch of fat, happy and relaxed cats. God save the cats."[78] The museum litigated the orders, arguing that the federal government's authority under the Commerce Clause didn't extend to the museum or to the cats. It lost on appeal.[79]

The federal government enacted another animal protection law in 1999, intended to criminalize "crush videos." Crush videos involve people torturing, mutilating, and killing small animals to satisfy sexual fetishes. The cruel acts are criminal in all fifty states. But videos made available on the Internet present jurisdictional problems for the states. This is why the federal government became involved.

The original federal law, which criminalized "depictions" of animal cruelty was invalidated by SCOTUS on First Amendment grounds.[80] The Court held that it was overbroad because it forbade the distribution of depictions of animal cruelty, not actual animal cruelty. In response to the decision, Congress amended the law to make it a crime to distribute videos that (1) depict actual conduct in which one or more non-human animals is intentionally crushed, burned, drowned, suffocated, impaled, or otherwise subjected to serious bodily injury and (2) is obscene. By narrowing the law to videos of genuine cruelty, not just depictions and by requiring that a video meet the test for obscenity, the amended law was upheld by a federal appellate court.[81]

To animal rights activists, however, the law didn't do enough because it only criminalized videos of cruelty, not the acts of cruelty themselves. In 2020, the Preventing Animal Cruelty and Torture Act (PACT) was enacted to address this concern. The law makes it a crime for a person to engage in crushing or to create a crush video. Crushing is defined as "actual conduct in which one or more living non-human mammals, birds, reptiles, or amphibians is purposely crushed, burned, drowned, suffocated, impaled, or otherwise subjected to serious bodily injury."

---

## Ethical Considerations

### The Special Obligations of Prosecutors

As discussed in Chapter 5, prosecutors hold a special place in the criminal justice system. A prosecutor's overarching obligation is to justice, and his client is the people. Both ethics rules and the Constitution impose obligations on prosecutors that are not equally borne by defense counterparts. The ABA Model Rules of Professional Conduct even have a rule (Rule 3.8) dedicated to prosecuting attorneys.

Although rare, serious violations of the standards by prosecutors occur. In 2006, an exotic dancer claimed that she had been sexually assaulted by several members of the Duke University lacrosse team. The allegation resulted in serious racial tensions because the accuser was black and the three accused students were white. Even though the DNA of several individuals was found on the accuser, none of the DNA matched the students. The prosecutor in the case, Mike Nifong, along with an employee of the testing site, made the decision not to provide the results to the defense.

After zealously prosecuting the men and insisting in numerous interviews that they were guilty, Nifong eventually filed a motion to dismiss the charges. Subsequently, the North Carolina State Bar filed an ethics complaint against Nifong, alleging prosecutorial misconduct.

The first charge against Nifong was for his decision not to provide exculpatory evidence to the defense (note that defense counsel is not required to disclose incriminating evidence to the prosecutor in most circumstances). The disclosure of exculpatory evidence by prosecutors is required by bar rules and by the Supreme Court's decision in *Brady v. Maryland*, 373 U.S. 83 (1963).

Nifong was also charged with misusing pretrial publicity. It appears that he was not shy when in the media spotlight. He gave many interviews with local and national news agencies. In these interviews, he made false allegations about racial epithets rendered by the defendants; he spoke in detail about the facts, as he knew them; and he expressed his personal opinion about the defendants and their guilt. North Carolina's rule concerning pretrial publicity is similar to Rule 3.6 of the Model Rules of Professional Conduct. It states that "[a] lawyer who is participating or has participated in the investigation or litigation of a matter shall not make an extrajudicial statement that the lawyer knows or reasonably should know will be disseminated by means of public communication and will have a substantial likelihood of materially prejudicing an adjudicative proceeding in the matter." The rule continues by excepting specific facts from its prohibition. None of those exceptions covered the kind of statements made by Nifong.

Ultimately, the bar found that Nifong should have known that his statements would prejudice the case. He was also found to have misled the court on several occasions. This included several instances when he stated to the court, or to opposing counsel in discovery, that he knew of no exculpatory evidence, even though he knew about the exculpatory DNA results. In 2007, Mr. Nifong was disbarred for his actions, and he resigned as district attorney.

# Key Terms

Brandenburg Test
breaches of the peace
bribery
contempt

fighting words
misprision of treason
perjury
prostitution

sodomy
subornation of perjury
tax evasion
tax fraud

# Review Questions

1. Andy approaches Roberta, who is standing on a street corner, and offers her $50 for sex. Roberta, an undercover vice officer, arrests Andy. What crime should he be charged with?

2. Is there a constitutional right to engage in homosexual conduct between mature, consenting adults?

3. When may a state regulate material that is thought to be sexually repulsive? What constitutional provision hinders governments from regulating such expression?

4. What are fighting words? Are they protected by the First Amendment?

5. Is proof that a driver's blood-alcohol level exceeded the statutory maximum the only way to prove that a driver was under the influence? Is it a valid defense for driver-defendants to claim that they could drive safely, even though their blood-alcohol level exceeded the amount allowed by statute?

6. What are the elements of Continuing Criminal Enterprise, and who is the statute aimed at?

7. What are the basic elements of bribery? The MPC recognizes two types of bribery. Name the two.

8. Distinguish criminal contempt from civil contempt. Do the same for direct contempt and indirect contempt.

9. Is this statement true? "Perjury is a law that applies only to judicial proceedings." Explain your answer.

10. What are the elements of indecent exposure?

11. What are the elements of treason?

12. Identify two ways that the Patriot Act of 2001 expanded the authority of federal officials to address terrorism.

# Problems & Critical Thinking Exercises

1. Are the following statutes constitutional? Explain, if not.

Statute One: Loitering

Any person who loiters in a place in an unusual manner for longer than 15 minutes and reasonably causes a person to be concerned for their safety must identify himself to police when requested. Any person who refuses to identify himself under these circumstances or takes flight when approached by a police officer is guilty of loitering.

Statute Two: Loitering

Any person who continually loiters in public parks without apparent employment or who lives off the handouts of others is guilty of loitering.

2. State law prohibits "hardcore pornography." Among the many prohibitions of the law is a provision making it a felony to possess or sell materials that are known to depict bestiality (sex between a human and an animal). Sam, a local adult bookstore owner, sold to Herb a magazine entitled *Wild on the Farm*. The magazine was sealed, and its contents were not visible. The magazine was delivered to Sam in error, part of a large shipment of magazines and books.

During a raid on Sam's establishment, the local police discovered the sales ticket reflecting Herb's purchase, his name, and his address. The police then obtained a search warrant for Herb's home and found the magazine during their search. Sam and Herb have both been charged with violating the state's obscenity law. Should they be convicted? Explain your answer.

3. Do you believe that acts that harm no one, but that most members of society find immoral, should be criminalized? Explain your position.

4. How has bribery been changed since it has become a statutory crime?

5–7. Classify each of the following as direct or indirect contempt and civil or criminal contempt.

5. During a personal injury trial, Noah told the judge to "kiss my ass" and then threw an apple, striking the judge in the head.

6. During a union dispute, a judge ordered striking employees back to work. They refused to comply with the order, and the judge ordered that each employee pay $50 per day until he or she returned to work.

7. Jon received a court order to tear down a fence he had constructed. The order was served by a sheriff. Immediately after the sheriff handed the order to him, Jon screamed, "Forget that idiot judge, I'm not tearing down the fence!" Jon never removed the fence, and the judge had him arrested and ordered him to remain in jail until he agreed to comply with the order.

8. Consider and discuss this statement:

Possession and use of drugs or alcohol should not be a crime. The only dangers presented from these substances arise when a person works, drives, or conducts some activity that requires the full use of the senses, while under their influence. Criminal statutes should be narrow and proscribe only the harm sought to be prevented. No harm is created by use in controlled environments, such as in the home. Accordingly, statutes should only proscribe engaging in certain undertakings while under the influence of alcohol or drugs.

9. Do you believe terrorists should be considered criminals (and handled by the criminal justice system) or combatants (and handled by the military)? Does it matter if the accused is a U.S. citizen?

# Endnotes

1. Model Penal Code § 251.2(5).
2. 18 U.S.C. § 2421.
3. The Court upheld a sodomy law in *Bowers v. Hardwick*, 478 U.S. 186 (1986) but explicitly reversed that decision in *Lawrence v. Texas*, 539 U.S. 558 (2003).
4. *Obergefell v. Hodges*, 576 U.S. 644 (2015).
5. 501 U.S. 560 (1991).
6. *Pap's v. City of Erie*, 529 U.S. 277 (2000)
7. Model Penal Code § 251.1.
8. 18 U.S.C. § 1461.
9. Anderson, "Mapplethorpe Photos on Trial," *A.B.A. J.* 28 (Dec. 1990).
10. There are other limits on First Amendment freedoms. Some of these are discussed in Chapter 8, in the constitutional defenses section. For more on the First Amendment, see Daniel E. Hall and John P. Feldmeier, *Constitutional Values: Governmental Powers and Individual Liberties*, chapters 10 and 11 (Upper Saddle River, NJ: Pearson Prentice Hall, 2009).
11. 378 U.S. 184 [1964]).
12. 354 U.S. 476 (1957).
13. *Manual Enterprises, Inc. v. Day*, 370 U.S. 478 (1962) (opinion by Justice Harlan).
14. 413 U.S. 15 (1973).
15. 50 Am. Jur. 2d *Lewdness, Indecency, etc.* 7 (1970).
16. See *Roth v. United States*, 354 U.S. 476, 487, n. 20 (1957).
17. *United States v. Guglielmi*, 819 F. 2d 451 (4th Cir. 1987).
18. See *New York v. Ferber*, 458 U.S. 747 (1982).
19. See *Capitol News Co. v. Metropolitan Government*, 562 S.W.2d 430 (Tenn. 1978).
20. 494 U.S. 103 (1990).

21. *Stanley v. Georgia*, 394 U.S. 557 (1969).

22. Model Penal Code § 251.4.

23. 143 *Cong. Rec.* E1633 (Sept. 3, 1997).

24. 110 Stat. 56.

25. 521 U.S. 844 (1997).

26. 47 U.S.C. § 231.

27. *Ashcroft v. ACLU* (2002).

28. 969 F. Supp. 160 (S.D. N.Y. 1997).

29. 553 U.S. 285 (2008).

30. MPC § 250.1.

31. 28 U.S.C. § 2101 and 2102.

32. *Champlinsky v. New Hampshire*, 315 U.S. 568 (1942).

33. 40 U.S. Code § 5104(e)

34. *Brandenburg v. Ohio*, 395 U.S. 444 (1969).

35. See Chapter 3 on personal status as an act.

36. 307 U.S. 174 (1939).

37. 445 U.S. 55 (1980).

38. See *Kolbe v Hogan*, 849 F.3d 114 (4th Cir. 2017). One possibility is that the Supreme Court will eventually identify a fundamental right to possession in the home, where strict scrutiny of restrictions will occur, and a lesser liberty right outside of the home where restrictions will be tested under the substantial relationship test.

39. *City of Seattle v. Evans*, 366 P.3d 906 (Wash. 2015)

40. *Mcdonald v. Chicago*, 561 U.S. 3025 (2010)

41. 26 U.S.C. § 5801 *et seq.*

42. 18 U.S.C. sec. 921.

43. *Id.*

44. *United States of America v. Mattis and Rahman*, Indictment dated June 11, 2020. Found at https://www.justice.gov/usao-edny/press-release/file/1285041/download on January 29, 2021.

45. 18 U.S.C. § 844.

46. Model Penal Code § 2.01(4).

47. *Robinson v. California*, 370 U.S. 660 (1962).

48. 21 U.S.C. § 848

49. *United States v. Brantley*, 733 F.2d 1429 (11th Cir. 1984).

50. 21 U.S.C. § 848(e).

51. 21 U.S.C. § 853(a).

52. Kenneth Johnson, "The Constitutionality of Drug Paraphernalia Laws," 81 *Columbia L. Rev.* 581 (1981).

53. *Posters 'N' Things, Ltd. v. United States*, 511 U.S. 513 (1994).

54. Conn. Gen. Stat. §53-392b

55. N.C. Gen. Stat. § 14-118.2

56. Model Penal Code § 224.8.

57. 26 U.S.C. § 7201 *et seq.*

58. Model Penal Code § 3.04(2)(a)(i).

59. 18 U.S.C. § 2381.

60. *Ex Parte Bollman and Ex Parte Swartwout*, 8 U.S. 75 (1807).

61. *Cramer v. United States*, 325 U.S. 1 (1945).

62. Kimberly Wehle, No, Flynn's Martial Law Plot Isn't Sedition. But It's Not Necessarily Legal Either. Politico. December 24, 2020. Retrieved from Politico.com on January 4, 2020.

63. *See* 70 Am. Jur. 2d 70.

64. 18 U.S.C. § 2384.

65. 18 U.S.C. § 2389.

66. See Oklahoma Department of Health, *Summary of Reportable Injuries in Oklahoma: Oklahoma City Bombing Injuries*, http://web.archive.org/web/20080110063748/ http://www.health.state.ok.us/PROGRAM/injury/Summary/bomb/OKCbomb.htm, retrieved January 10, 2011.

67. 33 USC § 407.

68. *Id.*

69. 33 U.S.C. § 1319(a).

70. 33 U.S.C. § 1319(c).

71. 42 U.S.C. § 7413.

72. 42 U.S.C. § 9603.

73. 42 U.S.C. § 6928.

74. 15 U.S.C. §§ 2614–15.

75. 7 U.S.C. § 136i–1(d).

76. 16 U.S.C. §§ 1531–1543.

77. 16 U.S.C. §§ 1361–1384, 1401–7.

78. Alvarez, L. "Cats at Hemingway Museum Draw Tourists, and Legal A Battle," New York Times, December 22, 2012. Retrieved from http://www.nytimes.com on February 24, 2021.

79. 907 Whitehead Street, Inc., d.b.a. *Ernest Hemingway Home and Museum, v. Gipson*, 701 F.3d 1345 (11th Cir. 2012)

80. *United States v. Stevens*, 559 U.S. 460 (2010)

81. *United States of America v. Richards*, 755 F.3d 269, 271, 273 (5th Cir. 2014)

# Chapter 7

# Parties and Incomplete Crimes

## Chapter Outline

Parties to Crimes

Incomplete Crimes
  Attempt
  Conspiracy
  Solicitation

Ethical Considerations: Judges Have Rules Too

## Parties to Crimes

Learning Objective: Define, describe, and apply the traditional four parties to crimes.

Not all crimes are committed by only one person. Not all planned crimes are completed. This chapter examines these phenomena. Those who participate in a crime are referred to as *parties*. Uncompleted crimes are referred to as *inchoate crimes*.

At common law, there were four parties to crimes: principals in the first degree; principals in the second degree; accessories before the fact; and accessories after the fact.

A **principal in the first degree** is the participant who actually committed the proscribed act. For example, three people (A, B, and C) agree to rob a grocery store. A enters the store, points a gun at a checker, and demands that money be placed in a bag. A is a principal in the first degree.

A **principal in the second degree** is a party who aids, counsels, assists, or encourages the principal in the first degree during commission of the crime. A party must be present during a crime to be a principal in the second degree. However, constructive presence is sufficient; a party who helps from a distance is a principal in the second degree. So, if B, from our hypothetical case, waits in the getaway car outside the store, B is a principal in the second degree. First-degree and second-degree principals are punished equally. Principals in the second degree are also referred to as *accomplices*, as are accessories before the fact. In many jurisdictions, accessories, particularly principals in the second degree, are liable for all crimes committed by the principal in the first degree. Other states, however, reject this approach and require the accomplice to either share in the principal's intent or they follow the **natural and probable consequences doctrine**, which limits a principal in the second degree's liability to the foreseeable acts of the principal in the first degree.

**principal in the first degree**
A person who commits the actus reus of a crime.

**principal in the second degree**
A person who is physically present and assists a principal in the first degree but does not commit the actus reus of the crime.

**natural and probable consequences doctrine**
A rule that holds that accomplices are criminally liable for the unplanned but foreseeable crimes of the principal in the first degree that are committed during the planned crime.

**accessory**

A person who helps to commit a crime without being present. An accessory before the fact is a person who, without being present, encourages, orders, or helps another to commit a crime. An accessory after the fact is a person who finds out that a crime has been committed and helps to conceal the crime or the criminal.

Anyone who aids, counsels, encourages, or assists in the preparation of a crime, but is not physically present during the crime, is an **accessory** before the fact. If C, an expert in bank security, assisted in planning the robbery, then C is an accessory before the fact. The primary distinction between a principal in the second degree and an accessory before the fact is the lack of presence during the crime of an accessory before the fact.

The states disagree over the mens rea of an accomplice (before and during a crime). One group of states requires accomplices to meet the target crime mens rea. Others permit less. For example, Shelly is asked by her wife, Roxanne, to kill a neighbor. Shelly doesn't share Roxanne's desire to kill the neighbor, but she helps Shelly by stealing the deadly poison from her employer. Assuming Roxanne is successful in her evil plan, she is guilty of intentional murder. In a jurisdiction that requires accomplices to possess the minimum required intent, Shelly isn't guilty of first degree murder, although she will be guilty of a lesser murder. In those jurisdictions that require only knowledge, Shelly is also guilty of first degree murder.

At common law, accessories could not be convicted until the principals were convicted. In addition, procedural rules made it more difficult to convict accessories than principals. These rules are no longer the law. Statutes commonly group principals in the first and second degree together with accessories before the fact and punish all equally. However, some jurisdictions condition the liability of accessories on the existence of a principal's liability (but not an actual conviction). In these states, if there is no principal liability, there is no accessory liability. This idea is the subject of your next Oyez.

## Oyez

### Dusenbery v. Virginia
#### 263 S.E.2d 392 (S. Ct. Va. 1980)

**PER CURIAM.**

Indicted for rape of "T... M... against her will and by force, in violation of Section 18.2-61" of the Code, William Donald Dusenbery was convicted in a bench trial and sentenced to confinement in the penitentiary for five years. Upon consideration of a presentence report, the trial court suspended the sentence and placed defendant on indefinite probation.

At approximately 10:30 P. M. on September 16, 1978, T... M... and J... G..., both 16 years of age, parked their car in a secluded area and partially undressed in preparation for sexual intercourse. Defendant, a part-time security guard wearing a uniform, badge, handcuffs, and a holstered pistol, appeared at the window with a flashlight, ordered the couple to get out, and demanded identification. Defendant told them that he would take them to the authorities or report their conduct to their parents unless they finished what they had started and allowed him to watch. The couple entered the back seat of the car, discussed the options, and agreed to attempt to perform the act in defendant's presence. Defendant watched as the couple undressed and the boy assumed the superior position. Complaining that the boy had not penetrated the girl, defendant thrust his head and shoulders through the open window, seized the boy's penis, and forced it "partially in" the girl's vagina.

Defendant contends that the evidence is insufficient to support his conviction under Code § 18.2-61 because "the evidence is clear that [he] did not 'carnally know' the alleged victim" within the meaning of that statute.

In felony cases, principals in the second degree and accessories before the fact are accountable "in all respects as if a principal in the first degree". Code § 18.2-18. But, by definition, there can be no accessory without a principal. Although *conviction* of a principal in the first degree is not a condition precedent to conviction of an accessory, Code § 18.2-21, "before the accessory to a crime can be convicted as such, it must be shown that the crime has been committed by the principal." Since the evidence fails to show that J... G... committed rape, defendant cannot be convicted as a principal in the second degree. The question remains whether the evidence is sufficient to prove that defendant committed that crime as a principal in the first degree.

With respect to certain crimes, the law regards a person who acts through an innocent agent as a principal in the first degree. In some jurisdictions, this rule has been applied in rape cases where the accused forced an innocent third party to have carnal knowledge of an unwilling victim. But the "innocent agent" rule cannot be applied here, for it is antithetical to the construction this Court has placed upon Virginia's rape statute.

(continued)

Our prior decisions establish that one element of rape is the penetration of the female sexual organ by the sexual organ of the principal in the first degree. Whether Dusenbery's conduct constituted an offense other than rape is not a question before us on appeal. We hold only that the evidence is insufficient to prove that defendant carnally knew the prosecutrix within the intendment of Code § 18.2-61 as construed by this Court, and the judgment must be reversed. The case will be remanded for further proceedings if the Commonwealth be so advised, provided that defendant may not be retried for rape. *Reversed and remanded.*

In some cases, the principal in the first degree may commit an offense but is not guilty of it. Justified crimes, such as self-defense, and excused crimes, such as those committed while insane, are examples. The states are split on whether an accomplice is culpable when the principal in the first degree committed a justified or excused crime. Accomplices are liable in some, not liable in others, and in a third variation, accomplices are liable if the principal's crime is excused but not liable if the principal's crime is justified.

Accessories after the fact continue to be treated differently. An actor is an accessory after the fact if

1. aid, comfort, or shelter is provided to a criminal

2. with the purpose of assisting the criminal in avoiding arrest or prosecution

3. after the crime is committed

4. and the accessory was not present during commission of the crime.

D is an accessory after the fact if A and B flee to D's house and D hides A and B from the police. It is possible to be an accessory both before and after the fact. Hence, if C were to hide A and B from the police, C would be an accessory both before and after the fact. Accessories after the fact are not punished as severely as the other three classifications of parties (Exhibit 7–1).

## Exhibit 7–1 Parties to a Burglary

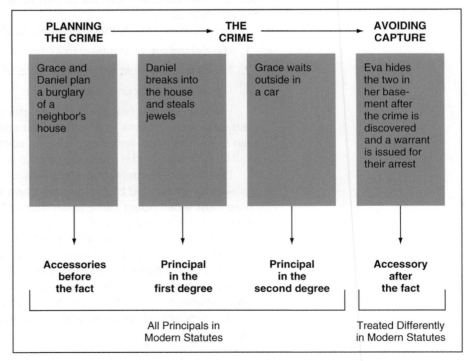

| PLANNING THE CRIME | THE CRIME | | AVOIDING CAPTURE |
|---|---|---|---|
| Grace and Daniel plan a burglary of a neighbor's house | Daniel breaks into the house and steals jewels | Grace waits outside in a car | Eva hides the two in her basement after the crime is discovered and a warrant is issued for their arrest |
| Accessories before the fact | Principal in the first degree | Principal in the second degree | Accessory after the fact |
| All Principals in Modern Statutes | | | Treated Differently in Modern Statutes |

The mental state required to prove that a person was an accessory after the fact is twofold: It must be shown first that the defendant was aware of the person's criminal status (scienter) and second that the defendant intended to hinder attempts to arrest or prosecute the criminal.

# Incomplete Crimes

Not all planned crimes are completed. Because of the danger posed by substantial planning, accompanied by an intent to carry out a plan, some uncompleted crimes may be punished. Unfinished crimes are known in criminal law as inchoate crimes.

Why punish acts that have not hurt anyone or anything? If the rule were otherwise, law enforcement officials would have no incentive to stop a crime before it is completed. By punishing attempt, conspiracy, and solicitation, police can prevent crime without risking losing a criminal conviction. Also, punishing incomplete crimes may deter people from starting wrongdoing in the first place.

## Attempt

Learning Objective: Define, describe, and apply the elements of attempt.

The are many reasons crimes go unfinished. Sometimes, law enforcement intervenes. If a police officer stops Penny from shooting Tom moments before she commits the act, should she be free from criminal liability because she was not successful? The law answers that question in the negative, referring to her crime as *attempt*.

**attempt**
An effort to commit a crime that goes beyond preparation and that proceeds far enough to make the person who did it guilty of an "attempt crime." For example, if a person fires a shot at another in a failed effort at murder, the person is guilty of *attempted murder*.

**Attempt** was not a crime at early Common Law; however, attempt cases do appear later in English common law. The first cases began to appear in the late 1700s and early 1800s.[1] Many of the early cases have been traced to an English court that is no longer in existence, the Star Chamber. Today, attempt is recognized in all jurisdictions.

The purpose of attempt laws is to deter people from planning to commit crimes, to punish those who intended to commit a crime, but who were unsuccessful, and to encourage law enforcement officers to prevent unlawful activity. The last may appear obvious; however, if it were not for making attempts illegal, police would have an incentive to permit illegal acts, so as to be able to punish the wrongdoer.

There are essentially three elements to all attempts.

1. The defendant must intend to commit a predicate (underlying) offense.
2. The defendant must act in furtherance of that intent.
3. The crime is not completed.

The first element requires that the defendant specifically intend to commit a predicate offense. Some jurisdictions limit attempt to specific predicate offenses, such as murder, rape, and theft; other jurisdictions permit attempt to be charged in all instances when the predicate offense is a felony or serious misdemeanor.

The second element, the actus reus of attempt, can be problematic. The problem is represented by this question: how close to completion of the intended crime must a defendant come to be guilty of attempt? It is well established that thoughts alone do not establish a crime; mere preparation without anything further does not amount to the crime of attempt. The failing student who sits at home and contemplates how to "do in" his or her criminal law instructor commits no crime. It is not until the student goes further that he or she can be liable for attempt.

Various tests are used to determine if an act is close enough to completion to permit an attempt conviction. The four commonly used tests are proximity, *res ipsa loquitur*, probable desistance, and the Model Penal Code's (MPC's) "substantial steps" test.

The *proximity test* examines what acts have been taken and what acts are left to be taken to complete the crime. Justice Holmes said that there "must be a dangerous proximity to success."[2] The test has been interpreted to require the actors to be very close to completing the crime. Consider, for example, *People v. Rizzo*.[3] Four men planned to rob a company, armed themselves, and drove to the location where they expected to find a company employee with payroll cash. The men were intercepted by police during their hunt for the employee. They were convicted of attempted robbery. On appeal, Rizzo's conviction was overturned because he didn't come within a dangerous proximity of completing the crime, even though the court concluded that "there is no doubt that he had the intention to commit robbery if he got the chance." The appellate court suggested that they would have crossed the line into attempt had they found and approached the employee.

The *res ipsa loquitur test* (also called the *unequivocality test*) looks at crimes individually and finds an act, a certain point in time, which indicates that the defendant has "no other purpose than the commission of that specific crime."[4] For example, most courts have held that once a defendant hires another to commit a crime, attempt has been committed. The step of hiring the person who will complete the crime crosses the line between mere preparation and illegal act.

The third test, *probable desistance*, focuses on the likelihood that the defendant would have followed through with the crime had the opportunity existed. The foundation of the theory is that all people may plan illegal acts at some time in life, but that there is a point where most stop. Any person who passes this line of demarcation has exhibited that the crime would have been completed, had the situation permitted. Critics have attacked this test, claiming that the determination of such a line, if it exists, is arbitrary.

The MPC uses a *substantial step* to completion test.[5] That is, one is guilty of attempt if substantial steps have been taken toward commission of a crime. The Code specifically states that the conduct in question must "strongly corroborate" the actor's criminal purpose. The Code goes further and lists acts that may constitute attempts, provided that they "strongly corroborate" an intent to commit a crime. That list includes:

1. Lying in wait or searching for the intended victim.

2. Enticing or seeking to entice the intended victim to go to the place where the crime will be committed.

3. Investigating the location where the crime is to be committed.

4. Unlawfully entering a structure where the crime is to be committed.

5. Possession of materials necessary to complete the crime, provided that the tools are specially designed for the commission of the crime.

6. Possession, collection, or fabrication of materials to be used in the crime, near the scene of the crime, when the materials serve no lawful purpose.

7. Soliciting someone to commit a crime.

See Exhibit 6-2 for a comparison of the various tests.

Keep in mind that different results are possible if these tests are applied to the same facts. In the *Murray* case, which appears in the next Oyez, the line between preparation and attempt is examined. Do you agree with the court?

Regardless of which test is applied, if a defendant has a change of heart and does not complete the crime, even after crossing the line, abandonment may be a valid defense.

Of course, the abandonment must be voluntary. Generally, any reason that causes a defendant to desist, other than the defendant's independent decision not to complete the crime, falls outside the defense. A criminal who chooses not to rob a store because a police officer arrives at the scene moments before the planned act was to occur is not entitled to the defense of abandonment.

## Exhibit 7–2 Attempt: Actus Reus Tests

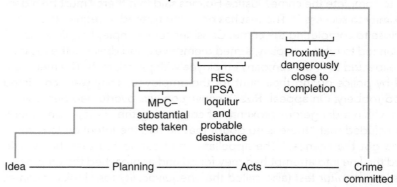

**legal impossibility**

A person who is unable to commit a crime because of legal impossibility cannot be convicted of a crime he or she intends or attempts.

Two other defenses that arise in the context of attempt are legal and factual impossibility. **Legal impossibility** refers to the situation when a defendant believes that his or her acts are illegal when they are not.

If defendants commit an act while believing it illegal when it is actually lawful, they are not liable. The law of attempt does not punish one for attempting to do a lawful thing, even if the person had an evil mind.

Factual impossibility refers to situations when people attempt to commit a crime, but it is impossible to do so. For example, John breaks into his friend's school locker to steal a virtual reality headset that he believes is in it, only to discover an empty locker. Distraught by the situation, John decides to relax by smoking marijuana. Unknown to John, the cigarette contains no marijuana or other illegal drug. John has made two factual errors. In both instances, John could be convicted because factual impossibility is not a defense. This rule is justified by the fact that the defendant possessed the required mens rea and took all the acts necessary to commit an attempted offense. The crime was not fully completed only because of an extraneous fact unknown to the defendant.

## Oyez

### People v. Murray
#### 15 Cal. 160 (1859)

**Field, C.J, delivered the opinion of the Court.**

The evidence in this case entirely fails to sustain the charge against the defendant of an attempt to contract an incestuous marriage with his niece. It only discloses declarations of his determination to contract the marriage, his elopement with the niece for that avowed purpose, and his request to one of the witnesses to go for a magistrate to perform the ceremony. It shows very clearly the intention of the defendant, but something more than mere intention is necessary to constitute the offense charged.

   Between preparation for the attempt and the attempt itself, there is a wide difference. The preparation consists of devising or arranging the means or measures necessary for the commission of the offense; the attempt is the direct movement toward the commission after the preparation is made. To illustrate: a party may purchase and load a gun, with the declared intention to shoot his neighbor; but until some movement is made to use the weapon upon the person of his intended victim, there is only preparation and not attempt. For the preparation, he may be held to keep the peace; but he is not chargeable with any attempt to kill. So, in the present case, the declarations, and elopement, and request for a magistrate, were preparatory to the marriage; but until the officer was engaged, and the parties stood before him, ready to take the vows appropriate to the contract of marriage, it cannot be said, in strictness, that the attempt was made. The attempt contemplated by the statute must be manifested by acts that would end in the consummation of the particular offence, but for the intervention of circumstances independent of the will of the party. [Conviction reversed.]

In the *Haines* case, a defendant appealed his conviction for attempted murder. He alleged that because of factual improbability, he did not take a "substantial step" toward completing a murder.

The Indiana Court of Appeals rejected factual impossibility (leaving open the issue of inherent factual impossibility) as a defense and rejected the factual assertion that AIDS cannot be transmitted through spitting and throwing blood on a person. Further, the court found that the acts of spitting and throwing blood on a person by a person with AIDS are substantial steps toward the commission of murder, thereby supporting an attempted murder conviction.

## Oyez

## State v. Haines
### 545 N.E.2d 834 (Ind. Ct. App. 1989)

**Buchanan, Judge**

On August 6, 1987, Lafayette, Indiana, police officers John R. Dennis (Dennis) and Brad Hayworth drove to Haines' apartment in response to a radio call of a possible suicide. Haines was unconscious when they arrived and was lying face down in a pool of blood. Dennis attempted to revive Haines and noticed that Haines' wrists were slashed and bleeding. When Haines heard the paramedics arriving, he stood up, ran toward Dennis, and screamed that he should be left to die because he had AIDS. Dennis told Haines they were there to help him, but he continued yelling and stated he wanted to [infect Dennis with the disease.] Haines told Dennis that he would "use his wounds" and began jerking his arms at Dennis, causing blood to spray into Dennis' mouth and eyes. Throughout the incident, as the officers attempted to subdue him, Haines repeatedly yelled that he had AIDS, that he could not deal with it, and that he was going to make Dennis deal with it.

Haines also struggled with emergency medical technicians Dan Garvey (Garvey) and Diane Robinson, threatening to infect them with AIDS, and began spitting at them. When Dennis grabbed Haines, Haines scratched, bit, and spit at him. At one point, Haines grabbed a blood-soaked wig and struck Dennis in the face with it. This caused blood again to splatter onto Dennis' eyes, mouth, and skin. When Dennis finally handcuffed Haines, Dennis was covered with blood. He also had scrapes and scratches on his arms and a cut on his finger that was bleeding.

When Haines arrived at the hospital, he was still kicking, screaming, throwing blood, and spitting at Dennis, Garvey, and another paramedic. . . . Haines again announced that he had AIDS and that he was going to show everyone else what it was like to have the disease and die. At one point Haines bit Garvey on the upper arm, breaking the skin. . . .

Haines was charged with three counts of attempted murder. At trial, medical experts testified that the virus could be transmitted through blood, tears, and saliva. They also observed that policemen, firemen, and other emergency personnel are generally at risk when they are exposed to body products. One medical expert observed that Dennis was definitely exposed to the HIV virus and others acknowledged that exposure of infected blood to the eyes and the mouth is dangerous, and that it is easier for the virus to enter the bloodstream if there is a cut in the skin.

Following a trial by jury, Haines was convicted of three counts of attempted murder on January 14, 1988. On February 18, 1988, Haines moved for judgment on the evidence as to the three counts of attempted murder, which the trial court granted. The trial court did enter judgment of conviction on three counts of battery as a class D felony. Haines was ordered to serve a two-year sentence on each count to run consecutively.

The only issue before us is whether the trial court erred in granting Haines' motion for judgment on the evidence and vacating the three counts of attempted murder.

## PARTIES' CONTENTIONS

The State maintains that the trial court erred in granting Haines' motion for judgment on the evidence because the trial judge misconstrued the requirements of proof necessary to constitute a substantial step in accordance with the law of attempt. Haines responds that his conduct did not constitute a substantial step toward murder as charged, because all evidence relating to the AIDS virus was introduced by the defense which led only to an inference in favor of Haines.

## CONCLUSION

The trial court erred in granting Haines' motion for judgment on the evidence.

(continued)

This appeal presents a novel question in Indiana.

■  ■  ■

Contrary to Haines' contention that the evidence did not support a reasonable inference that his conduct amounted to a substantial step toward murder, the record reflects otherwise. At trial, it was definitely established that Haines carried the AIDS virus, was aware of the infection, believed it to be fatal, and intended to inflict others with the disease by spitting, biting, scratching, and throwing blood. . . . His biological warfare with those attempting to help him is akin to a sinking ship firing on its rescuers.

Haines misconstrues the logic and effect of our attempt statute. . . .

"It is no defense that, because of a misapprehension of the circumstances, it would have been impossible for the accused person to commit the crime attempt". . . . [O]ur supreme court observed:

It is clear that section (b) of our statute rejects the defense of impossibility. It is not necessary that there be a present ability to complete the crime, nor is it necessary that the crime be factually possible. When the defendant has done all that he believes necessary to cause the particular result, regardless of what is actually possible under existing circumstances, he has committed an attempt. . . .

In accordance with [the statute], the State was not required to prove that Haines' conduct could actually have killed. It was only necessary for the State to show that Haines did all that he believed necessary to bring about an intended result, regardless of what was actually possible. . . . Haines repeatedly announced that he had AIDS and desired to infect and kill others. At the hospital, Haines was expressly told by doctors that biting, spitting, and throwing blood was endangering others.

While [the statute] rejects the defense of impossibility, some jurisdictions provide for the dismissal of a charge or reduction in sentence on the basis of "inherent impossibility" if the defendant's conduct was so inherently unlikely to result or culminate in the commission of a crime. . . .

While we have found no Indiana case directly on point, the evidence presented at trial renders any defense of inherent impossibility inapplicable in this case. . . .

In addition to Haines' belief that he could infect others, there was testimony by physicians that the virus may be transmitted through the exchange of bodily fluids. . . .

From the evidence in the record before us, we can only conclude that Haines had knowledge of his disease and that he unrelentingly and unequivocally sought to kill the persons helping him by infecting them with AIDS, and that he took a substantial step towards killing them by his conduct, believing that he could do so, all of which was more than a mere tenuous, theoretical, or speculative "chance" of transmitting the disease. From all of the evidence before the jury, it could have concluded beyond a reasonable doubt that Haines took a substantial step toward the commission of murder.

Thus, the trial court improperly granted Haines' motion for judgment on the evidence. . . . The trial court's judgment is reversed with instructions to reinstate the jury's verdict and resentence Haines accordingly.

# Conspiracy

Learning Objective: Define, describe, and apply the elements of conspiracy.

Sometimes punished more severely than the predicate crime itself and often easier to prove, the crime of conspiracy is a powerful and controversial tool in the prosecution toolbelt.

**Conspiracy** is

1. an agreement

2. between two or more persons

3. to commit an unlawful act or a lawful act in an unlawful manner.

The agreement is the actus reus of the crime, and the intent to commit an unlawful act or a lawful act in an unlawful manner is the mens rea.

As discussed in an earlier chapter, as of the time of the printing of this book, many of the actors who forcibly entered the U.S. Capitol on January 6, 2021, were facing a plethora of criminal charges. Of course, the charges varied because the participants' crimes varied from unlawful entry without force to violent entry and murder. Conspiracy is on the table for some of the participants. For those who broadcast their acts on social media, or who were otherwise recorded, the

**conspiracy**
A crime that may be committed when two or more persons agree to do something unlawful (or to do something lawful by unlawful means). The agreement can be inferred from the persons' actions.

predicate acts of conspiracy will not be difficult to prove. However, establishing an agreement between the insurrectionists may prove to be more difficult.

The federal government's general conspiracy statute, 18 U.S.C. § 371, declares it a crime "[i]f two or more persons conspire either to commit any offense against the United States, or to defraud the United States, or any agency thereof in any manner or for any purpose." Proving that individual insurrectionists intended to break windows, assault officers, steal items, commit illegal entry, the crimes of will be less difficult than proving more serious predicate offenses, such as sedition or terrorism. These crimes require evidence of an intent to be seditious or to threaten the population. The act of illegally entering the building will not be enough. Prosecutors will need statements or writings of the defendants, before, during, and after the riot to establish their specific intent.

In some jurisdictions, the conspiratorial agreement alone satisfies the actus reus. In others, an act must be taken in furtherance of the objective of the agreement. Although at least one jurisdiction requires the conspirators to take "substantial steps" to be liable for conspiracy, most require less; often proof of an "overt act" will sustain a conviction. Hence, although mere preparation is not sufficient to impose liability for attempt, it is sufficient in many jurisdictions to prove conspiracy.

Naturally, a conspiracy requires more than one person. One limitation on this rule is the **concert of action rule** (Wharton's Rule). Under this rule, two people cannot be charged with conspiracy when the underlying offense itself requires two people. For example, gambling is a crime that requires the acts of at least two people. Wharton's Rule prohibits convictions of both gambling and conspiracy. Adultery and incest are other examples. Wharton's Rule is limited, however, to two people. So, if three people agree to gamble, a conviction of gambling and conspiracy to commit gambling is permitted.

The mens rea of conspiracy has two aspects. First, conspirators must have an intent to enter into an agreement. Second, conspirators must possess a specific intent to commit an unlawful act or a lawful act in an unlawful manner. Note the use of the term "unlawful," not criminal. This is important because some acts, when taken by an individual, may lead to civil, but not criminal, liability. However, when the same acts are taken by a group, the law of conspiracy makes them criminal. This is common in the area of fraud.

The mens rea requirement of conspiracy is specific intent. Contrary to the general rule, mistake of law and fact are often accepted defenses. It is a defense for a party to have been under the mistaken belief that the group's actions and objectives were legal. This is because the conspiracy must be corrupt; the parties must have had an evil purpose for their union.

What if a party withdraws from the conspiracy while it is ongoing? As a general rule, withdrawal is not a defense because the crime was completed when the parties entered into the agreement. However, if the jurisdiction requires an agreement plus an overt act or substantial steps, and the withdrawal is made before those acts occur, there is no criminal liability on behalf of the withdrawn party. To determine when withdrawal occurrs, courts look to the defendants' actions. Withdrawal occurs at the time the acts would have conveyed to a reasonable person, standing in a co-conspirator's shoes, that they were abandoning the conspiracy. Additionally, the withdrawal must happen within a time that permits the other parties to abandon the objective. A last-second withdrawal, when it is too late to stop the wheels from turning, is not a defense. The MPC recognizes voluntary withdrawal as an affirmative defense.[6]

A few procedural issues are unique to conspiracy. As a whole, these rules favor prosecution. First, conspiracy is an independent crime. It does not merge into the intended offense. For example, if Amy and Ashley conspire to murder Elsa, they have committed two offenses: murder and conspiracy to murder. It is

**concert of action rule**
The rule that, unless a statute specifies otherwise, it is not a conspiracy for two persons to agree to commit a crime if the definition of the crime itself requires the participation of two or more persons. Also called *Wharton Rule* and *concerted action rule*.

not a violation of the Fifth Amendment's double jeopardy prohibition to punish both crimes (cumulative punishment). This is why conspiracy can be inchoate; it can be charged in cases where the objective is not met. If Amy and Ashley are not successful in their murderous plot, they are still liable for conspiracy to murder. One exception to the general rule of cumulative punishments is Wharton's Rule, which was discussed earlier.

Prosecutors must show an agreement between two or more parties to prove conspiracy. This creates some difficulties at trial. One difficulty concerns whether alleged co-conspirators should be tried together or separately. Because the U.S. Supreme Court has approved trial of all parties either at the location where the agreement was entered into or at any location where an act in furtherance of the conspiracy occurred, defendants are usually tried together.[7] It is possible for a defendant to be tried in a location where he or she has never been, and some argue that this practice is unconstitutional. In addition, critics argue that trying defendants together increases the likelihood of conviction because "guilt by association" can result.

**co-conspirator hearsay rule**
The principle that statements by a member of a proven conspiracy may be used as evidence against any of the members of the conspiracy.

**hearsay**
A statement about what someone else said (or wrote or otherwise communicated). *Hearsay evidence* is evidence, concerning what someone said outside of a court proceeding, that is offered in the proceeding to prove the truth of what was said. The *hearsay rule* bars the admission of hearsay as evidence to *prove the hearsay's truth* unless allowed by a hearsay exception.

Another procedural irregularity is the **co-conspirator hearsay rule**. **Hearsay** is an out-of-court statement. Although hearsay evidence is normally inadmissible at trial, the co-conspirator exception permits the statements of one party that are made out of court to be admitted. The rule is limited to statements made during planning and commission of the conspiracy; statements made after the conspiracy are inadmissible.

Because two people (or more) are required to have a conspiracy, if only two people are charged, and one is acquitted, the second defendant cannot be punished. For example, Edgar and Robert are charged and tried together for conspiring to rob a bank. If the jury acquits one, the other must also be acquitted. At least two people must be convicted. So, if a group of people are charged and the jury acquits all but two, the convictions stand.

Finally, many conspiracy laws are masquerading under other labels. You have already examined two federal conspiracy statutes, the Racketeer Influenced and Corrupt Organizations Act and Continuing Criminal Enterprise. In recent years there has been a rise in the number of conspiracy filings. This is largely the result of RICO and related statutes and because of the procedural advantages that prosecutors have, as discussed earlier.

## Solicitation

Learning Objective: Define, describe, and apply the elements of solicitation.

**solicitation**
Asking for; enticing; strongly requesting. This may be a crime if the thing being urged is a crime.

You have already encountered **solicitation** in the discussion of prostitution. But solicitation is much broader than attempting to engage someone in prostitution. Solicitation is the

1. encouraging, requesting, or commanding

2. of another

3. to commit a crime.

Solicitation is a specific-intent crime. The actor must intend to convince another to commit an offense. As you read earlier, solicitation is often associated with prostitution cases. But it isn't limited to prostitution. In some jurisdictions, any crime can be solicited. A few states limit the pool to felonies. The actus reus of the crime is the solicitation.

The crime of solicitation is different from attempt, because the solicitation itself is a crime, and no act to further the crime need be taken. Of course, if Gwen asks Tracy to kill Jeff, and the deed is completed, then Gwen is an accessory before the fact of murder, as well as a solicitor.

---

## Ethical Considerations

### Playing Both Sides of The Fence

Like the attorneys who appear before them, judges are bound by ethics rules. The ABA Model Code of Judicial Conduct, like its counterpart Model Rules of Professional Conduct for attorneys, has been adopted, in some form, in nearly every jurisdiction. The U.S. Courts have adopted a similar code. These rules require that judges maintain impartiality in the cases they hear; avoid impropriety and the appearance of impropriety; and refrain from political activity that is inconsistent with the integrity, independence, or impartiality of the judiciary. Federal judges are expected to refrain from politics altogether. The rule for state judges is broader because most state judges are elected. Federal judges, on the other hand, serve for life after having been nominated by the president and confirmed by the Senate. So, they have no reason to engage in politics.

In spite of these ethics rules, judges are infrequently held to account for misbehavior. With lifetime tenure, there is little that can be done to sanction ethics violations by federal judges. Colleagues can advise, guide, reprimand, and, in some cases, control the cases that are assigned to a judge. But removal can only occur through the difficult process of impeachment and removal by Congress. A case study in the challenges this can present is the impeachment and removal of Harry E. Claiborne, a federal district judge in Nevada. Mr. Claiborne was convicted of tax evasion and sentenced to two years in prison. Intending to return to the bench after his release, he didn't resign. Congress didn't get around to removing him from his post until after he was incarcerated.[8] So, the United States had a fully empowered federal judge who was also a federal prisoner.

Nearly 11,000 complaints were filed against federal judges between 2010 and 2018. Over 100 were terminated because of the retirement of the judge. In 33 cases, judges were censored, reprimanded, or had cases reassigned.[9] One was impeached and removed. Some commentators point to this data as evidence that ethics violations are not taken seriously. Judges point out that many of the complaints are filed by losing litigants and attorneys. The issue is the same in most states, where "judges judge judges." Concerns about the lack of impartial oversight have led to calls for reform, which will be an issue in years to come.

## Key Terms

accessory
attempt
co-conspirator hearsay rule
concert of action rule
conspiracy

hearsay
legal impossibility
natural and probable consequences
   doctrine
principal in the first degree

principal in the second degree
solicitation
Wharton's Rule

## Review Questions

1. Distinguish a principal in the first degree from a principal in the second degree. Which is punished more severely?

2. A person who helps principals prepare to commit a crime but is not present during the commission is called what?

3. Has Jan committed attempted murder if she decides to kill her sister and mentally works out the details of when, how, and where?

4. What are the elements of conspiracy?

5. What is hearsay? What is the co-conspirator hearsay rule?

6. What is meant by the phrase "inchoate crimes"?

7. What is the difference between solicitation and attempt?

## Problems & Critical Thinking Exercises

1. Use the following facts to answer problems 1 through 3: Abel and Baker were inmates sharing a cell in state prison. During their stay, they planned a convenience store robbery for after their release. They decided which store to rob, when they would rob it, and what method they would use. Having frequented the store on many occasions, Abel knew that the store had a safe and that the employees did not have access to its contents. Neither Abel nor Baker had any experience with breaking into safes and decided to seek help.

Accordingly, they sought out "Nitro," a fellow inmate who was a known explosives expert. They requested his assistance and promised to pay him one-third of the total recovery. He agreed. However, he would be able only to teach the two how to gain entry to the safe, because he was not scheduled for release until after the day they had planned for the robbery. He added that he owned a house in the area and that it would be available for them to use as a "hide-out until the heat was off."

The two were released as planned and drove to the town where the store was located. As instructed by Nitro, the two went to a store and purchased the materials necessary to construct an explosive, which was to be used to gain entry to the safe. That evening, Abel and Baker went to the convenience store with their homemade explosive. They left the car they were traveling in and went to the rear of the store to gain entry through a back door. However, as they entered the alley behind the store, they encountered a police officer. The officer, suspicious of them, examined their bag and discovered the bomb. Abel and Baker escaped from the officer and stayed in Nitro's house for three days before being discovered and arrested.

2. What crimes has Abel committed?

3. What crimes has Baker committed?

4. What crimes has Nitro committed?

5. John and Tyrone have a fight in a bar. Tyrone returns home, climbs into bed, and suffers a fatal heart attack. John, still angry from the earlier fight, climbs through a window into Tyrone's room and shoots Tyrone twice in the head. Has John committed a murder? Attempted murder? Explain your answer.

# Endnotes

1. See *Rex v. Scofield*, Cald. 397 (1784) and *Rex v. Higgins*, 2 East 5 (1801).

2. *Hyde v. United States*, 225 U.S. 347 (1912).

3. *People v. Rizzo*, 246 N.Y. 334 (N.Y. 1927)

4. Turner, "Attempts to Commit Crimes," 5 *Cambridge L.J.* 230, 236 (1934).

5. Model Penal Code § 5.01.

6. Model Penal Code § 5.03.

7. *Hyde v. United States*, 225 U.S. 347 (1912).

8. *The Impeachment Trial of Harry E. Claiborne (1986) U.S. District Judge, Nevada*. U.S. Senate. Retrieved from Senate.gov on January 29, 2021.

9. *Judges Policing Judges: True Disciplinary Actions Are Rare (1)*. Bloomberg Law. Retrieved from https://news.bloomberglaw.com/ on January 29, 2021.

# Chapter 8

# Factual and Legal Defenses

## Affirmative, Legal, and Factual Defenses

Learning Objective: Define and distinguish factual, legal, and affirmative defenses.

Criminal defendants commonly assert their innocence. A defendant's reason for claiming innocence is called a *defense*. Defenses can be factual: "I didn't do it!" They can also be legal: "I did it, but the case was filed after the statute of limitation expired." Many defenses developed under the common law; others, through legislation or the constitutions of the states and federal government. Defenses can be complete (perfect); that is, if they are successful, the defendant goes free. Other defenses are partial (imperfect); the defendant avoids liability on a higher charge but may be convicted of a lesser offense. This chapter examines several factual and statutory defenses. Chapter 9 discusses constitutional defenses.

In the United States, criminal defendants don't have to defend themselves. The Fifth Amendment's privilege against self-incrimination and the presumption of innocence allow a defendant to sit silent and to do nothing. Regardless, this is not always the best strategy, and defendants often present their own theories and evidence. Less frequently, they testify in their own defense.

**affirmative defense**
A defense that is more than a simple denial of the charges. It raises a new matter that may result in an acquittal or a reduction of liability. It is a defense that must be affirmatively raised, often before trial or it is lost.

**burden of proof**
The requirement that to win a point or have an issue decided in your favor in a lawsuit, you must show that the weight of evidence is on your side rather than "in the balance" on that question.

**burden of production**
The requirement that one side in a lawsuit produce evidence on a particular issue or risk losing on that issue.

**prima facie**
On first impression; sufficient evidence introduced early in a case to continue with a claim.

**burden of persuasion**
The duty to convince the fact finder or court of the truth of a fact or a legal position.

There is a special class of defenses known as **affirmative defenses**. Affirmative defenses go beyond a simple denial; they raise special or new issues that, if proven, can result in an acquittal or lesser liability. Challenging a defendant's mental state to commit a crime (e.g., insanity and intoxication), whether a defendant was justified or excused to commit the crime (e.g., self-defense), and in some states, alibi, are examples of affirmative defenses.

As a general rule, criminal defendants may sit passively during trial, as the prosecution bears the burden of proof. The **"burden of proof"** isn't one burden, but two: the burden of production and the burden of persuasion. The burden of production refers to raising an issue and to introducing evidence to establish the legitimacy of the issue. The burden of persuasion, on the other hand, refers to convincing the court that the issue raised is true. Because it is not practical to require prosecutors to prove that every defendant was sane, was not intoxicated, or did not have justification to use force, the burden for affirmative defenses operates differently than for the ultimate question of guilt. For an affirmative defense, the burden of proof "shifts" to the defendant.

How does this work? First, defendants have the duty of raising all affirmative defenses. In some cases, this means that defendants must inform the prosecutor and court of their intention to raise the defense early in the process. To be entitled to present the defense to the jury, a defendant must establish a **prima facie** case for the defense. This means the defendant must have evidence to support the defense. The amount is minimal; it only needs to raise a genuine question. The purpose of the prima facie process is to reduce waste of time and to prevent jury confusion. The prima facie decision is legal and therefore, it is made by the judge. If a prima facie case is established, the defendant is permitted to argue it to the jury. In some jurisdictions and depending on the specific defense, the burden of persuasion either remains with the jury or shifts back to the prosecutor. For example, most jurisdictions require the defendant to prove insanity to the jury by either a preponderance of evidence or the higher clear and convincing evidence standard.

After a defendant has met the burden of production, the **burden of persuasion** must be satisfied. There is a split among the states; some require the defendant to carry this burden, whereas others require it of the prosecution. If defendants have the burden, they must convince the fact finder that the defense is true. Defendants must prove this by a preponderance of evidence. In jurisdictions that require prosecutors to disprove an affirmative defense, there is again a split as to the standard of proof required. Some require proof by a preponderance, and others require proof beyond a reasonable doubt.

Some of the defenses covered in this chapter are affirmative defenses. It is necessary to research local law to determine which procedure is followed in a particular jurisdiction and what defenses are considered "affirmative."

# Insanity

Learning Objective: Define, compare, and contrast the M'Naghten, Irresistible Impulse, Durham, and Model Penal Code tests for insanity.

Few aspects of criminal law have received as much public attention as the insanity defense. The defense has also been the subject of considerable scholarly research and discussion. Some critics charge that the defense should not be available. Others are critical of the particular tests used to determine sanity. Despite its critics, the insanity defense is recognized in all but four states—Montana, Kansas, Utah, and Idaho.[1]

In reality, insanity is a mens rea defense. If a defendant was insane at the time of the crime, it is unlikely that they formed intent. It is generally held that one who is insane is incapable of forming a rational purpose or intent. In fact, in most jurisdictions, defendants may put on evidence to establish that insanity prevented the requisite mens rea from being formed. This is the defense of **diminished capacity**. It is a direct attack on the mens rea element of the crime, separate from the defense of insanity. If successful, the result could be conviction of a lesser, general-intent crime. However, a few states have made defendants choose between the insanity defense and the assertion of lack of mens rea due to insanity.

The theory underlying the insanity defense is that no penological purpose is satisfied by punishing the insane. Because insane persons have no control over their behavior, they cannot be deterred from similar future behavior. Similarly, no general deterrence will occur, as others suffering from a mental or physical disease of the mind are not likely to be deterred. The one purpose that may be served, incapacitation, is inappropriate if the defendants no longer suffer from a mental disease, or if the disease is now controlled. If the defendants continue to be dangerous, there is no need to use the criminal justice system to remove them from society, because this can be accomplished using civil commitment.

Criminal law has its own test (actually tests) of insanity. Other areas of law (e.g., civil commitment) use different tests, as do other professions (e.g., psychiatry). Between the states and territories, four tests are used to determine insanity, M'Naghten, irresistible impulse, Model Penal Code, and Durham.

**diminished capacity**
The principle that having a certain recognized form of *diminished mental capacity* while committing a crime should lead to the imposition of a lesser punishment or to lowering the degree of the crime.

## M'Naghten

In 1843, Daniel M'Naghten was tried for killing the British prime minister's secretary. M'Naghten was laboring under the paranoid delusion that the prime minister was planning to kill him, and he killed the minister's secretary, believing him to be the prime minister. The jury found M'Naghten not guilty by reason of insanity.[2] The decision created controversy, and the House of Lords asked the justice of the Queen's Bench to state the standards they used to acquit M'Naghten.[3] Those standards were attached to the decision and set forth the following standard, known as the **M'Naghten test**.

1. At the time that the act was committed
2. the defendant was suffering from a defect of reason, from a disease of the mind, that caused
3. the defendant to not know
   a. the nature and quality of the act taken or
   b. that the act was wrong.

The M'Naghten test is used by most jurisdictions today. First, the defendant must have suffered from a disease of the mind at the time the act occurred. *Disease of the mind* is not clearly defined, but it appears that any condition that causes one of the two events from the third part of the test satisfies this element. That is, any disease of the mind that causes a defendant to not know the quality of an act or that an act is wrong is sufficient. In at least one case, extremely low intelligence was found adequate.[4]

The phrase "*the defendant must not know the nature and quality of the act*" simply means that the defendant did not understand the consequences of his or her physical act. The drafters of the MPC gave the following illustration: A man who squeezes his wife's neck, believing it to be a lemon, does not know the nature and quality of his actions.[5]

**M'Naghten test**
A principle employed in some jurisdictions for determining whether criminal defendants had the capacity to form criminal intent at the time they committed the crime of which they are accused. The M'Naghten rule is also referred to as the M'Naghten test or the right-wrong test.

What is meant by "wrong," as used in the M'Naghten test? Courts have defined it two ways. One asks whether the defendant knew that the act was legally wrong, and the other asks whether the defendant knew that the act was morally wrong.

## Irresistible Impulse

**irresistible impulse**
The loss of control due to insanity that is so great that a person cannot stop from committing a crime.

Under the M'Naghten test, defendants who know that their actions are wrong but can not control their behavior because of a disease of the mind are not insane. This has led a few jurisdictions, which follow M'Naghten, to supplement the rule. These states continue to follow the basic rule but add that defendants are not guilty by reason of insanity if a disease of the mind caused the defendants to be unable to control their behavior. This is true even if the defendants understood the nature and quality of the act or knew that the behavior was wrong. This is known as **irresistible impulse**.

Irresistible impulse tests can be found in American cases as far back as 1863.[6] Of course, the largest problem with implementing the irresistible impulse test is distinguishing acts that can be resisted from those that cannot.

## Durham

**Durham rule**
The principle, used in *Durham v. United States* (214 F.2d. 862 (1954)), that defendants are not guilty of a crime because of insanity if they were "suffering from a disease or defective mental condition at the time of the act and there was a causal connection between the condition and the act."

In 1871, the New Hampshire Supreme Court rejected the M'Naghten test and held that a defendant was not guilty because of insanity if the crime was the "product of mental disease." No other jurisdictions followed New Hampshire's lead, until 1954, when the District of Columbia Court of Appeals handed down *Durham v. United States*, 214 F.2d 862 (D.C. Cir. 1954). Generally, the **Durham rule** requires an acquittal if defendants would not have committed the crime if they had not been suffering from a mental disease or mental defect.

*Durham* was overturned in 1972 by the District of Columbia Court of Appeals in favor of a modified version of the Model Penal Code test.[7] Today, Durham is only applied in the state of New Hampshire.

## The Model Penal Code Test

The Model Penal Code (MPC) contains a definition of insanity similar to, but broader than, the M'Naghten and irresistible impulse tests. This test is also referred to as the *substantial capacity test*. The relevant section of the Code reads:[8]

> A person is not responsible for criminal conduct if at the time of such conduct as a result of mental disease or defect he lacks substantial capacity either to appreciate the criminality [wrongfulness] of his conduct or to conform his conduct to the requirements of law.

The Code is similar to M'Naghten in that it requires that mental disease or defect impair a defendant's ability to appreciate the wrongfulness of his or her act. The final line, "conform his conduct to the requirements of law," incorporates the irresistible impulse concept.

The Code's approach differs from the M'Naghten and irresistible impulse test in two important regards: First, the Code requires only substantial impairment, whereas M'Naghten requires total impairment of the ability to know the nature or wrongfulness of the act. Second, the Code uses the term *appreciate*, rather than *know*. The drafters of the Code clearly intended more than knowledge, and, as such, evidence concerning the defendant's personality and emotional state are relevant.

The MPC test has been adopted by a few jurisdictions. The federal courts used the test until Congress enacted a statute that established a test similar to the M'Naghten test.[9] That statute places the burden of proving insanity, by clear and convincing evidence, on the defendant.

## Guilty but Mentally Ill (GBMI)

In 1981, John Hinckley attempted to assassinate President Ronald Reagan. The president was seriously wounded a Secret Service agent, and local police officer were shot, and Reagan's press secretary, James Brady, suffered permanent brain injury. It was later learned that Hinckley committed the act to impress actress Jodie

John Hinckley in front of the White House

Bettmann/Getty Images

Foster. At trial, Hinckley was found not guilty by reason of insanity. There was both public and legislative backlash to the decision and to the insanity defense. As a result, legislators throughout the nation moved to abolish or limit the scope of the insanity defense. Today, four states—Idaho, Montana, Utah, and Kansas—have abolished the defense altogether.[10]

Rather than abolishing the defense, other states sought to limit or alter its impact. One such measure was the establishment of the Guilty but Mentally Ill (GBMI) verdict. Pennsylvania's GBMI statute reads, in part, that a "person who timely offers a defense of insanity in accordance with the Rules of Criminal Procedure may be found 'guilty but mentally ill' at trial if the trier of facts finds, beyond a reasonable doubt, that the person is guilty of an offense, was mentally ill at the time of the commission of the offense and was not legally insane at the time of the commission of the offense."[11] As you can see, the GBMI verdict is a finding of mental illness at the time of the crime, but not insanity as defined by the applicable legal test. Unlike a defendant who is not guilty by reason of insanity, a defendant who is GBMI is both punished and treated. The defendant is sentenced as any other offender for the crime, but in addition the state provides mental health treatment.

## Constitutional Status of the Insanity Defense

James and Karen Kahler had been married for years, when in 2008, she expressed interest in having a sexual affair with her fitness instructor, Sunny Reese. Mr. Kahler consented to her experimentation. But by early 2009, Karen Kahler filed for divorce and took their two teenage daughters and 9-year-old son to her grandmother's home in Kansas. Mr. Kahler became increasingly distraught in the following months. On Thanksgiving weekend, he drove to the home of Karen's grandmother, walked in the back door, and saw Karen and his son. He shot Karen twice but permitted his son to run from the home. He then found and shot Karen's grandmother and both of his daughters. All four of his victims died. He was subsequently charged with the murders, to which he wanted to plead insanity. But he committed the crime in Kansas, a state that had abolished the insanity defense. He was convicted and appealed, alleging a right to put the insanity defense before the jury. The case eventually reached the Supreme Court.

In 2020, the Court decided that neither the Fourteenth Amendment's Due Process Clause, nor the Eighth Amendment's prohibition of cruel and unusual punishments, requires a defendant to know right from wrong in order to be criminally culpable, provided the defendant is allowed to present evidence that his mental illness prevented him from forming the requisite mens rea. In the case it reviewed, Kansas statutory law expressly recognized the absence of mens rea as a defense. Even more, mental illness could be considered a mitigating factor at sentencing. So, the defendant had no constitutional right to assert the insanity defense.[12]

## Procedures of the Insanity Defense

Insanity is an affirmative defense. In the federal system and in many states, defendants must provide notice to the court and government that insanity will be used as a defense at trial. These statutes usually require that the notice be filed a certain number of days before trial. This notice provides the prosecution with an opportunity to prepare to rebut the defense prior to trial.

In most instances, lay testimony is not adequate to prove insanity; psychiatric examination of defendants is necessary. The judge presiding over the case will appoint a psychiatrist or psychologist, who will conduct the exam and make the findings available to the judge. Often, defendants wish to have a psychiatrist of their own choosing perform an examination. This is not a problem if the defendant can afford to pay for the service. In the case of indigent defendants who desire an independent mental examination, statutes often provide reimbursement from the government for independent mental examinations. In the federal system, trial courts may approve up to $1,000 in defense-related services. Defendants who seek reimbursement for greater expenses must receive approval from the chief judge of the circuit.[13]

As with all affirmative defenses, the defendant bears the burden of production at trial. Generally, the defendant must present enough evidence to create some doubt of sanity. The states are split on the issue of persuasion. Some require that the prosecution disprove the insanity claim, usually beyond a reasonable doubt. In other jurisdictions, the defendant bears the burden of persuasion, usually by preponderance of the evidence. One exception is federal law, which requires the defendant to prove insanity by the higher standard—clear and convincing evidence.[14]

## Disposition of the Criminally Insane

Contrary to popular belief, those adjudged insane by a criminal proceeding are not automatically released. In most jurisdictions, after a defendant has been determined "not guilty by reason of insanity," the court (the jury in a few states) must make a determination of whether the person continues to be dangerous. If so, commitment is ordered. If the defendant is determined to not be dangerous, then release follows. A few jurisdictions have followed the MPC approach,[15] which requires automatic commitment following a finding of not guilty by reason of insanity. This is the rule in the federal system.[16]

In theory, those committed have a right to be treated for their mental disease. In reality, due to lack of funds, security concerns, and overcrowding problems in facilities, adequate treatment is often not provided.

Once a committed person is no longer a danger, release is granted. The determination of dangerousness is left to the judge, not hospital administrators or mental health professionals—an often-criticized practice. Patients, doctors, government officials, and even the judge can begin the process of release. Some states provide for periodic reviews of the patient's status in order to determine if they continue to present a threat to others. The relevant federal statute reads, in part:[17]

> When the director of the facility in which an acquitted person is hospitalized
> . . . determines that the person has recovered from his mental disease or defect
> to such an extent that his release, or his conditional release under a prescribed
> regimen of medical, psychiatric, or psychological care or treatment, would no
> longer create a substantial risk of bodily injury to another person or serious
> damage to property of another, he shall promptly file a certificate to that effect
> with the clerk of the court that ordered the commitment . . . The court shall
> order a discharge of the acquitted person or, on the motion of the attorney for
> the government or on its own motion, shall hold a hearing [to determine if the
> patient is dangerous].

At that hearing, the defendant has the burden of proving by clear and convincing evidence that a risk to people or property is not created by release.

Finally, as you learned earlier, some states have a "guilty but mentally ill" verdict. Juries may return such a verdict when the defendant's illness does not rise to the level of negating culpability but treatment should be provided in addition to incarceration (see Exhibit 8–1).

Sidebar

### The Realities of the Insanity Defense

In spite of the popular media attention it receives, and the strong feelings it engenders, the insanity defense is not widely asserted and rarely results in not guilty verdicts. One author notes that defense is raised in only 1% of felony cases in the United States, and it succeeds in only about 25% of the cases in which it is asserted. This computes to about 300 insanity pleas per state per year.[18] Another researcher examined nearly 1 million cases and found that insanity was claimed in about one in a thousand cases and was successful 29% of the time. It was discovered that when successful, it was rare for the jury to make the decision. In most cases, the decision was a product of negotiation among the defendant, police, and prosecutor.[19] Other researchers also have found that the vast majority of the individuals who assert insanity suffer from a mental illness that is so serious that prosecutors support pleas of not guilty by reason of insanity or guilty but mentally ill. In a study of criminal cases in Tennessee, researchers found that 7% of defendants were referred for mental examination, and of that 7%, 19% subsequently asserted the insanity defense, and of that number, the prosecutors supported the pleas in 72% of the cases (less than 1% of all cases).[20]

## Insanity at the Time of Trial

The Supreme Court has held that a defendant who is insane at the time of trial may not be tried.[21] The Court found that the Due Process Clauses of the Fifth and Fourteenth Amendments require that defendants be able to assist in their defense and understand the proceeding against them.

The test for determining insanity in this context is different from that discussed earlier. Insanity exists when defendants lack the capacity to understand the proceedings or to assist in their defense. This simply means that defendants must be rational, possess the ability to testify coherently, and be able to meaningfully discuss their cases with their lawyers. The burden of establishing incompetence is placed on the defendant in many jurisdictions. While this procedure comports with due process, requiring the defendant to establish incompetence by clear and convincing evidence does not. In *Cooper v. Oklahoma* (1996),[22] the Supreme Court held that the burden of proof can be placed on the defendant but that the standard of proof cannot exceed preponderance of evidence.

Typically, a defendant who is incompetent to stand trial is committed until competence is regained. Many statutes have mandatory commitment of defendants determined incompetent to stand trial. However, indefinite confinement is unconstitutional, based solely upon a finding of incompetence to stand trial. Generally, the Supreme Court has held that a lengthy (18 months or longer) detention (awaiting competence to stand trial) is tantamount to punishment and violative of the Due Process Clause.[23] In such cases, there must be a separate finding of dangerousness to continue to hold such persons.

A mistrial is to be declared in the event that a defendant becomes incompetent during a trial, and defendants who are sane at trial but become insane before sentencing should be sentenced to a psychiatric facility.

Last, the Supreme Court has held that a person who has become insane after being sentenced to death may not be executed until his or her sanity is regained.[24] The constitutional basis of the Court's decision was the Eighth Amendment's prohibition of cruel and unusual punishment. Thurgood Marshall penned, "It is no less abhorrent today than it has been for centuries to exact in penance the life of one whose mental illness prevents him from comprehending the reasons for the penalty or its implications."[25] Similarly, the Court has held that individuals who are developmentally disabled may not be executed.[26]

## Exhibit 8–1 Insanity and Criminal Procedure

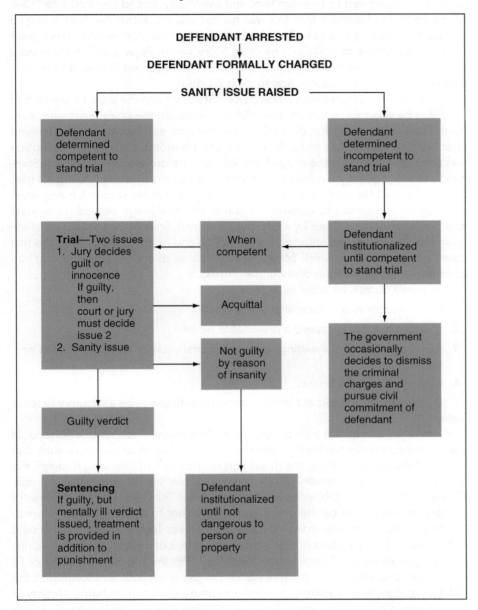

DEFENDANT ARRESTED

DEFENDANT FORMALLY CHARGED

SANITY ISSUE RAISED

Defendant determined competent to stand trial

Defendant determined incompetent to stand trial

**Trial**—Two issues
1. Jury decides guilt or innocence
   If guilty, then court or jury must decide issue 2
2. Sanity issue

When competent

Defendant institutionalized until competent to stand trial

Acquittal

Not guilty by reason of insanity

Guilty verdict

The government occasionally decides to dismiss the criminal charges and pursue civil commitment of defendant

**Sentencing** If guilty, but mentally ill verdict issued, treatment is provided in addition to punishment

Defendant institutionalized until not dangerous to person or property

Although not a defense, the issue of insanity during imprisonment and at the time of release is important. See Chapter 4 for a discussion of civil commitment of sex offenders and those who are dangerously mentally ill after release from prison.

# Duress and Necessity

Learning Objective: Define, describe, and apply the elements of the duress and necessity defenses.

A physician prescribed oxycodone, a controlled substance, to Brian Stannard for knee pain. Still in pain when his prescribed ended, Mr. Stannard bought, on credit, additional oxycodone from a drug dealer. When he failed to pay as promised, the dealer, Pops, threatened to hurt Stannard several times over a couple of months.

Stannard was so fearful that he and his mother moved. Pops and his accomplices found him, continued to threaten him, and eventually, forced him into a car. One of the men told Stannard that this was his last chance; either he "was going to pay up or [he] was going to be beat bad enough that his mom wouldn't recognize [him]." They drove to a Walgreens Drug Store where Pops handed Stannard a fake prescription, which was issued in his name, and ordered Stannard to go into Walgreens and fill the prescription to clear his debt.

Two of Pops's accomplices accompanied Stannard into the store to ensure that he did as he was told. Although they did not approach the pharmacist with Stannard, Stannard testified that they were watching him, and he was afraid. Stannard later testified that he was afraid for himself and his mother. After the prescription was filled, the men took the drugs from Stannard before they left the store. Stannard was subsequently arrested and charged with drug trafficking. During his trial, Stannard asked the trial judge to instruct the jury that he should be acquitted because he was forced to commit the crime. The trial judge denied his request and Stannard was convicted by a jury. But on appeal, Stannard won. The appellate court that heard his case reversed his conviction and returned the case to the trial court for a new trial, at which Stannard was entitled to ask the jury to acquit him because he committed the crime under **duress**.[27]

**duress**
Unlawful pressure on what a person would not otherwise have done. It includes force, threats of violence, physical restraint, etc.

To prove duress, an actor must show

1. that the actor was threatened

2. and that the threat caused a reasonable belief

3. that the only way of avoiding serious personal injury or death to oneself or others

4. was to commit the crime.

Duress was recognized at common law and continues to be a statutory defense today.

It must be shown that a threat was made. The threat must create a reasonable fear of immediate serious bodily harm or death. This fear must be reasonable; that is, even if the person making the threat had no intention of following through, the defense is still valid if a reasonable person would have thought the threat was real. Hence, even if a bank robber never intended to kill Terry, she has the defense of duress. Terry need not be the one threatened for her to be able to claim duress. So, if bank robber threatened to kill a customer unless Terry complied, Terry could claim duress. The fear must not only be reasonable, but it must also be of serious bodily injury or death. If bank robber exclaims, "Put the money in the bag or I'll smack you across the face," the threatened danger is not sufficient to support the defense of duress. In addition, the threat must be of imminent harm. Threats of future harms are not adequate duress. Courts define imminent differently. Consider the opening story to this discussion. Mr. Stannard was threatened in the moment, and he feared that Pops would hurt him or his mother tens of minutes, hours, or possibly days in the future. The appellate court held that a jury could plausibly find the threat to be imminent. Other courts could reach a different conclusion, in part because one could conclude that he could have sought help by telling the pharmacist or in some other way notifying police, during or immediately after the crime.

One limitation that is recognized nearly everywhere is that homicide is not justified by duress. This rule is criticized, rightfully so, because it does not account for those situations where taking one life may save many more. It is no defense to a crime to claim that one was only carrying out the orders of a superior, such as an employer or military superior. The immediacy of threat requirement of duress is explored in your next Oyez.

**necessity**
Often refers to a situation that requires an action that would otherwise be illegal or expose a person to tort liability.

**Necessity** is similar to duress. However, whereas duress is created by human pressures, necessity comes about by natural forces. When people are confronted with two choices, both causing harm, they choose the lesser harm. If they do, they may have the defense of necessity to the act taken. For example, a person may be justified in breaking into someone's cabin to avoid freezing to death. Or a captain of a ship may be justified in a trespassory use of another's dock, if setting ashore is necessary to save the ship and its passengers.

Necessity is a broad and amorphous concept. As a general proposition, it applies any time a person is confronted with the task of choosing between two or more evils. The harm avoided need not be bodily injury; it can also be harm to property. Of course, choosing property over life is never justified. Finally, if an alternative existed that involved less harm than the chosen act, the defense is invalid.

Duress and necessity are perfect defenses. When valid, they result in acquittal of all related charges.

## Oyez

### Howell v. Maryland
### Court of Appeals of Maryland (2019)

[Freddie Curry told Howell that he committed a murder. Howell testified to Curry's confession before the grand jury and he was subsequently called to testify at Curry's murder trial. Concerned that he could be implicated, Howell refused to testify invoking the Fifth Amendment privilege against self-incrimination. He was granted use and derivative use immunity from prosecution for his testimony and ordered to return to court to testify on March 10, 2016. On March 9, 2016 the *Baltimore Sun* published an article about the Curry trial wherein it disclosed that Howell intended to testify against Curry. While waiting to testify at Curry's trial, just a month later, Howell was attacked by five or six unidentified men who threatened him for snitching. One of the attackers told Howell that "[y]ou got to come out on the street sometime." The men were removed from the courthouse. Fearing for his life, Howell refused to testify. For his refusal, he was found guilty of criminal contempt by the trial judge. He appealed, claiming that his refusal was excused because he was under duress. He lost his first appeal and then appealed to the Maryland Court of Appeals, the state's highest court.]

**Opinion by McDonald, J.**

This Court recently defined duress as follows, citing various treatises and other states' formulations:

[T]o constitute a defense, the duress by another person on the defendant must be present, imminent, and impending, and of such a nature as to induce well grounded apprehension of death or serious bodily injury if the act is not done. It must be of such a character as to leave no opportunity to the accused for escape. Mere fear or threat by another is not sufficient nor is a threat of violence at some prior time. The defense cannot be raised if the apprehended harm is only that of property damage or future but not present personal injury. . . . [T]he defense cannot be claimed if the compulsion arose by the defendant's own fault, negligence or misconduct. . . .

. . . For the defense to be established, there must be a "present, immediate, and impending" threat that induces a well-grounded apprehension of death or serious bodily injury and no reasonable opportunity for escape.

The State argues that a duress defense should not be available to a witness charged with contempt for a refusal to testify in a criminal case for two reasons — one doctrinal, and the other policy-based. The doctrinal argument is that a recalcitrant witness inherently can never prove two elements of the duress defense — immediacy and the lack of any reasonable opportunity to escape. The policy argument is that, even if a recalcitrant witness could satisfy every element of the defense, there should be an exception similar to that for intentional murder because it would render the criminal justice system subservient to intimidation.

In particular, the criminal justice system has a duty to limit witness intimidation, which is "the supreme disgrace of our justice." Professor Wigmore distinguished between intimidation inside and outside of the courthouse. As for witness intimidation outside the courthouse, that is a "far more difficult and deep-rooted" problem. Professor Wigmore recommended that jurisdictions provide mechanisms for protecting witnesses and pass laws criminalizing witness intimidation, which Maryland has done.10 In practice, limiting witness intimidation and protecting threatened witnesses is a daunting task.

While some courts have entertained the possibility that a witness who refuses to testify out of a fear of reprisal may satisfy the duress defense, as the Court of Special Appeals accurately observed, the overwhelming majority of courts to address the issue have held that

(continued)

fear of reprisal does not provide a legal basis for a witness's refusal to testify. In any event, neither party has cited – and we have not found – any case that held that a witness who refused to testify out of a fear of reprisal generated a duress defense. . . .

As noted above, an essential element of a duress defense is that the threat be "present, immediate, and impending." Each of those adjectives, according to its common dictionary definition, connotes simultaneity, or something close to it. It is difficult to imagine circumstances in which a witness on the stand would face a "present, immediate, and impending" threat in a courtroom with no opportunity for escape. . . .

Mr. Howell's proffered evidence failed to generate that defense in this case because the alleged threat was not "present, imminent, and impending."

[The decision below is affirmed.]

# Use-of-Force Defenses

Learning Objective: Define, describe, and apply the elements of self-defense and defense of others, including the Retreat Doctrine, Castle Doctrine, and Stand Your Ground Doctrine.

A homicide on February 26, 2012 in Florida focused the nation's attention on several criminal justice problems, including race, the role of citizens in preventing and responding to crime, and the law of self-defense. George Zimmerman, a Hispanic 28-year-old community watch leader, shot and killed Treyvon Martin, a 17-year-old African American male.

On the night of the shooting, Martin was visiting with his father and his father's fiancée. While watching television, Martin left the home to walk to a convenience store. Martin trespassed through Zimmerman's neighborhood during his walk. Zimmerman observed Martin in the neighborhood during Martin's return from the store. Finding his presence suspicious, Zimmerman followed him, called the police, is alleged to have ignored a suggestion to discontinue the pursuit by the police dispatcher, and confronted and shot Martin. Zimmerman was charged with second degree murder, tried by jury, and acquitted.[28]

Claims that Zimmerman had a racial motivation for pursuing Martin contributed to making the incident a national cause célèbre. Of the many social and legal questions that the Treyvon Martin homicide raised, one concerns the nature of self-defense. The defense varies between the states.

All states permit the use of physical force against others in specific circumstances. Self-defense, defense of others, defense of property, and use of force to make arrests fall into this area. Self-defense, defense of others, and defense of property, when successful, are perfect defenses. Imperfect self-defense (including defense of another) does not lead to acquittal; however, it does reduce murder to manslaughter.

## Self-Defense

**self-defense**

Physical force used against a person who is threatening the use of physical force or using physical force.

To prove **self-defense**, it must be shown that the actor (1) was confronted with an unprovoked, (2) immediate threat of bodily harm, (3) that force was necessary to avoid the harm, (4) and that the amount of force used was reasonable.

One who initiates an attack on another cannot claim self-defense, as a general proposition. There are two exceptions to this rule. First, if attackers are met with excessive force in return, they may defend themselves. For example, Mike attacks Norm with his fists, and in defense Norm uses a deadly weapon. In such a circumstance, Mike may also use deadly force to protect himself. Second, if an attacker withdraws from the attack and is pursued by the intended victim, then he or she may claim self-defense. Suppose Randy attacks Sue with an intent to sexually assault her. After he grabs her, she displays a gun, and he runs. If Sue follows after him, intending to cause him harm, then he would be privileged to use force to defend himself.

The threat of harm must be immediate in most jurisdictions. Threat of future harm does not justify using force against another. To satisfy this requirement, the harm must be one that will occur unless force is used, and no other means of avoiding the harm exists. However, this principle is occasionally stretched. For example, some jurisdictions have permitted a jury to be instructed on the **battered spouse syndrome** defense. Under this defense, an individual who is constantly abused by their spouse may be justified in using force at a time when they are not strictly in "immediate danger." The theory is that an individual in this situation has two choices: either wait for their spouse to kill them or strike first in a form of offensive self-defense. Critics of this defense contend that because other remedies are available, such as leaving the spouse and obtaining a court order restraining the spouse, there is no immediate danger.

Finally, the force used to defend oneself must be reasonable. It would be unreasonable to knife a person who is attempting to slap one's hand. Deadly force may be used to defend against an attack that threatens serious bodily injury or death. Deadly force may not be used to defend against other attacks.

## Retreat, Castle, and Stand Your Ground

Many states require that a person retreat from an attack, if possible, before using deadly force. This is known as the **retreat to the wall doctrine** or simply the retreat doctrine. But there are exceptions.

The first exception is when retreating poses a danger to the victim of the attack. Another is for police officers, who are not required to retreat when performing their lawful duties. The MPC has a retreat provision that recognizes these exceptions:

> The use of deadly force is not justifiable . . . [if] the actor knows that he can avoid the necessity of using such force without complete safety by retreating or by surrendering possession of a thing to a person asserting a claim of right thereto or by complying with a demand that he abstain from any action which he has no duty to take, except that (1) the actor is not obliged to retreat from his dwelling or place of work, unless he was the initial aggressor.[29]

The Code provides that public officials need not retreat during the performance of their duties. There is no duty to retreat rather than using nondeadly force.

Also, notice that the Code requires not only retreat, but that "thing[s]" be surrendered and one comply with another's demands before deadly force is used. Of course, one can later use civil law to recover unlawfully taken items or to recover for complying with a demand that caused damage. The aggressor will be liable both civilly and criminally for such unlawful demands.

Most states do not require one to retreat from his or her home. This is known as the **castle doctrine**. The castle doctrine dates to the old Common Law. Indeed, the phrase "A man's home is his castle" is of ancient English origin. The castle doctrine reflects the idea that the home is a very special place, a venue that is inviolable by outsiders, and where the residents can feel their safest and live free from intrusion.

There are different versions of the castle doctrine between the states where it is recognized. Castle doctrine statutes commonly include one or more of the following:

1. Repeal of the common law retreat doctrine for lawful residents of homes who use deadly force against an intruder into the home.

**battered spouse syndrome**
Continuing abuse of a woman by a spouse or lover, and the resulting physical or psychological harm.

**retreat to the wall doctrine**
The doctrine that before a person is entitled to use deadly force in self-defense, he or she must attempt to withdraw from the encounter by giving as much ground as possible.

**castle doctrine**
An exception to the retreat doctrine, one has no obligation to retreat from his or her home before using deadly force to repel an intruder.

2. The creation of a presumption that intruders are a threat to life or limb.

3. Immunity from criminal and civil liability for residents of homes who use deadly force on intruders.

As to the first of these, there are common exceptions. For example, deadly force may not be used against people who have a lawful right to be on the premises. Police officers and family members are examples. This isn't to say that an ex-wife can't use deadly force against a homicidal ex-husband who happens to be a police officer. The statutes typically deny the castle doctrine defense to residents who use deadly force against individuals they should reasonably know are lawfully entering the premises.

Another variation on the home element of the castle doctrine is the inclusion of more than homes in its grasp. For example, Ohio has extended the castle doctrine to include automobiles. The applicable statute provides that "Every person accused of an offense is presumed innocent until proven guilty beyond a reasonable doubt, and the burden of proof for all elements of the offense is upon the prosecution. The burden of going forward with the evidence of an affirmative defense, and the burden of proof, by a preponderance of the evidence, for an affirmative defense, is upon the accused."[30]

**stand your ground doctrine**
A law that enables a person to use deadly force to repel an attack without first retreating.

One half of the states have enacted so-called **stand your ground** laws.[31] Florida, the location of the Zimmerman shooting of Martin, is such a state. Stand your ground laws are essentially an extension of the castle doctrine to public spaces. A victim of an attack that threatens life or limb in any space, not just the home or car, does not have a duty to retreat, even if a safe retreat is available. Florida's law provides, in part:

> A person who is not engaged in an unlawful activity and who is attacked in any other place where he or she has a right to be has no duty to retreat and has the right to stand his or her ground and meet force with force, including deadly force if he or she reasonably believes it is necessary to do so to prevent death or great bodily harm to himself or herself or another or to prevent the commission of a forcible felony.

As to the second dimension, reasonable force, states vary between requiring the use of deadly force to be objectively reasonable to creating a presumption of reasonable fear of life or limb by intruders in the home. The difference between the two is procedural. If the former, the law permits the use of deadly force without retreat, but the person who used the force may bear the burden of proving to the jury that her fear was reasonable. If the latter, the law presumes the fear was reasonable and the burden falls to the state to prove that was unreasonable. Florida shifts the burden to the state to prove that the fear was unreasonable:

1. A person is presumed to have held a reasonable fear of imminent peril of death or great bodily harm to himself or herself or another when using defensive force that is intended or likely to cause death or great bodily harm to another if:

   a. The person against whom the defensive force was used was in the process of unlawfully and forcefully entering, or had unlawfully and forcibly entered, a dwelling, residence, or occupied vehicle, or if that person had removed or was attempting to remove another against that person's will from the dwelling, residence, or occupied vehicle; and

   b. The person who uses defensive force knew or had reason to believe that an unlawful and forcible entry or unlawful and forcible act was occurring or had occurred.

2. A person who unlawfully and by force enters or attempts to enter a person's dwelling, residence, or occupied vehicle is presumed to be doing so with the intent to commit an unlawful act involving force or violence.[32]

The third dimension of most castle doctrine statutes is the creation of civil liability for individuals who use deadly force in a manner recognized by the statutes. Of course, liability may be found if the person using force is found to have acted outside the protection of the castle doctrine statute, for example, used force unreasonably.

The U.S. law of self-defense has evolved considerably since the old Common Law, and the variation between the states is considerable. See Exhibit 8–2 for a continuum of the right to use deadly force as a form of self-defense.

## Defense of Others

It is also a justified use of force to defend another. The rules are similar to that of self-defense: There must be a threat of immediate danger to the other person; the perception of threat must be reasonable; the amount of force used must be reasonable; and deadly force may be used only to repel a deadly attack.

At Common Law, one was privileged to defend only those with whom a special relationship existed, such as parent and child. Today, most jurisdictions permit any person to use force to protect another.

What happens when a person uses force to defend another who is *not* privileged to use force? For example, Perry is an undercover police officer attempting to arrest Norm, who is resisting. Randa observes what is happening and comes to Norm's defense, believing that Norm was being unlawfully attacked. There is a split of authority concerning this problem. Some jurisdictions limit the authority of the defender to use force to the privilege held by the person being attacked. Because Norm was not privileged to use force against the police officer, Randa is guilty of assault. Other states, however, use an objective test. Under such a test, if a reasonable person standing in Randa's shoes would have believed that force was justified, then he or she would be acquitted.

## Defense of Property and Habitation

At common law and by legislative enactment today, one may use force to defend property. As with defending oneself, only reasonable force may be used. Because property is not as valuable as life, deadly force may not be used to protect property. Thus, one must allow another to take or destroy property before killing to defend it. No force is reasonable if other methods of protecting the property were available. So, if one has ample time to seek assistance from the police or the courts, force would be unreasonable. In contrast, if an enemy appears at one's

## Exhibit 8–2 Deadly Force Continuum

| Least Protection | | Self-Defense | | Greatest Protection |
|---|---|---|---|---|
| Retreat to Wall | Castle Doctrine | Castle Doctrine Plus | Castle Doctrine Enhanced | Stand-Your-Ground |
| Duty to retreat, even in the home, before using deadly Force | Deadly Force may be used by residents of homes against intruders without first retreating. Person using deadly force may have to prove it was reasonable. | The use of deadly force by the resident of a home is presumed reasonable, unless the victim had right to enter premises. | Castle Doctrine is extended to cars or other venues. | Deadly Force may be used to repel an attacker in any location without first retreating, so long as reasonable attacker threatens life or limb. |

house and begins to destroy a car in the driveway, force would be permitted to protect the vehicle. An actor must have a reasonable belief that their property is in danger of trespass or destruction and that the force used was necessary to defend the property.

The basic rules concerning defense of property also apply to defense of habitation: One must have a reasonable belief that the property is threatened; only reasonable force may be used to protect the property; and other nonviolent remedies must be utilized before resorting to force. However, one difference between dwellings and other property is that deadly force may be used, under some circumstances, to protect one's home.

In early Common Law, the security of the home was as important as life itself. Therefore, people were permitted to use deadly force against any forcible intruder after warning the person not to enter. Today the rule has been narrowed, and statutes now commonly require that the occupant must believe that the intruder intends to commit a felony once inside before deadly force may be used.

The MPC allows the use of deadly force if either (1) the intruder is attempting to take the dwelling (with no legal claim to do so) or (2) the intruder is there to commit a crime (arson, burglary, theft) and has threatened deadly force or poses a substantial risk to those inside.[33]

This provision of the Code incorporates a self-defense concept. Remember, the rules of self-defense apply in the home also. So, any time a person's life (or another's) is threatened, deadly force may be used.

Some people choose to protect their property with man-made devices, such as electric fences and spring guns. Others have used natural protection, such as dogs and snakes. Whatever is used, the rules are the same. If the device employs nondeadly force, it is likely to be lawful. An electric fence that does not have sufficient electric current to kill is a justified use of force.

However, the result is often different when a property owner uses deadly force. There are two perspectives on the use of deadly traps to protect property. One permits the use of deadly force so long as those who set the trap would have been permitted to use such force themselves, if they had been present. So, if a murderer gains entry to a house and is killed by a spring gun, the occupant is not criminally liable because he or she would have been privileged to use deadly force against the murderer. The second perspective, adopted by the drafters of the MPC, rejects the use of deadly traps in all instances.[34] This position is sound, as deadly traps do not discriminate between the dangerous and the nondangerous. The occupant who sets such a trap is simply lucky if the intruder is a criminal and not a firefighter responding to a blaze in the home.

## Imperfect Self-Defense

The so-called imperfect self-defense is actually a mens rea defense. It applies to situations when people cannot make a successful self-defense (or defense of another) claim, but because they lacked malice aforethought (or purpose), the crime should not be murder but, rather, manslaughter. The defense applies only to homicides and is not recognized everywhere.

As stated, a person must have a reasonable belief that he or another is in danger of serious bodily injury or death before deadly force may be used. What if a person possesses a good-faith but unreasonable belief? Self-defense is unavailable, but because there is no malicious intent, purpose, or malice aforethought (depending on the jurisdiction's definition of murder), the crime is reduced to manslaughter. The defense is available in a second situation: whenever people who initiate an attack using nondeadly force later justifiably use deadly force to defend themselves.

# Arrests

Sometimes it is necessary for law enforcement officers to use force to execute their duties and to defend themselves. When a police officer uses force in defense of another's attack, the rules of self-defense that you have already learned apply. In addition, because the use of force is an integral part of law enforcement, it is often justified. However, a person making an arrest does not have an unlimited right to use force against an arrestee. This section examines a person's right to resist an unlawful arrest, the so-called citizen's arrest, and arrests by law enforcement officers.

## Resisting Unlawful Arrests

In some states, people may use force to resist an unlawful arrest. The amount of force is usually limited to nondeadly, although some jurisdictions permit one to use deadly force. Of course, if a person uses force against a lawful arrest, he or she is fully liable for whatever crime results (assault, battery, or murder), as well as for resisting a lawful arrest.

The rule permitting force to resist an unlawful arrest evolved during a time when arrestees were detained for long periods before appearing before a court, jail conditions were extremely poor, and no civil remedies existed for unlawful arrests. In light of these harsh facts, public policy was best served by permitting people to resist unlawful arrests.

Today, many jurisdictions have adopted an approach closer to the MPC's, which prohibits any resistance to an arrest by a law enforcement officer. This is the sensible approach, as the reasons for permitting resistance no longer exist: Arrestees must be promptly brought before judges and released if there is no probable cause. When available, bail is set immediately. Also, federal law now permits civil suits against law enforcement officers for violation of a person's civil rights. Prohibiting resistance advances two important public policy objectives: First, it fosters obedience to police, and, second, it reduces violence.

## Arrests by Law Enforcement Officers

A law enforcement officer is privileged to use reasonable force to apprehend criminals and to prevent those incarcerated from escaping. At Common Law, police could use all but deadly force to arrest misdemeanants and deadly force to arrest felons. This latter rule was justified by the fact that all felons were put to death at early Common Law.

In 1974, a Memphis, Tennessee, police officer shot and killed a 15-year-old male who was fleeing a burglary. The boy had stolen $40. The family of the deceased boy sued the police department in federal court for violating his constitutional rights. The case ended up before the U.S. Supreme Court.

In this case, *Tennessee v. Garner*, 471 U.S. 1 (1985), the Court held that the use of deadly force by a police officer is a "seizure" under the Fourth Amendment. Accordingly, the test used to determine whether the use of deadly force is proper is the Fourth Amendment's test: reasonability. The Court then held that the use of deadly force is reasonable only when the person fleeing is a dangerous felon. This finding invalidated the laws of many states that permitted the use of deadly force to stop all fleeing felons, including those who posed no threat to life or limb, such as thieves, extortionists, and those who tendered bad checks. The Court did not state what standard must be applied in cases of nondeadly force. Some courts applied a due process standard, others the Fourth Amendment's reasonableness standard.

In 1989, the Court handed down *Graham v. Connor*, 490 U.S. 386 (1989), in which the standard was set for all preconviction seizures, deadly and nondeadly. Through that decision, the Court held that all seizures are to be evaluated under the Fourth Amendment's objective reasonableness standard. Specifically, the Court held that courts must review challenged use of force from the perspective of a reasonable officer at the time the force was applied.

## Oyez

### Scott v. Harris
### 550 U.S. 372 (2007)

**Justice Scalia delivered the opinion of the Court.**

We consider whether a law enforcement official can, consistent with the Fourth Amendment, attempt to stop a fleeing motorist from continuing his public—endangering flight by ramming the motorist's car from behind. Put another way: Can an officer take actions that place a fleeing motorist at risk of serious injury or death in order to stop the motorist's flight from endangering the lives of innocent bystanders?

**I**

In March 2001, a Georgia county deputy clocked respondent's vehicle traveling at 73 miles per hour on a road with a 55-mile-per-hour speed limit. The deputy activated his blue flashing lights indicating that respondent should pull over. Instead, respondent sped away, initiating a chase down what is in most portions a two-lane road, at speeds exceeding 85 miles per hour. The deputy radioed his dispatch to report that he was pursuing a fleeing vehicle, and broadcast its license plate number. Petitioner, Deputy Timothy Scott, heard the radio communication and joined the pursuit along with other officers. In the midst of the chase, respondent pulled into the parking lot of a shopping center and was nearly boxed in by the various police vehicles. Respondent evaded the trap by making a sharp turn, colliding with Scott's police car, exiting the parking lot, and speeding off once again down a two-lane highway.

Following respondent's shopping center maneuvering, which resulted in slight damage to Scott's police car, Scott took over as the lead pursuit vehicle. Six minutes and nearly 10 miles after the chase had begun, Scott decided to attempt to terminate the episode by employing a "Precision Intervention Technique ('PIT') maneuver, which causes the fleeing vehicle to spin to a stop." Having radioed his supervisor for permission, Scott was told to " '[g]o ahead and take him out.' " *Harris v. Coweta County*, 433 F.3d 807, 811 (CA11 2005). Instead, Scott applied his push bumper to the rear of respondent's vehicle. As a result, respondent lost control of his vehicle, which left the roadway, ran down an embankment, overturned, and crashed. Respondent was badly injured and was rendered a quadriplegic.

Respondent filed suit against Deputy Scott and others under Rev. Stat. § 1979, 42 U.S.C. § 1983, alleging, *inter alia*, a violation of his federal constitutional rights, *viz*. use of excessive force resulting in an unreasonable seizure under the Fourth Amendment. In response, Scott filed a motion for summary judgment based on an assertion of qualified immunity. The District Court denied the motion, finding that "there are material issues of fact on which the issue of qualified immunity turns which present sufficient disagreement to require submission to a jury." On interlocutory appeal, the United States Court of Appeals for the Eleventh Circuit affirmed the District Court's decision to allow respondent's Fourth Amendment claim against Scott to proceed to trial (citation omitted). Taking respondent's view of the facts as given, the Court of Appeals concluded that Scott's actions could constitute "deadly force" under *Tennessee v.* Garner, 471 U.S. 1 (1985), and that the use of such force in this context "would violate [respondent's] constitutional right to be free from excessive force during a seizure. Accordingly, a reasonable jury could find that Scott violated [respondent's] Fourth Amendment rights." The Court of Appeals further concluded that "the law as it existed [at the time of the incident], was sufficiently clear to give reasonable law enforcement officers 'fair notice' that ramming a vehicle under these circumstances was unlawful." The Court of Appeals thus concluded that Scott was not entitled to qualified immunity. We granted certiorari and now reverse . . . .

**II**

In resolving questions of qualified immunity, courts are required to resolve a "threshold question: Taken in the light most favorable to the party asserting the injury, do the facts alleged show the officer's conduct violated a constitutional right? This must be the initial inquiry." *Saucier v. Katz*, 533 U.S. 194, 201 (2001). If, and only if, the court finds a violation of a constitutional right, "the next, sequential step is to ask whether the right was clearly established . . . in light of the specific context of the case." Although this ordering contradicts "[o]ur policy of avoiding unnecessary adjudication of constitutional issues," we have said that such a departure from practice is "necessary to set forth principles which will become the basis for a [future] holding that a right is clearly established." We therefore turn to the threshold inquiry: whether Deputy Scott's actions violated the Fourth Amendment.

**III**

**A**

The first step in assessing the constitutionality of Scott's actions is to determine the relevant facts. As this case was decided on summary judgment, there have not yet been factual findings by a judge or jury, and respondent's version of events (unsurprisingly) differs substantially from Scott's version. When things are in such a posture, courts are required to view the facts and draw reasonable inferences "in the light most favorable to the party opposing the [summary judgment] motion." In qualified immunity cases, this usually means adopting (as the Court of Appeals did here) the plaintiff's version of the facts.

There is, however, an added wrinkle in this case: existence in the record of a videotape capturing the events in question. There are no allegations or indications that this videotape was doctored or altered in any way, nor any contention that what it depicts differs from what actually happened. The videotape quite clearly contradicts the version of the story told by respondent and adopted by the Court of Appeals (citation omitted). For example, the Court of Appeals adopted respondent's assertions that, during the chase, "there was little, if any, actual threat to pedestrians or other motorists, as the roads were mostly empty and [respondent] remained in control of his vehicle." Indeed, reading the lower court's opinion, one gets the impression that respondent, rather than fleeing from police, was attempting to pass his driving test:

"[T]aking the facts from the non-movant's viewpoint, [respondent] remained in control of his vehicle, slowed for turns and inter-sections, and typically used his indicators for turns. He did not run any motorists off the road. Nor was he a threat to pedestrians in the shopping center parking lot, which was free from pedestrian and vehicular traffic as the center was closed. Significantly, by the time the parties were back on the highway and Scott rammed [respondent], the motorway had been cleared of motorists and pedestrians allegedly because of police blockades of the nearby intersections."

The videotape tells quite a different story. There we see respondent's vehicle racing down narrow, two-lane roads in the dead of night at speeds that are shockingly fast. We see it swerve around more than a dozen other cars, cross the double-yellow line, and force cars traveling in both directions to their respective shoulders to avoid being hit. We see it run multiple red lights and travel for considerable periods of time in the occasional center left-turn-only lane, chased by numerous police cars forced to engage in the same hazardous maneuvers just to keep up. Far from being the cautious and controlled driver the lower court depicts, what we see on the video more closely resembles a Hollywood-style car chase of the most frightening sort, placing police officers and innocent bystanders alike at great risk of serious injury.

. . .

Respondent's version of events is so utterly discredited by the record that no reasonable jury could have believed him. The Court of Appeals should not have relied on such visible fiction; it should have viewed the facts in the light depicted by the videotape.

**B**

Judging the matter on that basis, we think it is quite clear that Deputy Scott did not violate the Fourth Amendment. Scott does not contest that his decision to terminate the car chase by ramming his bumper into respondent's vehicle constituted a "seizure." "[A] Fourth Amendment seizure [occurs] . . . when there is a governmental termination of freedom of movement through means intentionally applied." It is also conceded, by both sides, that a claim of "excessive force in the course of making [a] . . . 'seizure' of [the] person . . . [is] properly analyzed under the Fourth Amendment's 'objective reasonableness' standard." *Graham v. Connor*, 490 U.S. 386, 388 (1989). The question we need to answer is whether Scott's actions were objectively reasonable.

Respondent urges us to analyze this case as we analyzed *Garner*. We must first decide, he says, whether the actions Scott took constituted "deadly force." (He defines "deadly force" as "any use of force which creates a substantial likelihood of causing death or serious bodily injury.") If so, respondent claims that *Garner* prescribes certain preconditions that must be met before Scott's actions can survive Fourth Amendment scrutiny: (1) The suspect must have posed an immediate threat of serious physical harm to the officer or others; (2) deadly force must have been necessary to prevent escape; and (3) where feasible, the officer must have given the suspect some warning. Since these *Garner* preconditions for using deadly force were not met in this case, Scott's actions were per se unreasonable.

Respondent's argument falters at its first step; *Garner* did not establish a magical on/off switch that triggers rigid preconditions whenever an officer's actions constitute "deadly force." *Garner* was simply an application of the Fourth Amendment's "reasonableness" test, to the use of a particular type of force in a particular situation. *Garner* held that it was unreasonable to kill a "young, slight, and unarmed" burglary suspect, by shooting him "in the back of the head" while he was running away on foot, and when the officer "could not reasonably have believed that [the suspect] . . . posed any threat," and "never attempted to justify his actions on any basis other than the need to prevent an escape." Whatever *Garner* said about the factors that might have justified shooting the suspect in that case, such "preconditions" have scant applicability to this case, which has vastly different facts. "*Garner* had nothing to do with one car striking another or even with car chases in general . . . . A police car's bumping a fleeing car is, in fact, not much like a policeman's shooting a gun so as to hit a person." Nor is the threat posed by the flight on foot of an unarmed suspect even remotely comparable to the extreme danger to human life posed by respondent in this case. Although respondent's attempt to craft an easy-to-apply legal test in the Fourth Amendment context is admirable, in the end we must still slosh our way through the factbound morass of "reasonableness." Whether or not Scott's actions constituted application of "deadly force," all that matters is whether Scott's actions were reasonable.

In determining the reasonableness of the manner in which a seizure is effected, "[w]e must balance the nature and quality of the intrusion on the individual's Fourth Amendment interests against the importance of the governmental interests alleged to justify the intrusion." Scott defends his actions by pointing to the paramount governmental interest in ensuring public safety, and respondent nowhere suggests this was not the purpose motivating Scott's behavior. Thus, in judging whether Scott's actions were reasonable, we must consider the risk of bodily harm that Scott's actions posed to respondent in light of the threat to the public that Scott was trying to eliminate. Although there is no obvious way to quantify the risks on either side, it is clear from the videotape that respondent posed an

(continued)

actual and imminent threat to the lives of any pedestrians who might have been present, to other civilian motorists, and to the officers involved in the chase. It is equally clear that Scott's actions posed a high likelihood of serious injury or death to respondent—though not the near certainty of death posed by, say, shooting a fleeing felon in the back of the head or pulling alongside a fleeing motorist's car and shooting the motorist. So how does a court go about weighing the perhaps lesser probability of injuring or killing numerous bystanders against the perhaps larger probability of injuring or killing a single person? We think it appropriate in this process to take into account not only the number of lives at risk, but also their relative culpability. It was respondent, after all, who intentionally placed himself and the public in danger by unlawfully engaging in the reckless, high-speed flight that ultimately produced the choice between two evils that Scott confronted. Multiple police cars, with blue lights flashing and sirens blaring, had been chasing respondent for nearly 10 miles, but he ignored their warning to stop. By contrast, those who might have been harmed had Scott not taken the action he did were entirely innocent. We have little difficulty in concluding it was reasonable for Scott to take the action that he did.

But wait, says respondent: Couldn't the innocent public equally have been protected, and the tragic accident entirely avoided, if the police had simply ceased their pursuit? We think the police need not have taken that chance and hoped for the best. Whereas Scott's action—ramming respondent off the road—was certain to eliminate the risk that respondent posed to the public, ceasing pursuit was not. First of all, there would have been no way to convey convincingly to respondent that the chase was off, and that he was free to go. Had respondent looked in his rear-view mirror and seen the police cars deactivate their flashing lights and turn around, he would have had no idea whether they were truly letting him get away, or simply devising a new strategy for capture. Perhaps the police knew a shortcut he didn't know, and would reappear down the road to intercept him; or perhaps they were setting up a roadblock in his path. Given such uncertainty, respondent might have been just as likely to respond by continuing to drive recklessly as by slowing down and wiping his brow (citation omitted).

Second, we are loath to lay down a rule requiring the police to allow fleeing suspects to get away whenever they drive so recklessly that they put other people's lives in danger. It is obvious the perverse incentives such a rule would create: Every fleeing motorist would know that escape is within his grasp, if only he accelerates to 90 miles per hour, crosses the double-yellow line a few times, and runs a few red lights. The Constitution assuredly does not impose this invitation to impunity-earned-by-recklessness. Instead, we lay down a more sensible rule: A police officer's attempt to terminate a dangerous high-speed car chase that threatens the lives of innocent bystanders does not violate the Fourth Amendment, even when it places the fleeing motorist at risk of serious injury or death.

The car chase that respondent initiated in this case posed a substantial and immediate risk of serious physical injury to others; no reasonable jury could conclude otherwise. Scott's attempt to terminate the chase by forcing respondent off the road was reasonable, and Scott is entitled to summary judgment.

The Court of Appeals' decision to the contrary is reversed.

High-speed police chases have received considerable public attention in recent years because they pose a threat not only to the police officer and the person fleeing, but to the general public. Whether *Garner* applied to these chases was not known until 2007.

Finally, note that police officers are often put into positions where they must defend themselves, such as during arrests. The same rules discussed earlier concerning self-defense apply in these situations, with one exception: Police officers are not required to retreat.

## Arrests by Citizens

At Common Law, private citizens were privileged to arrest those who committed a felony or misdemeanor (which amounted to a breach of the peace) in their presence. Some jurisdictions have retained this rule, and others have changed it by statute.

In jurisdictions that have changed the rule, it is common to permit so-called "citizens' arrests" any time probable cause exists to believe that the person has committed a felony. In most jurisdictions, a citizen may not arrest a misdemeanant unless the person making the arrest witnessed the crime. Even in such cases, only certain misdemeanors may lead to such an arrest.

The reason for these rules is to immunize citizens who make these arrests from civil and criminal prosecution. However, the citizen must be privileged to make the arrest and, even when privileged, a reasonable amount of force must be used.

In some jurisdictions, a private person making an arrest may use deadly force only when the person is in fact a felon. The jurisdictions employing this rule are split: Some permit the use of deadly force by private citizens to arrest for any felony and others only for specific felonies (e.g., murder and rape). These jurisdictions are similar in one important regard. The person against whom the deadly force is used must have *in fact* committed the crime. A reasonable, but incorrect, belief that the person has committed a crime is not a defense. So, if Pat kills Sam while attempting to arrest Sam for a crime he did not commit, Pat is liable for manslaughter, even though she had a reasonable belief that he committed the crime. Some states have followed the MPC approach, which prohibits the use of deadly force by private persons in all circumstances.[35]

The results are different if a private person is assisting a law enforcement officer. In fact, many states have statutes that require citizens to assist police officers upon order. In such cases, the private party is privileged to use whatever force is reasonable. In addition, a private person responding to a police officer's order to assist in an arrest is privileged, even if the police officer was exceeding his or her authority and had no cause to make the arrest. In such instances, the police officer may be liable for both his or her own actions and the actions of the private party summoned. Of course, there are limits to the rule. For example, a private person who obeys a police officer's order to strike an already apprehended and subdued criminal would not be privileged.

# Infancy

Learning Objective: Describe the evolution of how infancy impacted criminal culpability from the Common Law to modernity.

At common law, it was a perfect defense to a charge that the accused was a child under the age of 7 at the time the crime was committed. It was irrebuttably presumed that children under age 7 were incapable of forming the requisite mens rea to commit a crime. A rebuttable presumption of incapacity existed for those between 7 and 14 years of age. The presumption could be overcome if the prosecution could prove that the defendant understood that the criminal act was wrong.

Few minors are charged with crimes today. This is the result of the advent of the juvenile court systems in the United States. Currently, each state has a juvenile court system that deals with juvenile delinquency and neglected children.

Statutes vary, but it is common for juvenile courts to possess exclusive jurisdiction over criminal behavior of juveniles. However, some states give concurrent jurisdiction to criminal courts and juvenile courts. If concurrent, the juvenile court usually must waive jurisdiction before the criminal court can hear the case. Determining who is a juvenile also differs, with some jurisdictions utilizing a method similar to the Common Law (irrebuttable and rebuttable presumptions) and others simply setting an age cutoff, such as 14 or 16.

The purpose of the juvenile justice system differs from that of the criminal justice system. Whereas criminal law has punishment as one of its major purposes, the purpose of the juvenile system is not to punish but to reform the delinquent child.

# Intoxication

Learning Objective: Describe how intoxication during the commission of a crime affects criminal culpability.

*Intoxication* refers to all situations in which a person's mental or physical abilities are impaired by drugs or alcohol. Generally, voluntary intoxication is a defense if it has the effect of negating the required mens rea. In common law language, this means that if intoxication prevents a defendant from being able to form a specific intent, then the crime is reduced to a similar general intent crime. A number of states, however, no longer allow intoxication to be used to reduce mens rea. The Ohio criminal code, for example, states that "[v]oluntary intoxication may not be taken into consideration in determining the existence of a mental state that is an element of a criminal offense."[36] The question whether a defendant has a due process right to have an intoxication defense heard by a jury was answered in the negative by the Supreme Court in the 1996 case *Montana v. Engelhoff*.[37] The Court's rationale for rejecting the right focused on the scientific ambiguity of the impact of intoxication on mens rea and the lack of consensus among the states in recognizing the defense.

In the rare case of involuntary intoxication in jurisdictions that permit the defense, the defendant is relieved of liability entirely. To be successful with such a claim, the defendant is required to show that the intoxication had the same effect as insanity. In jurisdictions using the M'Naghten test for insanity, a defendant is required to prove that the intoxication prevented him or her from knowing right from wrong.

# Mistake

Learning Objective: Define, describe, and apply the elements of mistake of fact and mistake of law.

People may be mistaken in two ways. First, a person can make a mistake of law. This occurs when an actor believes that conduct is legal when it is not. Second, a person may not understand all the facts of a given situation. This is a mistake of fact. As a general proposition, mistake of fact is a defense, and mistake of law is not. However, many exceptions to each rule have been developed. A few of these exceptions are discussed here.

Mistake of fact is a defense whenever it negates the mens rea aspect of a crime. For example, an intent to steal another's property is an element of theft. If an attorney picks up a briefcase believing it to be their's when it is actually someone else's, it is not theft. The mistake negates the intent to steal. To be valid, mistakes must be made honestly and in good faith.

Although honest mistakes of fact usually constitute a defense, there are exceptions. One exception is obvious: strict liability crimes, because there is no requirement of mens rea to negate.

You may have heard it said that, "ignorance of the law is no excuse." Most of the time, this is true. The law presumes that everyone knows what is legal and what is not. Regardless, the MPC recognizes two situations when a person can make a mistake of law:

1. When the law wasn't published or made reasonably available to the public or

2. When the defendant relied on a statute, judicial decision, or official interpretation of the law by an appropriate public official, even though that law or interpretation is later found to be wrong.[38]

The first mistake of law exception is easy enough to understand. Fair notice that an act may be punished is a central feature of due process. The second exception to the rule that mistake of law is no defense exists when a person relies on statutes, judicial opinions, or certain administrative decisions that later turn out to be wrong. The advice must be rendered by a government official or agency that has the authority to enforce the law. Bad legal advice from a friend, a government official who is not responsible for giving the advice sought, or from an attorney is not adequate to establish the defense.

# Entrapment

Learning Objective: Define, compare, and contrast the subjective and objective entrapment defenses.

To what extent should police officers be permitted to encourage someone to commit a crime? This question underlies the defense of **entrapment.** Entrapment occurs when law enforcement officers encourage a person to commit a crime with the intent of arresting and prosecuting that person for the commission of that crime.

Perjury traps are another form of entrapment. Perjury traps are committed by prosecutors whenever they inquire of a witness as to matters that are tangential or peripheral to an investigation in order to catch the witness in perjury.[39]

Entrapment is a defense of recent development, although all states and the federal government recognize some form of the defense today. There is no constitutional basis for the entrapment defense, so each jurisdiction is free to structure the defense in any manner. Of course, a state may also do away with the defense, although none have done so. This is a sound policy decision, as most people would agree that there must be some limit on police conduct. However, where the line should be drawn is debated. Currently, two tests are used to determine whether a defendant was entrapped: the subjective and objective tests.

The test used in the federal system and most widely used by the states is the subjective test. The test attempts to distinguish between those who are predisposed to commit crime from those who are not. The test is subjective; the defendant's mental state at the time of the encouragement is determinative. A defendant is predisposed if he or she is ready to commit the crime and is only awaiting the opportunity. The Supreme Court has said that the subjective test is designed to draw a line between the "unwary innocent and the unwary criminal."[40]

Under the subjective approach, evidence of the defendant's criminal record may be relevant to show predisposition. For example, drug convictions may evidence a predisposition to enter into future drug purchases or sales. Also considered is the effort that had to be made by police to get the actor involved. The easier it is for the police to entice the actor, the more likely the actor was predisposed.

The second method of determining whether a person was entrapped is objective. The MPC[41] adopts this approach, as do a minority of states. The objective approach focuses on the State's conduct. It asks whether the police created a "substantial risk that an offense will be committed by persons other than those who are ready to commit it."[42]

The defendant's actual state of mind is not relevant to this inquiry, and, accordingly, evidence of a defendant's criminal history is irrelevant. Under this approach, a defendant may be acquitted even though they were predisposed to commit the crime. Suppose a police officer offers a prostitute $150,000 for sex. The prostitute would have agreed had the officer offered $50. Using the subjective approach, the prostitute would be convicted because they were predisposed to engage in prostitution. However, in jurisdictions using the objective test, the actor may have been entrapped, as people who do not normally sell sex might be encouraged to do so for $150,000.

In many states, entrapment may not be used to defend against crimes involving violence to people, such as battery and murder. The MPC also takes this view. See Exhibit 8-3 for a summary of entrapment.

# Alibi and Consent

Learning Objective: Define, describe, and apply the alibi and consent defenses.

Alibi and consent are two factual defenses. An **alibi** is a claim by a defendant that he or she was not present at the scene of the crime at the time it was committed.

**entrapment**
The act of government officials (usually police) or agents inducing a person to commit a crime that the person would not have committed without the inducement.

**alibi**
(Latin) "Elsewhere"; the claim that at the time a crime was committed a person was somewhere else. [pronounce: al-eh-bi]

## Exhibit 8–3 Comparison of Entrapment Tests

|  | Subjective | Objective |
| --- | --- | --- |
| Inquiry | Would a reasonable law-abiding person have committed the crime without the government's involvement? | Would a reasonable law-abiding person have been enticed into the crime by the government's actions? |
| What is the focus of the inquiry? | The defendant's predisposition to the crime. | The conduct of the police in encouraging or enticing the defendant. |
| What evidence is needed? | Defendant's criminal history and evidence of interest through preparation, statements, and conduct. | The government's offers, enticements, threats, or other coercion. |
| How common in the United States? | Majority of jurisdictions | Minority of jurisdictions |

Whenever defendants assert an alibi, they are simply refuting the government's factual claims. Alibi is an affirmative defense, and defendants are usually required to give the government notice of the alibi claim prior to trial. Alibi notice laws have been approved by the Supreme Court.[43] Of course, the government must prove the elements of the crime (e.g., presence at the crime) beyond a reasonable doubt. This means that the defendant bears no burden in an alibi defense.

**consent**
Voluntary and active agreement.

Victim **consent** is a defense to some crimes, such as rape or larceny. That is, if a person consents to sex or to give you his property, there is no crime. Consent is, however, not a defense to many crimes, such as statutory rape, incest, child molestation, battery, and murder.

## Statutes of Limitation

Many crimes must be prosecuted within a specified time after being committed. A **statute of limitation** sets the time limit. If prosecution is initiated after the applicable statute has expired, the case is dismissed.

**statute of limitation**
Federal and state statutes prescribing the maximum period of time during which various types of civil actions and criminal prosecutions can be brought after the occurrence of the injury or the offense.

Statutes vary in length, and serious crimes, such as murder, have no limitation. Generally, the higher the crime in the jurisdiction's classification system, the longer the statute. Statutes begin running when the crime occurs; however, statutes may be tolled in some situations. *Tolling* refers to stopping the clock. The time during which a defendant is a fugitive is commonly tolled. For example, assume that the limitation on felony assault is six years. The assault was committed on June 1, 2021. Normally, prosecution would have to be started by June 1, 2027. However, if the defendant was a fugitive from June 1, 2021, to June 1, 2023, then the statute would be tolled, and the new date of limitation would be June 1, 2030. There is no limit to how long a tolling period may run.

In 2005, a defendant in New York was tried for the second time for one of a series of rapes he committed in the 1970s. He became known as the Silver Springs rapist at the time of the attacks. His first trial had occurred 33 years earlier. It concluded with a hung jury, after which he fled the jurisdiction. This tolled the clock on the statute of limitation. While he was a fugitive, incriminating DNA evidence was recovered and DNA science developed into a reliable prosecution tool. He was eventually discovered and apprehended when he applied to purchase a gun in Georgia. He was extradited from Georgia to New York, where his DNA sample was collected. His sample not only connected him to the rapes in New York but to rapes in other states where DNA evidence existed. He was convicted at his second trial. Interestingly, the case caught the public's attention and was a catalyst to a change in statute of limitations law in New York. Today, there is no limitation in rape cases.[44]

At Common Law, there were no statutes of limitations, and they do not appear to have a constitutional underpinning. They are purely legislative creations. This being so, legislatures are free to alter or abolish statutes of limitation. If there is no limitation fixed, prosecution may occur any time after the crime.

Sometimes a prosecution for a serious crime may begin after the statute on a lesser included crime has expired. For example, battery is a lesser included crime of aggravated battery. Assume that aggravated battery has a six-year statute and battery three years. In most jurisdictions, a prosecutor may not circumvent the three-year statute by charging aggravated battery and including the lesser battery offense in the information or indictment. After the time has run out on the lesser offense, but not on the more serious offense, the defendant may be tried for the greater offense but not the lesser included. However, at least one jurisdiction does not follow this rule.[45]

## Ethical Considerations

### Playing both Sides of the Fence

Raleigh George Spain pled guilty and was convicted of burglary of a dwelling in a Texas Court in 1976. He was sentenced to 10 years' probation. Later, he violated the terms of his probation by committing the offenses of failing to report to his probation officer, changing his residence without notifying his probation officer, and failing to pay required fees. As a consequence, the district attorney filed a petition to revoke Spain's probation. He was found in violation of the terms of his probation at hearing, his probation was revoked, and he was sentenced to the remaining 8 years of his term of imprisonment.

This case would not be noteworthy except for one fact: The prosecuting attorney had been the defense counsel in the trial court. On appeal the revocation was reversed. The Court stated:

This duty to avoid a conflict of interest has long been imposed on the prosecutors of this State . . . .

Section 1.2 of the American Bar Association's Standards Relating to the Prosecution Function and the Defense Function provides that

(a)   A prosecutor should avoid the appearance or reality of a conflict of interest with respect to his official duties.

(b)   A conflict of interest may arise when, for example, . . .

   (iii)   a former client or associate is a defendant in a criminal case.

The commentary to this section states:

. . . When a conflict of interest may arise the prosecutor should recuse himself and make appropriate arrangements for the handling of the particular matter by other counsel . . . It is of the utmost importance that the prosecutor avoid participation in a case in circumstances where any implication of partiality may cast a shadow over the integrity of his office.

When a district attorney prosecutes someone whom he previously represented in the same case, the conflict of interest is obvious and the integrity of the prosecutor's office suffers correspondingly. Moreover, there exists the very real danger that the district attorney would be prosecuting the defendant on the basis of facts acquired by him during the existence of his former professional relationship with the defendant. Use of such confidential knowledge would be a violation of the attorney-client relationship and would be clearly prejudicial to the defendant. *See Gajewski v. United States*, 321 F.2d 261 (8th Cir. 1963). The prosecutor in this case should never have initiated or participated in the revocation proceedings.

When an appointed counsel has an actual conflict of interest, a defendant is denied his right of effective representation, without the necessity of a showing of specific prejudice . . . . We likewise conclude that when a prosecutor proceeds against a defendant whom he formerly represented as defense counsel in the same case, no specific prejudice need be shown by the defendant.

We hold that Article 2.01, *supra*, has been violated, and petitioner has been denied due process of law under the Fourteenth Amendment to the Constitution of the United States and Article I, Section 19 of the Texas Constitution.

As this case illustrates, ethical violations by prosecutors can transcend the applicable code of conduct; they can lead to constitutional, often due process, violations.

See *Ex parte Spain*, 589 S.W.2d 132 (Tex.Cr.App., 1979) and
*Ex parte Morgan*, 616 S.W.2d 625 (Tex.Cr.App., 1981).

# Key Terms

affirmative defense
alibi
battered woman syndrome
burden of persuasion
burden of production
burden of proof
castle doctrine

consent
diminished capacity
duress
Durham rule
entrapment
irresistible impulse
M'Naghten test

necessity
prima facie
retreat to the wall doctrine/retreat
  doctrine
self-defense
stand your ground doctrine
statute of limitation

# Review Questions

1. What are affirmative defenses? How do affirmative defenses differ from other defenses?

2. What are the elements of the M'Naghten test for insanity? Irresistible impulse? MPC?

3. What must be proven to support a claim of self-defense?

4. What is the retreat doctrine?

5. What is imperfect self-defense? When is it applicable?

6. When may a law enforcement officer use deadly force to stop a fleeing suspect?

7. What is entrapment? What are the two tests used to determine if a defendant was entrapped?

8. May an insane defendant be tried? If not, what standard is used to determine whether the defendant is insane?

9. What is a statute of limitations?

10. Distinguish legal from factual impossibility, and state whether a person is criminally culpable in both circumstances.

# Problems & Critical Thinking Exercises

1. Should law enforcement be permitted to encourage children to engage in criminal activity with the purpose of arresting and prosecuting the child? Should law enforcement be permitted to use family and friend relationships to induce another to engage in criminal activity with the purpose of arresting and prosecuting the family member or friend? How about preying on another's drug or alcohol addiction?

2. Ira stabbed his good friend, inflicting a fatal wound. At trial, a psychiatrist testified that Ira could not control his behavior, as he has a brain tumor that causes him to act violently. The doctor also testified that the condition did not impair Ira's ability to know what he was doing or that it was wrong. Assume that the jury believes the psychiatrist's explanation. Would Ira be convicted in a jurisdiction that uses the M'Naghten test? The irresistible impulse test? The MPC?

3. Jane was attacked by an unknown man. She was able to free herself and ran to a nearby house, with the man chasing close behind. She screamed and knocked at the door of the house. The occupants of the house opened the door, and she requested refuge. The occupant refused, but Jane forced her way into the house. To gain entry, Jane had to strike the occupant. Once inside, she used the telephone to contact the police, who responded within minutes. At the insistence of the occupants of the house, Jane has been charged with trespass and battery. Does she have a defense?

4. Gary and Gene were both drinking at a bar. Gary became angered after Gene asked Gary's wife to dance. Gary walked up to Gene and struck him in the face. Gene fell to the floor, and as he was returning to his feet, Gary hit him again. In response, Gene took a knife out of his pocket and attacked Gary with it. Gary then shot Gene with a gun he had hidden in his coat. The injury proved fatal. What crime has Gary committed?

# Endnotes

1. See Henry F. Fradella, "From Insanity to Beyond Diminished Capacity: Mental Illness and Criminal Excuse in the Post-Clark Era," 18 U. *Fla. J. L. & Pub. Pol'y* 7, 28 (2007); and Samuel J. Brakel, "Searching for the Therapy in Therapeutic Jurisprudence," 33 *New Eng. J. on Crim. & Civ. Confinement* 455, fn82 (2007).

2. *M'Naghten's Case*, 8 Eng. Rep. 718 (H.L. 1843).

3. LaFave & Scott, *Criminal Law* § 4.2A(a)(Hornbook Series, St. Paul, MN: West, 1986).

4. *State v. Johnson*, 290 N.W. 159 (Wis. 1940).

5. Model Penal Code, Tent. Draft 4, at 156.

6. LaFave & Scott at § 4.2(d).

7. *United States v. Brawner*, 471 F.2d 969 (D.C. Cir. 1972).

8. Model Penal Code § 4.01(1).

9. 18 U.S.C. § 17.

10. Justine A. Dunlap, "What's Competence Got to Do with It: The Right Not to Be Acquitted by Reason of Insanity," 50 *Okla. L. Rev.* 495 (1997).

11. 18 Pa. C.S.A. § 314.

12. *Kahler v. Kansas*, 589 U.S. __ (2020).

13. 18 U.S.C. § 3006A(e)(3).

14. 18 U.S.C. § 17.

15. Model Penal Code § 4.08.

16. 18 U.S.C. § 4243(a).

17. 18 U.S.C. § 4243(f).

18. Angela Paulsen, "Limiting the Scope of State Power to Confine Insanity Acquittees: *Foucha v. Louisiana*," 28 *Tulsa L. J.*, 537 (1993).

19. Callahan, L., Steadman, H., McGreevy, M., & Robbins, P., "The Volume and Characteristics of Insanity Defense Pleas: An Eight-State Study," *Bulletin of the American Academy of Psychiatry and the Law*, 19(4): 331–338 (1991). Other researchers have made similar findings. See Cirincione, C., Steadman, H., & McGreevy, M. (1995). "Rates of Insanity Acquittals and the Factors Associated with Successful Insanity Pleas," *Bulletin of the American Academy of Psychiatry and Law* 23, 399–409 (1995).

20. Conner, K., "Factors in a Successful Use of the Insanity Defense," *Internet Journal of Criminology* (2006).

21. *Dusky v. United States*, 362 U.S. 402 (1960).

22. 517 U.S. 348.

23. *Jackson v. Indiana*, 406 U.S. 715 (1972).

24. *Ford v. Wainwright*, 477 U.S. 399 (1986).

25. Id. at 417.

26. *Atkins v. Virginia*, 122 S. Ct. 2242 (2002).

27. *Stannard v. State*, 113 So. 3$^{rd}$ 929 (Fla: Dist. Court of Appeals, 5th Dist. 2013).

28. See New York Times: Times Topics at www.nytimes.com and search for Treyvon Martin.

29. Model Penal Code § 3.04(2)(b)(ii).

30. O.R.C. §2901.05.

31. There are 25 states with stand your ground laws according to the National Conference of State Legislatures; Self-Defense and "Stand Your Ground: retrieved at http://www.ncsl .org on December 26, 2020.

32. Fla. Stat. §776.012.

33. Model Penal Code § 3.06(d).

34. Model Penal Code § 3.06(5).

35. Model Penal Code § 3.07(2)(b)(ii).

36. O.R.C. §2901.21(E)

37. 518 U.S. 37 (1996).

38. Model Penal Code §2.04.

39. *See Vermont v. Tonzola*, 621 A.2d 243 (Vt. 1993).

40. *Sherman v. United States*, 356 U.S. 369 (1958).

41. Model Penal Code § 2.13.

42. Model Penal Code § 2.13(2).

43. *Williams v. Florida*, 399 U.S. 78 (1970).

44. Sources: Emily Jane Goodman, "State Removes Statute of Limitations for Rape Cases," *Gotham Gazette: New York City News and Policy*, June 2006; Fox News, November 10, 2005, and Julia Preston, "After Thirty-Two Years, Clothing Yields a DNA Key to Dozens of Rapes," *New York Times*, New York Region, April 27, 2005.

45. 21 Am. Jur. 2d 225 (1990); *State v. Borucki*, 505 A.2d 89 (Me. 1986).

# Chapter 9

# Constitutional Defenses

## Chapter Outline

## Introduction

By its nature, a constitutional right can be operationalized as a defense to a criminal charge. For example, if a state were to declare hate speech to be a crime, the First Amendment's Free Speech Clause would be used to defend against a prosecution under the law.

A few rights were included in the original Constitution, including habeas corpus, ex post facto, bills of attainder, privileges and immunities, and jury trial. But most of the rights that apply in criminal cases are found in the Bill of Rights. The Fourteenth Amendment's protection of due process and equal protection are also significant. Many criminal procedure rights are discussed in future chapters. These include, for example, the right to be free from unreasonable searches and seizures, to have a lawyer, to confront and cross-examine witnesses, and to a jury trial. Several rights that are not covered later are discussed in this chapter, such as double jeopardy, free speech, and religion.

The U.S. Constitution is the safety net of liberty. It provides a minimum level of protection for all people in the country. No government, at any level, may violate a rights protected by it. And when they do, it falls on the courts to hold the offending government accountable. This is done in a variety of ways. Illegally obtained evidence may be excluded from a defendant's trial, and an unconstitutional law may be stricken down or not enforced in a specific case.

The states are free to raise the net of liberty higher; they may expand liberties through their own constitutions and statutory law. With a few exceptions, the rights discussed in this text only restrict governments, not private individuals. This is known as the **State Action Doctrine**. Individuals are free to restrict speech in their homes or businesses, with a few exceptions, in ways governments may not. If it were different, a parent couldn't discipline a child's foul mouth and a business couldn't discipline an employee who offends customers. The State Action Doctrine isn't usually in question in criminal cases, because governments investigate and prosecute criminal cases.

During this discussion, you may want to refer to the U.S. Constitution, which is reprinted as Appendix A of this text. The discussion begins with the prohibition of being tried twice for the same crime.

**State Action Doctrine**
The rule that constitutional rights only limit governments, not private parties.

# Double Jeopardy

The Fifth Amendment to the U.S. Constitution provides that "no person shall be subject for the same offense to be twice put in jeopardy of life or limb." The principle of not punishing someone twice for the same act can be found as far back as Blackstone's *Commentaries* in the 1700s.[1] The **Double Jeopardy Clause** applies only to criminal proceedings.

A basic principle of due process is that the government doesn't get a second bite at the apple. An acquittal is final. There are two prohibitions in the Double Jeopardy Clause. It forbids: (1) a second prosecution for the same offense and (2) a second punishment for the same offense.

Often the legal question in double jeopardy cases is whether a prior "jeopardy" occurred. The manner in which a case proceeds determines when jeopardy "attaches." In cases that are disposed of by a guilty pleas, the prevailing rule is that a person has been put in jeopardy when the plea has been entered and accepted by a court. An unapproved plea does not suffice. In jury trials, jeopardy attaches once a jury has been selected and sworn. States treat bench trials differently, although the most common rule is that jeopardy attaches when the first witness has been sworn.

Once jeopardy attaches, the defendant may not be tried again. However, there are a few, narrowly defined exceptions. A defendant may be retried if the first trial was terminated by a properly declared mistrial. Mistrials may be declared when there is "manifest necessity." If a defendant objects to a government motion for a mistrial, there must be a "manifest necessity" (darn good reason) for the mistrial.[2] The inability of a jury to render a verdict—a hung jury—is manifest necessity warranting retrial. The extent to which the prosecution or defendant is responsible for the trial's defect is a factor. Prosecutorial misconduct rarely is treated as manifest necessity. Acts of nature outside of the control of the court or parties are legitimate reasons for mistrial resulting in a second trial. The death of the trial judge or one of the participating attorneys, for example. The same is true of prejudicial conduct of people outside of the control of the parties. A witness blurting out an answer that prejudices the jury before the judge has an opportunity to sustain an objection to the question is an example. The causes of a mistrial are endless. If an appellate court later determines that a mistrial should not have been declared, the defendant has been put into jeopardy. It is always proper to retry a defendant whose prior trial was declared a mistrial upon the defendant's motion.

It is also not a violation of the Fifth Amendment to prosecute a defendant who was previously charged but whose charges were dismissed prior to jeopardy attaching. Additionally, a defendant who prevails on appeal on a legal issue may be retried in a manner consistent with the appellate court's holding. However, if defendants are

**Double Jeopardy Clause**
A second prosecution by the same government against the same person for the same crime (or for a lesser included offense) once the first prosecution is totally finished and decided. This is prohibited by the U.S. Constitution.

acquitted on a serious charge and convicted on a lesser charge and then prevail on appeal, they may be retried only on the lesser charge. It is violative of the Fifth Amendment to retry the defendant on the more serious offense. Whether a defendant may be retried following government appeals has been an issue in many cases. Clearly, the government may not win a new trial following an acquittal. However, a conviction may be reinstated by an appellate court if a trial court's order setting aside the conviction is found invalid.[3] But an appellate court may not order a new trial where the trial judge entered a judgment of acquittal following a hung jury.[4] The outcomes in this area of law are dependent upon what judgment is first entered by the trial court. If it is a conviction, then an appellate court may tamper with trial judge reversals of convictions. If it is an acquittal, then double jeopardy bars acting further against the accused.

The Supreme Court has also held that double jeopardy does not bar correcting a sentence on appeal or rehearing because such a procedure is not retrial of an "offense." However, the outcome may be different if resentencing results in the application of the death penalty.[5]

The Fifth Amendment only forbids retrial for the same offense. Two offenses are the same unless one requires proof of a fact that the other does not.[6] This is also known as the "same evidence test."

The Double Jeopardy Clause is fully applicable to the states through the Fourteenth Amendment. However, the clause does not prevent second punishments for the same offense by different sovereigns. For example, a person who robs a federally insured bank may be prosecuted by both the state where the bank resides and the United States. This is true even though the offenses arise from the same acts. The Supreme Court affirmed the **dual sovereignty doctrine** in the 2019 case *Gamble v. United States*, featured in your next Oyez.

**dual sovereignty doctrine**
A second prosecution by a different government against the same person for the same crime (or for a lesser included offense) does not violate the Double Jeopardy Clause.

# Oyez

## Gamble v. United States
### 587 U.S. ___ (2019)

**Justice Alito delivered the opinion of the Court.**

We consider in this case whether to overrule a longstanding interpretation of the Double Jeopardy Clause of the Fifth Amendment. That Clause provides that no person may be "twice put in jeopardy" "for the same offence." Our double jeopardy case law is complex, but at its core, the Clause means that those acquitted or convicted of a particular "offence" cannot be tried a second time for the same "offence." But what does the Clause mean by an "offence"?

We have long held that a crime under one sovereign's laws is not "the same offence" as a crime under the laws of another sovereign. Under this "dual-sovereignty" doctrine, a State may prosecute a defendant under state law even if the Federal Government has prosecuted him for the same conduct under a federal statute.

Or the reverse may happen, as it did here. Terance Gamble, convicted by Alabama for possessing a firearm as a felon, now faces prosecution by the United States under its own felon-in-possession law. Attacking this second prosecution on double jeopardy grounds, Gamble asks us to overrule the dual-sovereignty doctrine. He contends that it departs from the founding-era understanding of the right enshrined by the Double Jeopardy Clause. But the historical evidence assembled by Gamble is feeble; pointing the other way are the Clause's text, other historical evidence, and 170 years of precedent. Today we affirm that precedent, and with it the decision below.

In November 2015, a local police officer in Mobile, Alabama, pulled Gamble over for a damaged headlight. Smelling marijuana, the officer searched Gamble's car, where he found a loaded 9-mm handgun. Since Gamble had been convicted of second-degree robbery, his possession of the handgun violated an Alabama law providing that no one convicted of "a crime of violence" "shall own a firearm or have one in his or her possession." Ala. Code §13A–11–72(a) (2015); see §13A–11–70(2) (defining "crime of violence" to include robbery). After Gamble pleaded guilty to this state offense, federal prosecutors indicted him for the same instance of possession under a federal law—one forbidding those convicted of "a crime punishable by imprisonment for a term exceeding one year . . . to ship or transport in interstate or foreign commerce, or possess in or affecting commerce, any firearm or ammunition." 18 U. S. C. §922(g)(1).

Gamble moved to dismiss on one ground: The federal indictment was for "the same offence" as the one at issue in his state conviction and thus exposed him to double jeopardy. . . .

(continued)

We start with the text of the Fifth Amendment. Although the dual-sovereignty rule is often dubbed an "exception" to the double jeopardy right, it is not an exception at all. On the contrary, it follows from the text that defines that right in the first place. "[T]he language of the Clause . . . protects individuals from being twice put in jeopardy 'for the same *offence*,' not for the same *conduct* or *actions* . . . And the term " '[o]ffence' was commonly understood in 1791 to mean 'transgression,' that is, 'the Violation or Breaking of a Law.' " As originally understood, then, an "offence" is defined by a law, and each law is defined by a sovereign. So where there are two sovereigns, there are two laws, and two "offences." The constitutional provision is not, that no person shall be subject, for the same act, to be twice put in jeopardy of life or limb; but for the same *offence*, the same *violation of law*, no person's life or limb shall be twice put in jeopardy". . . .

Faced with this reading, Gamble falls back on an episode from the Double Jeopardy Clause's drafting history. The first Congress, working on an earlier draft that would have banned " 'more than one trial or one punishment for the same offence,' " voted down a proposal to add " 'by any law of the United States.' " In rejecting this addition, Gamble surmises, Congress must have intended to bar successive prosecutions regardless of the sovereign bringing the charge.

Even if that inference were justified—something that the Government disputes—it would count for little. The private intent behind a drafter's rejection of one version of a text is shoddy evidence of the public meaning of an altogether different text. ("[F]ailed legislative proposals are a particularly dangerous ground on which to rest an interpretation of a prior statute" . . .

Besides, if we allowed conjectures about purpose to inform our reading of the text, the Government's conjecture would prevail. The Government notes that the Declaration of Independence denounced King George III for "protecting [British troops] by a mock Trial, from punishment for any Murders which they should commit on the Inhabitants of these States." The Declaration was alluding to "the so-called Murderers' Act, passed by Parliament after the Boston Massacre," a law that allowed British officials indicted for murder in America to be " 'tried in England, beyond the control of local juries.' " "During the late colonial period, Americans strongly objected to . . . [t]his circumvention of the judgment of the victimized community." Yet on Gamble's reading, the same Founders who quite literally *revolted* against the use of acquittals abroad to bar criminal prosecutions here would soon give us an Amendment allowing foreign acquittals to spare domestic criminals. We doubt it.

We see no reason to abandon the sovereign-specific reading of the phrase "same offence," from which the dual-sovereignty rule immediately follows. . . .

The judgment of the Court of Appeals [upholding both the federal and state prosecutions] for the Eleventh Circuit is affirmed.

### Justice Gorsuch, dissenting.

A free society does not allow its government to try the same individual for the same crime until it's happy with the result. Unfortunately, the Court today endorses a colossal exception to this ancient rule against double jeopardy. My colleagues say that the federal government and each State are "separate sovereigns" entitled to try the same person for the same crime. So if all the might of one "sovereign" cannot succeed against the presumptively free individual, another may insist on the chance to try again. And if both manage to succeed, so much the better; they can add one punishment on top of the other. But this "separate sovereigns exception" to the bar against double jeopardy finds no meaningful support in the text of the Constitution, its original public meaning, structure, or history. Instead, the Constitution promises all Americans that they will never suffer double jeopardy. I would enforce that guarantee. . . .

Enforcing the Constitution always bears its costs. But when the people adopted the Constitution and its Bill of Rights, they thought the liberties promised there worth the costs. It is not for this Court to reassess this judgment to make the prosecutor's job easier. Nor is there any doubt that the benefits the framers saw in prohibiting double prosecutions remain real, and maybe more vital than ever, today. When governments may unleash all their might in multiple prosecutions against an individual, exhausting themselves only when those who hold the reins of power are content with the result, it is "the poor and the weak," and the unpopular and controversial, who suffer first—and there is nothing to stop them from being the last. The separate sovereigns exception was wrong when it was invented, and it remains wrong today.

I respectfully dissent.

Justice Ginsburg, dissenting

■ ■ ■

I dissent from the Court's adherence to that misguided doctrine. Instead of "fritter[ing] away [Gamble's] libert[y] upon a metaphysical subtlety, two sovereignties," I would hold that the Double Jeopardy Clause bars "successive prosecutions [for the same offense] by parts of the whole USA.

Justification for the separate-sovereigns doctrine centers on the word "offence": An "offence," the argument runs, is the violation of a sovereign's law, the United States and each State are separate sovereigns, ergo successive state and federal prosecutions do not place a defendant in "jeopardy . . . for the same offence."

This "compact syllogism" is fatally flawed. The United States and its constituent States, unlike foreign nations, are "kindred systems," "parts of ONE WHOLE." They compose one people, bound by an overriding Federal Constitution. Within that "WHOLE," the Federal and State Governments should be disabled from accomplishing together "what neither government [could] do alone—prosecute an ordinary citizen twice for the same offence. . . .

In our "compound republic," the division of authority between the United States and the States was meant to operate as "a double security [for] the rights of the people." The separate-sovereigns doctrine, however, scarcely shores up people's rights. Instead, it invokes federalism to withhold liberty.

Although the Double Jeopardy Clause does not prohibit two sovereigns from prosecuting for the same offense, many states prohibit this by statute. Even where permitted, many prosecutors do not pursue a defendant who has been previously prosecuted in another jurisdiction for the same crime. The Model Penal Code incorporates this approach in certain circumstances.[7] Municipalities are not independent beings; they owe their existence not to the Constitution of the United States, but to a state. Accordingly, prosecutions by cities are treated as being brought by the state, and it is a violation of the Double Jeopardy Clause for a state and city to punish one for the same offense.

# Self-Incrimination

Learning Objective: Define and describe the right to be free of self-incrimination.

The Fifth Amendment also states that no person "shall be compelled in any criminal case to be a witness against himself." The following passage explains why the framers of the Constitution included a privilege against self-incrimination.

> Perhaps the best-known provision of the Fifth Amendment is the clause against forced "self-incrimination," whose origin goes back to England where persons accused of crimes before ecclesiastical courts were forced to take an ex officio oath. That is, they had to swear to answer all questions even if the questions did not apply to the case at trial. This requirement was later adopted by the Court of Star Chamber. One of the victims of the Court was a printer and book distributor named John Lilburne, charged in 1637 with treason for importing books "that promoted Puritan dissent." Lilburne told his accusers, "I am not willing to answer to you any more of these questions because I see you go about by this examination to ensnare me. For seeing the things for which I am imprisoned cannot be proved against me, you will get other material out of my examination; and therefore if you will not ask me about the thing laid to my charge, I shall answer no more. . . . I think by the law of the land, that I may stand upon my just defense." Lilburne was convicted, fined, whipped, pilloried, gagged, and imprisoned until he agreed to take the oath. . . .
>
> One notorious instance of forced self-incrimination in the American colonies occurred in the Salem witch trials. In 1692, Giles Corey, an elderly Massachusetts farmer, was accused of witchcraft. He knew whether he pleaded guilty or not guilty he would be convicted and executed and his property confiscated. So, to ensure that his heirs inherited his property, he refused to plead and thus could not be convicted. The judges ordered him strapped to a table, and stones were loaded upon his chest to force the plea out of him. Corey's final words were "more weight." Then his chest caved in.[8]

John Bradshaw, John Lilburne's attorney, stated the principle best when he said that "It is contrary to the laws of God, nature and the kingdom for any man to be his own accuser."

Generally, the Fifth Amendment prohibits the government from compelling people to testify when incrimination is possible. Most people have heard of "pleading the Fifth." However, if immunity from prosecution is granted to a witness, he or she may be compelled to testify. If a witness refuses to testify because of the fear of self-incrimination, the government may offer the witness immunity from prosecution so that the testimony may be compelled. There are two types of immunity: transactional and derivative use.

**Transactional immunity** shields witnesses from prosecution for all offenses related to their testimony. For example, if a witness testifies concerning a robbery,

**transactional immunity**
Freedom from prosecution for all crimes related to the compelled testimony, so long as the witness tells the truth.

the government may not prosecute the witness for that robbery, even though the government may have evidence of guilt independent of the witness's testimony. Transactional immunity gives more protection to the witness than is required by the Constitution, so when it is granted, a witness may be ordered to testify.

The minimum immunity that must be provided a witness to overcome a Fifth Amendment claim is derivative **use immunity.** This prohibits the government from using the witness's testimony or any evidence derived from that testimony to prosecute the witness. However, all evidence that is independently obtained may be used against the witness.

Use immunity only prohibits the government from using the witness's testimony against him or her. Statutes that provide only for use immunity are unconstitutional, as derivative use is the minimum protection required by the Fifth Amendment.

States vary in how immunity is granted. Some permit the prosecutor to give the immunity; others require both the request of the prosecutor and the approval of the trial judge.

A person may also waive the Fifth Amendment privilege against self-incrimination. Generally, once a person testifies freely, the privilege is waived as to the subject discussed during the same proceeding. A witness (or defendant) may not testify selectively concerning a subject. It is often said that testifying to a fact waives to the details. This principle prevents witnesses from testifying only to the information beneficial to one party and then refusing to testify further, even though they may have omitted important facts. However, a witness may not be compelled to testify if there is a chance of incriminating themselves beyond the original testimony.

The fact that a witness may waive the Fifth Amendment privilege against self-incrimination on one occasion does not mean it is waived forever. First, a defendant (or witness) may speak to the police during the investigative stage and later refuse to testify at trial, provided such testimony may be incriminating. Second, it is generally held that a person who testifies before a grand jury without claiming the Fifth does not waive the right to raise the defense at trial. Third, even within the same proceeding a person may invoke the Fifth Amendment privilege against self-incrimination if the two hearings are separate and distinct. For example, a defendant may testify at a suppression hearing without waiving the privilege not to testify at trial.

Finally, the Fifth Amendment applies to all proceedings, whether civil, criminal, or administrative.[9] Therefore, a person called to testify in a civil proceeding may invoke the Fifth Amendment's privilege and refuse to testify. Any person, not just a suspect or defendant, may invoke the privilege. In 2019, allegations of sexual assault against the actor Kevin Stacey were dismissed because the accuser pled the Fifth when asked questions about his possible destruction of evidence that would have been favorable to Spacey.

**use immunity**
Freedom from prosecution based on the compelled testimony and on anything the government learns from following up on the testimony.

# Due Process and Equal Protection

Learning Objective: Define and describe the substantive due process and equal protection rights of the Fifth and Fourteenth Amendments.

The Fifth Amendment to the U.S. Constitution prohibits the government from depriving a person of life, liberty, or property without due process of law. This amendment acts to constrain the power of the federal government. You have previously learned that the Fourteenth Amendment has identical language and constrains the power of state governments.

Due process requires the government to treat people fairly; therefore, whenever a law or other governmental action appears to be unfair, there is a due process issue. In a sense, due process is a safety net, protecting the individual when another specific constitutional provision doesn't.

On the surface, the Clause appears to be only about process. And indeed, it has been interpreted to impose meaningful procedural expectations on the state and courts when adjudicating criminal cases. For example, the Due Process Clause is the constitutional source of the **principle of legality**, which requires that criminal laws (and punishments) be written and enacted before an act may be punished.

But due process has a second dimension. It is the source of important substantive rights. The protection of privacy, discussed later in this chapter, is an example. You will learn later in this chapter that overly broad or vague laws may be violative of due process.

And it is through due process that most of the provisions of the Bill of Rights, which initially applied only against the federal government, have been extended to the states. Today, the Fourth Amendment's right to be free from unreasonable searches and seizures, the Fifth Amendment's right to be free from self-incrimination, the Sixth Amendment's right to counsel at critical stages of criminal adjudications, and the Eighth Amendment's prohibition of cruel and unusual punishment are among the many rights that are now available to defendants in state courts.

In some instances, due process or equal protection increases the scope of a right found in the Bill of Rights. For example, the Sixth Amendment's right to counsel is limited to the critical stages of criminal proceedings. Appeals are not critical stages, and therefore the Sixth Amendment does not mandate counsel. But the Supreme Court has held that if a state provides for felony appeals by right, then the Equal Protection Clause requires that indigent defendants receive appointed counsel. To hold otherwise would unfairly discriminate against the indigent.[10]

Although the Fourteenth Amendment is the source of the incorporation of most of the Bill of Rights, its importance extends further. Any time an issue of fairness surfaces, due process should be examined. If the issue concerns one of improper classifications, equal protection law should be considered. The Supreme Court stated of substantive due process:

> The inescapable fact is that adjudication of substantive due process claims may call upon the Court in interpreting the Constitution to exercise that same capacity which by tradition courts always have exercised: reasoned judgment. Its boundaries are not susceptible of expression as a simple rule. That does not mean we are free to invalidate state policy choices with which we disagree: yet neither does it permit us to shrink from the duties of our office. As Justice Harlan observed: "Due process has not been reduced to any formula: its content cannot be determined by reference to any code. The best that can be said is that through the course of this Court's decisions it has represented the balance which our Nation, built upon postulates of respect for liberty of the individual, has struck between that liberty and the demands of organized society."

The Fourteenth Amendment also expressly requires the states to extend equal protection of the laws to the people. There is no express equal protection clause in the Fifth Amendment, but the Supreme Court has found it to be implied in the Due Process Clause. Equal protection concerns classifications and discrimination.

Discrimination is not inherently evil. Students discriminate between professors, possibly due to grading policy or teaching skill, when deciding what courses to take. Governments also discriminate and make classifications, most of which are sensible and acceptable. For example, people who commit homicides are divided into groups: murderers, manslaughterers, and those who are excused or justified in killing. When classifications are based upon meaningful criteria (e.g., mens rea), the law is valid. However, our society has decided that certain classifications are improper and violative of equal protection. A classification between those who exercise a constitutional right and those who do not, if it results in prosecution

**principle of legality**
The procedural side of due process, which requires that criminal laws (and punishments) be written and enacted before an act may be punished.

or increased punishment for the former, is unconstitutional. Classifications based on race, religion, gender, and other immutable conditions are "suspect." You will return to this subject in the section below on analyzing due process and equal protection claims.

# Vagueness and Overbreadth

Learning Objective: Describe and provide examples of vague and overbroad criminal laws.

The Due Process Clauses of the Fifth and Fourteenth Amendments to the U.S. Constitution are the foundation of the void-for-vagueness and overbreadth doctrines.

A statute is void for **vagueness** whenever "men of common intelligence must necessarily guess at its meaning and differ as to its application."[11] But for the doctrine, legislatures could draft statutes so that everyone, law abiding and not, could be ensnared in the coils of the state.

It is evidence of vagueness if lower courts issue widely divergent interpretations of the same law.[12] The Supreme Court has held that uncertain statutes do not provide notice of what conduct is forbidden and are violative of due process. The Court has also found statutes that permit arbitrary or discriminatory enforcement void. That is, if the police or courts are given unlimited authority to decide who will be prosecuted, the statute is invalid.

A law that criminalizes "annoying conduct" is too vague to warn a person what specific conduct is prohibited. For the same reason, several vagrancy laws that forbade loitering, wandering without purpose, and other similarly worded prohibitions have been struck down for vagueness.

A closely related doctrine is **overbreadth.** A statute is overbroad if it includes within its grasp not only unprotected activity but also activity protected by the Constitution. For example, in one case a city ordinance made it illegal for "one or more persons to assemble" on a sidewalk and conduct themselves in an annoying manner. The U.S. Supreme Court found that the law was unconstitutional not only because it made unprotected activity illegal (fighting words or riotous activity) but also because it included activity that is protected by the First Amendment's free assembly and association provisions.[13] It is possible for a statute to be clear and precise (not vague) but overbroad.

**vagueness doctrine**
The rule that a criminal law may be unconstitutional if it does not clearly say what is required or prohibited, what punishment may be imposed, or what persons may be affected. A law that violates due process of law in this way is *void for vagueness*.

**overbreadth doctrine**
A law will be declared void for *overbreadth* if it attempts to punish speech or conduct that is protected by the Constitution and if it is impossible to eliminate the unconstitutional part of the law without invalidating the whole law.

# Analyzing Due Process and Equal Protection Claims

Learning Objective: Describe and apply the strict scrutiny, intermediate, and rational basis tests of constitutional review.

No right is absolute. Every right protected by the Constitution has limitations. But the Constitution doesn't detail these limits; they have been created by the courts. Judges don't make these decisions arbitrarily. A thousand years of the Common Law, the colonial experience, rules governing how to interpret the law, including the doctrine of stare decisis, and contemporary values all play a rule in interpreting the Constitution.

Due process and equal protection claims are analyzed using the same framework. The analysis balances the liberty interest of the individual against the government's interest in its regulation. Three standards, or tests, are employed. The first standard is **strict scrutiny**. A court applies the strict scrutiny in both of these circumstances:

**strict scrutiny test**
A test used to determine if due process or equal protection has been violated. Laws that burden fundamental rights or employ suspect classifications must be supported by a compelling interest, narrowly designed, and the least restrictive means to accomplish the state's objectives.

1. when the government burdens a fundamental right or

2. when the government groups people into suspect classes

As the first of the two, nearly all the rights found in the Constitution are "fundamental." Remember these standards as you read about the rights—e.g., speech, religion—discussed in this chapter.

Strict scrutiny is the hardest test for the government to pass; it is intended to favor liberties. To pass this test, the government must prove that it has a

1. compelling interest and

2. the law is narrowly tailored to satisfy its interest and

3. it is the least restrictive way to accomplish the government's objective.

The compelling interest prong demands more than a reasonable interest. The government must have a "damn good reason" for what it is doing. The government must also show that the law is narrowly tailored to achieve its objectives; that is, it is not overly broad. To illustrate, consider a law aimed at forbidding child pornography. The Supreme Court has recognized child pornography that involves an actual child to be unprotected by the First Amendment. But depictions of child pornography, where no child is involved, are protected expression. Therefore, a law that forbids all "photos, written descriptions, drawings, and video recording of a person under the age of 15 in a state of nudity or engaged in a sex act" is overbroad because it includes both obscene (sex acts involving children) and protected speech. Specifically, written depictions don't involve actual children and not every photo of a nude child is obscene. Consider, for example, a parent's photo of a toddler playing in a bathtub full of bubbles. A law may also be invalidated if there is another way for the government to accomplish its purpose without burdening a right exists.

The Equal Protection Clause applies the same test when a law uses **suspect classifications**. A trait is deemed suspect when there is a history of discrimination or it is immutable (inherent). Distinctions between people by race, religion, national origin, and, sometimes, alienage (citizenship) are tested under the strict scrutiny test.

Laws that don't burden individual rights and don't classify along suspect lines are tested under an easier standard, the **rational relationship test**. Under this test, a law is valid if *rationally related to a legitimate government objective*. This is the default standard.

A third "tweener" test between strict scrutiny and rational basis applies when rights, not deemed fundamental, are encroached up and when classifications are made upon criteria that have been the subject of discrimination, but not to the extent of race, ethnicity, or religion. Commercial speech, for example, is protected under the First Amendment, but not to the extent of political speech. In Equal Protection terms, gender, "legitimacy of birth," and sometimes alienage are examples of when the middle tier applies. Laws that fall into this category are analyzed under the **Substantial Relationship Test**, which requires a law

1. further a substantial/important governmental interest and

2. there be a substantial relationship between that interest and the law to be constitutional.

Most laws tested under scrutiny fail and most laws tested under rational relationship pass. But there are exceptions to both. An example of a statute that failed the rational relationship test was Ohio's sexual battery law, as applied to law enforcement officers generally. The law was aimed at defendants in certain professions, including *inter alia*, doctors and other health care workers, clerics, corrections officers, and police officers. To apply the heightened punishment under the law, the defendant must be in a position

**suspect classifications**
Laws that classify people by race, religion, national origin, and alienage must pass the strict scrutiny test to be valid.

**rational relationship test**
The default test used to determine if due process or equal protection has been violated. Laws must be rational to satisfy this test.

**Substantial Relationship Test**
A test used to determine if due process or equal protection has been violated. Laws that burden liberties not deemed fundamental and that classify according to sex and a few other classifications must be substantially related to a legitimate governmental interest to be valid.

of authority over the victim. However, the provision that applied to police officers had no such limitation. It applies to all instances of sexual battery on a minor by a police officer.

Matthew Mole, a police officer, aged 35, met and had sex with a minor, aged 14. The two met on a digital dating application. He didn't disclose that he was a police officer, and he never exercised any authority over the victim. He was charged with violating the peace officer prohibition in the law. He challenged the law as it applied to officers who didn't abuse their authority, and the Ohio Supreme Court of Ohio agreed, holding that the prohibition failed to rationally connect to its purposes, which were to hold officers to a high standard of conduct and to protect minors. Rejecting the State's first argument, the Court noted that many legitimate criminal statutes do single out police officers for special treatment, such as dereliction of duty, theft by public official, interfering with civil rights, and sexual battery on persons over whom they have authority. Further, they can be held to higher standards in employment. Mole, for example, could be fired for his conduct. The Court said of Ohio's two objectives that

> [a]fter all, the government has a valid interest in strictly controlling the immoral or unbecoming conduct of peace officers as employees. Mole resigned from his position at the Waite Hill Police Department immediately after he was criminally charged. Regardless of any causal connection between the conduct and the employment itself. That governmental interest, however, does not justify differential treatment under the criminal law of peace officers acting as private citizens when there is no connection between the criminalized conduct and the office, duties, or other aspects of the occupation of a peace officer. Peace officers must accept certain burdens as part of their employment in order to maintain the honor and privilege of being peace officers and to foster public trust. They do not lose all of their rights as ordinary citizens, including their constitutional right to be treated equally under the criminal law, simply because they have chosen the profession of peace officer. . . .

> Undeniably, the state has a valid, rational interest in proscribing the use of professional authority to sexually exploit minors or other vulnerable persons. And R.C. 2907.03(A) may have been born from the desire to prevent those in positions of authority or control from abusing that authority or control to sexually exploit vulnerable persons. But here, to obtain a conviction, the statute does not require the state to prove that Mole knew that J.S. was a minor or that Mole was reckless in not knowing that J.S. was a minor. Nor does it require the state to prove that Mole's sexual contact with J.S. had any connection to Mole's status as a peace officer. Thus, although the state's interest in protecting minors from sexual conduct is rational, the classification of peace officers in R.C. 2907.03(A)(13) is not. Indeed, the irrationality of the R.C. 2907.03(A)(13) classification is evident when considered in the larger context of the statutory scheme at issue here, which otherwise requires that there be a nexus between the offender's employment and the offender's illegal conduct with a child or other defenseless person.

> R.C. 2907.03(A)(13) omits any mention of a relationship between the conduct and the profession.

> To obtain a conviction under R.C. 2907.03(A)(13), the state does not need to prove the existence of any authoritative relationship. But in other sections of the statute, the state must demonstrate that the potential offenders used trickery or occupied a position of authority in order to make sexual conduct with the victim a crime under the statute. How is it rational to require that the state demonstrate that offenders in other professions that provide access to

## Exhibit 9–1 Constitutional Standards of Review

|  | Governmental Objective | Relationship to Objective | Does Least Restrictive Means/ Alternatives Test Apply? | Applies When? |
|---|---|---|---|---|
| Strict Scrutiny | Compelling | Directly Advance | Yes | 1. Fundamental right is burdened<br>2. Suspect classification |
| Substantial Relationship | Substantial/Important | Substantial | Yes/No | 1. Liberty not rising to fundamental right is burdened<br>2. Specific classifications |
| Rational Basis | Legitimate | Rational | No | Default for laws that don't fall into one of the above |

children, including coaches, teachers, clerics, employees of detention facilities, and scout leaders, used their professional capacity to exploit the victim, but to omit that requirement if the offender is a peace officer?[14]

See Exhibit 9–1 for a summary of the three constitutional standards of review.

# Ex Post Facto and Bills of Attainder

Learning Objective: Describe and offer examples of ex post facto laws and bills of attainder.

In England, Parliament is sovereign and supreme. Although less common today than in the past, Parliament can retroactively declare an act to be a crime and it can decide a person's guilt. The former is known as **ex post facto law** and the latter, a **bill of attainder**. The American colonists believed these actions to be so oppressive that they were two of many reasons the colonies declared their independence in 1776. Subsequently, the Framers of the Constitution prohibited both in Article I of the U.S. Constitution.

An ex post facto law is one that

1. makes an act illegal after the act was taken or

2. increases the punishment or severity of a crime after it occurred or

3. changes the procedural rules so as to increase the chances of conviction after the crime occurs

In short, a government may not make criminal law retroactive if doing so is detrimental to the defendant. However, changes that benefit a defendant may be applied retroactively. Retroactive changes that may benefit an accused or a prisoner come in many forms. One is procedural. Imagine, for example, that the law concerning the search of a cell phone changes after a defendant has been charged but before trial. If that change of law benefits the defendant, does it apply? What if the change occurs after conviction, during appeal or while the actor is in prison? Clearly, a legislature, or high court, can apply the change retroactively. Periodically, due process mandates retroactive application is a different and more complex question that is beyond this text.

A second form of change is legislative amnesty, also known as abatement. Amnesty provides people convicted under a law full legal forgiveness. They are released from prison, and other legal disabilities are removed. This may occur, for example, when an act is decriminalized.

In a third form of positive ex post facto, so-called legislative amelioration, something less than amnesty occurs. The reduction in a prison sentence is a common example. The mix of a less punitive attitude about marijuana and other drugs,

**ex post facto law**
(Latin) After the fact. An *ex post facto* law is one that retroactively attempts to make an action a crime that was not a crime at the time it was done, or a law that attempts to reduce a person's rights based on a past act that was not subject to the law when it was done.

**bill of attainder**
A legislative act pronouncing a person guilty (usually of treason) without a trial and sentencing the person to death and attainder. This is now prohibited by the U.S. Constitution.

the costs of high incarceration rates, and the racial inequity in the U.S. prison population have led many jurisdictions to decriminalize, or at least reduce the punishments for, many crimes. The states have been split in their application of these changes retroactively. In 2018, the Formerly Incarcerated Reenter Society Transformed Safely Transitioning Every Person Act (First Step Act) was enacted by Congress.[15] The law is intended to reduce both the federal prison population and recidivism. The Act provides for a number of inmate benefits, such as increased phone privileges, compassionate release for terminally ill inmates, and the possibility of being housed in an institution closer to home. It also establishes a program of incentives where inmates can reduce their sentences by completing coursework and programs intended to reduce recidivism.

A bill of attainder is a legislative act punishing a person without a judicial trial. This provision reinforces the concept of separation of powers. It is the duty of the legislative branch to make the laws, and it is the duty of the judicial branch to determine who has violated those laws. Alexander Hamilton, in support of the prohibition of bills of attainder, wrote:

> Nothing is more common than for a free people, in times of heat and violence, to gratify momentary passions by letting into the government principles and precedents which afterwards prove fatal to themselves. Of this kind is the doctrine of disqualification, disfranchisement, and banishment by acts of the legislature. The dangerous consequences of this power are manifest. If the legislature can disfranchise any number of citizens at pleasure by general descriptions, it may soon confine all the votes to a small number of partisans, and establish an aristocracy or an oligarchy; if it may banish at discretion all those whom particular circumstances render obnoxious, without hearing or trial, no man can be safe, nor know when he may be the innocent victim of a prevailing faction. The name of liberty applied to such a government would be a mockery of common sense.[16]

In a few instances, however, Congress may act in a judicial role. Congress may punish those who disrupt its functions for contempt. In addition, Congress is authorized by the Constitution to conduct impeachment hearings of the president, federal judges, and other federal officers and to discipline its own members.

# First Amendment and Religion

Learning Objective: Define and describe the two religion clauses of the First Amendment, offering examples of how they have been applied in criminal law.

Considered by many to be a first among equals (other rights), the First Amendment reads:

> Congress shall make no law respecting an establishment of religion, or prohibiting the free exercise thereof; or abridging the freedom of speech, or of the press; or the right of the people peaceably to assemble, and to petition the government for a redress of grievances.

It contains six rights:

1. speech
2. press
3. to choose and practice a religion (Free Exercise Clause)
4. to be free of an official religion (Establishment Clause)
5. to peaceably assemble
6. to petition the government to redress grievances

Although the First Amendment is directly applicable only against the national government, the Fourteenth Amendment extends its prohibitions to the states.

Concerning the freedom of religion, the right to one's own conscience and belief is, of course, absolute. Any law prohibiting a religious belief is void. However, the Supreme Court has held that some religious practices may be regulated.

To determine whether a specific religious act may be criminalized, the strict scrutiny test is applied. For example, it has been held that the Mormon practice of polygamy may be regulated.[17] Also, a parent who depends upon prayer to save a dying child may be charged with manslaughter for failing to seek competent medical care. In this instance, the state's interest in protecting the child's life outweighs the parent's interest in practicing his or her religion in such a manner.

The Supreme Court issued an important decision concerning the standard of review in Free Exercise cases in *Department of Human Resources v. Smith*, 494 U.S. 872 (1990). The case involved an appeal from a denial of unemployment benefits by Alfred Leo Smith. Mr. Smith's, a Native American, application for benefits was denied because he was dismissed from his job for using peyote, a hallucinogen that is used ritually by Native Americans. On appeal, he claimed that the government couldn't withhold a benefit from him because his use of the substance was protected by the Free Exercise Clause. Reversing an earlier decision, the Court decided that a neutral law of general applicability is to be reviewed under the Rational Basis Test, not strict scrutiny.

> [T]he right of free exercise does not relieve an individual of the obligation to comply with a valid and neutral law of general applicability on the ground that the law proscribes (or prescribes) conduct that his religion prescribes (or proscribes).

A law of general applicability is one that is not targeting any religion and applies to all people, generally. The Court held that controlling dangerous substances, through the Controlled Substances Act, is a legitimate governmental interest. Further, the law applies to everyone.

The Smith decision was not popular. Congress and the White House responded with two pieces of legislation. First, Native American use of peyote as a religious ritual was specifically exempted from the Controlled Substances Act. Second, the Religious Freedom Restoration Act (RFRA) was enacted.[18] Through this statute, courts are required to apply the strict scrutiny test when applying statutes of general applicability to religious practices. So, a government must demonstrate both a compelling reason and that there is no less restrictive way to accomplish the governmental objective. The new standard was applied in the following 2006 case.

## Oyez

### Gonzales V. O Centro Espirita Beneficente Uniao Do Vegetal
#### 546 U.S. 418 (2006)

**Chief Justice Roberts Delivered the Opinion of the Court.**

A religious sect with origins in the Amazon Rainforest receives communion by drinking a sacramental tea, brewed from plants unique to the region, that contains a hallucinogen regulated under the Controlled Substances Act by the Federal Government. The Government concedes that this practice is a sincere exercise of religion, but nonetheless sought to prohibit the small American branch of the sect from engaging in the practice, on the ground that the Controlled Substances Act bars all use of the hallucinogen. The sect sued to block enforcement against it of the ban on the sacramental tea, and moved for a preliminary injunction.

It relied on the Religious Freedom Restoration Act of 1993, which prohibits the Federal Government from substantially burdening a person's exercise of religion, unless the Government "demonstrates that application of the burden to the person" represents the least restrictive means of advancing a compelling interest. 42 U.S.C. § 2000bb—1(b). The District Court granted the preliminary injunction, and

(continued)

the Court of Appeals affirmed. We granted the Government's petition for certiorari. Before this Court, the Government's central submission is that it has a compelling interest in the *uniform* application of the Controlled Substances Act, such that no exception to the ban on use of the hallucinogen can be made to accommodate the sect's sincere religious practice. We conclude that the Government has not carried the burden expressly placed on it by Congress in the Religious Freedom Restoration Act, and affirm the grant of the preliminary injunction. . . .

O Centro Espírita Beneficente Uniã do Vegetal (UDV) is a Christian Spiritist sect based in Brazil, with an American branch of approximately 130 individuals. Central to the UDV's faith is receiving communion through *hoasca* (pronounced "wass-ca"), a sacramental tea made from two plants unique to the Amazon region. One of the plants, *Psychotria viridis*, contains dimethyltryptamine (DMT), a hallucinogen whose effects are enhanced by alkaloids from the other plant, *Banisteriopsis caapi*. DMT, as well as "any material, compound, mixture, or preparation, which contains any quantity of [DMT]," is listed in Schedule I of the Controlled Substances Act. § 812(c), Schedule I(c).

In 1999, United States Customs inspectors intercepted a shipment to the American UDV containing three drums of *hoasca*. A subsequent investigation revealed that the UDV had received 14 prior shipments of *hoasca*. The inspectors seized the intercepted shipment and threatened the UDV with prosecution.

The UDV filed suit against the Attorney General and other federal law enforcement officials, seeking declaratory and injunctive relief. The complaint alleged, *inter alia,* that applying the Controlled Substances Act to the UDV's sacramental use of *hoasca* violates RFRA. . . .

The Government's second line of argument rests on the Controlled Substances Act itself. The Government contends that the Act's description of Schedule I substances as having "a high potential for abuse," "no currently accepted medical use in treatment in the United States," and "a lack of accepted safety for use . . . under medical supervision," 21 U.S.C. § 812(b (1), by itself precludes any consideration of individualized exceptions such as that sought by the UDV. The Government goes on to argue that the regulatory regime established by the Act—a "closed" system that prohibits all use of controlled substances except as authorized by the Act itself. . . . Under the Government's view, there is no need to assess the particulars of the UDV's use or weigh the impact of an exemption for that specific use, because the Controlled Substances Act serves a compelling purpose and simply admits of no exceptions. . . .

RFRA, and the strict scrutiny test it adopted, contemplate an inquiry more focused than the Government's categorical approach. RFRA requires the Government to demonstrate that the compelling interest test is satisfied through application of the challenged law "to the person"—the particular claimant whose sincere exercise of religion is being substantially burdened. Under the more focused inquiry required by RFRA and the compelling interest test, the Government's mere invocation of the general characteristics of Schedule I substances, as set forth in the Controlled Substances Act, cannot carry the day. It is true, of course, that Schedule I substances such as DMT are exceptionally dangerous. Nevertheless, there is no indication that Congress, in classifying DMT, considered the harms posed by the particular use at issue here—the circumscribed, sacramental use of *hoasca* by the UDV. . . .

And in fact an exception has been made to the Schedule I ban for religious use. For the past 35 years, there has been a regulatory exemption for use of peyote—a Schedule I substance—by the Native American Church. See 21 CFR § 1307.31 (2005). In 1994, Congress extended that exemption to all members of every recognized Indian Tribe. See 42 U.S.C. § 1996a(b)(1). Everything the Government says about the DMT in *hoasca*—that, as a Schedule I substance, Congress has determined that it "has a high potential for abuse," "has no currently accepted medical use," and has "a lack of accepted safety for use . . . -under medical supervision," 21 U.S.C. § 812(b) (1)—applies in equal measure to the mescaline in peyote, yet both the Executive and Congress itself have decreed an exception from the Controlled Substances Act for Native American religious use of peyote. If such use is permitted in the face of the congressional findings in § 812(b)(1) for hundreds of thousands of Native Americans practicing their faith, it is difficult to see how those same findings alone can preclude any consideration of a similar exception for the 130 or so American members of the UDV who want to practice theirs. . . . [Therefore, the application of the Controlled Substances Act to UDV's religious use of hoasca is invalidated.]

Smith and the RFRA only apply when neutral laws are challenged. It is different when government targets a religion or its practices. In *Church of Lukumi Babalu Aye, Inc. v. Hialeah,* the Supreme Court invalidated several ordinances that prohibited the adherents of Santeria from sacrificing animals as part of their religious rites.

## Oyez

# Church of Lukumi Babalu Aye, Inc. v. Hialeah
## 508 U.S. 520 (1993)

This case involves practices of the Santeria religion, which originated in the nineteenth century. When hundreds of thousands of members of the Yoruba people were brought as slaves from eastern Africa to Cuba, their traditional African religion absorbed significant elements of Roman Catholicism. The resulting syncretion, or fusion, is Santeria, "the way of the saints." The Cuban Yoruba express their devotion to spirits, called *orishas*, through the iconography of Catholic saints, Catholic symbols are often present at Santeria rites, and Santeria devotees attend the Catholic sacraments. . . .

The Santeria faith teaches that every individual has a destiny from God, a destiny fulfilled with the aid and energy of orishas. The basis of the Santeria religion is the nurture of a personal relation with the orishas, and one of the principal forms of devotion is an animal sacrifice. . . . The sacrifice of animals as part of religious rituals has ancient roots. . . . Animal sacrifice is mentioned throughout the Old Testament . . . and it played an important role in the practice of Judaism before destruction of the second Temple in Jerusalem. . . . In modern Islam, there is an annual sacrifice commemorating Abraham's sacrifice of a ram in the stead of his son. . . .

According to Santeria teaching, the orishas are powerful but not immortal. They depend for survival on the sacrifice.

Santeria adherents faced widespread persecution in Cuba, so the religion and its rituals were practiced in secret. The open practice of Santeria and its rites remains infrequent. . . . The religion was brought to this Nation most often by exiles from the Cuban revolution. The District Court estimated that there are at least 50,000 practitioners in South Florida today.

Petitioner Church of Lukumi Babalu Aye, Inc. (Church), is a not-for-profit corporation organized under Florida law in 1973. The Church and its congregants practice the Santeria religion. The president of the Church is petitioner Ernesto Pichardo, who is also the Church's priest and holds the religious title of Italero, the second highest in the Santeria faith. In April 1987, the Church leased land in the city of Hialeah, Florida, and announced plans to establish a house of worship as well as a school, cultural center, and museum. Pichardo indicated that the Church's goal was to bring the practice of the Santeria faith, including its ritual of animal sacrifice, into the open.

The Church began the process of obtaining utility service and receiving the necessary licensing, inspection, and zoning approvals. Although the Church's efforts at obtaining the necessary licenses and permits were far from smooth . . . it appears that it received all needed approvals by early August 1987.

The prospect of a Santeria church in their midst was distressing to many members of the Hialeah community, and the announcement of the plans to open a Santeria church in Hialeah prompted the city council to hold an emergency public session on June 9, 1987. [The city council enacted ordinance] 87–66, which noted the "concern" expressed by residents of the city "that certain religions may propose to engage in practices which are inconsistent with public morals, peace or safety," and declared that "[t]he City reiterates its commitment to a prohibition against any and all acts of any and all religious groups which are inconsistent with public morals, peace or safety." Next, the council approved an emergency ordinance, Ordinance 87–40, that incorporated in full, except as to penalty, Florida's animal cruelty laws. . . . Among other things, the incorporated state law subjected to criminal punishment "[w]hoever . . . unnecessarily or cruelly . . . kills any animal."

[In September 1987, the city council adopted three additional ordinances prohibiting owning or possessing an animal for purpose of sacrifice and regulating the slaughtering of animals.] Violations of each of the four ordinances were punishable by fines not exceeding $500 or imprisonment not exceeding 60 days, or both.

Following enactment of these ordinances, the Church and Pichardo filed this action pursuant to 42 U.S.C. § 1983 in the United States District Court for the Southern District of Florida. Named as defendants were the city of Hialeah and its mayor and members of its city council in their individual capacities. [The defendants prevailed at the trial and appellate levels.] . . .

The city does not argue that Santeria is not a "religion" within the meaning of the First Amendment. Nor could it. Although the practice of animal sacrifice may seem abhorrent to some, "religious beliefs need not be acceptable, logical, consistent, or comprehensible to others in order to merit First Amendment protection. . . . Given the historical association between animal sacrifice and religious worship . . . petitioners' assertion that animal sacrifice is an integral part of their religion "cannot be deemed bizarre or incredible." . . . Neither the city nor the courts below, moreover, have questioned the sincerity of petitioners' professed desire to conduct animal sacrifices for religious reasons. We must consider petitioners' First Amendment claim.

In addressing the constitutional protection for free exercise of religion, our cases establish the general proposition that a law that is neutral and of general applicability need not be justified by a compelling governmental interest even if the law has the incidental effect of burdening a particular religious practice. . . . Neutrality and general applicability are interrelated, and, as becomes apparent in this case, failure to satisfy one requirement is a likely indication that the other has not been satisfied. A law failing to satisfy these requirements must be justified by a compelling governmental interest and must be narrowly tailored to advance the interest. These ordinances fail to satisfy the [constitutional] requirements. . . .

There are, of course, many ways of demonstrating that the object or purpose of a law is the suppression of religion or religious conduct. To determine the object of a law, we must begin with its text, for the minimum requirement of neutrality is that a law not discriminate on its face. A law lacks facial neutrality if it refers to a religious practice without a secular meaning discernable from the language or context. Petitioners contend that three of the ordinances fail this test of facial neutrality because they use the words "sacrifice" and "ritual," words with strong religious connotations. . . . We agree that these words are consistent with the claim of facial discrimination, but the argument is not conclusive. The words "sacrifice" and "ritual" have a religious origin, but current use admits also of secular meanings. . . .

We reject the contention advanced by the city . . . that our inquiry must end with the text of the laws at issue. Facial neutrality is not determinative. The Free Exercise Clause, like the Establishment Clause, extends beyond facial discrimination. The Clause "forbids subtle departures from neutrality." . . . The Free Exercise Clause protects against governmental hostility which is masked, as well as overt. "The

(continued)

Court must survey meticulously the circumstances of governmental categories to eliminate, as it were, religious gerrymanders." . . .

The record in this case compels the conclusion that suppression of the central element of the Santeria worship service was the object of the ordinances. First, though the use of the words "sacrifice" and "ritual" does not compel a finding of improper targeting of the Santeria religion, the choice of these words is support for our conclusion. . . . [One of the ordinances] recited that "residents and citizens of the City of Hialeah have expressed their concern that certain religions may propose to engage in practices which are inconsistent with public morals, peace or safety," and "reiterate[d]" the city's commitment to prohibit "any and all [such] acts of any and all religious groups." No one suggests, and on this record it cannot be maintained, that city officials had in mind a religion other than Santeria.

It becomes evident that these ordinances target Santeria sacrifice when the ordinances' operation is considered. Apart from the text, the effect of a law in its real operation is strong evidence of its object. To be sure, adverse impact will not always lead to a finding of impermissible targeting. . . .

It is a necessary conclusion that almost the only conduct subject to [the ordinances] is the religious exercise of Santeria Church members. The texts show that they were drafted in tandem to achieve this purpose. . . . [One of the ordinances] prohibits the sacrifice of animals but defines sacrifice as "to unnecessarily kill . . . an animal in a public or private ritual or ceremony not for the primary purpose of food consumption." The definition excludes almost all killings of animals except for religious sacrifice, and the primary purpose requirement narrows the proscribed category even further, in particular by exempting Kosher slaughter. . . .

The net result of the gerrymander is that few if any killings of animals are prohibited other than Santeria sacrifice, which is proscribed because it occurs during a ritual or ceremony and its primary purpose is to make an offering to the orishas, not food consumption. Indeed, careful drafting ensured that, although Santeria sacrifice is prohibited, killings that are no more necessary or humane in almost all other circumstances are unpunished.

Operating in similar fashion [is another ordinance] which prohibits the "possess[ion], sacrifice, or slaughter" of an animal with the inten[t] to use such animal for food purposes." This prohibition, extending to the keeping of an animal as well as the killing itself, applies if the animal is killed in "any type of ritual." . . . The ordinance exempts, however, "any licensed [food] establishment" with regard to "any animals which are specifically raised for food purposes," if this activity is permitted by zoning and other laws. This exception, too, seems intended to cover Kosher slaughter. Again, the burden of the ordinance, in practical terms, falls on Santeria adherents but almost no others. . . .

We also find significant evidence of the ordinances' improper targeting of Santeria sacrifice in the fact that they proscribe more religious conduct than is necessary to achieve their stated ends. . . .

The legitimate governmental interests in protecting the public health and preventing cruelty to animals could be addressed by restrictions stopping far short of a flat prohibition of all Santeria sacrificial practice. If improper disposal, not the sacrifice itself, is the harm to be prevented, the city could have imposed a general regulation on the disposal of organic garbage. It did not do so. Indeed, counsel for the city conceded at oral argument that, under the ordinances, Santeria sacrifices would be illegal even if they occurred in licensed, inspected, and zoned slaughterhouses. . . . Thus, these broad ordinances prohibit Santeria sacrifice even when it does not threaten the city's interest in the public health. . . .

Respondent claims that [the ordinances] advance two interests: protecting the public health and preventing cruelty to animals. The ordinances are underinclusive for those ends. They fail to prohibit nonreligious conduct that endangers these interests in a similar or greater degree than Santeria sacrifice does. The underinclusion is substantial, not inconsequential. Despite the city's proffered interest in preventing cruelty to animals, the ordinances are drafted with care to forbid few killings but those occasioned by religious sacrifice. Many types of animal deaths or kills for nonreligious reasons are either not prohibited or approved by express provision. For example, fishing . . . is legal. Extermination of mice and rats within a home is also permitted. Florida law incorporated by [the ordinances] sanctions euthanasia of "stray, neglected, abandoned, or unwanted animals . . . and the use of live animals "to pursue or take wildlife or to participate in any hunting." . . .

The ordinances are underinclusive as well with regard to the health risk posed by consumption of uninspected meat. Under the city's ordinances, hunters may eat their kill and fisherman may eat their catch without undergoing governmental inspection. . . .

A law burdening religious practice that is not neutral or not of general application must undergo the most rigorous of scrutiny. To satisfy the commands of the First Amendment, a law restrictive of religious practice must advance "interests of the highest order" and must be narrowly tailored in pursuit of those interests . . . The compelling interest standard [applies].

. . . As we have discussed . . . all four ordinances are overbroad or underinclusive in substantial respects. . . .

Respondent has not demonstrated, moreover, that, in the context of these ordinances, its governmental interests are compelling. . . .

The Free Exercise Clause commits government itself to religious tolerance, and upon even slight suspicion that proposals for state intervention stem from animosity to religion or distrust of its practices, all officials must pause to remember their own high duty to the Constitution and to the rights it secures. Those in office must be resolute in resisting importunate demands and must ensure that the sole reasons for imposing the burdens of law and regulation are secular. Legislators may not devise mechanisms, overt or disguised, designed to persecute or oppress a religion or its practices. The laws here in question were enacted contrary to these constitutional principles and they are void. Reversed.

One provision of the RFRA was invalidated by the Supreme Court in 1997 where it held that Congress lacked the authority under the Fourteenth Amendment to impose the strict scrutiny standard on state laws.[19] In response, many states enacted counterparts to the RFRA. Smith remains controversial, and it is possible that the Supreme Court may reconsider it in the 2020s.

The Free Exercise Clause was challenged in a new way during the COVID-19 pandemic. One of the many governmental responses to the fast-spreading and deadly disease was to limit public gatherings. Some jurisdictions banned large gatherings (10, for example) altogether and others mandated distancing that reduced the numbers of people who could meet. Fearing that the virus was more easily spread by singing and projecting when speaking, restrictions on these acts during religious services were also ordered in some states. Many of these measures were challenged as unduly restricting religious freedom. In the early months of the pandemic, courts gave governments considerable room to act. The Supreme Court, for example, in a 5-4 decision in *South Bay United Pentecostal Church v. Newsom* (Feb. 5, 2021),[20] upheld California's limitation of 25% of capacity at indoor services and its ban on singing at church services, although it issued an injunction against California's complete prohibition of indoor services in the regions of the state with the highest levels of infection. The decision was quickly made, and the majority decision wasn't fully explained.

But the situation changed by early 2021. Supreme Court Justice Ruth Bader Ginsburg, who died in September 2020, had been replaced by Justice Amy Comey Barrett; more was known about COVID-19; and the emergency measures that abridged individual rights were now many months old. Consequently, the Court began to review the restrictions on religious liberty more closely, invalidating many.[21]

Determining whether an act is a genuine exercise of religious beliefs is not always easy. The practices of a religion may appear unusual, or even bizarre, to outsiders. The *Hodges* case, found in your next Oyez, case both illustrates the sensitivity with which our society treats religion and stands as an example of an activity that is not a religion, although the opinion does not contain the latter finding, for reasons you will see.

How does a court distinguish between fraudulent and bona fide religious practices? First, it must be determined that the defendant is asserting a religious belief, not a personal or philosophical belief. If religious, several factors are considered. How well established is the religion in the world? If a defendant is the only adherent, or one of only a few followers, of a religion, it is less likely to be deemed legitimate. How old is the religion? How long has the defendant practiced the religion? What is the nature of the practice in question? How important is the practice to the religion? Once it is determined that a religious practice is being regulated by the state, then the state's interest in regulating the defendant's conduct must be weighed against the defendant's First Amendment interest. If the state's interest is compelling, then the conduct may be regulated.

## Oyez

### State v. Hodges
#### 695 S.W.2d 171 (Tenn. 1985)

**FONES, Justice.**

In January, 1983, defendant was charged in a multiple count indictment with tampering with utility metering devices. His lawyer appeared before the trial judge on February 22, 1983, asking for a trial date for the misdemeanors with which defendant was charged. The trial judge informed defendant's counsel on that occasion that he would not "put up with [defendant's] foolishness" and if "he comes in here dressed like a chicken, I am going to order him out of here under guard."

(continued)

On June 28, 1983, defendant appeared for trial, with the same counsel, and to say that he was dressed "like a chicken" as the trial judge had anticipated, is a mild description of the outrageous attire in which defendant barely covered himself. [In a footnote the court described his appearance. The "defendant appeared for trial dressed in a grossly shocking and bizarre attire, consisting of brown and white fur tied around his body at his ankles, loins and head, with a like vest made out of fur, and complete with eye goggles over his eyes. He had colored his face and chest with a very pale green paint for coloring. He had what appeared to be a human skull dangling from his waist and in his hand he carried a stuffed snake. . . .] (T)he so-called vest consisted of two pieces of fur that covered each arm but did not meet in front and back, leaving defendant's chest and back naked to his waist. His legs were also naked from mid-way between his knee and waist to his ankles. He appeared to be carrying a military gas mask and other unidentifiable ornaments."

The trial judge first addressed defendant's attorney and asked him to have his client appear in proper clothes. Defendant's attorney responded by informing the court that defendant wished to exercise his right of "freedom of expression." The trial judge then directed his remarks to defendant and ordered him to put on "regular clothes" for the trial scheduled that day. The trial judge sought a yes or no answer, but defendant responded with the following assertion:

"This is a spiritual attire and it is my religious belief and I have never worn anything else in court but this when I am on trial."

Whereupon, the trial judge found him to be in contempt of court, revoked his bond, and ordered him committed to jail for ten days or until he agreed to appear for trial in proper clothes.

Defendant's counsel asked the court to allow him to "build a record for appeal" which was denied. Motions were filed the following day, June 29, 1983, on behalf of defendant for a new trial, for reconsideration of the finding of contempt, and for bail pending appeal. At the hearing held the same day, defense counsel again sought an evidentiary hearing on the issue of defendant's religious belief which was again denied. . . . The court of Criminal Appeals reversed the contempt adjudication, holding that the trial judge erred in failing to inquire into the "nature and sincerity of appellant's beliefs, the denomination of his religion, its origin, organization and the length of time which appellant has espoused it."

We agree that the trial judge erred in failing to inquire into the religious belief of defendant and in failing to allow a full record to be developed for appeal. However, we think the intermediate court's instructions on remand, quoted above, may be misleading and not entirely in conformity with United States Supreme Court opinions.

A Rhode Island litigant appeared in court wearing a white, knitted skull cap and the trial judge ordered him to remove it or leave the courtroom and refused to consider the litigant's claim that he was a Sunni Muslim, that he was wearing a prayer cap that was a religious symbol of that sect, that indicated that the wearer was in constant prayer. . . . On appeal, the Supreme Court of Rhode Island accurately summarized the first amendment principle enunciated by the United States Supreme Court applicable where a religious belief or practice collides with a state law or regulation, as follows:

Despite the exalted status so rightly afforded to religious beliefs and activities that are motivated and embody those beliefs, the freedom of an individual to practice his religion does not enjoy absolute immunity from infringement by the state. Individuals have been subject to mandatory inoculations despite religious objections to such medical care. . . . Thus while the freedom to hold religious beliefs and opinions is absolute, the freedom to act in harmony with these religious beliefs and opinions is not beyond state regulation where such restriction serves the public interest by promoting public health and safety or preserving order. We must then accommodate the right to exercise the religious freedoms safeguarded by the first amendment with the right of the state to regulate those individual freedoms for the sake of societal interests. The problem is one of balance and degree—the courts are called upon to determine when the societal interest becomes so important as to justify an incursion by the state into religious activity that is otherwise protected by the free exercise clause of the first amendment. . . .

After discussion of the United States Supreme Court's application of the balancing test to the facts . . . the Supreme Court of Rhode Island continued as follows:

We believe that because petitioner claimed that his act was protected by the free exercise clause, in order to justifiably curtail the exercise of the alleged right the trial justice should have first allowed petitioner to display the sincerity of his religious belief, and then should have . . . [balanced] petitioner's first amendment right with the interest of the court in maintaining decorum in its proceedings by regulating dress in the courtroom. . . .

Thus, the threshold inquiry is whether or not the religious belief or practice asserted qualifies for the protection of the free exercise clause of the first amendment. The record in this case, though meager, clearly indicates that that issue may be decisive, particularly if it proves to be true that defendant is the sole adherent to his asserted religious belief and practice. . . .

Although a determination of what is a "religious" belief or practice entitled to constitutional protection may present a most delicate question, the very concept of ordered liberty precludes allowing every person to make his own standards of matters of conduct in which society as a whole has important interests. . . .

Paraphrasing an additional observation of the Court that involved Thoreau's isolation at Walden Pond, the Court made it clear that a belief which is philosophical and personal rather than religious, does not rise to the demands of the free exercise clause of the first amendment. . . .

Only beliefs rooted in religion are protected by the Free Exercise Clause, which, by its terms, gives special protection to the exercise of religion. . . . The determination of what is a "religious" belief or practice is more often than not a difficult and delicate task. . . . However, the resolution of that question is not to turn upon a judicial perception of the particular belief or practice in question; religious beliefs need not be acceptable, logical, consistent, or comprehensible to others in order to merit First Amendment protection.

One can, of course, imagine an asserted claim so bizarre, so clearly nonreligious in motivation, as not to be entitled to protection under the First Amendment. . . .

This case is clearly illustrative of what Mr. Justice Jackson had in mind when he said, "The price of freedom of religion or of speech or of the press is that we must put up with, and even pay for, a good deal of rubbish." . . .

The judgment of the Court of Criminal Appeals is affirmed and this case is remanded to the trial court for further proceedings consistent with this opinion.

# First Amendment and Speech

Learning Objective: Define and describe the Free Speech Clause of the First Amendment, offering examples of how it has been applied in criminal law.

"Congress shall make no law . . . abridging the freedom of speech." In spite of the plain language of this clause, several words mean something different than what appears to be "plain." First, the clause limits the authority of Congress, but in reality, it limits all three branches of the federal government. Because the Amendment has been incorporated, state and local governments are also prohibited from abridging free speech.

Second, the term "speech" is used. Regardless, the Supreme Court has held that more than the spoken word is protected. All forms of expression—nonverbal, artistic, written, digital, and visual—are protected. Sometimes, conduct is expressive. Pure conduct isn't speech and therefore, it is unprotected. But conduct that has an expressive quality is protected, but not to the same extent as pure speech. See Exhibit 9–2 for an illustration of the relationship between speech, conduct, and expressive conduct. Picketing is an example of protected expression, as is flag burning, which is the subject the next Oyez.

## Exhibit 9–2 Free Speech and Conduct

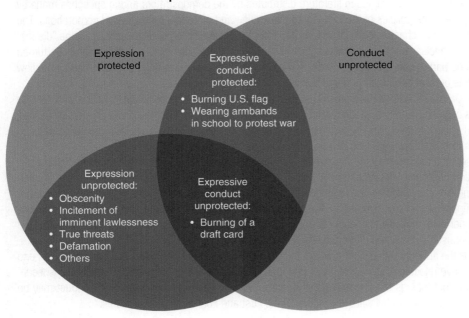

# Oyez

## Texas v. Gregory Lee Johnson
### 491 U.S. 397 (1989)

**Justice Brennan delivered the opinion of the Court.**

After publicly burning the American flag as a means of political protest, Gregory Lee Johnson was convicted of desecrating a flag in violation of Texas law. This case presents the question whether his conviction is consistent with the First Amendment. We hold that it is not.

Gregory Lee Johnson

Allan Tannenbaum/Archive Photos/Getty Images

While the Republican National Convention was taking place in Dallas in 1984, respondent Johnson participated in a political demonstration dubbed the "Republican War Chest Tour." As explained in literature distributed by the demonstrators and in speeches made by them, the purpose of this event was to protest the policies of the Reagan administration and of certain Dallas-based corporations. The demonstrators marched through the Dallas streets, chanting political slogans and stopping at several corporate locations to stage "die-ins" intended to dramatize the consequences of nuclear war. On several occasions they spray-painted the walls of buildings and overturned potted plants, but Johnson himself took no part in such activities. He did, however, accept an American flag handed to him by a fellow protester who had taken it from a flag pole outside one of the targeted buildings.

The demonstration ended in front of Dallas City Hall, where Johnson unfurled the American flag, doused it with kerosene, and set it on fire. While the flag burned, the protesters chanted, "America, the red, white, and blue, we spit on you." After the demonstrators dispersed, a witness to the flag-burning collected the flag's remains and buried them in his backyard. No one was physically injured or threatened with injury, though several witnesses testified that they had been seriously offended by the flag-burning. . . .

Johnson was convicted of flag desecration for burning the flag rather than for uttering insulting words. That fact somewhat complicates our consideration of his conviction under the First Amendment. We must first determine whether Johnson's burning of the flag constituted expressive conduct, permitting him to invoke the First Amendment. . . . If his conduct was expressive, we next decide whether the State's regulation is related to the suppression of free expression. If the State's regulation is not related to expression, then the less stringent standard . . . for regulations of noncommunicative conduct controls. . . . If it is, then we are outside of the *O'Brien* test, and we must ask whether this interest justifies Johnson's conviction under a more demanding standard. . . .

The First Amendment literally forbids the abridgment only of "speech," but we have long recognized that its protection does not end at the spoken or written word. While we have rejected "the view that an apparently limitless variety of conduct can be labeled 'speech' whenever the person engaging in the conduct intends thereby to express an idea," . . . we have acknowledged that conduct may be "sufficiently imbued with elements of communication to fall within the scope of the First and Fourteenth Amendments." . . .

In deciding whether particular conduct possesses sufficient communicative elements to bring the First Amendment into play, we have asked whether "[a]n intent to convey a particularized message was present, and [whether] the likelihood was great that the message would be understood by those who viewed it." . . . Hence, we have recognized the expressive nature of students' wearing of black armbands to protest American military involvement in Vietnam . . . of a sit-in by blacks in a "whites only" area to protest segregation. . . .

The expressive, overtly political nature of this conduct was both intentional and overwhelmingly apparent. At his trial, Johnson explained his reasons for burning the flag as follows:

"The American Flag was burned as Ronald Reagan was being nominated as President. And a more powerful statement of symbolic speech, whether you agree with it or not, couldn't have been made at that time. It's quite a just position [juxtaposition]. We had new patriotism and no patriotism." In these circumstances, Johnson's burning of the flag was conduct "sufficiently imbued with elements of communication." . . .

In order to decide whether the *O'Brien* test applies here, therefore, we must decide whether Texas has asserted an interest in support of Johnson's conviction that is unrelated to the suppression of expression. If we find that an interest asserted by the State is simply not implicated on the facts before us, we need not ask whether *O'Brien* applies. . . . The State offers two separate interests to justify his conviction: preventing breaches of the peace, and preserving the flag as a symbol of nationhood and national unity. We hold that the first interest is not implicated on this record and that the second is related to the suppression of expression. . . .

The State's position, therefore, amounts to a claim that an audience that takes serious offense at particular expression is necessarily likely to disturb the peace and that the expression may be prohibited on this basis. Our precedents do not countenance such a presumption. On the contrary, they recognize that a principal "function of free speech under our system of government is to invite dispute. It may indeed best serve its high purpose when it induces a condition of unrest, creates dissatisfaction with conditions as they are, or even stirs people to anger." . . .

The State also asserts an interest in preserving the flag as a symbol of nationhood and national unity. . . .

Johnson was not, we add, prosecuted for the expression of just any idea; he was prosecuted for his expression of dissatisfaction with the policies of this country, expression situated at the core of our First Amendment values. . . .

Moreover, Johnson was prosecuted because he knew that his politically charged expression would cause "serious offense." If he had burned the flag as a means of disposing of it because it was dirty or torn, he would not have been convicted of flag desecration under the Texas law; federal law designates burning as the preferred means of disposing of a flag "when it is in such condition that it is no longer a fitting emblem for display." . . .

If there is a bedrock principle underlying the First Amendment, it is that the Government may not prohibit the expression of an idea simply because society finds the idea itself offensive or disagreeable. . . .

We are tempted to say, in fact, that the flag's deservedly cherished place in our community will be strengthened, not weakened, by our holding today. Our decision is a reaffirmation of the principles of freedom and inclusiveness that the flag best reflects, and of the conviction that our toleration of criticism such as Johnson's is a sign and source of our strength. . . .

The way to preserve the flag's special role is not to punish those who feel differently about these matters. It is to persuade them that they are wrong. . . . And, precisely because it is our flag that is involved, one's response to the flag-burner may exploit the uniquely persuasive power of the flag itself. We can imagine no more appropriate response to burning a flag than waving one's own, no better way to counter a flag-burner's message than by saluting the flag that burns, no surer means of preserving the dignity even of the flag that burned than by—as one witness here did—according its remains a respectful burial. We do not consecrate the flag by punishing its desecration, for in doing so we dilute the freedom that this cherished emblem represents. . . . Justice Kennedy, concurring.

I write not to qualify the words Justice Brennan chooses so well, for he says with power all that is necessary to explain our ruling. I join his opinion without reservation, but with a keen sense that his case, like others before us from time to time, exacts its personal toll. This prompts me to add to our pages these few remarks.

The case before us illustrates better than most that the judicial power is often difficult in its exercise. We cannot here ask another branch to share responsibility, as when the argument is made that a statute is flawed or incomplete. For we are presented with a clear and simple statute to be judged against a pure command of the Constitution. The outcome can be laid at no door but ours.

The hard fact is that sometimes we must make decisions we do not like. We make them because they are right, right in the sense that the law and the Constitution, as we see them, compel the result. And so great is our commitment to the process that, except in the rare case, we do not pause to express distaste for the result, perhaps for fear of undermining a valued principle that dictates decision. This is one of those rare cases.

Our colleagues in dissent advance powerful arguments why respondent may be convicted for his expression, reminding us that among those who will be dismayed by our holding will be some who have had the singular honor of carrying the flag into battle. And I agree that the flag holds a lonely place of honor in an age when absolutes are distrusted and simple truths are burdened by unneeded apologetics.

With respect to those views, I do not believe the Constitution gives us the right to rule as the dissenting members of the Court urge, however painful this judgment is to announce. . . . It is poignant but fundamental that the flag protects those who hold it in contempt.

Police sometimes encounter expressive conduct that they find to be obstructive. For example, the practice of drivers flashing their lights to oncoming cars to warn that there are police ahead checking for speeders has been treated as criminal obstruction in several cases. Lower courts have consistently held, however, that the practice is protected under the First Amendment.[22] Similar decisions have been made about video and audio recording of police during the performance of their duties.

Third, as is true of all the amendments, there are exceptions—even though not recognized by the text of the Amendment. As you learned earlier in this chapter, any law that burdens speech must be narrowly tailored and it must be supported by a compelling governmental interest. Underlying the First Amendment's protection of speech is the philosophical belief that a free market of ideas will advance democracy, social and scientific development, and individual growth and autonomy. The price of free speech is the protection of provocative, annoying, offensive, ignorant, and insulting speech.

The default position under the First Amendment is that expression is protected. But no right is absolute. The Supreme Court has carved out several narrowly defined exceptions. Among them are the following:

- Speech that is directed at inciting, and is likely to cause, lawlessness
- Speech integral to criminal conduct
- Speech that threatens national security
- Obscenity
- True threats
- Defamation
- Time, place, and manner restrictions

Volumes have been written about free speech. All of the law of free expression can't be discussed in this chapter. True threats and obscenity were discussed in earlier chapters. Because of their significance to criminal law, incitement to lawlessness; speech integral to criminal conduct; and time, place, and manner restrictions will be briefly covered next. See Exhibit 9–3 for a summary of free speech and its limitations.

## Exhibit 9–3 Free Speech and Its Limitations

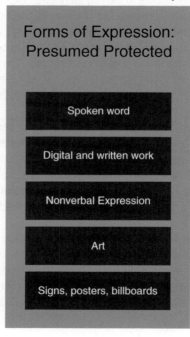

**Forms of Expression: Presumed Protected**

- Spoken word
- Digital and written work
- Nonverbal Expression
- Art
- Signs, posters, billboards

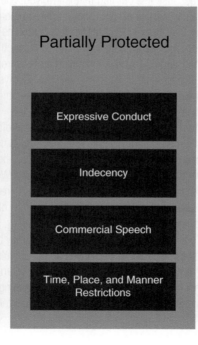

**Partially Protected**

- Expressive Conduct
- Indecency
- Commercial Speech
- Time, Place, and Manner Restrictions

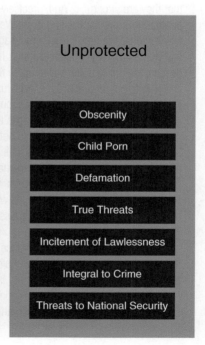

**Unprotected**

- Obscenity
- Child Porn
- Defamation
- True Threats
- Incitement of Lawlessness
- Integral to Crime
- Threats to National Security

In 1964, Clarence Brandenburg spoke at a meeting of the Ku Klux Klan in a field near Cincinnati, Ohio. His comments were recorded by members of the press, who he invited to attend. Brandenburg made overtly racist and anti-Semitic comments and expressed concern for the future of the "White Caucasian race" at the hands of the government. He also referenced the possibility of "revenge-ance" [sic] if the federal government and Supreme Court continued to "suppress the white, Caucasian race." Brandenburg was charged and convicted of violating Ohio's Criminal Syndicalism law, which made it a crime to "advocate . . . the duty, necessity, or propriety of crime, sabotage, or unlawful methods of terrorism as a means of accomplishing industrial or political reform." He was fined and sentenced to serve 1 to 10 years in prison. On appeal, the Supreme Court reversed his conviction because his speech was protected under the First Amendment. Speech that is alleged to have caused lawlessness may be regulated if it

1. is directed at inciting or producing

2. imminent lawless action and

3. it is likely to incite or produce such action.[23]

The standard presents a high hurdle for the government to jump. The first element, *directed at*, expresses a high level of mens rea. A defendant must have as her purpose, causing lawlessness. The second element demands that the lawlessness occur immediately following the speech. Although not precisely defined, in most cases this means minutes or tens of minutes—hours is questionable. Finally, the outcome must be probable. Mere possibility is inadequate. Words that create a likelihood of imminent lawlessness may be regulated because the government has a compelling interest in preventing law breaking.

Imagine, for example, two scenarios. In the first, Robert, a communist, addresses a convention of the American Society of Political Theorists. The group is composed of professors who research and teach political theory. During his presentation, he states that "Revolution is inevitable. The only way to break the bonds of capitalism is for the workers to violently overthrow their overlords, to take control of the factories and businesses owned by the rich and protected by the government. To this end, we must all commit ourselves. It will happen and I will, and you should, be there." His speech is protected because he has not called for imminent lawlessness, he uttered no details, such as the place or time anyone should act, and the context was an academic conference. The outcome would be different in a second scenario. Robert, a communist and worker, is standing in front of an angry group of co-workers who are picketing low wages and the recent death of a colleague who was killed in a workplace accident. He yells, "The owners and managers of this plant don't give a crap about you, your safety, or your families. They will keep killing us unless you take matters into your own hands. Let's go inside Now and teach our overseers a Lesson! Let's beat them and destroy their precious machines and the phones WE build – not them. I am with you, pick up a tool, a knife, whatever you can find. Go, go, go!"

Although inciting acts of violence are typically the "lawlessness" that is the subject of governmental regulation, there are examples of speech that may be prohibited because it creates a likelihood of imminent non-violent lawlessness. Encouraging jurors to not follow the law during deliberations is an example. The Julien Heicklen case illustrates the line between protected speech and jury tampering.

Closely related to the imminent lawless doctrine is the Fighting Words Doctrine. In 1940, Walter Chaplinsky, a Jehovah's Witness, distributed pamphlets and engaged with people on the streets about his religious beliefs. People complained to the town Marshal, reporting that Chaplinsky was causing a riot. After unsuccessfully calming the situation, the Marshal decided to remove Chaplinsky from the area. Chaplinsky yelled at the Marshal, "You are a God damned racketeer" and "a damned Fascist" and the said the whole government of Rochester were Fascists or agents of Fascists. For these statements, he was arrested and convicted under

## Oyez

# United States v. Julian Heicklen
### (Order Dismissing Indictment, U.S. District Court, S.D. NY April 19, 2012)

**Kimba M. Wood, Judge**

On November 18, 2010, a grand jury indicted Julian Heicklen, charging him with attempting to influence the actions or decisions of a juror of a United States Court, in violation of 18 U.S.C. § 1504, a federal jury tampering statute. The Indictment states that, from October 2009 through May 2010, in front of the entrance to the United States Court for the Southern District of New York (the "Courthouse"), Heicklen distributed pamphlets that advocated jury nullification. . . .

Heicklen advocates passionately for the right of jurors to determine the law as well as the facts. The Government states that, in advocating these views, Heicklen has on several occasions stood outside the entrance to the Courthouse, holding a sign reading "Jury Info" and distributing pamphlets from the Fully Informed Jury Association ("FIJA"). (Government's Memorandum of Law in Opposition to Defendant's Motions ("Govt.'s Mem.") at 1.) The pamphlets state that a juror has not just the responsibility to determine the facts of a case before her on the basis of the evidence presented, but also the power to determine the law according to her conscience.

In opposition to Heicklen's motion, the Government quotes an excerpt of a transcript of a recorded conversation that it alleges Heicklen had with an undercover agent from the Federal Bureau of Investigation ("FBI"), in which the agent specifically identified herself as a juror; the agent was not actually a juror. The Government alleges that Heicklen handed that "juror" a FIJA pamphlet and a single-sided, typewritten handout. The handout states in relevant part that "[i]t is not the duty of the jury to uphold the law.

It is the jury's duty to see that justice is done." The FIJA pamphlet is entitled "A Primer for Prospective Jurors" and contains 13 questions and answers for jurors regarding what FIJA characterizes as jurors' rights and responsibilities. . . .

The Court understands the statute [under which the defendant was charged] to contain three elements:

1.  that the defendant knowingly attempted to influence the action or decision of a juror of a United States court;
2.  that the defendant knowingly attempted to influence that juror (a) upon an issue or matter pending before that juror, or pending before the jury of which that juror is a member; or (b) pertaining to that juror's duties; and
3.  that the defendant knowingly attempted to influence that juror by writing or sending to that juror a written communication in relation to such issue or matter. . . .

The statute thus prohibits a defendant from trying to influence a juror upon any case or point in dispute before that juror by means of a written communication in relation to that case or that point in dispute. It also prohibits a defendant from trying to influence a juror's actions or decisions pertaining to that juror's duties, but only *if* the defendant made that communication in relation to a case or point in dispute before that juror. The statute therefore squarely criminalizes efforts to influence the outcome of a case, but exempts the broad categories of journalistic, academic, political, and other writings that discuss the roles and responsibilities of jurors in general, as well as innocent notes from friends and spouses encouraging jurors to arrive on time or to rush home, to listen closely or to deliberate carefully, but with no relation to the outcome of a particular case. Accordingly, the Court reads the plain text of the statute to require that a defendant must have sought to influence a juror through a written communication in relation either to a specific case before that juror or to a substantive point in dispute between two or more parties before that juror.

Although "political speech by its nature will sometimes have unpalatable consequences, . . . in general, our society accords greater weight to the value of free speech than to the dangers of its misuse." The First Amendment reflects "a profound national commitment to the principle that debate on public issues should be uninhibited, robust, and wide-open." "Indeed, the Amendment exists so that this debate can occur—robust, forceful, and contested. It is the theory of the Free Speech Clause that 'falsehood and fallacies' are exposed through 'discussion,' 'education,' and 'more speech.'" That is because "speech concerning public affairs is more than self-expression; it is the essence of self-government." . . .

Decisions applying the clear and present danger test articulated in *Bridges* and *Wood* have consistently held that speech may be restricted only if that speech "is directed to inciting or producing" a threat to the administration of justice that is both "imminent" and likely to materialize. . . .

The relevant cases establish that the First Amendment squarely protects speech concerning judicial proceedings and public debate regarding the functioning of the judicial system, so long as that speech does not interfere with the fair and impartial administration of justice. In *Wood*, the Supreme Court held that even speech to a grand juror may be protected by the First Amendment if it does not present a clear and present danger to the functioning of the courts (370 U.S. at 395). At the same time, the First Amendment does not create a right to influence juries outside of official proceedings because "[d]ue process requires that the accused receive a trial by an impartial jury free from outside influences." . . .

Based upon the plain meaning of the text of 18 U.S.C. § 1504, reinforced by relevant judicial interpretations and the doctrine of constitutional avoidance, the Court holds that a person violates the statute only when he knowingly attempts to influence the action or decision of a juror upon an issue or matter pending before that juror or pertaining to that juror's duties by means of written communication made in relation to *a specific case pending before that juror* or in relation to *a point in dispute between the parties before that juror*. . . .

Heicklen's alleged actions do not violate 18 U.S.C. § 1504. The Indictment alleges that Heicklen "distributed pamphlets urging jury nullification, immediately in front of an entrance to the United States District Court of the Southern District of New York."

Both pamphlets discuss the role of juries in society and urge jurors to follow their conscience regardless of instructions on the law. Heicklen's pamphlets self-evidently pertain to a "juror's duties," satisfying the requirements for liability under the second element of 18 U.S.C. § 1504. To satisfy the requirements for liability under the third element of 18 U.S.C. § 1504, however, the pamphlets must have been written or distributed in relation to an "issue or matter" pending before that juror. The two pamphlets do not relate to an "issue" pending before a juror, because a juror's duties are not a point in dispute between the parties to a suit.

Understanding "matter" to mean "case," the pamphlets could trigger liability under the statute's third element if they were distributed in relation to a particular case pending before a juror. But unlike in [a prior case], there is no allegation that Heicklen distributed the pamphlets in relation to a specific case. Indeed, the Government concedes that it "does not allege that the defendant targeted a particular jury or a particular issue."

The Court's holding merely maintains the existing balance that federal courts have found between freedom of speech and the administration of justice. Attempts to tamper with a jury in order to influence the outcome of a trial or a grand jury proceeding are still clearly prohibited under 18 U.S.C. § 1503 and 18 U.S.C. § 1504. Efforts to distribute leaflets to jurors in the immediate vicinity of courthouses may still be sanctioned through reasonable time, place, and manner restrictions such as those promulgated pursuant to 40 U.S.C. § 1315 and 41 C.F.R. § 102-74.415(c). The Court declines to stretch the interpretation of the existing statute prohibiting communications with a juror in order to cover speech that is not meant to influence the actions of a juror with regard to a point in dispute before that juror or the outcome of a specific case before that juror.

For the foregoing reasons, the Defendant's motion to dismiss the Indictment is GRANTED.

a law that forbade "any offensive, derisive or annoying word to any other person who is lawfully in any street or other public place," or "call him by any offensive or derisive name. On appeal before the Supreme Court, Chaplinsky claimed that his speech was protected by both the Free Speech and Free Exercise Clauses. The Court rejected his religion claim, finding that his words were not the exercise of religion. Affirming his conviction, the Court wrote that there are "limited classes of speech [that] include obscene (lewd) speech, slander and libel, and "fighting words" that aren't protected by the First Amendment. Fighting words are "those which by their very utterance inflict injury or tend to incite an immediate breach of the peace."

The Fighting Words Doctrine has been narrowed, if not de facto invalidated, by subsequent caselaw. For example, in the 1949 case, *Terminiello v. Chicago,*[24] the Court reversed a conviction for breach of the peace where the defendant delivered a provocative speech to over 800 people in an auditorium with 1,000 angry protestors outside. In the speech, he criticized various racial and political groups, and the mob that had gathered outside of the venue. Chicago police had a difficult time maintaining order among the protestors. Writing for the majoriy in its decision reversing the conviction, Justice William O. Douglas penned:

> The vitality of civil and political institutions in our society depends on free discussion. As Chief Justice Hughes wrote in *De Jonge v. Oregon*, 299 U.S. 353, 365, 260, it is only through free debate and free exchange of ideas that government remains responsive to the will of the people and peaceful change is effected. The right to speak freely and to promote diversity of ideas and programs is therefore one of the chief distinctions that sets us apart from totalitarian regimes

> Accordingly a function of free speech under our system of government is to invite dispute. It may indeed best serve its high purpose when it induces a

condition of unrest, creates dissatisfaction with conditions as they are, or even stirs people to anger. Speech is often provocative and challenging. It may strike at prejudices and preconceptions and have profound unsettling effects as it presses for acceptance of an idea. That is why freedom of speech, though not absolute, is nevertheless protected against censorship or punishment.

Another example of the Court receding from the Fighting Words Doctrine is *Cohen v. California* (1971).[25] Cohen was convicted of disturbing the peace for wearing a jacket with "Fuck the Draft" written on it in a courthouse. Again, the Court reversed the conviction, holding that fighting words were only "those personally abusive epithets which, when addressed to the ordinary citizen, are, as a matter of common knowledge, inherently likely to provoke violent reaction."

On year later, in *Gooding v. Wilson*,[26] the justices decided that a defendant's speech, "White son of a bitch, I'll kill you." "You son of a bitch, I'll choke you to death." and "You son of a bitch, if you ever put your hands on me again, I'll cut you all to pieces," directed at a police officer was protected.

Similarly, courts have held that speech with racially or sexually insulting content - so-called hate speech - to also be protected. Consequently, the punch has been taken out of the Fighting Words Doctrine. Regardless, police and prosecutors continue to enforce fighting words statutes and some lower courts continue to recognize the doctrine.

Speech that is integral to criminal conduct is also unprotected. The U.S. Supreme Court recognized the exception in *Giboney v. Empire Storage & Ice Co.*[27] According to constitutional scholar Eugene Volokh, this exception isn't one form of unprotected speech, it is many. It includes soliciting crime, speech that provokes violence, speech that incentivize crime, threats, and conspiracy.[28]

Let's look at conspiracy specifically. The conversation of co-conspirators in a plan to commit murder may be used in court to prove conspiracy to commit murder. In such a case, the speech of the co-conspirators is not only proof a crime but may be the actus reus (the evil act) of the crime. Some conspiracy laws require a physical act, even if minimal, beyond planning. Other laws treat the act of communicating as the actus reus and proof of the mens rea of the crime.

The speech integral to criminal conduct exception has also been applied to fraud, the distribution of child pornography, solicitation of co-conspirators, solicitation of prostitution, fighting words, sexting, and, in the case of *Giboney*, to illegal picketing and boycotting that was intended to coerce another to violate the law. The potential for this exception to include protected speech is significant, especially because the exception is not well developed. It is unclear when it may be applied to new cases.

In some instances, a state may regulate speech in public spaces, not because of its content but to protect the normal use of the space. Laws that are enacted for this purpose are known as time, place, and manner restrictions (TPM). All time, place, and manner restrictions must be viewpoint neutral, narrowly tailored, and not overly burden the speaker's rights. A regulation may not, for example, allow people who agree with a City's new policy on collecting taxes to speak between the hours of 8 a.m. and 8 p.m. and restrict the time of opponents of the policy to 8 p.m. to 10 p.m.

Beyond neutrality, a balancing of interests is conducted: does the government's interest in enforcing the statute outweigh the First Amendment interest? For example, it is unlawful to stand in the middle of the street to make a speech. The interest in maintaining a safe, consistent flow of traffic outweighs the speaker's First Amendment interest. However, the result would be different if a state attempted to prohibit all speeches made in a public place. Such a statute would be overbroad, as it includes not only activity that the state may regulate (standing in traffic) but also lawful activity. These are examples of common restrictions:

- Requiring speakers to respect the rights of others to use public property (e.g. no blocking of streets or sidewalks)
- A requirement that groups larger than 10 people obtain a permit to demonstrate in a public park, in order to inform the group of applicable laws and to enable the government to plan for security and other matters
- Sound and noise controls around courthouses or public schools where sound levels are important to the work that is conducted inside
- Sounds and noise controls in residential neighborhoods during the late evening and night

First Amendment free exercise of speech claims also arise in the context of hate crime legislation. Such legislation either makes it illegal to express prejudicial opinions or enhances the penalty for a crime that is motivated by prejudice. The former is unconstitutional. As to the latter, most states enhance the penalties for crimes such as trespass, assault, battery, and harassment if the motive of the crime was the victim's race, religion, color, or other characteristic.

Two Supreme Court opinions, only one year apart, set the limits of hate crime laws. Both are excerpted here. In the first, the Court held an ordinance unconstitutional. In the second, the Court upheld the law.

## Oyez

### R.A.V. v. City of St. Paul
### 505 U.S. 377 (1992)

**Justice Scalia delivered the opinion of the Court.**

In the predawn hours of June 21, 1990, petitioner and several other teenagers allegedly assembled a crudely-made cross by taping together broken chair legs. They then allegedly burned the cross inside the fenced yard of a black family that lived across the street from the house where petitioner was staying. Although this conduct could have been punished under any number of laws, one of the two provisions under which respondent city of St. Paul chose to charge petitioner (then a juvenile) was the St. Paul-Motivated Crime Ordinance, which provides:

> "Whoever placed on public property or private property a symbol, object, appellation, characterization or graffiti, including, but not limited to, a burning cross or Nazi swastika, which one knows or has reasonable grounds to know arouse anger, alarm or resentment in others on the basis of race, color, creed, religion or gender commits disorderly conduct and shall be guilty of a misdemeanor."

Petitioner moved to dismiss this count on the ground that the St. Paul ordinance was substantially overbroad and impermissibly content-based and therefore facially invalid under the First Amendment. The trial court granted this motion, but the Minnesota Supreme Court reversed. That court rejected petitioner's overbreadth claim because, as construed in prior Minnesota cases . . . the modifying phrase "arouses anger, alarm or resentment in others" limited the reach of the ordinance to conduct that amounts to "fighting words," . . . and therefore the ordinance reached only expression "that the first amendment does not protect." . . . The court also concluded that the ordinance was not impermissibly content-based because, in its view, "the ordinance is a narrowly tailored means toward accomplishing the compelling governmental interest in protecting the community against bias-motivated threats to public safety and order." . . .

Assuming, arguendo, that all of the expression reached by the ordinance is proscribable under the "fighting words" doctrine, we nonetheless conclude that the ordinance is facially unconstitutional in that it prohibits otherwise permitted speech solely on the basis of the subjects the speech addresses. . . .

The proposition that a particular instance of speech can be proscribable on the basis of one feature (e.g., obscenity) but not on the basis of another (e.g., opposition to the city government) is commonplace, and has found application in many contexts. We have long held, for example, that nonverbal expressive activity can be banned because of the action it entails, but not because of the ideas it expresses—so that burning the flag in violation of an ordinance against outdoor fires could be punishable, whereas burning a flag in violation of an ordinance against dishonoring the flag is not. . . .

(continued)

Similarly, we have upheld reasonable "time, place, or manner" restrictions, but only if they are "justified without reference to the content of the regulated speech." . . . And just as the power to proscribe particular speech on the basis of a noncontent element (e.g., noise) does not entail the power to proscribe it on the basis of a content element; so also, the power to proscribe it on the basis of one content element (e.g., obscenity) does not entail the power to proscribe it on the basis of other content elements.

In other words, the exclusion of "fighting words" from the scope of the First Amendment simply means that, for purposes of that Amendment, the unprotected features of the words are, despite their verbal character, essentially a "nonspeech" element of communication. Fighting words are thus analogous to a noisy sound truck: Each is, as Justice Frankfurter recognized, a "mode of speech," . . . both can be used to convey an idea; but neither has, in and of itself, a claim upon the First Amendment. As with the sound truck, however, so also with fighting words: The government may not regulate use based on hostility—or favoritism—towards the underlying message expressed. . . .

Applying these principles to the St. Paul ordinance, we conclude that, even as narrowly construed by the Minnesota Supreme Court, the ordinance is facially unconstitutional. Although the phrase in the ordinance, "arouses anger, alarm or resentment in others," has been limited by the Minnesota Supreme Court's construction to reach only those symbols or displays that amount to "fighting words," the remaining, unmodified terms make clear that the ordinance applies only to "fighting words" that insult, or provoke violence, "on the basis of race, color, creed, religion or gender." Displays containing abusive invective, no matter how vicious or severe, are permissible unless they are addressed to one of the specified disfavored topics. Those who wish to use "fighting words" in connection with other ideas—to express hostility, for example, on the basis of political affiliation, union membership, or homosexuality—are not covered. The First Amendment does not permit St. Paul to impose special prohibitions on those speakers who express views on disfavored subjects. . . .

In its practical operation, moreover, the ordinance goes even beyond mere content discrimination, to actual viewpoint discrimination. Displays containing some words—odious racial epithets, for example—aspersions upon a person's mother, for example—would seemingly be usable ad libitum in the placards of those arguing in favor of racial, color, etc. tolerance and equality, but could not be used by the speaker's opponents. One could hold up a sign saying, for example, that all "anti-catholic bigots" are misbegotten; but not that all "papists" are, for that would insult or provoke violence "on the basis of religion." St. Paul has no such authority to license one side of a debate to fight freestyle, while requiring the other to follow Marquis of Queensbury Rules. . . .

Let there be no mistake about our belief that burning a cross in someone's front yard is reprehensible. But St. Paul has sufficient means at its disposal to prevent such behavior without adding the First Amendment to the fire. . . .

## Oyez

# Wisconsin v. Mitchell
## 508 U.S. 476 (1993)

**Rehnquist, C. J., delivered the opinion for a unanimous Court.**

Respondent Todd Mitchell's sentence for aggravated battery was enhanced because he intentionally selected his victim on account of the victim's race. The question presented in this case is whether this penalty enhancement is prohibited by the First and Fourteenth Amendments. We hold that it is not.

On the evening of October 7, 1989, a group of young black men and boys, including Mitchell, gathered at an apartment complex in Kenosha, Wisconsin. Several members of the group discussed a scene from the motion picture "Mississippi Burning," in which a white man beat a young black boy who was praying. The group moved outside and Mitchell asked them: "Do you all feel hyped up to move on some white people?" . . . Shortly thereafter, a young white boy approached the group on the opposite side of the street where they were standing. As the boy walked by, Mitchell said: "You all want to fuck somebody up? There goes a white boy: go get him." . . . Mitchell counted to three and pointed in the boy's direction. The group ran towards the boy, beat him severely, and stole his tennis shoes. The boy was rendered unconscious and remained in a coma for four days.

After a jury trial in the Circuit Court for Kenosha County, Mitchell was convicted of aggravated battery. . . . That offense ordinarily carries a maximum sentence of two years imprisonment. . . . But because the jury found that Mitchell had intentionally selected his victim because of the boy's race, the maximum sentence for Mitchell's offense was increased to seven years under a [Wisconsin statute]. That provision enhances the maximum penalty for an offense whenever the defendant "[i]ntentionally selects the person against whom the crime . . . is committed . . . because of race, religion, color, disability, sexual orientation, national origin or ancestry of that person." . . .

The Circuit Court sentenced Mitchell to four years' imprisonment for the aggravated battery. . . .

Mitchell unsuccessfully sought postconviction relief in the Circuit Court. Then he appealed his conviction and sentence, challenging the constitutionality of Wisconsin's penalty-enhancement provision on First Amendment grounds. The Wisconsin Court of Appeals rejected Mitchell's challenge, but the Wisconsin Supreme Court reversed. The Supreme Court held that the statute "violates the First Amendment directly by punishing what the legislature has deemed to be offensive thought." . . . It rejected the State's contention "that the statute punishes only the conduct of intentional selection of a victim." According to the court, "[t]he statute punishes the 'because of' aspect of the defendant's selection, the reason the defendant selected the victim, the motive behind the selection." . . .

The Supreme Court also held that the penalty-enhancement statute was unconstitutionally overbroad. It reasoned that, in order to prove that a defendant intentionally selected his victim because of the victim's protected status, the State would often have to introduce evidence of the defendant's prior speech, such as racial epithets he may have uttered before the commission of the offense. . . .

We granted certiorari because of the importance of the question presented and the existence of a conflict of authority among the states' high courts on the constitutionality of statutes similar to Wisconsin's penalty-enhancement provision. . . . We reverse. . . .

Mitchell argues (and the Wisconsin Supreme Court held) that the statute violates the First Amendment by punishing offenders' bigoted beliefs.

Traditionally, sentencing judges have considered a wide variety of factors in addition to evidence bearing on guilt in determining what sentence to impose on a convicted defendant. . . . [T]he defendant's motive for committing the offense is one important factor. . . . Thus, in many states the commission of a murder, or other capital offense, for pecuniary gain is a separate aggravating circumstance under the capital-sentencing statute. . . .

But it is equally true that a defendant's abstract beliefs, however obnoxious to most people, may not be taken into consideration by a sentencing judge. . . . In [*Dawson v. Delaware*, 503 U.S. 159 (1992)] the State introduced evidence at a capital-sentencing hearing that the defendant was a member of a white supremacist prison gang. Because "the evidence proved nothing more than [the defendant's] abstract beliefs," we held that its admission violated the defendant's First Amendment rights. . . . In so holding, however, we emphasized that "the Constitution does not erect a per se barrier to the admission of evidence concerning one's beliefs and associations at sentencing simply because those beliefs and associations are protected by the First Amendment. . . . Thus, in *Barclay v. Florida*, 463 U.S. 939 (1983) . . . we allowed the sentencing judge to take into account the defendant's racial animus towards his victim. The evidence in that case showed that the defendant's membership in the Black Liberation Army and desire to provoke a "race war" were related to the murder of a white man for which he was convicted. . . . Because "the elements of racial hatred in [the] murder" were relevant to several aggravating factors, we held that the trial judge permissibly took his evidence into account in sentencing the defendant to death. . . .

Mitchell suggests that *Dawson* and *Barclay* are inapposite because they did not involve application of a penalty-enhancement provision. But in *Barclay* we held that it was permissible for the sentencing court to consider the defendant's racial animus in determining whether he should be sentenced to death, surely the most severe "enhancement" of all. And the fact that the Wisconsin Legislature has decided, as a general matter, that bias-motivated offenses warrant greater maximum penalties across the board does not alter the result here. For the primary responsibility for fixing criminal penalties lies with the legislature. . . .

Mitchell argues that the Wisconsin penalty-enhancement statute is invalid because it punishes the defendant's discriminatory motive, or reason, for acting. But motive plays the same role under the Wisconsin statute as it does under federal and state antidiscrimination laws, which we have previously upheld against constitutional challenge. . . . Title VII, for example, makes it unlawful for an employer to discriminate against an employee "because of such individual's race, color, religion, sex, or national origin." . . . In [another case] we rejected the argument that Title VII infringed employers' First Amendment rights. Nothing in our decision last Term in *R.A.V.* compels a different result here. That case involved a First Amendment challenge to a municipal ordinance prohibiting the use of "'fighting words' that insult or provoke violence, on the basis of race, color, creed, religion or gender." . . .

Finally, there remains to be considered Mitchell's argument that the Wisconsin statute is unconstitutionally overbroad because of the "chilling effect" on free speech. Mitchell argues (and the Wisconsin Supreme Court agreed) that the statute is "overbroad" because evidence of the defendant's prior speech or associations may be used to prove that the defendant intentionally selected his victim on account of the victim's protected status. Consequently, the argument goes, the statute impermissibly chills free expression with respect to such matters by those concerned about the possibility of enhanced sentences if they should in the future commit a criminal offense covered by the statute. We find no merit in this contention.

The sort of chill envisioned here is far more attenuated and unlikely than that contemplated in traditional "overbreadth" cases. We must conjure up a vision of a Wisconsin citizen suppressing his unpopular bigoted opinions for fear that if he later commits an offense covered by the statute, these opinions will be offered at trial to establish that he selected his victim on account of the victim's protected status, thus qualifying him for penalty-enhancement. To stay within the realm of rationality, we must surely put to one side minor misdemeanor offenses covered by the statute, such as negligent operation of a motor vehicle . . . for it is difficult, if not impossible, to conceive of a situation where such offenses would be racially motivated. We are left, then, with the prospect of a citizen suppressing his bigoted

(continued)

beliefs for fear that evidence of such beliefs will be introduced against him at trial if he commits a more serious offense against person or property. This is simply too speculative a hypothesis to support Mitchell's overbreadth claim.

The First Amendment, moreover, does not prohibit the evidentiary use of speech to establish the elements of a crime or to prove motive or intent. Evidence of a defendant's previous declarations or statements is commonly admitted in criminal trials subject to evidentiary rules dealing with relevancy, reliability, and the like. Nearly half a century ago, . . . we rejected a contention similar to that advanced by Mitchell here. Haupt was tried for the offense of treason, which, as defined by the Constitution, may depend very much on proof of motive. To prove that the acts in question were committed out of "adherence to the enemy" rather than "parental solicitude," . . . the Government introduced evidence of conversations that had taken place long prior to the indictment, some of which consisted of statements showing Haupt's sympathy with Germany and Hitler and hostility towards the United States. We rejected Haupt's argument that this evidence was improperly admitted. While "[s]uch testimony is to be scrutinized with care to be certain the statements are not expressions of mere proper appreciation of the land of birth," we held that "these statements . . . clearly were admissible on the question of intent and adherence to the enemy." . . .

For the foregoing reasons, we hold that Mitchell's First Amendment rights were not violated by the application of the Wisconsin penalty-enhancement provision in sentencing him. The judgment of the Supreme Court of Wisconsin is therefore reversed, and the case is remanded for further proceedings not inconsistent with this opinion.

R.A.V. and Mitchell establish that while bigoted expressions, so-called hate speech, themselves may not be prohibited (legislation aimed at content), bigotry as a motive may be considered at sentencing to enhance a penalty (legislation aimed at the motive of content). The Court pointed out in R.A.V. that the conduct itself could be punished under content neutral laws, such as prohibitions of open burning. These laws apply to all outside burning, not just those that are the product of a (racial) opinion or belief. The Court upheld the sentence enhancement in Mitchell because it didn't criminalize motive. Instead, content neutral behavior was criminalized. It also found that there has been a long history of allowing motives of all sorts to be considered at sentencing, so the law was upheld.

Subsequently, in a 2003 decision, Virginia v. Black, the Supreme Court upheld a Virginia statute that criminalized cross burning. The Supreme Court did not overrule R.A.V. Rather, it distinguished the Virginia statute from the challenged law in R.A.V. The distinguishing characteristic was Virginia's requirement that the burning occur with an intent to intimidate. There was no such element in the challenged law in R.A.V. The Court analogized intimidating cross burning to threatening speech, which it had previously determined could be regulated.[29]

# The Right to Privacy

Learning Objective: Describe the evolution of the right to privacy, including the specific rights that have been recognized by the Supreme Court.

Unlike some state constitutions, the U.S. Constitution does not expressly protect privacy. Many of the expressly stated rights in the Bill of Rights protect privacy, such as the Fourth Amendment, which has been interpreted as applying to searches that encroach upon a person's reasonable expectation to privacy.

The issue is whether the Constitution protects privacy to a greater extent than through its express provisions. Stated another way, is there an independent and inherent privacy right in the Constitution? If so, what is the textual source of that right?

The Supreme Court answered the former question affirmatively in 1965 in Griswold v. Connecticut.[30] In that case, a Connecticut statute that prohibited the use of contraceptives, even by married couples, was held unconstitutional as invasive of a right to privacy.

As to the second issue, the source of the right, the Court found that the right to privacy grows out of the First, Fourth, Fifth, Ninth, and Fourteenth Amendments. Justice William O. Douglas, writing for the Court, found the right to privacy to be a "penumbra" of these expressly protected rights. The Court stressed that the First Amendment's right to association protected the marriage relationship and that the intimate subject sought to be regulated was especially protected. The Court wrote that

> [Prior case law] suggests that specific guarantees in the Bill of Rights have penumbras, formed by emanations from those guarantees that help give them life and substance. . . . Various guarantees create zones of privacy. The right of association contained in the penumbra of the First Amendment is one, as we have seen. The Third Amendment in its prohibition against the quartering of soldiers "in any house" in time of peace without the consent of the owner is another facet of that privacy. The Fourth Amendment explicitly affirms the "right of the people to be secure in their persons, houses, papers, and effects, against unreasonable searches and seizures." The Fifth Amendment in its Self-Incrimination Clause enables the citizens to create a zone of privacy which government may not force him to surrender to his detriment. The Ninth Amendment provides: "The enumeration in the Constitution, of certain rights, shall not be construed to deny or disparage others retained by the people." . . .
>
> The present case, then, concerns a relationship lying within the zone of privacy created by several fundamental constitutional guarantees. . . .
>
> We deal with a right to privacy older than the Bill of Rights—older than our political parties, older than our school system. Marriage is a coming together for better or worse, hopefully enduring, and intimate to the degree of being sacred. It is an association that promotes a way of life, not causes; a harmony in living, not political faiths; a bilateral loyalty, not commercial or social projects. Yet it is an association for as noble a purpose as any involved in our prior decisions.

Privacy has also been an issue in abortion cases. Abortion cases involve a competing interest that did not exist in *Griswold,* that is, the interest of the state in protecting the fetus. In 1973, the U.S. Supreme Court handed down the landmark decision of *Roe v. Wade,* in which the Court declared that the right to privacy protects a woman's right to elect to abort a fetus in some situations.[31]

Specifically, the Court adopted a trimester analysis where the state's authority to regulate abortion increases as the pregnancy lengthens. During the first trimester, states could not regulate abortion. During the second trimester, states could regulate abortions insofar as necessary to protect the health and life of the woman. Finally, states could protect the fetus during the third trimester, including proscribing abortion, except in cases in which abortion was necessary to protect the life or health of the mother. The Court decided that the government's interest in protecting a fetus during the third trimester was compelling because it was viable at that time.

The trial court found Roe's right to privacy in the Ninth Amendment, but the Supreme Court refused to rely on the Ninth Amendment alone. Rather, the Court found the right to privacy to stem from the Fourteenth, Ninth, and other amendments.

The *Roe v. Wade* decision was the subject of intense political and legal controversy during the 1980s and 1990s. Certiorari was sought in several abortion-related cases during this period; so-called right-to-life groups believed that, with a more conservative Court than had existed since the *Roe v. Wade* decision issued, the chances of reversing the decision were good. The Court granted certiorari in

# Oyez

## Casey v. Planned Parenthood of Southeastern Pennsylvania
## 505 U.S. 833 (1992)

**Justice O'Connor, Justice Kennedy, and Justice Souter announced the judgment of the Court and delivered the opinion of the Court.**

Liberty finds no refuge in a jurisprudence of doubt. Yet 19 years after our holding that the Constitution protects a woman's right to terminate her pregnancy in its early stages, the respondents as amicus curiae, the United States, as it has done in five other cases in the last decade, again asks us to overrule *Roe*. . . .

At issue in these cases are five provisions of the Pennsylvania Abortion Control Act of 1982 as amended in 1988 and 1989. . . . The Act requires that a woman seeking an abortion give her informed consent prior to the abortion procedure, and specifies that she be provided with certain information at least 24 hours before the abortion is performed. For a minor to obtain an abortion, the Act requires the informed consent of one of her parents, but provided for [a] judicial bypass option if the minor does not wish to or cannot obtain a parent's consent. Another provision of the Act requires that, unless certain exceptions apply, a married woman seeking an abortion must sign a statement indicating that she has notified her husband of her intended abortion. . . .

Before any of these provisions took effect, the petitioners, who are five abortion clinics and one physician representing himself as well as a class of physicians who provide abortion services, brought this suit seeking declaratory and injunctive relief. Each provision was challenged as unconstitutional on its face. . . .

After considering the fundamental constitutional questions resolved by *Roe*, principles of institutional integrity, and the rule of stare decisis, we are led to conclude this: the essential holding of *Roe v. Wade* should be retained and once again reaffirmed.

It must be stated at the outset and with clarity that *Roe's* essential holding, the holding we reaffirm, has three parts. First is a recognition of the right of the woman to choose to have an abortion before viability and to obtain it without undue interference from the State. Before viability, the State's interests are not strong enough to support a prohibition of abortion or the imposition of a substantial obstacle to the woman's effective right to elect the procedure. Second is a confirmation of the State's power to restrict abortions after fetal viability, if the law contains exceptions for pregnancies which endanger a woman's life or health. And third is the principle that the State has legitimate interests from the outset of the pregnancy in protecting the health of the woman and the life of the fetus that may become a child. These principles do not contradict one another; and we adhere to each.

Constitutional protection of the woman's decision to terminate her pregnancy derives from the Due Process Clause of the Fourteenth Amendment. It declares that no State shall "deprive any person of life, liberty, or property, without due process of law." The controlling word in the case before us is "liberty." . . . We have held that the Due Process Clause of the Fourteenth Amendment incorporates most of the Bill of Rights against the States. . . . It is tempting, as a means of curbing the discretion of federal judges, to suppose that liberty encompasses no more than those rights already guaranteed to the individual against federal interference by the express provisions of the first eight amendments to the Constitution. . . . But of course this Court has never accepted that view. It is also tempting, for the same reason, to suppose that the Due Process Clause protects against government interference by other rules of law when the Fourteenth Amendment was ratified. . . . But such a view would be inconsistent with our law. It is a promise of the Constitution that there is a realm of personal liberty which the government may not enter. We have vindicated this principle before. Marriage is mentioned nowhere in the Bill of Rights and interracial marriage was illegal in most States in the 19th century, but the Court was no doubt correct in finding it to be an aspect of liberty protected against state interference by the substantive component of the Due Process Clause. . . . Neither the Bill of Rights nor the specific practices of States at the time of the adoption of the Fourteenth Amendment marks the outer limits of the substantive sphere of liberty which the Fourteenth Amendment protects. . . .

Our law affords constitutional protection to personal decisions relating to marriage, procreation, contraception, family relationships, child rearing, and education. . . . These matters, involving the most intimate and personal choices a person may make in a lifetime, choices central to personal dignity and autonomy, are central to the liberty protected by the Fourteenth Amendment. At the heart of liberty is the right to define one's own concept of existence, of meaning, of the universe, and of the mystery of human life. Beliefs about these matters could not define the attributes of personhood were they formed under compulsion of the State.

The consideration begins our analysis of the woman's interest in terminating her pregnancy but cannot end it, for this reason: though the abortion decision may originate within the zone of conscience and belief, it is more than a philosophic exercise. Abortion is a unique act. It is an act fraught with consequences for others: for the woman who must live with the implications of her decision; for the persons who perform and assist in the procedure; for the spouse, family and society which must confront the knowledge that these procedures exist, procedures some deem nothing short of an act of violence against innocent human life; and depending on one's beliefs, for the life or potential life that is aborted: Though abortion is conduct, it does not follow that the State is entitled to proscribe it in all instances. That is because the liberty of the woman is at stake in a sense unique to the human condition and so unique to the law. The mother who carries a child to full term is subject to anxieties, to physical constraints, to pain that only she must bear. . . .

No evolution of legal principle has left *Roe's* doctrinal footings weaker than they were in 1973. No development of constitutional law since the case was decided has implicitly or explicitly left *Roe* behind as a mere survivor of obsolete constitutional thinking. . . .

We have seen how time has overtaken some of *Roe's* factual assumptions: advances in maternal health care allow for abortions safe to the mother later in pregnancy than was true in 1973 . . . and advances in neonatal care have advanced viability to a point somewhat earlier. . . . But these facts go only to the scheme of the limits on the realization of competing interests, and the divergences from the factual premises of 1973 have no bearing on the validity of *Roe's* central holding, that viability marks the earliest point at which the State's interest in fetal life is constitutionally adequate to justify a legislative ban on nontherapeutic abortions. The soundness or unsoundness of that constitutional judgment in no sense turns on whether viability occurs at 23 to 24 weeks. . . . Whenever it may occur, the attainment of viability may continue to serve as the critical fact, just as it has done since *Roe* was decided; which is to say that no change in *Roe's* factual underpinnings has left its central holding obsolete, and none supports an argument for overruling it. . . .

Only where a state regulation imposes an undue burden on a woman's ability to make this decision does the power of the State reach into the heart of the liberty protected by the Due Process Clause. . . .

The very notion that the State has a substantial interest in potential life leads to the conclusion that not all regulations must be deemed unwarranted. Not all burdens on the right to decide whether to terminate a pregnancy will be undue. . . .

A finding of undue burden is a shorthand for the conclusion that a state regulation has the purpose or effect of placing a substantial obstacle in the path of a woman seeking an abortion of a nonviable fetus. A statute with this purpose is invalid. . . .

several abortion-related cases, but the cardinal principle announced in *Roe v. Wade* was reaffirmed again and again: The decision whether to abort a fetus is, in some circumstances, so private and intimate that it is protected by the Constitution from governmental intrusion. This occurred in *Casey v. Planned Parenthood*, where the Court reaffirmed a woman's right to end her pregnancy but set aside Roe's trimester analysis in favor an "undue interference" test. Applying this new test, a regulation is invalid if it unduly interferes with a woman's choice. Also, the Court reaffirmed the *Roe* holding that until a fetus is viable outside of the mother's womb, a state may not prohibit its abortion. Further, even after viability, abortion is permitted to save the life or health of the mother.

The Court examined the Pennsylvania statute and concluded that:

1. Requiring information concerning abortions and abortion procedures to be distributed to patients before the procedure is performed is not unduly burdensome.

2. Mandating 24-hour waiting periods between receipt of the information and performance of the procedure is not unduly burdensome.

3. Requiring parental consent (with a judicial bypass) by minor girls is not unduly burdensome.

4. Requiring spousal notification by married women is unduly burdensome, and therefore, invalid.[32]

The right to privacy applies outside the abortion context as well. For example, as the Court stated in *Casey*, the right to engage in an interracial marriage is also protected by the Fourteenth Amendment.[33] In *Eisenstadt v. Baird*,[34] the Supreme Court invalidated a statute that prohibited the sale and distribution of contraceptives to unmarried persons. The Court stated in that opinion, "If the right of privacy means anything, it is the right of the individual, married or single, to be free from unwarranted governmental intrusion into matter so fundamentally affecting a person as the decision whether to bear or beget a child."

Alex Wong/Getty Images News/Getty Images

Jim Obergefell, plaintiff in the Obergefell v. *Hodges* same-sex marriage case, in front of the Supreme Court

These are a few examples of how the power of the state to regulate conduct is limited by the right to privacy. Today, courts are likely to rely on the Fourteenth Amendment as the source of the right to privacy. Arguably, the privacy right has its roots in other amendments as well, such as the Ninth Amendment, which declares that the enumeration in the Constitution of certain rights shall not be construed as denying or disparaging others retained by the people. Although this amendment appears to be an independent source of rights, probably with natural rights origins, it has received little attention by the courts, and standing alone has never been relied upon by the Supreme Court to establish an unenumerated right.

The Supreme Court refused to extend the right to privacy to include a right for consenting adults to engage in "deviate sexual" behavior in its 1986 decision *Bowers v. Hardwick*,[35] where it upheld a Georgia statute that criminalized sodomy. But the Court reversed itself seven years later in *Lawrence v. Texas*[36] (see Chapter 6 for more on this subject). And in the 2015 decision, *Obergefell v. Hodges*,[37] the right of same-sex couples to have their marriages recognized by the state was recognized.

## Privileges and Immunities

Learning Objective: Describe the Privileges and Immunities Clause, including the specific rights that have been recognized by the Supreme Court.

Article IV, sec. 2 commands that "The Citizens of each State shall be entitled to all Privileges and Immunities of Citizens in the several States." The purpose of the clause is to prevent states from discriminating against citizens of other states. The clause applies only to the most fundamental of rights, and even then a state may overcome the prohibition if it can demonstrate a compelling reason.

Once a viable source of individual rights, the reach of the clause has been severely limited by the Supreme Court, which has increasingly turned to the

Fourteenth Amendment's Due Process Clause to protect unenumerated rights. One of the few rights protected by the Privileges and Immunities Clause is the right to travel freely between the states. The right to travel abroad is subject to reasonable restrictions and regulations[38] because of national security and foreign affairs concerns.

The Fourteenth Amendment contains a sister clause that forbids states from abridging the privileges or immunities of citizens of the United States. While the Fourth Amendment's Privileges and Immunities Clause forbids states from discriminating against each other's citizens, the Fourteenth Amendment's Privileges and Immunities Clause forbids the states from abridging any person, local or not, from exercising federally secured rights.

Any time a statute conflicts with a constitutionally protected activity, the statute will fail unless the government has a compelling interest. The defenses discussed in this chapter are only a few of the many constitutional defenses. Most, but not all, criminal constitutional defenses appear in the Bill of Rights.

This chapter does not exhaust all the nonconstitutional defenses that may be asserted. Do not forget that each state is free to design its criminal law in any manner it wishes, so long as its design is consonant with the U.S. Constitution. The most common factual, legislative, and constitutional substantive law defenses have been discussed. Many procedural defenses are examined in later chapters of this text.

---

## Ethical Considerations

### Are Federal Prosecutors Subject to State Ethics Rules?

In 1992, a federal grand jury indicted Joseph McDade for bribery. Four years later, he was acquitted on all charges. He claimed that during his prosecution, federal prosecutors violated well-established state ethics rules, including the no-contact rule. In both civil and criminal law, there is a general prohibition of counsel having direct contact with an opposing party without the consent and, if desired, presence of opposing counsel. In criminal cases, this rule is predicated upon the theory that without defense counsel, defendants could be subject to duress or overreaching by prosecutors. The rule applies to direct contact by attorneys or contact through agents and informants of prosecutors.

Even though this rule can be found in the ABA's Model Code of Professional Responsibility and exists in every state, the U.S. Department of Justice has resisted its application in federal prosecutions. Both the attorneys general of President George H. W. Bush (Richard Thornburgh) and President Bill Clinton (Janet Reno) were of the opinion that federal prosecutors are not subject to such state rules. Feeling persecuted and angry, McDade wanted to change the law—and he was in a better than average position to do so. McDade was a U.S. congressman (and attorney) from Pennsylvania (he served from 1962 to 1999). Following his acquittal, he proposed the Citizens Protection Act (CPA), a law that applies state ethics rules to federal prosecutors. The CPA further makes it clear that federal court rules also limit the authority of federal prosecutors. McDade testified at hearing about the law, lobbied his colleagues and the public, and eventually was successful in getting it enacted.

*Sources:* Brenna K. DeVaney, "The 'No-Contact' Rule: Helping or Hurting Criminal Defendants in Plea Negotiations," 14 *Geo. J. Legal Ethics* 933 (2001); and Fred C. Zacharias and Bruce A. Green, "The Uniqueness of Federal Prosecutors," 88 *Geo. L.J.* 207 (2000).

## Key Terms

bill of attainder
Double Jeopardy Clause
dual sovereignty doctrine
ex post facto law
overbreadth

principle of legality
rational relationship test
State Action Doctrine
strict scrutiny
Substantial Relationship Test

suspect classifications
transactional immunity
use immunity
vagueness

## Review Questions

1. Differentiate overbreadth from vagueness. Give an example of each.

2. Describe and differentiate a bill of attainder from an ex post facto law.

3. May racially derogatory statements be made criminal? May racial motives be used to enhance the punishment for crimes such as assault and battery?

4. Is a right to privacy specifically expressed in the U.S. Constitution?

5. Through what amendment are rights incorporated and applied against the states?

6. May religious beliefs be regulated by the state?

7. Which of the following is protected by the First Amendment's Free Speech Clause?

   a. A public flag burning in protest of a recently enacted law.

   b. An advertisement for potato chips found on a billboard.

   c. The placing of a hand over one's heart while the national anthem is played.

8. What are the three standards of constitutional review? To what cases does each apply?

## Problems & Critical Thinking Exercises

1. Senator Bob Kerry of Nebraska, a military veteran, was initially outraged by the *Texas v. Johnson* flag-burning decision. However, he later stated, "I was surprised to discover . . . [that the decision was] reasonable, under-standable and consistent with those values which I believe have made America wonderful." Do you agree with Senator Kerry? Explain your position.

2. State law requires that all children between the ages of 5 and 16 years attend an approved school. Defendants have been charged with violating the statute, as they do not permit their children to attend school. The defendants are Mennonites and claim that it would violate their First Amendment right to freely exercise their religion. The defendants teach their children in a manner consistent with their religious teachings. Should they be convicted?

3. Do you believe that a person should be subjected to two prosecutions, by different sovereigns, for the same offense? Support your answer.

4. State law forbids the "practice of any religion that teaches or has a tenet that the races of people vary in their intelligence or their inherent morality." If the law is challenged as violating the First Amendment's Free Exercise Clause, what standard of review would a court use to analyze the claim? Analyze the law using this standard. Explain your analysis and conclusion.

# Endnotes

1. David S. Rudstein, "Brief History of the Fifth Amendment Guarantee Against Double Jeopardy," 14 *Wm & Mary Bill of Rts. J.* 193, 204 (2005).

2. *Arizona v. Washington*, 434 U.S. 497 (1978).

3. *United States v. Dreitzler*, 577 F.2d 539 (9th Cir. 1978).

4. *United States v. Martin Linen Supply Co.*, 430 U.S. 564 (1977).

5. *See Monge v. California*, 524 U.S. 721 (1998).

6. *Blockburger v. United States*, 284 U.S. 299 (1932).

7. Model Penal Code § 1.10.

8. Passage taken from a 1991 calendar prepared by the Commission on the Bicentennial of the United States Constitution, Washington, D.C.

9. *Pillsbury v. Conboy*, 459 U.S. 248 (1983).

10. *Douglas v. California*, 372 U.S. 353 (1963).

11. *Connally v. General Construction Co.*, 269 U.S. 385 (1926).

12. *United States v. Cardiff*, 344 U.S. 174 (1952).

13. *Coates v. Cincinnati*, 402 U.S. 611 (1971).

14. *Ohio v. Mole*, 149 Ohio St.3d 215 (2016).

15. 18 U.S.C. § 3621(h).

16. See *United States v. Brown*, 381 U.S. at 444 (quoting John C. Hamilton, *History of the Republic of the United States* 34 (1859), who is *quoting* Alexander Hamilton).

17. *Reynolds v. United States*, 98 U.S. 145 (1878).

18. 42 U.S. sec. 2000bb.

19. *City of Boerne v. Flores*, 521 U.S. 507 (1997).

20. *South Bay United Pentecostal Church v. Newsom*, 592 U.S. __ (2021).

21. See, for example, *Roman Catholic Diocese of Brooklyn, New York v. Cuomo*, 592 U.S. ___ (2020).

22. See, for example, *Elli v. City of Ellisville*, 997 F. Supp. 2d 980 (U.S. Dist. E.D. Mo. 2014).

23. *Brandenburg v. Ohio*, 395 U.S. 444 (1969).

24. *Terminiello v. Chicago*, 337 U.S. 1 (1949).

25. *Cohen v. California*, 403 U.S. 15 (1971).

26. *Gooding v. Wilson*, 405 U.S. 518 (1972). See also *Hess v. Indiana*, 414 U.S. 105 (1973)

27. *Giboney v. Empire Storage*, 336 U.S. 490 (1949).

28. Eugene Volokh, The Speech Integral to Criminal Conduct Exception, 101 Cornell L. Rev. 981 (2016).

29. 538 U.S. 343 (2003).

30. 381 U.S. 479 (1965). The Supreme Court noted in *Roe v. Wade*, 410 U.S. 113 (1973), that the right to privacy may have been recognized by the Court as early as 1891, in *Union Pacific Railroad v. Botsford*, 141 U.S. 250 (1891), in which it held that a plaintiff in a tort action could not be compelled to submit to a medical examination because it would have been an invasion of privacy.

31. 410 U.S. 113 (1973).

32. *See also Webster v. Reproductive Health Services*, 492 U.S. 490 (1989).

33. *Loving v. Virginia*, 388 U.S. 1 (1967).
34. 405 U.S. 438 (1972).
35. 478 U.S. 186 (1986).
36. 539 U.S. 558 (2003).
37. *Obergefell v. Hodges*, 576 U.S. 644 (2015)
38. *Zemel v. Rusk*, 381 U.S. 1 (1965).

# 2

## Part

# Criminal Procedure

# Chapter 10

# The Criminal Justice System

## Chapter Objectives

After completing the chapter, you should be able to

- Describe and offer examples of the adversarial and accusatorial features of the U.S. criminal justice system.
- Describe Herbert Packer's criminal justice system models and explain where, and why,

the United States falls on the continuum between the two.

- Describe the roles and ethical responsibilities of prosecutors, defense attorneys, and judges.

The second section of this text addresses criminal procedure. *Criminal procedure*, as a field of law, describes the methods used in bringing an alleged criminal to justice. Criminal procedure puts substantive criminal law into action. It also includes the substantive rights of criminal defendants.

Each state and the federal government have their own procedural rules. In some instances, the variation is significant. For convenience, most references will be to federal procedure. Many federal procedural rules can be found in the U.S. Code. A good number of procedures are judicially created (and approved by Congress) and are found in the Federal Rules of Criminal Procedure (Fed. R. Crim. P.). Finally, the constitutions of the national government and the states play a major role in defining procedures of criminal adjudications.

What follows is a discussion of the constitutional and statutory aspects of criminal procedure; the process, from investigation to appeal; searches and seizures; arrests; confessions and admissions; and the right to counsel.

## A Common Law, Adversarial, and Accusatorial System

Learning Objective: Describe and offer examples of the adversarial and accusatorial features of the U.S. criminal justice system.

The British colonists brought with common law of England to America. The Common Law, which began with the Norman Conquest of England in 1066, is judge-made law, as opposed to law created by legislatures. When the Common Law began its development, there was no legislative body in England. Preexisting feudal laws, which varied throughout England in so-called hundreds and shires laws, were replaced, over time, with laws announced by judges as they heard cases. For example, at some point in history, a judge heard the first homicide case. The judge announced the killing of a human being with malice aforethought to be a felony, punishable by murder. That rule was affirmed by a higher court, and through the Doctrine of Stare Decisis, which translates to "let the decision stand," the law spread throughout England. Consequently, the murder rule became "common" to all people in England, and hence the name the Common Law.

The Common Law was in continuous evolution, as courts heard new cases that put a twist on rules that were announced in prior similar cases, known as precedent. For example, after the crime of murder was created, another case was heard where a man was accused of murder, but he asked for forgiveness because he committed the murder to protect his wife from a man who was attempting to sexually assault her. In that case, defending another from serious bodily harm was announced as a justification for murder and the man was set free. Today, England has Parliament to make laws, and the United States has Congress, state legislatures, and thousands of local lawmaking bodies. But the influence of judges in the interpretation of law and the influence of the old Common Law continues. The Common Law traveled with the British as it colonized much of the world. Although the British Empire has shrunk, the Common Law has remained rooted in its former colonies. Australia, New Zealand, Belize, Bahamas, Uganda, and the United States are a few examples. To make it more complex, subvariants of the British Common Law exist. For example, American Samoa, a territory of the United States, employs an British-American version of the Common Law. The same is true of Liberia because it was founded by freed American slaves.

The Common Law is contrasted with the Civil Law Family. The Civil Law has its roots in Rome and differs from the Common Law in important ways. In the seventh century, the Civil Law was created by groups of scholars appointed by the Roman Emperor to make law. In modern terms, legislatures make the law. In addition, judicial interpretation of the law is less important than in common law nations. In common law nations, precedent is often binding. In civil law, courts often interpret the law anew, without regard to earlier decisions about the meaning of the law. The civil law can be found in nearly two-thirds of the world: Italy, France, Spain, Japan, China, Ethiopia, and Chile are a few examples. Today, all jurisdictions in the United States, except Louisiana and Puerto Rico, which are a mix of the Common and Civil Law Families, are of the common law family.

In addition to being common law in nature, the legal system is **adversarial.** Adversarial adjudications resemble sporting events. There are two opposing parties and a neutral umpire. In criminal cases, these roles are played by the defendant, prosecutor, and judge. The judge in criminal adjudications is a passive participant, usually becoming involved only as needed by the parties or as required by law. Of course, the approach of judges varies; and some are more proactive than others. A pure adversarial system is not employed in the United States, and judges are expected to supervise the proceedings to ensure fairness. The **adversary system** is built upon the theory that the truth is more likely to be discovered when there are two competing parties, each conducting its own investigation of the facts, asserting differing theories of fact and law, and each presenting its own case to the court. Common law nations use, with variation, adversarial systems. Civil law jurisdictions, on the other hand, employ **inquisitorial systems**. In the inquisitorial model, the judge plays are more active role in the entire case. Judges may decide what theories will be explored and what evidence is to be collected. The process is far less formal and technical than the adversarial system.

Also, in the common law, judges are expected to remain impartial, neutral, and detached. This is believed to increase the fairness of the proceedings. In civil law jurisdictions, on the other hand, judges sometimes develop an opinion or theory, which may limit their consideration of alternatives and, accordingly, limit the facts

**adversarial**
A system of adjudication where the state and defendant are competitors with independent investigations and theories of the case. The two parties are active in the development of the case with the court in a more passive role, overseeing the process and ensuring due process. Common Law nations, such as the United States, use the adversarial system.

**adversary system**
The system of adjudication in the United States and other common law jurisdictions. The judge acts as the referee between opposite sides (between two individuals, between the state and an individual, etc.) rather than acting as the person who also makes the state's case or independently seeks out evidence.

**inquisitorial system**
The system of adjudication found in civil law jurisdictions. Less formal and technical than the adversarial model, a judge plays a prominent role in the gathering of evidence and the development of the case.

that are sought and the theories that are advanced. In the adversarial system, the parties are largely responsible for development of the case—that is, discovery of the evidence and, accordingly, the issues of law as well.

The adversarial system has its critics. Opponents contend that the truth is not found because the system encourages the opposing parties to present distorted, misleading, and sometimes untruthful accounts of the facts. The fact finder, who is not part of the investigative process, is often left to choose between polarized versions of the same event. The adversarial system is also challenged as being unfair because it assumes two equally competent competing parties. However, because of differences in the abilities of counsel and the respective resources and powers of the parties, this premise is questionable.

**accusatorial**
An element of the adversarial system that places the burden of production and proof on the state, and otherwise gives the benefit of doubt to the defendant.

In addition to being adversarial, the criminal justice system is **accusatorial**. This means that the government, as the accuser, bears the burden of proving a defendant's guilt. If the government fails in its burden, then a defendant is entitled to a directed verdict or a judgment of acquittal. The accusatorial nature of the system extends beyond placing the burden of proof on the government at trial. The entire process is designed to minimize the risk of convicting an innocent person. The philosophy that it is better to free several guilty persons than to convict one innocent person is a major theme of the U.S. criminal justice system. Accordingly, the system is designed so that the accused enjoys several advantages, the most critical one being the presumption of innocence; the freedom from self-incrimination, the right to a jury trial, and the right to counsel are others.

The fact that a defendant enjoys a few advantages does not mean that the defendant has the advantage on the whole. The government, state or federal, can commit substantial resources to a prosecution.

# The Due Process Model

Learning Objective: Describe Herbert Packer's criminal justice system models and explain where, and why, the United States falls on the continuum between the two.

Criminal justice systems are commonly characterized as falling on a continuum that is bracketed by Herbert Packer's *crime control* and the *due process models*.[1] The repression, detection, and efficient prosecution of crime is central to the crime control model. Failure to detect and successfully prosecute criminals is a failure. This failure reduces liberty because citizens live in constant fear of, and are actually subject to, criminal conduct. A secondary consequence is a loss of confidence in government by the public, thereby further hindering its ability to detect and prevent crime. Prosecution in such systems tends to be bureaucratic, that is, a form of "assembly-line" justice. Some civil law and socialist law nations fall closer to the crime control pole.

**factual guilt**
Whether a defendant committed the alleged crime.

**legal guilt**
A combination of factual guilt proven beyond a reasonable doubt, and a fair process.

The due process model places a premium on the integrity of individual rights and the fairness of process, as well as factual guilt. Efficiency (speed and expense) is a secondary concern. The balance is different in crime control systems. **Factual guilt** and efficiency are emphasized. Factual guilt refers to whether a defendant has in fact committed a crime. **Legal guilt** is concerned not only with factual guilt but also with whether the defendant's rights have been observed and respected by the government.

It is possible under the due process model to have sufficient evidence to prove a defendant factually guilty, but because of a civil rights violation, the defendant is acquitted. The due process model has little tolerance for conviction of the innocent; the crime control model equally abhors crimes going unsolved and defendants unpunished. Investigation and adjudication of defendants are less efficient and more costly under the due process model than under the crime control model. Said another way, the due process model occasionally sacrifices factual truth and punishing the guilty in favor of protecting liberty. The English jurist William Blackstone expressed it this way, in what is known as Blackstone's Ratio:

## Exhibit 10–1  Crime Control and Due Process Models Compared

|  | Crime Control | Due Process |
|---|---|---|
| Philosophy | Discovering, apprehending, and punishing offenders, and deterring crime, is a priority. Civil liberties are protected, but not to the extent they jeopardize social control. | Discovering, apprehending, and punishing offenders is balanced against civil liberties. In some instances, civil liberties will prevail and crimes will go unpunished. |
| Process | Mechanistic; efficiency is a high priority. The criminal justice system is a machine through which the government processes its cases. | Cumbersome; efficiency is not a high priority. The criminal justice system is not so much a machine but a maze through which the government must navigate to secure a conviction. |
| Conviction Standard | Actual guilt of accused is required for conviction. Government's burdens of proof and production are less than in systems emphasizing due process. | Legal and factual guilt are required for conviction. Government has high burdens of production and proof. |

The law holds that it is better that ten guilty persons escape, than that one innocent suffer.

This description is a simplification of the two models.[2] See Exhibit 10-1 for a comparison of the two models. No system falls squarely into one or the other, although most systems can be generally characterized as adhering to the principles of one more than the other. The United States most closely aligns the due process model. As you will learn in future chapters, due process is operationalized in the United States in many different ways. These include, inter alia:

- Presumption that criminal defendants are innocent
- **Rule of Lenity**, which requires ambiguous laws to be interpreted in a manner that benefits the defendant
- Proof beyond a reasonable doubt for conviction
- Freedom from unreasonable searches, to probable cause and warrants in some cases, and the exclusion of evidence that is illegally obtained by police
- Right to counsel
- Right to a jury trial and unanimous jury verdict for conviction
- Adequate notice of the charges and time to prepare a defense
- Right to be free from self-incrimination

**rule of lenity**
If there are two or more reasonable interpretations of a statute, the interpretation that most favors the defendant is to be adopted.

# The Players

Learning Objective: Describe the roles and ethical responsibilities of prosecutors, defense attorneys, and judges.

Besides the accused and witnesses, there are six major participants in criminal adjudications: law enforcement officers, prosecutors, judges, defense attorneys, victims, and jurors. What follows is a discussion of all of these participants, except jurors. Jurors are discussed later.

## Law Enforcement Officers

The television crime drama *Law and Order* opens each episode with a narrator stating that "[i]n the criminal justice system, the people are represented by two separate yet equally important groups: The police, who investigate crime, and the district attorneys, who prosecute the offenders. These are their stories." The statement is true. In the United States, the police and prosecution functions are independent. They work closely together, but neither oversees the other.

The front line of the criminal justice system is the *police*. Law enforcement officers exist at the national, state, and local levels. Federal law enforcement agencies include inter alia the Federal Bureau of Investigation; the Drug Enforcement Administration; Customs; the Coast Guard; U.S. Marshals; the Secret Service; and the Bureau of Alcohol, Tobacco, and Firearms.

Each state has a police department, and many have a counterpart to the FBI, such as the Kansas Bureau of Investigation (KBI). In addition, within each state, county sheriffs and municipal police departments enforce the laws of the state as well as the laws of their locality. There are more than 18,000 local law enforcement agencies in the United States. This includes 12,502 local police departments; 3,086 sheriffs' offices; 49 state police departments; and more than 700,000 sworn police officers and 300,000-plus civilian personnel. In addition, there were 105,000 federal officers who carry weapons and are authorized to make arrests in the 50 states and District of Columbia in 2004. Three-fourths of these officers work in the Department of Homeland Security. An additional 1,500 officers work in U.S. territories. Additional officers are stationed in foreign nations.[3]

## Discretion

Law enforcement personnel are expected to keep the peace, investigate wrongdoing, enforce the laws, and further crime prevention. Police don't have the resources to enforce the law in every case where a violation is suspected, nor is it fair to enforce the law in every case. Consequently, officers exercise considerable discretion. But police discretion is not unlimited. Police officers must comply with constitutional, statutory, and departmental standards.

## Ethics

As is true of prosecutors and defense attorneys, the police officer's paramount ethical code is the Constitution. Police officers have a legal and ethical obligation to keep themselves within constitutional limits when performing their duties.

The International Association of Chiefs of Police (IACP) has formulated a set of ethical principles intended to guide the law enforcement officer in the performance of his or her duties. The IACP has issued two ethics documents, the Law Enforcement Code of Ethics and the Police Code of Conduct. The Code of Ethics is a general statement of ethical responsibility that may be used as an oath of office.

The Code of Ethics recognizes that police officers hold a special public trust and that they have an obligation not to violate that trust.

Although substantially the same, the Police Code of Conduct is more specific than the Code of Ethics. The Code of Conduct prohibits discriminatory treatment of individuals based upon race, sex, religion, political belief, or aspiration; the unnecessary use of force; the infliction of cruel, degrading, or inhuman treatment; violation of confidences, except when necessary in the performance of duties or as required by law; bribery; the acceptance of gifts; refusals to cooperate with other law enforcement officials; and other unreasonable and inappropriate behavior. The Code of Conduct further qualifies the necessary force requirement by stating that force should be used "only with the greatest restraint and only after discussion, negotiation and persuasion have been found to be inappropriate or ineffective."

Officers are expected to behave in a manner that inspires confidence and respect for law enforcement officials. Further, police officers are to attempt to obtain maximum public cooperation and to enforce all laws with courtesy, consideration, and dignity. Although the IACP has no enforcement authority, the codes do provide an excellent standard for adoption by law enforcement agencies, as well as by individual officers.

In recent years, the role race plays in law enforcement has received increasing attention. The Equal Protection Clause applies to law enforcement at all levels of government. As was discussed in the last chapter, laws and departmental policies that have race-based classifications are subject to strict scrutiny review, and police conduct that is unconstitutionally motivated by race can result in the exclusion of evidence at trial and civil liability for the officer under 42 U.S.C. §1983. As you will learn later in this book, other constitutional rights offer protections against unreasonable searches and seizures and other police misconduct.

For the remainder of this book, references to police or law enforcement officers are to any one of the previously mentioned agencies.

# Prosecutors

*Prosecutors* are government attorneys responsible for prosecuting violators. This role includes preparing and filing documents; engaging in pretrial activity, such as discovery; and appearing in court. Prosecutors often also act as legal counsel to law enforcement officers, rendering advice on the law of searches, seizures, arrests, surveillance techniques, and similar matters. Prosecutors appear at grand jury hearings, where they present evidence and assist the jury in other ways. Finally, in some jurisdictions, prosecutors act in a supervisory capacity as the head of a law enforcement agency, such as the attorney general of the United States, who is the head of the Department of Justice.

At the federal level, the highest law enforcement official and prosecutor is the attorney general, who undergoes the presidential nomination and senatorial confirmation process. The attorney general is a cabinet member who heads the Department of Justice.

Within each judicial district is one U.S. attorney, a subordinate of the attorney general, who also is selected through the nomination and confirmation process. U.S. attorneys, with the aid of several assistant U.S. attorneys, are responsible for most federal prosecutions. In rare cases, however, another attorney from the Department of Justice may travel to a district to handle a case. Federal law also provides for the appointment of an independent counsel (special prosecutor) when government officials are suspected of violating the law.

Similar to the federal government, each state has an attorney general. The states vary in the structure of their prosecutorial agencies, but most have locally elected prosecutors, who may be titled *prosecutor*, *district attorney*, or *state attorney*. The degree to which these individuals answer to the state attorney general differs greatly. Additionally, local forms of government have attorneys. In some localities, these attorneys prosecute ordinance violations.

## Prosecutorial Discretion

Like the police, prosecutors enjoy a lot of discretion in the performance of their duties. The decision whether to prosecute an individual is one aspect of prosecutorial **discretion.** This charging decision is made by a prosecutor in most cases. In a small number of cases, however, the prosecutor may not make this decision, such as when a traffic ticket acts as the charging instrument and the case proceeds directly to court without the prosecutor's involvement. However, most cases are initiated directly by a prosecutor, grand jury, or, as is usually the case, the police (through the arrest and complaint procedure). A case may not proceed under a complaint; rather, the prosecutor must file an information (or an indictment issued by a grand jury), which replaces the complaint. If a prosecutor refuses, or files a **nolle prosequi,** the case proceeds no further.

There are at least two reasons prosecutorial discretion is important. First, the prosecutor's ethical obligation is to seek justice, not convictions. Prosecutors are not to maintain a prosecution simply because there is a probability of prevailing.

**discretion**
The power to act within general guidelines, rules, or laws, but without either specific rules to follow or the need to completely explain or justify each decision or action.

**nolle prosequi**
(Latin) The ending of a criminal case because the prosecutor decides or agrees to stop prosecuting.

Rather, the totality of the facts must be examined, and it must be determined that a prosecution is just. The justice obligation continues through the entire adjudicative process.

Economics is the second reason prosecutors cannot pursue every case. The resources of the prosecutor—and law enforcement agencies—are limited. Prosecutors must prioritize cases for prosecution. The decision whether to prosecute is influenced by many factors: the facts of the case; the accused's criminal, social, and economic history; the likelihood of success; the cost of prosecution, including the probable time investment; public opinion; the seriousness of the crime; the desires of the victims; police expectations and desires; political concerns; and whether the prosecution will further the administration of justice are all considered.

Although prosecutorial discretion is broad, it is not absolute. First, the authority to file a nolle prosequi, or dismissal, may be limited. The further along a case is in the process, the more involved the court becomes in the decision. Generally, the decision not to prosecute before the formal charge (information or indictment) is filed is left to the prosecutor without judicial intervention. However, a small number of states require judicial approval of nolle prosequi decisions.

Once the formal charge has been filed, judicial approval of dismissal is the rule rather than the exception. This is true in the federal system, which also requires leave of court to dismiss complaints.[4]

Second, decisions to prosecute that are motivated by improper criteria may violate equal protection. The Fourteenth Amendment prohibits each state from taking actions that "deny to any person within its jurisdiction the equal protection of the laws." Although the Fifth Amendment does not contain this language, the Supreme Court has interpreted the Fifth Amendment's Due Process Clause as requiring equal protection of the laws. A claim that it is unfair to prosecute a person because other known violators are not prosecuted will not be successful, unless it can be shown that the accused has been singled out for an improper reason.

Generally, three elements must be shown to establish improper, discriminatory prosecution. A defendant must prove

1. that other people similarly situated were not prosecuted and
2. the prosecutor intentionally singled out the defendant and
3. the selection was based upon an arbitrary classification.

As the Supreme Court stated in *Oyler v. Boles*,[5] for there to be an equal protection violation, it must be shown that "the selection was *deliberately* based upon an unjustified standard." What is an unjustified standard? Prosecutions based upon race, religion, and gender are examples. A prosecution intended to punish an individual for exercising a constitutional right is also improper. The Supreme Court discusses selective prosecution in *United States v. Armstrong* (1996) found in the Oyez feature.

To determine whether a classification is proper, equal protection analysis must be employed. Most decisions are tested under the rational relationship test. That is, if the decision to prosecute is rationally related to a legitimate governmental objective, it is valid. If a decision is based upon race or religion, or in retaliation for a person's exercise of a right, the decision is tested under the strict scrutiny test and is invalid unless it can be shown to further a compelling governmental interest. Finally, a few classifications, such as those based upon gender, are tested under a standard less demanding than strict scrutiny but more demanding than the rational relationship test. Such laws must bear a substantial relationship to a legitimate governmental interest. In reality, claims of selective enforcement are rarely successful.

## Ethics

All attorneys are bound by ethical rules. Two sets of rules are used in the United States: the Model Code of Professional Responsibility and the Model Rules of

# Oyez

## United States v. Armstrong
### 517 U.S. 456 (1996)

**Chief Justice Rehnquist delivered the opinion of the Court**

In this case, we consider the showing necessary for a defendant to be entitled to discovery on a claim that the prosecuting attorney singled him out for prosecution on the basis of his race. We conclude that respondents failed to satisfy the threshold showing: They failed to show that the Government declined to prosecute similarly situated suspects of other races.

In April 1992, respondents were indicted in the United States District Court for the Central District of California on charges of conspiring to possess with intent to distribute more than 50 grams of cocaine base (crack) and conspiring to distribute the same, in violation of 21 U.S.C. §§ 841 and 846 (1988 ed. and Supp. IV), and federal firearms offenses. For three months prior to the indictment, agents of the Federal Bureau of Alcohol, Tobacco, and Firearms and the Narcotics Division of the Inglewood, California, Police Department had infiltrated a suspected crack distribution ring by using three confidential informants. On seven separate occasions during this period, the informants had bought a total of 124.3 grams of crack from respondents and witnessed respondents carrying firearms during the sales. The agents searched the hotel room in which the sales were transacted, arrested respondents Armstrong and Hampton in the room, and found more crack and a loaded gun. The agents later arrested the other respondents as part of the ring.

In response to the indictment, respondents filed a motion for discovery or for dismissal of the indictment, alleging that they were selected for federal prosecution because they are black. In support of their motion, they offered only an affidavit by a "Paralegal Specialist," employed by the Office of the Federal Public Defender representing one of the respondents. The only allegation in the affidavit was that, in every one of the 24 § 841 or § 846 cases closed by the office during 1991, the defendant was black. Accompanying the affidavit was a "study" listing the 24 defendants, their race, whether they were prosecuted for dealing cocaine as well as crack, and the status of each case.

The Government opposed the discovery motion, arguing, among other things, that there was no evidence or allegation "that the Government has acted unfairly or has prosecuted nonblack defendants or failed to prosecute them." The District Court granted the motion. It ordered the Government (1) to provide a list of all cases from the last three years in which the Government charged both cocaine and firearms offenses, (2) to identify the race of the defendants in those cases, (3) to identify what levels of law enforcement were involved in the investigations of those cases, and (4) to explain its criteria for deciding to prosecute those defendants for federal cocaine offenses.

The Government moved for reconsideration of the District Court's discovery order. With this motion it submitted affidavits and other evidence to explain why it had chosen to prosecute respondents and why respondents' study did not support the inference that the Government was singling out blacks for cocaine prosecution. The federal and local agents participating in the case alleged in affidavits that race played no role in their investigation. An Assistant United States Attorney explained in an affidavit that the decision to prosecute met the general criteria for prosecution, because

> "there was over 100 grams of cocaine base involved, over twice the threshold necessary for a ten year mandatory minimum sentence; there were multiple sales involving multiple defendants, thereby indicating a fairly substantial crack cocaine ring; . . . there were multiple federal firearms violations intertwined with the narcotics trafficking; the overall evidence in the case was extremely strong, including audio and videotapes of defendants; . . . and several of the defendants had criminal histories including narcotics and firearms violations."

The Government also submitted sections of a published 1989 Drug Enforcement Administration report which concluded that "large-scale, interstate trafficking networks controlled by Jamaicans, Haitians and Black street gangs dominate the manufacture and distribution of crack."

In response, one of respondents' attorneys submitted an affidavit alleging that an intake coordinator at a drug treatment center had told her that there are "an equal number of caucasian users and dealers to minority users and dealers." Respondents also submitted an affidavit from a criminal defense attorney alleging that in his experience many nonblacks are prosecuted in state court for crack offenses, and a newspaper article reporting that federal "crack criminals . . . are being punished far more severely than if they had been caught with powder cocaine, and almost every single one of them is black."

The District Court denied the motion for reconsideration. When the Government indicated it would not comply with the court's discovery order, the court dismissed the case.

A divided three-judge panel of the Court of Appeals for the Ninth Circuit reversed, . . . A selective-prosecution claim is not a defense on the merits to the criminal charge itself, but an independent assertion that the prosecutor has brought the charge for reasons forbidden by the Constitution. Our cases delineating the necessary elements to prove a claim of selective prosecution have taken great pains to explain that the standard is a demanding one. These cases afford a "background presumption," that the showing necessary to obtain discovery should itself be a significant barrier to the litigation of insubstantial claims.

(continued)

A selective-prosecution claim asks a court to exercise judicial power over a "special province" of the Executive. The Attorney General and United States Attorneys retain "broad discretion" to enforce the Nation's criminal laws. They have this latitude because they are designated by statute as the President's delegates to help him discharge his constitutional responsibility to "take *Care that the Laws be* faithfully executed." U.S. Const., Art. II, § 3; see 28 U.S.C. §§ 516, 547. As a result, "the presumption of regularity supports" their prosecutorial decisions and, "in the absence of clear evidence to the contrary, courts presume that they have properly discharged their official duties." In the ordinary case, "so long as the prosecutor has probable cause to believe that the accused committed an offense defined by statute, the decision whether or not to prosecute, and what charge to file or bring before a grand jury, generally rests entirely in his discretion."

Of course, a prosecutor's discretion is "subject to constitutional constraints." One of these constraints, imposed by the equal protection component of the Due Process Clause of the Fifth Amendment, is that the decision whether to prosecute may not be based on "an unjustifiable standard such as race, religion, or other arbitrary classification." A defendant may demonstrate that the administration of a criminal law is "directed so exclusively against a particular class of persons . . . with a mind so unequal and oppressive" that the system of prosecution amounts to "a practical denial" of equal protection of the law.

In order to dispel the presumption that a prosecutor has not violated equal protection, a criminal defendant must present "clear evidence to the contrary." We explained in Wayte why courts are "properly hesitant to examine the decision whether to prosecute." Judicial deference to the decisions of these executive officers rests in part on an assessment of the relative competence of prosecutors and courts. "Such factors as the strength of the case, the prosecution's general deterrence value, the Government's enforcement priorities, and the case's relationship to the Government's overall enforcement plan are not readily susceptible to the kind of analysis the courts are competent to undertake." It also stems from a concern not to unnecessarily impair the performance of a core executive constitutional function. "Examining the basis of a prosecution delays the criminal proceeding, threatens to chill law enforcement by subjecting the prosecutor's motives and decision making to outside inquiry, and may undermine prosecutorial effectiveness by revealing the Government's enforcement policy." The requirements for a selective-prosecution claim draw on "ordinary equal protection standards." The claimant must demonstrate that the federal prosecutorial policy "had a discriminatory effect and that it was motivated by a discriminatory purpose." To establish a discriminatory effect in a race case, the claimant must show that similarly situated individuals of a different race were not prosecuted. This requirement has been established in our case law since *Ah Sin v. Wittman*, 198 U.S. 500, 49 L. Ed. 1142, 25 S. Ct. 756 (1905). Ah Sin, a subject of China, petitioned a California state court for a writ of habeas corpus, seeking discharge from imprisonment under a San Francisco County ordinance prohibiting persons from setting up gambling tables in rooms barricaded to stop police from entering. He alleged in his habeas petition "that the ordinance is enforced 'solely and exclusively against persons of the Chinese race and not otherwise.'" We rejected his contention that this averment made out a claim under the Equal Protection Clause, because it did not allege "that the conditions and practices to which the ordinance was directed did not exist exclusively among the Chinese, or that there were other offenders against the ordinance than the Chinese as to whom it was not enforced."

The similarly situated requirement does not make a selective-prosecution claim impossible to prove. Twenty years before *Ah Sin*, we invalidated an ordinance, also adopted by San Francisco, that prohibited the operation of laundries in wooden buildings. The plaintiff in error successfully demonstrated that the ordinance was applied against Chinese nationals but not against other laundry-shop operators. The authorities had denied the applications of 200 Chinese subjects for permits to operate shops in wooden buildings, but granted the applications of 80 individuals who were not Chinese subjects to operate laundries in wooden buildings "under similar conditions." We explained in *Ah Sin* why the similarly situated requirement is necessary:

> "No latitude of intention should be indulged in a case like this. There should be certainty to every intent. Plaintiff in error seeks to set aside a criminal law of the State, not on the ground that it is unconstitutional on its face, not that it is discriminatory in tendency and ultimate actual operation as the ordinance was which was passed on in the *Yick Wo* case, but that it was made so by the manner of its administration. This is a matter of proof, and *no fact should be omitted to make it out completely*, when the power of a Federal court is invoked to interfere with the course of criminal justice of a State." 198 U.S. at 508 (emphasis added).

Although *Ah Sin* involved federal review of a state conviction, we think a similar rule applies where the power of a federal court is invoked to challenge an exercise of one of the core powers of the Executive Branch of the Federal Government, the power to prosecute. . . .

Having reviewed the requirements to prove a selective-prosecution claim, we turn to the showing necessary to obtain discovery in support of such a claim. If discovery is ordered, the Government must assemble from its own files documents which might corroborate or refute the defendant's claim. Discovery thus imposes many of the costs present when the Government must respond to a prima facie case of selective prosecution. It will divert prosecutors' resources and may disclose the Government's prosecutorial strategy. The justifications for a rigorous standard for the elements of a selective-prosecution claim thus require a correspondingly rigorous standard for discovery in aid of such a claim.

The parties, and the Courts of Appeals which have considered the requisite showing to establish entitlement to discovery, describe this showing with a variety of phrases, like "colorable basis," "substantial threshold showing," "substantial and concrete basis," or "reasonable likelihood," Brief for Respondents Martin et al. 30. However, the many labels for this showing conceal the degree of consensus about the evidence necessary to meet it. The Courts of Appeals "require some evidence tending to show the existence of the essential elements of the defense," discriminatory effect and discriminatory intent.

In this case we consider what evidence constitutes "some evidence tending to show the existence" of the discriminatory effect element. The Court of Appeals held that a defendant may establish a colorable basis for discriminatory effect without evidence that the Government has failed to prosecute others who are similarly situated to the defendant. We think it was mistaken in this view. The vast majority of the Courts of Appeals require the defendant to produce some evidence that similarly situated defendants of other races could have been prosecuted, but were not, and this requirement is consistent with our equal protection case law. As the three-judge panel explained, "'selective prosecution' implies that a selection has taken place."

The Court of Appeals reached its decision in part because it started "with the presumption that people of *all* races commit *all* types of crimes—not with the premise that any type of crime is the exclusive province of any particular racial or ethnic group." It cited no authority for this proposition, which seems contradicted by the most recent statistics of the United States Sentencing Commission. Those statistics show: More than 90 percent of the persons sentenced in 1994 for crack cocaine trafficking were black, United States Sentencing Comm'n, 1994 Annual Report 107 (Table 45); 93.4 percent of convicted LSD dealers were white, and 91 percent of those convicted for pornography or prostitution were white. Presumptions at war with presumably reliable statistics have no proper place in the analysis of this issue.

The Court of Appeals also expressed concern about the "evidentiary obstacles defendants face." But all of its sister Circuits that have confronted the issue have required that defendants produce some evidence of differential treatment of similarly situated members of other races or protected classes. In the present case, if the claim of selective prosecution were well founded, it should not have been an insuperable task to prove that persons of other races were being treated differently than respondents. For instance, respondents could have investigated whether similarly situated persons of other races were prosecuted by the State of California and were known to federal law enforcement officers, but were not prosecuted in federal court. We think the required threshold—a credible showing of different treatment of similarly situated persons—adequately balances the Government's interest in vigorous prosecution and the defendant's interest in avoiding selective prosecution.

In the case before us, respondents' "study" did not constitute "some evidence tending to show the existence of the essential elements of" a selective- prosecution claim. The study failed to identify individuals who were not black and could have been prosecuted for the offenses for which respondents were charged, but were not so prosecuted. This omission was not remedied by respondents' evidence in opposition to the Government's motion for reconsideration. The newspaper article, which discussed the discriminatory effect of federal drug sentencing laws, was not relevant to an allegation of discrimination in decisions to prosecute. Respondents' affidavits, which recounted one attorney's conversation with a drug treatment center employee and the experience of another attorney defending drug prosecutions in state court, recounted hearsay and reported personal conclusions based on anecdotal evidence. The judgment of the Court of Appeals is therefore reversed, and the case is remanded for proceedings consistent with this opinion.

*It is so ordered.*

Professional Conduct. The two are similar, and every state has adopted some form of these rules. Ethical violations may result in discipline by the bar, an offended court, or both. Common sanctions include private and public reprimands, suspension, and disbarment. Under court rules and rules of procedure, other sanctions, such as monetary penalties, may be assessed. Also, all courts possess the authority to punish for contempt.

Prosecutors have special ethical responsibilities. You have already learned that the mission of the prosecutor is to achieve justice. The Model Code of Professional Responsibility states that the "responsibility of a public prosecutor differs from that of the usual advocate; his duty is to seek justice, not merely to convict."[6]

Prosecutors have an ethical obligation to be sure that a prosecution is warranted and to seek dismissal immediately upon discovering that one is not. Prosecutors are not to trump up charges to increase their power during plea negotiations. Prosecutors are only to request a fair sentence from a court. Of course, prosecutors may not use perjured or falsified evidence to obtain a conviction. In addition, you will learn later in this text that prosecutors have a constitutional duty to disclose exculpatory evidence.[7] Evidence that mitigates the degree of an offense or reduces a sentence must also be disclosed.[8] Further, prosecutors are not to avoid pursuing evidence because it may damage the government's case or assist the defendant.[9] Through discovery rules, prosecutors have a duty to disclose other evidence prior to or during trial. In short, prosecutors have an obligation to deal with defendants fairly.

On the other side, prosecutors have an obligation to pursue a prosecution when the facts of the case demand it. At trial, unless a prosecutor becomes convinced that the accused is innocent, the prosecutor is to zealously pursue a conviction.

Government officials, including law enforcement officers, prosecutors, and judges, are not above the law. Violation of an individual's rights by an official, even if during the performance of official duties, may lead to civil and criminal liability.[10] It is not in society's best interest, however, to create an environment where officials are threatened with civil or criminal liability for every incorrect decision and action, especially when they act in good-faith and after thoughtful consideration of alternatives and repercussions. In such a world, civil authorities would be afraid to act and government would be paralyzed. Therefore, the laws governing liability of government officials are designed to provide remedies only for acts that are outrageous, malicious, shocking, or in clear violation of established rights.

States have laws that may provide remedies to the victims of improper governmental conduct. A police officer who commits an unjustified assault, battery, or false imprisonment may be liable under traditional tort and criminal law theories. These and other actions may lead to civil and criminal liability under state civil rights laws.

In addition, violations of federally secured rights by state or federal officers can result in both civil and criminal prosecutions under federal civil rights statutes, including, as referenced before, civil lawsuits under 42 U.S.C. § 1983.[11] This law enables people to sue individuals acting under "color of state law" for violations of civil rights. Only individuals, not states, may be sued and only when the defendant has acted under the law of the state or local government. This clearly includes all state and local police when they are performing their duties. It doesn't include federal officials or the federal government, although Congress has, through other law, opened a small window of liability for federal officer misconduct. The federal government can be held liable for a battery, assault, false imprisonment, false arrest, and malicious prosecution by its officers.

The civil liability of officials is limited by immunity doctrines. Immunities developed at common law, and the U.S. Supreme Court has determined that Congress did not intend to abolish these immunities when it enacted the civil rights acts.[12] Therefore, governmental officials may assert immunity as a defense if sued under the federal civil rights statutes. Returning to Section 1983 specifically, the Supreme Court has interpreted the statute to create a qualified immunity for officers. Under the *qualified immunity doctrine*, Section 1983 liability is limited to instances when a *clearly established right* has been violated. The standard has been narrowly construed by lower courts, making it very difficult for civil rights victims to be successful. Recent concerns about police use of force, particularly in regards to racial minorities, have brought the qualified immunity standard out of the legal shadows and into the public consciousness. In early 2021, federal legislation was enacted that abolished the long-standing qualified immunity standard. A few courts have also begun interpreting qualified immunity is a less rigid way, making police liability more likely than in years past.

As is true of police, prosecutors who violate civil rights may be liable under federal law,[13] or a similar state law, or under a state tort theory. In fewer instances, judges may also be liable for their actions. Judges are protected by an even heartier immunity than police or prosecutors. Any action that is judicial in nature is shielded by *absolute immunity*. Because it is absolute, a government official is free from both suit and liability when performing judicial functions. Issuing orders (including warrants) and presiding over hearings are examples of judicial acts.

Most judicial acts are performed by judges, but not all. Prosecutors perform quasi-judicial acts and are shielded with absolute immunity for the performance of these acts. Appearing in court (including ex parte warrant application hearings) and complying with court orders are considered quasi-judicial acts. The Supreme Court has held that this immunity extends to the supervisory and training functions of prosecutors when the functions in question are intimately associated with the judicial phase of a case.[14] So, failure to supervise or properly train junior prosecutors in trial rules is immunized conduct. Other, more administrative conduct, such as recruitment, hiring, and awarding contracts, is not shielded. Similar to prosecutors, police officers are shielded with absolute immunity when enforcing court orders (including warrants) and when testifying in court but not when performing nonjudicial tasks.

In other situations, another form of immunity may apply. A person entitled to *qualified immunity* is free from liability but not necessarily free from suit. That means that the process of establishing nonliability may involve a greater commitment of time, energy, and money by a defendant. Under absolute immunity, issues of malice, intent, or the nature of the right alleged to be violated are immaterial, because the defendant is immune regardless. In contrast, whether an official acted with malice or whether the alleged right violated was clearly established at law are material in the qualified immunity case. Under some laws, an official is liable only if malice is shown, or, as required by federal law, a plaintiff can prove that a clearly established right was violated.

So, under federal law, although prosecutors are absolutely immune from civil liability for quasi-judicial acts, such as appearing in court and filing charges, they enjoy only a qualified immunity when performing other acts, such as rendering legal advice to law enforcement officers.[15] Similarly, judges are protected by qualified immunity when performing nonjudicial but work-related functions, such as making personnel decisions.[16] Police officers are shielded by qualified immunity when conducting investigations, making warrantless searches or seizures, and engaging in administrative and personnel matters.

Finally, the government itself may be sued in some circumstances. A serious obstacle, which must be overcome to establish governmental liability, is **sovereign immunity.** The doctrine of sovereign immunity holds that the government is immune from lawsuits. Therefore, governments must consent to be sued. This is true of both state and federal governments. Most states have abolished sovereign immunity to some degree, some by statute, and a few by judicial decision.

The federal government has consented to be sued under several laws. Through the Federal Tort Claims Act,[17] the United States has waived immunity from suit for a number of torts. In 1974, the statute was amended to permit suits based upon assault, battery, false imprisonment, false arrest, abuse of process, or malicious prosecution committed by federal law enforcement officers.

States may not be sued directly under federal civil rights statutes, nor may the federal government. However, local forms of government may be sued under federal civil rights laws if the acts alleged to have violated the plaintiff's civil rights were committed pursuant to an ordinance, regulation, policy, or decision of the locality.[18]

**sovereign immunity**
The government's freedom from being sued. In many cases, the U.S. government has waived immunity by a statute such as the Federal Tort Claims Act; states have similar laws.

## Judges

Judges are not executive branch officials, as are prosecutors and law enforcement officers. Judges are part of the judiciary, a separate and independent branch of government. Generally, the judiciary is responsible for the resolution of disputes and the administration of justice. In regard to criminal law, judges are responsible for issuing warrants, supervising pretrial activity, presiding over hearings and trial, deciding guilt or innocence in some cases, and passing sentence on those convicted.

A judge has the obligation to remain unbiased, fair, and impartial in all cases before the bar.

## Ethics

Like attorneys, judges are subject to a code of ethics. Most states have enacted the Code of Judicial Conduct. Judges are to be fair and impartial.[19] In criminal cases, judges must be sensitive to defendants' rights and be careful not to imply to a jury that a defendant is guilty.

# Defense Attorneys

Because of the complexity of the legal system and the advantage of having an advocate, competent legal counsel has become an important feature of the American system of criminal justice. The Sixth Amendment to the Constitution provides that all persons have a right to be represented by counsel in criminal cases. Today, indigent defendants have a right to counsel in all cases that may result in incarceration. Counsel for indigent defendants may be appointed from the private bar or, as is the case in most jurisdictions, a public defender will be assigned. Public defenders are provided to defendants at no cost. Regarding professional responsibility, defense counsel—whether a paid private defender or a public defender—owes his or her client the same loyalty and zeal in representation.

## Ethics

Defense attorneys have high, and sometimes morally challenging, ethical responsibilities. Unlike the prosecutor, whose duty is to see that justice is achieved, the defense attorney must zealously represent the accused, within the bounds of the law,[20] regardless of innocence or guilt.

This obligation is the cause of some public disrespect for the legal profession. Attorneys are perceived as hired guns, not as advocates of civil liberties. Defense lawyers are frequently asked how they can defend people they know are guilty. There are two responses to this inquiry. First, defense attorneys often do not know whether their clients are in fact guilty, as this question is rarely asked. Second, defense attorneys are not defending the actions that the defendant is accused of committing; rather, defense attorneys are defending the rights of the accused, specifically, the right to have the government prove its case beyond a reasonable doubt using lawfully obtained evidence. In defending the rights of one person against governmental oppression, the rights of all the people are defended.

This approach, which is a vital part of the U.S. criminal justice system, is often misunderstood by the public. The defense attorney who fulfills this constitutional and ethical mission is often the source of public animosity and ridicule.

Communications between attorneys and clients are confidential and privileged. Attorneys are generally prohibited from disclosing those communications.[21] In the *Belge* case, found in your next Oyez, an attorney was indicted for not revealing a client's privileged communication and was the subject of considerable public disdain. The indictment was dismissed in the interests of justice, namely, preservation of the attorney-client privilege. However, the court could do nothing to restore the attorney's good reputation and standing in his community.

*Belge* turned on the fact that the crimes had already occurred and the defendant posed no threat. An attorney is allowed, but not required, to report a client's intention to commit a crime.[22] Therefore, if a client informs his counsel that he intends to kill a witness if he is released on bond, the attorney may disclose this information without breaching any ethical obligations.

## Oyez

### People v. Belge
### 372 N.Y.S.2d 798 (1975)

**Ormand N. Gale, J.**

In the summer of 1973 Robert F. Garrow, Jr. stood charged in Hamilton County with the crime of murder. The defendant was assigned two attorneys, Frank H. Armani and Francis R. Belge. A defense of insanity had been interposed by counsel for Mr. Garrow. During the course of the discussions between Garrow and his two counsel, three other murders were admitted by Garrow, one being in Onondaga County. On or about September of 1973 Mr. Belge conducted his own investigation based upon what his client had told him and with the assistance of a friend the location of the body of Alicia Hauck was found in Oakwood Cemetery in Syracuse. Mr. Belge personally inspected the body and was satisfied, presumably, that this was Alicia Hauck that his client had told him he murdered.

This discovery was not disclosed to the authorities, but became public during the trial of Mr. Garrow in June of 1974, when, to affirmatively establish the defense of insanity, these three other murders were brought before the jury by the defense in the Hamilton County trial. Public indignation reached the fever pitch; statements were made by the District Attorney of Onondaga County relative to the situation and he caused the Grand Jury of Onondaga County, then sitting, to conduct a thorough investigation. As a result of this investigation Frank Armani was No Billed by the Grand Jury, but [an i]ndictment . . . was returned against Francis R. Belge, Esq., accusing him of having violated [the public health law], which, in essence, requires that a decent burial be accorded the dead, and . . . requires anyone knowing of the death of a person without medical attendance, to report the same to the proper authorities. Defense counsel moved for dismissal of the Indictment on the grounds that a confidential, privileged communication existed between him and Mr. Garrow, which should excuse the attorney from making full disclosure to the authorities. The National Association of Criminal Defense Lawyers, as Amicus Curiae . . . succinctly stated the issue in the following language:

> "If this indictment stands, the attorney-client privilege will be effectively destroyed. No defendant will be able to freely discuss the facts of his case with his attorney. No attorney will be able to listen to those facts without being faced with the Hobson's choice of violating the law or violating his professional code of Ethics."

Initially in England the practice of law was not recognized as a profession and certainly some people are skeptics today. However, the practice of learned and capable men appearing before the Court on behalf of a friend or an acquaintance became more and more demanding. Consequently, the King granted a privilege to certain of these men to engage in such practice. There had to be rules governing their duties. These came to be known as "Canons." The King has, in this country, been substituted by a democracy, but the "Canons" are with us today, having been honed and refined over the years to meet the changes of time. Most are constantly being studied and revamped by the American Bar Association and by the bar associations of the various states. While they are, for the most part, general by definition, they can be brought to bear in a particular situation. Among those is the [rule that] confidential communications between an attorney and his client are privileged from disclosure . . . as a rule of necessity in the administration of justice. . . .

The effectiveness of counsel is only as great as the confidentiality of its client-attorney relationship. If the lawyer cannot get all the facts about the case, he can only give his client half of a defense. . . .

When the facts of the other homicides became public, as a result of the defendant's testimony to substantiate his claim of insanity, "Members of the public were shocked at the apparent callousness of these lawyers with the public interest and with simple decency." A hue and cry went up from the press and other news media suggesting that the attorneys should be found guilty of such crimes as obstruction of justice or becoming an accomplice after the fact. From a layman's standpoint, this certainly was a logical conclusion. However, the constitution of the United States of America attempts to preserve the dignity of the individual and to do that guarantees him the services of an attorney who will bring to the bar and to the bench every conceivable protection from the inroads of the state against such rights as are vested in the constitution for one accused of a crime. Among those substantial constitutional rights is that a defendant does not have to incriminate himself. His attorneys were bound to uphold that concept and maintain what has been called a sacred trust of confidentiality.

The following language of the brief of the Amicus Curiae further points up the statements just made: "The client's Fifth Amendment rights cannot be violated by his attorney. . . . Because the discovery of the body of Alicia Hauck would have presented 'a significant link in the chain of evidence tending to establish his guilt' . . . Garrow was constitutionally exempt from any statutory requirement to disclose the location of the body. And Attorney Belge, as Garrow's attorney, was not only equally exempt, but under a positive stricture precluding such disclosure. Garrow, although constitutionally privileged against a requirement to compulsory disclosure, was free to make such a revelation if he chose to do so. Attorney Belge was affirmatively required to withhold disclosure. The criminal defendant's self-incrimination rights become completely nugatory if compulsory disclosure can be exacted through his attorney." . . .

It is the decision of this Court that Francis R. Belge conducted himself as an officer of the Court with all the zeal at his command to protect the constitutional rights of his client. Both on the grounds of a privileged communication and the interests of justice the Indictment is dismissed.[22]

Attorneys are generally obligated to represent criminal defendants when appointed by a court or upon request by a bar association. However, an attorney may be excused for compelling reasons. In no event is belief in a defendant's guilt or disgust with the alleged acts compelling.[23]

An interesting ethical dilemma is presented when a defense attorney knows (or has a strong belief) that either the client or one of the defense witnesses has given or intends to give false testimony. On the one hand, the attorney is an officer of the court and thus prohibited from defrauding the court. On the other hand, the defense attorney has an obligation to the client. There is a split in the jurisdictions concerning how this situation is to be handled. There are three possibilities. First, the most preferable, the defense attorney dissuades the client from committing perjury. Second, the attorney moves to withdraw from the case, keeping the reason secret. Third, the attorney discloses the client's intention to commit perjury to the court. The law in each jurisdiction must be examined to determine which of these options is permitted or preferred.

Defense attorneys are sometimes asked to represent codefendants. This can create a conflict of interest for a defense attorney if the defendants have conflicting or antagonistic defenses. Because of the inherent dangers of representing codefendants, many defense attorneys refuse joint representation. It is a violation of a defendant's Sixth Amendment right to the assistance of effective counsel to have a lawyer with divided loyalties.

Finally, trial counsel for criminal defendants have an obligation to continue on appeal unless new counsel is retained or the court has authorized withdrawal. This is different from civil cases, where there is no general obligation to continue after trial.

## Legal Assistants

Legal assistants are employed by both prosecutors and defense attorneys, with the latter being more common.[24] In the defense context, legal assistants may be asked to perform several tasks, including conducting initial interviews, conducting legal research, preparing drafts of motions and other documents, maintaining and organizing files, acting as a contact with incarcerated clients, assisting in preparing the defendant and other witnesses for trial, and preparing the defendant for the presentence investigation interview. Some paralegals are called upon to conduct investigations.

As employees of attorneys, legal assistants must also follow ethical guidelines and responsibilities. Although no state has yet established mandatory certification of legal assistants, and therefore there is no enforceable set of ethics rules, the National Federation of Paralegal Organizations and the National Association of Legal Assistants (NALA) have promulgated codes of ethics.

The NALA Code states that, first, legal assistants may not engage in the practice of law.[25] This includes rendering legal advice, establishing an attorney-client relationship, setting fees, and appearing in court on behalf of a client. Although some administrative agencies permit legal assistants to represent clients at hearings, this is never so in criminal law. The unauthorized practice of law is both criminal and unethical. Further, legal assistants are to act prudently in determining the extent to which a client may be assisted without the presence of a lawyer.[26] Finally, it is imperative that the attorney directly supervise the legal assistant's work in criminal law.[27]

Second, all employees of an attorney are bound by the confidentiality rule.[28] All communications made by a client to a legal assistant fall within the scope of the attorney-client privilege and may not be disclosed by the legal assistant.

Third, legal assistants must be careful not to suborn perjury when preparing the client and witnesses for trial. Instructing a witness in effective techniques, including dress and personal appearance, and methods of responding to inquiries (e.g., answer directly, honestly, and as succinctly as possible; look at the jury during your response) is proper. Suggesting, urging, encouraging, or directing a witness to lie or mislead a court is suborning perjury.

Fourth, legal assistants are bound through their attorney-supervisors by the American Bar Association's Model Rules of Professional Conduct and Model Code of Professional Responsibility.[29]

## Victims

Recall that the legal victim of a crime is the government. That is why criminal prosecutions are brought in the name of the government. However, most crimes have another victim, the victim-in-fact. This is the person assaulted, battered, raped, or robbed. Victims affect criminal adjudications in a number of ways.

First, law enforcement officers may decline to make an arrest or conduct an investigation if the victim is disinterested in having the matter pursued. Second, the prosecutor may file a nolle prosequi, if there has been an arrest, or otherwise refuse to proceed with a prosecution if that is the victim's desire. Third, if the matter proceeds to trial, the victim may be required to testify at both pretrial hearings and trial. A victim may choose to attend even if his or her testimony is not required. Fourth, the victim may participate in the sentencing portion of the trial. As you will learn, statements concerning how a victim and a victim's family have been affected may be considered by the judge and jury when passing sentence. Restitution is also made a condition of some sentences.

Victims' rights have received considerable attention since the mid-1980s. Victims' rights organizations have strenuously—and successfully—lobbied to introduce both state constitutional amendments and legislation concerning victims' rights. For example, the Arizona Constitution was amended to include a Victims' Bill of Rights. Through that amendment and its enabling legislation, crime victims are allowed to participate in the initial appearance, be heard on conditions of release, be present at all court proceedings, confer with the prosecutor concerning disposition of the case, refuse a defense interview or other discovery request, provide an impact statement for sentencing, receive restitution and other damages, receive notice of probation modifications of the perpetrator, and receive notice of the parole or death of the perpetrator.[30]

Rape shield legislation is another form of victims' rights laws. Rape shield laws exclude from trial evidence of a rape victim's sexual history (except evidence of sexual history with the accused) and reputation in the community. These laws were enacted to protect the rape victim from embarrassing, harassing, and intimidating inquiries that don't materially add to a jury's understanding of the facts of the case.

In most jurisdictions, victims' rights are a matter of statutory, not constitutional, law. Change came quickly in this area. In 1982, only 4 states had victims' bills of rights. That number increased to 44 by 1987, and today, all 50 states and the federal government have victims' rights laws. Similarly, **victim impact statements**, once constitutionally forbidden, are now permitted at sentencings in a majority of states.[31]

In addition to laws providing for victim participation in court proceedings, laws have been enacted for the protection of both victims and witnesses. These laws provide for the relocation of a witness or victim whose cooperation with an investigation or prosecution endangers his or her life. The federal law is well known. It provides for relocation of the victim or witness and his or her immediate family at taxpayer expense. Further, the United States provides the family with a new identity.[32]

**victim impact statement**
At the time of sentencing, a statement made to the court concerning the effect the crime has had on the victim or on the victim's family.

Victims are likely to have civil remedies against perpetrators under traditional civil law theories. Intentional tort actions for assault, battery, invasion of privacy, and conversion are examples.

Finally, *victim assistance organizations* are available in many jurisdictions. Some are independent, not-for-profit corporations, and others are governmental entities. These organizations provide information, counseling, and other assistance to victims. Also, most states have enacted *victim compensation programs*. In many instances, restitution proves inadequate, such as when the perpetrator is indigent. In these instances, a victim can request compensation from a state victim compensation fund. These programs reimburse victims for medical expenses and, sometimes, loss of income. Generally, they do not compensate victims for property losses.

---

## Ethical Considerations

### Attorney Compensation

Generally, attorneys get paid in one of several different ways. Salary, hourly, fixed, contingency, and court ordered are the most common methods. The first, salary, is common in corporations, not-for-profit, public service, and government settings. The attorney is hired, full- or part-time, and is paid salary and benefits regardless of time invested or success. The second, hourly, is common in simple transaction cases, such as negotiating a contract or drafting a legal document. It is also common when attorneys provide single-visit or transaction legal advice. Attorneys bill hours differently. Some record every minute of time spent on a case. This includes research, writing, investigation, and time with the client (including e-mail, telephone, or fax). Clients who pay hourly are often asked to provide a deposit, known as a retainer, from which the attorney draws compensation and expenses. Regardless of the form of compensation, clients typically are responsible for expenses. These include filing fees, discovery costs, exhibit production expenses, and other non-attorney expenses.

Fixed fees are often offered for classes of cases where an attorney has considerable experience and can predict the total time investment. A simple divorce case and the drafting of a will are examples. Fixed fee arrangements typically do not include expenses. So, the client will pay both the fixed fee and the expenses of litigation.

Attorneys may, in certain cases, accept contingency payment. Under a contingency fee arrangement, the attorney is paid only if there is a recovery. In most cases, the fee equals a percentage of the total recovery. Many states limit the percentage an attorney may recover, and that amount varies by the size of the recovery and the effort of the attorney. In some states, for example, the contingency fee increases as a case proceeds through litigation (pretrial, trial, appeal). With a few exceptions, clients remain responsible for litigation expenses. Contingency fee arrangements are beneficial to low-income clients who might not otherwise be able to prosecute legitimate claims.

The final form of payment is the statutorily ordered payment. In specific types of cases, such as some federal civil rights cases, the law requires losing defendants to pay the attorney's fees and costs of prevailing plaintiffs. In such cases, the court hearing the case determines the amount owed and issues an order for payment. While losing parties in some other nations are expected to pay the attorneys' fees and litigation expenses of their opponents, this is not the norm in the United States, where each party is expected to pay his or her own fees. This deviation from the American rule exists to encourage civil rights clients who could not otherwise afford to prosecute their cases, either because they lack the resources to hire an attorney or because the recovery is expected to be less than attorneys' fees and costs, to seek relief.

In criminal cases, contingency fee arrangements are not allowed. Instead, clients typically pay hourly or fixed fees. Attorneys in the United States have long provided free services, known as pro bono, to low-income clients. This is done in criminal as well as civil cases.

---

## Key Terms

| | | |
|---|---|---|
| accusatorial | factual guilt | rule of Lenity |
| adversarial | inquisitorial system | sovereign immunity |
| adversary system | legal guilt | victim impact statements |
| discretion | nolle prosequi | |

# Review Questions

1. What is the constitutional mission of a prosecutor?

2. What is the policy behind requiring defense attorneys to zealously represent guilty persons?

3. What is the attorney-client privilege?

4. Legal assistants and other nonlawyers are prohibited from practicing law. What acts constitute the practice of law?

5. Are legal assistants who are employed in law offices obligated to maintain client confidences?

6. What are victims' bills of rights? Name three rights typically included in such a law.

7. According to the Police Code of Conduct promulgated by the International Association of Chiefs of Police, when may force be used?

8. What do U.S.C. and Fed. R. Crim. P. represent?

# Problems & Critical Thinking Exercises

1. Create a set of facts under which codefendants could not be represented by the same attorney. Explain why separate counsel is necessary under your scenario.

2. Do you believe that a defense attorney should be required to zealously represent a client who has admitted guilt to the lawyer? What if the result is the release of a violent criminal (i.e., acquittal or dismissal of charges)? Can you suggest an alternative method?

3. Do you believe that police officers should arrest every violator they encounter, discover, or are made aware of? Support your answer. What factors should an officer consider when deciding whether to arrest or otherwise pursue a prosecution?

4. In some nations, prosecutors are required to file a criminal charge if sufficient evidence exists. What are the advantages of such a system? What are the disadvantages of such a system? Should this form of compulsory prosecution replace the U.S. model of prosecutorial discretion? Explain your answer.

5. In some nations, individual victims are permitted to file a criminal charge against the person(s) who committed the alleged act(s). In these nations, the victim may prosecute the case or a public prosecutor may prosecute on the victim's behalf. Should such a method be employed in the United States? Explain your answer.

# Endnotes

1. Herbert L. Packer, Two Models of the Criminal Justice Process, 113 U. Pa. L. Rev. 1 (1964).

2. For more information concerning the due process and crime control models, *see* N. Gary Holten & Lawson Lamar, *The Criminal Courts,* ch. 1 (New York: McGraw-Hill, 1991).

3. Bureau of Justice Statistics, Bulletin: *Federal Law Enforcement Officers,* 2004 (2006).

4. Fed. R. Crim. P. 48.

5. 368 U.S. 448 (1962).

6. Ethical Consideration (EC) 7-13.

7. *Id. See also Brady v. Maryland,* 373 U.S. 83 (1963).

8. Model Code of Professional Responsibility, Disciplinary Rule (DR) 7-103.

9. EC 7-13.

10. For a more thorough discussion of governmental liability, including the liability of government officials, *see* Daniel E. Hall, *Administrative Law: Bureaucracy in Democracy,* 7th ed. (Upper Saddle River, NJ: Pearson Prentice Hall, 2020).

11. *See* 42 U.S.C. § 1983; 18 U.S.C. § 241 *et seq.*

12. *See Burns v. Reed*, 111 S. Ct. 1934 (1991); *Pierson v. Ray*, 386 U.S. 547 (1967).

13. *See* 42 U.S.C. § 1983.

14. *Van de Kamp v. Goldstein*, 555 U.S. 335 (2009).

15. *See* Daniel Hall, supra, Ch. 11.

16. *Id.*

17. 28 U.S.C. §§ 1291, 1346, 1402, 1504, 2110, 2401–2402, 2411–2412, 2671–2678, and 2680.

18. *Monell v. Department of Social Services*, 436 U.S. 658 (1978). *Also see* Hall, *Administrative Law*, ch. 11, *supra*.

19. Code of Judicial Conduct, Canon 3.

20. EC 7-1; DR 7-101.

21. DR 4-101.

22. Model Code of Professional Responsibility, DR 4-101(c)(3); Model Rules of Professional Conduct 1.6(b)(1).

23. The decision was affirmed on appeal. *See* 376 N.Y.S.2d 771 (1975) and 390 N.Y.S.2d 867 (1976).

24. EC 2-29.

25. Approximately 13% of all paralegals in the United States work in criminal law. *See* Angela Schneeman, *Paralegals in American Law* (Lawyers Cooperative) (Albany, NY: Delmar Publishers 1994).

26. NALA Code of Ethics, Canons 1, 3, 4, and 6.

27. *Id.*, Canon 5.

28. *Id.*, Canon 2.

29. *Id.*, Canon 7.

30. *Id.*, Canon 12.

31. Christopher Johns, "Criminal Justice in America—Part One, The Costs of Victims' Rights," 29 *Arizona Attorney* 27 (Oct. 1992).

32. See National Center for Victims of Crime website, policy pages at victimsofcrime.org.

33. Victim and Witness Protection Act, 18 U.S.C. § 224.

# Chapter 11

# The Constitution and Criminal Procedure

## Chapter Objectives

After completing the chapter, you should be able to

- Define incorporation and identify what rights have, and have not, been incorporated.
- Describe how the rights applied in criminal law have expanded since they were adopted.
- Define, describe, and apply the exclusionary rule.

- Define, describe, and apply the fruit of the poisonous tree doctrine.
- Define, describe, and apply the standing doctrine.
- Describe the relationship, particularly the hierarchy, of the U.S. and state constitutions.

## Introduction

As you learned in Chapter 1, criminal justice belongs largely to the states. This is borne out in trial data; nearly 95% of all criminal prosecutions occur in state courts. Not only do the states conduct most criminal prosecutions, but each state is free, with few limitations, to design its criminal justice system in any manner it chooses. This was especially true in the early years of the United States. For the most part, the national government did not involve itself in state criminal law for 150 years.

This situation began to change in the 1950s, with significant changes occurring in the 1960s. Today, the United States plays a major role in defining the rights of criminal defendants in state prosecutions, as well as federal. The source of federal involvement is the U.S. Constitution. These three developments account for its increased role in state criminal law:

1. The reach of the Constitution has been extended to the states through what is known as *incorporation*.
2. The rights found in the Bill of Rights have significantly expanded.
3. The Exclusionary Rule.

Let's examine each of these, beginning with incorporation.

# Incorporation

Learning Objective: Define incorporation and identify what rights have, and have not, been incorporated.

Prior to the adoption of the Fourteenth Amendment, the Bill of Rights and the rights found in the original Constitution applied to the federal government, but not to the states.[1] Consequently, the fundamental rights that contemporary Americans take for granted, such as the right to counsel and the right to be free from unreasonable searches and seizures, were guaranteed to a defendant only when prosecuted in federal court. This meant little since nearly all prosecutions occurred, and continue to occur, in state courts. The protection of liberty was left to the states. And indeed, state constitutions and statutory law protected many rights. But the treatment of liberty varied between the states.

In 1868, the Fourteenth Amendment to the U.S. Constitution was adopted. One objective of the Fourteenth Amendment is to limit the authority of the states by protecting liberties that the Constitution previously only protected at the federal level. Section One of that amendment reads:

> All persons born or naturalized in the United States, and subject to the jurisdiction thereof, are citizens of the United States and of the State wherein they reside. No State shall make or enforce any law which shall abridge the privileges or immunities of citizens of the United States; nor shall any State deprive any person of life, liberty, or property, without due process of law; nor deny to any person within its jurisdiction the equal protection of the laws.

The language of the Fourteenth Amendment is similar to that found in the Fifth Amendment, insofar as they both contain a Due Process Clause. It is through the Due Process Clause and the Equal Protection Clause that the powers of the states are limited. However, what is meant by *due process* has been the subject of great debate.

Note that the language of the Fourteenth Amendment does not include any of the specific guarantees found in the Bill of Rights, except that it requires the states to afford due process whenever depriving a person of life, liberty, or property. Thus, one of the most important issues raised in the context of the Fourteenth Amendment is whether it includes the rights found in the Bill of Rights, such as the rights to counsel, to freedom of the press, to freedom of speech, to be free from self-incrimination, to be free of unreasonable searches and seizures, and to be free from cruel and unusual punishments, to trial by jury, and so on.

Today, the idea that the Fourteenth Amendment is a vehicle for the application of the Bill of Rights against the states is known as Incorporation. Eleven years after the adoption of the Fourteenth Amendment, the Supreme Court answered the incorporation question in the negative.[2] But the Court slowly changed its position. The first right to be incorporated was the Fifth Amendment's Takings Clause, in 1897.[3] The first application of incorporation in a criminal case occurred in 1925.[4]

In the years that followed, several theories concerning which rights applied to the states developed.

At one extreme is the *independent content approach*. Under this theory, the Fourteenth Amendment's Due Process Clause does not include any right found in the Bill of Rights; that is, due process does not overlap with the Bill of Rights. Rather, due process has an independent content, and none of the rights secured in the Bill of Rights apply against the states. The Supreme Court has never adopted this position.

At the other extreme is *total incorporation*. Proponents of total incorporation, who included Supreme Court Associate Justice Black, argue that the entire Bill of Rights is incorporated by the Fourteenth Amendment and that all the rights contained therein may be asserted by defendants in both state and federal courts. The incorporation occurs automatically, as the proponents of this position believe that the drafters of the Fourteenth Amendment intended to incorporate the entire Bill of Rights. Under this approach, however, the Due Process Clause was limited to recognizing rights contained in the Bill of Rights. Another group of jurists have been labeled *total incorporation plus,* because they suggest that the Due Process Clause not only incorporates the Bill of Rights but also secures additional independent rights. Neither of these positions has been adopted by the Supreme Court.

Another position, which was held by the Supreme Court until the 1960s, is known as *fundamental fairness.* Those rights that are "fundamental" and "essential to an ordered liberty" are incorporated through this approach. The fundamental fairness doctrine held that no relationship existed between the Bill of Rights and those deemed fundamental, although the rights recognized under the fundamental fairness doctrine may parallel rights recognized by the Bill of Rights.

The Supreme Court rejected the fundamental fairness doctrine in the 1960s and replaced it with the *selective incorporation doctrine.* Similar to the fundamental fairness doctrine, a right is incorporated under this doctrine if it is both fundamental and essential to the concept of ordered liberty. Like the fundamental fairness approach, independent rights are also recognized under selective incorporation analysis.

However, the two approaches differ in two major respects. First, under the fundamental fairness approach, cases were analyzed case by case. That is, it was possible to have essentially the same facts with different outcomes under the fundamental fairness doctrine. Critics charged that the approach was too subjective. Under the selective incorporation method, blanket rules are established to act as precedent for all similar cases in the future. In addition, the entire body of precedent interpreting a federal amendment becomes applicable to the states as a result of an amendment's incorporation. Exhibit 11–1 illustrates the incorporation process.

Second, selective incorporation gives special attention to the rights contained in the Bill of Rights. A right secured by the Bill of Rights is more likely to be protected by the Fourteenth Amendment's Due Process Clause than are other rights.

Nearly the entire Bill of Rights has been incorporated under the selective incorporation doctrine. The right to grand jury indictment has not been incorporated,[5] nor has the right to a jury trial in civil cases, nor the Eighth Amendment's right to be free from excessive bail. The right to bear arms was incorporated in 2010 and the Eighth Amendment's right to be free of excessive fines was extended to the states in 2019. The most recent right to be incorporated is a "sub right" of the Sixth Amendment's jury trial right. In the 2020 decision in *Ramos v. Louisiana*, the Court decided that convictions must be made by unanimous verdicts, overturning the laws of two states that permitted as few as 10 of 12 jurors to convict. The Court had previously held that juror unanimity was required in federal courts.

Exhibit 11–2 contains a chart of rights that have been incorporated.[6] Once incorporated, a right applies against the states to the extent and in the same manner as it does against the United States. Also, several independent due process rights have been declared. You will learn many of these in the following chapters.

## Exhibit 11–1 Incorporation Process

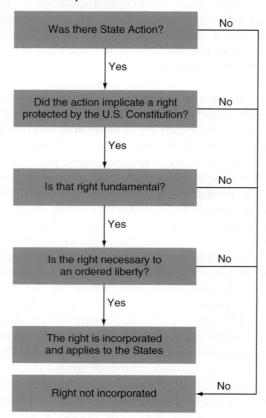

**Incorporation Process**

Was there State Action? — No

Yes ↓

Did the action implicate a right protected by the U.S. Constitution? — No

Yes ↓

Is that right fundamental? — No

Yes ↓

Is the right necessary to an ordered liberty? — No

Yes ↓

The right is incorporated and applies to the States

Right not incorporated — No

# Expansion of Rights

Learning Objective: Describe how the rights applied in criminal law have expanded since they were adopted.

Another major development in criminal procedure has been the expansion of many rights. The language of the Constitution is concise. It refers to "unreasonable searches and seizures," "due process," "equal protection," "speedy and public trial," and so on. The Constitution offers no further understanding of these provisions. But courts have to apply them in the criminal cases they hear. The process of determining their meaning is referred to as *constitutional interpretation*. It is possible to make each right ineffective by reading it narrowly. The opposite is also true.

Many rights were expanded by the Supreme Court during the 1960s under the leadership of Chief Justice Earl Warren, a period known as the "Warren Court." *Expansion* refers to extending a right beyond its narrowest reading. The effect of expansive interpretation is to increase defendants' rights. An example of an expansive interpretation is the *Miranda v. Arizona* decision, 384 U.S. 436 (1966). Although the language of the Fifth Amendment does not explicitly state that a defendant must be advised of the right to remain silent or to have the assistance of counsel, and so forth, the Court now requires that such admonishments be given because of an expanded interpretation of the Fifth Amendment.

## Exhibit 11–2 The Bill of Rights and Incorporation

| Right | Status |
|---|---|
| First Amendment speech | Incorporated in *Gitlow v. New York, 268 U.S. 652* (1925) |
| First Amendment—religion | Incorporated in *Everson v. Board of Education,* 330 *U.S. 1* (1947) and *Cantwell v. Connecticut,* 310 *U.S. 296* (1940) |
| First Amendment press | Incorporated in *Near v. Minnesota,* 283 *U.S. 697* (1931) |
| First Amendment assembly | Incorporated in *DeJonge v. Oregon,* 299 *U.S. 353* (1937) |
| First Amendment grievances | Incorporated in *Edwards v. South Carolina,* 372 U.S. 229 (1963) |
| Second Amendment—arms | Incorporated in *McDonald v. Chicago,* 561 U.S.3025 *(2010)* |
| Third Amendment | Not incorporated (lower courts have held that it is incorporated) |
| Fourth Amendment | Incorporated. Different requirements incorporated through several cases, including *Mapp v. Ohio,* 367 *U.S. 643* (1961) |
| Fifth Amendment—grand jury | Not incorporated |
| Fifth Amendment—self incrimination | Incorporated in *Malloy v. Hogan,* 378 *U.S. 1* (1964) |
| Fifth Amendment—double jeopardy | Incorporated in *Benton v. Maryland,* 395 *U.S. 784* (1969) |
| Fifth Amendment takings | Incorporated in *Chicago, Burlington & Quincy Railroad Co. v. City of Chicago,* 166 U.S. 226 (1897) |
| Fifth Amendment—due process | Fourteenth Amendment contains due process clause |
| Sixth Amendment—counsel | Incorporated in *Gideon v. Wainwright,* 372 *U.S. 335* (1963) |
| Sixth Amendment—public trial | Incorporated in *In re Oliver,* 333 *U.S. 257* (1948) |
| Sixth Amendment—jury trial | Incorporated in several cases upholding right to impartial jury, unanimous jury verdict, etc. |
| Sixth Amendment—speedy trial | Incorporated in *Klopfer v. North Carolina,* 386 *U.S. 213* (1967) |
| Sixth Amendment—confront accusers | Incorporated in *Pointer v. Texas,* 380 *U.S. 400* (1965) |
| Sixth Amendment—compulsory process | Incorporated in *Washington v. Texas,* 388 U.S. 14 (1967) |
| Sixth Amendment—notice of charge | Incorporated in *In re Oliver,* 333 U.S. 257 (1947) |
| Seventh Amendment | Not incorporated |
| Eighth Amendment—cruel punishments | Incorporated in *Robinson v. California,* 370 *U.S. 660* (1962) |
| Eighth Amendment—excessive bail<br>Eighth Amendment – excessive fines | Not incorporated (dicta in Supreme Court opinions indicate that it will be if the Court hears the issue)<br>Incorporated in *Timbs v. Indiana,* 586 U.S. __ (2019) |
| Ninth Amendment | Has never been used by Supreme Court to establish a right, although it has been cited as support for incorporated, unenumerated rights |
| Tenth Amendment | Not applicable |

Another example of a right that has grown considerably is the right to counsel. It has grown from applying in only a few cases to nearly every criminal case in the Nation. Exhibit 11–3 graphs the growth of the federal right to counsel from the adoption of the Bill of Rights until today.

As you learned earlier, the Framers didn't explicitly protect privacy. However, the Supreme Court has found a right to privacy to be implicit in the Constitution. The Court has held that the right to privacy protects a woman's right to abortion, in some circumstances,[7] a couple's right to use contraceptives,[8] the right to interracial marriage, and more. Many more expansions will be discussed later.

## Exhibit 11-3 The Evolution of the Federal Right to Counsel

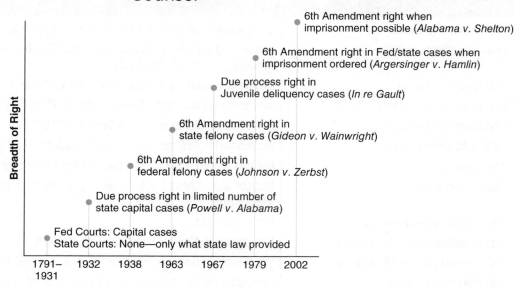

Breadth of Right

- 6th Amendment right when imprisonment possible (*Alabama v. Shelton*)
- 6th Amendment right in Fed/state cases when imprisonment ordered (*Argersinger v. Hamlin*)
- Due process right in Juvenile deliquency cases (*In re Gault*)
- 6th Amendment right in state felony cases (*Gideon v. Wainwright*)
- 6th Amendment right in federal felony cases (*Johnson v. Zerbst*)
- Due process right in limited number of state capital cases (*Powell v. Alabama*)
- Fed Courts: Capital cases
  State Courts: None—only what state law provided

1791–1931   1932   1938   1963   1967   1979   2002

## Exclusionary Rule

Learning Objective: Define, describe, and apply the exclusionary rule.

Another important constitutional development was the creation of the **Exclusionary Rule.** The rule is simple: Evidence that is obtained by an unconstitutional search or seizure is inadmissible at trial.

The rule was first announced by the Supreme Court in 1914.[9] However, at that time the rule had not been incorporated, so the rule did not apply to state court proceedings. This changed in 1961 when the Supreme Court declared that evidence obtained in violation of the Constitution could not be used in state or federal criminal proceedings. The case was *Mapp v. Ohio*, presented in the next Oyez.

There is no explicit textual language establishing the exclusionary rule in the Constitution. For that reason, critics contend that the Supreme Court exceeded its authority by creating it; that it is the responsibility of the legislative branch to make such laws.

On the other hand, the Constitution is silent on what is to happen, if anything, when the government violates the Bill of Rights. The Court rightly points out that it needs a remedy to enforce liberties, lest the Constitution will be reduced to a meaningless sheet of parchment. For example, why require the officers in the *Mapp* case to have a search warrant, yet permit them to conduct a warrantless search and use the evidence obtained against the defendant? These questions go to the purpose of the exclusionary rule: it discourages law enforcement personnel from engaging in unconstitutional conduct. The Court acknowledges the costs of the exclusionary rule; a few guilty may go free because the constable has blundered. This is not only unfair to the truth, it is argued, but potentially dangerous to the public. In reality, as discussed in the sidebar, The Exclusionary Rule in Practice, the exclusion of evidence rarely leads to freedom for offenders.

The Court has been criticized for creating such a rigid, single-remedy approach to police misconduct. In fact, most nations, including those in the Western world who share a legal heritage with the United States, do not employ the Exclusionary Rule.

# Oyez

## Mapp v. Ohio
### 367 U.S. 643 (1961)

**Mr. Justice Clark Delivered the Opinion of the Court.**

Appellant stands convicted of knowingly having had in her possession and under her control certain lewd and lascivious books, pictures, and photographs in violation [of Ohio law]. . . .

On May 23, 1957, three Cleveland police officers arrived at appellant's residence in that city pursuant to information that "a person [was] hiding out in the home, who was wanted for questioning in connection with a recent bombing." . . .

Upon their arrival at that house, the officers knocked on the door and demanded entrance but appellant, after telephoning her attorney, refused to admit them without a search warrant. They advised their headquarters of the situation and undertook a surveillance of the house.

The officers again sought entrance some three hours later when four or more additional officers arrived on the scene. When Miss Mapp did not come to the door immediately, at least one of the several doors to the house was forcibly opened and the policemen gained admittance. Meanwhile Miss Mapp's attorney arrived, but the officers, having secured their own entry, and continuing in their defiance of the law, would permit him neither to see Miss Mapp nor to enter the house. It appears that Miss Mapp was halfway down the stairs from the upper floor to the front door when the officers, in this highhanded manner, broke into the hall. She demanded to see the search warrant. A paper, claimed to be a warrant, was held up by one of the officers. She grabbed the "warrant" and placed it in her bosom. A struggle ensued in which the officers recovered the piece of paper and as a result of which they handcuffed appellant because she had been "belligerent" in resisting their official rescue of the "warrant" from her person. Running roughshod over appellant, a policeman "grabbed" her, "twisted [her] hand," and she "yelled [and] pleaded with him" because "it was hurting." Appellant, in handcuffs, was then forcibly taken upstairs to her bedroom where the officers searched a dresser, a chest of drawers, a closet and some suitcases. They also looked into a photo album and through personal papers belonging to the appellant. The search spread. . . . The obscene materials for possession of which she was ultimately convicted were discovered in the course of that widespread search.

At the trial no search warrant was produced by the prosecution, nor was the failure to produce one explained or accounted for. At best, "There is, in the record, considerable doubt as to whether there ever was any warrant for the search."

We hold that all evidence obtained by searches and seizures in violation of the Constitution is, by that same authority, inadmissible in a state court.

Since the Fourth Amendment's right of privacy has been declared enforceable against the States through the Due Process Clause of the Fourteenth, it is enforceable against them by the same sanction of exclusion as is used against the Federal Government. Were it otherwise, then, just as without the *Weeks* rule the assurance against unreasonable federal searches and seizures would be "a form of words," valueless and undeserving of mention in a perpetual charter of inestimable human liberties, so too, without that rule, the freedom from state invasions of privacy would be so ephemeral and so neatly severed from its conceptual nexus with the freedom from all brutish means of coercing evidence as not to merit this Court's high regard as a freedom "implicit in the concept of ordered liberty." At the time that the Court held in *Wolf* that the Amendment was applicable to the States through the Due Process Clause, the cases of this Court, as we have seen, had steadfastly held that as to federal officers the Fourth Amendment included the exclusion of the evidence seized in violation of its provisions. Even *Wolf* "stoutly adhered" to that proposition. The right to privacy, when conceded operatively enforceable against the States, was not susceptible of destruction by avulsion of the sanction upon which its protection and enjoyment had always been deemed dependent under the *Boyd, Weeks* and *Silverthorne* cases. Therefore, in extending the substantive protections of due process to all constitutionally unreasonable searches—state or federal—it was logically and constitutionally necessary that the exclusion doctrine--an essential part of the right to privacy—be also insisted upon as an essential ingredient of the right newly recognized by the *Wolf* case. In short, the admission of the new constitutional right by *Wolf* could not consistently tolerate denial of its most important constitutional privilege, namely, the exclusion of the evidence which an accused had been forced to give by reason of the unlawful seizure. To hold otherwise is to grant the right but, in reality, to withhold its privilege and enjoyment. Only last year, the Court itself recognized that the purpose of the exclusionary rule "is to deter—to compel respect for the constitutional guaranty in the only effectively available way--by removing the incentive to disregard it."

Indeed, we are aware of no restraint, similar to that rejected today, conditioning the enforcement of any other basic constitutional right. The right to privacy, no less important than any other right carefully and particularly reserved to the people, would stand in marked contrast to all other rights declared as "basic to a free society." *Wolf v. Colorado, supra*, at 27. This Court has not hesitated to enforce as strictly against the States as it does against the Federal Government the rights of free speech and of a free press, the rights to notice and to a fair, public trial, including, as it does, the right not to be convicted by use of a coerced confession, however logically relevant it be, and without regard to its reliability. *Rogers v. Richmond*, 365 U. S. 534 (1961). And nothing could be more certain than that, when a coerced confession is involved, "the relevant rules of evidence" are overridden without regard to "the incidence of such conduct by the

(continued)

police," slight or frequent. Why should not the same rule apply to what is tantamount to coerced testimony by way of unconstitutional seizure of goods, papers, effects, documents, etc.? We find that, as to the Federal Government, the Fourth and Fifth Amendments and, as to the States, the freedom from unconscionable invasions of privacy and the freedom from convictions based upon coerced confessions do enjoy an "intimate relation" in their perpetuation of "principles of humanity and civil liberty [secured] . . . only after years of struggle," They express "supplementing phases of the same constitutional purpose to maintain inviolate large areas of personal privacy." The philosophy of each Amendment and of each freedom is complementary to, although not dependent upon, that of the other in its sphere of influence—the very least that together they assure in either sphere is that no man is to be convicted on unconstitutional evidence.

Moreover, our holding that the exclusionary rule is an essential part of both the Fourth and Fourteenth Amendments is not only the logical dictate of prior cases, but it also makes very good sense. There is no war between the Constitution and common sense. Presently, a federal prosecutor may make no use of evidence illegally seized, but a State's attorney across the street may, although he supposedly is operating under the enforceable prohibitions of the same Amendment. Thus, the State, by admitting evidence unlawfully seized, serves to encourage disobedience to the Federal Constitution which it is bound to uphold.

There are those who say, as did Justice (then Judge) Cardozo, that, under our constitutional exclusionary doctrine, "[t]he criminal is to go free because the constable has blundered." In some cases, this will undoubtedly be the result. But, as was said in *Elkins*, "there is another consideration--the imperative of judicial integrity." The criminal goes free, if he must, but it is the law that sets him free. Nothing can destroy a government more quickly than its failure to observe its own laws, or worse, its disregard of the charter of its own existence. As Mr. Justice Brandeis, dissenting, said in *Olmstead v. United States*: "Our Government is the potent, the omnipresent teacher. For good or for ill, it teaches the whole people by its example. . . . If the Government becomes a lawbreaker, it breeds contempt for law; it invites every man to become a law unto himself; it invites anarchy." Nor can it lightly be assumed that, as a practical matter, adoption of the exclusionary rule fetters law enforcement. Only last year, this Court expressly considered that contention and found that "pragmatic evidence of a sort" to the contrary was not wanting. The Court noted that

"The federal courts themselves have operated under the exclusionary rule of *Weeks* for almost half a century; yet it has not been suggested either that the Federal Bureau of Investigation has thereby been rendered ineffective, or that the administration of criminal justice in the federal courts has thereby been disrupted. Moreover, the experience of the states is impressive. . . . The movement towards the rule of exclusion has been halting, but seemingly inexorable."

The ignoble shortcut to conviction left open to the State tends to destroy the entire system of constitutional restraints on which the liberties of the people rest. Having once recognized that the right to privacy embodied in the Fourth Amendment is enforceable against the States, and that the right to be secure against rude invasions of privacy by state officers is, therefore, constitutional in origin, we can no longer permit that right to remain an empty promise. Because it is enforceable in the same manner and to like effect as other basic rights secured by the Due Process Clause, we can no longer permit it to be revocable at the whim of any police officer who, in the name of law enforcement itself, chooses to suspend its enjoyment. Our decision, founded on reason and truth, gives to the individual no more than that which the Constitution guarantees him, to the police officer no less than that to which honest law enforcement is entitled, and, to the courts, that judicial integrity so necessary in the true administration of justice.

The judgment of the Supreme Court of Ohio is reversed, and the cause remanded for further proceedings not inconsistent with this opinion.

*Reversed and remanded.*

The Warren Court

Bettmann/Getty Images

Instead, they attempt to deter police misconduct in ways that have lesser social expense (e.g., releasing a dangerous individual back into the public as can occur following the suppression of key evidence in the United States). Administrative discipline, civil liability, and personal criminal liability for offending officers are examples of alternatives. Indeed, the Court has begun to soften the exclusionary rule, as evinced in the *Hudson* case.

## Oyez

### Hudson v. Michigan
### 547 U.S. 1096 (2006)

**Justice Scalia delivered the opinion of the Court, except as to Part IV.**

We decide whether violation of the "knock-and- announce" rule requires the suppression of all evidence found in the search.

Police obtained a warrant authorizing a search for drugs and firearms at the home of petitioner Booker Hudson. They discovered both. Large quantities of drugs were found, including cocaine rocks in Hudson's pocket. A loaded gun was lodged between the cushion and armrest of the chair in which he was sitting. Hudson was charged under Michigan law with unlawful drug and firearm possession.

This case is before us only because of the method of entry into the house. When the police arrived to execute the warrant, they announced their presence, but waited only a short time—perhaps "three to five seconds," before turning the knob of the unlocked front door and entering Hudson's home. Hudson moved to suppress all the inculpatory evidence, arguing that the premature entry violated his Fourth Amendment rights. . . .

The common-law principle that law enforcement officers must announce their presence and provide residents an opportunity to open the door is an ancient one. . . . [In a prior case] we were asked whether the rule was also a command of the Fourth Amendment. Tracing its origins in our English legal heritage . . . we concluded that it was.

We recognized that the new constitutional rule we had announced is not easily applied. *Wilson* and cases following it have noted the many situations in which it is not necessary to knock and announce. It is not necessary when "circumstances presen[t] a threat of physical violence," or if there is "reason to believe that evidence would likely be destroyed if advance notice were given," *id.*, at 936, or if knocking and announcing would be "futile," *Richards v. Wisconsin,* 520 U.S. 385, 394 (1997). We require only that police "have a reasonable suspicion . . . under the particular circumstances" that one of these grounds for failing to knock and announce exists, and we have acknowledged that "[t]his showing is not high."

When the knock-and-announce rule does apply, it is not easy to determine precisely what officers must do. How many seconds' wait are too few? Our "reasonable wait time" standard, see *United States v. Banks,* 540 U.S. 31, 41 (2003), is necessarily vague. *Banks* (a drug case, like this one) held that the proper measure was not how long it would take the resident to reach the door, but how long it would take to dispose of the suspected drugs—but that such a time (15 to 20 seconds in that case) would necessarily be extended when, for instance, the suspected contraband was not easily concealed. . . . Happily, these issues do not confront us here. From the trial level onward, Michigan has conceded that the entry was a knock-and- announce violation. The issue here is remedy. . . .

Suppression of evidence, however, has always been our last resort, not our first impulse. The exclusionary rule generates "substantial social costs," *United States v. Leon,* 468 U.S. 897, 907 (1984), which sometimes include setting the guilty free and the dangerous at large. We have therefore been "cautio[us] against expanding" it. . . .

We did not always speak so guardedly. Expansive dicta in *Mapp*, for example, suggested wide scope for the exclusionary rule. ("[A]ll evidence obtained by searches and seizures in violation of the Constitution is, by that same authority, inadmissible in a state court") was to the same effect. But we have long since rejected that approach. . . .

In other words, exclusion may not be premised on the mere fact that a constitutional violation was a "but-for" cause of obtaining evidence. Our cases show that but-for causality is only a necessary, not a sufficient, condition for suppression. . . .

Quite apart from the requirement of unattenuated causation, the exclusionary rule has never been applied except "where its deterrence benefits outweigh its 'substantial social costs,'" . . . The costs here are considerable. In addition to the grave adverse consequence that exclusion of relevant incriminating evidence always entails (viz., the risk of releasing dangerous criminals into society), imposing that massive remedy for a knock-and-announce violation would generate a constant flood of alleged failures to observe the rule. . . . The cost of entering this lottery would be small, but the jackpot enormous: suppression of all evidence, amounting in many cases to a

(continued)

get-out-of-jail-free card. Courts would experience as never before the reality that "[t]he exclusionary rule frequently requires extensive litigation to determine whether particular evidence must be excluded." Unlike the warrant or *Miranda* requirements, compliance with which is readily determined (either there was or was not a warrant; either the *Miranda* warning was given, or it was not), what constituted a "reasonable wait time" in a particular case . . . is difficult for the trial court to determine and even more difficult for an appellate court to review.

Another consequence of the incongruent remedy Hudson proposes would be police officers' refraining from timely entry after knocking and announcing. As we have observed, see *supra*, at 3, the amount of time they must wait is necessarily uncertain. If the consequences of running afoul of the rule were so massive, officers would be inclined to wait longer than the law requires—producing preventable violence against officers in some cases, and the destruction of evidence in many others. . . .

Next to these "substantial social costs" we must consider the deterrence benefits, existence of which is a necessary condition for exclusion. It is not, of course, a sufficient condition: "[I]t does not follow that the Fourth Amendment requires adoption of every proposal that might deter police misconduct." . . . To begin with, the value of deterrence depends upon the strength of the incentive to commit the forbidden act. Viewed from this perspective, deterrence of knock-and-announce violations is not worth a lot. Violation of the warrant requirement sometimes produces incriminating evidence that could not otherwise be obtained. But ignoring knock-and-announce can realistically be expected to achieve absolutely nothing except the prevention of destruction of evidence and the avoidance of life-threatening resistance by occupants of the premises—dangers which, if there is even "reasonable suspicion" of their existence, *suspend the knock-and-announce requirement anyway.* Massive deterrence is hardly required.

It seems to us not even true, as Hudson contends, that without suppression there will be no deterrence of knock-and-announce violations at all. Of course even if this assertion were accurate, it would not necessarily justify suppression. Assuming (as the assertion must) that civil suit is not an effective deterrent, one can think of many forms of police misconduct that are similarly "undeterred." When, for example, a confessed suspect in the killing of a police officer, arrested (along with incriminating evidence) in a lawful warranted search, is subjected to physical abuse at the station house, would it seriously be suggested that the evidence must be excluded, since that is the only "effective deterrent"? And what, other than civil suit, is the "effective deterrent" of police violation of an already-confessed suspect's Sixth Amendment rights by denying him prompt access to counsel? Many would regard these violated rights as more significant than the right not to be intruded upon in one's nightclothes—and yet nothing but "ineffective" civil suit is available as a deterrent. And the police incentive for those violations is arguably greater than the incentive for disregarding the knock-and- announce rule.

We cannot assume that exclusion in this context is necessary deterrence simply because we found that it was necessary deterrence in different contexts and long ago. That would be forcing the public today to pay for the sins and inadequacies of a legal regime that existed almost half a century ago. . . .

Dollree Mapp could not turn to 42 U.S.C. § 1983 for meaningful relief; *Monroe v. Pape,* which began the slow but steady expansion of that remedy, was decided the same Term as *Mapp.* It would be another 17 years before the § 1983 remedy was extended to reach the deep pocket of municipalities. Citizens whose Fourth Amendment rights were violated by federal officers could not bring suit until 10 years after *Mapp,* with this Court's decision in *Bivens v. Six Unknown Fed. Narcotics Agents,* 403 U.S. 388 (1971).

Hudson complains that "it would be very hard to find a lawyer to take a case such as this," but 42 U.S.C. § 1988(b) answers this objection. Since some civil-rights violations would yield damages too small to justify the expense of litigation, Congress has authorized attorney's fees for civil-rights plaintiffs. This remedy was unavailable in the heydays of our exclusionary-rule jurisprudence, because it is tied to the availability of a cause of action. . . .

Another development over the past half-century that deters civil-rights violations is the increasing professionalism of police forces, including a new emphasis on internal police discipline. Even as long ago as 1980 we felt it proper to "assume" that unlawful police behavior would "be dealt with appropriately" by the authorities . . . we now have increasing evidence that police forces across the United States take the constitutional rights of citizens seriously. There have been "wide-ranging reforms in the education, training, and supervision of police officers."

In sum, the social costs of applying the exclusionary rule to knock-and-announce violations are considerable; the incentive to such violations is minimal to begin with, and the extant deterrences against them are substantial—incomparably greater than the factors deterring warrantless entries when *Mapp* was decided. Resort to the massive remedy of suppressing evidence of guilt is unjustified.

When it applies, the exclusionary rule prevents the admission into evidence of any item, confession, or other thing that was obtained by law enforcement officers in an unconstitutional manner.

The excluded evidence must be obtained by the police in an unlawful manner. However, if a private citizen working on his or her own obtains evidence illegally and then turns it over to the police, it may be admitted.[10] People hired or authorized to assist the police are considered agents of the government, and therefore the exclusionary rule applies to their actions.

## Sidebar

### The Exclusionary Rule in Practice

Few topics in criminal procedure are as controversial and divisive as the exclusionary rule. Clearly, the public perception of the rule is that it is a device that frees the guilty, allowing murderers, rapists, and other miscreants to continue their carnage because of technicalities. Whether constraining the government to constitutional procedures should be characterized as "technical" is for each individual to decide.

In spite of its reputation, the exclusionary rule is not responsible for opening the door for countless criminals. In fact, less than 0.02% of all felony arrests in the United States are not prosecuted because of exclusionary rule problems. See Davies, "A Hard Look at What We Know (And Still Need to Learn) About the 'Costs' of the Exclusionary Rule," 1983 *A.B.F. Research* J. 611, 635, cited in *Commonwealth v. Edmunds,* 526 Pa. 374 (1991). The total number of cases not prosecuted and unsuccessfully prosecuted that are attributable to the exclusionary rule is estimated at between 0.6% and 2.35%. *Id.*

In another study of federal cases, searches and seizures were conducted in 30% of the prosecutions, and 11% of all defendants filed motions to suppress on Fourth Amendment grounds. Motions to suppress were granted in only 1.3% of the total number of cases, and half of the defendants who were successful in having evidence suppressed were convicted. In cases not prosecuted, exclusionary rule problems were the cause in only 0.4%. See Report of the Comptroller General, Impact of the Exclusionary Rule on Federal Criminal Prosecutions (1979).

The exclusionary rule does not apply to pretrial matters. A defendant may not challenge a grand jury indictment because the grand jury considered illegally obtained evidence. The defendant's remedy is at trial. In most cases, but not all, evidence obtained illegally may be used at sentencing.

Another important exception to the exclusionary rule allows the government to use illegally seized evidence to rebut statements made by a defendant.[11] However, this is only permitted if a defendant "opens the door." That is, the government may use the evidence if the defense refers to it in its case.

Most exclusionary rule issues are resolved prior to trial by way of a motion to suppress, or exclude, evidence. In some instances, the motion may be made at the moment the prosecutor attempts to introduce such evidence at trial. This is known as a *contemporaneous objection.*

# Fruit of the Poisonous Tree

Learning Objective: Define, describe, and apply the fruit of the poisonous tree doctrine.

The exclusionary rule applies to *primary evidence,* that is, evidence that is the direct result of an illegal search or seizure. Sometimes primary evidence leads police to other evidence. For example, suppose a special agent of the Federal Bureau of Investigation searches a home, in violation of the Fourth Amendment. The agent discovers on the homeowner's computer a plan to rob a federally insured bank. The plan includes a list of supplies that are needed and where they are hidden. Two of the items, a gun and a mask, are buried under a tree in a public park. The agent leaves the home, drives to the park, and digs up the items. Because the items were in a public space, the agent didn't need to obtain a warrant to search for them. But because they were found as a consequence of the illegal search, both the primary evidence (the plan) and the secondary or derivative evidence (the gun and mask) are inadmissible at trial. Such secondary evidence is known as **fruit of the poisonous tree.**

Generally, evidence that is "tainted" by the prior illegal conduct is inadmissible. The rule does not make all evidence later obtained by law enforcement inadmissible. In some instances, evidence may be admissible because the connection between the illegally seized evidence and the subsequently obtained evidence is marginal, or as the Supreme Court has stated it, "the causal connection . . . may have become so attenuated as to dissipate the taint."[12]

**fruit of the poisonous tree doctrine**

The rule that evidence gathered as a *result* of evidence gained in an illegal search or questioning cannot be used against the person searched or questioned even if the later evidence was gathered lawfully.

# Exceptions

Several exceptions to the exclusionary rule (and fruit of the poisonous tree) exist. First, such evidence is admissible at court hearings where determinations of guilt are not made, such as grand jury proceedings, pretrial hearings, and sentencing, for example. Second, if a defendant opens the door by referring to such evidence, a prosecutor may refer to it as well in rebuttal or to impeach the testimony of a defendant. This was the case in *Kansas v. Ventris* (2009),[13] where a confession was obtained illegally by a government informant. While such evidence could not be admitted at trial to prove guilt, the Supreme Court held that it could be used to impeach the defendant's testimony that he didn't commit the crime. The Court found the deterrent effect on police by excluding the evidence at trial to prove guilt was adequate and that the exclusion didn't need to extend to rebutting the defendant's testimony. In the Court's words, "[O]nce the defendant testifies inconsistently, denying the prosecution 'the traditional truth-testing devices of the adversary process,' is a high price to pay for vindicating the right to counsel at the prior stage. On the other hand, preventing impeachment use of statements taken in violation of *Massiah* would add little appreciable deterrence for officers, who have an incentive to comply with the Constitution, since statements lawfully obtained can be used for all purposes, not simply impeachment."

**independent source**

The general rule that if new evidence can be traced to a source completely apart from the illegally gathered evidence that first led to the new evidence, it may be used by the government in a criminal trial.

Third, illegally obtained evidence may be admitted when an independent source exists. An **independent source** must be an alternative, unconnected, and legal pathway to the same evidence. Consider the preceding bank robbery example. If a co-conspirator in the robbery also told the police where the money is, it is admissible regardless of the illegal confession, so long as the co-conspirator's admission was lawfully obtained.

**inevitable discovery doctrine**

The principle that even if criminal evidence is gathered by unconstitutional methods, the evidence may be admissible if it definitely would have come to light anyway.

Fourth, evidence that would have been inevitably discovered by law enforcement may also be admitted. This doctrine is similar to the independent source doctrine. However, police must actually obtain evidence from an untainted, lawful source to invoke the independent source doctrine. The **inevitable discovery doctrine** holds that evidence that is the fruit of an illegal search, seizure, or arrest may be admitted if it is probable that the evidence would have been obtained lawfully at a later date.

Fifth, in what is known as the Attenuation Doctrine, evidence that is illegally obtained may be admitted if the causal connection between the government's wrongful conduct and the resulting evidence has been severed by an intervening event. For example, in *Utah v. Strieff*, a suspect, Edward Strieff, was wrongfully stopped. During the Terry stop, the investigating officer discovered that there was an outstanding arrest warrant for Strieff. Consequently, Strieff was arrested and searched. Illegal drugs were discovered on his person. His motion to exclude the drugs was denied, he was convicted, and ultimately, his appeal was heard by the Supreme Court. The Court affirmed the use of the drugs at trial because the outstanding arrest warrant for Strieff's arrest is a critical intervening circumstance that is wholly independent of the illegal stop. The discovery of that warrant broke the causal chain between the unconstitutional stop and the discovery of evidence by compelling Officer Fackrell to arrest Strieff. And, it is especially significant that there is no evidence that Officer Fackrell's illegal stop reflected flagrantly unlawful police misconduct.[14]

A sixth limitation on the fruits doctrine is the admissibility of secondary or derivative evidence in cases where suspects have not been given *Miranda* warnings but have made voluntary statements leading to the seizure of secondary or derivative evidence. You will learn more about *Miranda* and this exception later.

Because the Constitution's individual rights only limit governmental authority, evidence that is obtained illegally by private individuals and turned over to law enforcement may be admitted. Of course, the individual who illegally obtained the evidence may be prosecuted for the underlying offense (e.g., trespass or theft). If the private individual was asked or encouraged to find the evidence by the government, the evidence will be excluded under agency doctrine (although not an employee, the individual was acting as an agent of the government).

# Standing

Learning Objective: Define, describe, and apply the standing doctrine.

A defendant must have **standing** before they may successfully have evidence suppressed. There are two aspects to standing. First, the person challenging the evidence must have an adversarial interest in the proceeding. Typically, only defendants in criminal cases may challenge evidence as seized in violation of the Fourth Amendment. A defendant's mother may not intervene in the criminal case and attempt to have evidence suppressed because her Fourth Amendment rights were violated by an illegal search and seizure—even if the claim is true. A mother lacks standing to make the claim.

The second aspect concerns the defendant's interest in the area searched or thing seized. A defendant must have either a reasonable expectation of privacy or a property interest for the protections of the Fourth Amendment to apply. To say it another way, a defendant can only assert their own rights, not the rights of others. Therefore, the defendant may not assert his mother's right to be free from illegal searches and seizures.

Note that in *Simmons v. United States*[15] (1968), the Supreme Court held that a defendant may testify at a suppression hearing without waiving the right not to testify at trial and that any testimony given at a suppression hearing by a defendant may not be used at trial.

*Simmons* eliminated the quandary many defendants had: Should they give incriminating evidence during a suppression hearing in hopes of having the evidence excluded? Of course, if the suppression claim was unsuccessful, then a defendant faced the incriminating testimony at trial. This put many defendants in a position of having to choose one right or another: the right to be free from self-incrimination versus the right to have illegally seized evidence excluded from trial. The Supreme Court held that defendants should be free from such dilemmas.

During the 1960s and early 1970s, some scholars predicted that the Supreme Court would become so involved with criminal procedure that it would, in effect, write its own "constitutional criminal procedure code." This prediction has not proven to be true; however, many areas of criminal procedure are greatly influenced by Supreme Court decisions. It is common to refer to the expansion of individual rights and the extension of those rights to the states as the *constitutionalization* of criminal procedure.

In recent years, though, there appears to be a trend away from expansive interpretation. This is largely because the composition of the Supreme Court is more conservative than it was during the 1960s. Some believe that the trend of increasing individual rights was hindering law enforcement and they welcome regression. Those who believe strongly in the rights of the individual point out that the Framers intended to create an inefficient government in favor of protecting liberties, and that it is better to free several guilty persons than to imprison one innocent person.

**standing**
A person's right to bring (start) or join a lawsuit or to raise a particular issue because he or she is directly affected by the issues raised.

# State Constitutions

Learning Objective: Describe the relationship, particularly the hierarchy, of the U.S. and state constitutions.

Each state has its own constitution. State constitutions typically differ from the U.S. Constitution in several ways. Most are longer than the U.S. Constitution. This is often a consequence of greater elaboration of governmental structures, often including how local forms of government are to be created and organized. It is also common for state constitutions to have more amendments than the federal Constitution. This is because amendment is easier in most states. In many, amendment can occur through public referendum. This leads to another difference between state and federal constitutions. Because state constitutions are easier to amend, they are more likely to address hot button and transient issues, and they are more likely to be internally inconsistent than is the federal Constitution.

One area where the two are very similar is in their respective bills of rights. Most states' bills of rights are identical, or nearly identical, in language to the national Constitution's Bill of Rights. There are exceptions, however. For example, several states protect privacy explicitly, while the federal Constitution does not. As you previously learned, though, privacy has been found to be an unenumerated federal right. States that explicitly protect privacy include Alaska, Arizona, California, Hawaii, Illinois, Louisiana, Montana, and Washington, D.C.. California's right, found in Art. I, § 1, reads:

> All people are by nature free and independent and have inalienable rights. Among these are enjoying and defending life and liberty, acquiring, possessing, and protecting property, and pursuing and obtaining safety, happiness, and privacy.

Montana's Constitution, at Art. II, § 10, provides that

> The right of individual privacy is essential to the well-being of a free society and shall not be infringed without the showing of a compelling state interest.

Until recently, state constitutions have not played an important role in defining civil liberties. This is because both state and federal courts have looked almost exclusively to the national Constitution to answer questions concerning civil liberties, particularly in criminal cases. It is also due to the tendency of state courts to interpret state constitutional rights as identical to those secured by the national Constitution.

Increasingly, this is not the case. In recent decades, commentators, judges, and attorneys have exhibited a renewed interest in state constitutional law. Concerned that the Supreme Court of the United States was backing away from the protections recognized by the Court in the 1960s, former Justice William Brennan of the U.S. Supreme Court urged states and their courts to turn to their own constitutions to protect liberties.[16]

The resurgence in state constitutional law is known as "New Constitutional Federalism." Of course, a state constitution cannot be used to limit or encroach on a federally secured right, but it can be used to extend the scope of a right.

An example is Pennsylvania, where its Supreme Court strongly asserted that its state's constitution has its own meaning separate and independent from the federal Constitution. In a 1991 case, that Court stated:

> [T]he decisions of the [U.S. Supreme] Court are not, and should not be, dispositive of questions regarding rights guaranteed by counter-part provisions of State Law. Accordingly, such decisions are not mechanically applicable to

state law issues, and state court judges and members of the bar seriously err if they so treat them. Rather, state court judges, and also practitioners, do well to scrutinize constitutional decisions by federal courts, for only if they are found to be logically persuasive and well-reasoned, paying due regard to precedent and the policies underlying specific constitutional guarantees, may they properly claim persuasive weight as guide posts when interpreting counter-part state guarantees.[17]

The California courts have taken a similar approach. Even if a provision's interpretation parallels national law, the courts favor citing state law over federal law.

Whether a state court depends on state or federal law in defining a right determines what court has the final word on the subject. If a right is founded upon federal law, the Supreme Court of the United States is the final arbiter. If a right is founded upon state law, the highest court of the state is the final arbiter, again assuming that no federal right is encroached upon by the state decision. This problem normally arises when one person's exercise of a right affects another person's rights. For example, if a state court were to find that a fetus has a right to life in every instance, the decision would be void as violative of the mother's privacy right to elect to end the pregnancy in some circumstances.

If a state court relies upon federal law when defining a right, the possibility of reversal by a federal court, usually the Supreme Court, exists. This is what occurred in California concerning the use of peyote, a drug made from cactus, by Native Americans. The Supreme Court of California decided in 1965 that the use of peyote by Native Americans during religious ceremonies was protected by the U.S. Constitution's First Amendment free exercise of religion clause.[18] That decision was not disturbed until 1990, when the Supreme Court of the United States decided that the regulation of peyote as a drug was a reasonable burden upon the First Amendment[19] and therefore overruled the 1965 California decision. Although the defendant asserted both the federal and state free exercise guarantees, the California Supreme Court relied entirely upon federal law in making its decision. Both Congress and the State of California subsequently recognized the right of Native Americans to use peyote.

## Oyez

### United States v. Leon
#### 468 U.S. 897 (1984)

**Justice White delivered the opinion of the Court.**

[Facially valid warrants were issued by a state judge. The searches conducted under the warrants produced narcotics and other evidence of narcotics violations.]

The respondents . . . filed motions to suppress the evidence seized pursuant to the warrant. The District Court held an evidentiary hearing and, while recognizing that the case was a close one, . . . granted the motions to suppress in part. It concluded that the affidavit was insufficient to establish probable cause. . . . In response to a request from the Government, the court made clear that Officer Rombach had acted in good faith. . . . [This decision was affirmed on appeal before the court of appeals.]

The Government's petition for certiorari expressly declined to seek review of the lower courts' determinations that the search warrant was unsupported by probable cause and presented only the question "[w]hether the Fourth Amendment exclusionary rule should be modified so as not to bar the admission of evidence seized in reasonable, good-faith reliance on a search warrant that is subsequently held to be defective." . . .

(continued)

[T]he exclusionary rule is designed to deter police misconduct rather than to punish the errors of judges and magistrates. . . .

If exclusion of evidence obtained pursuant to a subsequently invalidated warrant is to have any deterrent effect, therefore, it must alter the behavior of the individual law enforcement officers or the policies of their departments. One could argue that applying the exclusionary rule in cases where the police failed to demonstrate probable cause in the warrant application deters future inadequate presentations or "magistrate shopping" and thus promotes the ends of the Fourth Amendment. Suppressing evidence obtained pursuant to a technically defective warrant supported by probable cause also might encourage officers to scrutinize more closely the form of the warrant and to point out suspected judicial errors. We find such arguments speculative and conclude that suppression of evidence obtained pursuant to a warrant should be ordered only on a case-by-case basis and only in those unusual cases in which exclusion will further the purposes of the exclusionary rule.

We conclude that the marginal or nonexistent benefits produced by suppressing evidence obtained in objectively reasonable reliance on a subsequently invalidated search warrant cannot justify the substantial costs of exclusion. We do not suggest, however, that exclusion is always inappropriate in cases where an officer has obtained a warrant and abided by its terms. . . . [A]n officer's reliance on the magistrate's probable-cause determination and on the technical sufficiency of the warrant he issues must be objectively reasonable . . . and it is clear that in some circumstances the officer will have no reasonable grounds for believing that the warrant was properly issued.

# Oyez

## Commonwealth v. Edmunds
## 526 Pa. 374 (1991)

### Cappy, Justice

[Defendant who was convicted in the Court of Common Pleas, Criminal Division, of possession of marijuana and related offenses, appealed. The Superior Court affirmed the conviction.]

The issue presented to this court is whether Pennsylvania should adopt the "good faith" exception to the exclusionary rule as articulated by the United States Supreme Court in the case of *United States v. Leon*, 468 U.S. 897, 104 S. Ct. 3405, 82 L. Ed. 2d 677 (1984). We conclude that a "good faith" exception to the exclusionary rule would frustrate the guarantees embodied in Article I, Section 8, of the Pennsylvania Constitution. Accordingly, the decision of the Supreme Court is reversed. . . .

The trial court held that the search warrant failed to establish probable cause that the marijuana would be at the location to be searched on the date it was issued. The trial court found that the warrant failed to set forth with specificity the date upon which the anonymous informants observed the marijuana. . . . However, the trial court went on to deny the defendant's motion to suppress the marijuana. Applying the rationale of *Leon*, the trial court looked beyond the four corners of the affidavit, in order to establish that the officers executing the warrant acted in "good faith" in relying upon the warrant to conduct the search. . . .

We must now determine whether the good-faith exception to the exclusionary rule is properly part of the jurisprudence of this Commonwealth, by virtue of Article 1, Section 8 of the Pennsylvania Constitution. In concluding that it is not, we set forth a methodology to be followed in analyzing future state constitutional issues which arise under our own Constitution. . . .

This Court has long emphasized that, in interpreting a provision of the Pennsylvania Constitution, we are not bound by the decisions of the United States Supreme Court which interpret similar (yet distinct) federal constitutional provisions. . . . [T]he federal constitution establishes certain minimum levels which are "equally applicable to the [analogous] state constitutional provision." . . . However, each state has the power to provide broader standards, and go beyond the minimum floor which is established by the federal Constitution. . . .

Here in Pennsylvania, we have stated with increasing frequency that it is both important and necessary that we undertake an independent analysis of the Pennsylvania Constitution, each time a provision of that fundamental document is implicated. . . .

The recent focus on the "New Federalism" has emphasized the importance of state constitutions with respect to individual rights and criminal procedure. As such, we find it important to set forth certain factors to be briefed and analyzed by litigants in each case hereafter implicating a provision of the Pennsylvania constitution. The decision of the United States Supreme Court in *Michigan v. Long*, 463 U.S. 1032, 103 S. Ct. 3469, 77 L. Ed. 2d 1201 (1983), now requires us to make a "plain statement" of the adequate and independent state grounds upon which we rely, in order to avoid any doubt that we have rested our decision squarely on Pennsylvania jurisprudence. Accordingly, as a general rule it is important that litigants brief and analyze at least the following four factors:

1. Text of the Pennsylvania constitutional provision;
2. History of the provision, including Pennsylvania case-law;
3. Related case-law from other states;
4. Policy considerations, including unique issues of state and local concern, and applicability within modern Pennsylvania jurisprudence.

Depending on the particular issue presented, an examination of related federal precedent may be useful as part of the state constitutional analysis, not as binding authority, but as one form of guidance. . . . Utilizing the above four factors, and having reviewed *Leon*, we conclude that a "good faith" exception to the exclusionary rule would frustrate the guarantees embodied in Article I, Section 8 of our Commonwealth's Constitution. . . .

The United States Supreme Court in *Leon* made clear that, in its view, the sole purpose for the exclusionary rule under the 4th Amendment [to the Constitution of the United States] was to deter police misconduct. . . . The *Leon* majority also made clear that, under the Federal Constitution, the exclusionary rule operated as "a judicially created remedy designed to safeguard Fourth Amendment rights generally through its deterrent effect, rather than a personal constitutional right of the party aggrieved." . . .

[T]he exclusionary rule in Pennsylvania has consistently served to bolster the twin aims of Article I, Section 8, to wit, the safeguarding of privacy and the fundamental requirement that warrants shall only be issued upon probable cause. . . .

The linch-pin that has been developed to determine whether it is appropriate to issue a search warrant is the test of probable cause. . . . It is designed to protect us from unwarranted and even vindictive incursions upon our privacy. It insulates from dictatorial and tyrannical rule by the state, and preserves the concept of democracy that assures the freedom of citizens. This concept is second to none in its importance in deliniating [*sic*] the dignity of the individual living in a free society. . . .

Whether the United States Supreme Court has determined that the exclusionary rule does not advance the 4th Amendment purpose of deterring police conduct is irrelevant. Indeed, we disagree with the Court's suggestion in *Leon* that we in Pennsylvania have been employing the exclusionary rule all these years to deter police corruption. We flatly reject this notion. . . . What is significant, however, is that our Constitution has historically been interpreted to incorporate a strong right to privacy, and an equally strong adherence to the requirement of probable cause under Article I, Section 8. Citizens in this Commonwealth possess such rights, even where a police officer in "good faith" carrying out his or her duties inadvertently invades the privacy or circumvents the strictures of probable cause. To adopt a "good faith" exception to the exclusionary rule, we believe, would virtually emasculate those clear safeguards which have been carefully developed under the Pennsylvania Constitution over the past 200 years.

Although there has been an increase in the number of state courts that have turned to their own constitutions to protect liberties since Justice Brennan issued his famous challenge, the response hasn't been as significant as many civil libertarians had hoped.

The two Oyez cases above offer an illustration of New Constitutional Federalism. The *Leon* case, issued by the Supreme Court of the United States, recognized a good-faith exception to the exclusionary rule; the *Edmunds* decision, by the Supreme Court of Pennsylvania, expressly rejects the good-faith exception in state prosecutions.

As another example, several states have not followed the Supreme Court's lead in allowing statements made in violation of *Miranda* to be used by the prosecution in impeachment of a defendant.[20] These are but a few of the many instances in which a right has received greater protection under state law than under federal law.[21]

State laws may not reduce federally secured rights. Similarly, state laws may not enlarge federally secured rights. They may use state law to, enlarge rights also protected by federal law. In the following case, decided in 2008, the distinction that was just drawn was at issue.

# Oyez

## Virginia v. Moore
### Supreme Court of the United States (2008)

**Justice Scalia delivered the opinion of the Court.**

We consider whether a police officer violates the *Fourth Amendment* by making an arrest based on probable cause but prohibited by state law.

On February 20, 2003, two City of Portsmouth police officers stopped a car driven by David Lee Moore. They had heard over the police radio that a person known as "Chubs" was driving with a suspended license, and one of the officers knew Moore by that nickname. The officers determined that Moore's license was in fact suspended, and arrested him for the misdemeanor of driving on a suspended license, which is punishable under Virginia law by a year in jail and a $2,500 fine. The officers subsequently searched Moore and found that he was carrying 16 grams of crack cocaine and $516 in cash.

Under state law, the officers should have issued Moore a summons instead of arresting him. Driving on a suspended license, like some other misdemeanors, is not an arrestable offense except as to those who "fail or refuse to discontinue" the violation, and those whom the officer reasonably believes to be likely to disregard a summons, or likely to harm themselves or others. The intermediate appellate court found none of these circumstances applicable, and Virginia did not appeal that determination. . . .

[Moore was charged and convicted of possession of cocaine with an intent to distribute. His conviction was reversed by the Virginia court of appeals and Virginia Supreme Court because it found that the Fourth Amendment prohibited the search incident to arrest because Virginia law didn't authorize the arrest.]

In a long line of cases, we have said that when an officer has probable cause to believe a person committed even a minor crime in his presence, the balancing of private and public interests is not in doubt. The arrest is constitutionally reasonable. . . .

Our decisions counsel against changing this calculus when a State chooses to protect privacy beyond the level that the *Fourth Amendment* requires. We have treated additional protections exclusively as matters of state law. In *Cooper v. California*, *386 U.S. 58* (1967), we reversed a state court that had held the search of a seized vehicle to be in violation of the *Fourth Amendment* because state law did not explicitly authorize the search. We concluded that whether state law authorized the search was irrelevant. States, we said, remained free "to impose higher standards on searches and seizures than required by the Federal Constitution," but regardless of state rules, police could search a lawfully seized vehicle as a matter of federal constitutional law. . . .

In *California v. Greenwood*, *486 U.S. 35* (1988), we held that search of an individual's garbage forbidden by California's Constitution was not forbidden by the *Fourth Amendment*. "[W]hether or not a search is reasonable within the meaning of the *Fourth Amendment*," we said, has never "depend[ed] on the law of the particular State in which the search occurs." While "[i]ndividual States may surely construe their own constitutions as imposing more stringent constraints on police conduct than does the Federal Constitution," *ibid.*, state law did not alter the content of the *Fourth Amendment*. . . .

We have applied the same principle in the seizure context. *Whren v. United States*, *517 U.S. 806* (1996), held that police officers had acted reasonably in stopping a car, even though their action violated regulations limiting the authority of plainclothes officers in unmarked vehicles. We thought it obvious that the *Fourth Amendment's* meaning did not change with local law enforcement practices—even practices set by rule. While those practices "vary from place to place and from time to time," *Fourth Amendment* protections are not "so variable" and cannot "be made to turn upon such trivialities." . . .

If we concluded otherwise, we would often frustrate rather than further state policy. Virginia chooses to protect individual privacy and dignity more than the *Fourth Amendment* requires, but it also chooses not to attach to violations of its arrest rules the potent remedies that federal courts have applied to *Fourth Amendment* violations. Virginia does not, for example, ordinarily exclude from criminal trials evidence obtained in violation of its statutes. Moore would allow Virginia to accord enhanced protection against arrest only on pain of accompanying that protection with federal remedies for *Fourth Amendment* violations, which often include the exclusionary rule. States unwilling to lose control over the remedy would have to abandon restrictions on arrest altogether. This is an odd consequence of a provision designed to protect against searches and seizures. . . .

Finally, linking *Fourth Amendment* protections to state law would cause them to "vary from place to place and from time to time. . . ."

We conclude that warrantless arrests for crimes committed in the presence of an arresting officer are reasonable under the Constitution, and that while States are free to regulate such arrests however they desire, state restrictions do not alter the *Fourth Amendment*'s protections.

Moore argues that even if the Constitution allowed his arrest, it did not allow the arresting officers to search him. We have recognized, however, that officers may perform searches incident to constitutionally permissible arrests in order to ensure their safety and safeguard evidence. . . .

The Virginia Supreme Court may have concluded that *Knowles* required the exclusion of evidence seized from Moore because, under state law, the officers who arrested Moore should have issued him a citation instead. This argument might have force if the Constitution forbade Moore's arrest, because we have sometimes excluded evidence obtained through unconstitutional methods in order to deter constitutional violations. But the arrest rules that the officers violated were those of state law alone, and as we have just concluded, it is not the province of the *Fourth Amendment* to enforce state law. That Amendment does not require the exclusion of evidence obtained from a constitutionally permissible arrest.

## Ethical Considerations

### Should Judges Follow Public Opinion?

The Framers of the U.S. Constitution were fearful of centralized authority. James Madison penned, in *Federalist* No. 47, that the "[a] ccumulation of all power, legislative, executive and judiciary in the same hands, whether hereditary, self-appointed, or elective, may justly be pronounced the very definition of tyranny." Accordingly, the Framers designed a government with diffused and checked authorities. Laws are made by Congress, but the president has to endorse them before they become effective. A presidential veto, however, can be overridden by a two-thirds vote. The president is the chief executive of government and commander in chief of the military. But Congress establishes government agencies, gives them their charge, and funds them. Similarly, Congress declares war, funds the military, and makes the rules that govern the military. Both of these branches are political. The president, through the electoral college; and Congress, through direct election, are elected and accountable to the people.

The third branch of government is different. The Framers intended to have a federal judiciary that is insulated from political forces. To accomplish this, federal judges are endowed with lifetime tenure after appointment, which requires nomination by the president and confirmation by the Senate. Once appointed, they cannot have their pay reduced; and they leave office only through death, retirement, or impeachment. In this sense, our federal courts are counter-majoritarian. Justice Jackson said it well:

The very purpose of the Bill of Rights was to withdraw certain subjects from the vicissitudes of political controversy, to place them beyond the reach of majorities and officials and to establish them as legal principles to be applied by the courts. One's right to life, liberty, and property, to free speech, a free press, freedom of worship and assembly, and other fundamental rights may not be submitted to vote; they depend on the outcome of no elections.

This independence allows judges to be faithful to the law, even when their decisions are unpopular with elected officials or the public. This also advances the Model Code of Judicial Conduct canon requiring judges to avoid even the appearance of impropriety. Another canon states that judge shall not be swayed by partisan interests, public opinion, or fear of criticism.

While federal judges are well insulated from political forces, at least after appointment, judges in some state courts enjoy less independence. This is because judges are elected in most states. The method of election varies. Some are partisan, others nonpartisan, and in others, retention elections are held. In the latter, there are no opposing candidates. Whether a judge should be retained is asked. If a judge is not retained, then an appointment or election is held to determine the successor.

John Fabian documents several instances where the electoral process was used to remove a judge who made a correct legal judgment that was politically unpopular. His examples involve highly contentious issues, such as the death penalty. He also gives examples of judges who appeared to have catered to public opinion and political ambitions in their campaigns as well as examples of elected officials who exploited electoral vulnerabilities of judges. Individuals who support the notion that judges should reflect majoritarian views find nothing wrong in judges responding to public opinion or bowing to political pressures. Whether elected judges can maintain judicial integrity, avoid the appearance of impropriety, and remain fair in the cases they hear is a genuine issue in a system that requires their election and reelection.

*Source:* John Fabian, "The Paradox of Elected Judges: Tension in the American Judicial System," 15 *Geo. J. Legal Ethics* 155 (2001).

For more on the politics of federal judicial appointments and the relationship between public opinion and federal judicial decisions, see Lee Epstein and Jeffrey A. Segal, *Advice and Consent: The Politics of Judicial Appointments* (Oxford University Press 2005), and Cass Sunstein, *Are Judges Political? An Empirical Analysis of the Federal Judiciary* (Brookings Institution Press 2006).

## Key Terms

Exclusionary Rule
fruit of the poisonous tree

independent source
inevitable discovery doctrine

standing

## Review Questions

1. What is selective incorporation? Total incorporation? Which reflects current law?

2. Name three rights that have been incorporated and one that has not.

3. What is the exclusionary rule?

4. Give an example of when evidence would be fruit of the poisonous tree.

5. Name three exceptions to the fruit of the poisonous tree doctrine.

6. What is the "New Federalism" in the context of constitutional law?

## Problems & Critical Thinking Exercises

1. The Constitution of the United States significantly affects all criminal law. Why is that so when more than 95% of all prosecutions occur in state courts?

2. Do you believe that evidence that has been obtained by law enforcement in an unconstitutional manner should be inadmissible at trial? Explain your position.

3. England does not employ the exclusionary rule. Rather, police officers are subject to civil liability for illegal searches. Is this a satisfactory remedy that should be employed in the United States? Can you think of alternative remedies?

## Endnotes

1. *Barron ex rel. Tiernan v. Mayor of Baltimore*, 7 Pet. 243 (1833).

2. *United States v. Cruikshank*, 92 U.S.w42 (1876).

3. *Chicago, Burlington & Quincy Railroad Co. v. City of Chicago*, 166 U.S. 226 (1897).

4. *Gitlow v. New York*, 268 U.S. 652 (1925).

5. *Hurtado v. California*, 110 U.S. 516 (1884).

6. *McDonald v. Chicago*, 561 U.S. __ (2010).

7. *Roe v. Wade*, 410 U.S. 113 (1973).

8. *Griswold v. Connecticut*, 381 U.S. 479 (1965).

9. The rule, as it applied in federal courts, was announced in *Weeks v. United States*, 232 U.S. 383 (1914). However, it appears that the rule was applied in at least one case prior to that date. See LaFave & Israel, *Criminal Procedure* 78 (Hornbook Series) (St. Paul, MN: West, 1985).

10. *Burdeau v. McDowell*, 256 U.S. 465 (1921).

11. *Walder v. United States*, 347 U.S. 62 (1954); *United States v. Havens*, 446 U.S. 620 (1980).

12. *Nardone v. United States*, 308 U.S. 338 (1939).

13. 556 U.S. 586 (2009).

14. *Utah v. Strieff*, 579 U.S. , 136 S. Ct. 2056, 2061 (2016)

15. 390 U.S. 377.

16. William J. Brennan, Jr., *State Constitutions and the Protection of Individual Rights*, 90 Harv. L. Rev. 489 (1977).

17. *Commonwealth v. Ludwig*, 527 Pa. 472, 478 (1991).

18. *People v. Woody*, 61 Cal. 2d 716, 394 P.2d 813 (1965).

19. *Department of Human Resources v. Smith*, 494 U.S. 872 (1990).

20. See *People v. Disbrow*, 16 Cal. 3d 101, 545 P.2d 272 (1976) (California law); *State v. Santiago*, 53 Haw. 254, 492 P.2d 657 (1971) (Hawaii law); *Commonwealth v. Triplett*, 462 Pa. 244, 341 A.2d 62 (1975) (Pennsylvania law).

21. See Joseph Cook, *Constitutional Rights of the Accused*, 2d ed., § 1:8, n.16 (Lawyers Cooperative, 1989) for a more thorough list.

# Chapter 12

# Searches and Seizures: Fundamentals

## Chapter Outline

## Searches

Learning Objective: Define, describe, and apply the Fourth Amendment's rules for searches.

Searches and seizures are vital aspects of law enforcement. Because they involve significant invasions of individual liberties, limits on their use can be found in the constitutions, statutes, and other laws of the states and federal government.

The most important limitation is the Fourth Amendment of the U.S. Constitution. It reads:

> The right of the people to be secure in their persons, houses, papers, and effects, against unreasonable searches and seizures, shall not be violated, and no warrants shall issue but upon probable cause, supported by oath or affirmation, and particularly describing the place to be searched and the persons or things to be seized.

First, although the Amendment is a single sentence, not divided into clauses by periods or semicolons, it has been interpreted as having separate, albeit related, clauses. The baseline requirement of the Amendment is that *all* searches and seizures by the government be reasonable. Additional clauses require that some searches and seizures be supported by probable cause, but they can be warrantless, and a smaller number of searches and seizures can occur only if there is both probable cause and a warrant. In this chapter, you will learn when each of these standards applies. See Exhibit 12-1 for a graphical representation of the Fourth Amendment's reasonableness, probable cause, and warrant requirements.

**Exhibit 12–1** Fourth Amendment Requirements

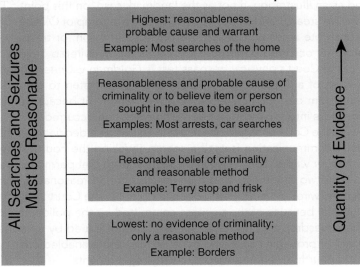

As you learned in Chapter 9, the State Action Doctrine limits the reach of the Fourth Amendment to state action. Evidence obtained by a private citizen, acting on his or her own, is not subject to the exclusionary rule. So, if Ira's neighbor illegally enters and searches his house, discovers evidence of a crime, and turns that evidence over to law enforcement, it may be used at trial. Of course, the result would be different if the neighbor was working under the direction (as an agent) of a government official.

## Defining Search: Privacy *and* Property

Learning Objective: Describe and apply the two tests, and the landmark case-law defining them, used to determine if a search has occurred under the Fourth Amendment.

The first question that must be answered in all Fourth Amendment cases is whether the Amendment applies at all. As mentioned above, the Framers of the Constitution only intended to limit *governmental authority* through the Bill of Rights. Accordingly, it must be determined if the act in question was taken under authority of law. In the criminal context, this translates to acts by law enforcement officers, both police and prosecutors, in most instances. However, any person who acts on the government's behalf is subject to the constraints of the Constitution. For example, a private individual who has access to another's private computer is a governmental agent if asked by police to access records on that computer.

The determination of state action is obvious in most cases, but it doesn't end the analysis. The Fourth Amendment applies to *searches* and *seizures* of persons, houses, papers, and effects. So, the second question is whether a search or seizure has occurred. Not all interactions between police and the public amount to a search or seizure under the Fourth Amendment. Let's begin with what qualifies as a search.

Clearly, the Framers intended to protect a person's body from unreasonable searches. With a few exceptions, a touching of a person's body by law enforcement officers triggers the protections of the Fourth Amendment. An example of an exception would be when an officer pulls a person out of harm's way.

In terms of the other three protected interests—houses, paper, and effects—the Fourth Amendment was strictly interpreted to protect "areas" until 1967. During this period, law enforcement officers had to commit a physical trespass of property for the Fourth Amendment to apply. *Olmstead v. United States*[1] is often used as an illustration, if not as the landmark case, on this point.[2] The Court decided in *Olmstead*, handed down in 1928, that a wiretap of Olmstead's phones did not constitute a search because no physical intrusion, or trespass, of Olmstead's property occurred during the installation of the wiretap devices. Another example of the Court's physical trespass test is *Goldman v. United States*,[3] where the placement of a "detectaphone" against a wall to listen to conversations in an adjacent room did not violate the Fourth Amendment because there was no physical trespass into the room where the conversation occurred.

However, the Court changed direction in 1967 when it decided that the capture of a person's communication is itself a search, invoking the Fourth Amendment. The case, *Berger v. New York*,[4] involved a state statute that permitted warrantless wiretaps up to two months in length when officers had reasonable suspicion to believe that the wiretap would yield evidence of crime. The Court found the statute unconstitutional because of the trespass committed by the police, the extended time of the eavesdropping, the absence of a warrant issued by a neutral magistrate, the lack of probable cause, and because the statute enabled broad searches, violating the Fourth Amendment's particularly requirements.

In 1967, the rule for determining whether a search occurred changed in *Katz v. United States*. In *this* landmark case, the Supreme Court held that the Fourth Amendment protects *people, not places*. To operationalize its decision, the Court established a two-part test to decide if the Fourth Amendment is implicated. First, an individual must have a subjective expectation to privacy. Second, that expectation must be objectively reasonable. The *Katz* "reasonable expectation of privacy" test continues to be a method of determining whether a search or seizure has occurred. Consistent with *Katz*, the Supreme Court has defined a search as "when an expectation of privacy that society is prepared to consider reasonable is infringed." In the same opinion, the court defined a *seizure* as a "meaningful interference with an individual's possessory interest" in property.[5]

## Oyez

## Katz v. United States
### 389 U.S. 347 (1967)

**MR. JUSTICE STEWART delivered the opinion of the Court.**

The petitioner was convicted in the District Court for the Southern District of California under an eight-count indictment charging him with transmitting wagering information by telephone from Los Angeles to Miami and Boston, in violation of a federal statute. At trial the Government was permitted, over the petitioner's objection, to introduce evidence of the petitioner's end of telephone conversations, overheard by FBI agents who had attached an electronic listening and recording device to the outside of the public telephone booth from which he had placed his calls. In affirming his conviction, the Court of Appeals rejected the contention that the recordings had been obtained in violation of the Fourth Amendment, because "[t]here was no physical entrance into the area occupied by [the petitioner]." We granted certiorari in order to consider the constitutional questions thus presented.

The petitioner has phrased those questions as follows:

A. Whether a public telephone booth is a constitutionally protected area so that evidence obtained by attaching an electronic listening and recording device to the top of such booth is obtained in violation of the right to privacy of the user of the booth.

B. Whether physical penetration of a constitutionally protected area is necessary before a search and seizure can be said to be violative of the Fourth Amendment to the United States Constitution.

We decline to adopt this formulation of the issues. In the first place, the correct solution of Fourth Amendment problems is not necessarily promoted by incantation of the phrase "constitutionally protected area." Secondly, the Fourth Amendment cannot be translated into a general constitutional "right to privacy." That Amendment protects individual privacy against certain kinds of governmental intrusion, but its protections go further, and often have nothing to do with privacy at all. Other provisions of the Constitution protect personal privacy from other forms of governmental invasion. But the protection of a person's *general* right to privacy—his right to be left alone by other people—is, like the protection of property and of his very life, left largely to the law of the individual States.

Because of the misleading way the issues have been formulated, the parties have attached great significance to the characterization of the telephone booth from which the petitioner placed his calls. The petitioner has strenuously argued that the booth was a "constitutionally protected area." The Government has maintained with equal vigor that it was not. But this effort to decide whether or not a given "area," viewed in the abstract, is "constitutionally protected" deflects attention from the problem presented by this case. For the Fourth Amendment protects people, not places. What a person knowingly exposes to the public, even in his own home or office, is not a subject of Fourth Amendment protection. . . . But what he seeks to preserve as private, even in an area accessible to the public, may be constitutionally protected. . . .

The Government stresses the fact that the telephone booth from which the petitioner made his calls was constructed partly of glass, so that he was as visible after he entered it as he would have been if he had remained outside. But what he sought to exclude when he entered the booth was not the intruding eye—it was the uninvited ear. He did not shed his right to do so simply because he made his calls from a place where he might be seen. No less than an individual in a business office, in a friend's apartment, or in a taxicab, a person in a telephone booth may rely upon the protection of the Fourth Amendment. One who occupies it, shuts the door behind him, and pays the toll that permits him to place a call is surely entitled to assume that the words he utters into the mouthpiece will not be broadcast to the world. To read the Constitution more narrowly is to ignore the vital role that the public telephone has come to play in private communication.

The Government contends, however, that the activities of its agents in this case should not be tested by Fourth Amendment requirements, for the surveillance technique they employed involved no physical penetration of the telephone booth from which the petitioner placed his calls. It is true that the absence of such penetration was at one time thought to foreclose further Fourth Amendment inquiry . . . for that Amendment was thought to limit only searches and seizures of tangible property . . . we have since departed from the narrow view on which that decision rested. Indeed, we have expressly held that the Fourth Amendment governs not only the seizure of tangible items, but extends as well to the recording of oral statements, overheard without any "technical trespass under . . . local property law." *Silverman v. United States,* 365 U.S. 505, 511. Once this much is acknowledged, and once it is recognized that the Fourth Amendment protects people—and not simply "areas"—against unreasonable searches and seizures, it becomes clear that the reach of that Amendment cannot turn upon the presence or absence of a physical intrusion into any given enclosure.

We conclude that the underpinnings of [prior decisions] have been so eroded by our subsequent decisions that the "trespass" doctrine there enunciated can no longer be regarded as controlling. . . .

[The Court then held that the warrantless search was conducted in violation of the Fourth Amendment.]

Applying the *Katz* privacy test, courts have held that the Fourth Amendment doesn't apply to open, public spaces, such as sidewalks, public parks, in public buildings, and on public roads. For this reason, police may observe people and cars that are in public spaces without a warrant or any evidence of wrongdoing. It is not a search for an officer to observe and "run" the license plate of a car when it is in public view. The same reasoning has been applied to odors that can be smelled in public spaces. A K-9 sniff of a person in a public space is not a Fourth Amendment search.[6]

That a space is open to the public isn't dispositive. The stall of a restroom on public land, for example, is a space where a person has a reasonable expectation to privacy. On the other hand, the shopping areas of a grocery store are privately owned, but there isn't a reasonable expectation to privacy in those spaces—even for the store's owner. The office and restrooms of the store, on the other hand, are different.

It was believed by many scholars, judges, and attorneys that the *Katz* privacy test replaced the property test. Then came *Jones v. United States* in 2012. Although the decision was unanimous, the justices split in their reasoning. What appears in your next Oyez are excerpts from the majority opinion and one of the two concurring opinions.

# Oyez

## Jones v. United States
### 565 U.S. 400 (2012)

**Justice Scalia delivered the opinion of the Court.**

We decide whether the attachment of a Global-Positioning-System (GPS) tracking device to an individual's vehicle, and subsequent use of that device to monitor the vehicle's movements on public streets, constitutes a search or seizure within the meaning of the Fourth Amendment.

In 2004 respondent Antoine Jones, owner and operator of a nightclub in the District of Columbia, came under suspicion of trafficking in narcotics and was made the target of an investigation by a joint FBI and Metropolitan Police Department task force. Officers employed various investigative techniques, including visual surveillance of the nightclub, installation of a camera focused on the front door of the club, and a pen register and wiretap covering Jones's cellular phone.

Based in part on information gathered from these sources, in 2005 the Government applied to the United States District Court for the District of Columbia for a warrant authorizing the use of an electronic tracking device on the Jeep Grand Cherokee registered to Jones's wife. A warrant issued, authorizing installation of the device in the District of Columbia and within 10 days.

On the 11th day, and not in the District of Columbia but in Maryland, agents installed a GPS tracking device on the undercarriage of the Jeep while it was parked in a public parking lot. Over the next 28 days, the Government used the device to track the vehicle's movements, and once had to replace the device's battery when the vehicle was parked in a different public lot in Maryland. By means of signals from multiple satellites, the device established the vehicle's location within 50 to 100 feet, and communicated that location by cellular phone to a Government computer. It relayed more than 2,000 pages of data over the 4-week period.

[Jones moved to suppress the data because it was obtained without a valid warrant. The motion was granted in part, much of the data was admitted, he was tried, convicted, charged and convicted on additional counts, and sentenced to life in prison.]

The Fourth Amendment provides in relevant part that "[t]he right of the people to be secure in their persons, houses, papers, and effects, against unreasonable searches and seizures, shall not be violated." It is beyond dispute that a vehicle is an "effect" as that term is used in the Amendment. We hold that the Government's installation of a GPS device on a target's vehicle, and its use of that device to monitor the vehicle's movements, constitutes a "search."

It is important to be clear about what occurred in this case: The Government physically occupied private property for the purpose of obtaining information. We have no doubt that such a physical intrusion would have been considered a "search" within the meaning of the Fourth Amendment when it was adopted. . . .

The text of the Fourth Amendment reflects its close connection to property, since otherwise it would have referred simply to "the right of the people to be secure against unreasonable searches and seizures"; the phrase "in their persons, houses, papers, and effects" would have been superfluous.

Consistent with this understanding, our Fourth Amendment jurisprudence was tied to common-law trespass, at least until the latter half of the 20th century. *Kyllo v. United States*, 533 U. S. 27, 31 (2001); Kerr, *The Fourth Amendment and New Technologies: Constitutional Myths and the Case for Caution*, 102 Mich. L. Rev. 801, 816 (2004). Thus, in Olmstead v. United States, 277 U. S. 438 (1928), we held that wiretaps attached to telephone wires on the public streets did not constitute a Fourth Amendment search because "[t]here was no entry of the houses or offices of the defendants," . . .

Our later cases, of course, have deviated from that exclusively property-based approach. In Katz v. United States, 389 U. S. 347, 351 (1967), we said that "the Fourth Amendment protects people, not places," and found a violation in attachment of an eavesdropping device to a public telephone booth. Our later cases have applied the analysis of Justice Harlan's concurrence in that case, which said that a violation occurs when government officers violate a person's "reasonable expectation of privacy."

The Government contends that the Harlan standard shows that no search occurred here, since Jones had no "reasonable expectation of privacy" in the area of the Jeep accessed by Government agents (its underbody) and in the locations of the Jeep on the public roads, which were visible to all. But we need not address the Government's contentions, because Jones's Fourth Amendment rights do not rise or fall with the Katz formulation. . . .

As explained, for most of our history the Fourth Amendment was understood to embody a particular concern for government trespass upon the areas ("persons, houses, papers, and effects") it enumerates. Katz did not repudiate that understanding. Less than two years later the Court upheld defendants' contention that the Government could not introduce against them conversations between other people obtained by warrantless placement of electronic surveillance devices in their homes. The opinion rejected the dissent's contention that there was no Fourth Amendment violation "unless the conversational privacy of the homeowner himself is invaded." "[W]e [do not] believe that Katz, by holding that the Fourth Amendment protects persons and their private conversations, was intended to withdraw any of the protection which the Amendment extends to the home. . . ."

More recently, in Soldal v. Cook County, 506 U. S. 56 (1992), the Court unanimously rejected the argument that although a "seizure" had occurred "in a 'technical' sense" when a trailer home was forcibly removed, id., at 62, no Fourth Amendment violation occurred because law enforcement had not "invade[d] the [individuals'] privacy, "Katz, the Court explained, established that "property rights are not the sole measure of Fourth Amendment violations," but did not "snuf[f] out the previously recognized protection for property." . . .

The concurrence begins by accusing us of applying "18th-century tort law." That is a distortion. What we apply is an 18th-century guarantee against unreasonable searches, which we believe must provide at a minimum the degree of protection it afforded when it was adopted. The concurrence does not share that belief. It would apply exclusively Katz's reasonable-expectation-of-privacy test, even when that eliminates rights that previously existed.

The concurrence faults our approach for "present[ing] particularly vexing problems" in cases that do not involve physical contact, such as those that involve the transmission of electronic signals. We entirely fail to understand that point. For unlike the concurrence, which would make Katz the exclusive test, we do not make trespass the exclusive test. Situations involving merely the transmission of electronic signals without trespass would remain subject to Katz analysis.

## Concurring Opinion by Justice Sotomayor

[Note: Jones raised the question whether the long-term monitoring of his movements constituted a search. The Court didn't answer this question because it found the placement of the GPS device on the vehicle was a search. Justice Sotomayor wrote this concurring opinion agreeing with the outcome but expressing concern about the monitoring question.]

I join the Court's opinion because I agree that a search within the meaning of the Fourth Amendment occurs, at a minimum, "[w] here, as here, the Government obtains information by physically intruding on a constitutionally protected area." In this case, the Government installed a Global Positioning System (GPS) tracking device on respondent Antoine Jones' Jeep without a valid warrant and without Jones' consent, then used that device to monitor the Jeep's movements over the course of four weeks. The Government usurped Jones' property for the purpose of conducting surveillance on him, thereby invading privacy interests long afforded, and undoubtedly entitled to, Fourth Amendment protection. . . .

Of course, the Fourth Amendment is not concerned only with trespassory intrusions on property. Rather, even in the absence of a trespass, "a Fourth Amendment search occurs when the government violates a subjective expectation of privacy that society recognizes as reasonable. . . .

Nonetheless, as Justice Alito notes, physical intrusion is now unnecessary to many forms of surveillance. With increasing regularity, the Government will be capable of duplicating the monitoring undertaken in this case by enlisting factory- or owner-installed vehicle tracking devices or GPS- enabled smartphones. . . .

As Justice Alito incisively observes, the same technological advances that have made possible nontrespassory surveillance techniques will also affect the Katz test by shaping the evolution of societal privacy expectations. Under that rubric, I agree with Justice Alito that, at the very least, "longer term GPS monitoring in investigations of most offenses impinges on expectations of privacy."

In cases involving even short-term monitoring, some unique attributes of GPS surveillance relevant to the Katz analysis will require particular attention. GPS monitoring generates a precise, comprehensive record of a person's public movements that reflects a wealth of detail about her familial, political, professional, religious, and sexual associations. . . .

[Disclosed in [GPS] data . . . will be trips the indisputably private nature of which takes little imagination to conjure: trips to the psychiatrist, the plastic surgeon, the abortion clinic, the AIDS treatment center, the strip club, the criminal defense attorney, the by-the-hour motel, the union meeting, the mosque, synagogue or church, the gay bar and on and on"). The Government can store such records and efficiently mine them for information years into the future. And because GPS monitoring is cheap in comparison to conventional surveillance techniques and, by design, proceeds surreptitiously, it evades the ordinary checks that constrain abusive law enforcement practices: "limited police resources and community hostility."

Awareness that the Government may be watching chills associational and expressive freedoms. And the Government's unrestrained power to assemble data that reveal private aspects of identity is susceptible to abuse. The net result is that GPS monitoring—by making available at a relatively low cost such a substantial quantum of intimate information about any person whom the Government, in its unfettered discretion, chooses to track—may "alter the relationship between citizen and government in a way that is inimical to democratic society."

I would take these attributes of GPS monitoring into account when considering the existence of a reasonable societal expectation of privacy in the sum of one's public movements. I would ask whether people reasonably expect that their movements will be recorded and aggregated in a manner that enables the Government to ascertain, more or less at will, their political and religious beliefs, sexual habits, and so on. . . .

More fundamentally, it may be necessary to reconsider the premise that an individual has no reasonable expectation of privacy in information voluntarily disclosed to third parties. This approach is ill suited to the digital age, in which people reveal a great deal of

(continued)

information about themselves to third parties in the course of carrying out mundane tasks. People disclose the phone numbers that they dial or text to their cellular providers; the URLs that they visit and the e-mail addresses with which they correspond to their Internet service providers; and the books, groceries, and medications they purchase to online retailers. Perhaps, as Justice Alito notes, some people may find the "tradeoff" of privacy for convenience "worthwhile," or come to accept this "diminution of privacy" as "inevitable," and perhaps not. I for one doubt that people would accept without complaint the warrantless disclosure to the Government of a list of every Web site they had visited in the last week, or month, or year. But whatever the societal expectations, they can attain constitutionally protected status only if our Fourth Amendment jurisprudence ceases to treat secrecy as a prerequisite for privacy. I would not assume that all information voluntarily disclosed to some member of the public for a limited purpose is, for that reason alone, disentitled to Fourth Amendment protection.

Resolution of these difficult questions in this case is unnecessary, however, because the Government's physical intrusion on Jones' Jeep supplies a narrower basis for decision. I therefore join the majority's opinion.

The type of telephone booth used by the defendant in the Katz case.

So, *Jones* makes clear that *both* the old property test and Katz's privacy test are applied to determine if the Fourth Amendment is triggered. To summarize, the Fourth Amendment applies when:

1. police trespass upon a legally recognized property interest and
2. when police conduct invades a space where a suspect has a reasonable expectation to privacy.

What constitutes a trespass or invasion of a reasonable expectation of privacy has been the subject of a lot of litigation. It is common to refer to the triggering decision as resting on "standing" law. Standing is the legal principle that a person must have a personal interest—"skin in the game"—to assert a legal right. In a strict sense, standing decides whether a court has jurisdiction (authority) to hear a case. Although convenient, the characterization is incorrect. The Katz and Jones tests are not about jurisdiction, even though they operate in the same way, and their outcomes are the same as if standing analysis were applied. Consequently, the shorthand "**standing**" is commonly used to describe whether a person has a Fourth Amendment right to challenge a search. You will see this use of standing in this discussion.

**standing**
A rule that requires a person to have either a property interest or a reasonable expectation of privacy in the area searched in order to have a Fourth Amendment right.

Every case presents different (and often unique) facts. Accordingly, the determination of whether a defendant's expectation to privacy is reasonable is fact sensitive. However, there are Supreme Court cases holding, as a matter of law, whether an expectation to privacy is reasonable in different contexts. Just as not all subjective beliefs of privacy are objectively reasonable, every touching of property by police doesn't constitute a search. Only those that "meaningful interfere" with a property interest trigger the Fourth Amendment. As to when physical contact of an "effect" by a law enforcement officer becomes a search, the Supreme Court has drawn the line in favor of individual liberty. In *Bond v. United States*,[7] for example, a border patrol officer's quick squeeze of a bus passenger's soft luggage was determined to be a search, even though there was considerable evidence that passengers commonly touched each other's luggage in a manner no less intrusive than that of the border patrol officer.

The Fourth Amendment distinguishes between commercial property and other private property. Generally, there is less legal right to privacy in commercial premises than in dwellings.[8] But the nature of the use of the premises must be considered.

The home is one of the most sacred Fourth Amendment spaces. The often quoted and famous English judge Sir Edward Coke wrote in a 1604 decision *domus sua cuique est tutissimum refugium*, which translates to every person's house is his safest refuge.[9] This and other language from the decision are commonly shortened to "A person's home is their castle." The notion that a person should be safe and secure in the home is universal, a product of natural law. For this reason, police must, absent exigent circumstances, have both probable cause and a warrant to enter the home. As recently as 2021, the Court reaffirmed the sanctity of the home. In *Caniglia v. Strom*, the Court wrote that there is an "unmistakable distinction" between the home and car, and it affirmed its policy of "repeatedly declin[ing] to expand the scope of . . . exceptions to the warrant requirement to permit warrantless entry into the home."

But not all residents of a home, or other property, are equal. Homeowners and long-term residents are fully protected by the Fourth Amendment. In a pre-Katz property-based decision, the Court extended full Fourth Amendment protection to a short-term resident of an apartment because he exercised lawful "dominion and control" over it. Specifically, the tenant, who was out of town, had given the defendant a key, and he had stayed overnight. But other short-term guests, business customers, and others don't always enjoy the same rights. In *Minnesota v. Olson* (1990), the Supreme Court held that an overnight guest may possess a reasonable expectation to privacy in the host's home.[10] Expanding on the reasoning in *Olson*, the defendant in *Minnesota v. Carter* (1998) presented in your next Oyez, asserted that a short-term guest—not an overnight resident—in another's home should also be protected by the Fourth Amendment. The Court rejected the claim.

A hotel is a public establishment, but the common purpose of the hotel business is to provide individuals with privacy, safety, and comfort when away from home. Therefore, hotel guests often have a reasonable expectation to privacy. But there are exceptions. Several factors are considered, including whether the defendant is a registered guest and if not, what his or her relationship to the registered

## Oyez

### Minnesota v. Carter
### 525 U.S. 83 (1998)

**Chief Justice Rehnquist delivered the opinion of the Court.**

Respondents and the lessee of an apartment were sitting in one of its rooms, bagging cocaine. While so engaged they were observed by a police officer, who looked through a drawn window blind. The Supreme Court of Minnesota held that the officer's viewing was a search which violated respondents' Fourth Amendment rights. We hold that no such violation occurred.

James Thielen, a police officer in the Twin Cities' suburb of Eagan, Minnesota, went to an apartment building to investigate a tip from a confidential informant. The informant said that he had walked by the window of a ground-floor apartment and had seen people putting a white powder into bags. The officer looked in the same window through a gap in the closed blind and observed the bagging operation for several minutes. He then notified headquarters, which began preparing affidavits for a search warrant while he returned to the apartment building. When two men left the building in a previously identified Cadillac, the police stopped the car. Inside were respondents Carter and Johns. As the police opened the door of the car to let Johns out, they observed a black zippered pouch and a handgun, later determined to be loaded, on the vehicle's floor. Carter and Johns were arrested, and a later police search of the vehicle the next day discovered pagers, a scale, and 47 grams of cocaine in plastic sandwich bags.

After seizing the car, the police returned to Apartment 103 and arrested the occupant, Kimberly Thompson, who is not a party to this appeal. A search of the apartment pursuant to a warrant revealed cocaine residue on the kitchen table and plastic baggies similar to those found in the Cadillac. Thielen identified Carter, Johns, and Thompson as the three people he had observed placing the powder into baggies. The police later learned that while Thompson was the lessee of the apartment, Carter and Johns lived in Chicago and had come to the apartment for the sole purpose of packaging the cocaine. Carter and Johns had never been to the apartment before and were only in the apartment for approximately 2½ hours. In return for the use of the apartment, Carter and Johns had given Thompson one-eighth of an ounce of the cocaine.

Carter and Johns were charged with conspiracy to commit controlled substance crime in the first-degree and aiding and abetting in a controlled substance crime in the first degree, in violation of [Minnesota statute]. They moved to suppress all evidence obtained from the apartment and the Cadillac, as well as to suppress several post arrest incriminating statements they had made. They argued that Thielen's initial observation of their drug packaging activities was an unreasonable search in violation of the Fourth Amendment and that all evidence obtained as a result of this unreasonable search was inadmissible as fruit of the poisonous tree. The Minnesota trial court held that since, unlike the defendant in *Minnesota v. Olson*, 495 U.S. 91, 109 L. Ed. 2d 85, 110 S. Ct. 1684 (1990), Carter and Johns were not overnight social guests but temporary out-of-state visitors, they were not entitled to claim the protection of the Fourth Amendment against the government intrusion into the apartment. The trial court also concluded that Thielen's observation was not a search within the meaning of the Fourth Amendment. After a trial, Carter and Johns were each convicted of both offenses. The Minnesota Court of Appeals held that the respondent Carter did not have "standing" to object to Thielen's actions because his claim that he was predominantly a social guest was "inconsistent with the only evidence concerning his stay in the apartment, which indicates that he used it for a business purpose—to package drugs." *Minnesota v. Carter*, 545 N.W.2d 695, 698 (1996). In a separate appeal, the Court of Appeals also affirmed Johns' conviction, without addressing what it termed the "standing" issue. A divided Minnesota Supreme Court reversed, holding that respondents had "standing" to claim the protection of the Fourth Amendment because they had "'a legitimate expectation of privacy in the invaded place.'" . . .

The Minnesota courts analyzed whether respondents had a legitimate expectation of privacy under the rubric of "standing" doctrine, an analysis which this Court expressly rejected 20 years ago in *Rakas* 439 U.S. at 139–140. In that case, we held that automobile passengers could not assert the protection of the Fourth Amendment against the seizure of incriminating evidence from a vehicle where they owned neither the vehicle nor the evidence. Central to our analysis was the idea that in determining whether a defendant is able to show the violation of his (and not someone else's) Fourth Amendment rights, the "definition of those rights is more properly placed within the purview of substantive Fourth Amendment law than within that of standing." Thus, we held that in order to claim the protection of the Fourth Amendment, a defendant must demonstrate that he personally has an expectation of privacy in the place searched, and that his expectation is reasonable; i.e., one which has "a source outside of the Fourth Amendment, either by reference to concepts of real or personal property law or to understandings that are recognized and permitted by society." The Fourth Amendment guarantees: "The right of the people to be secure in their persons, houses, papers, and effects, against unreasonable searches and seizures, shall not be violated, and no Warrants shall issue, but upon probable cause, supported by Oath or affirmation, and particularly describing the place to be searched, and the persons or things to be seized." The Amendment protects persons against unreasonable searches of "their persons [and] houses" and thus indicates that the Fourth Amendment is a personal right that must be invoked by an individual. But the extent to which the Fourth Amendment protects people may depend upon where those people are. We have held that "capacity to claim the protection of the Fourth Amendment depends . . . upon whether the person who claims the protection of the Amendment has a legitimate expectation of privacy in the invaded place."

The text of the Amendment suggests that its protections extend only to people in "their" houses. But we have held that in some circumstances a person may have a legitimate expectation of privacy in the house of someone else. In *Minnesota v. Olson*, 495 U.S. 91, 109 L. Ed. 2d 85, 110 S. Ct. 1684 (1990), for example, we decided that an overnight guest in a house had the sort of expectation of privacy that the Fourth Amendment protects. We said:

> "To hold that an overnight guest has a legitimate expectation of privacy in his host's home merely recognizes the everyday expectations of privacy that we all share. Staying overnight in another's home is a long-standing social custom that serves functions recognized as valuable by society. We stay in others' homes when we travel to a strange city for business or pleasure, we visit our parents, children, or more distant relatives out of town, when we are in between jobs, or homes, or when we house-sit for a friend. . . .

> "From the overnight guest's perspective, he seeks shelter in another's home precisely because it provides him with privacy, a place where he and his possessions will not be disturbed by anyone but his host and those his host allows inside. We are at our most vulnerable when we are asleep because we cannot monitor our own safety or the security of our belongings. It is for this reason that, although we may spend all day in public places, when we cannot sleep in our own home we seek out another private place to sleep, whether it be a hotel room, or the home of a friend."

In *Jones v. United States*, (1960), the defendant seeking to exclude evidence resulting from a search of an apartment had been given the use of the apartment by a friend. He had clothing in the apartment, had slept there " 'maybe a night,' " and at the time was the sole occupant of the apartment. But while the holding of *Jones*—that a search of the apartment violated the defendant's Fourth Amendment rights—is still valid, its statement that "anyone legitimately on the premises where a search occurs may challenge its legality," was expressly repudiated in *Rakas v. Illinois*. Thus an overnight guest in a home may claim the protection of the Fourth Amendment, but one who is merely present with the consent of the householder may not.

Respondents here were obviously not overnight guests, but were essentially present for a business transaction and were only in the home a matter of hours. There is no suggestion that they had a previous relationship with Thompson, or that there was any other purpose to their visit. Nor was there anything similar to the overnight guest relationship in *Olson* to suggest a degree of acceptance into the household. While the apartment was a dwelling place for Thompson, it was for these respondents simply a place to do business.

Property used for commercial purposes is treated differently for Fourth Amendment purposes than residential property. "An expectation of privacy in commercial premises, however, is different from, and indeed less than, a similar expectation in an individual's home." If we regard the overnight guest in *Minnesota v. Olson* as typifying those who may claim the protection of the Fourth Amendment in the home of another, and one merely "legitimately on the premises" as typifying those who may not do so, the present case is obviously somewhere in between. But the purely commercial nature of the transaction engaged in here, the relatively short period of time on the premises, and the lack of any previous connection between respondents and the householder, all lead us to conclude that respondents' situation is closer to that of one simply permitted on the premises. We therefore hold that any search which may have occurred did not violate their Fourth Amendment rights.

Because we conclude that respondents had no legitimate expectation of privacy in the apartment, we need not decide whether the police officer's observation constituted a "search." The judgment of the Supreme Court of Minnesota is accordingly reversed, and the cause is remanded for proceedings not inconsistent with this opinion.

It is so ordered. . . .

### Justice Ginsburg, with whom Justice Stevens and Justice Souter join, dissenting.

The Court's decision undermines not only the security of short-term guests, but also the security of the home resident herself. In my view, when a homeowner or lessor personally invites a guest into her home to share in a common endeavor, whether it be for conversation, to engage in leisure activities, or for business purposes licit or illicit, that guest should share his host's shelter against unreasonable searches and seizures. . . .

guest is, whether the defendant paid any of the hotel charges, the use of the room, and the total time the defendant spent in the room. The short-term use of a hotel room to conduct a drug transaction is different from the ordinary overnight guest.

Just one year after its 2012 *Jones* decision, the Court had the opportunity to apply the property test to a police dog sniff at the front door of a person's home in *Florida v. Jardines*.

# Oyez

## Florida v. Jardines
### 569 U.S. 1 (2013)

**Justice Scalia delivered the opinion of the Court.**

■ ■ ■

In 2006, Detective William Pedraja of the Miami-Dade Police Department received an unverified tip that marijuana was being grown in the home of respondent Joelis Jardines. One month later, the Department and the Drug Enforcement Administration sent a joint surveillance team to Jardines' home. Detective Pedraja was part of that team. He watched the home for fifteen minutes and saw no vehicles in the driveway or activity around the home, and could not see inside because the blinds were drawn. Detective Pedraja then approached Jardines' home accompanied by Detective Douglas Bartelt, a trained canine handler who had just arrived at the scene with his drug-sniffing dog. The dog was trained to detect the scent of marijuana, cocaine, heroin, and several other drugs, indicating the presence of any of these substances through particular behavioral changes recognizable by his handler.

Detective Bartelt had the dog on a six-foot leash, owing in part to the dog's "wild" nature, and tendency to dart around erratically while searching. As the dog approached Jardines' front porch, he apparently sensed one of the odors he had been trained to detect, and began energetically exploring the area for the strongest point source of that odor. As Detective Bartelt explained, the dog "began tracking that airborne odor by . . . tracking back and forth," engaging in what is called "bracketing," "back and forth, back and forth." Detective Bartelt gave the dog "the full six feet of the leash plus whatever safe distance [he could] give him" to do this—he testified that he needed to give the dog "as much distance as I can." And Detective Pedraja stood back while this was occurring, so that he would not "get knocked over" when the dog was "spinning around trying to find" the source.

After sniffing the base of the front door, the dog sat, which is the trained behavior upon discovering the odor's strongest point. Detective Bartelt then pulled the dog away from the door and returned to his vehicle. He left the scene after informing Detective Pedraja that there had been a positive alert for narcotics.

On the basis of what he had learned at the home, Detective Pedraja applied for and received a warrant to search the residence. When the warrant was executed later that day, Jardines attempted to flee and was arrested; the search revealed marijuana plants, and he was charged with trafficking in cannabis. . . .

The Fourth Amendment provides in relevant part that the "right of the people to be secure in their persons, houses, papers, and effects, against unreasonable searches and seizures, shall not be violated." The Amendment establishes a simple baseline, one that for much of our history formed the exclusive basis for its protections: When "the Government obtains information by physically intruding" on persons, houses, papers, or effects, "a 'search' within the original meaning of the Fourth Amendment" has "undoubtedly occurred." United States v. Jones . . . By reason of our decision in *Katz v. United States*, 389 U. S. 347 (1967), property rights "are not the sole measure of Fourth Amendment violations," *Soldal v. Cook County*, 506 U. S. 56, 64 (1992)—but though Katz may add to the baseline, it does not subtract anything from the Amendment's protections "when the Government does engage in [a] physical intrusion of a constitutionally protected area,"

That principle renders this case a straightforward one. The officers were gathering information in an area belonging to Jardines and immediately surrounding his house—in the curtilage of the house, which we have held enjoys protection as part of the home itself. And they gathered that information by physically entering and occupying the area to engage in conduct not explicitly or implicitly permitted by the homeowner.

The Fourth Amendment "indicates with some precision the places and things encompassed by its protections": persons, houses, papers, and effects. Fourth Amendment does not, therefore, prevent all investigations conducted on private property; for example, an officer may (subject to Katz) gather information in what we have called "open fields"—even if those fields are privately owned—because such fields are not enumerated in the Amendment's text.

But when it comes to the Fourth Amendment, the home is first among equals. At the Amendment's "very core" stands "the right of a man to retreat into his own home and there be free from unreasonable governmental intrusion." This right would be of little practical value if the State's agents could stand in a home's porch or side garden and trawl for evidence with impunity; the right to retreat would be significantly diminished if the police could enter a man's property to observe his repose from just outside the front window.

We therefore regard the area "immediately surrounding and associated with the home"—what our cases call the curtilage—as "part of the home itself for Fourth Amendment purposes. . . .

While the boundaries of the curtilage are generally "clearly marked," the "conception defining the curtilage" is at any rate familiar enough that it is "easily understood from our daily experience." Here there is no doubt that the officers entered it: The front porch is the classic exemplar of an area adjacent to the home and "to which the activity of home life extends. . . .

Since the officers' investigation took place in a constitutionally protected area, we turn to the question of whether it was accomplished through an unlicensed physical intrusion. While law enforcement officers need not "shield their eyes" when passing by the home "on public thoroughfares," an officer's leave to gather information is sharply circumscribed when he steps off those thoroughfares and enters the Fourth Amendment's protected areas. In permitting, for example, visual observation of the home from "public navigable airspace," we were careful to note that it was done "in a physically nonintrusive manner. . . .

"[O]ur law holds the property of every man so sacred, that no man can set his foot upon his neighbour's close without his leave." As it is undisputed that the detectives had all four of their feet and all four of their companion's firmly planted on the constitutionally protected extension of Jardines' home, the only question is whether he had given his leave (even implicitly) for them to do so. He had not. . . .

A license may be implied from the habits of the country," notwithstanding the "strict rule of the English common law as to entry upon a close." We have accordingly recognized that "the knocker on the front door is treated as an invitation or license to attempt an entry, justifying ingress to the home by solicitors, hawkers and peddlers of all kinds." This implicit license typically permits the visitor to approach the home by the front path, knock promptly, wait briefly to be received, and then (absent invitation to linger longer) leave. Complying with the terms of that traditional invitation does not require fine-grained legal knowledge; it is generally managed without incident by the Nation's Girl Scouts and trick-or-treaters. Thus, a police officer not armed with a warrant may approach a home and knock, precisely because that is "no more than any private citizen might do."

But introducing a trained police dog to explore the area around the home in hopes of discovering incriminating evidence is something else. There is no customary invitation to do that. An invitation to engage in canine forensic investigation assuredly does not inhere in the very act of hanging a knocker. To find a visitor knocking on the door is routine (even if sometimes unwelcome); to spot that same visitor exploring the front path with a metal detector, or marching his bloodhound into the garden before saying hello and asking permission, would inspire most of us to—well, call the police. The scope of a license—express or implied—is limited not only to a particular area but also to a specific purpose. Consent at a traffic stop to an officer's checking out an anonymous tip that there is a body in the trunk does not permit the officer to rummage through the trunk for narcotics. Here, the background social norms that invite a visitor to the front door do not invite him there to conduct a search. . . .

The government's use of trained police dogs to investigate the home and its immediate surroundings is a "search" within the meaning of the Fourth Amendment.

The lawfulness of a person's use of property is relevant to the Fourth Amendment trigger question, but it doesn't fully answer it. For example, a car thief doesn't have a Fourth Amendment interest in the car because the thief doesn't have a legally recognized property or privacy interest. But the driver of a rental car who is not listed as an authorized driver with the rental company, but who is driving with the authorization of the person listed on the rental agreement, does have a Fourth Amendment interest in the vehicle.[11]

The use of simple technology to enhance the senses has been held not to be a search. For example, a police officer may use a flashlight to look into a stopped car. However, the area where the enhancement is used, the sophistication of the technology, and the threat to privacy must all be considered. This was the issue in *Kyllo*, featured in your next Oyez where the Supreme Court invalidated the warrantless use of thermo-imaging on the exterior of a home.

## Oyez

### Kyllo v. United States
#### 533 U.S. 27 (2001)

**Justice Scalia delivered the opinion of the Court.**

This case presents the question whether the use of a thermal-imaging device aimed at a private home from a public street to detect relative amounts of heat within the home constitutes a "search" within the meaning of the Fourth Amendment.

In 1991 Agent William Elliott of the United States Department of the Interior came to suspect that marijuana was being grown in the home belonging to petitioner Danny Kyllo, part of a triplex on Rhododendron Drive in Florence, Oregon. Indoor marijuana growth typically

(continued)

requires high-intensity lamps. In order to determine whether an amount of heat was emanating from petitioner's home consistent with the use of such lamps, at 3:20 A.M. on January 16, 1992, Agent Elliott and Dan Haas used an Agema Thermovision 210 thermal imager to scan the triplex. Thermal imagers detect infrared radiation, which virtually all objects emit but which is not visible to the naked eye. The imager converts radiation into images based on relative warmth—black is cool, white is hot, shades of gray connote relative differences; in that respect, it operates somewhat like a video camera showing heat images. The scan of Kyllo's home took only a few minutes and was performed from the passenger seat of Agent Elliott's vehicle across the street from the front of the house and also from the street in back of the house. The scan showed that the roof over the garage and a side wall of petitioner's home were relatively hot compared to the rest of the home and substantially warmer than neighboring homes in the triplex. Agent Elliott concluded that petitioner was using halide lights to grow marijuana in his house, which indeed he was. Based on tips from informants, utility bills, and the thermal imaging, a Federal Magistrate Judge issued a warrant authorizing a search of petitioner's home, and the agents found an indoor growing operation involving more than 100 plants. Petitioner was indicted on one count of manufacturing marijuana. . . .

The Fourth Amendment provides that "[t]he right of the people to be secure in their persons, houses, papers, and effects, against unreasonable searches and seizures, shall not be violated." "At the very core" of the Fourth Amendment "stands the right of a man to retreat into his own home and there be free from unreasonable governmental intrusion." . . .

In assessing when a search is not a search, we have applied somewhat in reverse the principle first enunciated in *Katz v. United States,* (1967). Katz involved eavesdropping by means of an electronic listening device placed on the outside of a telephone booth—a location not within the catalog ("persons, houses, papers, and effects") that the Fourth Amendment protects against unreasonable searches. We held that the Fourth Amendment nonetheless protected Katz from the warrantless eavesdropping because he "justifiably relied" upon the privacy of the telephone booth. As Justice Harlan's oft-quoted concurrence described it, a Fourth Amendment search occurs when the government violates a subjective expectation of privacy that society recognizes as reasonable. . . .

The present case involves officers on a public street engaged in more than naked-eye surveillance of a home. We have previously reserved judgment as to how much technological enhancement of ordinary perception from such a vantage point, if any, is too much. While we upheld enhanced aerial photography of an industrial complex in *Dow Chemical,* we noted that we found "it important that this is *not* an area immediately adjacent to a private home, where privacy expectations are most heightened. . . .

The Government maintains, however, that the thermal imaging must be upheld because it detected "only heat radiating from the external surface of the house,". The dissent makes this its leading point, contending that there is a fundamental difference between what it calls "off-the-wall" observations and "through-the-wall surveillance." But just as a thermal imager captures only heat emanating from a house, so also a powerful directional microphone picks up only sound emanating from a house—and a satellite capable of scanning from many miles away would pick up only visible light emanating from a house. We rejected such a mechanical interpretation of the Fourth Amendment in *Katz,* where the eavesdropping device picked up only sound waves that reached the exterior of the phone booth. Reversing that approach would leave the homeowner at the mercy of advancing technology—including imaging technology that could discern all human activity in the home. While the technology used in the present case was relatively crude, the rule we adopt must take account of more sophisticated systems that are already in use or in development.

Where, as here, the Government uses a device that is not in general public use, to explore details of the home that would previously have been unknowable without physical intrusion, the surveillance is a "search" and is presumptively unreasonable without a warrant.

Since we hold the Thermovision imaging to have been an unlawful search, it will remain for the District Court to determine whether, without the evidence it provided, the search warrant issued in this case was supported by probable cause—and if not, whether there is any other basis for supporting admission of the evidence that the search pursuant to the warrant produced.

## Third-Party Doctrine

In the 1970s, the Supreme Court issued two decisions holding that a person doesn't have a Fourth Amendment privacy interest in information voluntarily given to third parties. Consequently, police don't have to obtain a warrant to obtain customer information from businesses. Even before the *Katz* decision, the Court made privacy-like decisions concerning evidence that was visible, or disclosed, to third parties. For example, it was decided in 1878 that it wasn't a search for postal inspectors to visually inspect the exterior of items placed in the mails.[12] But the most informative decisions for the modern era were *Miller v. United States* and *Smith v. Maryland.*[13] In the former, the Court decided that a customer lacks a privacy interest in bank records because they were disclosed to the bank. The same decision was made about the telephone call record by a defendant in the latter case.

The impact of these cases on privacy is more pronounced in the digital world. Today, smartphones are the gateway into the whole of a person's life—telephone conversations, location and travel, finances, web searches, and intimate information. And under the Third-Party Doctrine, none of this is protected by the Fourth Amendment because smartphones (and other digital devices) continuously ping towers that are owned by third parties, calls are made using third-party carriers, and documents are stored in third-party cloud companies. Concern about the continuous monitoring of a person's movement was addressed, albeit in a limited way, in the *Jones* case discussed earlier in this chapter. But that decision was limited to the trespassory placement of a tracker on a vehicle. The Court didn't address this question: does prolonged tracking of location provoke the Fourth Amendment? And more specifically, does the Third-Party Doctrine permit warrantless searches and seizures of location data? The Court addressed these questions in your next Oyez, *Carpenter v. United States*.

## Oyez

### Carpenter v. United States
### 585 U.S. ___ (2018)

**Chief Justice Roberts delivered the opinion of the Court.**

This case presents the question whether the Government conducts a search under the Fourth Amendment when it accesses historical cell phone records that provide a comprehensive chronicle of the user's past movements.

There are 396 million cell phone service accounts in the United States—for a Nation of 326 million people. Cell phones perform their wide and growing variety of functions by connecting to a set of radio antennas called "cell sites." Although cell sites are usually mounted on a tower, they can also be found on light posts, flagpoles, church steeples, or the sides of buildings. Cell sites typically have several directional antennas that divide the covered area into sectors.

Cell phones continuously scan their environment looking for the best signal, which generally comes from the closest cell site. Most modern devices, such as smartphones, tap into the wireless network several times a minute whenever their signal is on, even if the owner is not using one of the phone's features. Each time the phone connects to a cell site, it generates a time-stamped record known as cell-site location information (CSLI). . . .

Wireless carriers collect and store CSLI for their own business purposes, including finding weak spots in their network and applying "roaming" charges when another carrier routes data through their cell sites. In addition, wireless carriers often sell aggregated location records to data brokers, without individual identifying information of the sort at issue here. While carriers have long retained CSLI for the start and end of incoming calls, in recent years phone companies have also collected location information from the transmission of text messages and routine data connections. Accordingly, modern cell phones generate increasingly vast amounts of increasingly precise CSLI.

In 2011, police officers arrested four men suspected of robbing a series of Radio Shack and (ironically enough) T-Mobile stores in Detroit. One of the men confessed that, over the previous four months, the group (along with a rotating cast of getaway drivers and lookouts) had robbed nine different stores in Michigan and Ohio. The suspect identified 15 accomplices who had participated in the heists and gave the FBI some of their cell phone numbers; the FBI then reviewed his call records to identify additional numbers that he had called around the time of the robberies.

Based on that information, the prosecutors applied for court orders under the Stored Communications Act to obtain cell phone records for petitioner Timothy Carpenter and several other suspects. That statute, as amended in 1994, permits the Government to compel the disclosure of certain telecommunications records when it "offers specific and articulable facts showing that there are reasonable grounds to believe" that the records sought "are relevant and material to an ongoing criminal investigation." Federal Magistrate Judges issued two orders directing Carpenter's wireless carriers—MetroPCS and Sprint—to disclose "cell/site sector [information] for [Carpenter's] telephone [ ] at call origination and at call termination for incoming and outgoing calls" during the four-month period when the string of robberies occurred. The first order sought 152 days of cell-site records from MetroPCS, which produced records spanning 127 days. The second order requested seven days of CSLI from Sprint, which produced two days of records covering the period when Carpenter's phone was "roaming" in northeastern Ohio. Altogether the Government obtained 12,898 location points cataloging Carpenter's movements—an average of 101 data points per day.

(continued)

Carpenter was charged with six counts of robbery and an additional six counts of carrying a firearm during a federal crime of violence. Prior to trial, Carpenter moved to suppress the cell-site data provided by the wireless carriers. He argued that the Government's seizure of the records violated the Fourth Amendment because they had been obtained without a warrant supported by probable cause. The District Court denied the motion. . . .

Carpenter was convicted on all but one of the firearm counts and sentenced to more than 100 years in prison. . . .

The Court of Appeals for the Sixth Circuit affirmed. The court held that Carpenter lacked a reasonable expectation of privacy in the location information collected by the FBI because he had shared that information with his wireless carriers. Given that cell phone users voluntarily convey cell-site data to their carriers as "a means of establishing communication," the court concluded that the resulting business records are not entitled to Fourth Amendment protection. . . .

For much of our history, Fourth Amendment search doctrine was "tied to common-law trespass" and focused on whether the Government "obtains information by physically intruding on a constitutionally protected area." More recently, the Court has recognized that "property rights are not the sole measure of Fourth Amendment violations." In *Katz* v. *United States*, 389 U. S. 347, 351 (1967), we established that "the Fourth Amendment protects people, not places," and expanded our conception of the Amendment to protect certain expectations of privacy as well. . . .

Although no single rubric definitively resolves which expectations of privacy are entitled to protection,[1] the analysis is informed by historical understandings "of what was deemed an unreasonable search and seizure when [the Fourth Amendment] was adopted." On this score, our cases have recognized some basic guideposts. First, that the Amendment seeks to secure "the privacies of life" against "arbitrary power." Second, and relatedly, that a central aim of the Framers was "to place obstacles in the way of a too permeating police surveillance."

We have kept this attention to Founding-era understandings in mind when applying the Fourth Amendment to innovations in surveillance tools. As technology has enhanced the Government's capacity to encroach upon areas normally guarded from inquisitive eyes, this Court has sought to "assure[ ] preservation of that degree of privacy against government that existed when the Fourth Amendment was adopted." For that reason, we rejected in *Kyllo* a "mechanical interpretation" of the Fourth Amendment and held that use of a thermal imager to detect heat radiating from the side of the defendant's home was a search. Because any other conclusion would leave homeowners "at the mercy of advancing technology," we determined that the Government—absent a warrant—could not capitalize on such new sense-enhancing technology to explore what was happening within the home.

Likewise in *Riley*, the Court recognized the "immense storage capacity" of modern cell phones in holding that police officers must generally obtain a warrant before searching the contents of a phone. We explained that while the general rule allowing warrantless searches incident to arrest "strikes the appropriate balance in the context of physical objects, neither of its rationales has much force with respect to" the vast store of sensitive information on a cell phone. . . .

The question we confront today is how to apply the Fourth Amendment to a new phenomenon: the ability to chronicle a person's past movements through the record of his cell phone signals. Such tracking partakes of many of the qualities of the GPS monitoring we considered in *Jones*. Much like GPS tracking of a vehicle, cell phone location information is detailed, encyclopedic, and effortlessly compiled.

At the same time, the fact that the individual continuously reveals his location to his wireless carrier implicates the third-party principle of *Smith* and *Miller*. But while the third-party doctrine applies to telephone numbers and bank records, it is not clear whether its logic extends to the qualitatively different category of cell-site records. After all, when *Smith* was decided in 1979, few could have imagined a society in which a phone goes wherever its owner goes, conveying to the wireless carrier not just dialed digits, but a detailed and comprehensive record of the person's movements.

We decline to extend *Smith* and *Miller* to cover these novel circumstances. Given the unique nature of cell phone location records, the fact that the information is held by a third party does not by itself overcome the user's claim to Fourth Amendment protection. Whether the Government employs its own surveillance technology as in *Jones* or leverages the technology of a wireless carrier, we hold that an individual maintains a legitimate expectation of privacy in the record of his physical movements as captured through CSLI. The location information obtained from Carpenter's wireless carriers was the product of a search.

A person does not surrender all Fourth Amendment protection by venturing into the public sphere. To the contrary, "what [one] seeks to preserve as private, even in an area accessible to the public, may be constitutionally protected." A majority of this Court has already recognized that individuals have a reasonable expectation of privacy in the whole of their physical movements. Prior to the digital age, law enforcement might have pursued a suspect for a brief stretch, but doing so "for any extended period of time was difficult and costly and therefore rarely undertaken." For that reason, "society's expectation has been that law enforcement agents and others would not—and indeed, in the main, simply could not—secretly monitor and catalogue every single movement of an individual's car for a very long period."

Allowing government access to cell-site records contravenes that expectation. Although such records are generated for commercial purposes, that distinction does not negate Carpenter's anticipation of privacy in his physical location. Mapping a cell phone's location over the course of 127 days provides an all-encompassing record of the holder's whereabouts. As with GPS information, the time-stamped data provides an intimate window into a person's life, revealing not only his particular movements, but through them his "familial, political, professional, religious, and sexual associations." These location records "hold for many Americans the 'privacies of life.' And like GPS monitoring, cell phone tracking is remarkably easy, cheap, and efficient compared to traditional investigative tools. With just the click of a button, the Government can access each carrier's deep repository of historical location information at practically no expense.

In fact, historical cell-site records present even greater privacy concerns than the GPS monitoring of a vehicle we considered in *Jones*. Unlike the bugged container in *Knotts* or the car in *Jones*, a cell phone—almost a "feature of human anatomy," —tracks nearly exactly the movements of its owner. While individuals regularly leave their vehicles, they compulsively carry cell phones with them all the time. A cell phone faithfully follows its owner beyond public thoroughfares and into private residences, doctor's offices, political headquarters, and other potentially revealing locales. Accordingly, when the Government tracks the location of a cell phone it achieves near perfect surveillance, as if it had attached an ankle monitor to the phone's user.

Moreover, the retrospective quality of the data here gives police access to a category of information otherwise unknowable. In the past, attempts to reconstruct a person's movements were limited by a dearth of records and the frailties of recollection. With access to CSLI, the Government can now travel back in time to retrace a person's whereabouts, subject only to the retention polices of the wireless carriers, which currently maintain records for up to five years. Critically, because location information is continually logged for all of the 400 million devices in the United States—not just those belonging to persons who might happen to come under investigation—this newfound tracking capacity runs against everyone. Unlike with the GPS device in *Jones*, police need not even know in advance whether they want to follow a particular individual, or when.

Whoever the suspect turns out to be, he has effectively been tailed every moment of every day for five years, and the police may—in the Government's view—call upon the results of that surveillance without regard to the constraints of the Fourth Amendment. Only the few with- out cell phones could escape this tireless and absolute surveillance.

Accordingly, when the Government accessed CSLI from the wireless carriers, it invaded Carpenter's reason- able expectation of privacy in the whole of his physical movements.

The Government's primary contention to the contrary is that the third-party doctrine governs this case. In its view, cell-site records are fair game because they are "business records" created and maintained by the wireless carriers. The Government (along with Justice Kennedy) recognizes that this case features new technology, but asserts that the legal question nonetheless turns on a garden-variety request for information from a third-party witness. . . .

There is a world of difference between the limited types of personal information addressed in *Smith* and *Miller* and the exhaustive chronicle of location information casually collected by wireless carriers today. The Government thus is not asking for a straightforward application of the third-party doctrine, but instead a significant extension of it to a distinct category of information. . . .

We therefore decline to extend *Smith* and *Miller* to the collection of CSLI. Given the unique nature of cell phone location information, the fact that the Government obtained the information from a third party does not overcome Carpenter's claim to Fourth Amendment protection. The Government's acquisition of the cell-site records was a search within the meaning of the Fourth Amendment.

Our decision today is a narrow one. We do not express a view on matters not before us: real-time CSLI or "tower dumps" (a download of information on all the devices that connected to a particular cell site during a particular interval). We do not disturb the application of *Smith* and *Miller* or call into question conventional surveillance techniques and tools, such as security cameras. Nor do we address other business records that might incidentally reveal location information. Further, our opinion does not consider other collection techniques involving foreign affairs or national security. As Justice Frankfurter noted when considering new innovations in airplanes and radios, the Court must tread carefully in such cases, to ensure that we do not "embarrass the future."

Having found that the acquisition of Carpenter's CSLI was a search, we also conclude that the Government must generally obtain a warrant supported by probable cause before acquiring such records.

We decline to grant the state unrestricted access to a wireless carrier's database of physical location information. In light of the deeply revealing nature of CSLI, its depth, breadth, and comprehensive reach, and the inescapable and automatic nature of its collection, the fact that such information is gathered by a third party does not make it any less deserving of Fourth Amendment protection. The Government's acquisition of the cell-site records here was a search under that Amendment.

The judgment of the Court of Appeals is reversed, and the case is remanded for further proceedings consistent with this opinion.

In the cases discussed so far, police have targeted the geo-location or other data of a specific person. In a twist, police are now reverse investigating geo-location data at crime scenes. For example, it is suspected that federal investigators obtained cell phone tower data from the Capital area for the time during the January 6, 2021 assault on the Capitol Building. Investigators then targeted the people in the data set, which included both the innocent and guilty who were in the area, looking for other digital fingerprints, such as social media postings, texts, and email. This led to the prosecution of many suspects. Whether the collection of this type of aggregate data gives rise to privacy concerns under the Fourth Amendment is yet to be resolved.

# Probable Cause

Learning Objective: Define probable cause and explain when it is required and what forms of evidence may, and may not, be used to establish it.

## Probable Cause Defined

Recall that the baseline requirement of the Fourth Amendment is reasonableness; all searches and seizures must be reasonable. In some instances, reasonableness is enough. But in others, the Fourth Amendment requires more—the existence of **probable cause.** When a warrant is first obtained, the probable cause determination is made by a judge. In cases where a police officer acts without a warrant, the officer makes the probable cause determination. Either way, the probable cause decision is reviewable by a judge after the search. Judicial decisions of probable cause—when a warrant was obtained—are given more deference by a reviewing court than are police decisions.

Probable cause is the amount of evidence necessary for a search, seizure, or arrest to be proper under the Fourth Amendment. There is no one universal definition of probable cause. Probable cause is flexible; and it is contextual. In all situations, it is more than a hunch and less than the amount of evidence required to prove a defendant guilty at trial, beyond a reasonable doubt. As the Supreme Court has expressed, probable cause is present when the trustworthy facts within the officer's knowledge are sufficient in themselves to justify a "person of reasonable caution" in the belief that seizable property would be found or that the person to be arrested committed the crime in question.[14] The probable cause determination is made through the eyes of the officer at the time it is made. Neither hindsight nor the suspect's perspective is part of any subsequent review. To illustrate how "fluid" probable cause is, consider the following statement by the Court:

> A police officer has probable cause to conduct a search when "the facts available to [him] would 'warrant a [person] of reasonable caution in the belief '" that contraband or evidence of a crime is present. The test for probable cause is not reducible to "precise definition or quantification." "Finely tuned standards such as proof beyond a reasonable doubt or by a preponderance of the evidence . . . have no place in the [probable-cause] decision." All we have required is the kind of "fair probability" on which "reasonable and prudent [people,] not legal technicians, act." In evaluating whether the State has met this practical and common-sensical standard, we have consistently looked to the totality of the circumstances. We have rejected rigid rules, bright-line tests, and mechanistic inquiries in favor of a more flexible, all-things-considered approach. In Gates, for example, we abandoned our old test for assessing the reliability of informants' tips because it had devolved into a "complex superstructure of evidentiary and analytical rules," any one of which, if not complied with, would derail a finding of probable cause. We lamented the development of a list of "inflexible, independent requirements applicable in every case." Probable cause, we emphasized, is "a fluid concept—turning on the assessment of probabilities in particular factual contexts—not readily, or even usefully, reduced to a neat set of legal rules."[15]

Probable cause, while elastic itself, is one of many levels of proof that are used in criminal law. Reasonable suspicion, which is covered in greater detail in the next chapter, is expected to support temporary detentions and frisks; beyond a reasonable doubt is the standard for convictions; clear and convincing evidence and preponderance of the evidence are both required to establish some specific facts that arise during pretrial and trial proceedings. The only standard to have a precise numerical setting is preponderance of the evidence, which is quantified as more likely true than not or 51% confidence. Otherwise, the standards do not have precise levels of confidence. We only know how they related to one another (e.g., beyond a reasonable doubt conveys higher confidence in the truth of guilt than preponderance while reasonable suspicion represents less confidence than the preponderance standard). See Exhibit 12–2 for a visual depiction of the relationships between these standards.

When making the probable cause determination, an officer may rely on their own observations, hearsay evidence, and statements of witnesses, victims, and other law enforcement officers. The fact that evidence will be inadmissible at trial does not exclude it from the probable cause determination.

However, innuendo or conjecture that is not supported by facts may not be considered. Although the evidence does not have to rise to the level of being admissible at trial, it must have some credibility.

It is common for the police to depend on information from informants to obtain a search warrant. An informant is a person who has knowledge concerning a crime because of his or her involvement in crime. The reliability of such information (and whether it should be the basis of a warrant) is hotly debated.

In *Aguilar v. Texas,* 378 U.S. 108 (1964), the Supreme Court established a two-prong test for the use of such information (usually hearsay) when making a warrant determination. First, the affidavit had to contain information about the basis for the informant's information. This permitted the issuing judge to determine whether the informant's allegations were well founded. Second, the officer had to provide the judge with reasons for believing that the informant was reliable. This could be done, for example, by showing that the informant had been truthful in the past.

In *Illinois v. Gates,* 462 U.S. 213 (1983), the Court reversed position and adopted a "totality of the circumstances" test, thereby overruling *Aguilar*. However, the Court did not abandon the two prongs of *Aguilar*. Although the two prongs are no longer determinative, they continue to be important factors when examining the totality of the circumstances. The Court stated that:

> The task of the issuing magistrate is simply to make a practical, commonsense decision whether, given all the circumstances set forth in the affidavit before him, including the "veracity" and the "basis of knowledge" of persons supplying hearsay information, there is a fair probability that contraband or evidence of a crime will be found in a particular place. (*Gates* at 233)

This test does not require that the officer name the informant in the application for the warrant. All that is required is that the magistrate be given enough information to make his or her own determination concerning the credibility and reliability of the informant. The law of this area was discussed fully in the Supreme Court's opinion in *Florida v. J.L.* (2000) which you may read in the next Oyez.

## Exhibit 12–2 Standards of Proof

**Standards of Proof**

| | Frisks; Stops | Arrests Searches | Standard of proof in civil cases | Required to prove specific facts and in other circumstances | Required for conviction and punishment | |
|---|---|---|---|---|---|---|
| **0%** | | | **51%** | | | **100%** |
| **Confidence** | | | | | | **Confidence** |
| | Reasonable suspicion | Probable cause | Preponderance of evidence | Clear & convincing evidence | Beyond a reasonable doubt | |

*Sources:* Used to Establish Probable Cause.

## Oyez

### Florida v. J. L.
### 529 U.S. 266 (2000)

**JUSTICE GINSBURG delivered the opinion of the Court.**

The question presented in this case is whether an anonymous tip that a person is carrying a gun is, without more, sufficient to justify a police officer's stop and frisk of that person. We hold that it is not.

I

On October 13, 1995, an anonymous caller reported to the Miami-Dade Police that a young black male standing at a particular bus stop and wearing a plaid shirt was carrying a gun. . . . So far as the record reveals, there is no audio recording of the tip, and nothing is known about the informant. Sometime after the police received the tip—the record does not say how long—two officers were instructed to respond. They arrived at the bus stop about six minutes later and saw three black males "just hanging out [there]." One of the three, respondent J.L., was wearing a plaid shirt. Apart from the tip, the officers had no reason to suspect any of the three of illegal conduct. The officers did not see a firearm, and J.L. made no threatening or otherwise unusual movements. One of the officers approached J.L., told him to put his hands up on the bus stop, frisked him, and seized a gun from J.L.'s pocket. The second officer frisked the other two individuals, against whom no allegations had been made, and found nothing.

J.L., who was at the time of the frisk "10 days shy of his 16th birth [day]," was charged under state law with carrying a concealed firearm without a license and possessing a firearm while under the age of 18. He moved to suppress the gun as the fruit of an unlawful search, and the trial court granted his motion. The intermediate appellate court reversed, but the Supreme Court of Florida quashed that decision and held the search invalid under the Fourth Amendment. Anonymous tips, the Florida Supreme Court stated, are generally less reliable than tips from known informants and can form the basis for reasonable suspicion only if accompanied by specific indicia of reliability, for example, the correct forecast of a subject's " 'not easily predicted' " movements. The tip leading to the frisk of J.L., the court observed, provided no such predictions, nor did it contain any other qualifying indicia of reliability. Two justices dissented. The safety of the police and the public, they maintained, justifies a "firearm exception" to the general rule barring investigatory stops and frisks on the basis of bare-boned anonymous tips.

Seeking review in this Court, the State of Florida noted that the decision of the State's Supreme Court conflicts with decisions of other courts declaring similar searches compatible with the Fourth Amendment. We granted certiorari, and now affirm the judgment of the Florida Supreme Court.

II

Our "stop and frisk" decisions begin with *Terry v. Ohio*, (1968). This Court held in *Terry*:

"[W]here a police officer observes unusual conduct which leads him reasonably to conclude in light of his experience that criminal activity may be afoot and that the persons with whom he is dealing may be armed and presently dangerous, where in the course of investigating this behavior he identifies himself as a policeman and makes reasonable inquiries, and where nothing in the initial stages of the encounter serves to dispel his reasonable fear for his own or others' safety, he is entitled for the protection of himself and others in the area to conduct a carefully limited search of the outer clothing of such persons in an attempt to discover weapons which might be used to assault him."

In the instant case, the officers' suspicion that J.L. was carrying a weapon arose not from any observations of their own but solely from a call made from an unknown location by an unknown caller. Unlike a tip from a known informant whose reputation can be assessed and who can be held responsible if her allegations turn out to be fabricated, anonymous tip alone seldom demonstrates the informant's basis of knowledge or veracity. As we have recognized, however, there are situations in which an anonymous tip, suitably corroborated, exhibits "sufficient indicia of reliability to provide reasonable suspicion to make the investigatory stop." The question we here confront is whether the tip pointing to J.L. had those indicia of reliability.

In *White*, the police received an anonymous tip asserting that a woman was carrying cocaine and predicting that she would leave an apartment building at a specified time, get into a car matching a particular description, and drive to a named motel. Standing alone, the tip would not have justified a *Terry* stop. Only after police observation showed that the informant had accurately predicted the woman's movements, we explained, did it become reasonable to think the tipster had inside knowledge about the suspect and therefore to credit his assertion about the cocaine. Although the Court held that the suspicion in *White* became reasonable after police surveillance, we regarded the case as borderline. Knowledge about a person's future movements indicates some familiarity with that person's affairs, but having such knowledge does not necessarily imply that the informant knows, in particular, whether that person is carrying hidden contraband. We accordingly classified *White* as a "close case."

The tip in the instant case lacked the moderate indicia of reliability present in *White* and essential to the Court's decision in that case. The anonymous call concerning J.L. provided no predictive information and therefore left the police without means to test the informant's knowledge or credibility. That the allegation about the gun turned out to be correct does not suggest that the officers, prior to the frisks, had a reasonable basis for suspecting J.L. of engaging in unlawful conduct: The reasonableness of official suspicion must be measured by what the officers knew before they conducted their search. All the police had to go on in this case was the bare report of an unknown, unaccountable informant who neither explained how he knew about the gun nor supplied any basis for believing he had inside information about J.L. If *White* was a close case on the reliability of anonymous tips, this one surely falls on the other side of the line.

Florida contends that the tip was reliable because its description of the suspect's visible attributes proved accurate: There really was a young black male wearing a plaid shirt at the bus stop. The United States as *amicus curiae* makes a similar argument, proposing that a stop and frisk should be permitted "when (1) an anonymous tip provides a description of a particular person at a particular location illegally carrying a concealed firearm, (2) police promptly verify the pertinent details of the tip except the existence of the firearm, and (3) there are no factors that cast doubt on the reliability of the tip. . . ." These contentions misapprehend the reliability needed for a tip to justify a *Terry* stop.

An accurate description of a subject's readily observable location and appearance is of course reliable in this limited sense: It will help the police correctly identify the person whom the tipster means to accuse. Such a tip, however, does not show that the tipster has knowledge of concealed criminal activity. The reasonable suspicion here at issue requires that a tip be reliable in its assertion of illegality, not just in its tendency to identify a determinate person. . . .

A second major argument advanced by Florida and the United States as *amicus* is, in essence, that the standard *Terry* analysis should be modified to license a "firearm exception." Under such an exception, a tip alleging an illegal gun would justify a stop and frisk even if the accusation would fail standard pre-search reliability testing. We decline to adopt this position.

Firearms are dangerous, and extraordinary dangers sometimes justify unusual precautions. Our decisions recognize the serious threat that armed criminals pose to public safety; *Terry's* rule, which permits protective police searches on the basis of reasonable suspicion rather than demanding that officers meet the higher standard of probable cause, responds to this very concern. But an automatic firearm exception to our established reliability analysis would rove too far. Such an exception would enable any person seeking to harass another to set in motion an intrusive, embarrassing police search of the targeted person simply by placing an anonymous call falsely reporting the target's unlawful carriage of a gun. Nor could one securely confine such an exception to allegations involving firearms. . . .

Finally, the requirement that an anonymous tip bear standard indicia of reliability in order to justify a stop in no way diminishes a police officer's prerogative, in accord with *Terry*, to conduct a protective search of a person who has already been legitimately stopped. We speak in today's decision only of cases in which the officer's authority to make the initial stop is at issue. In that context, we hold that an anonymous tip lacking indicia of reliability of the kind contemplated in *Adams* and *White* does not justify a stop and frisk whenever and however it alleges the illegal possession of a firearm.

The judgment of the Florida Supreme Court is affirmed.

Probable cause may be established by an animal as well as a human. Police, border, and customs officers use dogs to detect drugs, bombs and explosives, and contraband, and to track fugitives.

As you learned earlier, the Supreme Court has stated that the act of having a dog sniff a person or thing is not a search.[16] The question then becomes whether a dog's indication (a dog alert) that contraband is present is probable cause. The Supreme Court answered this as a conditional yes in the 2014 case *Florida v. Harris*,[17] where the Court held that the totality of circumstances around the reliability of a K-9's alert are to be considered. The dog's training, history of accuracy, the handler's behavior, and other factors are considered. If reliable, a dog alert can furnish probable cause for a warrant or a warrantless search.

## Good-Faith Reliance on a Warrant

Judges can differ in opinion. Judges can make mistakes. What happens if a judge finds that probable cause exists and accordingly issues a warrant, only to have the probable cause finding reversed later? Should the evidence discovered during the search be excluded?

The Supreme Court has answered this question in the negative. The Court found, in *United States v. Leon*, 468 U.S. 897 (1984), that the exclusionary rule does not apply to evidence seized by a police officer, acting in good-faith reliance on the warrant, while executing a facially valid warrant. In the words of the Court:

> We conclude that the marginal or nonexistent benefits produced by suppressing evidence obtained in objectively reasonable reliance on a subsequently invalidated search warrant cannot justify the substantial costs of exclusion. We do not suggest, however, that exclusion is always inappropriate in cases where an officer has obtained a warrant and abided by its terms. . . . [A]n officer's reliance on the magistrate's probable-cause determination and on the technical sufficiency of the warrant he issues must be objectively reasonable . . . and it is clear that in some circumstances the officer will have no reasonable grounds for believing that the warrant was properly issued.

The Court found that exclusion of evidence when an officer is relying on a judicially issued warrant would not advance the objective of the exclusionary rule; it would not deter future police misconduct.

For *Leon* to apply, an officer's reliance must be in good faith. An officer who misleads a judge to obtain a warrant is not acting in good faith. Further, the warrant must be facially valid. If a reasonable officer should know that a warrant is facially defective, then any evidence obtained under it must be excluded. Examples of facially invalid warrants include unsigned warrants, warrants that contain an inadequate description of the place or thing to be searched or seized, failure of the magistrate to require the supporting affidavit to be under oath, and such a lack of evidence that an officer could not in reasonable, good-faith believe that probable cause exists. An officer may, however, rely on a warrant that contains mere technical and typographical errors, unless the errors are so fundamental that they render some element of the warrant (e.g., description) defective.

*Leon* is applicable only to searches and seizures that occur pursuant to warrants. An officer's good-faith, but mistaken, belief that probable cause exists to conduct a warrantless search or to make a warrantless seizure does not justify the admission of evidence obtained as a result thereof. As discussed previously in this text, several state courts have refused to follow the *Leon* holding when interpreting their state constitutions.

The *Leon* reasoning has been extended to a court official's negligent false report to police that a warrant exists[18] and to situations in which police officers act in good faith reliance upon a statute.[19] The same standards apply as in *Leon;* that is, the statute relied upon must be facially valid.

## The Search Warrant

Learning Objective: Define, describe, and apply the Fourth Amendment's warrant requirement.

Depending upon the circumstances, a search may be conducted with or without a warrant. The Supreme Court has expressed that there is a strong preference for the use of warrants, when possible, over warrantless actions.[20] The warrant preference serves an important purpose: It protects citizens from overzealous law enforcement practices.

> The presence of a search warrant serves a high function. Absent some grave emergency, the Fourth Amendment has interposed a magistrate between the citizen and police. This was done not to shield criminals nor to make the home a safe haven for illegal activities. It was done so that an objective mind might weigh the need to invade the privacy in order to enforce the law. The right of privacy was deemed too precious to entrust to the discretion of those whose job is the detection of crime and the arrest of criminals.[21]

Accordingly, a search conducted pursuant to a valid search warrant is per se reasonable. Warrantless searches are permitted only in special circumstances, and it is the responsibility of the government to prove that the facts of the case fit into one of the exceptions to the warrant requirement.

To give this preference some "teeth," the Supreme Court, in *Aguilar v. Texas*, 378 U.S. 108, 111 (1964), announced that, "when a search is based upon a magistrate's, rather than a police officer's determination of probable cause," reviewing courts are to accept lesser competent evidence than if the officer made the determination personally, so long as there was a "substantial basis" for the magistrate's decision. To say it another way, less evidence is required to sustain a search if a warrant was obtained prior to the search.

"Reviewing courts" are referred to because the determination that probable cause exists by a magistrate when issuing a warrant is not final. A defendant may later attack any evidence seized pursuant to a warrant through a motion to suppress. As stated, determinations by a magistrate are less likely to be overturned than those made by police officers.

## Requirements for Obtaining a Warrant

The Fourth Amendment enumerates the requirements that must be met before a warrant can be issued. It is the responsibility of the law enforcement officer requesting the warrant to establish these elements to the judge making the warrant determination. An example of criminal complaint and supporting affidavit appears in Exhibit 12–3.

First, the evidence presented must establish probable cause to believe that within the area to be searched, the items sought will be found. Second, there must be probable cause to believe that the items sought are connected to criminal activity.

Third, the area to be searched and any item to be seized must be described with particularity. The amount of specificity required varies from case to case. A warrant that authorizes a police officer to search a particular home for "unauthorized contraband" clearly violates the Fourth Amendment, whereas a warrant authorizing a search of the same home for a "nine-inch knife with an ivory handle" is valid, provided the warrant is valid in all other respects (probable cause, etc.).

Warrants for the seizure of items that are illegal in themselves do not have to be as particular as others. For example, a warrant to search for a book must be more specific than one for drugs. The description "book" is clearly insufficient, whereas a warrant to search for "cocaine" probably is sufficient.

As to location, a street address is normally sufficient. If there is no street address, the warrant should describe the location, owner, color, and architectural style of the property. Of course, any additional information that aids in describing property should be included. If the building to be searched is an apartment building or similar multiunit structure, the specific subunit to be searched must be stated in the warrant.

Fourth, the facts that are alleged to establish probable cause must be "supported by Oath or affirmation." In the typical case, this means that the government will produce one or more affidavits to prove the alleged crime has occurred or that the evidence will be found in the location to be searched. Note that the sample application for a search warrant (Exhibit 12–3) provides space for a supporting affidavit.

Finally, the warrant must be issued by a neutral and detached magistrate. Although judges are most commonly given the authority to issue warrants, a state may grant this authority to others. However, the Supreme Court has stated that the person authorized must be neutral and detached and be capable of determining whether probable cause exists.

## Exhibit 12–3 Criminal Complaint and Supporting Affidavit

### UNITED STATES DISTRICT COURT

for the

District of Columbia

| | |
|---|---|
| United States of America | ) |
| v. | ) Case: 1:21-mj-00271 |
| Shane Jenkins | ) Assigned To : Harvey, G. Michael |
| | ) Assign. Date : 03/02/2021 |
| | ) Description: Complaint w/ Arrest Warrant |
| | ) |
| _____ | ) |
| *Defendant* | ) |

### ARREST WARRANT

To:    Any authorized law enforcement officer

**YOU ARE COMMANDED** to arrest and bring before a United States magistrate judge without unnecessary delay

*(name of person to be arrested)*                                        Shane Jenkins                                        .

who is accused of an offense or violation based on the following document filed with the court:

❏ Indictment        ❏ Superseding Indictment        ❏ Information        ❏ Superseding Information        ☒ Complaint

❏ Probation Violation Petition        ❏ Supervised Release Violation Petition        ❏ Violation Notice        ❏ Order of the Court

This offense is briefly described as follows:

18 U.S.C. § 111(a)(1) and (b) - Assault on Federal Officer;
18 U.S.C. § 231(a)(3) - Obstruction of Law Enforcement During Civil Disorder;
18 U.S.C. § 1361 - Damage to Federal Property;
18 U.S.C. § 1752(a)(1) - Knowingly Entering or Remaining in any Restricted Building or Grounds Without Lawful Authority;
18 U.S.C. § 1752(a)(2) - Disorderly and Disruptive Conduct in a Restricted Building or Grounds;
18 U.S.C. § 1752(a)(4) - Knowingly Entering or Remaining in any Restricted Building or Grounds Without Lawful Authority.

Date:    03/02/2021                                        Digitally signed by G. Michael Harvey
                                                       Date: 2021.03.02 13:30:54 -05'00'
                                        _____
                                        *Issuing officer's signature*

City and state:        Washington, D.C.                G. Michael Harvey, U.S. Magistrate Judge
                                        *Printed name and title*

---

| **Return** |
|---|
| This warrant was received on *(date)* _____ , and the person was arrested on *(date)* _____ |
| at *(city and state)* _____ . |
| |
| Date: _____                    _____ |
| *Arresting officer's signature* |
| |
| _____ |
| *Printed name and title* |

Thus, a state law permitting a state's attorney general, who had investigated the crime and would later be responsible for its prosecution, to issue a warrant was invalid.[22] In another case, a court clerk was found sufficiently detached, neutral, and capable to issue a warrant because the clerk worked for a court and was under the supervision of a judge.[23] See Exhibit 12–4 for the federal application for search warrant.

## Scope of Warrants

Warrants may be issued to search and seize any item that constitutes evidence of a crime, is the fruit of a crime, is contraband, or is used to commit a crime.[24] A warrant may be issued to search or seize any place or property, whether belonging to a suspected criminal or an innocent third party. A warrant may be prospective. That is, it may be written to be executed when a triggering event occurs. An anticipatory warrant of this nature must comply with the probable cause and particularity requirements of the Fourth Amendment. For example, a warrant to search a suspect's home at the time a package of child pornography was delivered was upheld. The package was ordered by the suspect from an undercover officer and the warrant described it, limited execution of the warrant to when the package was received and taken into the home, and described the suspect's home. The application for the warrant detailed how the suspect had ordered the items.[25]

The particularity requirement acts to limit the breadth of a search. If an officer searches beyond the scope of a warrant, the exclusionary rule will make the fruits from the forbidden area inadmissible at trial.

In some circumstances, the particularity requirement is heightened. For example, because of the importance of protecting the press from government intrusion, warrants to search newsrooms or similar areas must be drafted with "particular exactitude."[26] The same is true if a search will probe into confidential information, such as client records of attorneys and physicians.

As a general proposition, a warrant to search premises does not authorize the police to search the occupants of the premises.[27] Of course, a search may be conducted if an independent basis exists justifying the action. Generally, the occupants of an area to be searched may be detained until the search is complete. However, occupants cannot be detained for an "unduly prolonged" period of time.[28] Once the evidence sought is found or the threat of loss or destruction of evidence by an occupant has passed, he or she should be released.

## Executing Warrants

The warrant may direct a particular officer or an entire unit of police officers to conduct the search. The language of the warrant itself contains the duties of the officers executing the warrant, as well as their limitations.

As a general proposition, warrants are to be executed during the day. This is because a nighttime search is considered to be more intrusive than a daytime search[29] and because the probability of resistance is greater at night.

To conduct a nighttime search, a specific request for a warrant authorizing such must be made. To receive a warrant permitting a nighttime search, an officer must present the magistrate with facts evidencing the necessity for a nighttime search, usually including proof that a daytime search will not be successful. An anticipated nighttime delivery of illegal goods justifies a nighttime warrant, as does a concern that evidence of a crime will be destroyed in the night.

Most states have statutes requiring that warrants be executed within a specific amount of time after issuance. Warrants issued under federal law must be executed within 10 days of issuance.[30]

In all cases, the search must be conducted when there is probable cause. If an officer fails to execute a warrant before probable cause has dissipated, then any

**Exhibit 12–4** Federal Search Warrant Application And Warrant

AO 106 (Rev. 04/10) Application for a Search Warrant

# UNITED STATES DISTRICT COURT

for the

In the Matter of the Search of )
*(Briefly describe the property to be searched* )
*or identify the person by name and address)* )  Case No.
)
)
)

## APPLICATION FOR A SEARCH WARRANT

I, a federal law enforcement officer or an attorney for the government, request a search warrant and state under penalty of perjury that I have reason to believe that on the following person or property *(identify the person or describe the property to be searched and give its location)*:

located in the _____ District of _____ , there is now concealed *(identify the person or describe the property to be seized)*:

The basis for the search under Fed. R. Crim. P. 41(c) is *(check one or more)*:

❑ evidence of a crime;

❑ contraband, fruits of crime, or other items illegally possessed;

❑ property designed for use, intended for use, or used in committing a crime;

❑ a person to be arrested or a person who is unlawfully restrained.

The search is related to a violation of:

*Code Section*                                      *Offense Description*

The application is based on these facts:

❑ Continued on the attached sheet.

❑ Delayed notice of _____ days (give exact ending date if more than 30 days: _____ ) is requested under 18 U.S.C. § 3103a, the basis of which is set forth on the attached sheet.

_____
*Applicant's signature*

_____
*Printed name and title*

Sworn to before me and signed in my presence.

Date: _____

_____
*Judge's signature*

City and state: _____         _____
*Printed name and title*

| Print | Save As... | Attach | Reset |

resulting search is violative of the Fourth Amendment, and the fruits thereof are subject to the exclusionary rule. This is true even if the search is conducted within the period of time set by law.

At the premises of a search, the police must knock and announce their purpose before entering the premises. This is true whether entry is gained through the use of force or not. Your next Oyez, *Richards v. Wisconsin*, addresses this rule. However, to prevent the destruction of evidence or injury to the officers, judges may issue "no-knock" warrants if the facts indicate that one or the other is likely to occur. The decision to issue a no-knock warrant must be based on the evidence. The Supreme Court has ruled that blanket exceptions to the knock-and-announce rule are violative of the Fourth Amendment. Instead, judges and police must make no-knock decisions based on the facts of each case.

## Oyez

### Richards v. Wisconsin
### 520 U.S. 385 (1997)

**Justice Stevens delivered the opinion of the Court.**

In *Wilson v. Arkansas*, (1995), we held that the Fourth Amendment incorporates the common-law requirement that police officers entering a dwelling must knock on the door and announce their identity and purpose before attempting forcible entry. At the same time, we recognized that the "flexible requirement of reasonableness should not be read to mandate a rigid rule of announcement that ignores countervailing law enforcement interests and left "to the lower courts the task of determining the circumstances under which an unannounced entry is reasonable under the Fourth Amendment."

In this case, the Wisconsin Supreme Court concluded that police officers are never required to knock and announce their presence when executing a search warrant in a felony drug investigation. In so doing, it reaffirmed a pre-*Wilson* holding and concluded that *Wilson* did not preclude this *per se* rule. We disagree with the court's conclusion that the Fourth Amendment permits a blanket exception to the knock-and-announce requirement for this entire category of criminal activity. But because the evidence presented to support the officers' actions in this case establishes that the decision not to knock and announce was a reasonable one under the circumstances, we affirm the judgment of the Wisconsin court.

On December 31, 1991, police officers in Madison, Wisconsin, obtained a warrant to search Steiney Richards's hotel room for drugs and related paraphernalia. The search warrant was the culmination of an investigation that had uncovered substantial evidence that Richards was one of several individuals dealing drugs out of hotel rooms in Madison. The police requested a warrant that would have given advance authorization for a "no-knock" entry into the hotel room, but the magistrate explicitly deleted those portions of the warrant.

The officers arrived at the hotel room at 3:40 a.m. Officer Pharo, dressed as a maintenance man, led the team. With him were several plainclothes officers and at least one man in uniform. Officer Pharo knocked on Richards's door and, responding to the query from inside the room, stated that he was a maintenance man. With the chain still on the door, Richards cracked it open. Although there is some dispute as to what occurred next, Richards acknowledges that when he opened the door he saw the man in uniform standing behind Officer Pharo. He quickly slammed the door closed and, after waiting two or three seconds, the officers began kicking and ramming the door to gain entry to the locked room. At trial, the officers testified that they identified themselves as police while they were kicking the door in. When they finally did break into the room, the officers caught Richards trying to escape through the window. They also found cash and cocaine hidden in plastic bags above the bathroom ceiling tiles.

Richards sought to have the evidence from his hotel room suppressed on the ground that the officers had failed to knock and announce their presence prior to forcing entry into the room. The trial court denied the motion, concluding that the officers could gather from Richards's strange behavior when they first sought entry that he knew they were police officers and that he might try to destroy evidence or to escape. . . . The judge emphasized that the easily disposable nature of the drugs the police were searching for further justified their decision to identify themselves as they crossed the threshold instead of announcing their presence before seeking entry. . . . Richards appealed the decision to the Wisconsin Supreme Court and that court affirmed. . . .

In reaching this conclusion, the Wisconsin court found it reasonable—after considering criminal conduct surveys, newspaper articles, and other judicial opinions—to assume that all felony drug crimes will involve "an extremely high risk of serious if not deadly injury to the police as well as the potential for the disposal of drugs by the occupants prior to entry by the police."

We recognized in *Wilson* that the knock-and-announce requirement could give way "under circumstances presenting a threat of physical violence," or "where police officers have reason to believe that evidence would likely be destroyed if advance notice were given."

(continued)

It is indisputable that felony drug investigations may frequently involve both of these circumstances. The question we must resolve is whether this fact justifies dispensing with case-by-case evaluation of the manner in which a search was executed.

The Wisconsin court explained its blanket exception as necessitated by the special circumstances of today's drug culture, and the State asserted at oral argument that the blanket exception was reasonable in "felony drug cases because of the convergence in a violent and dangerous form of commerce of weapons and the destruction of drugs." But creating exceptions to the knock-and-announce rule based on the "culture" surrounding a general category of criminal behavior presents at least two serious concerns.

First, the exception contains considerable overgeneralization. For example, while drug investigation frequently does pose special risks to officer safety and the preservation of evidence, not every drug investigation will pose these risks to a substantial degree. . . .

A second difficulty with permitting a criminal category exception to the knock-and-announce requirement is that the reasons for creating an exception in one category can, relatively easily, be applied to others. Armed bank robbers, for example, are, by definition, likely to have weapons, and the fruits of their crime may be destroyed without too much difficulty. If a *per se* exception were allowed for each category of criminal investigation that included a considerable—albeit hypothetical—risk of danger to officers or destruction of evidence, the knock-and-announce element of the Fourth Amendment's reasonableness requirement would be meaningless.

Thus, the fact that felony drug investigations may frequently present circumstances warranting a no-knock entry cannot remove from the neutral scrutiny of a reviewing court the reasonableness of the police decision not to knock and announce in a particular case. Instead, in each case, it is the duty of a court confronted with the question to determine whether the facts and circumstances of the particular entry justified dispensing with the knock-and-announce requirement.

In order to justify a "no-knock" entry, the police must have a reasonable suspicion that knocking and announcing their presence, under the particular circumstances, would be dangerous or futile, or that it would inhibit the effective investigation of the crime by, for example, allowing the destruction of evidence. This standard—as opposed to a probable cause requirement—strikes the appropriate balance between the legitimate law enforcement concerns at issue in the execution of search warrants and the individual privacy interests affected by no-knock entries. . . .

Although we reject the Wisconsin court's blanket exception to the knock-and-announce requirement, we conclude that the officers' no-knock entry into Richards's hotel room did not violate the Fourth Amendment. We agree with the trial court, and with Justice Abrahamson, that the circumstances in this case show that the officers had a reasonable suspicion that Richards might destroy evidence if given further opportunity to do so.

The judge who heard testimony at Richards's suppression hearing concluded that it was reasonable for the officers executing the warrant to believe that Richards knew, after opening the door to his hotel room the first time, that the men seeking entry to his room were the police. Once the officers reasonably believed that Richards knew who they were, the court concluded, it was reasonable for them to force entry immediately given the disposable nature of the drugs. In arguing that the officers' entry was unreasonable, Richards places great emphasis on the fact that the magistrate who signed the search warrant for his hotel room deleted the portions of the proposed warrant that would have given the officers permission to execute a no-knock entry. But this fact does not alter the reasonableness of the officers' decision, which must be evaluated as of the time they entered the hotel room. At the time the officers obtained the warrant, they did not have evidence sufficient, in the judgment of the magistrate, to justify a no-knock warrant. Of course, the magistrate could not have anticipated in every particular the circumstances that would confront the officers when they arrived at Richards's hotel room. These actual circumstances—petitioner's apparent recognition of the officers combined with the easily disposable nature of the drugs—justified the officers' ultimate decision to enter without first announcing their presence and authority.

After a search is completed, the officers are required to inventory items seized. Federal rules require that the owner of the property be given a receipt for the goods taken.[31] Property unlawfully taken must be returned to the owner, unless it is unlawful in itself, such as drugs. In *Hudson v. Michigan*, 547 U.S. 586 (2006), the Supreme Court decided that the remedies for violations of the knock-and-announce requirement do not exclude exclusion of any evidence obtained following an unannounced entry. The Court found that the societal costs of such a remedy outweigh the benefits. Other remedies, such as civil suits against the officers, were found by the Court to be adequate to preserve the right.

## Search Incident to Arrest and Protective Sweep

Searches and arrests can be volatile and dangerous events. Police have a variety of strategies intended to manage the risk. One is to secure the person arrested and the area of the search or arrest.

The issue of searching the defendant's person was addressed in *United States v. Robinson,* 414 U.S. 260 (1973), in which the Court held that, after a lawful arrest, the defendant's person may be fully searched without first obtaining a warrant. The Court held that to require officers to obtain a warrant would needlessly endanger their lives and would increase the possibility of evidence being destroyed by the defendant. Search incident to arrest includes a full search of the defendant's clothing. The search automatically attends the arrest; no suspicion of dangerousness is required. And, as you will learn in the next chapter, any evidence found during a search incident to arrest, even if unrelated to the cause of the arrest, is admissible in court.

But a search of an arrestee may not be enough to protect the arresting officers. The driver of an automobile may have a gun hidden under the seat of the car, and the homeowner may have weapon within reach. So, the second question is whether police may extend the safety search beyond the body of an arrestee. The landmark case in this area is *Chimel v. California.*

## Oyez

### Chimel v. California
### 395 U.S. 752 (1969)

**MR. JUSTICE STEWART delivered the opinion of the Court.**

This case raises basic questions concerning the permissible scope under the Fourth Amendment of a search incident to a lawful arrest.

The relevant facts are essentially undisputed. Late in the afternoon of September 13, 1965, three police officers arrived at the Santa Ana, California, home of the petitioner with a warrant authorizing his arrest for the burglary of a coin shop. The officers knocked on the door, identified themselves to the petitioner's wife, and asked if they might come inside. She ushered them into the house, where they waited 10 to 15 minutes until the petitioner returned home from work. When the petitioner entered the house, one of the officers handed him the arrest warrant and asked for permission to "look around." The petitioner objected, but was advised that "on the basis of the lawful arrest," the officers would nonetheless conduct the search. No search warrant had been issued.

Accompanied by the petitioner's wife, the officers then looked through the entire three-bedroom house, including the attic, the garage, and a small workshop. In some rooms the search was relatively cursory. In the master bedroom and sewing room, however, the officers directed the petitioner's wife to open drawers and "to physically remove contents of the drawers from side to side so that [they] might view items that would have come from [the] burglary." After completing the search, they seized numerous items—primarily coins, but also several medals, tokens, and a few other objects. The entire search took between 45 minutes and an hour. . . .

When an arrest is made, it is reasonable for the arresting officer to search the person arrested in order to remove any weapons that the latter might seek to use in order to resist arrest or effect his escape. Otherwise, the officer's safety might well be endangered, and the arrest itself frustrated. In addition, it is entirely reasonable for the arresting officer to search for and seize any evidence on the arrestee's person in order to prevent its concealment or destruction. And the area into which an arrestee might reach in order to grab a weapon or evidentiary items must, of course, be governed by a like rule. A gun on a table or in a drawer in front of one who is arrested can be as dangerous to the arresting officer as one concealed in the clothing of the person arrested. There is ample justification, therefore, for a search of the arrestee's person and the area "within his immediate control"—construing that phrase to mean the area from within which he might gain possession of a weapon or destructible evidence.

There is no comparable justification, however, for routinely searching any room other than that in which an arrest occurs—or, for that matter, for searching through all the desk drawers or other closed or concealed areas in the room itself. Such searches, in the absence of well-recognized exceptions, may be made only under the authority of a search warrant. . . .

Application of sound Fourth Amendment principles to the facts of this case produces a clear result. . . . The scope of the search was . . . "unreasonable" under the Fourth and Fourteenth Amendments, and the petitioner's conviction cannot stand.

Reversed.

*Chimel* significantly changed the law, as before *Chimel* was decided officers had the authority to search a much greater area as incident to arrest. The "within the defendant's immediate control" test continues to be the governing law. As with any other lawful search and seizure, any evidence obtained may be used to prosecute the defendant.

The search incident to arrest doctrine does not consider the possibility that other potentially dangerous persons may be present, but out of sight, when an arrest is made. Must police take the risk that no other dangerous persons are on the premises when making a lawful arrest? This question was answered by the Supreme Court in *Maryland v. Buie* featured in your next Oyez.

## Oyez

### Maryland v. Buie
#### 494 U.S. 325 (1990)

**Justice WHITE delivered the opinion of the Court.**

A "protective sweep" is a quick and limited search of a premises, incident to an arrest and conducted to protect the safety of police officers or others. It is narrowly confined to a cursory visual inspection of those places in which a person might be hiding. In this case we must decide what level of justification is required by the Fourth and Fourteenth Amendments before police officers, while effecting the arrest of a suspect in his home pursuant to an arrest warrant, may conduct a warrantless protective sweep of all or part of the premises. . . .

On February 3, 1986, two men committed an armed robbery of a Godfather's Pizza restaurant in Prince George's County, Maryland. One of the robbers was wearing a red running suit. The same day, Prince George's County police obtained arrest warrants for respondent Jerome Edward Buie and his suspected accomplice in the robbery, Lloyd Allen. Buie's house was placed under police surveillance.

On February 5, the police executed the arrest warrant for Buie. They first had a police department secretary telephone Buie's house to verify that he was home. The secretary spoke to a female first, then to Buie himself. Six or seven officers proceeded to Buie's house. Once inside, the officers fanned out through the first and second floors. Corporal James Rozar announced that he would "freeze" the basement so that no one could come up and surprise the officers. With his service revolver drawn, Rozar twice shouted into the basement, ordering anyone down there to come out. When a voice asked who was calling, Rozar announced three times: "this is the police, show me your hands." Eventually, a pair of hands appeared around the bottom of the stairwell and Buie emerged from the basement. He was arrested, searched, and handcuffed by Rozar. Thereafter, Detective Joseph Frolich entered the basement "in case there was someone else" down there. . . . He noticed a red running suit lying in plain view on a stack of clothing and seized it.

The trial court denied Buie's motion to suppress the running suit, stating in part: "The man comes out from a basement, the police don't know how many other people are down there." . . .

It goes without saying that the Fourth Amendment bars only unreasonable searches and seizures. . . . Our cases show that in determining reasonableness, we have balanced the intrusion on the individual's Fourth Amendment interests against its promotion of legitimate governmental interests. . . . Under this test, a search of the house or office is generally not reasonable without a warrant issued on probable cause. There are other contexts, however, where the public interest is such that neither a warrant nor probable cause is required. . . .

The *Terry* case is most instructive for present purposes. There we held that an on-the-street "frisk" for weapons must be tested by the Fourth Amendment's general proscription against unreasonable searches because such a frisk involves "an entire rubric of police conduct—necessarily swift action predicated upon the on-the-spot observations of the officer on the beat—which historically has not been, and as a practical matter could not be, subjected to the warrant procedure." . . .

The ingredients to apply the balance struck in *Terry* and *Long* are present in this case. Possessing an arrest warrant and probable cause to believe Buie was in his home, the officers were entitled to enter and to search anywhere in the house in which Buie might be found. Once he was found, however, the search for him was over, and there was no longer that particular justification for entering any rooms that had not yet been searched.

That Buie had an expectation of privacy in those remaining areas of his house, however, does not mean such rooms were immune from entry. In *Terry* and *Long* we were concerned with the immediate interest of the police officers in taking steps to assure themselves that the persons with whom they were dealing were not armed with or able to gain immediate control of a weapon that could unexpectedly and fatally be used against them. In the instant case, there is an analogous interest of the officers in taking steps to assure themselves that the house in which the suspect is being or has just been arrested is not harboring other persons who are dangerous and who could

> unexpectedly launch an attack. The risk of danger in the context of an arrest in the home is as great as, if not greater than, it is in the on-the-street or roadside investigatory encounter. . . .
>
> We should emphasize that such a protective sweep, aimed at protecting the arresting officers, if justified by the circumstances, is nevertheless not a full search of the premises, but may extend only to a cursory inspection of those spaces where a person may be found. The sweep lasts no longer than is necessary to dispel the reasonable suspicion of danger and in any event no longer than it takes to complete the arrest and depart from the premises. . . .
>
> The Fourth Amendment permits a properly limited protective sweep in conjunction with an inhome arrest when the searching officer possesses a reasonable belief based on specific and articulable facts that the area to be swept harbors an individual posing a danger to those on the arrest scene.

The protective sweep may not be automatically conducted by the police, unlike a search incident to arrest. An officer must have a reasonable belief, supported by specific and articulable facts, that a dangerous person may be hiding in the home, before a protective sweep may be conducted. There need not be a belief of dangerousness to conduct a search incident to arrest.

A protective sweep must be limited to searching those areas where a person might be hiding. Justice Brennan, dissenting in *Buie*, wrote:

> Police officers searching for potential ambushers might enter every room including basements and attics, open up closets, lockers, chests, wardrobes, and cars; and peer under beds and behind furniture. The officers will view letters, documents and personal effects that are on tables or desks or are visible inside open drawers; books, records, tapes, and pictures on shelves; and clothing, medicines, toiletries and other paraphernalia not carefully stored in dresser drawers or bathroom cupboards. While perhaps not a "full-blown" or "top-to-bottom" search . . . a protective sweep is much closer to it than to a "limited patdown for weapons" or a "frisk" [as authorized by *Terry v. Ohio*].

Similarly, safety concerns are the reason officers are permitted to detain occupants of a house during a search. The Court went so far as to approve a two- to three-hour detention of the occupants of a home in handcuffs during a search.[32]

Finally, "when a policeman has made a lawful custodial arrest of the occupant of an automobile, he may, as a contemporaneous incident of that arrest, search the passenger compartment of that automobile," including the contents of any containers found in that area.[33]

# Seizures

Learning Objective: Define, describe, and apply the Fourth Amendment's rules for arrests.

Recall that the Fourth Amendment applies to both searches *and* seizures of houses, persons, papers, and effects. Many seizures are obvious, such as when a police officer takes a suspect's cell phone, file folder, gun, or poster and when an officer "arrests" a suspect. But there are situations that are less clear, such as when an officer asks a person to stop for a moment to ask a question.

One of the most serious interferences with a person's liberty is to be physically seized by a government. The Fourth Amendment regulates seizures of the person.

## Defining Seizure: Arrests and Less

Searches don't always involve touching a person or property. In *Katz*, for example, police conducted a search of a conversation. Seizures, on the other hand, involve touching or the capture of digital data. A seizure of property occurs when police interfere with a person's possessory interests, as recognized by property law. But Katz expands the Fourth Amendment beyond possessory interests to any action that interferes with a person's reasonable expectation to privacy.

There are different forms of seizure of the person. For example, there are lower forms of seizure that don't require a warrant, or even probable cause. An example is the brief encounter known as the "stop and frisk." At the higher end is the full arrest—a seizure that is longer in duration and involves taking a person into custody. In between these two are seizures that require probable cause but not a warrant. You will learn a lot more about this subject in the next chapter.

The seizure of the person occurs whenever (1) there is a show of force or authority by police and (2) a reasonable person believes that he or she is not free to leave. The totality of the circumstances is examined to determine if a seizure occurred. Obviously, any person who is physically restrained by police is seized. Beyond physical restraint, the number of officers; the officers' presence, attitude, and voice; the location of the encounter; the length of the encounter; the circumstances surrounding the encounter; and the age, intelligence, and the ability of the suspect to understand the nature of the encounter are all factors. Consider location, for example. Normally, it is more intimidating to be interviewed in a small room of a police station than in one's living room. An officer's words are also important. A direction to remain in place is a seizure, if the suspect complies. However, a suspect who immediately flees is not seized. Whether a suspect who flees after being shot by police is seized is the issue in your next Oyez, *Torres v. Madrid*.

## Oyez

### Torres v. Madrid
### 592 U.S. ___ (2021)

**Chief Justice Roberts delivered the opinion of the Court.**

The Fourth Amendment prohibits unreasonable "seizures" to safeguard "[t]he right of the people to be secure in their persons." Under our cases, an officer seizes a person when he uses force to apprehend her. The question in this case is whether a seizure occurs when an officer shoots someone who temporarily eludes capture after the shooting. The answer is yes: The application of physical force to the body of a person with intent to restrain is a seizure, even if the force does not succeed in subduing the person.

At dawn on July 15, 2014, four New Mexico State Police officers arrived at an apartment complex in Albuquerque to execute an arrest warrant for a woman accused of white collar crimes, but also "suspected of having been involved in drug trafficking, murder, and other violent crimes." What happened next is hotly contested. We recount the facts in the light most favorable to petitioner Roxanne Torres because the court below granted summary judgment to Officers Janice Madrid and Richard Williamson, the two respondents here.

The officers observed Torres standing with another person near a Toyota FJ Cruiser in the parking lot of the complex. Officer Williamson concluded that neither Torres nor her companion was the target of the warrant. As the officers approached the vehicle, the companion departed, and Torres—at the time experiencing methamphetamine withdrawal—got into the driver's seat. The officers attempted to speak with her, but she did not notice their presence until one of them tried to open the door of her car.

Although the officers wore tactical vests marked with police identification, Torres saw only that they had guns. She thought the officers were carjackers trying to steal her car, and she hit the gas to escape them. Neither Officer Madrid nor Officer Williamson, according to Torres, stood in the path of the vehicle, but both fired their service pistols to stop her. All told, the two officers fired 13 shots at Torres, striking her twice in the back and temporarily paralyzing her left arm.

Steering with her right arm, Torres accelerated through the fusillade of bullets, exited the apartment complex, drove a short distance, and stopped in a parking lot. After asking a bystander to report an attempted carjacking, Torres stole a Kia Soul that happened to be idling nearby and drove 75 miles to Grants, New Mexico. The good news for Torres was that the hospital in Grants was able to airlift her to another hospital where she could receive appropriate care. The bad news was that the hospital was back in Albuquerque, where the police arrested her the next day. She pleaded no contest to aggravated fleeing from a law enforcement officer, assault on a peace officer, and unlawfully taking a motor vehicle.

Torres later sought damages from Officers Madrid and Williamson under 42 U. S. C. §1983, which provides a cause of action for the deprivation of constitutional rights by persons acting under color of state law. She claimed that the officers applied excessive force, making the shooting an unreasonable seizure under the Fourth Amendment. The District Court granted summary judgment to the officers, and the Court of Appeals for the Tenth Circuit affirmed on the ground that "a suspect's continued flight after being shot by police negates a Fourth Amendment excessive-force claim." The court relied on Circuit precedent providing that "no seizure can occur unless there is physical touch or a show of authority," and that "such physical touch (or force) must terminate the suspect's movement" or otherwise give rise to physical control over the suspect.

The Fourth Amendment protects "[t]he right of the people to be secure in their persons, houses, papers, and effects, against unreasonable searches and seizures." This case concerns the "seizure" of a "person," which can take the form of "physical force" or a "show of authority" that "in some way restrain[s] the liberty" of the person. *Terry* v. *Ohio.* The question before us is whether the application of physical force is a seizure if the force, despite hitting its target, fails to stop the person.

We largely covered this ground in *California* v. *Hodari D.* (1991). There we interpreted the term "seizure" by consulting the common law of arrest, the "quintessential 'seizure of the person' under our Fourth Amendment jurisprudence." As Justice Scalia explained for himself and six other Members of the Court, the common law treated "the mere grasping or application of physical force with lawful authority" as an arrest, "whether or not it succeeded in subduing the arrestee." . . .

The common law distinguished the application of force from a show of authority, such as an order for a suspect to halt. The latter does not become an arrest unless and until the arrestee complies with the demand. As the Court explained in *Hodari D.,* "[a]n arrest requires *either* physical force . . . *or,* where that is absent, *submission* to the assertion of authority."

*Hodari D.* articulates two pertinent principles. First, common law arrests are Fourth Amendment seizures. And second, the common law considered the application of force to the body of a person with intent to restrain to be an arrest, no matter whether the arrestee escaped. We need not decide whether *Hodari D.,* which principally concerned a show of authority, controls the outcome of this case as a matter of *stare decisis,* because we independently reach the same conclusions. . . .

The common law rule identified in *Hodari D.*—that the application of force gives rise to an arrest, even if the officer does not secure control over the arrestee—achieved recognition to such an extent that English lawyers could confidently (and accurately) proclaim that "[a]ll the authorities, from the earliest time to the present, establish that a corporal touch is sufficient to constitute an arrest, even though the defendant do not submit." The slightest application of force could satisfy this rule. . . .

Early American courts adopted this mere-touch rule from England, just as they embraced other common law principles of search and seizure. . . .

This case, of course, does not involve "laying hands," but instead a shooting. Neither the parties nor the United States as *amicus curiae* suggests that the officers' use of bullets to restrain Torres alters the analysis in any way. And we are aware of no common law authority addressing an arrest under such circumstances, or indeed any case involving an application of force from a distance. . . .

The closest decision seems to be *Countess of Rutland's Case* (Star Chamber 1605). In that case, serjeants-at-mace tracked down Isabel Holcroft, Countess of Rutland, to execute a writ for a judgment of debt. They "shewed her their mace, and touching her body with it, said to her, we arrest you, madam." We think the case is best understood as an example of an arrest made by touching with an object, for the serjeants-at-mace announced the arrest at the time they touched the countess with the mace. . . .

The dissent (though not the officers) argues that the common law limited arrests by force to the literal placement of hands on the suspect, because no court published an opinion discussing a suspect who continued to flee after being hit with a bullet or some other weapon. . . .

We will not carve out this greater intrusion on personal security from the mere-touch rule just because founding-era courts did not confront apprehension by firearm. While firearms have existed for a millennium and were certainly familiar at the founding, we have observed that law enforcement did not carry handguns until the latter half of the 19th century, at which point "it bec[a]me possible to use deadly force from a distance as a means of apprehension." So it should come as no surprise that neither we nor the dissent has located a common law case in which an officer used a gun to apprehend a suspect. . . .

We stress, however, that the application of the common law rule does not transform every physical contact between a government employee and a member of the public into a Fourth Amendment seizure. A seizure requires the use of force *with intent to restrain.* Accidental force will not qualify. Nor will force intentionally applied for some other purpose satisfy this rule. In this opinion, we consider only force used to apprehend. We do not accept the dissent's invitation to opine on matters not presented here—pepper spray, flash-bang grenades, lasers, and more.

Moreover, the appropriate inquiry is whether the challenged conduct *objectively* manifests an intent to restrain, for we rarely probe the subjective motivations of police officers in the Fourth Amendment context. Only an objective test "allows the police to determine in advance whether the conduct contemplated will implicate the Fourth Amendment." While a mere touch can be enough for a seizure, the amount of force remains pertinent in assessing the objective intent to restrain. A tap on the shoulder to get one's attention will rarely exhibit such an intent.

(continued)

Nor does the seizure depend on the subjective perceptions of the seized person. Here, for example, Torres claims to have perceived the officers' actions as an attempted carjacking. But the conduct of the officers—ordering Torres to stop and then shooting to restrain her movement—satisfies the objective test for a seizure, regardless whether Torres comprehended the governmental character of their actions.

The rule we announce today is narrow. In addition to the requirement of intent to restrain, a seizure by force—absent submission—lasts only as long as the application of force. That is to say that the Fourth Amendment does not recognize any "*continuing* arrest during the period of fugitivity." The fleeting nature of some seizures by force undoubtedly may inform what damages a civil plaintiff may recover, and what evidence a criminal defendant may exclude from trial. But brief seizures are seizures all the same.

Applying these principles to the facts viewed in the light most favorable to Torres, the officers' shooting applied physical force to her body and objectively manifested an intent to restrain her from driving away. We therefore conclude that the officers seized Torres for the instant that the bullets struck her. . . .

We hold that the application of physical force to the body of a person with intent to restrain is a seizure even if the person does not submit and is not subdued. Of course, a seizure is just the first step in the analysis. The Fourth Amendment does not forbid all or even most seizures—only unreasonable ones. All we decide today is that the officers seized Torres by shooting her with intent to restrain her movement. We leave open on remand any questions regarding the reasonableness of the seizure, the damages caused by the seizure, and the officers' entitlement to qualified immunity.

The judgment of the Court of Appeals is vacated, and the case is remanded for further proceedings consistent with this opinion.

## The Arrest Warrant

Searches must be conducted pursuant to a valid warrant, unless an exception to the warrant requirement can be shown. Arrests are quite different. Rather than a requirement for a warrant, in most instances, there is simply a preference for one. The "informed and deliberate determinations of magistrates empowered to issue warrants . . . are to be preferred over the hurried action of officers."[34] As is the case with warrantless searches, probable cause determinations by magistrates will be supported on appeal with less evidence than those made by police officers.

Notwithstanding the preference, most arrests are made without first obtaining a warrant. The authority to make warrantless arrests has a long history. Under the common law, a law officer could arrest whenever he had reasonable grounds to believe that a defendant committed a felony. Misdemeanants who breached the peace could be arrested without warrant if the crime was committed in the presence of an officer.

*United States v. Watson*, 423 U.S. 411 (1976), was the case in which the Supreme Court recognized that warrantless arrests in public places, based upon probable cause, did not violate the Fourth Amendment. There is no constitutional requirement that an officer obtain a warrant to effect an arrest in a public place—even if the officer has adequate time to get the warrant prior to making the arrest. However, the Fourth Amendment does require that probable cause exist before an arrest can be made.

For a warrantless arrest in a public place to be upheld, it must be shown that the officer who made the arrest (1) had probable cause to believe that a crime was committed, and (2) that the person arrested committed that crime. As with searches and seizures, probable cause can be established in a number of ways: statements from victims and witnesses, personal knowledge and observations of the officer, reliable hearsay, and informant tips.

Most, if not all, states permit officers to arrest without a warrant if there is probable cause to believe that the suspect committed a felony. States vary in their treatment of misdemeanors, but most permit warrantless arrest only for a misdemeanor committed in an officer's presence. Some states have a broader rule that permits the arrest of a misdemeanant, even if the crime was not committed in the presence of an officer, provided there is both probable cause and an exigent circumstance.

An officer's determination of probable cause may later be challenged by the defendant. If the officer was wrong, then the defendant may be successful in obtaining his or her freedom or suppressing any evidence that is the fruit of the illegal arrest.

When an officer does seek an arrest warrant, the requirements previously discussed concerning search warrants apply. That is, the warrant must be issued by a neutral and detached magistrate upon a finding of probable cause, supported by oath or affirmation. See Exhibit 12–5 for the formal federal arrest warrant.

## Arrests in Protected Areas

So far, the discussion of arrests has been confined to arrests made in public. If the arrest is to be made in an area protected by the Fourth Amendment, such as a person's home, a warrant must be obtained, unless an exception exists.

In *Payton v. New York*, 445 U.S. 573 (1980), it was held that a valid arrest warrant implicitly carries with it a limited right to enter the suspect's home to effect the arrest, provided there is reason to believe the suspect is within. Under *Payton*, the search must be limited to areas where the suspect may be hiding. Because the entry is lawful, any evidence discovered in plain view may be seized.

Arrest warrants do not authorize entry into the private property of third persons. In the absence of consent or exigent circumstances, a search warrant must be obtained before a search of a third person's home or property may be conducted.[35]

The warrant requirement is obviated if the occupant gives consent to the search. Exigent circumstances, such as hot pursuit, also justify warrantless entries into homes to effect an arrest.

## Misdemeanor Arrests

The authority of law enforcement officers to arrest in cases where probable cause exists to believe an individual has committed a felony is clear. Similarly, the authority to arrest misdemeanants who breach the peace has been clear since the early common law. However, whether the arrest authority extends to minor misdemeanors was not addressed by the Supreme Court until 2001. This is discussed by the Supreme Court in the *Atwater* case, which appears in your next Oyez.

As you learned earlier in this chapter, an officer may fully search an arrestee as incident to arrest. In addition, the area within the arrestee's immediate control may also be searched. The scope of a search incident to arrest, however, is limited to areas where a weapon might be obtained by the person arrested. Clearly, a search of any room other than the one where a defendant is being held is not supported by the doctrine of search incident to arrest. Also, recall that police may conduct a sweep of a home during and immediately following an arrest, for the safety of the officers and other people who are present.

## Executing Arrest Warrants

Arrest warrants may be executed at the officer's discretion. There are limitations on executing warrants during the night, particularly in homes, in many jurisdictions. When possible, police should obtain night time authorization from a judge.

## **Exhibit 12–5** Warrant for the Arrest of a Capitol Rioter

UNITED STATES DISTRICT COURT

for the

District of Columbia

FILED
UNITED STATES DISTRICT COURT
DENVER, COLORADO
11:20 am, Feb 17, 2021
JEFFREY P. COLWELL, CLERK

United States of America
v.
Glenn Wes Lee Croy
*Defendant*

Case No. 1:21 MJ 234

Colorado Case: 21-mj-00024-NRN

**ARREST WARRANT**

To: Any authorized law enforcement officer

**YOU ARE COMMANDED** to arrest and bring before a United States magistrate judge without unnecessary delay

*(name of person to be arrested)* Glenn Wes Lee Croy,

who is accused of an offense or violation based on the following document filed with the court:

❒ Indictment ❒ Superseding Indictment ❒ Information ❒ Superseding Information ☒ Complaint
❒ Probation Violation Petition ❒ Supervised Release Violation Petition ❒ Violation Notice ❒ Order of the Court

This offense is briefly described as follows:

18 U.S.C. § 1752(a)(1) and (2)- Unlawful Entry on Restricted Buildings or Grounds;
40 U.S.C. § 5104(e)(2)(D) and (G)- Violent Entry and Disorderly Conduct on Capitol Grounds

Date: 02/16/2021

Digitally signed by G. Michael Harvey
Date: 2021.02.16 09:12:25 -05'00'

*Issuing officer's signature*

City and state: Washington, D.C.

G. Michael Harvey U.S. Magistrate Judge
*Printed name and title*

**Return**

This warrant was received on *(date)* 2/16/2021, and the person was arrested on *(date)* 2/17/2021

at *(city and state)* Colorado Springs, CO.

Date: 2/17/2021

*Arresting officer's signature*

Holly Andersen, Special Agent FBI
*Printed name and title*

Source: https://www.uscourts.gov/forms/law-enforcement-grand-jury-and-prosecution-forms/arrest-warrant

## Oyez

# Atwater v. City Of Lago Vista, Et Al.
## 532 U.S. 318 (2001)

**JUSTICE SOUTER delivered the opinion of the Court.**

In Texas, if a car is equipped with safety belts, a front-seat passenger must wear one, Tex. Tran. Code Ann. § 545.413(a) (1999), and the driver must secure any small child riding in front. Violation of either provision is "a misdemeanor punishable by a fine not less than $25 or more than $50." Texas law expressly authorizes "any peace officer [to] arrest without warrant a person found committing a violation" of these seatbelt laws, § 543.001, although it permits police to issue citations in lieu of arrest.

In March 1997, Petitioner Gail Atwater was driving her pickup truck in Lago Vista, Texas, with her 3-year-old son and 5-year-old daughter in the front seat. None of them was wearing a seatbelt. Respondent Bart Turek, a Lago Vista police officer at the time, observed the seatbelt violations and pulled Atwater over. According to Atwater's complaint (the allegations of which we assume to be true for present purposes), Turek approached the truck and "yelled" something to the effect of "we've met before" and "you're going to jail." He then called for backup and asked to see Atwater's driver's license and insurance documentation, which state law required her to carry. When Atwater told Turek that she did not have the papers because her purse had been stolen the day before, Turek said that he had "heard that story two-hundred times."

Atwater asked to take her "frightened, upset, and crying" children to a friend's house nearby, but Turek told her, "you're not going anywhere." As it turned out, Atwater's friend learned what was going on and soon arrived to take charge of the children. Turek then handcuffed Atwater, placed her in his squad car, and drove her to the local police station, where booking officers had her remove her shoes, jewelry, and eyeglasses, and empty her pockets. Officers took Atwater's "mug shot" and placed her, alone, in a jail cell for about one hour, after which she was taken before a magistrate and released on $310 bond.

Atwater was charged with driving without her seatbelt fastened, failing to secure her children in seatbelts, driving without a license, and failing to provide proof of insurance. She ultimately pleaded no contest to the misdemeanor seatbelt offenses and paid a $50 fine; the other charges were dismissed.

Atwater and her husband, petitioner Michael Haas, filed suit in a Texas state court under 42 U.S.C. § 1983 against Turek and respondents City of Lago Vista and Chief of Police Frank Miller. So far as concerns us, petitioners (whom we will simply call Atwater) alleged that respondents (for simplicity, the City) had violated Atwater's Fourth Amendment "right to be free from unreasonable seizure," . . . [the plaintiffs lost in the trial court, prevailed before a three-judge panel in the appellate court, and subsequently, the full appellate court sitting en banc reversed the three-judge panel.]

We granted certiorari to consider whether the Fourth Amendment, either by incorporating common-law restrictions on misdemeanor arrests or otherwise, limits police officers' authority to arrest without warrant for minor criminal offenses. We now affirm.

The Fourth Amendment safeguards "the right of the people to be secure in their persons, houses, papers, and effects, against unreasonable searches and seizures." In reading the Amendment, we are guided by "the traditional protections against unreasonable searches and seizures afforded by the common law at the time of the framing," since "an examination of the common-law understanding of an officer's authority to arrest sheds light on the obviously relevant, if not entirely dispositive, consideration of what the Framers of the Amendment might have thought to be reasonable." Thus, the first step here is to assess Atwater's claim that peace officers' authority to make warrantless arrests for misdemeanors was restricted at common law (whether "common law" is understood strictly as law judicially derived or, instead, as the whole body of law extant at the time of the framing). Atwater's specific contention is that "founding-era common-law rules" forbade peace officers to make warrantless misdemeanor arrests except in cases of "breach of the peace," a category she claims was then understood narrowly as covering only those nonfelony offenses "involving or tending toward violence." . . .

We begin with the state of pre-founding English common law and find that, even after making some allowance for variations in the common-law usage of the term "breach of the peace," the "founding-era common-law rules" were not nearly as clear as Atwater claims; on the contrary, the common-law commentators (as well as the sparsely reported cases) reached divergent conclusions with respect to officers' warrantless misdemeanor arrest power. Moreover, in the years leading up to American independence, Parliament repeatedly extended express warrantless arrest authority to cover misdemeanor-level offenses not amounting to or involving any violent breach of the peace. . . .

On one side of the divide there are certainly eminent authorities supporting Atwater's position. In addition to Lord Halsbury, quoted in *Carroll*, James Fitzjames Stephen and Glanville Williams both seemed to indicate that the common law confined warrantless misdemeanor arrests to actual breaches of the peace.

Sir William Blackstone and Sir Edward East might also be counted on Atwater's side, although they spoke only to the sufficiency of breach of the peace as a condition to warrantless misdemeanor arrest, not to its necessity. Blackstone recognized that at common law

(continued)

"the constable . . . hath great original and inherent authority with regard to arrests," but with respect to nonfelony offenses said only that "he may, without warrant, arrest any one for breach of the peace, and carry him before a justice of the peace." Not long after the framing of the Fourth Amendment, East characterized peace officers' common-law arrest power in much the same way: "A constable or other known conservator of the peace may lawfully interpose upon his own view to prevent a breach of the peace, or to quiet an affray. . . ." The great commentators were not unanimous, however, and there is also considerable evidence of a broader conception of common-law misdemeanor arrest authority unlimited by any breach-of-the-peace condition. . . . We thus find disagreement, not unanimity, among both the common-law jurists and the text-writers who sought to pull the cases together and summarize accepted practice. Having reviewed the relevant English decisions, as well as English and colonial American legal treatises, legal dictionaries, and procedure manuals, we simply are not convinced that Atwater's is the correct, or even necessarily the better, reading of the common-law history. . . .

A second, and equally serious, problem for Atwater's historical argument is posed by the "divers Statutes," M. Dalton, Country Justice ch. 170, § 4, p. 582 (1727), enacted by Parliament well before this Republic's founding that authorized warrantless misdemeanor arrests without reference to violence or turmoil. Quite apart from Hale and Blackstone, the legal background of any conception of reasonableness the Fourth Amendment's Framers might have entertained would have included English statutes, some centuries old, authorizing peace officers (and even private persons) to make warrantless arrests for all sorts of relatively minor offenses unaccompanied by violence. The so-called "nightwalker" statutes are perhaps the most notable examples. From the enactment of the Statute of Winchester in 1285, through its various readoptions and until its repeal in 1827, night watchmen were authorized and charged "as . . . in Times past" to "watch the Town continually all Night, from the Sun-setting unto the Sun-rising" and were directed that "if any Stranger do pass by them, he shall be arrested until Morning. . . ."

Nor were the nightwalker statutes the only legislative sources of warrantless arrest authority absent real or threatened violence, as the parties and their *amici* here seem to have assumed. On the contrary, following the Edwardian legislation and throughout the period leading up to the framing, Parliament repeatedly extended warrantless arrest power to cover misdemeanor-level offenses not involving any breach of the peace. . . .

An examination of specifically American evidence is to the same effect. Neither the history of the framing era nor subsequent legal development indicates that the Fourth Amendment was originally understood, or has traditionally been read, to embrace Atwater's position.

Nor does Atwater's argument from tradition pick up any steam from the historical record as it has unfolded since the framing, there being no indication that her claimed rule has ever become "woven . . . into the fabric" of American law. The story, on the contrary, is of two centuries of uninterrupted (and largely unchallenged) state and federal practice permitting warrantless arrests for misdemeanors not amounting to or involving breach of the peace. . . .

Finally, both the legislative tradition of granting warrantless misdemeanor arrest authority and the judicial tradition of sustaining such statutes against constitutional attack are buttressed by legal commentary that, for more than a century now, has almost uniformly recognized the constitutionality of extending warrantless arrest power to misdemeanors without limitation to breaches of the peace. . . .

Small wonder, then, that today statutes in all 50 States and the District of Columbia permit warrantless misdemeanor arrests by at least some (if not all) peace officers without requiring any breach of the peace, as do a host of congressional enactments. . . .

Accordingly, we confirm today what our prior cases have intimated: the standard of probable cause "applies to all arrests, without the need to 'balance' the interests and circumstances involved in particular situations." If an officer has probable cause to believe that an individual has committed even a very minor criminal offense in his presence, he may, without violating the Fourth Amendment, arrest the offender. . . .

The Court of Appeals's en banc judgment is affirmed.

In *Ker v. California*, 374 U.S. 23 (1963), an unannounced entry into a person's home was found to be violative of the Fourth Amendment. Therefore, the general rule is that officers must knock and announce their reason for being there. A number of exceptions to this rule have been recognized, including

1. When the safety of the police or others will be endangered by the announcement.

2. When the announcement will allow those inside to destroy evidence or escape.

3. When the occupants know the purpose of the officers.

The Court has said that the knock-and-announcement requirement applies whether the police gain entry by force or not. It is not important whether the police gain entry through using a key, opening an unlocked door, smashing a window, or breaking a door down. Police may obtain no-knock warrants in exceptional circumstances.

## Illegal Arrests

Does the exclusionary rule apply to people as it does to things? That is, should a defendant be excluded from trial because he or she has been arrested unlawfully? Generally, the Supreme Court has answered "no."[36] Therefore, the fact that a defendant is kidnapped has no bearing on whether the criminal proceeding will continue.

There may be an exception to this rule. If the conduct of the government is outrageous, shocking, and a gross invasion of a defendant's constitutional rights, he or she may be set free. This is known as a *Toscanino* case, named after the defendant in a Supreme Court case involving such a claim.

Later, the Second Circuit Court of Appeals reiterated that the *Toscanino* reasoning applies only to situations in which the government's conduct is both shocking and outrageous, as was true of the allegations in *Toscanino*.[37] Be aware that not all courts have followed the Second Circuit's lead. Rather than deal with the thorny legal issue, most courts factually distinguish their cases from *Toscanino*. The Supreme Court has not yet addressed the issue.

### Oyez

### United States v. Toscanino
### 500 F.2d 267 (2d Cir. 1974)

**Mansfield, Circuit Judge**

Francisco Toscanino appeals from a narcotics conviction entered against him in the Eastern District of New York. . . .

Toscanino does not question the sufficiency of the evidence or claim any error with respect to the conduct of the trial itself. His principal argument . . . is that the entire proceedings in the district court against him were void because his presence within the territorial jurisdiction of the court had been illegally obtained. . . . He offered to prove the following:

"On or about January 6, 1973 Francisco Toscanino was lured from his home in Montevideo, Uruguay by a telephone call. This call has been placed by or at the direction of Hugo Campos Hermedia. Hermedia was at that time and still is a member of the police in Montevideo, Uruguay. . . .

"The telephone call ruse succeeded in bringing Toscanino and his wife, seven months pregnant at the time, to an area near a deserted bowling alley in the City of Montevideo. Upon their arrival there Hermedia together with six associates abducted Toscanino. This was accomplished in full view of Toscanino's terrified wife by knocking him unconscious with a gun. . . .

"At no time had there been any formal or informal request on the part of the United States or the government of Uruguay for the extradition of Francisco Toscanino nor was there any legal basis to justify this rank criminal enterprise. . . .

"Later that same day Toscanino was brought to Brasilia. . . . For seventeen days Toscanino was incessantly tortured and interrogated. Throughout this entire period the United States government and the United States Attorney for the Eastern District of New York . . . did in fact receive reports as to its progress. . . . [Toscanino's] captors denied him sleep and all forms of nourishment for days at a time. Nourishment was provided intravenously in a manner precisely equal to an amount necessary to keep him alive. Reminiscent of the horror stories told by our military men who returned from Korea and China, Toscanino was forced to walk up and down a hallway for seven or eight hours at a time. When he could no longer stand he was kicked and beaten but all in a manner contrived to punish without scarring. When he could not answer, his fingers were pinched with metal pliers. Alcohol was flushed into his eyes and nose and other fluids . . . were forced up his anal passage. Incredibly, these agents of the United States government attached electrodes to Toscanino's earlobes, toes, and genitals. Jarring jolts of electricity were shot throughout his body, rendering him unconscious for indeterminate periods of time but again leaving no physical scars. . . .

[Toscanino was eventually drugged and brought to the United States to stand trial.]

Since *Frisbie,* the Supreme Court in what one distinguished legal luminary describes as a "constitutional revolution," . . . has expanded the interpretation of "due process." No longer is it limited to the guarantee of "fair" procedure at trial. In an effort to deter police misconduct, the term has been extended to bar the government from realizing directly the fruits of its own deliberate and unnecessary lawlessness in bringing the accused to trial. . . .

Accordingly, we view due process as now requiring a court to divest itself of jurisdiction over the person of a defendant where it has been acquired as the result of the government's deliberate, unnecessary and unreasonable invasion of the accused's constitutional rights.

Even though a defendant's person may not be excluded because of an illegal arrest, the evidence obtained pursuant to that arrest may be. For example, if there is a causal connection between an illegal arrest and a subsequent confession, then the statement must be excluded.[38] Or, if evidence is obtained through a search incident to an illegal arrest, it must also be suppressed. In short, any evidence obtained as a result of an illegal arrest must be excluded, unless an independent basis for its discovery can be shown by the government.

## Analyzing Fourth Amendment Problems

Search and seizure problems can be complex. This area of the law is highly fact-sensitive. It is also an area where one must be precise in analysis. Often a single case will have several interrelated and interdependent search and seizure problems.

Fourth Amendment analysis is methodical (Exhibit 12–6). In many instances, the validity of a search or seizure will depend on the validity of an earlier search or seizure. Therefore, if the government fails at an earlier stage, it may likely fail again later. For example, the police arrest Barry Burglar and conduct a search incident to arrest. During that search they discover burglar tools and other evidence of the alleged burglary. If it is determined that the arrest was invalid, then the fruits of the search incident to arrest must be suppressed. If the evidence discovered from the search led to other evidence, it may also be excluded.

### Exhibit 12–6 Fourth Amendment Analysis

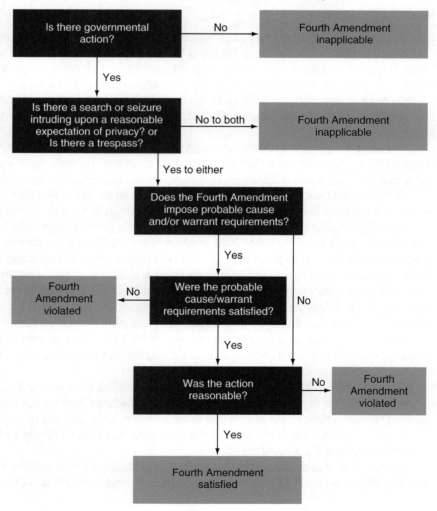

Often, officers obtain evidence in stages—each stage increasing the governmental interest in crime control, and concurrently increasing the officer's suspicion—thereby permitting a greater invasion of a person's privacy.

Even though search and seizure laws can be complex and sometimes nuanced, a little common sense goes a long way. The exceptions to the search warrant requirement are not surprising (Exhibit 12–3); common sense tells a person that an officer may continue to pursue a fleeing murderer into the suspect's home without first obtaining a warrant. Similarly, it is not shocking that illegally obtained evidence may not be used to convict a defendant.

Two important, sometimes competing, policy objectives are at play in Fourth Amendment problems: crime detection and prevention versus the citizen's right to be free from intrusive governmental behavior. Consider these interests when analyzing Fourth Amendment problems.

## Remedying Fourth Amendment Violations

Several remedies are available to the defendant whose Fourth Amendment rights have been violated by the government. First, as you learned earlier, illegally seized evidence can't be used to convict a defendant. Concerns about illegally seized evidence are normally reviewed pretrial through a motion to suppress (or exclude) evidence.

Second, the warrant itself can be overturned if it was based on false information. The Supreme Court decided in *Franks v. Deleware*[39] that a defendant is entitled to a hearing on the legitimacy of a warrant when they can make a (1) substantial preliminary showing that a false statement knowingly and intentionally, or with reckless disregard for the truth, was offered by police and (2) the statement was essential to the judge's issuance of the warrant. If these elements are satisfied, the trial court must conduct an evidentiary hearing on the matter. This is known as a **Franks hearing**. At the hearing, the defendant must prove, by preponderance of the evidence, the

**Franks hearing**
The right of a defendant who can make a preliminary showing that false evidence was used to obtain a warrant to a hearing to decide the truth of the allegation.

---

## Ethical Considerations

### Police Ethics

Law enforcement officers are bound by departmental rules and local, state, and federal laws. The Constitution itself plays a role in defining police ethics. For example, the exclusionary rule is both an evidentiary rule and an ethical directive.

In addition to the above laws, the International Association of Chiefs of Police has promulgated a model policy of ethical standards. Although not binding, these standards are widely recognized by police agencies as good guidance.

The model policy provides, inter alia, that officers:

- shall obey the law.
- shall not behave in unbecoming ways.
- shall respect other officers, be truthful, cooperate with internal investigations, and not interfere with investigations.
- shall report any convictions to their superior.
- shall not harass, intimidate, or demean others.
- shall adhere to use-of-force policies and respect civil rights.
- shall not be under the influence of alcohol or drugs while on duty or in a public place at any time.
- shall not accept gifts or gratuities or otherwise financially benefit from their position, except to receive compensation.
- shall not use their official powers to resolve personal disputes.
- shall not commence a personal relationship with the target of an investigation and other specific individuals.
- shall follow state law concerning political activities. Where silent, officers shall not engage in political activities, including campaigning, soliciting support, or posting notices, while on duty or in uniform.

falsity of the evidence. If proven, the trial judge will then determine if probable cause still exists. If so, the evidence remains admissible. If not, it is excluded.

The third remedy is to sue the offending officer for the civil rights violation under state and federal civil rights statutes, under constitutional tort theory,[40] and under traditional state tort theory. Fourth, individuals can request criminal prosecution by state and federal authorities for civil rights violations, assault, battery, trespass, or other crimes by officers. Finally, harmed individuals can complain to an officer's department or to other officials (e.g., some state officials have the authority to revoke a police officer's peace officer status), with resulting administrative discipline.

## Key Terms

Franks hearing                    probable cause                    standing

## Review Questions

1. In what way did *Katz v. United States* (1967) change Fourth Amendment law?

2. What is the relationship of *Jones v. United States* (2012) to *Katz v. United States* (1967)?

3. What are the basic requirements for obtaining a search warrant?

4. Ling is a suspect in an embezzlement investigation. The police believe that she has hidden evidence in her neighbor's house, without the neighbor's consent. The neighbor will not consent to a search. Can the police obtain a search warrant for the non-suspect's home?

5. Police Officer Brown observes Cassandra steal a cell phone from a man's pocket. As Brown approaches Cassandra, she darts off. He draws his baton and throws it at her feet, intending to stop her. Brown's aim is bad and he hits her in the head. She is dazed and bleeding but escapes. She suffers a concussion and nearly dies in the hospital two days later. Cassandra sues Brown, alleging that he used excessive force under the Fourth Amendment. Brown moves to dismiss her lawsuit on the theory

that the Fourth Amendment doesn't apply because she wasn't seized. Should Brown's motion be dismissed or granted? Explain your answer.

6. A police officer is approached by a man on the street who tells the officer that he was just robbed. The man points out the robber, who is standing in a park just across the street. Must the officer obtain a warrant to make the arrest?

7. A police officer is approached by a man on the street who tells the officer that he was just robbed. Although he did not see where the robber fled, he knew the assailant's name and address, as the two men "grew up together." The officer and the victim went to the police station and completed an incident report. After a telephone call to one of suspect's neighbors, they learned that he was at home. Must the officer obtain a warrant to make the arrest?

8. The same facts as in question 7, except that the victim points to a fleeing suspect. The officer chases the suspect to a house, where the officer sees the suspect enter with the use of a key. Must the officer end the chase and obtain a warrant?

## Problems & Critical Thinking Exercises

1. Assume that officers have a valid search warrant for the defendant's apartment. The warrant specifies that the officers may search for a stolen bicycle. May the officers do the following?

2. Search the defendant's desk drawers in his study?

3. Search the defendant's closets in his bedroom?

4. Search the defendant's body?

5. Seize a transparent bag of cocaine found lying on the defendant's dining room table?

# Endnotes

1. 277 U.S. 438 (1928).

2. Interestingly, one scholar believes that no trespass test ever existed, even though he, like his contemporaries, taught and wrote about it. Believing it true but unimportant because it had been replaced by the privacy test, he only researched the question and came to his conclusion after the trespass test was "revived" in the 2012 *Jones* decision. See Orin S. Kerr, *The Curious History of Fourth Amendment Searches*, Supreme Court Review, *George Washington University Law Review*, March 26, 2013, available at http://papers.ssrn.com/sol3/papers.cfm?abstract_id=2154611

3. 316 U.S.129 (1942).

4. 388 U.S. 41(1967).

5. *United States v. Jacobsen*, 466 U.S. 109, 113 (1984).

6. See, for example, *United States v. Place*, 462 U.S. 696 (1983).

7. 529 U.S. 334 (2000).

8. *New York v. Burger*, 482 U.S. 691 (1987).

9. *Sir Edward Coke Declares That Your House Is Your "House and Fortress."* Online Library of Liberty. Retrieved from oll.libertyfund.org on April 30, 2021.

10. *Minnesota v. Olson*, 495 U.S. 91 (1990).

11. *Byrd v. United States*, 584 U.S. __ (2018).

12. *Ex parte Jackson*, 96 U.S. 727 (1878). The Court did find, however, that the contents of mail are protected by the Fourth Amendment.

13. *United States v. Miller*, 425 U.S. 435 (1976); *Smith v. Maryland*, 442 U.S. 735 (1979).

14. *Carroll v. United States*, 267 U.S. 132 (1934).

15. *Florida v. Harris*, 568 U.S. 237 (2013).

16. *United States v. Place*, 462 U.S. 696 (1983). A dog sniff of a person or thing, assuming no more intrusion, is not a search under the Fourth Amendment because no reasonable expectation of privacy has been violated. See also *Illinois v. Caballes*, 543 U.S. 405 (2005).

17. *Harris*, supra.

18. *Herring v. United States*, 555 U.S. 135 (2009).

19. See *Michigan v. DeFillippo*, 443 U.S. 31 (1979); *Illinois v. Krull*, 480 U.S. 340 (1987).

20. *Beck v. Ohio*, 379 U.S. 89 (1964).

21. *McDonald v. United States*, 335 U.S. 451, 455–56 (1948).

22. *Coolidge v. New Hampshire*, 403 U.S. 443 (1971).

23. *Shadwick v. Tampa*, 407 U.S. 345 (1972).

24. Fed. R. Crim. P. 41(b).

25. *United States v. Grubbs*, 547 U.S. 90 (2006).

26. *Zurcher v. Stanford Daily*, 436 U.S. 547 (1978).

27. *Ybarra v. Illinois*, 444 U.S. 85 (1979).

28. *Michigan v. Summers*, 452 U.S. 692 (1981).

29. *Jones v. United States*, 357 U.S. 493 (1958).

30. Fed. R. Crim. P. 41(c)(1).

31. Fed. R. Crim. P. 41(d).

32. *Muehler v. Mena*, 544 U.S. 93 (2005).

33. *New York v. Belton*, 453 U.S. 454 (1981).

34. *Aguilar v. Texas*, 378 U.S. 108, 110–11 (1964).

35. *Stealgald v. United States*, 451 U.S. 204 (1981).

36. *Frisbie v. Collins*, 342 U.S. 519 (1952).

37. *United States ex rel. Lujan v. Gengler*, 510 F.2d 62 (2d Cir.), *cert. denied*, 421 U.S. 1001 (1975).

38. *Taylor v. Alabama*, 457 U.S. 687 (1982).

39. *Franks v. Delaware*, 438 U.S. 154 (U.S. 1978).

40. *Bivens v. Six Unknown Named Agents*, 403 U.S. 388 (1971).

# Chapter 13

# Searches and Seizures: Exceptions

## Chapter Outline

Learning Objective: Identify and describe, including landmark cases, the exceptions to the Fourth Amendment's warrant and probable cause requirements.

In the last chapter, you learned the fundamentals of searches and seizures. This included the reasonableness, probable cause, and warrant requirements, Fourth Amendment analysis, and the remedies for Fourth Amendment violations. This chapter expands on that knowledge by examining the Fourth Amendment in action. Specifically, when police are expected to satisfy the Fourth Amendment's greatest demands—reasonability, probable cause, and a warrant. And, you will learn when less is required: those instances when police don't have to have a warrant, or even probable cause, to conduct a search or seizure. There are many of these "exceptions." The discussion begins with the exception, consent.

## Consent Searches

A voluntary **consent** to a search obviates the Fourth Amendment's requirements of suspicion and a warrant. The only requirement is reasonableness, which is satisfied when a competent person voluntarily consents.

There is no requirement that police officers inform a person that they may refuse to consent.[1] The scope of the search is limited by the person consenting.

**consent**
Voluntary and active agreement.

Absent special circumstances, a consent to search may be terminated at any time by the person giving consent.

Courts examine the totality of the circumstances when determining whether a consent was voluntary. The following factors are among those that are considered, but none are individually dispositive:

1. The suspect's knowledge of the right to refuse.

2. The age, intelligence, and language skills of the suspect.

3. The degree of cooperation exhibited by the suspect.

4. The suspect's attitude about the likelihood of discovering contraband during the search.

5. The length of detention.

6. The nature of the detention, including the nature of the questions and whether police intimidated the suspect or coerced the statements.[2]

Police must respect any limitations placed on a suspect's consent. So, if a suspect indicates that police may search the family room of a house, but no more, any evidence discovered in another room of the house would be excluded. Also, consent may be revoked at any time before the search is completed. Prosecutors bear the burden of establishing that consents are voluntary by a preponderance of the evidence.

Of course, a defendant who is threatened or coerced into consenting has not voluntarily consented. It is not coercion for a person to be told that if they do not consent, a warrant will be obtained authorizing the desired search. But it is coercion for officers to tell a person that if they do not consent to a search, a warrant will be obtained and the officers will ransack the home.[3]

Consent is invalid if it is obtained by a mistaken belief that the officer had a legal right to conduct the search. For example, if Officer Frisk tells Patty Pat-Down that he has a warrant, or that the law does not require that he have one, and she acquiesces, the search is invalid if he had no warrant or legal right to conduct the search.

The same is true when officers use fraud or deceit to obtain consent. For example, in one case a defendant was arrested and interrogated. He gave no incriminating information during the questioning. The following day the officers went to the home of the defendant and told his wife that he had confessed to the crime and had sent the police to seize the contraband. Based upon these statements, the defendant's wife consented to a search by the officers. The state court found that this tactic led to an involuntary consent and that the evidence seized was inadmissible at trial.[4]

The facts of that case raise another issue: third-party consent. This arises often in cases where many people share a single dwelling or room, such as families, fraternities, and dormitories. In *United States v. Matlock* (1974),[5] the Supreme Court found that a third party may consent so long as the parties share access, control, and use of the property. If coinhabitants section off a dwelling, with each tenant having exclusive control over a specific area, then only the tenant in control of an area may consent to its search. If closets, desks, or similar areas are reserved for one person's private use, only that person may consent. Also, if coinhabitants are both present, either one may refuse consent for a search. If, however, police remove the coinhabitant from the premises before consent is refused, then the remaining coinhabitant's consent is adequate.[6]

Having a property interest does not always give one a right to consent to a search of the property. The Supreme Court has said that neither landlords nor hotel managers may consent to the search of their tenants' rooms.[7] They may have a property interest, but the privacy interest rests with the tenants.

A search conducted upon a mistaken, but reasonable, belief that a person has the authority to consent is valid. In *Illinois v. Rodriguez*, police responded to a call by a woman who alleged that she had been beaten by the defendant. She led them from one residence to another, used a key to open the door, and referred to the apartment as "ours." The police found both the defendant and drugs in the apartment. He challenged the entry on the theory that the woman didn't have common control over the property because she had moved out weeks before. While it was true that she lacked the authority to consent, the Supreme Court found the officers' reliance on her consent to be reasonable.[8]

## Stop and Frisk

The landmark stop and frisk case, *Terry v. Ohio*, appears in the next Oyez. The facts that gave rise to the case occurred on October 31, 1963, when a *Cleveland, Ohio,* police detective observed three men standing on a street corner. Suspicious of the men, the detective positioned himself to watch their behavior. After some time, the officer concluded that the men were "casing a job, a stick-up."

The officer approached the men, identified himself, and asked them to identify themselves. After the men "mumbled something," the officer grabbed one of the men, John Terry, and conducted a frisk, or a patdown, of the man's clothing. The officer felt a pistol in the man's coat pocket. He removed the gun from his coat and then patted down the other two men. Another gun was discovered during those frisks.

Protestor of the New York City Stop and Frisk Program.

# Oyez

## TERRY v. OHIO
### 392 U.S. 1 (1968)

**MR. CHIEF JUSTICE WARREN delivered the opinion of the Court.**

This case presents serious questions concerning the role of the Fourth Amendment in the confrontation on the street between the citizen and the policeman investigating suspicious circumstances.

Petitioner Terry was convicted of carrying a concealed weapon and sentenced to the statutorily prescribed term of one to three years in the penitentiary. Following the denial of a pretrial motion to suppress, the prosecution introduced in evidence two revolvers and a number of bullets seized from Terry and a codefendant, Richard Chilton, by Cleveland Police Detective Martin McFadden. At the hearing on the motion to suppress this evidence, Officer McFadden testified that, while he was patrolling in plain clothes in downtown Cleveland at approximately 2:30 in the afternoon of October 31, 1963, his attention was attracted by two men, Chilton and Terry, standing on the corner of Huron Road and Euclid Avenue. He had never seen the two men before, and he was unable to say precisely what first drew his eye to them. However, he testified that he had been a policeman for 39 years and a detective for 35, and that he had been assigned to patrol this vicinity of downtown Cleveland for shoplifters and pickpockets for 30 years. He explained that he had developed routine habits of observation over the years, and that he would "stand and watch people or walk and watch people at many intervals of the day." He added: "Now, in this case, when I looked over, they didn't look right to me at the time."

His interest aroused, Officer McFadden took up a post of observation in the entrance to a store 300 to 400 feet away from the two men. "I get more purpose to watch them when I seen their movements," he testified. He saw one of the men leave the other one and walk southwest on Huron Road, past some stores. The man paused for a moment and looked in a store window, then walked on a short distance, turned around and walked back toward the corner, pausing once again to look in the same store window. He rejoined his companion at the corner, and the two conferred briefly. Then the second man went through the same series of motions, strolling down Huron Road, looking in the same window, walking on a short distance, turning back, peering in the store window again, and returning to confer with the first man at the corner. The two men repeated this ritual alternately between five and six times apiece—in all, roughly a dozen trips. At one point, while the two were standing together on the corner, a third man approached them and engaged them briefly in conversation. This man then left the two others and walked west on Euclid Avenue. Chilton and Terry resumed their measured pacing, peering, and conferring. After this had gone on for 10 to 12 minutes, the two men walked off together, heading west on Euclid Avenue, following the path taken earlier by the third man.

By this time, Officer McFadden had become thoroughly suspicious. He testified that, after observing their elaborately casual and oft-repeated reconnaissance of the store window on Huron Road, he suspected the two men of "casing a job, a stick-up," and that he considered it his duty as a police officer to investigate further. He added that he feared "they may have a gun." Thus, Officer McFadden followed Chilton and Terry and saw them stop in front of Zucker's store to talk to the same man who had conferred with them earlier on the street corner. Deciding that the situation was ripe for direct action, Officer McFadden approached the three men, identified himself as a police officer and asked for their names. At this point, his knowledge was confined to what he had observed. He was not acquainted with any of the three men by name or by sight, and he had received no information concerning them from any other source. When the men "mumbled something" in response to his inquiries, Officer McFadden grabbed petitioner Terry, spun him around so that they were facing the other two, with Terry between McFadden and the others, and patted down the outside of his clothing. In the left breast pocket of Terry's overcoat, Officer McFadden felt a pistol. He reached inside the overcoat pocket, but was unable to remove the gun. At this point, keeping Terry between himself and the others, the officer ordered all three men to enter Zucker's store. As they went in, he removed Terry's overcoat completely, removed a .38 caliber revolver from the pocket and ordered all three men to face the wall with their hands raised. Officer McFadden proceeded to pat down the outer clothing of Chilton and the third man, Katz. He discovered another revolver in the outer pocket of Chilton's overcoat, but no weapons were found on Katz. The officer testified that he only patted the men down to see whether they had weapons, and that he did not put his hands beneath the outer garments of either Terry or Chilton until he felt their guns. So far as appears from the record, he never placed his hands beneath Katz' outer garments. Officer McFadden seized Chilton's gun, asked the proprietor of the store to call a police wagon, and took all three men to the station, where Chilton and Terry were formally charged with carrying concealed weapons.

On the motion to suppress the guns, the prosecution took the position that they had been seized following a search incident to a lawful arrest. The trial court rejected this theory, stating that it "would be stretching the facts beyond reasonable comprehension" to find that Officer McFadden had had probable cause to arrest the men before he patted them down for weapons. However, the court denied the defendants' motion on the ground that Officer McFadden, on the basis of his experience,

> . . . had reasonable cause to believe . . . that the defendants were conducting themselves suspiciously, and some interrogation should be made of their action.

Purely for his own protection, the court held, the officer had the right to pat down the outer clothing of these men, who he had reasonable cause to believe might be armed. The court distinguished between an investigatory "stop" and an arrest, and between a "frisk" of the

(continued)

outer clothing for weapons and a full-blown search for evidence of crime. The frisk, it held, was essential to the proper performance of the officer's investigatory duties, for, without it, "the answer to the police officer may be a bullet, and a loaded pistol discovered during the frisk is admissible." [They were convicted, sentenced, and lost their appeal before the Supreme Court of Ohio.]

We would be less than candid if we did not acknowledge that this question thrusts to the fore difficult and troublesome issues regarding a sensitive area of police activity—issues which have never before been squarely presented to this Court. Reflective of the tensions involved are the practical and constitutional arguments pressed with great vigor on both sides of the public debate over the power of the police to "stop and frisk"—as it is sometimes euphemistically termed—suspicious persons.

On the one hand, it is frequently argued that, in dealing with the rapidly unfolding and often dangerous situations on city streets, the police are in need of an escalating set of flexible responses, graduated in relation to the amount of information they possess. For this purpose, it is urged that distinctions should be made between a "stop" and an "arrest" (or a "seizure" of a person), and between a "frisk" and a "search." Thus, it is argued, the police should be allowed to "stop" a person and detain him briefly for questioning upon suspicion that he may be connected with criminal activity. Upon suspicion that the person may be armed, the police should have the power to "frisk" him for weapons. If the "stop" and the "frisk" give rise to probable cause to believe that the suspect has committed a crime, then the police should be empowered to make a formal "arrest," and a full incident "search" of the person. This scheme is justified in part upon the notion that a "stop" and a "frisk" amount to a mere "minor inconvenience and petty indignity," which can properly be imposed upon the citizen in the interest of effective law enforcement on the basis of a police officer's suspicion.

On the other side, the argument is made that the authority of the police must be strictly circumscribed by the law of arrest and search as it has developed to date in the traditional jurisprudence of the Fourth Amendment. It is contended with some force that there is not -- and cannot be -- a variety of police activity which does not depend solely upon the voluntary cooperation of the citizen, and yet which stops short of an arrest based upon probable cause to make such an arrest. The heart of the Fourth Amendment, the argument runs, is a severe requirement of specific justification for any intrusion upon protected personal security, coupled with a highly developed system of judicial controls to enforce upon the agents of the State the commands of the Constitution. . . .

Our first task is to establish at what point in this encounter the Fourth Amendment becomes relevant. That is, we must decide whether and when Officer McFadden "seized" Terry, and whether and when he conducted a "search." There is some suggestion in the use of such terms as "stop" and "frisk" that such police conduct is outside the purview of the Fourth Amendment because neither action rises to the level of a "search" or "seizure" within the meaning of the Constitution. We emphatically reject this notion. It is quite plain that the Fourth Amendment governs "seizures" of the person which do not eventuate in a trip to the stationhouse and prosecution for crime—"arrests" in traditional terminology. It must be recognized that, whenever a police officer accosts an individual and restrains his freedom to walk away, he has "seized" that person. And it is nothing less than sheer torture of the English language to suggest that a careful exploration of the outer surfaces of a person's clothing all over his or her body in an attempt to find weapons is not a "search." Moreover, it is simply fantastic to urge that such a procedure performed in public by a policeman while the citizen stands helpless, perhaps facing a wall with his hands raised, is a "petty indignity." It is a serious intrusion upon the sanctity of the person, which may inflict great indignity and arouse strong resentment, and it is not to be undertaken lightly. . . .

In this case, there can be no question, then, that Officer McFadden "seized" petitioner and subjected him to a "search" when he took hold of him and patted down the outer surfaces of his clothing. We must decide whether, at that point, it was reasonable for Officer McFadden to have interfered with petitioner's personal security as he did. And, in determining whether the seizure and search were "unreasonable," our inquiry is a dual one -- whether the officer's action was justified at its inception, and whether it was reasonably related in scope to the circumstances which justified the interference in the first place. . . .

If this case involved police conduct subject to the Warrant Clause of the Fourth Amendment, we would have to ascertain whether "probable cause" existed to justify the search and seizure which took place. However, that is not the case. We do not retreat from our holdings that the police must, whenever practicable, obtain advance judicial approval of searches and seizures through the warrant pro-cedure, *see, e.g., Katz v. United States* . . . or that, in most instances, failure to comply with the warrant requirement can only be excused by exigent circumstances. But we deal here with an entire rubric of police conduct -- necessarily swift action predicated upon the on-the-spot observations of the officer on the beat -- which historically has not been, and, as a practical matter, could not be, subjected to the warrant procedure. Instead, the conduct involved in this case must be tested by the Fourth Amendment's general proscription against unreasonable searches and seizures. . . .

Nonetheless, the notions which underlie both the warrant procedure and the requirement of probable cause remain fully relevant in this context. In order to assess the reasonableness of Officer McFadden's conduct as a general proposition, it is necessary "first to focus upon the governmental interest which allegedly justifies official intrusion upon the constitutionally protected interests of the private citizen," for there is . . .

> . . . no ready test for determining reasonableness other than by balancing the need to search [or seize] against the invasion which the search [or seizure] entails.

And, in justifying the particular intrusion, the police officer must be able to point to specific and articulable facts which, taken together with rational inferences from those facts, reasonably warrant that intrusion. The scheme of the Fourth Amendment becomes meaningful only when it is assured that, at some point, the conduct of those charged with enforcing the laws can be subjected to the more detached, neutral scrutiny of a judge who must evaluate the reasonableness of a particular search or seizure in light of the particular circumstances. And, in making that assessment, it is imperative that the facts be judged against an objective standard: would the facts available to the officer at the moment of the seizure or the search "warrant a man of reasonable caution in the belief" that the action taken was appropriate? Anything less would invite intrusions upon constitutionally guaranteed rights based on nothing more substantial than inarticulate hunches, a result this Court has consistently refused to sanction. And simple

> "good faith on the part of the arresting officer is not enough." . . . If subjective good faith alone were the test, the protections of the Fourth Amendment would evaporate, and the people would be "secure in their persons, houses, papers, and effects," only in the discretion of the police.

Applying these principles to this case, we consider first the nature and extent of the governmental interests involved. One general interest is, of course, that of effective crime prevention and detection; it is this interest which underlies the recognition that a police officer may, in appropriate circumstances and in an appropriate manner, approach a person for purposes of investigating possibly criminal behavior even though there is no probable cause to make an arrest. It was this legitimate investigative function Officer McFadden was discharging when he decided to approach petitioner and his companions. He had observed Terry, Chilton, and Katz go through a series of acts, each of them perhaps innocent in itself, but which, taken together, warranted further investigation. There is nothing unusual in two men standing together on a street corner, perhaps waiting for someone. Nor is there anything suspicious about people in such circumstances strolling up and down the street, singly or in pairs. Store windows, moreover, are made to be looked in. But the story is quite different where, as here, two men hover about a street corner for an extended period of time, at the end of which it becomes apparent that they are not waiting for anyone or anything; where these men pace alternately along an identical route, pausing to stare in the same store window roughly 24 times; where each completion of this route is followed immediately by a conference between the two men on the corner; where they are joined in one of these conferences by a third man who leaves swiftly, and where the two men finally follow the third and rejoin him a couple of blocks away. It would have been poor police work indeed for an officer of 30 years' experience in the detection of thievery from stores in this same neighborhood to have failed to investigate this behavior further.

The crux of this case, however, is not the propriety of Officer McFadden's taking steps to investigate petitioner's suspicious behavior, but, rather, whether there was justification for McFadden's invasion of Terry's personal security by searching him for weapons in the course of that investigation. We are now concerned with more than the governmental interest in investigating crime; in addition, there is the more immediate interest of the police officer in taking steps to assure himself that the person with whom he is dealing is not armed with a weapon that could unexpectedly and fatally be used against him. Certainly it would be unreasonable to require that police officers take unnecessary risks in the performance of their duties. American criminals have a long tradition of armed violence, and every year in this country many law enforcement officers are killed in the line of duty, and thousands more are wounded. Virtually all of these deaths and a substantial portion of the injuries are inflicted with guns and knives.

In view of these facts, we cannot blind ourselves to the need for law enforcement officers to protect themselves and other prospective victims of violence in situations where they may lack probable cause for an arrest. When an officer is justified in believing that the individual whose suspicious behavior he is investigating at close range is armed and presently dangerous to the officer or to others, it would appear to be clearly unreasonable to deny the officer the power to take necessary measures to determine whether the person is, in fact, carrying a weapon and to neutralize the threat of physical harm. . . .

The scope of the search in this case presents no serious problem in light of these standards. Officer McFadden patted down the outer clothing of petitioner and his two companions. He did not place his hands in their pockets or under the outer surface of their garments until he had felt weapons, and then he merely reached for and removed the guns. He never did invade Katz' person beyond the outer surfaces of his clothes, since he discovered nothing in his pat-down which might have been a weapon. Officer McFadden confined his search strictly to what was minimally necessary to learn whether the men were armed and to disarm them once he discovered the weapons. He did not conduct a general exploratory search for whatever evidence of criminal activity he might find.

We conclude that the revolver seized from Terry was properly admitted in evidence against him. At the time he seized petitioner and searched him for weapons, Officer McFadden had reasonable grounds to believe that petitioner was armed and dangerous, and it was necessary for the protection of himself and others to take swift measures to discover the true facts and neutralize the threat of harm if it materialized. The policeman carefully restricted his search to what was appropriate to the discovery of the particular items which he sought. Each case of this sort will, of course, have to be decided on its own facts. We merely hold today that, where a police officer observes unusual conduct which leads him reasonably to conclude in light of his experience that criminal activity may be afoot and that the persons with whom he is dealing may be armed and presently dangerous, where, in the course of investigating this behavior, he identifies himself as a policeman and makes reasonable inquiries, and where nothing in the initial stages of the encounter serves to dispel his reasonable fear for his own or others' safety, he is entitled for the protection of himself and others in the area to conduct a carefully limited search of the outer clothing of such persons in an attempt to discover weapons which might be used to assault him. Such a search is a reasonable search under the Fourth Amendment, and any weapons seized may properly be introduced in evidence against the person from whom they were taken.

■    ■    ■

## Sidebar

### New York City Stop and Frisk

New York City is home to a large and controversial stop and frisk program. Relying on the law established in *Terry*, New York established a program of aggressively stopping individuals who are suspected of criminality. Included in the program is Operation Clean Halls, a practice that enables owners of apartment houses and managers of public housing units to invite police into the public spaces of their buildings and to stop people who are suspected of criminality, including trespass. The program is large. More than 3,000 private housing units were enrolled in the program and over 600,000 people were stopped in 2011 alone. The program was challenged as violative of the Fourth Amendment, and because of the disproportionate number of minorities stopped, as violative of equal protection as well. A federal district court found the program unconstitutional in 2013.[9] The number of stop and frisks has steadily declined since that time.

The officer testified that he conducted the frisks because he believed the men were carrying weapons. At trial, Terry was convicted of carrying a concealed weapon and was subsequently sentenced to one to three years in prison. His appeal made it to the U.S. Supreme Court.

In one of the most significant Fourth Amendment decisions the Court has ever issued, the justices emphasized that officers don't have carte blanche to stop and frisk. Although probable cause is not required, officers must have a "reasonable suspicion" that the person to be stopped has just committed, is committing, or is about to commit a crime. The officer's suspicion must be supported by "specific and articulable facts which, taken together with rational inferences from those facts, reasonably warrant that intrusion."[10] An officer's hunch doesn't ever, by itself, justify a *Terry* stop. When reviewing an officer's reasonable suspicion decision, a court is to examine the "totality of the circumstances" as known to the officer at the time of the encounter. The determination is dependent on the factual and practical considerations of everyday life on which reasonable and prudent men, not legal technicians, act.

The temporal requirement, that the crime be "afoot," is narrow. The crime must have been committed only moments before, or will be committed in moments, or it must be under way. The Supreme Court has carved out an exception in cases where an officer has reasonable suspicion to believe a suspect has committed a felony in the past.[11]

Facts that may not be admissible at trial may be considered.[12] Most commonly, an officer will personally observe the facts that create reasonable suspicion. However, the Supreme Court has held "that reasonable cause for a[n investigative stop] can only be based on the officer's personal observation, rather than on information supplied by another person."[13] A 911 call from a driver who reported being run off the road by a truck, with a detailed description of the truck and the location where it occurred, was adequate evidence to justify a *Terry* stop of the truck minutes later.[14] Even a confidential informant's information is sufficient, if reliable. Also, one police department may treat another department's wanted notice as reasonable suspicion to stop a suspect who meets the description in the notice.

In *Terry*, the facts that established reasonable suspicion included the officer's personal observation of the defendant and another man pacing near a business, repeatedly looking into the business's window, and briefly encountering and conferring with a third man. In addition, the Court noted that the detective who stopped Terry had 39 years of experience in policing, and the officer testified that in his experience the men appeared to be "casing" the business. While the Court stressed that an officer's intuition alone is insufficient to establish reasonable cause, it can be relied upon in conjunction with specific facts to support a temporary detention.

Another example of how much evidence is required to establish reasonable suspicion can be found in the 2000 Supreme Court case *Illinois v. Wardlow*. In *Wardlow*, a defendant, who was in a high crime area, took flight immediately upon seeing police officers. The Court stated that even though a person's presence in a high crime area is not enough to establish reasonable suspicion, that fact combined with the defendant's unprovoked flight is enough.[15]

Not all contacts between an officer and a citizen amount to a seizure. A seizure occurs anytime a reasonable person believes that he or she is not free to leave. There need not be an attempt to leave. A person may feel restrained by physical contact from a police officer, tone of voice, threatening language, or the intimidating presence of many officers.[16]

Mere questioning of a citizen by a police officer is not a detention. The questions, however, must probe the reason for the stop. Questions that wander into other matters are not permitted. Also, if the interrogation becomes accusatory or its duration lengthy, the Fourth Amendment may be triggered. A Texas statute that required an individual to comply with a police officer's order to identify himself, even though there was no basis to believe criminal activity was afoot, was held unconstitutional by the Supreme Court in 1979.[17] The Court held that the Fourth Amendment prohibits the police from temporarily detaining a person and demanding identification without at least a reasonable suspicion to believe the individual has committed, or is engaged in committing, a crime. However, if a *Terry* stop is justified, a statute may require the individual to produce identification, and if refused, the individual may be arrested, charged, and convicted for the refusal. In the 2004 decision in *Hiibel v. Sixth Judicial District,* 544 U.S. 177 (2004), the Court stated:

> Obtaining a suspect's name in the course of a *Terry* stop serves important government interests. Knowledge of identity may inform an officer that a suspect is wanted for another offense, or has a record of violence or mental disorder. On the other hand, knowing identity may help clear a suspect and allow the police to concentrate their efforts elsewhere. Identity may prove particularly important in cases such as this, where the police are investigating what appears to be a domestic assault. Officers called to investigate domestic disputes need to know whom they are dealing with in order to assess the situation, the threat to their own safety, and possible danger to the potential victim. . . . Petitioner argues that the Nevada statute circumvents the probable cause requirement, in effect allowing an officer to arrest a person for being suspicious. According to petitioner, this creates a risk of arbitrary police conduct that the Fourth Amendment does not permit. Brief for Petitioner 28–33. These are familiar concerns; they were central to the opinion in *Papachristou,* and also to the decisions limiting the operation of stop and identify statutes in *Kolender* and *Brown.* Petitioner's concerns are met by the requirement that a *Terry* stop must be justified at its inception and "reasonably related in scope to the circumstances which justified" the initial stop. 392 U.S., at 20. Under these principles, an officer may not arrest a suspect for failure to identify himself if the request for identification is not reasonably related to the circumstances justifying the stop.

A motorist may be temporarily detained under *Terry.* Also, the Supreme Court has said that once a person is lawfully pulled over and probable cause exists to believe a crime, including a traffic violation, has occurred, he or she may be ordered out of the vehicle, even though there is no reason to believe that the driver is a threat. There will be a more thorough discussion of automobiles and the Fourth Amendment later in this chapter.

In addition to requiring reasonable suspicion, the *Terry* Court also stated that stops are to "last no longer than is necessary," and the investigative methods employed during the stop should be the "least intrusive means reasonably available to verify or dispel the officer's suspicion in a short period of time." If an officer detains a person longer than necessary, the investigatory detention turns into a full seizure (arrest), and the probable cause requirement of the Fourth Amendment applies.

It is not always easy to distinguish stops from arrests. But the distinction is important because of the differing legal standards, reasonable suspicion, and probable cause. *Florida v. Royer*, 460 U.S. 491 (1983), provides an example of the distinction between an investigatory detention and an arrest. The defendant, a suspected drug dealer, was questioned in a public area of an airport. After a few minutes, he was taken 40 feet to a small police office, where he consented to a search of his luggage. The Court concluded that the search was the product of an illegal arrest, as less-intrusive methods of investigation were available. As alternatives, the Court mentioned that the officers could have used narcotics dogs to inspect the luggage or could have immediately requested consent to search the defendant's luggage. The act of requiring the defendant to accompany the officers to a small room 40 feet away transformed the detention from a *Terry* stop to an arrest, which was violative of the Fourth Amendment because it was not supported by probable cause. In another case from a federal appellate court, that the police drew their guns on, and handcuffed, a driver and the car's occupant did not convert the *Terry* stop into a full seizure requiring probable cause. But the court acknowledged that the distinction between full seizures and *Terry* stops is often hard to draw.[18]

The fact that there has been a lawful stop does not itself justify a frisk. The purpose behind permitting investigatory stops is the advancement of crime detection and prevention. Frisks, on the other hand, are permitted to protect officers and others from the person stopped.

To conduct a frisk, an officer must have a reasonable belief that the person is armed and dangerous. Again, the officer must be able to point to facts to support this conclusion. An officer may draw on his or her experience as a police officer in making the decision. Again, however, intuition (suspicion not supported by any facts) alone is not adequate.

Full searches require probable cause. A *Terry* frisk requires less, and, accordingly, the permitted intrusion is less. The search must be limited to the outer clothing. A search of interior clothing or pockets is improper.

If the defendant is in an automobile, the officer may search those areas within the person's immediate control.[19] Once any lawful stop of a vehicle is made, the driver may be ordered out of the vehicle. However, to frisk an occupant of a vehicle, the *Terry* standard must be met.

If during a patdown an officer feels an item that may be a weapon, then the officer may reach into the clothing of the citizen to seize the item. Any item seized, whether a weapon, contraband, or other item associated with a crime, may be used as evidence.

If the officer does not feel an item that may be a weapon, the search can go no further. If the officer feels evidence of another crime, the intrusion may continue under the "plain feel" doctrine.

## Plain Feel

You have learned both the plain view doctrine and the *Terry* exception to the warrant and probable cause requirements of the Fourth Amendment. The plain feel doctrine is the product of their joining. That is, what happens when an officer who is conducting a *Terry* patdown discovers, through the sense of touch, not a weapon, but contraband? May this information be used to establish probable cause allowing a more intrusive search? This question was answered in *Minnesota v. Dickerson*, 508 U.S. 366 (1993), where the Supreme Court held that evidence felt during a *Terry* frisk may be used to establish probable cause to support retrieving an item, as long as the incriminating character of the evidence is immediately apparent.

The rules set out in *Terry* apply. First, stops must be supported by reasonable suspicion. Second, patdowns may be conducted only when an officer possesses a reasonable suspicion based on specific and articulable facts that the suspect may

## Exhibit 13–1  Terry Stop and Frisk Encounters.

```
[Does officer have reasonable suspicion of criminality, supported by specific & articulable facts?] --Yes--> [Is the stop limited in duration & manner?] --Yes--> [Has the investigation discovered probable cause of criminality?] --Yes--> [Arrest]
         |No                                    |No                                      |                                              ^Yes
         v                                      v                                        v                                              |
  [Stop not permitted]              [4th Amendment Violated]                    [Stop must end]                               [Does item establish probable cause of criminality?]
         |
         v
  [Does officer have a reasonable suspicion of dangerousness?] --Yes--> [Does a frisk of outer clothing reveal weapon or contraband?] --Yes--> [Item may be retrieved] --> [Does item establish probable cause of criminality?]
         |No                                         |No                                                                                          |No
         v                                           v                                                                                            v
  [No frisk permitted]                       [Search must end]                                                               [If weapon can be held until encounter ends, then returned unless suspect arrested]
```

be armed and dangerous. Third, the patdown must be limited. Exploration of the clothing beyond what is necessary to determine dangerousness is not permitted, unless probable cause to believe that there is contraband is created through the officer's sense of touch.

## Plain View

Another exception to the warrant requirement is the **plain view doctrine.** Under this rule, a warrantless seizure of evidence by an officer who is lawfully in a position to see the evidence is valid.

A large body of cases discuss the plain view doctrine. From those cases, it can be gleaned that for a seizure to be lawful under the doctrine, the following must be shown: (1) the officer must lawfully be in an area (2) from which the object to be seized is in plain view, and (3) the officer does in fact see the item; (4) there is probable cause to believe the object is connected to a crime, and (5) the officer has a right to access the object itself.

First, the officer must be in a place where he or she has a right to be. An officer, as is true of anyone, has a right to be in public places. Thus, evidence seen in a public park, on the street, or in a business open to the public may be seized without a warrant.

Evidence located on private property is different. As a general rule, the police have no right to enter private property to seize evidence that was in plain view from a public area. In such a case, the officer is expected to obtain a warrant; the officer's observation provides the requisite probable cause. However, if an exception applies, such as preventing the destruction of the evidence, the officer may immediately seize the evidence.

If an officer is on private property for a lawful reason, then the officer may seize evidence in plain view without first obtaining a warrant. There are many reasons that an officer may be in a position to see evidence. Many of these were discussed

**plain view doctrine**
The rule that if police officers see or come across something while acting lawfully, that item may be used as evidence in a criminal trial even if the police did not have a search warrant.

in *Coolidge.* An officer who has to enter a home to execute an arrest warrant is not expected to overlook illegal objects in plain sight. The same is true if the officer is executing a search warrant, is in hot pursuit, is responding to an emergency, or is conducting a stop and frisk.

Plain view doesn't apply when a police officer is otherwise violating the Fourth Amendment. For example, if an officer has a warrant to search a defendant's garage, any evidence obtained from the defendant's home, even if in plain view, may not be used at trial.

Second, the evidence seized must be in plain view. Only the senses of sight and touch may be used to establish plain view. Use of the sense of touch is discussed later. Of course, whether an item is in plain sight depends on the scope of the officer's authority. An officer who has a search warrant authorizing the search of a closet for a gun may seize cocaine lying on the floor of the closet. The same is not true if the warrant did not authorize a search of the closet. In any case, the item must be plainly visible from a place where the officer has a right to be.

If an officer moves something with the intent of gaining a better vantage of the item, it is not in plain view. In one case, the movement of a stereo to record its serial number was considered an illegal search because the officers were on the premises for another reason. The Court noted in that case that merely observing the stereo, which was in plain view, was legal. If the serial number had been visible without moving the stereo, recording its number would not have been violative of the Fourth Amendment. But moving the stereo constituted a "new invasion" of the defendant's rights.[20]

Officers may use mechanical or electrical aids to see evidence, so long as they are in a place where they have a right to be. Flashlights and binoculars are examples of such aids.

Third, the officer must see the item. In *Coolidge,* the Court stated that

> . . . the discovery of evidence in plain view must be inadvertent. The rationale of the exception to the warrant requirement, as just stated, is that a plain-view seizure will not turn an initially valid (and therefore limited) search into a "general" one, while the inconvenience of procuring a warrant to cover an inadvertent discovery is great. But where the discovery is anticipated, where the police know in advance that location of the evidence and intend to seize it, the situation is altogether different. The requirement of a warrant imposes no inconvenience whatever.[21]

In *Horton v. California,* 496 U.S. 128 (1990), the Supreme Court reversed itself in part by eliminating inadvertence as a requirement of plain view. The Court recognized that discoveries will be inadvertent in most instances but found requiring inadvertence unworkable. In *Horton,* an officer sought a search warrant for both the proceeds of a robbery and the weapons used during the robbery. The warrant was issued, but only for the proceeds. During the search, the officer discovered the weapon, as expected, in plain view. The Court held that even though expected, the gun was properly seized.

Fourth, the officer must have probable cause to believe that the object is subject to seizure, or, as the Court stated in *Horton,* the incriminating character of the object must be immediately apparent. Contraband (an item that is illegal itself, such as drugs) can be seized, as can property that is used to commit crimes, has been used in a crime, or has been stolen.

Fifth, the officer must be located such that he or she had a legal right to access the object. If not, the officer must obtain a warrant.

## Search Incident to Arrest and the Protective Sweep

Earlier, you learned another exception, the protective sweep. You may recall that in the interests of officer and bystander safety, police officers may conduct a quick search of a home during an arrest. The objective is to determine if there are dangerous occupants. The sweep is limited to areas where a person may hide.

## Exigent Circumstances: Preservation of Evidence

Several exceptions to the warrant and probable cause requirements fall into a bucket broadly referred to as **exigent circumstances**. These include preventing the destruction of evidence, stopping fleeing suspects, and the protection of life and property from imminent harm.

In some instances, evidence may be destroyed before a warrant can be obtained. In such cases, an officer may make a warrantless search and seizure. In the 1973 case *Cupp v. Murphy*,[22] for example, the warrantless scraping of a fingernail for dried blood, supported by probable cause, was upheld because the blood could be so easily removed. Indeed, the suspect put his hands in his pocket during his detention and the officers heard a metallic sound, indicating to them that he may have been using his car keys or another item to destroy the evidence. Although the typical case involves the intentional destruction of evidence by a suspect, the preservation-of-evidence theory also has been applied to evanescent evidence (evidence that may vanish on its own). For example, in one case a defendant who had been arrested for drunk driving was subjected to a warrantless blood alcohol test. The Court concluded that the test was reasonable.

> The officer in the present case, however, might reasonably have believed that he was confronted with an emergency, in which the delay necessary to obtain a warrant, under the circumstances, threatened "the destruction of evidence." . . . We are told that the percentage of alcohol in the blood begins to diminish shortly after drinking stops, as the body functions to eliminate it from the system. Particularly in a case such as this, where time had to be taken to bring the accused to the hospital and to investigate the scene of the accident, there was no time to seek out a magistrate and secure a warrant. Given these special facts, we conclude that the attempt to secure evidence of blood-alcohol content in this case was an appropriate incident to petitioner's arrest.[23]

So, any evidence that may be destroyed, intentionally or not, before a warrant is obtained can be the foundation of a warrantless search and seizure under the preservation-of-evidence exception to the Fourth Amendment's warrant requirement. See Chapter 13 for more on this subject.

## Exigent Circumstances: Emergency Responses and Hot Pursuit

One of the many responsibilities of being a police officer is to respond to emergencies and to assist those in danger. Police officers are permitted to enter areas protected by the Fourth Amendment without a warrant if there is an emergency. For example, an officer may respond to cries for help from within a home or may enter a building that is on fire to assist firefighters. While the cause for entry must be genuine, it need not rise to the level of threatening life. In *Brigham City v. Stuart*, 547 U.S. 398 (2006), the warrantless police entry of a home, following an announcement that they were entering, to quell a fight between four adults and a juvenile was upheld. During the fight, the juvenile punched one of the adults in the face, causing him to spit blood into a sink. The Court found that the officers were objectively reasonable in assuming the adult might need assistance and that the fight could escalate, leading

**exigent circumstances**
A situation where law enforcement officers must act so quickly to prevent the destruction of evidence, the successful flight of a suspect, or serious injury or death to any person, that there isn't time to obtain a warrant. Warrantless searches that occur when exigent circumstances exist are valid.

to more serious injuries. Connecting to what you learned earlier, any evidence in plain view may be seized. Also, officers may remedy any immediate problems, secure the premises, and then obtain a warrant before proceeding further.

It has been argued that the government has such a great interest, especially in murder cases, in having immediate access to crime scenes that the warrant requirement should be dispensed with. The Supreme Court rejected that position in *Mincey v. Arizona*, 437 U.S. 385 (1978), in which a warrantless four-day search of an apartment where a police officer was murdered was held violative of the Fourth Amendment.

Similar to the emergency exception is the hot pursuit exception. An officer who is chasing a suspect does not have to end the pursuit at the door of a home or business. The normally unlawful entry into the structure is permitted to catch the defendant. Again, once inside, the plain view exception applies.

The Supreme Court addressed whether a police officer may continue a hot pursuit into the home of a misdemeanant in the 2021 case *Lange v. California*. In *Lange*, the justices are tasked with deciding whether the hot pursuit doctrine allows officers to chase a minor misdemeanant into his home. The defendant, Mr. Lange, was observed by a California Highway Patrol officer driving with loud music and honking his horn for no apparent reason, both minor misdemeanors. The officer followed Lange to his house and turned on his overhead lights as Mr. Lange pulled into his driveway. Mr. Lange opened the door to the garage attached to his home using a remote opener and pulled inside. The officer exited his car and put his foot under the garage door as it was closing, activating a sensor that reopened the door. The officer engaged Mr. Lange, determined he was intoxicated, and arrested him. Mr. Lange's blood alcohol level was determined to be three times the legal limit. The Court decided against creating a categorical rule forbidding or permitting hot pursuits into homes for misdemeanor suspects. Instead, each case is to be reviewed independently to determine if an exigent circumstance, e.g. potential harm to others, destruction of evidence, or future escape from the home, exists that justifies a warrantless entry.

## Community Caretaking

Related to exigent circumstances is the so-call "community caretaking" exception. This exception is unconnected to the criminal justice function of policing. This refers to situations when police perform social welfare duties, such as searching for missing persons and welfare checks on the elderly, mentally ill, and shut-ins. The exception was first recognized in a case—*Cady v. Dombrowski*—where police searched an impounded vehicle that belonged to a police officer. The purpose of the search was to locate the officer's service revolver, which they believed would present a danger to the public if it were left in the car. During the search, the officers discovered evidence of a murder. The Court upheld the search because the intention of the officers, who knew nothing about the murder at the time of the search, was to protect the public.[24]

A *Terry* standard is applied. An officer must have a reasonable belief, supported by specific and articulable facts, that the welfare action is needed to assist a person in distress. The public welfare concern must be genuine, and if it is used as pretext to conduct an investigatory search, found evidence will be excluded.

Subsequently, lower courts have stretched the application of the caretaking exception. In the 2021 case *Caniglia v. Strom*, the Supreme Court refused to extend the case to the search of a home where there was no exigent circumstance, e.g. immediate threat to life. The case involved a police a welfare check of a husband whose wife had reported that he might be suicidal. The man voluntarily agreed to leave the home to undergo a psychiatric evaluation, on the condition that the police wouldn't enter the home to seize his guns. Regardless, the police entered the home and seized two guns after he left for the hospital. Subsequently, he and his wife were unsuccessful in recovering the guns, and they sued the police for violating his Fourth Amendment rights. The Court emphasized the primacy of the home in Fourth Amendment terms, refusing to extend the *Cady* automobile caretaking exception to homes. In dicta and through concurring opinions, several justices recognized that warrantless entries in homes might be justified in some circumstances, such as when an objectively reasonable belief that an occupant is about to commit suicide or in need of urgent medical care. Justice Samuel Alito suggested that state legislatures establish rules for the issuance of warrants in these circumstances.

## Open Fields

The open fields doctrine is not, technically, an exception to the search warrant requirement. That is because, to be an exception to the Fourth Amendment warrant requirement, the Fourth Amendment must apply to the conduct of the officers. The Supreme Court has held that the "open fields" around one's home are not protected by the Fourth Amendment, so officers are free to intrude upon such areas without first obtaining a warrant. In addition, officers will not be liable for trespass if they make such an intrusion while performing a lawful duty.[25]

Open fields are not protected, due to the language of the Fourth Amendment itself: "The right of the people to be secure in their persons, houses, papers, and effects. . . ." The Supreme Court has found that this language extends the Fourth Amendment's protection only to a person's home and the curtilage of that home.

*Curtilage* is the area directly around one's home. It is treated as part of the home, as the Court has recognized that a person's privacy interest does not end at the front door of the home. Determining whether an area is curtilage, and protected, or an open field, and unprotected, can be troublesome. In *United States v. Dunn*,[26] the high Court held that a barn located 60 yards from a house was not within the curtilage, even though a fence enclosed the barn. In that opinion, the Court stated four factors that should be considered when making an open fields determination:

1. The proximity of the area claimed to be curtilage from the home.
2. Whether the area enclosed is enclosed with the home.
3. The nature of the use of the area.
4. The attempts of the residents to keep the area private.

The proximity of the area in question to the home, the fact that it is enclosed by fencing, that it is commonly used by the residents, and that the residents have taken measures to ensure privacy in the area, all increase the probability that the area will be determined to be curtilage. The issue is whether the residents have a reasonable expectation of privacy in the area.

Planes and drones have made it possible for law enforcement officers to see what once was unseeable. The question in the Fourth Amendment context is, a person has a reasonable expectation of privacy in areas observable from the air, but not from the ground?

One federal district court outlined five factors to be considered when examining the validity of aerial surveillance:

1. The height of the aircraft.
2. The size of the objects viewed.
3. The nature of the use of the area.
4. The number of flights over the area.
5. The frequency and duration of the aerial surveillance.[27]

Structures, even though in an open field, may be protected if it appears that one took measures to ensure privacy.[28] However, the fact that an area is curtilage does not mean that a warrantless aerial observation is unreasonable. In a 1986 case, the Supreme Court upheld an aerial observation of a backyard that was surrounded by a fence and not visible from the street.[29] In another twist of facts, a Wisconsin court upheld a trespassory installation of cameras in an open field by police. The images of the defendants growing marijuana were admitted at trial.[30]

Finally, although the Fourth Amendment speaks of "houses," its protection extends to businesses and other structures as well. However, privacy expectations and trespass rules vary in businesses, depending on their use. The public area of a restaurant is different from the office or the owner's living quarters located in the back.

## Border Searches and Profiles

It is a long-standing principle of international and U.S. law that a nation's authority to protect itself is at its zenith at its borders. For this reason, searches at the borders of the United States do not require probable cause. In fact, no suspicion is required whatsoever. However, border searches must comply with the reasonableness requirement of the Fourth Amendment.[31] This rule applies to searches of both luggage and persons.[32] It also applies to vehicles that cross the border. For example, border agents may remove, inspect, and reassemble a car's gas tank with no suspicion of wrongdoing.[33]

In recent years, border agents have seized and searched the contents of cell phones and other digital devices. Cursory examinations of the devices are consistent with the caselaw. But a search of the contents of a digital device is more invasive than the standard border search. The Supreme Court recognized this concern in the search incident to arrest context in *Riley v. California*,[34] and at least one federal appellate court found the practice to be violative of the Fourth Amendment by 2021.[35] Given the rise in the number of cell phone seizures by border and immigration officers, this is an area of law that will likely see considerable development in the upcoming years.

For a strip search to be conducted, a customs official must have a "real suspicion" that illegality is afoot. As for more invasive searches, such as cavity searches, more suspicion is required. A customs official must be aware of a "clear indication" of illegality before such searches are conducted. Further, these searches must be conducted in a private and medically safe environment. A *clear indication* is less than probable cause, but more than either the *Terry* reasonable suspicion or the border strip-search "real suspicion" standards.

The border search exception to the Fourth Amendment extends beyond the actual border. For example, first arrival ports in the United States of international flights are treated as borders for purposes of the Fourth Amendment. The Department of Homeland Security claims a 100-mile zone of authority extending inward from the exterior boundary of the nation. That places most of the states of Connecticut, Delaware, Florida, Hawaii, Maine, Massachusetts, New Hampshire, New Jersey, New York, Rhode Island, and Vermont in the zone. Because of the nation's sizeable coastal population, 200 million of the roughly 330 million people who live in the United States are within the zone.[36] Roadblock-style checkpoints miles from a border intended to discover illegal aliens have been approved,[37] but the authority to search is more limited than at the border. Officers may not search the occupants of the vehicles stopped at these checkpoints without probable cause.[38] Random stops of vehicles away from the border must be supported by reasonable suspicion because they are treated as *Terry* detentions.

Customs officials commonly use profiles to determine who to detain and search. A *profile* is an established set of criteria that are believed to indicate a probability that a person is involved in illegal activity. For example, a person who makes frequent trips between the United States and Colombia (a nation noted for its drug production and exportation), who carries little or no luggage, who has paid

Passengers in TSA security line at Denver International Airport.

for airline tickets with cash, whose visits to Colombia are for short periods of time (e.g., 48 hours), and who behaves nervously at the customs desk, would meet a drug courier profile. Similar profiles have been used to stop motorists in Florida suspected of transporting and trafficking drugs.

Two issues are raised by profiles: first, whether a profile may be used to establish a reasonable suspicion, thereby permitting a *Terry* stop; and second, whether profiles justify searches.

As to the first question, the answer is yes. However, a profile must be reasonable. Courts examine the totality of the circumstances when examining the validity of a profile. Although no one factor in a profile may justify a temporary detention, the whole picture may. Although race may be a factor in the decision, the Supreme Court held in *United States v. Brignoni-Ponce*[39] that race alone may not establish reasonable suspicion, even if the detention occurs near the Mexican border and the occupants appear to be of Mexican ancestry. The Court enumerated factors that may be taken into account:

1. The characteristics of the area, including the proximity to the border, the usual patterns of traffic on the road, and experience with alien traffic.
2. Information concerning recent illegal border crossings in the area.
3. The driver's behavior, such as erratic driving and obvious attempts to evade officers.
4. The type of vehicle, such as a station wagon with large compartments, which are frequently used for transporting concealed aliens.
5. Whether the vehicle appears heavily loaded or has an extraordinary number of occupants.
6. Whether passengers are attempting to hide.
7. The characteristics of persons living in Mexico, including mode of dress and hair styles.
8. Other meaningful factors in light of the officers' experiences in detecting illegal aliens.

This list is not exclusive, and profiles vary depending upon the situation. Nevertheless, the *Brignoni-Ponce* decision provided a basis upon which law enforcement agencies can create profiles and courts can assess the validity of those profiles.

This leads to the second question: May profiles be used to justify searches? Recall that at borders no suspicion is necessary to conduct general searches of persons and things. However, to conduct body searches, a "real suspicion" must exist, and to conduct more invasive searches, there must be a "clear indication" of some illegality. Although a profile may satisfy the real suspicion test, it does not, acting alone, justify more invasive searches.

Outside the border areas, profiles may be used to conduct *Terry* stops, but no more. To conduct a frisk of the persons detained, a reasonable belief as to dangerousness must exist. Probable cause is required if a full search of a person, vehicle, or other things is conducted.

Finally, although profiles may be used to support detentions, they may not be used at trial to establish guilt.[40]

## Automobiles and Roadblocks

Privacy in automobiles is protected by the Fourth Amendment. However, the Supreme Court has not extended full Fourth Amendment protection to the occupants of automobiles. The Court's rationale for decreased protection is twofold. First, due to the mobile nature of automobiles, evidence can disappear quickly. Second, automobiles are used on the public roads where they and their occupants are visible to the public; thus, an occupant of an automobile has a lesser expectation of privacy than does the occupant of a home.

### Car Stops

Of course, a motorist may be stopped if an officer has probable cause. In addition, a *Terry* stop may be made if there is reasonable suspicion that an occupant has committed a crime or that contraband will be found. As discussed earlier, *Terry* stops must be limited in duration and reasonable in method, and a frisk of the occupant is permissible only if the officer possesses a reasonable belief that the individual may have a weapon. If a stop is arbitrary (e.g., not supported by reasonable suspicion, probable cause, or for another legitimate road safety or traffic management reason), it violates the Fourth Amendment, as found in the *Prouse* case.

## Oyez

### Delaware v. Prouse
#### 440 U.S. 648 (1979)

**MR. JUSTICE WHITE delivered the opinion of the Court.**

At 7:20 P.M. on November 30, 1976, a New Castle County . . . patrolman in a police cruiser stopped the automobile occupied by respondent. The patrolman smelled marihuana smoke as he was walking toward the stopped vehicle, and he seized marihuana in plain view on the car floor. Respondent was subsequently indicted for illegal possession of a controlled substance. At a hearing on respondent's motion to suppress the marihuana seized as a result of the stop, the patrolman testified that prior to stopping the vehicle he had observed neither traffic or equipment violations nor any suspicious activity, and that he made the stop only in order to check the driver's license and registration. The patrolman was not acting pursuant to any standards, guidelines, or procedures pertaining to document spot checks, promulgated by either his department or the State Attorney General. Characterizing the stop as "routine," the patrolman explained, "I saw the car in the area and wasn't answering any complaints, so I decided to pull them off." The trial court granted the motion to suppress, finding the stop and detention to have been wholly capricious and therefore violative of the Fourth Amendment. . . .

The Delaware Supreme Court affirmed. . . .

But the State of Delaware urges . . . these stops are reasonable under the Fourth Amendment because the State's interest in the practice as a means of promoting public safety upon its roads more than outweighs the intrusion entailed. Although the record discloses no statistics concerning the extent of the problem of highway safety, in Delaware or in the Nation as a whole, we are aware of danger to life and property posed by vehicular traffic and the difficulties that even a cautious and experienced driver may encounter. We agree that the States have a vital interest in ensuring that only those qualified to do so are permitted to operate motor vehicles, that these vehicles are fit for safe operation, and hence that licensing, registration, and vehicle inspection requirements are being observed. . . .

The question remains, however, whether in the service of these important ends the discretionary spot check is a sufficiently productive mechanism to justify the intrusion upon Fourth Amendment interests which stops entail. On the record before us, that question must be answered in the negative. Given the alternative mechanisms available, both those in use and those that might be adopted, we are unconvinced that the incremental contribution to highway safety of the random spot check justifies the practice under the Fourth Amendment.

The foremost method of enforcing traffic and vehicle safety regulations, it must be recalled, is acting upon observed violations. Vehicle stops for traffic violations occur countless times each day; and on these occasions, licenses and registration papers are subject to inspection and drivers without them will be ascertained. Furthermore, drivers without licenses are presumably the less safe drivers whose propensities may well exhibit themselves. . . .

Much the same can be said about the safety aspects of automobiles as distinguished from drivers. Many violations of minimum vehicle-safety requirements are observable, and something can be done about them by the observing officer, directly and immediately. Furthermore, in Delaware, as elsewhere, vehicles must carry and display current license plates, which themselves evidence that the vehicle is properly registered; and, under Delaware law, to qualify for annual registration a vehicle must pass the annual safety inspection and be properly insured. . . .

The marginal contribution to roadway safety possibly resulting from a system of spot checks cannot justify subjecting every occupant of every vehicle on the roads to a seizure—limited in magnitude compared to other intrusions but nonetheless constitutionally cognizable—at the unbridled discretion of law enforcement officials. To insist neither upon an appropriate factual basis for suspicion directed at a particular automobile nor upon some other substantial and objective standard or rule to govern the exercise of discretion "would invite intrusions upon constitutionally guaranteed rights based on nothing more substantial than inarticulable hunches. . . ." This kind of standardless and unconstrained discretion is the evil the Court has discerned when in previous cases it has insisted that the discretion of the official in the field be circumscribed, at least to some extent. . . ."

Accordingly, we hold that except in those situations in which there is at least articulable and reasonable suspicion that a motorist is unlicensed or that an automobile is not registered, or that either the vehicle or an occupant is otherwise subject to seizure for violation of law, stopping an automobile and detaining the driver in order to check his driver's license and the registration of the automobile are unreasonable under the Fourth Amendment. This holding does not preclude the State of Delaware or other States from developing methods for spot checks that involve less intrusions or that do not involve unconstrained exercise of discretion. Questioning of all oncoming traffic at roadblock-type stops is one possible alternative. We hold only that persons in automobiles on public roadways may not for that reason alone have their travel and privacy interfered with at the unbridled discretion of police officers. The judgment below is affirmed.

In 2020, the Supreme Court decided that it is reasonable, absent contrary information, for a police officer to assume that the driver of a vehicle is the person to whom it is registered. The case involved a man who was driving a truck on a suspended license. An officer stopped the vehicle after running the license plate and discovering that the registrant had a suspended license. The officer concluded that he had reasonable suspicion to believe the driver was the registrant. The Court said of the officer's stop that

> [b]efore initiating the stop, Deputy Mehrer observed an individual operating a 1995 Chevrolet 1500 pickup truck with Kansas plate 295ATJ. He also knew that the registered owner of the truck had a revoked license and that the model of the truck matched the observed vehicle. From these three facts, Deputy Mehrer drew the commonsense inference that Glover was likely the driver of the vehicle, which provided more than reasonable suspicion to initiate the stop.

The fact that the registered owner of a vehicle is not always the driver of the vehicle does not negate the reasonableness of Deputy Mehrer's inference. Such is the case with all reasonable inferences. The reasonable suspicion inquiry "falls considerably short" of 51% accuracy, for, as we have explained, "[t]o be reasonable is not to be perfect . . . combining database information and commonsense judgments in this context is fully consonant with this Court's Fourth Amendment precedents

Had the driver been of a different race or sex than the registrant, the outcome would have been different. Similarly, an officer's reasonable mistake of law or fact may not invalidate a stop. In *Heien v. North Carolina*,[41] an officer stopped a car that had a broken brake light. But the officer was mistaken; state law only required one brake light to be working. Regardless, the stop was deemed legitimate because the law was confusing and the officer's mistake was objectively reasonable.

Car stops are limited to the time needed to cite the driver for the traffic violation or to determine if probable cause exists for some other crime. Extending the time of a stop to conduct a search, including to wait for a K-9 to inspect the car, violates the Fourth Amendment.[42] Because the sniff of the exterior of a car stopped on a public road by a K-9 isn't a search, there is no Fourth Amendment violation if the dog sniff can occur within the time frame of a routine traffic stop.

Fourth Amendment issues also arise in the context of roadblocks, which are used by law enforcement officers in two situations. First, roadblocks are used to find fleeing suspects. Second, in serving the regulatory function of protecting the public from unsafe drivers, officers may stop vehicles to determine if the car satisfies the state's safety requirements, whether the driver is properly licensed, and whether the vehicle is properly registered. Regarding the former, reasonable suspicion is required before a stop can be made. As to the latter, temporary regulatory detentions are permitted so long as they are both objectively random and reasonable. That is, the police must use an objective system in deciding what automobiles will be stopped. Every car, or every tenth car, or some similar method is permissible.

The Supreme Court has also upheld roadblocks intended to discover drunk drivers. *Michigan State Police v. Sitz* (1990)[45] upheld a highway sobriety checkpoint program where 126 vehicles passed through the checkpoint, the average delay for each vehicle was 25 seconds, and two intoxicated drivers were arrested. The Court found that the stops were seizures under the Fourth Amendment, but that they were reasonable. In support of this conclusion, the Court stressed that the stops were of limited duration; that drunk drivers are a serious problem in the nation, and accordingly Michigan had a compelling interest in performing the sobriety checks; that all stops were governed by objective guidelines; that the guidelines required all vehicles to be stopped, thereby preventing arbitrary decisions by individual officers; that all officers were fully uniformed, thereby lessening motorists' concerns; and finally, that data support the conclusion that sobriety checkpoints are effective in apprehending drunk drivers.

In the 2000 Supreme Court decision, *City of Indianapolis v. Edmond,* the Court reviewed a different type of checkpoint: one intended to intercept illegal drugs. You can read an excerpt of this case in your next Oyez.

## Sidebar

### Drones

The use of unmanned aerial vehicles by the U.S. military is widely known. The military has used drones for surveillance, in combat, and to execute terrorists. Drones are attractive surveillance and fighting weapons because they are fast, inexpensive, they can survey and record images, and can track persons and objects from great distances using cameras, thermal detection devices, radar, and other equipment. Because they don't require a human pilot, they pose little risk to life. Drones can be as small as an insect and as large as a jet. For all their benefits, they also pose a serious threat to privacy. For this reason, the use of drones by police and other government agencies for criminal surveillance, to monitor borders, and for other purposes, as well as by private individuals, has begun to garner the public's attention.

Many people are concerned that an impending loosening of federal restrictions (2015) coupled with the low cost of drones will lead to a proliferation of the vehicles. The Federal Aviation Administration has predicted that 30,000 drones will be flying in the United States before 2023.[43] In response to the threat to privacy, many states have preemptively enacted laws restricting their use. By September 2013, nine states had laws restricting the use of drones. Most of those laws restricted use by law enforcement only, one restricted use by both private persons and law enforcement, and one state restricts individual use but not police use.[44]

Use by the police raises Fourth Amendment concerns that the courts will have to address in the years to come. Existing Fourth Amendment law defining aerial searches by traditional aircraft and defining open fields and curtilage may prove outdated when examined in the context of drones.

## Oyez

### City Of Indianapolis v. Edmond
### 531 U.S. 32 (2000)

**JUSTICE O'CONNOR delivered the opinion of the Court.**

In *Michigan Dept. of State Police v. Sitz*, 496 U.S. 444 (1990), and *United States v. Martinez-Fuerte*, 428 U.S. 543 (1976), we held that brief, suspicionless seizures at highway checkpoints for the purposes of combating drunk driving and intercepting illegal immigrants were constitutional. We now consider the constitutionality of a highway checkpoint program whose primary purpose is the discovery and interdiction of illegal narcotics.

In August 1998, the city of Indianapolis began to operate vehicle checkpoints on Indianapolis roads in an effort to interdict unlawful drugs. The city conducted six such roadblocks between August and November that year, stopping 1,161 vehicles and arresting 104 motorists. Fifty-five arrests were for drug-related crimes, while 49 were for offenses unrelated to drugs. The overall "hit rate" of the program was thus approximately nine percent.

The parties stipulated to the facts concerning the operation of the checkpoints by the Indianapolis Police Department (IPD) for purposes of the preliminary injunction proceedings instituted below. At each checkpoint location, the police stop a predetermined number of vehicles. Approximately 30 officers are stationed at the checkpoint. Pursuant to written directives issued by the chief of police, at least one officer approaches the vehicle, advises the driver that he or she is being stopped briefly at a drug checkpoint, and asks the driver to produce a license and registration. The officer also looks for signs of impairment and conducts an open-view examination of the vehicle from the outside. A narcotics-detection dog walks around the outside of each stopped vehicle.

The directives instruct the officers that they may conduct a search only by consent or based on the appropriate quantum of particularized suspicion. The officers must conduct each stop in the same manner until particularized suspicion develops, and the officers have no discretion to stop any vehicle out of sequence. The city agreed in the stipulation to operate the checkpoints in such a way as to ensure that the total duration of each stop, absent reasonable suspicion or probable cause, would be five minutes or less.

The affidavit of Indianapolis Police Sergeant Marshall DePew, although it is technically outside the parties' stipulation, provides further insight concerning the operation of the checkpoints. According to Sergeant DePew, checkpoint locations are selected weeks in advance based on such considerations as area crime statistics and traffic flow. The checkpoints are generally operated during daylight hours and are identified with lighted signs reading, "NARCOTICS CHECKPOINT___MILE AHEAD, NARCOTICS K-9 IN USE, BE PREPARED TO STOP." Once a group of cars has been stopped, other traffic proceeds without interruption until all the stopped cars have been processed or diverted for further processing. Sergeant DePew also stated that the average stop for a vehicle not subject to further processing lasts two to three minutes or less.

Respondents James Edmond and Joell Palmer were each stopped at a narcotics checkpoint in late September 1998. Respondents then filed a lawsuit on behalf of themselves and the class of all motorists who had been stopped or were subject to being stopped in the future at the Indianapolis drug checkpoints. . . .

The Fourth Amendment requires that searches and seizures be reasonable. A search or seizure is ordinarily unreasonable in the absence of individualized suspicion of wrongdoing. While such suspicion is not an "irreducible" component of reasonableness, *Martinez-Fuerte*, 428 U.S., at 561, we have recognized only limited circumstances in which the usual rule does not apply. For example, we have upheld certain regimes of suspicionless searches where the program was designed to serve "special needs, beyond the normal need for law enforcement." We have also allowed searches for certain administrative purposes without particularized suspicion of misconduct, provided that those searches are appropriately limited. We have also upheld brief, suspicionless seizures of motorists at a fixed Border Patrol checkpoint designed to intercept illegal aliens, and at a sobriety checkpoint aimed at removing drunk drivers from the road. In addition, in *Delaware v. Prouse*, 440 U.S. 648, 663 (1979), we suggested that a similar type of roadblock with the purpose of verifying drivers' licenses and vehicle registrations would be permissible. In none of these cases, however, did we indicate approval of a checkpoint program whose primary purpose was to detect evidence of ordinary criminal wrongdoing.

In *Martinez-Fuerte*, we entertained Fourth Amendment challenges to stops at two permanent immigration checkpoints located on major United States highways less than 100 miles from the Mexican border. We noted at the outset the particular context in which the constitutional question arose, describing in some detail the "formidable law enforcement problems" posed by the northbound tide of illegal entrants into the United States. . . . In *Martinez-Fuerte*, we found that the balance tipped in favor of the Government's interests in policing the Nation's borders. . . .

In *Sitz*, we evaluated the constitutionality of a Michigan highway sobriety checkpoint program. The *Sitz* checkpoint involved brief suspicionless stops of motorists so that police officers could detect signs of intoxication and remove impaired drivers from the road. Motorists who exhibited signs of intoxication were diverted for a license and registration check and, if warranted, further sobriety tests.

(continued)

This checkpoint program was clearly aimed at reducing the immediate hazard posed by the presence of drunk drivers on the highways, and there was an obvious connection between the imperative of highway safety and the law enforcement practice at issue. The gravity of the drunk driving problem and the magnitude of the State's interest in getting drunk drivers off the road weighed heavily in our determination that the program was constitutional. In *Prouse*, we invalidated a discretionary, suspicionless stop for a spot check of a motorist's driver's license and vehicle registration. The officer's conduct in that case was unconstitutional primarily on account of his exercise of "standardless and unconstrained discretion." We nonetheless acknowledged the States' "vital interest in ensuring that only those qualified to do so are permitted to operate motor vehicles, that these vehicles are fit for safe operation, and hence that licensing, registration, and vehicle inspection requirements are being observed." Accordingly, we suggested that "[q]uestioning of all oncoming traffic at roadblock-type stops" would be a lawful means of serving this interest in highway safety. We further indicated in *Prouse* that we considered the purposes of such a hypothetical roadblock to be distinct from a general purpose of investigating crime. . . . Not only does the common thread of highway safety thus run through *Sitz* and *Prouse*, but *Prouse* itself reveals a difference in the Fourth Amendment significance of highway safety interests and the general interest in crime control. . . .

It is well established that a vehicle stop at a highway checkpoint effectuates a seizure within the meaning of the Fourth Amendment. The fact that officers walk a narcotics-detection dog around the exterior of each car at the Indianapolis checkpoints does not transform the seizure into a search. Just as in *Place*, an exterior sniff of an automobile does not require entry into the car and is not designed to disclose any information other than the presence or absence of narcotics. Like the dog sniff in *Place*, a sniff by a dog that simply walks around a car is "much less intrusive than a typical search." Rather, what principally distinguishes these checkpoints from those we have previously approved is their primary purpose.

As petitioners concede, the Indianapolis checkpoint program unquestionably has the primary purpose of interdicting illegal narcotics. . . .

We have never approved a checkpoint program whose primary purpose was to detect evidence of ordinary criminal wrongdoing. Rather, our checkpoint cases have recognized only limited exceptions to the general rule that a seizure must be accompanied by some measure of individualized suspicion. We suggested in *Prouse* that we would not credit the "general interest in crime control" as justification for a regime of suspicionless stops. Consistent with this suggestion, each of the checkpoint programs that we have approved was designed primarily to serve purposes closely related to the problems of policing the border or the necessity of ensuring roadway safety. Because the primary purpose of the Indianapolis narcotics checkpoint program is to uncover evidence of ordinary criminal wrongdoing, the program contravenes the Fourth Amendment.

Petitioners propose several ways in which the narcotics-detection purpose of the instant checkpoint program may instead resemble the primary purposes of the checkpoints in *Sitz* and *Martinez-Fuerte*. Petitioners state that the checkpoints in those cases had the same ultimate purpose of arresting those suspected of committing crimes. Securing the border and apprehending drunk drivers are, of course, law enforcement activities, and law enforcement officers employ arrests and criminal prosecutions in pursuit of these goals. If we were to rest the case at this high level of generality, there would be little check on the ability of the authorities to construct roadblocks for almost any conceivable law enforcement purpose. Without drawing the line at roadblocks designed primarily to serve the general interest in crime control, the Fourth Amendment would do little to prevent such intrusions from becoming a routine part of American life.

Petitioners also emphasize the severe and intractable nature of the drug problem as justification for the checkpoint program. There is no doubt that traffic in illegal narcotics creates social harms of the first magnitude. The law enforcement problems that the drug trade creates likewise remain daunting and complex, particularly in light of the myriad forms of spinoff crime that it spawns. The same can be said of various other illegal activities, if only to a lesser degree. But the gravity of the threat alone cannot be dispositive of questions concerning what means law enforcement officers may employ to pursue a given purpose. Rather, in determining whether individualized suspicion is required, we must consider the nature of the interests threatened and their connection to the particular law enforcement practices at issue. We are particularly reluctant to recognize exceptions to the general rule of individualized suspicion where governmental authorities primarily pursue their general crime control ends.

Nor can the narcotics-interdiction purpose of the checkpoints be rationalized in terms of a highway safety concern similar to that present in *Sitz*. The detection and punishment of almost any criminal offense serves broadly the safety of the community, and our streets would no doubt be safer but for the scourge of illegal drugs. Only with respect to a smaller class of offenses, however, is society confronted with the type of immediate, vehicle-bound threat to life and limb that the sobriety checkpoint in *Sitz* was designed to eliminate.

Petitioners also liken the anticontraband agenda of the Indianapolis checkpoints to the antismuggling purpose of the checkpoints in *Martinez-Fuerte*. . . .

The primary purpose of the Indianapolis narcotics checkpoints is in the end to advance "the general interest in crime control," We decline to suspend the usual requirement of individualized suspicion where the police seek to employ a checkpoint primarily for the ordinary enterprise of investigating crimes. We cannot sanction stops justified only by the generalized and ever-present possibility that interrogation and inspection may reveal that any given motorist has committed some crime.

Of course, there are circumstances that may justify a law enforcement checkpoint where the primary purpose would otherwise, but for some emergency, relate to ordinary crime control. For example, as the Court of Appeals noted, the Fourth Amendment would almost certainly permit an appropriately tailored roadblock set up to thwart an imminent terrorist attack or to catch a dangerous criminal who is likely to flee by way of a particular route. . . .

Petitioners argue that our prior cases preclude an inquiry into the purposes of the checkpoint program. For example, they cite *Whren v. United States,* 517 U.S. 806 (1996), and *Bond v. United States,* 529 U.S. 334 (2000), to support the proposition that "where the government articulates and pursues a legitimate interest for a suspicionless stop, courts should not look behind that interest to determine whether the government's 'primary purpose' is valid." These cases, however, do not control the instant situation.

It goes without saying that our holding today does nothing to alter the constitutional status of the sobriety and border checkpoints that we approved in *Sitz* and *Martinez-Fuerte,* or of the type of traffic checkpoint that we suggested would be lawful in *Prouse.* The constitutionality of such checkpoint programs still depends on a balancing of the competing interests at stake and the effectiveness of the program. When law enforcement authorities pursue primarily general crime control purposes at checkpoints such as here, however, stops can only be justified by some quantum of individualized suspicion.

Our holding also does not affect the validity of border searches or searches at places like airports and government buildings, where the need for such measures to ensure public safety can be particularly acute. Nor does our opinion speak to other intrusions aimed primarily at purposes beyond the general interest in crime control. Our holding also does not impair the ability of police officers to act appropriately upon information that they properly learn during a checkpoint stop justified by a lawful primary purpose, even where such action may result in the arrest of a motorist for an offense unrelated to that purpose. Finally, we caution that the purpose inquiry in this context is to be conducted only at the programmatic level and is not an invitation to probe the minds of individual officers acting at the scene.

Because the primary purpose of the Indianapolis checkpoint program is ultimately indistinguishable from the general interest in crime control, the checkpoints violate the Fourth Amendment. The judgment of the Court of Appeals is accordingly affirmed.

Although systematic roadblocks are proper, discretionary spot checks are not. In the *Prouse* case, the Supreme Court held that arbitrary stops of automobiles by law enforcement officers violate the Fourth Amendment.

Finally, note that profiles are used by some law enforcement agencies to establish a reasonable suspicion to stop motorists. As examples, drug courier profiles are used in Florida and illegal alien profiles are used by the Border Patrol. See earlier in this chapter for a more thorough discussion of the use of profiles. The Supreme Court has also held that the validity of a stop is determined by whether probable cause exists to believe a traffic violation has occurred, not the motives of the police. In *Whren v. United States* (1996),[46] the Court rejected a defendant's claim that a police officer who stops an individual who has violated a traffic law with the genuine purpose of investigating another crime (e.g., drug possession) has violated the Fourth Amendment, so long as the officer had probable cause to believe the driver has committed a traffic offense.

Avoiding a driving under the influence (DUI) checkpoint by turning around or turning away gives rise to police suspicion. Although this conduct doesn't establish probable cause to believe a driver is intoxicated, it create a reasonable suspicion of it. So, absent contrary state law, officers may conduct a *Terry* stop of a car that turns to avoid a checkpoint. The same is true of a person who breaks into a run when encountering a police officer.

## Car Searches

One area where the Fourth Amendment's warrant requirement rarely applies is in the context of automobile searches and seizures. In *Carroll v. United States,* 267 U.S. 132 (1925), it was announced that a warrantless search of a vehicle stopped on a public road is reasonable, provided the officer has probable cause to believe that an object subject to seizure will be found in the vehicle. The existence of probable cause is the key to the search, and no exigency has to exist for a police officer to conduct such a warrantless search.[47] This authority has been extended to permit the search to continue after the vehicle is impounded.[48] The Supreme Court has also validated warrantless seizures of vehicles when probable cause exists to believe the vehicle itself is forfeitable because the automobile had been used to traffic drugs.[49] The Court also affirmed the entry into a car and the moving of papers to read the Vehicle Identification Number (VIN), located on the interior dash, of a lawfully stopped vehicle.[50]

**automobile exception**
The rule that warrantless searches of cars and their contents are permitted by the Fourth Amendment, provided probable cause exists.

This so-called "**automobile exception**" to the warrant requirement is quite broad. A police officer may search any area of a car where probable cause to believe contraband exists. This includes the glove box, trunk, and closed containers found in the car.[51] But probable cause must exist to believe the specific item sought will be found in the area searched. [52] Thus, if an officer has probable cause to believe that a shotgun used in a crime will be found in a car, a search of the glove box is improper. The opposite would be true if the item sought was a piece of jewelry, such as a ring. Once the sought-after item is found, the search must cease.

An automobile may be searched incident to the arrest of its driver. This includes situations where arrestees have exited their cars, were immediately arrested, and the car is still within a reasonable proximity of the location of the arrest.[53] The purpose of this exception is to protect officers and others from hidden weapons. Accordingly, if a driver has been arrested and can no longer access the automobile, a warrantless search is not justified. The intersection of the search incident to arrest doctrine and the automobile exception are discussed in *Arizona v. Gant* in your next Oyez.

# Oyez

## Arizona v. Gant
### 556 U.S. 332 (2009)

**Justice Stevens delivered the opinion of the Court.**

On August 25, 1999, acting on an anonymous tip that the residence at 2524 North Walnut Avenue was being used to sell drugs, Tucson police officers Griffith and Reed knocked on the front door and asked to speak to the owner. Gant answered the door and, after identifying himself, stated that he expected the owner to return later. The officers left the residence and conducted a records check, which revealed that Gant's driver's license had been suspended and there was an outstanding warrant for his arrest for driving with a suspended license.

When the officers returned to the house that evening, they found a man near the back of the house and a woman in a car parked in front of it. After a third officer arrived, they arrested the man for providing a false name and the woman for possessing drug paraphernalia. Both arrestees were handcuffed and secured in separate patrol cars when Gant arrived. The officers recognized his car as it entered the driveway, and Officer Griffith confirmed that Gant was the driver by shining a flashlight into the car as it drove by him. Gant parked at the end of the driveway, got out of his car, and shut the door. Griffith, who was about 30 feet away, called to Gant, and they approached each other, meeting 10 to 12 feet from Gant's car. Griffith immediately arrested Gant and handcuffed him.

Because the other arrestees were secured in the only patrol cars at the scene, Griffith called for backup. When two more officers arrived, they locked Gant in the backseat of their vehicle. After Gant had been handcuffed and placed in the back of a patrol car, two officers searched his car: One of them found a gun, and the other discovered a bag of cocaine in the pocket of a jacket on the backseat.

Gant was charged with two offenses—possession of a narcotic drug for sale and possession of drug paraphernalia (*i.e.*, the plastic bag in which the cocaine was found). He moved to suppress the evidence seized from his car on the ground that the warrantless search violated the Fourth Amendment. Among other things, Gant argued that *Belton* did not authorize the search of his vehicle because he posed no threat to the officers after he was handcuffed in the patrol car and because he was arrested for a traffic offense for which no evidence could be found in his vehicle. When asked at the suppression hearing why the search was conducted, Officer Griffith responded: "Because the law says we can do it. . . .

In *Chimel*, we held that a search incident to arrest may only include "the arrestee's person and the area 'within his immediate control'—construing that phrase to mean the area from within which he might gain possession of a weapon or destructible evidence." That limitation, which continues to define the boundaries of the exception, ensures that the scope of a search incident to arrest is commensurate with its purposes of protecting arresting officers and safeguarding any evidence of the offense of arrest that an arrestee might conceal or destroy. If there is no possibility that an arrestee could reach into the area that law enforcement officers seek to search, both justifications for the search-incident-to-arrest exception are absent and the rule does not apply. . . .

Although it does not follow from Chimel, we also conclude that circumstances unique to the vehicle context justify a search incident to a lawful arrest when it is "reasonable to believe evidence relevant to the crime of arrest might be found in the vehicle. . . .

Police may search a vehicle incident to a recent occupant's arrest only if the arrestee is within reaching distance of the passenger compartment at the time of the search or it is reasonable to believe the vehicle contains evidence of the offense of arrest. When these justifications are absent, a search of an arrestee's vehicle will be unreasonable unless police obtain a warrant or show that another exception to the warrant requirement applies. The Arizona Supreme Court correctly held that this case involved an unreasonable search. Accordingly, the judgment of the State Supreme Court is affirmed.

For the search incident to arrest to apply, the arrestee must not only have access to the space, but there must be an arrest. A warrantless search of an automobile after issuing a traffic ticket to the driver is violative of the Fourth Amendment— even though the officer could have arrested the driver and then searched the car incident to the arrest.[54] Note that *Gant* contains a second important principle; it authorizes warrantless searches, even if the driver doesn't have access to the automobile, if officers have reason to believe the evidence that is the subject of the arrest will be found inside. May the occupants of a vehicle be searched incident to a proper search of the vehicle? The answer is no[55]—unless an officer has probable cause to believe that one of the occupants has hidden contraband on his or her person. Or, if an officer has a reasonable belief that one of the occupants may be armed, a frisk of the outer clothing is permitted to ensure officer safety.[56] In 2018, the Supreme Court decided that the Automobile Exception doesn't permit the warrantless search, even with probable cause, of a vehicle that is found in the curtilage of a home.[57]

## Car Occupants

Concerning the occupants of lawfully stopped cars, the Supreme Court has held that both driver and passengers may be ordered to exit the car without cause to believe they hold contraband, a threat to the officer, or act out of fear of flight. The Court held that it may be done routinely to protect the safety of police officers.[58]

## Car Inventory Searches

Police officers may impound vehicles whenever the driver or owner is arrested. *Impoundment* means towing the vehicle to a garage or parking lot for storage.

Although the decision to impound a vehicle is generally left to the discretion of the police officer, an officer may not refuse a less-intrusive manner of caring for the vehicle. For example, if a husband and wife are riding together, and the husband is arrested for drunk driving, the wife is to be permitted to drive the vehicle home, provided she is capable.

Once impounded, an inventory search may be conducted. The purpose of an inventory search is to protect the owner of the vehicle from vandalism, protect the safety of the officers and others, and protect the police department from claims of theft.

Because inventory searches are not conducted with an intent to discover evidence, there is no requirement of probable cause. If the facts of a case show that the police impounded a vehicle for the purpose of searching it, the search is improper.

Inventory searches are limited in scope. Although it is reasonable to search unlocked glove compartments and trunks, it is unreasonable under the Fourth Amendment if they are locked. A search of a vehicle's seats, floor area, and dashboard are routine. The Supreme Court has also stated that closed items found in impounded vehicles are subject to inventory searches.[59]

To avoid arbitrary inventory searches, police departments are expected, if not required, to establish an inventory search policy and procedure. All items discovered during an inventory search are to be recorded. See Exhibit 13–2 for a summary of the most prominent Supreme Court Fourth Amendment automobile cases.

## Exhibit 13–2 Summary of Fourth Amendment Issues and Automobiles

| Subject | Case |
| --- | --- |
| **Stops and Arrests** | |
| Stops may not be arbitrary. | *Delaware v. Prouse* (1979) |
| Stops may occur without suspicion if systematic. | *Michigan v. Sitz* (1990) |
| The motives of police are not relevant when determining if a stop is lawful. | *Whren v. United States* (1996) |
| The issue is whether there is probable cause to believe a traffic violation has occurred. | |
| States may delegate the discretion to arrest for misdemeanors, including traffic violations, to police. | *Atwater v. City of Lago Vista* (2001) |
| Systematic stops to intercept illegal drugs violate Fourth Amendment. | *Indianapolis v. Edmond* (2000) |
| Absent contrary data, police may assume driver of vehicle is the person to whom it is registered. | *Kansas v. Glover* (2020) |
| **Occupants** | |
| Drivers and passengers are seized when pulled over, and therefore they may challenge the stop and search. | *Brendlin v. California* (2007) |
| Drivers of lawfully stopped auto mobiles may be ordered out without specific cause. | *Pennsylvania v. Mimms* (1977) |
| Occupants of lawfully stopped auto mobiles may be ordered out without specific cause. | *Maryland v. Wilson* (1997) |
| Occupants of automobiles may not be searched as incident to lawful search of automobiles—probable cause to believe sought item will be found on person required. | *United States v. DiRe, 332 U.S. 581* (1948) |
| Drivers and occupants may be frisked if officer has reasonable belief of dangerousness | *Arizona v. Johnson* (2009) |
| Warrantless blood draw of driver arrested for DUI only reasonable if exigency exists. | *Schmerber v. California* (1966) |
| Warrantless breath test of driver arrested for DUI reasonable | *Birchfield v. North Dakota* (2016) |
| **Searches** | |
| Warrantless search of automobile valid if probable cause exists to believe item sought will be found in automobile. No exigency required if probable cause exists. | *Carroll v. United States* (1925) *Maryland v. Dyson* (1999) |
| Warrantless searches of closed container in automobile valid if probable cause exists to believe item sought will be found in container. | *California v. Acevedo* (1991) |
| Entry into lawfully stopped vehicle to read the VIN legitimate. | *New York v. Class* (1986) |
| Warrantless search of personal item in automobile (e.g., purse) valid if there is probable cause to search for an item that may be concealed there. | *Wyoming v. Houghton* (1999) |
| Warrantless search of automobile invalid if probable cause exists to search container in automobile only. | *California v. Acevedo* (1991) |
| Warrantless search of recent occupant arrestee's automobile that is within his or her control is valid. | *Thornton v. United States* (2004) |
| Warrantless search of automobile of suspect arrested in an officer's cruiser invalid because car was outside of his control; warrantless search of car valid if reasonable belief evidence that is subject of arrest will be found within. | *Arizona v. Gant* (2009) |
| Warrantless search of automobile parked in the curtilage of a home violates the Fourth Amendment, even though probable cause to believe the vehicle was involved in a crime exists. | *Collins v. Virginia* (2018) |
| Extending the time of a car stop to conduct a dog sniff violates the Fourth Amendment. | *Rodriguez v. United States* (2015) |
| Warrantless search of automobile by officer who issued ticket but chose not to arrest driver is violative of the Fourth Amendment. | *Knowles v. Iowa* (1998) |
| Inventory searches of automobiles including containers—are valid if systematic. | *Colorado v. Bertine, 479 U.S. 367* (1987) |
| Properly framed profile may be used to stop an automobile, but searches and arrests require more. | *United States v. Brignoni-Ponce* (1975) |
| Automobile may be seized without a warrant if probable cause exists to believe it is contraband. | *Florida v. White* (1999) |

# Boats

As effects, boats are protected by the Fourth Amendment. Like automobiles, boats are mobile. They can, therefore, confound normal policing techniques. Also, like automobiles, they typically operate in the public view—lakes, rivers, and upon the ocean. For these reasons, having a reduced Fourth Amendment expectation, as is true with automobiles, is to be expected. But they differ from automobiles in ways that impact the Fourth Amendment analysis. One is that determining compliance with registration and safety requirements is harder for boats than for cars. Another difference is history. Boats have a long treatment in the law, and it isn't one that favors privacy. Authorities in the United States, and around the world, have a history of freely boarding and inspecting watercraft.

All of these factors converge to reduce the Fourth Amendment's expectations of the government to less than required of automobiles. Boats may be stopped, boarded, and searched without a warrant or any suspicion. The Supreme Court expressly rejected the suggestion that Coast Guard officers must have reasonable suspicion of criminality to board an inland vessel in 1983.[60] The reasonableness limit of the Fourth Amendment applies. Whether a more privacy-protecting standard will be found in specific cases, such as enclosed sleeping areas of boats, is to be seen.

# Prisoners

The law generally distinguishes between pretrial detainees and convictees. The former includes individuals who have been arrested but not convicted. Because pretrial detainees have not been convicted, they may not be punished or rehabilitated. Instead, the objective of their detention is to ensure their appearance at trial. Because they have not been convicted, pretrial detainees are not protected by the Eighth Amendment's prohibition of cruel and unusual punishments. But they are protected by due process.[61] In some instances, the protections mirror one another. In others, they do not.

Local jails, which commonly house both pretrial detainees and convictees sentenced to a year or less, must, at times, distinguish in the treatment of the two populations. The most obvious difference is that pretrial detainees may not be subjected to forms of punishment, such as a program of hard labor or shaming. Another example concerns legal materials. In order for pretrial detainees to properly prepare for trial, they have greater privacy rights to their papers and access to counsel than do convictees. Of course, jailers must maintain order, prevent escapes, and provide for the safety of everyone in the jail setting. Rules that advance these objectives may be applied to all inmates, pretrial and convictees. Whether pretrial detainees can be subjected to systematic but suspicionless strip searches at the time of first admission to a facility was the question in the 2012 case *Florence v. Board of Chosen Freeholders*.[62]

Albert Florence and his family were stopped by the police for a traffic offense committed by his wife, who was driving their vehicle. Police checked both Florence and his wife for warrants. The computer database erroneously indicated that there was an outstanding arrest warrant for Florence. He was arrested, transported to a jail, booked, and subjected to a strip search. Unable to secure his immediate release, he was still in jail six days later when he was moved to a second jail, where another strip search was conducted. Florence sued under 42 U.S.C. §1983, alleging that suspicionless searches of persons charged with minor misdemeanors violated due process and the Fourth Amendment. The Court rejected Florence's claim in a decision exhibiting substantial deference to corrections authorities:

> Maintaining safety and order at (detention) institutions requires the expertise of correctional officials, who must have substantial discretion to devise reasonable solutions to the problems they face" . . . (T)he seriousness of an offense is a poor predictor of who has contraband."

Although a small number of pretrial detainees are housed in prisons, most inmates of these facilities are convictees. The Fourth Amendment is not fully applicable in prisons, for two reasons. First, security and order concerns are significant. Second, loss of privacy is considered by our society to be an attribute of confinement and punishment.

Hence, the Fourth Amendment is not implicated in the search of an inmate's cell, as there is no reasonable expectation of privacy in that area. The Supreme Court stated:

> A prison "shares none of the attributes of privacy of a home, an automobile, an office, or a hotel room." . . . We strike the balance in favor of institutional security, which we have noted is "central to all other correctional goals." . . . A right of privacy in traditional Fourth Amendment terms is fundamentally incompatible with the close and continual surveillance of inmates and their cells required to ensure institutional security and internal order. We are satisfied that society would insist that the prisoner's expectation of privacy always yield to what must be considered the paramount interest in institutional security. We believe that it is accepted by our society that "[l]oss of freedom of choice and privacy are inherent incidents of confinement."[63]

Although the Fourth Amendment does not apply to searches of inmates' cells, it does apply to searches of their persons. However, the probable cause and warrant requirements are dispensed within the prison context. Rather, they are tested by the Fourth Amendment's reasonableness provision. Prisoners may be searched without any particular suspicion if the search is part of a routine system. Analogous to roadblocks, if the custodians search every prisoner, or every other prisoner, or use some other system, no suspicion is required. Prisoners may also be searched without suspicion if they have recently come into contact with visitors. In *Bell v. Wolfish*,[64] the Supreme Court held that strip searches of prisoners, conducted after they have contact with visitors or upon their return to the institution from outside, are permissible even without individualized suspicion. Otherwise, individual searches of inmates are allowed only when an officer has a reasonable suspicion that the inmate possesses contraband.

Although searches of inmates' cells are not included within the grasp of the Fourth Amendment, repeated searches intended to harass an inmate may be violative of the Eighth Amendment's prohibition of cruel and unusual punishment, as may searches of an inmate's person.

## Probationers and Parolees

Because probationers and parolees have a lesser expectation to privacy, searches of their persons, effects, and homes do not have to be supported by probable cause. Nor do searches have to be authorized by a warrant. In 1987, the Court approved a state policy that empowered a probation officer to search the homes of a probationer if "reasonable grounds" existed to believe contraband would be found.[65] In *United States v. Knights*,[66] the rule concerning searches of probationers was announced. The Court held that warrantless searches of probationers are reasonable so long as reasonable suspicion exists. The Court left open the question of searches without reasonable suspicion where a probationer consents to such searches at the time of sentencing.

In 2006, this decision was extended to parolees in *Samson v. California*,[67] where the Supreme Court held that the Fourth Amendment does not prohibit suspicionless, warrantless searches of parolees. On the continuum of punishment, the Court noted, a parolee enjoys less privacy than probationers and only slightly more than prisoners. Significant to the Court in *Samson* was the consent of the parolees, who were given the option of remaining in prison; the large number of parolees at large; the interest of the state in monitoring parolees for reintegration; and recidivism. The Court pointed to the likelihood of recidivism, as opposed to the general population, in its *Knights* opinion as further support for the decision to subject probationers to greater oversight.

## Administrative and School Searches

Although outside the content of this text, be aware that administrative searches often require less than probable cause and a warrant. The rationale for the lower standard is that the purpose of such searches is not to detect and punish criminals. It is to protect the public from health and welfare threats, the violation of which are typically punished with fines, the disciplining of a license, or a similar noncriminal sanction. For example, warrantless inspections of restaurants, groceries, public school students, and the work areas of public employees must be reasonable under the Fourth Amendment, even though probable cause is not required for any of them.

In most instances, the Fourth Amendment's reasonableness requirement is satisfied in the administrative context if there is either (1) reasonable suspicion or (2) a comprehensive regulatory scheme in place. If the latter, the scheme shall define the authority of inspectors, define the inspection itself, and provide a rationale for the inspection.[68] "Precompliance review" or the opportunity of a business to challenge a search must be offered. The challenge must be heard by a neutral person, but it need not be a judge. An administrative law judge or an agency official who is not connected to the investigation is adequate. Also, probable cause is not required.

In the 2015 case *Los Angeles v. Patel*,[69] the high court decided that an ordinance requiring hotel operators to maintain and turn over guest records to the police on demand was facially invalid under the Fourth Amendment. Although probable cause and a traditional warrant aren't required to obtain the information and the Court validated the ordinance's record-keeping requirement, the Court imposed the standard administrative search expectations, including the existence of a legislative scheme authorizing the police demand and the opportunity for hotel operators to challenge it before compliance.

So-called closely regulated industries enjoy less Fourth Amendment protection than other businesses. These businesses may be inspected without the opportunity for precompliance review. To date, the Supreme Court has identified four closely regulated businesses. They are liquor and firearms sales, mining, and automobile junkyards. State courts have found many more, including energy producers, pharmacies, massage parlors, and childcare facilities.

Just as public school students "do not shed their constitutional rights to freedom of speech and expression at the schoolhouse gate,"[70] they don't shed their protection from unreasonable searches at the schoolhouse gate. But the academic, noncriminal objectives of school, the need to maintain discipline, and the immaturity of students justify a reduction in the warrant and probable cause requirements. Searches are measured by the reasonableness standard.

In *New Jersey v. T.L.O.*,[71] it was decided that a search be reasonable at its inception (i.e., there must be reasonable grounds for suspecting that the search will turn up evidence that the student has violated or is violating either the law or the rules of the school). The search must also be reasonably related in scope to the circumstances justifying the interference, and not excessively intrusive in light of the age and sex of the student and the nature of the infraction. Applying these rules, the Court upheld as reasonable the search of *T.L.O.*'s purse for cigarettes, which were prohibited by the school. The cigarettes found in her purse were held to be admissible in her juvenile delinquency hearing.

*Safford Unified School District #1 v. Redding*[72] is an example of an unreasonable school search. Redding, a 13-year-old girl, had been reported by another student as the source of ibuprofen, a non-prescription pain killer, which was prohibited by school policy. School officials searched her outer clothing and backpack. No pills were discovered. The student was then taken to another location where a school official and nurse had her strip to her underwear and pull her bra and panties out, so those areas could be inspected for the pills. Again, no pills were found. The student sued, alleging a Fourth Amendment violation. The Supreme Court found the search of Redding's outer clothing and backpack reasonable, but the quasi–strip search unreasonable. The absence of evidence that the pills might be found under her clothing, the low risk presented by ibuprofen, the indignity of a strip search, and the risk of emotional distress all were factors in the Court's conclusion.

## Exhibit 13–3 Summary of Warrant Rules and Exceptions

---

**SEARCHES**

RULE: Pursuant to the Fourth and Fourteenth Amendments, in both federal and state cases, a warrant to search must be obtained, unless one of the following exceptions is established.

EXCEPTIONS and LIMITATIONS:

1. Consent
2. *Terry* frisks
3. Plain view
4. Plain feel
5. Incident to arrest
6. Preservation of evidence
7. Emergencies and hot pursuit
8. Community Caretaking
9. Borders
10. Motor vehicles
11. Vehicle inventories
12. Prisoners, probationers, and parolees
13. Protective sweeps
14. Open fields
15. Administrative inspections

**ARRESTS**

RULE: The Fourth and Fourteenth Amendments govern arrests by both federal and state officials. Arrests in public areas may be warrantless. Arrests made in the home or other property of the defendant must be supported by either an arrest warrant or a search warrant for the defendant's person. Arrests in the homes or other property of third parties must be supported by a search warrant authorizing the search for the defendant at the particular property.

---

## Ethical Considerations

### The Racial Profiling Controversy

In recent years, the use of race as a factor in law enforcement and corrections officer's decision making has been the subject of considerable controversy. Many scholars and commentators have asserted that it is common for police officers to stop black motorists simply because of their skin color. This phenomenon has become known as "driving while black." Similarly, police use of force, particularly on African Americans, has received considerable attention in recent years. In addition to traditional policing, race is used as a factor at borders to decide what bags and persons should be searched.

Racial profiling was already the subject of considerable debate when the United States was attacked on September 11, 2001, by 19 Muslim terrorists. Several hijackings in the 1970s and 1980s, the 1993 World Trade Center bombing, the 1996 bombing of a U.S. military site in Saudi Arabia, the bombings of two U.S. embassies in 1996, the attack on the naval ship U.S.S. *Cole* in 2000, and other attacks on U.S. citizens and interests were all committed by Muslim extremists. In the wake of these events, many people called for increased scrutiny of people who appeared to be of Arab descent or who appeared to be Muslim. Others contended that such profiling was inherently wrong.

In an effort not to engage in "racial profiling," U.S. Secretary of Transportation Norman Mineta ordered that race not be used as a factor by airport security officers when making decisions to search baggage or persons. This policy had many critics, who contended that ethnicity and dress were legitimate characteristics given the nature of threat to the United States.

The Supreme Court of the United States has found a middle ground. The Court has held that race, ethnicity, religion, skin color, and similar characteristics may not be the sole basis upon which a person is searched or seized. However, the Court held in *United States v. Brignoni-Ponce* (1975) that race may be one of many factors law enforcement officers may consider when stopping motorists or conducting border searches, provided that race can be connected with criminality in the particular circumstances in which the officers are operating.

## Key Terms

automobile exception

consent

exigent circumstances

plain view doctrine

## Review Questions

1. Officer Duright observes a woman holding what appears to be a severed, bloody human hand. As he approaches the vehicle, the woman makes a furtive gesture toward the floorboard of the car. May the officer order the woman out of the car? May he search it for the hand without a warrant? Explain your answers.

2. Ling is a suspect in an embezzlement investigation. The police believe that she has hidden evidence in her neighbor's house, without the neighbor's consent. The neighbor will not consent to a search. Can the police obtain a search warrant for the non-suspect's home, and if so, what is required?

3. What is the plain view doctrine?

4. What is curtilage? Open fields? Why are the concepts important in criminal law?

5. Distinguish an investigatory stop from an arrest; a frisk from a search.

6. A police officer is approached by a man on the street who tells the officer that he was just robbed. The man points out the robber, who is standing in a park just across the street. Must the officer obtain a warrant to make the arrest? Explain your answer.

7. A police officer is approached by a man on the street who tells the officer that he was just robbed. Although he did not see where the robber fled, he knew the assailant's name and address, as the two men "grew up together." The officer and the victim went to the police station and completed an incident report. After a telephone call to one of the suspect's neighbors, they learned that he was at home. Must the officer obtain a warrant to make the arrest?

8. The same facts as in question 7, except that the victim points to a fleeing suspect. The officer chases the suspect to a house, where the officer sees the suspect enter with the use of a key. Must the officer end the chase and obtain a warrant?

9. What is a protective sweep?

# Problems & Critical Thinking Exercises

1. Tommy Transmitter planned to burglarize a local audio/video dealer. On the night he intended to commit the burglary, Tommy was observed standing in an alley behind the shop by a police officer. It was 11:50 a.m. on a June evening, and Tommy was wearing a pair of jeans, tennis shoes, and a shirt.

   After 5 minutes, the officer approached Tommy and asked him "what he was doing in the alley at such a late hour." Tommy responded that he lived only a few blocks away, was suffering from insomnia, and had decided to take a walk. He produced identification that confirmed that he lived a short distance from the store. The officer then grabbed Tommy, swung him around, pushed him against the wall of the store, and "frisked him." After feeling a hard object in Tommy's back pocket, the officer reached in and discovered a small 3 × 3-inch container full of locksmith tools. He then arrested Tommy for possession of burglary tools and conducted a search incident to arrest. During that search, he discovered a diagram of the audio/video store hidden in Tommy's pants.

   Tommy was subsequently charged with attempted burglary and possession of burglary tools. He has filed a motion to suppress the tools and diagram, as well as a motion to dismiss. Should the motions be granted? Discuss.

   **2–5.** Assume that officers have a valid search warrant for the defendant's apartment. The warrant specifies that the officers may search for stolen stereos. May the officers do the following?

2. Search the defendant's desk drawers in his study?

3. Search the defendant's closets in his bedroom?

4. Search the defendant's body?

5. Seize a transparent bag of cocaine found lying on the defendant's dining room table?

6. Do you agree with Justice Brennan that the protective sweep goes beyond the *Terry v. Ohio* decision? Explain your position.

7. In *United States v. Leon*, the Supreme Court created a good-faith exception to the probable cause requirement of the Fourth Amendment. Under *Leon*, evidence seized in good-faith pursuant to a search warrant is admissible at trial, even though it is later determined that probable cause was lacking. Should this exception be extended to warrantless searches when an officer has a good-faith belief that probable cause exists?

8. Do you believe that the exclusionary rule is required under the Fourth Amendment? Can you suggest alternatives to the rule? Explain your answers.

# Endnotes

1. *Schneckloth v. Bustamonte,* 412 U.S. 218 (1973).

2. *See* Jeremy Calsyn et al., "Investigation and Police Practices: Warrantless Searches and Seizures," 86 *Geo. L.J.* 1214, 1249–51 (1998).

3. *United States v. Kampbell,* 574 F.2d 962 (8th Cir. 1978).

4. *Commonwealth v. Wright,* 190 A.2d 709 (Pa. 1963).

5. 415 U.S. 164.

6. *Georgia v. Randolph,* 547 U.S. 103, 126 U.S. 1515 (2006).

7. For a discussion of landlord–tenant situations, *see Stoner v. California,* 376 U.S. 483 (1964).

8. *Illinois v. Rodriguez,* 497 U.S. 177 (1990).

9. See Floyd v. New York, 959 F. Supp. 2d 540 (S.D.N.Y. 2013) and NYPD patrols inside private buildings; residents say they are unfairly stopped. Fox News, found at http://www.foxnews.com/us/2013/03/11/nypd-program- patrols-inside-private-buildings-residents-say-theyre-unfairly/ and also http://www.nyclu.org/news/judge-finds-nypd-routinely-makes-unconstitutional-street-stops-outside-clean-halls-buildings

10. *Terry,* 392 U.S. at 21.

11. *United States v. Hensley,* 469 U.S. 221 (1985).

12. *United States v. Arvizu,* 122 S. Ct. 744 (2002).

13. *Adams v. Williams*, 407 U. S. 143, 147 (1972).

14. *Navarette v. California*, 572 U.S. 393 (2014).

15. *Illinois v. Wardlow*, 528 U.S. 119 (2000).

16. *United States v. Mendenhall*, 466 U.S. 544 (1980), and *United States v. Drayton*, 536 U.S. 194 (2002).

17. *Brown v. Texas*, 443 U.S. 47 (1979).

18. *United States v. Johnson*, No. 09-2245, 2010 U.S. App. LEXIS (3rd Cir. Decided January 27, 2010).

19. *Michigan v. Long*, 463 U.S. 1032 (1983).

20. *Arizona v. Hicks*, 480 U.S. 321 (1987).

21. 403 U.S. at 470–71.

22. *Cupp v. Murphy*, 412 U.S. 291 (1973)

23. *Schmerber v. California*, 384 U.S. 757, 770–71 (1966).

24. *Cady v. Dombrowski*, 413 U.S. 433 (1973).

25. *Oliver v. United States*, 466 U.S. 170 (1984).

26. 480 U.S. 294 (1987).

27. *United States v. Bassford*, 601 F. Supp. 1324, 1330 (D. Mass. 1985).

28. *United States v. Broadhurst*, 612 F. Supp. 777 (C.D. Cal. 1985).

29. *California v. Ciraolo*, 476 U.S. 207 (1986).

30. Timothy Lee, Police Allowed to Install Cameras on Private Property Without Warrant, May 12, 2013, found at http://arstechnica.com/tech-policy/2012/10/police-allowed-to-install-cameras-on-private-property-without-warrant/

31. See Torcia, *Wharton's Criminal Evidence* § 733 (13th ed.) (New York: Lawyers Co-operative, 1986 Supp.).

32. *United States v. Ramsey*, 431 U.S. 606 (1977).

33. *United States v. Flores-Montano*, 541 U.S. 149 (2004).

34. *Riley v. California*, 573 U.S. 373 (2014).

35. *Alasaad v. Mayorkas* (1st Cir. Feb 9, 2021).

36. *The Constitution in the 100 Mile Border Zone.* American Civil Liberties Union. Retrieved from ACLU.org on May 1, 2021.

37. *United States v. Martinez-Fuerte*, 428 U.S. 543 (1976).

38. *United States v. Ortiz*, 422 U.S. 891 (1975).

39. *United States v. Brignoni-Ponce*, 422 U.S. 873 (1975).

40. *United States v. Hernandez-Cuartas*, 717 F.2d 552 (11th Cir. 1983).

41. *Heien v. North Carolina*, 574 U.S. 54 (2014).

42. *Rodriguez v. United States*, 575 U.S. 348 (2015).

43. Richard M. Thompson, II. *Drones in Domestic Surveillance Operations: Fourth Amendment Implications and Legislative Responses.* Congressional Research Service. April 3, 2013. Can be found at http://www.a51.nl/storage/pdf/R42701.pdf

44. Liebelson, D. "Map: Is Your State a No-Drone Zone?" *Mother Jones*, September 30, 2013. Can be found at http://www.motherjones.com/politics/2013/09/map-are-drones-illegal-your-state

45. 496 U.S. 444.

46. 517 U.S. 806 (1996).

47. *Maryland v. Dyson*, 527 U.S. 465 (1999).

48. *Florida v. White*, 526 U.S. 559 (1999).

49. *Chambers v. Mahoney*, 399 U.S. 42 (1970).

50. *New York v. Class*, 475 U.S. 106 (1986).

51. *California v. Acevedo*, 500 U.S. 565 (1991).

52. *United States v. Ross*, 456 U.S. 798 (1982).

53. See *Thornton v. U.S.*, 541 U.S. 615 (2004).

54. *Knowles v. Iowa*, (1998).

55. *United States v. DiRe*, 332 U.S. 581 (1948).

56. *Arizona v. Johnson*, 555 U.S. 323 (2009).

57. *Collins v. Virginia*, 584 U.S. (2018).

58. *Pennsylvania v. Mimms*, 434 U.S. 106 (1977), and *Maryland v. Wilson*, 117 S. Ct. 882 (1997).

59. *Colorado v. Bertine*, 479 U.S. 367 (1986).

60. *United States v. Villamonte-Marquez*, 462 U.S. 579 (1983).

61. *Bell v. Wolfish*, 441 U.S. 520 (1979).

62. 566 U.S. 318 (2012).

63. *Hudson v. Palmer*, 468 U.S. 517 (1984).

64. Bell infra.

65. *Griffin v. Wisconsin*, 483 U.S. 868 (1987).

66. 534 U.S. 112 (2001).

67. 547 U.S. 843 (2006).

68. For more on this topic, see Daniel E. Hall, *Administrative Law: Bureaucracy in a Democracy*, 7th ed. (Upper Saddle River, NJ: Prentice Hall, 2020).

69. *Los Angeles v. Patel*, 576 U.S. 409 (2015).

70. *Tinker v. Des Moines Independent Community School District*, 393 U.S. 503 (1969).

71. *New Jersey v. T.L.O.*, 469 U.S. 325 (1985).

72. *Safford Unified School District #1 v. Redding*, 557 U.S. 364 (2009).

# Chapter 14

# Interrogation, Surveillance, and Forensic Practices

## Chapter Outline

## Interrogations and Confessions

Learning Objectives: Define, describe, and apply the Fifth Amendment's privilege against self-incrimination to police interrogations.

**interrogation**
Questioning by police, especially of a person suspected or accused of a crime. A *custodial interrogation* involves a restraint of freedom, so it requires a *Miranda* warning. A routine *investigatory interrogation* involves no restraint and no accusation of a crime.

**confession**
A voluntary statement by a person that he or she is guilty of a crime.

**admission**
A voluntary statement that a fact or a state of events is true.

Police routinely question suspects and witnesses. An **interrogation** occurs whenever officers question a suspect. A **confession** is a statement made by a person claiming that he or she has committed a crime. A statement that has incriminating facts but doesn't amount to a confession is an **admission**.

    The use of interrogations, confessions, and admissions to prove guilt is controversial. British courts viewed them with suspicion for hundreds of years, as did America's founders. More recently, the U.S. Supreme Court has said that confessions are highly suspect, particularly when solely relied upon to obtain a conviction. For example, the Court has opined that a "system of criminal law enforcement which comes to depend on the 'confession' will, in the long run, be less reliable and more subject to abuses than a system which depends on extrinsic evidence independently" obtained through other law enforcement practices. [1]

    The first generation of interrogation techniques that raised legal concerns is known as the "third degree." The third degree refers to the use of physical coercion to extract confessions. Striking suspects, sometimes with rubber hoses to minimize bruising and scarring, is a third-degree technique.

Historically suspect in state and lower federal courts, the third degree was eventually invalidated by the Supreme Court. Consequently, some police officers turned to a combination of environmental and psychologically manipulative interrogation methods to extract confessions. Desmond S. O'Neill refers to this second-generation of interrogation as "accusatory." This approach has been dominated by the Reid Technique for decades. This method, first developed by John Reid and Fred Inbau in the 1940s, begins with an "interview," through which the interrogator determines, through both a suspect's answers and behavioral queues, whether the suspect is likely to be guilty. If determined to be not guilty, the suspect is released. If guilt is presumed by the interrogator, the interview morphs into an interrogation.[2] The interrogation is premised on creating a tense, high-pressure environment followed by a process of trust building with offers of support and expressions of sympathy and understanding. The key is that the interrogator offer these things in exchange for a confession. During the interrogation, the suspect is interrogated in uncomfortable or intimidating surrounding; subjected to harsh and aggressive questioning; isolated from family, friends, and legal counsel; interrogated for long periods of time; and deprived of sleep and water.

During the trust-building stage, interrogators affirm a suspect's anger and feelings, tell a suspect that they have their best interests at heart, suggest that a suspect will benefit from telling their story, and capitalize on a suspect's moralistic or religious values.

Another modern technique is the use of telling and retelling, which is discussed later in the context of the *Miranda* case. Lying to a suspect is an important aspect of the Reid Technique. A suspect may be told that a co-conspirator has implicated him, that his fingerprint of DNA was found at the scene of the crime, or that he failed a polygraph. The Supreme Court has affirmed the use of factual deception in the interrogation room.[3] However, lying to a suspect about his legal rights, such as his right to remain silent, is not permitted. The Reid method is credited by some with reducing physically abusive practices by offering an effective alternative. Today, however, some departments have abandoned or moderated the technique in response to concerns that the probability of eliciting false confessions is too high.

The evolution of the law of confessions and admissions roughly coincides with the evolution in police interrogation practices. The three stages of the law of confessions are voluntariness, *Miranda*, and post-*Miranda*.

## Voluntariness Requirement

At the Common Law, a confession, or admission, was legitimate only if it was given voluntarily. This principle found its way into colonial America and subsequently, state laws. The Supreme Court first recognized voluntariness in the 1896 case *Wilson v. United States*,[4] where it stated that "the true test of admissibility is that the confession is made freely, voluntarily, and without compulsion or inducement of any sort." This decision, however, wasn't based on a constitutional right. The Court made the decision in its supervisory role over the federal courts. However, one year later, the Court explicitly held that confessions must be voluntary to satisfy the Fifth Amendment's due process expectation in *Bram v. United States*.[5] This right was extended to state prosecutions in *Brown v. Mississippi* in 1936.[6]

As you have seen in other contexts, the totality of the circumstances test is used to determine if an admission was voluntary. Police officers do not have to physically coerce a confession for it to be involuntary. Mental or emotional coercion by law enforcement also violates a defendant's due process rights. The Supreme Court has held that a defendant's silence during questioning by police without an affirmative declaration of the exercise of the right to be free from self-incrimination may be admitted as evidence of guilt.[7] An exception to this rule is at trial. Concerned that a defendant's refusal to take the stand is so prejudicial that it violates the privilege against self-incrimination, prosecutors are forbidden from calling defendants to testify and from commenting on their silence to juries.

Involuntary confessions are to be excluded at trial. For years, the admission of a coerced confession resulted in an automatic reversal of conviction. This was changed in *Arizona v. Fulminante* (1991),[8] where the Supreme Court decided that a conviction is not to be automatically reversed because a coerced confession was admitted at trial. Rather, the Court held that if the prosecution can show beyond a reasonable doubt that the trial court error was harmless, the conviction is to be affirmed. That is, if there was sufficient other evidence to sustain the conviction, then it stands.

## McNabb-Mallory Rule

An old British rule required that arrestees be brought quickly before a magistrate to determine the legitimacy of the detention, and to otherwise ensure that the individual's rights were protected. As a matter of evidence law, admissions or confessions are admissible, even through hearsay, as statements against interest.[9]

The Supreme Court instituted this practice, in part, to limit the opportunity for police to coerce a confession before the defendant appeared in court. The rule is not constitutionally based. Instead, the Court announced the rule in its supervisory role over the nation's federal courts. It is called the McNabb-Mallory Rule, named for the two Supreme Court cases from which it sprang.[10] Although it existed at Common Law and was affirmed by Congress, neither provided a remedy for violations. So, the Court created one. Specifically, it held that a confession that occurred during a period of unreasonable delay in presenting the defendant in court is to be excluded. Congress reacted to McNabb-Mallory and *Miranda* by enacting a statute requiring the admission of voluntary confessions if obtained within six hours of arrest. In *Corley v. United States*,[11] it was held that if there is a delay in presenting a suspect to a judge longer than six hours, the old McNabb-Mallory exclusionary rule applies if the delay is unreasonable.

Today, interrogations, confessions, and admissions are governed by these rules, as well as two broader rights: the Fifth Amendment right to be free from self-incrimination and the Sixth Amendment right to counsel.

## Miranda

The next major step in the development of the law of confessions occurred in 1966 when the Supreme Court issued its decision in *Miranda v. Arizona*. As a consequence of its frequent portrayal in streaming crime dramas, films, and detective novels, *Miranda* has become part of the American consciousness. Read *Miranda* in your next Oyez.

## Oyez

### Miranda v. Arizona
### 384 U.S. 436 (1966)

**MR. CHIEF JUSTICE WARREN delivered the opinion of the Court.**

[The Supreme Court consolidated appeals from several individuals who had been convicted at trials where their confessions were entered into evidence. Ernesto Miranda, for whom the case is named, was arrested for rape and kidnapping. He was interrogated at a police station. He was not advised of his constitutional rights, he never requested to see an attorney, and he never refused to discuss the allegations with the officers. He only had contact with the police during the interrogation. After two hours he signed a written confession to the rape. He also attested to the voluntariness of his confession in the document. He was convicted, appealed, and lost in Arizona's appellate courts. Chief Justice Earl Warren delivered the Court's opinion.]

(continued)

The cases before us raise questions that go to the roots of our concepts of American criminal jurisprudence: the restraints society must observe consistent with the Federal Constitution in prosecuting individuals for crime. More specifically, we deal with the admissibility of statements obtained from an individual who is subjected to custodial police interrogation and the necessity for procedures which assure that the individual is accorded his privilege under the Fifth Amendment to the Constitution not to be compelled to incriminate himself. . . .

Our holding will be spelled out with some specificity in the pages which follow but briefly stated it is this: the prosecution may not use statements, whether exculpatory or inculpatory, stemming from custodial interrogation of the defendant unless it demonstrates the use of procedural safeguards effective to secure the privilege against self-incrimination. By custodial interrogation, we mean questioning initiated by law-enforcement officers after a person has been taken into custody or otherwise deprived of his freedom of action in any significant way. As for the procedural safeguards to be employed, unless other fully effective means are devised to inform accused persons of their right of silence and to assure a continuous opportunity to exercise it, the following measures are required. Prior to any questioning, the person must be warned that he has a right to remain silent, that any statement he does make may be used as evidence against him, and that he has a right to the presence of an attorney, either retained or appointed. The defendant may waive effectuation of these rights, provided the waiver is made voluntarily, knowingly, and intelligently. If, however, he indicates in any manner and at any stage of the process that he wishes to consult with an attorney before speaking there can be no questioning. Likewise, if the individual is alone and indicates in any manner that he does not wish to be interrogated, the police may not question him. The mere fact that he may have answered some questions or volunteered some statements on his own does not deprive him of the right to refrain from answering any further inquiries until he has consulted with an attorney and thereafter consents to be questioned.

The constitutional issue we decide in each of these cases is the admissibility of statements obtained from a defendant questioned while in custody or otherwise deprived of his freedom of action in any significant way. In each, the defendant was questioned by police officers, detectives, or a prosecuting attorney in a room in which he was cut off from the outside world. In none of these cases was the defendant given a full and effective warning of his rights at the outset of the interrogation process. In all of the cases, the questioning elicited oral admissions, and in three of them, signed statements as well, which were admitted at their trials. They all thus share salient features—incommunicado interrogation of individuals in a police-dominated atmosphere, resulting in self-incriminating statements without full warnings of constitutional rights.

An understanding of the nature and setting of this in-custody interrogation is essential to our decisions today. The difficulty in depicting what transpires at such interrogations stems from the fact that in this country they have largely taken place incommunicado. From extensive factual studies undertaken in the early 1930s . . . it is clear that police violence and the "third degree" flourished at that time. In a series of cases decided by the Court long after those studies, the police resulted to physical brutality—beating, hanging, whipping—and to sustained and protracted questioning incommunicado in order to extort confessions. . . .

Again we stress that the modern practice of in-custody interrogation is psychologically rather than physically oriented. As we have stated before, ". . . this court has recognized that coercion can be mental as well as physical, and that the blood of the accused is not the only hallmark of an unconstitutional inquisition.". . .

The circumstances surrounding in-custody interrogation can operate very quickly to overbear the will of one merely made aware of his privilege [against self-incrimination] by his interrogators. Therefore, the right to have counsel present at the interrogation is indispensable to the protection of the Fifth Amendment privilege under the system we delineate today. Our aim is to assure that the individual's right to choose between silence and speech remains unfettered throughout the interrogation process. A once-stated warning, delivered by those who will conduct the interrogation, cannot itself suffice to that end among those who most require knowledge of their rights. A mere warning given by the interrogators is not alone sufficient to accomplish that end. Prosecutors themselves claim that the admonishment of the right to remain silent without more "will benefit only the recidivist and the professional." Even preliminary advice given to the accused by his own attorney can be swiftly overcome by the secret interrogation process. . . . Thus, the need for counsel to protect the Fifth Amendment privilege comprehends not merely a right to consult with counsel prior to questioning, but also to have counsel present during any questioning if the defendant so desires.

The presence of counsel at the interrogation may serve several significant subsidiary functions as well. If the accused decides to talk to his interrogators, the assistance of counsel can mitigate the dangers of trustworthiness. With a lawyer present the likelihood that the police will practice coercion is reduced, and if coercion is nevertheless exercised the lawyer can testify to it in court. The presence of a lawyer can also help to guarantee that the accused gives a fully accurate statement to the police and that the statement is rightly reported to the prosecution.

[Miranda's case was remanded, he was retried, his confession was excluded, and he was again convicted. Although sentenced to twenty to thirty years in prison, he was paroled in 1972. Subsequently, he found himself in trouble on several occasions, one leading to revocation of his parole. He spent another year in prison, was released, and was stabbed to death in a bar room fight in 1976. Several Miranda Warning Cards, which he had been autographing and selling, were found on his person at the time of his death. The man alleged to have killed Miranda was arrested, read his Miranda rights, invoked his right to remain silent, was released, and fled. The Miranda murder was never prosecuted.]

Police investigator interrogating a suspect.

Although *Miranda* concerns the rights of suspects to counsel in certain circumstances, it is not a Sixth Amendment right to counsel case. Instead, the right to an attorney springs out of the Fifth Amendment's right to be free from self-incrimination. Simply stated, the Court found that to meaningfully implement the right to be free from self-incrimination, suspects must be informed of both their right to remain silent and to the assistance of legal counsel before they are questioned.

## The Warnings

The heart of the *Miranda* decision is the warnings. These are:

1. The right to remain silent.
2. Any statements made may be used against the defendant to gain a conviction.
3. The right to consult with a lawyer and to have a lawyer present during questioning.
4. For the indigent, a lawyer will be provided without cost.

The warnings are to be read to all persons in custody who are to be interrogated. The law does not presume that any person, including an attorney, knows these rights. The warnings should be presented in a timely manner and read at such a speed that the arrestee has the opportunity and time to comprehend them.

Specific language doesn't have to be used, so as long as the defendant is fully and effectively apprised of each right. For example, the Court approved the following language against the defendant's claim that it conveyed the idea that he had a right to speak to his attorney before questioning but not during questioning.

> "You have the right to talk to a lawyer before answering any of our questions" and "[y]ou have the right to use any of these rights at any time you want during this interview."

The words, the Court found, "were not the *clearest possible* formulation of *Miranda*'s right-to-counsel advisement, they were sufficiently comprehensive and comprehensible when given a commonsense reading."[12]

Many law enforcement agencies have made it a policy to record (video/audio or audio only) the giving of the warnings and any waiver of rights to eliminate any question concerning whether the warnings were given and whether coercion was used to gain a waiver.

## Custodial Interrogation

Not all questioning by law enforcement officers must be preceded by the *Miranda* warnings. Two conditions must be present before police are required to deliver the *Miranda* warnings. Specifically, a suspect must be in

1. custody and
2. subjected to interrogation.

This is commonly known as the "custodial interrogation" requirement.

The Court used the phrase "taken into custody or otherwise deprived of his freedom of action in any significant way" to define the custody element of *Miranda*. An objective test is used to determine if a suspect is in custody; the suspect's and interrogating officer's subjective beliefs about the status of the suspect are not dispositive.[13] Instead, the test is whether a reasonable person would have felt free to leave. Although a statement by a police officer to a suspect that he is not under arrest is not dispositive, it may be considered. Of course, a person is in custody if an officer announces that an arrest is being made or that the person is not free to leave. The Court made it clear that the in-custody element may be satisfied anywhere. The defendant need not be at the police station or in a police cruiser to be in custody.

Typically, a brief encounter between a citizen and a police officer is not custodial. All of the surrounding facts must be considered in making the custody determination. The location of the interrogation is very important. There is a greater chance of finding a person in custody if the questioning takes place in a police station or prosecutor's office rather than the suspect's home or in public. The presence of other persons during the interrogation decreases the odds of the suspect being in custody. The Court found the fact that the suspects in *Miranda* were "cut off from the outside world" troubling. The length and intensity of the questioning are also relevant.

The Supreme Court found age to be a factor in a case where police interrogated a 13-year-old boy who was enrolled in special education classes outside the presence of his guardians and without *Mirandizing* him. The Court concluded that the child's age and maturity impacted his perception of whether he was free to leave, as well as his ability to develop sound judgment.[14]

Whether a prisoner who is interrogated about a crime unrelated to the reason they are incarcerated is in "custody" for *Miranda* purposes is confounding. This was the issue in the *Howes v. Fields* case, presented in the following Oyez.

## Oyez

### Howes v. Fields
### 565 U.S. 499 (2012)

**Justice Alito delivered the opinion of the Court.**

■ ■ ■

While serving a sentence in a Michigan jail, Randall Fields was escorted by a corrections officer to a conference room where two sheriff's deputies questioned him about allegations that, before he came to prison, he had engaged in sexual conduct with a 12-year-old boy. In order to get to the conference room, Fields had to go down one floor and pass through a locked door that separated two sections of the facility. Fields arrived at the conference room between 7 p.m. and 9 p.m. and was questioned for between five and seven hours.

At the beginning of the interview, Fields was told that he was free to leave and return to his cell. Later, he was again told that he could leave whenever he wanted. The two interviewing deputies were armed during the interview, but Fields remained free of handcuffs and other restraints. The door to the conference room was sometimes open and sometimes shut.

About halfway through the interview, after Fields had been confronted with the allegations of abuse, he became agitated and began to yell. Fields testified that one of the deputies, using an expletive, told him to sit down and said that "if [he] didn't want to cooperate, [he] could leave." Fields eventually confessed to engaging in sex acts with the boy. According to Fields' testimony at a suppression hearing, he said several times during the interview that he no longer wanted to talk to the deputies, but he did not ask to go back to his cell prior to the end of the interview.

When he was eventually ready to leave, he had to wait an additional 20 minutes or so because a corrections officer had to be summoned to escort him back to his cell, and he did not return to his cell until well after the hour when he generally retired. At no time was Fields given Miranda warnings or advised that he did not have to speak with the deputies.

The State of Michigan charged Fields with criminal sexual conduct. Relying on Miranda, Fields moved to suppress his confession, but the trial court denied his motion. [He was convicted and sentenced to 10 to 15 years in prison.]

As used in our Miranda case law, "custody" is a term of art that specifies circumstances that are thought generally to present a serious danger of coercion. In determining whether a person is in custody in this sense, the initial step is to ascertain whether, in light of "the objective circumstances of the interrogation," a "reasonable person [would] have felt he or she was not at liberty to terminate the interrogation and leave. And in order to determine how a suspect would have "gauge[d]" his "freedom of movement," courts must examine "all of the circumstances surrounding the interrogation." Relevant factors include the location of the questioning, its duration, statements made during the interview, the presence or absence of physical restraints during the questioning, and the release of the interviewee at the end of the questioning. . . .

Determining whether an individual's freedom of movement was curtailed, however, is simply the first step in the analysis, not the last. Not all restraints on freedom of movement amount to custody for purposes of Miranda. We have "decline[d] to accord talismanic power" to the freedom-of-movement inquiry, and have instead asked the additional question whether the relevant environment presents the same inherently coercive pressures as the type of station house questioning at issue in Miranda. "Our cases make clear . . . that the freedom-of-movement test identifies only a necessary and not a sufficient condition for Miranda custody."

There are at least three strong grounds for [the conclusion that prisoners will not feel in custody]. First, questioning a person who is already serving a prison term does not generally involve the shock that very often accompanies arrest. In the paradigmatic Miranda situation—a person is arrested in his home or on the street and whisked to a police station for questioning—detention represents a sharp and ominous change, and the shock may give rise to coercive pressures. A person who is "cut off from his normal life and companions," and abruptly transported from the street into a "police-dominated atmosphere," may feel coerced into answering questions.

By contrast, when a person who is already serving a term of imprisonment is questioned, there is usually no such change. "Interrogated suspects who have previously been convicted of crime live in prison." For a person serving a term of incarceration, we reasoned in Shatzer, the ordinary restrictions of prison life, while no doubt unpleasant, are expected and familiar and thus do not involve the same "inherently compelling pressures" that are often present when a suspect is yanked from familiar surroundings in the outside world and subjected to interrogation in a police station.

Second, a prisoner, unlike a person who has not been sentenced to a term of incarceration, is unlikely to be lured into speaking by a longing for prompt release. When a person is arrested and taken to a station house for interrogation, the person who is questioned may be pressured to speak by the hope that, after doing so, he will be allowed to leave and go home. On the other hand, when a prisoner is questioned, he knows that when the questioning ceases, he will remain under confinement.

Third, a prisoner, unlike a person who has not been convicted and sentenced, knows that the law enforcement officers who question him probably lack the authority to affect the duration of his sentence. . . .

In short, standard conditions of confinement and associated restrictions on freedom will not necessarily implicate the same interests that the Court sought to protect when it afforded special safeguards to persons subjected to custodial interrogation. Thus, service of a term of imprisonment, without more, is not enough to constitute Miranda custody. . . .

When a prisoner is questioned, the determination of custody should focus on all of the features of the interrogation. These include the language that is used in summoning the prisoner to the interview and the manner in which the interrogation is conducted. An inmate who is removed from the general prison population for questioning and is "thereafter . . . subjected to treatment" in connection with the interrogation "that renders him 'in custody' for practical purposes . . . will be entitled to the full panoply of protections prescribed by Miranda." . . .

The record in this case reveals that respondent was not taken into custody for purposes of Miranda. To be sure, respondent did not invite the interview or consent to it in advance, and he was not advised that he was free to decline to speak with the deputies. The following facts also lend some support to respondent's argument that Miranda's custody requirement was met: The

(continued)

interview lasted for between five and seven hours in the evening and continued well past the hour when respondent generally went to bed; the deputies who questioned respondent were armed; and one of the deputies, according to respondent, "[u]sed a very sharp tone,"...

These circumstances, however, were offset by others. Most important, respondent was told at the outset of the interrogation, and was reminded again thereafter, that he could leave and go back to his cell whenever he wanted ("I was told I could get up and leave whenever I wanted"). Moreover, respondent was not physically restrained or threatened and was interviewed in a well-lit, average-sized conference room, where he was "not uncomfortable." He was offered food and water, and the door to the conference room was sometimes left open. "All of these objective facts are consistent with an interrogation environment in which a reasonable person would have felt free to terminate the interview and leave."

Because he was in prison, respondent was not free to leave the conference room by himself and to make his own way through the facility to his cell. Instead, he was escorted to the conference room and, when he ultimately decided to end the interview, he had to wait about 20 minutes for a corrections officer to arrive and escort him to his cell. But he would have been subject to this same restraint even if he had been taken to the conference room for some reason other than police questioning; under no circumstances could he have reasonably expected to be able to roam free. And while respondent testified that he "was told . . . if I did not want to cooperate, I needed to go back to my cell," these words did not coerce cooperation by threatening harsher conditions. ("I was told, if I didn't want to cooperate, I could leave"). Returning to his cell would merely have returned him to his usual environment.

Taking into account all of the circumstances of the questioning—including especially the undisputed fact that respondent was told that he was free to end the questioning and to return to his cell—we hold that respondent was not in custody within the meaning of Miranda.

In addition to being in custody, a defendant must be subjected to an interrogation before *Miranda* applies. Clearly, interrogation includes questioning by law enforcement officers, but this is not all. In *Rhode Island v. Innis*, 446 U.S. 291 (1980),[15] the Supreme Court held that any "functional equivalent" to express questioning is also interrogation. That is, all actions or words by police officers that can reasonably be expected to elicit an incriminating response are interrogation. The facts of *Innis* illustrate a functional equivalence. Innis had been arrested for a robbery that was committed using a shotgun. The gun hadn't been found by police. In response to his Miranda warnings, Innis said he wanted to speak to an attorney. Respecting *Miranda*, the officers ceased their interrogation. But with Innis in the back seat of their squad car, the two arresting officers engaged in a colloquy where one noted that handicapped children were playing near the site of the robbery. In response, the other officer commented, "God forbid . . . they might hurt themselves." Out of a concern for the children, Innis led the officers to the weapon. Finding the officers' statements to be the equivalent of an interrogation, they ordered that his admission be excluded from trial.

The nature of the information elicited is not relevant; the *Miranda* court stated that the decision applies to both inculpatory and exculpatory statements. Accordingly, *Miranda* is effective whether a defendant confesses or simply makes an admission.

## Waiver

A defendant may waive the right to have the assistance of counsel and/or to remain silent. The waiver must be made voluntarily and knowingly. In *Miranda*, the Supreme Court said that the "heavy burden" of proving that a defendant made a knowing and voluntary waiver rests with the prosecution; courts are to presume no waiver.

In determining whether there has been a waiver, the totality of the circumstances is considered. The actions of the police, as well as the defendant's age, intelligence, and experience, are all relevant to this inquiry.

An express waiver, preferably written or recorded, is best for the prosecution. Although more difficult for prosecutors to defend, unrecorded verbal waivers are also valid. On the other hand, a suspect who knowingly and voluntary speaks to police following the Miranda warnings waives the right to counsel.

In the same case, *Berghuis v. Thompkins* (2010), the Court held that police do not have an obligation to obtain a waiver of *Miranda* following the warnings. Instead, they may begin an interrogation and must stop only if the suspect unambiguously invokes the right to remain silent or asks for an attorney. Further, silence by a suspect after receiving the warnings is not the same as an invocation of the rights. If a suspect's statement is ambiguous or equivocal, the police may continue the interrogation.

In the context of public employment, a waiver that is coerced through fear of employment discipline or termination is not valid. So, police officers who were *Mirandized* but told they would be terminated if they didn't respond to questions about traffic ticket fixing were entitled to have their admissions excluded when they were later tried for crimes arising out of the investigation.[16]

## Exceptions to Miranda

Not every communication between a police officer and a suspect amounts to an interrogation under *Miranda*. First, volunteered statements are not the product of interrogation. The *Miranda* decision explicitly states that officers are under no duty to interrupt a volunteered confession to read a confessor his or her *Miranda* rights.

Second, routine questions that are purely informational, and normally do not lead to incriminating responses, need not be preceded by a reading of the *Miranda* warnings. Questions about one's name, age, address, and employment are examples. So, a statute that requires individuals who have been legitimately arrested or detained by police to produce identification is valid because a person's name, standing alone, is not incriminating in most circumstances.[17]

Third, questions made by officers in the interest of public safety need not be preceded by a *Miranda* warning. In one case, a woman told two police officers that she had just been raped by a man carrying a gun and that the rapist had gone into a nearby grocery. The officers went to the store and arrested the man. However, he did not have the gun on his person. One of the police officers asked the arrestee where the gun was, and the arrestee responded by indicating the location where the gun was hidden in the store. The justices rules that even though the officer's question satisfied the interrogation element, the defendant was in custody, and the defendant had not been *Mirandized*, the evidence could be used at trial. The Court recognized that in such situations, when there is a danger to the officers or the public, officers must be permitted to extinguish the public threat. Thus, the relatively rigid *Miranda* rules are relaxed when there is a public safety exigency that was the impetus of a brief and limited interrogation designed to meet that exigency.[18]

The public safety exception came into full focus following the bombings at the 2013 Boston Marathon. The government announced that it would invoke the public safety exception and not immediately *Mirandize* the suspect Dzhokhar Tsarnaev. The decision was guided by a U.S. Department of Justice Memorandum entitled *Custodial Interrogation for Public Safety and Intelligence-Gathering Purposes of Operational Terrorists Inside the United States.*[19] The memorandum advised federal agents who arrest terrorist suspects of the following:

(1) If applicable, agents should ask any and all questions that are reasonably prompted by an immediate concern for the safety of the public or the arresting agents without advising the arrestee of his *Miranda* rights.

(2) After all applicable public safety questions have been exhausted, agents should advise the arrestee of his Miranda rights and seek a waiver of those rights before any further interrogation occurs, absent exceptional circumstances described below.

(3) There may be exceptional cases in which, although all relevant public safety questions have been asked, agents nonetheless conclude that continued unwarned interrogation is necessary to collect valuable and timely intelligence not related to any immediate threat, and that the government's interest in obtaining this intelligence outweighs the disadvantages of proceeding with unwarned interrogation.

The determination of whether particular unwarned questions are justified on public safety grounds must always be made on a case-by-case basis, examining the totality of the circumstances based on all the facts and circumstances. In light of the magnitude and complexity of the threat often posed by terrorist organizations, particularly international terrorist organizations, and the nature of their attacks, the circumstances surrounding an arrest of an operational terrorist may warrant significantly more extensive public safety interrogation without Miranda warnings than would be permissible in an ordinary criminal case. Depending on the facts, such interrogation might include, for example, questions about possible impending or coordinated terrorist attacks; the location, nature, and threat posed by weapons that might post an imminent danger to the public; and the identities, locations, and activities or intentions of accomplices who may be plotting additional imminent attacks.

Tsarnaev was apprehended in a national manhunt that involved shoot-outs, the murder of a police officer, and a lock down (public transit and schools were closed and residents were asked to lock themselves at home) of a city. Tsarnaev was injured during the ordeal and taken to hospital where law enforcement officers conducted un-*Mirandized* interrogations of the suspect from the time of his arrest until his first appearance before a judge 16 hours later. The judge *Mirandized* Tsarnaev during the hearing, at which time he stopped talking.[20] No doubt Tsarnaev was asked if other explosives had been built or hidden, whether he had hidden or mislaid any weapons during the manhunt, or any question concerning the immediate public safety. But it is not clear that questions beyond these matters, even if related to his alleged terrorist crimes, fall into the public safety exception.

Fourth, related to the public safety exception is spontaneous questioning by police. If a question is asked spontaneously and reflexively, such as in response to an emergency, there is no interrogation. For example, if an officer were to return to a room where he has placed two arrestees to find one dead, it would not be an interrogation if the officer were to excitedly utter, "Oh my, what happened here?"

Fifth, the *Miranda* warnings do not have to be given by undercover officers because there is no custody, no "police-dominated atmosphere."[21] However, once criminal charges have been filed, undercover officers may not be used to extract information from a defendant.[22]

Sixth, *Miranda* warnings do not have to be recited during routine traffic stops, even though an interrogation occurs. The Court concluded that even though traffic stops are seizures for Fourth Amendment purposes, they are not custodial for Fifth Amendment purposes. The "noncoercive aspect of ordinary traffic stops prompts us to hold that persons temporarily detained pursuant to such stops are not 'in custody' for the purposes of *Miranda*." This includes answering field sobriety questions.[23]

## Multiple Interrogations and Reinterrogation

*Miranda* clearly states that once a defendant invokes the right to remain silent, whether before or during questioning, the interrogation must stop. The same is true when a suspect asks for an attorney. If the defendant's attorney is not available, the police are to respect the defendant's right to remain silent and not question him or her until the attorney arrives. However, ambiguous references to an attorney do not invoke a suspect's right to be free of questioning. A suspect's request must be clear enough that a reasonable officer would believe that the suspect wanted to see counsel.[24] A defendant's invocation must be unambiguous, and in the 2010 case *Berghuis v. Thompkins* the Supreme Court held that silence during a long interrogation is not an invocation of the Fifth Amendment right to remain silent. So, a *Mirandized* suspect who remained silent for a long period and then made a single short admission was unsuccessful in having the admission excluded.

Under very limited circumstances, police officers may reattempt to interrogate a defendant who has invoked the right to remain silent. Although multiple attempts to interrogate an arrestee about the same crime are not permitted, it has been determined that a second interrogation about a separate and unrelated crime may be valid.[25]

Reinterrogations when a long period of time has passed between the two, with intervening circumstances, are permitted. In *Maryland v. Shatzer*, a 2010 Supreme Court case, a prisoner who was interrogated by police about a new crime invoked his *Miranda rights*, resulting in a cessation of the interrogation, and the investigation was closed. The case was reopened three years later, the prisoner was interrogated after waiving his *Miranda* rights, and his incriminating statements were used to gain a conviction for sexual child abuse. He later asserted that his initial invocation of *Miranda* should have carried forward to the interrogation three years later. The Court rejected his argument, finding that his return to the general population of the prison and the three-year period constituted a break in *Miranda* custody.

*Miranda* clearly stated that once an accused has invoked the right to counsel, the police are prohibited from interrogating him or her until he or she has conferred with counsel. *Miranda* did not answer this question: May police reinterrogate a defendant without counsel present once the defendant has consulted with a lawyer? The answer is found in *Minnick v. Mississippi*. *Minnick* makes it clear that once an accused has asserted a right to counsel, all police-initiated interrogations must occur with defense counsel present.

## Oyez

### Minnick v. Mississippi
#### 498 U.S. 146 (1990)

**Justice KENNEDY delivered the opinion of the Court.**

To protect the privilege against self-incrimination guaranteed by the Fifth Amendment, we have held that the police must terminate interrogation of an accused in custody if the accused requests the assistance of counsel. *Miranda v. Arizona*, 384 U.S. 436, 474 (1966). We reinforced the protections of *Miranda in Edwards v. Arizona*, 451 U.S. 477, 484–485 (1981), which held that once the accused requests counsel, officials may not reinitiate questioning "until counsel has been made available" to him. The issue in the case before us is whether *Edwards* protection ceases once the suspect has consulted with an attorney.

Petitioner Robert Minnick and fellow prisoner James Dyess escaped from a county jail in Mississippi and, a day later, broke into a mobile home in search of weapons. In the course of the burglary they were interrupted by the arrival of the trailer's owner, Ellis Thomas, accompanied by Lamar Lafferty and Lafferty's infant son. Dyess and Minnick used the stolen weapons to kill Thomas and the senior Lafferty. Minnick's story is that Dyess murdered one victim and then forced Minnick to shoot the other. Before the escapees could get away, two young women arrived at the mobile home. They were held at gunpoint, then bound by hand and foot. Dyess and Minnick fled in Thomas' truck, abandoning the vehicle in New Orleans. The fugitives continued to Mexico, where they fought, and Minnick then proceeded alone to California. Minnick was arrested in Lemon Grove, California, on a Mississippi warrant, some four months after the murders.

(continued)

The confession at issue here resulted from the last interrogation of Minnick while he was held in the San Diego jail, but we first recount the events which preceded it. Minnick was arrested on Friday, August 22, 1986. Petitioner testified that he was mistreated by local police during and after the arrest. The day following the arrest, Saturday, two FBI agents came to the jail to interview him. Petitioner testified that he refused to go to the interview, but was told he would "have to go down or else.". . . The FBI report indicates that the agents read petitioner his *Miranda* warnings, and that he acknowledged he understood his rights. He refused to sign a rights waiver form, however, and said he would not answer "very many" questions. Minnick told the agents about the jail break and the flight, and described how Dyess threatened and beat him. Early in the interview, he sobbed "[i]t was my life or theirs," but otherwise he hesitated to tell what happened at the trailer. The agents reminded him he did not have to answer questions without a lawyer present. According to the report, "Minnick stated, 'Come back Monday when I have a lawyer,' and stated that he would make a more complete statement then with his lawyer present.". . .

After the FBI interview, an appointed attorney met with petitioner. Petitioner spoke with the lawyer on two or three occasions, though it is not clear from the record whether all of these conferences were in person.

On Monday, August 25, Deputy Sheriff J.C. Denham of Clarke County, Mississippi, came to the San Diego jail to question Minnick. Minnick testified that his jailers again told him he would "have to talk" to Denham and that he "could not refuse.". . . Denham advised petitioner of his rights, and petitioner again declined to sign a rights waiver form. Petitioner told Denham about the escape and then proceeded to describe the events at the mobile home. . . .

Minnick was tried for murder in Mississippi. He moved to suppress all statements given to the FBI or other police officers, including Denham. The trial court denied the motion with respect to petitioner's statements to Denham, but suppressed his other statements. Petitioner was convicted on two counts of capital murder and sentenced to death.

On appeal, petitioner argued that the confession to Denham was taken in violation of his rights to counsel under the Fifth and Sixth Amendments. The Mississippi Supreme Court rejected the claims. . . .

The Mississippi Supreme Court relied on our statement in *Edwards* that an accused who invokes his right to counsel "is not subject to further interrogation by the authorities until counsel has been made available to him. . . ." 451 U.S., at 484–485. We do not interpret this language to mean, as the Mississippi court thought, that the protection of *Edwards* terminates once counsel has consulted with the suspect. In context, the requirement that counsel be "made available" to the accused refers to more than an opportunity to consult with an attorney outside the interrogation room.

In *Edwards*, we focused on *Miranda's* instruction that when the accused invokes his right to counsel, the "interrogation must cease until an attorney is *present* during custodial interrogation. . . ." In the sentence preceding the language quoted by the Mississippi Supreme Court, we referred to the "right to have counsel *present* during custodial interrogation.". . .

In our view, a fair reading of *Edwards* and subsequent cases demonstrates that we have interpreted the rule to bar police-initiated interrogation unless the accused has counsel with him at the time of questioning. Whatever the ambiguities of our earlier cases on this point, we now hold that when counsel is requested, interrogation must cease, and officials may not reinitiate interrogation without counsel present, whether or not the accused has consulted with his attorney.

Another twist on multiple interrogations was introduced by the police practice of eliciting a confession without the benefit of *Miranda* warning, following that confession with the warning, and then attempting to elicit the confession again. Apparently, there are two factors at play. First, *Miranda* prevents some suspects from confessing. Second, once a suspect confesses, the psychological gates have been opened in such a way that the suspect is more likely to repeat the confession, even if the *Miranda* warnings are interposed. With this knowledge, police across the nation began seeking confessions they knew were inadmissible, only to then *Mirandize* their suspects in hope of obtaining a second confession (see Exhibit 14–1). This practice was invalidated as violating the Fifth Amendment in *Missouri v. Seibert*, 542 U.S. 600 (2004),[26] where the Court wrote:

Strategists dedicated to draining the substance out of Miranda cannot accomplish by training instructions [what this Court said] Congress could not do by statute. Because the question-first tactic effectively threatens to thwart *Miranda's* purpose of reducing the risk that a coerced confession would be admitted, and because the facts here do not reasonably support a conclusion that the warnings given could have served their purpose, [the defendant's] postwarning statements are inadmissible.

## Exhibit 14–1  Summary of Significant Miranda Cases

| Rule | Case |
|---|---|
| Suspects in custody and subject to an interrogation must be advised of their rights to remain silent, that statements may be used to prove guilt at trial, to the assistance of counsel, and for the indigent, counsel must be provided. | *Miranda v. Arizona* (1966) |
| A suspect is in custody if a reasonable person would have believed he or she was not free. The subjective beliefs of the suspect and officers are immaterial. | *Stansbury v. CA* (1994) |
| Volunteered statements, responses to routine questions, and responses to questions concerning immediate public safety do not have to follow *Miranda* warnings to be admissible. | |
| Questioning by undercover officers does not need to be *Mirandized*. | *Illinois v. Perkins* (1990) |
| Suspect silence is not an invocation of *Miranda*; a suspect's invocation must be unambiguous. | *Berghuis v. Thompkins* (2010) |
| Reinterrogation for the same crime after a suspect has invoked and consulted with an attorney can only occur with suspect's attorney present. | *Minnick v. Mississippi* (1990) |
| Interrogation of suspect for separate and unrelated crime after suspect invoked *Miranda* for different crime is permitted, subject to *Miranda* again. | *Michigan v. Mosely* (1975) |
| Police technique of eliciting non-*Mirandized* confessions followed by *Miranda* warnings and reinterrogation is invalid. | *Missouri v. Seibert* (2004) |
| A break in custody allows reinterrogation without the presence of counsel, even if *Miranda* was previously invoked. | *Maryland v. Shatzer* (2010) |
| The age and maturity of a minor are factors in custody determinations. | *JBD v. North Carolina* (2010) |
| Precise words are not required for warnings so long as rights are communicated. | *Florida v. Powell* (2010) |
| Prisoners not automatically in Miranda custody; separate custodial determination is made. | *Howes v. Fields* (2012) |

The many exceptions the Court has found to Miranda, and the continuous evolution of interrogation techniques, have put the law into a post-*Miranda* era. It is likely that the Reid Technique and other developments in interrogation will be scrutinized more closely in the years to come.

## Violating Miranda

Any statement obtained in violation of *Miranda* is inadmissible at trial to prove guilt. The defendant ordinarily raises the issue prior to trial through a motion to suppress.

Although statements that are illegally obtained may not be admitted to prove a defendant's guilt, the Supreme Court has held that illegally obtained statements may be admitted, under certain circumstances, to impeach the defendant.[27] Therefore, if a defendant's testimony at trial is different from an earlier confession that was suppressed as violative of *Miranda*, the confession may be admitted to rebut the defendant's in-court testimony.

Also, the question concerning the application of the fruits of the poisonous tree doctrine to evidence obtained through a non-*Mirandized* confession was open for many years. For example, a murder suspect confesses and points the police to the location where the dead body is buried. Without the *Miranda warnings*, the confession is out. But what about the body? Some lower courts decided that the secondary evidence should be excluded. A minority of lower courts disagreed. The Supreme Court resolved this issue in *United States v. Patane*,[28] where it held that physical fruits of a non-*Mirandized* confession are not to be suppressed at trial. Justice Thomas, writing for the majority, penned:

> [T]he core protection afforded by the Self-Incrimination Clause is a prohibition on compelling a criminal defendant to testify against himself at trial. . . . The Clause can-not be violated by the introduction of nontestimonial evidence obtained as a result of voluntary statements. . . . It follows that police do not violate a suspect's constitutional rights (or the *Miranda* rule) by negligent or even deliberate failures to provide the suspect with the full panoply of warnings prescribed by *Miranda*. Potential violations occur, if at all, only upon the admission of unwarned statements into evidence at trial. And, at that point, "[t]he exclusion of unwarned statements . . . is a complete and sufficient remedy" for any perceived *Miranda* violation. . . . Thus, unlike unreasonable searches under the Fourth Amendment or actual violations of the Due Process Clause or the Self-Incrimination Clause, there is, with respect to mere failures to warn, nothing to deter. There is therefore no reason to apply the "fruit of the poisonous tree" doctrine. . . . But *Dickerson's* characterization of *Miranda* as a constitutional rule does not lessen the need to maintain the closest possible fit between the Self-Incrimination Clause and any judge-made rule designed to protect it. And there is no such fit here. Introduction of the nontestimonial fruit of a voluntary statement, such as respondent's Glock, does not implicate the Self-Incrimination Clause. The admission of such fruit presents no risk that a defendant's coerced statements (however defined) will be used against him at a criminal trial. In any case, "[t]he exclusion of unwarned statements . . . is a complete and sufficient remedy" for any perceived *Miranda* violation. . . .

This limitation on Miranda only applies to voluntary admissions. The physical evidence that results from a coerced confession is not admissible under the Voluntariness Doctrine.

The Court's decision in *Patane* has been interpreted by some state courts as a retraction of a constitutional right. The Ohio Supreme Court, for example, held that fruits resulting from unwarned statements are to be excluded. In its 2006 decision, *State v. Farris*,[29] that court stated

> The Ohio Constitution "is a document of independent force. In the areas of individual rights and civil liberties, the U.S. Constitution, where applicable to the states, provides a floor below which state court decisions may not fall. As long as state courts provide at least as much protection as the United States Supreme Court has provided in its interpretation of the federal Bill of Rights, state courts are unrestricted in according greater civil liberties and protections to individuals and groups". . . . In general, when provisions of the Ohio Constitution and U.S. Constitution are essentially identical, we should harmonize our interpretations of the provisions, unless there are persuasive reasons to do otherwise. . . . To hold that the physical evidence seized as a result of unwarned statements is inadmissible, we would have to hold that section 10, Article I of the Ohio Constitution provides greater protection to criminal defendants than the Fifth Amendment to the U.S. Constitution. We so find here.
> Only evidence obtained as the direct result of statements made in custody without the benefit of a Miranda warning should be excluded. We believe that to hold otherwise would encourage law-enforcement officers to withhold Miranda

warnings and would thus weaken section 10, Article I of the Ohio Constitution. In cases like this one, where possession is the basis for the crime and physical evidence is the keystone of the case, warning suspects of their rights can hinder the gathering of evidence. When physical evidence is central to a conviction and testimonial evidence is not, there can arise a virtual incentive to flout Miranda. We believe that the overall administration of justice in Ohio requires a law-enforcement environment in which evidence is gathered in conjunction with Miranda, not in defiance of it. We thus join the other states that have already determined after Patane that their state constitutions' protections against self-incrimination extend to physical evidence seized as a result of pre-Miranda statements.

## Sixth Amendment

*Miranda* is triggered as soon as a person is in custody and is subject to interrogation. This can occur long before or directly before the filing of a formal charge. Once the adversary judicial proceeding has begun, the primary source of protection changes from the Fifth Amendment (*Miranda*), which continues in effect though, to the Sixth Amendment.

The reading of the *Miranda* warnings is sufficient for protecting a defendant's Sixth Amendment rights, so police, courts, or prosecutors are not required to inform a defendant of the independent Sixth Amendment right, although it is often done. In practice, the Sixth Amendment and Fifth Amendment rights are nearly identical, although small differences in their application exist.[30]

# Electronic Surveillance

Learning Objective: Define and describe the elements of the Federal Wiretap Act.

A perennial challenge for law enforcement in a free republic is to stay current with, if not ahead of, the changes in the way people steal from and hurt one another. Generally, police are more reactive than proactive in a free society. Historically, this has meant that harm must occur before the law becomes involved. Modern technology puts this dynamic on steroids. The Internet and social media enable fast, widespread harm in new ways. Even more, if the old reactive model is applied, the precise technology used to commit the crime can be changed by the time the problem is identified and law enforcement develops a solution. These challenges are pushing Americans to be more proactive in crime control. This concern, and general crime control objectives, has caused police to use modern technology in ways that pose serious privacy concerns. Continuous tracking of devices, monitoring people through cameras in public and private spaces, and digging into the contents of cell phones are examples of modern surveillance techniques frame the new world of policing.

Underpinning much of digital privacy law is the distinction between content and non-content data. Content data refers to the words, ideas, and substance of a communication. Non-content data is information about communication, such as the telephone numbers of calls placed or received, location data, connections (pings) to cell towers, and other similar data that doesn't reveal the substance of a communication. Most of the time, content data is more protected than non-content data. The rationale is that content data, by its nature, involves more private information than non-content data. A secondary rationale is that non-content data has been shared with a third-party, such as a communications company, while content data has not. The law often treats third-party disclosures as waivers of Fourth Amendment protections. But contemporary technology is challenging these assumptions. Two other important distinctions are between episodic and continuous data collection and short-term and long-term storage.

What appears here is a basic overview of the law of electronic surveillance, both constitutional and statutory. The landmark federal statute in this area of the law is Title III of the Omnibus Crime Control Act and Safe Streets Act of 1968. See Exhibits 14–2 and 14–3. Let's begin the discussion by taking a step back in time with a discussion of older, but still used, forms of surveillance: wiretaps and pen registers.

## Wiretap Act

Title III of the Omnibus Crime Control Act and Safe Streets Act of 1968[31] is a federal statute that regulates the use of electronic surveillance. It is also known as Title III and the Federal Wiretap Act. The Wiretap Act has been amended on several occasions. The Act permits the states to enact similar legislation. State laws may not lessen, although they may increase, the requirements for obtaining a warrant and they must mimic the federal laws in other ways. Today, most states have such legislation. Federal law requires state officials to report their wiretap and other electronic surveillance to the federal government for purposes of monitoring and the prevention of abuse. Exhibit 14–2 summarizes the requirements to conduct electronic surveillance.

The Wiretap Act prohibits wiretapping, bugging, or other electronic surveillance of a conversation when the parties to that conversation possess a reasonable expectation of privacy. The parties to a conversation possess independent privacy rights under the law, so one party to a conversation may not consent to a third party eavesdrop or recording. Violation of the act may result in civil and criminal penalties. Evidence obtained in violation of the act is excluded at trial. The suppression provision does not, however, apply to e-mail.

The statute permits states to enact their own electronic surveillance laws; however, those laws cannot provide less protection of individual rights than the federal statute. A state may, however, provide greater protection of individual rights through its surveillance law than does the federal statute. The USA Patriot Act amended existing surveillance statutes.

## Exhibit 14–2 Summary of Requirements to Conduct Electronic Surveillance

| Form of Surveillance | Requirements for Governmental Surveillance | Remedies for Violations |
| --- | --- | --- |
| Wiretap | Super-warrant | Criminal and civil. Except for e-mail, illegally obtained evidence is excluded at trial. Service providers are exempt when acting in course of employment. |
| Tracking device | Applies to non-content location data. Warrant supported by probable cause. | Traditional liability |
| Stored communication | Applies to content and non-content data. *180 days or less:* Warrant supported by probable cause. *181 days or more:* Notice to subscriber, administrative subpoena, and specific and articulable facts with reasonable grounds to believe data sought will be relevant and material to ongoing investigation. | Criminal (lesser penalties than for Wiretap Act) and civil. Service providers absolutely immune for violations. No suppression of illegally obtained evidence in criminal proceedings. |
| Pen register/ Trap and trace | Applies to non-content call data. Government certifies relevance to investigation. Court to issue order without independent judgment of relevance. | No civil or criminal remedies. No suppression of illegally obtained evidence. |

When the Fourth Amendment and these statutes are viewed as a whole, electronic and wire surveillance can be divided into four categories, each with a different level of privacy protection. They are

1. Wiretaps

2. Tracking devices

3. Stored communications and subscriber information

4. Pen registers and trap devices

Law enforcement officers may not intercept telephone conversations or the content of other electronic messages (e.g., e-mail) without a warrant.[32] Because Congress deemed intrusions into telephone conversations to be significant invasions of privacy, the Wiretap Act requires more than the Fourth Amendment for this form of surveillance. The high standards for issuing a wiretap warrant have led to it being dubbed a "super-warrant." One way that wiretap warrants are more limited than standard warrants is the crimes to which they apply. Standard warrants may be issued for any crime whatsoever. Congress, however, has limited wiretaps to a list of crimes. Over time, the list has grown very large. Espionage, treason, murder, kidnapping, robbery, extortion, mail and wire fraud, drug crimes, gambling, racketeering, bribery of public officials, and terrorism are but a few of the crimes in the list.

To obtain a wiretap order, a high-level official in the U.S. Department of Justice must either apply or authorize another official to apply for an order. Additionally, Title III empowers states to designate high-level prosecutors who may apply for a wiretap order. Such designations must appear in statute. Most states have designated their elected prosecutors and state attorneys general. The application, which shall be supported by oath or affirmation, must contain the following:[33]

1. The identity of the official applying for the order and the official authorizing the application.

2. Evidence establishing probable cause to believe that the person whose communication is to be intercepted has committed, is committing, or is about to commit one of the named crimes.

3. Evidence establishing probable cause to believe that the communication to be intercepted concerns the crime.

4. A statement that other normal investigative procedures have been tried and failed, or that no other procedure is available.

5. The time period during which the interception will occur.

6. A full description of the location where the interception will take place.

7. A statement reflecting all prior attempts to obtain a similar order for any of the same places or persons.

Wiretap applications may be made to federal judges, or if authorized by state statute, to state criminal courts. If the judge grants the application, the order must specify the person whose communication is to be intercepted, the location of the interception, the nature of the communication to be intercepted, the crime involved, and the duration of the interception. Because of the ongoing nature of such investigations, wiretap orders are sealed. In all cases, the surveillance is to cease once the desired information has been seized (recorded). After the interception has ended, the recording is to be given to the judge who issued the order, for safekeeping. See the sidebar for data on the number of wiretap orders issued in 2019.

## Execution of Wiretap Warrants

The statute provides that all communications intercepted shall, if possible, be recorded. The method of recording is to protect against editing and other alterations. The purpose of this requirement is obvious: to preserve the integrity of the evidence.

The statute also requires that all interceptions of irrelevant information be minimized. Said another way, if an officer intercepting a conversation knows that it is unrelated to the investigation, the officer is to stop listening and recording. The minimization requirement is no more than a codification of the Fourth Amendment's reasonableness requirement.

Of course, determining whether an interception is related to the offense under investigation is not always easy, and courts tend to defer to the judgment of the intercepting officer in close cases. The following factors are considered by a reviewing court when a claim is made that interceptions were not properly minimized:

1. The percentage of calls that were related to the investigation. The lower the percentage, the greater the likelihood that the government did not properly minimize its interceptions.

2. The number of calls that were one-time only.

3. The length of the calls intercepted. The shorter the calls, the less opportunity the government had to determine whether the interception was proper.

4. The nature of the calls. The more ambiguous the call, the greater the government's interest in prolonging its interception.[34]

Other factors may also be important to the inquiry. For example, if a known co-conspirator makes frequent calls, interception of all the calls is probably valid, even though most of the suspect's conversations do not concern the conspiracy. Each case must be examined on its own facts to determine whether Title III or the Fourth Amendment has been violated.

Implicit in court orders under this statute is the authority to enter premises to install listening devices. Courts have held that it would be nonsensical to give an officer the authority to conduct surveillance but not to enter the premises of the defendant to install the necessary device. The court order does not have to specifically give this authority; it is implicit in the order itself. Of course, where an officer may go depends on the facts of each case.

The statute authorizes judges to order third parties, such as telephone company personnel, to assist law enforcement officers in executing an electronic surveillance order. Third parties must be compensated for their assistance.

Within 90 days after the expiration of the order, the target of a wiretap order, who is not always the criminal suspect, must be sent notice and an inventory of what was tapped. Judges have the discretion to order that notices also be sent to third parties whose communications were intercepted. Some states, such as California,

## Sidebar

### Crime Stats: Wiretap Orders

There were 2,377 wiretap authorizations in 2020. Most were for phones, portable devices, and apps. Drug crimes, conspiracy, and murder were the three most common crimes to be wiretapped. Most were issued at the state level. Unsurprisingly, the greatest number of wiretap orders were issued in New York and California. The average length of original wiretap authorizations was 30 days. Most order were extended, with a typical length of about two months. All were decoded. Intercepts are costly, averaging nearly $119,418 each. One narcotics wiretap in 2019 led to 17 arrests and one conviction at the time of this writing. It cost nearly $2 million.

*Source:* 2020 Report of the Director of the Administrative Office of the United States Courts on Applications for Orders Authorizing or Approving Interceptions of Wire, Oral, or Electronic Communications.

require that the order itself also be provided. In cases where an ongoing investigation would be jeopardized by the notice, the government may apply to the issuing court for an extension of time to send it.

### Exceptions to the Wiretap Act

In a number of situations, a court order is not required to intercept an electronic communication. Several exceptions are discussed here.

First, be aware that the act tracks the privacy aspect of the *Katz* decision; that is, only communications for which a person has a reasonable expectation of privacy are protected. Because Title III does not expand the privacy protection aspect of the Fourth Amendment, decisions concerning whether a person has a reasonable expectation of privacy under the Fourth Amendment are applicable to Title III.

Second, any employee of a communications company who intercepts an incriminating communication while engaged in the normal course of employment (i.e., maintenance) may disclose such information to the authorities, and it may be used at trial.

Third, officers need not obtain a court order when engaged in certain national security investigations.

Fourth, in emergency situations, when an officer does not have time to obtain a court order, the interception may begin immediately, but an application must be made within 48 hours. If the judge determines that there was no emergency justifying a warrantless tap, then any evidence obtained must be suppressed. However, the statute excludes unlawfully obtained e-mail from the suppression rule.

Finally, parties to conversations or e-mail exchanges may consent to surveillance. So, law enforcement officers and individuals working with law enforcement can record or allow others to listen or read their communications without the consent of the other party.

## Pen Registers and Trap Devices

A pen register is a device that is attached to a telephone line to record the numbers of outgoing calls. A trap and trace device record the numbers of incoming calls. Neither of these devices records or accesses the content of telephone conversations. Because they do not access content, they are not governed by the Fourth Amendment or by the 1968 Title III act. Further, the Supreme Court had held that a person does not possess a privacy interest in the numbers that he or she dials.[35] Even though not required by the Fourth Amendment, the 1986 ECPA[36] requires federal and state law enforcement officers to obtain a court order to install such a device. However, the standard for issuance of the order is relatively low. An officer only needs to certify that the information likely to be obtained is "relevant" to an ongoing criminal investigation. The court to which the application for the order is made does not make an independent decision. Once certified, the court must issue the order. The statute specifically authorizes ex parte issuance of such orders.

Because the Act was adopted before the advent of e-mail, the legal requirements for identifying the recipients and senders of e-mail were unknown until 2001. The Patriot Act answered this question by expanding the definition of pen registers to include computer software that records identifying information of e-mail, such as Internet protocol addresses. Further, the authority of court orders for computer information was expanded to include the entire nation. Previously, such orders could be executed only in the federal district where they were issued. Given the national nature of Internet communications, law enforcement officials often had to seek multiple warrants during a single investigation.

# Stored Communications and Subscriber Records

The Stored Communications Act[37] amendment to Title III authorizes government access to information stored by telecommunications, cable, and Internet provider companies. This includes voice mail and e-mail.

The Stored Communications Act differentiates between information stored for less than 6 months and information stored for longer periods. The greater protection is afforded to communications stored less than 6 months. If 180 days or less, a warrant, supported by probable cause, is required. If 181 days or longer, either a warrant supported by probable cause or in the alternative, notice must be provided to the subscriber; a court order, administrative order, or trial or grand jury subpoena must be issued. Instead of probable cause, these orders may be issued upon a showing of specific and articulable facts that show that reasonable grounds exist to believe the data sought are relevant and material to an ongoing investigation.

The statute also requires a communications provider to give the government access to client information, including name, address, telephone address, session information, and means of payment data (e.g., credit card number). Probable cause and a warrant are not required for this disclosure. Instead, the requirement is for specific and articulable facts supporting a reasonable belief that the records sought are relevant to an ongoing investigation. In counterintelligence and terrorism investigations, the government can obtain stored information simply by certifying that the records are relevant to the investigation.

Violators of the Stored Communications Act are subject to both civil and criminal penalties, although the prison terms and fines are lesser than for violations of the Wiretap Act. Unlike the Wiretap Act, data obtained in violation of the Stored Communications Act are admissible in a criminal prosecution of the accused. Service providers who violate the Stored Communications Act are shielded with absolute immunity from liability. This provision is substantially different from the "acting in the normal course of employment" immunity for violations of the Wiretap Act.

## Tracking and Geo-location Data

Law enforcement authority to use a tracking device is lower than for wiretaps, but higher than for stored communication and pen registers. Standard Fourth Amendment probable cause and particularity requirements are applied to tracking devices. Recall from *United States v. Jones* (2012), discussed in the Chapter 12, that a trespass upon a car to mount a tracking device triggers Fourth Amendment protection. Although the majority based their decision on trespass, Justice Sotomayer raised a concern about the privacy issues that attend continuous tracking, even in the absence of a trespass. The historic rule that a person may be followed by police in public spaces doesn't translate well to the digital age. Historically, officers were limited in their surveillance. It was impossible and cost-prohibitive to follow a person indefinitely. Also, police were limited to public spaces. But digital technology enables 24/7 surveillance that is unlimited by location, is limitless in storage, and costs nearly nothing. The Fourth Amendment limits on the collection of this form of information are still being defined.

The 2018 decision *Carpenter v. United States*, also discussed in an earlier chapter, established that police must have a warrant to obtain customer location data from communication providers, when the data covers a week or longer. Presumably, this will apply to other data as well. You may recall that the Court expressly chose not to extend the Third-Party Doctrine to location information. Equally important, it decided that a person has a privacy interest in location data extending a week or longer. Specifically, the Court wrote that

> The question we confront today is how to apply the Fourth Amendment to a new phenomenon: the ability to chronicle a person's past movements through the record of his cell phone signals. Such tracking partakes of many of the

qualities of the GPS monitoring we considered in *Jones*. Much like GPS tracking of a vehicle, cell phone location information is detailed, encyclopedic, and effortlessly compiled. . . .

A person does not surrender all Fourth Amendment protection by venturing into the public sphere. To the contrary, "what [one] seeks to preserve as private, even in an area accessible to the public, may be constitutionally protected." A majority of this Court has already recognized that individuals have a reasonable expectation of privacy in the whole of their physical movements. Prior to the digital age, law enforcement might have pursued a suspect for a brief stretch, but doing so "for any extended period of time was difficult and costly and therefore rarely undertaken." For that reason, "society's expectation has been that law enforcement agents and others would not—and indeed, in the main, simply could not—secretly monitor and catalogue every single movement of an individual's car for a very long period."

Allowing government access to cell-site records contravenes that expectation. Although such records are generated for commercial purposes, that distinction does not negate Carpenter's anticipation of privacy in his physical location. Mapping a cell phone's location over the course of 127 days provides an all-encompassing record of the holder's whereabouts. As with GPS information, the time-stamped data provides an intimate window into a person's life, revealing not only his particular movements, but through them his "familial, political, professional, religious, and sexual associations." These location records "hold for many Americans the 'privacies of life.' " And like GPS monitoring, cell phone tracking is remarkably easy, cheap, and efficient compared to traditional investigative tools. With just the click of a button, the Government can access each carrier's deep repository of historical location information at practically no expense.

In fact, historical cell-site records present even greater privacy concerns than the GPS monitoring of a vehicle we considered in *Jones*. Unlike the bugged container in *Knotts* or the car in *Jones*, a cell phone—almost a "feature of human anatomy," —tracks nearly exactly the movements of its owner. While individuals regularly leave their vehicles, they compulsively carry cell phones with them all the time. A cell phone faithfully follows its owner beyond public thoroughfares and into private residences, doctor's offices, political headquarters, and other potentially revealing locales. See *id.*, at ___ (slip op., at 19) (noting that "nearly three-quarters of smart phone users report being within five feet of their phones most of the time, with 12% admitting that they even use their phones in the shower"); contrast *Cardwell v. Lewis*, 417 U. S. 583, 590 (1974) (plurality opinion) ("A car has little capacity for escaping public scrutiny."). Accordingly, when the Government tracks the location of a cell phone it achieves near perfect surveillance, as if it had attached an ankle monitor to the phone's user.

Moreover, the retrospective quality of the data here gives police access to a category of information otherwise unknowable. In the past, attempts to reconstruct a person's movements were limited by a dearth of records and the frailties of recollection. With access to CSLI, the Government can now travel back in time to retrace a person's whereabouts, subject only to the retention polices of the wireless carriers, which currently maintain records for up to five years. Critically, because location information is continually logged for all of the 400 million devices in the United States—not just those belonging to persons who might happen to come under investigation—this newfound tracking capacity runs against everyone. Unlike with the GPS device in *Jones*, police need not even know in advance whether they want to follow a particular individual, or when.

Whoever the suspect turns out to be, he has effectively been tailed every moment of every day for five years, and the police may—in the Government's view—call upon the results of that surveillance without regard to the constraints of the Fourth Amendment. Only the few with- out cell phones could escape this tireless and absolute surveillance.

New technology continually challenges the Fourth Amendment. For example, in recent years, border officers have been seizing cell phones, searching their contents, and in some cases, holding them for days—without warrants. Border officers are analogizing the devices as luggage, which they are free to inspect without any individualized suspicion.

This issue will likely see appellate, if not Supreme Court, review in the early 2020s. Another new police technique is geofence searching. A **geofence search** consists of the police obtaining cell phone tower pings, Google use, and similar data for a targeted area around where a crime occurred, during the time of the crime. For example, although unconfirmed at the time this material was written, there were rumors that federal investigators sought records of digital activity in the area around the U.S. Capitol Building during the insurrection of January 6, 2021. Other than location and time, these searches are not particular to any person. In fact, that is the point. They are used to identify suspects. The anonymous data that is received is used to identify specific devices for which the government wants names and account information. At least one federal trial court refused to issue a geofence warrant on the grounds that it failed to meet the particularity and probable cause requirements of the Fourth Amendment. This case featured in the next Oyez.

**geofence search**
The police practice of obtaining location and use data from all devices in the area of a crime during the period of the crime.

# Oyez

## In the Matter of Information Stored at Premises Controlled by Google
### In the United States District Court of the Northern District of Illinois
### Eastern Division (August 24, 2020)

Hon. Gabriel A. Fuentes

### Introduction

While investigating the suspected theft of prescription medications, the government has developed evidence indicating that an unknown individual ("the Unknown Subject") entered two physical locations to receive and ship the stolen medication at specific times. To try to identify the Unknown Subject, the government wants to know which mobile or smartphone devices that transmit their location information to service provider Google, Inc. ("Google") can be known by Google to have been at those two locations at the times when the Unknown Subject was there. The government has proposed a "geofence" search warrant to obtain Google's historical information about what devices were at those locations at those times.

The idea behind a geofence warrant is to cast a virtual net – in the form of the geofence – around a particular location for a particular time frame. The government seeks to erect three geofences. Two would be at the same location (but for different time frames), and one would be at a second location. The window for each geofence is a 45-minute time period on a particular day. As to each of these geofences, the government proposes that Google be compelled to disclose a list of unique device identifiers for devices known by Google to have traversed the respective geofences. The purpose of the geofences is to identify the devices known by Google to have been in the geofences during the 45-minute time frames around the Unknown Subject's appearances on surveillance video entering the two locations on three occasions. By identifying the cell phones that traversed any of the geofences, the government hopes to identify the person suspected in the theft of the pharmaceuticals, under the theory that at least one of the identified devices might be associated with the Unknown Subject. . . .

According to the Amended Application, Google collects location information data from sources including GPS data, cell-site information, wi-fi access points, and Bluetooth beacons within range of a given mobile device. Google offers an operating system known as Android for mobile devices, and devices using the Android operating system have associated Google accounts. Devices that do not run the Android operating system, such as Apple devices, also communicate with Google through Google applications that are available on Apple products. When a device user enables Google's "location services" on an Android device, or a "location sharing" (with Google) feature on a non-Android device, Google collects and retains location data from that device. The location data can show that a certain device was located at a particular place at a particular point in time. From this information, the government can seek to identify the device's user, from information the user may have provided to Google. . . .

The Fourth Amendment bars unreasonable searches and seizures. U.S. Const. amend. IV. In describing the Fourth Amendment as a protection of people and not places, the U.S. Supreme Court has stated that what a person "seeks to preserve as private, even in an area accessible to the public, may be constitutionally protected." *Katz v. United States* . . . The Supreme Court also has recognized that an intrusion need not be "trespassory" to be considered a search for Fourth Amendment purposes. See *United States v. Jones* . . . .

In *Carpenter*, the Supreme Court extended the warrant requirement to "cell-site location information" or "CSLI" maintained by cellular service providers, reasoning that the privacy interest in one's movements, as discoverable through the CSLI, was an interest that modern society was prepared to recognize as reasonable. The Supreme Court in Carpenter spoke of the device holder's "anticipation of privacy in his physical location":

> Mapping a cell phone's location over the course of 127 days provides an all encompassing record of the holder's whereabouts. As with GPS information, the time-stamped data provides an intimate window into a person's life, revealing not only his particular movements, but through them his "familial, political, professional, religious, and sexual associations." These location records "hold for many Americans the 'privacies of life.'"

quoting, among other authorities, *Riley v. California*. In *Riley*, the Court held that a search warrant is required to conduct a search, incident to arrest, of the contents of a suspect's cellular telephone. . . .

*Carpenter* also held that the government's retrieval of CSLI from a third-party service provider qualified as a search for Fourth Amendment purposes, notwithstanding the "third-party" doctrine . . .

## The Fourth Amendment's Probable Cause And Particularity Requirements

Probable cause is "a fair probability that contraband or evidence of a crime will be found in a particular place." Illinois v. Gates, 462 U.S. 213, 238 (1983). Probable cause is a "practical, nontechnical conception" based on "common-sense conclusions about human behavior," and courts determine its existence by analyzing the totality of the circumstances surrounding the proposed intrusion. Id. at 231, 238. The Fourth Amendment also requires that any warrant must "particularly describe[] the place to be searched, and the persons or things to be seized." U.S. Const. amend. IV. The Court will discuss the particularity requirement in somewhat greater detail.

The particularity requirement operates as a protection against arbitrary government intrusions, as the Fourth Amendment's very purpose is "to safeguard the privacy and security of individuals against arbitrary invasions by governmental officials." The Fourth Amendment has its roots in colonial resistance to "the reviled 'general warrants' and 'writs of assistance' of the colonial era, which allowed British officers to rummage through homes in an unrestrained search for evidence of criminal activity." In 1965, the U.S. Supreme Court commented that its past recitations of "the detailed history of the use of general warrants as instruments of oppression from the time of the Tudors, through the Star Chamber, the Long Parliament, the Restoration, and beyond" was so well-trodden that to review it again would be "a needless exercise in pedantry." The Court nonetheless recounted:

> In Tudor England officers of the Crown were given roving commissions to search where they pleased in order to suppress and destroy the literature of dissent, both Catholic and Puritan. In later years warrants were sometimes more specific in content, but they typically authorized of all persons connected of the premises of all persons connected with the publication of a particular libel, or the arrest and seizure of all the papers of a named person thought to be connected with a libel.

. . . General warrants permit "a general, exploratory rummaging in a person's belongings," an "evil" that the Fourth Amendment addresses by requiring a particular description of the things to be seized in the search. The particularity requirement's bar on general warrants protects not only the sanctity of a person's home but also "the privacies of life." . . .

## Fourth Amendment Analysis of the Amended Application

Probable Cause Determination

First, as to the proposed warrant's requested authority for disclosure of just the anonymized information and not the actual subscriber records disclosing the identities of the account holders for those devices, the Court sees no practical difference between a warrant that harnesses the technology of the geofence, easily and cheaply, to generate a list of device IDs that the government may easily use to learn the subscriber identities, and a warrant granting the government unbridled discretion to compel Google to disclose some or all of those identities. . . . The proposed warrant, and the application of the geofence technology embedded in it, therefore give the government all the tools it needs to learn individuals' location histories, which, as we have said, are treated here – in the government's search warrant application – as information that cannot be obtained without full Fourth Amendment compliance. . . .

(continued)

Second, with the Amended Application seeking a form of authority that will harness geofence technology to cause the disclosure of the identities of various persons whose Google connected devices entered the geofences, the government must satisfy probable cause as to those persons. On the Amended Application now before the Court, along with the related briefing, the government has not established probable cause to believe that evidence of a crime will be found in the location history and identifying subscriber information of persons other than the Unknown Subject. There is likely a fair probability that the Amended Application's proposed warrant will generate location information, and device IDs that are the functional equivalent of the identities of the device users, that will include the identification of the Unknown Subject and will thus include evidence of the crime, but it will include other information as well: The location information of persons not involved in the crime.

The Seventh Circuit has not yet spoken explicitly on "all persons" warrants, but Ybarra remains good law and remains instructive in the analysis of whether a warrant allowing a seizure of information about all persons who traverse the three geofences can pass constitutional muster. In Ybarra, police obtained a warrant to search a public tavern and the bartender for narcotics, but the police expanded the warrant's terms and searched a bar patron who was present there. The Supreme Court held that a search of everyone in the bar, including the patron, violated the Fourth Amendment, concluding:

> [A] person's mere propinquity to others independently suspected of criminal activity does not, without more, give rise to probable cause to search that person. Where the standard is probable cause, a search or seizure of a person must be supported by probable cause particularized with respect to that person. This requirement cannot be undercut or avoided by simply pointing to the fact that coincidentally there exists probable cause to search or seize another or to search the premises where the person may happen to be.

In effect, the government in the Amended Application seeks the same type of authority, based only on device users' "propinquity" to the crime scenes or to the Unknown Subject, that Ybarra held was not supported by individualized probable cause.

Particularity Determination

. . . the [requested] warrant puts no limit on the government's discretion to select the device IDs from which it may then derive identifying subscriber information from among the anonymized list of Google-connected devices that traversed the geofences. A warrant that meets the particularity requirement leaves the executing officer with no discretion as to what to seize, Stanford, 379 U.S. at 485, but the warrant here gives the executing officer unbridled discretion as to what device IDs would be used as the basis for the mere formality of a subpoena to yield the identifying subscriber information, and thus, those persons' location histories. . . .

It is also possible to imagine other applications of geofence technology that might comport with Fourth Amendment standards. Say, for example, that the government develops information supporting probable cause to believe that its geofences will not capture the information of uninvolved persons, such as a scenario in which the government can establish independently that only the suspected offender(s) would be found in the geofence, or where probable cause to commit an offense could be found as to all present there. . . . But the proposed warrant would grant the government far greater discretion, namely, to sort through the location information and derivative identifying information of multiple people to identify the suspect by process of elimination. This amount of discretion is too great to comply with the particularity requirement . . .

## Conclusion
\* \* \*

For the foregoing reasons, and by applying the Fourth Amendment to the government's proposed warrant in the Amended Application, the Court must deny the Amended Application and the warrant requested under it.

# National Security Surveillance

In 2013, Edward Snowden, an employee of the National Security Agency (NSA), the lead U.S. agency responsible for collecting foreign intelligence and for securing U.S. intelligence systems, disclosed sensitive information to the press. The United States charged him with espionage and theft of government property; he fled the United States and was eventually awarded temporary asylum by Russia.[38] His case became an international media sensation, provoking discussions around the world about data collection by governments, democratic governance (privacy versus national security), international relations, and about the specific information that was disclosed, much of it embarrassing to the United States. But Snowden's case wasn't the first to raise the questions about information collection in the post–9/11 United States. There were other disclosures and discoveries, by federal government employees and others, that caused many people to worry about the erosion of privacy and abuses of power by federal officials. Indeed, the Department of Justice acknowledged that the NSA collected private data in violation of the law, although rarely.[39] As you will see below, at least one federal court has also found that the NSA violated national security law in its collection of data on U.S. persons in its Terrorist Surveillance Program.

Earlier, you learned some of the criminal laws of national security, laws of sedition, treason, and terrorism. National security is receiving special attention in this book because the rise in the terror threat in the United States has resulted in greater surveillance and detention authority by federal officials and because there has been a rapid increase in technology that enables surveillance into nearly every corner of life and mind.

National security law is highly complicated, spanning criminal law, administrative law, and constitutional law. The most significant legislation is the Foreign Intelligence Surveillance Act of 1978 (FISA).[40] FISA regulates the collection of foreign intelligence by government officers, whether through wiretaps, pen registers, trap devices, and other electronic means, The 1978 FISA Act, which was enacted in response to intelligence gathering by the President Nixon administration, was substantively amended by the United and Strengthening America by Providing Appropriate Tools Required to Intercept and Obstruct Terrorism Act of 2001 (aka the Patriot Act) and again in 2007 and 2008. These amendments widened the authority of federal officials to gather intelligence, often without court order.

Balancing the need for oversight and for secrecy, Congress provided in FISA for the establishment of the Foreign Intelligence Surveillance Court (FISC) and the Foreign Intelligence Act Court of Review (FIACR). These courts are staffed by Article III federal judges who are appointed to the courts by the Chief Justice of the U.S. Supreme Court. FISC has the responsibility of issuing surveillance orders and reporting on its activities to Congress. FIACR acts as FISC's appellate court. FIACR's decisions may be appealed to the U.S. Supreme Court. In the interests of national security, both courts meet in secret. Although its hearings and deliberations are secret, the membership of the courts and their annual reports to Congress are available to the public. Select FISC orders, particularly those interpreting FISA, have been made public. In addition to FISC's reports, the Department of Justice issues an annual report to Congress summarizing its FISA activities, including its applications for FISC orders, surveillance conducted without FISC order, and summaries of surveillance conducted.

FISA, and many judicial decisions that predated FISA, is constructed around the idea that the Fourth Amendment distinguishes standard criminal cases from national security cases. Criminal investigations are aimed at preventing, discovering, and punishing crime, typically targeting persons in the United States, while national security cases are aimed at preventing attacks and protecting the political, economic, and social interests of the United States through surveillance of foreign governments and their agents. At the highest levels, the distinction is clear. Closer to the ground, in individual cases, it is more difficult to discern. The legal distinction is significant.

In an attempt to preserve the balance between privacy of U.S. persons and the need to gather data threatening the security of the nation, FISA initially authorized the United States to "spy" on two targets: foreign powers and agents of foreign powers. Foreign governments, officers of foreign governments, and entities doing the work of foreign governments are all foreign powers. Agents of foreign powers include anyone, except U.S. citizens and permanent residents, who act on behalf of foreign governments in clandestine information gathering in the United States. So, the original FISA applied to foreign governments and their spies.

Through the Patriot Act and other amendments to FISA, the definition of foreign power has been expanded to include groups engaged in international terrorism, foreign political groups that are not substantially composed of U.S. persons, and entities not substantially composed of U.S. persons engaged in the international proliferation of weapons of mass destruction. Agents of foreign powers have also been expanded to include non–U.S. persons engaged in international terrorism or the international proliferation of weapons of mass destruction, even if unconnected to a foreign power.

FISA applies to the collection of foreign intelligence. The provisions of FISA authorizing the United States to collect data apply only if it can be shown that the data relate to, or are necessary to prevent, attacks or other grave hostile acts upon the United States by a foreign power or agents of foreign powers, the proliferation of weapons of mass destruction, spying on the United States, or espionage, or are needed to advance foreign affairs or the security of the nation.

Generally, an FISC order is required for the federal government to conduct foreign intelligence surveillance. FISC must find that probable cause exists to believe that the target of the surveillance is a foreign power or an agent of a foreign power and that the form of communication to be intercepted is in the foreign power's control. Business records orders are easier for the government to obtain. The government only has to show that the records are relevant to an ongoing investigation.

During ordered surveillance, FISA requires the attorney general to "minimize" the acquisition, retention, and dissemination of records about U.S. persons. In cases where intelligence officers and law enforcement officers are working together, a "wall" must be created, keeping records acquired during foreign surveillance from criminal investigators. That evidence must be obtained by criminal investigators by other means.

There are two instances where an FISC order is not required for surveillance. The president may authorize surveillance if the attorney general certifies, under oath, that the communication devices to be monitored belong to foreign powers or that it is "technical intelligence" from a foreign power being sought. The law is clear that U.S. persons are not to be targets: "There is no substantial likelihood that the surveillance will acquire the contents of any communication to which a U.S. person is a party." Additionally, the attorney general is to minimize and report these activities. Since an amendment to FISA in 1995, the president is also authorized to order the intrusion of physical spaces controlled by foreign governments in order to collect intelligence. FISC has the same authority.

The 1978 version of FISA required that *the purpose of foreign surveillance* be the collection of foreign intelligence. In a highly criticized change, the Patriot Act softened *the purpose* requirement to *significant purpose*, thereby permitting the government to have other primary objectives, such as gathering criminal evidence.

Generally, the president is authorized, through the attorney general, to collect foreign intelligence information from foreign governments for as long as a year. If the target is an agent of a foreign government, the attorney general must petition FISC for an order.

FISA also empowers the government to obtain data from third parties, typically communication companies. In some instances, third parties have voluntarily provided information or access to their systems for the government to collect data. In others, the government has obtained FISC orders. In recent years, third-party authority has been scrutinized in the context of metadata, or non-content information. An example of metadata is the government's collection of phone numbers dialed but not the content of those conversations. In its review of an application for an order to capture a huge amount of "telephony metadata," FISC ruled in 2013 that such intelligence gathering is analogous to the phone records sought in *Smith v. Maryland*.[41] In that case, the Supreme Court held that when an individual dials a phone number he is transmitting the data to a third party, the telephone company, and as a consequence loses his privacy in the number he dialed. For this reason, the acquisition of the number dialed, but not the content of the call, does not implicate the Fourth Amendment. FISC held that this conclusion is not changed because of the size of the data request.[42] The amendments to the FISA mentioned earlier empowered the FISC to review and approve programs that collect metadata, in addition to individual orders of surveillance.

One particularly controversial authority created by the Patriot Act is the National Security Letter (NSL). Without subpoena, the government is empowered to demand non-content data from Internet service providers, communication companies, universities, libraries, and businesses about their clients. Again, non-content data include websites visited, telephone numbers called, and e-mail addresses. Thousands—in some years, tens of thousands—of NSLs have been issued yearly since 9/11. NSLs come with a "gag" order. That is, the recipient of the NSL is ordered, under criminal penalty, to not disclose to anyone, including the target of the NSL, that the letter has been received. A federal district judge found this and other provisions of the NSL law to be contrary to the First Amendment's protection of free speech and the Fourth Amendment in 2013.[43]

FISC is aimed at foreign governments and its agents, abroad. As you can see, the authority of the United States to spy on U.S. persons abroad is limited to when U.S. persons are acting as foreign agents and when engaged in terrorism. If the United States wants to conduct a search within the United States, the Fourth Amendment and the Title III rules you have already learned apply, even if the underlying offense is a violation of a national security law. If the government acquires otherwise-protected information during an otherwise legitimate surveillance, the information is to be destroyed unless the contents indicate a threat of serious bodily harm or death to any person.

An extended discussion of national security law is beyond the scope of a criminal law and procedure text. Be aware, however, that many other statutes, executive orders, and judicial decisions exist defining this rapidly evolving area of law.

# Pretrial Identification Procedures

Learning Objective: Define, describe, and apply the constitutional rules governing pretrial identification.

Law enforcement officers use a variety of techniques to identify a person as a criminal, such as eyewitness identifications, fingerprinting, blood tests, and, recently, deoxyribonucleic acid (DNA) tests. The use of any of these procedures raises certain constitutional issues, such as the right to be free from self-incrimination and the right to counsel.

There is also another concern: reliability. Eyewitness identification, though powerful, has inherent problems. First, each person will testify to his or her perception of an event, and people often perceive the same event differently. Second, not every person will use the same language to describe what was witnessed. Third, a witness may simply have a faulty memory and unintentionally testify to an untruth. Fourth, for a variety of reasons, a witness may intentionally lie.

Scientific testing may also prove to be invalid or unreliable. How accurate is the test when performed properly? Was the test performed properly in this case? Is the evidence tested actually the defendant's? These types of questions are asked of expert witnesses who testify to the results of scientific testing. This discussion begins with eyewitness identification procedures.

## Eyewitness Identification

Learning Objective: Explain what social science has discovered about the fallibility of eyewitness identifications and how the law attempts to mitigate the risk of misidentification.

An eyewitness's identification of an offender is often a key piece of evidence in criminal cases. It is generally regarded that eyewitness testimony is one of the most persuasive forms of evidence that can be presented to jurors.

## Fairness in Identification

There are two competing values concerning the reliability of evidence at trial. The first concerns the nature of the jury trial. The adjudicatory system is constructed around the jury as the finder of fact. In the extreme, jurors should hear all evidence and be trusted to distinguish between the reliable and unreliable. The other value is one of fair process, as enshrined in the due process clauses. Due process demands that seriously unreliable evidence be withheld from a jury.

The Supreme Court has issued several decisions that are intended to gauge the balance of these competing values. In *Stoval v. Denno,* 388 U.S. 293 (1967), the Supreme Court found that the Due Process Clauses of the Fifth and Fourteenth Amendments prohibit identifications that are so *unnecessarily suggestive* that there is a real chance of misidentification. In addition to being impermissibly suggestive, an identification must be *unreliable* to be excluded.[44] *Wade* the case in the next Oyez, illustrates these concepts as applied to lineups.

Evidence is not automatically excluded even when police employ an identification procedure that is unnecessarily suggestive. Instead, the trial court is to make an independent determination of whether the process was unreliable (e.g., created a *substantial likelihood of misidentification*). If so, the identification is to be excluded. When making the decision of substantial likelihood of misidentification, a court is to examine the "totality of the circumstances" surrounding the identification. Examples of impermissibly suggestive were mentioned in the *Wade* opinion. For example, if a witness states that a white male committed a crime, it would be improper to exhibit four black men and one white man in a lineup.

## Oyez

### United States v. Wade
### 338 U.S. 218 (1967)

**MR. JUSTICE BRENNAN delivered the opinion of the Court.**

The question here is whether courtroom identifications of an accused at trial are to be excluded from evidence because the accused was exhibited to the witness before trial at a post-indictment lineup conducted for identification purposes without notice to and in the absence of the accused's appointed counsel.

The federally insured bank in Eustace, Texas, was robbed on September 21, 1964. A man with a small strip of tape on each side of his face entered the bank, pointed a pistol at the female cashier and the vice president, the only persons in the bank at the time, and forced them to fill a pillowcase with the bank's money. The man then drove away with an accomplice who had been waiting in a stolen car outside the bank. On March 23, 1965, an indictment was returned against respondent, Wade, and two others for conspiring to rob the bank, and against Wade and accomplice for the robbery itself.

Wade was arrested on April 2, and counsel was appointed to represent him on April 26. Fifteen days later an FBI agent, without notice to Wade's lawyer, arranged to have the two bank employees observe a lineup made up of Wade and five or six other prisoners and conducted in a courtroom of the local county courthouse. Each person in the line wore strips of tape such as allegedly worn by the robber and upon direction each said something like "put the money in the bag," the words allegedly uttered by the robber. Both bank employees identified Wade in the lineup as the bank robber.

At trial, the two employees, when asked on direct examination if the robber was in the courtroom, pointed to Wade. The prior lineup identification was then elicited from both employees on cross examination. . . . But the confrontation compelled by the State between the accused and the victim or witnesses to a crime to elicit identification evidence is peculiarly riddled with innumerable dangers and variable

(continued)

factors which might seriously, even crucially, derogate from a fair trial. The vagaries of eyewitness identification are well-known; the annals of criminal law are rife with instances of mistaken identification. . . . The identification of strangers is proverbially untrustworthy. . . . A major factor contributing to the high incidence of miscarriage of justice from mistaken identification has been the degree of suggestion inherent in the manner in which the prosecution presents the suspect to witness for pretrial identification. A commentator has observed that "[t]he influence of improper suggestion upon identifying witnesses probably accounts for more miscarriages of justice than any other single factor—perhaps it is responsible for more such errors than all other factors combined.". . . Suggestion can be created intentionally or unintentionally in many subtle ways. And the dangers for the suspect are particularly grave when the witness' opportunity for observation was insubstantial, and thus his susceptibility to suggestion the greatest.

> Moreover, "[i]t is a matter of common experience that, once a witness has picked out the accused at the lineup, he is not likely to go back on his word later on, so that in practice the issue of identity may (in the absence of other relevant evidence) for all practical purposes be determined there and then, before the trial.". . .

> What facts have been disclosed in specific cases about the conduct of pretrial confrontations for identification illustrate both the potential for substantial prejudice to the accused at that stage and the need for its revelation at trial. A commentator provides some striking examples:

> > In a Canadian case . . . the defendant had been picked out of a lineup of six men, of which he was the only Oriental. In other cases, a black-haired suspect was placed among a group of light-haired persons, tall suspects have been made to stand with short non-suspects, and, in a case where the perpetrator of the crime was known to be a youth, a suspect under twenty was placed in a lineup with five other persons, all of whom were forty or over.

> Similarly, state reports, in the course of describing prior identifications admitted as evidence of guilt, reveal numerous instances of suggestive procedures, for example, that all in the lineup, but the suspects were known to the identifying witness, that the other participants in a lineup were grossly dissimilar in appearance to the suspect, that only the suspect was required to wear distinctive clothing which the culprit allegedly wore. . . .

> > Since it appears that there is grave potential for prejudice, intentional or not, in the pretrial lineup, which may not be capable of reconstruction at trial, and since presence of counsel can often avert prejudice and assure a meaningful confrontation at trial, there can be little doubt that for Wade the post--indictment lineup was a critical stage of the prosecution at which [he] was [entitled to counsel]. . . .

> > [The Court then concluded that in-court identifications must be excluded if they follow a lineup at which a defendant is not permitted counsel, unless the in-court identification has an independent origin.]

*Wade, Stoval,* and other decisions defining this area of law were issued in the 1970s. Subsequently, a wealth of research in human memory has called the reliability of eyewitness identification into question. The problems of unconscious bias, blurred memory, the ways in which memories are stored and retrieved, and the phenomena of reconstructed memory all make memory fallible and often unreliable.

The advent of forensic identification procedures that are highly accurate, such as DNA testing, have been used to establish the innocence of many people whose convictions were based, often largely, on eyewitness identification. Eyewitness identification played a role in the conviction of as many as 75% of convictions that were overturned through DNA testing.[45] The problem of wrongful convictions, because of eyewitness misidentification and other causes, is so acute that a nonprofit group, the Innocence Project, was formed to raise funds, provide legal defense, and support research. The Innocence Project reports that more than 250 people have been exonerated using DNA testing since 1989.[46]

Consequently, many people have called for a more critical review of eyewitness testimony than required by the 1970s' decisions. The Court rejected this position in *Perry v. New Hampshire* (2012). The defendant in this case urged the Court to modify the test from its requiring proof that police created a suggestive situation to any suggestive circumstance, police created or not. The defendant pointed to the large number of studies that demonstrate the unreliability of eyewitness identifications in support of his position. Rejecting the proposition, the Court found that (1) one of the purposes of the unnecessarily suggestive rule it had created was to deter police misconduct and that extending the protection in the manner suggested would not achieve this goal; (2) juries should be trusted to determine the reliability of evidence in all but the most extreme cases; (3) trial judges have the authority, both constitutionally and through rules of evidence, to exclude evidence that is misleading or prejudicial; and (4) the trial judge will instruct the jury in how to evaluate the reliability of the eyewitness testimony.

## Lineups and Showups

A **lineup** is where the police exhibit a group of people, among whom is the suspect, to a witness or victim for identification as the criminal. A one-man **showup** is an exhibition of one person to a witness or victim for identification as the criminal.

In practice, police first conduct a lineup and then, if the suspect is identified, the witness is asked at trial to testify that he or she identified the perpetrator of the crime at the lineup. Therefore, if the initial identification is faulty, the subsequent in-court identification is also faulty. Even if the witness is asked to identify anew the perpetrator of the crime, such an identification is tainted by the witness's earlier identification.

One-man showups, obviously, are more suggestive of guilt than lineups are. As such, they should be used with caution. Generally, a one-man showup should occur soon after the crime (minutes or hours). If there is time to organize a lineup, this is the preferable method of identification procedure.

## The Right to Counsel

*Wade* mandates that counsel be provided at pretrial lineups and showups. For years, it was unknown whether this meant all pretrial lineups and showups or just those after the Sixth Amendment attaches. *Kirby v. Illinois*, (1972)[47] resolved this dispute by requiring counsel only after initiation of "adversary judicial proceedings—whether by way of formal charge, preliminary hearing, indictment, information, or arraignment."

## Self-Incrimination

It is not violative of the Fifth Amendment's privilege against self-incrimination for a defendant to be compelled to appear in a lineup. The privilege against self-incrimination applies to "testimony" and not to physical acts, such as walking, gesturing, measuring, or speaking certain words for identification purposes.[48] If a defendant has changed in appearance, he or she may be made to shave, to don a wig or hairpiece, or wear a certain article of clothing.

The question under the Fifth Amendment is whether the act requested is "communicative." If so, then the defendant may not be compelled to engage in the act. If not, the opposite is true.

Today, witness identification through photo arrays is more common than using lineups. The due process test discussed earlier applies to the use of photos; that is, the event must not be impermissibly suggestive and unreliable. The showing of one picture is likely to be determined improper, absent an emergency. As is true of lineups, the people in the photos should be similar in appearance. Also, a "mug shot" (a picture taken by law enforcement agencies after arrest) of the accused should not be mixed with ordinary photos of nonsuspects. Nor should the photos be presented in such a manner that the defendant's picture stands out.

The Supreme Court has determined that there is no right to counsel at a photo identification session, either before initiation of the adversary judicial proceeding or thereafter.

**lineup**
A group of persons, placed side by side in a line, shown to a witness of a crime to see if the witness will identify the person suspected of committing the crime. A *lineup* should not be staged so that it is suggestive of one person.

**showup**
A pretrial identification procedure in which only one suspect and a witness are brought together.

# Forensic Evidence

Learning Objective: Describe the tests used to determine the validity and reliability of evidence.

Law enforcement officials may use scientific methods of identification to prove that a defendant committed a crime. Fingerprinting, blood tests, genetic tests (deoxyribonucleic acid, or DNA, testing), voice tests, and handwriting samples are examples of such techniques.

Such tests are not critical stages of the criminal proceedings, and, accordingly, there is no right to counsel. There is also no right to refuse to cooperate with such testing on Fifth Amendment grounds, because the defendant is not being required to give testimony. However, if a test involves an invasion of privacy, then the Fourth Amendment requires probable cause before the procedure may be forced on an unwilling defendant.

Confrontation and cross-examination clause issues are raised when forensic experts testify as to what other experts have found or analyzed. See Chapter 15 for a more thorough discussion of these issues.

## Validity and Reliability

Scientific evidence must be reliable before it may be introduced at trial. In a landmark case, *Frye v. United States*, 293 F. 1013 (D.C. Cir. 1923), it was held that scientific techniques must be generally accepted as valid and reliable by the scientific community to be admissible. *Frye* was the law from 1923 until the Supreme Court issued *Daubert v. Merrell Dow Pharmaceuticals*, 113 S. Ct. 2786 (1993). *Daubert* changed the standard of admissibility from acceptance in the scientific community to scientific validity. Under this new standard, the trial judge is required to make a preliminary determination that

Crime scene marked by forensic investigators

Digital Storm/Shutterstock.com

the proffered evidence is valid before it may be presented to a jury. In making this decision, the trial judge is to consider the following factors:

1. Whether the evidence or theory has, or can be, tested.
2. Whether it has been reviewed and tested by other scientists.
3. Whether the method has been published and the quality of the publication(s) in which it is found.
4. Whether its error rate and other potential defects are known.
5. Whether standards and protocols for its use have been established.
6. Whether its use is widely accepted in the relevant scientific community.

Techniques that are experimental and not highly reliable are not admissible. A few common scientific techniques are discussed here. Note that the results of a specific test may be denied admission, even if the scientific basis of the testing is valid, if the test is administered incorrectly. Further, scientific testing also raises Fourth, Fifth, Sixth, and Fourteenth Amendments issues, some of which are discussed later.

### Fingerprinting

A fingerprint consists of several identifiable characteristics, such as loops, arches, whorls, islands, and bifurcations. The arrangement, frequency, and design of these features are among the many characteristics used to distinguish prints from one another. See Exhibit 14–3 for a fingerprint and a fingerprint

## Exhibit 14–3 A Fingerprint and Fingerprint Card

© Seth Joel/Digital Vision/Getty Images

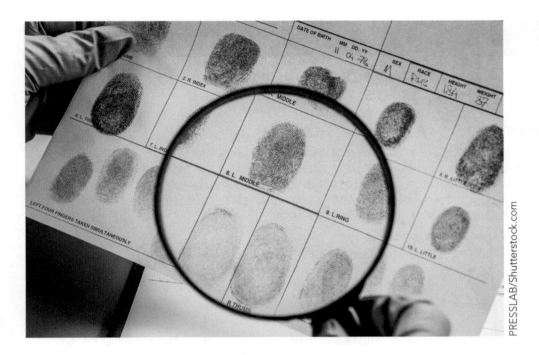

card. Although it is common to state that every person has a unique set of prints, there is a possibility of duplication. However, the odds of that occurring have been estimated to be as low as 1 in 64 billion.[49]

Fingerprint identification is a highly accurate science and is universally accepted by federal and state courts.[50] Federal and state law enforcement agencies, as well as international agencies, possess libraries of fingerprints. Through the use of computers, fingerprints lifted from crime scenes, weapons, and other objects can be matched to a particular individual's fingerprints in a matter of minutes. Lifted prints may be matched to a print already on file or to a print taken from a suspect.

The taking of fingerprints does not implicate the Fifth Amendment, because the accused is not compelled to give testimony. Further, it is not a search to take a suspect's fingerprints. This being so, neither probable cause nor a warrant is required to take the suspect's prints. Courts have analogized fingerprints to physical characteristics such as hair and eye color. Because it is not an invasion of a reasonable expectation to privacy (search) for an officer to visually observe a defendant, courts have reasoned that it is not an invasion of privacy to observe and record a suspect's fingerprints.

## Blood Testing

Blood testing is commonly employed and universally accepted by courts in the United States. Although the science of blood testing is generally beyond scrutiny, individual blood tests are not. Laboratories make mistakes, and both the defense and the prosecution may challenge a particular test.

Securing a suspect's blood is different from rolling a fingerprint. The process of withdrawing blood involves a bodily invasion and the possibility of pain and infection. Therefore, a person's expectation of privacy is higher when the government seeks blood rather than fingerprints. In *Schmerber v. California*,[51] *the Supreme Court decided that the* withdrawal of blood, as well as other bodily intrusive procedures, constitutes a search under the Fourth Amendment. Probable cause is required, as is a warrant, unless exigent circumstances, such as those in *Schmerber,* justify bypassing the warrant requirement. In addition, such procedures must be conducted in a safe, discrete, medical environment. Read the *Schmerber* case in the Oyez feature.

# Oyez

## Schmerber v. California
### 384 U.S. 757 (1966)

**MR. JUSTICE BRENNAN delivered the opinion of the Court.**

Petitioner was convicted in Los Angeles Municipal Court of the criminal offense of driving an automobile while under the influence of intoxicating liquor. He had been arrested at a hospital while receiving treatment for injuries suffered in an accident involving the automobile that he was apparently driving. At the direction of a police officer, a blood sample was then withdrawn from petitioner's body by a physician at the hospital. The chemical analysis of this sample revealed a percent by weight of alcohol in his blood at the time of the offense which indicated intoxication, and the report of this analysis was admitted in evidence at trial. . . .

### II. THE PRIVILEGE AGAINST SELF- INCRIMINATION CLAIM

. . . We . . . must now decide whether the withdrawal of the blood and admission in evidence of the analysis involved in this case violated petitioner's privilege. We hold that the privilege protects an accused only from being compelled to testify against himself, or otherwise provide the State with evidence of a testimonial or communicative nature, and that the withdrawal of blood and use of the analysis in question in this case did not involve compulsion to these ends. . . .

### IV. THE SEARCH AND SEIZURE CLAIM

The overriding function of the Fourth Amendment is to protect personal privacy and dignity against unwarranted intrusion by the State. . . .

The values protected by the Fourth Amendment thus substantially overlap those the Fifth Amendment helps to protect. . . .

Because we are dealing with intrusions into the human body rather than with state interferences with property relationships or private papers—"house, papers, and effect"—we write on a clean slate. . . .

In this case, as will often be true when charges of driving under the influence of alcohol are pressed, these questions arise in the context of an arrest made by an officer without a warrant. Here, there was plainly probable cause for the officer to arrest petitioner and charge him with driving an automobile while under the influence of intoxicating liquor. The police officer who arrived at the scene shortly after the accident smelled liquor on petitioner's breath, and testified that petitioner's eyes were "bloodshot, watery, sort of a glassy appearance." The officer saw petitioner again at the hospital, within two hours of the accident. There he noticed similar symptoms of drunkenness. He thereupon informed petitioner "that he was under arrest and that he was entitled to the services of an attorney, and that he could remain silent, and that anything he told me would be used against him in evidence." . . .

Although the facts which established probable cause to arrest in this case also suggested the required relevance and likely success of a test of petitioner's blood for alcohol, the question remains whether the arresting officer was permitted to draw these inferences himself, or was required instead to procure a warrant before proceeding with the test. Search warrants are ordinarily required for searches of dwellings, and, absent an emergency, no less could be required where intrusions of the human body are concerned. . . . The importance of informed, detached and deliberate determinations of the issue whether or not to invade another's body in search of evidence of guilt is indisputable and great.

The officer in the present case, however, might reasonably have believed that he was confronted with an emergency, in which the delay necessary to obtain a warrant, under the circumstances, threatened "the destruction of evidence." . . . We are told that the percentage of alcohol in the blood begins to diminish shortly after drinking stops, as the body functions to eliminate it from the system. Particularly in a case such as this, where time had to be taken to bring the accused to a hospital and to investigate the scene of the accident, there was no time to seek out a magistrate and secure a warrant. . . .

Finally, the records show that the test was performed in a reasonable manner. Petitioner's blood was taken by physician in a hospital environment according to accepted medical practices. We are thus not presented with the serious questions which would arise if a search involving use of a medical technique, even of the most rudimentary sort, were made by other than medical personnel or in other than a medical environment—for example, if it were administered by police in the privacy of the stationhouse. To tolerate searches under these conditions might be to invite an unjustified element of personal risk of infection and pain.

The Supreme Court refused to create a per se rule out of the *Schmerber* decision in the 2013 case *Missouri v. McNeely.* In that case, Missouri argued that the inherently evanescent nature of alcohol justified, per *Schmerber,* the routine warrantless drawing the blood of drivers who refuse to submit to breath testing and where police have probable cause to believe the drivers have been driving while intoxicated. The Court penned the following:

It is true that as a result of the human body's natural metabolic processes, the alcohol level in a person's blood begins to dissipate once the alcohol is fully absorbed and continues to decline until the alcohol is eliminated. . . . But it does not follow that we should depart from careful case-by-case assessment of exigency and adopt the categorical rule proposed by the State and its amici. In those drunk-driving investigations where police officers can reasonably obtain a warrant before a blood sample can be drawn without significantly undermining the efficacy of the search, the Fourth Amendment mandates that they do so.

The context of blood testing is different in critical respects from other destruction-of-evidence cases in which the police are truly confronted with a "'now or never'" situation. In contrast to, for example, circumstances in which the suspect has control over easily disposable evidence, BAC evidence from a drunk-driving suspect naturally dissipates over time in a gradual and relatively predictable manner. Moreover, because a police officer must typically transport a drunk-driving suspect to a medical facility and obtain the assistance of someone with appropriate medical training before conducting a blood test, some delay between the time of the arrest or accident and the time of the test is inevitable regardless of whether police officers are required to obtain a warrant.

The State's proposed per se rule also fails to account for advances in the 47 years since *Schmerber* was decided that allow for the more expeditious processing of warrant applications, particularly in contexts like drunk-driving investigations where the evidence offered to establish probable cause is simple. The Federal Rules of Criminal Procedure were amended in 1977 to permit federal magistrate judges to issue a warrant based on sworn testimony communicated by telephone. As amended, the law now allows a federal magistrate judge to con- sider "information communicated by telephone or other reliable electronic means." Fed. Rule Crim. Proc. 4.1. States have also innovated. Well over a majority of States allow police officers or prosecutors to apply for search warrants remotely through various means, including telephonic or radio communication, electronic communication such as e-mail, and video conferencing. And in addition to technology-based developments, jurisdictions have found other ways to streamline the warrant process, such as by using standard-form warrant applications for drunk-driving investigations.

The extent of the intrusion into the body, the medical risk of the intrusion, and the likelihood of the evidence being lost to delay are all factors in the decision whether a warrant must be obtained. Requiring a driver arrested for driving under the influence to submit to a breath test, for example, was upheld because it is less invasive than a blood test.[52] Also, as you read in the last chapter, the warrantless scraping of blood from the fingernail of an accused murderer was upheld by the Supreme Court because it involved no medical risk and the risk of destruction of the evidence was large.[53]

But the opposite conclusion was reached in *Winston v. Lee*,[54] where the Supreme Court employed the analysis outlined in *Schmerber* and concluded that a defendant accused of armed robbery could not be compelled to undergo surgery to remove a bullet from his chest. The Court held that the suspect's interest in his health and bodily privacy outweighed the government's interest in obtaining the evidence. Also important to the Court was the fact that the government had other evidence to prove the defendant's guilt. This lowered the government's interest in having the bullet removed. If the bullet had been critical to the government's case, the result might have been different.

## DNA Testing

*Deoxyribonucleic acid* (DNA) is a complex compound with two strands that spiral around one another, forming a double helix. Within the helix are molecules, called

## **Exhibit 14–4** A DNA Strand

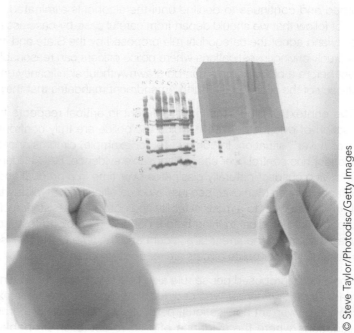

Steve Taylor/Photodisc/Getty Images

**DNA printing**

Comparing body tissue samples (such as blood, skin, hair, or semen) to see if the genetic materials match. The process is used to identify criminals by comparing their DNA with that found at a crime scene, and it is used to identify a child's parent. Most states allow its use as evidence.

*nucleotide bases,* that connect the strands. There are four bases, identified by the letters A, T, G, and C. The A base of one strand attaches to the T base of its counterpart strand. In the same manner, the G base of one strand connects to the C base of the opposing strand. There are more than 3 billion base pairs in human DNA. However, only 3 million of these differ from person to person. The precise vertical ordering of these pairs determines a person's genetic code. See Exhibit 14–4.

Through biological specimens, such as hair, blood, tissue, and semen, evidence from crime scenes can be compared with specimens from suspects. This testing is known as **DNA printing** or *genetic fingerprinting.* DNA printing compares the codes and determines if they are from the same individual. DNA testing is sophisticated, and if properly performed, testing nearly conclusively establishes identity. The possibility of a chance match, assuming perfect testing, has been estimated to be 1 in 3 trillion.[55]

DNA has proven to be an effective weapon for both prosecutors and defendants. In recent years, several convicted felons have used DNA testing to prove their innocence and secure their release. This has occurred, for example, in rape cases where blood and semen were used as prosecution evidence, but DNA testing was unavailable. After their conviction, and from prison, these men used DNA testing to establish their innocence and set aside their verdicts. Prosecutors are increasingly relying on DNA evidence to prove their cases. DNA evidence was first used in a criminal prosecution in the United States in 1987. Forty-two percent of prosecutors reported having used DNA evidence by 1994, and the number rose to 68% by 2001. DNA evidence is most commonly used in sexual assault and murder cases. Overall, conviction rates in cases where prosecutors have introduced DNA evidence are high.

DNA testing is not perfect. The testing method is sophisticated, and errors can be made. For instance, methodology was hotly contested in the O. J. Simpson murder trial of 1995. Further, interpretations of test results differ. It is, therefore, imperative that a reliable laboratory be selected. Further, in some cases, the defense and prosecution may have independent DNA testing conducted. Despite the possibility of error (false positive and false negative findings), courts have generally held that DNA evidence is sufficiently reliable for admission into evidence. The parties may, of course, challenge the accuracy of a particular DNA test.[56]

In recent years the federal government and several states have enacted legislation concerning the use of DNA in criminal proceedings. For example, Congress authorized the creation of a national DNA database (CODIS) in 1994. Ironically, however, the statute did not authorize the collections of samples; CODIS remained unused until 2000, when federal law was changed to require the collection of samples from all individuals convicted of federal crimes.

Today, statutes in all 50 states authorize state and local officials to collect DNA samples from individuals convicted of terrorism acts and violent, sexual, and some property crimes. These samples are entered in CODIS. In 2006, the federal DNA Fingerprint Act of 2005 became effective.[57] This law expands collection of DNA samples to include individuals arrested and detained by federal authorities. However, DNA samples are to be destroyed and records expunged for individuals whose cases have been dismissed.

In many states and the federal government, another recent change in law has been the use of DNA evidence to toll the applicable statute of limitation. In these jurisdictions, law enforcement may use the DNA fingerprint in lieu of a name to file the charge and obtain an arrest warrant for the individual identified by the DNA. Once the warrant is issued, the statute of limitation is tolled. A few states, including Colorado, have gone so far as to automatically toll the statute after a suspect has been identified by DNA evidence.[58]

An open question is whether police must have probable cause or obtain a warrant before conducting noninvasive DNA tests, such as cheek swabs. Also, the right of a suspect to counsel at pretrial noninvasive DNA testing hasn't been answered by the Supreme Court. At least one state court has determined that only reasonable suspicion is required, no warrant must be obtained, and there is no right to counsel during DNA cheek swabs.[59]

The practice of systematically taking DNA samples from felony arrestees was upheld the Supreme Court in *Maryland v. King* (2013). The Court reasoned that the many benefits of the testing, the reliability and validity of the science, and the minimal invasion of a cheek swab justified the practiced.

## Voice Tests

Compelling a suspect to speak for the purposes of audio identification is not violative of the Fifth Amendment's prohibition against compelled self-incrimination. This is because the purpose in compelling the statements is identification, not to secure testimony. Again, the voice is considered a physical characteristic that is readily observable to the ordinary person; accordingly, it is not a search under the Fourth Amendment to compel a suspect to speak.

Voice is also at issue whenever a party intends to introduce audio records that purport to be a particular individual's, such as the defendant. For example, assume John is charged with murdering Henry. The police have in their possession a tape from John's telephone answering machine. The tape contains a threat to Henry's life that the government claims was made by John. To prove that John made the threat, the prosecutor plans to introduce voice spectrographic identification evidence.

This test involves a comparison of the recording and a voice sample provided by the defendant. It compares the complex sound waves of the two for similarity. The accuracy of voice spectrographics is questionable, and therefore this type of evidence is not universally accepted by courts. In some jurisdictions, admissibility is prohibited, whereas in others the decision is left to the trial judge.

## Polygraph Tests

Polygraph testing, also known as lie detection testing, measures a subject's physical responses, such as heartbeat, blood pressure, and perspiration, during questioning. This is not a new concept. The Chinese monitored the heartbeat of suspects as long as 4,000 years ago. If a suspect's heartbeat increased during a response, he was presumed to have lied. Until recently, courts have held that the results of polygraph evidence are too unreliable to be admitted at trial, unless the parties have stipulated to admission. Today, however, a few jurisdictions permit the introduction of polygraph evidence if it is determined reliable. That is, polygraph evidence is not automatically excluded, but it may be if found to be unreliable in a specific case. In *United States v. Scheffer* (1998),[60] the Supreme Court held that defendants do not have a right to introduce the results of a polygraph examination over the objection of the prosecution and where evidentiary rules preclude polygraph results. The Court found that the right of defendants to present evidence has been limited historically to that which is reliable. The Court found that the scientific community is divided on the reliability of polygraph exams and asserts; the results of such exams may be excluded at trial.

In addition to the issue of reliability, a Fifth Amendment self-incrimination issue surfaces when a prosecutor seeks an order requiring a defendant to undergo a polygraph examination.[61] The Supreme Court has stated in dictum, and the lower courts have similarly ruled directly, that lie detector tests involve communications and, accordingly, that the Fifth Amendment applies. Defendants may refuse to respond to questions when the answers may be incriminating, and *Miranda*-type warnings should be given before the test begins, assuming that custody exists. Further, a prosecutor may not refer to a defendant's refusal to submit to polygraph testing at trial.

## Chain of Custody

**chain of custody**
The chronological list of those in continuous possession of a specific physical object. A person who presents physical evidence (such as a gun used in a crime) at a trial must account for its possession from the time of receipt to time of trial in order for the evidence to be "admitted" by the judge. It must thus be shown that the *chain of custody* was unbroken.

To ensure that physical evidence discovered during an investigation remains unchanged and is not confused with evidence from other investigations, police must maintain **chain of custody**. The officer who discovered the evidence must mark it; and all subsequent contacts with the evidence, such as by forensics officers, must be recorded. This creates a record known as the chain of custody. Chain-of-custody records must be kept from the time the evidence is seized until it is introduced at trial. Breaks in the chain of custody may result in exclusion of the evidence at trial.

In some instances, evidence may be admitted even though the chain of custody has been broken. If evidence is easily identified by a witness, such as its owner, then proving the chain of custody may not be necessary. This may also be true if an item is unique and can be precisely identified by its characteristics (e.g., serial and model numbers). Even in these cases, chain of custody is sometimes required, and the best practice is for the police to maintain a chain in every instance.

The burden of establishing the chain of custody rests with the party seeking admission. The standard of proof is characterized differently among the states, but usually amounts to a preponderance of the evidence. In some jurisdictions, proof of police policy, custom, and practice may be used to prove chain of custody.

# Exclusion of Improper Identifications

The consequences of not providing counsel during an identification procedure after the adversary judicial proceeding has begun were discussed in *Wade*. First, testimony about an illegal identification must be excluded at trial. Second, in-court identifications may be excluded if tainted by the pretrial identification. However, if the government can show, by clear and convincing evidence, that an in-court identification has a source independent of the illegal pretrial identification, then it is to be allowed. The *Wade* Court said the following factors are to be considered when making the taint or no taint determination:

1. The prior opportunity to observe the criminal act.
2. The difference between a witness's pre-lineup description and actual description of an accused.
3. Whether the witness identified another person as the criminal before the lineup.
4. Whether the witness identified the accused by photograph prior to the lineup.
5. Whether the witness was unable to identify the accused on a previous occasion.
6. The lapse of time between the crime and the identification.

In most cases, a court will find an independent source for an in-court identification and will allow a witness to identify the defendant during trial, while prohibiting mention of the pretrial identification.

The same rules apply to identifications that are impermissibly suggestive and unreliable. They must be excluded, as must the fruits thereof, unless an independent basis for an in-court identification can be shown.

## Ethical Considerations

### Legal Advice as War Crime?

In response to a request from then White House Counsel (and soon to be attorney general) Roberto Gonzales, two Department of Justice attorneys—John Yoo, deputy assistant attorney general, and Jay S. Bybee, assistant attorney general (soon to be U.S. district judge)—drafted a memorandum in 2002 addressing questions that the Central Intelligence Agency had concerning interrogation methods that may be used in the War on Terror. Specifically, the definition of torture was sought. The memo, commonly known as the "torture memo," defined torture as

> Physical pain [the] equivalent in intensity to the pain accompanying serious physical injury, such as organ failure, impairment of bodily function, or even death. . . . We conclude that the statute, taken as a whole, makes plain that it prohibits only extreme acts.

The memo went on to conclude that to qualify as mental torture, treatment "must result in significant psychological harm of significant duration, e.g., lasting for months or even years."

Many scholars and commentators have criticized the memo, alleging that it was not well reasoned and because it was relied on by the White House, abuses of detainees of the War on Terror resulted. Yoo, who has been a vocal defender of the memo, contends that the definition was largely driven by Congress' definition of torture, which was developed when Congress ratified the United Nations Convention Against Torture.

Some scholars have moved beyond criticizing Bybee and Yoo for their analysis; instead, they claim the authors violated their ethical responsibilities as lawyers in rendering the opinion. So much so, some have charged—including Milan Markovic—they were reckless and complicit in war crimes. According to Markovic, that they did not torture anyone themselves is not dispositive. Recklessness is the mens rea of aiding and abetting the international war crime of abusing detainees. He contends that the International Criminal Court, of which the United States is not a member, as well as other nations, has jurisdiction to try the men.

It is highly unlikely that either attorney will be charged, domestically or abroad. It is also unlikely that their bar memberships will be challenged. However, as international accountability grows, these questions will occur more frequently, and the attorney's role and responsibilities in public international law will likely change.

See Milan Markovic, "Can Lawyers Be War Criminals?" 20 *Geo. J. Legal Ethics* 347 (2007); John Yoo, *The Powers of War and Peace* (Chicago: University of Chicago Press, 2005); and John Yoo, "Behind the 'torture memos,'" *UCBerkeleyNews*, January 4, 2005. *http://www.berkeley.edu*

## Key Terms

admission
chain of custody
confession

DNA printing
geofence search
interrogation

lineup
showup

## Review Questions

1. List the rights included in the *Miranda* warnings. When must they be read to a defendant?

2. What happens if an officer fails to read a defendant his or her rights before obtaining a confession?

3. Is it a violation of the Federal Wiretap Law (Title III of the Omnibus Crime Control and Safe Streets Act) for Gary to allow law enforcement officers to listen to a telephone conversation between himself and Terry without Terry's knowledge? If so, what happens if Terry makes incriminating statements?

4. Does a defendant have a right to counsel at a lineup? If so, what is the source of that right?

5. Does a defendant have a right to counsel at a photograph identification session? If so, what is the source of that right?

6. Why must law enforcement officers obtain a court order to intercept a telephone conversation using traditional line phones and not a conversation using a cordless phone?

7. What is chain of custody?

8. Assume that a prosecutor wants a defendant to submit to genetic testing to compare the defendant's DNA with that of hair found on a victim. Does the defendant have a Fourth Amendment challenge? A Fifth?

## Problems & Critical Thinking Exercises

1. While on patrol, Officer Norman heard a scream from the backyard of a house. The officer proceeded to the back of the house, where he observed two people—a badly beaten victim and a young man (Tom) standing over her. Shocked by the sight of the victim, the officer exclaimed, "What happened here?" Tom responded, "I killed her and threw the baseball bat over the fence." Officer Norman restrained the young man, called for an ambulance, and retrieved the bat. While waiting for the ambulance to arrive, Officer Norman asked the young man what his motive was for injuring the woman. Tom explained his motive to the officer. The officer never *Mirandized* Tom. A motion to suppress the statement, "I killed her and threw the baseball bat over the fence," as well as the statement explaining his motive, has been filed. Additionally, Tom claims that the bat should be excluded because it is a fruit of an illegal interrogation. What should be the outcome? Explain your answer.

2. An officer has made application for a court order approving electronic surveillance of Defendant. The order is granted, stating: "From June 1 to June 7, Officer X, having established probable cause, is granted the authority to intercept the wire communications of Defendant." The officer proceeded to enter Defendant's house, without a warrant, to install the listening device. Eventually, a recording is made of Defendant discussing his illegal activities with a friend. Defendant is arrested, charged, and has filed a motion to suppress the interception. Defendant asserts that the entry into his house was illegal. Discuss.

3. Why are the rules concerning the admissibility of confessions more stringent than for other forms of evidence?

4. Do you believe that it is self-incrimination to give blood, hair, and other such items that might prove one's guilt?

5. Describe a pretrial identification which you believe is unduly suggestive. Explain why it is too suggestive of guilt.

# Endnotes

1. *Escobedo v. Illinois* 378 U.S. 478 (1964).
2. Desmond S. O'Neill, *From Third-Degree to Third-Generation Interrogation Strategies: Putting Science into the Art of Criminal Interviewing.* Thesis in Support of Master's Degree. Naval Graduate School. March 2017.
3. See *Frazier v. Cupp*, 394 U.S. 731 (1969), *State v. Cobb*, 115 Ariz. 484; 566 P.2d 285 (AZ 1977), and *State v. Jackson*, 308 N.C. 549 (1983).
4. *Wilson v. United States*, 162 U.S. 613 (1896).
5. *Bram v. United States*, 168 U.S. 532 (1897). See also *Ziang Sung Wan v. United States*, 266 U.S. 1 (1924).
6. *Brown v. Mississippi*, 297 U.S. 278 (1936).
7. *Salinas v. Texas* 570 U.S. 178 (2013).
8. 499 U.S. 279.
9. Fed. R. Evid. 804(b)(5).
10. *McNabb v. United States*, 318 U.S. 332 (1943), and *Mallory v. United States*, 354 U.S. 449 (1957).
11. *Corley v. United States*, 556 U.S. 303 (2009).
12. *Florida v. Powell*, 559 U.S. 50 (2010).
13. *Stansbury v. California*, 511 U.S. 318 (1994).
14. *J.D.B. v. North Carolina*, 564 U.S. 261 (2011).
15. 446 U.S. 291 (1980).
16. *Garrity v. New Jersey*, 385 U.S. 493 (1967).
17. See *Hiibel v. Sixth Judicial District*, 542 U.S. 177 (2004).
18. *New York v. Quarles*, 467 U.S. 649 (1984).
19. Found at http://www.nytimes.com/2011/03/25/us/25miranda-text.html (May 16, 2013).
20. *Boston bombing suspect stops talking after being read Miranda rights.* Associated Press, April 15, 2013. Found at http://www.nj.com/news/index.ssf/2013/04/ boston_bombing_suspect_stops_t.html
21. *Illinois v. Perkins*, 496 U.S. 292 (1990).
22. *Massiah v. United States*, 377 U.S. 201 (1964).
23. *Pennsylvania v. Bruder*, 488 U.S. 9 (1988).
24. *Davis v. United States*, 512 U.S. 452 (1994).
25. *Michigan v. Mosley*, 423 U.S. 96 (1975).
26. 542 U.S. 600 (2004)
27. *Oregon v. Haas*, 420 U.S. 714 (1975).
28. *United States v. Patane*, 542 U.S. 630 (2004).
29. 109 Ohio St. 3d 519 (2006).
30. See *Montejo v. Louisiana*, 556 U.S. 778 (2009).
31. 18 U.S.C. § 2510 et seq.
32. Although the U.S. Supreme Court has not fully addressed the e-mail issue, see *United States v. Councilman*, 418 F.3d67 (1st Cir. 2005).
33. 18 U.S.C. § 2518.
34. *Scott v. United States*, 436 U.S. 128 (1978).
35. *Smith v. Maryland*, 442 U.S. 735 (1979).
36. 18 U.S.C. § 2511.
37. 18 U.S.C. §§ 2701 et. seq.

38. Max Ehrenfreund, Asylum for NSA Leaker Edward Snowden a Challenge to U.S.–Russia Relations. *Wall Street Journal*, August 2, 2013. Can be found at Washingtonpost.com

39. Eva Perez and Shiobhan Gorman, NSA Exceeds Legal Limits in Eavesdropping Program. *Wall Street Journal*, April 16, 2013. Found at http://online.wsj.com/news/articles/SB123985123667923961

40. 50 U.S.C. sec. 36 et seq. and 36 U.S.C. sec 1801 et seq.

41. 442 U.S. 735 (1979).

42. *In Re Application of the FBI for an Order, Amended Memorandum Opinion.* Foreign Intelligence Surveillance Court. Docket No. 13-109. August 29, 2013.

43. Ellen Nakashima, *FBI Surveillance Tool Ruled Unconstitutional. Washington Post,* March 15, 2013. This can be found by searching Washingtonpost.com

44. *Manson v. Braithwaite,* 432 U.S. 98 (1977).

45. *Eyewitness Identification: a policy review.* Found at innocenceproject.org

46. Innocenceproject.org.

47. 406 U.S. 682.

48. *Schmerber v. California,* 384 U.S. 757 (1966).

49. Braun, "Quantitative Analysis and the Law: Probability Theory as a Tool of Evidence in Criminal Trials," 1982 *Utah L. Rev.* 41, 57 n.82.

50. For a case where a U.S. district judge questioned whether the science of fingerprinting was adequately developed to satisfy the *Daubert* test, see *United States v. Llerla Plaza,* 179 F.Supp.2d 492 (E.D. Pa. 2002).

51. *Schmerbe v. California,* 384 U.S. 757 (1966),

52. 136 S. Ct. 2160 (2016).

53. 412 U.S. 291 (1973).

54. 470 U.S. 753 (1985).

55. Dodd, "DNA Fingerprinting in Matters of Family and Crime," 26 *Med. Sci. L.* 5 (1986).

56. Morland, *An Outline of Scientific Criminology,* 59–60 (2nd ed., 1971). Jeffrey M. Prottas & Alice A. Noble, "Use of Forensic DNA Evidence in Prosecutors' Offices," 35 *J.L. Med. & Ethics,* 310, 311–13 (2007).

57. The law can be found in 42 U.S.C. § 14135a.

58. See, for example, Colo. Rev. Stat. § 16-5-401 (8)(a.5) (2006).

59. *Arturo Garcia-Torres v. Indiana, No. 64A03-0812-CR-630,* In App.Ct. (Sept. 30, 2009).

60. 523 U.S. 303.

61. *Schmerber v. California,* 384 U.S. 757, 764 (1966).

# Chapter 15

# The Pretrial Process

## Chapter Outline

This chapter presents an outline of the basic process a criminal case goes through, from before arrest until trial. The next chapter is devoted to the criminal trial. As you learned earlier in this book, the United States doesn't have one criminal justice system. Each state, territory, and the federal government have different processes. The federal process is used for illustration. Exhibit 15–1 provides a visual summary of the entire process. You may find it helpful to refer to it as you learn the different stages of the process.

## Investigation and Arrest

Learning Objective: Describe the investigative stage of a criminal case, including the elements of a criminal complaint.

The process begins when law enforcement officials learn of a crime that has been committed (or is being, or about to be, committed). Police learn of criminal activity in two ways: they may discover it themselves, or it is reported to them.

Once police are aware of criminal activity, the pre-arrest investigation begins. There are two objectives to this stage. First, police must determine whether a crime has been committed. Second, if a crime has been committed, police attempt to gather sufficient evidence to charge and convict the person believed to have committed the crime.

# Exhibit 15–1 Visual Summary of The Basic Criminal Process

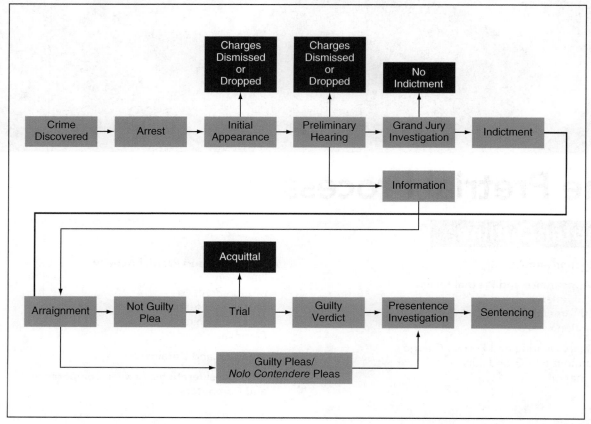

**arrest**
The official taking of a person to answer criminal charges. This involves at least temporarily depriving the person of liberty and may involve the use of force. An arrest is usually made by a police officer with a warrant or for a crime committed in the officer's presence.

When enough evidence is discovered to establish probable cause, **arrest** often follows. However, in some misdemeanor cases, a defendant is asked to come to the police station (to "surrender" themself), and an arrest is not made unless the defendant refuses. The arrest may be made without an arrest warrant in some situations. In others, an ex parte hearing may be held to determine if probable cause exists to believe the suspect committed the crime. If so, the judge may issue an arrest warrant.

At the time of arrest, police ordinarily search the defendant. Once at the police station, the defendant is "booked." *Booking* consists of obtaining biographical information about the defendant (name, address, etc.), fingerprinting the defendant, and taking the defendant's photograph, commonly known as a "mug shot." The defendant is usually permitted to make a telephone call at this stage.

The defendant is then searched (sometimes deloused and showered) and held in jail until further arrangements are made. For minor offenses, the defendant may be able to post bail prior to appearing before a judge. In such cases, defendants are out of jail within hours. All others wait for a judge to set a bail amount at an initial appearance. During and after this stage, law enforcement investigation and gathering of evidence may continue.

## The Complaint

**complaint**
A *criminal complaint* is a formal document that charges a person with a crime.

At this stage, a police officer, or less often a prosecutor, files a **complaint**, which acts as the initial charging instrument. Fed. R. Crim. P. 3 states: "The complaint is a written statement of the essential facts constituting an offense charged. It shall be made upon oath before a magistrate." The officer who creates the complaint doesn't have to have personal knowledge about the crime. The officer may rely on hearsay and circumstantial evidence. Also, the evidence detailed in the complaint doesn't have to be admissible at trial. Affidavits from those who have personal knowledge, such as witnesses and victims, are often attached to the complaint.

When a warrant is sought to arrest a defendant, the complaint is often produced in support of the request for a warrant. This occurs at the ex parte hearing mentioned earlier. Federal law requires that a warrant be issued if probable cause is established by the complaint and its accompanying affidavits. Upon the request of the government, a summons (an order to appear) may be issued rather than an arrest warrant.[1]

If the defendant was arrested without a warrant, the complaint serves as the charging document at the initial appearance or preliminary hearing.

For traffic violations and some lesser misdemeanors, the complaint, a ticket for traffic violations, acts as both a summons to appear in court and the charging document. In such cases, the defendant appears in court on only one occasion, and the ticket is used in place of an information or indictment. Exhibit 15–2 shows the first two pages of the federal complaint filed against Ethan Nordean, a defendant in the January 6, 2021, U.S. Capitol insurrection. The complaint is much longer and can be easily found in the FBI website. In these first two pages, however, you will see the basic format of a complaint.

# Initial Appearance and Pretrial Release

Learning Objective: Describe the initial appearance and detail the forms of pretrial release and the causes to deny pretrial release.

After arrest, the defendant is taken "without unnecessary delay" before the nearest available federal magistrate.[2] In most cases, this means that a defendant will be brought before the judge within 24 hours. However, if a defendant is arrested on a weekend, it may be the following Monday before the defendant has the initial appearance, unless a weekend session of court is held.

The first appearance is brief. If the arrest was executed under an arrest warrant, it is the duty of the judge to confirm that the person arrested is the person named in the warrant. The defendant is also informed of various rights, such as the rights to remain silent and to have the assistance of counsel. If the defendant is indigent, the court will appoint counsel. The right to counsel is discussed more fully later. If the arrest was warrantless, an initial probable cause determination must occur.

In 1991, the U.S. Supreme Court examined the need for prompt probable cause determinations in warrantless arrest situations. In *County of Riverside v. McLaughlin*,[3] the Court held that persons arrested without a warrant must have a probable cause determination within 48 hours after arrest or quicker if reasonable. A defendant who asserts unreasonable delay, but was held less than 48 hours before a probable cause hearing was conducted, bears the burden of proving that the delay was unreasonable under the Fourth Amendment. If a defendant is held longer than 48 hours without a probable cause hearing, the burden of showing a bona fide emergency or other extraordinary circumstance falls on the government.

Time to gather additional evidence, ill will, and the fact that the defendant was arrested on a weekend are not sufficient to delay the probable cause determination longer than 48 hours.

Finally, a preliminary hearing date is set, and if the defendant is in jail, the court determines whether he or she should be released prior to trial.

## Exhibit 15–2 Criminal Complaint

AO 91 (Rev. 08/09)  Criminal Complaint

# UNITED STATES DISTRICT COURT
for the

District of Columbia

United States of America
v.
ETHAN NORDEAN
also known as "Rufio Panman"
▉▉▉▉▉▉▉▉▉

Case No.

_____
*Defendant(s)*

**CRIMINAL COMPLAINT**

I, the complainant in this case, state that the following is true to the best of my knowledge and belief.

On or about the date(s) of _____ January 6, 2021 _____ in the county of _____ in the

_____ District of ___ Columbia ___, the defendant(s) violated:

| Code Section | Offense Description |
|---|---|
| 18 U.S.C. § 1361 and 2 | Aid and Abet Injury or Depredation Against Government Property |
| 18 U.S.C. § 1512(c)(2) | Obstruct or Impede an Official Proceeding. |
| 18 U.S.C. Section 1752(a) | Knowingly Entering or Remaining in Restricted Building or Grounds. |
| 40 U.S.C. §§ 5104(e)(2)(D)and G) | Violent Entry and Disorderly Conduct on Capitol Grounds. |

This criminal complaint is based on these facts:

See the attached affidavit, which is incorporated herin by reference.

❏ Continued on the attached sheet.

▉▉▉▉▉▉▉▉▉▉▉▉▉▉▉
▉▉▉▉▉▉▉▉▉▉▉▉▉▉▉
▉▉▉▉▉▉▉▉▉▉▉▉▉▉▉
▉▉▉▉▉▉▉▉▉▉▉▉▉▉▉

*Printed name and title*

Sworn to before me and signed in my presence.

Date: _____ 02/02/2021 _____

2021.02.02
22:09:59 -05'00'

*Judge's signature*

City and state: _____ Washington, D.C. _____

Zia M. Faruqui, U.S. Magistrate Judge
*Printed name and title*

**Exhibit 15–2** *(Continued)*

## AFFIDAVIT IN SUPPORT OF A CRIMINAL COMPLAINT

I, ███████████ , being first duly sworn, hereby depose and state as follows:

### PURPOSE OF AFFIDAVIT

1.      This Affidavit is submitted in support of a Criminal Complaint charging Ethan Nordean ("NORDEAN"), also known as "Rufio Panman," with violations of 18 U.S.C. § 1512(c)(2), 18 U.S.C. §§ 1361, 2, 18 U.S.C. § 1752(a), and 40 U.S.C. §§ 5104(e)(2)(D) and (G), in connection with his actions at and inside the U.S. Capitol on or about January 6, 2021. I respectfully submit that this Affidavit establishes probable cause to believe that NORDEAN (i) corruptly did obstruct, influence, or impede an official proceeding before Congress—that is, the certification of the Electoral College; (ii) did aid and abet others, both known and unknown, to forcibly enter the Capitol and thereby cause damage to the building in an amount more than $1,000—that is, NORDEAN aided and abetted individuals who removed barricades and broke windows to storm the Capitol building; (iii) did knowingly enter or remain in a restricted building or grounds, *i.e.*, the U.S. Capitol, without lawful authority, or did knowingly, and with intent to impede or disrupt the orderly conduct of Government business or official functions, engage in disorderly or disruptive conduct; and (iv) did willfully and knowingly engage in disorderly or disruptive conduct, at any place in the Grounds or in any of the Capitol Buildings with the intent to impede, disrupt, or disturb the orderly conduct of a session of Congress or either House of Congress, or the orderly conduct in that building of any deliberations of either House of Congress.

### BACKGROUND OF AFFIANT

2.      I am a Special Agent with the Federal Bureau of Investigation (FBI) and have been so since February 2019. As such, I am an officer of the United States who is empowered by law

## Pretrial Release

In old England, jail conditions were unsanitary and inmates often died from disease, malnutrition, or abuse before trial. For this reason, release pending trial became the norm. The Framers operationalized practice by including the Eighth Amendment's Bail Clause in the Bill of Rights. Although not yet incorporated, it is treated as a fundamental right by all states and courts. In many cases, defendants are released prior to trial. A court may order many types of release, but the most common methods are cash bail, surety bond, property bond, and personal recognizance.

**bail**

The money or property given as security for a defendant's appearance in court. The money, often in the form of a bail bond, may be lost if the released defendant does not appear in court.

Posting **bail** is a common way for a defendant to secure their release. Bail is money a defendant deposits with a court to secure their pretrial freedom. If the arrestee appears in court as required, the money is returned. The money is forfeited if the defendant runs from the law. A defendant who has the resources may simply pay into the court the amount of the bail.

Many defendants don't have the cash to pay the full amount of bail. They either remain in jail pending trial, borrow the money from a family member or friend, offer collatoral (e.g. a home or car), or they secure a bail bond. A bail bond is a form of insurance. The defendant pays a fee (commonly 8%—10% of the bail amount) to a bond agent who acts as a surety (insurance) with the court. If the defendant doesn't appear in court, the bail agent pays the court the full amount of the bail. If the defendant appears, the bail agent keeps the fee.

For many misdemeanors and a few felonies, a defendant may be released on personal recognizance. A defendant needs only promise to appear.

Regardless of the type of release, courts frequently impose conditions upon the defendant. Defendants who arrested, intimidate witnesses or others involved in the prosecution, destroy evidence, possess a firearm, or violate protective orders may be jailed until trial.

## Eighth Amendment

The Eighth Amendment proscribes the imposition of "excessive bail." This provision may be applicable to the states through the Fourteenth Amendment. The purpose of imposing money bail is to ensure the defendant's appearance at trial, not to inflict punishment. Bail set higher than necessary to accomplish this purpose is deemed excessive.[4] In practice, courts have significant discretion in setting bail and are rarely reversed.

The Supreme Court has held that the mere fact that a defendant cannot pay the amount set by a court does not make it excessive. Additionally, the Court has stated that not all defendants have a right to bail. Defendants who are a danger to the community or unlikely to appear for trial may be held without bail.

The exact meaning of the Eighth Amendment has not been spelled out by the Supreme Court. Whether pretrial detention laws, especially those that create a presumption of detention, are constitutional remains to be seen.

## Detention

Although pretrial release is the default, all jurisdiction permit the detention of some defendants prior to trial. Pretrial detention may not be used to punish a person. To do so violates a person's due process right to be free from punishment without a fair trial. However, pretrial detention is permitted if the defendant

1. presents a flight risk or
2. is a danger to themselves or others or
3. will obstruct justice, such as intimidating witnesses, jurors, or officials.

In the federal system, the defendant is entitled to an adversary hearing concerning pretrial detention, and the government must prove by clear and convincing evidence that the defendant is either dangerous or unlikely to appear for trial.[5] The adversary hearing must be held at the initial appearance, or, upon the motion of the defendant or the government, it may be continued.

Although the general rule is that the government bears the burden of proving that a defendant must be detained, there are exceptions. There are two classes of presumptions in the federal statute. One presumes that certain defendants will not appear for trial, and another presumes that certain defendants are a danger to the community. For example, defendants charged with crimes of violence who have a prior conviction for a crime of violence, which was committed while the defendant was released pending trial, are presumed to be dangerous to the community. It is also presumed that defendants charged with drug crimes that carry 10 years or more imprisonment will flee. These presumptions also apply to many other defendants.[6] The presumption is rebuttable, and the defendant has the burden of disproving it. Some question the constitutionality of such presumptions, and it remains to be seen whether such statutes will be reversed or upheld.

Many states have statutes that require detention of persons charged with crimes punishable by life imprisonment or death, provided that the proof of guilt is great.

# Preliminary Hearing and Formal Charge

Learning Objective: Describe the preliminary hearing and the two formal methods of charging a defendant.

The defendant's second appearance before a judge is the **preliminary hearing**. How this stage is handled by the states varies significantly. At the preliminary hearing, the court determines if probable cause exists to believe the accused committed the crime. If probable cause is found, the defendant is "bound over" to the next stage of the process. The next stage is either trial or review by grand jury. If probable cause is not established, the defendant is released.

If indictment by grand jury is required, the case is bound over to the grand jury. The grand jury is not bound by the judge's decision that probable cause exists; it makes an independent decision whether to charge the defendant. If grand jury review is not required, the defendant is bound over for trial.

The purpose of the preliminary hearing is to have an impartial third party review the facts to be sure that probable cause exists. There is no constitutional requirement for a preliminary hearing.[7] However, many states do provide for preliminary hearings.

It is common to permit prosecutors to bypass the preliminary hearing either by submitting the case to a grand jury or by directly filing an information. Defendants often waive the preliminary hearing. In some states, prosecutors may demand a preliminary hearing over the objection of the defendant.

The preliminary hearing can be quite lengthy compared to a defendant's initial appearance. The hearing is adversarial. Witnesses are called, and the attorneys are allowed to make arguments. Rules of evidence are applied in modified form, so hearsay and illegally obtained evidence are often considered. Defendants have a right to counsel and may also be allowed to cross-examine the prosecution witnesses and to present defense witnesses. The right to counsel is a matter of federal constitutional law. The other two rights are granted by state laws. The preliminary hearing can be an important asset to both prosecution and defense, as it can serve as a source of discovery.

The preliminary hearing is different from the initial probable cause determination required by *County of Riverside v. McLaughlin*. The initial determination is constitutionally required, whereas the preliminary hearing is not. Further, although the same terminology is used (i.e., probable cause), less evidence is needed to satisfy the government's obligation at the initial determination than at the preliminary

**preliminary hearing**
The first court proceeding on a criminal charge, in federal courts and many state courts, by a magistrate or a judge to decide whether there is enough evidence for the government to continue with the case and to require the defendant to post bail or be held for trial.

hearing. Probable cause at the initial hearing equates with the probable cause required to obtain a warrant, which is generally recognized as requiring less proof than does probable cause at the later preliminary hearing. Also in contrast is the fact that the probable cause hearing required by *County of Riverside* will likely be one-sided. That is, only the government will present evidence. Some states, however—such as California—permit defendants to present evidence at preliminary hearings.

Fed. R. Crim. P. 5 requires that the date for "preliminary examination" be scheduled at the defendant's initial appearance. It shall be held within 10 days of the initial appearance if the defendant is in custody and within 20 days if the defendant has been released.

In federal courts and in many states, probable cause may be founded upon hearsay evidence.[8] Motions to suppress illegally seized evidence are made after the preliminary hearing, so such evidence may be considered at the preliminary examination stage. If a grand jury has issued an indictment, the preliminary hearing may be dispensed within the federal system.[9] Many states have a similar rule.

There are two formal charges: the **information** and the **indictment**. Informations are charges filed by prosecutors. Indictments are charges issued by grand juries. Once filed, an information or indictment replaces the complaint and becomes the formal charging instrument.

## Indictment and Grand Jury

### Purpose of the Grand Jury

In early American history, **grand juries** were used to guard against unfair and arbitrary government prosecutions and to preserve the reputation of a person investigated—the **target**—but who is not ultimately charged. The Framers of the U.S. Constitution thought grand jury review so important that it is included in the Fifth Amendment: "[N]o person shall be held to answer for a capital, or otherwise infamous, crime, unless on a presentment or indictment of a Grand Jury." However, the right to be charged by grand jury has not been incorporated. Connecticut, Pennsylvania, Washington D.C., and the territories do not have grand juries with charging authority. Connecticut and Pennsylvania, however, allow prosecutors to use grand juries to investigate crimes. The other 48 states employ grand juries as charging bodies, but only about half of the states require their use.

Grand juries consist of 12 to 23 persons who are usually selected in the same method as petit juries (juries that determine guilt or innocence). Grand juries sit for longer periods of time and are called to hear cases as needed.

In practice, grand juries serve two purposes. First, they perform investigations. Operating in secrecy and with the power to subpoena evidence, they can be powerful investigative tools. Second, they act as accusatory bodies. In this role, they determine if there is probable cause to believe a crime has been committed. The Fifth Amendment requires that serious federal cases be charged by grand jury—not by a prosecutor alone. So, the grand jury is an indispensable gatekeeper in the federal system.

### Procedures of the Grand Jury

First, grand juries are closed. The public, including the defendant, is not entitled to attend. Second, the prosecutor runs the show before the grand jury. No judge is present and the defendant has no right to present evidence or to make a statement. Third, the actions of grand juries are secret. Those who attend are not permitted to disclose what transpires. Defendants have no right to know

---

**information**
A formal accusation of a crime made by a proper public official such as a prosecuting attorney.

**indictment**
A sworn, written accusation of a crime, made against a person by a prosecutor to a *grand jury*.

**grand jury**
Persons who receive complaints and accusations of crime, hear preliminary evidence on the complaining side, and make formal accusations or indictments.

**target**
A person investigated by a grand jury.

what evidence is presented to a grand jury, unless it is exculpatory (tends to prove the defendant's innocence). Fourth, those who testify before the grand jury are not entitled to have counsel in the jury room.[10] In most states, witnesses are permitted to leave the proceeding to confer with counsel waiting directly outside. Because statements made to a grand jury can be used later, the Fifth Amendment right to be free from self-incrimination is available to witnesses. Grand juries can overcome Fifth Amendment claims (refusals to testify) by granting witnesses immunity from prosecution. Also, witnesses may not refuse to testify because the inquiry is the result of illegally seized evidence. To permit refusal or exclusion would not further the objective of the exclusionary rule (to deter police misconduct) and would substantially interfere with the grand jury process.[11]

Grand juries possess the power to order people to appear, to subpoena documents, to hold people in contempt, and to grant immunity in order to procure testimony.

For the most part, grand juries convene only when called by the prosecutor. The prosecutor decides who will be called to testify and who should be given immunity. Nearly all people targeted (the person the prosecutor believes guilty) by prosecutors are indicted. Many criticize the grand jury system for this reason: The government has too much control over the grand juries. The argument is reasonable when one considers the historical purpose of grand jury review.

The proponents of abolishing the grand jury system argue that grand juries have not only lost their independence, but they also now act to the benefit of prosecutors by allowing discovery of information that may otherwise have been unavailable.

## The Indictment

After a grand jury has completed its investigation, a vote on whether to charge is taken. In the federal system, grand juries consist of 16 to 23 people. At least 12 must vote for indictment.[12] In many cases, indictments are sealed until the indicted defendant is arrested. A synonym for indictments is **true bill**.

The Constitution requires that all federal prosecutions for capital and infamous crimes be by indictment. However, if a defendant waives the right to grand jury review, he or she may be charged by information. Crimes punishable by 1 year or longer in prison are "infamous."[13] A defendant may not waive indictment in federal capital cases. It is always proper to charge corporations by information, as imprisonment is not possible.

The U.S. Supreme Court has ruled that grand jury review is not a fundamental right; therefore, the Fifth Amendment requirement for indictment is not applicable against the states. However, many states have grand juries and require that serious charges be brought by indictment.

Indictments must be written and state in "plain and concise" terms the essential facts constituting the offense charged.[14] Indictments are liberally read, and technical errors do not make them invalid. However, an indictment must contain all the essential elements of the crime charged. If an indictment charges more than one crime, each crime must be made a separate count.[15] Jurisdiction must be noted, and the law upon which the charge is made must be cited. Earlier you saw the complaint filed against Ethan Nordean. See Exhibit 15-3 for a shortened version of the indictment that replaced the complaint. The indictment was filed against Mr. Nordean and three alleged co-conspirators.

If a defendant believes that an indictment is fatally deficient, it may be attacked by a **motion** to **quash**. Indictments are not quashed because of technical errors. An example of a valid reason to quash is failure to allege an essential element of

**true bill**
A grand jury indictment.

**motion**
A request that a judge make a ruling or take some other action.

**quash**
Overthrow; annul; completely do away with. *Quash* usually refers to a court stopping a subpoena, an order, or an indictment.

**Exhibit 15–3** Indictment of Ethan Nordean.

**UNITED STATES DISTRICT COURT**
**FOR THE DISTRICT OF COLUMBIA**

Holding a Criminal Term

Grand Jury Sworn in on January 8, 2021

| | | |
|---|---|---|
| UNITED STATES OF AMERICA | : | **CRIMINAL NO. 21-cr-175 (TJK)** |
| | : | |
| v. | : | **MAGISTRATE NOS.** |
| | : | **21-mj-126, 21-mj-195** |
| **ETHAN NORDEAN,** | : | |
| also known as "Rufio Panman," | : | **VIOLATIONS:** |
| (Counts 1, 2, 3, 4, 5, 6) | : | **18 U.S.C. § 371** |
| | : | **(Conspiracy)** |
| **JOSEPH BIGGS,** | : | |
| (Counts 1, 2, 3, 4, 5, 6) | : | **18 U.S.C. §§ 1512(c)(2), 2** |
| | : | **(Obstruction of an Official Proceeding and** |
| **ZACHARY REHL, and** | : | **Aiding and Abetting)** |
| (Counts 1, 2, 3, 4, 5, 6) | : | |
| | : | **18 U.S.C. §§ 231(a)(3), 2** |
| **CHARLES DONOHOE,** | : | **(Obstruction of Law Enforcement During** |
| (Counts 1, 2, 3, 4, 5, 6) | : | **Civil Disorder and Aiding and Abetting)** |
| | : | |
| | : | **18 U.S.C. §§ 1361, 2** |
| **Defendants.** | : | **(Destruction of Government Property and** |
| | : | **Aiding and Abetting)** |
| | : | |
| | : | **18 U.S.C. § 1752(a)(1)** |
| | : | **(Entering and Remaining in a Restricted** |
| | : | **Building or Grounds)** |
| | : | |
| | : | **18 U.S.C. § 1752(a)(2)** |
| | : | **(Disorderly Conduct in a Restricted** |
| | : | **Building or Grounds)** |

**FIRST SUPERSEDING INDICTMENT**

The Grand Jury charges that, at all times material to this Indictment, on or about the dates
and at or about the times stated below:

**Exhibit 15–3** *(Continued)*

<u>Introduction</u>

***The 2020 United States Presidential Election and the Official Proceeding on January 6, 2021***

1.      The 2020 United States Presidential Election occurred on November 3, 2020.

2.      The United States Electoral College ("Electoral College") is a group required by the Constitution to form every four years for the sole purpose of electing the president and vice president, with each state appointing its own electors in a number equal to the size of that state's Congressional delegation.

3.      On December 14, 2020, the presidential electors of the Electoral College met in the state capital of each state and in the District of Columbia and formalized the result of the 2020 U.S. Presidential Election: Joseph R. Biden, Jr. and Kamala D. Harris were declared to have won sufficient votes to be elected the next president and vice president of the United States.

4.      On January 6, 2021, a Joint Session of the United States House of Representatives and the United States Senate ("the Joint Session") convened in the United States Capitol ("the Capitol") to certify the vote of the Electoral College of the 2020 U.S. Presidential Election ("the Electoral College vote").

***The Proud Boys***

5.      The Proud Boys describes itself as a "pro-Western fraternal organization for men who refuse to apologize for creating the modern world; aka Western Chauvinists." Proud Boys members routinely attend rallies, protests, and other events, some of which have resulted in violence involving members of the group. There is an initiation process for new members of the Proud Boys, and members often wear black and yellow polo shirts or other apparel adorned with Proud Boys logos to public events.

6.      The Proud Boys organization has a national chairman, referred to here as Proud Boys Chairman, and is led by group of individual members known as the "Elders" chapter.

# Exhibit 15–3 *(Continued)*

Throughout the United States, there are local Proud Boys chapters, which are typically led by chapter "presidents."

### *Conspirators*

7.  ETHAN NORDEAN, also known as "Rufio Panman," is a 30-year-old resident of Auburn, Washington. NORDEAN is a member of Proud Boys Elders chapter and president of his local chapter.

8.  JOSEPH BIGGS, also known as "Sergeant Biggs," is a 37-year-old resident of Ormond Beach, Florida. BIGGS is a member of the Proud Boys and a self-described organizer of certain Proud Boys events.

9.  ZACHARY REHL is a 35-year-old resident of Philadelphia, Pennsylvania. REHL is the president of his local chapter of Proud Boys.

10. CHARLES DONOHOE is a 33-year-old resident of Kenersville, North Carolina. DONOHOE is the president of his local chapter of Proud Boys.

### *The Attack at the U.S. Capitol on January 6, 2021*

11. On December 19, 2020, plans were announced for a Stop the Steal protest event in Washington, D.C. on January 6, 2021, which protest would coincide with Congress's certification of the Electoral College vote.

12. On December 29, 2020, Proud Boys Chairman posted a message on social media that read, in part, that the Proud Boys planned to "turn out in record numbers on Jan 6th but this time with a twist . . . . We will not be wearing our traditional Black and Yellow. We will be incognito and we will be spread across downtown DC in smaller teams. And who knows . . . we might dress in all BLACK for the occasion." At different times, NORDEAN, BIGGS, REHL, and DONOHOE reiterated that Proud Boys members should avoid wearing Proud Boys colors on January 6, 2021.

3

**Exhibit 15–3** *(Continued)*

A TRUE BILL

FOREPERSON

*Channing D. Phillips / jt*

CHANNING D. PHILLIPS
ACTING U.S. ATTORNEY FOR THE UNITED STATES
IN AND FOR THE DISTRICT OF COLUMBIA

the crime charged. It is not violative of the Fifth Amendment's Double Jeopardy Clause for a grand jury to issue a second indictment after the first has been quashed or dismissed.

In some jurisdictions, a prosecutor may refuse to prosecute, even though an indictment has been issued. In that situation, the prosecutor must assist the jury in preparing the document and must usually explain why a prosecution will not be maintained. In other instances, the prosecutor *must* pursue the case. The former situation represents federal law. The federal prosecutor may refuse to prosecute a case, even though the grand jury has found probable cause.[16]

## Information

The second formal method of charging someone with a crime is by information. Informations are filed by prosecutors without grand jury review. The current trend is away from indictments in favor of charging by information.

If a defendant has been initially charged by complaint, the prosecutor must independently review the evidence and determine whether a prosecution is warranted. If not, a prosecutor may file a nolle prosequi. If so, the information is filed.

Informations serve the same function as indictments. Under the federal rules, informations must take the same form as indictments. They must be plain, concise, and in writing. All essential elements, as well as the statute relied upon by the government, must be included.[17] (See the sample criminal information in Chapter 4.) As is true of an indictments, an information must be filed with the appropriate court.

A defendants may seek to have a defective information quashed or dismissed. The rules regarding defectiveness are the same for both formal charging instruments. Technical errors are not fatal.

## Arraignment and Pretrial Activity

Learning Objective: Describe arraignment, motion practice, and plea negotiations.

After the formal charge has been filed, the defendant is brought to the trial court for **arraignment**. This is the hearing where the defendant is read the formal charge and is asked to enter a **plea**.

Defendants may plead guilty, not guilty, nolo contendere, or Alford. By pleading guilty, a defendant admits all the charges contained in the charging document, unless a plea agreement has been reached with the government. A **plea agreement**, also known as a *plea bargain*, is the product of negotiations between the prosecutor and the defendant. It is common for the prosecution to dismiss one or more charges of a multi-count charge or to reduce a charge in exchange for a defendant's plea of guilty. Judges are not permitted to participate in plea negotiations, and a judge's involvement, including urging a defendant to plead guilty, can be cause for a reversal of a conviction.[18]

Plea bargaining is an important aspect of criminal procedure. More than 90% of all felony cases are disposed of by pleas of guilty. Most guilty pleas are the result of plea bargaining.

By pleading guilty, defendants waive a host of rights. The right to a jury trial and to be proven guilty beyond a reasonable doubt are two. Due to the significance of such waivers, courts must be sure that guilty pleas are given knowingly and voluntarily. To be knowing, a defendant must understand his or her rights and that he or she is waiving them by making the plea. The plea must be free of

**arraignment**
The hearing at which a defendant is brought before a judge to hear the charges and to enter a plea (guilty, not guilty, etc.).

**plea**
The *defendant's* formal answer to a criminal charge. The defendant says "guilty," "not guilty," or "nolo contendere" (no contest).

**plea bargain (plea agreement)**
Negotiations between a prosecutor and a criminal defendant's lawyer, in the attempt to resolve a criminal case without trial.

coercion or duress to be voluntary. Offers by prosecutors to reduce and eliminate charges made during plea negotiations are not considered coercion.

The court must also find that a factual basis exists before a plea of guilty can be accepted. This means there must be sufficient facts in the record to support the conclusion that the defendant committed the crime. A defendant has no right to plead guilty to a crime he or she did not commit. The factual basis may be established by the testimony of the investigating officer or by the defendant recounting what transpired. Once the plea is taken, the court will either impose sentence or set a future date for sentencing.

If a defendant enters a not guilty plea, the court will set a trial date. In some instances, courts will set a pretrial schedule, which will include a pretrial conference date and a deadline for filing pretrial motions.

Finally, a plea of nolo contendere may be entered. **Nolo contendere** is a Latin phrase that translates to "I do not contest it." The defendant who pleads nolo contendere neither admits nor denies the charges and has no intention of defending himself or herself.

Nolo contendere is treated as a plea of guilty. That is, the government must establish that a factual basis exists to believe the defendant committed the offense, and the court accepting the plea must be sure that the plea is made voluntarily and knowingly. In most jurisdictions, a defendant may plead nolo contendere only with the court's approval. This is true in the courts of the United States.[19]

The advantage of a no-contest plea over a guilty plea is that the no-contest plea cannot be used in a later civil proceeding against the defendant, whereas a guilty plea may be used. If the case is not disposed of by a plea of guilty or nolo contendere, the parties begin preparing for trial.

A fourth option is the **Alford Plea**. In the Alford, a defendant pleads guilty but maintains her innocence. The guilty plea is offered because the defendant agrees that she is likely to be convicted by a jury. Most jurisdictions permit Alford pleas, at the discretion of the trial judge. Where allowed, an Alford may only be entered when

1. the defendant "intelligently concludes" that the plea is the best strategic decision, and
2. the evidence strongly indicates that the defendant is guilty.

## Discovery

**Discovery** refers to a process of exchanging information between the prosecution and defense. Discovery is not as broad in criminal cases as in civil.

The amount of discovery that should be allowed is heavily debated. Those favoring broad discovery contend that limited discovery leads to "trial by ambush," which is not in the best interests of justice. The purpose of a trial is to discover the truth and achieve justice, not to award the better game player. Proponents of this position claim that unexpected evidence at trial is inefficient, costly, and unfair. It is inefficient because trials often have to be delayed to give one party time to prepare a response to the unexpected evidence. Such tactics lead to time problems for the parties as well as the trial court. They may also be unfair. Evidence that was once available may not be so at trial. If the party surprised at trial had known about the unexpected evidence, other contrary evidence could have been secured, and a proper defense or response could have been prepared.

Finally, it appears unfair to subject defendants to the possibility of surprise when the government is insulated from certain surprises. For example, affirmative defenses must be specially pled. Intent to rely on alibi and insanity defenses must be provided to the government in most jurisdictions, often with strict enforcement

**nolo contendere**
A plea of no-contest to a charge. The plea operates as a guilty plea, although it may not be used in subsequent civil litigation as proof of guilt.

**Alford Plea**
A guilty plea that is accompanied with an assertion of innocence.

**discovery**
The formal and informal exchange of information between the prosecution and the defense.

of time requirements. The purpose of these rules is to prevent surprises to the government at trial. Those who support expanded discovery feel that it is unfair to place such requirements upon defendants but not upon the government.

Those opposed contend that expansive discovery increases the likelihood that defendants will manipulate the system. In particular, defendants might intimidate government witnesses. Additionally, opponents contend that it is easier for a defendant to skillfully plan his or her testimony, even if false, if a defendant knows the government's entire case. For example, if a defendant originally planned to assert an alibi but finds out through discovery that the government has a witness placing him at the location of the crime, he has been provided an opportunity to change his defense. Today, discovery in criminal proceedings is quite limited in many jurisdictions, including federal courts. A few states have enlarged what information may be obtained prior to trial.

What follows is an examination of the federal rules, as well as constitutional requirements for discovery.

## Bill of Particulars

**bill of particulars**
A detailed, formal, written statement of charges or claims by a plaintiff or the prosecutor (given upon the defendant's formal request to the court for more detailed information).

One method that defendants have to obtain information about the government's case is through a **bill of particulars**. The purpose of bills of particulars is to make general indictments and informations more specific. Fed. R. Crim. P. 7(f) allows district courts to order prosecutors to file a bill of particulars.

Bills of particulars are not true discovery devices. If the charging instrument is sufficiently clear and detailed, the court will not grant a defense motion for particularization of the charge. A bill of particulars is intended to provide a defendant with details about the charges that are necessary for the preparation of a defense and to avoid prejudicial surprise at trial.[20] The test is not whether the indictment is sufficiently drawn; the question is whether the information is necessary to avoid prejudice to the defendant.

## Statements of the Defendant

Fed. R. Crim. P. 16(a) (1) (A) states that upon request the government must allow the defendant to inspect, copy, or photograph all prior relevant written and recorded statements made by the defendant. This includes testimony that defendants give before grand juries—an exception to the rule of secrecy of grand jury proceedings.

Prosecutors are required to allow inspection of all statements made by the defendant that are in the possession of the prosecution or that may be discovered through due diligence. Hence, if a defendant makes a statement to an arresting officer and the statement is recorded or reduced to writing, the prosecutor must allow defense inspection even though the statement may be in the possession of the officer and not the prosecutor.

In addition to recorded statements and writings, the government is required to inform the defendant of "the substance of any oral statement that the government intends to offer in evidence." This means that statements made by a defendant that are summarized by the police (or other government agent), but not verbatim or signed by the defendant, are also discoverable. However, such evidence is discoverable only if the prosecution intends to use it at trial. This is not true of written and recorded statements of a defendant.

## Criminal Record of the Defendant

Fed. R. Crim. P. 16 also requires prosecutors to furnish a copy of the defendant's criminal record to the defendant. This includes not only the records known to the prosecutor but also those that can be discovered through due diligence.

## Documents and Tangible Objects

Under Rule 16, defendants are also entitled to inspect and copy photographs, books, tangible objects, papers, buildings, and places that are in the possession of the government if:

1. The item is material to preparation of the defendant's defense, or

2. The item is going to be used by the government at trial, or

3. The item was obtained from, or belongs to, the defendant.

The situations in which this rule might apply are countless. For example, if the police take pictures of the scene of a crime, this provision allows the defendant to view and copy those pictures prior to trial. Or, if the police seize a building that was used to manufacture drugs, the defendant can invoke this rule to gain access to the premises.

This section of Rule 16 has a reciprocal provision. That is, defendants must allow the government to inspect and copy defense items. However, the rule is not as broad for government discovery. Defendants only have to permit inspection and copying of those items intended to be used at trial.

## Scientific Reports and Tests

All scientific reports and tests in the possession of the government (or that can be discovered through due diligence) must be turned over to the defendant, if requested.

This provision includes reports and conclusions of mental examinations of the defendant, autopsy reports, drug tests, fingerprint analysis, blood tests, DNA (genetic) tests, ballistic tests, and other related tests and examinations.

The defendant must accord the government reciprocity, if requested. For example, if a defendant undergoes an independent mental examination, the government is entitled to review the report of the evaluator prior to trial.

## Statements of Witnesses/Jencks Act

Many jurisdictions require that the prosecution, and in some the defense, provide a list of intended trial witnesses. It is common to require additional information about expert witnesses, such as background and reports they have prepared.

In the federal system, defendants are not entitled to inspect or copy statements of prosecution witnesses prior to trial. However, a federal statute, commonly known as the Jencks Act,[21] permits a defendant to review a prior written or recorded statement after the witness has testified for the government. Reviewing such statements may prove important to show that a witness is inconsistent, biased, or has a bad memory.

This procedure often causes trial delay, as defendants usually request time between direct examination and cross-examination to review such statements. For this reason, some federal prosecutors provide such information prior to trial. The Jencks Act is a matter of federal statutory law and does not apply in state criminal prosecutions.

## Depositions

A **deposition** is oral testimony given under oath, not in a court. In civil procedure, depositions are freely conducted. Upon notice to a party or subpoena to a witness, an attorney can call a person to testify prior to trial. This is not so in criminal practice.

Fed. R. Crim. P. 15 allows depositions only when "exceptional circumstances" exist. Expected absence of a witness at trial is an example of an exceptional circumstance. If such a circumstance is shown, the deposition may be ordered by the trial court, and the deposition may be used at trial. Of course, both the defendant and government have the opportunity to question the witness at the deposition.

**deposition**
The process of taking a witness's sworn out-of-court testimony. The questioning is usually done by a lawyer, and the lawyer from the other side is given a chance to attend and participate.

## Brady Doctrine

Although most discovery occurs under the authority of statutes and court rules, the Constitution also requires disclosure of information by the government in some situations. In *Brady v. Maryland*, the Supreme Court announced what is now referred to as the Brady doctrine.

Obviously, *Brady* applies to both state and federal prosecutions. Note that only exculpatory evidence must be provided. Evidence that tends to prove a defendant's innocence is exculpatory. *Brady* does not stand for the proposition that prosecutors must reveal incriminating evidence to defendants. Failure to disclose to a defendant will result in reversal of a conviction if there is a reasonable probability that the likelihood of a different result is great enough to undermine confidence in the outcome of the trial.[22]

In most situations, disclosure at trial will satisfy *Brady*. However, if disclosure at trial would prejudice a defendant, pretrial disclosure may be constitutionally required. As is sometimes the case with Jencks Act materials, prosecutors may provide such information prior to trial as a courtesy.

In a case related to *Brady*, the Supreme Court found that it is violative of due process for prosecutors to use perjured testimony or to deceive juries. This is true even if the perjury was unsolicited by the prosecuting attorney. As such, a prosecutor has a duty to correct any testimony of a witness that he or she knows is false.[23]

Although *Brady* and related cases are law in both state and federal prosecutions, the other discovery rules differ. Be sure to check local law to determine what your client has a right to discover.

## Oyez

### Brady v. Maryland
### 373 U.S. 83 (1962)

**Opinion of the Court by MR. JUSTICE DOUGLAS, announced by MR. JUSTICE BRENNAN.**

Petitioner and companion, Boblit, were found guilty of murder in the first degree and were sentenced to death. . . . Their trials were separate, petitioner being tried first. At his trial Brady took the stand and admitted his participation in the crime, but he claimed that Boblit did the actual killing. And, in his summation to the jury, Brady's counsel conceded that Brady was guilty of murder in the first degree, asking only that the jury return that verdict "without capital punishment." Prior to the trial petitioner's counsel had requested the prosecution to allow him to examine Boblit's extrajudicial statements. Several of those statements were shown to him; but one dated July 9, 1958, in which Boblit admitted the actual homicide, was withheld by the prosecution and did not come to petitioner's notice until after he had been tried, convicted, and sentenced, and after his conviction had been affirmed.

Petitioner moved the trial court for a new trial based on the newly discovered evidence that had been suppressed by the prosecution. Petitioner's appeal from a denial of that motion was dismissed by the Court of Appeals without prejudice to relief under the Maryland Post Conviction Procedures Act. . . . The petition for post-conviction relief was dismissed by the trial court; and on appeal the Court of Appeals held that suppression of the evidence by the prosecution denied petitioner due process of law and remanded the case for a retrial of the question of punishment, not the question of guilt. . . .

We now hold that the suppression by the prosecution of evidence favorable to an accused upon request violates due process where the evidence is material either to guilt or to punishment, irrespective of the good faith or bad faith of the prosecution.

[This principle] is not punishment of society for misdeeds of a prosecutor but avoidance of an unfair trial to the accused. Society wins not only when the guilty are convicted but when criminal trials are fair; our system of the administration of justice suffers when any accused is treated unfairly. An inscription on the walls of the Department of Justice states the proposition candidly for the federal domain: "The United States wins its point whenever justice is done its citizens in the courts." A prosecution that withholds evidence on demand of an accused which, if made available, would tend to exculpate him or reduce the penalty helps shape a trial that bears heavily on the defendant. That casts the prosecutor in the role of an architect of a proceeding that does not comport with standards of justice.

## Freedom of Information Laws

The federal government and most, if not all, states have statutes requiring the public disclosure of files, documents, and other information in the possession of the government.[24] The federal statute is known as the Freedom of Information Act (FOIA).[25]

There are nine exemptions to the federal FOIA. If a request for information falls into one of the nine exemptions, the government may withhold disclosure. Otherwise, disclosure is mandated.

One of the exemptions provides that law enforcement records may be withheld if disclosure will:

1. Interfere with enforcement proceedings.
2. Deprive a person of a fair trial or an impartial adjudication.
3. Constitute an unwarranted invasion of personal privacy.
4. Disclose the identity of a confidential source.
5. Disclose investigative techniques and procedures.
6. Endanger the life or physical safety of law enforcement personnel.

The FOIA is not a discovery device. It is a statute of general applicability, and any person may request inspection or production of documents under its authority. The purpose of the FOIA, which is unrelated to litigation, is the promotion of democracy by having an informed citizenry; it keeps the governors accountable to the governed.

Even though the FOIA was not specifically intended to be used for discovery in litigation, it does not foreclose that use. However, although the FOIA may be used to obtain information, it is not intended to displace or supplement the recognized forms of discovery.[26] Nor shall the process of obtaining information through the FOIA be cause for delaying a criminal proceeding. Therefore, requests for information under the FOIA are separate from a defendant's discovery requests in a criminal case.[27]

Hence, defendants may seek information under the FOIA, but such requests are not part of the criminal discovery process, and criminal proceedings will not be delayed to wait for such requests to be answered or disputes over disclosure to be adjudicated.

The same principles apply to other disclosure laws. For example, the federal Privacy Act[28] provides that individuals have a right to discover the contents of files containing information about them. Again, requests for information under this law are aside from, not in addition to, criminal discovery rules.

## Reciprocal Discovery

The Fifth Amendment's freedom from self-incrimination clause, as well as due process, greatly limits what can be expected of defendants in discovery. Requiring defendants to give notice of affirmative defenses, such as alibi and insanity, is common and constitutional. Many jurisdictions also expect defendants to provide witness lists, pretrial statements of the witnesses, and to detail expert testimony and reports that will be offered at trial.

# Motion Practice

In both civil and criminal practice, a motion is a request made to a court for it to do something. In most cases, a party that files a motion is seeking an order from the court. Generally, when a person desires something from a court, a formal motion must be filed and copies sent to opposing counsel. On occasion, oral motions are made. This is most common during trials and hearings. Some of the most common motions are discussed here.

## Motion to Dismiss/Quash

If a defendant believes that the indictment or information is fatally flawed, the appropriate remedy is a motion to dismiss. In some jurisdictions, this would be called a motion to quash. Examples of fatal flaws in the charging instrument are as follows: the court lacks jurisdiction; the facts alleged do not amount to a crime; an essential element is not charged; or the defendant has a legal defense, such as double jeopardy.

If the form of the charging instrument is attacked, courts often permit prosecutors to amend the charge rather than dismissing it entirely. Dismissal of an indictment or information does not mean that the defendant cannot be recharged. A person is not in "jeopardy" under the Fifth Amendment until later in the proceeding.

## Motion to Suppress

You have already learned that evidence obtained in an unconstitutional manner may not be used at trial. Objection at trial to the admission of such evidence is one method of excluding such evidence. Another is by way of a motion to suppress prior to trial.

A separate hearing is conducted prior to trial to determine whether the motion to suppress should be granted. Defendants may testify at suppression hearings, and their testimony may not be used against them at trial.[29] To allow a defendant's testimony from a suppression hearing to be used at trial would place the defendant in a position of choosing between the right to suppress evidence and the right to be free from self-incrimination. The best alternative is to allow the defendant to testify and to prohibit that testimony from being used later.

Who has the burden of proof in suppression hearings varies by jurisdiction and on what the defendant wishes to be suppressed. For example, most jurisdictions place the burden of proving that a search pursuant to a warrant was unconstitutional on the defendant. The opposite is true if there was no warrant; the government bears the burden of proving the propriety of the search. Most jurisdictions also place the burden of proving that a confession was voluntary upon the prosecution.

## Motion for Change of Venue

*Venue* means "place for trial." In state criminal proceedings, venue usually lies in the county where the crime occurred. In federal proceedings, venue lies in the district where the crime occurred. Many federal crimes are interstate in character, and the charges may be filed in any district where the crime took place.

Fed. R. Crim. P. 21 permits transfer of a case from one district to another if "the defendant cannot obtain a fair and impartial trial" at the location where the case is pending. In addition, a district judge may transfer a case if it is most convenient for the defendant and witnesses.

Pretrial publicity of criminal matters may be cause to transfer a case (change venue in state proceedings). If a defendant receives considerable negative media coverage, it may be necessary to try the defendant in another location. Several factors are taken into consideration when a defendant moves for a change of venue due to excessive negative publicity, including the total amount of coverage, whether media attention had increased or waned since the case first became public, the length of time between first coverage and trial, the extent to which the coverage itself directly accused or implied guilt, and the nature of the facts that had been brought to light.

On May 25, 2020, in Minneapolis, Minnesota, a store clerk who believed George Floyd had used a counterfeit $20 bill to pay for cigarettes went outside of the store, with other employees, to retrieve the cigarettes. Mr. Floyd refused to surrender them, prompting the clerk to call the police. The clerk reported to dispatch that Mr. Floyd was drunk and not in control of himself. Eventually, four police officers arrived. After several minutes of discussion and conflict, Minneapolis police officer Derek Chauvin pinned Mr. Floyd to the ground with his knee on his neck. Ignoring Mr. Floyd's pleas, and those of bystanders, Mr. Chauvin maintained this hold for over nine minutes. Mr. Floyd subsequently died. The incident precipitated demonstrations, some which devolved into riots, across the nation. The situation in Minneapolis was particularly tense and at times, violent.

The four officers at the scene were charged with murder. Mr. Chauvin, the first to be tried, was convicted of three counts of homicide on April 20, 2021. Before his trial, he moved for a change of venue, alleging that the intensity of the feelings and widespread press and social media coverage in Minneapolis made it impossible for him to receive a fair trial. The trial court denied the motion. The trial judge's order appears in your next Oyez.

## Oyez

### State of Minnesota v. Chauvin, Thao, Lane, Kueng
#### District Court (Fourth Judicial District Nov. 4, 2020)

**Judge Cahill**

A criminal case should be tried in the county in which the offense was allegedly committed. Venue may, however, be transferred to a different county for trial under certain circumstances. Minn. R. Crim. P. 25.02 lists the grounds for transferring venue to another county:

The case may be transferred to another county:

a. If the court is satisfied that a fair and impartial trial cannot be had in the county in which the case is pending;

b. For the convenience of parties and witnesses;

c. In the interests of justice;

d. As provided by Rule 25.02 governing prejudicial publicity.

As noted above, Minn. R. Crim. P. 25.02 governs motions for continuance or change of venue on the grounds of prejudicial publicity. The rule sets out the type of proof that may be submitted in support of a motion, but the proof basically may be anything with probative value. Under Rule 25.02, a motion for change of venue "must be granted whenever potentially prejudicial material creates a reasonable likelihood that a fair trial cannot be had. Actual prejudice need not be shown." When a motion is made pre-trial, the motion must be decided before the jury is sworn. Even then, a prior denial of a change of venue motion does not prohibit reconsideration and the court granting a change of venue, even after the jury has been sworn.

In these cases, whether the analysis is under Minn. R. Crim. P. 24.03 subd. 1(a) or Minn. R. Crim. P. 25.02, this Court must determine if a fair and impartial trial cannot be had in Hennepin County. On the current record, the Court believes a fair and impartial trial in Hennepin County can be had. Thus, Defendants' motions for change of venue should be denied unless and until probative evidence is developed to the contrary.

#### Safety Concerns

Both Defendants Thao and Kueng cite public safety concerns as one reason to change venue. Kueng notes that the attorneys and defendants were physically and verbally harassed following the September 11, 2020, hearing and that a defense attorney was verbally harassed when he stopped on the skyway level of the Hennepin County Government Center to give a statement to the media after the October 15, 2020, hearing. Also, a protester in the Government Center was arrested with a gun on that day. Thao argues that a Hennepin jury might convict out of concern that an acquittal would rekindle riots in Minneapolis.

The safety concerns expressed by Defendants do not argue for a change of venue, but for better safety planning, planning the Court and the Hennepin County Sheriff's Office are currently conducting. The lesson learned from having the September 11, 2020, hearing at the Hennepin County Family Justice Center is that effective security measures are more difficult to put in place in a smaller courthouse

(continued)

with limited entrances and exits. For that reason, if the trial remains in Hennepin County, the trial will take place in the Hennepin County Government Center with floor access and movement of both defendants and attorneys tightly controlled. Moving venue to a smaller county will not assuage the defendants' security concerns but instead

Is likely to heighten those concerns because the relevant courthouse would certainly be smaller than the Hennepin County Government Center. The Court believes that safety issues can be mitigated to the point that a fair and safe trial may be had in Hennepin County and a jury can be insulated from outside influence and remain impartial.

### Prejudicial Publicity

All Defendants have cited the overwhelming amount of pretrial publicity these cases have generated and argue that the tremendous amount of publicity has tainted a pool of potential jurors in Hennepin County such that a fair trial before an impartial jury cannot be had in Hennepin County.

In evaluating a similar claim in *State v. Parker*, the Minnesota Supreme Court affirmed the Court of Appeals' decision to uphold a defendant's second-degree murder conviction where the trial court had denied defendant's motion to change venue.[11] The defendant had asserted that a fair trial was impossible due to a "feeding frenzy" of pretrial publicity that served to amplify the prosecution's comments about the victim being a "good Samaritan."[12] The district court reasoned that because the allegedly prejudicial information was found on the internet, there was no other venue in the state that would prove to be a better alternative, stating that "people in every corner could have been exposed to [the pretrial publicity] so I'm not sure where in Minnesota someone would not have been exposed to[it] if the material was prejudicial, where we would move venue, given the type of coverage." . . . While none of the jurors in *Parker* claimed to have any knowledge of the case during voir dire, the Court said that even if the jurors had prior knowledge, their exposure alone to pretrial publicity would not show that they had been prejudiced by it. Instead, the Court said that prejudice is shown when a juror is unable to "set aside his impression or opinion" to "render an impartial verdict."

In *State v. Warren*, the defendant had been convicted on three counts of first-degree murder.[17] The Minnesota Supreme Court reviewed a defendant's postconviction petition alleging denial of a fair trial due to pretrial publicity. The Court upheld the district court's decision to deny the defense motion for change of venue despite the fact that fourteen of the fifteen jurors chosen had been exposed to pretrial publicity giving accounts of the murders through television and newspapers. The Court stated that the mere fact a juror was exposed to pretrial publicity reporting on "factual accounts of the crime" does not suffice to show prejudice, concluding that a defendant must demonstrate that pretrial publicity "affect[ed] the minds of the specific jurors involved in the case". . . .

In *State v. Blom*, the Minnesota Supreme Court held that the trial court did not abuse its Discretion in denying defendant's motion for a second venue change. In *Blom*, the defendant kidnapped, murdered, and burned the remains of his victim near Moose Lake, Minnesota. Criminal charges were filed in Carlton County, and the trial court granted defendant's first motion for a change of venue, transferring venue to the City of Virginia in St. Louis County—65 miles from Moose Lake. During jury selection in Virginia, the defendant made a second motion for change of venue, citing concerns about bias of individual jurors and the Virginia community at large, as well as the potential for jury exposure to prejudicial publicity. In denying the second motion, the district court acknowledged that although pretrial publicity was extensive, "no evidence had been provided to indicate that any part of Minnesota had been shielded from such publicity." The district court stated that it "could not conclude that the jury had been adversely affected by any exposure to publicity or inadmissible evidence, or that the jury would be unfair," but would "reconsider Blom's motion if it became necessary." The Supreme Court affirmed, concluding the district court acted appropriately in ascertaining that the seated jurors would be fair and impartial.

Here, even more so than in *Blom*, no corner of the State of Minnesota has been shielded from pretrial publicity regarding the death of George Floyd. Because of that pervasive media coverage, a change of venue is unlikely to cure the taint of potentially prejudicial pretrial publicity. Nevertheless, this is only a preliminary ruling and the parties are free to present the evidence from public opinion surveys they are presently conducting. In addition, this Court is planning to issue jury summonses earlier than usual and to require summoned jurors to fill out questionnaires well before trial to gauge their knowledge of the case and any potential bias. These questionnaires, directed only to members of the actual jury pool summoned for the trial, will certainly be more probative than surveys of the general population of Hennepin County.

Because this Court is not persuaded at this moment that a change of venue is necessary to ensure a fair trial before an impartial jury for the Defendants, the defense motions for a change of venue are denied, although the Court will reconsider as the case develops if circumstances warrant.

Because of the First Amendment free press issue, judges are generally prohibited from excluding the press or public from hearings.[30] In some instances, judges may order the attorneys involved in a case not to provide information to anyone not involved in the proceeding.

## Motion for Severance

Fed. R. Crim. P. 8 permits two or more defendants to be charged in the same information or indictment if they were involved in the same crime. That rule also permits joinder of two offenses by the same person in one charging instrument, provided they are similar in character or arise out of the same set of facts.

In some situations, severance of the two defendants may be necessary to ensure fair trials. For example, if two defendants have antagonistic defenses, severance must be granted. Defenses are *antagonistic* if the jury must disbelieve one by believing the other. For example, if Defendant A denies being at the scene of a crime, and Defendant B claims that they were both there, but also claims that A forced him to commit the crime, their defenses are antagonistic.

If a defendant is charged with two or more offenses, it may be necessary to sever them to have a fair trial. For example, if a defendant plans to testify concerning one charge and not the other, severance is necessary.

## Motion in Limine

Prior to trial, both the defendant and the prosecution may file motions in limine. This is a request that the court order the other party not to mention or attempt to question a witness about some matter. A motion in limine is similar to a motion to suppress, except that it encompasses more than admission of illegally seized evidence.

For example, if one anticipates that the opposing counsel will attempt to question a witness about evidence that is inadmissible under the rules of evidence (e.g., hearsay), a motion in limine may be filed to avoid having to object at trial. This is important, as often a witness may blurt out the answer before an attorney has had an opportunity to object. In addition, knowing whether the judge will permit the admission of evidence prior to trial helps an attorney to plan the case.

## Other Motions

A variety of other motions may be filed. If the prosecution fears that revealing information required under a discovery rule will endanger the case or a person's life, a motion for a protective order may be filed. In such cases, the trial court reviews the evidence **in camera** and decides if it is necessary to keep it from the defendant. If so, the judge will enter a protective order so stating.

**in camera**
A meeting with a judge in private, typically in chambers.

Motions for continuance of hearings and trial dates are common. In criminal cases, courts must be careful not to violate speedy trial requirements.

If two defendants have been charged jointly, one or both may file a motion for severance of trial. If defense counsel believes that the defendant is not competent to stand trial, a motion for mental examination may be filed.

# Pretrial Conference

Sometime prior to trial, the court will hold a pretrial conference. This may be weeks or only days before trial.

At this conference, the court will address any remaining motions and discuss any problems the parties have. In addition, the judge will explain his or her method of trying a case, such as how the jury will be selected. The next stage is trial.

# Plea Bargaining

Statistics vary, but it is widely accepted that approximately 90% of all felony cases end with guilty pleas. The number is probably higher for misdemeanors. There is no question that plea bargaining greatly reduces the amount of time expended on trials. It is so important that the Supreme Court has stated that it "is not only an essential part of the process but a highly desirable part."[31]

In *Boykin v. Alabama* (1969),[32] it was decided that a guilty plea is legitimate only if it is given voluntarily and knowingly. To be knowing, a defendant must understand the rights that she is waiving by entering a plea of guilty.

The plea negotiation involves the defendant and the prosecutor. Judges do not participate in plea negotiations. Some defendants plead "straight up," or without negotiating the outcome with the prosecutor. A defendant may do this when he is overwhelmed with guilt or he believes that by not resisting the charge, the judge will be lenient in sentencing. In most cases, a defendant will bargain with the prosecutor for an agreement to be recommended to the court. Typically, prosecutors have three tools in their negotiation belt; the dismissal of one or more charges, the reduction of one or more charges, and a specific sentencing recommendation.

After a bargain is reached, it is presented to the trial court. The court may then accept the agreement and sentence the defendant accordingly. With good cause, the court may also reject the agreement. Some states permit defendants to withdraw their guilty pleas if the judge rejects the bargain. In others, the judge has the discretion of allowing the defendant to withdraw the guilty plea or sentencing the defendant contrary to the bargain.

The fairness of plea bargaining has come under scrutiny in recent years. This is in part due to an increased criminalization of the nation. There are more crimes than in the past and punishments for most crimes have increased. The War on Drugs was a large factor in this development. The outcome of the combination of prosecutorial discretion and increased criminalization is a system of plea bargaining that disadvantages defendants. The threat of being tried and punished for a more serious crime if trial is chosen over plea bargaining is known as the trial **penalty**.

**penalty**
The risk of greater punishment that a defendant assumes by electing to go to trial on greater charges rather than accepting an offer to plea to guilty to lesser charges or a recommendation for a lesser punishment.

## Removal

Congress has provided that, in certain circumstances, criminal cases may be removed from state courts to federal courts. Removal is premised upon the principle that certain cases are more properly adjudicated in a federal, rather than state, court. The purpose of removal is to preserve the sovereignty of the federal government by ensuring a fair trial to particular criminal defendants. Otherwise, the states could interfere with the functioning of the federal government by harassing federal officials through criminal proceedings.

Statute 28 U.S.C. § 1442 provides that a federal official who is sued in state court, whether the action is civil or criminal, may remove the case to the federal district court where the action is pending, if the suit concerns the performance of his or her official duties. Similarly, 28 U.S.C. § 1442(a) provides for removal of cases, civil or criminal, filed against members of the U.S. armed forces for actions taken in the course of their duties. 28 U.S.C. § 1443 provides for removal of certain civil rights cases.

Removal of criminal cases is the same as for civil: The defendant must file a notice of, and petition for, removal.[33] Improperly removed actions are remanded to the state court from which they came.[34]

## **Extradition and Detainers**

Learning Objective: Define extradition and detainer and offer an example of both.

**extradition**
One country (or state) giving up a person to a second country (or state) when the second requests the person for a trial on a criminal charge or for punishment after a trial.

If wanted persons are located outside the jurisdiction where they are, or will be, charged, **extradition** is one method of securing their presence in the charging jurisdiction. *Extradition* is the surrender of a person from one jurisdiction to another where the person has been charged or convicted of a crime.

Extradition usually occurs under the provisions of a treaty. Extradition includes transfers between states, as well as between nations. Extradition, especially international, is as much a political decision as a legal one.

Pursuant to the Uniform Interstate Criminal Extradition Act, which has been adopted by 47 states,[35] the request for extradition is made between governors. If a governor determines that the person sought should be delivered, an arrest warrant is issued by that governor.

Once seized, the arrestee is brought before a judge and may file a petition for writ of habeas corpus. During the proceedings, release on bail is permitted, unless the crime charged is one punishable by death or life imprisonment in the state where the crime was committed. If the person sought is under charge in the sending state, the governor may order his or her surrender immediately or may wait until the prosecution and punishment are completed in the first state.

Generally, the guilt or innocence of the accused may not be considered by the governor or courts during the proceedings; that issue is left to the requesting jurisdiction. It is the obligation of the governor and courts of the sending state to be sure that the correct person is seized and that proper procedures are followed.

Defendants may waive extradition. This waiver must be made in court, and defendants must be informed of their rights, including habeas corpus, for waivers to be valid.

The law permits arrests by police officers from outside a state in hot-pursuit situations. If an arrest is made in hot pursuit, the officer is to bring the accused before a local court, which is to order the defendant held, or released on bail, until an extradition warrant is issued by the governor.

The Supreme Court has held that the exclusionary rule does not exclude persons who have been illegally seized from trial. In *Frisbie v. Collins*, 342 U.S. 519 (1952), the fact that Michigan police officers kidnapped a defendant from Illinois and returned him to Michigan, disregarding extradition laws, did not affect the court's jurisdiction to try the defendant. The same result was reached in a case in which international extradition laws were not followed.[36] Today, if the government's conduct in seizing a defendant were outrageous or shocking, there is a possibility that a court would bar prosecution.[37]

You may recall from discussion of double jeopardy earlier in this text that the Fifth Amendment's Double Jeopardy Clause does not prevent two sovereigns from charging an individual for the same crime or two crimes arising from the same facts. Accordingly, one state may grant immunity to an individual and then extradite that individual to another state to be tried for the immunized crime.

A **detainer** is a request (or order) for the continued custody of a prisoner. For example, suppose federal charges are pending against a Utah prisoner. The United States would issue a detainer requesting that Utah hold the prisoner after his or her sentence is completed, so that the United States may take custody. This situation does not raise jurisdictional issues, as federal authorities have nationwide jurisdiction. As to interstate detention, the detainer is used in conjunction with extradition.

Pursuant to the Interstate Agreement on Detainers, a state may request the temporary custody of a prisoner of another state in order to try the person. Once the trial is completed, the prisoner is returned, regardless of the outcome. If the prisoner is convicted, a detainer is issued and he or she is again returned after the sentence is completed in the sending state.

The Agreement also provides that prisoners are to be notified of any detainers against them. Further, if a state issues a detainer for a prisoner, that prisoner may request to be temporarily transferred to that state for final disposition of that case. A request for final disposition by a prisoner is deemed a waiver of extradition to and from the sending state. Also, it is deemed a waiver of extradition to the receiving state to serve any resulting sentence after the sentence in the sending state is completed.

**detainer**

A warrant or court order to keep a person in custody when that person might otherwise be released. This is often used to make sure a person will serve a sentence or attend a trial in one state at the end of a prison term in another state or in a federal prison.

It is a common practice for jail and prison officials to conduct warrant checks before releasing or transferring prisoners. The importance of this practice was highlighted by the tragic events leading to the death of 6-year-old Jake Robel. On February 20, 2000, a local jail in Missouri released Kim Davis. Within hours of his release, Davis carjacked an automobile owned by Christy Robel. Christy's son, Jake Robel, was in the automobile at the time Kim Davis stole the car. Ms. Robel attempted to remove her son from the car, but he became entangled in the seatbelt and her pleas to Kim Davis to stop were ignored. She was dragged for a short distance before she lost her grip of the car. Tangled in the seatbelt and hanging out of the car, Jake Robel was dragged five miles by Kim Davis while driving at speeds reaching 80 miles per hour. Jake was dead by the time Kim Davis was forced to stop the vehicle. It was discovered that there was an outstanding warrant for the arrest of Kim Davis when he was released and that a warrants check had not been conducted by jail officials. Kim Davis was subsequently convicted of second-degree murder and sentenced to life imprisonment. In response to the records check oversight, Missouri enacted "Jake's Law," a statute requiring records checks of individuals scheduled for release from jails and prison in Missouri.

## Ethical Considerations

### Lawyer Competence and Computers

Section 1.1 of the ABA Model Rules of Professional Conduct require attorneys to provide competent representation. Section 1.6 requires attorneys to maintain the confidences of their clients. There are obvious applications of these rules. An attorney may not, for example—and with few exceptions—reveal the content of a client's statements, such as a confession, to any person. The rule is clear. How far an attorney must go in protecting client information from theft and unintended disclosures is not. The advent of mass data storage and the use of the Internet to access client information have raised new questions about the obligation to preserve client confidentiality.

Must an attorney lock client files when they are not in use? May an attorney send confidential information by e-mail? May confidential data be stored on a mass storage device? If so, must it be encrypted? The State Bar of Arizona addressed just such a question in 2005 where it held that lawyers must take reasonable and competent steps to avoid disclosure of client confidences through theft or accidental disclosure. The Arizona bar went further by requiring attorneys who do not have the technical expertise to ensure the confidentiality of client data to secure the services of a computer security expert. This ruling, of course, requires a financial investment in the security expert as well as in software and hardware.

The ABA has not gone as far as the Arizona bar in its interpretation of Sections 1.1 and 1.6. In 1999, it interpreted these rules to not require encryption, or other increased security, of e-mail correspondence containing client information. However, as state bar authorities increase their expectations and as computer theft and crime increase, the likelihood increases that ABA will elaborate a more sophisticated and security conscious set of rules.

*Source:* John D. Comerford, "Competent Computing: A Lawyer's Ethical Duty to Safeguard the Confidentiality and Integrity of Client Information Stored on Computers and Computer Networks," 19 *Geo. J. Legal Ethics* 629 (2006).

## Key Terms

| | | |
|---|---|---|
| Alford Plea | discovery | *nolo contendere* |
| arraignment | extradition | plea |
| arrest | grand juries | plea bargain (plea agreement) |
| bail | in camera | preliminary hearing |
| bill of particulars | indictment | quash |
| complaint | information | target |
| deposition | motion | true bill |
| detainer | | |

# Review Questions

1. For what two reasons may a defendant be detained prior to trial?

2. What is the difference between an indictment and an information?

3. What are the purposes of indictments and informations?

4. If a defendant needs more information than appears in the indictment to prepare a defense, what should be done?

5. What advantage does a plea of nolo contendere have over a guilty plea?

6. Kevin has been charged with murder. He believes a weapon that the prosecutor plans on using at trial was unconstitutionally seized from his home. How can he raise this issue prior to trial?

7. Place the following in the proper order of occurrence: preliminary hearing; formal charge; initial appearance; arraignment; trial; and complaint.

8. What is the Brady doctrine?

9. When is removal from state to federal court allowed?

10. What is extradition?

# Problems & Critical Thinking Exercises

1. What is the historical purpose of the grand jury? Many feel that grand juries should be abolished. Why?

2. Discovery in civil cases is very broad. Fed. R. Civ. P. 26 permits discovery of anything "reasonably calculated to lead to the discovery of admissible evidence." Should discovery in criminal cases be broader? Explain your position.

3. Do you believe that indictment by grand jury should be incorporated? Explain your position.

# Endnotes

1. Fed. R. Crim. P. 4.
2. Fed. R. Crim. P. 5.
3. 500 U.S. 44 (1991).
4. *Stack v. Boyle*, 342 U.S. 1 (1951).
5. 18 U.S.C. § 3142(f).
6. 18 U.S.C. § 3142(e), (f).
7. *Gerstein v. Pugh*, 420 U.S. 103 (1975).
8. Fed. R. Crim. P. 5.1; 18 U.S.C. § 3060.
9. 18 U.S.C. § 3060(e).
10. *United States v. Mandujano*, 425 U.S. 564 (1976).
11. *United States v. Calandra*, 414 U.S. 338 (1974).
12. Fed. R. Crim. P. 6.
13. *Ex parte Wilson*, 114 U.S. 417 (1884). *See also* Fed. R. Crim. P. 7.
14. Fed. R. Crim. P. 7(c).
15. Fed. R. Crim. P. 8(a).
16. *See United States v. Cox*, 342 F.2d 167 (5th Cir.), *cert. denied*, 381 U.S. 935 (1965).
17. Fed. R. Crim. P. 7(c).
18. See *United States v. Davila*, U.S. (2013).
19. Fed. R. Crim. P. 11.
20. *United States v. Diecidue*, 603 F.2d 535 (5th Cir.), *cert. denied*, 445 U.S. 946 (1979).
21. 18 U.S.C. § 3500.

22. *Smith v. Cain*, 564 U.S. (2012).

23. *Mooney v. Holohan*, 294 U.S. 103 (1935).

24. See Daniel Hall, *Administrative Law: Bureaucracy in a Democracy,* 7th ed., ch. 10 (Upper Saddle River, NJ: Pearson: Prentice Hall, 2020), for a more thorough discussion of the Freedom of Information Act.

25. 5 U.S.C. § 552.

26. *John Doe Corp. v. John Doe Agency*, 493 U.S. 146 (1989).

27. *North v. Walsh*, 881 F.2d 1088 (D.C. Cir. 1989).

28. 5 U.S.C. § 552(a).

29. *Simmons v. United States*, 390 U.S. 377 (1968).

30. *Richmond Newspapers, Inc. v. Virginia*, 448 U.S. 555 (1980).

31. *Santobello v. New York*, 404 U.S. 257, 261 (1971)

32. *Boykin v. Alabama*, 395 U.S. 238 (1969)

33. 28 U.S.C. § 1446.

34. 28 U.S.C. § 1447.

35. Rhonda Wasserman, "The Subpoena Power: *Pennoyer's* Last Vestige," 74 *Minn. L. Rev.* 37 (1989).

36. *Ker v. Illinois*, 119 U.S. 436 (1886).

37. *See United States v. Toscanino*, 500 F.2d 267 (2d Cir. 1974).

# Chapter 16

# Trial

Previous chapters discussed the many rights that protect suspects during the investigatory and early stages of the adjudicatory process. This chapter covers the rare, but important, step in the process: trial. The discussion begins with trial rights and concludes with trial process. Trial rights can be found in several provisions of the Constitution. But the most important source of trials rights is the Sixth Amendment. It reads:

> In all criminal prosecutions, the accused shall enjoy the right to a speedy and public trial, by an impartial jury of the State and district wherein the crime shall have been committed, which district shall have been previously ascertained by law, and to be informed of the nature and cause of the accusation; to be confronted with the witnesses against him; to have compulsory process for obtaining witnesses in his favor, and to have the Assistance of Counsel for his defence.

See Exhibit 16-1 for an illustration of the rights protected by the Sixth Amendment. Let's begin with the right to counsel.

**Exhibit 16–1** Sixth Amendment Rights

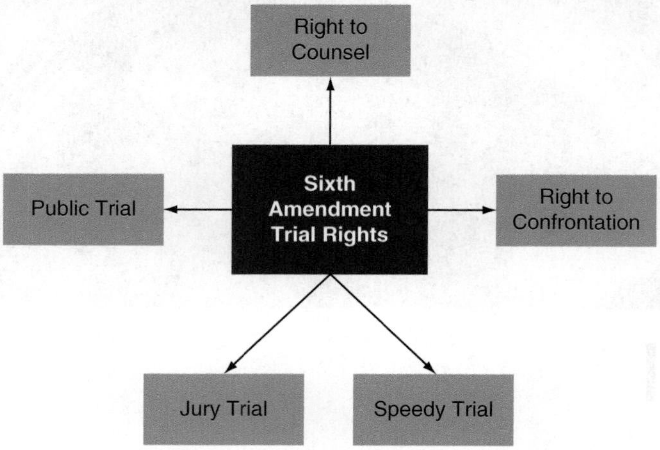

# Trial Right: Counsel

Learning Objective: Describe the Sixth Amendment's right to counsel, including the landmark cases that define the right.

Several provisions of the Constitution contain trial rights. The most significant is the Sixth Amendment.

The final clause of this Amendment provides that "in all criminal prosecutions, the accused shall enjoy the right . . . to have the Assistance of Counsel for his defense." The right to counsel is one of the most fundamental rights guaranteed to criminal defendants and is fully applicable to the states.

The right to the assistance of counsel is found not only in the Sixth Amendment but also in the Fifth and Fourteenth Amendments. These alternative sources are discussed later in the particular contexts within which they apply.

## Indigency

Criminal defendants have long had the right to retain the attorney of their choice-at their own expense. It was not until 1923 that the U.S. Supreme Court recognized a constitutional right to appointed counsel for indigent defendants in *Powell v. Alabama*, 287 U.S. 45 (1923).

In the *Powell* case (commonly known as the Scottsboro case), nine young black males were charged with the rape of two white women. Within one week of arrest, the defendants were tried. Eight of the so-called "Scottsboro Boys" were convicted and sentenced to death. The defendants appealed, alleging that they should have been provided counsel. The Supreme Court agreed.

However, the right to appointed counsel in *Powell* was not found in the Sixth Amendment, but in the Fourteenth. The Court reasoned that the absence of counsel deprived the defendants of a fair trial. The decision was narrow in its precedential effect. It applied only to a capital case where a defendant was incapable of preparing an adequate defense, and did not have the resources to hire an attorney.

The due process right to counsel was subsequently extended to other cases where the absence of counsel would result in unfairness. The determination of whether counsel was required was made on a case-by-case basis, after an examination of the "totality of facts." If denial of counsel was "shocking to the universal sense of justice," then the defendant's right to a fair trial, as guaranteed by the

## Oyez

### Gideon v. Wainwright
### 372 U.S. 335 (1963)

**MR. JUSTICE BLACK delivered the opinion of the Court.**

Petitioner was charged in Florida state court with having broken and entered a poolroom with intent to commit a misdemeanor. This offense is a felony under Florida law. Appearing in court without funds and without a lawyer, petitioner asked the court to appoint counsel for him, whereupon the following colloquy took place:

THE COURT: Mr. Gideon, I am sorry, but I cannot appoint Counsel to represent you in this case. Under the laws of the State of Florida, the only time the Court can appoint Counsel to represent a defendant is when that person is charged with a capital offense. I am sorry, but I will have to deny your request to appoint Counsel to defend you in this case.

THE DEFENDANT: The United States Supreme Court says I am entitled to be represented by Counsel.

Put to trial before a jury, Gideon conducted his defense about as well as could be expected from a layman. He made an opening statement to the jury, cross-examined the State's witnesses, presented witnesses in his own defense, declined to testify himself, and made a short argument "emphasizing his innocence to the charge contained in the Information filed in this case." The jury returned a verdict of guilty, and petitioner was sentenced to five years in the state prison. Since 1942, when *Betts v. Brady*, 316 U.S. 455, was decided by a divided Court, the problem of a defendant's federal constitutional right to counsel in a state court has been a continuing source of controversy and litigation in both state and federal courts. . . . Since Gideon was proceeding in forma pauperis, we appointed counsel to represent him and requested both sides to discuss in their briefs and oral arguments the following: "Should this Court's holding in *Betts v. Brady* . . . be reconsidered? . . .

Governments, both state and federal, quite properly spend vast sums of money to establish machinery to try defendants accused of crime. Lawyers to prosecute are everywhere deemed essential to protect the public's interest in an orderly society. Similarly, there are few defendants charged with crime, few indeed, who fail to hire the best lawyers they can get to prepare and present their defenses. That government hires lawyers to prosecute and defendants who have the money to hire lawyers to defend are the strongest indications of the widespread belief that lawyers in criminal courts are necessities, not luxuries. The right of one charged with crime to counsel may not be deemed fundamental and essential to fair trials in some countries, but it is in ours. From the very beginning, our state and national constitutions and laws have laid great emphasis on procedural and substantive safeguards designed to assure fair trials before impartial tribunals in which every defendant stands equal before the law. This noble idea cannot be realized if the poor man charged with crime has to face his accusers without a lawyer to represent him. . . . The Court in *Betts v. Brady* departed from sound wisdom upon which the Court's holding in *Powell v. Alabama* rested. Florida, supported by two other States, has asked that *Betts v. Brady* be left intact. Twenty-two states, as friends of the Court, argue that *Betts* was "an anachronism when handed down" and that it should now be overruled. We agree. . . . Reversed.

Fourteenth Amendment, was violated.[1] The Court refused to extend the right to counsel to all state criminal proceedings in *Betts v. Brady*. Cases that involved complex legal issues and where a defendant was incapable of adequately representing himself (e.g., low intelligence, juvenile) were the types of situations that required the appointment of counsel under the *Betts* due process standard.

In 1938, the Court decided *Johnson v. Zerbst*, 304 U.S. 458 (1938), which held that the Sixth Amendment guarantees counsel. The Sixth Amendment right to counsel was found to be broader than the due process right to counsel announced in *Powell*, as it applied to all criminal prosecutions. However, *Zerbst* did not apply to state proceedings. Eventually, the Sixth Amendment right to counsel was extended to all state felony proceedings, in *Gideon v. Wainwright*, found in the Oyez above.

Subsequently, the right to counsel was again extended to include all criminal cases punished with a jail term. Whether the crime is labeled a misdemeanor or felony is not dispositive of the right-to-counsel issue.[2] In the 2002 case, *Alabama v. Shelton*, the Supreme Court extended the right again. In *Shelton*, the right to counsel was found for a convictee who was sentenced to imprisonment, even though the entire sentence was suspended to probation. This is the state of the law today. All criminal defendants who are facing a single day in jail are entitled to appointed counsel. Read why the Court extended the right further in your next Oyez.

In some cases, it may be to the prosecution's advantage for a defendant to have counsel, even though a sentence of imprisonment is not available for a first conviction but is available for subsequent convictions. This is because a sentence may not be enhanced to include jail time based on a prior conviction where the defendant possessed a right to but was denied counsel.[3] For example, the penalty for first-offense drunk driving is not punished by a term in jail; however, subsequent violations are. If Jack is arrested and convicted without counsel for his first offense, he may not be sentenced to jail time for his second drunk driving conviction, because he did not have counsel during his first trial.

To qualify for appointed counsel, a defendant does not have to be financially destitute. It need only be shown that the defendant's financial situation will prevent him or her from being able to retain an attorney. An indigent defendant does not have a right to choose the appointed attorney; this decision falls within the discretion of the trial court.

## Effective Assistance of Counsel

Not all attorneys are equal and good attorneys make mistakes. Beyond simply being represented, a defendant is entitled to the "effective assistance of counsel."

## Oyez

### Alabama v. Shelton
### 535 U.S. 654 (2002)

**JUSTICE GINSBURG delivered the opinion of the Court.**

This case concerns the Sixth Amendment right of an indigent defendant charged with a misdemeanor punishable by imprisonment, fine, or both, to the assistance of court-appointed counsel. Two prior decisions control the Court's judgment. First, in *Argersinger v. Hamlin*, (1972), this Court held that defense counsel must be appointed in any criminal prosecution, "whether classified as petty, misdemeanor, or felony," . . . "that actually leads to imprisonment even for a brief period," . . . Later, in *Scott v. Illinois*, the Court drew the line at "actual imprisonment," holding that counsel need not be appointed when the defendant is fined for the charged crime, but is not sentenced to a term of imprisonment.

Defendant-respondent LeReed Shelton, convicted of third-degree assault, was sentenced to a jail term of 30 days, which the trial court immediately suspended, placing Shelton on probation for two years. The question presented is whether the Sixth Amendment right to appointed counsel, as delineated in *Argersinger* and *Scott*, applies to a defendant in Shelton's situation. We hold that a suspended sentence that may "end up in the actual deprivation of a person's liberty" may not be imposed unless the defendant was accorded "the guiding hand of counsel" in the prosecution for the crime charged.

After representing himself at a bench trial in the District Court of Etowah County, Alabama, Shelton was convicted of third-degree assault, a class A misdemeanor carrying a maximum punishment of one year imprisonment and a $2000 fine . . . He invoked his right to a new trial before a jury in Circuit Court. . . . where he again appeared without a lawyer and was again convicted. The court repeatedly warned Shelton about the problems self-representation entailed, but at no time offered him assistance of counsel at state expense.

The Circuit Court sentenced Shelton to serve 30 days in the county prison. As authorized by Alabama law, however, . . . the court suspended that sentence and placed Shelton on two years' unsupervised probation, conditioned on his payment of court costs, a $500 fine, reparations of $25, and restitution in the amount of $516.69.

Shelton appealed his conviction and sentence on Sixth Amendment grounds. . . .

. . . A suspended sentence is a prison term imposed for the offense of conviction. Once the prison term is triggered, the defendant is incarcerated not for the probation violation, but for the underlying offense. The uncounseled conviction at that point "result[s] in imprisonment. . . . This is precisely what the Sixth Amendment, as interpreted in *Argersinger* and *Scott*, does not allow. . . .

Satisfied that Shelton is entitled to appointed counsel at the critical stage when his guilt or innocence of the charged crime is decided and his vulnerability to imprisonment is determined, we affirm the judgment of the Supreme Court of Alabama. *It is so ordered.*

On appeal, defendants may challenge their convictions by claiming that at a lower level (trial or appellate) they did not have effective counsel.

To succeed with an ineffective counsel claim, two facts must be shown. First, the representation must have been extremely inadequate. Second, the defendant must demonstrate actual harm. So, if an appellate court determines that a defendant would have been convicted with the best of attorneys, the defendant's claim of inadequate counsel fails.

A Sixth Amendment claim of ineffective assistance of counsel can take many forms. Incompetence of counsel is often claimed, but rarely successful. Attorneys are expected to make the legal and tactical decisions of the defense. The fact that defense counsel rendered incorrect legal advice is not determinative. The issue is whether the defendant's representation was shockingly substandard.

A defendant also has a right to the "undivided loyalty" of defense counsel. Hence, it is common to have ineffective assistance of counsel claims where one attorney is representing codefendants. In *Cuyler v. Sullivan*, 446 U.S. 335 (1980), it was held that an ineffective assistance of counsel claim based upon an alleged conflict of interest will succeed only if the defendant can show that the conflict "adversely affected" his or her rights.

Also, the accused has a right to confer with counsel to prepare a defense. If a court denies a defendant access to his or her counsel, a Sixth Amendment claim may be made.

Governmental eavesdropping on a defendant's conversation with his or her counsel is also improper and violative of the Sixth Amendment.

## The Right to Self-Representation

In *Faretta v. California*, 422 U.S. 806 (1975), the right to self-representation was established. The Supreme Court recognized that the assistance of trained legal counsel is essential to preparing and presenting a defense. However, in balance, the Court found that a defendant's right to represent themselves (referred to as pro se) trumps the benefits of forcing appointed counsel.

The record must clearly show that a defendant who has chosen to proceed pro se has done so voluntarily and knowingly. At a Faretta hearing, named for the case just discussed, the defendant "must be made aware of the dangers and disadvantages of self-representation." Whether the defendant possesses any legal training or education is not relevant.

Pro so defendants are notoriously difficult. Most often they are unfamiliar with evidence law and trial procedures. In some instances, they are unruly, and in others, they have a change of heart when they realize they can't adequately defend themselves. To avoid unnecessary mistrials or later reversals, trial judges are permitted to appoint "standby counsel." This attorney attends the trial and is available to provide advice to the defendant or take over the defense, if necessary. The Supreme Court has approved the practice of appointing standby counsel over the objection of the defendant. This is routinely done in felony cases. The right to self-representation is not absolute. A defendant who engages in disruptive behavior during the proceeding may be relieved of pro se status.

## The Scope of the Right

Through *Gideon*, the right to counsel in criminal prosecutions was extended to the states. *Argersinger* made it clear that counsel must be provided in all cases in which the defendant is sentenced to actual imprisonment. But when does the right begin?

The Supreme Court has held that the Sixth Amendment right to counsel applies to all critical stages of a criminal prosecution. This definition requires that a "prosecution" be initiated before the right to counsel, under the Sixth Amendment, attaches. Accordingly, the Sixth Amendment does not apply to juvenile proceedings, or to administrative hearings such as parole determination and revocation.

The right starts whenever the "adversary judicial proceeding" is initiated. Police contacts prior to the initiation of an adversary judicial proceeding are not covered by the Sixth Amendment.

In determining what constitutes a critical stage, courts focus on "whether substantial rights of the defendant may be affected." The greater the contact between the prosecutor and the defendant, the more likely the event is at a critical stage. The first critical stage is normally the initial appearance or the arraignment. Courts have also determined that a defendant may be entitled to counsel at a police lineup, sentencing, preliminary hearing, and during a probation revocation hearing. Once charges are filed, all interrogations of the defendant by the government are critical stages.

The Sixth Amendment is not the only constitutional provision ensuring counsel. As you learned earlier, the Fifth Amendment's right to be free from self-incrimination also guarantees counsel in some instances, as does the Fourteenth Amendment's Equal Protection Clause and Due Process Clause.

# Trial Right: A Jury of Impartial Peers

Learning Objective: Describe the Sixth Amendment's right to be tried by a jury of peers, including the landmark cases that define the right.

A trial is a method of determining guilt or innocence. In medieval England, trials by ordeal, combat, and compurgation were used.

Trial by ordeal was devine; that is, God rendered the verdict. There were two ordeals: by water and fire, with two versions of the water ordeal. In the first, the accused was thrown into a body of water. If he sank, he was innocent; if he floated, he was guilty. In the second water ordeal, the accused's arm was submerged in boiling water. The defendant had to survive unhurt to be proven innocent. The fire ordeal was similar, the accused having to walk over fire or grasp hot irons.

Trial by jury was known to the British as early as the Norman Conquest of 1066, or possibly earlier. Its inclusion in the Magna Carta (1215) demonstrates how important juries were to the nobility of the period. However, equality in the eyes of the law had not yet taken hold; only the nobility benefited from Magna Carta's protections. The Magna Carta and other legal protections of liberties subsequent to it were so much a part of the legal landscape in America that the Framers protected the right in the Constitution itself. Article III requires that "Trial of all Crimes, except in Cases of Impeachment, shall be by Jury." The Sixth Amendment restated the right, with details added.

The Sixth Amendment has been interpreted to mean that defendants have a right to a jury trial for all offenses that may be punished with six months' imprisonment or more. Most crimes that have as their maximum punishment less than six months are "petty offenses," and there is no right to trial by jury.[4]

Note that the term "most" is used. Possibly, when a fine becomes large enough, a person is entitled to a jury trial, regardless of possible jail time. The same argument can be made about crimes that were indictable at common law. The Supreme Court has not answered these questions, and the lower courts are are split.

The maximum *possible* penalty determines if a crime is petty, not the actual sentence. For example, if a crime is punishable by from three months to one year in jail, the defendant is entitled to a jury, even if the trial judge routinely sentences those convicted to three months for the offense. Some crimes do not have a legislatively established punishment, such as contempt. In such cases, the issue is whether the defendant is sentenced to more than six months in jail. If so, the defendant is entitled to a jury.

Although the right to a jury trial for non-petty offenses nearly always attaches, there are a few exceptions. There is no right to a jury in military trials. In addition,

O.J. Simpson trying on gloves in his 1995 jury trial for murder.

those appearing in juvenile court (delinquency proceedings) are not entitled to a jury trial.[5] Of course, juveniles who are tried as adults are entitled to the same rights as adults, including the right to have a jury trial.

Juries sit as fact finders. A defendant may be entitled to have a jury decide guilt or innocence, and as you learn in the next chapter, there is also a right to have juries decide the facts that are essential to passing sentence. Some jurisdictions have the jury impose sentence, or make a sentence recommendation to the trial court; however, this is not usually the practice and there is no federal constitutional reason for it.

The Sixth Amendment doesn't mention jury size, but 12 is the most common number of jurors in criminal cases. The number of twelve jurors is of ancient origin. The Welsh king Morgan of Glamorgan, who established trial by jury in A.D. 725, is said to have declared, "For as Christ and his 12 apostles were finally to judge the world, so human tribunals should be composed of the king and 12 wise men." Even though the 12 member jury was the standard at the old Common Law and in the colonies of the United States, the Supreme Court has held that there is no constitutional requirement for 12 jurors, referring to the number 12 as a "historical accident."[6] Juries as small as six are used by several jurisdictions in misdemeanor cases, and at least one state, Florida, uses six jurors in noncapital offense felonies.

The use of less than 12 jurors is criticized as elevating efficiency and money above justice. Research has demonstrated, for example, that larger juries are more likely to deliberate longer, to recall evidence with greater accuracy, and to be more diverse. At least one study found that discussion is more inhibited in smaller juries, where jurors with strong personalities can overwhelm their peers.

For a long period of time, the Supreme Court held that the Constitution didn't require juror unanimity. Until 2020, two states permitted convictions with as few as 10 of 12 jurors. The Court reversed itself in the 2020 case *Ramos v. Louisiana*, featured in your next Oyez.

A defendant cannot be penalized for choosing to proceed to trial rather than pleading guilty. In *United States v. Jackson*, 390 U.S. 570 (1968), the Supreme Court found that a statute making the death penalty available for those who were tried and not for those who pled guilty was violative of the Sixth Amendment.

# Oyez

## Ramos v. Louisiana
### 590 U.S. _____ (2020)

**Justice Gorsuch announced the judgment of the Court . . . .**

Accused of a serious crime, Evangelisto Ramos insisted on his innocence and invoked his right to a jury trial. Eventually, 10 jurors found the evidence against him persuasive. But a pair of jurors believed that the State of Louisiana had failed to prove Mr. Ramos's guilt beyond reasonable doubt; they voted to acquit.

In 48 States and federal court, a single juror's vote to acquit is enough to prevent a conviction. But not in Louisiana. Along with Oregon, Louisiana has long punished people based on 10-to-2 verdicts like the one here. So instead of the mistrial he would have received almost anywhere else, Mr. Ramos was sentenced to life in prison without the possibility of parole.

Why do Louisiana and Oregon allow nonunanimous convictions? Though it's hard to say why these laws persist, their origins are clear. Louisiana first endorsed nonunanimous verdicts for serious crimes at a constitutional convention in 1898. According to one committee chairman, the avowed purpose of that convention was to "establish the supremacy of the white race," and the resulting document included many of the trappings of the Jim Crow era: a poll tax, a combined literacy and property ownership test, and a grandfather clause that in practice exempted white residents from the most onerous of these requirements.

Nor was it only the prospect of African-Americans voting that concerned the delegates. Just a week before the convention, the U. S. Senate passed a resolution calling for an investigation into whether Louisiana was systemically excluding African-Americans from juries. Seeking to avoid unwanted national attention, and aware that this Court would strike down any policy of overt discrimination against African-American jurors as a violation of the Fourteenth Amendment,[3] the delegates sought to undermine African-American participation on juries in another way. With a careful eye on racial demographics, the convention delegates sculpted a "facially race-neutral" rule permitting 10-to-2 verdicts in order "to ensure that African-American juror service would be meaningless."

Adopted in the 1930s, Oregon's rule permitting nonunanimous verdicts can be similarly traced to the rise of the Ku Klux Klan and efforts to dilute "the influence of racial, ethnic, and religious minorities on Oregon juries."[5] In fact, no one before us contests any of this; courts in both Louisiana and Oregon have frankly acknowledged that race was a motivating factor in the adoption of their States' respective nonunanimity rules.

We took this case to decide whether the Sixth Amendment right to a jury trial—as incorporated against the States by way of the Fourteenth Amendment—requires a unanimous verdict to convict a defendant of a serious offense. . . .

The Sixth Amendment promises that "[i]n all criminal prosecutions, the accused shall enjoy the right to a speedy and public trial, by an impartial jury of the State and district wherein the crime shall have been committed, which district shall have been previously ascertained by law." The Amendment goes on to preserve other rights for criminal defendants but says nothing else about what a "trial by an impartial jury" entails.

Still, the promise of a jury trial surely meant *something*—otherwise, there would have been no reason to write it down. Nor would it have made any sense to spell out the places from which jurors should be drawn if their powers as jurors could be freely abridged by statute. Imagine a constitution that allowed a "jury trial" to mean nothing but a single person rubberstamping convictions without hearing any evidence—but simultaneously insisting that the lone juror come from a specific judicial district "previously ascertained by law." And if that's not enough, imagine a constitution that included the same hollow guarantee *twice*—not only in the Sixth Amendment, but also in Article III. . . .

Wherever we might look to determine what the term "trial by an impartial jury trial" meant at the time of the Sixth Amendment's adoption—whether it's the common law, state practices in the founding era, or opinions and treatises written soon afterward—the answer is unmistakable. A jury must reach a unanimous verdict in order to convict.

The requirement of juror unanimity emerged in 14th- century England and was soon accepted as a vital right protected by the common law. As Blackstone explained, no person could be found guilty of a serious crime unless "the truth of every accusation . . . should . . . be confirmed by the unanimous suffrage of twelve of his equals and neighbors, indifferently chosen, and superior to all suspicion." A " 'verdict, taken from eleven, was no verdict' " at all.

This same rule applied in the young American States. . . .

It was against this backdrop that James Madison drafted and the States ratified the Sixth Amendment in 1791. By that time, unanimous verdicts had been required for about 400 years.[15] If the term "trial by an impartial jury" carried any meaning at all, it surely included a requirement as long and widely accepted as unanimity.

Influential, postadoption treatises confirm this understanding. For example, in 1824, Nathan Dane reported as fact that the U. S. Constitution required unanimity in criminal jury trials for serious offenses.[16] A few years later, Justice Story explained in his Commentaries on the Constitution that "in common cases, the law not only presumes every man innocent, until he is proved guilty; but unanimity in the verdict of the jury is indispensable." Similar statements can be found in American legal treatises throughout the 19th century. . . .

[The Court then acknowledged it was its own "badly fractured" precedent that caused the two states to retain their nonunanimous practices.]

Sensibly, Louisiana doesn't dispute that the common law required unanimity. Instead, it argues that the drafting history of the Sixth Amendment reveals an intent by the framers to leave this particular feature behind. The State points to the fact that Madison's proposal for the Sixth Amendment originally read: "The trial of all crimes . . . shall be by an impartial jury of freeholders of the vicinage, with the requisite of unanimity for conviction, of the right of challenge, and other accustomed requisites. . . ." Louisiana notes that the House of Representatives approved this text with minor modifications. Yet, the State stresses, the Senate replaced "impartial jury of freeholders of the vicinage" with "impartial jury of the State and district wherein the crime shall have been committed" and also removed the explicit references to unanimity, the right of challenge, and "other accustomed requisites." In light of these revisions, Louisiana would have us infer an intent to abandon the common law's traditional unanimity requirement.

But this snippet of drafting history could just as easily support the opposite inference. Maybe the Senate deleted the language about unanimity, the right of challenge, and "other accustomed prerequisites" because all this was so plainly included in the promise of a "trial by an impartial jury" that Senators considered the language surplusage. The truth is that we have little contemporaneous evidence shedding light on why the Senate acted as it did. So rather than dwelling on text left on the cutting room floor, we are much better served by interpreting the language Congress retained and the States ratified. And, as we've seen, at the time of the Amendment's adoption, the right to a jury trial *meant* a trial in which the jury renders a unanimous verdict.

[The Court addressed and dismissed the argument that stare decisis should bind the court to its earlier decisions permitted convictions with less than 12 jurors.]

[conviction] Reversed

Justice Alito, with whom The Chief Justice joins, and with whom Justice Kagan joins as to all but Part III–D, dissenting.

The doctrine of *stare decisis* gets rough treatment in today's decision. Lowering the bar for overruling our precedents, a badly fractured majority casts aside an important and long-established decision with little regard for the enormous reliance the decision has engendered. If the majority's approach is not just a way to dispose of this one case, the decision marks an important turn.

Nearly a half century ago in *Apodaca v. Oregon*, 406 U.S. 404 (1972), the Court held that the Sixth Amendment permits non-unanimous verdicts in state criminal trials, and in all the years since then, no Justice has even hinted that *Apodaca* should be reconsidered. Understandably thinking that *Apodaca* was good law, the state courts in Louisiana and Oregon have tried thousands of cases under rules that permit such verdicts. But today, the Court does away with *Apodaca* and, in so doing, imposes a potentially crushing burden on the courts and criminal justice systems of those States. The Court, however, brushes aside these consequences and even suggests that the States should have known better than to count on our decision.

To add insult to injury, the Court tars Louisiana and Oregon with the charge of racism for permitting non- unanimous verdicts—even though this Court found such verdicts to be constitutional and even though there are entirely legitimate arguments for allowing them.

I would not overrule *Apodaca*. Whatever one may think about the correctness of the decision, it has elicited enormous and entirely reasonable reliance. And before this Court decided to intervene, the decision appeared to have little practical importance going forward. Louisiana has now abolished non-unanimous verdicts, and Oregon seemed on the verge of doing the same until the Court intervened. . . .

If Louisiana and Oregon originally adopted their laws allowing non-unanimous verdicts for these reasons,[2] that is deplorable, but what does that have to do with the broad constitutional question before us? The answer is: nothing.

For one thing, whatever the reasons why Louisiana and Oregon originally adopted their rules many years ago, both States readopted their rules under different circumstances in later years. Louisiana's constitutional convention of 1974 adopted a new, narrower rule, and its stated purpose was "judicial efficiency." "In that debate no mention was made of race."

The more important point, however, is that today's decision is not limited to anything particular about Louisiana or Oregon. The Court holds that the Sixth Amendment requires jury unanimity in all state criminal trials. If at some future time another State wanted to allow non-unanimous verdicts, today's decision would rule that out—even if all that State's lawmakers were angels. . . .

I begin with the question whether *Apodaca* was a precedent at all. It is remarkable that it is even necessary to address this question, but in Part IV–A of the principal opinion, three Justices take the position that *Apodaca* was never a precedent. The only truly fitting response to this argument is: "Really?"

Consider what it would mean if *Apodaca* was never a precedent. It would mean that the entire legal profession was fooled for the past 48 years. Believing that *Apodaca* was a precedent, the courts of Louisiana and Oregon tried thousands of cases under rules allowing conviction by a vote of 11 to 1 or 10 to 2, and appellate courts in those States upheld these convictions based on *Apodaca*. But according to three Justices in the majority, these courts were deluded.

This Court, for its part, apparently helped to perpetuate the illusion, since it reiterated time and again what *Apodaca* had established.

Even though there may not be an explicit penalty for invoking the right to a jury trial, the plea bargaining system creates a de facto penalty. As discussed earlier in the book, it is a common practice for prosecutors to charge stack (charge every possible crime) to encourage defendants to plead guilty. Defendants who opt for trial face conviction for all the charged offenses, as well as little or no leniency by prosecutors when making sentencing recommendations.

An interesting question that has received considerable attention from the Supreme Court in recent years is exactly what facts must be found by a jury. As you will learn in the next chapter, the responsibility of juries extends beyond the guilt decision. They must also find all facts that are essential to the sentencing decision.

Beyond having peers sit in judgment, an accused is entitled to an impartial jury. The Sixth Amendment specifically requires an impartial jury. The Due Process Clause and Equal Protection Clause do the same. Impartiality has two dimensions; the jury selection process must be designed to create a pool, known as a **venire**, that reasonably reflects the diversity of the community, and the conduct of a selected jury must be unbiased.

**venire**
The pool of prospective jurors.

As to the first, the systematic exclusion of a "distinctive" group violates the Sixth Amendment, and possibly the Equal Protection Clause. The rule doesn't require the final jury to reflect the diversity of the community, only that the venire panel be drawn from a cross-section of the community. A law, for example, that excluded women from jury service was invalidated.[7] Similarly, a system that gave women an automatic exemption from service, and thereby yielded a grossly disproportionate male pool of juror candidates, was stricken.[8] The Supreme Court held as early as the late 1800s that the systematic exclusion of African Americans from both grand jury and petit jury service violated equal protection.[9] To establish a prima facie case that there is an unfair cross-section of the community, a defendant must show

1. that the group alleged to be excluded is a "distinctive" group in the community;
2. that the representation of this group in venires from which juries are selected is not fair and reasonable in relation to the number of such persons in the community; and
3. that this underrepresentation is due to systematic exclusion of the group in the jury selection process.

If a defendant proves these three elements, the burden shifts to the government to justify the underrepresentation. This is a high hurdle, but not impossible. For example, a defendant convicted of violating federal narcotics laws in Washington, D.C., alleged that he had a partial jury because most of his jurors were employees of the government. But given the large number of federal government employees in the nation's capital, his claim was rejected.[10]

At trial, the voir dire process is also limited by equal protection principles. A lawyer, for example, can't exercise a peremptory challenge to remove a juror because of the person's race or sex.[11]

Beyond a fair selection process, selected jurors are expected to be unbiased. Jurors must express that they will set aside personal opinions and render their votes on the facts, as presented during the trial, and that they will follow the law. If a juror is unable to do this, the trial judge is to excuse the juror for cause. For example, a juror who indicates that he has a moral objection to the death penalty and could never vote to convict a capital defendant must be excused. Undue influence, coercion, and threats to jurors are all valid reasons for a trial judge to declare a mistrial and to start again with a new jury.

To promote full and honest discussion, jury deliberations are secret, and for centuries, a no-impeachment rule has prevented challenging jury verdicts because of statements made in the jury room. The rule once forbade all inquiries into jury deliberations. The Supreme Court carved out an exception to the no-impeachment rule for juror racial animus in the 2017 case *Pena-Rodriguez v. Colorado*.

## Oyez

## Pena-Rodriguez v. Colorado
### 580 U.S. __ (2017)

**Justice Kennedy delivered the opinion of the Court.**

The jury is a central foundation of our justice system and our democracy. Whatever its imperfections in a particular case, the jury is a necessary check on governmental power. The jury, over the centuries, has been an inspired, trusted, and effective instrument for resolving factual disputes and determining ultimate questions of guilt or innocence in criminal cases. Over the long course its judgments find acceptance in the community, an acceptance essential to respect for the rule of law. The jury is a tangible implementation of the principle that the law comes from the people.

In the era of our Nation's founding, the right to a jury trial already had existed and evolved for centuries, through and alongside the common law. The jury was considered a fundamental safeguard of individual liberty. See The Federalist No. 83, p. 451 (B. Warner ed. 1818) (A. Hamilton). The right to a jury trial in criminal cases was part of the Constitution as first drawn, and it was restated in the Sixth Amendment. Art. III, §2, cl. 3; Amdt. 6. By operation of the Fourteenth Amendment, it is applicable to the States. *Duncan v. Louisiana*, 391 U. S. 145 –150 (1968).

Like all human institutions, the jury system has its flaws, yet experience shows that fair and impartial verdicts can be reached if the jury follows the court's instructions and undertakes deliberations that are honest, candid, robust, and based on common sense. A general rule has evolved to give substantial protection to verdict final-ity and to assure jurors that, once their verdict has been entered, it will not later be called into question based on the comments or conclusions they expressed during deliberations. This principle, itself centuries old, is often referred to as the no-impeachment rule. The instant case presents the question whether there is an exception to the no-impeachment rule when, after the jury is discharged, a juror comes forward with compelling evidence that an-other juror made clear and explicit statements indicating that racial animus was a significant motivating factor in his or her vote to convict.

State prosecutors in Colorado brought criminal charges against petitioner, Miguel Angel Peña-Rodriguez, based on the following allegations. In 2007, in the bathroom of a Colorado horse-racing facility, a man sexually assaulted two teenage sisters. The girls told their father and identified the man as an employee of the racetrack. The police located and arrested petitioner. Each girl separately identified petitioner as the man who had assaulted her.

The State charged petitioner with harassment, unlawful sexual contact, and attempted sexual assault on a child. Before the jury was empaneled, members of the venire were repeatedly asked whether they believed that they could be fair and impartial in the case. A written questionnaire asked if there was "anything about you that you feel would make it difficult for you to be a fair juror." The court repeated the question to the panel of prospective jurors and encouraged jurors to speak in private with the court if they had any concerns about their impartiality. Defense counsel likewise asked whether anyone felt that "this is simply not a good case" for them to be a fair juror. None of the empaneled jurors expressed any reservations based on racial or any other bias. And none asked to speak with the trial judge.

After a 3-day trial, the jury found petitioner guilty of unlawful sexual contact and harassment, but it failed to reach a verdict on the attempted sexual assault charge. When the jury was discharged, the court gave them this instruction, as mandated by Colorado law:

"The question may arise whether you may now discuss this case with the lawyers, defendant, or other persons. For your guidance the court instructs you that whether you talk to anyone is entirely your own decision. . . . If any person persists in discussing the case over your objection, or becomes critical of your service either before or after any discussion has begun, please report it to me."

Following the discharge of the jury, petitioner's counsel entered the jury room to discuss the trial with the jurors. As the room was emptying, two jurors remained to speak with counsel in private. They stated that, during deliberations, another juror had expressed anti-Hispanic bias toward petitioner and petitioner's alibi witness. Petitioner's counsel reported this to the court and, with the court's supervision, obtained sworn affidavits from the two jurors.

The affidavits by the two jurors described a number of biased statements made by another juror, identified as Juror H. C. According to the two jurors, H. C. told the other jurors that he "believed the defendant was guilty because, in [H. C.'s] experience as an ex-law enforcement officer, Mexican men had a bravado that caused them to believe they could do whatever they wanted with women." The jurors reported that H. C. stated his belief that Mexican men are physically controlling of women because of their sense of entitlement, and further stated, " 'I think he did it because he's Mexican and Mexican men take whatever they want.' " According to the jurors, H. C. further explained that, in his experience, "nine times out of ten Mexican men were guilty of being aggressive toward women and young girls." Finally, the jurors recounted that Juror H. C. said that he did not find petitioner's alibi witness credible because, among other things, the witness was " 'an illegal.' " (In fact, the witness testified during trial that he was a legal resident of the United States.)

After reviewing the affidavits, the trial court acknowledged H. C.'s apparent bias. But the court denied petitioner's motion for a new trial, noting that "[t]he actual deliberations that occur among the jurors are protected from inquiry under [Colorado Rule of Evidence]

(continued)

606(b)." Like its federal counterpart, Colorado's Rule 606(b) generally prohibits a juror from testifying as to any statement made during deliberations in a proceeding inquiring into the validity of the verdict. . . .

[T]he Court has addressed the precise question whether the Constitution mandates an exception to it in just two instances.

In its first case, *Tanner*, 483 U. S. 107 , the Court rejected a Sixth Amendment exception for evidence that some jurors were under the influence of drugs and alcohol during the trial. Central to the Court's reasoning were the "long-recognized and very substantial concerns" supporting "the protection of jury deliberations from intrusive inquiry." The *Tanner* Court echoed [the concern of another case], if attorneys could use juror testimony to attack verdicts, jurors would be "harassed and beset by the defeated party," thus destroying "all frankness and freedom of discussion and conference. . . .

The second case to consider the general issue presented here was *Warger*, 574 U. S. ___. The Court again rejected the argument that, in the circumstances there, the jury trial right required an exception to the no-impeachment rule. *Warger* involved a civil case where, after the verdict was entered, the losing party sought to proffer evidence that the jury forewoman had failed to disclose prodefendant bias during *voir dire*. As in *Tanner*, the Court put substantial reliance on existing safeguards for a fair trial. The Court stated: "Even if jurors lie in *voir dire* in a way that conceals bias, juror impartiality is adequately assured by the parties' ability to bring to the court's attention any evidence of bias before the verdict is rendered, and to employ nonjuror evidence even after the verdict is rendered." 574 U. S., at ___ .

In *Warger*, however, the Court did reiterate that the no-impeachment rule may admit exceptions. As in *Reid* and *McDonald*, the Court warned of "juror bias so extreme that, almost by definition, the jury trial right has been abridged. . . .

It must become the heritage of our Nation to rise above racial classifications that are so inconsistent with our commitment to the equal dignity of all persons. This imperative to purge racial prejudice from the administration of justice was given new force and direction by the ratification of the Civil War Amendments.

"[T]he central purpose of the Fourteenth Amendment was to eliminate racial discrimination emanating from official sources in the States." In the years before and after the ratification of the Fourteenth Amendment, it became clear that racial discrimination in the jury system posed a particular threat both to the promise of the Amendment and to the integrity of the jury trial. "Almost immediately after the Civil War, the South began a practice that would continue for many decades: All-white juries punished black defendants particularly harshly, while simultaneously refusing to punish violence by whites, including Ku Klux Klan members, against blacks and Republicans." To take one example, just in the years 1865 and 1866, all-white juries in Texas decided a total of 500 prosecutions of white defendants charged with killing African-Americans. All 500 were acquitted. . . .

The duty to confront racial animus in the justice system is not the legislature's alone. Time and again, this Court has been called upon to enforce the Constitution's guarantee against state-sponsored racial discrimination in the jury system. Beginning in 1880, the Court interpreted the Fourteenth Amendment to prohibit the exclusion of jurors on the basis of race. . . . The unmistakable principle underlying these precedents is that discrimination on the basis of race, "odious in all aspects, is especially pernicious in the administration of justice. . . .

This case lies at the intersection of the Court's decisions endorsing the no-impeachment rule and its decisions seeking to eliminate racial bias in the jury system. The two lines of precedent, however, need not conflict.

Racial bias of the kind alleged in this case differs in critical ways from the compromise verdict in *McDonald*, the drug and alcohol abuse in *Tanner*, or the pro-defendant bias in *Warger*. The behavior in those cases is troubling and unacceptable, but each involved anomalous behavior from a single jury—or juror—gone off course. Jurors are presumed to follow their oath), and neither history nor common experience show that the jury system is rife with mischief of these or similar kinds. To attempt to rid the jury of every irregularity of this sort would be to expose it to unrelenting scrutiny. "It is not at all clear . . . that the jury system could survive such efforts to perfect it." *Tanner*, 483 U. S., at 120.

The same cannot be said about racial bias, a familiar and recurring evil that, if left unaddressed, would risk systemic injury to the administration of justice. This Court's decisions demonstrate that racial bias implicates unique historical, constitutional, and institutional concerns. An effort to address the most grave and serious statements of racial bias is not an effort to perfect the jury but to ensure that our legal system remains capable of coming ever closer to the promise of equal treatment under the law that is so central to a functioning democracy.

Racial bias is distinct in a pragmatic sense as well. In past cases this Court has relied on other safeguards to protect the right to an impartial jury. Some of those safeguards, to be sure, can disclose racial bias. *Voir dire* at the outset of trial, observation of juror demeanor and conduct during trial, juror reports before the verdict, and nonjuror evidence after trial are important mechanisms for discovering bias. Yet their operation may be compromised, or they may prove insufficient. . . .

For the reasons explained above, the Court now holds that where a juror makes a clear statement that indicates he or she relied on racial stereotypes or animus to convict a criminal defendant, the Sixth Amendment requires that the no-impeachment rule give way in order to permit the trial court to consider the evidence of the juror's statement and any resulting denial of the jury trial guarantee.

Not every offhand comment indicating racial bias or hostility will justify setting aside the no-impeachment bar to allow further judicial inquiry. For the inquiry to proceed, there must be a showing that one or more jurors made statements exhibiting overt racial bias that cast serious doubt on the fairness and impartiality of the jury's deliberations and resulting verdict. To qualify, the statement must tend to show that racial animus was a significant motivating factor in the juror's vote to convict. Whether that threshold showing has been satisfied is a matter committed to the substantial discretion of the trial court in light of all the circumstances, including the content and timing of the alleged statements and the reliability of the proffered evidence.

In this case the alleged statements by a juror were egregious and unmistakable in their reliance on racial bias. Not only did juror H. C. deploy a dangerous racial stereotype to conclude petitioner was guilty and his alibi witness should not be believed, but he also encouraged other jurors to join him in convicting on that basis.

The Nation must continue to make strides to overcome race-based discrimination. The progress that has already been made underlies the Court's insistence that blatant racial prejudice is antithetical to the functioning of the jury system and must be confronted in egregious cases like this one despite the general bar of the no-impeachment rule. It is the mark of a maturing legal system that it seeks to understand and to implement the lessons of history. The Court now seeks to strengthen the broader principle that society can and must move forward by achieving the thoughtful, rational dialogue at the foundation of both the jury system and the free society that sustains our Constitution.

The judgment of the Supreme Court of Colorado is reversed, and the case is remanded for further proceedings not inconsistent with this opinion.

# Trial Right: A Public Trial

Learning Objective: Describe the Sixth Amendment's right to a public trial, including the landmark cases that define the right.

In addition to a jury trial, the Sixth Amendment guarantees a public trial. This right applies throughout the trial, from openings to return of the verdict; it also applies to many pretrial hearings, such as suppression hearings. The presence of the public is intended to keep prosecutions "honest." As the Supreme Court stated in *Estes v. Texas*, 381 U.S. 532 (1965): "History has proven that secret tribunals were effective instruments of oppression."

The right to a public hearing does not mean that everyone who wishes to attend has a right to attend. The trial judge is responsible for maintaining order in the courtroom and may require the doors to be shut when all of the seats have been filled. Also, a disruptive observer may be removed.

The defendant's right to a public trial is not absolute. Trial judges, acting with extreme caution, may order that a hearing be conducted in private. Facts that support excluding the public are rare. An example of when exclusion of the public may be justified is when an undercover law enforcement agent testifies, and public exposure would put the officer's life in jeopardy.

If a court closes a hearing (or trial) without justification, the defendant is entitled to a new hearing, regardless of whether the defendant was actually harmed. The 1998 First Circuit Court of Appeals case, *United States v. DeLuca*, which appears in the next Oyez, addressed both the presumption of innocence and the right to a public trial in what are rather unusual circumstances.

Generally, members of the press have no greater right to attend a hearing than do other members of the public. However, many judges provide special seating for reporters.

# Trial Right: Confrontation and Cross-Examination

Learning Objective: Describe the Sixth Amendment's right to cross-examination and confrontation, including the landmark cases that define the right.

The Sixth Amendment also contains a right to confront one's accusers. Confrontation includes the right to cross-examine the prosecution's witnesses. The right only applies at trial, not pretrial hearings. Each state drafts its own rules of evidence; however, it may not enact a rule of evidence that conflicts with a defendant's right to confrontation.

## Oyez

### United States v. Deluca
### 137 F.3d 24 (1st Cir. 1998)

**Cyr, Senior Circuit Judge.**

[Defendants were tried and convicted of extortion. Because of fears of juror tampering and intimidation, the trial judge ordered that the identity of the jurors be kept anonymous. The judge also permitted the U.S. Marshal to screen trial spectators. The defendants appealed several issues, including whether an anonymous jury violates the presumption of innocence and whether the screening violated the Sixth Amendment right to a public trial.]

### A. THE ANONYMOUS JURY EMPANELMENT

Appellants first contend that the decision to empanel an anonymous jury constituted an abuse of discretion. . . . We disagree.

Although the empanelment of an anonymous jury should be recognized as an extraordinary protective device, especially if it tends to suggest that the jurors may have something to fear from the accused, thereby conceivably encroaching upon the presumption of innocence, it is a permissible precaution where (1) there are strong grounds for concluding that it is necessary to enable the jury to perform its factfinding function, or to ensure juror protection; and (2) reasonable safeguards are adopted by the trial court to minimize any risk of infringement upon the fundamental rights of the accused.

Our review takes into account not only the evidence available at the time the anonymous empanelment occurred, but all relevant evidence introduced at trial. We conclude that the record as a whole affords sufficient foundation for empaneling an anonymous jury both as a prudent safety precaution and a means of ensuring unfettered performance of the factfinding function.

First, the record links appellants to organized crime, a factor which strongly indicated that clandestine "outside" assistance might be brought to bear in any effort to intimidate or punish jurors. Moreover, Ouimette's capacity and readiness to enlist criminal confederates in jury tampering plans was supported by actual precedent.

Second, both Ouimette and DeLuca Sr. have long been involved in violent crimes, including robbery, assault with a dangerous weapon, larceny in a dwelling, and conspiracy to commit murder, not to mention their violent extortions in the instant case.

Third, appellants also attempted to tamper with witnesses and to suborn perjury in the instant case. DeLuca Sr. and Ouimette, through intermediaries, pressured prospective prosecution witnesses, Paula Coppola and Robert Buehne, to perjure themselves, and offered $5,000 to another prospective government witness, David Duxbury, to abscond prior to trial. Thereafter, when Duxbury nevertheless showed up at a pretrial hearing, Ouimette told an associate: "If we can't get [Duxbury], we'll get one of his kids."

Fourth, both Ouimette and DeLuca were confronting mandatory lifetime sentences upon conviction, which surely provided a strong inducement to resort to extreme measures in any effort to influence the outcome of their trial. Moreover, their trial was prominently and extensively covered by local print and electronic media (e.g., several lengthy front-page stories in the *Providence Journal*), to the degree that any public disclosure of the jurors' identities would have enhanced the practicability, hence the likelihood, of efforts to harass, intimidate, or harm the jurors.

Finally, the district court adopted prudent measures designed to safeguard defendants' constitutional rights by informing the members of the jury that their identities would not be disclosed, so as to ensure that no extrajudicial information could be communicated to them during trial, either by the public or by media representatives. Thus, the court explained, the constitutional right of each defendant to a jury trial, based exclusively on the evidence, would be preserved.

In our view, the district court thereby satisfactorily averted any unacceptable risk of intrusion upon the constitutional rights of the individual defendants by diverting juror attention from the possible perception that anonymous empanelment was a safeguard against defendants' dangerousness. Accordingly, given the demonstrated need, coupled with the cautionary instruction fashioned by the district court, the anonymous jury empanelment did not constitute an abuse of discretion.

### B. THE PROCEDURAL IMPEDIMENTS TO COURTROOM ACCESS BY SPECTATORS

The United States Marshal, acting sua sponte on the first day of trial, established a screening and identification procedure whereby each would—be spectator was required to present written identification before being allowed to enter the courtroom. Deputy marshals examined whatever written identification was presented, then recorded the type of identification and the bearer's name, address and birth date. The recorded information was retained by the United States Marshal for use in determining whether the bearer had a criminal background or any connection with a defendant on trial, such as might indicate a courtroom security risk. On the second day of trial the district court ratified the spectator screening procedure over appellants' objections.

Appellants contend on appeal that the screening procedure violated their Sixth Amendment right to a public trial. . . .

The Sixth Amendment right to a public trial enures to the benefit of the criminal justice system itself as well as the defendant, by enhancing due process, encouraging witnesses to come forward, and enabling the public at large to confirm that the accused are dealt with fairly and that the trial participants properly perform their respective functions. Due to the important individual rights and public interests at stake, an alleged violation of the Sixth Amendment right to a public trial resulting from a "total" closure is not subject to "harmless error" analysis. Nevertheless, the Sixth Amendment right to a public trial is not absolute and must on occasion yield to competing interests in the fair and efficient administration of justice.

The government initially urges, as a matter of law, that the Sixth Amendment right to a public trial was never implicated in the present case because the challenged screening procedure effected neither a total nor a partial closure. According to the government, a "closure" occurs only if the trial court unconditionally excludes persons from the courtroom, but not if it simply imposes universal preconditions on courtroom access which have the incidental effect of barring only those persons who elect not to comply. To cite an obvious example, magnetometer screenings are designed to prevent armed spectators from entering the courtroom, yet no one would suggest that conditioning spectator access on submission to reasonable security screening procedures for dangerous weapons violates the Sixth Amendment right to a public trial. Furthermore, the government correctly notes, no authority squarely holds that such "universal" preconditions to courtroom access constitute a Sixth Amendment "closure." We need not opt for the broad rule urged by the government, however, since the security screening procedure utilized below amounted at most to a permissible "partial" closure.

Although we have yet to rule on the matter, cf. *Martin v. Bissonette*, 118 F.3d 871, 874 (1st Cir. 1997), several other courts of appeals have held that the Sixth Amendment test laid down in *Waller*, 467 U.S. at 48, need be less stringent in the "partial" closure context; that is to say, a "substantial reason," rather than an "overriding interest," may warrant a closure which ensures at least some public access. These courts essentially conclude that a less stringent standard is warranted in the "partial" closure context provided the essential purposes of the "public trial" guarantee are served and the constitutional rights of defendants are adequately protected. As yet, no court of appeals has held otherwise.

Unlike the "total" closure in *Waller*, 467 U.S. at 42, which excluded all persons (other than court personnel, witnesses, parties and trial counsel) throughout the entire suppression hearing, the screening and identification procedure employed below effected at most a "partial" closure, as it (1) barred only those would-be spectators who opted not to submit written identification, and (2) presumably may have "chilled" attendance by some potential spectators who opted not to present themselves at the courthouse. Cf. *Woods*, 977 F.2d at 74 (finding "partial" closure where members of defendant's family were excluded while particular witness testified). Moreover, the district court supportably found that members of the general public, as well as members of the defendants' families, attended throughout the seven-day trial, as did credentialed representatives of the print and electronic media, see *Douglas v. Wainwright*, 714 F.2d 1532, 1541 (11th Cir. 1983) (noting that media presence and coverage renders court order one for "partial" closure rather than total, by increasing the likelihood that witnesses with material evidence who are unknown to the parties may learn of perjured testimony through media reports even though they themselves do not attend the trial), vacated and remanded. . . .

Relying on the requirement that a closure be "no broader than necessary" to promote the asserted justification, *Waller*, 467 U.S. at 48, appellants suggest, alternatively, that (1) the anonymous empanelment and partial sequestration adequately addressed any legitimate security concerns, or (2) the court could have resorted to less restrictive security measures, such as installing magnetometers immediately outside the courtroom. In addressing these contentions, we note at the outset that since the spectator-screening procedure resulted at most in a "partial" closure, the government was not required to establish that it furthered a "compelling" interest but simply a "substantial" one.

Although anonymous empanelment and partial sequestration may afford jurors significant protections beyond the confines of the courtroom, prophylactic procedures of an entirely different nature may be required to safeguard against attempts to intimidate jurors and witnesses in the performance of their courtroom responsibilities. These difficult judgments are matters of courtroom governance which require "a sensitive appraisal of the climate surrounding a trial and a prediction as to the potential security or publicity problems that may arise during the proceedings[.]" Thus, in our view an appellate court should be hesitant to displace a trial court's judgment call in such circumstances. ("The trial court's choice of courtroom security procedures requires a subtle reading of the immediate atmosphere and a prediction of potential risks—judgments nearly impossible for appellate courts to second-guess after the fact."); see also *United States v. Brooks*, 125 F.3d 484, 502 (7th Cir. 1997) ("The decisions of a district court concerning security in the courtroom are reviewed deferentially."); *Elledge v. Dugger*, 823 F.2d 1439, 1456 (11th Cir. 1987) ("We generally defer to a trial court's discretion in courtroom-security decisions."); cf. In re *San Juan Star Co.*, 662 F.2d 108, 117 (1st Cir. 1981) (noting that appellate court "must defer to the [district] court's . . . close familiarity with the nature of the [trial] publicity involved").

As the Eleventh Circuit acknowledged recently in relation to another spectator-screening procedure, given their many coincident duties trial judges cannot be expected to scan their courtrooms efficiently on a continuous basis for spectators whose very demeanor might represent an attempt to intimidate a witness or juror. See *Brazel*, 102 F.3d at 1155 (addressing "fixed stares" directed at witnesses by courtroom spectators). Similarly, in the circumstances presented here we cannot agree that prudent identification procedures suitably focused at deterring would-be trial spectators who may pose unacceptable risks—either to the security of the courtroom or the integrity

(continued)

of the factfinding process—need be held in abeyance pending evidence of an actual attempt to influence or harm a witness or juror in the case on trial. Therefore, though we cannot endorse the unilateral action by the United States Marshal, we hold that it did not strip away the substantial deference due the district court's subsequent assessment that the screening procedures were warranted.

These appellants either were directly associated with prior efforts to obstruct fair factfinding through untruthful trial testimony, or were found to possess the present means as well as ample inducement (viz., avoidance of potential life sentences) to sponsor similar efforts in the case at bar, see *supra* Section II.A. Moreover, the challenged spectator-screening procedure was reasonably designed to respond to these concerns, as it plainly alerted would-be spectators that their courtroom conduct would be closely monitored, thereby efficiently focusing the desired deterrent effect principally upon those most likely to impede a fair and orderly trial—particularly appellants' criminal associates. Thus, the challenged screening procedure represented a permissible response to defendants' demonstrated capacity and motivation to undermine the administration of justice at their trial.

Finally, as the district court supportably found, their extensive criminal histories (not to mention the violent criminal activity alleged in the pending indictment) generated realistic concerns that appellants might circumvent normal courtroom security procedures, as by attempting to coerce or bribe authorized personnel to facilitate the introduction of weapons into the courtroom or elsewhere in the courthouse.

In our view, therefore, the district court order ratifying these screening procedures adequately addressed and significantly minimized the demonstrated potential for harassment and intimidation of jurors and witnesses by would-be trial spectators, for many of the same reasons that warranted the anonymous empanelment and partial jury sequestration. Although any courtroom closure represents a serious undertaking which ought never be initiated without prior judicial authorization, we conclude that the partial closure in this case did not contravene the Sixth Amendment, given the strong circumstantial and historical evidence that precautionary security measures were well warranted and the essential constitutional guarantees of a public trial were preserved.

For example, a state procedure permitting government witnesses to refuse to identify themselves was found violative of the Sixth Amendment.[12] The Supreme Court reasoned that the procedure was invalid because it did not permit the defendant to conduct his or her own investigation into the credibility of government witnesses.

Statutes allowing victims to testify remotely, such as by closed-circuit television, also raise confrontation issues. However, the Supreme Court has stated that the Confrontation Clause does not per se prohibit child witnesses in child abuse cases from testifying outside the defendant's physical presence by one-way closed-circuit television. Before such a procedure is used, however, the court must examine the facts of the case and determine that remote testimony is necessary.[13] Failure to make such a finding (e.g., the child fears the defendant) can lead to reversal.[14]

The Confrontation Clause does not give defendants carte blanche to probe any area on cross-examination. If a state can show a compelling reason, it may prohibit cross-examination of a subject. For example, rape shield laws prohibit defendants from inquiring into a rape victim's sexual background in most cases. Courts have affirmed these laws, finding that the protection of the rape victims from unwarranted personal attacks is a legitimate reason to limit defense cross-examination.

The Confrontation Clause also restricts the government's use of hearsay evidence. *Hearsay* is a statement made by a person out of court that is intended to *prove the matter asserted*. To prove the matter asserted means, in plain language, that the out-of-court statement must prove, or support, the matter fact that the attorney is trying to make. For example, in a trial of Samuel for murder, it is hearsay for him to testify that a third person, Ambrose, told him that he observed Samuel commit the murder because the purpose of the testimony is to prove the matter asserted (e.g., Samuel committed the murder). The prosecutor in this instance must find and call Ambrose to testify.

There are exceptions to the hearsay rule, and hearsay is commonly admitted in civil trials. However, the Confrontation Clause limits the admissibility of hearsay in criminal trials. To be admissible, it must be shown that

1. the witness is unavailable at trial and
2. the defendant had a prior opportunity to examine the witness.

This standard was announced by the Court in *Crawford v. Washington,* a case where a wife's statement to police that incriminated her husband had committed a crime was determined to be inadmissible because she was unavailable at trial to the prosecutor because of the marital privilege. The Court limited its Confrontation Clause protection to hearsay—evidence that is introduced to prove the matter asserted. Since the matter at hand in *Crawford* was intended to prove the guilt of the husband, the wife's incriminating statements to the police were excluded. As you will learn in a moment, the exception for non-testimonial statements will prove significant in a later case.[15]

The Confrontation Clause implicitly includes a right of a defendant to be at the trial. This right includes the entire trial, from selection of the jury to return of the verdict. It also includes many pretrial matters, such as suppression hearings. Of course, defendants have a right to be present at both sentencing and probation revocation hearings. Although the right to be present during one's trial is fundamental, it may be lost by disruptive behavior.

There is a long and widely accepted exception to evidence and Confrontation Clause rules that permit purely scientific evidence to be admitted through a report. Unless a defendant had evidence to challenge the validity of such a test, courts in most states and in the federal system admit scientific reports without requiring the scientist or lab attendant to testify. The Supreme Court appeared to have altered this long-standing practice in two cases, *Melendez-Diaz* and *Bullcoming*. The former case is presented in Oyez. Note that a strongly worded dissent by four justices criticized the majority for setting aside over 200 years of evidentiary law that permitted the admission of scientific testing through authenticated reports, citing the concern that the requirement of having analysts testify in all cases where scientific reports are introduced will be burdensome, expensive, and often difficult to implement.

## Oyez

### Melendez-Diaz v. Massachusetts
### 577 U.S. 305 (2009)

**Justice Scalia delivered the opinion of the Court.**

The Massachusetts courts in this case admitted into evidence affidavits reporting the results of forensic analysis which showed that material seized by the police and connected to the defendant was cocaine. The question presented is whether those affidavits are "testimonial," rendering the affiants "witnesses" subject to the defendant's right of confrontation under the Sixth Amendment.

In 2001, Boston police officers received a tip that a Kmart employee, Thomas Wright, was engaging in suspicious activity. The informant reported that Wright repeatedly received phone calls at work, after each of which he would be picked up in front of the store by a blue sedan, and would return to the store a short time later. The police set up surveillance in the Kmart parking lot and witnessed this precise sequence of events. When Wright got out of the car upon his return, one of the officers detained and searched him, finding four clear white plastic bags containing a substance resembling cocaine. The officer then signaled other officers on the scene to arrest the two men in the car—one of whom was petitioner Luis Melendez-Diaz. The officers placed all three men in a police cruiser. During the short drive to the police station, the officers observed their passengers fidgeting and making furtive movements in the back of the car. After depositing the men at the station, they searched the police cruiser and found a plastic bag containing 19 smaller plastic bags hidden in the partition between the front and back seats. They submitted the seized evidence to a state laboratory required by law to conduct chemical analysis upon police request.

Melendez-Diaz was charged with distributing cocaine and with trafficking in cocaine in an amount between 14 and 28 grams. At trial, the prosecution placed into evidence the bags seized from Wright and from the police cruiser. It also submitted three "certificates of analysis" showing the results of the forensic analysis performed on the seized substances. The certificates reported the weight of the seized bags and stated that the bags "[h]a[ve] been examined with the following results: The substance was found to contain: Cocaine." The certificates were sworn to before a notary public by analysts at the State Laboratory Institute of the Massachusetts Department of Public Health, as required under Massachusetts law.

(continued)

Petitioner objected to the admission of the certificates, asserting that our Confrontation Clause decision in *Crawford* v. *Washington*, 541 U.S. 36 (2004), required the analysts to testify in person. [the objection was overruled and the defendant was convicted.] . . .

There is little doubt that the documents at issue in this case fall within the "core class of testimonial statements" . . . The "certificates" are functionally identical to live, in-court testimony, doing "precisely what a witness does on direct examination. . . .

In short, under our decision in *Crawford* the analysts' affidavits were testimonial statements, and the analysts were "witnesses" for purposes of the Sixth Amendment. Absent a showing that the analysts were unavailable to testify at trial *and* that petitioner had a prior opportunity to cross-examine them, petitioner was entitled to " 'be confronted with' " the analysts at trial. . . .

Respondent claims that there is a difference, for Confrontation Clause purposes, between testimony recounting historical events, which is "prone to distortion or manipulation," and the testimony at issue here, which is the "resul[t] of neutral, scientific testing. . . . Nor is it evident that what respondent calls "neutral scientific testing" is as neutral or as reliable as respondent suggests. Forensic evidence is not uniquely immune from the risk of manipulation. According to a recent study conducted under the auspices of the National Academy of Sciences, "[t]he majority of [laboratories producing forensic evidence] are administered by law enforcement agencies, such as police departments, where the laboratory administrator reports to the head of the agency." And "[b]ecause forensic scientists often are driven in their work by a need to answer a particular question related to the issues of a particular case, they sometimes face pressure to sacrifice appropriate methodology for the sake of expediency." A forensic analyst responding to a request from a law enforcement official may feel pressure—or have an incentive—to alter the evidence in a manner favorable to the prosecution.

Confrontation is one means of assuring accurate forensic analysis. . . .

Confrontation is designed to weed out not only the fraudulent analyst, but the incompetent one as well. Serious deficiencies have been found in the forensic evidence used in criminal trials. One commentator asserts that "[t]he legal community now concedes, with varying degrees of urgency, that our system produces erroneous convictions based on discredited forensics." . . .

The Sixth Amendment does not permit the prosecution to prove its case via *ex parte* out-of-court affidavits, and the admission of such evidence against Melendez-Diaz was error.

In spite of the strongly worded dissent, the Court reaffirmed *Melendez-Dias* in the 2011 case *Bullcoming v. New Mexico*, where the use of a surrogate lab technician who testified on behalf of the technician who conducted a blood alcohol test was invalidated by the Court as contrary to the Confrontation Clause. The Court found that the analyst who conducted the test had to testify at trial or be available pretrial to testify and be subjected to cross-examination by the defendant.[16]

What appeared to be clear and settled law was dealt a confusing blow in 2012. In a 5-4 decision with no one rationale commanding a majority of justices, the Court decided in *Williams v. Illinois*[17] that the testimony of a forensic DNA expert who testified that the DNA of semen taken from a vaginal swab of a rape victim and analyzed at a private lab, Cellmark, which matched the defendant, was admissible. This expert did not conduct the testing and most likely had never been in the Cellmark lab.

Because the justices were divided, it is difficult to identify exactly how they distinguished the case from *Crawford, Melendez-Diaz,* and *Bullcomings.* But a few ideas can be extracted from the opinions. First, the testing occurred before the defendant had been identified as a suspect. The DNA profile had been built in order to identify an unknown rapist. Accordingly, the profile was not aimed at the defendant, and accordingly, the important purpose of enabling defendants to cross-examine witnesses "against them" would not have been satisfied by prohibiting the expert's testimony.

Second, the expert's statements were not hearsay. She didn't testify to prove the matter asserted—that is, she didn't testify as to the testing or the contents of the testing report. The Court summarized the expert's testimony as such:

In order to assess petitioner's Confrontation Clause argument, it is helpful to inventory exactly what Lambatos said on the stand about Cellmark. She testified to the truth of the following matters: Cellmark was an accredited lab; the ISP occasionally sent forensic samples to Cellmark for DNA testing; according to shipping manifests admitted into evidence, the ISP lab sent vaginal swabs taken from the victim to Cellmark and later received those swabs back from Cellmark; and, finally, the Cellmark DNA profile matched a profile produced by the ISP lab from a sample of petitioner's blood. Lambatos had personal knowledge of all of these matters, and therefore none of this testimony infringed petitioner's confrontation right.

Third, the case was tried before a judge. The law assumes that judges have a better understanding of the law and are better at categorizing evidence and not considering it for purposes beyond what is permitted than are jurors. In this case, the expert's testimony was not admitted to prove the quality of the testing, and the judge is presumed to have not considered it for such purposes. Whether the decision would have been different if the case had been tried before a jury is unclear. But it is easy to imagine that many jurors would interpret the testimony as proving the guilt of the defendant. The full impact of this decision will be revealed in the years to come.

# Trial Right: Presumption of Innocence/ Beyond a Reasonable Doubt

Learning Objective: Describe the due process right to the presumption of innocence and proof beyond a reasonable doubt, including the landmark cases that define the right.

One of the most basic rights underlying the right to a fair trial is the presumption of innocence. Every person accused of a crime must be proven guilty by the government. Criminal defendants have no duty to defend themselves and may remain silent throughout the trial. In fact, the government is prohibited from calling a defendant to testify, and defendants cannot be made to decide whether they will testify at the start of the trial.[18] Furthermore, a defendant's decision to not testify may not be mentioned by the prosecutor to the jury. Defendants may testify in their own behalf. If so, they are subject to full cross-examination by the prosecutor. The Fifth Amendment right to be free from self-incrimination is discussed more fully in Chapter 9.

The standard imposed upon the government in criminal cases is to prove guilt **beyond a reasonable doubt**. A doubt that would cause a reasonable or prudent person to question the guilt of the accused is a reasonable doubt. Although not precisely quantified, beyond a reasonable doubt is greater than the civil preponderance (51% likely) and less than absolute (100% confidence of guilt). See the standards of proof graphic in Chapter 12 to refresh your understanding of the different standards that are employed in criminal law. The prosecution must prove every element of the charged crime beyond a reasonable doubt. The reasonable doubt standard is an important feature of the accusatorial system of the United States and is required by due process.[19] A juror must vote for acquittal if he or she harbors a reasonable doubt.

To further the presumption of innocence, judges must be careful not to behave in a manner that implies to a jury that a defendant is guilty.

Also, The court must guard against unconscious, nonverbal signals of guilt. The Supreme Court has stated that the presence of a defendant at a jury trial in prison clothing is prejudicial.[20] In the *Young* case, in your next Oyez, a federal appellate court reviewed the use of "prisoner docks" for a Sixth Amendment violation. Similarly, a criminal defendant also has a right to be free from appearing before the jury in handcuffs or shackles. But the rule isn't absolute. The government's needs are balanced against the defendant's interests. In *Holbrook v. Flynn*, 475 U.S. 560 (1986), the Court stated that not all practices that single out the defendant are excessively prejudicial. The question is whether there is unacceptable prejudice that is not justified by governmental necessity. Using this standard, the Court allowed a conviction to stand where the defendant objected to the presence of four police officers in the first row of the spectator gallery, directly behind the defendant, during trial.

**beyond a reasonable doubt**
The level of proof required to convict a person of a crime. Precise definitions vary, but moral certainty and firm belief are both used. Beyond a reasonable doubt is not absolute certainty. This is the highest level of proof required in any type of trial.

## Oyez

### Young v. Callahan
### 700 F.2d 32 (1st Cir. 1983)

[The Court included a footnote which stated that a *prisoner dock* is "a box approximately four feet square and four feet high. It is open at the top so that the defendant's head and shoulders can be seen when he or she is seated. The dock is placed typically at the center of the bar enclosure which separates the spectator's section from that portion of the courtroom reserved for trial principals. The dock is usually fifteen to twenty feet behind counsel table, and is sometimes on a raised platform."]

#### Coffin, Chief Judge

In January of 1979 appellant was tried in Massachusetts Superior Court on one count of assault and battery with a dangerous weapon and two counts of murder. The jury returned a guilty verdict on the assault and battery but was unable to reach a verdict on the two murder indictments. In a new trial in February of 1979, appellant was found guilty of second-degree murder on both counts. These convictions were affirmed by the Massachusetts Supreme Judicial Court. . . .

Prior to appellant's second trial, counsel moved that he be allowed to sit at counsel table rather than in the prisoner's dock on the grounds that "forcing him to sit in the prisoner's dock would deprive him of his constitutional rights to a fair trial, to the presumption of innocence, to access to counsel, non-suggestive eyewitness identifications, and due process of law." That motion was accompanied by an affidavit from appellant's trial counsel averring, based on his own observations and those of corrections officers during appellant's two years of incarceration and on appellant's conduct at the first trial, that "allowing [appellant] to sit at counsel table will not present any hazards to the orderly judicial process or to the security of its personnel," and that the trial of the case would involve a substantial amount of testimony concerning acts and conduct of the appellant over a several-day period and would thus "require consultation with the defendant." . . .

In once again evaluating for constitutional error the confinement of an accused to the prisoner's box, we reiterate . . . that such confinement, like appearance in prison attire, is a "constant reminder of the accused's condition" which "may affect a juror's judgment," eroding the presumption of innocence which the accused is due. . . .

The prisoner's dock, like other physical restraints, should thus be employed only when "the trial judge has found such restraint reasonably necessary to maintain order" and when cured by an instruction to the "jurors that such restraint is not to be considered in assessing the proof and determining guilty."

Trial judges also have a responsibility to monitor private conduct in the courtroom to ensure unacceptable unfairness to the defendant does not happen. For example, spectators are not permitted to express opinions about the case to jurors. Whether more subtle behaviors, such as wearing a button with a photo of the victim, are unacceptably prejudicial remains to be seen.[21]

This right to be free of restraint is not absolute. Judges have the authority to take whatever measures are necessary to ensure safety in the courtroom and to advance the administration of justice. Accordingly, a defendant who is disorderly may be expelled from the trial. However, before exclusion is ordered, the Court should consider other alternatives. Defendants who are threatening may be restrained, and those who verbally interfere with the proceeding may be gagged.[22]

## Trial Right: Speedy Trial

Learning Objective: Describe the Sixth Amendment right to speedy trial, including the landmark cases that define the right.

In old England, defendants would be jailed before trial for long periods of time. The jails were dank and unsanitary, and prisoners malnourished. Pretrial release (bail) and speedy trial both developed to counter the ill effects of prolonged pretrial detention. The right to speedy trial has a history dating back to at least the Magna Carta. The Framers included it in the Sixth Amendment.

To date, the U.S. Supreme Court has not set a specific time period for speedy trial. Rather, the Court said in *Barker v. Wingo* that four factors must be considered when determining if a defendant has enjoyed a speedy trial. First, the length of the delay; second, the reason for the delay; third, whether the defendant has asserted the right to a speedy trial; fourth, how seriously the defendant was prejudiced.[23]

Time for speedy trial begins once the defendant is arrested or formally charged.[24] If a defendant is charged by sealed indictment, speedy trial does not start until the indictment has been opened.

Dismissal with prejudice is the remedy for violation of speedy trial. That is, the charge is dismissed and may not be refiled by the prosecutor.

All the states and the national government have enacted speedy trial acts. The Speedy Trial Act of 1974[25] is the federal statute. That act requires that individuals be formally charged within 30 days from the date of arrest and tried within 70 days of the filing date of the information or indictment, or of the date the defendant had the initial appearance before the court that will try the case, whichever is later.

To avoid prejudice by having a trial before a defendant has had an opportunity to prepare a defense, the statute provides that trial shall not occur for 30 days, unless the defendant consents to an earlier date.

The statute specifies certain delays that are excluded from computing time for purpose of speedy trial. A few of the periods excluded by the Speedy Trial Act of 1974 are when the defendant is a fugitive; when trial is delayed because an issue is on appeal; when delays are caused by motions of the parties; and when delays result from mental examinations of the defendant.

The Speedy Trial Act of 1974 gives the trial court the discretion to decide whether violation of its provisions justifies a dismissal with or without prejudice. Factors that must be considered are the seriousness of the offense, the reason for delay, other facts of the case, and the impact of reprosecution on the administration of justice.[26]

Because the U.S. Supreme Court has not established specific time requirements for speedy trial, each state has its own time requirements. Of course, states must comply with the requirements of *Barker v. Wingo*. Most states have speedy trial provisions in their constitutions, which are similar, if not identical, to the Sixth Amendment. Other states set their speedy trial requirements out in statute or court rules. Time requirements differ, but trial within six months is common.

# Trial Procedure

Learning Objective: Describe the procedural steps of a trial from voir dire to verdict and judgment.

## Voir Dire

The first stage of trial is the **voir dire**. This is a French phrase that translates "look speak" (to speak the truth). Voir dire is also known as *jury selection*.

The jury selection process varies across the states. In all jurisdictions, prospective jurors are asked questions bearing upon their individual ability to serve fairly and impartially. Each state differs in how this information is obtained. In many, the judge is responsible for asking most of the questions. In others, the judge makes only a few brief inquiries, and the lawyers do most of the questioning.

There are two ways to eliminate a prospective juror, known as a venireperson. First, if one of the attorneys believes that a juror could not be fair and impartial, the juror can be **challenged for cause**. If the judge agrees, the venireperson is released. An unlimited number of prospective jurors may be eliminated for cause.

**voir dire**
(French) "To see, to say"; "to state the truth." The preliminary in-court questioning of a prospective witness (or juror) to determine competency to testify (or suitability to decide a case). [pronounce: vwahr deer]

**challenge for cause**
A formal objection to the qualifications of a prospective juror or jurors.

**Exhibit 16–2** Sixth Amendment Right to Counsel

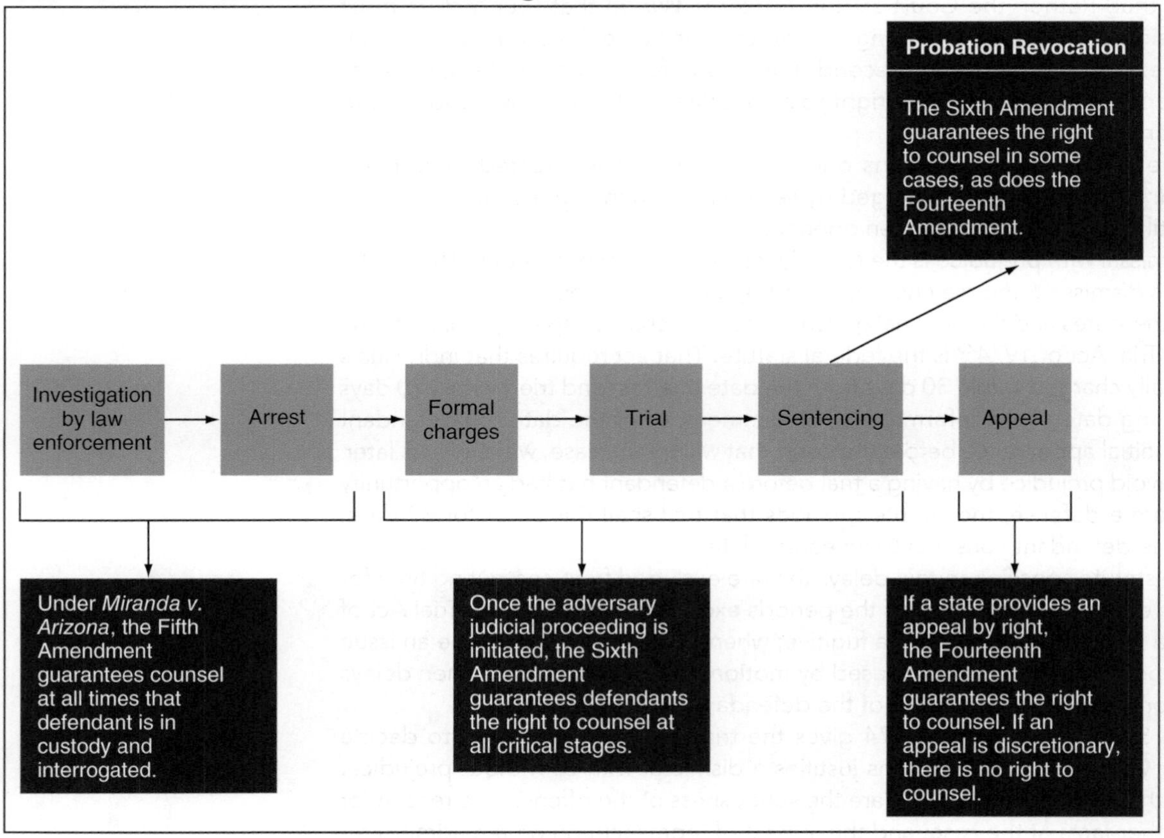

**Probation Revocation**

The Sixth Amendment guarantees the right to counsel in some cases, as does the Fourteenth Amendment.

Investigation by law enforcement → Arrest → Formal charges → Trial → Sentencing → Appeal

Under *Miranda v. Arizona*, the Fifth Amendment guarantees counsel at all times that defendant is in custody and interrogated.

Once the adversary judicial proceeding is initiated, the Sixth Amendment guarantees defendants the right to counsel at all critical stages.

If a state provides an appeal by right, the Fourteenth Amendment guarantees the right to counsel. If an appeal is discretionary, there is no right to counsel.

**peremptory challenge**
The automatic elimination of a potential juror by one side before trial without needing to state the reason for the elimination.

In addition to challenges for cause, a venireperson may be eliminated by a party using a **peremptory challenge**. Each party is given a specific number of peremptory challenges at the start of the trial and may strike jurors until that number is exhausted. A party is free to eliminate, without stating a reason, any potential juror. However, a juror may not be eliminated because of race.[27]

In the federal system, both defendant and prosecutor have 20 peremptory strikes in death cases and 3 in misdemeanors; in noncapital felony cases the defendant gets 10 and the government 6.[28] States have similar rules. Although the parties have broad authority in the use of their peremptory challenges, year read earlier that two limitations exist - they may not be used to eliminate a prospective juror because of race and sex. Other than these limitations, parties often go to great lengths to try to understand the psychological profile of prospective jurors. When resources permit, experts are retained who make recommendations about whether venireman should be retained or struck using models that predict how a prospective juror will react to the facts of the case.

In addition to challenging individual jurors, entire jury panels may be challenged. For example, a defendant may challenge the method used to select prospective jurors if the method does not select individuals who represent a fair cross section of the community. In many instances, these challenges concern race or ethnicity.

## Preliminary Instructions

The next stage in the trial proceeding is for the judge to give preliminary instructions to the jury. The trial judge explains to the jury what its obligation is and gives a brief introduction to the law and facts of the case. The judge may read the formal charge verbatim to the jury or may summarize its contents.

The presumption of innocence is explained, and the judge admonishes the jury not to discuss the case prior to deliberating. Jurors are told not to read newspaper articles or watch television reports concerning the trial. In rare cases, it may be necessary to keep the jurors' identities secret and to conduct the voir dire in private. Threat to the safety of the jurors is an example of such an instance. This method is to be used cautiously, as it encroaches upon First Amendment rights of media and of the defendant to a public trial. Moreover, when using this method, the trial judge should be careful not to prejudice the jury. If the reason for secrecy is a perceived threat, the judge should instruct the jury as to another reason, such as concern over pretrial publicity.[29]

## Opening Statements

After the judge has given the preliminary instructions, the parties address the jury. These statements are commonly known as *opening statements*. The purpose of opening statements is to acquaint the jury with the basic facts of the case. Opening statement is not the time for counsel to argue the law; only the facts expected to be presented should be mentioned.

In some cases, the defense attorney may be permitted to wait until after the prosecution has put on its case before giving an opening statement. Because the purpose of opening statements is to present the facts surrounding the charge to the jury, opening statements are often waived in bench trials.

## The Prosecution's Case in Chief

The United States employs an adversarial system of adjudication. In adversarial systems, the parties take the lead, not the court, in the development of the facts and theories of the case. At trial, the parties are responsible for introducing the evidence, calling and examining the witnesses, and presenting theories to juries. Judges occasionally ask questions of witnesses and even less often, call witnesses. Historically, jurors have been expected to sit silently during trials. They do not call or questions witnesses. In recent years, there has been a small movement in the direction of jury participation. Arizona, Florida, and a few other states, for example, now permit jurors to ask questions of witnesses. State rules vary in how this happens. It is common, for example, to require questions to be submitted to the Court for review. In some jurisdictions, the parties are permitted to review and object to questions. It is common for the judge to ask the questions that are approved.

Because the government has brought the charges, the government puts its case on first. This consists of calling witnesses to testify and producing exhibits.

All jurisdictions have rules of evidence that govern procedure and the admissibility of evidence. The Federal Rules of Evidence are used in the federal courts, and many states have modeled their rules after the federal ones.

Many evidentiary questions can be resolved prior to trial through a motion **in limine**. Those arising during trial are handled through **objections**. Any time an attorney believes that a question, statement, or action of the opposing lawyer is improper, he or she may object. The court will then rule on the objection, and the trial will continue. In some instances, the attorneys will want to argue the objection outside the hearing of the jury. In such cases, a **sidebar** may be held, or the judge may order that the jury be removed until the matter is resolved.

The Confrontation Clause assures the defendant of the right to cross-examine the prosecution's witnesses. Normally, cross-examination is limited to matters raised during the prosecution's direct examination. The defense also has the right to review an exhibit before it is shown to the jury.

**in limine**
(Latin) "At the beginning"; preliminary. A motion in limine is a (usually pretrial) request that prejudicial information be excluded as trial evidence.

**objections**
A claim that an action by your adversary in a lawsuit (such as the use of a particular piece of evidence) is improper, unfair, or illegal, and you are asking the judge for a ruling on the point.

**sidebar**
An in-court discussion among lawyers and the judge that is out of the hearing of witnesses and the jury. Sidebar conferences are usually *on* the record.

The Supreme Court has held that prosecutors may not call defendants to testify. While a defendant may assert the privilege and refuse to testify once called, the Court has found that to demand this of a defendant creates an appearance of guilt. Furthermore, prosecutors may not refer to a defendant's failure to testify in closing arguments. Of course, a prosecutor may cross-examine a defendant who chooses to testify. However, in the 2013 case *Salinas v. Texas,*[30] the Supreme Court held that a defendant's silence in response to a question during a voluntary interview by police may be mentioned by a prosecutor as evidence of guilt to a jury.

### Directed Verdict and Judgment of Acquittal

After the government has rested (finished its case), the defendant may move for a directed verdict or, as it is also known, a judgment of acquittal. Upon such motion, the trial judge reviews the evidence presented by the government. If the evidence to support a conviction is insufficient, the judge will enter a directed verdict favoring the defendant. A directed verdict may never be entered favoring the government.

The prosecution's evidence is insufficient if reasonable persons could not conclude that the defendant is guilty. If the trial court grants a motion for directed verdict, the jury never deliberates and is discharged. Directed verdicts are rarely granted, as most judges prefer to have the jury return a verdict.

## The Defense Case

If the motion for directed verdict is denied, the defense may put on its case. The defendant is not required to put on a defense, and juries are instructed not to infer guilt by the absence of a defense.

If a defendant chooses to present a defense, the rules are the same as for the prosecution. The defendant may call witnesses and introduce exhibits, as limited by the rules of evidence. Defense witnesses are subject to cross-examination by the prosecutor. Defendants do not have to testify but may choose to do so. If a defendant does testify, he or she is subject to cross-examination by the prosecutor.

## Rebuttal

After the defense has concluded, the prosecution may call rebuttal witnesses in an effort to disprove the evidence of the defense. No new issues may be raised during rebuttal. The defense is then permitted to rebut the prosecution's rebuttal evidence.

## Closing Arguments

After the evidentiary stage of the trial has concluded, the parties present their closing arguments. The length of closing arguments is left to the discretion of the trial judge.

Attorneys may argue both the facts and the law during closing arguments. However, an attorney may not argue law different from what the judge will express to the jury as controlling in the case. Closing arguments give the parties an opportunity to summarize the evidence and explain their positions to the jury.

Attorneys must not make incorrect factual or legal statements to the jury. Objections to such statements may be made. If an objection is sustained, the jury will be instructed by the judge to disregard the statement. Prosecutors must be especially careful not to make inflammatory remarks about the defendant or defense counsel. Such remarks, if extreme, can lead to mistrial.

## Final Instructions

After closing arguments are completed, the judge will instruct the jury. Through these instructions, the judge explains the law to the jury. The information contained in the judge's instructions includes the prosecutorial burden, the standard of proof, the elements of the charged crime, how to weigh and value evidence, and rules for reaching a verdict.

## Jury Deliberations and Verdict

After receiving its instructions, the jury goes into deliberations. Jury deliberations are secret in all cases.

Generally, no person has contact with the jury when it is deliberating. If the jury has a question for the judge, the jury is escorted into the courtroom, where all the parties may hear the question. Some judges, but not all, permit juries to take the exhibits and instructions with them into the jury room.

As mentioned earlier, juror unanimity is required a guilty verdict. On occasion, a jury may communicate to the judge that a verdict cannot be reached. Some courts will then give the jury an *Allen* charge. Also known as the dynamite and shotgun instruction, the Allen charge directs the jurors in the minority to reexamine their position during continued deliberations. The charge gets its name from *Allen v. United States*, 164 U.S. 492 (1896), wherein the Supreme Court approved its use. Courts must be careful with such charges, but they are not violative of the U.S. Constitution. However, some states have banned the *Allen* charge.

In the event of a **hung jury**, the court will declare a mistrial and set a new trial date. Due to the expense and inconvenience of trying cases a second time, plea bargains are often reached.

If a verdict is reached, the parties are summoned to the courtroom and the jury verdict is read. The parties may request that the jury be polled. **Polling the jury** involves asking each juror how he or she voted. If there has been an error, the judge may order the jury to return to deliberations or may declare a mistrial.

Jurors have an obligation to follow the law, as interpreted by the trial judge, when rendering a verdict.[31] Trial judges instruct jurors in this obligation. Further, the trial judge is not to instruct the jury, nor the parties to encourage the jury in closing arguments, to disregard the law. This rule affects the defense, not the prosecution. That is, if a law (defining a crime or punishment) is harsh or unfavorable, defendants have an interest in arguing that a jury should disregard the law and acquit, notwithstanding guilt. This is not permitted in most, if not all, jurisdictions. Accordingly, a defendant has no right to insist that a jury be instructed that it has the authority to nullify the law.[32]

In 2012, a professor in Manhattan was charged with obstructing justice for standing outside a courthouse with a sign that read "Jury Information" and distributed pamphlets encouraging jurors who disagree with a law to disregard it and acquit the defendants charged under it. The charges were dismissed by the trial court, finding that his general pleas were not intended to influence jurors in specific cases, as required by the statute.[33] The case also raises First Amendment Free Speech questions.

In reality, though, juries can and may disregard the law—even though unlawful. When a jury retires, its deliberations are secret; and each juror, while feeling bound by the law, also feels bound by personal conscience. A jury does not have to support its verdict with a statement of its findings and conclusions. An acquittal, even if the result of nullification, is valid. Accordingly, although the trial judge may comment on the evidence to the jury before it retires to deliberate, a judge may not instruct a jury that the government has met its burden and that the jury must return a guilty verdict.[34]

**hung jury**
A jury that cannot reach a verdict (decision) because of disagreement among jurors.

**polling the jury**
Individually asking each member of a jury what his or her decision is. Polling is done by the judge, at the defendant's request, immediately after the verdict.

## JNOV/New Trial

If the jury returns a verdict of guilty, the defendant may move for a judgment notwithstanding the verdict (**JNOV**). This is similar to a directed verdict, in that the defendant is asserting that the evidence is insufficient to support a guilty verdict.

In addition to JNOV, a defendant may file a motion for a new trial. The common law equivalent of a motion for a new trial was the *writ of error coram nobis*. *Coram nobis* is still recognized in a few states.

The motion for a new trial is different from the JNOV because the defendant is not claiming that the evidence was insufficient, but rather that the trial was flawed. For example, if a defendant believes that evidence was admitted that should have

**JNOV**
A request by a defendant convicted by a jury for the court to set aside the verdict as unsupported by the evidence.

been excluded and that he or she was denied a fair trial because of the admission of the evidence, he or she may file a motion for new trial. A motion for new trial may also be made because of new evidence discovered after the trial.

---

## Ethical Considerations

### Disclosing Intended Client Perjury

As you have learned, attorneys have an obligation to zealously represent their clients. They also have a duty to be loyal to their clients and not to disclose the content of their client's statements. There are limits to these responsibilities, however. For example, the ABA Model Rules of Professional Responsibility allow (but do not require) an attorney to reveal client information, if such a disclosure will prevent death or substantial injury to another, will prevent the client from committing fraud that will lead to substantial financial harm to another, and in other specific situations (see Rule 1.6). Note, however, that an attorney may not disclose a client's confession for past acts or a statement of intention to commit a lesser crime.

A particularly thorny issue concerns client perjury. Model Rule 3.3 addresses this topic.

As provided in the ABA rules an attorney may not intentionally use false evidence. As such, an attorney may not call a witness that he or she reasonably believes will commit perjury. If a witness surprises an attorney on the stand by testifying falsely on material (important) facts, the attorney has an obligation to take "remedial" measures to correct the misinformation. Any remedial measure is acceptable—including inter alia, informing the court, calling a contrary witness, and questioning the witness further. In cases where notifying the court is the only solution open to an attorney, the court will react by instructing the jury to ignore the testimony, receiving more evidence on the subject, or, if the prejudice cannot be remediated, by declaring a mistrial.

The situation is more challenging if the perjury is committed by a client. The governing rule specifically distinguishes client perjury in criminal cases from civil cases. Defense attorneys may refuse to question a witness, other than the defendant, about matters where perjury is reasonably expected or to otherwise offer evidence that is reasonably believed to be false. If an attorney believes a client intends to commit perjury, the attorney has an obligation to attempt to dissuade the client. This is known as the remonstration requirement. In the remonstration, the attorney is to emphasize that the client has a legal obligation to testify truthfully, that the judge can consider a defendant's perjury at sentencing, that perjury can be prosecuted, that such perjury could hurt the defense case, and that defense counsel may withdraw if the client continues.

If the client is not dissuaded, it is generally agreed that an attorney must withdraw if he or she has knowledge of the client's intended perjury. If the attorney has only a reasonable belief, however, withdrawal is optional. Even when withdrawal is sought, it is not always granted. This is because of the prejudice to the defendant, both in front of the jury—who may be suspicious of the sudden, mid-trial change—and because it leaves a defendant without counsel at a critical time in the proceedings. Even if a motion to withdraw is denied, the attorney remains obligated not to present false evidence. To solve this conundrum, many jurisdictions have developed the "narrative" solution. In these cases, the attorney advises the client to call him- or herself to the witness stand. The attorney then questions the client in such a manner that the specific false evidence is not adduced; but instead, the door is opened for the client to provide testimony in narrative form. References to the false evidence are then omitted from the attorney's closing statements. While this method has been criticized by the ABA and the U.S. Supreme Court as a passive form of introducing false evidence, many jurisdictions have seen it as the compromise position that allows defense attorneys to remain loyal to their clients while not presenting false evidence. While no solution has presented itself, there is no doubt that a better one needs to be identified.

---

## Key Terms

| | | |
|---|---|---|
| beyond a reasonable doubt | JNOV | sidebar |
| challenge for cause | objections | venire |
| hung jury | peremptory challenge | voir dire |
| in limine | polling the jury | |

# Review Questions

1. What rights are encompassed by the Confrontation Clause?

2. What is the standard of proof in criminal cases? Define that standard.

3. How soon after arrest must a defendant be tried to comply with the Sixth Amendment's speedy trial clause?

4. What is jury nullification? May a prosecutor ask a jury to nullify? May defense counsel?

5. Distinguish challenging a prospective juror for cause from using a peremptory challenge.

6. Does a defendant have a right to self-representation?

7. What must a defendant show on appeal to be successful with a claim of ineffective assistance of counsel at trial?

# Problems & Critical Thinking Exercises

1. Does each of the following defendants have a right to a jury trial? Explain your answer.

1. A juvenile delinquency proceeding has been initiated against John because of his involvement with drugs. For more than a year, he has been dealing drugs, a crime punishable by as much as five years in prison in his state.

2. Jane is charged with simple assault. In her state, that crime is punishable by a maximum fine of $2,500 and 12 months imprisonment. However, the judge assigned to her case has never sentenced a person to more than 4 months and customarily suspends that sentence to probation.

3. Nick is 16 years old. He is charged with murder in state trial court. Murder in his state is punished with life imprisonment or death.

4. Norm, an officer in the military, has been charged with raping a female officer. Rape is punished with 10 years to life imprisonment in the military.

# Endnotes

1. *Betts v. Brady*, 316 U.S. 455 (1942).

2. *Argersinger v. Hamlin*, 407 U.S. 25 (1972).

3. *Burgett v. Texas*, 389 U.S. 109 (1962).

4. *Baldwin v. New York*, 399 U.S. 66 (1970).

5. *McKeiver v. Pennsylvania*, 403 U.S. 528 (1971).

6. *Williams v. Florida*, 399 U.S. 78 (1970).

7. *Taylor v. Louisiana*, 419 U. S. 522 (1975).

8. *Duren v. Missouri*, 439 U.S. 357 (1979).

9. *Strauder v. West Virginia*, 100 U. S. 303–309 (1880). See also *Norris v. Alabama*, 294 U.S. 587 (1935). This case involved one of the Scottsboro Boys, a group of young African American men and boys who were tried for the rape of two white women in one of the most notorious racially motivated prosecutions in U.S. history.

10. *Frazier v. United States*, 335 U.S. 497 (1948).

11. *Batson v. Kentucky*, 476 U.S. 79 (1986) and *J.E.B. v. Alabama*, 511 U.S. 127 (1994).

12. *Smith v. Illinois*, 390 U.S. 129 (1968).

13. *Maryland v. Craig*, 497 U.S. 836 (1990).

14. *Cumbie v. Singletary*, 991 F.2d 715 (11th Cir. 1993).

15. *Crawford. v. Washington*, 541 U.S. 36 (2004).

16. 564 U.S. 647 (2011).

17. 567 U.S. 50 (2012).
18. *Brooks v. Tennessee*, 406 U.S. 605 (1972).
19. *Johnson v. Louisiana*, 406 U.S. 356 (1972).
20. *Estelle v. Williams*, 425 U.S. 501 (1976).
21. *See Carey v. Musladin*, 549 U.S. 70 (2006).
22. *Stewart v. Corbin*, 850 F.2d 492 (9th Cir. 1988).
23. *Barker v. Wingo*, 407 U.S. 514 (1972).
24. *United States v. Marion*, 404 U.S. 307 (1971).
25. 18 U.S.C. § 3161.
26. 18 U.S.C. § 3162.
27. *Batson v. Kentucky*, 476 U.S. 79 (1986).
28. Fed. R. Crim. P. 24(b).
29. *United States v. Locascio*, 6 F.3d 924 (2d Cir. 1993).
30. 570 U.S. 178 (2013).
31. *See United States v. Avery*, 717 F.2d 1020 (6th Cir. 1983).
32. *United States v. Newman*, 743 F. Supp. 533 (M.D. Tenn. 1990).
33. Benjamin Weiser, Jury Statute Not Violated by Protestor, Judge Rules, *The New York Times*, April 19, 2012.
34. *See Sparf v. United States*, 156 U.S. 51 (1895); *United States v. Martin Linen Supply Co.*, 430 U.S. 564 (1977).

# Chapter 17

# Sentencing and Appeal

## Chapter Outline

If there is a conviction, verdict and judgment aren't the end of the process. Sentencing, which occurs later most of the time, and appeals to higher courts follow. This chapter details sentencing and briefly introduces the appellate process.

# Sentencing

Learning Objective: Describe the sentencing hearing procedure and applicable rights, including counsel, cross-examination, jury, and whether victim impact evidence may be considered.

After conviction, sentence must be imposed. For many misdemeanors and nearly all infractions, sentence is imposed immediately. For felonies and some misdemeanors, trial and sentencing are bifurcated—they occur at different times.

In most cases, sentence is imposed by the trial judge. A few jurisdictions provide for a jury sentence recommendation, and even fewer actually permit the jury to impose sentence. Juries always play a role in deciding whether death should be imposed. In all jurisdictions, due process and jury trial right empower juries to find the facts, called an aggravating factor, that are required in capital cases.

The legislature determines how a crime should be punished. Legislatures normally set ranges within which judges may punish violators. In recent years, there has been a substantial movement to limit the discretion of judges. This has been done in the federal system and in many states.

The authority of the legislative branch in this area is curbed by the Eighth Amendment, which prohibits "cruel and unusual punishment." The protection of the Eighth Amendment has been extended to state proceedings through the Fourteenth Amendment. However, legislatures enjoy wide discretion in deciding how to punish criminals.

## The Sentencing Hearing

### The Presentence Investigation/No Right to Counsel

After a defendant is determined guilty, a sentencing date is set. For most felonies and misdemeanors, the date will be set far enough in the future to permit the probation officer to complete a presentence investigation. Speedy trial only applies to the trial phase. There is no Sixth Amendment right to a speedy sentencing. However, several justices have signaled that a lengthy delay between judgment and sentencing could be a due process violation.[1]

The investigation typically begins with an interview of the defendant. Information concerning the defendant's drug habits, criminal history, family, employment history, education, medical and psychological problems, and personal finances is obtained. The defendant is also permitted to give his or her version of the facts surrounding the offense. There appears to be no right to counsel during this interview,[2] although most courts and probation officers permit attorneys to attend. The Seventh Circuit Court of Appeals held that the Sixth Amendment right to counsel does not apply at presentence interviews by probation officers. The court reasoned that because probation officers are neutral judicial employees and not law enforcement officers, interviews conducted by them are not critical stages of an *adversarial* proceeding.[3] The Seventh Circuit, like other courts that have considered the issue, thus determined that the presentence interview is a neutral, nonadversarial meeting between the probation officer and the defendant. This is so even though the defendant may be in custody and admissions could lead to greater punishment.

Three facts support the conclusion that there is no right to counsel during a presentence investigation interview. First, the objective of the interview is to gather information to assist the sentencing court, not to establish that the defendant committed a crime. Second (and related to the first), a probation officer is not, strictly speaking, a law enforcement officer. Third, the questions asked at the interview are routine, and defense counsel can properly advise the client of his or her rights before the interview occurs.

In addition to conducting an interview of the defendant, the probation officer will obtain copies of vital documents, such as the defendant's "rap sheet" and relevant medical records. The probation officer will attempt to verify the information provided by the defendant through these documents and other investigatory processes.

When the probation officer has completed the investigation, a presentence report is prepared. This report reflects the information discovered during the investigation and is used by the court in determining what sentence should be imposed. Often, the prosecutor and law enforcement officers involved in prosecuting the defendant, the family members of the defendant, and the victim of the crime are permitted to make statements that are incorporated into the report.

There is no constitutional right to the preparation of a presentence report; however, most jurisdictions have followed the lead of the federal government, which requires a presentence report unless the record contains information sufficient to enable the meaningful exercise of sentencing discretion.[4]

In the federal system, the defendant is entitled to review the presentence report prior to sentencing. This is true in most states as well, but the right is not absolute. For example, the recommendation of the probation officer may be kept confidential.[5]

At the sentencing hearing, the defendant may disprove factual statements contained in the report. To this end, witnesses may be called and exhibits introduced.

### The Sentencing Hearing

The next stage in the process is the sentencing hearing. Sentencing hearings are adversarial. Witnesses may be called, other evidence introduced, and arguments made. In most instances, the hearing is before a judge, not a jury, and accordingly the rules of evidence are relaxed. When the hearing is before a jury, such as in capital cases, the rules of evidence are fully effective. This is a critical stage under the Sixth Amendment, and therefore there is a right to counsel. As is true for defendants at earlier stages of the process, convictees are entitled to more than a warm body; they are entitled to effective assistance of counsel. To prove ineffective assistance of counsel, it must be shown that the attorney's representation fell below an objective standard of reasonableness and that the defendant was genuinely prejudiced. The following case, which involves the sentencing of a man for a brutal rape and murder, is an example of ineffective counsel at sentencing.

## Oyez

### Sears v. Upton
### 561 U.S. 945 (2010)

**Per Curiam**

In 1993, a Georgia jury convicted Sears of armed robbery and kidnaping with bodily injury (which also resulted in death), a capital crime under state law. During the penalty phase of Sears' capital trial, his counsel presented evidence describing his childhood as stable, loving, and essentially without incident. Seven witnesses offered testimony along the following lines: Sears came from a middle-class background; his actions shocked and dismayed his relatives; and a death sentence, the jury was told, would devastate the family. Counsel's mitigation theory, it seems, was calculated to portray the adverse impact of Sears' execution on his family and loved ones. But the strategy backfired. The prosecutor ultimately used the evidence of Sears' purportedly stable and advantaged upbringing against him during the State's closing argument. With Sears, the prosecutor told the jury, "[w]e don't have a deprived child from an inner city; a person who[m] society has turned its back on at an early age. But, yet, we have a person, privileged in every way, who has rejected every opportunity that was afforded him."

The mitigation evidence that emerged during the state postconviction evidentiary hearing, however, demonstrates that Sears was far from "privileged in every way." Sears' home life, while filled with material comfort, was anything but tranquil: His parents had a physically abusive relationship, and divorced when Sears was young, he suffered sexual abuse at the hands of an adolescent male cousin, his mother's "favorite word for referring to her sons was 'little mother fuckers,'" and his father was "verbally abusive," and disciplined Sears with age-inappropriate military-style drills. Sears struggled in school, demonstrating substantial behavior problems from a very young age. For example, Sears repeated the second grade, and was referred to a local health center for evaluation at age nine. By the time Sears reached high school, he was "described as severely learning disabled and as severely behaviorally handicapped."

Environmental factors aside, and more significantly, evidence produced during the state postconviction relief process also revealed that Sears suffered "significant frontal lobe abnormalities." Two different psychological experts testified that Sears had substantial deficits in mental cognition and reasoning—*i.e.*, "problems with planning, sequencing and impulse control,"—as a result of several serious head injuries he suffered as a child, as well as drug and alcohol abuse. Regardless of the cause of his brain damage, his scores on at least two standardized assessment tests placed him at or below the first percentile in several categories of cognitive function, "making him among the most impaired individuals in the population in terms of ability to suppress competing impulses and conform behavior only to relevant stimuli." The assessment also revealed that Sears' "ability to organize his choices, assign them relative weight and select among them in a deliberate way is grossly impaired." From an etiological standpoint, one expert explained that Sears' "history is replete with multiple head trauma, substance abuse and traumatic experiences of the type expected" to lead to these significant impairments.

Whatever concern the dissent has about some of the sources relied upon by Sears' experts— informal personal accounts,—it does not undermine the well-credentialed expert's assessment, based on between 12 and 16 hours of interviews, testing, and observations, that Sears suffers from substantial cognitive impairment. Sears performed dismally on several of the forensic tests administered to him to assess his frontal lobe functioning. On the Stroop Word Interference Test, which measures response inhibition, 99.6% of those individuals in his cohort (which accounts for age, education, and background) performed better than he did. On the Trail-Making B test, which also measures frontal lobe functioning, Sears performed at the first (and lowest) percentile. Based on these results, the expert's first-hand observations, and an extensive review of Sears' personal history, the expert's opinion was unequivocal: There is "clear and compelling evidence" that Sears has "pronounced frontal lobe pathology."

(continued)

Further, the fact that Sears' brother is a convicted drug dealer and user, and introduced Sears to a life of crime, actually would have been consistent with a mitigation theory portraying Sears as an individual with diminished judgment and reasoning skills, who may have desired to follow in the footsteps of an older brother who had shut him out of his life. And the fact that some of such evidence may have been "hearsay" does not necessarily undermine its value—or its admissibility—for penalty phase purposes.

Finally, the fact that along with this new mitigation evidence there was also some adverse evidence is unsurprising, given that counsel's initial mitigation investigation was constitutionally inadequate. Competent counsel should have been able to turn some of the adverse evidence into a positive—perhaps in support of a cognitive deficiency mitigation theory. In particular, evidence of Sears' grandiose self-conception and evidence of his magical thinking, were features, in another well-credentialed expert's view, of a "profound personality disorder." This evidence might not have made Sears any more likable to the jury, but it might well have helped the jury understand Sears, and his horrendous acts—especially in light of his purportedly stable upbringing.

Because they failed to conduct an adequate mitigation investigation, *none* of this evidence was known to Sears' trial counsel. It emerged only during state postconviction relief.

Unsurprisingly, the state postconviction trial court concluded that Sears had demonstrated his counsel's penalty phase investigation was constitutionally deficient. . . .

What is surprising, however, is the court's analysis regarding whether counsel's facially inadequate mitigation investigation prejudiced Sears. . . .

A proper analysis of prejudice under Strickland would have taken into account the newly uncovered evidence of Sears' "significant" mental and psychological impairments, along with the mitigation evidence introduced during Sears' penalty phase trial, to assess whether there is a reasonable probability that Sears would have received a different sentence after a constitutionally sufficient mitigation investigation.

[Accordingly, the Court remanded the case for a full analysis of whether the ineffective assistance of counsel at sentencing actually prejudiced the outcome of the sentence. Be aware that Justices Scalia and Thomas issued a sharply worded dissent in this case.]

---

**victim impact statement**
At the time of sentencing, a statement made to the court concerning the effect the crime has had on the victim or on the victim's family.

In most instances, sentencing facts are established by preponderance of the evidence and are found by the sentencing judge. In rare instances, however, clear and convincing evidence or proof beyond a reasonable doubt is required. Death cases are an example. This issue has also arisen in the context of sentence enhancements. For example, due process requires that any fact that increases the penalty for a crime beyond the prescribed statutory maximum, other than the fact of a prior conviction, must be submitted to a jury and proven beyond a reasonable doubt. So, a sentencing scheme that increases the punishment for a racially motivated second-degree murder beyond the limits set by the second-degree murder statute is invalid unless the racial motive is proved to the jury beyond a reasonable doubt.[6]

One issue that has received considerable attention, and contradictory treatment, from the Supreme Court is the use of **victim impact statements** at sentencing. A *victim impact statement* is an oral or written statement to the sentencing judge explaining how the crime has affected the victim and, possibly, the victim's family. In 1987, the Supreme Court handed down *Booth v. Maryland*, 482 U.S. 496 (1987), wherein it invalidated a state statute requiring sentencing judges to consider victim impact statements in capital cases. The Court determined that the use of victim impact statements could prejudice the proceeding by injecting irrelevant, but inflammatory, evidence into the sentencing determination.

Only four years later, though, the Supreme Court overruled *Booth in Payne v. Tennessee*. Thus, victim impact evidence may be admitted, even if it is not related to the facts surrounding the crime. The decision concerning admissibility must be made on a case-by-case basis, and it is a violation of due process to admit evidence that is so prejudicial that the sentencing becomes fundamentally unfair. Read the Payne case in Oyez.

On the other side of the coin, defendants have wide latitude in the presentation of evidence at sentencing. This right is constitutionally mandated in capital cases; the Supreme Court has said that a state cannot preclude a defendant from proffering evidence in support of a sentence less than death.[7]

# Oyez

## Payne v. Tennessee
### 501 U.S. 808 (1991)

**CHIEF JUSTICE REHNQUIST delivered the opinion of the Court.**

In this case we reconsider our holdings in *Booth v. Maryland* . . . that the Eighth Amendment bars the admission of victim impact statement evidence during the penalty phase of a capital trial.

The petitioner, Pervis Tyrone Payne, was convicted by a jury on two counts of first-degree murder and one count of assault with intent to commit murder in the first degree. He was sentenced to death for each of the murders, and to 30 years in prison for assault.

The victims of Payne's offenses were 28-year-old Charisse Christopher, her 2-year-old daughter Lacie, and her 3-year-old son Nicholas. The three lived together . . . across the hall from Payne's girlfriend, Bobbie Thomas. On Saturday, June 27, 1987, Payne visited Thomas's apartment several times in expectation of her return from her mother's house in Arkansas, but found no one at home. One visit, he left his overnight bag, containing clothes and other items for his weekend stay, in the hallway outside Thomas's apartment. With the bag were three cans of malt liquor.

Payne passed the morning and early afternoon injecting cocaine and drinking beer. Later, he drove around the town with a friend in the friend's car, each of them taking turns reading a pornographic magazine. Sometime around 3 p.m., Payne returned to the apartment complex, entered the Christophers' apartment, and began making sexual advances toward Charisse. Charisse resisted and Payne became violent. A neighbor who resided in the apartment directly beneath the Christophers heard Charisse screaming, "'Get out, get out,' as if she were telling the children to leave." The noise briefly subsided and then began "horribly loud." The neighbor called the police after she heard a "bloodcurdling scream" from the Christopher apartment. . . .

When the first police officer arrived at the scene, he immediately encountered Payne, who was leaving the apartment building, so covered with blood that he appeared to be "sweating blood." The officer confronted Payne, who responded, "I'm the complainant." . . . When the officer asked, "What is going on up there?" Payne struck the officer with the overnight bag, dropped his tennis shoes, and fled.

Inside the apartment, the police encountered a horrifying scene. Blood covered the walls and floor throughout the unit. Charisse and her children were lying on the floor in the kitchen. Nicholas, despite several wounds inflicted by a butcher knife that completely penetrated through his body from front to back, was still breathing. Miraculously, he survived. . . . Charisse and Lacie were dead.

Charisse's body was found on the kitchen floor on her back, her legs fully extended. . . . None of the 84 wounds inflicted by Payne were individually fatal; rather, the cause of death was most likely bleeding from all of the wounds. She had suffered stab wounds to the chest, abdomen, back, and head. The murder weapon, a butcher knife, was found at her feet. Payne's baseball cap was snapped on her arm near her elbow. Three cans of malt liquor bearing Payne's fingerprints were found near her body, and a fourth empty was on a landing outside the apartment door.

Payne was apprehended later that day. . . .

[T]he jury returned guilty verdicts against Payne on all counts.

During the sentencing phase of the trial, Payne presented the testimony of four witnesses, his mother and father, Bobbie Thomas, and Dr. John T. Huston, a clinical psychologist specializing in criminal court evaluation work. Bobbie Thomas testified that she met Payne at church, during a time when she was being abused by her husband. She stated that Payne was a very caring person, and that he devoted much time and attention to her three children, who were being affected by her marital difficulties. She said that the children had come to love him very much and would miss him, and that he "behaved just like a father that loved his kids." She asserted that he did not drink, nor did he use drugs, and that it was generally inconsistent with Payne's character to have committed these crimes. . . .

The State presented the testimony of Charisse's mother, Mary Zvolanek. When asked how Nicholas had been affected by the murder of his mother and sister, she responded:

> He cries for his mom. He doesn't seem to understand why she doesn't come home. And he cries for his sister Lacie. He comes to me many times during the week and asks me, Grandma, do you miss Lacie. And I tell him yes. He says, I'm worried about my Lacie.

In arguing for the death penalty during closing argument, the prosecutor commented on the continuing effects of Nicholas's experience, stating:

> But we do know that Nicholas was alive. And Nicholas was in the same room. Nicholas was still conscious. His eyes were open. He responded to the paramedics. He was able to follow their directions. He was able to hold his intestines in as he was carried to the ambulance. So he knew what happened to his mother and baby sister. . . .

(continued)

Somewhere down the road Nicholas is going to grow up, hopefully. He's going to want to know what happened. And he is going to know what happened to his baby sister and mother. He is going to want to know what type of justice was done. He is going to want to know what happened. With your verdict, you will provide the answer. . . .

In the rebuttal to Payne's closing argument, the prosecutor stated:

You saw the videotape this morning. You saw what Nicholas Christopher will carry in his mind forever. When you talk about cruel, when you talk about atrocious, and when you talk about heinous, that picture will always come into your mind, probably throughout the rest of your lives.

■  ■  ■

No one will ever know about Lacie Jo because she never had a chance to grow up. Her life was taken from her at the age of two years old. . . . His mother will never kiss [Nicholas] good night or pat him as he goes off to bed, or hold him and sing him a lullaby. [Petitioner's attorney] wants you to think about a good reputation, people who love the defendant and things about him. He doesn't want you to think about the people who loved Charisse Christopher, her mother, and daddy who loved her. The people who loved little Lacie Jo, the grandparents who are still here. The brother who mourns for her every single day and wants to know where his best little playmate is. He doesn't have anybody to watch cartoons with him, a little one. These are the things that go into why it is especially cruel, heinous, and atrocious, the burden that child will carry forever.

The jury sentenced Payne to death on each of the murder counts. The Supreme Court of Tennessee affirmed the conviction and sentence. . . .

We granted certiorari . . . to reconsider our holdings in *Booth* . . . that the Eighth Amendment prohibits a capital sentencing jury from considering "victim impact" evidence relating to the personal characteristics of the victim and the emotional impact of the crimes on the victim's family. . . .

Under our constitutional system, the primary responsibility for defining crimes against state law, fixing punishments for the commission of these crimes, and establishing procedures for criminal trials rests with the States. The state laws respecting crimes, punishments, and criminal procedure are of course subject to the overriding provisions of the United States Constitution. . . .

Within the constitutional limitations defined in our cases, the States enjoy their traditional latitude to prescribe the method by which those who commit murder should be punished. . . . The states remain free, in capital cases, as well as others, to devise new procedures and new remedies to meet felt needs. Victim impact evidence is simply another form or method of informing the sentencing authority about the specific harm caused by the crime in question, evidence of a general type long considered by sentencing authorities. [The] *Booth* Court was wrong in stating that this kind of evidence leads to the arbitrary imposition of the death penalty. In the majority of cases, and in this case, victim impact evidence serves entirely legitimate purposes. In the event that evidence is introduced that is so unduly prejudicial that it renders the trial fundamentally unfair, the Due Process Clause of the Fourteenth Amendment provides a mechanism for relief. . . . Courts have always taken into consideration the harm done by the defendant in imposing sentence, and the evidence adduced in this case was illustrative of the harm caused by Payne's double murder.

We are now of the view that a State may properly conclude that for the jury to assess meaningfully the defendant's moral culpability and blameworthiness, it should have before it at the sentencing phase evidence of the specific harm caused by the defendant. "[T]he State has a legitimate interest in counteracting the mitigating evidence which the defendant is entitled to put in, by reminding the sentencer that just as the murderer should be considered an individual, so too the victim is an individual whose death represents a unique loss to society and in particular to his family." . . . By turning the victim into a "faceless stranger at the penalty phase of a criminal trial" . . . *Booth* deprives the State of the full moral force of its evidence and may prevent the jury from having before it all the information necessary to determine the proper punishment for a first-degree murder.

The present case is an example of the potential for such unfairness. The capital sentencing jury heard testimony from Payne's girlfriend that they met at church, that he was affectionate, caring, kind to her children. . . . Payne's parents testified that he was a good son, and a clinical psychologist testified that Payne was an extremely polite prisoner and suffered from a low IQ. None of this testimony was related to the circumstances of Payne's brutal crimes. . . . The Supreme Court of Tennessee in this case obviously felt the unfairness of the rule pronounced in *Booth* when it said "[i]t is an affront to the civilized members of the human race to say that at sentencing in a capital case, a parade of witnesses may praise the background, character and good deeds of the defendant (as was done in this case), without limitation as to relevancy, but nothing may be said that bears upon the character of, or the harm imposed, upon the victims." . . .

We thus hold that if the State chooses to permit the admission of victim impact evidence and prosecutorial argument on that subject, the Eighth Amendment erects no per se bar.

## Punishing Acquitted Crimes

Historically, judges have held considerable discretion in sentencing. The rules of evidence are relaxed, and judges may hear evidence that is otherwise inadmissible. Victim impact evidence, family history, medical history, mental health history, employment history, and criminal history are examples of the type of evidence that is considered at sentencing.

Additionally, the nature of the crime committed and the particular manner in which it was committed are considered. In some cases, evidence concerning the nature and manner of the offense may include evidence of other crimes that were committed in conjunction with the offense under sentence. An interesting question concerns whether a defendant may have a sentence increased for acquitted crimes. This issue was before the Supreme Court in *United States v. Watts* (1997).[8] Police discovered both cocaine and guns in a search of Watts's property, and he was subsequently charged and tried for possession of cocaine and possession of a gun in relation to a drug offense. The jury convicted him of the former charge and acquitted him of the latter charge. At sentencing, however, the trial judge found that Watts did use the gun in relation to a drug offense and, accordingly, increased his sentence for the cocaine possession conviction.

On appeal, the Supreme Court affirmed the sentence enhancement. The Court stressed that judges have historically had significant discretion in sentencing and that the enhancement was not punishment for an acquitted offense but instead was an enhanced punishment for the manner in which the defendant committed the crime of conviction. Also important are the differing standards of proof between conviction and sentencing. Conviction requires a finding beyond a reasonable doubt, while sentencing requires proof by preponderance of the evidence. The high standard of proof for conviction, according to the Court, means that an acquittal cannot be interpreted as a finding of fact. An acquittal means that the government has not proved its case, not that the defendant did not commit the act in question. However, for reasons to be discussed, the status of *Watts* is unknown.

## Proving Facts for Sentencing

In a practice similar to using acquitted crimes to enhance a sentence, judges have historically used facts not presented to the trial jury to increase sentences. If there is a plea of guilty, the judge must find that the essential elements of the crime were committed. This usually involves a recitation of the facts by the defendant. If there has been a trial, the judge is armed with the findings of the jury; or in the case of a bench trial, of the trial judge. Once the facts have been established at trial, whether by confession or a finding of fact, additional evidence must be received at sentencing. However, that evidence is limited to the facts that are relevant to the sentencing decision. For over 150 years, trial judges routinely found sentencing facts, often by a preponderance of the evidence. However, judges have always been restricted by jury decisions. That is, a jury's fact-finding cannot be set aside by a judge. For example, if a jury finds a defendant guilty of possession of a specific amount of cocaine, a sentencing judge is prohibited from increasing the sentence because the judge finds that the defendant possessed a greater amount of cocaine.

However, judges would commonly find other facts that affected the final sentence—for example, whether a defendant possessed a weapon while engaged in a drug deal in a case where the defendant was charged only with dealing drugs, not possession of the weapon. Often, these facts were proved by the preponderance standard.

In recent years, however, a new body of law has developed around the Sixth Amendment's jury trial right. In short, these cases require that all findings that are used to support the sentence must be heard by a jury and found to be true beyond a reasonable doubt.[9] In *Blakely*, the defendant had been charged with first-degree kidnapping. He and the state reached a plea agreement that reduced the charges to second-degree kidnapping involving domestic violence and the use of a firearm. Pursuant to the plea agreement, the state recommended a sentence of between 49 and 53 months. The judge, however, found that the crime involved deliberate cruelty and enhanced the sentence to 90 months. After the defendant objected, the judge conducted a three-day fact hearing on the deliberate cruelty question. The judge again sentenced the defendant to 90 months, having found deliberate cruelty following the hearing.

The Supreme Court reversed, finding that it was not possible for the judge to justify the enhanced sentence solely because of the facts admitted in the guilty plea. While the defendant admitted to kidnapping and the use of a gun, he did not provide evidence that he acted with deliberate cruelty. Accordingly, the judge had to find facts the trial jury was not charged with determining. This effort is proved by the judge's need to conduct a three-day sentencing hearing. Because the Sixth Amendment guarantees individuals the right to have all facts essential to sentencing heard by a jury, using the reasonable doubt standard, the trial judge erred. Whether the judge had charged the trial jury to make the deliberate cruelty finding or had empaneled a jury at sentencing to make the finding, the sentence would not have violated the Sixth Amendment. Similarly, in the 2007 *Cunningham* case, the Court invalidated a California law that created an upper range of 12 years in prison for the crimes covered by the jury's verdict but allowed the judge to sentence the offender to an additional 4 years for facts the judge could find, by preponderance of the evidence, at a sentencing hearing. Later, in the discussion of the federal sentencing guidelines, you may read an excerpt of the Supreme Court's decision *United States v. Booker*, wherein the right to have facts decided by a jury under the Sixth Amendment was used to invalidate the mandatory nature of the federal sentencing guidelines. The relationship between *Booker* and *Watts* is not clear. *Watts* may be overruled altogether. At the least, *Booker* demands that the conduct for which the defendant was acquitted be found by a jury before a judge may rely upon them at sentencing.

Death can only be imposed if a jury finds that murder was committed with aggravating circumstances. That the victim was a minor, tortured, or sexually assaulted are examples. Not only must a jury find an aggravating circumstance, but it must find it beyond a reasonable doubt.[10] Judges may still be empowered to decide whether to impose death or a lesser punishment, but death is only an option if the jury finds an aggravating factor. Some states have delegated the aggravating factor decision to juries and left the final sentence to the judge, and others have handed the jury both the aggravating factor and the sentencing decisions.

## Forms of Punishment

The legislature determines what type of sentence may be imposed; judges impose sentences. The Eighth Amendment establishes boundaries, but they are loose and widely drawn. Few punishments are cruel or excessive.

### Capital Punishment

In early American history, capital punishment was commonly used. During the nineteenth century, use of the death penalty greatly declined. Today, more than half the states provide for the death penalty, and its use has regained popular support. Although the number of inmates actually executed every year is small, the number is increasing.

The suggestion that the death penalty is inherently cruel and unusual under the Eighth Amendment has been rejected. Indeed, it is a hard case to make, given that the Constitution itself recognizes the government's power to take life. The Due

Process Clause, for example, requires due process when taking *life*, liberty, and property. However, the Court has struggled, as have state courts and legislatures, with establishing standards for its use.

One concern is equality. In *Furman v. Georgia*, 408 U.S. 238 (1972), the Court held that the death penalty cannot be imposed under a sentencing procedure that creates a substantial risk of being implemented in an arbitrary manner. It found that Georgia's law permitted arbitrary decisions and so declared it void. *Furman* required that the sentencer's discretion be limited by objective standards to eliminate unfairness—specifically, to eliminate racial and other bias from death sentence decisions.

States responded to *Furman* in various ways. Some chose to eliminate discretion entirely by mandating capital punishment for certain crimes. The Supreme Court invalidated mandatory capital punishment laws in *Locket v. Ohio*, 438 U.S. 586 (1978). In *Locket,* the Court held that individualized sentencing was constitutionally required. The Court stated that any law prohibiting a sentencer from considering "as a mitigating factor, any aspect of a defendant's character or record and any circumstances of the offense that the defendant proffers as a basis for a sentence less than death" creates an unconstitutional risk that the "death penalty will be imposed in spite of factors which may call for a less severe penalty."[11]

However, Georgia's new death penalty legislation was upheld in *Gregg v. Georgia*, 428 U.S. 153 (1976). The new law provided that the jury must find, in a sentencing hearing separate from the trial, an aggravating circumstance before the death penalty can be imposed. The statute enumerated possible aggravating circumstances. By requiring a jury to find an aggravating circumstance, arbitrariness is believed to be lessened. Indeed, today the decision to impose death must be made by a unanimous jury, and defendants must be given the opportunity to present mitigating evidence. A statute that mandates death in all cases is invalid. A statute may, however, require death if a jury finds that the mitigating factors do not outweigh the aggravating factors.[12]

*Furman, Gregg, Locket*, and their progeny stand for the principle that a sentencing statute cannot totally eliminate discretion nor grant so much discretion that the death penalty can be imposed arbitrarily. These concepts of individualized sentencing and minimized discretion in sentencing are somewhat antithetical. The Supreme Court itself recognizes that a tension exists between the two goals and has struggled to establish procedures and standards to successfully implement them. "Experience has shown that the consistency and rationality promised in *Furman* are inversely related to the fairness owed the individual when considering a sentence of death. A step toward consistency is a step away from fairness."[13]

The death penalty issue has been divisive to the Court. Some justices have so strongly believed that the death penalty is unconstitutional (either inherently or as administered) that they have refused to acquiesce to notions of stare decisis on the issue. Justice Thurgood Marshall, for example, dissented in every capital punishment case, including both denials of petitions of certiorari and cases under review, because of his firmly held belief that capital punishment was unconstitutional.

Until 1994, Justice Harry Blackmun held that the death penalty was not inherently unconstitutional. However, in *Callins v. Collins*, he made the following statement:

> Courts are in the very business of erecting procedural devices from which fair, equitable, and reliable outcomes are presumed to flow. Yet, in the death penalty area, this Court, in my view, had engaged in a futile effort to balance these constitutional demands, and now is retreating not only from the *Furman* promise of consistency and rationality, but from the requirement of individualized sentencing as well. Having virtually conceded that both fairness and rationality cannot be achieved in the administration of the death penalty . . . the Court has chosen to deregulate the entire enterprise, replacing, it would seem,

substantive constitutional requirements with mere aesthetics, and abdicating its statutorily and constitutionally imposed duty to provide meaningful judicial oversight to the administration of death by the States. From this date forward, I no longer shall tinker with the machinery of death. For more than 20 years I have endeavored—indeed, I have struggled—along with a majority of this Court, to develop procedural and substantive rules that would lend more than the mere appearance of fairness to the death penalty endeavor. Rather than continue to coddle the Court's delusion that the desired level of fairness has been achieved and the need for regulation eviscerated, I feel morally and intellectually obligated simply to concede that the death penalty experiment has failed. It is virtually self-evident to me now that no combination of procedural rules or substantive regulations ever can save the death penalty from its inherent constitutional deficiencies. The basic question—does the system accurately and consistently determine which defendants "deserve" to die?—cannot be answered in the affirmative. It is not simply that this Court has allowed vague aggravating circumstances to be employed . . . relevant mitigating evidence to be disregarded . . . and vital judicial review to be blocked. . . . The problem is that the inevitability of actual, legal, and moral error gives us a system that we know must wrongly kill some defendants, a system that fails to deliver the fair, consistent, and reliable sentences of death required by the Constitution. . . . Perhaps one day this Court will develop procedural rules or verbal formulas that actually will provide consistency, fairness, and reliability in a capital-sentencing scheme. I am not optimistic that such a day will come. I am more optimistic, though, that this Court eventually will conclude that the effort to eliminate arbitrariness while preserving fairness "in the infliction of [death] is so plainly doomed to failure that it—and the death penalty—must be abandoned altogether." . . . I may not live to see that day, but I have faith that eventually it will arrive. The path the Court has chosen lessens us all. I dissent.[14]

One decision that bothered Justice Blackmun was *McCleskey v. Kemp*, 481 U.S. 279 (1987), where the Court refused to set aside a death sentence even though the defendant presented reliable statistical data supporting the conclusion that race continues to be a significant factor in the application of capital punishment. The Court held that statistical evidence could not be used to invalidate an entire sentencing scheme; rather, the burden falls on each individual defendant to prove that race was a factor in his or her sentence. Justice Blackmun argued that the Court was thereby abandoning the *Furman* requirement of consistency and rationality.

The definition of cruelty is an evolving concept. The Supreme Court opined in 1878 that beheading, drawing and quartering, burning alive, and dissection were cruel and unusual.[15] Electrocution, hanging, and shooting are all approved methods of executing a prisoner. In 2008, the Supreme Court decided that Kentucky's lethal injection process was constitutional in *Baze v. Rees*.[16]

The Eighth Amendment has been interpreted to prohibit sentences that are disproportionate to the crime committed. In this vein, the Supreme Court has held that capital punishment may not be imposed for the crime of raping an adult woman.[17] In *Kennedy v. Louisiana*, found in the next Oyez, the long-standing question whether child rapists could be put to death was answered in the negative.

The Court was careful to note that the decision was limited to crimes against the person, not crimes against the State (e.g., terrorism, treason).

In another case, it was decided that a person may not be put to death for aiding in a felony that results in murder, unless there was an intent to kill.[18] Subsequently, the Court modified this decision to permit the execution of felony murderers who exhibited a reckless disregard for human life.[19]

## Sidebar

### Crime Stats: Capital Punishment in the United States

In 2020, the laws of 28 states and the federal government authorized capital punishment. Alaska, Colorado, Connecticut, Delaware, Hawaii, Illinois, Iowa, Maine, Maryland, Massachusetts, Michigan, Minnesota, New Hampshire, New Jersey, New Mexico, New York, North Dakota, Rhode Island, Vermont, Washington, West Virginia, and Wisconsin were the states without the death penalty. Also, there was no death penalty in the District of Columbia.

There were 2,591 people were awaiting execution in 2021. In 2020, 17 individuals were executed, 10 by the federal government and 7 by the states.

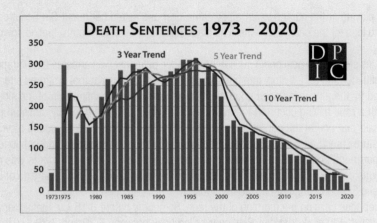

Source: Death Penalty Information Center 2020 Report, available at deathpenaltyinfo.org.

## Oyez

### Kennedy v. Louisiana
### 558 U.S. 1 (2008)

**Justice Kennedy delivered the opinion of the Court.**

Petitioner's crime was one that cannot be recounted in these pages in a way sufficient to capture in full the hurt and horror inflicted on his victim or to convey the revulsion society, and the jury that represents it, sought to express by sentencing petitioner to death. At 9:18 A.M. on March 2, 1998, petitioner called 911 to report that his stepdaughter, referred to here as L. H., had been raped. He told the 911 operator that L. H. had been in the garage while he readied his son for school. Upon hearing loud screaming, petitioner said, he ran outside and found L. H. in the side yard. Two neighborhood boys, petitioner told the operator, had dragged L. H. from the garage to the yard, pushed her down, and raped her. Petitioner claimed he saw one of the boys riding away on a blue 10-speed bicycle.

When police arrived at petitioner's home between 9:20 and 9:30 A.M., they found L. H. on her bed, wearing a T-shirt and wrapped in a bloody blanket. She was bleeding profusely from the vaginal area. Petitioner told police he had carried her from the yard to the bathtub and then to the bed. Consistent with this explanation, police found a thin line of blood drops in the garage on the way to the house and then up the stairs. Once in the bedroom, petitioner had used a basin of water and a cloth to wipe blood from the victim. This later prevented medical personnel from collecting a reliable DNA sample.

L. H. was transported to the Children's Hospital. An expert in pediatric forensic medicine testified that L. H.'s injuries were the most severe he had seen from a sexual assault in his four years of practice. A laceration to the left wall of the vagina had separated her cervix

(continued)

from the back of her vagina, causing her rectum to protrude into the vaginal structure. Her entire perineum was torn from the posterior fourchette to the anus. The injuries required emergency surgery.

At the scene of the crime, at the hospital, and in the first weeks that followed, both L. H. and petitioner maintained in their accounts to investigators that L. H. had been raped by two neighborhood boys. One of L. H.'s doctors testified at trial that L. H. told all hospital personnel the same version of the rape, although she reportedly told one family member that petitioner raped her. L. H. was interviewed several days after the rape by a psychologist. The interview was videotaped, lasted three hours over two days, and was introduced into evidence at trial. On the tape one can see that L. H. had difficulty discussing the subject of the rape. She spoke haltingly and with long pauses and frequent movement. Early in the interview, L. H. expressed reservations about the questions being asked:

"I'm going to tell the same story. They just want me to change it. . . . They want me to say my Dad did it. . . . I don't want to say it. . . . I tell them the same, same story."

She told the psychologist that she had been playing in the garage when a boy came over and asked her about Girl Scout cookies she was selling; and that the boy "pulled [her by the legs to] the backyard," where he placed his hand over her mouth, "pulled down [her] shorts," and raped her.

Eight days after the crime, and despite L. H.'s insistence that petitioner was not the offender, petitioner was arrested for the rape. The State's investigation had drawn the accuracy of petitioner and L. H.'s story into question. Though the defense at trial proffered alternative explanations, the case for the prosecution, credited by the jury, was based upon the following evidence: An inspection of the side yard immediately after the assault was inconsistent with a rape having occurred there, the grass having been found mostly undisturbed but for a small patch of coagulated blood. Petitioner said that one of the perpetrators fled the crime scene on a blue 10-speed bicycle but gave inconsistent descriptions of the bicycle's features, such as its handlebars. Investigators found a bicycle matching petitioner and L. H.'s description in tall grass behind a nearby apartment, and petitioner identified it as the bicycle one of the perpetrators was riding. Yet its tires were flat, it did not have gears, and it was covered in spider webs. In addition police found blood on the underside of L. H.'s mattress. This convinced them the rape took place in her bedroom, not outside the house.

Police also found that petitioner made two telephone calls on the morning of the rape. Sometime before 6:15 A.M., petitioner called his employer and left a message that he was unavailable to work that day. Petitioner called back between 6:30 and 7:30 A.M. to ask a colleague how to get blood out of a white carpet because his daughter had "'just become a young lady.'" At 7:37 A.M., petitioner called B & B Carpet Cleaning and requested urgent assistance in removing bloodstains from a carpet. Petitioner did not call 911 until about an hour and a half later.

About a month after petitioner's arrest L. H. was removed from the custody of her mother, who had maintained until that point that petitioner was not involved in the rape. On June 22, 1998, L. H. was returned home and told her mother for the first time that petitioner had raped her. And on December 16, 1999, about 21 months after the rape, L. H. recorded her accusation in a videotaped interview with the Child Advocacy Center.

The State charged petitioner with aggravated rape of a child under La. Stat. Ann. §14:42 (West 1997 and Supp. 1998) [which provided for death or life imprisonment at hard labor. Kennedy was convicted and a sentencing hearing was conducted, at which the jury heard about prior unreported child rapes the defendant had committed. He was sentenced to death].

The Eighth Amendment, applicable to the States through the Fourteenth Amendment, provides that "[e]xcessive bail shall not be required, nor excessive fines imposed, nor cruel and unusual punishments inflicted." . . . The Amendment "draw[s] its meaning from the evolving standards of decency that mark the progress of a maturing society." This is because "[t]he standard of extreme cruelty is not merely descriptive, but necessarily embodies a moral judgment. The standard itself remains the same, but its applicability must change as the basic mores of society change.

Applying this principle, we held in *Roper* and *Atkins* that the execution of juveniles and mentally retarded persons are punishments violative of the Eighth Amendment because the offender had a diminished personal responsibility for the crime. The Court further has held that the death penalty can be disproportionate to the crime itself where the crime did not result, or was not intended to result, in death of the victim. In *Coker*, 433 U.S. 584, for instance, the Court held it would be unconstitutional to execute an offender who had raped an adult woman. And in *Enmund v. Florida*, 458 U.S. 782 (1982), the Court overturned the capital sentence of a defendant who aided and abetted a robbery during which a murder was committed but did not himself kill, attempt to kill, or intend that a killing would take place. On the other hand, in *Tyson v. Arizona*, 481 U.S. 137 (1987), the Court allowed the defendants' death sentences to stand where they did not themselves kill the victims but their involvement in the events leading up to the murders was active, recklessly indifferent, and substantial . . . .

In these cases the Court has been guided by "objective indicia of society's standards, as expressed in legislative enactments and state practice with respect to executions." *Roper*, 543 U.S., at 563; see also *Coker*, supra, at 593–597 (plurality opinion) (finding that both legislatures and juries had firmly rejected the penalty of death for the rape of an adult woman); *Enmund, supra*, at 788 (looking to "historical development of the punishment at issue, legislative judgments, international opinion, and the sentencing decisions juries have made"). The inquiry does not end there, however. Consensus is not dispositive. Whether the death penalty is disproportionate to the crime committed depends as well upon the standards elaborated by controlling precedents and by the Court's own understanding and interpretation of the Eighth Amendment's text, history, meaning, and purpose. . . .

In 1925, 18 States, the District of Columbia, and the Federal Government had statutes that authorized the death penalty for the rape of a child or an adult. See *Coker, supra*, at 593 (plurality opinion). Between 1930 and 1964, 455 people were executed for those crimes. See 5 Historical Statistics of the United States: Earliest Times to the Present, pp. 5–262 to 5–263 (S. Carter et al. eds. 2006) (Table Ec343–357). To our knowledge the last individual executed for the rape of a child was Ronald Wolfe in 1964. . . .

. . . 44 States have not made child rape a capital offense. As for federal law, Congress in the Federal Death Penalty Act of 1994 expanded the number of federal crimes for which the death penalty is a permissible sentence, including certain nonhomicide offenses; but it did not do the same for child rape or abuse. . . .

The evidence of a national consensus with respect to the death penalty for child rapists, as with respect to juveniles, mentally retarded offenders, and vicarious felony murderers, shows divided opinion but, on balance, an opinion against it. Thirty-seven jurisdictions—36 States plus the Federal Government—have the death penalty. As mentioned above, only six of those jurisdictions authorize the death penalty for rape of a child. Though our review of national consensus is not confined to tallying the number of States with applicable death penalty legislation, it is of significance that, in 45 jurisdictions, petitioner could not be executed for child rape of any kind. That number surpasses the 30 States in *Atkins* and *Roper* and the 42 States in *Enmund* that prohibited the death penalty under the circumstances those cases considered.

[The Court recognized that there was a small trend in the direction of reinstituting death for child rape in several states. But the Court found the trend inconclusive.]

As we have said in other Eighth Amendment cases, objective evidence of contemporary values as it relates to punishment for child rape is entitled to great weight, but it does not end our inquiry. "[T]he Constitution contemplates that in the end our own judgment will be brought to bear on the question of the acceptability of the death penalty under the Eighth Amendment. . . .

Consistent with evolving standards of decency and the teachings of our precedents we conclude that, in determining whether the death penalty is excessive, there is a distinction between intentional first-degree murder on the one hand and nonhomicide crimes against individual persons, even including child rape, on the other. The latter crimes may be devastating in their harm, as here, but "in terms of moral depravity and of the injury to the person and to the public," they cannot be compared to murder in their "severity and irrevocability. . . ."

[The Court also discussed how imposing death could cause a rise in underreporting of the crime and could increase the number of raped children who are murdered. For the above reasons, the Court held that child rapists may not be punished with death.]

Mental capacity, both at the time of crime and at the time of execution, is also an issue. Generally, it is cruel and unusual to execute a person who doesn't understand the nature of their acts or who can't understand why the state is killing them.

In 1986, the Supreme Court stated that defendants who are incapable of understanding why they are being executed because of insanity may not be executed until they regain their faculties.[20] In *Atkins v. Virginia*[21] (2002), the Court applied similar reasoning to reach the same conclusion about individuals who are cognitively disabled. However, a person who can reach a rational understanding of the reason for their execution may be executed even if brain damage or mental illness leaves them with no memory of the crime.[22] In 2005, the Supreme Court extended the protection from capital punishment to convictees who were juveniles (persons under 18) when they committed their crimes.[23] See Exhibit 17-1 for a listing of the Supreme Court's most significant death penalty decisions.

## Corporal/Physical Punishment

The Eighth Amendment limits the use of physical punishment. Punishment is not, however, unconstitutional simply because it involves pain. The question is whether the pain is excessive. Pain is excessive when it exceeds the quantity necessary to achieve a legitimate penological purpose, such as rehabilitation or retribution. Generally, hard labor is not per se cruel.[24] If the labor is beyond the physical limits of the inmate, or involves unnecessary pain, it is unconstitutional.

**Exhibit 17–1** Death Penalty Decisions by the Supreme Court

| Subject | Case | Holding |
|---|---|---|
| Capacity | | |
| | *Madison v. Alabama* (2019) | A person who doesn't recall the crime because of brain damage or mental illness may be executed provided he understands the reason for his execution. |
| | *Atkins v. Virginia* (2002) | A person who doesn't understand why they are being executed because of cognitive disability or insanity at the time of execution may not be executed. |
| | *Roper v. Simmons* (2005) | Juveniles may not be executed. |
| Proportionality | | |
| | *Enmund v. Florida* (1982) | Intent to cause death is required; death for aiding and abetting a crime that results in murder is disproportionate and not permitted. However, this decision was modified by *Tison v. Arizona.* |
| | *Tison v. Arizona* (1987) | Reckless indifference to life is adequate mens rea to impose death on felony murderer. |
| | *Kennedy v. Louisiana* (2008) | Death for rape of a child is disproportionate and not permitted. |
| | *Coker v. Georgia* (1977) | Death for the rape of an adult is disproportionate and not permitted. |
| Process | | |
| | *Ring v. Arizona* (2002) | Jury must find aggravating factor, not the judge. |
| Method | | |
| | *Glossip v. Gross* (2005) *& Baze v. Rees* (2008) | Lethal injection isn't per se a cruel method. |
| | *Wilkerson v. Utah* (1878) | Shooting and hanging are not cruel. Beheading, disembowelment, drawing and quartering, public dissection, and burning alive are cruel. |
| Equal Protection/Due Process | | |
| | *McCleskey v. Kemp* (1987) | Statistical evidence of racial disparity in capital punishment not enough to set aside sentence; proof of purposeful discrimination required. |
| | *Locket v. Ohio* (1978) | Ohio's response to Furman, which was to eliminate discretion by mandating death, was stricken. |
| | *Gregg v. Georgia* (1976) | Georgia's response to Furman was upheld. The new law required a finding of aggravating circumstances to impose death. |
| | *Furman v. Georgia* (1972) | Capital punishment not per se unconstitutional. But there were few boundaries in all of the existing systems, enabling arbitrary and capricious, often racially based, decisions. This decision effectively stopped executions for a several years. |

Whipping has been held both constitutional[25] and unconstitutional[26] by lower courts. The Supreme Court has not decided the issue.[27] Solitary confinement may be used in some circumstances, such as when a prisoner is disruptive or is highly dangerous. The use of prolonged solitary confinement for other prisoners is of questionable constitutionality.

The basic medical and nutritional needs of inmates must be satisfied by the government. Deliberately disregarding the medical or nutritional needs of inmates, or in some other manner imposing cruel or unusual punishment, can lead to liability under 42 U.S.C. § 1983.

## Sidebar

### Race and Cocaine

When Congress established the penalties for powder and rock cocaine crimes (possession, distribution) in the 1980s, it was assumed that rock cocaine was more dangerous, and as such, the punishment for rock cocaine crimes was more severe than for powder cocaine crimes. In the years that followed, the experience of law enforcement personnel, courts, and drug treatment experts brought that assumption into question. Even more, a racial disparity was discovered. Rock cocaine proved to be more commonly used by African Americans and powder cocaine by European Americans. Therefore, African Americans, mostly men, were disproportionately represented in the prison population for cocaine offenses. The problem was recognized by the U.S. Sentencing Commission, and subsequently Congress, at the urging of President Barack Obama, enacted the Fair Sentencing Act of 2010.[28] The Act amended the Controlled Substances Act to harmonize the punishment of powder and rock cocaine offenses.

The Supreme Court has said that the Eighth Amendment is to be interpreted consistent with society's evolving standards of decency. Therefore, although some courts have approved sterilization, and many states are considering chemical castration of men who commit sexual assault, there is a possibility that such practices could be found inconsistent with the Eighth Amendment.

## Incarceration

Restraint is an effective method of dealing with dangerous persons. Incarceration serves this purpose, and in some cases, the offender is also rehabilitated. Regrettably, because rehabilitation is rare and (contrary to popular belief) prison conditions are often poor, many offenders leave prison angry, no more educated or employable, and occasionally more dangerous.

Nevertheless, incarceration continues to be the most common method of punishing violent offenders. Offenders may be committed to prisons, camps, or local jails. Those sentenced to short terms (one year or less) are usually housed in a local jail. Individuals sentenced to longer terms are committed to prisons.

Like capital punishment, the Eighth Amendment's prohibition of cruel and unusual punishments establishes boundaries. The cruelty provision impacts the conditions of confinement.

The principle of keeping punishments proportional to crimes is not significant to incarceration as a form of punishment. The Court has given legislatures wide berth when setting terms of imprisonment for all crimes. Some justices, such as Antonin Scalia, reject the notion of proportionality altogether, and as was famously suggested by Justice Stevens, Justice Scalia would permit life imprisonment for a parking ticket. *Harmelin v. Michigan*[29] is an example. The Court, in a divided opinion, upheld life imprisonment with no possibility of parole for possession of cocaine.

The Court has recognized a few limits for defendants of special populations. In the 2010 case *Graham v. Florida*, for example, the Court held that a juvenile may not be sentenced to life imprisonment without parole for a non-homicide crime. The Court extended this reasoning to murder by juveniles in *Miller v. Alabama*.

## Shaming

Using shame to punish has a long history, memorialized in the Nathaniel Hawthorne book and later the film of the same name, *The Scarlet Letter*. Shaming was a common punishment in colonial America but declined in popularity in favor of imprisonment. Judges, citizens, and sometimes offenders, disillusioned with

# Oyez

## Miller v. Alabama
### 567 U.S. 460 (2012)

**Justice Kagan delivered the opinion of the Court.**

In November 1999, petitioner Kuntrell Jackson, then 14 years old, and two other boys decided to rob a video store. En route to the store, Jackson learned that one of the boys, Derrick Shields, was carrying a sawed-off shotgun in his coat sleeve. Jackson decided to stay outside when the two other boys entered the store. Inside, Shields pointed the gun at the store clerk, Laurie Troup, and demanded that she "give up the money." Troup refused. A few moments later, Jackson went into the store to find Shields continuing to demand money. At trial, the parties disputed whether Jackson warned Troup that "[w]e ain't playin'," or instead told his friends, "I thought you all was playin'." When Troup threatened to call the police, Shields shot and killed her. The three boys fled empty-handed.

Arkansas law gives prosecutors discretion to charge 14-year-olds as adults when they are alleged to have committed certain serious offenses. [The defendant was convicted and sentenced to life imprisonment without the possibility of parole. The sentencing court noted that the punishment was the only one available to it.]

The cases before us implicate two strands of precedent reflecting our concern with proportionate punishment. The first has adopted categorical bans on sentencing practices based on mismatches between the culpability of a class of offenders and the severity of a penalty. So, for example, we have held that imposing the death penalty for nonhomicide crimes against individuals, or imposing it on mentally retarded defendants, violates the Eighth Amendment. See Kennedy v. Louisiana, 554 U. S. 407 (2008); Atkins v. Virginia, 536 U. S. 304 (2002). Several of the cases in this group have specially focused on juvenile offenders, because of their lesser culpability. Thus, Roper held that the Eighth Amendment bars capital punishment for children, and Graham concluded that the Amendment also prohibits a sentence of life without the possibility of parole for a child who committed a nonhomicide offense. Graham further likened life without parole for juveniles to the death penalty itself, thereby evoking a second line of our precedents. In those cases, we have prohibited mandatory imposition of capital punishment, requiring that sentencing authorities consider the characteristics of a defendant and the details of his offense before sentencing him to death. Here, the confluence of these two lines of precedent leads to the conclusion that mandatory life-without-parole sentences for juveniles violate the Eighth Amendment.

To start with the first set of cases: Roper and Graham establish that children are constitutionally different from adults for purposes of sentencing. Because juveniles have diminished culpability and greater prospects for reform, we explained, "they are less deserving of the most severe punishments." Those cases relied on three significant gaps between juveniles and adults. First, children have a " 'lack of maturity and an underdeveloped sense of responsibility,' " leading to recklessness, impulsivity, and heedless risk-taking. Second, children "are more vulnerable . . . to negative influences and outside pressures," including from their family and peers; they have limited "contro[l] over their own environment" and lack the ability to extricate themselves from horrific, crime-producing settings. And third, a child's character is not as "well formed" as an adult's; his traits are "less fixed" and his actions less likely to be "evidence of irretrievabl[e] deprav[ity]. . . .

Our decisions rested not only on common sense—on what "any parent knows"—but on science and social science as well. In Roper, we cited studies showing that " '[o]nly a relatively small proportion of adolescents' " who engage in illegal activity " 'develop entrenched patterns of problem behavior.' . . . and in Graham, we noted that "developments in psychology and brain science continue to show fundamental differences between juvenile and adult minds"—for example, in "parts of the brain involved in behavior control." We reasoned that those findings—of transient rashness, proclivity for risk, and inability to assess consequences—both lessened a child's "moral culpability" and enhanced the prospect that, as the years go by and neurological development occurs, his " 'deficiencies will be reformed.' . . .

Roper and Graham emphasized that the distinctive attributes of youth diminish the penological justifications for imposing the harshest sentences on juvenile offenders, even when they commit terrible crimes. Because " '[t]he heart of the retribution rationale' " relates to an offender's blameworthiness . . .

Most fundamentally, Graham insists that youth matters in determining the appropriateness of a lifetime of incarceration without the possibility of parole. . . .

But the mandatory penalty schemes at issue here prevent the sentencer from taking account of these central considerations. By removing youth from the balance— by subjecting a juvenile to the same life-without-parole sentence applicable to an adult—these laws prohibit a sentencing authority from assessing whether the law's harshest term of imprisonment proportionately punishes a juvenile offender. That contravenes Graham's (and also Roper's) foundational principle: that imposition of a State's most severe penalties on juvenile offenders cannot proceed as though they were not children. . . .

Graham, Roper, and our individualized sentencing decisions make clear that a judge or jury must have the opportunity to consider mitigating circumstances before imposing the harshest possible penalty for juveniles. By requiring that all children convicted of homicide receive lifetime incarceration without possibility of parole, regardless of their age and age- related characteristics and the nature of their crimes, the mandatory sentencing schemes before us violate this principle of proportionality, and so the Eighth Amendment's ban on cruel and unusual punishment.

prison as a form of punishment, are increasingly returning to shaming. Consider the following examples:

- A federal judge ordered a mail thief to stand in front of a post office in San Francisco for 8 hours wearing a sign that read "I stole mail. This is my punishment." The sentence was upheld on appeal.[30]

- A woman who regularly drove onto a sidewalk to avoid a school bus was ordered to stand on a public street wearing a sign that read "Only an idiot would drive on a sidewalk to avoid a school bus."[31]

- Drunk drivers have been required to put license plates on their cars that identify them as having been convicted of a DUI.

- Sexual offenders are required to register with local law enforcement after release and their locations are made known to the general public.

- A woman was required to place an advertisement in her local newspaper declaring that she purchased drugs in the presence of her children.

- One judge offered thieves probation if they permitted their victims to take one item each from the offenders' homes.

- A man who was convicted of assaulting his wife was ordered to allow her to spit in his face.[32]

## Indeterminate and Determinate Sentencing

The **indeterminate sentence** gives corrections officials the greatest amount of control over an inmate's sentence. Under an indeterminate sentence, the judge sets a minimum and maximum period to be served, and the corrections agency determines the actual date of release. Once common in the United States, indeterminate sentencing has fallen into disfavor.

In **determinate sentencing** schemes, the sentencing judge is given discretion to set a fixed sentence from within a range set by the legislature. The determinate sentence is fixed, and there is no possibility of early release.

**indeterminate sentence**
A sentence having a minimum and maximum, with the decision of how long the criminal will serve depending on the criminal's behavior in prison and other things.

**determinate sentence**
An exact penalty set by law.

## Definite and Indefinite Sentencing

Unlike with determinate sentencing, in definite sentencing, the sentencing judge has no discretion. Rather, the legislature establishes the specific penalty to be imposed for each crime, and there is no possibility of early release. Definite sentencing reduces sentencing disparity. However, it is criticized for not allowing the particular facts of each case to be taken into consideration.

Indefinite sentencing incorporates both judicial and corrections agency discretion. It is the antithesis of definite sentencing. The sentencing judge is given a range from which to impose sentence, and the corrections agency is delegated the authority to grant early releases.

## Presumptive Sentencing

In many instances, when a legislature gives the sentencing judge discretion, it also establishes a *presumptive sentence*. That is, the legislature states what sentence should be imposed from within a range, absent **aggravating circumstances** or **mitigating circumstances**. Circumstances upon which the judge relies to increase the presumptive sentence are aggravating; those used to justify a sentence below a presumption are mitigating.

If a judge deviates from a presumptive sentence, the aggravating or mitigating circumstances justifying the departure must be made part of the record. For example, an assault statute may call for one to three years' punishment with a presumptive sentence of 18 months. If the judge sentences the defendant to more or less than 18 months, the reasons must be reflected on the record. Of course, even when deviating from a presumption, the sentencing judge must remain within the statutory limits.

**aggravating circumstances**
Actions or occurrences that increase the seriousness of a crime but are not part of the legal definition of that crime.

**mitigating circumstances**
Facts that provide no justification or excuse for an action but that can lower the amount of moral blame and thus lower the criminal penalty or civil damages for the action.

What constitutes an aggravating or mitigating circumstance is often expressed in the statute. Examples of aggravating circumstances are injury, torture, or death of the victim; use of a weapon during commission of the crime; whether the crime involved a child; and whether the defendant violated a trust. Examples of mitigating circumstances are physical disability of the defendant; whether the defendant has dependents; a crime committed in a nonviolent manner; and the defendant's acting in good faith.

## Suspended Imposition of Sentence

For some misdemeanors and infractions, judges are sometimes permitted to *suspend imposition of sentence* (SIS), also known as *diversion*. SIS is one of many forms of community-based correction, a term that refers to several varieties of nonincarceration correctional programs, such as probation, restitution, halfway houses, and parole. (Some of these other forms of community-based correction are discussed later.)

SIS is different from suspended sentencing. In SIS, a judge not only withholds sentencing the defendant but also refrains from entering a judgment of conviction until some future date. If the defendant complies with imposed conditions until that date, the prosecution is dismissed and the defendant is freed from having a criminal record. Suspended sentences, in contrast, involve conviction and imposition of sentence, but the defendant is relieved of actually serving the sentence so long as conditions are satisfied.

Where available, SIS is usually limited to nonviolent misdemeanors and infractions and is available to first-time offenders only.

## Concurrent and Consecutive Sentencing

**concurrent sentences**
Prison terms that run at the same time.

**consecutive sentences**
An additional prison term given to a person who is already convicted of a crime; the additional term is to be served after the previous one is finished.

If a defendant is already serving a sentence for another crime, or is convicted of two related crimes, the sentencing judge may impose **concurrent sentences** or **consecutive sentences**. If two sentences are concurrent, it is said that they "run together." That is, a defendant who receives two 5-year sentences will actually spend 5 years incarcerated. If the sentences are consecutive, the defendant will spend a total of 10 years incarcerated.

## Parole

**parole**
Early release from prison or jail. Parole is usually granted with conditions such as requiring the parolee to refrain from communicating with the victim of the crime that led to the confinement and remaining free of criminality while on parole. If the conditions of parole are violated, parole may be revoked and the parolee may be returned to confinement to complete the original sentence.

After committing a defendant to a correctional institution, the judge loses control and responsibility over that defendant, unless a statute provides otherwise. In many states, **parole** is available to prison inmates. *Parole*, an early release from prison, is used to encourage inmates to stay out of trouble and engage in rehabilitative efforts while in prison. Parole decisions are made by corrections officials (i.e., a parole board). Similar to probation, an offender must comply with certain conditions while on parole. Conditions routinely include not possessing a gun; not contacting witnesses, judge, jurors, or prosecutors associated with the offender's conviction; and not becoming involved in further criminal activity. Violation of a condition of parole may result in recommitment to prison.

Parole has fallen into disfavor in recent years. The result has been to limit the availability of parole in many situations. Parole has been eliminated for those convicted of crimes against the United States.

## The Federal Guidelines

In November 1987, the Federal Sentencing Guidelines became effective. The guidelines are a milestone in federal criminal law. Their purpose is twofold: (1) to reduce sentencing disparity and (2) to achieve "honesty in sentencing."[33] Prior to the Guidelines, judges were given a large penalty range from which a defendant could be sentenced. The result of this discretion was that defendants similarly situated were often sentenced very differently. One goal of the Guidelines is to reduce such disparity in sentencing.

The second goal, honesty in sentencing, concerns parole. Prior to the Guidelines, defendants could be released on parole, in some cases, after only one-third of the imposed sentence had been served. In addition, prisoners complained that parole was arbitrarily and inconsistently applied. Accordingly, Congress eliminated parole, and the guidelines now reflect the time that will be served, less 54 days of good time that may be earned yearly (after the first year).

To achieve the first goal—the reduction of sentencing disparity—the Guidelines greatly limit the discretion of the judge in sentencing. To determine what sentence should be imposed, the offender's criminal history category and offense level must be determined. The criminal history category is simply determined by the number of prior convictions of the offender.

Finding an offender's offense level is more complex. First, the crime is assigned a base offense number. That number is then increased by "specific offense characteristics." Adjustments to this figure are then made for mitigating or aggravating circumstances. This final figure is the offense level.

Once the criminal history category and offense level are determined, the court looks to the sentencing table. This table provides a small range (the top figure never exceeds 25% of the bottom figure) from which the judge is to sentence the defendant. Only in rare instances may a judge deviate from the proscribed sentencing range.

The Guidelines continue to permit judges to suspend sentences to probation for offenses at the low end of the sentencing table. For offenses just above the probation cutoff, judges may sentence an offender to probation, provided some form of confinement is ordered, such as house arrest or community confinement. There is also a third layer of offenses, for which the judge may order a "split sentence." This is where one-half or more of the sentence must be served in prison, and the remaining amount may be served in another form of confinement.

The Guidelines have been the subject of much controversy. Federal judges themselves have been very critical of the Guidelines. Many contend that the reason judges are complaining is simply their loss of authority. Though this may be true, there also appear to be problems caused by the rigidity of the Guidelines.

The drafters of the Guidelines knew that all factors that should be considered in sentencing could not be anticipated (or quantified). As such, provisions are made to permit deviation from the Guidelines. However, deviation is rarely permitted. This practice has led to some absurd results. For example, one 21-year-old honor student, with no prior record, was sentenced to 10 years in prison for his involvement in one drug transaction.[34] At least one federal district judge has resigned because of dissatisfaction with the guidelines.

The guidelines were mandatory for nearly 20 years, surviving many constitutional challenges. Then, in 2005, the Supreme Court decided that the mandatory nature of the guidelines violated the Sixth Amendment's jury trial requirement in *United States v. Booker*.

# Oyez

## United States v. Booker
### 543 U.S. 220 (2005)

**JUSTICE STEVENS DELIVERED THE OPINION OF THE COURT IN PART.**

The question presented in each of these cases is whether an application of the Federal Sentencing Guidelines violated the Sixth Amendment. In each case, the courts below held that binding rules set forth in the Guidelines limited the severity of the sentence that the judge could lawfully impose on the defendant based on the facts found by the jury at his trial. In both cases the courts rejected, on the basis of

(continued)

our decision in *Blakely v. Washington*, 542 U.S. _____ (2004), the Government's recommended application of the Sentencing Guidelines because the proposed sentences were based on additional facts that the sentencing judge found by a preponderance of the evidence. We hold that both courts correctly concluded that the Sixth Amendment as construed in *Blakely* does apply to the Sentencing Guidelines. In a separate opinion authored by Justice Breyer, the Court concludes that in light of this holding, two provisions of the Sentencing Reform Act of 1984 (SRA) that have the effect of making the Guidelines mandatory must be invalidated in order to allow the statute to operate in a manner consistent with congressional intent.

Based upon Booker's criminal history and the quantity of drugs found by the jury, the Sentencing Guidelines required the District Court Judge to select a "base" sentence of not less than 210 nor more than 262 months in prison. See United States Sentencing Commission, Guidelines Manual §§ 2D1.1(c)(4), 4A1.1 (Nov. 2003) (hereinafter USSG). The judge, however, held a post-trial sentencing proceeding and concluded by a preponderance of the evidence that Booker had possessed an additional 566 grams of crack and that he was guilty of obstructing justice. Those findings mandated that the judge select a sentence between 360 months and life imprisonment; the judge imposed a sentence at the low end of the range. Thus, instead of the sentence of 21 years and 10 months that the judge could have imposed on the basis of the facts proved to the jury beyond a reasonable doubt, Booker received a 30-year sentence. . . .

It has been settled throughout our history that the Constitution protects every criminal defendant "against conviction except upon proof beyond a reasonable doubt of every fact necessary to constitute the crime with which he is charged." *In re Winship*, 397 U.S. 358, 364 (1970). It is equally clear that the "Constitution gives a criminal defendant the right to demand that a jury find him guilty of all the elements of the crime with which he is charged." *United States v. Gaudin*, 515 U.S. 506, 511 (1995). These basic precepts, firmly rooted in the common law, have provided the basis for recent decisions interpreting modern criminal statutes and sentencing procedures. . . .

In *Apprendi v. New Jersey*, 530 U.S. 466 (2000), the defendant pleaded guilty to second-degree possession of a firearm for an unlawful purpose, which carried a prison term of 5-to-10 years. Thereafter, the trial court found that his conduct had violated New Jersey's "hate crime" law because it was racially motivated, and imposed a 12-year sentence. This Court set aside the enhanced sentence. We held: "Other than the fact of a prior conviction, any fact that increases the penalty for a crime beyond the prescribed statutory maximum must be submitted to a jury, and proved beyond a reasonable doubt." The fact that New Jersey labeled the hate crime a "sentence enhancement" rather than a separate criminal act was irrelevant for constitutional purposes. As a matter of simple justice, it seemed obvious that the procedural safeguards designed to protect Apprendi from punishment for the possession of a firearm should apply equally to his violation of the hate crime statute. Merely using the label "sentence enhancement" to describe the latter did not provide a principled basis for treating the two crimes differently.

In *Ring v. Arizona*, 536 U.S. 584 (2002), we reaffirmed our conclusion that the characterization of critical facts is constitutionally irrelevant. There, we held that it was impermissible for "the trial judge, sitting alone" to determine the presence or absence of the aggravating factors required by Arizona law for imposition of the death penalty. "If a State makes an increase in a defendant's authorized punishment contingent on the finding of a fact, that fact—no matter how the State labels it—must be found by a jury beyond a reasonable doubt." Our opinion made it clear that ultimately, while the procedural error in Ring's case might have been harmless because the necessary finding was implicit in the jury's guilty verdict, "the characterization of a fact or circumstance as an 'element' or a 'sentencing factor' is not determinative of the question 'who decides,' judge or jury," . . .

In *Blakely v. Washington*, 542 U.S. _____ (2004), we dealt with a determinate sentencing scheme. . . .

For reasons explained in *Jones, Apprendi*, and *Ring*, the requirements of the Sixth Amendment were clear. The application of Washington's sentencing scheme violated the defendant's right to have the jury find the existence of "'any particular fact'" that the law makes essential to his punishment. . . .

If the Guidelines as currently written could be read as merely advisory provisions that recommended, rather than required, the selection of particular sentences in response to differing sets of facts, their use would not implicate the Sixth Amendment. We have never doubted the authority of a judge to exercise broad discretion in imposing a sentence within a statutory range. Indeed, everyone agrees that the constitutional issues presented by these cases would have been avoided entirely if Congress had omitted from the SRA the provisions that make the Guidelines binding on district judges; it is that circumstance that makes the Court's answer to the second question presented possible. For when a trial judge exercises his discretion to select a specific sentence within a defined range, the defendant has no right to a jury determination of the facts that the judge deems relevant.

The Guidelines as written, however, are not advisory; they are mandatory. . . .

[The Court concluded by invalidating the mandatory provision of the statute and thereby rendering the guidelines advisory. Judges, of course, remain obligated to sentence offenders within the statutory range and to refer to the advice of the guidelines.]

The impact of *Booker* on sentencing has not been significant. The vast majority of convictees have continued to be sentenced within the ranges established by the guidelines after *Booker* was decided. The patterns of sentencing, even within the guidelines, were largely unchanged. Also, differences in sentencing (e.g., by region) that existed before *Booker* continued post–*Booker*.[35]

The federal government was not the first to enact sentencing guidelines. At least two states, Minnesota and Washington, were using guidelines when the federal version became law. It is probable that more jurisdictions will contemplate similar reform in the future.

## Probation and Revocation

A popular alternative to incarceration is probation, also known as a **suspended sentence**. Probation is not always an alternative and is rarely available for crimes that are punished with life imprisonment or death. While on probation, the defendant is released from custody but must comply with conditions imposed by the court during the probationary period. Each defendant is placed under the supervision of a probation officer during this period. The probation officer is an officer of the court, not of the corrections system.

Typical conditions of probation include a requirement of steady employment, refraining from other unlawful conduct, not carrying a firearm or other weapon, and not leaving the jurisdiction of the court. A judge may tailor conditions to fit the circumstances of each case. For example, a child molester may be prohibited from obtaining employment that requires working around children.

Some judges make consent to search by a probation officer a condition of probation. This may include search of the person as well as property. In some cases, judges impose the search requirement independently; in others, the defendant and prosecutor stipulate to the searches through a plea agreement. In either situation, are there limits to this authority? May a probation officer search a probationer at any time, in any manner, and without any cause to believe that mischief is afoot? Further, can a defendant who is facing incarceration as an alternative give meaningful consent to such a condition? This is the subject of the *Consuelo-Gonzalez* case, in which the court decided that probationers are entitled to full Fourth Amendment protection as to law enforcement officers generally. Searches by police officers of probationers must satisfy the usual Fourth Amendment requirements.

**suspended sentence**
A sentence (usually "jail time") that the judge allows the convicted person to avoid serving (usually if the person continues on good behavior, completes community service, etc.).

## Sidebar

### Crime Stats: Prisoners in the United States

Lack of space in U.S. prisons is an ever-increasing concern. Most prisons are overcrowded, often housing double or triple the intended capacity; this leads to serious problems for both prison administrators and inmates. If prison conditions are extremely bad, an inmate may succeed in an Eighth Amendment lawsuit against prison authorities.

The total number of adults under state and federal correctional supervision in 2019 was 1,430,800. That equated to 419 of every 100,000 adults. There were 1,096 black prisoners for every 100,000 black residents, 525 Hispanic prisoners for every 100,000 Hispanic residents, and 214 white prisoners for every 100,000 white residents. Men represented 92% of the prison population; 88% of inmates were in state facilities.

The number of incarcerated decreased from 2018 to 2019, as it had for 10 consecutive years before. Declines fell in reverse order of rate of incarceration by race (e.g., black prisoners saw the greatest decrease, with Hispanics and whites following in that order).

*Source: Prisoners in 2019. Bureau of Justice Statistics (Oct. 2020).*

# Oyez

## United States v. Consuelo-Gonzalez
### 521 F.2d 259 (9th Cir. 1975)

**Sneed, Circuit Judge**

Consuelo-Gonzalez appeals from a conviction under 21 USC § 841(a)(1) for possession of heroin with intent to distribute. We reverse.

Between November 15, 1972, and December 18, 1972, agents of the Federal Bureau of Narcotics and Dangerous Drugs received information from four different sources that Virginia Consuelo-Gonzalez was actively engaged in the importation and sale of heroin. A check of the records at the United States Attorney's Office on December 12, 1972, revealed to the agents that Virginia Consuelo-Gonzalez had previously been convicted of heroin smuggling under the name of Virginia Cardenas and was currently on probation. At this time, the agents were also apprised that it was a condition of Consuelo-Gonzalez's probation that she submit her person and property to search at any time upon request by a law enforcement officer. On December 14, 1972, an independent verification was made of the fact that Virginia Cardenas and Virginia Consuelo-Gonzalez were one and the same person; and on December 19, 1972, the agents reconfirmed the probationary status and condition that she submit to search.

On the morning of December 19, 1992, . . . federal and local law enforcement officers approached the Consuelo-Gonzalez residence for purposes of conducting a search of the premises. When they arrived, they found the front door of the house ajar. The agents knocked on the door and waited for Consuelo-Gonzalez to appear. When she did so, the lead agent showed her his identification, informed her that he was aware of her probation and the conditions which had been attached to it, and indicated his intention to enter the residence and conduct a search. Consuelo-Gonzalez responded to his request by stepping back and saying "Sure, search my purse." Upon entering the house, the lead agent made a cursory search of her handbag to determine whether it contained weapons. None were found. The handbag was then placed beside a chair in which Consuelo-Gonzalez was asked to sit.

A thorough search of Consuelo-Gonzalez's person and residence was then commenced. In the bedroom, the agents found a narcotics injection outfit in a dresser; and on a shelf in the living room they discovered a paper sack containing a bundle of notebook papers with brown debris on them. Both of these items were seized. A second search of Consuelo-Gonzalez's handbag revealed two coin purses, inside of which the agents found two white paper bindles and seven rubber condoms containing a total of 11.7 grams of brown powder, later proven to be heroin. This evidence was also seized, and subsequently used to provide the basis for the present conviction.

In a timely and appropriate manner, counsel for Consuelo-Gonzalez moved to suppress this evidence. However, the trial judge denied the motion to suppress, relying specifically upon the authorization to search which had been made a condition of the probation. . . . Thereafter, defendant was found guilty of possession of heroin with intent to distribute. . . .

In this appeal, defendant asserts that the trial court erred in failing to suppress the evidence on the ground that the condition of probation requiring her to "submit to search of her person or property at any time when requested by a law-enforcement" officer was improper and thus could not serve to make the search lawful. It is argued that the Fourth Amendment requires this result.

While we are not prepared to embrace the full reach of defendant's argument, we do believe that the condition employed in the instant case is not in keeping with the purposes intended to be served by the Federal Probation Act. It is our view that, even though the trial judge has very broad discretion in fixing the terms and conditions of probation, such terms must be reasonably related to the purposes of the Act. In determining whether a reasonable relationship exists, we have found it necessary to give consideration to the purposes sought to be served by probation, the extent to which the full constitutional guarantees available to those not under probation should be accorded probationers, and the legitimate needs of law enforcement. Having done so, we have concluded that Consuelo-Gonzalez could have been required to submit her person and property to search by a probation officer. We have further concluded that any search made pursuant to the condition included in the terms of probation must necessarily meet the Fourth Amendment's standard of reasonableness. . . .

Although it is doubtful that any formulation of a condition relating to the search of a probationer's person or property can be drafted that will provide unambiguous guidance to both the probationer and the probation officer, it is suggested that the following condition would properly reflect the views expressed herein:

That she submit to search of her person or property conducted in a reasonable manner and at a reasonable time by a probation officer.

. . . [W]e hold that the search in this case was improper and that the motion to suppress should have been granted. . . .

The guiding principle which has emerged in construing the Probation Act is that the only permissible conditions are those that, when considered in context, can reasonably be said to contribute significantly both to the rehabilitation of the convicted person and to the protection of the public. . . .

This guiding interpretive principle plainly suggests the manner in which the Act's administration should be accommodated to the constitutional guarantees of the Bill of Rights. While it must be recognized that probationers, like parolees and prisoners, properly are subject to limitations from which ordinary persons are free, it is also true that these limitations in the aggregate must serve the ends of probation. . . . [I]t is necessary to recognize that when fundamental rights are curbed it must be done sensitively and with a keen appreciation that the infringement must serve the broad purposes of the Probation Act. This burden cannot be avoided by asserting either that the probationer has voluntarily waived his rights by not objecting in a proper manner to the conditions imposed upon him or that he must accept any condition the court "deems best" as a consequence of being "in custody."

Turning to the Fourth Amendment rights that Consuelo-Gonzalez insists were infringed, two things are obvious. The first is that some forms of search by probation officers are not only compatible with rehabilitation, but, with respect to those convicted of certain offenses such as possession and distribution of narcotics; are also essential to the proper functioning of a probationary system. The second is that the condition imposed on Consuelo-Gonzalez literally permits searches which could not possibly serve the ends of probation. For example, an intimidating and harassing search to serve law enforcement ends totally unrelated to either her prior conviction or her rehabilitation is authorized by the terms of the condition. Submission to such searches should not be the price of probation. A probationer, like the parolee, has the right to enjoy a significant degree of privacy. . . .

Probation authorities also have a special and unique interest in invading the privacy of probationers. This special and unique interest does not extend to law enforcement officers generally. . . . Inasmuch as the search of Consuelo-Gonzalez's residence and handbag occurred neither during the course of a probation visit by a probation officer nor pursuant to a proper warrant, the evidence must be suppressed. . . .

[I]t may well be necessary during the course of a probation visit to conduct a pat-down search for weapons or contraband, to examine the probationer's arms to ascertain whether drugs are being used, or take the probationer into custody. When done reasonably and humanely by probation officers, no question concerning the appropriateness of their actions should arise. Moreover, a thorough search of a probationer's residence incident to, or following, a probation visit is not dependent upon the establishment of probable cause. A reasonable belief on the part of the probation officer that such a search is necessary to perform properly his duties is sufficient. As we said [in a prior case], this belief may be based on a "hunch" having its origin in what the probation officer has learned or observed about the behavior and attitude of the probationer.

Probationers are also protected by the Fourth Amendment's reasonableness requirement in regard to searches by probation officers. However, the standards are lowered, as the public has a greater interest in searching the probationer and the probationer has a lessened expectation to privacy. Also, probation officers do have a penal objective; in fact, they should have the welfare of their probationers in mind.

Therefore, probation officers may search a probationer's person or property with reasonable grounds; no warrant is required, although the search must be conducted in a reasonable manner. These conclusions have also been reached by the Supreme Court.[36] As a condition of probation, a search condition must be reasonably related to the probation, or it is invalid. Therefore, if a person is convicted of embezzlement, a condition providing for searches of the person would be unreasonable. The result would, of course, be different if the offense were possession of a firearm or drugs.

Finally, any other condition of probation that encroaches upon a constitutional guarantee is suspect. For example, a condition that restricts free speech is unconstitutional in most circumstances.[37] However, the right to travel freely and to bear arms are examples of constitutionally preserved rights that are commonly restricted during probation and parole.

A defendant who violates a condition of probation may be disciplined. Generally, the decision about whether any action should be taken for a violation is made by the probation officer. If a violation is extreme, the probation officer may file a petition to revoke probation. The sentencing court then holds a **revocation hearing**. If the petition is granted, the defendant is taken off probation and incarcerated.

At the revocation hearing, the defendant may be entitled to counsel. As a general rule, the right is not found in the Sixth Amendment, as the "critical stages" of trial have passed. In one rare case, the Supreme Court held that a Sixth Amendment right to counsel did exist at a revocation hearing. In *Mempa v. Rhay*, 389 U.S. 128 (1967), the trial judge withheld sentencing, placed the defendant on probation,

**revocation hearing**
The due process hearing required before the government can revoke a privilege it has previously granted.

and did not pronounce sentence until after the defendant violated his probation and then had it revoked. Because the revocation hearing turned out to be the defendant's sentencing hearing, where there is a right to counsel under the Sixth Amendment, the Court found that the Sixth Amendment applied.

The Due Process Clauses of the Fifth and Fourteenth Amendments may also provide a right to counsel at a revocation hearing. If a substantial question of law or fact must be resolved at the hearing, counsel must be appointed for the indigent defendant so that the issues can be fully explored and developed. If revocation is obvious, though, counsel need not be allowed.

## Community Service

One alternative to incarceration for nonviolent offenders is community service. In such a program, a defendant's sentence is suspended, and the completion of a stated number of community service hours is a condition of the defendant's probation.

In most instances, the probation officer works with the probationer to find an appropriate job. However, the judge may require that a specific job be performed.

The requirements of community service range from unskilled to professional. For example, a judge may require that a professional, such as a physician or attorney, work in a clinic that provides services to the poor. The same person may be expected to pick up trash from local roads. Clearly, the former makes best use of the defendant's skills and benefits the community the most.

## Restitution

The purpose of restitution is to compensate the victim, not to punish the offender. As such, restitution is not a substitute for other forms of punishment.

Restitution is limited to the actual amounts resulting from the offenses convicted.[38] Said another way, restitution is limited to losses resulting from the specific conduct that formed the basis of the conviction.[39] However, an agreement between the government and the defendant to pay a higher amount may be constitutional.[40]

Restitution may be made a condition of probation. A probationer's refusal to pay restitution can result in a revocation of probation. However, when a fine or restitution is imposed as a condition of probation, and "the probationer has made all reasonable efforts to pay . . . yet cannot do so through no fault of his own, it is fundamentally unfair to revoke probation automatically without considering whether adequate alternative methods of punishing the defendant are available."[41]

## Fines

Unlike the goal of restitution, the purpose of a fine is to punish the offender. Accordingly, restitution monies are paid to victims, and fines end up in the public treasury. Fines are a common method of punishing misdemeanants. Serious crimes are frequently punished with both a fine and incarceration. Any fine imposed must be reasonable; that is, the amount must be within the financial means of the offender. Excessive fines are prohibited by the Eighth Amendment.

It is a violation of equal protection to sentence individuals without means to pay a fine to longer periods of incarceration than those received by individuals who can pay a fine. In *Williams v. Illinois*,[42] a defendant was sentenced to a maximum one year in prison and a $500 fine for petty theft. Illinois statute provided that if at the end of the year, the fine (and court costs) were not paid, the defendant was to remain in jail for a time to satisfy the debt. This sentence was calculated at $5.00 per day. The Court found that because Williams was indigent, the statute violated the Equal Protection Clause by improperly sentencing defendants according to economic status. Of course, a defendant who has the financial means to pay a fine and does not pay may have probation revoked or incarceration increased.

## Forfeiture

Forfeitures are similar to fines in that they involve the taking of property and money to punish defendants. A forfeiture is, however, not directed at the defendant's pocketbook in general, as is a fine. Rather, forfeiture focuses on taking the property owned by a defendant that is in some manner connected with the crimes. Automobiles, airplanes, or boats used to transport drugs are an example. Forfeiture has become an increasingly popular tool amongst law enforcement agencies.

Procedurally, forfeiture may occur within and as part of a criminal proceeding. In addition, many laws permit forfeiture to occur in a separative in rem civil proceeding. Most statutes allow law enforcement officers to make seizures based upon probable cause, to be immediately followed by the filing of a forfeiture proceeding.[43] Of course, seizure can also occur later in the proceedings. Under federal law, if a seizure was proper (i.e., based upon probable cause), the burden of proof falls on a claimant to establish that the property is not subject to seizure. The claimant must prove this by a preponderance of the evidence.[44]

Under federal law, forfeiture is provided for in several instances, including violations of the Racketeer Influenced and Corrupt Organizations Act (RICO) and under the so-called drug kingpin statute, the Continuing Criminal Enterprise law.[45]

There are limits to the use of forfeiture. In *United States v. James Daniel Good Real Property*,[46] the Supreme Court determined that the Due Process Clause requires the government to provide notice and a preseizure hearing when it intends to forfeit real property, unless exigent circumstances justify an immediate seizure. There is no requirement of preseizure notice in cases where property can disappear. The Court stated that in cases where property is movable, immediate seizure, without notice or a hearing, is necessary to "establish the court's jurisdiction over the property" and to guard against someone absconding with the property.

A critical issue concerns the relationship between the crime and the property forfeited. Forfeiture of all property associated with a crime can be troubling. Forfeiting a boat that was purchased with drug money and is used to transport drugs from Colombia to the United States is not problematic. But is it constitutionally sound to forfeit a home because one joint of marijuana is discovered inside? Does the Eighth Amendment's Excessive Fines Clause limit the use of forfeitures? In *Austin v. United States*, the Supreme Court examined this issue.

## Oyez

### Austin v. United States
### 509 U.S. 602 (1993)

**JUSTICE BLACKMUN delivered the opinion of the Court.**

In this case, we are asked to decide whether the Excessive Fines Clause of the Eighth Amendment applies to forfeitures of property under 21 U.S.C. §§ 881(a)(4) and (a)(7). We hold that it does and therefore remand the case for consideration of the question whether the forfeiture at issue here was excessive.

On August 2, 1990, petitioner Richard Lyle Austin was indicted on four counts of violating South Dakota's drug laws. Austin ultimately pleaded guilty to one count of possessing cocaine with intent to distribute and was sentenced by the state court to seven years' imprisonment. On September 7, the United States filed an in rem action in the United States District Court for the District of South Dakota seeking forfeiture of Austin's mobile home and auto body shop under 21 U.S.C. §§ 881(a)(4) and (a)(7) [these laws provide for the forfeiture of property in drug cases]. Austin filed a claim and an answer to the complaint.

On February 4, 1991, the United States made a motion, supported by an affidavit from Sioux Falls Police Officer Donald Satterlee, for summary judgment. According to Satterlee's affidavit, Austin met Keith Engebretson at Austin's body shop on June 13, 1990, and

(continued)

agreed to sell cocaine to Engebretson. Austin left the shop, went to his mobile home, and returned to the shop with two grams of cocaine which he sold to Engebretson. State authorities executed a search warrant on the body shop and mobile home the following day. They discovered small amounts of marijuana and cocaine, a .22 caliber revolver, drug paraphernalia, and approximately $4,700 in cash. In opposing summary judgment, Austin argued that forfeiture of the properties would violate the Eighth Amendment. The District Court rejected this argument and entered summary judgment for the United States.

The United States Court of Appeals for the Eighth Circuit "reluctantly agree[d] with the government" and affirmed. . . . Although it thought that "the principle of proportionality should be applied in civil actions that result in harsh penalties," . . . and that the Government was "exacting too high a penalty in relation to the offense committed . . . the court felt constrained from holding the forfeiture unconstitutional." . . .

Austin contends that the Eighth Amendment's Excessive Fines Clause applies to in rem civil forfeiture proceedings. . . . In [an earlier case] we held that the Excessive Fines Clause does not limit the award of punitive damages to a private party in a civil suit when the government neither has prosecuted the action nor has any right to receive a share of the damages. . . . The Court concluded that both the Eighth Amendment and § 10 of the Bill of Rights of 1689, from which it derives, were intended to prevent the government from abusing its power to punish . . . and therefore "that the Excessive Fines Clause was intended to limit only those fines directly imposed by, and payable to, the government." . . .

We found it unnecessary to decide . . . whether the Excessive Fines Clause applies only to criminal cases. . . . The United States now argues that

> any claim that the government's conduct in a civil proceeding is limited by the Eighth Amendment generally, or by the Excessive Fines Clause in particular, must fail unless the challenged action, despite its label, would have been recognized as a criminal punishment at the time the Eighth Amendment was adopted.

■  ■  ■

It further suggests that the Eighth Amendment cannot apply to a civil proceeding unless that proceeding is so punitive that it must be considered criminal. . . .

Some provisions of the Bill of Rights are expressly limited to criminal cases. . . . The text of the Eighth Amendment includes no similar limitation.

Nor does the history of the Eighth Amendment require such a limitation. Justice O'Connor noted in *Browning-Ferris*: "Consideration of the Eighth Amendment immediately followed consideration of the Fifth Amendment. After deciding to confine the benefits of the Self-Incrimination Clause of the Fifth Amendment to criminal proceedings, the Framers turned their attention to the Eighth Amendment. There were no proposals to limit that Amendment to criminal proceedings. . . ."

The purpose of the Eighth Amendment, putting the Bail Clause to one side, was to limit the government's power to punish. . . . The Cruel and Unusual Clause is self-evidently concerned with punishment. The Excessive Fines Clause limits the Government's power to extract payments, whether in case or in kind, "as punishment for some offense." . . . "The notion of punishment, as we commonly understand it, cuts across the division between civil and criminal law." . . . "It is commonly understood that civil proceedings may advance punitive and remedial goals, and conversely, that both punitive and remedial goals may be served by criminal penalties." . . . Thus, the question is not, as the United States would have it, whether forfeiture . . . is civil or criminal, but rather whether it is punishment.

In considering this question, we are mindful of the fact that sanctions frequently serve more than one purpose. We need not exclude the possibility that a forfeiture serves remedial purposes to conclude that it is subject to the limitations of the Excessive Fines Clause. We, however, must determine that it can be explained as serving in part to punish. . . . We turn, then, to consider whether, at the time the Eighth Amendment was ratified, forfeiture was understood at least in part as punishment and whether forfeiture under §§ 881(a)(4) and (a)(7) should be so understood today.

Three kinds of forfeiture were established in England at the time the Eighth Amendment was ratified in the United States: deodand, forfeiture upon conviction for a felony or treason, and statutory forfeiture. . . . Each was understood, at least in part, as imposing punishment.

■  ■  ■

The First Congress passed laws subjecting ships and cargos involved in customs offenses to forfeiture. . . . Indeed, examination of those laws suggests that the First Congress viewed forfeiture as punishment. . . . It is also of some interest that "forfeit" is the word Congress used for fine. . . .

We turn next to consider whether forfeitures under 21 U.S.C. §§ 881(a)(4) and (a)(7) are properly considered punishment today. We find nothing in these provisions or their legislative history to contradict the historical understanding of forfeiture as punishment. . . .

The legislative history of § 881 confirms the punitive nature of these provisions. When it added subsection (a)(7) to § 881 in 1984, Congress recognized "that the traditional criminal sanctions of fine and imprisonment are inadequate to deter or punish the enormously profitable trade in dangerous drugs." . . . It characterized the forfeiture of real property as "a powerful deterrent." . . .

We therefore conclude that forfeiture under these provisions constitutes "payment to a sovereign as punishment for some offense," . . . and, as such, is subject to the limitations of the Eighth Amendment's Excessive Fines Clause.

The *Austin* Court held that the Eighth Amendment's Excessive Fines Clause applies to civil in rem forfeiture proceedings. Accordingly, a forfeiture must be proportional to the offense. A fine or forfeiture that is grossly larger than the underlying offense is excessive and violative of the Eighth Amendment. The fine at issue in *United States v. Bajakajian* is an example of an excessive fine.

## Oyez

### United States v. Bajakajian
### 524 U.S. 321 (1998)

**Justice Thomas delivered the opinion of the Court:**

Respondent Hosep Bajakajian attempted to leave the United States without reporting, as required by federal law, that he was transporting more than $10,000 in currency. Federal law also provides that a person convicted of willfully violating this reporting requirement shall forfeit to the government "any property . . . involved in such offense." 18 U.S.C. § 982 (a)(1). The question in this case is whether forfeiture of the entire $357,144 that respondent failed to declare would violate the Excessive Fines Clause of the Eighth Amendment. We hold that it would, because full forfeiture of respondent's currency would be grossly disproportional to the gravity of his offense.

On June 9, 1994, respondent, his wife, and his two daughters were waiting at Los Angeles International Airport to board a flight to Italy; their final destination was Cyprus. Using dogs trained to detect currency by its smell, customs inspectors discovered some $230,000 in cash in the Bajakajians' checked baggage. A customs inspector approached respondent and his wife and told them that they were required to report all money in excess of $10,000 in their possession or in their baggage. Respondent said that he had $8,000 and that his wife had another $7,000, but that the family had no additional currency to declare. A search of their carry-on bags, purse, and wallet revealed more cash; in all, customs inspectors found $357,144. The currency was seized and respondent was taken into custody.

A federal grand jury indicted respondent on three counts. Count One charged him with failing to report, that he was transporting more than $10,000 outside the United States, and with doing so "willfully." Count Two charged him with making a false material statement to the United States Customs Service. Count Three sought forfeiture of the $357,144 pursuant to 18 U.S.C. § 982 (a)(1), which provides: "[A] person or an agent or bailee of the person shall file a report . . . when the person, agent, or bailee knowingly—" (1) transports, is about to transport, or has transported, monetary instruments of more than $10,000 at one time—"(A) from a place in the United States to or through a place outside the United States. . . ."

"The court, in imposing sentence on a person convicted of an offense in violation of § . . . 5316, . . . shall order that the person forfeit to the United States any property, real or personal, involved in such offense, or any property traceable to such property."

Respondent pleaded guilty to the failure to report in Count One; the Government agreed to dismiss the false statement charge in Count Two; and respondent elected to have a bench trial on the forfeiture in Count Three. After the bench trial, the District Court found that the entire $357,144 was subject to forfeiture because it was "involved in" the offense. The court also found that the funds were not connected to any other crime and that respondent was transporting the money to repay a lawful debt. The District Court further found that respondent had failed to report that he was taking the currency out of the United States because of fear stemming from "cultural differences": Respondent, who had grown up as a member of the Armenian minority in Syria, had a "distrust for the Government." Although § 982 (a)(1) directs sentencing courts to impose full forfeiture, the District Court concluded that such forfeiture would be "extraordinarily harsh" and "grossly disproportionate to the offense in question," and that it would therefore violate the Excessive Fines Clause. The court instead ordered forfeiture of $15,000, in addition to a sentence of three years of probation and a fine of $5,000—the maximum fine under the Sentencing Guidelines—because the court believed that the maximum Guidelines fine was "too little" and that a $15,000 forfeiture would "make up for what I think a reasonable fine should be."

The United States appealed, seeking full forfeiture of respondent's currency as provided in § 982 (a)(1). The Court of Appeals for the Ninth Circuit affirmed.

The Eighth Amendment provides: "Excessive bail shall not be required, nor excessive fines imposed, nor cruel and unusual punishments inflicted." U.S. Const., Amdt. 8. This Court has had little occasion to interpret, and has never actually applied, the Excessive Fines Clause. We have, however, explained that at the time the Constitution was adopted, "the word 'fine' was understood to mean a payment to a sovereign as punishment for some offense." The Excessive Fines Clause thus "limits the government's power to extract payments, whether in cash or in kind, 'as punishment for some offense.'" Forfeitures—payments in kind—are thus "fines" if they constitute punishment for an offense.

(continued)

We have little trouble concluding that the forfeiture of currency ordered by § 982 (a)(1) constitutes punishment. The statute directs a court to order forfeiture as an additional sanction when "imposing sentence on a person convicted of" a willful violation of § 5316's reporting requirement. The forfeiture is thus imposed at the culmination of a criminal proceeding and requires conviction of an underlying felony, and it cannot be imposed upon an innocent owner of unreported currency, but only upon a person who has himself been convicted of a § 5316 reporting violation. The United States argues, however, that the forfeiture of currency under § 982 (a)(1) "also serves important remedial purposes." The Government asserts that it has "an overriding sovereign interest in controlling what property leaves and enters the country." It claims that full forfeiture of unreported currency supports that interest by serving to "dete[r] illicit movements of cash" and aiding in providing the Government with "valuable information to investigate and detect criminal activities associated with that cash." Deterrence, however, has traditionally been viewed as a goal of punishment, and forfeiture of the currency here does not serve the remedial purpose of compensating the Government for a loss. . . . Although the Government has asserted a loss of information regarding the amount of currency leaving the country, that loss would not be remedied by the Government's confiscation of respondent's $357,144. . . .

Traditional in rem forfeitures were thus not considered punishment against the individual for an offense. . . . The forfeiture in this case does not bear any of the hallmarks of traditional civil in rem forfeitures. The Government has not proceeded against the currency itself, but has instead sought and obtained a criminal conviction of respondent personally. The forfeiture serves no remedial purpose, is designed to punish the offender, and cannot be imposed upon innocent owners.

§ 982 (a)(1) thus descends not from historic in rem forfeitures of guilty property, but from a different historical tradition: that of in personam, criminal forfeitures. Such forfeitures have historically been treated as punitive, being part of the punishment imposed for felonies and treason in the Middle Ages and at common law. Although in personam criminal forfeitures were well established in England at the time of the Founding, they were rejected altogether in the laws of this country until very recently.

The Government specifically contends that the forfeiture of respondent's currency is constitutional because it involves an "instrumentality" of respondent's crime. According to the Government, the unreported cash is an instrumentality because it "does not merely facilitate a violation of law," but is "the very sine qua non of the crime." . . .

Acceptance of the Government's argument would require us to expand the traditional understanding of instrumentality forfeitures. This we decline to do. Instrumentalities historically have been treated as a form of "guilty property" that can be forfeited in civil in rem proceedings. In this case, however, the Government has sought to punish respondent by proceeding against him criminally, in personam, rather than proceeding in rem against the currency. It is therefore irrelevant whether respondent's currency is an instrumentality; the forfeiture is punitive, and the test for the excessiveness of a punitive forfeiture involves solely a proportionality determination.

Because the forfeiture of respondent's currency constitutes punishment and is thus a "fine" within the meaning of the Excessive Fines Clause, we now turn to the question of whether it is "excessive."

The touchstone of the constitutional inquiry under the Excessive Fines Clause is the principle of proportionality: The amount of the forfeiture must bear some relationship to the gravity of the offense that it is designed to punish. . . . Until today, however, we have not articulated a standard for determining whether a punitive forfeiture is constitutionally excessive. We now hold that a punitive forfeiture violates the Excessive Fines Clause if it is grossly disproportional to the gravity of a defendant's offense.

The text and history of the Excessive Fines Clause demonstrate the centrality of proportionality to the excessiveness inquiry; nonetheless, they provide little guidance as to how disproportional a punitive forfeiture must be to the gravity of an offense in order to be "excessive." Excessive means surpassing the usual, the proper, or a normal measure of proportion. The constitutional question that we address, however, is just how proportional to a criminal offense a fine must be, and the text of the Excessive Fines Clause does not answer it.

Nor does its history. The Clause was little discussed in the First Congress and the debates over the ratification of the Bill of Rights. As we have previously noted, the Clause was taken verbatim from the English Bill of Rights of 1689. That document's prohibition against excessive fines was a reaction to the abuses of the King's judges during the reigns of the Stuarts but the fines that those judges imposed were described contemporaneously only in the most general terms. Similarly, Magna Charta—which the Stuart judges were accused of subverting—required only that amercements (the medieval predecessors of fines) should be proportioned to the offense and that they should not deprive a wrongdoer of his livelihood:

"A Free-man shall not be amerced for a small fault, but after the manner of the fault; and for a great fault after the greatness thereof, saving to him his contenement; (2) and a Merchant likewise, saving to him his merchandise; (3) and any other's villain than ours shall be likewise amerced, saving his wainage." Magna Charta, 9 Hen. III, ch. 14 (1225), 1 Stat. at Large 6–7 (1762 ed.).

None of these sources suggests how disproportional to the gravity of an offense a fine must be in order to be deemed constitutionally excessive. We must therefore rely on other considerations in deriving a constitutional excessiveness standard, and there are two that we find particularly relevant. The first, which we have emphasized in our cases interpreting the Cruel and Unusual Punishments Clause, is that judgments about the appropriate punishment for an offense belong in the first instance to the legislature. The second is that any judicial determination regarding the gravity of a particular criminal offense will be inherently imprecise. Both of these principles counsel against requiring strict proportionality between the amount of a punitive forfeiture and the gravity of a criminal offense, and we therefore adopt the standard of gross disproportionality articulated in our Cruel and Unusual Punishments Clause precedents. In applying this standard, the district courts in the first instance, and the courts of appeals, reviewing the proportionality determination *de novo*, the amount of the forfeiture to the gravity of the defendant's offense. If the amount of the forfeiture is grossly disproportional to the gravity of the defendant's offense, it is unconstitutional.

Under this standard, the forfeiture of respondent's entire $357,144 would violate the Excessive Fines Clause. Respondent's crime was solely a reporting offense. It was permissible to transport the currency out of the country so long as he reported it. Section 982 (a)(1) orders currency to be forfeited for a "willful" violation of the reporting requirement. Thus, the essence of respondent's crime is a willful failure to report the removal of currency from the United States. Furthermore, as the District Court found, respondent's violation was unrelated to any other illegal activities. The money was the proceeds of legal activity and was to be used to repay a lawful debt. Whatever his other vices, respondent does not fit into the class of persons for whom the statute was principally designed: He is not a money launderer, a drug trafficker, or a tax evader. See Brief for United States 2–3. And under the Sentencing Guidelines, the maximum sentence that could have been imposed on respondent was six months, while the maximum fine was $5,000. Such penalties confirm a minimal level of culpability.

The harm that respondent caused was also minimal. Failure to report his currency affected only one party, the Government, and in a relatively minor way. There was no fraud on the United States, and respondent caused no loss to the public fisc. Had his crime gone undetected, the Government would have been deprived only of the information that $357,144 had left the country. The Government and the dissent contend that there is a correlation between the amount forfeited and the harm that the Government would have suffered had the crime gone undetected. We disagree. There is no inherent proportionality in such a forfeiture. It is impossible to conclude, for example, that the harm respondent caused is anywhere near - 30 times greater than that caused by a hypothetical drug dealer who willfully fails to report taking $12,000 out of the country in order to purchase drugs.

Comparing the gravity of respondent's crime with the $357,144 forfeiture the Government seeks, we conclude that such a forfeiture would be grossly disproportional to the gravity of his offense. It is larger than the $5,000 fine imposed by the District Court by many orders of magnitude, and it bears no articulable correlation to any injury suffered by the Government. . . .

■  ■  ■

For the foregoing reasons, the full forfeiture of respondent's currency would violate the Excessive Fines Clause. The judgment of the Court of Appeals is Affirmed.

Similarly, even though forfeiture may be characterized as civil, the exclusionary rule applies to bar illegally seized evidence in quasi-criminal forfeiture cases.[47] This is contrary to the rule that the exclusionary rule is not applied in civil and administrative cases.

## Modern Sentencing Alternatives

In recent years, many new alternatives to incarceration have been developed. Such alternatives are actually forms of probation and as such are administered by courts and probation officers.

For the nonviolent criminal, work release is an alternative. Offenders in these programs live in jail but are allowed to leave to work. Work release has many advantages. The defendant continues to earn a living. This is particularly important if the defendant has dependents. Also, it is good for the self-esteem of offenders; they continue to feel they are a useful part of the community. The final advantage is true of many sentencing alternatives: The cost to the public is lower because the offender is often required to pay, in whole or part, for participation in the program.

For those convicted of some alcohol and drug offenses, courts have turned to alcohol and drug treatment over imprisonment. These programs vary greatly. For first-time drunk driving convictions, offenders may be required to do one or more of the following, in addition to traditional conditions of probation:

1. Participate in an alcohol treatment program, such as Alcoholics Anonymous.

2. Report for periodic urine or blood tests to detect the presence of alcohol.

3. Take a drug such as Antabuse, which makes a person ill if alcohol is ingested.

4. Participate in a defensive/safe-driving school.

If a defendant has a previous drunk driving conviction, he or she is likely to receive some "executed time" or jail time, in addition to some or all of the previously listed conditions. A few courts have tried a form of shock treatment. For example, a defendant may be required to meet with drunk drivers who are responsible for killing someone and discuss that experience. In another example, at least one judge has required that a drunk driver work in a hospital emergency room so that the defendant would be exposed to alcohol-related injuries and deaths.

First-time drug users may also be placed on probation, subject to conditions similar to those previously listed: periodic urinalysis or blood screening and drug counseling and treatment. This form of probation is not available to drug dealers.

Two other forms of probation that may be used independently or mixed with one or more of the others are house arrest and halfway houses. If a defendant is sentenced to house arrest, he or she may not leave the home without prior permission of the probation officer, except in emergencies.

Today, the use of electronic shackles makes enforcement of house arrests easier. These devices are attached to the probationer's leg, and through the transmission of a radio signal, it can be determined if the defendant is at home.

**halfway house**

A facility in which persons recently discharged from a rehabilitation center or prison live for a time and are given support and assistance in readjusting to society at large.

**Halfway houses** are minimum security homes located in the community. Generally, they serve two groups of offenders: those making the transition from prison to the community and those who need some confinement, but not jail or prison.

Halfway houses are commonly used in conjunction with work release programs. The residents are given some freedom to leave the home but are restricted in their travel. Often, such homes provide drug and alcohol counseling and treatment and vocational training.

Yet another community-based correction program is the boot camp or "shock incarceration" program. Boot camps are gaining in popularity as a method of reforming youthful offenders. As of early 1994, nearly 30 states were operating prison boot camps.[48]

The typical boot camp experience involves 90 to 180 days of "rigid military-training atmosphere followed by intensive community supervision." Boot camp programs are usually limited to first-time offenders who have been sentenced to a term of imprisonment. Most programs are designed to accommodate individuals sentenced to prison, but a growing number of jails are using boot camps as an alternative to traditional confinement.[49]

This is not by any means an exhaustive list of alternative punishments. The list is limited only by the U.S. Constitution and the imagination of judges. For example, one Florida judge required those convicted of drunk driving to place bumper stickers on their cars warning of their convictions. This requirement was upheld by the Florida Court of Appeals.[50]

## Habitual Offender Statutes

The career criminal or repeat offender is now subject to extreme penalty in most jurisdictions. These statutes are referred to as *recidivist* or **habitual offender laws**.

**habitual offender statutes**

Laws that may apply to a person who has been convicted of as few as two prior crimes (often violent or drug-related crimes) and that greatly increase the penalties for each succeeding crime.

Most statutes provide for an increased penalty if a defendant has been convicted of a stated number of felonies, often three, within a certain period of time, such as 10 years. These are popularly known as the "three strikes and you're out" laws.

To prevent unfair prejudice to the defendant, the jury usually does not know about the habitual criminal charge until it has reached a verdict in the underlying charge. So, if Pam is charged with murder and of being a habitual criminal, the jury would initially know only of the murder charge. If the jury comes back with an acquittal, the habitual criminal charge is dismissed. If the verdict is guilty, the jury is then told that it must also determine if the defendant is a habitual criminal. This is known as a bifurcated procedure.

To prove the habitual criminal charge, the prosecutor will introduce court records reflecting the prior convictions and, in some instances, call the prosecutors involved in the prior convictions to attest that the defendant was indeed convicted.

**A Sentencing Story**

Willie Smith was convicted of the extortion and assault of a 93-year-old woman confined to a wheelchair. He was also convicted of resisting arrest, counterfeiting food stamps, and mugging.

During sentencing, the trial judge told the defendant that he was irritated by the defendant's constant claims of police brutality and left the bench, approached the defendant, and punched him in the nose. While the defendant was on the floor of the courtroom, the judge kicked and punched him. The judge then returned to the bench and stated to the defendant, "That, Mr. Smith, is a sample of real, honest-to-goodness police brutality."

Habitual criminal laws have been attacked as violative of the Double Jeopardy Clause. Such claims have not been successful, as they are not considered a second punishment of one of the earlier offenses. Rather, evidence of a criminal record provides a reason to increase the penalty for the most recent offense.

# Postconviction Remedies

Learning Objective: Distinguish and explain the fundamental processes of appeal and habeas corpus.

Technically, motions for new trials are postconviction remedies. Other than such motions, there are two major methods of attacking a conviction or other decision at the trial level: appeal and habeas corpus.

## Appeal

The Constitution of the United States does not expressly confer a right to appeal.[51] Regardless, every state provides for appeal either through statute or constitution. Once a state establishes a right to appeal, the U.S. Constitution requires that appellate procedure not violate the Fourteenth Amendment's Due Process Clause or Equal Protection Clause.

Appeals from federal district courts go to the U.S. Courts of Appeals (circuit courts). From there, appeal is taken to the U.S. Supreme Court. In state cases, appeal is taken to the state intermediate appellate court, if any. Appeal from that court is taken to the state high court, usually named the Supreme Court of the state. All issues, federal and state, are heard by those courts. Issues of state law may not be appealed any further. If the defendant wishes to appeal a decision of the state high court concerning an issue of federal law, the appeal is taken to the U.S. Supreme Court.

## Filing the Appeal

Because the right to appeal is purely statutory, it may be lost if it is not timely filed. The federal rules require that appeals be filed within 10 days of the date of judgment.[52] The government is given 30 days in those instances where it may appeal. Appeals from state courts to the U.S. Supreme Court must be filed within 90 days of the entry of judgment.[53]

Procedures vary, but it is common to require the appellant to file several documents to begin the appeal. The first document is a notice or petition of appeal. This simply informs all the parties, as well as the trial judge, that the case is being appealed. A designation of record will also be filed by the parties. Through this document, the parties select the portions of the trial record that they desire to be sent to the appellate court. A statement of issues that must be resolved on appeal may also be filed by the appellant. Finally, a filing fee must be paid. Appellants who cannot afford it may seek relief from the filing fee requirement.

After the necessary documents are filed, the parties brief the issues for the appellate court. The appellate court, in its discretion, may hear oral arguments.

Because the penalty for untimely filings is harsh (dismissal of the appeal), most courts recognize constructive filings. This is particularly true for incarcerated defendants who rely on counsel or prison officials in preparing or filing an appeal.

Note that most jurisdictions provide for the possibility of bail pending appeal. This is most often available in misdemeanor cases; however, it may be granted in felony cases also.

## The Scope of Review

**final judgment (order)**
The last action of a court; the one upon which an appeal can be based.

To avoid unnecessary delay, only **final orders** may be appealed. Therefore, erroneous pretrial decisions are not corrected until appeal is taken, after the case is completed. Orders that may not be reviewed until after final judgment are those relating to the suppression of evidence, discovery, and the sufficiency of the charging instruments.

There are a few exceptions to the final judgment rule. The most prominent exception is the collateral order doctrine. Under this doctrine, orders that are independent of the criminal case may be immediately appealed. The appeal proceeds concurrently with the underlying criminal case.

**interlocutory appeal**
The *Interlocutory Appeals* Act (28 U.S.C. 1292 (1948)) is a federal law that provides for an appeal while a trial is going on if the trial judge states in writing: (1) A legal question has come up that directly affects the trial. (2) There are major questions as to how that point of law should be resolved. (3) The case would proceed better if the appeals court answers the question.

Appeals taken from ongoing litigation (where no final order has been issued) are called **interlocutory appeals**. Orders holding a defendant incompetent to stand trial, denying bail, and denying a defendant's double jeopardy claim have been held collateral and immediately appealable.[54] Certain orders that occur after judgment, such as revocation of probation, are also immediately appealable.

Remember, cases are not retried on appeal. Appellate courts review the record for errors of law, not fact. That means the appellate court will not examine the evidence and substitute its judgment for that of the trial court (or jury). However, the court will examine the record to make sure that sufficient evidence exists to support the judgment. So long as sufficient evidence can be found, the appellate court will not reverse, even if it would have decided the case differently. Issues of law are reviewed anew (de novo).

**prejudicial error**
A trial court mistake that impacted the outcome of the case. It may be reversed or otherwise changed by a higher court.

Not every trial court error leads to a reversal. Only when an error prejudices the defendant is reversal required. A mistake that changed the outcome of the case is **prejudicial error**. If the mistake doesn't change the outcome, it is **harmless error**. Prejudicial error can cause the trial court's judgment to be reversed. Harmless error doesn't, although it could lead to a remand with orders to the court to do something less than retrial or dismiss the earlier judgment. The appellant bears the burden of proving that he or she was prejudiced by the error of the trial court.

**harmless error**
A trial court mistake that doesn't change the outcome of the case and therefore does not result in reversal.

Some error is so violative of the Constitution that it is irrebuttably presumed prejudicial, so reversal is automatic. An order denying defense counsel at trial is never harmless error.[55]

The law distinguishes between fact and law. Alleged factual errors are treated differently than legal errors. Most of the time, factual decisions are given deference because it is the trial court's responsibility, not the appellate court's, to find the facts. It is the trial judge that is most intimate with the facts of the case. The trial judge—and jury—observes the demeanor of witnesses; watches and hears witnesses, videos, and audio recordings; and sees the physical and other evidence. It, therefore, is in a better place to weigh the value evidence and assess the credibility of witnesses. The role of an appellate court is to review the record of the trial court for error. No new factual evidence is presented on appeal. The judges rely exclusively on the written and digital record. Accordingly, appellate courts employ several deferential standards of review, depending on the question, to questions of fact. Without detailing the various review standards, it is enough for this discussion to say that the factual decisions are affirmed, unless they are very wrong.

On the other hand, appellate courts review legal questions de novo. If the trial judge is only slightly wrong, an appellate court will reverse it. The impact of legal decisions can affect more than the case that is under review. Obviously, the new law will impact cases in the future. But what about cases that are pending when the new rule is announced, or cases from the past? In what is known as the Teague Doctrine, new constitutional rules of criminal procedure are not retroactive unless they are "watershed" and fundamental to fairness. But substantive constitutional decisions are applied retroactively, provided they benefit the convictee. Any rule that disadvantages the individual would be ex post facto and a violation of due process.

Why don't all changes in constitutional law apply backwards? The Court has identified several reasons. First, the importance of finality. At some point, it is best for the people involved and the predictability and stability of law for decisions to be final. Second, comity, or respect for the states. Third, efficiency and fairness. Retrying cases is expensive, and the possibility that evidence has been lost or become stale or that witnesses have died or become unavailable for other reasons must be balanced against the convictee's interest in having the new rule applied in a retrial.

The following are examples of new rules that were and weren't retroactively applied:

*Edwards v. Vannoy*, 590 U.S. __ (2021)

> The Court's early decision that guilty verdicts must be unanimous not to be applied retroactively.

*Hurst v. Florida*, 577 U. S. 92 (2016)

> A state law that permitted judges, not juries, to determine if an aggravating factor in a capital case violated the right to a jury trial applied retroactively.

*Montgomery v. Louisiana*, 577 U. S. 190 (2016)

> Mandatory life sentence for a juvenile was cruel and unusual punishment applied retroactively.

*Welch v. United States*, 578 U. S. 120 (2016)

> An unconstitutionally vague statute violated due process is applied retroactively.

*Teague v. Lane*, 489 U.S. 288 (1989)

> The decision that prosecutors may not use peremptory challenges to eliminate prospective jurors because of race is a procedural right, and thereby it doesn't apply to cases already completed.

## Prosecution/Defense Appeals

Because of the Double Jeopardy Clause, defendants have a broader right to appeal than the government. A defendant who is tried and convicted is free to appeal any factual or legal error. However, this right may be limited by a requirement of *preservation*. To satisfy this rule, the defendant must raise the issue at the trial level. This gives the trial judge an opportunity to avoid error.

Failure to raise the issue results in a waiver. For example, a defendant who does not challenge the sufficiency of an indictment at the trial level may not raise the issue for the first time before the appellate court. The same is true of evidentiary matters. The defendant must object to the admission of evidence that he or she believes should be excluded to preserve the issue for appeal.

The prosecution has a limited right to appeal. Because of the prohibition on trying a person twice for the same offense, the government has no right to appeal acquittals. However, most states permit the government to appeal certain orders issued before jeopardy attaches. Orders dismissing charging instruments, suppressing evidence prior to trial, and releasing the defendant before trial may be appealed. These interlocutory appeals do not violate the Fifth Amendment's Double Jeopardy Clause, because jeopardy does not attach until a jury has been impaneled or the first witness is sworn in a nonjury trial. See Chapter 9 for a more thorough discussion of double jeopardy and appeals.

### The Right to Counsel on Appeal

There is no Sixth Amendment right to counsel on appeal. The Sixth Amendment right begins once a defendant is charged and continues, at all critical stages, through trial and sentencing. In some instances, it is in effect at probation revocation. It does not ever include appeals.

The right to counsel on appeal can be found, however, in the Equal Protection Clause of the Fourteenth Amendment. The Supreme Court said, in *Douglas v. California*,[56] that indigent defendants convicted of a felony have a right to appointed counsel on appeal, provided that the appeal is by right. *By right* means that the defendant's appeal must be heard by the appellate court. Most, if not all, states have provided for appeal by right.

If an appeal is discretionary, the Equal Protection Clause of the Fourteenth Amendment does not compel the state to provide counsel.

As is true at trial, the defendant is entitled to effective counsel. The appointed attorney has an ethical obligation to zealously pursue the defendant's appeal. Because of the large number of frivolous appeals, the Supreme Court has stated that an appointed attorney may be allowed to withdraw. However, the following must be done: first, the attorney must request withdrawal from the appellate court; second, a brief must be filed explaining why the attorney believes the appeal to be wholly without merit. In that brief, all potential issues must be outlined for the court's review. If the appellate court agrees that there are no valid issues, the attorney may withdraw. If the court finds an issue that has some merit, the lawyer must continue to represent the defendant.

## Habeas Corpus

Both the states and federal governments have habeas corpus relief. Here we discuss federal habeas corpus relief, particularly federal habeas corpus in state criminal proceedings. Although habeas corpus relief is available at any stage of a criminal proceeding, most habeas corpus petitions are filed after conviction. The discussion here is limited to such postconviction petitions.

Through habeas corpus proceedings, an individual may attack the lawfulness of confinement, whether it be substantive or procedural in nature. Further, the conditions of confinement and the lawfulness of an imposed punishment may be reviewed by a habeas court.

### History

Translated, *habeas corpus* means "you have the body." In action, the writ is used to order someone who has custody of another to bring that person before the court. Any person who believes that he or she is being detained illegally may use the writ to gain his or her freedom. Because of the significant power of the writ, it has come to be known as the "Great Writ of Liberty."

The writ has ancient origin, dating back as far as the twelfth century. Habeas corpus was often used to enforce provisions of the Magna Carta. The success of the writ in protecting liberty in England influenced the drafters of the U.S. Constitution. The result is Article I, § 9, clause 2, which states: "The Privilege of the Writ of Habeas Corpus shall not be suspended unless when in Cases of Rebellion or Invasion the Public Safety may require it."

Federal habeas corpus is important in criminal law because it is used to challenge state court convictions. That is, if a defendant believes that his or her federal constitutional rights were violated in a state court, he or she may attack the conviction through federal habeas corpus.

Habeas corpus has had congressional authorization since 1789. The first statute made habeas corpus available only to federal prisoners. This was changed by the Habeas Corpus Act of 1867, which extended habeas corpus to any person "restrained of his or her liberty in violation of the constitution, or of any treaty or law of the United States." The 1867 act continues to be in effect, with some modifications.

## Scope of Review

The current habeas corpus statutes are found at 28 U.S.C. §§ 2241–2255. Section 2254 provides habeas corpus relief to state prisoners. Under § 2255, federal prisoners are to move to vacate or set aside their sentences, in a procedure nearly identical to § 2254. Relief under this section must be sought before a federal prisoner can bring habeas corpus. Even then, the statute states that habeas corpus shall not be issued if the prisoner was unsuccessful with a § 2255 claim, unless that proceeding was "inadequate or ineffective." A biased judge is an example of when habeas corpus may be issued after a § 2255 motion has been denied.

The federal courts continued to have little involvement with state proceedings, even after the 1867 act extended the reach of federal habeas corpus to state prisoners. This was largely due to Supreme Court decisions limiting the review of federal habeas corpus to questions of jurisdiction.

The scope of review was enlarged in *Brown v. Allen*, 344 U.S. 443 (1953), in which it was held that federal habeas corpus could be used to relitigate all issues of federal law. This decision significantly increased the power of federal habeas corpus and resulted in increased intervention of federal courts in state criminal proceedings.

The Supreme Court has since narrowed habeas corpus relief by decision. For example, a state prisoner may not use federal habeas corpus to relitigate Fourth Amendment claims (search and seizure), provided the defendant was provided a "full and fair litigation" in state court. Also, the Court has emphasized that the purpose of habeas corpus is to provide relief to persons imprisoned in violation of the laws of the United States, not to relitigate or correct factual errors. Accordingly, a claim of innocence, even when supported by new evidence, is not alone sufficient to confer habeas jurisdiction upon a court. An independent constitutional claim must be made for a court to examine such a petition.[57]

## Exhaustion of Remedies

Before a state prisoner can seek the aid of a federal court, he or she must satisfy certain procedural requirements. First, the defendant must use all means available in the state system to correct the alleged error. This is the doctrine of **exhaustion of remedies**. Section 2254(b) states:

> An application for a writ of habeas corpus in behalf of a person in custody pursuant to the judgment of a State court shall not be granted unless it appears that the applicant has exhausted the remedies available in the courts of the State, or that there is either an absence of available corrective process or the existence of circumstances rendering such process ineffective to protect the rights of the prisoner.

The remedies that must be exhausted depend on what is available in the state system, such as motions for new trial, state habeas corpus relief, and appeals. Of course, if no remedy is available, the defendant may immediately petition for habeas corpus relief.

**exhaustion of remedies**
A person must usually take all reasonable steps to get satisfaction from a state or federal government before seeking judicial relief.

If a remedy is available, but it would be futile to exhaust it, habeas corpus may be brought without exhaustion. For example, assume the state Supreme Court has previously addressed the legal issue raised by the defendant, and its decision is contrary to the defendant's claim. Unless there is reason to believe that the court will reconsider its decision, there is no need to exhaust this remedy. Excessive delay in the state proceedings may also be a basis for bringing habeas corpus before the state remedies have been exhausted, provided the state does not have a remedy for such delays (e.g., mandamus).

The fact that a defendant has failed to timely appeal (or file a motion for new trial, etc.) does not mean that habeas corpus is unavailable. The question is: Are state remedies available? If a defendant has missed the right to appeal under state law, and no other remedy is available, then habeas corpus may be used to resolve his or her federal constitutional claims. However, defendants who deliberately bypass state procedures may be denied habeas relief.[58]

## The Custody Requirement

The Habeas Corpus Act speaks of prisoners "in custody." However, this has been interpreted to include all wrongful restraints of liberty. The Supreme Court has said that persons who are subject to "restraints not shared by the public generally" are entitled to habeas corpus protection, even though they may not be in the physical custody of the government.

Under this interpretation, persons placed on probation and parole have been held to be in custody, as have defendants released on bail.[59] Habeas corpus protection is also available to a defendant who has served his or her entire sentence, because the restraint of liberty includes not only incarceration but also collateral loss of civil liberties (e.g., right to carry a weapon), injury to reputation, and the possibility of an increased penalty for a later conviction.

A defendant who is lawfully detained may use habeas corpus to challenge his or her sentence if he or she believes it is excessive. Also, if he or she was convicted of several crimes and was sentenced to consecutive sentences, he or she need not wait until the lawful sentence expires before petitioning for habeas corpus. It appears that an invalid sentence may be attacked even though it runs concurrently with a valid sentence. Again, the collateral effects of the conviction are the rationale.

## Procedure

The following rules were established by the U.S. Supreme Court to implement 22 U.S.C. § 2254.[60] The petition for habeas corpus relief is filed in the federal district within which the prisoner is being held. The petition shall name the person who has custody of the applicant as the respondent. Indigent persons may file a motion to proceed in forma pauperis, which relieves such persons from paying the filing fee.

Immediately after the petition is filed, the district judge will examine the petition. If the petition is "plainly" invalid, the court will dismiss it. If not, the court will direct the respondent to answer the petition.

Counsel may be appointed and discovery is available, with leave of the district court. After the petition has been answered and appropriate discovery conducted, the district court may hold an evidentiary hearing and issue an opinion or rule from the record without a hearing. Habeas corpus decisions may be appealed.

## The Right to Counsel

To date, the Supreme Court has not found a constitutional right to the assistance of counsel in preparing and presenting a petition for habeas corpus.

In some instances, the district court may have to hold an evidentiary hearing. It is possible that in such instances a due process right to counsel exists to ensure that the hearing is fair. The issue is not of critical importance presently, because federal habeas corpus rules require the appointment of counsel for such hearings. Additionally, the rules give the district court the discretion to appoint counsel earlier, if necessary.

Although there may be no right to counsel, there is a right to "access to the courts." Therefore, prisoners must be furnished with paper, pens, stamps, and access to a law library. Further, unless a prison provides adequate legal assistance to its prisoners, so-called jailhouse lawyers may not be prohibited from assisting other inmates in the preparation of legal documents.

# Appealing Outside the Courts

Learning Objective: Define pardon, reprieve, commutation, and legislative amelioration.

The courts aren't the only recourse to correct an injustice. In 2014, President Barack Obama commuted a man's sentence from 15 years of imprisonment to 11.5 to correct an error in the calculation of his sentence that was made at the time of sentencing. The convictee's attorney discovered the error years later and attempted to correct it in court. But the judge rejected the request, referring to the expiration of the 1-year limitation on correcting sentencing errors. President Obama's Press Secretary said of the decision, "[g]iven the circumstances of this case and the manifest injustice of keeping a person in federal prison for an extra three and a half years because of a typographical mistake, the president wanted to act as quickly as possible. . . . This is a matter of basic fairness and it reflects the important role of clemency as a fail-safe in our judicial system."[61]

In most states and the federal government, the chief executive (i.e., the governor or the president) possesses several powers concerning criminal convictions and sentences. One such power is executive clemency. To forgive or, more commonly, to reduce a punishment is an act of clemency. To reduce a prisoner's sentence from death to life imprisonment is an example of clemency. The reduction of a sentence is also known as **commutation of sentence**. Commutation is used when the executive believes a person is guilty, but also believes the sentence is disproportionate. In 1993, the Supreme Court ruled that a prisoner who is sentenced to death who claims to have new evidence of innocence does not possess the right to federal review in all instances. The court indicated that executive clemency, not judicial action, is the system's fail-safe to guard against unwarranted executions.

The **pardon** is similar to commutation of sentence in that both relieve a person of punishment. However, the pardon is different in one important respect: It also relieves the defendant of the conviction. With the pardon, the conviction is erased and treated as though it never occurred. Pardons are granted when the executive believes there was an error concerning the defendant's guilt.

Finally, a **reprieve** is a stay or delay of execution of sentence. Reprieves are used to give the executive or a court the opportunity to further review the case.

The governor has the sole authority to grant clemency in most states; a handful rest the authority in clemency boards; a few have clemency boards make recommendations to their respective governors; and in Rhode Island, the governor can grant clemency only with the consent of that state's senate.

In addition to executive action, legislatures have the authority to ameliorate punishment (e.g., reduce sentences or free offenders altogether). This power is legislative, not judicial. So, a legislature may not free or reduce the sentence of an individual, but it may for a class of people who are convicted of the same crime or subject to the same form of punishment. As discussed earlier in this text, the rise in the decriminalization of marijuana has resulted in ameliorations of convicted marijuana users at the federal and state levels.

**commutation of sentence**
Changing a criminal punishment to one less severe.

**pardon**
A president's or governor's release of a person from punishment for a crime.

**reprieve**
Holding off on enforcing a criminal sentence for a period of time after the sentence has been handed down.

---

## Ethical Considerations

### Attorney Discipline by the Numbers

According to the American Bar Association, there were 1,257,772 attorneys in the United States in 2018. In that year, the state bar authorities collectively received 83,073 complaints against attorneys and had 24,527 pending from prior years; 53,478 complaints were investigated with 6,356 attorneys charged after probable cause was found. Also in that year, 4,704 attorneys were privately sanctioned and 2,872 were publicly sanctioned, with 378 involuntarily disbarred, 253 consented to disbarment, 1,054 had their practices suspended, 1,007 received a public censure, and 339 were placed on probation. Many were ordered to pay restitution to their clients and the costs of the disciplinary action.

Today, many states have online databases that permit attorney discipline records to be investigated. These databases often indicate whether an attorney has been disciplined; and if so, the nature of the violation, the date, and the discipline imposed.

*Source of filings data:* American Bar Association, Center for Professional Responsibility,
Survey on Lawyer Discipline Systems (2018).

---

## Key Terms

| | | |
|---|---|---|
| aggravating circumstances | habitual offender statutes | parole |
| commutation of sentence | halfway houses | prejudicial error |
| concurrent sentences | harmless error | reprieve |
| consecutive sentences | indeterminate sentence | revocation hearing |
| determinate sentencing | interlocutory appeal | suspended sentence |
| exhaustion of remedies | mitigating circumstances | victim impact statement |
| final judgment | pardon | |

## Review Questions

1. What is a presentence investigation? Who conducts the investigation, and what is its purpose?

2. What are aggravating and mitigating circumstances in sentencing?

3. What is the final judgment rule?

4. Does a defendant have a right to appointed counsel on appeal?

5. What is habeas corpus?

6. Distinguish harmless from prejudicial error.

7. May victim impact evidence be considered by sentencing courts?

8. Which of the following punishments has the Supreme Court held to be inherently cruel and unusual?
   a. Death by hanging
   b. Death by starvation
   c. Flogging
   d. Solitary confinement
   e. Imprisonment without lighting or a bed

9. Differentiate a suspended imposition of sentence from a sentence suspended to probation.

## Problems & Critical Thinking Exercises

1–4. Kevin, an attorney, has been indicted for embezzlement. After his preliminary hearing, he filed a motion to suppress a confession he believes was illegally obtained. A hearing was conducted, and the trial court granted his motion. The evidence was vital to the prosecution.

Kevin's attorney has also requested that the trial be continued because he claims that Kevin is not competent to stand trial. The judge ordered a mental evaluation, held a hearing, and found Kevin competent to stand trial.

The defense also requested that the court order a number of police officers to submit to depositions prior to trial. The court denied the motion.

At trial, the defendant objected to the introduction of a document that he believed was unconstitutionally obtained during a search of his office. The judge overruled the objection and admitted the confession into evidence.

Answer the following questions using these facts.

1. The prosecution strongly believes that the documents that were suppressed are admissible. The prosecutor objects on the record to the judge's order and then appeals the issue after Kevin is acquitted. What should be the outcome on appeal?

2. Kevin disagrees with the trial court finding of competency. What is his remedy?

3. Believing that Kevin cannot have a fair trial without the depositions, his attorney filed an interlocutory appeal seeking an order from the appellate court requiring the trial judge to provide for the depositions. What should be the outcome?

4. Kevin appealed the trial court's decision denying his motion to suppress the document. The appellate court affirmed the trial court, and Kevin filed a habeas corpus petition in federal court, claiming that his federal constitutional rights were violated by admission of the evidence. What should be the outcome?

# Endnotes

1. *Betterman v. Montana*, 578 U. S. 437 (2016).
2. The Supreme Court has not yet answered this question. *See also United States v. Rogers*, 921 F.2d 957 (10th Cir. 1990), *cert. denied*, 111 S. Ct. 113 (1991).
3. *United States v. Jackson*, 886 F.2d 838 (7th Cir. 1989).
4. Fed. R. Crim. P. 32(c)(1).
5. Fed. R. Crim. P. 32(c)(3).
6. *Apprendi v. New Jersey*, 530 U.S. 466 (2000).
7. *Eddings v. Oklahoma*, 455 U.S. 104 (1982).
8. *United States v. Watts*, 519 U.S. 148 (1997).
9. *See Apprendi v. New Jersey*, 530 U.S. 466 (2000); *Blakely v. Washington*, 542 U.S. 296 (2004); *United States v. Booker*, 543 U.S. 220 (2005); and *Cunningham v. California*, 549 U.S. 270 (2007).
10. *Ring v. Arizona*, 536 U.S. 584 (2002). See also *Hurst v. Florida*, 577 U. S. 92 (2016).
11. *Locket v. Ohio*, 438 U.S. at 604–05.
12. *See Kansas v. Marsh*, 548 U.S. (2006).
13. *Callins v. Collins*, 510 U.S. 1141 (1994) 114 S. Ct. 1127, 1132 (1994) (Blackmun, J., dissenting).
14. 114 S. Ct. at 1129–30.
15. *Wilkerson v. Utah*, 99 U.S. 130 (1878)
16. 553 U.S. 35 (2008).
17. *Coker v. Georgia*, 433 U.S. 584 (1977).
18. *Enmund v. Florida*, 458 U.S. 782 (1972).
19. *Tison v. Arizona*, 481 U.S. 137 (1987).
20. *Ford v. Wainwright*, 477 U.S. 399 (1986).
21. *Atkins v. Virginia*, 536 U.S. 304 (2002).
22. *Madison v. Alabama*, 586 U.S. ___ (2019).
23. *See Roper v. Simmons*, 543 U.S. 551 (2005).
24. *Pervear v. Commonwealth*, 72 U.S. (5 Wall) 475 (1867); *Wing Wong v. United States*, 163 U.S. 228 (1896); *Kehrli v. Sprinkle*, 524 F.2d 328 (10th Cir. 1975).
25. *Delaware v. Cannon*, 55 Del. 587, 190 A.2d 574 (1963).
26. *Jackson v. Bishop*, 404 F.2d 571 (8th Cir. 1968).

27. For a thorough discussion of the constitutionality of whipping, see Daniel E. Hall, "When Caning Meets the Eighth Amendment: Whipping Offenders in the United States," 4 *Widener J. Pub. L.* 403 (1995).

28. 21 *U.S.C.* 841(b)(1).

29. 501 U.S. 957 (1991).]

30. United States v. Gementera, 379 F.3d 596 (9th Cir. 2004).

31. Laura Edwins, *10 Weird Criminal Sentences*, The Christian Science Monitor. Found on May 15, 2013 at csmonitor.com

32. All the examples with the exception of the first and second come from Jan Hoffman, *Crime and Punishment: Shame Gains Popularity, The New York Times.* January 16, 1997. Found at http://www.nytimes.com/1997/01/16/us/crime-and-punishment-shame-gains-popularity.html?pagewanted=all&src=pm

33. Breyer, "The Federal Sentencing Guidelines and the Key Compromises Upon Which They Rest," 17 *Hofstra L. Rev.* 4 (1988).

34. Federal Judges Association, *In Camera* (Dec. 1990).

35. Final Report on the Impact of the *United States v. Booker* on Federal Sentencing, United States Sentencing Commission, March 2006.

36. *Griffin v. Wisconsin*, 483 U.S. 868 (1987).

37. *Porth v. Templar*, 453 F.2d 330 (10th Cir. 1971).

38. *United States v. Green*, 735 F.2d 1203 (9th Cir. 1984).

39. *Hughey v. United States*, 495 U.S. 411 (1990).

40. *Phillips v. United States*, 679 F.2d 192 (9th Cir. 1982).

41. *Bearden v. Georgia*, 461 U.S. 660, 668–69 (1983).

42. 399 U.S. 235 (1970).

43. *See*, for example, 21 U.S.C. § 881.

44. 19 U.S.C. § 1615.

45. *See* 21 U.S.C. § 853.

46. *United States v. James Daniel Good Real Property*, 510 U.S. 43 (1993).

47. *One 1958 Plymouth v. Pennsylvania*, 380 U.S. 693 (1965).

48. *The Growing Use of Jail Boot Camps: The Current State of the Art* (Washington, DC: National Institute of Justice, October 1993).

49. Belinda McCarthy and Bernard McCarthy, *Community-Based Corrections*, 2nd ed. (Belmont, CA: Brooks/Cole, 1991), p. 128.

50. *Goldschmitt v. State*, 490 So. 2d 123 (Fla. Dist. Ct. App.), *review denied*, 496 So. 2d 142 (Fla. 1986).

51. *McKane v. Durston*, 153 U.S. 684 (1894).

52. Fed. R. Crim. P. 37.

53. Supreme Ct. R. 11.1.

54. W. Lafave and J. Israel, *Criminal Procedure* § 26.2(c). (Hornbook Series; St. Paul, MN: West, 1985).

55. *Gideon v. Wainwright*, 373 U.S. 335 (1963).

56. 372 U.S. 353 (1963).

57. *Herrera v. Collins*, 113 S. Ct. 853 (1993).

58. *Fay v. NOIA*, 372 U.S. 391 (1963).

59. *Jones v. Cunningham*, 371 U.S. 236 (1963); *Hensley v. Municipal Court*, 411 U.S. 345 (1973).

60. *See Rules Governing Section 2254 Cases in the United States District Courts* (February 1989). These rules also contain the forms necessary to petition for habeas corpus relief in the district court of the United States.

61. Nedra Pickler, *Obama Commutes Sentence Made Longer by Typo.* April 15, 2014. Retrieved from HeraldNet.com on May 15, 2021.

# Appendix

# The Constitution of the United States of America

We the People of the United States, in Order to form a more perfect Union, establish Justice, insure domestic Tranquility, provide for the common defence, promote the general Welfare, and secure the Blessings of Liberty to ourselves and our Posterity, do ordain and establish this Constitution for the United States of America.

## Article I

### Section 1.

All legislative Powers herein granted shall be vested in a Congress of the United States, which shall consist of a Senate and House of Representatives.

### Section 2.

1) The House of Representatives shall be composed of Members chosen every second Year by the People of the several States, and the Electors in each State shall have the Qualifications requisite for Electors of the most numerous Branch of the State Legislature.

2) No Person shall be a Representative who shall not have attained to the age of twenty-five Years, and been seven Years a Citizen of the United States, and who shall not, when elected, be an Inhabitant of that State in which he shall be chosen.

3) Representatives and direct Taxes shall be apportioned among the several States which may be included within this Union, according to their respective Numbers, which shall be determined by adding to the whole Number of free Persons, including those bound to Service for a Term of Years, and excluding Indians not taxed, three fifths of all other Persons. The actual Enumeration shall be made within three Years after the first Meeting of the Congress of the United States, and within every subsequent Term of ten Years, in such Manner as they shall by Law direct. The Number of Representatives shall not exceed one for every thirty Thousand, but each State shall have at Least one Representative; and until such enumeration shall be made, the State of New Hampshire shall be entitled to chuse three, Massachusetts eight, Rhode Island and Providence Plantations one, Connecticut five, New York six, New Jersey four, Pennsylvania eight, Delaware one, Maryland six, Virginia ten, North Carolina five, South Carolina five, and Georgia three.

4) When vacancies happen in the Representation from any State, the Executive Authority thereof shall issue Writs of Election to fill such Vacancies.

5) The House of Representatives shall chuse their Speaker and other Officers; and shall have the sole Power of Impeachment.

### Section 3.

1) The Senate of the United States shall be composed of two Senators from each State, chosen by the Legislature thereof, for six Years; and each Senator shall have one Vote.

2) Immediately after they shall be assembled in Consequence of the first Election, they shall be divided as equally as may be into three Classes. The Seats of the Senators of the first Class shall be vacated at the Expiration of the Second Year, of the second Class at the Expiration of the fourth Year, and of the third Class at the Expiration of the sixth Year, so that one third may be chosen every second Year; and if Vacancies happen by Resignation,

or otherwise, during the Recess of the Legislature of any State, the Executive thereof may make temporary Appointments until the next Meeting of the Legislature, which shall then fill such Vacancies.

3) No Person shall be a Senator who shall not have attained to the Age of thirty Years, and been nine Years a Citizen of the United States, and who shall not, when elected, be an Inhabitant of that State for which he shall be chosen.

4) The Vice President of the United States shall be President of the Senate, but shall have no Vote, unless they be equally divided.

5) The Senate shall chuse their other Officers, and also a President pro tempore, in the Absence of the Vice President, or when he shall exercise the Office of the President of the United States.

6) The Senate shall have the sole Power to try all Impeachments. When sitting for that Purpose, they shall be on Oath or Affirmation. When the President of the United States is tried, the Chief Justice shall preside: And no Person shall be convicted without the Concurrence of two thirds of the Members present.

7) Judgment in Cases of Impeachment shall not extend further than to removal from Office, and disqualification to hold and enjoy any Office of honor, Trust or Profit under the United States: but the Party convicted shall nevertheless be liable and subject to Indictment, Trial, Judgment and Punishment, according to Law.

### Section 4.

1) The Times, Places and Manner of holding Elections for Senators and Representatives, shall be prescribed in each State by the Legislature thereof; but the Congress may at any time by Law make or alter such Regulations, except as to the Places of chusing Senators.

2) The Congress shall assemble at least once in every Year, and such Meeting shall be on the first Monday in December, unless they shall by Law appoint a different Day.

### Section 5.

1) Each House shall be the Judge of the Elections, Returns and Qualifications of its own Members, and a Majority of each shall constitute a Quorum to do Business; but a smaller Number may adjourn from day to day, and may be authorized to compel the Attendance of absent Members, in such Manner, and under such Penalties as each House may provide.

2) Each House may determine the Rules of its Proceedings, punish its Members for disorderly Behaviour, and, with the Concurrence of two thirds, expel a Member.

3) Each House shall keep a Journal of its Proceedings, and from time to time publish the same, excepting such Parts as may in their Judgment require Secrecy; and the Yeas and Nays of the Members of either House on any question shall, at the Desire of one fifth of those Present, be entered on the Journal.

4) Neither House, during the Session of Congress, shall, without the Consent of the other, adjourn for more than three days, nor to any other Place than that in which the two Houses shall be sitting.

### Section 6.

1) The Senators and Representatives shall receive a Compensation for their Services, to be ascertained by Law, and paid out of the Treasury of the United States. They shall in all Cases, except Treason, Felony and Breach of the Peace, be privileged from Arrest during their Attendance at the Session of their respective Houses, and in going to and returning from the same; and for any Speech or Debate in either House, they shall not be questioned in any other Place.

2) No Senator or Representative shall, during the Time for which he was elected, be appointed to any civil Office under the Authority of the United States, which shall have been created, or the Emoluments whereof shall have been encreased during such time; and no Person holding any Office under the United States, shall be a Member of either House during his Continuance in Office.

### Section 7.

1) All Bills for raising Revenue shall originate in the House of Representatives; but the Senate may propose or concur with Amendments as on other Bills.

2) Every Bill which shall have passed the House of Representatives and the Senate, shall, before it become a Law, be presented to the President of the United States; If he approve he shall sign it, but if not he shall return it, with his Objections to that House in which it shall have originated, who shall enter the Objections at large on their Journal, and proceed to reconsider it. If after such Reconsideration two thirds of that House shall agree to pass the Bill, it shall be sent, together

with the Objections, to the other House, by which it shall likewise be reconsidered, and if approved by two thirds of that House, it shall become a law. But in all such Cases the Votes of both Houses shall be determined by Yeas and Nays, and the Names of the Persons voting for and against the Bill shall be entered on the Journal of each House respectively. If any Bill shall not be returned by the President within ten Days (Sunday excepted) after it shall have been presented to him, the Same shall be a Law, in like Manner as if he had signed it, unless the Congress by their Adjournment prevent its Return, in which Case it shall not be a Law.

3) Every Order, Resolution, or Vote to which the Concurrence of the Senate and House of Representatives may be necessary (except on a question of Adjournment) shall be presented to the President of the United States; and before the Same shall take Effect, shall be approved by him, or being disapproved by him, shall be repassed by two thirds of the Senate and House of Representatives, according to the Rules and Limitations prescribed in the Case of a Bill.

*Section 8.*

1) The Congress shall have Power To lay and collect Taxes, Duties, Imposts and Excises, to pay the Debts and provide for the common Defence and general Welfare of the United States; but all Duties, Imposts and Excises shall be uniform throughout the United States;

2) To borrow Money on the credit of the United States;

3) To regulate Commerce with foreign Nations, and among the several States, and with the Indian Tribes;

4) To establish an uniform Rule of Naturalization, and uniform Laws on the subject of Bankruptcies throughout the United States;

5) To coin Money, regulate the Value thereof, and of foreign Coin, and to fix the Standard of Weights and Measures;

6) To provide for the Punishment of counterfeiting the Securities and current Coin of the United States;

7) To establish Post Offices and post Roads;

8) To promote the Progress of Science and useful Arts, by securing for limited Times to Authors and Inventors the exclusive Right to their respective Writings and Discoveries;

9) To constitute Tribunals inferior to the supreme Court;

10) To define and punish Piracies and Felonies committed on the high Seas, and Offenses against the Law of Nations;

11) To declare War, grant Letters of Marque and Reprisal, and make Rules concerning Captures on Land and Water;

12) To raise and support Armies, but no Appropriation of Money to that Use shall be for a longer Term than two Years;

13) To provide and maintain a Navy;

14) To make Rules for the Government and Regulation of the land and naval Forces;

15) To provide for calling forth the Militia to execute the Laws of the Union, suppress Insurrections and repel Invasions;

16) To provide for organizing, arming, and disciplining, the Militia, and for governing such Part of them as may be employed in the Service of the United States, reserving to the States respectively, the Appointment of the Officers, and the Authority of training the Militia according to the discipline prescribed by Congress;

17) To exercise exclusive Legislation in all Cases whatsoever, over such District (not exceeding ten Miles square) as may, by Cession of particular States, and the Acceptance of Congress, become the Seat of the Government of the United States, and to exercise like Authority over all Places purchased by the Consent of the Legislature of the State in which the Same shall be, for the Erection of Forts, Magazines, Arsenals, dock-Yards, and other needful Buildings;—And

18) To make all Laws which shall be necessary and proper for carrying into Execution the foregoing Powers, and all other Powers vested by this Constitution in the Government of the United States, or in any Department or Officer thereof.

*Section 9.*

1) The Migration or Importation of such Persons as any of the States now existing shall think proper to admit, shall not be prohibited by the Congress prior to the Year one thousand eight hundred and eight, but a Tax or Duty may be imposed on such Importation, not exceeding ten dollars for each Person.

2) The Privilege of the Writ of Habeas Corpus shall not be suspended unless when in Cases of Rebellion or Invasion the public Safety may require it.

3) No Bill of Attainder or ex post facto Law shall be passed.

4) No Capitation, or other direct, Tax shall be laid, unless in Proportion to the Census or Enumeration herein before directed to be taken.

5) No Tax or Duty shall be laid on Articles exported from any State.

6) No Preference shall be given by any Regulation of Commerce or Revenue to the Ports of one State over those of another; nor shall Vessels bound to, or from, one State, be obliged to enter, clear or pay Duties in another.

7) No Money shall be drawn from the Treasury, but in Consequence of Appropriations made by Law; and a regular Statement and Account of the Receipts and Expenditures of all public Money shall be published from time to time.

8) No Title of Nobility shall be granted by the United States: And no Person holding any Office of Profit or Trust under them, shall, without the Consent of the Congress, accept of any present, Emolument, Office, or Title, of any kind whatever, from any King, Prince or foreign State.

*Section 10.*

1) No State shall enter into any Treaty, Alliance, or Confederation; grant Letters of Marque and Reprisal; coin Money; emit Bills of Credit; make any Thing but gold and silver Coin a Tender in Payment of Debts; pass any Bill of Attainder, ex post facto Law, or Law impairing the Obligation of Contracts, or grant any Title of Nobility.

2) No State shall, without the Consent of Congress, lay any Imposts or Duties on Imports or Exports, except what may be absolutely necessary for executing its inspection Laws: and the net Produce of all Duties and Imposts, laid by any State on Imports or Exports, shall be for the Use of the Treasury of the United States; and all such Laws shall be subject to the Revision and Controul of the Congress.

3) No State shall, without the Consent of Congress, lay any Duty of Tonnage, keep Troops, or Ships of War in time of Peace, enter into any Agreement or Compact with another State, or with a foreign Power, or engage in War, unless actually invaded, or in such imminent Danger as will not admit of Delay.

## Article II

*Section 1.*

1) The executive Power shall be vested in a President of the United States of America. He shall hold his Office during the Term of four Years, and, together with the Vice President, chosen for the same Term, be elected, as follows:

2) Each State shall appoint, in such Manner as the Legislature thereof may direct, a Number of Electors, equal to the whole Number of Senators and Representatives to which the State may be entitled in the Congress: but no Senator or Representative, or Person holding an Office of Trust or Profit under the United States, shall be appointed an Elector.

The Electors shall meet in their respective States, and vote by Ballot for two Persons, of whom one at least shall not be an Inhabitant of the same State with themselves. And they shall make a List of all the Persons voted for, and of the Number of Votes for each; which List they shall sign and certify, and transmit sealed to the Seat of the Government of the United States, directed to the President of the Senate. The President of the Senate shall, in the presence of the Senate and House of Representatives, open all the Certificates, and the Votes shall then be counted. The Person having the greatest Number of Votes shall be the President, if such Number be a Majority of the whole Number of Electors appointed; and if there be more than one who have such Majority, and have an equal Number of Votes, then the House of Representatives shall immediately chuse by Ballot one of them for President; and if no Person have a Majority, then from the five highest on the List the said House shall in like Manner chuse the President. But in chusing the President, the Votes shall be taken by States, the Representation from each State having one Vote; a quorum for this Purpose shall consist of a Member or Members from two thirds of the States, and a Majority of all the States shall be necessary to a Choice. In every Case, after the Choice of the President, the Person having the greatest Number of Votes of the Electors shall be the Vice President. But if there should remain two or more who have equal Votes, the Senate shall chuse from them by Ballot the Vice President.

3) The Congress may determine the Time of chusing the Electors, and the Day on which they shall give their Votes; which Day shall be the same throughout the United States.

4) No Person except a natural born Citizen, or a Citizen of the United States, at the time of the Adoption of this Constitution, shall be eligible to the Office of President; neither shall any Person be eligible to that Office who shall not have attained to the Age of thirty-five Years, and been fourteen Years a Resident within the United States.

5) In Case of the Removal of the President from Office, or of his Death, Resignation, or Inability to discharge the Powers and Duties of the said Office, the Same shall devolve on the Vice President, and the Congress may by Law provide for the Case of Removal, Death, Resignation or Inability, both of the President and Vice President, declaring what Officer shall then act as President, and such Officer shall act accordingly, until the Disability be removed, or a President shall be elected.

6) The President shall, at stated Times, receive for his Services, a Compensation, which shall neither be increased nor diminished during the Period for which he shall have been elected, and he shall not receive within that Period any other Emolument from the United States, or any of them.

7) Before he enter on the Execution of his Office, he shall take the following Oath or Affirmation:—"I do solemnly swear (or affirm) that I will faithfully execute the Office of President of the United States, and will to the best of my Ability, preserve, protect and defend the Constitution of the United States."

### Section 2.

1) The President shall be Commander in Chief of the Army and Navy of the United States, and of the Militia of the several States, when called into the actual Service of the United States; he may require the Opinion, in writing, of the principal Officer in each of the executive Departments, upon any Subject relating to the Duties of their respective Offices, and he shall have Power to grant Reprieves and Pardons for Offenses against the United States, except in Cases of Impeachment.

2) He shall have Power, by and with the Advice and Consent of the Senate, to make Treaties, provided two thirds of the Senators present concur; and he shall nominate, and by and with the Advice and Consent of the Senate, shall appoint Ambassadors, other public Ministers and Consuls, Judges of the supreme Court, and all other Officers of the United States, whose Appointments are not herein otherwise provided for, and which shall be established by Law: but the Congress may by Law vest the Appointment of such inferior Officers, as they think proper, in the President alone, in the Courts of Law, or in the Heads of Departments.

3) The President shall have Power to fill up all Vacancies that may happen during the Recess of the Senate, by granting Commissions which shall expire at the End of their next Session.

### Section 3.

He shall from time to time give to the Congress Information of the State of the Union, and recommend to their Consideration such Measures as he shall judge necessary and expedient; he may, on extraordinary Occasions, convene both Houses, or either of them, and in Case of Disagreement between them, with Respect to the Time of Adjournment, he may adjourn them to such Time as he shall think proper; he shall receive Ambassadors and other public Ministers; he shall take Care that the Laws be faithfully executed, and shall Commission all the Officers of the United States.

### Section 4.

The President, Vice President and all Civil Officers of the United States, shall be removed from Office on Impeachment for, and Conviction of, Treason, Bribery, or other high Crimes and Misdemeanors.

## Article III

### Section 1.

The judicial Power of the United States, shall be vested in one supreme Court, and in such inferior Courts as the Congress may from time to time ordain and establish. The Judges, both of the supreme and inferior Courts, shall hold their Offices during good Behaviour, and shall, at stated Times, receive for their Services, a Compensation, which shall not be diminished during their Continuance in Office.

### Section 2.

1) The judicial Power shall extend to all Cases, in Law and Equity, arising under this Constitution, the Laws of the United States, and Treaties made, or which shall be made, under their Authority;—to all Cases affecting Ambassadors, other public Ministers and Consuls;— to all Cases of admiralty and maritime Jurisdiction;— to Controversies to which the United States shall be a party;—to Controversies between two or more States;—between a State and Citizens of another State;— between Citizens of different States;—between Citizens of the same State claiming Lands under Grants of different States, and between a State, or the Citizens thereof, and foreign States, Citizens or Subjects.

2) In all Cases affecting Ambassadors, other public Ministers and Consuls, and those in which a State shall be Party, the supreme Court shall have original Jurisdiction. In all the other Cases before mentioned, the supreme Court shall have appellate Jurisdiction, both as to Law and Fact, with such

Exceptions, and under such Regulations as the Congress shall make.

3) The Trial of all Crimes, except in Cases of Impeachment, shall be by Jury; and such Trial shall be held in the State where the said Crimes shall have been committed; but when not committed within any State, the Trial shall be at such Place or Places as the Congress may by Law have directed.

### Section 3.

1) Treason against the United States, shall consist only in levying War against them, or in adhering to their Enemies, giving them Aid and Comfort. No Person shall be convicted of Treason unless on the Testimony of two Witnesses to the same overt Act, or on Confession in open Court.

2) The Congress shall have Power to declare the Punishment of Treason, but no Attainder of Treason shall work Corruption of Blood, or Forfeiture except during the Life of the Person attainted.

## Article IV

### Section 1.

Full Faith and Credit shall be given in each State to the public Acts, Records, and judicial Proceedings of every other State. And the Congress may by general Laws prescribe the Manner in which such Acts, Records and Proceedings shall be proved, and the Effect thereof.

### Section 2.

1) The Citizens of each State shall be entitled to all privileges and Immunities of Citizens in the several States.

2) A Person charged in any State with Treason, Felony, or other Crime, who shall flee from Justice, and be found in another State, shall on Demand of the executive Authority of the State from which he fled, be delivered up, to be removed to the State having Jurisdiction of the Crime.

3) No Person held to Service of Labour in one State, under the Laws thereof, escaping into another, shall, in Consequence of any Law or Regulation therein, be discharged from such Service or Labour, but shall be delivered up on Claim of the Party to whom such Service or Labour may be due.

### Section 3.

1) New States may be admitted by the Congress into this Union; but no new State shall be formed or erected within the Jurisdiction of any other State;

nor any State be formed by the Junction of two or more States, or Parts of States, without the Consent of the Legislatures of the States concerned as well as of the Congress.

2) The Congress shall have power to dispose of and make all needful Rules and Regulations respecting the Territory or other Property belonging to the United States; and nothing in this Constitution shall be so construed as to Prejudice any Claims of the United States, or of any particular State.

### Section 4.

The United States shall guarantee to every State in this Union a Republican Form of Government, and shall protect each of them against Invasion; and on Application of the Legislature, or of the Executive (when the Legislature cannot be convened) against domestic Violence.

## Article V

The Congress, whenever two thirds of both Houses shall deem it necessary, shall propose Amendments to this Constitution, or, on the Application of the Legislatures of two thirds of the several States, shall call a Convention for proposing Amendments, which, in either Case, shall be valid to all Intents and Purposes, as Part of this Constitution, when ratified by the Legislatures of three fourths of the several States, or by Conventions in three fourths thereof, as the one or the other Mode of Ratification may be proposed by the Congress; Provided that no Amendment which may be made prior to the Year One thousand eight hundred and eight shall in any Manner affect the first and fourth Clauses in the Ninth Section of the first Article; and that no State, without its Consent, shall be deprived of its equal Suffrage in the Senate.

## Article VI

1) All Debts contracted and Engagements entered into, before the Adoption of this Constitution, shall be as valid against the United States under this Constitution, as under the Confederation.

2) This Constitution, and the Laws of the United States which shall be made in Pursuance thereof; and all Treaties made, or which shall be made, under the Authority of the United States, shall be the supreme Law of the Land; and the Judges in every State shall be bound thereby, any Thing in the Constitution or Laws of any State to the Contrary notwithstanding.

3) The Senators and Representatives before mentioned, and the Members of the several State Legislatures, and all executive and judicial Officers,

both of the United States and of the several States, shall be bound by Oath or Affirmation, to support this Constitution; but no religious Test shall ever be required as a Qualification to any Office or public Trust under the United States.

## Article VII

The Ratification of the Conventions of nine States, shall be sufficient for the Establishment of this Constitution between the States so ratifying the Same.

## ARTICLES IN ADDITION TO, AND AMENDMENT OF, THE CONSTITUTION OF THE UNITED STATES OF AMERICA, PROPOSED BY CONGRESS, AND RATIFIED BY THE SEVERAL STATES, PURSUANT TO THE FIFTH ARTICLE OF THE ORIGINAL CONSTITUTION

### Amendment I (1791)

Congress shall make no law respecting an establishment of religion, or prohibiting the free exercise thereof; or abridging the freedom of speech, or of the press; or the right of the people peaceably to assemble, and to petition the Government for a redress of grievances.

### Amendment II (1791)

A well regulated Militia, being necessary to the security of a free state, the right of the people to keep and bear Arms, shall not be infringed.

### Amendment III (1791)

No Soldier shall, in time of peace be quartered in any house, without the consent of the Owner, nor in time of war, but in a manner to be prescribed by law.

### Amendment IV (1791)

The right of the people to be secure in their persons, houses, papers, and effects, against unreasonable searches and seizures, shall not be violated, and no Warrants shall issue, but upon probable cause, supported by Oath or affirmation, and particularly describing the place to be searched, and the persons or things to be seized.

### Amendment V (1791)

No person shall be held to answer for a capital, or otherwise infamous crime, unless on a presentment or indictment of a Grand Jury, except in cases arising in the land or naval forces, or in the Militia, when in actual service in time of War or public danger; nor shall any person be subject for the same offence to be twice put in jeopardy of life or limb; nor shall be compelled in any criminal case to be a witness against himself, nor be deprived of life, liberty, or property, without due process of law; nor shall private property be taken for public use, without just compensation.

### Amendment VI (1791)

In all criminal prosecutions, the accused shall enjoy the right to a speedy and public trial, by an impartial jury of the State and district wherein the crime shall have been committed, which district shall have been previously ascertained by law, and to be informed of the nature and cause of the accusation; to be confronted with the witnesses against him; to have compulsory process for obtaining witnesses in his favor, and to have the Assistance of Counsel for his defence.

### Amendment VII (1791)

In Suits at common law, where the value in controversy shall exceed twenty dollars, the right of trial by jury shall be preserved, and no fact tried by a jury, shall be otherwise re-examined in any Court of the United States, than according to the rules of the common law.

### Amendment VIII (1791)

Excessive bail shall not be required, nor excessive fines imposed, nor cruel and unusual punishments inflicted.

### Amendment IX (1791)

The enumeration in the Constitution, of certain rights, shall not be construed to deny or disparage others retained by the people.

### Amendment X (1791)

The powers not delegated to the United States by the Constitution, nor prohibited by it to the States, are reserved to the States respectively, or to the people.

### Amendment XI (1798)

The Judicial power of the United States shall not be construed to extend to any suit in law or equity, commenced or prosecuted against one of the United States by Citizens of another State, or by Citizens or Subjects of any Foreign State.

### Amendment XII (1804)

The Electors shall meet in their respective states and vote by ballot for President and Vice-President, one of whom, at least, shall not be an inhabitant of the same state with themselves; they shall name in their ballots the person voted for as President, and in distinct ballots the person voted for as Vice-President, and they shall make distinct lists of all persons voted for as President, and of all persons voted for as Vice-President, and of the number of votes for each, which lists they shall sign and certify, and transmit sealed to the seat of the government of the United States, directed to the President of the Senate;—The President of the Senate shall, in the presence of the Senate and House of Representatives, open all the certificates and the votes shall then be counted;—The person having the greatest number of votes for President, shall be the President, if such number be a majority of the whole number of Electors appointed; and if no person have such majority, then from the persons having the highest numbers not exceeding three on the list of those voted for as President, the House of Representatives shall choose immediately, by ballot, the President. But in choosing the President, the votes shall be taken by states, the representation from each state having one vote; a quorum for this purpose shall consist of a member or members from two-thirds of the states, and a majority of all the states shall be necessary to a choice. And if the House of Representatives shall not choose a President whenever the right of choice shall devolve upon them, before the fourth day of March next following, then the Vice-President shall act as President, as in the case of the death or other constitutional disability of the President—The person having the greatest number of votes as Vice-President, shall be the Vice-President, if such number be a majority of the whole number of Electors appointed, and if no person have a majority, then from the two highest numbers on the list, the Senate shall choose the Vice-President; A quorum for the purpose shall consist of two-thirds of the whole number of Senators, and a majority of the whole number shall be necessary to a choice. But no person constitutionally ineligible to the office of President shall be eligible to that of Vice-President of the United States.

## Amendment XIII (1865)

*Section 1.*

Neither slavery nor involuntary servitude, except as a punishment for crime whereof the party shall have been duly convicted, shall exist within the United States, or any place subject to their jurisdiction.

*Section 2.*

Congress shall have power to enforce this article by appropriate legislation.

## Amendment XIV (1868)

*Section 1.*

All persons born or naturalized in the United States and subject to the jurisdiction thereof, are citizens of the United States and of the State wherein they reside. No State shall make or enforce any law which shall abridge the privileges or immunities of citizens of the United States; nor shall any State deprive any person of life, liberty, or property, without due process of law; nor deny to any person within its jurisdiction the equal protection of the laws.

*Section 2.*

Representatives shall be apportioned among the several States according to their respective numbers, counting the whole number of persons in each State, excluding Indians not taxed. But when the right to vote at any election for the choice of electors for President and Vice-President of the United States, Representatives in Congress, the Executive and Judicial officers of a State, or the members of the Legislature thereof, is denied to any of the male inhabitants of such State, being twenty-one years of age, and citizens of the United States, or in any way abridged, except for participation in rebellion, or other crime, the basis of representation therein shall be reduced in the proportion which the number of such male citizens shall bear to the whole number of male citizens twenty-one years of age in such State.

*Section 3.*

No person shall be a Senator or Representative in Congress, or elector of President and Vice-President, or hold any office, civil or military, under the United States, or under any State, who, having previously taken an oath, as a member of Congress, or as an officer of the United States, or as a member of any State legislature, or as an executive or judicial officer of any State, to support the Constitution of the United States, shall have engaged in insurrection or rebellion against the same, or given aid or comfort to the enemies thereof. But Congress may by a vote of two-thirds of each House, remove such disability.

*Section 4.*

The validity of the public debt of the United States, authorized by law, including debts incurred for payment of pensions and bounties for services in suppressing insurrection or rebellion, shall not be questioned. But neither the United States nor any State shall assume or pay any debt or obligation incurred in aid of insurrection or rebellion against the United States, or any claim for the loss or emancipation of any slave; but all such debts, obligations and claims shall be held illegal and void.

*Section 5.*

The Congress shall have power to enforce, by appropriate legislation, the provisions of this article.

## Amendment XV (1870)

*Section 1.*

The right of citizens of the United States to vote shall not be denied or abridged by the United States or by any State on account of race, color, or previous condition of servitude.

*Section 2.*

The Congress shall have power to enforce this article by appropriate legislation.

## Amendment XVI (1913)

The Congress shall have power to lay and collect taxes on incomes, from whatever source derived, without apportionment among the several States, and without regard to any census or enumeration.

## Amendment XVII (1913)

The Senate of the United States shall be composed of two Senators from each State, elected by the people thereof, for six years; and each Senator shall have one vote. The electors in each State shall have the qualifications requisite for electors of the most numerous branch of the State legislatures.

When vacancies happen in the representation of any State in the Senate, the executive authority of such State shall issue writs of election to fill such vacancies: *Provided*, That the legislature of any State may empower the executive thereof to make temporary appointments until the people fill the vacancies by election as the legislature may direct.

This amendment shall not be so construed as to affect the election or term of any Senator chosen before it becomes valid as part of the Constitution.

## Amendment XVIII (1919)

*Section 1.*

After one year from the ratification of this article the manufacture, sale, or transportation of intoxicating liquors within, the importation thereof into, or the exportation thereof from the United States and all territory subject to the jurisdiction thereof for beverage purposes is hereby prohibited.

*Section 2.*

The Congress and the several States shall have concurrent power to enforce this article by appropriate legislation.

*Section 3.*

This article shall be inoperative unless it shall have been ratified as an amendment to the Constitution by the legislatures of the several States, as provided in the Constitution, within seven years from the date of the submission hereof to the States by the Congress.

## Amendment XIX (1920)

The right of citizens of the United States to vote shall not be denied or abridged by the United States or by any State on account of sex.

Congress shall have power to enforce this article by appropriate legislation.

## Amendment XX (1933)

*Section 1.*

The terms of the President and Vice President shall end at noon on the 20th day of January, and the terms of Senators and Representatives at noon on the 3d day of January, of the years in which such terms would have ended if this article had not been ratified; and the terms of their successors shall then begin.

*Section 2.*

The Congress shall assemble at least once in every year, and such meeting shall begin at noon on the 3d day of January, unless they shall by law appoint a different day.

*Section 3.*

If, at the time fixed for the beginning of the term of the President, the President elect shall have died, the Vice President elect shall become President. If a President shall not have been chosen before the time fixed for the beginning of his term, or if the President elect shall have failed to qualify, then the Vice President elect shall act as President until a President shall have qualified; and the Congress may by law provide for the case wherein neither a President elect nor a Vice President elect shall have qualified, declaring who shall then act as President, or the manner in which one who is to act shall be selected, and such person shall act accordingly until a President or Vice President shall have qualified.

*Section 4.*

The Congress may by law provide for the case of the death of any of the persons from whom the House of Representatives may choose a President whenever the right of choice shall have devolved upon them, and for the case of the death of any of the persons from whom the Senate may choose a Vice President whenever the right of choice shall have devolved upon them.

*Section 5.*

Sections 1 and 2 shall take effect on the 15th day of October following the ratification of this article.

*Section 6.*

This article shall be inoperative unless it shall have been ratified as an amendment to the Constitution by the legislatures of three-fourths of the several States within seven years from the date of its submission.

## Amendment XXI (1933)

*Section 1.*

The eighteenth article of amendment to the Constitution of the United States is hereby repealed.

*Section 2.*

The transportation or importation into any State, Territory or possession of the United States for delivery or use therein of intoxicating liquors, in violation of the laws thereof, is hereby prohibited.

*Section 3.*

This article shall be inoperative unless it shall have been ratified as an amendment to the Constitution by conventions in the several States, as provided in the Constitution, within seven years from the date of the submission hereof to the States by the Congress.

## Amendment XXII (1951)

*Section 1.*

No person shall be elected to the office of the President more than twice, and no person who has held the office of President, or acted as President, for more than two years of a term to which some other person was elected President shall be elected to the office of the President more than once. But this Article shall not apply to any person holding the office of President when this Article was proposed by the Congress, and shall not prevent any person who may be holding the office of President, or acting as President, during the term within which this Article becomes operative from holding the office of President or acting as President during the remainder of such term.

*Section 2.*

This Article shall be inoperative unless it shall have been ratified as an amendment to the Constitution by the legislatures of three-fourths of the several States within seven years from the date of its submission to the States by the Congress.

## Amendment XXIII (1961)

*Section 1.*

The District constituting the seat of Government of the United States shall appoint in such manner as the Congress may direct:

A number of electors of President and Vice President equal to the whole number of Senators and Representatives in Congress to which the District would be entitled if it were a State, but in no event more than the least populous State; they shall be in addition to those appointed by the States, but they shall be considered, for the purposes of the election of President and Vice President, to be electors appointed by a State; and they shall meet in the District and perform such duties as provided by the twelfth article of amendment.

*Section 2.*

The Congress shall have power to enforce this article by appropriate legislation.

## Amendment XXIV (1964)

*Section 1.*

The right of citizens of the United States to vote in any primary or other election for President or Vice President, for electors for President or Vice President, or for Senator or Representative in Congress, shall not be denied or abridged by the United States or any State by reason of failure to pay any poll tax or other tax.

*Section 2.*

The Congress shall have power to enforce this article by appropriate legislation.

## Amendment XXV (1967)

*Section 1.*

In case of the removal of the President from office or of his death or resignation, the Vice President shall become President.

*Section 2.*

Whenever there is a vacancy in the office of the Vice President, the President shall nominate a Vice President who shall take office upon confirmation by a majority vote of both Houses of Congress.

*Section 3.*

Whenever the President transmits to the President pro tempore of the Senate and the Speaker of the House of Representatives his written declaration that he is unable to discharge the powers and duties of his office, and until he transmits to them a written declaration to the contrary, such powers and duties shall be discharged by the Vice President as Acting President.

*Section 4.*

Whenever the Vice President and a majority of either the principal officers of the executive departments or of such other body as Congress may by law provide, transmit to the President pro tempore of the Senate and the Speaker of the House of Representatives their written declaration that the President is unable to discharge the powers and duties of his office, the Vice President shall immediately assume the powers and duties of the office as Acting President.

Thereafter, when the President transmits to the President pro tempore of the Senate and the Speaker of the House of Representatives his written declaration that no inability exists, he shall resume the powers and duties of his office unless the Vice President and a majority of either the principal officers of the executive department or of such other body as Congress may by law provide, transmit within four days to the President pro tempore of the Senate and the Speaker of the House of Representatives their written declaration that the President is unable to discharge the powers and duties of his office. Thereupon Congress shall decide the issue, assembling within forty-eight hours for that purpose if not in session. If the Congress, within twenty-one days after receipt of the latter written declaration, or, if Congress is not in session, within twenty-one days after Congress is required to assemble, determines by two-thirds vote of both Houses that the President is unable to discharge the powers and duties of his office, the Vice President shall continue to discharge the same as Acting President; otherwise, the President shall resume the powers and duties of his office.

## Amendment XXVI (1971)

*Section 1.*

The right of citizens of the United States, who are eighteen years of age or older, to vote shall not be denied or abridged by the United States or by any State on account of age.

*Section 2.*

The Congress shall have power to enforce this article by appropriate legislation.

## Amendment XXVII (1992)

No law varying the compensation for the services of the senators and representatives shall take effect, until an election of representatives shall have intervened.

# Glossary

## A

**accessory** A person who helps to commit a crime without being present. An accessory before the fact is a person who, without being present, encourages, orders, or helps another to commit a crime. An accessory after the fact is a person who finds out that a crime has been committed and helps to conceal the crime or the criminal.

**accusatorial** An element of the adversarial system that places the burden of production and proof on the state, and otherwise gives the benefit of doubt to the defendant.

**actus reus** (Latin) An act. For example, an *actus reus* is a "wrongful deed" (such as killing a person), which, if done with mens rea, a "guilty mind" (such as *malice aforethought*), is a crime (such as *first-degree* murder).

**admission** A voluntary statement that a fact or a state of events is true.

**adversarial** A system of adjudication where the state and defendant are competitors with independent investigations and theories of the case. The two parties are active in the development of the case with the court in a more passive role, overseeing the process and ensuring due process. Common Law nations, such as the United States, use the adversarial system.

**adversary system** The system of adjudication in the United States and other common law jurisdictions. The judge acts as the referee between opposite sides (between two individuals, between the state and an individual, etc.) rather than acting as the person who also makes the state's case or independently seeks out evidence.

**affirmative defense** A defense that is more than a simple denial of the charges. It raises a new matter that may result in an acquittal or a reduction of liability. It is a defense that must be affirmatively raised, often before trial or it is lost.

**aggravating circumstances** Actions or occurrences that increase the seriousness of a crime but are not part of the legal definition of that crime.

**Alford plea** A guilty plea that is accompanied with an assertion of innocence.

**alibi** (Latin) "Elsewhere"; the claim that at the time a crime was committed a person was somewhere else. [pronounce: *al*-eh-bi]

**appellate court** A higher court that can hear appeals from a lower court.

**arraignment** The hearing at which a defendant is brought before a judge to hear the charges and to enter a plea (guilty, not guilty, etc.).

**arrest** The official taking of a person to answer criminal charges. This involves at least temporarily depriving the person of liberty and may involve the use of force. An arrest is usually made by a police officer with a warrant or for a crime committed in the officer's presence.

**arson** The malicious and unlawful burning of a building.

**assault** An intentional threat, show of force, or movement that could reasonably make a person feel in danger of physical attack or harmful physical contact.

**attempt** An effort to commit a crime that goes beyond preparation and that proceeds far enough to make the person who did it guilty of an "attempt crime." For example, if a person fires a shot at another in a failed effort at murder, the person is guilty of *attempted murder*.

**attendant circumstances** Facts or conditions that must be proven, along with the mens rea and actus reus, for a defendant to be convicted.

**automobile exception** The rule that warrantless searches of cars and their contents are permitted by the Fourth Amendment, provided probable cause exists.

## B

**bail** The money or property given as security for a defendant's appearance in court. The money, often in the form of a bail bond, may be lost if the released defendant does not appear in court.

**battered spouse syndrome** Continuing abuse of a woman by a spouse or lover, and the resulting physical or psychological harm.

**battery** An intentional, unconsented to, physical contact by one person (or an object controlled by that person) with another person.

**beyond a reasonable doubt** The level of proof required to convict a person of a crime. Precise definitions vary, but moral certainty and firm belief are both used. Beyond a reasonable doubt is not absolute certainty. This is the highest level of proof required in any type of trial.

**bill of attainder** A legislative act pronouncing a person guilty (usually of treason) without a trial and sentencing the person to death and attainder. This is now prohibited by the U.S. Constitution.

**bill of particulars** A detailed, formal, written statement of charges or claims by a plaintiff or the prosecutor (given upon the defendant's formal request to the court for more detailed information).

**Bill of Rights** The first 10 amendments (changes or additions) to the U.S. Constitution.

**Brandenburg Test** An exception to free speech. Speech that is directed at causing imminent lawless action and is likely to cause such action may be regulated.

**breaches of the peace** A vague term for any illegal public disturbance; sometimes refers to the offense known as "disorderly conduct." It is defined and treated differently in different states.

**bribery** The offering, giving, receiving, or soliciting of anything of value in order to influence the actions of a public official.

**brief** A written document filed with a court through which a party presents a legal claim, legal theory, supporting authorities, and requests some form of relief.

**burden of persuasion** The duty to convince the fact finder or court of the truth of a fact or a legal position.

**burden of production** The requirement that one side in a lawsuit produce evidence on a particular issue or risk losing on that issue.

**burden of proof** The requirement that to win a point or have an issue decided in your favor in a lawsuit, you must show that the weight of evidence is on your side rather than "in the balance" on that question.

**burglary** Unlawfully entering the house of another person with the intention of committing a felony (usually theft).

# C

**castle doctrine** An exception to the retreat doctrine, one has no obligation to retreat from his or her home before using deadly force to repel an intruder.

**certiorari** (Latin) "To make sure." A request for certiorari (or "cert." for short) is like an appeal, but one that the higher court is not required to take for decision. It is literally a writ from the higher court asking the lower court for the record of the case.

**chain of custody** The chronological list of those in continuous possession of a specific physical object. A person who presents physical evidence (such as a gun used in a crime) at a trial must account for its possession from the time of receipt to time of trial in order for the evidence to be "admitted" by the judge. It must thus be shown that the *chain of custody* was unbroken.

**challenge for cause** A formal objection to the qualifications of a prospective juror or jurors.

**civil liberties** Individual liberties guaranteed by the Constitution and, in particular, by the Bill of Rights.

**co-conspirator's hearsay rule** The principle that statements by a member of a proven conspiracy may be used as evidence against any of the members of the conspiracy.

**Commerce Clause** Found in Article I, sec. 8 of the Constitution, this clause empowers the federal government to regulate commerce between the states, with foreign governments, and Indian tribes.

**common law** The legal system that originated in England and is composed of case law and statutes that grow and change, influenced by ever-changing custom and tradition.

**commutation of sentence** Changing a criminal punishment to one less severe.

**compensatory damages** Damages awarded for the actual loss suffered by a plaintiff.

**complaint** A *criminal complaint* is a formal document that charges a person with a crime.

**concert of action rule** The rule that, unless a statute specifies otherwise, it is not a conspiracy for two persons to agree to commit a crime if the definition of the crime itself requires the participation of two or more persons. Also called *Wharton Rule* and *concerted action rule*.

**concurrent jurisdiction** Two or more jurisdictions or courts possessing authority over the same matter.

**concurrent sentences** Prison terms that run at the same time.

**confession** A voluntary statement by a person that he or she is guilty of a crime.

**consecutive sentences** An additional prison term given to a person who is already convicted of a crime; the additional term is to be served after the previous one is finished.

**consent** Voluntary and active agreement.

**conspiracy** A crime that may be committed when two or more persons agree to do something unlawful (or to do something lawful by unlawful means). The agreement can be inferred from the persons' actions.

**constructive intent** Inferred, implied, or presumed from the circumstances.

**contempt** A willful disobeying of a judge's command or official court order. Contempt can be *direct* (within the judge's notice) or *indirect* (outside the court and punishable only after proved to the judge). It can also be *civil contempt* (disobeying a court order in favor of an opponent) or *criminal contempt*.

**contract** An agreement that affects or creates legal relationships between two or more persons. To be a *contract*, an agreement must involve at least one promise, consideration, persons legally capable of making binding agreements, and a reasonable certainty about the meaning of the terms.

**conversion** Any act that deprives an owner of property without that owner's permission and without just cause.

**cooperative federalism** A model of governance where the federal government and the states share in governing.

**corporate liability** The liability of a corporation for the acts of its directors, officers, shareholders, agents, and employees.

**corpus delicti** (Latin) "The body of the crime." The material substance upon which a crime has been committed; for example, a dead body (in the crime of murder) or a house burned down (in the crime of arson).

**counterfeiting** The creation or passing of an imitation.

**court of general jurisdiction** Another term for trial court; that is, a court having jurisdiction to try all classes of civil and criminal cases except those that can be heard only by a court of limited jurisdiction.

**court of limited jurisdiction** A court whose jurisdiction is limited to civil cases of a certain type, or that involve a limited amount of money, or whose jurisdiction in criminal cases is confined to petty offenses and preliminary hearings.

**court of record** Generally, another term for trial court.

**court rules** Rules promulgated by the court, governing procedure or practice before it.

**criminal coercion** A synonym for extortion.

**criminal law** The branch of the law that specifies what conduct constitutes crime, sets out the defenses to criminal accusations, and establishes punishments for such conduct.

**criminal procedure** The rules of procedure by which criminal prosecutions are governed.

**culpable** Blamable; at fault. A person who has done a wrongful act (whether criminal or civil) is described as "culpable."

**Cyberstalking** Cyberstalking is the crime of using communication technology to transmit obscene, abusive, or harassing language intended to harass or threaten another person.

# D

**damages** Money that a court orders paid to a person who has suffered damage (a loss or harm) by the person who caused the injury (the violation of the person's rights).

**deadly weapon doctrine** A rule that permits juries to infer an actor's intent to cause the death of a victim when an instrument of death has been used in a manner that is likely to cause death or serious bodily injury.

**de novo** Anew. For a case to be tried again as if there had not been a prior trial.

**deposition** The process of taking a witness's sworn out-of-court testimony. The questioning is usually done by a lawyer, and the lawyer from the other side is given a chance to attend and participate.

**detainer** A warrant or court order to keep a person in custody when that person might otherwise be released. This is often used to make sure a person will serve a sentence or attend a trial in one state at the end of a prison term in another state or in a federal prison.

**determinate sentence** An exact penalty set by law.

**deterrence** To prevent an individual from committing a crime.

**diminished capacity** The principle that having a certain recognized form of *diminished mental capacity* while committing a crime should lead to the imposition of a lesser punishment or to lowering the degree of the crime.

**discovery**    The formal and informal exchange of information between the prosecution and the defense.

**discretion**    The power to act within general guidelines, rules, or laws, but without either specific rules to follow or the need to completely explain or justify each decision or action.

**DNA Printing**    Comparing body tissue samples (such as blood, skin, hair, or semen) to see if the genetic materials match. The process is used to identify criminals by comparing their DNA with that found at a crime scene, and it is used to identify a child's parent. Most states allow its use as evidence.

**double jeopardy clause**    A second prosecution by the same government against the same person for the same crime (or for a lesser included offense) once the first prosecution is totally finished and decided. This is prohibited by the U.S. Constitution.

**Dual federalism**    A model of governance where the federal government and states have distinct, separate authorities.

**dual sovereignty doctrine**    A second prosecution by a different government against the same person for the same crime (or for a lesser included offense) does not violate the Double Jeopardy Clause.

**dual Sovereignty**    When multiple governments have concurrent authority over people or policy.

**due process**    The *due process* clauses of the Fifth and Fourteenth Amendments to the U.S. Constitution require that no persons be deprived of life, liberty, or property without having notice and a real chance to present their side in a legal dispute.

**duress**    Unlawful pressure on what a person would not otherwise have done. It includes force, threats of violence, physical restraint, etc.

**Durham rule**    The principle, used in *Durham v. United States* (214 F.2d. 862 (1954)), that defendants are not guilty of a crime because of insanity if they were "suffering from a disease or defective mental condition at the time of the act and there was a causal connection between the condition and the act."

# E

**element analysis**    The assignment of separate mens rea to each element of an offense.

**embezzlement**    The fraudulent and secret taking of money or property by a person who has been trusted with it. This usually applies to an employee's taking money and covering it up by faking business records or account books.

**entrapment**    The act of government officials (usually police) or agents inducing a person to commit a crime that the person would not have committed without the inducement.

**exclusionary rule**    "The exclusionary rule" often means the rule that illegally gathered evidence may not be used in a criminal trial. The rule has several exceptions, such as when the evidence is used to impeach a defendant's testimony and when the evidence was gathered in a good-faith belief that the process was legal.

**exhaustion of remedies**    A person must usually take all reasonable steps to get satisfaction from a state or federal government before seeking judicial relief.

**exigent circumstances**    A situation where law enforcement officers must act so quickly to prevent the destruction of evidence, the successful flight of a suspect, or serious injury or death to any person, that there isn't time to obtain a warrant. Warrantless searches that occur when exigent circumstances exist are valid.

**ex post facto law**    (Latin) After the fact. An *ex post facto* law is one that retroactively attempts to make an action a crime that was not a crime at the time it was done, or a law that attempts to reduce a person's rights based on a past act that was not subject to the law when it was done.

**extortion**    To acquire property or money using threats of harm to person, property, or reputation.

**extradition**    One country (or state) giving up a person to a second country (or state) when the second requests the person for a trial on a criminal charge or for punishment after a trial.

# F

**factual guilt**    Whether a defendant committed the alleged crime.

**false imprisonment**    The unlawful restraint by one person of the physical liberty of another.

**false pretenses**    A lie told to cheat another person out of his or her money or property. It is a crime in most states, though the precise definition varies.

**federalism**    A system of political organization with two or more levels of government (e.g., city, state, and national) coexisting in the same area, with the lower levels having some independent powers.

**felony murder**    All co-felons are responsible for all homicides that occur during their crime, regardless of who committed the homicide and their individual mens rea.

**fighting words**    Speech that is not protected by the First Amendment to the U.S. Constitution because it is likely to cause violence by the person to whom the words are spoken.

**final judgment (order)**    The last action of a court; the one upon which an appeal can be based.

**first-degree murder**    The highest form of homicide. The killing of another person with malice and premeditation, cruelty, or done during the commission of a major felony is typically murder in the first degree.

**foreseeable**    The degree to which the consequences of an action *should* have been anticipated, recognized, and considered beforehand. *Not* hindsight.

**forfeiture**    A deprivation of money, property, or rights, without compensation, as a consequence of a default or the commission of a crime.

**forgery**    Making a fake document (or altering a real one) with intent to commit a fraud.

**forum analysis**    A framework for deciding whether an individual possesses free speech or association rights on public property.

**Franks hearing**    The right of a defendant who can make a preliminary showing that false evidence was used to obtain a warrant to a hearing to decide the truth of the allegation.

**fruit of the poisonous tree doctrine**    The rule that evidence gathered as a *result* of evidence gained in an illegal search or questioning cannot be used against the person searched or questioned even if the later evidence was gathered lawfully.

# G

**general intent**    The desire to commit a prohibited act but not the outcome of that act.

**Geofence search**    The police practice of obtaining location and use data from all devices in the area of a crime during the period of the crime.

**grand jury** Persons who receive complaints and accusations of crime, hear preliminary evidence on the complaining side, and make formal accusations or indictments.

# H

**habitual offender statutes** Laws that may apply to a person who has been convicted of as few as two prior crimes (often violent or drug-related crimes) and that greatly increase the penalties for each succeeding crime.

**halfway house** A facility in which persons recently discharged from a rehabilitation center or prison live for a time and are given support and assistance in readjusting to society at large.

**harmless error** A trial court mistake that doesn't change the outcome of the case and therefore does not result in reversal.

**hearsay** A statement about what someone else said (or wrote or otherwise communicated). *Hearsay evidence* is evidence, concerning what someone said outside of a court proceeding, that is offered in the proceeding to prove the truth of what was said. The *hearsay rule* bars the admission of hearsay as evidence to *prove the hearsay's truth* unless allowed by a hearsay exception.

**hung jury** A jury that cannot reach a verdict (decision) because of disagreement among jurors.

# I

**identity theft** The act of assuming another person's identity by fraud.

**in camera** A meeting with a judge in private, typically in chambers.

**independent source** The general rule that if new evidence can be traced to a source completely apart from the illegally gathered evidence that first led to the new evidence, it may be used by the government in a criminal trial.

**indeterminate sentence** A sentence having a minimum and maximum, with the decision of how long the criminal will serve depending on the criminal's behavior in prison and other things.

**indictment** A sworn, written accusation of a crime, made against a person by a prosecutor to a *grand jury*.

**inevitable discovery rule** The principle that even if criminal evidence is gathered by unconstitutional methods, the evidence may be admissible if it definitely would have come to light anyway.

**inference** A fact (or proposition) that is *probably* true because a true fact (or proposition) leads you to believe that the *inferred* fact (or proposition) is also true.

**inferior court** A court with special, limited responsibilities, such as a probate court.

**information** A formal accusation of a crime made by a proper public official such as a prosecuting attorney.

**injunctions** A judge's order to a person to do or to refrain from doing a particular thing.

**in limine** (Latin) "At the beginning"; preliminary. A motion in limine is a (usually pretrial) request that prejudicial information be excluded as trial evidence.

**inquisitorial system** The system of adjudication found in civil law jurisdictions. Less formal and technical than the adversarial model, a judge plays a prominent role in the gathering of evidence and the development of the case.

**intentional** Determination to do a certain thing.

**interlocutory appeal** The *Interlocutory Appeals* Act (28 U.S.C. 1292 (1948)) is a federal law that provides for an appeal while a trial is going on if the trial judge states in writing: (1) A legal question has come up that directly affects the trial. (2) There are major questions as to how that point of law should be resolved. (3) The case would proceed better if the appeals court answers the question.

**interpret** Studying a document *and* surrounding circumstances to decide the document's meaning.

**interrogation** Questioning by police, especially of a person suspected or accused of a crime. A *custodial interrogation* involves a restraint of freedom, so it requires a *Miranda* warning. A routine *investigatory interrogation* involves no restraint and no accusation of a crime.

**intervening cause** A cause of an accident or other injury that will remove the blame from the wrongdoer who originally set events in motion.

**irresistible impulse** The loss of control due to insanity that is so great that a person cannot stop from committing a crime.

# J

**JNOV** A request by a defendant convicted by a jury for the court to set aside the verdict as unsupported by the evidence.

**judicial review** The authority of a court to review and invalidate legislation and executive action that are unlawful.

**jurisdiction** The geographical area within which a court (or a public official) has the right and power to operate. Or the persons about whom and the subject matters about which a court has the right and power to make decisions that are legally binding.

# K

**kidnapping** Taking away and holding a person illegally, usually against the person's will or by force.

**knowingly** With full knowledge and intentionally; willfully.

# L

**larceny** Stealing of any kind. Some types of larceny are specific crimes, such as *larceny by trick* or grand larceny.

**legal cause** The proximate cause of an injury; probable cause; cause that the law deems sufficient.

**legal guilt** A combination of factual guilt proven beyond a reasonable doubt, and a fair process.

**legal impossibility** A person who is unable to commit a crime because of legal impossibility cannot be convicted of a crime he or she intends or attempts.

**legislative history** The background documents and records of hearings related to the enactment of a bill.

**lesser included offense** A crime whose elements are found completely within the elements of a more serious crime. If the more serious offense is proven, the lesser included offense merges into it and only the more serious offense is punished.

**lineup**   A group of persons, placed side by side in a line, shown to a witness of a crime to see if the witness will identify the person suspected of committing the crime. A *lineup* should not be staged so that it is suggestive of one person.

# M

**malicious (malicious) mischief**   The criminal offense of intentionally destroying another person's property.

**manslaughter**   A crime, less severe than murder, involving the wrongful but nonmalicious killing of another person.

**mayhem**   The crime of violently, maliciously, and intentionally giving someone a serious permanent wound. In some states, a type of aggravated assault. Once, the crime of permanently wounding another (as by dismemberment) to deprive the person of fighting ability.

**mens rea**   (Latin) A state of mind that produces a crime.

**merger**   When a person is charged with two crimes (based on exactly the same acts), one of which is a lesser included offense of the other. The lesser crime *merges* because, under the prohibition against double jeopardy, the person may be tried for only one crime.

**Misprision of Treason**   The crime of failing to report known treason to authorities.

**mitigating circumstances**   Facts that provide no justification or excuse for an action but that can lower the amount of moral blame and thus lower the criminal penalty or civil damages for the action.

**Model Penal Code**   A proposed criminal code prepared jointly by the Commission on Uniform State Laws and the American Law Institute.

**motion**   A request that a judge make a ruling or take some other action.

**motive**   The reason why a person does something.

**M'Naghten test**   A principle employed in some jurisdictions for determining whether criminal defendants had the capacity to form criminal intent at the time they committed the crime of which they are accused. The M'Naghten rule is also referred to as the M'Naghten test or the right-wrong test.

# N

**National Crime Information Center**   Computerized records of criminals, warrants, stolen vehicles, etc.

**Natural and Probable Consequences Doctrine**   A rule that holds that accomplices are criminally liable for the unplanned but foreseeable crimes of the principal in the first degree that are committed during the planned crime.

**necessity**   Often refers to a situation that requires an action that would otherwise be illegal or expose a person to tort liability.

**negligence**   Under the MPC, a defendant acts negligently when the resulting harm or material element of a crime occurs because of the defendant has taken a substantial and unjustifiable risk, even if the risk is not perceived, so long as the risk involves a gross deviation from the standard of conduct that a law-abiding person would observe.

**nolle prosequi**   (Latin) The ending of a criminal case because the prosecutor decides or agrees to stop prosecuting.

**nolo contendere**   A plea of no-contest to a charge. The plea operates as a guilty plea, although it may not be used in subsequent civil litigation as proof of guilt.

# O

**objections**   A claim that an action by your adversary in a lawsuit (such as the use of a particular piece of evidence) is improper, unfair, or illegal, and you are asking the judge for a ruling on the point.

**offense analysis**   The assignment of a single mens rea to an offense.

**omission**   Failing to do something that is required by law.

**ordinance**   A local or city law, rule, or regulation.

**overbreadth doctrine**   A law will be declared void for *overbreadth* if it attempts to punish speech or conduct that is protected by the Constitution and if it is impossible to eliminate the unconstitutional part of the law without invalidating the whole law.

# P

**pardon**   A president's or governor's release of a person from punishment for a crime.

**parole**   Early release from prison or jail. Parole is usually granted with conditions such as requiring the parolee to refrain from communicating with the victim of the crime that led to the confinement and remaining free of criminality while on parole. If the conditions of parole are violated, parole may be revoked and the parolee may be returned to confinement to complete the original sentence.

**peremptory challenge**   The automatic elimination of a potential juror by one side before trial without needing to state the reason for the elimination.

**perjury**   Lying while under oath, especially in a court proceeding. It is a crime.

**plain view doctrine**   The rule that if police officers see or come across something while acting lawfully, that item may be used as evidence in a criminal trial even if the police did not have a search warrant.

**plea**   The *defendant's* formal answer to a criminal charge. The defendant says "guilty," "not guilty," or "nolo contendere" (no contest).

**plea bargain (plea agreement)**   Negotiations between a prosecutor and a criminal defendant's lawyer, in the attempt to resolve a criminal case without trial.

**police power**   The government's authority and power to set up and enforce laws to provide for the safety, health, and general welfare of the people.

**polling the jury**   Individually asking each member of a jury what his or her decision is. Polling is done by the judge, at the defendant's request, immediately after the verdict.

**precedent**   Prior decisions of the same court, or a higher court, that a judge must follow in deciding a subsequent case presenting similar facts and the same legal problem, even though different parties are involved and many years have elapsed.

**predicate offense**   An act or offense that is an element of another crime.

**prejudicial error**   A trial court mistake that impacted the outcome of the case. It may be reversed or otherwise changed by a higher court.

**preliminary hearing**   The first court proceeding on a criminal charge, in federal courts and many state courts, by a magistrate or a judge to decide whether there is enough evidence for the government to continue with the case and to require the defendant to post bail or be held for trial.

**presumption**   A presumption *of law* is an automatic assumption required by law that whenever a certain set of facts shows up, a court must automatically draw certain legal conclusions.

**presumption of innocence doctrine**  In the United States and many other nations, the state has the obligation to prove a defendant's guilt. In the United States, the state must prove every element of the crime beyond a reasonable doubt. A defendant begins the process as innocent and is not obliged to put on a defense.

**prima facie**  On first impression; sufficient evidence introduced early in a case to continue with a claim.

**Principal in the First Degree**  A person who commits the actus reus of a crime.

**Principal in the Second Degree**  A person who is physically present and assists a principal in the first degree but does not commit the actus reus of the crime.

**principle of legality**  The procedural side of due process, which requires that criminal laws (and punishments) be written and enacted before an act may be punished.

**probable cause**  The U.S. Constitutional requirement that law enforcement officers present sufficient facts to convince a judge to issue a search warrant or an arrest *warrant*, and the requirement that no warrant should be issued unless it is more likely than not that the objects sought will be found in the place to be searched or that a crime has been committed by the person to be arrested.

**prostitution**  A person offering their body for sexual purposes in exchange for money. A crime in most states.

**provocation**  An act by a victim that reasonably causes another to respond with violence. Provocation has the effect of mitigating a crime.

**proximate cause**  The "legal cause" of an accident or other injury (which may have several actual causes). The *proximate cause* of an injury is not necessarily the closest thing in time or space to the injury, and not necessarily the event that set things in motion, because "proximate cause" is a legal, not a physical concept.

**punitive damages**  Damages that are awarded over and above compensatory damages or actual damages because of the wanton, reckless, or malicious nature of the wrong done by the plaintiff.

**purposely**  Intentionally; knowingly.

# Q

**quash**  Overthrow; annul; completely do away with. *Quash* usually refers to a court stopping a subpoena, an order, or an indictment.

# R

**Racketeer Influenced and Corrupt Organizations Act**  (19 U.S.C. 1961). A broadly applied 1970 federal law that creates certain "racketeering offenses" that include participation in various criminal schemes and conspiracies and that allows government seizure of property acquired in violation of the act.

**rape**  The crime of imposing sexual intercourse by force or otherwise without legally valid consent.

**rational relationship test**  The default test used to determine if due process or equal protection has been violated. Laws must be rational to satisfy this test.

**receiving stolen property**  The criminal offense of getting or concealing property known to be stolen by another.

**recklessness**  Indifference to consequences; indifference to the safety and rights of others. Recklessness implies conduct amounting to more than ordinary negligence.

**record on appeal**  A formal, written account of a case, containing the complete formal history of all actions taken, papers filed, rulings made, opinions written, and so forth.

**regulation**  Law created by governmental administrative agencies.

**remand**  The return of a case from a higher court to a lower court with instructions for the lower court to act in some manner, e.g., conduct a new trial or rehear an issue.

**reprieve**  Holding off on enforcing a criminal sentence for a period of time after the sentence has been handed down.

**retreat to the wall doctrine**  The doctrine that before a person is entitled to use deadly force in self-defense, he or she must attempt to withdraw from the encounter by giving as much ground as possible.

**revocation hearing**  The due process hearing required before the government can revoke a privilege it has previously granted.

**robbery**  The illegal taking of property from the person of another by using force or threat of force.

**rule of lenity**  If there are two or more reasonable interpretations of a statute, the interpretation that most favors the defendant is to be adopted.

# S

**scienter**  (Latin) Knowingly; with guilty knowledge. [pronounce: si-*en*-ter]

**second-degree murder**  Murder without premeditation.

**self-defense**  Physical force used against a person who is threatening the use of physical force or using physical force.

**separation of powers**  Division of the federal government (and state governments) into legislative (lawmaking), judicial (law interpreting), and executive (law enforcement) branches.

**Sextortion**  The use of sexual images of a person to commit extortion.

**shield laws**  A state law that prohibits use of most evidence of a rape (or other sexual crime) victim's past sexual conduct at trial.

**showup**  A pretrial identification procedure in which only one suspect and a witness are brought together.

**sidebar**  An in-court discussion among lawyers and the judge that is out of the hearing of witnesses and the jury. Sidebar conferences are usually *on* the record.

**social contract**  An implied agreement between all people that they will obey the laws and relinquish a measured amount of liberty in exchange for security.

**sodomy**  A general word for an "unnatural" sex act or the crime committed by such act. While the definition varies, *sodomy* can include oral sex, anal sex, homosexual sex, or sex with animals.

**solicitation**  Asking for; enticing; strongly requesting. This may be a crime if the thing being urged is a crime.

**sovereign immunity**  The government's freedom from being sued. In many cases, the U.S. government has waived immunity by a statute such as the Federal Tort Claims Act; states have similar laws.

**specific intent**  An intent to commit the exact crime charged or the precise outcome of the act, not merely an intent to commit the act without an intention to cause the outcome.

**stalking**  The crime of repeatedly following, threatening, or harassing another person in ways that lead to a legitimate fear of physical harm. Some states define *stalking* more broadly as any conduct with no legitimate purpose that seriously upsets a targeted person, especially conduct in violation of a protective order.

**standing**  A person's right to bring (start) or join a lawsuit or to raise a particular issue because he or she is directly affected by the issues raised.

**standing**    A rule that requires a person to have either a property interest or a reasonable expectation of privacy in the area searched in order to have a Fourth Amendment right.

**stand your ground doctrine**    A law that enables a person to use deadly force to repel an attack without first retreating.

**stare decisis**    Latin for "let the decision stand." The doctrine that judicial decisions stand as precedents for cases arising in the future.

**state action doctrine**    The rule that constitutional rights only limit governments, not private parties.

**statute**    A law passed by a legislature.

**statute of limitation**    Federal and state statutes prescribing the maximum period of time during which various types of civil actions and criminal prosecutions can be brought after the occurrence of the injury or the offense.

**statutory construction**    Guidelines employed by judges in the interpretation of statutes that have developed and evolved over hundreds of years.

**statutory rape**    The crime of having sexual intercourse with a person under a certain state-set age, regardless of consent.

**strict liability**    The legal responsibility for damage or injury, even if you are not at fault or negligent.

**strict liability crimes**    Crimes or offenses in which mens rea or criminal intent is not an element.

**strict scrutiny test**    A test used to determine if due process or equal protection has been violated. Laws that burden fundamental rights or employ suspect classifications must be supported by a compelling interest, narrowly designed, and the least restrictive means to accomplish the state's objectives.

**subornation of perjury**    The crime of asking or forcing another person to lie under oath.

**substantial relationship test**    A test used to determine if due process or equal protection has been violated. Laws that burden liberties not deemed fundamental and that classify according to sex and a few other classifications must be substantially related to a legitimate governmental interest to be valid.

**suspect classifications**    Laws that classify people by race, religion, national origin, and alienage must pass the strict scrutiny test to be valid.

**suspended sentence**    A sentence (usually "jail time") that the judge allows the convicted person to avoid serving (usually if the person continues on good behavior, completes community service, etc.).

# T

**target**    A person investigated by a grand jury.

**tax evasion**    The deliberate nonpayment or underpayment of taxes that are legally due. Criminal tax evasion has higher fines than civil fraud and the possibility of a prison sentence upon the showing of "willfulness."

**tax fraud**    The deliberate nonpayment or underpayment of taxes that are legally due.

**terrorism**    The definition of terrorism is the subject of ongoing debate. However, one federal statute defines it as activities that involve violence or acts dangerous to human life that are violations of law and appear to be intended to intimate or coerce a civilian population, to influence a policy of government by intimidation or coercion, or to affect the conduct of government through mass destruction, assassination, or kidnapping. 18 U.S.C. §2331.

**tort**    A civil (as opposed to a criminal) wrong, other than a breach of contract.

**transactional immunity**    Freedom from prosecution for all crimes related to the compelled testimony, so long as the witness tells the truth.

**transferred intent**    The principle that if an unintended illegal act results from the intent to commit a crime, that act is also a crime.

**trespass**    The unlawful touching of personal property or entry onto, or remaining on, real property.

**trial court**    A court that hears and determines a case initially, as opposed to an appellate court. A court of general jurisdiction.

**true bill**    A grand jury indictment.

**true threat**    A threatening statement that is not protected by the Free Speech Clause of the First Amendment.

# U

**use immunity**    Freedom from prosecution based on the compelled testimony and on anything the government learns from following up on the testimony.

# V

**vagueness doctrine**    The rule that a criminal law may be unconstitutional if it does not clearly say what is required or prohibited, what punishment may be imposed, or what persons may be affected. A law that violates due process of law in this way is *void for vagueness*.

**venire**    The pool of prospective jurors.

**vicarious liability**    Legal responsibility for the acts of another person because of some relationship with that person.

**victim impact statement**    At the time of sentencing, a statement made to the court concerning the effect the crime has had on the victim or on the victim's family.

**voir dire**    (French) "To see, to say"; "to state the truth." The preliminary in-court questioning of a prospective witness (or juror) to determine competency to testify (or suitability to decide a case). [pronounce: vwahr deer]

# Index